LEO BAECK INSTITUTE
YEAR BOOK
1980

Speakers at the Oxford Seminar of the Leo Baeck Institute, 8th to 12th July 1979, at Lady Margaret Hall and Yarnton Manor

PUBLICATIONS OF THE
LEO BAECK INSTITUTE

YEAR BOOK XXV

1980

SECKER & WARBURG · LONDON
PUBLISHED FOR THE INSTITUTE
LONDON · JERUSALEM · NEW YORK

FOUNDER EDITOR: ROBERT WELTSCH
CO-EDITOR: ARNOLD PAUCKER

OFFICES OF THE
LEO BAECK INSTITUTE

JERUSALEM (ISRAEL): 33 Bustanai Street
LONDON: 4 Devonshire Street, W.1
NEW YORK: 129 East 73rd Street

THE LEO BAECK INSTITUTE
was founded in 1955 by the
COUNCIL OF JEWS FROM GERMANY
for the purpose of collecting material on and sponsoring research into the history of the Jewish Community in Germany and in other German-speaking countries from the Emancipation to its decline and new dispersion. The Institute is named in honour of the man who was the last representative figure of German Jewry in Germany during the Nazi period.

The Council of Jews from Germany was established after the war by the principal organisations of Jews from Germany in Israel, USA and UK for the protection of their rights and interests.

THIS PUBLICATION WAS SUPPORTED
BY A GRANT FROM THE
MEMORIAL FOUNDATION FOR JEWISH CULTURE

© Leo Baeck Institute 1980
Published by Martin Secker & Warburg Limited
54 Poland Street, London WIV 3DF
SBN 436 24433 0
*Printed in Great Britain by Richard Clay (The Chaucer Press), Limited,
Bungay, Suffolk*

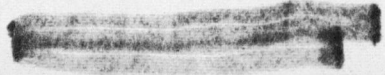

Contents

Preface by Arnold Paucker VII
Introduction by Ismar Schorsch: The Leo Baeck Institute: Continuity amid
Desolation IX

I. RELIGION AND SECULARISATION

ISMAR SCHORSCH: The Religious Parameters of Wissenschaft – Jewish
    Academics at Prussian Universities 3
VERNON LIDTKE: Social Class and Secularisation in Imperial Germany –
    The Working Classes 21
GEOFFREY G. FIELD: Religion in the German Volksschule, 1890–1928 .. 41
FRITZ STERN: Comments on the Papers of Ismar Schorsch, Vernon Lidtke and
    Geoffrey G. Field 73

II. ENLIGHTENMENT AND REFORM

NEHAMA REZLER-BERSOHN: Isaac Satanow – An Epitome of an Era .. 81
MICHAEL A. MEYER: The Orthodox and the Enlightened – An Unpublished
    Contemporary Analysis of Berlin Jewry's Spiritual Condition in the
    Early Nineteenth Century 101

III. FROM THE WILHELMINIAN ERA TO NAZI RULE

PETER PULZER: Why was there a Jewish Question in Imperial Germany? 133
MARJORIE LAMBERTI: Liberals, Socialists and the Defence against Anti-
    semitism in the Wilhelminian Period 147
MAX P. BIRNBAUM: On the Jewish Struggle for Religious Equality in Prussia
    1897–1914 163
HERMANN GREIVE: Zionism and Jewish Orthodoxy 173
WALTER ZWI BACHARACH: Jews in Confrontation with Racist Antisemitism,
    1879–1933 197
PAUL YOGI MAYER: Equality – Egality – Jews and Sport in Germany .. 221
CARL J. RHEINS: The Verband nationaldeutscher Juden 1921–1933 .. 243
LAWRENCE BARON: Erich Mühsam's Jewish Identity 269

IV. MARTIN BUBER

ARTHUR A. COHEN: Martin Buber and Judaism 287
NAHUM N. GLATZER: Reflections on Buber's Impact on German Jewry .. 301

V. IN THE THIRD REICH

HERBERT A. STRAUSS: Jewish Emigration from Germany – Nazi Policies and
Jewish Responses (I) 313

VI.   BIBLIOGRAPHY 363

VII.	LIST OF CONTRIBUTORS	473
VIII.	INDEX	477

Illustrations

Speakers at Oxford Seminar, 1979	Frontispiece
Eduard Rosenbaum Ernest Hamburger	} following preface
Joseph Wolff's treatise	opp. p. 116
Alfred Flatow and gymnastics team, Athens 1896, Ellen Preiss, Ilona Elek-Schacherer, Helene Mayer, Berlin 1936 Gretel Bergmann, Helene and Eugen Mayer, Daniel Prenn, Martel Jacob Makkabi and Schild championship German Makkabi team at Maccabiah, Tel-Aviv, Football at Theresienstadt	} between pp. 228–229
Max Naumann	opp. p. 260
Mühsam brothers Erich Mühsam	} between pp. 276–277

Preface

With this issue the Leo Baeck Institute celebrates both its twenty-fifth anniversary and that of the Year Book. There is an anecdote which has been handed down within the Institute that when the idea of an annual publication was first mooted in 1955 it was Martin Buber who predicted for the Year Book the limited life span its very name denotes. So it seems appropriate that we remember with affection the benevolent scepticism of Martin Buber whose memory is honoured in Year Book XXV by the papers of Arthur Cohen and Nahum Glatzer, delivered at a Symposium of the New York Leo Baeck Institute in October 1978, to mark the centenary of his birth.

In recent years the activities of our Institute have become increasingly diversified and it says much for the position that the New York Institute has attained in the American academic world that for some years now it has conducted sessions together with the American Historical Association at their Annual Meetings. This Year Book records yet another joint venture, the session on 'Religion and Secularization in German Society during the 19th and 20th Centuries' at the AHA's 93rd Annual Meeting in San Francisco in December 1978, which constitutes an innovation inasmuch as two of these papers are more within the field of general German history. Although Vernon Lidtke also touches on Eastern Jewish workers in Germany and Geoffrey Field dwells in some detail on the Jewish *Volksschule* their essays do, of course, transcend the terms of reference so far established by the Year Book. Yet we print the San Francisco session in full, not only because it was sponsored by the Leo Baeck Institute, but also because it reveals so clearly the barriers existing even within the labour movement, and in secondary education, which prevented the achieving of a truly secular state and shows too the general failure of the pluralistic society – and thus gives much of the essential background against which the Jewish Question in Germany is set.

In July 1979 the Leo Baeck Institute held its third international conference on the history of German Jewry when the London working centre organised a Seminar on 'Revolution and Evolution in German-Jewish History. 1848 in Historical Perspective' at Lady Margaret Hall and Yarnton Manor, Oxford. While some of the papers given at the Jerusalem Conference in 1970 (on Research into the History of Central European Jewry from the Emancipation to its Destruction) were printed in successive Year Books, and all the papers and commentaries given at the Arden House Conference in 1973 (Exploring a Typology of German Jewry), were published in Year Book XIX, the complete proceedings of the Oxford Seminar could not possibly be accommodated in this way. A separate conference volume will therefore be published in 1981 and it will be the first English-language volume in our *Schriftenreihe*.

A further AHA session sponsored by the Leo Baeck Institute, 'Ethnic Minorities and the Jews in Imperial Germany' at the 94th Annual Meeting in New

York in December 1979 is scheduled for inclusion in Year Book XXVI, and as to our future programme we will continue to try to extend our scope still further. Both volumes XXV and XXVI allot considerable space to Jewish life under the Nazi régime and to Jewish reactions to persecution, as well as placing greater emphasis on minority groups and trends within the Jewish community; topics to which hitherto we have perhaps paid insufficient attention.

An anniversary volume like this calls for many acknowledgments and space permits only a few, associated with the more recent Year Books. But Bertha Cohn must be singled out here for our special gratitude, as for twenty-four years until her retirement she has with great skill and devotion produced the annual Bibliography which has become such an essential tool for the student of the history of German-speaking Jewry; the Bibliography is now being continued by Irmgard Foerg, Locarno and Annette Pringle of the London Leo Baeck Institute. To Lux Furtmüller, our translator of long standing, we owe the elegant English versions of the essays of our German contributors. Sylvia Gilchrist of the London Leo Baeck Institute, Pauline Paucker and Ilse Shindel have been of great assistance in preparing the Year Book for the printers and seeing it through all the stages of its production. The proximity of the Wiener Library with its resources and its ever-helpful staff has been of course invaluable.

For some years now the Year Book has been largely written by a new generation of historians, Judaists, social scientists and Germanists and it seems only fitting that Ismar Schorsch, as a representative of those who have now come to the fore, introduces this volume to the readers. It is to the authors of this younger group in particular that thanks are due for their enthusiastic collaboration and unremitting support which makes the task of editing so enjoyable and rewarding. Yet it is also significant that on their part many of them have asked me to take advantage of the occasion of this twenty-fifth anniversary of the Leo Baeck Institute to pay homage, on behalf of us all, to the man who founded the Year Book in 1956. This jubilee volume is our tribute to Robert Weltsch.

Arnold Paucker

EDUARD ROSENBAUM
(1887–1979)

Eduard Rosenbaum, Member of the Executive of the London Board of the Leo Baeck Institute, died on 22nd May 1979 in London in his 92nd year. An economist and sociologist, he held distinguished posts in Germany, among them that of Syndikus of the Hamburg Chamber of Commerce and Director of its Commerzbibliothek. He served as a member of the German Delegation to the Versailles Peace Conference. After his emigration to England he was from 1935 to 1952 Acquisitions Librarian of the London School of Economics. Eduard Rosenbaum was a versatile writer who also contributed many essays to the Year Book. An English edition of his last book *M. M. Warburg & Co. 1798–1938* appeared shortly after his death. A dazzling conversationalist and a sparkling wit, he graced the meetings of the London Board of the Leo Baeck Institute which he had helped to found and of which he was Honorary Treasurer until 1975

ERNEST HAMBURGER
(1890–1980)

Ernest Hamburger, Member of the Executive of the New York Board of the Leo Baeck Institute, died on 3rd April 1980 in his 90th year. In the Weimar Republic he held high office in the Prussian Ministry of the Interior and was a Socialist Deputy in the Prussian Diet from 1924 until the advent of Nazi rule. After his emigration he became, in Paris, Lecturer of Comparative Law and Editor of *Cahiers de la Presse*; and later in New York Professor at the Ecole Libre des Hautes Etudes. From 1946 to 1958 he was Consultant and First Officer at the United Nations Secretariat and for many years Editor of the *UN Yearbook on Human Rights*. In 1968 the Leo Baeck Institute published Ernest Hamburger's opus magnum *Juden im öffentlichen Leben Deutschlands. Regierungsmitglieder, Beamte und Parlamentarier in der monarchischen Zeit*, on which subject his is the standard work. He had all but completed a second volume on Weimar Germany when his death deprived the Institute of a distinguished scholar and a humane and wise counsellor

The Leo Baeck Institute:
Continuity amid Desolation

BY ISMAR SCHORSCH

The twenty-fifth anniversary of the founding of the Leo Baeck Institute provides an appropriate occasion to ponder the source of its remarkable achievement, for in that time the Institute has attained an undisputed presence in the fractious world of academia. In a world that accords recognition primarily for creativity rather than longevity, the international reputation of the Institute rests firmly on a quarter-century of undiminished productivity. Twenty-five volumes of the English Year Book, thirty-six volumes of the *Schriftenreihe wissenschaftlicher Abhandlungen*, seventeen volumes of the German Bulletin, twenty-one volumes of biographies and memoirs in the Deutsche Verlags-Anstalt series, plus a number of special publications, which includes the incomparable Goldschmidt *Mahzor*, constitutes an unmatched scholarly output of well over 100 books, or an average of at least four books a year.

That publishing record in three languages (German, English and Hebrew) has tended to overshadow the Institute's other major accomplishment: the creation in New York of the single largest library and archive pertaining to central European Jewry anywhere in the world. In retrospect, and without exaggeration, the Institute has succeeded beyond the most audacious fantasies of its founders. Intent to compile data and stimulate research with a view towards an eventual comprehensive history of the Jewish experience in modern Germany, the Institute has spawned a flourishing sub-speciality of abiding interest to both Jewish and German historians.

A quick glance at the change in the composition of Year Book contributors conveys a sense of the vitality of the field. As the following table suggests, the ranks of the founders were gradually revitalised by a new generation of professional historians.

Year Book	Contributors	Ph.D.s	Academics	Average Age
1956	22	11	6	60
1966	13	7	6	53
1978	18	15	13	48·5

Furthermore, the contents of the Year Book show that the continued fascination with German-Jewish history goes well beyond a quest for the roots of the Holocaust to a desire to understand the complex and paradigmatic nature of the German-Jewish confrontation with modernity. Today the Year Book serves as the international forum in which young American, Israeli, German and English academics, whose own historical experience lies this side of 1933, exhibit and test the products of their craft.

The explanation for this track-record, I believe, abounds in paradox. Without doubt, an acute sense of discontinuity, a painful realisation that the Nazis had abruptly and brutally terminated a uniquely creative symbiosis stirred the founders to action. Yet the surprising success of their efforts is a direct function of continuity. They transcended the chaos of discontinuity precisely because they embodied the values, culture and style of German Jewry at its best. Beyond the proverbial German addiction to work and thoroughness, that continuity expressed itself in at least three identifiable ways.

In terms of organisational structure, the Institute was as comprehensive and flexible an institution as the German *Kultusgemeinde*. It too aspired to organisational unity by appreciating the reality and benefit of diversity. The Institute was able to harness the disparate and far-flung remnants of German Jewry because it allowed for geographic, political and religious diversity. Three working centres in the dominant areas of German-Jewish immigration coordinated their individual agenda through the annual meetings of a central board. Within that structural framework, an atmosphere obtained which induced German Jews of all persuasions, Zionist and non-Zionist, religious and secular, orthodox and liberal, to cooperate in the sacred task of preserving the past. The Institute never became the preserve of a single faction nor was any one facet of German-Jewish life ever programmatically ignored, though to be sure many still await their historian. Diversity within unity was part of the communal ethos which the founders of the Institute had absorbed while still in Germany.

Equally important, continuity expressed itself also in terms of personnel. It did not take a generation before qualified historians would emerge to implement the Institute's threefold programme of gathering material for the intellectual, social and institutional history of German Jewry. From the outset, the Institute benefited from the energetic involvement of an extraordinary cluster of Jewish scholars trained in German universities and steeped in *Jüdische Wissenschaft*. In fact, most had already made their mark in the world of Jewish scholarship. Their knowledge, vision and scholarship informed the Institute's collective judgment and elevated its publications to the highest standards.

Beyond that academic nucleus, the Institute galvanised the support of a significant circle of lettered Jews. Well educated, once prominent in some phase of organised Jewish life in Germany, and often with a keen eye sharpened by dislocation for that which was distinctive in German Jewry, they were eager and able to record their experiences and reflections. By publishing in German, the Institute spared them the anxiety and shame of writing in a language not their own and thus kept them from falling silent, the usual lot of literary men and women forced to relocate into another cultural orbit. Future historians of German Jewry will be the richer for this policy.

At the centre of this galaxy of academics and literati stood Robert Weltsch, the founder and editor of the Year Book. A product of the cultural fertility and Zionist idealism of Habsburg Prague and editor of the *Jüdische Rundschau* during its final two decades, Weltsch possessed a panoramic yet profound knowledge of Central European Jewry based on tumultuous experience tempered by voracious reading. His wisdom and integrity projected the distance so necessary for writing history at such close range. He demanded balance and empathy and repeatedly warned against writing history backwards or imposing simple-minded deterministic interpretations on complex developments often confounded by the fortuitous. His own corpus of introductions to the Year Book, his German essays and regular Hebrew articles for *Ha'aretz* constitutes a sophisticated exposition of the dominant features of Central European Jewish history in the modern era. Weltsch's powerful presence graced the Year Book with stability, direction and standards.

The third and final manifestation of continuity is perhaps the least tangible, yet, I believe, also the most decisive. The achievement of the Institute derives ultimately from a well-developed sense of history, cultivated for more than a century in Germany by *Wissenschaft des Judentums*. The programme to understand the totality of Judaism historically, initiated by Leopold Zunz in 1818 and gradually implemented by an ever widening circle of scholars down to 1939, eventually shaped the conceptual equipment and self-definition of nearly every sector of the community. During the disorientating experience after 1933, *Wissenschaft des Judentums* became a major source of consolation in the organised effort at spiritual resistance. The nearly 100 small volumes of the famous *Bücherei des Schocken Verlags* are moving testimony to the vital communal role of *Jüdische Wissenschaft* in those final difficult years. Yet no academic discipline can ever be enlisted as a social force in times of stress unless its method and meaning have not already gained some prior resonance outside the "ivory tower".

The historical consciousness of German Jewry likewise did not ignore the millennial presence of Jews in Central Europe. Since the early days of his *Monatsschrift*, Zacharias Frankel had encouraged his colleagues and students to study the origins of Jewish settlements in medieval German towns. The subject quickly received the competent attention of engaged *Wissenschaft* scholars, and by the end of the Weimar period the field of German-Jewish history could boast of a unique national archive, a special journal and a formidable amount of finished research.

In consequence, the founders of the Institute were imbued by a rich historiographical legacy marked by a lively sense of time and place and especially attuned to the distinctiveness of German Jewry. Both the nature and success of their enterprise had deep roots in their own cultural ambience.

On a concrete level, this connection is transparent. The Institute reissued a few scholarly books whose entire printing had been confiscated by the Nazis. More important, the Institute acted, where possible, to complete the pre-war agenda of a rejuvenated *Wissenschaft* movement as it pertained to the history of German Jewry. With the turn of the century, a circle of young scholars had begun to wrest control of the movement from the hands of a more apologetic, pulpit-orientated leadership. High on their priority list was the systematic search for new sources. While some of the projects inspired by this effort were completed before the war, most notably those of the young Yizhak Baer, others still required large investments of time and money. The support and publication of the two volumes of the *Germania Judaica* and the eight volumes of Selma Stern's *Der*

Preussische Staat und die Juden are a lasting tribute to the Institute's sense of responsibility and historical judgment.

On the deepest level, the founders of the Institute like the founders of the *Wissenschaft* movement were impelled by the same poignant need: to explain themselves to an alien world. Emancipation, no less than the Holocaust, had brought to an end, albeit differently, the conditions that had sustained a distinctive and vibrant community. In each case, an élite of proud but self-conscious survivors refused to abdicate the preservation of their past and the exposition of their heritage to uninformed and even hostile outsiders. The inevitable estrangement inflicted by homelessness had in fact invigorated their powers of self-perception, and the best of their work pulsated with insight and vitality. A tenacious effort at perpetuation by a cluster of visionaries had not only helped to transcend the personal reality of chaos and anomie, but also to enhance the prospects for collective Jewish survival, for self-renewal has always depended on creative cultural transmission.

Religion and Secularisation

The Religious Parameters of Wissenschaft
Jewish Academics at Prussian Universities

BY ISMAR SCHORSCH

Jewish emancipation is a classic case of secularisation. The revolutionary decision to abandon an entrenched policy of segregation for integration signalled a determination to resolve the question of Jewish status free of religious constraints. It bespoke the courage to fly in the face of a millennial Christian tradition which had progressively relegated the locus of Jewish existence to the periphery of society as separate and unequal. To invite Jews to enter society as equals meant to remove one more issue of public policy from church domination.[1]

But as an isolated measure emancipation was doomed to fail. It required the backing of a state prepared to restrict the institutional power of Christianity on a wide front. For what emancipation needed above all else was a social matrix in which religion had been neutralised. As long as religious interests retained the political capacity to shape policy in major sectors of society, Jews stood little chance of gaining legal equality or social integration. Long before Bruno Bauer concluded in 1842 that Jewish emancipation was unattainable in a state still dominated by Christianity, Moses Mendelssohn had foreseen that integrating Jews was predicated on transforming religion into a private matter. It was this realisation which prompted him to devote the first half of his emancipation tract *Jerusalem* to an elaborate theoretical argument for removing religion from the public arena.[2]

The zigzag course of emancipation in Prussia and Germany down to 1914 amply confirms Mendelssohn's political sagacity. Its piecemeal extension and administrative subversion testify to the sad fact that governments eager to shore up their eroding position with the romantic ideology of the Christian state were singularly ill-equipped to carry out a Jewish policy inherently secular.

The self-contradictory nature of Prussian policy on Jews in the first half of the nineteenth century is especially manifest in the question of university employment. The liberal spirit which informed the famous emancipation edict of 1812 had, among many innovations, also declared Jews eligible for academic posts, a measure in full accord with the new secular ethos of *Wissenschaft* as embodied two years earlier in the University of Berlin. Unlike older surviving universities, its statutes enunciated no religious requirements for those invited to join its facul-

---

[1]The conception of secularisation which informs this paragraph derives from Peter S. Berger, *The Sacred Canopy*, Anchor Books Edition, Garden City 1969, p. 107. The following abbreviations will be used throughout this essay:
  CAHJP – The Central Archives for the History of the Jewish People, Jerusalem
  DZAM – Deutsches Zentralarchiv, Merseburg
[2]Moses Mendelssohn, *Jerusalem: oder über religiöse Macht und Judenthum*, Frankfurt a. Main-Leipzig, 1787. For Bauer's views see his *Die Judenfrage*, Braunschweig 1843, pp. 19–20, 59–62.

ties. Similarly the statutes of the new interdenominational (*paritätische*) University of Breslau, which like those of Berlin were issued in 1816, stipulated no general religious conditions for its teaching personnel, though they did contain instructions to maintain a Catholic and Evangelical theology faculty as well as to appoint both a Catholic and Evangelical professor of philosophy.[3] At least in theory then, the revitalised Prussian university was to integrate a broad conception of scholarship with participatory learning in an atmosphere free of denominationalism.

During the ensuing decades, young Jews, often with little formal *Gymnasium* training, streamed into the universities, and most faculties of medicine and philosophy quickly divested commencement exercises of their religious character to award degrees to Jewish students. In consequence, by mid-century the percentage of Jews in German universities was already twice that of their percentage in the general population.[4] What often frustrated the upward mobility of Jewish graduates in Prussia and elsewhere was the absence of career opportunities in the public sector. Even the edict of 1812 had preferred to restrict state employment of Jews for the time being to the field of education, which below the university level, of course, was still conducted wholly along confessional lines and hence effectively closed to Jews.[5]

Thus when King Friedrich Wilhelm III personally decided on 18th August 1822 to deny Eduard Gans, the brilliant disciple of Hegel and intimate friend of Leopold Zunz, an appointment as associate professor of law, the last portal to the public sector was sealed. The promise of academic appointments to Jews, he stated cryptically, could not be effected "without great disruption" and should be withdrawn.[6]

In 1826 the ministry of education informed all Prussian universities that the King's decision applied even to the lowest rung of the academic ladder, the unsalaried position of instructor (*Privatdozent*), although that rank did not technically constitute a government appointment. The occasion was an enquiry from the Berlin philosophy faculty regarding Marcus Leo Frankenheim whom it had

---

[3]Ismar Freund, *Die Emanzipation der Juden in Preussen*, 2 vols., Berlin 1912, II, p. 456. The statutes of Berlin and Breslau were printed in Johann F. W. Koch, *Die Preussischen Universitäten*, 2 vols., Berlin–Posen–Bromberg 1839–1840, I, pp. 41 ff. and pp. 318 ff. Although Bonn was founded in 1818 during the tail end of the liberal era, its statutes were not issued till 1827. Not surprisingly, therefore, they stress to a much greater extent than those of Berlin and Breslau the religious mission of the university and the connection of the Evangelical faculty to the church. (Koch, *op. cit.*, I, pp. 190–191, 219–220.)

[4]Monika Richarz, *Der Eintritt der Juden in die akademischen Berufe. Jüdische Studenten und Akademiker in Deutschland 1678–1848*, Tübingen 1974 (Schriftenreihe wissenschaftlicher Abhandlungen des Leo Baeck Instituts 28), p. 93.

[5]Freund, *op. cit.*, II, p. 456.

[6]A copy of the King's order to Chancellor Hardenberg, Gans's benefactor, may be found in CAHJP, P17-634. The decisive German phrase reads

"nicht ohne grosse Missverhältnisse zu veranlassen". On the episode see Hanns Günther Reissner, *Eduard Gans. Ein Leben im Vormärz*, Tübingen 1965 (Schriftenreihe wissenschaftlicher Abhandlungen des Leo Baeck Instituts 14), pp. 91–93. The phrase quoted by Reissner (p. 92) actually comes from the proclamation by the *Königliches Geheimes Staatsministerium* on 4th December 1822 and not the King's order of 18th August. The text of the proclamation was published by M. Kalisch, *Die Judenfrage*, Leipzig 1860, pp. 3–4.

promoted in 1823. The faculty was now prepared to appoint him as an instructor in physics and mathematics, provided the step did not conflict with the spirit of the royal cabinet order of 18th August. The answer was unequivocal: "as long as he professes the Jewish religion, he may not be admitted to habilitate as an instructor".[7] The unrelenting enforcement of that policy for the next two decades prompted one contemporary to quip that in Prussia Jews were not even allowed to starve as *Privatdozenten*.[8]

The government, however, did unhappily allow the Academy of Sciences in 1842 to elect its first Jewish member since Mendelssohn to its section of physics and mathematics, a Dr. Riess, whose father was a Berlin banker. Although that honour carried with it the right to deliver lectures at the universities of Bonn and Berlin, thereby colliding with current policy, Eichhorn, the autocratic minister of education, felt quite certain that Riess had no intention of doing so. More important, in urging the King's approval, Eichhorn drew a basic distinction. Whereas religion was of little consequence for the Academy whose members engaged mainly in research in the natural sciences, it remained a prerequisite for the proper training of young men for a career in state service or in the church, which continued to be the primary function of university professors.[9] In sum, as long as that traditional view of the university prevailed, Jews could not advance beyond the level of students.

The issue was reopened by the government itself in 1847 as part of the new comprehensive Jewry law intended to complete, albeit in a restricted sense, the work of 1812.[10] The controversy set off by this issue alone deserves separate study because it illuminates such a broad horizon: the bureaucratic style of Prussian absolutism, the anti-Jewish animus of the professoriate, the Christian tone of the Prussian university and the religious parameters of its *Wissenschaft*.

The original impetus to reconsider Jewish suitability for academic office came paradoxically from no less a source than King Friedrich Wilhelm IV. An adherent of Karl Ludwig von Haller, the formidable theoretician of the medieval patrimonial state, the King came to the throne determined to hold the swelling forces of liberalism at bay by reinvigorating the alliance between throne and altar. Public life would be restored to a Christian foundation and Jews returned to a corporate status on the edge of Christian society.[11] Nevertheless, in reactivating

---

[7]The documents were published by Kalisch, pp. 4–5. Frankenheim was the first Jew to earn a doctorate from Berlin's philosophy faculty. By 1827 he had converted to Christianity, a step which eventually paid off in an associate professorship in mathematics at Breslau. (Richarz, *op. cit.*, p. 99, n. 40; Nahum N. Glatzer, *Leopold and Adelheid Zunz. An Account in Letters 1815–1885*, London 1958. Publication of the Leo Baeck Institute, p. 53; Heinrich Wuttke, ed., *Jahrbuch der deutschen Universitäten*, I, Leipzig 1842, p. 82.)

[8]Richarz, *op. cit.*, pp. 210–211. On the plight of Prussia's *Privatdozenten*, see Erich G. C. Hahn, 'The Junior Faculty in "Revolt": Reform Plans for Berlin University in 1848', *The American Historical Review*, vol. 82 (1977), pp. 875–895.

[9]The relevant documents were published by Kalisch, *op. cit.*, pp. 5–10.

[10]The best treatment of the involved and protracted drafting of the Jewry law is by Horst Fischer, *Judentum, Staat und Heer in Preussen im frühen 19. Jahrhundert. Zur Geschichte der staatlichen Judenpolitik*, Tübingen 1968 (Schriftenreihe wissenschaftlicher Abhandlungen des Leo Baeck Instituts 20), pp. 151–190.

[11]Ernst Rudolph Huber, *Deutsche Verfassungsgeschichte seit 1789*, 4 vols., Stuttgart 1957–1969, II, pp. 256–257; Fischer, *op. cit.*, pp. 151–157.

the machinery to prepare a uniform Jewry law for the entire realm in 1841, he expressed a willingness to accord Jews a measure of reward for their academic achievements. Specifically, he raised the possibility of admitting them to the faculties of medicine and philosophy.[12] The royal cabinet (*Staatsministerium*) was less than enthusiastic with the idea. By a six-to-five vote it accepted the principle of admitting Jews to academic office.[13] What eventually emerged from the laborious and protracted preparation of the draft of the Jewry law was an elliptic concession hedged with restrictions. In those universities which by statute did not insist on religious qualifications, Jews could serve as instructors and associate professors in the fields of mathematics, science and medicine.[14]

In the course of presenting the final draft for consultation in June 1847 to the United Diet, Prussia's first half-hearted stab at representative rule, the government spelled out the implications and rationale of this concession. The function of the university was not to transmit bare facts but to nurture spiritual growth. It enshrined the cultural treasures of a national life permeated by Christianity. Accordingly, four types of limitations were built into the text. First, no university would be compelled to violate its own statutes. The law would constitute no more than a recommendation. In fact, the government was fairly certain that of the six universities operating in Prussia, only the statutes of Berlin did not preclude employing Jews. Second, faculties of law and theology were not under discussion, since their subject matter self-evidently disqualified Jews. They could not teach church law, which the doctorate of jurisprudence included, nor even German law, which sprang from Christian roots, for genuine understanding was a function of spiritual kinship as well as intellect. Third, within the faculty of philosophy, Jews could not be entrusted with teaching classics, history or philosophy, subjects whose ultimate meaning could be grasped only from a Christian point of view. Finally, Jews were still barred from the rank of professor in order to deny them access to the positions of dean or rector in which they would exercise authority over Christians. Just in case anyone thought otherwise, the draft reiterated explicitly that the rest of the educational system would continue to remain inaccessible to Jews. In essence, what was being offered amounted to an empty gesture, signifying neither a viable career option for aspiring Jewish scholars nor the slightest compromise of the Christian character of the Prussian educational system.[15]

In their deliberations on the provisions of this paragraph, both curiae of Prussia's first "*Reichstag*" found them too restrictive.[16] The conservative upper house of lords, while respecting existing university statutes, proposed to allow Jews also to teach philology and to attain the rank of full professor.[17] In contrast, the

---

[12]DZAM, *Geheimes Zivilkabinett*, 2.2.1, Nr. 23680.
[13]DZAM, Rep. 90a, BIII2b, Nr. 6, Bd. 55.
[14]The draft submitted by the government to the United Diet was printed at the beginning of *Vollständige Verhandlungen des ersten Vereinigten Preussischen Landtages über die Emancipationsfrage der Juden*, Berlin 1847, pp. I–X. Paragraph 35 included stipulations regarding university teaching (pp. V–VI).
[15]*Ibid.*, pp. XXXVII–XXXIX, 98–99, 328–333.
[16]The designation "Reichstag" is applied by Reinhart Koselleck, *Preussen zwischen Reform und Revolution*, Stuttgart 1967, pp. 367–368.
[17]*Vollständige Verhandlungen*, pp. 110–114.

rebellious lower house led by *Landrat* Georg von Vincke of Westphalia and the Rhenish manufacturer and intellectual Gustav Mevissen, both of whom had previously advocated the extension of full emancipation, took the position that Jews be granted the right to teach all disciplines, except those which presupposed adherence to Christianity, and to fill all academic posts from instructor to rector. Mevissen, a self-educated Hegelian and co-founder of the radical *Rheinische Zeitung*, denounced the government for betraying Germany's greatest achievement in the modern era: the freeing of *Wissenschaft* from the tyranny of religious dogmatism.

> "Free scholarship exists only when it tosses aside all restraints, all presuppositions in its research, when it recognises as correct and true only that which it has found by way of free inquiry."[18]

Equally defiant was the lower house's unexpected vote to establish a chair for Jewish theology at a Prussian university. According Judaism its legitimate place in the cosmopolitan world of *Wissenschaft* would redound to the benefit of both.[19]

The stage was now set for one of the more bizarre episodes in the long and tortuous history of the Prussian bureaucracy. On 9th July 1847, several weeks before the actual promulgation of the new Jewry law in a version which did incorporate many of the modifications suggested by the more trustworthy upper house of the Diet, the senate and rector of the University of Berlin rushed off an apprehensive petition to the minister of education. The restrictive nature of university statutes throughout Prussia threatened to transform the magnanimous grant of university employment to Jews into a piece of special legislation pertaining only to Berlin. Since its statutes alone did not preclude hiring Jews *de jure*, Berlin would soon be overrun by young Jews bent on a career in the one public sector open to them. The consequences would aggravate an already troublesome situation. A falling enrolment coupled with an inflated teaching corps had reduced the student–teacher ratio to an all-time low of 8:1. That ratio, implied the petition, cut deeply into the faculty fees so vital to augmenting the inadequate salaries paid by the government. Moreover, Berlin would be denied the training benefits fostered by the mobility built into the *Privatdozent* system. It would become host to a growing number of Jewish instructors unable to teach elsewhere and with little prospect of advancement in Berlin. The time had come to raise the practice of *Wissenschaft* above the confines of religious parochialism. Certainly the University of Berlin, contended the senate, had nothing to regret in having adhered to that principle by appointing worthy Catholic scholars. Specifically, the senate called on Eichhorn to bring all university statutes into harmony with the intent of the new law.[20]

---

[18]*Ibid.*, p. 341. On Vincke and Mevissen, see their admiring younger contemporary Rudolf Haym, *Reden und Redner des ersten Vereinigten Preussischen Landtags*, Berlin 1847, pp. 55 ff. and 225 ff. Haym reprinted their addresses on the Jewry law (pp. 132–143, 253–259).

[19]*Vollständige Verhandlungen*, p. 343. Ludwig Geiger's doubts as to whether a vote in plenum was ever taken on this proposal derived from a careless reading of the protocols. The text is unambiguous. (Ludwig Geiger, 'Zunz im Verkehr mit Behörden und Hochgestellten', *Monatsschrift für Geschichte und Wissenschaft des Judentums*, vol. LX [1916], p. 334.)

[20]Published by Kalisch, *op. cit.*, pp. 66–71.

Indeed, the decision to open the academic market even partially to Jewish applicants could not have come at a more inopportune time. Prussian universities were still reeling from the sudden drop in student attendance which struck in the mid-1830s after nearly two decades of exhilarating growth. From 1829 to 1838 the total student population fell from 6,154 to 4,480.[21] In the winter semester of 1833–1834 student attendance at Berlin peaked at 2,001, a figure not attained again until the winter of 1862–1863.[22] By the summer of 1847, the number of matriculated students at Berlin had declined to 1,378.[23] Hardest hit were the faculties of law and theology which soon began to lose their numerical advantage. The fate of theology at Berlin was typical, declining from an enrolment of 641 students in the winter of 1830–1831 to 214 in the summer semester of 1847.[24] Unable to absorb the graduates of these faculties in the crowded and unexpanding field of state service, the government took a variety of steps to curtail the overproduction of an academic proletariat.[25]

The inevitable consequence was an excess of university teachers even in the more stable faculties of medicine and philosophy. As early as 1843 the Berlin senate had vigorously protested to Eichhorn over the harmful results. It pleaded at that time to be consulted about future appointments, as it had not been in the past, and proposed to stiffen the qualifications for the rank of instructor. Still more radical was the suggestion to introduce a "numerus clausus" governing the number of instructors in each faculty. Eichhorn's agreement to the first two requests temporarily improved the stormy relations between the minister and the university.[26] Four years later the prospect of opening a tight market to Jewish competition threatened to aggravate a chronic condition.

Nevertheless, Eichhorn chose to react to the Berlin petition of 1847 with uncharacteristic restraint. He simply ignored its appeal for firm government intervention. Instead he handled the paragraph in question as a recommendation and proceeded to solicit the opinion of the entire academic establishment on two questions: to what extent did the statutes of one's university accord with the provisions of the new Jewry law, and, if not, was it advisable to change them? Eichhorn felt that the importance of the subject warranted a three-tier response from each university: first the individual opinion of each full professor, then the collective opinion of each faculty and finally the collective opinion of the senate. Thus, during the autumn and winter months of 1847–1848, the entire upper echelon of the Prussian professoriate was compelled to set aside time to formulating its views on Jews and Judaism, the university and *Wissenschaft*.[27] Ironically, a law intended to end the panoply of conflicting regulations pertaining to Jewish

---

[21]Koselleck, *op. cit.*, p. 440, n. 174.
[22]Max Lenz, *Geschichte der Königlichen Friedrich-Wilhelms-Universität zu Berlin*, 4 vols., Halle 1910–1918, II, pt. 1, p. 406.
[23]Kalisch, *op. cit.*, p. 67.
[24]Lenz, *op. cit.*, II, pt. 2, p. 105.
[25]On the overproduction of university graduates, see Koselleck, *op. cit.*, pp. 438–440 and Lenore O'Boyle, 'The Problem of an Excess of Educated Men in Western Europe, 1800–1850', *Journal of Modern History*, vol. XLII (1970), pp. 471–478.
[26]Lenz, *op. cit.*, II, pt. 2, pp. 71–73.
[27]Kalisch, *op. cit.*, pp. 71–74.

status throughout the country was so worded as to preserve that confusion in university life.

The government's own deep-seated ambivalence on the wisdom of allowing Jews to teach prompted an extraordinary display of diffidence towards an institution it generally dominated. Friedrich Wilhelm IV's campaign against "atheistic" Hegelianism had repeatedly violated the academic freedom of the university. In March 1842 Eichhorn revoked the right of Bruno Bauer to teach as an instructor in the Protestant theological faculty of Bonn after the talented but temperamental scholar had produced the first part of a Hegelian study repudiating the synoptic Gospels as valid evidence for the historical Jesus. Prior to the dismissal, Eichhorn had requested, for the first time ever, the written opinion of all six Protestant theological faculties in Prussia and then promptly ignored the results, which favoured not removing Bauer by a margin of sixteen to eleven. Still more ominous for the survival of academic freedom was the prescription to all Protestant theological faculties which followed. Eichhorn reminded them of their primary responsibility to train pastors, and therefore the eternal truths of the Evangelical church would define the boundaries of their research and teaching.[28] Bauer supplied the epitaph:

> "Precisely there where the labour of investigation is warranted, research is forbidden. Only in peripheral and unessential subjects is it permitted. The prisoner may stroll around in his prison; but the very idea that he might be in prison is prohibited."[29]

A few months later Eichhorn turned his fire on Hoffmann von Fallersleben. A full professor of German language and literature at Breslau since 1835, Hoffmann was summarily dismissed without pension for the political intent of his artless verse. In 1844, Karl Nauwerck, a *Privatdozent* in Berlin's philosophy faculty, met the same fate for his unwelcome political views, despite the strenuous effort of his colleagues to defend him.[30] Finally, mention should be made of Karl Schwarz, a young erstwhile Hegelian, who was suspended by Eichhorn from the theology faculty of Halle in February 1846 for speaking at a meeting of Protestant Friends in Halle and espousing the right to study the Bible without theological preconceptions.[31] In light of this record, respect for the academic integrity of the university was a sentiment in which the government indulged only when indifferent or uncertain.

The unprecedented enquiry on Jews as academics generated nearly 280 separate opinions, many of considerable length. Largely unpublished, this body of material represents a unique if unwieldy treasure-trove of attitudes on Jews and

---

[28]Ernst Barnikol, *Bruno Bauer. Studien und Materialien*, Assen, Niederlande 1972, pp. 150, 157, 500–502. The entire episode was exhaustively studied by Barnikol, cf. pp. 136 ff.
[29]Bruno Bauer, *Die gute Sache der Freiheit*, Zürich–Winterthur 1842, p. 11. To counter public anger at Bauer's removal and to reaffirm the principle of free enquiry, the ministry of education permitted the Evangelical theological faculty of Bonn to publish all opinions submitted (Barnikol, *op. cit.*, pp. 174–175). See *Gutachten der Evangelisch-theologischen Facultäten*, Berlin 1842.
[30]On Hoffmann, see his autobiography *Mein Leben*, 6 vols., Hannover 1868, IV, pp. 1–35. On Nauwerck, see Lenz, *op. cit.*, II, pt. 2, pp. 77–83.
[31]See the exhaustive monograph by Ernst Barnikol, 'Karl Schwarz (1812–1885) in Halle vor und nach 1848', *Wissenschaftliche Zeitschrift der Martin-Luther-Universität Halle-Wittenberg*, X (1961), pp. 550–558.

Judaism held by the most educated of all Prussian élites.[32] Mostly men of humble origin who were the first to benefit when talent became the key to an academic career, they were now asked whether that same criterion should be extended to the members of another disadvantaged group.[33] Beyond pique and prejudice stood the basic issues of the nature of *Wissenschaft* and the function of the university, topics that could hardly be treated without relating to the political philosophy of the government. Professors must have realised all too well that the survey gave the ministry of education a superb opportunity for scanning their political views. Consequently, it is hard to judge how many must have been cowed into muting or concealing their genuine feelings. Nor was the audience for which they wrote exactly intransitive. The unduly liberal views expressed by most members of Breslau's Evangelical theology faculty evoked a prompt enquiry by Eichhorn. He was quickly reassured that by the time the vote had reached the senate, several men had reconsidered.[34]

Nor was there any mistaking the government's political philosophy, for immediately after the deliberations of the Diet on the Jewry law, Friedrich Julius Stahl, its premier ideological apostle, published a series of essays in the *Evangelische Kirchenzeitung* expounding the conception of the Christian state and its relation to deism and Judaism. Reissued as a book, the text was referred to by several respondents.[35] Against the inroads of atheistic individualism from across the French border, Stahl defended a traditional political culture in which the ethos of biblical Christianity sanctified and guided the existing monarchical and corporate structures. State institutions were to manifest their Christian character, and political rights as opposed to civil rights could be extended only to believers. To call for a chair of Jewish theology was to request the state to disseminate religious error. Jews were thus disqualified from full participation on principle, not prejudice. The farrago that passed for Reform Judaism was neither tenable nor acceptable. Assimilation and conversion were the only road to equality. Till then, the only state service open to them would be as university teachers of indisputably non-Christian subjects. Like Prussian Jewry, the humanities remained unemancipated.[36]

In order to quantify the cumbersome results of Eichhorn's survey it is necessary to translate the original two-fold question, which delicately focused on the statutes of the university, into the unambiguous question whether Jews should be admitted according to the modest terms of the new law; that is, as instructors, associate, and full professors in the fields of medicine, mathematics, natural sci-

---

[32]An instructive and representative selection was published by Kalisch, *op. cit.*, pp. 84–232. However, the bulk remains buried in the files of the Prussian *Kultusministerium* preserved in Merseburg. My discovery of them in July 1977 provided the impetus for this essay.

[33]On the change in the social origins of German scholars in the first half of the nineteenth century, see Franz Schnabel, *Deutsche Geschichte im neunzehnten Jahrhundert*, 4 vols., Freiburg im Breisgau 1933–1937, III, pp. 129–130, and Alexander Busch, *Die Geschichte des Privatdozenten*, Stuttgart 1959, pp. 43–53.

[34]Kalisch, *op. cit.*, pp. 192–193.

[35]For example, Voigt of Königsberg's philosophical faculty. See DZAM, Rep. 76Va, Sekt. 1, Tit. IV, Gen., Nr. 2a, Bd. II, pp. 66–71.

[36]Friedrich Julius Stahl, *Der christliche Staat und sein Verhältniss zu Deismus und Judenthum. Eine durch die Verhandlungen des Vereinigten Landtags hervorgerufene Abhandlung*, Berlin 1847, especially pp. 20–30.

ence, geography and philology?[37] Since the government knew precisely the contents of all university statutes – in fact they had been published just a few years before in an exhaustive collection of statutes and regulations pertaining to the conduct of Prussian universities – the first question was substantively gratuitous.[38] Functionally, however, it gave many a chance to objectify and obscure their personal opposition by interpreting the statutes negatively. As Planck of Greifswald's legal faculty astutely observed, form and content were inseparable:

> ". . . if one finally wants progress in the matter, the form can no longer stand in its way, just as the introduction of a new law cannot be impeded by the existence of an older, contradictory one."[39]

But judgment is called for in yet another way. Quite a few opinions, while espousing noble sentiments, were hedged with so many qualifications and preconditions that they amounted to a negative vote. For example, the senate of Greifswald conceded that its statutes did not explicitly exclude Jews. Nor was it necessary that every teacher be Christian in order to preserve the Christian character of the university. Yet by insisting that for every discipline in which a Jew be appointed, a Christian should be too, thereby guaranteeing students a choice, the senate actually answered the question negatively.[40] In short, my statistical analysis rests inescapably on a subjective though not arbitrary base.

In 1847 Prussia had six universities located in Berlin, Bonn, Breslau, Greifswald, Halle and Königsberg, and a Catholic academy in Münster with but two faculties, altogether a total of twenty-eight faculties. In terms of individual professors, 141 voted in favour of accepting Jews as colleagues, while 102, or 44 per cent of those voting, came out against. Broken down by universities, the individual vote favoured Jews at Berlin (47–15), Bonn (30–9), Greifswald (16–9) and Königsberg (19–9) but not at Breslau (18–21), Halle (11–29) or Münster (0–10). In terms of the collective vote of faculties, eleven favoured admitting Jews, while fourteen, or 50 per cent of all Prussian faculties, rejected the idea. Three faculties split. Broken down by disciplines, the negative vote consisted of all three Catholic theological faculties, three Evangelical, four legal, two medical and two philosophical faculties. Conversely, three Evangelical, one legal, two medical and five philosophical faculties voted to accept Jews. Finally, at the senate level, only Berlin, Bonn and Königsberg stood ready to live with the new law, while the senates of Breslau, Greifswald, Halle and Münster were not.[41]

---

[37]The stages in the emergence of the final text are laid out in the *Allgemeine Zeitung des Judentums*, 1847, pp. 443, 510.
[38]Koch, *op. cit.*, I, *passim*.
[39]Rep. 76Va, Sekt. 1, Tit. IV, Gen., Nr. 2a, Bd. I, pp. 43–44. Planck was even ready to open the legal faculty to Jewish scholars, for if the study of law required religious affinity, how could Christian savants presume to understand Roman law? (pp. 40–43).
[40]Kalisch, *op. cit.*, pp. 154–158.
[41]This statistical summary is based on the *Gutachten* published by Kalisch, pp. 84–232 as well as those preserved in the following files in Merseburg: Rep. 76Va, Sekt. 1, Tit., IV, Gen., Nr. 2, Bd. I & II and Rep. 76Va, Sekt. 1, Tit. IV, Gen., Nr. 2a, Bd. I & II. Henceforth, when referring to this material, I will give only the number, volume and page. Kalisch attempted no statistical analysis and erred in the case of Halle, which he thought refused to submit any *Gutachten*. Contemporary Jewish newspapers carried brief and sporadic, but generally accurate reports of the voting in different faculties and universities. (See *Die Allgemeine Zeitung des Judentums*, 1847, pp. 757, 759; and

The outcome can hardly be called a resounding vote of approval for the government's modest proposal, or for that matter for the principle of unfettered objective scholarship. With legal faculties tending to vote against and philosophical faculties in favour, a conflicted professoriate emerged even more conservative than the government. The unqualified stance of Cruse, of Königsberg's medical faculty, found only muted resonance among his colleagues.

> "In no religion, no country, no estate are outstanding minds so numerous as to make it possible to value faith, nationality, and estate when it comes to advancing scholarship and to disseminating it for the good of mankind."[42]

Of course, many who favoured the government's move were spared the need to expound their personal views. Their assignment was over when they took the position that the statutes of their university posed no obstacle.

In terms of a content analysis, it is possible to identify a medley of arguments brought forth in favour. First, the presence of a few Jews will not endanger the Christian character of the university.[43] Second, the step will serve to reduce the differences dividing a heterogeneous population.[44] Third, the history of Jewish suffering warrants compassion and Christian amends.[45] Fourth, the degree of assimilation generated by partial emancipation confirms the belief that Jewish defects were externally induced.[46] Fifth, the opportunity will help divert Jews from business.[47] Sixth, Jews have the talent to contribute; witness their achievements in Spain and the accomplishments of Spinoza and Mendelssohn.[48] Seventh, the law will reduce the career frustrations which drive bright young

---

1848, pp. 27, 71, 94.) Lenz's slanted discussion of the entire episode is restricted to Berlin. (*Op. cit.*, II, pt. 2, pp. 168–172.)

[42] Kalisch, *op. cit.*, p. 199.

[43] *Ibid.*, pp. 105–106 (Stahl), 188 (Berlin, phil. fac.). The view of Christian Julius Braniss, a Hegelian philosopher at Breslau and the teacher of Heinrich Graetz and other Jewish students preparing for the rabbinate, deserves special attention. He firmly advocated allowing Jews to teach at Breslau precisely because of his conviction that *Wissenschaft* was an inherently Christian mode of intellectual creativity. No Jew, no matter how distant from the dogmas of a church, could engage in *Wissenschaft* without being transformed by its essentially Christian spirit. (Nr. 2a, Bd. I, p. 275.) On Braniss's possible influence on Graetz, see Hans Liebeschütz, *Das Judentum im deutschen Geschichtsbild von Hegel bis Max Weber*, Tübingen 1967 (Schriftenreihe wissenschaftlicher Abhandlungen des Leo Baeck Instituts 17), pp. 139–140.

[44] Kalisch, *op. cit.*, p. 188 (Berlin, phil. fac.); Nr. 2, Bd. I, pp. 196–197 (Königsberg Evang. fac.).

[45] Kalisch, *op. cit.*, pp. 183–184; Nr. 2a, Bd. I, pp. 335–336 and Bd. II, pp. 80–81.

[46] Nr. 2a, Bd. II, pp. 80–81.

[47] Nr. 2a, Bd. II, pp. 129–130 (Christian A. Brandis).

[48] Nr. 2a, Bd. I, p. 226 (Heinrich Middeldorpf of Breslau's Evang. fac. See his equally liberal defence of Bruno Bauer in *Gutachten*, pp. 72–77). Also Bd. II, pp. 123–124 (Georg W. Freytag). The favourable opinion of Freytag, the renowned Arabist and teacher of Abraham Geiger, Salomon Munk, Jacob Bernays and other Jewish students, graphically illustrates the complexity of separating *Wissenschaft* from theology in an institution which served both of these jealous masters. While scholarship could only applaud the advantages to be gained from having Jews teach Hebrew, Freytag was quick to point out that Christian interests precluded any possibility of allowing them to explicate texts drawn from the Old Testament. Indeed, there was widespread apprehension at the thought of admitting Jews generally into *"sprachwissenschaftliche Lehrfächer"*, because of the perceived interrelatedness of philology, exegesis and *"Gesinnung"*. (Nr. 2a, Bd. I, p. 119.)

Jews to the left.⁴⁹ Eighth, no one should be disadvantaged because of his religion.⁵⁰ And finally, *Wissenschaft* itself must be emancipated from religion.⁵¹ What did unite many government supporters with their colleagues on the other side, however, was a robust antipathy for Jews and Judaism and a conviction that their mutual disappearance must be the ultimate consequence of emancipation.⁵²

The arguments against implementation were usually delivered with more passion and at greater length. They are noteworthy not for their originality but for their advocates.⁵³ The evidence accords with the unbroken history of antisemitism in modern Germany: education had little impact on prejudice. To begin with, the policy of piecemeal emancipation itself provided a convenient dodge. Legal faculties refused to countenance Jews teaching in their ranks as long as they were denied access to state service in general and the judiciary in particular. ⁵⁴ Conversely, Protestant universities like Halle, whose statutes required that professors adhere to the Augsburg Confession, preferred to delay action until the effect of the new law on other universities became apparent.⁵⁵ Also widespread was the revulsion aroused by the perception of Jews as a hermetically insulated, tenaciously egoistic and unalterably alien nation.⁵⁶ This spectre drove some despondent critics to advocate complete emancipation as the only remedy.⁵⁷

Whatever Jews did opened them to attack. The orthodox were abused for subservience to the Talmud with its anti-Christian animus, degenerate morality and obsessive ritualism.⁵⁸ The enlightened were deemed as dangerous atheists, men without character who dominated the press, polemicised against Christianity and led the destructive movements of the day.⁵⁹

Throughout these sundry objections against appointing Jews reverberated the conception of the university as a *corpus ecclesiasticum* whose ethical and scholarly message could be mediated only in a Christian atmosphere. Learning took place

---

⁴⁹Kalisch, *op. cit.*, p. 225; Nr. 2, Bd. I, pp. 216–217.
⁵⁰Nr. 2a, Bd. II, p. 90.
⁵¹Kalisch, *op. cit.*, pp. 131, 198–199; Nr. 2a, Bd. I, p. 115 and Bd. II, p. 137.
⁵²Kalisch, *op. cit.*, pp. 99–100; Nr. 2, Bd. I, pp. 196–197, 307; Nr. 2a, Bd. I, pp. 335–347 and Bd. II, pp. 86, 91, 160. The key word regarding ultimate expectations was "*Verschmelzung*".
⁵³The same and similar arguments abound in Eleonore Sterling, *Judenhass. Die Anfänge des politischen Antisemitismus in Deutschland (1815–1850)*, Frankfurt a. Main 1969.
⁵⁴Nr. 2, Bd. I, pp. 109–111, 201–202; Nr. 2a, Bd. I, p. 265; Kalisch, *op. cit.*, p. 91.
⁵⁵Nr. 2, Bd. I, pp. 287, 319; Nr. 2a, Bd. I, p. 124.
⁵⁶The opinion of Gaupp of Breslau's legal faculty was typical.
"Die Juden erscheinen aber nun vor allen Dingen als ein besonderes, durch ein Jahrhunderte lang geschlossenes Connubium nur in sich selbst fortgepflantztes Volk; ein Stückchen Orient was die Vorsehung in alle Länder des Occidents gestreut hat, was aber noch immer den Typus des Orients bewahrt." (Nr. 2a, Bd. I, p. 327.)
His colleague Purkinje of the medical faculty regarded the Jews as a race: "In anthropologischer Hinsicht betrachte ich die Juden als eine selbständige Race . . ." (Kalisch, *op. cit.*, p. 168.) See also Nr. 2a, Bd. II, pp. 36, 160.
⁵⁷Nr. 2a, Bd. I, p. 265.
⁵⁸Nr. 2, Bd. I, pp. 232–234 (Catholic fac. of Bonn), 281; Nr. 2a, Bd. II, pp. 62–71.
⁵⁹Kalisch, *op. cit.*, pp. 88 (Neander), 109; Nr. 2, Bd. I, p. 233; Nr. 2a, Bd. I, pp. 35–36, 317–320; Nr. 2a, Bd. II, pp. 62–71, 86.

only when student and teacher shared the same religion, and the pursuit of knowledge required a Christian disposition.[60]

Yet the Prussian university was less Christian than Protestant, for Catholics were almost as disadvantaged as Jews. Of the seven Catholic universities (Trier, Bonn, Köln, Münster, Paderborn, Erfurt and Breslau) operating at the end of the eighteenth century on land now belonging to Prussia, only a truncated Münster with faculties of theology and philosophy remained a Catholic institution.[61] Outside the Catholic theological faculties, Bonn and Breslau were hardly inter-denominational. In 1842 the philosophy faculty at Bonn had a staff of nineteen full professors; exactly one was a Catholic. History, philosophy, Oriental languages and philology were taught exclusively by Protestants.[62] At Berlin, Franz Bopp, who pioneered the comparative study of Sanskrit, was one of the few Catholic professors.[63] From Königsberg and Halle, Catholics were excluded by statute and from Greifswald until the 1840s by practice.[64] Shortly before Eichhorn's poll of the professoriate, the senate of Königsberg had dismissed a *Privatdozent* for joining the ranks of the German Catholic movement.[65]

This pervasive exclusion of Catholics complicated the Jewish issue in two ways. Some professors at Halle and Königsberg were horrified by the idea of

---

[60]The psychological case was put succinctly by Wilhelm Esser, a professor of philosophy and classical philology at Münster.
"Der Mensch lernt am besten von solchen Menschen, zu denen er sich hingezogen fühlt, bezüglich am besten von solchen, die in Ansehung der wichtigsten und heiligsten Dinge mit ihm dieselben Ueberzeugungen theilen." (Nr. 2a, Bd. I, p. 199.)
Julius A. S. Wegscheider, Halle's most famous rationalist theologian, did advocate a change in the statutes of his university despite grave reservations: an observant Jew could never carry out the obligations of full membership in a Christian academic body while an irreligious Jew would exert a deleterious influence on students (Nr. 2, Bd. I, p. 281).
His conservative colleague, Friedrich A. G. Tholuck, whose vote was negative, felt that no Jew, whatever his ilk, could teach history or philosophy.
"Kann ein Jude, ohne sein Judenthum aufzugeben, mit Hegel das Christenthum für den Wendepunkt der Weltgeschichte, mit Schiller für die grösste welthistorische Begebenheit erklären? Und auch diejenigen, welche ihren religiösen Grundsätzen nach verpflichtet sind, das Christenthum nur als eine Verirrung der Menschheit zu betrachten, sollten von einem christlichen Staate als Lehrer der Geschichte und Philosophie angestellt werden können?" (Nr. 2, Bd. I, p. 283.)
Georg F. Pohl, a professor of physics at Breslau, was equally adamant about their inability to teach the natural sciences properly.
"Es wird hier hinreichend sein, zu bemerken, dass Natur und Geschichte, wie Körper und Seele, so innig miteinander verbunden sind, dass wer die Geschichte nicht versteht, noch weniger dahin zu gelangen vermag, die Natur würdig zu begreifen und zu deuten ... Eine jüdische Lebensanschauung ist eines solchen zum wirklichen Fortschritt erforderlichen Naturverständnisses noch weniger als des Verständnisses der Geschichte mächtig; sie löst ohne zu erlösen, sie zerstreut statt zu sammeln, sie führt statt zur Einigung, zum Zerwürfniss und Verfall, und die höheren christlichen Lehranstalten, welche die Stimme dieser Anschauung unter sich aufnehmen und walten lassen, werden, je weniger sie es vielleicht ahnen um so entschiedener die Blüthe ihrer Wirksamkeit dem Todeshauche des inneren Unterganges opfern." (Nr. 2a, Bd. I, pp. 271–272.)
See also Nr. 2a, Bd. I, pp. 18, 280–282, 287–288 and Kalisch, *op. cit.*, pp. 87–88.
[61]Nr. 2a, Bd. I, p. 247.
[62]Friedrich von Bezold, *Geschichte der Rheinischen Friedrich-Wilhelms-Universität*, Bonn 1920, p. 351.
[63]Lenz, *op. cit.*, II, pt. 1, pp. 281–282.
[64]Several professors commented on the growth in the number of Catholic academics at Greifswald under Eichhorn's régime. See Nr. 2a, Bd. I, pp. 35–36, 118.
[65]His name was Hiabowski. See Nr. 2a, Bd. II, p. 13.

opening their ranks to Jews while still excluding Catholics and insisted that both be admitted simultaneously.[66] But that meant entangling the Jewish proposal in a web of other animosities. On the other hand, Catholic professors, in addition to giving vivid expression to a traditional abhorrence of Judaism, feared that Jewish advances would come at their expense. One informed Catholic theologian at Breslau claimed that the ratio of Protestant to Catholic academics in Prussia was 10:1, whereas the ratio in the population stood at 3:2. Thus if the exclusivist statutes of other universities were allowed to stand, Jews would be appointed only at the inter-denominational schools, thereby eroding the Catholic position still further. The total number of Catholic *Privatdozenten* at Prussia's six universities did not exceed the number at Münster or Trier at the turn of the century.[67]

But Protestant professors feared the spectre of Jewish competition no less than their Catholic colleagues. Certain code words recurred throughout the opinions. The moral indictment of Jewish egotism, arrogance, vanity, drive, industry and pushiness masked economic anxiety.[68] In particular, the large Jewish population in Breslau and Silesia unnerved many academics at the provincial university there.[69] In 1840 the philosophy faculty had reinstituted a Christian oath prior

---

[66] For example, Gebser, Sieffert and Lehnerdt of the Evangelical theological faculty at Königsberg (Nr. 2a, Bd. II, pp. 1–17) and De Witte, Henke and Wunderlich of Halle's legal faculty (Nr. 2, Bd. I, pp. 288–291). The following declaration by Sieffert is representative:
"Übrigens versteht es sich von selbst, dass bei einer etwaigen Aufhebung oder Modifizirung des Par. 105 unserer Statuten diese Modifizirung nicht etwa bloss zu Gunsten der Juden geschehen kann, sondern dann so gefasst werden muss, dass auch katholischen Dozenten zu den Stellen, welche nicht ihrer wesentlichen Natur und Bestimmung nach die evangelische Confession voraussetzen, der Zutritt offen sein muss, indem es eine schmähliche Herabwürdigung des einen Theils der christlichen Kirche durch den andern wäre, die dem Christenthum überhaupt beharrlich widerstrebenden Elemente unserer Staatsgesellschaft uns für verwandter und befreundeter zu erachten als die im Wesentlichen auf derselben christlichen Grundlage stehenden." (Nr. 2a, Bd. II, p. 11.)

[67] This instructive *Gutachten* by Franz Karl Movers, professor of Old Testament exegesis, presented a cogent case against Prussian partiality. The fact that not a single Catholic university had survived Prussian expansion epitomised the fate of Catholicism in the Prussian state. See Nr. 2a, Bd. I, pp. 247–248. Dieters of the legal faculty at Bonn claimed that young Catholics were avoiding an academic career for lack of opportunity. (Nr. 2a, Bd. II, pp. 105–106.) The scanty information available on the systematic exclusion of Catholics from an academic career in Prussia prior to 1870 was collected by Wilhelm Lossen, *Der Anteil der Katholiken am akademischen Lehramte in Preussen*, Köln 1901, pp. 4–11, 16–27, 162–164.

[68] One typical example of this rhetoric should suffice. Gerlach of Halle's philosophical faculty reluctantly voted to implement the new law, but he feared the impact on the university of a style peculiar to Jews.
"... sondern es wäre auch zu befürchten, dass unsere Universitäten bei der bekannten Industrie des jüdischen Volks und bei der kecken Zudringlichkeit und Eitelkeit, die sich schon jetzt nicht selten an jungen jüdischen Literaten bemerklich macht, in kurzer Zeit von einem Geiste würden durchdrungen werden, der je rein jüdischer er ist, um so mehr zu dem christlichen in Antipathie steht." (Nr. 2, Bd. I, p. 300.)

[69] Hans K. L. Barkow of Breslau was so firmly opposed to admitting Jews to his medical faculty that he wrote twice on the matter. As the following choice passage makes clear, it was Jewish style backed by Jewish power which frightened him.
"Ich halte die Ansicht nur zu begründet, dass die Fakultät jüdisch werden wird, wenn die Schranken gelockert werden sollten, so lange der jetzige Geist unter den Juden fortdauert, und ich kann für ihre Zulassung nicht stimmen, so lange unausstehliche Arroganz und Eitelkeit, und eine Betriebsamkeit, welche zur Erreichung ihres vorgesteckten Ziels keine humane Rücksicht

to awarding the doctorate in order to reduce its Jewish enrolment.[70] In the medical faculty Jews constituted some 60 per cent of the student population and Jews dominated the medical profession in Breslau.[71] In his statement the rector of the university, who personally favoured implementing the provisions of the Jewry law, summarised the concern which prompted the majority of his men to vote against the government. The talent, wealth and communal backing which Jewish academics enjoyed would quickly lead to a disruption of the harmony which prevailed in the faculties of medicine and philosophy.[72] It is quite clear that the response from Breslau betrayed the mentality of a guild. In less than half a century the opponents of emancipation had been forced by the pace of Jewish assimilation to switch their arguments from inferiority to superiority.

In sum, the survey of 1847 revealed the Prussian professoriate to be as ambivalent about Jewish emancipation as the rest of Prussian society. The mixed results suggest no widespread challenge to the cautious and equivocal approach set down by the government, with a sizeable preference for even greater caution. Axiomatic to the entire discussion were the convictions that the university was a Christian institution and *Wissenschaft* a Christian enterprise. Jewish participation was by sufferance, not principle.

Events overtook the cumbersome review process even before the last of the opinions was submitted. By the time the rector and senate of Bonn convened on 4th April 1848 to formulate their views, Berlin was host to its first revolution, the King had withdrawn to Potsdam, recalled the United Diet and was about to issue some liberal guidelines for a future constitution. Paragraph five of the proclamation of 6th April promised that political rights would no longer be restricted by religious considerations.[73] The Gordian knot had been cut. Not only were

---

und keine Pietät kennt, bei ihnen vorwaltend ist, weil ich die Überzeugung habe, dass die Fakultät es nicht mit einzelnen Persönlichkeiten, sondern mit der Judenschaft zu thun haben wird." (Kalisch, *op. cit.*, p. 186.)

[70]Kalisch, *op. cit.*, pp. 10–21.

[71]*Ibid.*, pp. 163, 176.

[72]Nr. 2, Bd. I, p. 170. The historian Heinrich Leo spoke at length of the unscrupulous style of Eduard Gans to underscore the dangers inherent in opening the academic market place to Jews. An erstwhile Hegelian, bitter critic of Ranke and author of a history of the Jews, Leo had been at Berlin until 1827, when he secured a post in Halle. Though typical, his envious testimony betrays deep personal wounds.

". . . weil ein längeres freundliches Verhältniss zu dem verstorbenen Prof. Gans in Berlin mir einen deutlichen Einblick gewährt hat in die Mittel, deren ein Mann jüdischer Art, sobald er nicht wirklich im innersten Sinne sich mit christlichen und deutschen Empfindungen identificirt hat, fähig ist, um Anderen mit denen er concurrirt, das Feld zu verderben. Wie dieser es gegen Freunde ganz offen aussprach, dass er *à tout prix* Zuhörer neben Herrn von Savigny haben müsse, und er gegen seine Freunde gar kein Hehl hatte, dass er sowohl was den Geldpunkt betreffe es jedem annehmlicher zu machen suche bei ihm als bei einem Anderen zu hören, – als was das wissenschaftliche Object anbetraf, es geradehin aussprach, dass Zuhörer durch spannenden unterhaltenden Vortrag herbei gezogen werden müssten selbst wenn der Gegenstand des Vortrags dabei etwas zu kurz komme – so würden es mehr oder weniger alle jüdischen Docenten *vis à vis* ihrer christlichen Concurrenten machen . . . Ich sehe in Folge der Zulassung von Juden allmälig eine völlige Degeneration der jetzigen academischen Stellungen kommen."

(*Ibid.*, p. 309. On Leo, see Lenz, *op. cit.*, II, pt. 1, pp. 277–279. On Gans's skill as a lecturer, *ibid.*, p. 495.)

[73]Freund, *op. cit.*, II, p. 520.

universities no longer closed to Jewish academics, the emancipation struggle itself seemed over. In July the ministry of education circulated a rescript to the effect that Jews henceforth were eligible for all academic posts except those which necessitated a Christian occupant.[74]

The appointment of three Jews as instructors during the same period of time seemed to confirm that law indeed governed reality. In October 1847, Berlin's medical faculty welcomed Robert Remak, a scientific polymath, who had been turned down four years earlier. In 1848 Jacob Bernays, a classical philologist, habilitated at Bonn and Joseph Saalschütz, a rabbi and Orientalist, did likewise at Königsberg, both in the faculty of philosophy.[75]

Yet once the régime had weathered the revolution, law and reality were quickly forced apart. In 1850 the legal faculties of Breslau and Berlin reiterated the long-standing objections to awarding a doctorate in jurisprudence to a Jew. The degree certified not only academic mastery of both civil and church law, but also moral commitment and spiritual kinship. To confer the doctorate on Jews would be to de-christianise the discipline. Civil servants represented merely the external dignity of the state, but the doctor of law embodied the inner dignity of the secular and religious legal systems.[76]

An equally specious distinction was made by the ministerial cabinet at its meeting of 9th September 1851. It acknowledged that the royal proclamation of 6th April 1848 assured Jews of the opportunity to prepare themselves adequately for state service. But having demonstrated competence by passing a state examination gave them no right to any specific state job. The decision to appoint or reject an applicant lay entirely within the jurisdiction of the department chief, who of course was to assess qualifications irrespective of religion. That logical legerdemain would be invoked by Prussian officials well into the twentieth century in order to restrict the number of Jews entering state service to a trickle.[77]

[74]Kalisch, *op. cit.*, p. 240.
[75]*Der Orient*, 1847, p. 357; Lenz, *op. cit.*, II, pt. 2, pp. 166–168; Busch, *op. cit.*, pp. 153–154; Richarz, *op. cit.*, pp. 210–212. Related developments in Austria allow for an instructive comparison with Prussia. On 31st March 1848 the Austrian government issued an edict that henceforth no qualified person would be denied a university post because of religion. By September 1849 Wolfgang Wessely, probably the first Jew to earn a doctorate from the Catholic University of Prague, received an appointment as its associate professor of Hebrew language and literature with a salary of 600 florin. Two years later he received yet a second appointment to the university's legal faculty as an associate professor of law. By 1861 he reached the rank of full professor. In December 1849 Saul Isaak Kaempf, the *Prediger* of Prague's reform synagogue, became a *Privatdozent* at the university in ancient Hebrew and Oriental languages. (Guido Kisch, *Die Prager Universität und die Juden 1348–1848*, Mährisch-Ostrau 1935, pp. 60–68.) The contrast with Prussia is striking. Whereas the philosophical faculty of Berlin turned down Zunz's well-known appeal of 25th July 1848 to create a professorship of Jewish history and literature, its Catholic counterpart in Prague saw fit to invite two men to cover the field. (Geiger, *op. cit.*, pp. 334–347.)
[76]Nr. 2, Bd. II, p. 9 ff.
[77]Nr. 2, Bd. II. The minutes read:
". . . dass aber die Erlangung dieser Qualification überhaupt noch kein Recht auf die Verleihung eines bestimmten Staatsamtes begründe, dass es vielmehr der Beurtheilung des betreffenden Departements Chefs bei Bewerbungen um ein bestimmtes Amt vorbehalten bleiben müsse, ob der Bewerber, ganze abgesehen von seinem religiösen Bekenntnisse, sich seiner Persönlichkeit und seinen Fähigkeiten nach für dieses Amt eigne."
The policy was publicly restated in the Prussian Chamber of Deputies by the minister of justice in 1901. (See my *Jewish Reactions to German Anti-Semitism, 1870–1914*, New York–London 1972, p. 151.)

As for academic employment, the fate of Jacob Bernays provides a poignant dénouement. The son of the orthodox if modern rabbi of Hamburg, Bernays was acknowledged to be among the most promising young classicists in all Germany. Immediately after having earned his doctorate at Bonn in 1848, he was invited by the faculty of philosophy to become an instructor, counter to its own regulations which required at least a two-year interval. During the next four years the faculty interceded annually with the government on his behalf for a special subvention to mitigate his poverty. The quality of his scholarship so impressed England's leading classicist that Oxford University invited him to prepare a new edition of Lucretius with a Latin commentary. By 1852 Bernays's meteoric career forced an inescapable test of the government's intention to abide by the provisions of the Jewry law of 1847 and the principles of 1848, though the reactionary climate was hardly conducive to a favourable outcome.

Bernays's letters of recommendation for promotion to the rank of associate professor were worthy of his impeccable credentials. One came from the King's long-time friend and ambassador to England, Freiherr Christian K. G. von Bunsen, who had been Bernays's host in London in 1851, and the other from Christian A. Brandis, his teacher and colleague at Bonn. Both men knew Bernays intimately and praised his piety and character as well as his scholarship. They stressed his religious orthodoxy, his respect for and knowledge of Christianity, his abhorrence of shallow rationalism and his political conservatism.[78]

Unable to avoid a decision, the King turned in April 1852 to his minister of education, Karl Otto von Raumer, for counsel. By the end of June, Raumer obliged with a reasoned negative response. To his credit, he averred and recounted Bernays's ample qualifications. His objections rested on other grounds. With three full and two associate professors, the field of classical philology at Bonn was already crowded. More fundamental, however, Raumer argued for the Christian character of the Prussian university. If not explicitly expressed in the university's statutes, the relationship was always spelled out in its ancient documents of incorporation, and the mission of every university as a training ground for civil servants for church and state certainly implied it. The primary function of the classical philologist was to train the teachers of Prussia's Gymnasia. On both levels of education classical literature had to be Christianised by teaching it in such a way as not to undermine the Christian value system and thought patterns of the young. To assign that responsibility to a Jew was a dereliction of duty.[79] Denied promotion, Bernays went off reluctantly to Breslau

---

[78]Copies of the letters of recommendation are in Nr. 2, Bd. II, pp. 29–30. The biographical information is drawn primarily from these letters and the subsequent opinion of von Raumer. See also Hans I. Bach, *Jacob Bernays. Ein Beitrag zur Emanzipationsgeschichte der Juden und zur Geschichte des deutschen Geistes im neunzehnten Jahrhundert*, Tübingen 1974 (Schriftenreihe wissenschaftlicher Abhandlungen des Leo Baeck Instituts 30), pp. 108–117. Senate requests of the government for financial assistance for Bernays may be found in DZAM, Rep. 76Va, Sekt. 3, Tit. IV, Nr. 45, Bd. II, pp. 16, 119, 180.

[79]DZAM, Rep. 76Va, Sekt. 3, Tit. IV, Nr. 45, Bd. II, pp. 51–54. Since this important memorandum was unknown to Bach, it is worthwhile quoting the crucial passage in the original.

"Die Hauptaufgabe eines Professors der alten Sprachen besteht in Ausbildung der Philologen und Theologen, welche dereinst als Lehrer an unseren Gymnasien wirken sollen; der Unterricht in den alten Sprachen ist die Hauptbasis der Gymnasial-Bildung und wird es, das hoffe ich, bleiben, trotz der Angriffe, die er von realistisch-lichtfreundlicher wie von katholischer Seite mit

to join the faculty of Zacharias Frankel's recently-opened rabbinical seminary, a tiny haven for a handful of frustrated Jewish academics.[80]

With Raumer's policy statement we have come full circle. Though major consumers of *Wissenschaft*, Jews were denied the chance to become its producers and purveyors. Decades later, when academic employment did become available on a restricted basis, Jews were still systematically excluded throughout Germany from the rank of full professor and from the fields of law, literature, history, philosophy, classics and Oriental studies.[81] The university as the apex of the educational system could not transcend its pervasive confessional character, and as a state institution it was often shackled by governments intent on exploiting religion to bolster their authority. In consequence, German governments repeatedly promised Jews in law what they would not deliver in practice and duplicity became normative. The duplicity which eventually facilitated the Nazi execution of the "Final Solution" had ample precedent in the history of the German bureaucracy's treatment of Jews. More basic, the continued centrality of religion in public life proved a potent factor in subverting emancipation and preserving the problematic status of Jews.

---

gleicher Stärke zu erdulden hat. Von höchster Bedeutung ist es aber, dass der Unterricht der alten Sprachen auf Universitäten wie auf Gymnasien in einer Weise stattfinde, welche der klassischen Bildung in dem Erziehungsgange der Jugend die rechte Stellung sichert, nicht als Gegensatz christlicher Gesinnung und Denkart sondern als ein wesentliches Moment ihrer Kräftigung. Bei aller Anerkennung, welche dem persönlichen Charakter eines Dozenten jüdischer Konfession zu zollen sein mag, kann ich nicht annehmen, dass er jenen Anforderungen zu entsprechen im Stande sey? Ich würde es vielmehr für höchst bedenklich erachten, durch Anstellung eines jüdischen Professors der alten Sprachen auf viele Jahre hin die Ausbildung von Gymnasiallehrern in einer Provinz in eine Hand zu legen, welche sonstiger Vorzüge ungeachtet, doch ausser Stande ist, für die Ausbildung christlicher Lehrer an christlichen Gymnasien die nöthigen Garantien zu geben." (pp. 53-54.)

[80]Bach, *op. cit.*, pp. 117-119.

[81]See the important statistics collected by Bernhard Breslauer, *Die Zurücksetzung der Juden an den Universitäten Deutschlands*, Berlin 1911, and the recent essay by David L. Preston, 'The German Jews in Secular Education, University Teaching, and Science: A Preliminary Inquiry', *Jewish Social Studies*, XXXVIII (1976), pp. 99-116. Friedrich Paulsen, the noted German authority on higher education at the end of the century, was distressed by "the strong preponderance of Jews at the universities". (*The German Universities*, New York 1906, pp. 158-159.) In his autobiography Paulsen related that the philosophy faculty of Berlin diverted him from philosophy into education with an enticing offer as associate professor to forestall the unwelcome appointment of Moritz Lazarus to the field as full professor. (*An Autobiography*, New York 1938, p. 253.)

Social Class and Secularisation in Imperial Germany

The Working Classes

BY VERNON LIDTKE

The purpose of this paper is to explore the dynamics and the variations of secularisation among the working classes in Imperial Germany. The goal is far more difficult to attain than the simplicity of the statement suggests. The first hurdle is the term "secularisation" itself. It is loaded with ambiguities, ideological connotations and far-reaching social implications. Since the middle of the seventeenth century, when it was first used to refer specifically to the appropriation of ecclesiastical property by secular political authorities, its meaning has broadened dramatically. One can no longer assume that any consensus exists on how the term is to be defined.[1] Moreover, how people define secularisation is related directly to what they understand by religion and on this issue there is an equally broad, if not broader spectrum of learned opinion.[2] These definitional problems could preoccupy us for a long time, as they have others, but I want to move on to the historical substance, and therefore offer two definitions to guide this exploration. By secularisation I mean a two-fold process whereby religious thinking, practice

---

[1] The original meaning of secularisation has little relevance today. It does not appear in the list of six definitions given by Larry Shiner, 'The Concept of Secularization in Empirical Research', *Journal for the Scientific Study of Religion*, VI, No. 2 (Autumn 1967), pp. 207-220. Some definitions of secularisation are so broad that they identify it with social change generally, as in Bernard Eugene Meland, *The Secularization of Modern Cultures*, New York 1966, p. 3. The social implications of "secularisation" still arouse considerable antagonism in some. One opponent of the term has argued that it is "less a scientific concept than a tool of counter-religious ideologies". David Martin, 'Toward Eliminating the Concept of Secularization', in Julius Gould (ed.), *Penquin Survey of the Social Sciences 1965*, Baltimore 1965, pp. 169-182. On the other hand, secularisation in modern culture, especially in the United States, has gone so far that certain scholars have concluded that some theology has lost its essential religious substance, that theology itself has been secularised. See Peter Berger, 'A Sociological View of the Secularization of Theology', *Journal for the Scientific Study of Religion*, VI, No. 1 (1967). Directions in research on secularisation is the topic of one entire issue of *Social Compass*, XX, No. 4 (1973). Cf. also Eric S. Waterhouse, 'Secularism', *Encyclopaedia of Religion and Ethics*, Edinburgh 1920, XI, pp. 347-350; and 'Säkularisation', *Die Religion in Geschichte und Gegenwart*, Tübingen 1913, V, cols. 167-173.

[2] Cf. Ernest Krausz, 'Religion and Secularization. A Matter of Definition', *Social Compass*, XVIII, No. 2 (1971), pp. 203-212, who offers a critical evaluation of definitions of both concepts. Some definitions and usages tend to dissolve the traditional distinction between what is religious and what is secular as, for example, in the notion of "secular religion". Concepts such as "political religion" and "civil religion" carry essentially the same meaning as "secular religion" – without, to be sure, the special ironic twist – and are more precise for analytical purposes. See Robert Bellah's explication of "civil religion" as he applies it to the United States, in 'Civil Religion in America', *Daedalus*, vol. 96, No. 1 (Winter 1967), pp. 1-21, and in *The Broken Covenant. American Civil Religion in Time of Trial*, New York 1975.

and institutions lose social and personal significance and a new vocabulary is acquired which provides a medium for asking and answering questions about the meaning of life.[3] By religion I mean a system of values or beliefs that includes concepts of the supernatural and of the sacred.[4]

Secularisation among the lower classes in Imperial Germany shared many of the dynamics and qualities that pertained to other social groups, but it also displayed unique dimensions. Among all social groups, secularisation came about as part of long-range cultural, social, economic and political developments that converged in Germany with special force after the middle of the nineteenth century. The intellectual challenge to religious orthodoxies launched under the aegis of the Enlightenment, furthered by such currents as the Biblical criticism of the early nineteenth century, received a powerful new thrust from Darwinian biology and its philosophical and social interpreters who used it to lash out at religion in the name of science. The defensive posture of many Christians, especially Pius IX's frantic assault on all modernism, only helped to persuade the antagonists that they had the upper hand.[5] By mid-century, intellectual currents that advanced secularism were far more pervasive among Germany's *Bildungsbürgertum* than among its handicraftsmen, urban workers and rural labourers. Concomitantly, however, the consequences of industrialisation, urbanisation and national unification converged with intellectual and cultural trends to bring about a multi-dimensional and intensified challenge to institutional religion. To some degree, all aspects of the process affected the lower classes. But the socioeconomic dimension in particular affected workers and became a more important secularising dynamic for them than the purely intellectual or political factors.[6]

Secularisation developed gradually and unevenly among the German working classes. Workers did not move uniformly as a unit away from religious practices and belief. Differences in confessional backgrounds, clerical personalities and practices in individual parishes, educational opportunities, occupational training (or lack of it), regional economic development, class relationships, the aggressiveness of local Social Democratic organisations and still other variables could

---

[3]This combines a slight modification of the definition used by Bryan Wilson, *Religion in Secular Society*, London 1966, p. xiv, with ideas drawn from Alasdair MacIntyre, *Secularization and Moral Change*, London 1967, pp. 30–31.

[4]I am using a substantive rather than a functional definition because it facilitates making distinctions that are appropriate to the historical context of Imperial Germany. A helpful discussion of substantive and functional definitions of religion is in Karel Dobbelaere and Jan Lauwers, 'Definition of Religion – a Sociological Critique', *Social Compass*, XX, No. 4 (1973), pp. 535–551.

[5]Cf. Owen Chadwick, *The Secularization of the European Mind in the Nineteenth Century*, Cambridge 1975; Theodor Steinbüchel, *Zerfall des christlichen Ethos im XIX. Jahrhundert*, Frankfurt a. Main 1951; and Alfred Armach-Müller, *Das Jahrhundert ohne Gott*, Stuttgart 1959.

[6]Some scholars have made a one-to-one casual connection between industrialisation and secularisation. "When a factory is built in a region of strong religious practice," Boulard writes of conditions in France, "it introduces a tendency to religious indifference." F. Boulard, *An Introduction to Religious Society*, London 1960, p. 16. That the process is more complicated is stressed by René Rémond, 'Die Entchristlichung. Gegenwärtiger Stand der Frage und der Arbeiten in Französischer Sprache', *Concilium. Internationale Zeitschrift für Theologie*, I, No. 7 (August/September 1965), pp. 611–615, and is also shown by the detailed analysis of François-André Isambert, *Christianisme et classe ouvrière*, Paris 1961.

influence the quality and the degree of secularisation among workers as well as other social groups.[7] Fluctuating combinations of these variables affected workers at different times, explaining the fact that one can find a wide spectrum of opinion, from those who remained devoutly religious at one end, to the highly secularised on the other. The great mass of workers were not at either extreme of the spectrum, but reflected varying mixtures of religiosity and secularity. Because workers were frequently bunched together in growing industrial centres and because they seemed to abandon outward religious practice more readily than people from other social classes, their alienation from institutionalised religion was easily noticed and caused consternation among clergymen already by the middle of the nineteenth century.[8] The decline in outward religious practice, such as church attendance, led to the conclusion that Christianity had lost its spiritual influence with a large percentage of German workers. The impression seemed correct, but it was not easy to demonstrate because just as regular religious practice on the part of respectable burghers or tradition-bound aristocrats may have camouflaged deep-seated scepticism and intellectual secularism, so genuine personal religiosity in shabbily-clad workers could go undetected when they failed to manifest their sentiments through participation in formal religious practices.[9] Despite this obvious pitfall, the outward signs must be examined as a first step in trying to establish the extent and quality of secularisation among German workers.

A few outward signs would suggest that a nearly-universal religiosity prevailed in Imperial Germany. Church membership is an example. As late as the 1860s and 1870s, most German states legally bound their subjects to membership in a church. Legislative changes in most states then made it possible, but not particularly easy, for people to sever all ecclesiastical ties.[10] Very few Germans

---

[7]Along with industrialisation and urbanisation, Wilhelm Brepohl notes that in the Ruhr among working people the *Kulturkampf* and Socialism contributed to secularisation. He also emphasises, however, that religious convictions remained stronger among workers than has generally been recognised, especially among those who migrated into the Ruhr from the East. Wilhelm Brepohl, *Industrievolk im Wandel von der agraren zur industriellen Daseinsform, dargestellt am Ruhrgebiet*, Tübingen 1957, pp. 185–190. In a related article Brepohl stresses that traditional piety remained strong among many workers throughout most of the nineteenth century, but concludes, significantly, that by the beginning of the twentieth century modernism and secularism were already dominant. 'Christlicher Glaube in der werdenden Industriegesellschaft', *Die Mitarbeit. Evangelisches Monatsheft zur Gesellschaftspolitik*, XII, No. 7/8 (July/August 1963), pp. 305, 308–309.

[8]William O. Shanahan, *German Protestants Face the Social Question*. Vol. I: *The Conservative Phase, 1815–1870*, Notre Dame 1954, pp. 70–91.

[9]In an amusing essay, Wilhelm Heinrich Riehl described what he called this "pseudo-Faith" (*Scheinglaube*) in a fictional South German Baron, an essentially secular person living with the appearance of religiosity for strictly social and political reasons. 'Problem der Konfessionsstatistik', in W. H. Riehl, *Religiöse Studien eines Weltkindes*, 3rd edn., Stuttgart 1895, pp. 241–251. One Dr. Johannes Müller who spent much time trying to win educated people back to an active Christian faith, reported that he found a "deep-rooted loathing" against everything that had to do with the church among "elements of educated society . . ." Those who remained in the church did so, he said, out of "reason of state" (*Staatsraison*). Johannes Müller, *Die Evangelisation unter den Entkirchlichten. Nach Beobachtungen und Erfahrungen*, Leipzig 1895, p. 89.

[10]On the various legal prescriptions covering church membership and procedures on disaffiliation, see Arthur B. Schmidt, *Der Austritt aus der Kirche. Eine Kirchenrechtliche und Kirchenpolitische Abhandlung*, Leipzig 1893, pp. 29–161.

availed themselves of the opportunity despite continuous agitation against church membership by freethinkers. As late as 1905, of 60,691,278 Germans, 62·03 per cent were officially Protestant, 36·51 were Catholic, 0·43 were classified as "other Christians" (that included Greek Orthodox, Church of England, Church of Scotland, Baptists, Methodists, *Herrnhuter*, Quakers, *Deutschkatholiken* and Mennonites), 1·0 per cent were Jewish and 0·03 per cent were in a miscellaneous category that included those for whom no information was available as well as those officially "without confession".[11] Taken in isolation, the data on church membership would lead one to conclude that essentially all Germans were religious and the search for secularisation could be closed.

Participation in ecclesiastical life-cycle ceremonies is still another instance in which the data would suggest widespread religiosity. Cultural tradition, social expectations and family custom all exerted enormous pressure on Germans to participate in baptism, confirmation and ecclesiastical marriage and burial rites. On the average, in the years between 1876–1880, 1891–1895 and 1906–1908, 94 to nearly 97 per cent of the children born to Prussian Protestant parents were baptised. The percentage in Catholic families was even higher. Participation in confirmation was equally high. Among Saxon Protestants between 1881 and 1900 only one out of every 10,000 declined to be confirmed.[12] One contemporary expert on German religious practices remarked as late as 1912 that "even the most passionate foe of the church will hardly [wish to] hurt his child by keeping [the child] from kneeling at the altar with the others . . ."[13] Prussian Protestant couples overwhelmingly favoured religious vows: 88·22 per cent between 1876–1880; 93·60 per cent between 1890–1895; and 90·51 per cent between 1906–1908. Even in Berlin, one of the most secularised of German cities, the percentages, though much lower, show a preference for religious marriage: there was a low of 35·85 per cent in 1876–80, but that rose to 64·61 per cent in 1890–1895, and dropped slightly to 58·28 per cent in 1906–1908.[14] Among Catholics participation in life-cycle ceremonies was always higher, reaching substantially 100 per cent in the country and small towns.[15] These figures certainly give no

---

[11]See Appendix I.
[12]Mulert, 'Kirchlichkeit', *Die Religion in Geschichte und Gegenwart*, III, col. 1487.
[13]*Ibid.*
[14]*Ibid.*, col. 1488. In Barmen, workers stayed within the church, passed through baptism, confirmation, marriage and burial, as a formality that had little meaning for them, is the conclusion of Wolfgang Köllmann, *Sozialgeschichte der Stadt Barmen*, Tübingen 1960, pp. 206–207.
[15]In the Catholic diocese of Regensburg, the following figures apply for the calendar year 1910: 99·9 per cent of the children born to Catholic parents were baptised as Catholics (31,701 out of 31,742); 99·7 per cent of babies born out of wedlock were baptised Catholic (3,499 out of 3,508); 73·2 per cent of babies born to mixed marriages were baptised Catholic (306 out of 418). In the same year, there were 5,689 marriages of persons of Catholic confession, and no less than 5,685 of them were celebrated in religious ceremonies; only 16 out of 22,641 Catholics who died did not have a Catholic funeral. Cf. *Kirchliches Handbuch für das katholische Deutschland*, edited by H. A. Krose, Freiburg im Breisgau 1911, III (1910–1911), p. 270–273.

The data from the diocese of Münster are particularly interesting because it included the industrial towns of Recklinghausen, Duisburg and Hamborn. The following figures for Recklinghausen are from 1912: all children born to Catholic parents were baptised as Catholic; 174 out of 285 babies born to mixed marriages were baptised Catholic; all babies born to unwed Catholic mothers were baptised; out of 1,076 marriages involving two Catholics, only 23 did not have a Catholic

clear indication of far-reaching secularisation. But the evidence needs to be understood within the context of a society that assumed an inevitable and automatic participation in life-cycle ceremonies. Participation might or might not indicate religious feeling. The difficulty is that from these figures alone we have no way of distinguishing the one from the other.

Only when we look at other evidence can we surmise that many who went through life-cycle ceremonies were already spiritually estranged from Christianity. In contrast to the high participation in life-cycle ceremonies, the number of Protestants partaking in Holy Communion dropped substantially. Some sample figures for 1906–1908 from selected states and provinces illustrate the point. Moving from high to low, the percentage of members taking communion appear as: 70 in Waldeck and Schaumburg-Lippe; 63 in Bavaria; 46·32 in Baden; 38·59 in the Kingdom of Saxony; 31 in Mecklenburg-Schwerin; and only 19 in Mecklenburg-Strelitz. In cities the percentage of communicants was markedly lower: about 15 in Berlin and Lübeck; 9·33 in Bremen; 8·26 in Hamburg; 7·6 in Altona; and 6·8 in Kiel.[16] Although data on normal church attendance are scattered, uneven and often questionable, they suggest massive indifference in some regions and in most cities. In Baden, beginning in 1872, Protestant clergymen took one of the few systematic annual counts of church attendance. The count was taken between Easter and Pentecost. They recorded that 29·1 per cent of Prostestants attended in 1872, dropping to 20·7 by 1907. In Schleswig-Holstein, around 1912, one calculation indicates that no more than 3·06 per cent of Protestant population attended Sunday services, rising only to 8·23 on Holy Days (*Festtage*).[17]

Such apathy required no effort, but to disaffiliate officially from one of the confessions required self-confidence and a measure of individual courage as well as effort. People who were apathetic, indifferent or ambivalent felt no need to make an official break with their traditional church. Germans who disaffiliated were not ambivalent, though their reasons for disaffiliation might vary considerably. They were breaking with tradition and cultural pressure, standing against conformity and adaptation. In Imperial Germany, they were in the forefront of the trend towards secularisation.[18] They constituted, however, only a small minority.

In the two decades between 1884 and 1905, the annual number of disaffiliations ranged between 1,800 and 6,300, generally averaging slightly under 4,000. Those are minuscule numbers in a country with over fifty-five million church members. In 1906 the number of disaffiliations rose sharply to 17,400 and, from

---

marriage ceremony; and it appears that all those who died had a Catholic burial. From *ibid.*, IV (1912–1913), pp. 236–237.

[16] Mulert, 'Kirchlichkeit', col. 1489. In 1912, the Catholic diocese of Regensburg had 888,468 members, of whom 686,080, or well over 75 per cent took Easter Communion, and during the year there were 4,734,346 communicants, an average of seven communions annually per church member. Cf. *Kirchliches Handbuch für das katholische Deutschland*, IV (1912–1913), p. 232–234.

[17] Mulert, 'Kirchlichkeit', cols. 1489–1490.

[18] Cf. Bruno Violet, *Die Kirchenaustrittsbewegung*, Berlin 1914, pp. 3–17.

then to 1914 fluctuated between 14,300 and 29,300 annually.[19] The absolute numbers were still not large, but the sudden jump aroused great concern in the Evangelical Church which suffered the greatest losses since only small numbers disaffiliated from the Catholic Church. Moreover, there was good reason to believe that most of those who did leave the Catholic Church were actually transferring to another confession, not disengaging themselves completely from institutionalised Christianity.[20]

The search for the causes of the increased number of disaffiliations led first to the observation that they were concentrated in urban and industrialising areas and, second, to the hypothesis that the overwhelming majority of the departees were from the working classes. Detailed local investigations generally confirmed the accuracy of the hypothesis. In answer to a questionnaire distributed in 1908, Evangelical pastors in Westphalia reported that most of the separationists were workers and that Social Democratic agitation had been responsible in great part for decisions to leave the church.[21] Writing in 1909, Paul Göhre concluded that the new wave of disaffiliation was carried "exclusively by workers", and that religious sceptics and educated disbelievers remained in the church as a bulwark to their social and economic interests.[22] Wilhelm Schneemelcher, General Secretary (1903–1923) of the *Evangelisch-Sozialer Kongreß* also concluded that the "educated and propertied circles" were remaining loyal to the church, while workers were severing their ties.[23] Pastor Ernst Bittlinger, after analysing the records of his own parish in Berlin, concluded that "in terms of occupation most of the departees are factory workers. Factories are the breeding places of anti-church propaganda."[24] Of the 76 in his parish who had left the Evangelical church, 24 were unskilled workers, 30 were skilled handicraftsmen, and the other 22 included 2 domestic servants, 2 shop assistants, a machinist, an electrician and people from several middle-class professions.[25]

The related issue of whether workers who left the Evangelical church may

---

[19] P. Ziegler, 'Kirchenaustrittsbewegung in Deutschland', *Die Religion in Geschichte und Gegenwart*, 3rd edn. 1958, III, p. 1344. For a statistical report on the history of church membership in Germany between 1917 and 1958, see Norbert Greinacher, 'The development of applications to leave the Church and the transfer from one Church to another, and its causes', *Social Compass*, VIII (1961), pp. 61–72.

[20] 'Kirchenaustritt', *Lexikon für Theologie und Kirche*, 2nd edn., Freiburg im Breisgau 1933, V, cols. 987–988.

[21] 'Fragebogen betr. Austrittsbewegung infolge kirchenfeindlicher, atheistischer Propaganda (Freidenkertum)', in Landeskirchliches Archiv Bielefeld, Generalia 1909, 0, 1–110.

[22] Paul Göhre, *Die neueste Kirchenaustrittsbewegung aus den Landeskirchen in Deutschland*, Jena 1909, pp. 16–17.

[23] W. Schneemelcher, 'Kirchenaustritte in Berlin 1912', *Evangelisch-Sozial*, 22, Folge X, No. 10 (October 1913), pp. 318–319. In an earlier analysis he located the concentration of disaffiliations in cities and industrial centres. He noted that owing to its faults the Evangelical Church shared much of the responsibility for the estrangement of people from Christianity, but thought that Social Democracy was a more important cause. W. Schneemelcher, 'Austritte aus den Landeskirchen', *Evangelisch-Sozial*, 18. Folge, VI, No. 12 (December 1909), pp. 395–397; 19. Folge, VII, No. 1 (January 1910), pp. 25–29); 19. Folge, VII, No. 2 (February 1910), pp. 57–64; 19. Folge, VII, No. 5 (May 1910), pp. 156–164.

[24] Ernst Bittlinger, 'Vom Kirchenaustritt in Berlin', *Evangelisch-Sozial*, 22. Folge, X, No. 10 (October 1913), pt. 2 of the article is in the same volume, No. 11 (November 1913), pp. 325–333.

[25] *Ibid.*

have transferred membership to another religious group needs to be considered briefly. For the most part, local registries on Church membership distinguished clearly between cases of permanent disaffiliation (*Austritt*) and transfer (*Übertritt*). Since transfers were made explicit there is no reason to suspect a sustained or hidden religious attachment among those who specifically dropped church membership. There were workers among those who transferred membership from one confession to another. Paul Göhre, an informed and perceptive observer of German religious practices, believed that certain people from the "working classes" found what he called the "imported sects" appealing and sometimes transferred their church membership accordingly. He also surmised that some sectarian workers were simultaneously "fellow-travellers" (*Mitläufer*) of the Social Democratic labour movement, at least to the point of voting for Socialists.[26] Unfortunately, Göhre did not substantiate his impressions with specific evidence on the working classes in the sectarian movements. Others tend to agree that sectarian congregations appealed to the lower classes, but these generalisations have not yet been tested by a close examination of local membership records.[27] Köllmann found that in Barmen sectarian congregations were especially supported by "Handwerker und Heimgewerbetreibenden", but he does not explicitly argue that the majority of sectarians were workers or that a majority of the workers in Barmen were sectarians.[28] Certainly, people from the lower classes constituted a substantial part of sectarian movements, but until we have detailed sociological investigations there is no way to determine what portion were workers.

[26] Göhre, *Die neuste Kirchenaustrittsbewegung*, pp. 13–14.
[27] Various leaders of The Free Religious Congregations (Die *Freireligiösen Gemeinden*), including Carl Scholl (1820–1907) and later Bruno Wille, were themselves at one time or another close to Social Democracy and tried to make their congregations appealing to members of the labour movement. A Federation of Free Religious Congregations (*Bund freireligiöser Gemeinden*) had been formed in 1859 as a union of *Lichtfreunde* and a segment of the German Catholics (*Deutschkatholiken*); both were movements of advanced liberal views in theology. The movement remained small and there is no reason to conclude that it attracted more than a handful of workers who broke with the Evangelical Church. Cf. Carl Scholl, *Die freien religiösen Gemeinden und Sozialdemokratie*, Heidelberg 1977; Carl Mirbt, 'Lichtfreunde', *Realencyklopädie für protestantische Theologie und Kirche*, 3rd edn., 1902, XI, pp. 465–474. Even the Proletarian Freethinkers' Federation (*Zentralverband proletarischer Freidenker*), which considered itself a part of the Social Democratic labour movement, enrolled only a small number of workers. By 1914 it had 115 clubs with a total membership of 6,400, about 75 per cent of whom were actually workers. Leaders complained that workers thought of the organisation as simply another sect. Cf. Konrad Beisswanger, *50 Jahre Freidenkertum*, Nuremberg [1930], pp. 27–29, 32, and Beisswanger, 'Freidenkertum und Arbeiterbewegung', *Der Atheist*, IV, No. 2 (12th January 1908), p. 14. The German Salvation Army asserted that people from the working classes made up its following, but specific data are not given. Cf. Max Gruner, *Revolutionäres Christentum. 50 Jahre Geschichte der Heilsarmee in Deutschland*, Band I: *1886 bis 1914*, Berlin–Steglitz and Bochum–Gerthe [about 1952], pp. 47, 52, 188–210. That Pietism in the eighteenth century enjoyed widespread popularity among the "lower classes" has been argued by Koppel S. Pinson, *Pietism as a Factor in the Rise of German Nationalism*, New York 1934, pp. 26, 69–70, 108–117, but the situation in the nineteenth century is unclear. My perusal of secondary literature on other denominations and sects, including Pentecostals, such as the *Mülheimer Bewegung*, has not turned up specific information about their social compositions.
[28] Köllmann, *Sozialgeschichte der Stadt Barmen*, pp. 208–211. On this issue there is, unfortunately, no specific data in Herwart Vorländer, *Evangelische Kirche und soziale Frage in der werdenden Industriegrossstadt Elberfeld*, Düsseldorf 1963.

Several interim observations need to be stressed at this point. Regardless of inner sentiments, substantially all Germans had a minimal formal connection with religious institutions and, for the overwhelming majority, religious rites were still a regular part of their lives. The data presented thus far also support the general assumption of many commentators in the nineteenth century that the lower classes, especially workers in urban areas, were more deeply alienated from institutional Christianity than other Germans. In Catholic communities, religion exerted a more pervasive influence on the population, including workers, than in Protestant areas. In varying degrees all German workers matured in a cultural environment in which a religious presence was abundantly evident.[29] This was reinforced by an elementary school system that allotted considerable instructional time to religion.[30] What cannot be avoided is the recognition that most Germans, including many workers drawn to the Social Democratic labour movement, retained, to some degree, a religious component in their lives. They were somewhere in the middle of the spectrum.

By turning our attention to workers at opposite ends of the spectrum we can bring into clearer focus the varying types of worker relationship to religion. It is easier to locate and describe secularised workers at the turn of the century than workers who remained faithful Christians. Clergymen, social reformers, politicians and Social Democrats all showed, for differing reasons, special interest in workers who were losing their religious faith.

In response to surveys and other enquiries, workers themselves expressed their diverse, but often intense feelings about religious beliefs and practices. Two such surveys are of particular interest. Late in the 1890s, Pastor Martin Rade sent out a short questionnaire to forty-eight workers, about half of them Socialists; the other half he described as "moderates" and "God-fearing". A decade later, Alfred Levenstein included questions on religious habits as part of an extensive questionnaire sent to metalworkers, miners and textile workers who belonged to the Social Democratic labour movement. On religion, Levenstein posed one central question with three parts: "Do you believe in God, or have you left the state church [*Landeskirche*] and for what reasons?" ("Glauben Sie an den lieben Gott, oder sind Sie und aus welchen Gründen aus der Landeskirche ausgetreten?") Keeping in mind the religiously-influenced cultural environment of Imperial Germany, a strikingly high number of respondents disavowed all belief in God. Of the miners, 43·8 per cent did not believe in God, and only 17·6 per cent did; of the textile workers, 61·6 per cent did not believe, and only 6·9 per cent said they did; and of the metal workers, 50·1 per cent declared for atheism, while only 12·1 per cent had retained a faith in God. Averaged out, that means that 50·2 per cent of the respondents were avowed atheists, with only 13·3 per cent believers in God. (The remainder did not answer the question.) Equally reveal-

---

[29]On the basis of an examination of workers' memoirs, one scholar concluded that they were reared in environments that were "permeated throughout by belief and piety", in considerable part because so many workers were born in villages or small towns. Susanne Hirschberg, *Das Bildungsschicksal des gewerblichen Proletariats im Lichte der Arbeiterautobiographie*, Cologne 1928, p. 52.

[30]*Ibid.*, 53. In Prussian *Volksschulen* four to six hours weekly were devoted to systematic instruction in religion, in addition to which religious themes were also integrated into other subjects. Cf. W. Lexis (ed.), *Das Volksschulwesen und das Lehrerbildungswesen im Deutschen Reich*, Berlin 1904, p. 111.

ing is the contrasting fact that only a small percentage of the respondents had gone to the trouble to leave the church: Only 7·3 per cent of the miners, 3·9 per cent of the textile workers and 6·2 per cent of the metalworkers.[31] Respondents gave the following explanations for leaving the church: (1) to avoid paying church taxes; (2) because the church served capitalism; (3) because clergy do not practise what they preach; (4) for general moral reasons; (5) because spiritually they had broken with the church; and finally, (6) because the church makes people stupid.[32]

If such a large percentage of the respondents no longer believed, why did they fail to leave the churches? The reasons given all reveal that even Social Democratic workers gave way to social pressure. They feared that their families would suffer discrimination from various authorities, that teachers would mistreat their children or, if they still faced military service, that army officers would abuse them with impunity. For others there were family pressures, usually from mothers, wives or sisters, who themselves were either believers or dreaded the possibility that they would be looked upon as pariahs. The fact that the Social Democratic Party did not pressure its followers to break with the church, but took the official position that "religion is a private matter", allowed workers to feel that no principle was violated by remaining church members. Some workers failed to leave because they objected to the fact that in certain states one had to pay a disaffiliation fee. Others simply procrastinated, felt so totally apathetic that it did not matter whether they were in or out of the church, or they were ignorant about how to withdraw their membership.[33] Lethargy played an important role. As one atheistic worker confessed: "I am, like so many hundred thousands, a hypocrite in this matter."[34] Workers were not alone in being lethargic or hypocritical. Germany's most eminent freethinker, materialist and monist, Ernst Haeckel, did not withdraw his membership from the Evangelical Church until 1910. In the following year, he was one of the leaders, along with Ostwald, of the newly-founded "Non-Confessional Committee" (*Komitee Konfessionslos*) which, by 1913 launched a more vigorous campaign, joined by individual Social Democrats, but not by the Party, to get people out of the churches.[35] Viewed from this perspective, workers who had disaffiliated earlier were indeed unique and had shown personal courage in leaving the church.

Organised workers were unanimous in condemning church and clergy in re-

---

[31]Appendix II.
[32]Alfred Levenstein, *Die Arbeiterfrage*, Munich 1912, pp. 336, 343, 353.
[33]The reasons compiled from: *Ibid.*, pp. 326, 334, 341, 346, 347; and 'Die Kirchenaustrittsbewegung', *Evangelisch-Sozial*, 23. Folge, XI, No. 2 (February 1914). It should be noted, as well, that as late as 1908 the states of Schwarzburg–Rudolstadt, Schaumburg–Lippe, Lippe–Detmold, Lübeck and Bremen required some kind of religious affiliation. Cf. 'Die deutschen Kirchenaustritts-Gesetze', *Der Atheist*, IV (13th December 1908), p. 396. In Schwarzburg–Sondershausen there was a particularly aggravating situation because the fee for leaving the church could range from 10 to 100 Marks, averaging usually about 13 to 14 Marks. 'Der Kirchenaustritt vor dem Landtag von Schwarzburg–Sondershausen', *Der Atheist*, VIII, No. 15 (14th April 1912), pp. 109–110.
[34]Levenstein, *Die Arbeiterfrage*, p. 349.
[35]Violet, *Die Kirchenaustrittsbewegung*, pp. 3–4; *Der Atheist*, VII, No. 10 (1st January 1911), pp. 3–5; 'Die Kirchenaustrittsbewegung', *Evangelisch-Sozial*, 23. Folge, XI, No. 2 (February 1914), pp. 58–60.

sponse to questions from Pastor Martin Rade. All but a few discounted the Biblical story of creation as an ignorant myth; Darwinist influence manifested itself in their language.[36] While some organised workers denounced the Bible as the worst book on the face of the earth, a far greater number viewed it as a major contribution to cultural history and some even allowed that it might contain kernels of moral truth.[37] A few believed in God; a few were confused by the issue; some were agnostics or pantheists, but the largest number dismissed God as a fiction.[38] Baptism and confirmation were viewed with open disdain, but some believed church weddings were preferable to civil ceremonies. Religious burial came in for intense criticism because pastors received special honoraria for their services. Even organised workers were generally favourable to religious holidays, but not for religious reasons. Religious holidays gave them a few days of rest. Aspects of religion, that is, could be preserved when they served beneficial secular functions.[39]

An element of residual Christianity seems most evident in the fact that with only one exception, the Socialist workers surveyed by Rade expressed admiration and respect for Jesus. But here too the explanation is that they offered an essentially secular interpretation of Jesus. They saw him as a friend of "poor people", a "true workers' friend" and an "ideal human". The same worker who could declare that "there is no God" could also write that Jesus was a "man who was called upon to shake the world to its foundations, who was not understood however in his time and even today would perhaps not be understood". Jesus was taken by organised workers to have been an "insurrectionist", a "revolutionary" whose very life stood as a biting indictment of institutional Christianity. They identified Jesus with their own labour movement, one saying that were Jesus alive "today he would certainly be a Social Democrat, maybe even a leader and a *Reichstag* deputy".[40] Clergymen took comfort in the fact that even organised workers honoured the name of Jesus, but they did so by mistake. Organised workers had stripped Jesus of everything supernatural and sacred and thought of him fundamentally as a secular reformer.

At the opposite end of the spectrum, loyal Christian workers still constituted a sizeable body at the turn of the century. They were mostly Catholic, though a small number of Evangelical workers also held to their church. For many Catholic workers, industrialisation and urbanisation did not lead to estrangement from the larger religious community. German Catholicism had created its own social–cultural milieu, similar in form but not in content, to the milieu that had taken shape around the Social Democratic labour movement in the latter third

---

[36]Martin Rade, 'Die sittlich-religiöse Gedankenwelt unserer Industriearbeiter', *Die Verhandlungendes neunten Evangelisch-sozialen Kongresses, abgehalten in Berlin am 2. und 3. Juni 1898*, Göttingen 1898, pp. 111–112.
[37]*Ibid.*, pp. 100–101.
[38]*Ibid.*, pp. 109–110.
[39]*Ibid.*, pp. 95–99.
[40]*Ibid.*, pp. 102–105. One respondent even ventured a mild criticism of Jesus for not having gone into a secular field: "He [Jesus] would have accomplished more, if he had gone into an economic or scientific field instead of religion" (p. 104). Attitudes on Jesus similar to those reported by Rade can be found in Paul Göhre, *Drei Monate Fabrikarbeiter*, pp. 109, 174, 190.

of the nineteenth century.⁴¹ Within the social–cultural milieu of Catholicism, workers, as well as others, found not only religious worship, but most of the ingredients for a way of life. The Catholic social–cultural milieu was an ingenious amalgam of religious and secular elements, fused together by tradition and in considerable part by a hostile political environment. Piety, sobriety and success were not preconditions for belonging; ritual observance, communal approval and even poverty would do. Although the milieu included many classes, workers could also feel that they belonged.⁴²

By contrast, such a social–cultural milieu did not exist for workers from Protestant backgrounds.⁴³ Even when well-intentioned Protestant clergymen and reformers sought to create a movement within which Evangelical workers could find a religiously-influenced associational life, their efforts were undermined by the intrinsic nature and the social structure of the very institution they hoped to support.⁴⁴ Evangelical workers' clubs were founded in the early 1880s at the same time that Catholics too established clubs designed to include all "workers" in contrast to earlier organisations that had limited membership to artisans.⁴⁵ By

---

⁴¹Similarities and contrasts between Social Democratic and Catholic "social milieus" are highlighted by Rainer Lepsius, 'Parteiensystem und Sozialstruktur. Zum Problem der Demokratisierung der deutschen Gesellschaft', in Wilhelm Abel (ed.), *Wirtschaft, Geschichte und Wirtschaftsgeschichte. Festschrift zum 65. Geburtstag von Friedrich Lütge*, Stuttgart 1966, pp. 388–389.

⁴²In Düsseldorf, stable, native Catholic workers were understandably more firmly integrated into the social–cultural milieu than were migrants who moved into the city. Migrant Catholic workers moved into the Social Democratic orbit as well as into the Catholic milieu. Cf. Mary Nolan, *The Socialist Movement in Düsseldorf, 1890–1914*, Dissertation, Columbia University, 1975, ch. II, pp. 28, 32–33, 35, 37.

⁴³Lepsius, 'Parteiensystem' (pp. 385–386) points out the lack of that kind of cohesive social–cultural milieu among Protestants. This was reflected, for example, in the fact that Protestants were dispersed among several Conservative and Liberal parties, none of which, incidentally, appealed to workers.

⁴⁴The social gap separating much of the Evangelical clergy from the lower classes in Germany was an important factor. A recent socio-historical study of the Evangelical clergy in Württemberg, covering 1700–1965, shows how the gap had become very marked by the eighteenth century. The clergy acquired the features of a separate *Stand*. One important dimension of this was recruitment from the families of clergymen, of teachers (in higher schools as well as in elementary education) and of senior civil servants. Recruitment of the Catholic clergy contrasted sharply: whereas, at the beginning of the twentieth century, 76·2 per cent of the Catholic clergy in Württemberg came from the rural population, only 21·5 per cent of the Evangelical clergy did. Between 1871 and 1911, 37 per cent of Catholic theological students were peasants' sons; among Evangelicals peasants' sons made up only 3 per cent. See, Günther Bormann, 'Studien zu Berufsbild und Berufswirklichkeit evangelischer Pfarrer in Württemberg. Die Herkunft der Pfarrer. Ein geschichtlich-statistischer Überblick von 1700–1965', *Social Compass*, XIII, No. 2 (1966), pp. 95–137. Owing to the fact that German industry grew in rural areas and small towns as well as in large cities and that so much of the labour force came from the countryside, the peasant background of Catholic clergymen brought them closer to most workers than did the higher, urban professional backgrounds of Evangelical clergy. The fact that Germany's *Bildungsbürgertum* was overwhelmingly Protestant made the gap between the bourgeois constituency of the Evangelical Church and the workers all the more evident. Cf. Klaus Vondung, 'Zur Lage der Gebildeten in der wilhelminischen Zeit', in Klaus Vondung (ed.), *Das wilhelminische Bildungsbürgertum*, Göttingen 1976, pp. 26–27. Many of these factors are also treated by Günter Brakelmann, *Die soziale Frage des 19. Jahrhunderts*, 3rd ed., Witten/Ruhr 1966, pp. 111–113, 174, 177, 185.

⁴⁵Preceding the founding of the Catholic Workers' Clubs (*Katholische Arbeiter-Vereine*), there had been a tradition of Catholic Journeymen's Clubs (*Katholische Gesellenvereine*) since the early 1850s. Cf. Andr. Brüll, 'Gesellenvereine (katholische)', *Handwörterbuch der Staatswissenschaften*, 2nd edn., 1900,

32   *Vernon Lidtke*

1912, there were no less than 3,301 Catholic Workers' Clubs with 442,418 members, while in 1911 the Evangelical Workers' Clubs numbered 644 with only 106,339 members, only two-thirds of which, even by the broadest definition, were workers.[46] Working-class consciousness began to manifest itself in the Catholic Workers' Clubs by the turn of the century, but had no place in the Protestant movement.[47] Clergymen played important roles in both movements, but in Catholic clubs, workers themselves took over many functions, especially as intermediaries (*Vertrauensmänner*) between the organisations and local neighbourhoods.[48] Both organisations sponsored a variety of activities, including entertainments and festivities, but Evangelicals, holding firmly to puritanical ethics, worked on the principle that all "pleasure seeking" should be excluded. They were the only workers' clubs in all of Germany to ban dancing at festivals.[49] They believed that a workers' confessional club should above all be

---

pp. 199–200. Later, the Catholic social movement developed other organisations. Particularly important was the founding, in 1868, of the Christian-Social Party (*Christlich-soziale Partei*). Throughout the 1870s and 1880s, its official publication, the *Christlich-soziale Blätter*, reflected a strong preference of artisans, an underlying mistrust of factory workers, an open antisemitism, a deep hatred of Social Democracy and the assumption that without Christianity there could be no solution to the social question. As late as 1885, a leading article declared that "handicraft [das Handwerk] is thus the true Christian trade [*Gewerbe*], and through religion and the Church artisans defend their existence". 'Handwerk und Christenthum', *Christlich-soziale Blätter*, XVIII (1885), p. 189 (signed J.A.). On the Christian-Social Party's early development, see the critical socialist evaluation by August Erdmann, *Die Christliche Arbeiterbewegung in Deutschland*, 2nd edn., Stuttgart 1909, pp. 75–86, and the sympathetic account included in Hermann Deite, 'Die katholisch-soziale Bewegung in Deutschland, nach ihrer Literatur geschildert', *Jahrbuch für Gesetzgebung, Verwaltung und Volkswirtschaft im deutschen Reich*, XXXII (1908), pp. 957–982.

[46] Appendices III and IV. The size of the regional federations of Evangelical Workers' Clubs is given in Appendix V.

[47] A handbook for the Catholic clubs contrasted "old style" and "new style" Catholic workers. The "old style" had been dominant through the 1880s, lacked a "genuine class consciousness", waited for other *Stände* to do good works and had no idea that workers could help themselves. "New style" workers joined others to strengthen all workers, grasped the necessary "intellectual weapons" and looked upon their club as a "conquering troop, a battle brigade, a leadership troop". *Arbeiter-Taschenbuch für das Jahr 1905*, edited by the *Verbände katholischer Arbeitervereine West- und Süddeutschlands*, Berlin [1905], pp. 31–33.

[48] On the role of the Vertrauensmänner, J. Giesberts, 'Die innere Organisation unserer Arbeitervereine', in *ibid*., pp. 46–49, where it is stressed that such intermediaries are the life-blood of the individual clubs and of the whole movement.

[49] Most Evangelical Workers' Clubs specifically proscribed dancing in their statutes, and others practised the prohibition. They also took a strict stand against drinking at club affairs. A. Just, *Der Gesamtverband der evang. Arbeitervereine Deutschlands, seine Geschichte und seine Arbeiten* (no place, no date, but *c*. 1904), pp. 62–63. As an earlier supporter of the Evangelical Workers' Clubs wrote: "There is no doubt about the fact that the flesh is denied where Evangelical Christians are together." That also meant the exclusion of theatrical performances in Evangelical Workers' Clubs. Deutelmoser, *Die evangelischen Arbeitervereine in Westfalen*, Magdeburg 1886, p. 20. The principles of the Evangelical Workers' Clubs of the Rhineland and Westphalia were spelled out in the statutes as follows: "1. The club stands on the Evangelical confession, seeks to awaken and strengthen Evangelical consciousness among fellow believers and is loyal to *Kaiser* and *Reich*. 2. The club strives to encourage and preserve harmony between employers and employees. 3. Whoever has given the degrading promise of handing his children over to the Catholic Church shall be, apart from certain exceptions, excluded from membership. Whether such an exception pertains is a decision of the Executive. 4. Dancing is prohibited at club festivities." *Statut des Verbandes evangelischer Arbeitervereine Rheinlands und Westfalens*, Essen [*c*. 1887], p. 1.

religious. Within the context of German Protestantism that meant that they also had to be patriotic, monarchical and in favour of social harmony.[50] Catholic clubs could emphasise secular activities because their members lived within a milieu strongly influenced and held together by confessional consensus. By contrast, Evangelical Workers' Clubs were outposts of Protestantism, designed to preserve a measure of confessional commitment among workers who otherwise lived in a predominantly secular world scarcely touched by religious influences. Under these conditions, Evangelical Workers' Clubs assumed that they could not fulfill their purpose without making religion and patriotism uppermost.[51] That limited their appeal to only a handful of workers.

The situation among the small number of Jewish workers in Imperial Germany emphasises the significance of the social–cultural environment. Jewish workers were almost exclusively immigrants from the East; by 1910 they numbered from 20,000 to 30,000.[52] They faced some unique obstacles when they sought integration in some segment of existing German society. They shared the lot of Eastern Jews generally who were not readily absorbed into existing German-Jewish religious communities and for workers such integration was even more difficult. At the same time, immigrant Jewish workers did not fit easily into an advanced industrial economy and native German workers often viewed them with suspicion or hostility. Coming from less-advanced economies these immigrant workers "shied away from heavy industry, readily accepted low status jobs, innovated in the delivery of new goods and services, and tended to seek work permitting self-employment".[53] These tendencies were reinforced because German Gentile employers normally expected their employees to work a six-day week, including thus the Jewish Sabbath. Despite their comparative isolation, Jewish immigrant workers appear not to have formed many of their own voluntary associations. Organisations of Jewish Socialist immigrants were founded in a number of cities – Berlin, Leipzig, Gera, Munich, Offenbach, Mannheim, Karlsruhe and Baden-Baden – but they were very small, included only a small portion of all Jewish workers, were incapable of providing members with important services and showed more interest in anti-Tsarism than in the political prob-

[50]Support of the Evangelical faith and the monarchical state was combined with a trenchant identification of the movement's enemies: "Therefore we combat the red and the black and the gold internationals as diabolical powers of selfishness and hold high our banner: the Evangelical faith." *Handbuch für Evangelische Arbeitervereine*. Edited by the *Evangelischer Bund zur Wahrung der deutschprotestantischen Interessen*, Leipzig 1892, p. 63.

[51]Lectures on religion, morality, patriotism, social reform, the fight against Social Democracy, along with occasional evenings of entertainment, constituted the main activities of the clubs, as reported by D. Weber, *Bericht über die Evangelische Arbeitervereinssache für 1912/13* (no place [1913]). Viewing the work of the clubs from a different perspective, Brepohl takes the position that socialising among members was more important in the Evangelical Workers' Clubs than religious instruction and concludes therefore that the clubs reflected the process of secularisation. Brepohl, *Industrievolk*, p. 132.

[52]Jack L. Wertheimer, *German Policy and Jewish Politics. The Absorption of East European Jews in Germany (1868–1914)*, Ph.D. Dissertation, Columbia University, 1978, p. 402. I am indebted to Dr. Wertheimer for making sections of his dissertation available to me.

[53]*Ibid.*, p. 252.

lems of Imperial Germany.[54] The sparsity of information and research on Jewish immigrant workers makes it difficult to specify the range of religious belief and practice among them. We can surmise that those in the Socialist organisations were likely to be most inclined towards secularism.

The discussion thus far has stressed the range and diversity that prevailed in the matter of secularisation among German workers. To highlight the main tendencies, I want to present a five-part typology that will both summarise and systematise the findings.

I. Religious type: Characteristics: traditionalist; believed and practised fundamentals of a faith; basic harmony between external behaviour and internal values; lived, intellectually, in a world heavily influenced by religious symbols; could be either Catholic or Evangelical, but more of the former.

II. Religious type, with marked secular infusion. Characteristics: lax in practice; occasional doubts about doctrine; had criticisms of church and clergy, but did not express them freely; if Catholic, would live close to the Catholic social milieu; if Evangelical, lived largely in secular environment; in both cases the world they knew had a mix of religious tradition and secular language; they would not normally explain things by appeal to the supernatural.

III. Apathetic type. Characteristics: church member, but completely indifferent to regular practice and belief; familial participation in life-cycle ceremonies; attitudes towards church and clergy ranged from critical to bitter cynicism; did not think of themselves as atheists, agnostics or anything else; did not care; largely from Protestant backgrounds.

IV. Secular, with religious residue. Characteristics: still officially a church member; out of custom, participation in life-cycle religious ceremonies; sceptical about Christian doctrine, but retained respect for the ethical values; could admire the historical Jesus; intellectual world shaped largely by secular language and symbols.

V. Secular type. Characteristics: left the church, or intended to do so; deeply sceptical and hostile to all religion; no practice, unless strong compulsion for occasional familial participation in life-cycle ceremonies; openly antagonistic to the clergy; had found a secular substitute for religion; strongly sympathic to Socialist labour movement; intellectual world formed by secular symbols and language.[55]

---

[54]*Ibid.*, pp. 398–401. Fragmentary information on Jewish immigrant workers also from S. Adler-Rudel, *Ostjuden in Deutschland 1880–1940. Zugleich eine Geschichte der Organisationen, die sie betreuten*, Tübingen 1959 (Schriftenreihe wissenschaftlicher Abhandlungen des Leo Baeck Instituts 1), pp. 25–27, and Robert S. Wistrich, 'German Social Democracy and Jewish Nationalism', in *LBI Year Book XXI* (1976), pp. 109–142.

[55]Without elaborating a formal typology, Brepohl nonetheless identifies four categories to describe workers in the Ruhr with respect to religion and secularisation from the late nineteenth century to the 1950s. "One part is believing and Christian, another outwardly Christian, a further is rationalist and also socialist and still another introduces eschatological impulses into this so-called political movement . . ." Brepohl, *Industrievolk*, p. 187.

Like most typologies, this one runs the risk of oversimplifying past reality in order to give it structure. It approximates reality, but does not duplicate it. It is an exploration that stresses qualities rather than quantities. Whole groups of workers may have fitted several types in a lifetime. But it should not be assumed that they travelled along a road from the first to the fifth type. The typology is not a chronological scheme, but a set of differentiations.

The typology helps to highlight several important points about workers and secularisation. Alasdair MacIntyre has argued, persuasively I think, that completion of the secularisation process depends upon the possession of a different vocabulary in which questions about the meaning of life can be asked and answered. Until people find and internalise a different language, they are likely to continue, despite apathy, indifference and all the outward signs to the contrary, to think about the meaning of life in terms that they learned as part of a Christian heritage.[56] Three of the five types used a Christian framework when confronted with large questions of meaning. In this sense, the typology emphasises that a complete shift to secularism can be clearly identified among only a minority of workers, those in type five. They had not only abandoned Christianity but found a new vocabulary.

Most secularised workers took their new idiom from the rhetoric of the Socialist labour movement. That distinguished them from other secularised Germans for whom other vocabularies, drawn, for example, from natural science, provided the language for discussing meaning.[57] In other respects, secularised workers had much in common with other secularised Germans. But Social Democracy, it should be stressed, was seldom if ever the primary cause for the alienation of workers from Christianity as many clergymen mistakenly assumed. True, it encouraged secularisation because it provided one possible secular frame of reference in which the meaning of life could be discussed. In that sense, Social Democracy served as a secular substitute for religion. Some interpreters have even argued that Social Democracy not only took the place of Christianity, but that it was itself a religion.[58] Such interpretations usually rest upon very broad definitions of religion, much broader than have been used in this article. Although Social Democratic doctrine reflected some of the modes of Christian thought, it lacked a crucial ingredient of religion – a sense of the sacred.

Workers in Imperial Germany were, nonetheless, so accustomed to living in a culture in which religious form played a constant role that only gradually could they move completely away from the language and intellectual scaffolding created by that environment. Even secularised workers, when they wanted to tell others how much their new secularist-socialist outlook meant to them, were likely to use religious terms which connoted great esteem and respect. Workers who experienced secularisation in their own lifetimes could not yet explain what had

[56] MacIntyre, *Secularization and Moral Change*, pp. 30–31.
[57] Relevant in this connection is the discussion in Karl Kupisch, 'Bürgerliche Frömmigkeit im Wilhelminischen Zeitalter', in Hans Joachim Schoeps (ed.), *Das Wilhelminische Zeitalter*, Stuttgart 1967, pp. 40–59.
[58] For example, Gustave Le Bon, *The Psychology of Socialism*, 1899; Henry de Man, *The Psychology of Socialism*, New York [1929], pp. 125–166; and Werner Sombart, *Der Proletarische Sozialismus* ('Marxismus'), 10th edn., Jena 1924, I, pp. 226–254.

happened to them in strictly secular terms. On the other hand, workers who experienced secularisation only in limited ways, found it more and more difficult to comprehend the changing world around them in traditional Christian terms. The key to their continued religious affiliation is to be found, not in the persuasiveness of Christian doctrine, but in the existence of a social–cultural milieu in which traditional sentiments were constantly reinforced. And the converse is also true. The key to the workers who moved towards secularisation is not to be found in their perception of the intellectual weaknesses of Christianity, but in the fact that their particular environments lacked a larger sense of community that owed anything to religious impulses. Those who were alienated from Christianity could make the final move to secularisation when they were drawn into an environment, such as that of the Socialist labour movement, that provided not only a new vocabulary for dealing with questions of meaning but also a sense that they belonged to a larger community that would sustain them.

APPENDIX I

Distribution of Population by Religious Affiliation: Imperial Germany, 1905[a]

State	Evangelical	Roman Catholic	Other Christians[b]	Israelites	Misc.[c]
Prussia	23,341,502	13,352,444	182,533	409,501	7,344
Bavaria	1,844,736	4,612,920	9,641	55,341	1,734
Saxony	4,250,059	269,872	22,858	14,697	515
Württemberg	1,582,745	696,031	10,883	12,053	467
Baden	769,866	1,206,919	7,449	25,893	601
Hesse	803,195	372,894	8,010	24,696	380
Mecklenburg-Schwerin	609,914	12,835	715	1,482	99
Saxe-Weimar	367,789	18,049	771	1,421	65
Mecklenburg-Strelitz	100,314	2,627	196	298	16
Oldenburg	339,916	96,067	1,310	1,493	70
Brunswick	455,680	26,304	1,900	1,815	59
Saxe-Meiningen	262,243	4,870	478	1,256	69
Saxe-Altenburg	200,511	5,449	393	131	24
Saxe-Coburg-Gotha	237,187	3,897	605	714	29
Anhalt	311,999	13,493	1,008	1,460	69
Schwarzburg-Sondershausen	83,389	1,521	43	195	4
Schwarzburg-Rudolstadt	95,641	994	115	82	3
Waldeck	56,341	1,890	259	629	8
Reuß older line	68,549	1,205	791	54	4
Reuß younger line	140,640	2,806	822	290	26
Schaumburg-Lippe	43,888	653	193	246	12
Lippe-Detmold	139,127	5,481	229	735	5
Lübeck	102,484	2,467	231	638	37
Bremen	240,041	19,655	1,334	1,432	978
Hamburg	807,429	40,639	3,112	19,602	4,096
Elsass-Lorraine	391,067	1,387,462	3,838	31,708	489
Total	37,676,852	22,159,644	259,717	607,862	17,203
Percentage of German Population	62·03%	36·51%	0·43%	1·0%	0·03%

Total for Germany 60,691,278   100%

[a] From: *Die Religion in Geschichte und Gegenwart*, Tübingen 1912, I, col. 2128.

[b] Includes Greek Orthodox, Evangelical Brethren, (*Herrnhuter*), Baptists, Methodists, Quakers, Mennonites, German Catholics (*Deutschkatholiken*), Church of England, Church of Scotland, as well as other sects and Christian communities.

[c] Includes non-Christian groups (apart from Jewish), those of unknown confession and those who had declared that they were "without confession".

APPENDIX II
Organised Workers on God and the Church[a]

	Miners		Textile workers		Metal workers		Total	
	Number	%	Number	%	Number	%	Number	%
Believe in God	370	17·6	79	6·9	219	12·1	668	13·3
Do not believe in God	914	43·8	711	61·6	905	50·1	2,530	50·2
Left the Church	148	7·3	45	3·9	112	6·2	305	6·0
Did not answer question	652	31·3	318	27·6	567	31·6	1,537	30·5
TOTAL	2,084	(100%)	1,153	(100%)	1,803	(100%)	5,040	(100%)

[a] Compiled from Alfred Levenstein, *Die Arbeiterfrage*, Munich 1912, pp. 335, 343, 353. The workers surveyed on religion were identical with those surveyed on all other topics by Levenstein. He sent out 3,000 questionnaires to miners in the Ruhr, the Saarland and Silesia, of which 2,084 were returned. To textile workers in Berlin and Forst he sent 2,000 questionnaires; 1,153 were returned. And of 3,000 questionnaires sent to metalworkers in Berlin, Solingen and Oberstein, 1,803 were returned (pp. 9–10). The question posed by Levenstein read as follows: "Glauben Sie an den lieben Gott, oder sind Sie und aus welchen Gründen aus der Landeskirche ausgetreten?"

APPENDIX III[a]
Growth of the Three Regional Associations of Catholic Workers' Clubs

	Verband süddeutscher kath. Arbeitervereine[b]		Verband kath. Arbeitervereine Westdeutschlands[c]		Verband der kath. Arbeitervereine (Sitz Berlin)[d]	
Year	Clubs	Members	Clubs	Members	Clubs	Members
1891	27	5,984				
1895	92	22,285				
1900	372	58,339				
1904			344	74,530	c.500	70,000
1907			720	130,000		
1909					988	123,000
1910	926	102,357	961	171,302		
1911					1,199	129,000
1912	978	108,250	1,041	189,979	1,200	130,000

[a] Dieter Fricke, 'Katholische Arbeitervereine', in Dieter Fricke (ed.), *Die bürgerlichen Parteien in Deutschland*, Berlin (DDR) 1968, II, pp. 255–256. The figures for 1912 are from *Arbeiter-Taschenbuch für das Jahr 1913*, edited by the *Kartellverband katholischer Arbeitervereine, West-, Süd- und Ostdeutschlands*, Berlin [1913], pp. 217, 228, 244.

[b] This federation established 1891, in Munich. Publication organ was *Der Arbeiter*, also founded in 1891.

[c] Established in 1904 in Mönchen-Gladbach as a federation of many existing workers' clubs and took as its publication organ the *Westdeutsche Arbeiter-Zeitung*, which had been started in 1899.

[d] Originally established in 1897 as the *Verband katholischer Arbeitervereine Nord-und Ostdeutschlands*; reorganised in 1903 with the above name. Its members were concentrated in the dioceses of Trier and Breslau with a sprinkling throughout North Germany. Publication was *Der Arbeiter (Berlin)*, founded in 1897.

In addition to the three main federations of Catholic Workers' Clubs, there were several smaller federations and organisations for women workers: *Verband der katholischen Vereine polnischer Arbeiter* (31,948 members in 1911); *Ostdeutscher Verband der katholischen Arbeitervereine* (Sitz Neisse) (founded in 1910 with 80 clubs and about 14,000 members; *Verband katholischer Vereine erwerbstätiger Frauen und Mädchen Deutschlands* (founded in 1905, with 160 clubs and 22,500 members by 1908); *Verband süddeutscher katholischer Arbeiterinnenvereine* (founded in 1906 in Munich, with 136 clubs and 20,000 members by 1912/13); From Fricke, as in note a, and 'Mehr Zentralisation der katholischen Arbeitervereine', *Westdeutsche Arbeiter-Zeitung*, XIII, No. 29 (22nd July 1911), p. 169.

APPENDIX IV[a]

Growth of the National Federation of Evangelical Workers' Clubs of Germany
(Gesamtverband Evangelischer Arbeitervereine Deutschlands)

Year[b]	Clubs	Membership
1890	—	20,000
1893	—	44,000
1897	—	56,000
1899	—	70,000
1901	401	81,677
1904	400	72,000
1905	402	81,137
1908	475	92,000
1911	644	106,339
1914	1,080	142,000

[a] From Dieter Fricke, 'Gesamtverband evangelischer Arbeitervereine Deutschlands', in Fricke (ed.), *op. cit.*, II, p. 150. Official organ of the federation was the *Evangelischer Arbeiterbote*, founded in 1885 and published in Hattingen in the Ruhr.

[b] Before the formation of the national federation in 1890, a provincial federation of Evangelical Workers' Clubs in Rhineland-Westphalia reported the following members: in 1885, 25 clubs with 11,700 members; in 1887, 44 clubs with 17,000 members; and in 1890, 95 clubs with 28,000 members. *Ibid.*, p. 151. Another source gives the following membership figures for the early nineties: for Rhineland-Westphalia, 80 clubs with 20,710 members in 1891; for Saxony, 18 clubs with about 2,000 members in 1891; and for Bavaria 41 clubs in 1890 and 50 in 1892. This source estimates that as of 1891 there were, in all of Germany, 251 Evangelical Workers' Clubs with 105,000 members. These figures given by Otto Märker, *Evangelische Arbeitervereine*, Stuttgart 1892, pp. 5–6.

One group, known as the "Bochumer Richtung" seceded officially from the *Gesamtverband evangelischer Arbeitervereine* in September 1901. The secession included 38 clubs with a total of 7,792 members. From Fricke, *op. cit.*, p. 154.

Protestants were slower than Catholics in forming organisations for women workers. A report from 1911 shows that there was a national Federation of Evangelical Women's Worker Clubs (*Verband ev. Arbeiterinn.-Vereine*) with 21 clubs and 2,145 members. The same report indicates that there were 1,033 women in the Rhineland-Westphalian Federation, 88 in the North Elbe Federation, 8 women's clubs with 798 members in the Hanover Federation, 296 women in the Middle Rhine Federation and 132 in a women's division of a club in Baden. The total female membership cannot be calculated from these figures because it is not clear whether some are listed twice, in the national federation and in connection with local associations. From the *Kirchlich-soziale Blätter*, XIV, No. 11 (November 1911), as reprinted in W. Schneemelcher, 'Christlichnationale Arbeiterbewegung', *Evangelisch-Sozial*, 21. Folge, IX, No. 1 (January 1912), p. 19.

APPENDIX V
Regional Federations of Evangelical Workers' Clubs, 1900/1901[a]

Name		Clubs	Membership
Norddeutscher Verband		18	
Workers (Arbeiterstand)	970		
Artisans (Handwerkerstand)	230		
Other (andere Stände)	200		
Male	c. 1,300		
Female	c. 100		
Evangelischer Arbeiter-Verein Berlin		—	—
Altpreußischer Verband		12	2,597
Schlesischer Verband Evangelischer Arbeiter-Vereine		6	3,375
Kurhessischer Verband		3	910
Mitteldeutscher Verband		3	—
Norddeutscher Verband der christlich gesinnten Arbeitervereine		10	1,666
Rheinisch-Westfälischer Verband		100/110	20,000
Kreisverband Dortmund-Holde		15	4,300
Kreisverband Gelsenkirchen II		8	600
Württemb. Landesverband ev. Arbeitervereine		48	3,714
Verband der protestantischen Arbeitervereine der Pfalz		29	5,000
Landesverband evangel. Arbeitervereine im Königreich Sachsen		37	14,500
Badischer Verband		—	3,632
Mitteldeutscher Verband		18	2,498
Workers (Arbeiterstand)	1,279		
Artisans (Handwerkerstand)	633		
other (andere Stände)	586		
Verband evangel. Arbeitervereine an der Saar		24	4,314

[a] From Fr. Arndt, *Bericht über die evangelische Arbeitervereinssache vom 1. April 1900 bis 31. März 1901*, Hattingen: C. Hundt [1901], pp. 3–22.

Religion in the German Volksschule, 1890–1928

BY GEOFFREY G. FIELD

Compared to France, elementary education and the campaign for its emancipation from religious control have until recently received scant attention from historians of Germany. While universities and Gymnasia, the shaping institutions of the German élite, have long been the subjects of searching analysis, no comparable body of research in quantity or quality exists for the *Volksschule* which boasted over eight million pupils and about 190,000 teachers in 1914. Fictional and real-life accounts of French *instituteurs*, descriptions of their social standing and political influence, of their stereotypical role as secularists and dogged adversaries of the local *curé*, trigger in our minds no picture of equal richness and clarity when we contemplate the German scene.[1] Yet, as a number of recent monographs and essays have shown, the sources for a comprehensive study of primary schooling are abundant and can enrich our understanding of such aspects of German life as: the character of confessional and class antagonisms; the transmission of political, social, religious and moral values from one generation to the next; concepts of authority, parental attitudes and the culture of youth; the social history of teachers; and the conceptually elusive but interrelated processes of modernisation and secularisation.

Central to all discussion of the *Volksschule* in Imperial and Weimar Germany is the issue of religion and clerical power over education. Proposals for reforms in pedagogy, for a remoulding of elementary education and an expansion of secondary institutions; demands for more professional recognition by schoolmasters and debates about the role and responsibilities of parents, all invariably led back to the same point of contention: the relationship of Church and school. Within the compass of a brief essay, all aspects of this relationship cannot be treated adequately. What follows, therefore, is a first exploration of the terrain, an attempt to illuminate the nature of German *Schulpolitik* from around 1890 to the last years of Weimar by viewing it as one almost continuous struggle. The final portion of the essay ponders briefly some of the consequences of this conflict for both Jews and Christians in Germany.

I

Willy Hellpach, the Democratic Party's candidate for the Presidency of the Weimar Republic in 1925, once characterised German education as "practical

---

[1]For example, I know of no German equivalent of Roger Thabault's fascinating study of the primary school at Mazières-en-Gatine, *Education and Social Change in a Village Community*, New York

Christianity for the masses, classical humanism for the cultured classes". His description was apt, capturing at once the system's rigid dualism and its emphasis upon religious and moral training as the cornerstone of public elementary instruction. Since schools were administered by the separate *Länder* there were regional variations but, in general, the system was the same throughout the Wilhelminian *Reich*. The children of the middle classes either went first to private schools or, in some cases, attended the first three grades of the *Volksschule* or special three year preparatory schools (*Vorschulen*) before transferring to a *Gymnasium* or some other secondary institution. For the overwhelming majority of Germans, however, education meant eight years in an overcrowded *Volksschule* sometimes followed by a brief period in a trade school. Thus, it has been estimated that in 1885 about 7·5 million pupils attended *Volksschule* as compared to 238,000 at secondary schools and 27,000 students enrolled in universities.[2] A comparison of schools in terms of state subsidies per pupil reflects in startling fashion the educational priorities inherent in this system: in 1900 in Bremen, for example, the figures for *Gymnasium*, *Realschule* and *Volksschule* were respectively 467·40, 205·87 and 57·72 Marks.[3] Almost entirely closed to the lower classes, secondary education opened the door to privileged positions in society and the coveted *Abitur* was required not only for university entrance but even for minor posts in the civil service.

The overwhelming majority of *Volksschulen* were organised on a confessional basis, although in Baden, Hesse and some parts of Prussia "common" or non-denominational schools existed in which pupils of different faiths were taught together and only separated for religious instruction. In these *Simultanschulen* as they were called lay the hopes of liberal Germans and advocates of a unified, national system. School inspection in most of the *Reich* was in the hands of the clergy and the curriculum, burdened by heavy doses of memorisation, consisted of religion, basic skills in reading, writing and arithmetic, and hymn singing. The avowed goal was character development and discipline rather than intellectual stimulation and student recollections – admittedly often from men who later became engaged in the labour movement and were sharply critical – dwell mostly on the daily drudgery of rote learning, the bombastic patriotism of schoolmasters, moralistic stories and written exercises, and on what Friedrich Paulsen called "the gabbling of the catechism and a few Bible texts and hymns".[4] The same narrow priorities governed the selection of teachers who

---

1971. For a recent, provocative discussion of education in France see: Theodore Zeldin, *France 1848–1945. Intellect, Taste, Anxiety*, Oxford 1977, especially ch. 4.

[2]Fritz K. Ringer, 'Higher Education in Germany in the Nineteenth Century', *Journal of Contemporary History*, 2 (1967), p. 132. For further information on German education and social mobility see Ringer's *Education and Society in Modern Europe*, Indiana 1979.

[3]Dirk Hagener, *Radikale Schulreform zwischen Programmatik und Realität. Die schulpolitischen Kämpfe in Bremen vor dem Ersten Weltkrieg und in der Entstehungsphase der Weimarer Republik*, Bremen 1973, p. 17.

[4]Friedrich Paulsen, *German Education, Past and Present*, New York 1908, p. 142. I was not able to obtain Alfred Graf (ed.), *Schülerjahre. Erlebnisse und Urteile namhafter Zeitgenossen*, Berlin 1912; August Winnig, *Frührot. Eine Buch von Heimat und Jugend*, Hamburg 1950; J. M. Olsen, *The Prussian Volksschule 1890–1914. A Study of the Social Implications of the Extension of Elementary Education*, New York University, Ph.D. Diss. 1971.

were themselves mostly graduates of the *Volksschulen*. "The authorities have not chosen you for your deep scholarly attainments, nor for your extensive learning," admitted one director of a training seminary: "No, but because you were sober and have shown yourselves humble and true believing Christians."[5]

There were wide variations in the size and quality of elementary institutions quite apart from differences based on religion. In the rural east of Prussia, for example, schools were typically badly financed, housed in ramshackle buildings with eighty or more pupils crammed into a single room with one teacher – usually an inexperienced recent graduate who had not yet managed to be transferred to a less isolated and more desirable post. Such schools were frequently closed owing to shortages of fuel and supplies, inclement weather, or the schoolmaster being called away to attend to other sexton's duties associated with the parish church. In 1906 a third of Prussian *Volksschulen*, the majority in the East, still had a single class with up to eighty pupils of all ages; the average class size in Prussia a few years later was fifty-six as compared to just under twenty-one for secondary schools. Urban schools usually had three or more classes and were better financed, equipped and staffed than those in the countryside, although demographic changes sometimes caused serious overcrowding as was the case in some Catholic *Volksschulen* in towns with large numbers of Polish immigrants and in areas of rapid urbanisation where the confessional balance suddenly shifted. Towns in Prussia and some other states also provided a form of secondary training at "middle schools" (*Mittelschulen*) but only a small percentage of the population were enrolled in them prior to 1914. Indeed, even when city authorities and teachers pressed for a broader curriculum and a higher school-leaving age, they often found their efforts restrained by the apathy or hostility of parents and employers.[6]

By the 1890s, as part of a wider process of national self-questioning, large numbers of Germans were engaged in a heated debate over the merits and purposes of the existing educational system. One part of this reappraisal of schools is well known, namely the growing expression of dissatisfaction with the overloaded syllabus of the *Gymnasium* and demands that more attention be devoted to fostering creativity and to teaching "modern" subjects.[7] But equally controversial was the future of the *Volksschulen*. For some they were a glaring symbol of the pervas-

---

[5]Quoted by F. Nyssen, 'Das Sozialisationskonzept der Stiehlschen Regulative und sein historischer Hintergrund', in K. Hartmann, *et al.* (eds.), *Schule und Staat im 18. und 19. Jahrdundert*, Frankfurt a. Main 1974, p. 305.

[6]E. N. Anderson, 'The Prussian Volksschule in the Nineteenth Century', in G. A. Ritter (ed.), *Entstehung und Wandel der modernen Gesellschaft. Festschrift für Hans Rosenberg zum 65. Geburtstag*, Berlin 1970, pp. 261–279; Rainer Bölling, *Volksschullehrer und Politik. Der Deutsche Lehrerverein 1918–1933*, Göttingen 1978, p. 17; Detlev K. Müller, *Sozialstruktur und Schulsystem. Aspekte zum Strukturwandel des Schulwesens im 19. Jahrhundert*, Göttingen 1977; D. Crew, 'Definitions of Modernity. Social Mobility in a German Town, 1880–1901', *The Journal of Social History*, 7, No. 1 (1973), p. 63–64. Describing the plight of rural schools in the *Reichstag* in 1900, Bebel reported that "the school at Oberlessnitz had to be closed because of the dilapidation of its quarters; the teacher was compelled to find employment elsewhere ... The community was responsible for levying money for a new building, but because they were poor day labourers they needed at least seven years to raise the small sum of 2,700 marks." Quoted in K. Hartmann, *et al.* (eds.), *op cit.*, pp. 369–370.

[7]Most recently: J. C. Albisetti, *Kaiser, Classicists and Moderns. Secondary School Reform in Imperial Germany*, Yale University Ph.D. Diss. 1976.

ive illiberalism of German society, a powerful brake upon social mobility which helped solidify class barriers and widen support for socialist extremism. For others anti-clericalism or anti-Catholicism lay at the root of their desire for reform, or nationalist conviction that a unified school system was necessary to offset the deep confessional and regional divisions between Germans. Also widespread was the belief that the *Volksschulen* in their existing form were totally inadequate training for the vast majority of citizens in a fast-expanding modern state. Huge numbers of *Angestellte* were required as technicians, supervisors and office personnel by an increasingly bureaucratised and commercialised economy while the rise of new and technologically more sophisticated industries required a more literate, responsible and adaptable workforce.[8] In primary education, as in much else, the 1890s ushered in an intensified discussion of priorities: were the chief duties of the *Volksschulen* social control or social advancement, a fostering of national unity or the preservation of religion, the training of the mind or the character?

Against the advocates of change were arrayed a conservative coalition of landowners, right-wing state officials and churchmen who guarded jealously their power over local school boards and anticipated severe social consequences from any meddling with mass education. These groups had always been ambivalent about elementary education, torn between their conviction that it was inevitable in a modern state and their disquiet at its social consequences. The widespread mistrust of schoolmasters had gained great and lasting stimulus from their outspoken identification with liberalism in 1848 after which Frederick Wilhelm IV chastised them "for all the misery visited upon Prussia" and for "the irreligious mass learning . . . through which you have eradicated the beliefs and loyalties of my subjects".[9] Admittedly in 1871 the refrain was different, Sedan and Königgrätz being claimed as victories for public education as well as the German nation; but, on balance, distrust persisted as typified by one *Konsistorialrat* Munchmeyer who in 1878 admonished: "Where there is no desire for reading, don't stimulate it! It is not desirable that peasants read newspapers."[10] In general, resistance to school reform should be placed in the context of anti-modernism and fears of social levelling; it was one element in an arsenal of conservative ideas, joined to hatred of mass politics and reflective of a general conviction that the *Reich*, beneath its show of wealth and technical progress, was suffering from

[8] Hartmut Titze, *Die Politisierung der Erziehung*, Frankfurt a. Main 1973. The relationship between economic growth and educational opportunity has attracted detailed research in recent years. P. Lundgreen argues that very little of the impressive rate of economic growth in nineteenth-century Germany appears directly attributable to developments in education; see his 'Educational Expansion and Economic Growth in Nineteenth Century Germany', in L. Stone (ed.), *Schooling and Society. Studies in the History of Education*, Baltimore 1976. See also R. H. Samuel and R. H. Thomas, *Education and Society in Modern Germany*, London 1949, and E. Spranger, *Zur Geschichte der deutschen Volksschule*, Heidelberg 1949.

[9] F. Kreppel, 'Der Lehrer in der Zeitgeschichte', in H. J. Schoeps (ed.), *Zeitgeist im Wandel*, vol. 1, Stuttgart 1967, p. 205. Also, Thomas Nipperdey, 'Volksschule und Revolution in Vormärz', in K. Kluxen and W. J. Mommsen (eds.), *Politische Ideologien und nationalstaatliche Ordnung. Festschrift für Theodor Schieder*, Munich 1968; Anthony J. LaVopa, 'Status and Ideology. Rural Schoolteachers in Pre-March and Revolutionary Prussia', *Journal of Social History*, 12, No. 3 (Spring 1979).

[10] K. Hartmann, *et al.* (eds.), *op. cit.*, p. 331 (essay by F. Wenzel, 'Sicherung von Massenloyalität und Qualifikation der Arbeitskraft als Aufgabe der Volksschule').

moral and spiritual decline. The Conservative Tivoli programme of December 1892 expressed this attitude succinctly: "The Christian *Volksschule*", it insisted, was "the most important guarantee against the increasing degeneration of the masses and the progressive dissolution of all the bonds of society". The next sentence, as is well known, deplored the obtrusive and divisive influence of Jews in the *Volksschulen* and demanded "Christian teachers for Christian pupils".[11]

It was "Jewish influence" in its broadest and vaguest sense that was meant here for, as was immediately apparent to anyone who investigated the matter, Jews formed only a minute fraction of the teaching staff in public schools. Other fears were more direct and tangible: in speeches and essays we repeatedly come across concern about Freethinking, Monism and other surrogate religions; there are laments that in the pitiful existence of slum families "nobody brings a child nearer to his God or teaches him to practise the virtues of a Christian"; and fears are often expressed that improved reading skills, where divorced from clerical guidance, merely promoted the readership of socialist newspapers and enlarged the pool of potential agitators.[12] It was the challenge of Social Democracy above all that shaped Prussian school legislation after 1890: the legislative tightening of confessional controls over the next two decades was guided by the belief that the *Volksschule* was a crucial locus of the class struggle and that to implant Christian principles was the best deterrent against revolutionary politics. Kaiser Wilhelm II sounded the alarm in May 1889 when his Cabinet Order urged that teachers "strive to create among youth the conviction that the teachings of Social Democracy not only contradict the divine commandments and Christian moral teaching, but are actually impracticable and are equally pernicious in their consequences both for the individual and the whole society". The royal pronouncement precipitated a national debate about political education focusing attention on schools and teachers as a front line in the battle against Marxism.[13]

If anything, it was the forces of conservatism that inflamed the school issue in the 1890s. The Social Democrats possessed no detailed school policy until 1906 and there are signs that in many areas the party preferred to tread lightly in questions of religion where workers' loyalties were divided. While Bebel might predict to the *Reichstag* in 1872: "If we bury heaven and its authority, then earthly authority soon collapses," some twenty years later in the Erfurt programme the party quietly acknowledged that religion was a private concern and Liebknecht insisted that "those among us who declare war on religion . . . do but strengthen the enemy". Not until 1905, with controversy mounting over the Prussian school bill and a turn towards socialism among a small but vocal group of teachers, did the party engage the *Volksschule* issue more directly.[14]

[11]F. Salomon, *Die Deutschen Parteiprogramme*, Leipzig 1907–1930, vol. 2, pp. 71–72. See also: R. S. Levy, *The Downfall of the Anti-Semitic Parties in Imperial Germany*, New Haven 1975, ch. 3.
[12]See, for example: *Pädagogischer Jahresbericht*, 61 (1908) pp. 1–9, 64 (1911) p. 1. Franz Wenzel, *loc. cit.*, p. 338; H. Titze, *op. cit.*, pp. 179–180.
[13]Gerhardt Giese, *Quellen zur deutschen Schulgeschichte seit 1800*, Berlin–Frankfurt a. Main 1961, p. 194. See also: W. C. Langsam, 'Nationalism and History in the Prussian Elementary Schools', in E. M. Earle (ed.) *Nationalism and Internationalism. Essays Inscribed to Carlton J. H. Hayes*, New York 1950.
[14]Owen Chadwick, *The Secularization of the European Mind in the Nineteenth Century*, Cambridge 1975, pp. 80–82. Also, Leo Arons, *Die Preussische Volksschule und die Sozialdemokratie*, Berlin 1905.

Most *Volksschullehrer* were from peasant, artisan and skilled worker backgrounds, though an increasing number were sons of minor officials and white collar employees as the century progressed. They were largely graduates of the *Volksschule* who at the age of fourteen were selected for six years of further training, three in a preparatory school and three at a teachers' seminary. Instruction was narrow and confessionally segregated, a large proportion of their time being devoted to just that corpus of knowledge necessary for the *Volksschule* curriculum plus additional study of the Bible, church history, prayers, drawing and hymns.[15] "The bedrock of all pedagogic virtue is true, unfeigned piety", declared a Catholic text for teaching candidates in 1896, "the teacher must regard his occupation as one of service to God".[16] At the seminaries this injunction to be a model of Christian behaviour was translated into endless restrictions upon personal freedom, prolonged afterwards by close supervision during a period of apprentice teaching. The Catholic and Protestant churches examined prospective religion teachers for their orthodoxy, clerics served as local school inspectors in most of the *Reich* and played a leading role on school boards and in poorer, rural areas schoolteachers were often obliged to perform a variety of menial duties at the local church. Their pay was generally low – figures for 1872 show their salaries about one third of those of secondary teachers – and until the 1880s little provision was made for retirement pensions. It is hardly surprising that the children of *Volksschullehrer* seldom followed in their footsteps although a large percentage went into "academic professions" where the social prestige was higher.[17]

It was this marked subordination at every stage of their career to the authority of the pastorate that more than anything irked *Volksschullehrer* and encouraged their efforts for greater professional recognition and educational reform. As early as the 1830s attempts were made to organise teachers but a new era dawned with the foundation of the *Deutsche Lehrerverein* (DLV) in December 1871. Conditions were favourable: a dramatic increase in the German population created a shortage of teachers which lasted till the end of the century; the presence of Falk at the Prussian *Kultusministerium* opened an era of steady improvement in teachers' pay and conditions; and, as we have seen, the rapid expansion of socialism helped focus attention on the *Volksschule* as a critical repository of "German values".[18] Membership in the DLV rose steadily from 5,000 in 1874 to over 100,000 in 1900, while smaller competing organisations developed mostly with confessional ties but also in answer to the needs of a growing number of women

---

[15] R. Bölling, *Volksschullehrer und Politik*, Göttingen 1978; Karl Bungardt, *Die Odyssee der Lehrerschaft. Sozialgeschichte eines Standes*, Frankfurt a. Main 1959; I. L. Kandel, *The Training of Elementary School Teachers in Germany*, New York 1910; J. M. Olsen, 'The Social Views of Prussian Primary School Teachers During the Wilhelminian Era', *Paedagogica Historica*, 15, No. 1 (1975).
[16] M. Heinemann (ed.), *Der Lehrer und seine Organisation*, Stuttgart 1977, p. 43.
[17] Bölling, *op. cit.*, pp. 22–24; E. Cloer, 'Sozialgeschichtliche Aspekte der Solidarisierung der preussischen Volksschullehrerschaft im Kaiserreich und in der Weimarer Republik', in M. Heinemann (ed.), *op. cit.*, for details on Prussian wage scales, etc. Also, Folkert Meyer, *Schule der Untertanen. Lehrer und Politik in Preussen*, Hamburg 1976.
[18] R. Rissmann, *Geschichte des Deutschen Lehrervereins*, Leipzig 1908; C. L. A. Pretzel, *Geschichte des Deutschen Lehrervereins in den ersten fünfzig Jahren seines Bestehens*, Leipzig 1921.

teachers.[19] Even in an age of pressure groups and *"Vereinsmeierei"*, elementary schoolteachers were notable for their high degree of organisation: some 92 per cent belonged to a professional association in 1914 and almost 65 per cent to the DLV alone.[20] Further research about the regional growth and activities of these *Vereine* is needed before the role of teachers in educational reform and in the larger process of secularisation can be fully evaluated. One group, for example, which is largely unstudied but for whom materials are abundant, is schoolmistresses whose organisations figure importantly in both the history of schools and of feminism. Generally from more middle-class backgrounds, women teachers encountered strong opposition from male colleagues – a mixture of sexual prejudice and social resentment, coupled with fears that employment of women would drive down wages and injure their social status. Female competition strengthened occupational solidarity among males in this as in other spheres.[21]

Autobiographies and reflections on schooldays in Wilhelminian Germany often depect the typical *Volksschullehrer* as a harsh disciplinarian, fiercely patriotic and anti-socialist, a civilian drillmaster and pillar of the *status quo*. How valid this depiction is requires further study; certainly, it embodies at best a small part of the truth filtered through the memories of the teacher's natural classroom antagonists. The many journals, books and speeches published in defence of the teacher's movement tell another story: of mounting discontent and pressure for reform, of anti-clericalism and a hardening conviction that changes in primary education must be predicated upon a wider process of political liberalisation. Books by DLV spokesmen like Karl Fischer and Robert Rissmann reveal *Volksschule* masters as an upwardly mobile, status conscious group, insistent upon their importance to society and resentful of the inferior status accorded them by the clergy and *Bildungsbürgertum*. Socially they occupied an intermediary position, linked firmly to the middle class in values and pretensions, emphatic about the social distance between themselves and most of the population they served, but committed to radical changes in the education of the poor. "The German *Volksschule* teacher", Fischer asserts, "may today expect to be numbered among the cultivated classes", because of his "breadth of learning". But, he adds, low salaries often force him to marry uneducated, lower-class women to the detriment of his community position and prevent him from having a home which – like the Evangelical parsonage – could offer a model of Christian comfort and respectability. Their ideology exemplified their position between classes: a curious blend of snobbishness towards the lower orders, anger at a class structure

---

[19]Bölling, *op. cit.*, p. 36; also, Ilse Gahlings, *Die Volksschullehrer und ihre Berufsverbände*, Neuwied–Berlin 1967.

[20]The DLV had about four times the number of members enrolled in the confessional associations that competed with it. For the Catholic organisations see: Ernst Cloer, *Sozialgeschichte, Schulpolitik und Lehrerfortbildung der katholischen Lehrerverbände*, Ratingen 1975.

[21]Ilse Gahlings and Elle Moering, *Die Volksschullehrerin. Sozialgeschichte und Gegenwartslage*, Heidelberg 1961; Gertrud Bäumer, *Lebensweg durch eine Zeitenwende*, Tübingen 1933; Helene Lange, *Lebenserinnerungen*, Berlin 1921. For teachers and other aspects of German feminism: R. J. Evans, *The Feminist Movement in Germany 1894–1933*, London 1976; Amy Hackett, *The Politics of Feminism in Wilhelmine Germany 1890–1918*, Ph.D. Diss. Columbia University 1976. I was not able to obtain: Helmut Beilner, *Die Emanzipation der bayerischen Lehrerin, aufgezeigt an der Arbeit des bayerischen Lehrerinnenvereins 1898–1933*, Munich 1971.

which thwarted their efforts to rise, and pride in their allotted task of integrating the rural and urban masses into one German culture.[22]

As the chief voice of the *Volksschullehrer* the DLV campaigned for a whole programme of reforms in pay and privileges as well as for structural changes in education. In the years after 1900 it focused increasingly upon the issue of church influence and drew up a list of goals including: the abolition of clerical *Schulaufsicht* and a limitation of church authority in the selection of classroom materials; the training of teachers at universities; curricula changes involving less memorisation and less religious instruction; and, most important, the reorganisation of education to create an "integral" school or *Einheitsschule* which would abolish the existing social and confessional segregation of children. These remained the basic goals of the teachers' movement throughout Weimar, although there was considerable difference of opinion about the specific details of each. Some envisioned a wholly secular education, others wished to retain a strong Christian emphasis. The relationship of teacher training to the rest of university curricula was a subject of disagreement, as was the optimum length of the "common" education before streaming of pupils. Not wishing to alienate any portion of its following the DLV leadership endeavoured to hold a middle course which among other things meant firm support of the *Simultan* model of Hesse and Baden.[23]

After 1905 passions over schools were greatly inflamed by the growing agitation of the radical wing of the teachers' movement especially active in Bremen, Hamburg and Saxony. These urban teachers were more independent and more politicised than their rural counterparts, although many had begun their careers in small communities and nursed vivid memories of clerical oversight. In Bremen a series of disputes with school authorities, culminating in disciplinary action against a teacher who had written a Nietzschean-style attack on religion, provoked a storm of protest and demands in September 1905 for a complete separation of church and school.[24] Shortly thereafter teachers in Hamburg – a town with a tradition of radical *Volksschullehrer* reaching back to 1848 – campaigned for completely secular education, the *Einheitsschule*, and the abolition of private elementary schools.[25] In both places, the rapid growth of labour coupled with socialist election successes had set off a wave of alarm among the ruling élites, while strikes and pressure for franchise reform thickened the atmosphere of social

---

[22]Konrad Fischer, *Geschichte des Deutschen Volksschullehrerstandes*, Hannover 1892; reprint Leipzig 1969, vol. 2, pp. 410–428. The best source for teachers is the DLV's *Pädagogische Zeitung* (after 1919: *Allgemeine Deutsche Lehrerzeitung*). Otto Buchheit *Die pädagogische Tagespresse in Deutschland 1871–1914*, Würzburg 1939; Otto Menne, *Die Autobiographie des deutschen Volksschullehrers im 19. Jahrhundert*, Ph.D. Diss. Frankfurt a. Main 1925, was not available to me.

[23]Johannes Tews, *Die Deutsche Einheitsschule. Freie Bahn jedem Tüchtigen*, Leipzig 1916; idem., *Aus Arbeit und Leben*, Berlin 1921; T. R. Hanshew, *The German Volksschullehrer and the Weimar Republic. A Study of the Deutscher Lehrerverein*, Ph.D. Diss. University of Nebraska 1975.

[24]Hagener, *op. cit.*, p. 31 ff. (Wilhelm Scharrelmann's book was titled *Blätter aus unseren Herrgotts Tagebuch*, 1904).

[25]See the excellent study by Hildegard Milberg, *Schulpolitik in der pluralistischen Gesellschaft. Die politischen und sozialen Aspekte der Schulreform in Hamburg 1890–1935*, Hamburg 1970. See also Friedrich Gansberg, *Religionsunterricht? Achtzig Gutachten*, Leipzig 1906, containing the views of well-known educators petitioned by a group of Bremen teachers.

and political tension. Agitation over a new Prussian school law had also reached a climax at this time further politicising the teachers' movement and causing a sizeable minority, in Bremen especially, to advocate closer ties with Social Democracy. Schoolteachers' aims, they concluded, were realisable only in a new social order "where the lower classes who have a definite interest in the *Volksschule*, exert a dominant influence over the legislative authorities". In fact, as we have noted, the SPD had done little until this time to elaborate a programme for secular education, but at the Mannheim Congress of 1906 a committee was established – led by Clara Zetkin and Heinrich Schulz, a former Bremen teacher – to draw up more concrete proposals.[26]

The Bremen and Hamburg disputes received wide publicity in the national press but still greater was the public furor over events in Saxony where the tightly knit *Lehrerverein* – with some 14,000 members in 240 local branches – voted overwhelmingly for sweeping reforms at its annual meeting at Zwickau in 1908. In brief, the "Zwickau Theses" called for an end to clerical inspection, non-confessional Christian instruction for all students, a drastic revision of materials used in religion classes, greater efforts to harmonise religion and the results of modern science and corresponding changes in teacher training. The Saxon solution was more radical than the *Simultanschule*, where separate confessional religious teaching was given, but stopped short of the Bremen demands for total secularisation.

Already in Hamburg *Volksschule* controversies had mobilised groups of clergy and Lutheran parents in favour of stricter doctrinal controls. Now, in Saxony, the Synod of the *Landeskirche*, with only one dissenting voice, quickly condemned the Zwickau proposals and the Evangelical *Schulverein* began to marshal opposition across the state. Literally dozens of polemical books and hundreds of articles contributed to the agitation; many localities sponsored public debates between pastors and schoolmasters, and a flood of protests reached the *Kultusministerium* from both sides. The issue stirred the whole intellectual community and one professor after another entered the fray. In the event the campaign produced no major reforms and liberal attempts in the *Landtag* to abolish clerical inspection were smothered by the government; but Zwickau revealed more clearly than before how widespread dissatisfaction with the *status quo* had become and demonstrated at least the possibility of forging a broad based liberal and anticlerical movement for school reform. No detailed scrutiny has been made of this whole debate, yet it would tell us much about the politicisation of education and would illuminate pre-war attitudes in Saxony, so crucial for developments there after 1918.[27]

The undisguised alarm which school disputes created in the Evangelical churches is a measure of the degree to which they felt themselves on the defensive against the secularising trends of modern society and weakened by internal divi-

[26] Karl Christ, *Sozialdemokratie und Volkserziehung. Die Bedeutung des Mannheimer Parteitages der SPD im Jahre 1906 für die Entwicklung der Bildungspolitik und Pädagogik der deutschen Arbeiterbewegung vor dem ersten Weltkrieg*, Bern 1975. *Pädagogische Reform*, Hamburg, 15th June 1905, quoted by Milberg, *op. cit.*, p. 20.

[27] A. B. Show, *The Movement for Reform in the Teaching of Religion in the Public Schools of Saxony*, U.S. Bureau of Education, Bulletin No. 1, Washington 1910.

sions between Liberals and Conservatives over social outlook. Pessimistic about the ability or willingness of the state to guarantee the faith, anxious over the pivotal position in politics achieved by Catholicism and the widening appeal of modernist theology among Protestants, the conservative groups that dominated the *Landeskirchen* manifested a kind of "siege" mentality.[28] Other symptoms of this embattled outlook, outside school issues, are not hard to find: the succession of heresy trials conducted in the Prussian church and elsewhere after 1900, culminating in disciplinary actions against Karl Jatho and Gottfried Traub; the manipulation of nationalism and militant anti-Catholicism as a way of diverting attention from political and spiritual divisions among Protestants; and stepped up campaigns against Monism and anti-clerical groups like the *Deutsche Kulturpartei*. Despite a large and nominally stable church membership, the influence of religion in everyday life was assumed to have waned sharply. Church attendance statistics were rarely taken and available records are subject to considerable error, but Protestant periodicals widely agreed that a precipitous decline had occurred since the 1860s. Probably 5 to 10 per cent of church members attended services with any regularity, though regional variations were large with Darmstadt as high as 12·4 per cent in 1913 and Berlin as low as 1 to 3 per cent.[29] Clearly, while local conditions were varied, the Protestant clergy were generally faced with the fact that their formal contact with a large number of Germans was increasingly limited to three occasions: baptism, marriage and burial. Recognition of this made the teacher and the schoolhouse all the more vital to the preservation of a Christian state and the dissemination of Protestant values.[30]

There were, of course, liberal Protestants who favoured reform and insisted that children were estranged from the faith by poor instruction and outmoded pedagogic methods. They sympathised with the moderates among schoolteachers, regarding the *Simultanschule* as the best means of fostering national unity in confessionally mixed areas; but their power within the Prussian and other state churches should not be exaggerated and while the number of interconfessional schools in Prussia increased rapidly after 1890, they still accounted for only 4 per cent of the total in 1911. Petitions to the Evangelical *Oberkirchenrat* included a steady stream of complaints about nondenominational schooling.[31]

The Catholic Church did not face a comparable protest movement in its confessional schools, although, as the researches of Ernst Cloer demonstrate, friction was not absent between church and teachers.[32] One factor in the generally better

---

[28]The literature on German Protestantism is enormous. For a recent, important study of Prussia, see: Arnold M. Horowitz, *Prussian State and Protestant Church in the Reign of Wilhelm II*, Ph.D. Diss. Yale University 1976.

[29]Daniel R. Borg, 'Volkskirche, "Christian State" and the Weimar Republic', *Church History* (1966), p. 188, n. 5. Some figures are contained in the *Kirchliches Jahrbuch*.

[30]Adolf Levenstein, *Die Arbeiterfrage unter besonderer Berücksichtigung der sozialpsychologischen Seite des modernen Grossbetriebes und der psycho-physischen Einwirkungen auf die Arbeiter*, Munich 1912, pp. 323–353. I was not able to obtain: Ermel Horst, *Die Kirchenaustrittsbewegung im deutschen Reich*, Cologne Univ. Diss. 1971.

[31]*Statistisches Jahrbuch für das Deutsche Reich* (1911). Gottfried Traub began a *Blätter für religiöse Erziehung* in October 1907 committed to reform of religious instruction and associated with the *Verein für religiöse Erziehung* (400 members).

[32]Cloer, *op. cit.*

relations may have been social: priests and teachers came from similar backgrounds whereas the Protestant pastorate was drawn from solidly middle-class and professional families, adding social distance to the occupational tensions that arose. In any case, on the necessity of confessional education Catholic teachers' groups, clergy and Centre were united and firm. The memory of the *Kulturkampf* remained vivid and uncertainty about church schools and clerical rights in school appointments and syllabi continued to plague the episcopate and Centre Party leadership. Through a variety of Catholic, occupational, political and recreational associations which provided for the spiritual and material needs of the faithful, the Church had developed its own complex subculture as all-embracing as that of the Social Democrats. And while recent research on the Centre after 1890 has tended to de-emphasise the clerical nature of the party and point to its focus on social and material rather than sectarian themes, such "de-Catholicisation" should not be exaggerated. Party and clergy continued to work closely; indeed, in several areas, partly in response to secularising pressures and the aggressively anti-Catholic campaigns of the anti-clericals and the *Evangelische Bund*, there seems to have been a resurgence of Catholic *Kulturpolitik* after 1900. Thus, in Bavaria, as Robin Lenman has shown, Catholic populism waged a furious struggle against "urban decadence" and the artistic avant garde of Munich; also, in Baden and Württemberg, Catholic solidarity and the mobilisation of a confessional vote was facilitated by liberal and socialist proposals for raising the school leaving age and limiting church authority over instruction. Such issues counteracted divisive tendencies within the Catholic electorate over social policy.[33]

In Prussia also the Centre gave highest priority to preserving the confessional character of schools in Catholic districts. Windthorst recognised the integrative power of the school issue and used it effectively in, for example, the *Landtag* elections of 1888 when Catholics were admonished to support only candidates who endorsed a greater church role in the appointment of teachers and the selection of reading texts. In 1890–1892 and again in 1904–1906 the Centre summoned all its energies for the task of obtaining a satisfactory school law. The first attempt ended in defeat when, after a storm of protests and petitions from Liberals, Socialists, Jewish organisations, academics and local authorities, the Zedlitz–Trützschler bill was abandoned. The genesis of this bill and its failure has been fully analysed by J. A. Nicholls and requires no further comment here, except to say that it intended a substantial increase of clerical power and a firm check to further expansion of the *Simultanschule*. By requiring that *all* teachers wherever possible be of the same confession as the majority of their pupils, it

---

[33] R. Morsey, 'Die deutschen Katholiken und der Nationalstaat zwischen Kulturkampf und dem ersten Weltkrieg', *Historisches Jahrbuch* (1970); Ronald J. Ross, *Beleaguered Tower. The Dilemma of Political Catholicism in Wilhelmine Germany*, Notre Dame 1976; David G. Blackbourn, 'Class and Politics in Wilhelmine Germany. The Center Party and the Social Democrats in Württemberg', *Central European History*, 9 (1976); idem., 'The Problem of Democratisation. German Catholics and the Role of the Center Party', in R. J. Evans (ed.), *Society and Politics in Wilhelmine Germany*, London–New York 1978; R. Lenman, 'Politics and Culture. The State and the Avant-Garde in Munich 1888–1914', in R. J. Evans (ed.), *op. cit.*; C. H. E. Zangerl, 'Courting the Catholic Vote. The Center Party in Baden, 1903–1913', *Central European History*, 10 (1977); *Pädagogischer Jahresbericht*, 61 (1908), p. 112; 63 (1910) No. 8.

threatened – in the eyes of critics – to saturate all instruction with the spirit of confessionalism. Furthermore, the setback to conservative and clerical aspirations was only shortlived: over the next years secret agreements with Prussian officials gave the Catholic hierarchy *de facto* control over its school appointments and in July 1906 the conservative–clerical alliance succeeded in passing a new school law that contained most of the Zedlitz proposals. This Prussian legislation showed again how meagre were the chances of achieving liberal school reform via the institutions of the *Kaiserreich*. In retrospect, despite all the efforts of teachers and reformers, the period after 1900 – at least in terms of tangible, legislative results – appears mostly as a time of reaction.[34]

In Prussia then, as in the other German states, the prevailing theme in *Volksschule* education prior to 1914 was conservatism. A Württemberg school ordinance of 1729 argued: "Schools are not to be regarded as a mere preparation for civic life but as workshops of the Holy Spirit, because the Lord is best served not with skilled people but with pious ones."[35] It was a viewpoint that showed staying power, and religion, taught according to confession, remained central to the curriculum. But the battle lines were drawn before 1914. Among the reformers it was the DLV that took the lead, enlisting wherever possible the support of Liberals and Left-Liberals but always suspicious of socialism. Its capacity to effect change, while arguably significant in such matters as pay, privileges and the status of *Volksschullehrer*, was small when it came to issues of a structural and curricula nature. By the outbreak of war it was evident that substantial reform depended upon further democratisation of German society; this alone would shake the tenacious hold conservative forces maintained over schools. Education, secularisation, political and social power were, in practice, inseparable; but, while discontent with the existing school system was widespread, it also encompassed a multiplicity of views and what remained very questionable was whether a common programme, a successful compromise, could be devised to accommodate these opinions – even if general conditions became more hospitable to change.

II

The defeat of Germany and the collapse of the monarchy altered completely the prospects for school reform. The Social Democrats and Independent Socialists supported firmly a separation of Church and State, the abolition of religious instruction, and the establishment of a free, compulsory and socially integrated school system. Liberals, or most of them, desired nondenominational schools, as did the majority of teachers. And while the Centre, the DNVP and the churches remained steadfast against any basic change in the pre-war system, the new

---

[34] John K. Zeender, *The German Center Party 1890–1906*, Transactions of the American Philosophical Society, vol. 66, pt. 1, Philadelphia 1976; J. Alden Nichols, *Germany After Bismarck. The Caprivi Era 1890–1894*, Harvard 1958, ch. 5. For the whole subject see: E. C. Helmreich, *Religious Education in German Schools. An Historical Approach*, Harvard 1959.

[35] A. B. Show, 'Historical Significance of the Religious Problem in the German Schools', reprint from *Education*, March 1911, p. 11.

political constellation of November 1918 seemed bound to produce far-reaching reorganisation. In fact the early euphoria in the ranks of school reformers proved false as the conflicts of the Republic forestalled decisive action and allowed a reassertion of much of the traditional order in education as in so many other spheres. Already by the end of 1920 the main wave of reform was halted; the statistics for 1931 illustrate concisely the limits of Weimar's achievement – 80 per cent of *Volksschulen* were still confessional and only 5·5 per cent of the pupils in secondary schools were listed as children of industrial and "other" workers.[36]

What accounts for this failure? Part of the answer lies with the adroit manoeuvring of the churches and the right who skillfully exploited moderate fears of revolution and social levelling. The continuation of Wilhelminian civil servants in many instances had an obstructive and conservative effect. But more important perhaps, were the sharp disagreements over aims and tactics that cut across the groups advocating reform. These schisms – between Liberals and Socialists, parents and teachers, and within the teaching profession – were not new but in the context of the Republic, with the larger opportunities it afforded, they became especially crippling. The fragmentation of the Left after November 1918 and the failure to build a solid bridge between Social Democracy and the German bourgeoisie undermined the cause of school reform; the Centre Party's growing power in the shifting coalitions of Weimar did the rest. The result is a commentary not so much upon the failings of the Republic as on the immensity of its tasks. There were no easy solutions or straightforward alternatives to the policies pursued: the school issue, like so many others, was encumbered with the conflicts and prejudices of the past.

Roughly speaking, there were three distinct stages in the *Volksschule* controversy that raged during the first decade of the Republic: (a) 1918–1920, a period of rapid reform in the states and immobility at the *Reich* level, concluding with a vague School Compromise enshrined in the Weimar Constitution; (b) 1920–1925, a time of intense controversy during which the contradictions of the constitutional settlement were tested and school practice brought into line with the emerging balance of power in Weimar; in general this period saw on all sides the retreat of reformism; (c) 1925–1928: in these years the defenders of religious education recaptured the offensive making strong efforts to secure national legislation satisfactory to confessional schools. After 1928 political and economic instability overshadowed education as a priority for the republican régime.

The first weeks of the Revolution brought a spontaneous wave of reforms at the state and local levels as revolutionary councils and newly constituted *Land* governments moved swiftly to decree the separation of Church and State, deprive clerics of their accustomed places as school inspectors and to revise or abolish altogether the teaching of religion. Discussions about curricula and the responsibilities of parents, proposals for the election of school principals, collegial review and teacher training were pursued energetically across the *Reich*. In Bavaria, Johannes Hoffmann introduced sweeping changes; the new Saxon government moved at once to implement the 1908 Zwickau programme; and in such

[36]Fritz Ringer, *Education and Society in Modern Europe*, Indiana 1979, p. 286. The sons of artisans, tradesmen and white-collar workers made the largest gains in secondary education during Weimar.

centres of pre-war agitation as Bremen, Hamburg and the Thuringian states, radical schoolteachers made their presence felt on Soldiers and Workers' Councils. Most significant of all, the SPD–USPD coalition in Prussia placed the *Kultusministerium* in the hands of Konrad Haenisch and Adolf Hoffmann ("Ten Commandments" Hoffmann who had introduced a bill for abolishing all subsidies to churches into the Prussian *Landtag* during the war). It was Hoffmann (USPD) who forced the pace, often over the objections of Haenisch, pushing through a series of measures by administrative decree: on 15th November instructions were issued allowing dissenters to withdraw their children from religion classes, then came the abolition of clerical *Schulaufsicht*, and on 27th November a more comprehensive set of directives further delimiting the role of religion in education. The DLV welcomed these developments and the stage seemed set for the establishment of the *Einheitsschule*.[37]

After their first stunned reactions to the sudden demise of the old order, the Catholic and Protestant churches rallied quickly demonstrating their power to mobilise a broad protest movement around a crusade against "atheistic socialism". The leaders of both confessions denounced the abrogation of their traditional privileges and waged a vigorous campaign, conducted by church groups, clergy, school parents' associations and confessional teacher *Vereine*, to rescue German *Kultur* from the avalanche of extremism. Over 800 protests reached the Prussian government alone from church associations, the *Reich* administration received some 3,000 separate petitions in a matter of months, and early in 1919 the Evangelical Church mounted a signature drive in support of Christian education which by April had gathered 6½ million names. Through its network of auxiliary associations – the *Volksverein für das katholische Deutschland* alone boasted 800,000 members in 1914 – the Catholic church particularly was well prepared to arouse the collective consciousness of its members, their fears of a renewed *Kulturkampf*, their small-town abhorrence of urban values and socialism, and longstanding distrust of centralised administration. The Protestant churches, less unified and more loosely structured, had greater difficulty adjusting to their new situation and lacked a political voice comparable to the Centre.

The impact of the religious campaign was soon evident in the actions and rhetoric of Majority Socialists and Liberals in the weeks prior to the election of the National Assembly. In Berlin, religious protests culminated in a demonstration of some 60,000 people against Hoffmann's decrees. This, coupled with separatist threats among the Catholic population in the Rhineland, brought conciliatory gestures. Haenisch and others began to delete references to secular education from their speeches; earlier decrees were modified or suspended in areas where opposition was greatest and promises were given that decisions over the separation of Church and State and over education would be deferred until a National Assembly could meet. Similarly, in Bremen and Hamburg where revolutionary councils had abolished religion in schools, spokesmen for the DDP and SPD began to shift their ground in response to the tide of protests from

---

[37]Helmreich, *op. cit.*, pt. 3, ch. 7; Giese, *op. cit.*, p. 234 ff.; Hermann Gieseke, 'Zur Schulpolitik der Sozialdemokraten in Preussen und im Reich 1918–1919', *Vierteljahrshefte für Zeitgeschichte* (1965), pp. 162–177; D. Hagener and H. Milberg, *op. cit.*

church congregations and parents' groups.[38] Through meetings and lectures, as well as at Sunday sermons, the clergy were active campaigners making candidates specify their views on religious and educational issues, paying special attention to newly enfranchised women voters, and in some cases assembling their congregations for a brief service before marching together to the polling booths. And while it is impossible to gauge closely their impact on the pattern of voting, to all appearances education and religion were among the earliest and most effective rallying points in the *fronde* against the new republic. But, while a non-socialist majority was returned to the Assembly, most delegates favoured a national school system based on nondenominational institutions; the SPD and DDP together polled 19·5 out of 30 million votes and gained 262 seats, on the face of things still a commanding position from which to continue the process of reform.

During the early months of 1919, while educational disputes at the state level remained intense, attention began to shift to the constitutional debates in Weimar, where schools emerged as among the most divisive problems under discussion. In fact, it proved easier to negotiate a compromise over the corporate status and privileges of the churches than to resolve the question of religion in the *Volksschule*. It was the Centre which took the initiative in defence of confessional schools, entering the first Weimar government and using its position in the Constitutional Committee on education to exploit the tensions between its coalition partners. Prospects for success in these efforts were uncertain for while opinion was mixed about the merits of a common school system (*Einheitsschule*) and secular education, about two-thirds of the Assembly accepted the *Simultanschule* as a basic model. What altered the situation overnight was a dramatic shift of power within the *Reich* administration caused by the resignation of the Democrats in June 1919. Their refusal to accept the Versailles peace terms left the SPD reliant on Catholic support, the price of which was substantial concessions over schools. The result was two hastily patched up School Compromises, worked out by Heinrich Schulz who had framed the SPD programme for secular education in 1906. The choice between confessional, nondenominational and secular schools was largely passed over to parents. In the first compromise all three school types were given equal status but so great was the uproar at this formula that it was quickly withdrawn. Much of the Left, Liberals and teachers condemned the plan as an unprecedented betrayal of principle – an "internal Versailles" in the words of Paul Oestreich – and defections ran high among the SPD rank and file (35 voted in support, 25 against and 104 abstained). The second compromise, for which a portion of the Democrats were won over, declared the *Simultanschule* to be the norm but permitted secular and confessional schools to exist at parents' request. This rather vague prescription was in-

---

[38]J. R. C. Wright, "*Above Parties*". *The Political Attitudes of the German Protestant Church Leadership 1918–1933*, Oxford 1974, pp. 17–18; K. W. Dahm, *Pfarrer und Politik*, Cologne 1965; Jochen Jacke, *Kirche zwischen Monarchie und Republik*, Hamburg 1976. By far the best study of the Centre in the post-war period is Günther Grünthal, *Reichsschulgesetz und Zentrumspartei in der Weimarer Republik*, Düsseldorf 1968.

corporated into the constitution adopted by the Assembly on 31st July 1919; it had been the final issue postponing ratification.[39]

With respect to the *Volksschule* the salient feature of the new constitution was confusion: it bore all the marks of hard bargaining and serious disagreement. Briefly stated, it called for a public school system to be developed as an "organic whole" (the meaning of which was left obscure) with a common course of instruction for all children. The length of this common *Grundschule* was a subject of marked dispute – the DLV, for example, favoured six years but the figure eventually accepted was four. Elementary schooling was made free and compulsory, religion was included as a subject of regular instruction but both pupils and teachers were permitted to withdraw from it. Special *Vorschulen* were to be abolished, so were private schools at a later, unspecified date, while public assistance was to be made available to poor students to obtain a secondary education. State authority over schools was affirmed and inspection given over to trained officials, but the question of the degree of church influence in instructional materials and on school boards was left in doubt. While the *Simultanschule* was described as the "norm", there was little agreement as to what that meant in practice and provision was made for other types of institutions as well (RV 146, 2). And then, most confusing of all, RV 174 prescribed that until the enactment of a *Reich* school law "the present legal status shall continue". This clause effectively ensured that three-quarters of the German elementary schools remained confessional and placed a serious obstacle in the way of converting them to other types. Thus the plan for a unitary system had been reduced to a four-year common curriculum administered in three distinct kinds of school. Moreover, the status of changes made by individual states since November 1918 was unclear; whether they fell under the protection of RV 174 was left to the courts to decide.[40] If not, then secular schools were obviously unlawful since none had existed prior to 1918. Soon after, in the *Reich* School Conference of 1920, the concept of a unitary system met with further opposition, this time from secondary schoolteachers assiduous in protecting the privileges of their schools and their own higher social prestige.

The first stage of the Weimar school battle ended with the *Reichstag* elections of June 1920 and a decided shift to the Right by voters. The Democratic Party, with which the DLV had closest personal and political ties, suffered most, declin-

[39]Christoph Führ, *Zur Schulpolitik der Weimarer Republik*, Weinheim 1970; L. Albertin, *Liberalismus und Demokratie am Anfang der Weimarer Republik*, Düsseldorf 1972, pp. 287–289. For Oestreich, see: W. Böhm, 'Paul Oestreich und das Problem der sozialistischen Pädagogik in der Weimarer Republik', in M. Heinemann (ed.), *Sozialisation und Bildungswesen in der Weimarer Republik*, Stuttgart 1976. He was the founder of the Socialist *Bund der entschiedenen Schulreformer*.

A comment on terminology is called for here. Strictly speaking the interdenominational schools after 1919 were titled *Gemeinschaftsschulen*. In theory, at least, they were religiously neutral and non-Christian faiths were on a par with the Christian confessions. The pre-war *Simultanschulen*, in contrast, were based on the two Christian confessions. In fact, the difference was very small, especially in view of the fact that resistance to the appointment of non-Christian teachers continued. In this essay, for the sake of convenience, I have used the term *Simultan* throughout, as did most contemporaries.

[40]Giese, *op. cit.*, p. 240 ff. The constitutional provisions became the basis for the so-called Basic School Law (*Grundschulgesetz*) of April 1920, which was to serve until a new, national law was devised. In fact it was never superseded and remained the basis of Weimar education.

ing from 5·6 to 2·3 million votes, a setback from which it never recovered. The SPD also sustained heavy losses and soon decided to leave the cabinet. Henceforth *Volksschullehrer* depended on the SPD and DVP to champion reform, never a very satisfactory situation since most teachers nursed strong anti-socialist opinions and the DVP was always divided and potentially unreliable on educational issues. Discord was also evident among teachers for, while average salaries rose, the drop in *Volksschule* enrollments (from 9 million in 1921 to 6·7 million in 1926) and the increasing number of women entering the profession intensified job competition. In 1926, it is estimated, there were 30,000 unemployed teachers in Prussia alone; "proletarianisation" (*Lehrerproletariat*) was a term bandied about in the press and "as poor as a schoolmaster" was a graphic phrase, then as now. Not surprisingly younger teachers began to found their own organisations, placing more emphasis on union tactics and envisioning the possibility of strikes. In these circumstances it became more difficult for the DLV leadership to offer clear direction.[41]

Over the next years controversy raged at *Reich*, state and local levels simultaneously as opposing groups tested the ambiguities of the constitutional settlement. Only the major themes can be outlined here but abundant materials exist for closer study of regional variations.

The educational aims of the Catholic Church and the Protestant *Landeskirchen* overlapped in many respects, although the Protestant leadership was suspicious and not a little resentful of the political power Catholicism had attained in Weimar. Both confessions desired a clearer legal foundation for the denominational school, a formal admission of its equality with the *Simultanschule*, teacher training on confessional lines and the recognition of church jurisdiction in matters of religious texts and appointments. At Fulda in November 1920 the Catholic episcopate declared that it was the duty of all Catholic parents to see that their children went to confessional schools; a year later the Bishop of Münster decreed that those who sent their children to secular schools should be refused holy sacraments.[42] In most areas the clergy argued strongly for parents' rights: on this ground, for example, the Catholic Church pressed for confessional schools in the traditional *Simultan* regions. Elsewhere, however, especially in industrial centres where popular pressure favoured secular education, the clergy stood firm on RV 174 ("the present legal status") and received powerful backing when the *Reichsgericht* in 1920 nullified reforms enacted by radical governments in Bremen, Hamburg and Saxony.[43]

Even where the constitution was crystal clear, as with the liberty of teachers to refuse religious instruction, it could not guarantee compliance since community pressure often made the right little more than semantic. Thus, frequently, in rural districts, there was nobody else available to conduct the lessons and school authorities simply refused to hire or keep refractory schoolmasters. In some in-

[41]*Statistisches Jahrbuch für das Deutsche Reich*, 1921–1922, 1926–1927; Volker Hoffmann, 'Lehrer und Gewerkschaft. Die preussische Junglehrerbewegung in den ersten Jahren der Weimarer Republik', in M. Heinemann (ed.), *Sozialisation und Bildungswesen*, especially pp. 254–255.
[42]Cloer, *op. cit.*, p. 108 n.
[43]Georg Schreiber, *Zwischen Demokratie und Diktatur*, Regensburg 1949, p. 60; Hagener, *op. cit.*, p. 217 ff.; Milberg, *op. cit.*, p. 264 ff.; Walther Landé, *Die Schule in der Reichsverfassung*, Berlin 1929.

stances harassment became extreme: one teacher reported to the *Sozialistische Erzieher* in 1920 that his food supplies had been stolen, his vegetable patch plundered and threatening notes left behind, that stones had been thrown at him by unseen enemies, and that local sources of fuel to heat the schoolroom were finally cut off forcing closure of the building. "The situation", he acknowledged, "has now become intolerable, so that I am compelled to seek a transfer ... the fanatical intolerance of the inhabitants knows no bounds." As for the local school board and inspector, he added, they sympathised with his tormentors.[44] Another case which received extensive publicity occurred in the Catholic schools of the Westphalian mining town of Herne in the summer of 1920 where a six-week strike involving as many as 6,000 children was launched to secure the dismissal of three teachers who refused to teach religion.[45] Clerics took striking pupils on nature walks and students paraded through the town waving the black, white and red flag of the monarchy, a symbol of their defiance of the constitution. The Rhineland Westphalian mining districts, with their long tradition of church influence on communal life and, more recently, growing leftist agitation, were particularly militant and strikes and withdrawals occurred in Solingen, Cologne, Düsseldorf and many other towns. In other parts of Prussia as well protests and demonstrations erupted against alterations in the composition of school boards or, in some cases, in opposition to secular schools. Parents' associations, elected in many regions in 1919, frequently became embroiled in these disputes. While in some cases they worked well, in others schoolteachers, who before 1914 had often urged greater public participation, now found themselves vexed at the constraints these committees imposed on them. Sometimes parents seemed too conservative and pro-clerical, at others – especially in Berlin and other large towns – too radical: the extremes rather than the middle seemed to dominate in this turbulent period. The DLV was adamant that "clerical and political parties shall not misuse" parents' rights "to destroy the unity of German popular education", but its own efforts at mobilising parental support were slow and largely ineffectual when compared to the *Katholische Schulorganisation* and the Protestant *Reichselternbund* (the latter estimated to have over 2 million supporters).[46]

In Saxony and Thuringia leftist régimes backed by the trade unions made determined efforts to introduce the *Einheitsschule* and to impose a policy of secularisation, encountering fierce opposition from a broad alliance of clergy, secondary school teachers, state bureaucrats, middle-class parents' groups and various associations of professional and technical people. Saxony, as we have seen, had long been a centre of radicalism among *Volksschullehrer* and the tradition continued during Weimar. Early in 1920 the Saxon *Lehrerverein* – in contrast to most of the DLV – affirmed strike action and began to organise a strike fund; at

[44]Helmut König (ed.), *Monumenta Paedagogica*, vol. 4, *Beiträge zur Bildungspolitik und Pädagogik der revolutionären deutschen Arbeiterbewegung in der Zeit der Novemberrevolution und der revolutionären Nachkriegskrise 1918–1923*, Berlin 1968, p. 210, from the *Sozialistischer Erzieher* 27th February 1920 (this was the organ of the *Verband sozialistischer Lehrer und Lehrerinnen Deutschlands und Deutsch-Österreichs*).
[45]Konrad Haenisch, *Neue Bahnen der Kulturpolitik*, Stuttgart 1921, p. 74; *Monumenta Paedagogica*, vol. 4, pp. 222–223.
[46]Breslau meeting of DLV in June 1924, *Educational Yearbook of the International Institute of Teachers' College 1924*, New York 1925, p. 282.

national conferences they championed the secular school and locally urged members to refuse to give classes in religion.[47] Thus, in 1923 some 13 per cent of *Volksschule* pupils – a very high figure compared to other states – were withdrawn from religion classes, while almost 35 per cent of teachers refused to teach it, and of the rest 45 per cent pronounced their support of the Zwickau programme of 1908.[48] This can be contrasted with Westphalia where almost 94 per cent of teachers favoured the retention of religion in 1920.[49] State efforts in Saxony to convert denominational schools met with stubborn resistance from church and right-wing political groups, but the *Simultan* model made consistent headway throughout the years of the Republic.

In Thuringia a Socialist government embarked on a series of reforms 1921–1923 to establish an integral school system.[50] It aroused the same opposition as in Saxony and was faced with numerous acts of defiance as when the régime's abolition of school religious holidays was met with widespread absenteeism. "In Jena," commented one local journal with obvious approval, "pupils in the upper classes of the secondary schools have taken a step toward self help; they have stayed away from classes and participated in an impressive religious service held at their request ... by a former pastor".[51] Pockets of resistance to the radical drift of most schoolmasters in the area were also evident in the *völkisch* teachers' groups that sprang up, among whom the Nazis made early progress.[52]

In Bremen and Hamburg, for which detailed local studies exist, it was clearly not religion alone that mobilised local opposition to school reforms: until Weimar both areas had a record of tolerance and moderation with respect to religious instruction. But the social levelling implied by a unitary school system sent tremors of alarm through the ranks of *Oberlehrer*, middle-class parents and public officials who were products of the old structure. Religious instruction and denominational schools often provided a convenient and disguised way of rejecting proposals that were socially repugnant. Support for the Protestant *Reichselternbund*, as Hildegard Milberg has shown, was less symptomatic of a resurgence of religious piety than of social disquiet among Hamburg's *Bürgertum*, the threat they perceived to their control of higher learning, and their determination to resist plans for the closure of private academies which many of their children attended.[53] Efforts to make the *Grundschule* work and to reform secondary education were impeded at every turn; private institutions continued and found

[47] Bölling, *op. cit.*, pp. 90, 99–101.
[48] *Christliche Welt* (1923), p. 125.
[49] Bölling, *op. cit.*, p. 254, n. 155.
[50] G. Witzmann, *Thüringen von 1918 bis 1933*, Meisenheim am Glan 1958, pp. 67–76; Donald R. Tracey, *Thuringia under the Early Weimar Republic, 1919–24. A Study in Reform and Reaction*, University of Maryland Ph.D. Diss. 1967; idem., 'Reform in the Early Weimar Republic. The Thuringian Example', *Journal of Modern History*, 44, No. 2 (1972), pp. 195–212. I was not able to obtain: Paul Mitzenheim, *Die Greilsche Schulreform in Thüringen*, Jena 1965, and, by the same author, 'Die schulpolitische Situation in den Thüringer Kleinstaaten vor der Novemberrevolution 1918', *Jahrbuch für Erziehungs-und Schulgeschichte*, 5–6 (1965–1966).
[51] *Christliche Welt* (1921), p. 847.
[52] Chaim Seeligmann, 'Vorläufer des Nationalsozialistischen Lehrerbundes', and W. Breyvogel, 'Volksschullehrer und Faschismus', in M. Heinemann (ed.), *Der Lehrer und seine Organisation*, Stuttgart 1977.
[53] Milberg, *op. cit.*, p. 206.

patrons not only among the established upper bourgeoisie, but also among upwardly mobile *Mittelstand* families. An echo of this may perhaps be seen in the denunciation of local *Volksschulen* by the Retailers Chamber of Hamburg in 1924, which called them "a mere experimental ground for Social Democracy".[54] The levelling effects of the inflation and the Depression probably did more to desegregate Hamburg schools than any reform measures enacted by the Senate.

In regions of Communist and Socialist strength community pressure mobilised behind *"weltlich"* or secular schools in which religion was replaced by classes in ethics and contemporary moral problems. They were the focus of much agitation, being regarded by important elements within the churches as contrary to RV 174. Demands by leftist parents and unions for the creation of such schools – in Prussia the government got around the constitutional tangle by simply permitting children who had been withdrawn from religion classes to be grouped into separate *Sammelschulen* or "assembled schools" staffed by volunteer teachers – usually produced confrontations with conservative officials and clergymen. Local records and newspaper files will reveal more about the evolution of these local clashes and their politicising effect on communities: East German research records numerous protests and demonstrations in Erfurt, Gelsenkirchen, Düsseldorf, Elberfeld, the working-class suburbs of Spandau, Wedding and Moabit in Berlin and many more. We learn, for example, of 700 pupils on strike for a week in Gladbach in April 1921, and more serious unrest in Düsseldorf in the same year: "We have been on strike since 13th September for a secular school", reported two activist pupils, "the Free School Society is leading the strike. At first we marched through the town and sang splendid songs of struggle. Now we are holding our classes in the rooms of inns."[55]

Fear of the polarisation of schools and of Communist infiltration was widespread. Not only in towns like Berlin and Hamburg but also in Württemberg where all *Volksschulen* were confessional, state and police authorities brooded about the presence of such groups as the *Jung Spartakusbund*.[56] In Prussia it would seem that clerical opinion altered somewhat over time, viewing the secular institutions more and more as a convenient means of displacing politically disruptive and insubordinate elements from the religious schools. The Social Democrats for their part favoured the *Sammelschulen* as a victory for gradualism, the wedge of a slowly emerging new secular system. Among Communists, however, opinion became divided with some deeply troubled by the "quarantining" of leftist pupils and teachers so that they could have little impact on the rest.[57]

For all the publicity about them, the significance of the *weltlich* schools should not be overestimated. Most were in Prussia (289 of 295 in the *Reich*), but even there they represented only 0·48 per cent of the total *Volksschulen* in 1931. As was to be expected, given the tighter hold of the Catholic church over its congregants, some five and a half times more Protestants were enrolled in them. With-

[54]*Ibid.*, p. 191.
[55]König (ed.), *op. cit.*, p. 231 (from *Der junge Genosse*, 15th May 1921).
[56]Hauptstaatsarchiv, Stuttgart, E 151c (Abt. III) Württemberg Innenministerium, No. 223: 29th December 1925, 14th January 1926, 3rd March 1926, 7th December 1926 (Klaiber to Min. of Interior).
[57]König (ed.), *op. cit.*, p. 235; *Die Rote Fahne* (Berlin), 22nd April 1921.

drawal of pupils from religion classes was more common, at least in traditionally radical areas. In Saxony 13 per cent opted to withdraw, in Berlin just under 7 per cent, while in Bremen and Hamburg in 1921 (just after religion was reintroduced) we find figures as high as 33 and 40 per cent respectively; but in the nation as a whole estimates place the number at 1 per cent or less.[58]

The local struggles discussed here took place within the context of a national debate over a new school law. The constitutional settlement had left education largely in the hands of the States, thereby increasing regional contrasts, and in areas where opinion was deeply split – in Brunswick, for example – each new administration brought disruptive shifts in policy.[59] But the constitution also called for the speedy enactment of a national school system and, while it is impossible here to offer an adequate analysis of the *Reichstag* and *Länder* debates, their broad contours should be sketched to illustrate both the steady retreat of the school reformers and the paralysis of the Republic over issues where the *Länder* were deadlocked.

During 1921 discussions of a school bill focused upon a proposal drawn up by Heinrich Schulz (SPD) and Erich Koch-Weser (DDP) which, after several delays, reached the *Reichstag* floor in January of the following year. It represented the most that Schulz believed attainable, little more in fact than the *status quo*, i.e., nondenomination, the "norm" with provision for other types of school at parental request. The bill may well have reflected accurately the political balance of the time but since the existing situation was unacceptable to almost everyone, the prospects for the Koch–Schulz formula were very poor from the outset. It was a measure, noted the DNVP deputy, Richard Mumm, with some disdain, that was framed by a Socialist who believed in secular schools, under a Minister of the Interior who advocated the *Simultanschule*, in the administration of a man who championed confessional education. As such it drew fire from all sides. The Centre remained firm over its definition of denominational schools and wanted recognition of their complete equality; the DNVP demanded safeguards for private institutions; and fierce opposition arose among Democrats, teachers, and the far Left who refused to tolerate a measure that perpetuated educational diversity, left secondary schools untouched and sanctioned confessional control of over 80 per cent of the *Volksschulen*. None of the interested groups was prepared to forsake their larger goals at this stage and the bill was finally sent to committee for revision where, after another 160 meetings, it was

---

[58] *Statistisches Jahrbuch für das Deutsche Reich*, 1931; Hagener, *op. cit.*, p. 218. If anything, parents seemed more ready to contract out of the churches themselves and thus avoid additional taxes than to intervene in their child's education. This may denote indifference in some cases or, perhaps, fear of singling out their child in the eyes of the authorities and the community. See also, for the Wilhelminian period, the remarks of Adolf Levenstein, *op. cit.*, p. 326; D. R. Borg, *loc. cit.*, p. 187, notes that 4·05 per cent of the membership of the Prussian church and 4·03 per cent of the membership of all Evangelical churches contracted out between 1919 and 1927, thus avoiding payment of church taxes levied by the state.

[59] Ernst-August Roloff, *Braunschweig und der Staat von Weimar*, Brunswick 1964; Wright, *op. cit.*, p. 56. The NSDAP gained office as early as October 1930 in Brunswick and immediately turned to a purge of the school system – the eradication of "Marxism" in the schools was calculated to win the sympathies of the bourgeoisie: see, Ernst-August Roloff, *Bürgertum und Nationalsozialismus, 1930–1933. Braunschweigs Weg ins Dritten Reich*, Hannover 1961, pp. 29–33.

abandoned altogether at the end of 1923. In retrospect, the Koch–Schulz formula may well have been – as Schulz later insisted – the last real opportunity of achieving a national law which gave precedence to the nondenominational school. But few could have foreseen the political instability of the next years and the basic change in voting patterns which fragmented and weakened the Liberals, bringing a succession of minority governments.[60]

After 1925 teachers and school reformers were clearly on the defensive.[61] The general shift of the Republic to the Right encouraged the Catholic Centre and Protestant interests to campaign hard for a law that would abolish the nominal precedence given to interconfessional schools and redefine clerical powers of surveillance. A major triumph in this direction was the Bavarian Concordat of January 1925 (followed soon after by agreements with the Protestant churches) which gave the Catholic church extensive privileges over schools and almost total veto power over their teaching staffs in all subjects. For Liberals, Socialists and teachers this was a clear affront to the principle of state authority over education and an outright rejection of the constitutional injunction that a national system of schools be introduced. While actual conditions in Bavarian schools were probably little changed, the wider implications of this clerical victory helped regalvanise the Liberal–Socialist school alliance; indeed, so great was the indignation of non-Catholics that the Conservative cabinet of Hans Luther which had been tinkering with a school bill very favourable to confessional interests, abandoned its plans and postponed indefinitely the negotiations it had begun for a national Concordat with the Papacy.[62]

The final effort to pass a school law – and the one which came closest to success – occurred in 1927 with the formation of the Marx–Keudell *Bürgerblock* cabinet, a shaky coalition of Nationalists, DVP and Catholic parties. Whereas during the early years of the Republic the Centre had formed coalitions with the SPD and DDP as the best means of protecting Catholic interests and restraining anti-clericalism, it now looked to alliance with the Right to safeguard its interests; the explosion of anger among Liberals and Socialists at the announcement of the Bavarian Concordat was proof enough that the Centre's programme for a national concordat and a favourable education law would never receive sympathy in those quarters. In January 1927, certainly, education was one of the chief considerations in the Centre's decision to participate in the cabinet and the

---

[60]Heinrich Schulz, *Der Leidensweg des Reichsschulgesetzes*, Berlin 1926; Grünthal, *op. cit.*, ch. 4, 5. Marx, Rheinländer and other Centre leaders were at first inclined to accept the proposal, tempted by the concession that all teaching in confessional schools would be "in the spirit of the confession"; but vehement opposition among the episcopate to any measure that accepted the *Simultan* model as the "norm" convinced Centre leaders to refuse the Schulz–Koch–Weser bill. In a blistering attack on Schulz, Clara Zetkin called the bill: "the rotten fruit from the rotten tree of the School Compromise of 1919". It was, she added, a complete betrayal of the ideas Schulz had espoused before the war and symbolised the larger treason of the Socialists to the ideas of the German Revolution – Clara Zetkin, *Ausgewählte Reden und Schriften*, vol. 2, pp. 476–495. See also the speech of DLV leader R. Seyfert at the Stuttgart Lehrertag in June 1921 in *Christliche Welt* (1921), p. 506 ("The *Einheitsschule* is dead, even before it could be born.").

[61]See Carl Weiss in *Pfälzische Lehrerzeitung* (1929), p. 222, as quoted by F. Kreppel, 'Der Lehrer in den zwanziger Jahren', in H. J. Schoeps (ed.), *Zeitgeist im Wandel*, vol. 2, Stuttgart 1968, p. 152.

[62]Grünthal, *op. cit.*

Nationalist Minister of the Interior, Keudell, began immediately to reorganise his ministry and prepare a bill. First came an unsuccessful attempt to extend the life of private schools, then a draft for a comprehensive school bill which represented considerably more than the churches had obtained in the constitutional negotiations of 1919. Briefly, it proposed the complete equality of confessional, secular and nondenominational schools, strongly affirmed parents' rights, and while verbally affirming the state's responsibility for education, gave the clergy wide powers over religious instruction and the choice of teachers.[63]

Months before the Keudell bill reached the *Reichstag* in October 1927 the national press was full of polemics and passionate appeals from its supporters and opponents. The *Volksschule* question had lost none of its intensity since 1919. Advocates of the bill included a wide range of church and parents' groups, confessional teachers' organisations, conservative academics and business interests. Some liberal Protestants worried that it might augment unwisely dogmatic and conservative tendencies in public education, but most religious journals gave the bill full support.[64] On the other side, the DLV – deeply shaken by the Bavarian Concordat and anxious about job security – summoned all its energies for a national campaign to obstruct the legislation. It worked for amendments and pressured parties at the state and national levels, arranged protests, petitions and lectures, and began mobilising support among parents. The key to success or failure was the DVP, a member of the governing coalition but always divided and unpredictable over educational issues; here the DLV strove to improve ties and to strengthen the resolve of DVP groups within the *Simultan* areas who spearheaded the resistance to Keudell.[65]

How effective the DLV's activities were cannot be gauged since many factors shaped the outcome; but the rank and file of the Peoples' Party refused to accept the bill unamended and despatched it to committee for revisions. A further two months of negotiations failed to break the deadlock and the cabinet collapsed under the strain. The Centre, as Ellen Evans has shown, preferred to kill the measure altogether rather than accept modifications for it feared that these would jeopardise advantages already achieved at the state level, particularly in Bavaria. And while some contemporaries misguidedly concluded that the school issue was a mere pretext for scuttling the coalition, in fact it had been the chief impetus for the formation of the *Bürgerblock* government.[66]

---

[63]*Ibid.*; R. Bölling, *op. cit.*, pp. 154–161. W. Offenstein, *Der Kampf um das Reichsschulgesetz. Die Entwürfe der Jahre 1925 und 1927*, Düsseldorf 1928.

[64]The reception of the Keudell bill by the Protestant press is discussed in F. J. Gordon, *The Evangelical Churches and the Weimar Republic*, University of Colorado Ph.D. Diss. 1977, although the account offers little by way of interpretation.

[65]Bölling, *op. cit.*, pp. 161–168.

[66]Ellen L. Evans, 'The Center Wages *Kulturpolitik*. Conflict in the Marx–Keudell-Cabinet of 1927', *Central European History*, 2 (1969), pp. 139–158. Evans points out that in states like Baden and Prussia the Centre had cooperated with the Socialists regularly, obtaining religious concessions in return. Thus, in Prussia, Josef Hess, the Centre leader in the *Landtag*, worked quite smoothly with Minister-President, Otto Braun, and his Minister of Education, Carl Becker, notwithstanding their opposing views on schools. What it meant, according to Braun, was that the Socialists gained almost a free hand in predominantly Protestant areas, while in Catholic regions the *status quo* was strictly observed. Lacking a powerful political voice – the DNVP was divided on religious issues and

So ended the last effort to pass a national school law during Weimar. Both the proponents of confessional and nondenominational schools were, so it appeared, capable of frustrating the intentions of their adversaries but unable to realise their own aims. When liberal reformers were in the ascendant, clerical forces had rallied successfully to defeat their proposals. By 1927 when the Centre looked like achieving a notable victory, it was snatched away by a temporary alliance of liberal and leftist groups. Past conflicts weighed too heavily upon the republican present to allow a compromise. Impasse on this issue also provides an illuminating parallel for the larger fate of the Republic: for failure in education contributed not a little to Catholic and Protestant disillusionment with the democratic system and greatly diminished the loyalty that *Volksschullehrer* felt towards Weimar.[67]

III

The weakening of religious controls over education is part of a broader process of secularisation in modern society. Admittedly, "secularisation" is a much more complicated notion than this essay implies.[68] Employed in a variety of ways and laden with all kinds of evaluative overtones and implications, the term has even been boycotted by some writers who argue that it no longer fulfils the function of a verbal sign being almost unintelligible and little more than a repository for all manner of ill-framed assumptions about religiosity and progress. Aware of the many disagreements about the word, I have chosen to rely on a rather bland and broad definition, i.e., "the process by which sectors of society are removed from the domination of religious institutions and symbols".[69] Clearly, the disengagement of society from religion, in education and other spheres, embraces both structural and what we might call intellectual–existential changes and there is

---

contained a strongly anti-clerical wing – the Protestant churches found it difficult to resist these pressures and, for example, by 1931 almost 34 per cent of Protestant *Volksschule* children were enrolled in nonconfessional schools as compared to 12·5 per cent of Catholics.

[67]Lack of space prevents me from discussing either the political affiliations of *Volksschullehrer* or the various gains they made under the Republic. With respect to the latter the results were fragmentary: in some states like Bavaria and Württemberg the Imperial system remained largely intact; elsewhere, sympathetic education ministers made headway in founding new secondary schools, allowing greater school autonomy, expanding nondenominational schooling and improving teacher training. As yet little is known about divisions within the ranks of teachers, the degree to which they were anti-clerical, or their relationship to clergy and parents during Weimar in small town, metropolis or rural environment. By the end of the 1920s teachers were, as a group, hard pressed: chronic inflation and then depression wiped out the gains achieved in salaries; government retrenchment jeopardised many, and a slowing of the birth rate reduced employment possibilities for younger teachers.

[68]See, for example, Peter E. Glasner, *The Sociology of Secularisation. A Critique of a Concept*, London 1977.

[69]Peter L. Berger, *The Sacred Canopy. Elements of a Sociological Theory of Religion*, New York 1969, p. 107.

frequently an asymmetry between the two. Lags and contradictions occur between legal and institutional developments and transformations in – to use too simple a term – the mental climate of a time. The history of the *Volksschulen*, then, reflects Church–State relations, the public authority of the churches and the intensity of religious belief among Germans – but not in any straightforward and obvious way. For one thing the role of schools in shaping cultural values and social change is so complex, a process so deeply entangled in the entire life of a society, that some historians despair of ever being able to say much about it.

Yet, if the impact of primary education on pupils and the significance of religious instruction for the wider process of secularisation are issues full of ambiguities and difficulties for historians, they were less problematical for most Germans discussed in this essay. What the passionate disputes from the 1890s to the 1920s illustrate, if nothing else, is that large numbers of Germans held firmly to the conviction that schools were a crucial formative agency in shaping national spirit, religious outlook and social values. This was true of the conservative and clerical defenders of the *Volksschule* before 1914, and also underlay the eagerness for sweeping reform during the early stages of the Republic. In a nation torn by deep political, social and ideological divisions, education was widely perceived as an antidote, a means of unifying and giving direction to society and of fostering loyalty to its political structures. Not surprisingly, in view of its vast numbers of pupils, the *Volksschule* became a focus for all the explosive tensions in German society.

Much more research on primary education is needed; the present essay, I am well aware, does little more than skim the surface. A few conclusions may be drawn nonetheless from the evidence surveyed here.

As we have seen, in 1933 over 80 per cent of *Volksschulen* were still confessionally organised. The Weimar Republic had failed either to establish a national, secular system of education akin to the French or to overcome religious divisions as was possible in England at a much earlier date. The continuation of close bonds between church and school was not merely an outcome of clever manœuvring by the clergy or the manipulative finesse of conservative interests, though both were important. The religious basis of elementary education could not have been prolonged had it not drawn strength from the religious and sectarian convictions of a great many Germans. While it is difficult to assess the weight of sheer indifference or inertia or to distinguish at times between anti-clericalism and rejection of religion *in toto*, the bitter quarrels provoked by the *Volksschule* seem to indicate strong religious attachments among Germans, attachments not easily measured by church attendance and similar statistics. Often historians slip easily into the assumption that religion from the 1870s was losing ground rapidly under the combined assault of rationalism, science and a host of new secular faiths; certainly, the "crisis of religion" was a theme that echoed through contemporary journals and speeches, but for all that the trend should not be exaggerated. While clergymen might lament the secular mood of the times, the fact remains that within a very short period after November 1918 they were able to mobilise a mass protest movement in defence of religion and confessional schools. "Parents' rights" in large areas of the *Reich* became almost synonymous with a religious education and the numbers of pupils kept away from classes in religion always remained small. Further research should tell us much more about the complex religious sociology of Germany, about regional and class variations beyond the basic divide between Protestant and Catholic. Admittedly, such information is hard to gather and to evaluate, but gradually a richer and more detailed mosaic can be pieced together. Clearly, the industrial strongholds of the Left were the places where rejection of religion was most pronounced; the prevalence of belief among workers and bourgeoisie in such towns seems markedly different. But we know relatively little about differences between men and women, between generations, or about the range of social, job and family pressures in small or large communities that dissuaded some from breaking with the church. In general, it appears that many working-class parents, while critical of clerical dogmatism, probably viewed a Christian ethical training as a necessary part of a decent upbringing. It was, for example, a check on youthful spirits and stopped children from "getting into bad ways" – in this regard one thinks of the British Socialist George Lansbury whose mother took him to a Methodist chapel if he were ill-behaved, for there he would be sure to hear of Hell.[70] Exactly what "religion" consisted of, is also unclear: a worker was probably more concerned with morals than metaphysics; religion might be subsumed under a vague sense of the purposiveness of life or might imply merely a reverence for Christ as an ethical exemplar; some undoubtedly claimed that science had replaced religion and yet acknowledged also the importance of living a Christian life – whatever the case, these shades of opinion and feeling are an important element of workers' culture and its relationship to the dominant culture.

If church attendance was not an accurate barometer of religious feeling in Germany, nominal religious affiliation was undeniably powerful in shaping a whole range of social and cultural attitudes. The history of primary education reconfirms this, especially with respect to German Catholics. Indeed, it would not be an exaggeration to say that Germany's confessional geography during the *Kaiserreich* and Republic was more significant in determining views about the *Volksschule* than any other single factor. In education, as in much else, Protestants and Catholics formed two cultures existing alongside each other. In comparison with the Protestant churches, Catholicism was everywhere more successful in safeguarding confessional schools and in maintaining its authority over teachers. Even after 1945 the Catholic episcopate remained "obsessed" with confessional schooling and as late as 1961 some 40 per cent of *Volksschulen* were Catholic, as compared to 17 per cent Protestant and 40 per cent interconfessional.[71] This meant that the vast majority of Catholic children were in Catholic schools, and only in the mid-1960s, despite a massive last-ditch advertising and pressure campaign by the bishops, did Catholic parents desert them in large numbers. What this reminds us is that while populations may be geographically close and contemporaneous in many respects, they can also display a differential temporality, so to speak; among Protestants the loosening of the bonds that connected them to their church and clergy occurred a full generation or more earlier.

[70]Chadwick, *op. cit.*, p. 106.
[71]Frederic Spotts, *The Churches and Politics in Germany*, Wesleyan Univ. Press 1973, p. 219.

Confessional distinctiveness in education is equally evident when one examines the German-Jewish community.* Representing in 1906 less than 1 per cent of the German population and only about 0·5 per cent of the total *Volksschule* pupils, it was seldom that Jews could gain much prominence for their priorities and aims in elementary education. As a result they have so far been omitted from this analysis of the national debate; but a few comments are necessary to complete the picture. In 1871 the long and widely debated process of Jewish emancipation was completed with the grant of full equality under the new federal constitution. And yet, as has been made clear, education remained indelibly Christian in character, confirming both the centrality of religion in German public life and bearing out what Uriel Tal and others have written about the deep and stubborn resistance to pluralism at so many levels in German society.[72] With regard to elementary schools the traditional distinction between "approved" and "tolerated" religious communities was carefully preserved. In Wilhelminian Prussia, for example, while religion was made a required part of school curricula, it was only Christian instruction that was obligatory; the responsibility for Jewish children was left to Jewish congregations, a heavy burden for some of the smaller and poorer ones in rural areas. Similarly, although public subsidies were provided in some states for Jewish schools, the vast majority of them were funded by private subscription and grants from the Jewish communities, not out of public taxes. Efforts to achieve more equable treatment met with repeated failure, serving – as Marjorie Lamberti has convincingly shown – to stimulate more intensive Jewish political lobbying.[73] Thus, during the Prussian school debates of 1904–1906 efforts by the *Verband der Deutschen Juden* and other organisations to obtain public provision of Jewish religious instruction, protection for Jewish schools and the appointment of Jewish teachers at all schools in subjects other than religion, were mostly disregarded.[74] After 1918, assuredly, the situation improved somewhat, but the heavily Christian character of *Volksschule* education remained unchanged and the bias of most public officials against Jews teaching Christian pupils was still very marked.

As several historians have noted, the urbanisation and integration of Jews into the emergent industrial society of Germany proceeded rapidly after 1830 but was uneven, producing a heterogeneous community rich in contrasts.[75] Focusing so heavily upon the cultural and political life of Jews in the big cities, for example,

---

*In addition to the literature quoted below see also the contribution by Max P. Birnbaum, 'On the Jewish Struggle for Religious Equality in Prussia 1897–1914', and the essay by Peter Pulzer, 'Why was there a Jewish Question in Imperial Germany?', pp. 144–145, in this volume of the Year Book – (Ed.).

[72]Uriel Tal, *Christians and Jews in Germany. Religion, Politics, and Ideology in the Second Reich, 1870–1914*, Ithaca–New York 1974.

[73]Marjorie Lamberti, *Jewish Activism in Imperial Germany and the Struggle for Civil Equality*, New Haven 1978.

[74]Ismar Freund, *Die Rechtstellung der Juden im preussischen Volksschulrecht*, Berlin 1908; S. Adler, *Das Schulunterhaltungsgesetz und die preussischen Bürger jüdischen Glaubens*, Frankfurt a. Main 1905. For comments on the Keudell bill of 1927 see: I. Freund, *Reichsschulgesetzentwurf und Judentum*, Berlin 1928.

[75]For example: Steven M. Lowenstein, 'The Pace of Modernisation of German Jewry in the Nineteenth Century', in *LBI Year Book XXI* (1976), pp. 41–56.

we often forget how many also lived in rural and small town areas.⁷⁶ Elementary education was an early and potent force in shaping the consciousness of Jews, in moulding their religious identity and their national self-image as Germans. And, as might be expected, the evolution of Jewish education mirrors both the contrasts within the community and the varying pace of its modernisation and assimilation. In the 1830s most Jewish children attended separate schools, but in the next decades, especially in large towns like Berlin, their enrolment dropped rapidly. In Prussia itself we find a steady decline: 318 schools in 1886, 244 in 1901, 219 in 1911, 153 in 1921 and 96 in 1926. In addition the number of pupils in each school decreased sharply as more and more families moved to larger urban areas or opted for better funded and better equipped Christian schools as giving a more promising start in life. Of 247 Jewish *Volksschulen* investigated in the *Reich* in 1913, Lamberti observes, some ninety-four had less than ten pupils.⁷⁷ Without any doubt discriminatory practices by public officials and the refusal in Prussia to grant state funds to indigent Jewish communities for schooling accelerated this decline; but, in general, it attests the vigorous "assimilationist" drive of the "modernised" sector of German Jewry. By 1901 only 37·7 per cent of Jewish *Volksschüler* in the State went to separate Jewish schools, 36 per cent attended Protestant ones and 21·5 per cent were registered in *Simultanschulen*.⁷⁸ Equally instructive in terms of Jewish distinctiveness is the fact that only 43·7 per cent of Jewish schoolchildren were enrolled in *Volksschulen* at all, as compared with 92·7 per cent of Christians.⁷⁹ Their numbers in secondary and private institutions were disproportionately high, testimony both to the bourgeois social character of German Jewry and its eagerness to seize new opportunities.

A growing cleavage between liberal and traditionalist Jews was also reflected in the decline of separate Jewish schools. Those who remained loyal to them were the orthodox, recently arrived *Ostjuden* who were in the first phase of assimilation, and rural Jews especially in the South-West; the majority of the Jewish bourgeoisie tended to regard them as retrogressive, a self-inflicted "ghettoisation" that could only impede the progress of successful integration. The debates over the Prussian school bill of 1906, already referred to, illustrate this split vividly. Thus, whereas liberal Jews focused chiefly upon the threats posed by the legislation to the *Simultanschule* and the situation of Jewish children in Christian schools, the orthodox protest was motivated by the danger posed to the future of Jewish schools. Unable to agree, the two sides lodged separate petitions of protest with the Prussian government.⁸⁰

During Weimar the decay of Jewish schools continued. In theory the constitution placed Jewish confessional education on a par with Christian, but failure to pass a national school law meant that Jewish schools were not established by the

---

⁷⁶In Württemberg, for example 21·52 percent of Jews in 1933 lived in villages and small towns. See Werner J. Cahnman, 'Village and Small-Town Jews in Germany. A Typological Study', in *LBI Year Book XIX* (1974), p. 107.
⁷⁷Lamberti, *op. cit.*, pp. 165–166.
⁷⁸J. Thon and A. Ruppin, *Der Anteil der Juden am Unterrichtswesen in Preussen*, Berlin 1905, p. 24.
⁷⁹*Ibid.*, p. 24.
⁸⁰Lamberti, *op. cit.*; also, most recently by the same author: 'The Jewish Struggle for Legal Equality of Religions in Imperial Germany', in *LBI Year Book XXIII* (1978), pp. 101–116.

states except where that was possible before 1919. In 1921 in Prussia only 3,921 children attended Jewish schools and 11,625 were registered in non-Jewish ones; moreover, between 1921 and 1926 the number of Jewish schools in the *Reich* plummeted from 207 to 124.[81] Only in 1933 did the Jewish school regain a vital place in the Jewish community as a whole.

This is not the place to make an appraisal of the consequences for Jews of attending schools that were permeated by Christian values and attitudes in a period when antisemitism was so virulent. The prevalence of anti-Jewish sentiments in both Catholic and Protestant churches, most recently explored by Hermann Greive and Richard Gutteridge, requires no additional comment here; clearly, from the 1890s to the end of Weimar, there were large numbers of Gentiles for whom the word "Jew" expressed in a vague cultural shorthand a whole cluster of values antithetical to the spirit of Christianity.[82] Jews themselves were deeply troubled by the presence of racial and religious prejudice in schools. The *C.V.-Zeitung*, *Jüdische Schulzeitung*, and other periodicals contain many reports on the increasing politicisation of elementary schools, especially during electoral campaigns, and the tension generated between Gentiles and Jews.[83] Fears that Jewish children were growing up divorced from their own religion and traditions coexisted with anxieties that they were ostracised and psychically impaired by Christian education. As for the Jewish schools, they occasioned their own worries: about both the character and quality of the education they offered and also the long-term results of such early segregation. Before historians can even speculate about the social and psychological impact of the *Volksschulen* in this regard we need to know much more about the interaction of school and society, conditions within schools and the behaviour of teachers. The recent spate of books on "socialisation" and education has ignored the topic altogether, and the whole subject of Jewish schooling in this period awaits proper treatment.[84] It has often been argued that *Volksschullehrer*, despite their liberal orientation over schools, were strongly attracted to *völkisch* and racialist ideas.[85] Individuals come

---

[81]Max Gruenewald, 'The Jewish Teacher', in *LBI Year Book XIX* (1974), p. 67; 'Zum jüdischen Volksschulwesen in Deutschland', in *Monatsschrift für Geschichte und Wissenschaft des Judentums* (1931), pp. 144–145.

[82]Hermann Greive, *Theologie und Ideologie. Katholizismus und Judentum in Deutschland und Österreich 1918–1935*, Heidelberg 1969; Richard Gutteridge, *The German Evangelical Church and the Jews, 1879–1950*, New York 1976.

[83]E.g., *C.V.-Zeitung*, 15th January 1926, pp. 1–3; 19th February 1926, pp. 6–7.

[84]To date historians have concentrated mostly on Jewish schools in the earlier part of the nineteenth century. See: A. Kober, 'Emancipation's Impact on the Education and Vocational Training of German Jewry', in *Jewish Social Studies*, January/April 1954; B. Stern, 'Die Stellung der Juden im öffentlichen Volksschulwesen in Preussen in ihrer Entwicklung vom Beginne der Emanzipation bis heute', in *Festschrift für Jacob Rosenheim*, Frankfurt a. Main 1931; Mordechai Eliav, *Jewish Education in Germany in the Period of the Enlightenment and the Emancipation* (in Hebrew), Jerusalem 1960. An important source for this whole subject is the *Jüdische Schulzeitung* (1925–1938), microfilm. Archives of the New York Leo Baeck Institute.

[85]See for example the comments of Werner Jochmann in 'Struktur und Funktion des deutschen Antisemitismus', in *Juden im Wilhelminischen Deutschland 1890–1914*. Ein Sammelband herausgegeben von Werner E. Mosse unter Mitwirkung von Arnold Paucker, Tübingen 1976 (Schriftenreihe wissenschaftlicher Abhandlungen des Leo Baeck Instituts 33), pp. 411, 422, 430–431. Also F. Neumann, *Behemoth. The Structure and Practice of National Socialism 1933–1944*, New York 1966, pp. 377–380.

immediately to mind – Adolf Damaschke, Julius Streicher and Hans Schemm, to name only three – but detailed study of a large sample would be necessary to assess how far this *Mittelstand* group converted its frustration and ultimately disillusion with Weimar into antisemitic passion.

Elementary teaching was not a profession that attracted large numbers of Jewish recruits. Those who became schoolteachers had much in common with their Christian counterparts being largely from village and small town backgrounds and eager for social mobility and recognition. Their frustrations were also similar. They were often burdened with extra duties as cantors, helpers at religious and community services and *Schochtim*; their pay was meagre; and they chafed at their subordination to the rabbi, much as the Christian teacher resented the interference of the pastorate. "If a *Hauptlehrer* of a state school", Max Gruenewald observed in understated fashion, "had the bad luck to have to contend with an antisemitic *Schulrat* on the one side and with an overbearing rabbi on the other, his life would be miserable."[86] Sometimes these shared occupational grievances did create bonds of friendship – the memoirs recently published by Monika Richarz include a touching example of a Christian and a Jewish teacher in a small Hessian village who exchanged the *Preussische Lehrerzeitung* and met regularly to bewail their lot, pulling closed the windows lest their grumblings be overheard.[87] But, whatever the relationships between individuals, the school system as a whole discriminated heavily against Jewish teachers, revealing again how far official practice fell short of official commitment to civic equality. Understandably the continuous decline of Jewish schools raised great concern among schoolmasters and made increasingly urgent the question of whether they could be hired in institutions that were largely Christian to give instruction in subjects other than religion. The figures were not very encouraging: in Prussia in 1901 there were 407 Jewish teachers (male and female) in Jewish schools, 78 in *Simultanschulen* and none in Christian confessional schools.[88] Also, in 1913, so the Jewish *Lehrerverband* claimed, only 112 out of 1,568 *Simultanschulen* had Jews on their faculty.[89] As for Jewish schoolmistresses, the non-denominational school was just about their only hope: of 56 in Prussia in 1901, 47 were in *Simultan* schools – 42 of them in Berlin.[90] Not surprisingly, while theoretically inclined to support nonconfessional education, Jewish teachers turned increasingly to defence of the Jewish school, having little faith that "common" education would mean equality in practice for Jews and Judaism.

During Weimar, the situation of Jewish teachers improved in some areas but the overall picture remained grim. Their total numbers declined by 25 per cent during the first decade of the Republic, as compared to a 10 per cent decline for

---

[86]Gruenewald, *loc. cit.*, pp. 67–68.
[87]Monika Richarz, *Jüdisches Leben in Deutschland. Selbstzeugnisse zur Sozialgeschichte im Kaiserreich*, Stuttgart 1979, Veröffentlichung des Leo Baeck Instituts, pp. 159–165.
[88]Thon and Ruppin, *op. cit.*, p. 47; also Ernest Hamburger, *Juden im öffentlichen Leben Deutschlands. Regierungsmitglieder, Beamte und Parlamentarier in der monarchischen Zeit 1848–1918*, Tübingen 1968 (Schriftenreihe wissenschaftlicher Abhandlungen des Leo Baeck Instituts 19), pp. 61–62.
[89]Lamberti, *op. cit.*, p. 163.
[90]Thon and Ruppin, *op. cit.*, p. 47.

the *Volksschullehrer* as a whole.[91] Moreover, those appointed to Christian schools during the extraordinary circumstances of the war were mostly replaced in subsequent years, and in answer to a formal enquiry in 1922 the Prussian Minister of Education announced that Jewish instructors could not be hired in *Simultanschulen* where no Jewish pupils attended.[92] In consequence, the percentage of Jewish *Volksschullehrer* became steadily smaller: 0·75 per cent in 1886, 0·44 per cent in 1901 and 0·28 per cent in 1931.[93] Not surprisingly, in this atmosphere of general decline, neither Jewish schools nor Jewish teachers, as Jochanan Ginat has observed, played much of a role in the new pedagogy of the 1920s.[94]

The plight of Jewish schools and teachers brings us back to our central theme: the ingrained resistance to genuine pluralism in German society. This, perhaps more than the rivalry between the States and the *Reich* or the party political squabbles of the 1920s, doomed efforts to achieve a unified national school system. The reform proposals formulated before 1914 were frustrated during the years of the Republic. Not that gains were absent – interconfessional schools made some headway, secondary schools expanded and progress occurred in pedagogy and teacher training. But the results were meagre compared to the expectations. Koppel S. Pinson once suggested that "perhaps the most serious charge against the Socialists and their bourgeois allies is that they failed to effect any significant change in education".[95] This is possibly too harsh and one may well doubt whether things could have been otherwise at least with respect to the *Volksschulen* after 1920. Certainly the continuities with the Wilhelminian system were very strong: church and school were not separated, and "parity" meant at best equality of numbers not that religion was reduced to a private affair. Early hopes that national unity and social consensus could be built via a more secular school remained mere dreams which dissolved altogether with the resurgence of the Right, the rift in the Left and the fissuring of German Liberals. Weimar never managed to harness the public school for its ideals, never realised what Durkheim viewed as the task of education in a republic: to make "a child understand his country and times, to make him aware of its needs, to initiate him into its life, and in this way to prepare him for the collective tasks awaiting him".[96]

[91]'Zum jüdischen Volksschulwesen in Deutschland', *loc. cit.* The number of Jewish children in *Volksschulen* also fell, by 15 per cent between 1921 and 1926. See also: *Im deutschen Reich*, 26 (1920), pp. 154–157, 312, 390–392; 27 (1921), pp. 63–64.
[92]*Im deutschen Reich*, 25 (1919), pp. 362–366. Also Helmreich, *op. cit.*, pp. 146–147.
[93]These figures are for Prussia, see J. Thon and A. Ruppin, *op. cit.*, and *Statistisches Jahrbuch für das Deutsche Reich* (1930). Also Helmreich, *op. cit.*, figures on p. 136.
[94]Jochanan Ginat, 'The Jewish Teacher in Germany', in *LBI Year Book XIX* (1974), p. 75.
[95]K. S. Pinson, *Modern Germany*, New York 1968, p. 414.
[96]E. Durkheim, *Moral Education. A Study in the Theory and Application of the Sociology of Education*, New York 1961, trans. E. K. Wilson and H. Schnurer.

Comments on the Papers of Ismar Schorsch, Vernon Lidtke and Geoffrey G. Field

BY FRITZ STERN

To talk of secularisation, to take stock of lingering Christianity in modern Germany, is a study of potential pitfalls, but our distinguished speakers demonstrate that these can be avoided.* It is important to remember the obvious: the form of religion cannot be taken for substance, the continued attachment of Germans to certain religious forms need not bespeak a high degree of actual credence; by the same token, a good deal of religious consciousness and sentiment can live on without necessarily finding expression in socially observable or sanctioned conduct.

The three papers deal with the role of the Christian religion in Germany and with the process of de-Christianisation; they deal, then, with some of the most profound and complicated problems in modern history. The process of de-Christianisation took place elsewhere, too, but it was of a particularly important character in Germany, in part because it became entangled with the continued division of Protestants and Catholics, in part because the development of higher criticism, itself a celebrated aspect of German scholarship, had so diverse an impact on German religious thought and practice. De-Christianisation and the fear of it also became entangled with the condition of the large and prominent Jewish minority in Germany. The process of secularisation cuts across the history of modern Germany, it cuts across the development of German thought and sentiment – and yet historians who have fastened on so many important subjects have done relatively little to probe the fundamental if elusive questions concerning religious consciousness and conduct in modern Germany.

The three papers have a common core. They ask what was the religious element and to what uses might it have been put at various times and by various people. Much can be learned from these papers, all of which bear witness to the vitality and the promise of our field. Our authors tried to find new material in order to ask new questions. We need to know not only what people and classes did or said, but also their "unspoken assumptions"; we need to know much more about the beliefs and ideas of Germans and of these none would be more important or elusive than questions about the great riddles: God, the meaning of life, the goal of life and self, the search for transcendence. German history has not only and at last discovered Jews, it is discovering as well certain hidden subjects, such as feelings and anxieties, such as questions of religious consciousness. French historians have pointed to the neglected subject, even if their approach may at

*These comments were delivered orally at the session on 'Religion and Secularization in German Society during the 19th and 20th Centuries' at the 93rd Annual Meeting of the American Historical Association in San Francisco in December 1978.

times be narrow. I am referring to their studies of *mentalité*, which need to be duplicated in our field, and perhaps supplemented by what might be called the iconography of daily life. If one deals with the church and with schools in the last century, one clearly touches on the formation of sentiments and values. There is obviously a constant interplay between social and intellectual change and religious consciousness; the change in idiom or vocabulary, as Vernon Lidtke suggests, is a major indicator of change, but that very change has of course its own social context, which needs to be explored.

Our three authors showed admirable restraint in not citing the all-too-familiar passage of Nietzsche; I shall not emulate their restraint, for the passage is the central text of our subject. It is in *Zarathustra* that he wrote:

> "God is Dead! God remains Dead! And we have killed him! ... The most holy and powerful the world has yet owned, it has bled to death under our knives – who will wipe this blood off us? The tremendous event is still on its way ... it has not yet reached the ears of man. Lightning and thunder require time, the light of stars requires time, deeds require time, even after they are done, before they are seen and heard. This deed is still farther from them than the farthest star – and yet they have done it themselves."

Nietzsche understood the magnitude of the cultural change; it was at the root of much of his thought. I would also recall to you his ever timely "untimely meditation" on David Friedrich Strauss, his magnificent diatribe against the trivialisers who would not recognise the enormity of the challenge of life without God, without Christianity.

I believe Nietzsche's attacks on Christianity and his warnings about life without it point to a fundamental characteristic of the process of secularisation in modern Germany. Much more than in France, in Germany in the last two centuries the process was one of *concealment*, not *confrontation*; in the Germanies there was no great indigenous struggle over the remaining Church lands or property, there was no *écrasez l'infame*, no fight – till very late in the day, as Geoffrey Field makes clear – over separation between Church and State, no sharp division or traditional hostility between teachers and priests. The one obvious exception was the *Kulturkampf*, which was directed against the Roman Church and often deplored by strict Protestants who saw in it an attack on all religions. But even the *Kulturkampf* – perhaps because of its divergent sponsors, i.e., the state and the liberals – carried with it an element of concealment. There was repression but little discussion or comprehension of fundamentals. Its importance in preserving an embattled religious minority in the *Reich* was considerable. The process of what J. V. L. Casserley has called *The Retreat from Christianity* takes specific forms in each national culture, its own particular mixture of religion and irreligion. The German experience can usefully be compared to the French or to the very different history of nineteenth-century England, where Victorian morality and the role of Methodism, for example, offered yet another variant.

Let me try to suggest what I mean by relative concealment: on the one hand, as Vernon Lidtke makes clear there was no major exodus from the Church. For the *Bildungsbürgertum* in particular there were two ways of sliding away from the stricter forms of religion. To certain elements of the secular world could be brought the veneration and the awe that at an earlier time had been reserved principally for the religious. I am referring here to what the Germans have called *Kulturreligion*, the particular veneration brought to education; the university became a temple of knowledge. Endowing secular life with transcendental values was one way of continuing a religious sense in life. It has often been pointed out, perhaps in too facile a way, that nationalism had certain religious attributes as well. In the German development in particular I would say there was a secularisation of awe, a transference of awe; there was also a recurrent effort at finding a communal form of exaltation, such as the youth movement of the 1890s demonstrated.

I would suggest yet another manner of concealing a degree of secularisation beneath the form of continued religious structure and sentiment. Franz Schnabel already pointed to the importance in the nineteenth century, especially for Protestants, of having the important religious ceremonies performed at home – away from the awesomeness of the Church: the "better classes" began to hold baptisms, marriages and even funerals at home. I believe this was true for Jews as well. Indeed the great question of the nineteenth century might be: for how long were Jews Jews or Germans Christians: for how long did they cherish beliefs and a sense of identity that would justify speaking of them as being Jews or Protestants?

The relative concealment of the struggle over religious commitment must also have bred hypocrisy and enhanced anxiety. Almost a decade and a half ago Ralf Dahrendorf coined the felicitous phrase about "the cartel of anxiety" that governed Germany. As Geoffrey Field makes clear that cartel included the Churches, indeed institutionalised Christianity; for obvious reasons, the degree of anxiety rose appreciably during Weimar. But even before Weimar, the unacknowledged uncertainty about one's commitment to Christianity or God probably bred a double anxiety: an anxiety about one's own self and an anxiety – itself quite old – about the social consequences of others, especially of the lower classes, falling away from Christianity. To what extent custom and credence coincided is a very difficult question; I would cite the poignant observation of Lionel Trilling about our own culture as a text for the observation of an earlier culture as well: ". . . it is characteristic of the intellectual life of our culture that it fosters a form of assent which does not involve actual credence".

The three papers suggest that organised Christianity, and especially Protestantism, had become part of the established order – and of course never more so than during the First World War. The Churches fought hard for certain institutional privileges, most notably in the field of primary education. But Christianity could also be invoked as a cloak for material interests. In the class struggle, the equation socialism qua atheism – an equation which it could always be said Karl Marx had himself propounded – gave a fine cover for the anti-socialist forces. Ismar Schorsch reminds us that the appeal to Christianity could be functional as well in contending with Jewish aspirants to true emancipation or equality. The usefulness of the religious argument, its effectiveness as an ideological buttress of privilege, may have been an additional factor in what I have suggested was a concealed or disguised retreat from the stricter Christianity of an earlier period.

Let me now turn to some specific comments concerning the three papers.

Ismar Schorsch's study is exemplary in its specificity and suggestiveness; we are much indebted to him for discovering so rich a mine of information. I would have some questions: Did German professors at that time define science differently, i.e., disinterestedly, in other contexts? What do we know about Christian attitudes towards the large number of Jewish students? How did Jewish academics fare in other countries, were they not also denied posts – and for even longer than in Germany? I was impressed by the evidence of Christian anxiety about Jewish colleagues and about the strong element of antipathy towards Jews at the time; certainly these reports by individual professors would bear out Felix Gilbert's recent contention that antisemitism was an important element in German society well before 1873. At the same time I must say I am struck by the liberality of some professors favouring Jewish employment, even in the face of government reluctance and a precarious job market. I would have wished that Ismar Schorsch might have had the time to elaborate on his statement that emancipation "required the backing of a government prepared to restrict the institutional power of Christianity on a wide front". To what extent did the institutional Church deny or inhibit emancipation? Would the example of nineteenth-century Britain in this regard be of some interest? Finally – and this is perhaps quite a trivial point – I am curious whether the enquiry and its results became public knowledge – and whether the whole question might have been raised in the private correspondence of academics, some of which might have been published by now.

Vernon Lidtke's valuable contribution particularly impressed me by its common-sensical typology of a sliding scale from a religious to a secular person. I accept his scepticism about Social Democracy as a secular religion. I would be interested whether we know much about the oft-quoted poll-takers, Göhre and Levenstein: what were their presuppositions, how sophisticated were their techniques? I thought Vernon Lidtke's analysis of why the working classes would be more likely to be estranged from the Churches than other classes very persuasive. His study does remind one that after the mid-century there were fewer religious crises of the kind we encounter in Bismarck. Yet there is some evidence that some of the Socialists did endure a comparable struggle. Here I would refer as one instance to the confrontation between the twenty-year-old Ernst Reuter and his pious, nationalistic mother: "My religious views have not changed, but are changing; for I am far from finished and must still go a long way before I attain full clarity. Christ is not God but man for me, I can believe in but one God, not two." As if to underscore the Protestant idealistic element in German Social Democracy before the First World War, Reuter, in announcing his active role in the party to his parents, cites the old defiant phrase: "Here I stand. I can do no other." I would suspect that Reuter's experience was far from unique; further studies might yield other clues concerning the religious convictions of some of the young socialists.

I learned a great deal from Geoffrey Field's paper as well. He presents us with a fascinating study of the *Volksschule*, of social discrimination, of hobbling talent. I would have wanted to know even more about the character of the denominational schools in Weimar; what did they hope to achieve and how did they go about realising their aim? What went on in religious instruction, how "modern" or how fundamentalist was it, how hostile to outsiders? I thought his critical assessment of much of the recent literature particularly valuable.

Let me conclude by making two further remarks. One of the inherent difficulties of this topic is the fact that the religious and the secular are so inextricably intertwined; they remain so even in present-day Germany. Let me remind you of what may well have been the two most important moments in what might be called the moral rehabilitation of the Federal Republic in Europe. The Franco-German reconciliation was consecrated in the Cathedral at Rheims and the decisive encounter between Poles and Germans was marked by Willy Brandt's kneeling in contrition before the ghetto memorial in Warsaw. The invocation of the religious on both occasions – one deliberate and manifest, the other more spontaneous and less obvious – suggests that the questions raised by our speakers shed light not only on the past, but on the present too – as so much of history does.

Finally let me thank the sponsoring organisation of this session, the Leo Baeck Institute of London, New York and Jerusalem. Their archival riches are well known to historians and the present papers are eloquent testimony to the largeness of perspective which characterises the Institute.

Enlightenment and Reform

Isaac Satanow

An Epitome of an Era

BY NEHAMA REZLER-BERSOHN

It was more than two centuries ago that Isaac Satanow (1732–1804),* the most prolific Hebrew writer of the Berlin *Haskalah*, published his first book.[1] Ever since, his personality has continued to capture the interest and imagination of Jewish scholars. Attitudes towards him shifted from contempt for his way of life[2] and criticism of his habit of attributing his own writings to authors long dead,[3] to a tendency to see the more positive side of Satanow.[4] It is the contention of this study that the main reason for the continuous interest in this man, who was neither an original thinker nor an influential figure, has been that perhaps more than anybody else he was the prototype of the moderate *Maskil* in Germany; his background and ideology epitomised his era – of rationalism in the European world and of transition in Jewish life.

The son of Moses ha-Levi,[5] born 1732 in the city of Satanow in Podolia, Poland, Isaac Satanow spent there his formative years. He studied the Torah, at the age of fifteen started writing, married at the age of eighteen and at the age of twenty became a merchant. Three times a year he used to travel to Frankfurt a.d. Oder, famous for its fairs, and three times to the Ukraine. Lack of details about his trade suggest that it was undertaken only out of necessity to support a family and that he considered writing his main avocation, as he himself testifies ". . . even in those days he never stopped writing. He used to carry an ink horn with him and whenever he took a rest he used to put into writing the ideas that came into his mind during the daytime."[6]

---

*This work was supported by a grant from The Jewish Memorial Foundation.
[1]Isaac Satanow, *Iggeret Eder ha-Yeqar*, Berlin 1772. Satanow's books are extremely scarce. Most of those which have survived can be found in the Jewish National and University Library in Jerusalem.
[2]S. Bernfeld in *Dor Tahapukhot*, Warsaw 1897, p. 10, calls him libertine.
[3]A. Wolfsohn, *Hame'asef*, VII, Berlin 1797, pp. 252–253, 396; M. Mendelson (Hamburg), *Pnei Tevel*, Amsterdam 1872, p. 251; J. S. Reggio, *Iggeret Yashar El Ahad mi-Me'yuda'av*, I, Vienna 1834, 6; P. E. Hurevitz, *Sefer ha -Berith ha-Shalem*, Warsaw 1876, p. 112; Y. L. Kantor, 'Dor ha-Me'asfim', *Hame'asef le Mefitzei Haskalah be-Russia*, (addition to *he-Asif*, 1887), p. 4; I. Zinberg, *Toledot Sifrut Yisrael*, vol. 5, trans. from Yiddish by B. Karu, Tel-Aviv 1959, p. 118; N. H. Shapiro, *Toledot ha-Sifrut ha-Ivrit ha-Hadasha*, Tel-Aviv, p. 315.
[4]F. Delitzsch, *Zur Geschichte der Jüdischen Poesie*, Leipzig 1836, p. 115; J. Klausner, *Historia Shel ha-Sifrut ha-Ivrit ha-Hadasha*, I, Jerusalem 1960, p. 167; F. Lachover, *Toledot ha-Sifrut ha-Ivrit ha-Hadasha*, Tel-Aviv 1963, p. 81; S. Verses, 'Al Yitzhaq Satanow ve-Hiburo *Mishlei Asaf*', *Tarbitz*, LII, Jerusalem 1962–1963, p. 371; Alexander Altmann, *Moses Mendelssohn. A Biographical Study*, University of Alabama Press 1973, pp. 353–354.
[5]S. J. Fin, *Knesset Yisrael*, Warsaw 1876, p. 643.
[6]Satanow, *Minhat Biqqurim*, Berlin 1797, p. 11.

In the year 1772, when Satanow was forty he moved to Berlin.[7] In that year Poland was partitioned for the first time and the Ukraine was annexed by Russia. As a result, the area of Satanow's commercial activities was greatly reduced. This may have been the decisive factor in his move to Berlin. Except for one son, Dr. Scheinmann who became a physician and practised in Dresden,[8] Satanow's wife and children did not follow him to Berlin,[9] and Satanow used to visit them in Podolia.[10] Satanow frequently used Scheinmann's name as a pen name, especially when he participated in polemics and, for various reasons, preferred not to use his own name.[11]

Satanow's move to Berlin was not an isolated phenomenon, but reflected a general trend in Jewish life of that time. Commercial connections between Poland and Prussia increased during the rule of Frederick II, resulting in closer ties between the two Jewish communities. Numerous Jews began to find their way into Germany. There were scholars looking for a new livelihood, Jewish intellectuals dissatisfied with traditional education, Jewish merchants hoping for better prospects in the West, and Frankists fleeing from persecution, trying to establish a new centre. These Jews had a disturbing and agitating effect on the established German Jewry. The fermentation and unrest they caused may have hastened the process of change in the Jewish community of Germany, and ultimately, in the new arrivals themselves. Satanow the Polish Jew, a merchant and a traditional scholar no longer satisfied with what Jewish education alone had to offer, typifies the new elements. Even his outward appearance – a German outfit under a Polish kaftan[12] – symbolised the split personality of a Polish Jew in Berlin.

Satanow describes his early life in Berlin in a book written in the third person and attributed to his son.

> "When he was forty years old, he came to the city of Berlin. There he invested his money in business (lent it on interest), which left him free to dedicate himself to spiritual matters. He devoted his days and nights to the holy undertaking of editing his own works, and slept no more than three or four hours a night. He lived in such a manner for a number of years, until he lost his wealth as a result of a bad business deal with two dishonest merchants from the city of Satanow, and because of some other misfortunes that befell him."[13]

After his financial débâcle, he had to depend on the benevolence of the Jewish

---

[7] Moses Mendelson (son of the Hamburg rabbi, Menahem Mendel Frankfurter), *Pnei Tevel*, Amsterdam 1872, p. 251; D. Kassel, *Qorot Am Yeshurun*, trans. by D. Radner, Vilno 1887, p. 562. According to Satanow's introduction to his book, *Megillat Hasidim*, Berlin 1802, he came to Berlin forty years earlier but the number forty is usually merely a symbolic number.

[8] A. Wolfsohn in *Hame'asef*, VII, Berlin 1797, p. 396.

[9] *Minhat Biqqurim*, p. 11. It is possible that his family did not follow him to Berlin because of the restrictive laws against Jewish settlement there. (See R. Mahler, *Divrei Yemei Yesrael, Dorot Aharonim*, Merhavia 1954, II, p. 16.) However, there might have been other reasons (S. Maimon's wife refused to follow him; see S. Maimon, *An Autobiography*, ed. M. Hadas, New York 1967, p. 102).

[10] See H. D. Friedberg, *Toledot ha-Defus ha-Ivri be-Polania*, Tel-Aviv 1950, p. 74, n. 2.

[11] For example, in *Minhat Biqqurim* which engaged in polemic with the *Me'asfim* 'Midarkhei ha-Lashon ve-Hameliza' in *Hame'asef*, Berlin 1788, pp. 82–95, which deals with controversial reforms in the Hebrew language.

[12] Delitzsch, *op. cit.*, p. 115.

[13] *Minhat Biqqurim*, p. 11. It appears that unlike Shlomo Maimon or even Moses Mendelssohn, Satanow had no financial problems when he first came to Berlin. See Maimon's *Autobiography*, pp. 79, 96, and I. Euchel, *Toledot hu-Rambaman*, Vienna 1814, p. 139.

rich, a fate he shared with many others. This relationship between *Maskilim* and rich Jewish benefactors was then not unusual. The Jewish magnates, bankers, industrialists, army purveyors, etc., who prospered at that time, strove for emancipation; but even though some individual rich Jews were granted certain privileges, they could not hope to achieve full emancipation except together with the rest of the Jews.[14] However, despite the enlightened ideas then prevalent, the non-Jewish society did not consider the Jews fit for emancipation in view of their current state of backwardness and their distinctive life style. Thus not only from altruistic motives, the Jewish magnates set out to change the Jews and make them fit to become equal citizens. For this they needed people versed in both Jewish and secular knowledge to educate the masses and that is why *Maskilim* like Wessely, Euchel and Satanow could always count on their support.

Among Satanow's major benefactors were the Jewish banker Daniel Itzig (for whose seventy-sixth birthday Satanow composed a poem and a prayer)[15] and Itzig's son-in-law David Friedländer. Together with the famous physician and philosopher Marcus Herz, they belonged to a philanthropic group with the Hebrew name *Marpeh la-Nefesh*, which assigned Satanow to the reissuing of old Hebrew classics. Satanow worked for a while as a director of the publishing house of the Berlin *Freischule* sponsored by Itzig and Friedländer. He held this position until 1788 when Isaac Euchel came from Königsberg to Berlin and took over. Satanow continued to work there as a printer, and most of his own books[16] were published by them.

In Berlin Satanow devoted himself to secular studies, such as philosophy, science and Hebrew grammar. These interests are strongly reflected in his writings. He also came to know most of the *Maskilim* of his time. For example, the poet laureate of the period, Naphtali Herz Wessely, dedicated a poem to him,[17] and it was Satanow who persuaded Moses Mendelssohn, in whose house he was a frequent visitor, to intervene in a case of blood libel in Poland.[18] He also became acquainted with the *Me'asfim* (the contributor to the periodical *Hame'asef*) and became one of them, but in the course of time his good relations with his colleagues became strained, as they suspected him of being the author of a book *Ein Mishpat* which was critical of the *Me'asfim*.[19] Satanow's literary activities included not only books and articles admittedly his own, but also some which were considered forgeries. However, these forgeries were not common plagiarism but original works by Satanow which he presented as the work of earlier writers. He justified this practice by arguing that the Jewish audience is more influenced by authorities of olden times than by scholars of the present day.[20] This unusual

---

[14] David Friedländer, *Akten-Stücke die Reform der jüdischen Kolonieen betreffend, in den Preussischen Staaten*, Berlin 1793, Erste Betrachtung, 'Über die solidarische Verbindung der Juden', pp. 84, 95, 96, 98, 122, 150.
[15] Satanow, *Shir Yedidut*, Berlin 1799.
[16] D. Kassel, *Qorot*, p. 562.
[17] N. H. Wessely, Introduction to Satanow's *Sefer ha-Hizzayon*, Berlin 1775.
[18] I. Euchel, *Toledot*, p. 132; Satanow, *Mishlei Asaf*, Berlin 1797, ch. 42, commentary to sen. 17; Altmann, *Moses Mendelssohn*, p. 354.
[19] I. Zinberg, *Toledot Sifrut Yisrael*, Tel-Aviv 1959, vol. 5, p. 71; A. Wolfsohn in *Hame'asef*, Berlin 1797, p. 301.
[20] *Mishlei Asaf*, ch. 33, sen. 5 (also commentary, ch. 23, com. 24); *Minhat Biqqurim*, p. 6.

practice, which certainly proved Satanow's great talent for imitation, caused controversy nevertheless among his colleagues and historians of modern Hebrew literature.[21]

Despite his failing health and even blindness Satanow's preoccupation with books continued until the very end of his life.[22] He died on 24th December 1904, and was buried without honour. Some years later Leopold Zunz erected a tombstone on his grave.[23] The flowery epitaph on his tombstone may be translated as follows:

> "A writer who never ceased studying and who continued to write until the day of his death."[24]

Satanow's writings reflect the eighteenth century of rationalism with its admiration for knowledge and science, and its preoccupation with the relationship between man and mankind, man and state, religion and tolerance, reforms in education and in the social, political and economic spheres. His starting point was rooted in the general thinking of the time but his final goal was much more parochial; to educate the Jewish masses and help improve their economic, social and political situation.

Satanow directed his arguments on behalf of "wisdom" (namely secular knowledge) and science primarily towards the Hebrew-reading orthodox Jews who distrusted ideas and ideologies acquired from the non-Jewish world. Satanow divided this audience into two groups: the more liberal orthodox Jews and *Mordei Or* (rejectors of light), whom he considered beyond redemption, and felt that trying to convince them would be a waste of time and possibly dangerous.[25] He hoped to persuade the former that enlightenment and wisdom did not contradict religion. Secular knowledge and religion are actually very much interrelated: "Both religion and knowledge are desirable because they both reflect truth and justice."[26] Therefore, each person should enquire after and search for wisdom, and every generation has the right to his own interpretation of the Torah according to his understanding based on the newly acquired wisdom. Even the sages understood the importance and necessity of research for a true understanding of the law and said that "It is desirable to examine and probe with wisdom everything done in the name of religion."[27] Religious law, Satanow concedes, should be practised in the way prescribed by tradition, but secular

---

[21] See notes 3 and 4. Tuvia Feder in *Lahat ha-Herev ha-Mithapekhet*, Vilno 1866, p. 15, says that Satanow's books were burnt in public but this has not been corroborated by other sources.
[22] *Megillat Hasidim*, front page.
[23] S. Bernfeld, *Dor Tahapukhot*, Warsaw 1897, p. 10.
[24] S. J. Fin, *Knesset Yisrael*, p. 645.
[25] Satanow, *Gam Elleh Mishlei Asaf*, Berlin 1792, ch. 69, sen. 9–10; ch. 73, commentary 22. Other Jewish writers drew similar distinctions. See Lazarus Bendavid, *Etwas zur Characteristik der Juden*, Leipzig 1793, p. 47 ff.; Aaron Wolfsohn, *Jeschurun*, Breslau 1804, pp. 111–116; David Friedländer, *Sendschriften . . . an Teller*, Berlin 1799; Isaac Euchel, *Hame'asef*, Berlin 1788, Introduction, p. 1.
[26] *Gam Elleh*, ch. 64, sen. 15–16.
[27] Satanow, *Divrei Rivot*, Berlin [1800?], II, pp. 19, 54.

knowledge must be the subject of the human intellect and research.[28] An enlightened person sees the benefits of wisdom both in its practical as well as its intellectual contributions to man; it helps man to acquire a livelihood and to conduct himself in the proper way, and also enables him to study natural phenomena.[29] Following ancient and medieval customs, Satanow even compares wisdom to God. Just as every believer recognised the existence of God, even though there may be some differences in the understanding of His essence and will, everyone admits the existence of wisdom, though people may differ in their views of its essence. Some believe that it is piety, others claim it is cleverness while ignorant people call their ignorance wisdom.[30] For the enlightened person sources of wisdom are irrelevant. Like Rabbi Meir who justified his studies with the heretic, Elisha B. Avuya, Satanow says:

> "Buy pearls from whoever sells them and knowledge from whoever is knowledgeable. Respect wisdom and ask for it from anybody, whether he is important or not.[31] The light of the candle of intellect which lightens the darkness through wisdom does not increase if it is lightened by a pious man, and does not decrease if it is held by a criminal ... as Maimonides said ... when it comes to truth I do not care if it was said by a prophet or by a Samaritan. The sages also said that the truth should be accepted from whoever tells it ... 'who is the wise man? The one who learns from everybody.'"[32]

Wisdom separates man from the animal, and unites all human beings in their parallel attempts to learn and understand the acts of God in the world.[33]

Echoing the traditional Jewish view, Satanow apparently admits that piety must precede wisdom because, "Piety is the teaching of man while wisdom is the teaching of God",[34] but this also means that wisdom is the ultimate goal of piety.[35] He reveals his true self when he levels criticism against piety, claiming that the pious shy away from research from fear that it may harm their belief in God, forgetting that the sages also advocated secular wisdom.

Satanow admits that there are people who while pretending to be enlightened forsake the Torah; however, these people, he declares, are really ignoramuses who are neither familiar with secular knowledge nor do they know Hebrew. Those who abandoned religion after acquiring wisdom were not fit for this wisdom, because their lapse was their own fault and not the result of wisdom as

---

[28] *Holekh Tamim*, Berlin 1795, p. 9. Satanow's approach to the problem of the relationship between religion and secular knowledge is reminiscent of the approach of the medieval and renaissance protagonists of the "double truth" doctrine. See E. Cassirer, *The Renaissance Philosophy of Man*, Chicago 1948, p. 12. See also E. Gilson, *Reason and Revelation in the Middle Ages*, New York 1938, pp. 67–99. Like Isaac Albalag of the thirteenth century, Eliyahu Delmedigo of the fifteenth and Yashar of Candia of the seventeenth century, Satanow thought that faith and philosophy must be separated. See I. Zinberg, *Toledot*, pp. 99–100; J. Guttman, *Philosophy of Judaism* (Hebrew), trans. by Y. H. Barukh, Jerusalem 1951, pp. 184, 234, 236.
[29] *Divrei Rivot*, I, pp. 12–13.
[30] Satanow, *Imrei Binah*, Berlin 1784, p. 6. See also Maimonides, *Moreh Nevukhim*. Joseph Kaspi, commentator (Solomon Herblinner publication, 1848), p. 98.
[31] *Mishlei Asaf*, ch. 1, commentary on sen. 10. It was said about R. Meir that he found a pomegranate, ate its inside and threw away its outside. See *Hagigah* 15:10.
[32] Satanow, *Sefer ha-Midot*, Berlin 1784, p. 105.
[33] *Holekh Tamim*, p. 3.
[34] *Megillat Hasidim*, ch. 4, commentary on sen. 1. He uses the terminology of N. H. Wessely in *Divrey Shalon ve-Emet*.
[35] *Mishlei Asaf*, ch. 1, commentary to sen. 10.

some mistakenly thought. Those who maintain that religion and wisdom cannot co-exist, imply that religion was given only to fools. Also, it is God who created wisdom and one cannot suspect God of creating anything in vain. Anybody who hates wisdom hates also its creator – God, who expects people to make use of it. That is why the greatest of our rabbis and prophets acquired wisdom.[36]

Satanow is fascinated by science. Scientific details appear in all his eclectic major works. In *Divrei Rivot* he enumerates some of the areas of study that he advises people to pursue which include politics, geometry, hydrology, optics, astronomy, dioptrics, logic and medicine. In whole chapters of his *Megillat Hasidim* he preaches the importance of acquiring wisdom and the learning of science. The sciences recommended most frequently were optics, hydrostatics and chemistry. He explains the function of a prism, the physical qualities of light and the way a magnet works. He devotes portions of *Asaf* to a description of the various branches of science as well as to the praise of science in general. *Eder ha-Yeqar* explains among other things the qualities of parallel lines and discusses the movement of the moon and the moon's spots. *Sefer ha-Midot* which is basically a book of ethics also deals with hydraulics, optics, the telescope, the Milky Way, light reflection, the earth's gravitation, blood circulation, the causes of fainting and a comparison between mental and physical illnesses. He explains that the rabbis knew about light reflection, colours, camera obscura and perhaps even a little bit about gravitation. He also maintains that the reason the Temple was never hit by lightning was because the rabbis knew about the lightning rod and had one made of gold to protect it. In *Imrei Binah* (1784) he discusses light, the prism and the phenomenon of camera obscura.

Satanow's sources for all the scientific details scattered in his books probably came from the wealth of material available in this time of unprecedented interest in science. He probably did not read most of the material in the original, because the greater part of the scientific works of the period were written in English, French and Latin, languages which he apparently did not know, or he would have mentioned it in his writings. However, the gist of these articles appeared in *Hame'asef*.[37] Another important source of Satanow's knowledge was the Hebrew discussions of scientific subjects that existed at this time, such as *Zemah David* (1592) by David Gans who in the introduction to the book wrote about geometry quoting Euclid, also the *Elim* (Amsterdam 1628–1629) by Yashar of Candia which dealt with the discoveries of his time and other contemporary scientific books in Hebrew.[38] Satanow's son, who as a physician probably knew

---

[36] Satanow, *Sefer Ha-Hizzayon*, Berlin 1775, pp. 6, 7, 8–9; *Mishlei Asaf*, ch. 25, sen. 12.

[37] *Hame'asef* (Nisan 1784), pp. 120–124 (Tishrei 1785), pp. 5–15 (Tishrei 1789), pp. 3–9 and many more.

[38] Other available scientific books in Hebrew were: A. Anschel b. Wolf Worms, *Mafte'ah ha-Algebra ha-Hadasha*, Frankfurt a. Main 1721; Rafael Levi, *Tekhunot Shamayim* (Astronomy), Altona 1755; Gumpel Schnaber published an article in London under the name 'Ma'amar ha-Torah ve-ha-Hokhmah, in which he explains basic physics, mathematics and astronomy, *Hame'asef*, 1784, pp. 183–186; also *Sefer Shvilei Rakia* by Aliyahu Mehris, Prague 1784, Introduction to *Sefer Merkevet ha-Mishneh* by Shlomo of Chelm, *Mlekhet Mahshevet* by Eliyahu of Pinchev, Berlin 1765; *Sefer Kelil Heshbon* by David Friesenhausen, Berlin 1796; *Or Olam* and *Beit Midot* by J. L. Margolioth, 1777; *Amudei Shameyim* by Barukh of Shklov, Berlin 1766–1767; *Ma'ase Tovia* by Tovia ha-Rofeh, Venice 1707, and others.

Latin, could also have helped him, or possibly someone like Marcus Herz who attended secular universities and was friendly with many people familiar with new discoveries.[39] In sum, despite Satanow's admiration for science, his actual knowledge was apparently limited and he had to write about various scientific discoveries in their popularised form.

While advocating secular knowledge and the study of science, Satanow also expressed great admiration for Kabbalah. His apparent preoccupation with Kabbalah is a puzzling aspect of Satanow's thought. Many scholars tend to dismiss it as not genuine, even a pretence aimed at convincing Kabbalists, through Kabbalah, to accept the principles of the Enlightenment. These scholars believed that it is impossible for a person to believe in Kabbalah and be a rationalist at the same time.[40] However, such a viewpoint may be too simplistic. No negative attitude towards Kabbalah can be found in Satanow's works. On the contrary, he was the publisher of the books of Hayim Vital.[41] It is hard to believe that an opponent of Kabbalah would help to spread it, even for the sake of earning money, especially if as a *Maskil* he believed that Kabbalah contributed to ignorance. Judging by his own writings Satanow attributed great importance to the main text of Kabbalah, the *Zohar*, one of the books he chose to imitate, and bestowed high praise on it.[42] Also, in a reply to criticism on Satanow's own *Zohar Tinyana* he implies that not to appreciate the *Zohar* represents a flaw in one's intellectual ability.[43] In contrast to Emden he claims that the whole *Zohar* was written by Bar Yohai and Moses De Leon had nothing to do with its writing. He also rejects Emden's claim that in the *Zohar* there are words against the Talmud, and promises to "consult the *Zohar* and prove that all its words are right and truthful, none of them is crooked".[44] Most baffling is Satanow's explanation of events and names mentioned in the *Zohar* which belong to a period much later than that of Bar Yohai, its alleged author. He says: "It is possible that the spirit of God spoke from the mouth of the people of the *Zohar* and God's word was on their tongue. Through the spirit of God they discovered then all that scholars will teach later on."[45] Pious though this explanation appears it is difficult to treat it seriously in the case of a rationalist like Satanow, who may have revealed his true opinion about the authenticity of the *Zohar* in the following: "Every clever preacher uses different devices to bring his words into the heart of his listeners . . ."[46] This implies that he was not really interested in the question of authenticity but in the teaching rather than the teacher, and in this respect he considered the *Zohar* of great value. Thus, while he probably paid only lip service to the authenticity of the *Zohar*, his admiration for the deep meaning of the *Zohar* seems genuine.

[39]Marcus Herz lectured in Berlin about science. See Klausner, *Historia*, I, p. 35.
[40]M. Mendelson (Hamburg), *Pnei Tevel*, p. 252.
[41]H. Vital, *Etz Hayim*, ed. by I. Satanow, Koretz 1782; *Torat Etz Hayim*, ed. by I. Satanow, Koretz 1782.
[42]*Imrei Binah*, p. 12.
[43]*Minhat Biqqurim*, p. 11.
[44]Satanow, *Zohar Tinyana*, Berlin 1783, pp. 25, 26. See also J. Emden, *Mitpahat Sefarim*, Lwow 1831, pp. 2, 3, 7.
[45]*Zohar Tinyana*, p. 26.
[46]*Ibid.*

Taken at face value, Satanow's writings would seem to indicate that he held the Kabbalah in general in great esteem and considered it the highest stage of philosophy. Satanow assumes a parallelism exists between the so-called upper and lower worlds. Thus a mastery of the "upper" world's knowledge through Kabbalah may elucidate the knowledge of our own world.[47] Whether facetious or serious, Satanow asserts that in view of the parallelism between the upper and lower domains of beings and the expertness of Kabballists in the mysteries of the former, they discovered the secrets of the supernal worlds long before scientists discovered the secrets on earth. Moreover, the Kabbalists may therefore be able to foretell things about our world which have not yet been discovered by modern science.[48] Nevertheless, he argues that:

> "One may conclude that anyone who wants to study Kabbalah cannot succeed unless he understands something of the wisdom which God used in his creation of the sensual world. This sensual wisdom should serve as an example of the wisdom in the intellectual world which is the origin of our world, the sensual one..."[49]

This type of double talk leads to the conclusion that though Satanow might have admired the teaching of the *Zohar* he used the Kabbalah mainly for the same reason he used his forgeries, namely, to diffuse science and rationalism. However, his keen interest in Kabbalah as an intellectual phenomenon, his extensive use of Kabbalistic books mentioned in his own books, indicate that even if he did not believe in Kabbalah in its popular mystical form, it nevertheless formed a substantial part of his spiritual and intellectual world. Moreover, Satanow's personality and interests may be understood not only from the books he wrote but also from the books he published and certainly he wrote and published books of Kabbalah. His writings and publications confirm the mystical side of his personality which to some extent may be attributed to the influence of Kabbalah during his early life in Podolia. Thus a man with his background could talk at the same time about the importance of secular knowledge ("wisdom"), science and Kabbalah and try to compromise between them.

It is unlikely that Satanow ever read the works of John Locke, Henri Grégoire or other eighteenth-century thinkers. Yet, their ideas which were a part of "the spirit of the time", travelled and were discussed in enlightened circles, literary salons and cafés.[50] Satanow was quick to transform the general subject of "Man

---

[47] *Imrei Binah*, p. 25; see also M. Isserles, *Torat ha-Olah*, I, ch. 2, where he compromises between Kabbalah and philosophy giving the upper hand to Kabbalah saying at the same time that Kabbalah is the true philosophy (*Torat ha-Olah*, III, ch. 4); also J. S. Del Medigo, *Matzref la-Hokhma*, Odessa 1864, pp. 21–23, discusses a compromise between Kabbalah and philosophy and mentions the idea of upper and lower worlds. Everything in the lower world has its roots in the upper world.
[48] *Imrei Binah*, pp. 12, 17.
[49] Satanow, *Zemirot Asaf*, Berlin 1793, ch. 5, commentary 6.
[50] More frequently than in any previous period, the Jew also was included in the thought of the time. See I. Barzilay, 'The Jew in the Literature of the Enlightenment', *Jewish Social Studies*, vol. XVIII (1956), pp. 243–261; John Locke, in 'A Letter Concerning Toleration', in *The Works of John Locke*, vol. VI, London 1823, p. 9, expressed the general idea that "the care of every man's soul belongs unto himself". Thus, on p. 59 he says, "Neither a Pagan nor Mohammedan nor Jews ought to be excluded from the civil rights of the commonwealth because of his religion." Henri Grégoire, in *Essai sur la Régénération Physique, Morale, et Politique des Juifs*, Metz 1789, pp. 11–112, said openly

and Society" into a more specific one, namely "Jews and Society". He was no doubt also acquainted with the controversy around Christian Wilhelm Dohm and indeed many of his arguments about Jews and society echo Dohm's treatise *Über die bürgerliche Verbesserung der Juden*.[51] Satanow's basic beliefs and views which reflect the thinking and attitude of the general enlightenment can be summarised as follows: (a) Man is free by nature; (b) every man ought to treat his fellow human beings fairly, regardless of religious views; (c) a man should be allowed to dispose of his property however he wishes; (d) a man cannot harm his body which is a part of the state, and is needed for the state's benefit, but his soul is free; (4) a man should not force others to convert from one religion to another.[52]

Satanow believed in the Aristotelian view that every human being had three concerns: himself, his household and family, and his country. In other words, it is the responsibility of every person to take care of his own conduct, the conduct of his household and the affairs of the state.[53] As a social being, it is natural for man to live within the framework of a state, because "a wild animal stays in the wilderness and a human being in a state so that he can find support when needed".[54] The state is the social structure in which a human being can be happiest. Even the purpose of the Torah is to keep and preserve the state.[55] On the other hand, the state's main function is to regulate human society in such a way that its members will contribute their utmost to the well-being of the state and through it, to that of the individual. For this purpose, society is also divided accordingly: "Divide your people into different classes, some of them should till the soil, some should be artisans, and others merchants, soldiers and scientists, so that they can help each other and be able to do everything that is worthwhile doing."[56] The social classes should be evaluated in accordance with their contribution to the good of the state. Thus, the upper class ought to be exempted from all taxes, while the middle class, consisting of artisans and tradesmen, should only pay for land tenancy, and provide soldiers for the state. The Jews also should be a part of this structure, and should have the same obligations as their Christian counterparts. This means that only the Jewish middle class should pay taxes, and not more than the Christians. A Jewish third class of farmers and peasants, which at that time was not in existence, should be created. The state should give this group special consideration, exempting the first two generations

---

that the Jews, once emancipated, "will become attached to the state by ties of pleasure, liberty and life of ease".

[51] Satanow, *Divrei Rivot*, I, p. 40. These words are almost quotations from Christian Dohm, of whose work here and later an English version is used, *Concerning the Amelioration of the Civil Status of the Jews*, trans. by H. Lederer, Cincinnati 1957, pp. 10–14. About the controversy, see Altmann, *Mendelssohn*, pp. 459–461.

[52] *Divrei Rivot*, I, p. 37. Some of these ideas are found in M. Mendelssohn's *Jerusalem*, Berlin 1783, where he also quotes J. Locke's 'Letter on Tolerance'. See Moses Mendelssohn, *Jerusalem and Other Jewish Writings*, trans. by A. Jospe, New York 1969, pp. 15–18.

[53] *Hizzayon*, p. 3.

[54] *Gam Elleh*, ch. 4, sen. 13.

[55] *Mishlei Asaf*, ch. 19, commentary 21.

[56] *Minhat Biqqurim*, ch. 8, sen. 9–11.

from the army. Only the third generation should serve in the army, but they must be allowed to maintain their religion.[57]

Satanow envisions yet another stratification of society. In *Megillat Hasidim* he depicts a society made up of four classes based on the intellectual abilities of its members. In this society the lower class are farmers and peasants. Above them are the "God-fearing people"; a still higher level is made up of wise men, and on the highest level are the prophets.[58] Obviously this is an intellectual rather than a social stratification. The low position he assigns to the farmer in his model societies is worth noting. This is quite different from the view of the later *Maskilim* in Galicia and Russia who idealised the agriculturists.

The second half of the eighteenth century was to bring about, of course, that time of deep transformation in the life of the Jews in Germany, intellectually, socially and economically which engaged all Jewish reformers and thinkers. Satanow divided the political, social and economic problems of this transitory period into two; those which appeared within the Jewish community itself and those imposed on the Jews by the Christian world.

A subject which frequently occupied Satanow and his contemporaries was the relationship between the communal Jewish leadership and the Jewish masses. In moving from Poland to Germany Satanow discovered to his great disappointment that Jewish communal life hardly differed from East to West:

> "In truth the Polish Jewish *Qahal* was in every respect as autocratic as the Jewish government of the West. Property qualifications determined franchise [in both places]. The principal officers of the *Qahal*, with their immense power to influence the courts and the excise Commissions, were very often wealthy tyrants who shifted the burden of taxation onto their disenfranchised impoverished brethren."[59]

Some of the families who controlled the Jewish Community in Berlin, such as Friedländer and his father-in-law Itzig, were, as we have seen, among Satanow's benefactors. However, being patrons of culture did not prevent them from exploiting the masses. This exploitation was common not only in Berlin but throughout the Jewish communities in Germany. Rabbi Jonathan Eybeschütz complained that "because of our numerous sins, most of the leaders and the respectable men of the community failed in their duties [towards the community], especially when it came to taxation".[60] Jacob Emden used even darker language to describe the situation.[61]

Satanow was no doubt aware of this problem as it existed in Poland as well as Germany. Being a *Maskil* he must have considered it his duty to press for reforms. However, since he was a beneficiary of the same system that Emden

---

[57] *Divrei Rivot*, I, 48; see also Friedländer, *Akten-Stücke*, pp. 91, 92, 158–160.
[58] *Megillat Hasidim*, ch. 24, commentary 15–23; J. Ha-Levi also puts the prophet at the upper social level, see *Kuzari* 1:43.
[59] M. H. Sachar, *The Course of Modern Jewish History*, Dell publ., 1963, p. 32. On the relationship between the community and its leadership in Germany, see also A. Schohat, *Im Hilufei Tequfot*, pp. 72–74, 113–117, 192–200. However, David Friedländer believed that the life of the Polish Jew was worse than that of the German Jew. See *Akten-Stücke*, p. 13.
[60] J. Eybeschütz, *Ya'arat Devash*, Karlsruhe 1779, vol. II, p. 17.
[61] J. Emden, *Megillat Sefer*, Warsaw 1897, p. 133.

complained about, he could not afford to press the point too hard. Nevertheless, he raised the problem in several of his books. For example, he said that:

> "When a man becomes a *Parnas* he does not consider his goal to benefit the community [as it should be] but to enhance his wealth, to benefit his friends and take revenge on his enemies. Therefore justice becomes meaningless, and the masses, instead of getting help from the *Parnasim* are wronged by them."[62]

An even sharper criticism of the communal leadership appeared in *Beit ha-Tefilah*:

> "Because of our sins this plague of taxation has spread in some communities. The country is full of evil, the important people of the community do not pay taxes as they should and they 'trample on the faces of the poor and pull the skin off their bones'. They close their ears and do not listen to the cry of the downtrodden."[63]

Heavy taxation is cited also by Friedländer as a reason for the poverty of the Jewish communities in Germany. Both Friedländer and Satanow say communities are forced to borrow to redeem Jews from death or captivity, and to pay the heavy taxes for the poor members of the community who cannot pay themselves.[64] However, Satanow considers as the core of the problem not just the taxation but also its uneven distribution by the leadership. The powerful *Parnasim* were part of the old ghetto establishment, but modern times have worsened the situation and made it more unbearable.[65] Other reasons for Jewish economic misery, mentioned by Satanow, are the Jewish love of luxury and a tendency to exhibitionism.[66]

More decisive for the state of German Jewry was, of course, the negative attitude of the government. It found its expression in an elaborate system of legal enactments aimed at restricting the numbers of Jews in Germany and their economic activities, restrictions which affected occupation, habitation and the social contacts of Jews outside the Jewish community. Satanow believed that this was partly responsible for Jewish misery.

One of the most common notions in the political and economic thought of the eighteenth century was that the size of the population was an essential element in the strength and wealth of a state. Satanow, like both Mendelssohn and Dohm, was well acquainted with that view, and wondered why Jews were restricted in habitation and trade:

> "I went through many cities in the kingdom and there were no Jews there. I asked for the reason and was told that no Jew had permission to dwell there, and in some of the cities where Jews do live, there are limitations on their trade..."[67]

---

[62] *Minhat Biqqurim*, p. 41.
[63] Satanow, *Iggeret Beit Tefilah*, Berlin 1793, p. 28. Some of Satanow's idioms are taken from *Amos* 2:7. See also *Divrei Rivot*, I, p. 49.
[64] Friedländer, *Akten-Stücke*, pp. 54, 57, 81–84; *Divrei Rivot*, I, p. 44.
[65] R. Mahler, *Divrei Ye'mei Yisrael*, Merhavia 1954, vol. II, pp. 35, 37–38; *Mishlei Asaf*, ch. 25, commentary 9; A. Schohat, *Im Hilufei Tequfot*, pp. 117, 118.
[66] *Divrei Rivot*, I, p. 44. See also A. Schohat, *Im Hilufei Tequfot*, pp. 35–37. C. S. Ibn Verga, *Shevet Yehuda*, Jerusalem 1946–1947, p. 30.
[67] *Divrei Rivot*, I, p. 49. He also writes: the Jews are treated as foreigners in your country... You do not help them as you should. You prohibit them from participating in arts and trades, and you teach your children to call them names as if they were thieves. See also Dohm, *Concerning the Amelioration*, pp. 1, 2.

This is an echo of an exhaustive study of the situation by Dohm who found that the special restrictions were based on antiquated laws. "The kings in the past distinguished you from other nations by putting upon you heavy taxes ... and they made a law that passing travellers must pay ransom to the lord of the land as if they were cattle",[68] which reminds us of Mendelssohn's famous story where he describes his own experience of having to pay ransom, as if he were an ox brought from Poland. High interest rates are cited as another cause of poverty, both for individual Jews and communities.[69] Worth noting, however, and reflecting the spirit of the time, is Satanow's general attitude towards money-lending and interest. The rise of capitalism increased dependency on credits and loans, resulting in a more positive attitude towards interest. Dohm tells us that ". . . lending out money was [formerly] regarded almost as a dishonest business deal ... nowadays this prejudice is no longer prevalent".[70] Satanow echoes this opinion:

> "There is no evil in collecting interest as long as it is done properly, that is to say, when the borrower gets out of the money as much as the lender does, because ... money-lending is really like business."[71]

Nevertheless, Satanow is still sensitive to the Gentile condemnation of the Jews as usurers. That is why he tries to explain the roots of this practice. Like Friedländer, he believes that it is the economic restrictions imposed on the Jews that forced them to turn to usury. A human being, he asserts, will turn to dishonest practices when forced by hunger.[72]

In *Divrei Rivot* Satanow analysed the arguments of Gentiles against granting civil rights to the Jews: (a) Jews are not capable of accepting the responsibilities that come with civil rights; (b) Jews are so sly that if they are allowed to own real estate they will eventually take over the entire land; (c) Jews hide their criminals and do not bring them to justice, therefore if Jews were appointed to the court the number of murders in the state will increase. He refuted those claims though he admitted that the Jews may be "sick". However, "the main reason for the general sickness of the Jews is the hatred toward them which exists in the heart of the multitude". Echoing Gentiles, he admits that the present "sick" generation may not be ready for civil rights, but he argues on behalf of future generations.[73] The "sickness of the Jews" is also manifested by their lack of secular knowledge and their pacifism. Even though ". . . the rulers wanted to teach the Jews war so that they would be able to defend themselves . . . they opposed it saying that it prevents them from studying the Torah; as a result they were killed in pogroms".[74] He argues that ". . . the Torah does not oppose self-

[68] *Divrei Rivot*, I, p. 40.
[69] *Ibid.*
[70] Dohm, *Concerning the Amelioration*, p. 4.
[71] *Divrei Rivot*, I, p. 34.
[72] These arguments were mentioned already by John Toland in *Reasons for Naturalizing the Jews in Great Britain and Ireland, on the Same Foot with all Other Nations. Containing also a Defence of the Jews Against all Vulgar Prejudices in all Countries*, London 1714, p. 56. See also Simhah Luzzato, *Ma'amar al Yehudei Venezia*, trans. from the Italian by Don Latès, Jerusalem 1941, pp. 109–110. See also L. Modena, *Riti*, Venice 1658, pp. ii, 3, 5. See also Satanow, *Divrei Rivot*, I, p. 34; Friedländer, *Akten-Stücke*, p. 35. C. to Dohm, *Concerning the Amelioration*, p. 5.
[73] *Divrei Rivot*, I, pp. 5, 38, 48. See also Friedländer, *Akten-Stücke*, pp. 91, 92.
[74] *Ibid.*, p. 47.

defence, and all those laws which restrict the learning of self-defence are late laws, which express mere cowardice".[75] In more than one place he repeats the common accusation that Jews are cowards. However,

> "... there is also an advantage in this situation, because other nations decrease in numbers because of wars, while Jews increase."[76]

To cure all the above-mentioned evils, Satanow suggests that there should not be any difference between Jews and other people, they should be allowed to live everywhere and participate in any trade ... the only thing that should separate people should be wisdom and eloquence. Ways to prevent antisemitism and suspicions about the Jews are: (1) Jews should invite Christians to their houses; (2) Christian mothers should not teach their children to hate Jews; (3) Proper education will take care of all kinds of poverty, poverty of the mind as well as material poverty. Many of Satanow's arguments on behalf of social, political and economic reforms in the situation of the Jews were similar to Dohm's; however, Satanow's focal point differed from Dohm's. The latter's primary interest was the State and he advocated political, social and economic improvement of the Jews only in so far as it was for the benefit of the State. Satanow's major intent was the improvement of the situation of the Jews, and he utilised contemporary theories of economics as an instrument to achieve that goal.

The issue of education was a major topic for many of the great thinkers of the time, such as John Locke, Rousseau, Diderot, Montesquieu, Voltaire, Leibniz, Helvétius and Condillac. Education is of paramount importance in the *Haskalah* literature.[77] *Hame'asef*, the mouthpiece of the Hebrew *Maskilim*, is filled with suggestions for reforms, demanding new curricula and methods.[78] The *Maskilim* composed new textbooks according to many of the new suggestions.[79]

Satanow was also part of this trend. Though he did not write textbooks, he participated actively in the criticism of contemporary Jewish education and put forward some suggestions of his own. He accepted Wessely's division of the educational process, but while Wessely believed secular studies should precede religious studies because the former prepares one for the latter, Satanow suggested the opposite. He recommended that natural sciences be taught only after the completion of Jewish education and only as a supplement to the latter. However, Satanow believed that after studying nature one should return again to Scriptures because by then one will be better equipped to understand the Bible.[80] He was among the first *Maskilim* to try to define the word *Hinukh* (education) as a combination of training and teaching, and said that both must be done grad-

---

[75]*Ibid.*
[76]*Ibid.*, p. 5.
[77]M. Eliav, *ha-Hinukh ha-Yehudi be-Germania*, p. 24; M. Stern, 'Der Jugendunterricht in der Berliner jüdischen Gemeinde während des achtzehnten Jahrhunderts', *Jahrbuch der Literarischen Gesellschaft*, 1928–1929; *Beiträge zur Geschichte der Gemeinde*, Berlin, Heft 5, Berlin 1934, p. 34.
[78]J. Rachenow in *Hame'asef*, Berlin 1789, pp. 32, 154, 171–187 and more.
[79]I. Barzilay, 'The Ideology of the Berlin Haskalah', Proceedings of the American Academy for Jewish Research, vol. XXV (1956), p. 33.
[80]*Divrei Rivot*, I, pp. 11–12; *Divrei Rivot*, II, p. 29. See also Wessely, *Divrei Shalom*, pp. 3–4.

ually.[81] Aware of the new pedagogical approaches of the time, Satanow understood the effectiveness of reward and punishment and advised educators to use this principle in education. A person should teach his children ethics and morals without frightening them. Teachers and nurses who frighten little children make cowards out of them, and those who teach children by scaring them with untruthful stories teach them to be liars. On the other hand, teachers should not be too permissive because that might spoil and weaken the children's character.[82]

Fables and proverbs were a popular genre of the time. Satanow considered it one of the best educational methods.

> "When a *Maskil* wants to teach the public or educate people with profound thoughts, he does it through proverbs [*Mashal* is translated both as fable and proberb], epigrams and riddles which enable them to grasp the deeper moral of the story ... Fables were created by God to enable man to understand a desired teaching the same way that a sailor builds a small model of a boat to teach his son how to navigate a big one."[83]

Satanow advises teachers not to teach by orders and commands, but by being a model and setting an example for emulation by the children. Above all, he insists that teachers be fully qualified and reports in *Hame'asef* (1785) that in the city of Mainz the Jewish teachers were required to pass a municipal examination to prove their qualifications. Teachers should prove their knowledge in the spoken language and Latin, and their familiarity with some astronomy and natural science.

In his book *Divrei Rivot* he suggested an interesting curriculum of study where in every city there should be three teachers. During the first ten years the day should be divided into three parts. During the first portion the children would learn the Bible, language, calligraphy, ethics and religious commandments. During the next portion they should study foreign languages with the second teacher while the third part of the day should be spent with the third teacher in studying arithmetic, geometry, geography, astronomy and some natural and empirical sciences. In the tenth year the boys should be examined to determine the quality of each boy. Any boy with a strong and skilful mind should continue his studies, choose his own subjects and study them with appropriate professors. Boys incapable of study and understanding should learn arts and crafts in wood, metal and stone, or choose any other occupation according to their preference.

Along with this general plan, Satanow also suggests a specific programme of Hebrew studies. Insisting that Hebrew studies cannot be done in translation, he divides the educational process into stages. In the first stage the child should simultaneously learn reading, writing, vocalisation and correct pronunciation. In the second stage he should learn the different meanings of roots and their synonyms. In the third stage grammar, correct accent and tropes. In the fourth stage the child should learn logic in its Jewish form, namely, the thirteen *Midot* (rules of deducing laws) of Rabbi Ishmael and the thirty-two of Rabbi Jose the Gallilean. Only after those four stages have been completed, should the child be

---

[81] *Gam Elleh*, ch. 65, commentary 15; *Megillat Hasidim*, ch. 18, sen. 1; ch. 37, sen. 6–8.
[82] *Mishlei Asaf*, ch. 40, sen. 1–10 and commentaries 3, 4. Also, *Gam Elleh*, ch. 37, sen. 7–10.
[83] *Divrei Rivot*, II, p. 38. Satanow must have read Eliezer Ashkenazi's book *Ma'ase Adonai* (1540), Lwow 1948, where Ashkenazi speaks about the fable as an educational tool (Introduction, p. 4) and uses the same example of the sailor and his son, p. 17.

introduced to the study of the Bible, according to the simple meaning of the text, based on a correct understanding of grammar. After the child has acquainted himself with the Bible, the study of Talmud and "Pilpul" may begin. However, "Pilpul" should not be used for the sake of mental exercise but for a better understanding of Jewish law.[84]

Satanow's writings on education as on other subjects, consist of criticism of the prevailing condition and of suggestions for reforms which will lead to the ultimate goal of forming a better Jew who would become an integral part of the general society. Defining the function of religion and tolerance had also the same purpose.

Following his contemporaries, Satanow tried to define the general function of religion as aiming to increase love among people and to help nature to benefit mankind in cases where nature by itself is incapable of doing so.[85] However, Satanow found fault with the undesirable results of religious fanaticism which breeds hatred. He pleads that all religious disputations over the so-called true religion, be abandoned and proofs left for the next world. He argues further that since no religion can be proven to be the true one, religion should not be used as a criterion for bestowing privileges.[86] Yet, despite his call for an end to religious polemics Satanow, like Mendelssohn, emphasises the supremacy of the Jewish religion. He points out that Judaism in contrast to Christianity does not contradict reason and, in fact, is based on it: "The argument that reason rejects faith is a Christian argument, because their faith is contrary to reason. However, Judaism is based on rationalism."[87]

Following the trends of the time, Satanow preached tolerance and was against religious persecution. He turned to history and tried to show the destructiveness of religious persecution, pointing out that it was cyclical – those who persecute today were persecuted in the past. Religious intolerance is as ancient as religion itself because

> "Since man recognised the existence of God, different religions have multiplied and caused hatred to flourish among mankind. Hatred separated people one from another and resulted in the murder of innocent people."[88]

Intolerance exists also among various religious sects. Though the Jews, more than any other people, suffered the ills of intolerance, they themselves, Satanow admits, were not free from the evil.[89] Satanow, no doubt, thought of the Jews of

---

[84] *Divrei Rivot*, I, p. 11. It might be interesting to compare Satanow's curriculum with Leibniz's memorandum to Peter the Great as is quoted by Smith in his book *History*, II, p. 437. The memorandum proposed a course of studies which Leibniz considered the best for moulding a man of the world.
[85] *Mishlei Asaf*, ch. 31, sen. 10, 11, 12.
[86] *Ibid.*, ch. 21, sen. 6–9; *Divrei Rivot*, I, p. 38.
[87] Mendelssohn, *Jerusalem*, p. 27, 'On Judaism and Christianity', from a letter to Karl-Wilhelm, Hereditary Prince of Braunschweig-Wolfenbüttel; *Jerusalem*, pp. 123–129; *Holekh Tamim*, p. 9. See also *Divrei Rivot*, I, p. 24; and *Mishlei Asaf*, ch. 47, commentary 2.
[88] *Mishlei Asaf*, ch. 31, sen. 6–9; commentary 6.
[89] *Zemirot Asaf*, ch. 45, commentary to sen. 13. This may be an allusion to the struggle between *Hasidim* and their opponents.

his day and the injustices perpetrated against them by Christians when he writes of religious intolerance and its by-products:

> "Religious hatred is the primary hatred among human beings and ... any member of one religion believes that it is a good deed to murder a member of another religion, take away his money, to enslave his sons, to cheat him, and to prevent him from deriving any benefit from agriculture, art and certain trades."[90]

The notion of the "evil priests" was common in the eighteenth century. Satanow follows the popular arguments by saying that because the priests were interested in money, they were not sensitive to the truth but enacted laws which would enable them to acquire fortunes. He even adduces some evidence from contemporary events to uphold this view that the clergy is the source of religious hatred:

> "The advice of the priests was that killing a member of a different religion is according to the wish of God. Some time ago several Greek priests were arrested for encouraging and arming their parishioners to murder the Jews and the noblemen of the town. However, the good Lord cancelled their scheme and revealed their plan and they were punished..."[91]

Another concept, popular at the time, was that of natural religion as opposed to revealed one. Satanow used the concept in his arguments against intolerance. The acquired religion in contrast to the natural one changes according to time and the nature of the land. Therefore, members of different religions should not hate each other because the variation in religions is the will of God. And if it is the will of God then religious tolerance is logical.[92]

He realised that rationalism cannot abolish religious fanaticism as long as every member of a creed says that his faith is on a higher plane than the human intellect and the human mind is incapable of judging its truth. However, if a man can admit that all nations are equal except for their religion, then he should also realise that there is no reason for mutual hatred because of differences in religion. For Satanow as well as for other Jews of his time a crusade for religious tolerance was both urgent and practical. They saw it as a way to improve their social and economic standing. Religious toleration also meant the final repudiation of the infamous blood accusation that still haunted Jewish life in Poland, as well as a way to lessen the pressure on the Jews to convert to Christianity. Satanow asserted that converts are dishonest, their conversion is not genuine, and they actually remain in the fold of their original religion. Moreover, they use their new religion as a means to attain influence in society. Those who are converted by force are even worse, because one cannot impose ideas by coercion, and the forced convert will use flattery to save himself, but he is far from becoming a true believer. Often when he has the opportunity he will return to his original religion.[93] Forced conversion is the result of religious fanaticism, and Satanow as a rationalist and a Jew rejected it vehemently.

---

[90] *Ibid.*

[91] *Divrei Rivot*, I, pp. 17, 24. See also *Gam Elleh*, ch. 18, commentary 17. The specific event to which Satanow refers is not clear.

[92] *Gam Elleh*, ch. 39, commentary 76 and ch. 42, sen. 6–9. See also Mendelssohn, 'A Letter to Karl-Wilhelm', in *Jerusalem*, p. 127; also *Jerusalem*, II, pp. 68–69.

[93] *Divrei Rivot*, I, pp. 5, 6, 7 and *Gam Elleh*, ch. 39, commentary 9.

A substantial portion of the book *Gam Elleh Mishlei Asaf* deals with the issue of conversion. Following his argument that different religions depend on different geographical and historical circumstances, Satanow says that any conversion is undesirable because laws of every religion are made to fit the nature of the people and the land where they were given and therefore it is also impossible that there will ever be a universal religion. That is why anybody who converts, be it to Judaism or Christianity is a very undesirable addition to his new religion. His arguments against conversion can be traced to the writings of both Mendelssohn and Dohm. However, his profound interest in that particular subject might be also linked to the mass conversion of Frankists in his time.

The link between Frankism and the Jewish enlightenment in Germany has not yet been fully explored. Both Jakob Frank and the *Maskilim* expressed similar ideas most of which were prevalent in the general enlightenment. However, in view of the fact that Satanow was not just a contemporary but also a compatriot of Frank, a brief comparison between some of their ideas and opinions is appropriate.

Many thinkers of the time expressed preference for modern rather than ancient ideas, as the new inventions and discoveries gave rise to a sense of pride and confidence in the human mind on the one hand, and to contempt for the sages of the past on the other hand. Frank said that "anyone who emulates manners and attitudes or reads books that were written in the past is like one who turns his eyes backward and looks at dead things . . . but the eyes of the wise man are always . . . in front of him".[94] Satanow also believed that the present and the future are more important than the past. Later generations are wiser than earlier ones because every day the understanding of God's wisdom increases; therefore the future generations will be even wiser than the present ones. The preference for the present over the past is a common theme in Satanow's writings. He said that even if Aristotle and the old sages of antiquity came back to life, they would have felt like ants comparing their knowledge to the present knowledge, because many scientific facts, unknown to the ancients, were now known. Satanow expressed the same view in *Gam Elleh Mishlei Asaf*: "Not all the ancients inherited wisdom and not all the moderns inherited stupidity; fathers were not clear of folly and sons did not lack advice."[95]

Frank wished to weaken the hold of religion on his people and bring them closer to the culture of the time. Much of Satanow's works aimed at a similar goal; to bring the spirit and ideas of the general enlightenment to the Jewish people and awaken them from their religious stagnation. Frank, like Satanow, did not believe in the superiority of one religion over another: "When people change their religion it is like pouring oil from one receptacle into another."[96] However, their conclusions were different. Frank believed that it was not only

---

[94] A. Kraushaar, *Frank ve-Adato*, trans. by N. Sokolow, I, Warsaw 1895, p. 119.

[95] *Sefer ha-Midot*, p. 92 and *Mishlei Asaf*, ch. 38, sen. 8; ch. 33, sen. 11, 14, 15; about the advantage of later generations in regard to knowledge see also A. De Rossi, *Me'or Einayim*, Berlin 1784, ch. 11, p. 56.

[96] Kraushaar, *Frank ve-Adato*, pp. 20, 225.

not harmful to change one's religion (as in fact he had done) but it is even necessary from time to time. Satanow, on the other hand, though agreeing that all religions are essentially the same, believed that a man should remain in his father's faith because it is the most suitable for him.

According to Kraushaar, Frank had one goal which he never forsook, and that was to put an end to the depressed condition of the Jews in the lands of their exile, a goal that was shared by the *Haskalah*. Most *Maskilim* saw Jewish military service as a prerequisite to attaining full civil rights. Frank preached Jewish militarism, which to him meant changing the image of the Jew from a coward into a warrior. He said: "What has happened happened, but now new things are coming. We will not deal anymore with what we dealt with in the past, from now on we will only learn war strategy."[97] Satanow also writes extensively on the idea and strongly advocates Jewish participation in the army, not only for the sake of civil rights but also as a means of insuring their own safety. Apparently referring to the recent Haydamak massacres in Poland, he questions why the Jews did not resist. His answer that it was their cowardliness and their lack of military knowledge is reminiscent of Ibn Verga's explanation for the defeat the Jews suffered in the great rebellion against the Romans.[98]

Satanow also preached the full enjoyment of life. A wise man should be joyous because there is no pleasure in the grave and no enjoyment after death: one should enjoy oneself while one is alive. One should not worry too much because:

> "Whatever has happened has already passed and what will happen does not yet exist and what exists at the moment, vanishes in the next moment. In the meantime, man should enjoy worldly pleasures because God did not create pleasure in vain. He created it for enjoyment. A man should enjoy the pleasures of the flesh as well as good food. Moreover, one should always find new pleasures because the newer the pleasure, the more enjoyable it is. One should also indulge in sex because it was not created in vain."[99]

Satanow's call for a life of pleasure and enjoyment was indicative of the life style of Frank and his followers. In this passage Satanow emerges as a man of this world, a lover of life and its pleasures and a seeker of enjoyment and gaiety. Moreover, his own life style was referred to by some as libertine.

While Satanow's critics considered him a libertine, and, some of his work seems reminiscent of Frankish ideology, including his apparent admiration for the *Zohar*, yet he was not Frankist. In several passages, he refutes Frankist ideology and life style. He condemns Frankists whom he identifies with Sabbataians for loose morals; in a commentary in *Asaf* he writes, "the stupid people like the sect of Sabbatai Zwi, may the name of the wicked rot, with their mouth they make sensual love poems and with their sex organs they engage in indecent coitus claiming that all their deeds are secrets and mysteries of wisdom".[100] He blames them for distorting the scripture, ". . . many support their false ideas with the Torah, like the sects of Sabbatai Zwi, may the name of the wicked rot. Many

---

[97]*Ibid.*, p. 285.
[98]*Divrei Rivot*, I, pp. 46, 47; S. Ibn Verga, *Shevet Yehudah*, Jerusalem 1947, p. 44; Friedländer in *Akten-Stücke*, pp. 91, 159, was only lukewarm to Jewish military service.
[99]*Mishlei Asaf*, ch. 31, sen. 17; ch. 36, sen. 11–12; ch. 49, sen. 3.
[100]*Ibid.*, ch. 13, commentary 27; *Gam Elleh*, ch. 65, commentary 14; *Zemirot Asaf*, ch. 5, commentary 5; ch. 43, commentary 9.

are preoccupied with unimportant concepts and ideas and some, like the sect of Sabbatai Zwi (may the name of the wicked rot) are occupied with false ideas deluding themselves that they come closer to God through these false ideas."[101]

One of the principles of Frankism, as formulated in the platform they submitted for the disputation at Lwow was a negative attitude to the Talmud and the national belief of restoration of Zion. Indeed, even before the Frankists turned their back on Judaism they already called themselves opponents of the Talmud. Many of the *Maskilim* of the time were rather cool to the Talmud. They considered it a major barrier between Jews and Gentiles. Satanow's instead was an entirely positive approach. Comparing the Sabbataians and Frankists to Karaites because of their rejection of the Talmud, he wrote:

> "If these [Frankists] sinners believe in Karaite doctrine, one should try to show them the greatness of the wisdom of our sages . . . proving to them that there is no other way than the way of the Talmud, because the oral law was received at Sinai the same way as the written law was."[102]

He recognises the importance of the Talmud for Jewish law, and admires its methods of reasoning and inference. In *Imrei Binah* Satanow says that all the commandments of the Torah cannot be fully understood without the commentaries of the great Talmud, as there can be no true faith without the Talmudic commentary. Satanow implied that the Talmud is a necessity for understanding of Biblical law. This is of course the traditional approach to the Talmud, an approach that was often abandoned by the *Maskilim*, but preferred by Satanow. It is possible that this Podolian Jew who was a witness to the harm caused by Frankist accusations against the Talmud had more reasons than others to come to its defence.

Satanow's time and place of birth, together with the direct references to the sectarian Jews strengthen the possibility that he was familiar with Frankist ideology, and to some extent was even influenced by it as his way of life and some of his writings suggest. It is expressed both directly, in the form of similar ideas and opinions, and indirectly, by his choice of specific topics of discussion and subjects of polemic against Frankist ideology. However, there is nothing there to indicate that he was a Frankist or even a sympathiser.

Certainly Isaac Satanow, the Jew who wandered from Poland to Germany, the man who was captivated by the spirit of the enlightenment yet could not shake off his training in Kabbalah, characterises his period. He touched on all the subjects that were popular in the age of reason. He was preoccupied with knowledge and science, with man in relation to society, with religion and mankind, and with social, political and economic problems and their solutions. Satanow – a contemporary of both Jakob Frank and Moses Mendelssohn – is the very embodiment of his time, this great era of transition in the history of the German Jews.

[101] *Midot*, p. 90. See also *Hizzayon*, p. 6; *Imrei Binah*, p. 12; *Divrei Rivot*, II, p. 12.
[102] *Midot*, p. 90. See also p. 89.

The Orthodox and the Enlightened

An Unpublished Contemporary Analysis of Berlin Jewry's Spiritual Condition in the Early Nineteenth Century

BY MICHAEL A. MEYER

The Prussian edict of 11th March 1812, which granted nearly equal civil status to Prussian Jewry, left the matter of its religious organisation unresolved. The final paragraph of the edict, Paragraph 39, indicated that the government preferred for the present to postpone "the necessary regulations regarding the ecclesiastical status of the Jews and the improvement of their education". Men of the Jewish faith who, on account of their knowledge and probity, enjoyed public trust were to be consulted and their opinions heard.[1]

Shortly after the edict was promulgated, David Friedländer, whose past efforts on behalf of Jewish emancipation and whose status as an elder of the Berlin Jewish community gave considerable justification for regarding himself as an adviser of the type envisioned by the edict, set forth in outline his own plan of communal reform. In an anonymously published pamphlet of forty-seven pages,[2] Friedländer argued that the new political status and cultural integration of the Jews made their traditional forms of worship and education antiquated. Noting an increasing indifference to religion among enlightened Jews, he proposed a solemn and dignified religious service in a language comprehensible to the worshippers. Jewish education was to focus on the fundamental tenets of the faith, abandoning the study of Hebrew except for those who intended to become teachers or scholars.

As soon became evident, Friedländer's proposals were too radical, not only for the conservative Prussian monarch Frederick William III,[3] but also for most of Prussian Jewry. The Berlin Jewish community did not elect him as one of its two representatives to advise the government in planning reorganisation.[4] Two leaders of Silesian Jewry, Lewin Benjamin Dohm, syndic of the Breslau community, and Abraham Muhr, a wealthy businessman in Pless, published anonymous replies to Friedländer's pamphlet. While sympathetic to the need for reform in the worship service, each defended the role of the Hebrew language both in the synagogue and in the school.[5] The Hebraist and *dayan* (religious judge) of the

---

[1] Ismar Freund, *Die Emanzipation der Juden in Preussen*, Berlin 1912, II, p. 459.
[2] *Ueber die, durch die neue Organisation der Judenschaften in den Preussischen Staaten nothwendig gewordene, Umbildung (1) ihres Gottesdienstes in den Synagogen, (2) ihrer Unterrichts-Anstalten, und deren Lehrgegenstände, und (3) ihres Erziehungs-Wesens überhaupt. Ein Wort zu seiner Zeit*, Berlin 1812.
[3] See the documentation in Ludwig Geiger, *Geschichte der Juden in Berlin*, Berlin 1871, II, pp. 212–216.
[4] *Idem.*, 'Nach dem Edikt vom 11 März 1812', *Gemeindeblatt der jüdischen Gemeinde zu Berlin*, 9th August 1912, p. 104.
[5] [L. B. Dohm], *Etwas zum Schutz des angegriffenen Gebrauchs der ebräischen Sprache bei den Gebeten der Juden in den Koenigl. Preuss. Staaten*, Breslau 1812; [Abraham Muhr], *Jerubaal oder über die religiöse*

Breslau community, Salomon Pappenheim, though likewise at least recognising the need for an authoritative reform of certain religious practices, was even more vigorous in his critique of Friedländer's radicalism.[6] Only Gotthold Salomon, later to become one of the preachers in the Hamburg Temple, wrote enthusiastically about Friedländer's proposal, but even he was forced to recognise that Friedländer spoke for only a small minority of Prussian Jewry.[7] These four pamphlets were the only published responses to Friedländer's plan of reform. None of them came from Berlin. With the exception of Salomon, the writers all concentrated on the issue of Hebrew. Though they disagreed with Friedländer's specific proposals, they did not question his basic assumption that a single plan of reform for all of Prussian Jewry was possible and desirable. None of them sought to analyse the religious composition of contemporary Prussian Jewry in order to judge whether any unified programme would be feasible.

In the following years the question of carrying out Paragraph 39 remained in abeyance. The government preferred to leave the specifically religious status of the Jews very much as it had been before the 1812 edict. The public debate seems to have begun and ended with Friedländer's plan and the immediate responses to it. Those Berlin Jews in favour of reform soon chose to act independently of the community and to create their own modernised religious services even as a generation earlier the enlightened devotees of Moses Mendelssohn had established an independent *Freischule* with a curriculum that stressed secular studies. But the question of a comprehensive reform of religious services and education for all of Berlin or Prussian Jewry remained a live issue, especially after the Prussian government forced the Berlin reformers to abandon their independent worship in the house of Jacob Herz Beer, and once the lines of opposition were clearly drawn between orthodox and reformers both in Berlin and in Hamburg.[8]

It was doubtless the added experience of the years following 1812 – the pressure for reform, the opposition, and the actual institution of modernised services – that, even for radical reformers, eventually raised questions of a different sort regarding Friedländer's plan. It ceased to be a matter of whether specific proposals in the programme were desirable or undesirable, but whether a comprehensive plan of reform was at all feasible given the divisions within Prussian Jewry. An anonymous manuscript has only now come to light which takes issue with Friedländer precisely on this point. More than just a critique of Friedlän-

---

Reform der Juden in preussischen Staaten, Breslau 1813. These two men were to represent Silesian Jewry at the advisory conference called by Minister of the Interior von Schuckmann. The conference was not held because the French defeat in Russia in the winter of 1812–1813 directed governmental attention to foreign affairs. See M. Brann, 'Abraham Muhr. Ein Lebensbild', *Jüdischer Volks- und Haus-Kalender*, 1891, pp. 68–84.

[6]*Freymüthige Erklärung über die erst jüngst rege gewordene Kritik des Gottesdienstes der Juden und deren Erziehung der Jugend*, Breslau 1813. Geiger (*op. cit.*, pp. 218–219) saw this pamphlet and briefly described its contents and character. However, I have been unable to locate a copy.

[7]*Licht und Wahrheit die Umbildung des Israelitischen Kultus betreffend*, Leipzig 1813.

[8]On the conflict over religious reform in Berlin see my 'The Religious Reform Controversy in the Berlin Jewish Community, 1814–1823', in *LBI Year Book XXIV* (1979), pp. 139–151; on that in Hamburg, my 'The Establishment of the "Temple" in Hamburg' (in Hebrew), *Jacob Katz Festschrift* (forthcoming).

der, it presents a remarkable analysis of the religious character of Berlin Jewry in the second decade of the nineteenth century.

The manuscript is entitled *Status causae et controversiae in Sachen der Israeliten in Berlin, die deutsche Synagoge betreffend. Frei und unparteiisch von einem alten Israeliten*. It is part of the large Jacob Jacobson collection acquired by the Leo Baeck Institute and is contained in its archives in New York. As Jacobson was head of the *Gesamtarchiv der deutschen Juden* before the Second World War, it is possible that the manuscript is one of the remnants of that archive, or, more likely, it was part of his extensive personal collection. The manuscript runs to ninety-one octavo pages and includes writing in various German hands. It is undated and there is no explicit indication of authorship. The first manuscript page is preceded by a printed memorial service of four pages which almost precisely corresponds to that contained in the Hamburg *Neue–Tempel–Verein* prayerbook of 1819.[9] There follows a preface and then a series of ten imaginary letters from one friend to another. The preface and the first page of the first letter (a total of sixteen pages with the memorial service) are unnumbered and written carefully on greenish paper in a neat, apparently professional hand. The following text, on numbered off-white pages beginning with page seventeen and running through to page eighty, is in a far more hasty and uneven handwriting, apparently that of the author himself. The last eleven pages, eighty-one to ninety-one, this time numbered, are again in the first hand and on the tinted paper. So, too, is the title page, which is wrapped around the entire manuscript. Though there are spelling variations between the two hands, the uniformity of style and expression leaves no doubt that, despite the scribal difference, the manuscript is the work of a single author. In the margins of the middle section, however, there are occasional notes in at least one other hand, which seems to be that of an editor or critic to whom the work was at some time submitted for review. Interspersed within the text and in the margins are occasional Hebrew terms, phrases and quotations written in Hebrew block letters. In a number of instances Hebrew words are spelled incorrectly. The Hebrew appears to be entirely the work of a single writer, almost certainly the author himself. With the manuscript is a covering note which reads:

---

[9] The service is entitled "Hascarot N'chamot. Todten-Feyer". The Hamburg prayerbook, in which the service appears on pp. 279 to 282, differs only in that the Hebrew title is given in Hebrew characters rather than in Latin ones. The transliteration here is surprising in two respects: the use of the plural in the first word (perhaps intentional, perhaps an error) and the transliteration of the "sh" sound as "ch", the latter possibly under French influence. The memorial service was probably written by the preacher Eduard Kley, who was first associated with the Berlin reform congregation and later with the Hamburg Temple. However, it was not included in the German prayerbook which Kley issued together with C. S. Günsburg, *Die deutsche Synagoge*, 2 vols., Berlin 1817–1818. He must have written it shortly thereafter, either while still in Berlin or after his removal to Hamburg. It was apparently used in Berlin as a supplement to the regular prayerbook. On the origins and development of the modern memorial service in Judaism, of which this is the first example, see Jakob J. Petuchowski, *Prayerbook Reform in Europe*, New York 1968, pp. 329–333. The service may have been attached to the manuscript as an example of the liturgy used by the reformers in Berlin. There is no reference to the service in the manuscript itself.

"The attached treatise: Status causae et controversiae in Sachen der Israeliten in Berlin, die deutsche Synagoge betreffend, which was furnished to me by Dr. Wolff, is to be placed in the files of the Bureau until further notice or request for it since Dr. Wolff presented it to me only for my personal use. The royal decision, made since then, has in fact ended all deliberation regarding this matter.
Berlin, 23 April 1824

Altenstein"

This note helps greatly to put the manuscript into context. Altenstein is Karl von Altenstein, the minister in charge of religions in the Prussian government. Together with Friedrich von Schuckmann, the Minister of the Interior, he had dealt with the Berlin Jewish community during the controversy over religious reform that ended with Frederick William's decree of 9th December 1823 prohibiting any religious innovation whatever. The manuscript in its final form must therefore have originated no later than the last phase of this dispute and been submitted to Altenstein at that time in the hope that it would influence the minister or even the King. It is more difficult to determine a *terminus a quo*. Within the preface itself are references to two earlier strata. Its opening lines state that the manuscript was composed "several years ago". It was at that time intended for publication especially on account of the appearance of a volume entitled *Dibor Habrit* [sic], a collection of responsa, properly entitled *Eleh Divre Haberit*, which was gathered by the three *dayanim* of Hamburg in opposition to the temple there and was published in 1819. The preface itself is an attack on the orthodox party in Hamburg and especially on the *dayanim*. But at the end of the preface our author tells us that the collection of letters which follows originated in the year 1812 in response to David Friedländer's pamphlet. This would lead us to the conclusion that the body of the manuscript represents the first stratum (1812), the preface and perhaps the final eleven pages in the neat hand were added in 1819 and re-worked, with the opening sentence added, in 1822 or 1823. However, even that section of the letters themselves which is in the presumed handwriting of the author refers to such later institutions and events as the private services in Berlin (1815), the Hamburg Temple (1818) and Isaak Levin Auerbach's published defence of the vernacular in prayer (1818).[10] Thus it is possible only to reach the tentative conclusion that a probable first version of the manuscript came into existence in 1812, that it was re-done in 1819–1820 with the addition of the preface dealing with *Eleh Divre Haberit*, and that at least the preface and the final segment were re-copied in the neater hand and possibly re-worked in 1822 or 1823, the first lines of the preface being added. From this last stage we also have a marginal note in the neater hand on the second-to-last page which specifically refers to the "recently formed" Berlin society for the conversion of the Jews, unquestionably that group which received royal sanction on 9th February 1822.

According to his covering memorandum, Altenstein was given the "treatise" by a Dr. Wolff. On the basis of internal evidence it is possible to determine that this Dr. Wolff was likewise the author and to establish definitely his identity. Almost at the very end of the manuscript we find: "That which I said at the

---

[10] *Sind die Israeliten verpflichtet, ihre Gebete durchaus in der hebräischen Sprache zu verrichten? Aus den Quellen des Talmuds und der späteren Gesetzlehrer erörtert*, Berlin 1818.

conclusion of a small pamphlet which I published in 1791 on such an occasion I can repeat here: may dungeon, chains and hangman protect me from such people." With slight variation these are the concluding words of a pamphlet published in Halle in 1792 (not 1791!) entitled *Freymüthige Gedanken über die vorgeschlagene Verbesserung der Juden in den Preussischen Staaten*. It appeared anonymously – "By a Jew with Additions by a Christian" – but it was already attributed by Kayser to "Sabattja Jos. Wolf" [sic].[11]

Unfortunately, little is known about Sabattia (or Sabattja) Joseph Wolff. He is not mentioned in any of the standard Jewish reference works. L. M. Landshuth,[12] in presenting the inscription on Wolff's gravestone, tells us that he was born in Berlin in 1757 and died there as a Jew in 1832, that he was a physician, and that he was a friend of Salomon Maimon, in 1813 publishing episodes from the philosopher's life in a book called *Maimoniana*. His ancestors, including a rabbi, were among the Jews expelled from Vienna in 1670, who founded the modern Jewish community of Berlin the following year. To this information Jacob Jacobson[13] adds that Wolff completed his medical studies in Frankfurt a.d. Oder and that he married in Berlin in 1801. Finally, an archival document of 15th April 1823 reveals that he was one of 151 signatories to a petition sent to the Elders of the Berlin community by defenders of the German services, requesting that the Elders press the petitioners' case as effectively as possible with the government authorities.[14] For anything of significance beyond these bare biographical facts one must rely on Wolff's published writings.

During his lifetime Wolff published more than a dozen works.[15] Of these, three dealt wholly with Jewish matters.[16] In addition, the above-mentioned *Maimoniana* – the best known of Wolff's works today – devoted considerable attention to the philosopher's Jewish characteristics.[17] The remainder of his writings, judging from the titles and the one work available to me, consist mostly of witty

[11] Christian Gottlob Kayser, *Vollständiges Bücherlexicon*, vol. VI, Leipzig 1836, p. 280. The same attribution is given in Volkmar Eichstädt, *Bibliographie zur Geschichte der Judenfrage*, Hamburg 1938, p. 45.
[12] *Vollständiges Gebet- und Andachtsbuch*, Berlin 1867, p. 8.
[13] *Jüdische Trauungen in Berlin 1759–1813*, Berlin 1968, p. 432. Jacobson, who had our manuscript in his possession, makes no reference to it in his entry on Wolff. A probably contemporary reference occurs in a series of entries in Giacomo Meyerbeer's diary during the summer of 1813. The diary mentions two visits the young composer paid to a Dr. Wolff of Berlin then residing briefly in Vienna. It is indeed most likely that Wolff was close to the Beer family. See Giacomo Meyerbeer, *Briefwechsel und Tagebücher*, vol. I, ed. Heinz Becker, Berlin 1960, p. 226.
[14] The petition, bearing *inter alia* the signature "S. J. Wolff Doctor Med.", is in the Berlin collection (KGe 2/81) of the Central Archives for the History of the Jewish People, Jerusalem.
[15] Kayser, *loc. cit.*; Wilhelm Hensius, *Allgemeines Bücher-Lexicon*, Erstes Supplement, Leipzig 1798, p. 473. Additional titles are on a handwritten list in Meyer Kayserling's copy of *Maimoniana* in the library of the Hebrew Union College-Jewish Institute of Religion, Cincinnati.
[16] The above-mentioned *Freymüthige Gedanken*; *Sendschreiben eines Christen an einen hiesigen Juden, über den Verfasser der Schrift: wider die Juden*, Berlin 1803; and *Wieder Juden, Sendschreiben an Herrn Julius v. Voss, veranlasst durch die, von ihm mir gewidmete, Schrift die Hep Heps, zur Vertheidigung der Christen*, Berlin im September 1819. The last was reviewed in *Sulamith*, vol. 6/1 (1820), pp. 28–29. It is briefly quoted by Heinrich Graetz in his *Geschichte der Juden*, vol. XI, Leipzig 1870, p. 366.
[17] From the contents of this volume, published in 1813, we may conclude that Wolff was a rather close associate of Maimon. He took meals with him regularly over a number of years and often spent afternoons and evenings with him. They visited one another's homes and went for walks together. Maimon called Wolff: "my future biographer". Wolff was a staunch defender of Maimon and much angered that, thirteen years after Maimon's death, his heretic's grave in Gross-Glogau

sayings and anecdotes intended to entertain sophisticated, enlightened readers, whether they be Jews or Christians. In one of them, published in his own name when he was fifty-eight years old, Wolff baldly asserted his own lack of faith. "Mein Glaubensbekenntniss in 3 Worten: Ich glaube Nichts. Erklärung in 10 Worten: Wer seiner Sach gewiss ist, Der nicht zu glauben braucht."[18] Wolff did not reject the existence of a deity, but his God was that of Spinoza: "Nicht für jedermann geschrieben: Im göttlichen Spinoza hab ich Gott erkannt, In Spinoza's Gott habe ich Spinoza erkannt."[19]

The *Freymüthige Gedanken*, with which Wolff began his literary career in 1792, was published in the midst of an extended effort to improve Jewish civil status in Prussia that began with the death of Frederick the Great. Like David Friedländer, who led this campaign,[20] Wolff was convinced that a change in the Jews' political situation would likewise require a change in their religious beliefs and practices. Wolff called for a "reformation" that would involve the gradual abandonment of certain laws and ceremonies irreconcilable with reason, while at the same time forcefully rejecting the view that Jews could be improved only through conversion. With regard to the religious service, Wolff here already proposed the introduction of a moral sermon and the elimination of prayers not understood by most of the worshippers. As in the much later "Status causae", Wolff here, too, takes issue with Friedländer (though his name remains unmentioned) and his supporters for insufficiently understanding the complexities of the Jewish situation. How can a Jew become apprentice to a Christian master, he asks, without violating Jewish laws or coming into conflict with him? How can he compete fairly in his trade with Christians when his faith requires far larger expenditures of time and money? For Wolff the answer lies in a comprehensive reform of Jewish education which will produce a new generation that no longer regards observance of all ceremonials as essential to Judaism. Only then will occupational integration become possible. To press for it under present circumstances would mean to pressure the observant Jews to give up practices against their conviction for the sake of material or civil advantage. Such a forced integration would encourage opportunism and destroy what for Wolff was most essential to religion: moral and intellectual integrity. The result would be a wholly unprincipled, frightening creature always seeking only its own advantage, one truly deserving of "dungeon, chains, and hangman".

Wolff's other two published works relating to the Jews are both written in their defence. The first was occasioned by Grattenauer's immensely popular racially antisemitic pamphlet, *Wider die Juden*, in 1803, the second by the hep-hep riots of 1819. In the second pamphlet, Wolff presents a most interesting analysis of the antisemite: he is not a faithful Christian but either a dissipator envious of the Jews' capacity to hold on to their money, a dishonest official, a failed businessman or simply an economic competitor. In defending the Jews

---

still had no gravestone. Wolff offered to pay for one, if only the Jewish burial society there would allow its erection.

[18] *Tripotage*, Berlin 1815, p. 158.
[19] *Ibid.*, p. 190. In a section of our manuscript omitted below, Wolff speaks of "Rabbi Spinoza".
[20] See his *Akten-Stücke die Reform der jüdischen Kolonieen in den Preussischen Staaten betreffend*, Berlin 1793.

from attack, Wolff sees no need to write about religious reforms. In part this is due to his belief that orthodox Judaism, despite all of his criticism of it, does not warrant Christian opposition to the Jews' civil integration. But in part it is no doubt also due to the fact that at just about the time he was publishing this defence he was likewise preparing a revised and expanded version of his letters on religious reform – our manuscript, the *Status causae et controversiae*.

Wolff's "letters" begin by agreeing with Friedländer regarding the need for religious and educational reform,[21] but pointing out his neglect of the difficulties posed by the divisions within Prussian Jewry. There are, in fact, four classes, each with its own particular characteristics. The first, according to Wolff, consists of the learned orthodox, the second of their unlearned imitators, the third of the learned, heterodox enlightened, and the fourth of the unlearned imitators of the enlightened. Wolff takes it upon himself to characterise each of these classes in colourful detail, for he believes that ignoring the profound differences between them makes any reform plan unlikely to succeed.

Wolff's description of the first class is surprisingly sympathetic, especially after his castigation of the Hamburg *dayanim* in the preface. He genuinely respects their remarkable learning, however inappropriate it may be to contemporary realities. In their own severely limited discipline they have achieved extraordinary expertise. Most importantly, they continue to enjoy considerable influence within their communities. The would-be reformer ignores them at his peril. Yet at first glance they appear wholly intractable, suspicious of any and every effort to bring about change. Are they so in fact? Wolff believes not. In private they recognise that some customs and ceremonies possess no genuine religious value or are inappropriate in present circumstances. They even violate certain traditions, because unlike the second class, they know them to be insignificant. But they do not dare to raise their voices out of fear that they will lose status in the eyes of their followers or that the removal of a single stone will lead to the extraction of others, until at length the entire structure will collapse. Thus it is not obstinacy (*Eigensinn*) but self-interest (*Eigennutz*) combined with religious apprehension (that "the baby might be thrown out with the bathwater") which has restrained them. They can be co-opted, Wolff suggests, if only one approaches them in the right way and does not cast them aside as superfluous.

The second class presents a far greater problem. Wolff pictures these imitators of the first class as ignorant pietists who lack any real knowledge of Judaism and so cling that much the more to all manner of inessentials and superstitions, "the husk without the kernel". For them he has only scorn and sarcasm. Not used to reasoning either in a Talmudic context or in a modern one, they are least susceptible to rational arguments. Ask them why they observe a particular custom and the *warum* will produce only a *darum*. They are those most needful of reform, yet they will cause the most trouble.

---

[21]Thus it was not inconsistent for his name to appear among the 136 Berlin community members who signed a letter of 12th November 1812 to the Elders supporting religious and educational reform in the spirit of Friedländer's pamphlet. The signature in this case is "Joseph Wolff Dr. med." but, according to Jacobson, *op. cit.*, Wolff sometimes used only one of his first names. Letter and signatures are in Moritz Stern, *Beiträge zur Geschichte der Jüdischen Gemeinde zu Berlin*, Heft 6, Berlin 1934, pp. 19–21.

The third class is the smallest in size. It is composed of the truly enlightened. Its members are universalists; they are rationalists whose natural religion is not based on denominational distinctions. Orthodox Jews pushed them aside except when their money was needed for the community treasury. In such instances they were even given communal office, but they could accomplish no reforms since they remained a minority. Frustrated, they withdrew from religious life, abandoning the synagogue to the orthodox. What kept them from conversion? Wolff refuses to give a direct answer. He suggests only indirectly, through a quotation from the French writer La Beaumelle and references to Mendelssohn, Spinoza and Schleiermacher, that conversion without conviction is an act of intellectual dishonesty.

The last class is by far the most pernicious. They possess neither religion nor enlightenment; they have cast off religious observance not on account of principle but out of convenience. Yet they have not succeeded in emancipating themselves completely from the ceremonial law. Wolff describes their religious condition as utterly chaotic. Everyone has made his own compromises, arrived at his own personal style of partial observance. Some go to the synagogue only once a year, others three times, etc. There is neither rhyme nor reason to their pattern of observance or lack thereof.[22] They neglect certain biblical prohibitions which interfere with their moral or business lives while clinging to far less significant practices. Wolff dwells on the resulting ludicrous combinations: they ardently kiss their ritual fringes at early morning prayer, but then have the barber apply a razor to their beards, put on garments containing wool and linen and enjoy a pork chop for breakfast. They surreptitiously whisper the grace over their non-kosher meals. Families are divided as each member makes his own religious rules. What is sacred to one is nonsense to another. Parents refuse to eat in their children's homes and vice versa. Worse yet are the cases in which some family members have converted to Christianity, while others have remained faithful to Judaism. Such families are no longer bound by a spiritual bond of common religious values. In its state of religious disorganisation, this class alone constitutes a danger to the moral welfare of society.

Given such fragmentation, Wolff is convinced that no comprehensive reform is possible, neither according to Friedländer's plan nor any other. The orthodox cannot be persuaded by Talmudic arguments; they will simply resort to counter-arguments, textual proof against textual proof. Success can be achieved only if the government cooperates. Under government pressure, and in council with their colleagues, the learned orthodox will be more likely to allow reforms. Wolff cites no less orthodox an authority than the *Chatam Sofer* to the effect that such a learned assembly under the aegis of European rulers could determine whether changes in practice might be made without violating Jewish law.

In a final section Wolff suggests that his fourfold classification is helpful not only in dealing with religious reform, but also in understanding the still apparent

---

[22]Another reflection of this chaos is the gross inconsistency between word and deed which bothered Jost when he attended the modernised services in Jacob Herz Beer's home in Berlin. See Nahum N. Glatzer, 'On an Unpublished Letter of Isaak Markus Jost', in *LBI Year Book XXII* (1977), pp. 129–137.

The Orthodox and the Enlightened

animosities between Christians and Jews. His point is that this animosity stems from the second and fourth classes among Jews and their equivalents in Christianity. These imitators, ignorant of the essentials of their own faith, have no understanding whatever of the religion of others.[23] Wolff ends with the pious wish that all men might in the course of time become either genuinely orthodox or genuinely enlightened. Apparently he has come to the conclusion that orthodoxy will not easily be swept away.

Wolff's characterisation of Berlin Jewry recalls an earlier division, likewise into four classes. In 1793, a year after Wolff's *Freymüthige Gedanken*, Lazarus Bendavid published his *Etwas zur Charackteristick der Juden*. In the context of plans for improving Prussian Jewry's civil status which were projected at that time, Bendavid laid out the principal Jewish faults which would have to be corrected, including the "shameful, senseless ceremonial law". He then said the Jews were divided into four groups: the superstitious, religiously incorrigible but often good-hearted wholly observant ones; the dissipators (*Wüstlinge*) who abandon the ceremonial law as a burden and engage in a dissolute style of life; the "good people" who remain observant only out of fear that immorality is the necessary concomitant of religious laxity; and the few truly enlightened adherents of natural religion in a particular manifestation called "the pure doctrine of Moses". Wolff refers to Bendavid both in his *Maimoniana* and in the *Status causae*. Undoubtedly he had read his pamphlet and was influenced by it.[24] Roughly speaking, Wolff's orthodox imitators correspond to Bendavid's superstitious believers, his imitators of the enlightened to Bendavid's dissipators, and each man's truly enlightened class is the same. The major difference between the two classifications lies in the remaining class. While for Bendavid it consists of those who remained orthodox half-heartedly, only out of apprehension, for Wolff this group is replaced by the learned orthodox. Writing at least twenty years later, Wolff has come to the conclusion that Berlin Jewry is better understood as divided into two élite groups each grounded in its own independent (and contradictory) principles, with the masses unreflectively gravitating to the one or to the other, identifying with the model while in effect creating its parody. In recognising – albeit grudgingly and inconsistently – this enduring dichotomy, Wolff's "letters" were reflecting the continued resilience that orthodoxy had still been able to muster.

In his preface Wolff says that several considerations had restrained him from publication. Since he does not go on to elaborate, it may be appropriate at this point to speculate about what they were. First, the similarity to Bendavid's pamphlet would have been evident to many readers and have detracted from Wolff's work. Second, the "letters" are not that well written. They are repetitive,

---

[23] In *Wieder Juden*, pp. 37–39, Wolff relates that since his youth he had regularly visited Christian churches in order to listen to the sermons. Never had he heard the preachers express any intolerance towards the Jews. He wished only that they would add the word *damalige* when referring (not so tolerantly!) to Jews at the time of Jesus, for not all their listeners added that adjective. This they could do legitimately since, were Christ alive today, Jews would treat him quite differently.

[24] Other classifications, made by David Friedrichsfeld and Saul Ascher, are too cursory and too much at variance to be regarded as an influence on Wolff. See D. Michman, 'David Friedrichsfeld. A Fighter for Enlightenment and the Emancipation of the Jews' (in Hebrew), *Studies on the History of Dutch Jewry*, ed. Jozeph Michman, Jerusalem 1975, I, p. 168.

include some material that would be known to fellow Jews but perhaps of interest to Christians, other sections that could only interest Jews. Third, what could Wolff really hope to accomplish? He presented no concrete plan. Far better at description than prescription, he vacillated between the hope that the orthodox would under certain circumstances agree to some modifications and his conviction that the orthodox and the enlightened would have to go their separate ways. But perhaps what most restrained him was the realisation that the letters were too revealing of the inner chaos within German Jewry. Wolff was well aware of the resentment against the newly emancipated Jews which grew in the years after 1812, finding expression in greater social exclusiveness, in anti-Jewish tracts and plays and eventually in the hep-hep riots. Under such circumstances to publish so unflattering, even self-mocking a portrait of Berlin Jewry would serve to supply ammunition to the Jews' enemies. Even if the author himself was not concerned by this consideration, others must have prevailed upon him. So Wolff put aside his manuscript, probably showing it to friends now and then, and finally submitting it to Altenstein in the vain hope that it would influence the King's decision.

Status causae et controversiae in Sachen der Israeliten in Berlin, die deutsche Synagoge betreffend

*Frei und unparteiisch
von
einem alten Israeliten*

Erstes Schreiben[25]

Herzlichen Dank für die mir überschickte Schrift.[26] Seit langer Zeit habe ich nichts begieriger, nichts mit mehr Interesse gelesen. Ich stimme ganz mit Dir überein, dass die Vortrefflichkeit des Styls, die klare und deutliche Auseinandersetzung des Gegenstandes, die herzliche Theilnahme an dem wahren Wohl der Nation,[27] die überall hervorleuchtet, den Verfasser gar bald als einen Mann darstellt, der über die Angelegenheit seiner Nation nicht zum ersten Mal das Wort nimmt, sondern vielmehr als einen Mann, der schon über diesen Gegenstand gedacht, und der mit erforderlichen Kenntnissen ausgerüstet, auftritt; und was das Vorzüglichste ist, der durch Sanftmuth und Bescheidenheit einzunehmen weiss, so dass ihn jeder Unbefangner liebgewinnen muss.

Sanftmuth, Bescheidenheit, Geduld und Beharrlichkeit sind Tugenden, die als nothwendige Bedingungen bei dem vorausgesetzt werden müssen, der als Reformator auftritt, der grau gewordenes Vorurtheil entwurzeln, und Licht an der Stelle der Egyptischen Finsterniss verbreiten will.

Der Arzt, der über einen Kranken, weil der trotz der ihm gereichten guten Medizin nicht geneset, zürnen könnte, so dass er ihm nun aus Verdruss gar nichts mehr reichen, und ihn umkommen lassen will, der wäre nicht nur ein Thor, sondern er wäre auch ein Barbar.

Ich gestehe es Dir, Freund, dass mich besonders folgende Stelle sehr entzückt hat. "Der Verfasser, heisst es, will nicht zu seiner Meinung bereden, er hat

---

[25] The original spellings, grammatical forms and punctuation found in the manuscript, even when in error, have been retained. The words in brackets are marginal comments which appear definitely not to be by the author. Limitation of space allows the printing of only selected portions of the manuscript. In the here omitted Preface, Wolff has taken issue with the rabbis who wrote responsa for *Eleh Divre Haberit*. To Wolff's mind these men are still living in the Talmudic age, oblivious to the world around them. He is especially critical of the Hamburg *dayanim*, who in their questions made it appear as if the reformers were motivated only by irreligiosity and a passion for novelty – instead of by genuine religious concern about the growing indifference which these religious leaders themselves noted but ignored. This indifference, according to Wolff, is caused by the lack of proper religious instruction, the inappropriate and unimpressive services and the lack of moral sermons.

[26] This is, of course, a reference to Friedländer's above-mentioned pamphlet.

[27] In this period even enlightened Jews continued to refer to the Jewish "nation", a term which did not necessarily imply lack of political loyalty to Prussia.

keinen Streit mit irgend einer andern Religions-Parthey, auch mit keinem seiner Mitbrüder, der eine andere Ansicht über diese Angelegenheit hat. Er referirt nach seinem Gewissen, nach seiner Ueberzeugung, nach seiner geringen Kenntniss der Sache u.s.w."[28] Das ist die Sprache, die Männer führen denen das wahre Wohl ihrer Mitbrüder am Herzen liegt, die ohne Anmassung auftreten, die sich selbst von dem Undank der sie erwartet, nicht abschrecken lassen, sondern standhaft beharren, und ihren Eifer für die gute Sache bei jeder sich darbietenden Gelegenheit mit jeder sich ihnen entgegenstellenden Schwierigkeit verdoppeln.

Ich gestehe es ferner, dass diese Stelle es war, die mir den Muth gab, meine Gedanken über diesen so wichtigen Gegenstand aufzuzeichnen, und sie Dir zur Beurtheilung vorzulegen. Ich habe Schwierigkeit gegen Schwierigkeit erwogen; Gewinn gegen Verlust genau berechnet; ich habe mir den Gegenstand klar und deutlich zu machen gesucht; und ich stellte vor allem folgende Fragen auf.

I. Ist dem Uebel allgemein abzuhelfen? ist eine allgemeine Verbesserung zu fassen und zu erwarten?

II. Und wie ist dem Uebel allgemein abzuhelfen, und eine Besserung zu hoffen? wie ist sie zu bewerkstelligen?

Du siehst, lieber Freund, dass ich mit dem würdigen Verfasser darüber einverstanden bin, dass eine Umbildung, besonders in Rücksicht des öffentlichen Gottesdienstes nicht nur nothwendig geworden, sondern durchaus unentbehrlich sey; ob ich aber in Rücksicht der Ausführung mit ihm übereinstimme, davon zweifele ich gar sehr, weil ich mir die Ausführung weit schwieriger denke, als man gewöhnlich glaubt.

Die Schwierigkeit, die sich mir darstellt, liegt darin, dass ich mir in dieser Hinsicht die Juden überhaupt und überall in 4 Klassen getheilt denke, und zwar glaube ich sie auch so eintheilen zu müssen.

Zur *ersten Klasse*, rechne ich die gelehrten Orthodoxen.

Zur *zweiten*, ungelehrte doch aber Orthodoxen, man nenne sie Nachahmer.

Zur *dritten*, gelehrte Aufgeklärte, Heterodoxen.

Zur *vierten* endlich, ungelehrte Aufgeklärte oder Nachahmer.

Diese in der That bestehende Eintheilung giebt, wie mich dünkt, hinreichend zu erkennen, welch ein schwieriges Unternehmen es sey, eine allgemeine Umbildung überhaupt zu bewerkstelligen; klar und deutlich aber geht daraus hervor, dass ohne Rücksicht auf diese verschiedenen Klassen sich eben so wenig eine bedeutende Abänderung erwarten, als hoffen lässt; und dass es sich vorzüglich darauf gründet, wenn alle bisherigen Versuche misslungen, und gescheitert sind, denn diese Kluft ist zu gross und nicht zu umgehen, wie wir auch bei näherer Beleuchtung sehen werden.

Wir wollen uns daher vor allem erst diese 4 Klassen, wie sich jede an und für sich verhält, und dann ihr Verhältniss unter und zu einander deutlich zu machen suchen; dieses ist durchaus nöthig, wenn wir uns nicht selbst täuschen, und zu falschen Schlüssen verleitet zu werden in Gefahr gerathen wollen, da aus eben diesen Verhältnissen hervorgehen soll, dass eine allgemeine Umbildung ohne alle Rücksicht darauf ein Unding ist und seyn muss. Für heute genug. Gott segne Dich.

[28]Pp. 5–6 with insignificant variations.

Zweites Schreiben

Liebster Freund. Ich will Dich heute mit der ersten Klasse unterhalten. Zu dieser Klasse habe ich die gelehrten Orthodoxen gerechnet, deren Anzahl gegenwärtig hier und überall zwar nicht mehr so zahlreich als ehedem ist, aber immer zahlreich genug, als dass man, ohne Rücksicht auf sie, mit gutem Erfolg etwas anfangen könnte. Und zwar schon darum nicht, weil wie ich dies bald zeigen werde, die 2te Klasse, die weit bedeutender in dieser Hinsicht ist, und aus festen wie wohl blinden aber desto treueren Anhängern derselben besteht.

Zu dieser ersten Klasse gehören, seltene Ausnahmen abgerechnet, alle Rabbiner, Assessoren [oder Beisitzer *dayanim*] [29] und solche Privatpersonen, die diese Art Gelehrsamkeit betreiben, und zwar bei letzteren nicht als Hauptgeschäft, nicht die Gelehrsamkeit der Gelehrsamkeit willen, noch weniger um etwa darin weitere Fortschritte zu machen, nein! weil sie es als ein verdienstvolles heiliges Geschäft, als ein Gott gefälliges Werk ansehen, womöglich Tag und Nacht sich damit zu beschäftigen, weil sie sich dadurch zugleich einige Achtung erwerben. (Nach dem Psalm, du sollst Tag und Nacht darin trachten – *vehigiti* [sic] *vo yom valaila*[30]).

Diese gelehrten Orthodoxen haben bisher noch immer in der Gemeinde selbst die bedeutendsten Rollen gespielt, sie wurden zu allen öffentlichen Aemtern gewählt; bisweilen musste bei ihnen die Orthodoxie die Gelehrsamkeit ersetzen, und hier und dort wurde mancher, mehr seiner Frömmigkeit als seiner Gelehrsamkeit wegen gewählt, mit einem Wort, sie machten und machen noch gleichsam den Stamm aus. Diese Klasse enthält mitunter Männer, die einen Umfang von Gelehrsamkeit im Talmud und allem dazu gehörigen besitzen (und das will wahrlich sehr viel sagen) das in der That ans Unglaubliche gränzt; der grösste Theil der Juden sowohl als der Christen hat gar keinen Begriff davon, was dazu gehört und lässt sich von dem Scharfsinn nichts träumen, der in solchen Schriften gefunden wird. Sie verbinden mit dieser Gelehrsamkeit einen sehr hohen Grad von Witz und Scharfsinn, am bewundernswürdigsten aber ist ein unbeschreibliches Gedächtniss das doch äusserst selten mit Witz und Scharfsinn vereint zu seyn pflegt, so dass sich Männer finden die den ganzen Talmud von Wort zu Wort auswendig wissen: man kann sie fragen wonach man will, so können sie Ort und Stelle, was vorher steht, und was darauf folgt, ganz genau angeben. Sie sind jedoch hierin nicht gleich, sondern pflegen sich einander zu übertreffen, daher die verschiedenen Nahmen oder Ehrentitel als da sind: *lamdan, talmud* [sic] *chacham, baki, charif, shinana, shanun, gaon, hamaor hagadol, oker harim* u.s.w. Eben so wenig gleichen sie sich einander in der Frömmigkeit, und einer

---

[29] The manuscript here and elsewhere uses Hebrew characters. As Hebrew type is not available, I have rendered the Hebrew, when the manuscript does not supply its own transliteration, in modern "Sephardi" form, realising that this is not the way it would have been pronounced in nineteenth-century Germany. Transliterations in the manuscript are here printed in roman type, those I have substituted are in italics.

[30] The quotation is inaccurate. Closest to it is Joshua 1:8, which corresponds to Wolff's German, but not his Hebrew. The closest Psalms verse is Psalms 77:13.

sucht darin den anderen zu übertreffen, daher gleichfalls die verschiedenen Nahmen: *tzadik, chasid, ish tam veyashar* oder mitunter auch verschiedene Sekten.

Andre Gelehrsamkeit, als diejenige, die zu dem Talmud u.s.w. gehört, findet man unter ihnen höchst selten, und sie ist eine so seltene Erscheinung, wie der Phönix unter den Vögeln; ja oft sind sie nicht einmal der ächten hebräischen Sprache so mächtig, als man zu glauben berechtigt wäre – und es wohl von ihnen fordern könnte. Fremde Sprachen verstehen sie gar nicht, selbst die Landessprache ist ihnen gewöhnlich fremd. Ich will gelinde verfahren und daher nicht sagen der grösste Theil, sondern nur ein grosser Theil von ihnen kann weder lesen noch schreiben, was auch in ihrem Verhältnisse und wie die Sachen bis jetzt standen, weder möglich noch so höchst nöthig war; daher das schöne Anekdötchen welches allgemein bekannt ist. Ein solcher jüdischer Assessor bekam eine Zuschickung vom Kammergericht, der Bothe wollte sie ihm eigenhändig abgeben, da jener den Empfang schriftlich bescheinigen musste. Die Frau nahm es mit der Bemerkung ab, ihr Mann sey ein jüdischer Gelehrer, er könne weder lesen noch schreiben.

Und diese gelehrten Orthodoxen sind es, wie schon gesagt, die den eigentlichen Stamm der Nation ausmachen, die die Religion aufrecht zu halten und zu verbreiten suchen; sie selbst weichen kein Haarbreit von den Mosaischen sowohl als von den talmudistischen Gesetzen ab. Moses und die sämmtlichen Propheten, der Talmud und alles dazu gehörige, Ceremonien und Gebete, alles ist ihnen gleich heilig, alles greift bei ihnen in einander und untereinander so ein, dass nach ihrer Meynung alles dieses zu dem Wesentlichen der Religion gehört, und als etwas Göttliches geachtet und festgehalten werden muss. Man frage sie über ein noch so unbedeutendes Gesetz, Gebot oder Verboth, Formel, Ceremonie, Sitte oder Gebrauch, sie werden mit gar wenig Mühe, freylich auf ihre eigne Art, die Göttlichkeit desselben beweisen. Bald wenden sie die heilige Schrift dazu an, um Kleinigkeiten aus dem Talmud zu erklären, bald zwingen sie Kleinigkeiten des Talmuds in die heilige Schrift hinein, um so das Göttliche zu beweisen; so ist alles ein künstliches Gewebe, oder ein mechanisches Uhrenwerk, wo jedes Stiftchen seine Bestimmung hat, und so unbedeutend es an und für sich, doch zum Ganzen nothwendig ist, und daher nicht fehlen darf.

Nicht wahr? Schon nach der oberflächlichen Schilderung dieser Klasse verzweifelst Du, dass es je möglich seyn wird irgend eine Verbesserung für dieselbe in Vorschlag zu bringen; es liegt ja in der Natur der Sache, höre ich Dich sagen, dass sie weder einen Vorschlag zu irgend einer Verbesserung anhören, noch annehmen können, sie werden auch nicht das allerunbedeutendste weder an Zeremonie, noch an Gottesdienst, noch weniger irgend ein noch so unbedeutendes Gesetz, wenn gleich talmudistischen Ursprungs, fahren lassen, sie können und dürfen es an und für sich nicht, und werden es aber besonders darum nicht thun, weil sie es nicht glauben werden, dass der Endzweck bei der Umbildung des Gottesdienstes zum Beyspiel der sey, das Wesentliche der Religion zu heben, dass der Endzweck der sey, statt der Gebete, die der grösste Theil nicht versteht, daher weder etwas dabei denken, noch weniger etwas fühlen kann, andre bessere einzuführen, oder dieselben zum Theil in eine verständliche Sprache zu übertragen, um den Geschmack, der ganz verloren gegangen ist, wieder zu beleben. Sie werden es nicht glauben, dass eine gute moralische Predigt in unsrer Synagoge darum wünschenswerth ist, weil man in unsren bisherigen sogenannten Predigten das Moralische zu wenig, oder gar nicht beachtete, solche gelehrte Abhandlungen vortrug, wovon der grösste Theil wenig oder nichts verstand. Sie werden glauben und zugleich fürchten, dass man nur damit den Anfang machen wolle, der Religion selbst den Fall vorzubereiten, und natürlicher Weise werden sie mit aller Macht dagegen streben.

Deine Furcht, liebster Freund, ist zum Theil nicht ohne Grund, in mehreren Hinsichten bist Du dazu berechtigt, ich bin dessen ohngeachtet doch nicht der Meynung, dass diese Klasse als die grösste Schwierigkeit einzusehen ist, vielmehr befürchte ich die grösste Schwierigkeit in der 2ten Klasse anzutreffen. Meine Gründe dazu sollst Du hören, wenn ich erst die 2te Klasse werde dargestellt haben ...

Drittes Schreiben

Liebster Freund. Die 2te Klasse habe ich ungelehrte Orthodoxen oder blosse Nachahmer genannt, weil sie bloss von der Macht der Gewohnheit zu Orthodoxen gebildet sind, von ihren Eltern, die gewöhnlich zu dieser Klasse gehört haben, oder noch gehören, dazu bloss abgerichtet worden. Sie besitzen in der Regel weder jüdische noch andere Gelehrsamkeit oder Kenntniss, höchstens etwa von jüdischen unbedeutenden leicht geschriebenen Büchern; so kennen sie auch leichte unbedeutende Sentenzen aus dem Talmud, womit sie bei jeder Gelegenheit um sich werfen, solche sehr oft ganz unpassend anbringen, und womit sie sich gegen diejenigen brüsten, die auf einer noch niedrigeren Stufe als sie selbst stehen. Sie bedienen sich dergleichen allgemeine Sentenzen etwa so, wie sich der gemeine Mann der Sprichwörter bedient, nemlich da, wo sie gar nicht passen, und dadurch suchen sie sich mehr als die Gelehrten selbst geltend zu machen.

Diese überall der Anzahl nach sehr grosse Klasse enthällt eigentlich diejenigen, die durch ihre grundlose Andächteley und Afterfrömmigkeit die Religion selbst verunstaltet haben. Weil sie das Wesentliche derselben gar nicht kennen, kleben sie an Vorurtheilen, an Aberglauben aller Art, den sie als etwas Wesentliches verehren und sehr fest daran halten.

Sie ahmen dem Gelehrten in allem ihren Thun und Lassen nach, und beeifern sich sogar, es ihm in der Frömmigkeit zuvor zu thun, sie plappern mit grossem Enthusiasmus alle Gebete her, die sie nicht nur nicht verstehen, sondern die sie oft kaum lesen können, was auch bey der Geschwindigkeit und der Unordnung, die dabei herrscht, nicht gut möglich ist, und so bringen sie statt Gotteslob unwissend öffentliche Gotteslästerung hervor. Falsche Frömmigkeit ist gefährlich, besser ist, gar keine haben. Andächteley und falsche Frömmigkeit verunstalten jede Religion, und man hat am Ende blosse Schale ohne Kern, und es wäre zu wünschen, dass die Zeit schon da wäre, wo man nicht mehr die Wahrheit um Fabeln willen verlässt, wie Paulus sagt.[31]

[31] In II Timothy 4:4.

Diese Klasse ist es vorzüglich, die man bey einer Umbildung vor Augen haben muss, für sie ist eigentlich eine gänzliche Umbildung höchst nothwendig, sie kann und darf nicht in diesem Zustand länger verbleiben; sie ist es aber auch, die die meisten Schwierigkeiten entgegen setzen wird, und das aus folgenden Gründen.

Wir haben die erste Klasse als Gelehrte wenigstens in allen Arten der jüdischen Gelehrsamkeit aufgestellt. Ein grosser Theil derselben kennt das Wesentliche der Religion sehr wohl, weiss von allem seiner Thun und Lassen Gründe anzugeben, und man findet unter denen, die dazu gehören, die besten, hellsten und sehr scharfsinnige Köpfe, so dass man sich ohne Bedenken in aller und jeder Angelegenheit bey ihnen Raths erholen kann; und mag man auch dagegen sagen, was man will, so glaube ich doch behaupten zu können, dass dies eine Frucht des talmudistischen Studiums sey, weil in demselben, manche Sophistereyen und Schnurren abgerechnet, ein ganz origineller Geist herrscht. Diese in der That in mancher Hinsicht achtungswerthe Männer erkennen im Stillen so manche Mängel, erkennen so manches als Vorurtheil und Aberglauben, erkennen so manches als lästig und unnütz; erkennen so manche Ceremonie als für unsere Zeit ganz unpassend und unnütz, eben so den grössten Theil der Gebetsformeln zum öffentlichen Gottesdienst als entbehrlich, besonders, da sie es sehr wohl wissen, dass der grösste Theil oder der grosse Haufen überall fast gar nichts davon versteht, daher sich der Kopf dabey nichts denken, und das Herz nichts fühlen kann. Aber sie wagen es nicht dagegen aufzutreten, und zwar aus mehr als einer Ursache: erstens fürchten sie ihrem eignen Ansehen bey ihren Anhängern und blinden Nachahmern dadurch einen Stoss zu geben, zweitens darum nicht, weil sie die Gefahr fürchten in einem alten Gebäude auch nur einen Stein zu lösen: denn, sagen sie sich, würde man es auch wol bey einem Steine bewenden lassen? wird man nicht bald weiter gehen? und das Gebäude stürzt ganz ein! Sie sind weise genug, es einzusehen, dass die Menschen nie recht verstehen, Maass und Ziel zu halten, dass sie von einem Extrem zum andern gern überspringen, und gar bald geschieht mehr, als man wollte. Du erkennst, liebster Freund, daraus meine Meinung, dass von der einen Seite wahre Frömmigkeit, und von der andern Seite Eigennütz (von ihrem Ansehen nichts zu verlieren) es war, was diese Klasse abhielt, in irgend eine Abänderung zu willigen, dass man ihnen offenbar Unrecht gethan, wenn man es ihrem Eigensinn zuschob. Wenn dieser gleich das seinige auch mit dazu beitragen mag, so muss doch immer als Hauptgrund angesehen werden, der erwähnte Eigennutz – man könnte es auch Eigenliebe nennen, – und die Furcht, dass man die Sachen zu weit treiben möchte, sie fürchten selbst das Unwesentliche, zur wahren Religion von ihnen ins Geheim als entbehrlich anerkannte antasten zu lassen, weil dadurch das Wesentliche der Religion erschüttert werden könnte, oder, wie man sagt, weil dadurch das Kind mit dem Bade ausgeschüttet werden könnte. Sie ahmen in diesen Stücken ganz den Talmudisten nach, bey denen man eine sehr grosse Menge von Verbothen antrifft, die nicht deswegen erlassen sind weil die verbothene Sache selbst an und für sich als etwas sündliches angesehen wird, sondern diese Gesetzgeber hatten gewöhnlich ganz andre Dinge im Sinne, aber um diese Dinge sicher zu stellen, verbothen sie eine Menge von andern Dingen,

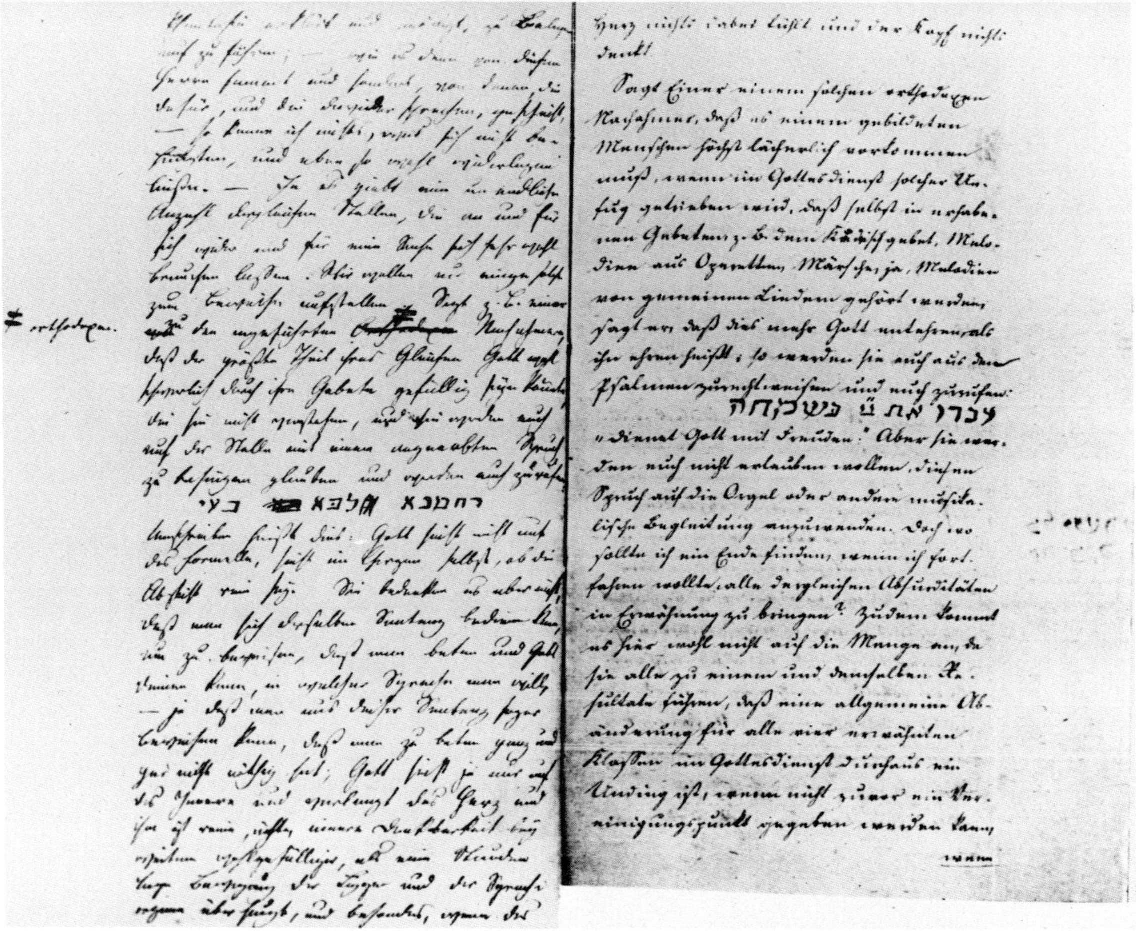

Pages from Sabattia Joseph Wolff's treatise

From the Archives of the Leo Baeck Institute, New York

die nur auf die entfernteste Weise zur Verletzung desjenigen, was sie bezweckten, führen konnten ...

Unsere Gelehrte sehen daher alle diese Verbothe mit ganz anderen Augen an, als die Ungelehrten, die Nachahmer, mit einem Wort der grosse Haufen. Sie sind daher bey weitem nicht so difficil bey manchen Dingen, als jene; sie können daher, wenn sie anders wollen, sowohl anderen als sich selbst so manches erlauben, wie es denn auch bisweilen geschieht. Der Gelehrte kann daher so manches begehen, das dem Ungelehrten oder dem grossen Haufen eine Sünde zu seyn scheint, ihn in Erstaunen setzen kann und muss, wie das denn auch irgendwo im Talmud ein weiser Rabbi zu bemerken scheint, und wie mich dünkt, gegen diesen Verstoss warnet, wenn er sagt: "Siehst Du einen Weisen bey Nacht sündigen so verurtheile ihn nicht hinterher am Tage."[32]

Aus dem allen, dünkt mich, geht es hervor, dass diese Klasse weit eher zu gewissen Abänderungen, zu Verbesserungen, die dem Zeitgeiste angemessen sind, stimmen würde, wenn man es nur am rechten Ende anzufangen weiss, – weil, wie schon gesagt, Männer von Kopf und Geist diese Klasse ausmachen, – und die Erfahrung lehrt es ja, dass man einem Klugen eher etwas abgewinnen kann, als einem minder Klugen. Zudem können wir hiervon mehrere Beyspiele anführen, wo sie in neueren Zeiten, zu ihrem Lobe sey es gesagt, schon so manches nachgeben. Es ist noch gar nicht sehr lange her, wo es als eine grosse Sünde angesehen wurde, am Osterfest Kartoffeln zu geniessen, es wurden ihnen vernünftige Gründe angegeben, und sie erlaubten es ohne Ausnahme zum Trost der Armen, diese Speise geniessen zu dürfen.[33] Eben so wurde noch ganz neulich von Rabbinen erlaubt, Ostern Reiss und davon bereitete Speisen zu geniessen, durch Doctor Bloch[34] mehrere Fischarten: dies mag der Beyspiele genug seyn, dass wenn man nur diese Klasse recht zu nehmen weiss, wenn man nicht glaubt, sie als überflüssig vorbeigehen zu dürfen – dass sich von ihnen und durch sie vieles erwarten lässt; doch wie es anzugreifen? davon in diesem Briefe nichts, da meine Briefe Dir ohnehin schon viel zu lang sind. Gott erhalte Dich ...

Fünftes Schreiben[35]

... Unter der dritten Klasse verstehe ich die wahren Aufgeklärten unserer Nation, die überall nur den kleinsten Theil ausmachen, Männer, die sich durch

---

[32] Berachot 19a. Wolff omits the continuation of the saying: "Perhaps he has repented".
[33] My colleague Alexander Guttmann has called my attention to several rabbinic responsa dealing with the permissibility of eating potatoes at Passover. Jacob Emden, in his *She'elat Yavetz*, Part Two, Altona 1770, Responsum 147, reports: "When I was in Mannheim, there was an attempt to prohibit the vegetables called *Erdäpfel* or *Kartoffeln* because they are used for flour. However, I opposed [the proponents of the prohibition], for the community cannot live without [these vegetables]: they are a food of the poor ... It would be wonderful if all the sages of our time agreed, but I doubt that the matter will be settled in this generation in which zealotry has increased and people are more respectful of customs than they are of the essentials of Torah." This is certainly an attitude most congenial to Wolff's point of view.
[34] Mordechai Bloch (1723–1799) practised medicine in Berlin and was a renowned icthyologist.
[35] The intervening fourth letter focuses in greater detail upon the second class. A typical member knows only what is permitted and prohibited, but not why. Though sometimes even more punctili-

das Studium sehr guter Schriften und eignes Nachdenken aufgeklärte, helle Begriffe über das wahre Wesen ihrer Religion sowohl, als über Religion überhaupt verschafft haben.

Ihre eigne Religion, d.h. die Religion, in der sie geboren und erzogen sind, hat bey ihnen keinen Vorzug vor jeder andern, die eine ist ihnen so viel werth als die andere. – Werden sie von der ersten Klasse dafür erkannt, wie dies gewöhnlich der Fall ist, so werden sie zugleich auch verkannt, wie es auch bey allen andern Religionspartheyen der Fall war, man nennt sie bald Deisten, bald Apicorsim (soll wol heissen Epicursim von Epicur), und so zog sich denn diese Klasse zurück, da man sie gewöhnlich nur dann duldete, wenn man sie dulden musste, nur dann achtete, wenn man sie achten musste, und dies war der Fall, wenn es vermögende Männer waren, mit deren man als dann auf einem politischen Fuss umging, weil sie zur Erhaltung des Ganzen unentbehrlich waren. Man muss von jenen solidarischen Verbindungen unterrichtet seyn, wie sie damals Statt fanden, weil es der Staat so haben wollte. – Gott sey dank, dass es nicht mehr so ist; ich sage es frey und dreist, unter allen Grausamkeiten, die man am Juden geübt, war keine so gross als diese (der würdige Stadt-Rath und Assessor Friedländer hat dieses auch in seinen Aktenstücken[36] sehr kräftig gerügt). Und in diesen Fällen musste man sie sogar zu Ehrenposten zulassen und wählen, und solche wurden ihnen sogar aufgedrungen, wenn sie dieselben nicht annehmen wollten. [Die Rabbiner mussten wie man zu sagen pflegt, ein Auge zu drücken, und gute Miene, zum bösen Spiel machen, auch ihre eigene ökonomische Umständen heischten dies –.]

Da nun diese Ehrenposten und Vorsteherstellen gewöhnlich besetzt waren von Männern aus der ersten Klasse, aus der 2ten, wenn sie Vermögen hatten, und wenn zur Bestreitung aller Abgaben, die der Gemeinde aufgelegt wurden ihr Beitrag nicht zu entbehren war, aus der dritten Klasse aus eben demselben Grunde, und zuletzt auch von Männern aus der 4ten Klasse, die wir bald werden näher kennen lernen; so ist es leicht einzusehen, was bey einer solchen Ungleichheit der Köpfe, die an die Spitze gestellt wurden, zu erwarten seyn konnte, wenn die Zeitumstände eine Veränderung, eine Verbesserung, und war sie auch noch so unbedeutend, erforderten, nicht einzusehen, wenn auch von dem Einen oder dem Andern die Rede war, doch nie etwas zu Stande kommen konnte. Und um nun bey dergleichen Gelegenheiten, wo man nicht unter sich einig werden konnte, von der Stelle zu kommen, glaubte man es als dann dadurch zu bewerkstelligen, dass man gewöhnlich eine Anzahl von 18 Männern, und bey sehr bedeutenden Dingen, von 32 oder 62 zusammen kommen liess, wodurch dann das schon Schlimme noch bey weitem verschlimmert wurde, denn da dergleichen Männer durch das Loos gewählt wurden, so wurde dieser Mischmasch von Köpfen nur noch vergrössert, – und ich denke mir dergleichen Sitzungen wie ehedem die polnischen Reichstage, wo ein jeder noch so einfältige

---

ous in his observance than the learned Jew, he succeeds only in earning the latter's contempt as an *am ha'aretz*, an ignoramus.

[36] See above, n. 20.

das Recht hatte, sich des Ausrufs Nie poz wolam[37] als Argument zu bedienen.

Was blieb der dritten Klasse wohl übrig, wenn sie sich bey jeder dergleichen Gelegenheiten, wo etwa gegen Vorurtheil, Aberglauben, Ceremoniell einer oder der andern auch wirklich auftrat, wenn sie sich jedes Mal überstimmt sah? sich mit den Nahmen Gottesleugner, Sünder, Bösewicht und so weiter beehrt sah? (*kalim, meshumadim, kofrim, apikorsim, posh'e yisraelim*) was blieb ihr anders übrig, wenn sie sich stets verkannt sah, als sich zurückzuziehen und nach und nach kalt und gleichgültig gegen alles zu werden, und alles so gehen zu lassen wie es geht, – da sie es wol ein sehen, dass dergleichen Versuche unter solchen Umständen offenbar mehr schaden als nützen; denn die andern Klassen drängten sich nach jedem misslungenen Versuche nur noch enger zusammen, wie etwa die Einwohner einer Stadt, der sich ein Feind nähert, um sie anzugreifen.

Natürlicher Weise konnte diese Klasse aufgeklärter Männer am wenigsten an dem gewöhnlichen Gottesdienst den geringsten Antheil nehmen. Die Gebete und Ceremonien sind weder dem Zeitgeiste noch der Zeit selbst anpassend; selbst die gelehrten Orthodoxen achten den grössten Theil derselben wenig oder gar nicht; nicht selten sieht man diese Gelehrten ein oder das andere Buch studieren, während sie den grossen Haufen diese oft ganz sinnlosen Gebete herplappern lassen. Und so überliess man denn die Synagoge mit allem, was dazu gehörte, der 1sten und 2ten Klasse, die denn bey ihrem alten Schlendrian blieben. (Darum hörte man auch diese Klassen von *ihren* Synagogen sprechen, als wenn sie ein ausschliessliches Recht daran hätten.) Wie konnte dies auch anders seyn, den gebildeten, aufgeklärten Theil hörte man nicht, und die orthodoxen Gelehrten wollten aus mehreren Gründen, die wir ja zum Theil schon kennen, nicht die mindeste Abänderung und lachten wol gar ins Fäustchen, wenn diese aufgeklärten Männer hier oder dort von Veränderungen oder Verbesserungen sprachen, weil sie es wohl wussten, dass nichts zu Stande kommen kann, oder jemals unter solchen Umständen zu Stande kommen wird. Sie hielten es bisweilen nicht einmal der Mühe werth, ein Wörtchen darüber zu sagen; und eine schöne Politik! bey solchen warlich nicht unwichtigen Gelegenheiten den Neutralen zu spielen, und zu schweigen, sich mit der Sentenz durch zu helfen: Sejak lechochma Schtika [etwa die ächte Klugheit schweigt] *seyag lachochmah shetikah*.[38]

[Aber auch dies kann einigerweisen entschuldigt werden, weil ihre ganze Subsistenz, von einer solche politische Neutralität abhängt – –.]

So stand nun die 3te Klasse ganz isolirt da, diese Männer machten unter sich kein Ganzes aus, sie lebten ohne alles Formelle und Ceremonielle, ohne Synagoge und öffentlichen Gottesdienst dennoch als moralisch gute Menschen. Sie nahmen an allem Guten ohne Unterschied der Religionsparthey, Antheil. Selbst ihre Kinder würden auf dieselbe Art erzogen. An Religionsunterricht war bey denselben nicht zu denken, eben so wenig an einen Katechismus, und alle Versuche zu dergleichen machten wenig oder gar keinen Eindruck, am wenigsten auf jene Klassen, auf die am meisten dabey gesehen wurde. Gab es Gelegenheiten, wo man aus Rücksichten so manches mitmachen musste, zum Beyspiel

---

[37] The *liberum veto* by which any member of the Polish diet was able to nullify a decision of the majority by saying: "I do not allow!"

[38] Mishnah Avot 3:13.

bey Trauungen, Begräbnissen, Beschneidungen, oder sich Neujahr und *Langenacht*[39] wenigstens in der Synagoge sehen zu lassen, so wurde dies natürlicher Weise als etwas sehr lästiges betrachtet, als ein nothwendiges Uebel angesehen. Und so seufzte dann im Stillen eine zwar nicht so zahlreiche aber doch immer bedeutende und schätzenswerthe Klasse.

Warum aber, fragt man gewöhnlich, gingen aus dieser Klasse die Reicheren, die von ökonomischen und Familienverhältnissen nicht zurückgehalten wurden, warum gingen sie nicht samt und sonders zu der so reinen christlichen Religion über?

Warum machten sie sich nicht von einer Religion los, von der sie fast nur den Nahmen und nichts weiter führten, von einer Religion, in der sie ohnehin von allen Seiten so viel Ungemach zu erdulden hatten? Waren sie so aufgeklärte und geschickte Männer, wie sie hier geschildert werden, was konnte sie sonst abhalten, wenn es ihre ökonomische Umstände nicht thaten, sich und ihre Familien glücklich und zu brauchbaren Mitgliedern des Staates zu machen? Was sie bloss des Nahmens wegen nicht werden konnten, warum duldeten sie so viel Ungemach um nichts? Es kann mit dieser Aufklärung wohl nicht ganz richtig seyn, hörte man oft von Männern sagen, von denen man es kaum erwartet hätte; diese Frage kann in verschiedener Rücksicht aufgeworfen und eben so verschieden beantwortet werden, – ich lasse mich daher gegenwärtig auf keine eigentliche Antwort ein, da mich dieses zu weit führen würde; – statt dessen will ich eine Stelle aus einem alten Schriftsteller, in dem ich gar vortreffliche Sachen gefunden habe hersetzen. Er sagt:

> Derjenige Hofmann, welcher die Religion seines Herrn annimmt, thut ein demselben schimpfliches Opfer, – insonderheit, wenn der Weg von der Religion, die er verlässt zu derjenigen, so er annimmt von weniger Wichtigkeit ist: denn, wenn die beyden Religionen von einander sehr unterschieden wären, so könnte man das jenige einem im Gewissen liegenden Bewegungsgrunde zuschreiben, was in dem anderen Falle ganz augenscheinlich das Werk einer knechtlichen Gefälligkeit ist.
>
> Ein Mensch (fährt er fort) kann das Unglück, alle Religionen mit einem gleichgültigen Auge anzusehen, und den Unverstand, sich in alle Religionen zu schicken, haben, und dennoch berechtigt seyn, die Wechselung der Religion seiner Väter zu verweigern. Die Gerechtsame des Gewissens sind so heilig, dass selbst derjenige, der kein Gewissen hat, sich darauf berufen kann. Die Annehmung der herschenden Religion zu verweigern, ist nicht allein eben so gut, als wenn man ein Heuchler zu werden abschlägt, sondern man erhält sich auch dadurch das allerwesentlichste Vorrecht der Freiheit. [Beiträge zu den Gedanken des L. v. Beaumelle u.s.w.][40]

Ich hoffe, dass diese Stelle einen Theil, der diese Frage aufzuwerfen pflegt, als Antwort genügen wird; so wie ich dem einem andre Theil mit Moses Mendels-

---

[39] Yom Kippur, the Day of Atonement.
[40] Wolff may have quoted from the German translation: Angliviel v. Beaumelle, *Gedanken, nebst Beiträgen zu denselben*, Glogau 1754. This edition was not available to me.

sohns Jerusalem antworte – und einem Dritten mit Spinoza, oder auch mit einer vortrefflichen Abhandlung von S-r: Ueber Religion, *Reden an die Gebildeten unter ihren Verächtern*,[41] da wohl keine ausführliche Antwort von mir gefordert werden möchte, nach hierher gehört. Lass uns, Freund, mit dieser Klasse schliessen, und in meinem nächsten Schreiben will ich die 4te und letzte Klasse darstellen. Gott erhalte Dich.

Sechstes Schreiben

Werthester Freund!
Wie die 2te Klasse, die wir ungelehrte Orthodoxen, oder blinde Nachahmer genannt haben, sich zu der ersten von uns aufgeführten Klasse, nemlich orthodoxen Gelehrten, verhält; so ungefähr verhält sich diese 4te und letzte Klasse zu der 3ten, oder den gelehrten Aufgeklärten, jedoch mit dem Unterschiede, dass diese letzte Klasse, die wir die ungelehrten Aufgeklärten, oder Nachahmer genannt haben, bey weitem schädlicher als jene ist. Diese sind wahre monströse Geburten in der Religion so wohl als in der Aufklärung. Sie besitzen grösstentheils auch nicht die mindesten Kenntnisse; ihre Afteraufklärung ist weder die Frucht eignes Nachdenkens, noch etwa herbeygeführt durch das Lesen solcher Schriften, die zu Irreligiosität leiten, sondern sie finden es bloss behaglich, das Joch der Religion abzuschütteln; sie ahmen blindlings den aufgeklärten Gelehrten darin nach, dass ihnen alle Religionen gleich viel, oder vielmehr gleich wenig sind; Gründe haben sie nicht und können sie nicht haben; und so zahlreich diese Klasse auch ist, so sind sie sich selbst nicht gleich, und stehen nicht nur mit den andren Klassen, sondern mit ihrer eignen Klasse und mit sich selbst in beständigem Widerspruch.

Gleich sind sie sich nur darin, dass sie alle weder feste Religion, noch feste Aufklärung haben, aber das sind sie nicht alle in gleichem Grade; – so dass sich ein jeder eine beliebige sogenannte Religion bildet, dies oder jenes wird von diesem oder jenem geachtet, von jenem wieder verachtet. Man kann sich keine tollern, inconsequentern, possierlichere Carrikaturen denken, als man unter ihnen findet.

So giebt es denn unter ihnen Eintags-Juden, die bloss die Langenacht als Juden leben; Dreitags-Juden, die die beyden Neujahrstage noch dazu nehmen; Viertags-Juden, die Hoschaino Rabbo[42] mitmachen; Sechstags-Juden, die noch den ersten Zeliches Tag und Eref Rosch Haschana[43] mit machen zu müssen glauben; Achttags-Juden, die das Osterfest in so fern halten, dass sie kein un-

---

[41] Schleiermacher's "Fifth Speech", though viciously derisive of Judaism, argues against uniformity in religion. But perhaps Wolff was thinking more of Schleiermacher's response to Friedländer's offer of conversion made to Probst Teller in 1799. In his *Briefe bei Gelegenheit der politisch-theologischen Aufgabe und des Sendschreibens jüdischer Hausväter*, which appeared in the same year as his *Reden*, the young Protestant theologian objected to half-hearted conditional conversions such as Friedländer and his associates were proposing at that time.

[42] Hoshana Rabba, the seventh and last day of the Sukkot festival.

[43] The Sunday before the New Year, when the penitential prayers, *selichot*, are first said, and the eve of the New Year.

gesäuertes Brod und dergleichen Getränk zu sich nehmen; Monaths-Juden, die vom Monat Ellel[44] an bis nach der Langenacht den Gesetzen gemäss leben, u.s.w. Welcher Anblick! wenn man diese Menschen an einem ganz unbedeutenden Gesetze, was selbst die gelehrten Orthodoxen für unbedeutend ausgeben würden, wenn man diese Menschen daran mit Leib und Seele hängen sieht, indem sie 100 andere, bey weitem wichtigere, ganz kalt mit Füssen treten, weil ihnen dies zur Aufklärung ihrer Art nöthig scheint. Ob ich gleich gestehen muss, dass es mich anekelt, Beyspiele dieser Art hier anzuführen, so will ich es doch thun, um das Lächerliche recht lebhaft darzustellen.

Es ist nichts seltenes, dass der eine oder der andere um alles in der Welt es nicht unterlässt, des Morgens beym Aufstehen sich die schon oben angeführten Denkfäden anzuziehen, den Segen darüber zu sprechen, sie recht brünstig zu küssen, eben so sich der andern Denkzeichen unter dem Nahmen Tephillim, *tefilin* wie der grösste Orthodoxe zu bedienen. Nicht lange nachher tritt der Barbier herein, (wenn sie das Geschäft desselben nicht selbst verrichten können) und ohne alle Umstände wird der Bart mit dem Rasiermesser abgenommen, ohne dass man daran im mindesten denkt, dass die Sünde die dadurch begangen wird in gar keinem Verhältnisse steht mit der frommen Handlung der Hersagung der Gebete und der Anlegung der Denkfäden, die sie kurz zuvor gethan haben. Diese Handlung nemlich gehört bloss zum Ceremoniel, ist höchstens als Symbol zu betrachten, aber sich den Bart mit dem Scheermesser abnehmen zu lassen, ist unmittelbar von Gott durch sein Propheten Moses verbothen worden. Doch wir wollen dieser Sünde, die fast allgemein unter ihnen gleichsam das Bürgerrecht bekommen hat, so dass sie kaum noch für eine Sünde gehalten wird, nicht bedenken. Es giebt offenbar solche Sünden, die das Bürgerrecht bekommen haben, z.B. keine Wolle und Leinewand zusammen zu tragen, d.h. sich nicht damit zu bekleiden, wurde ebenfalls von Gott unmittelbar durch Moses befohlen, aber man küsset die Denkfäden, und kleidet sich gleich darauf in Kleidern, die dem göttlichen Verbothe zuwider sind. Aber wie? wenn wir diese Menschen, die so eben so andächtig gebetet, die wir so eben die Denkfäden brünstig haben küssen gesehen, wenn wir diese Menschen beym Frühstück mit einer Schweins-Carbonade, oder einen Schinken u.s.w. antreffen? wenn wir sie des Mittags alle Speisen, die die Küche hergiebt, geniessen sehen? ohne sich daran zu kehren, dass ihnen ebenfalls diese von Gott unmittelbar durch seinen Propheten Moses verbothen sind? Ja wenn man unter ihnen sogar solche verschrobene Köpfe findet, die selbst beym Genusse solcher verbothenen Speisen die Segenssprüche vor und nach dem Mahle wohl ins Geheim hersagen (sie fühlen wahrscheinlich unter solchen Umständen wol das Lächerliche daran). Andere wieder modeln und bilden sich den Sabbath ganz nach ihrer Bequemlichkeit, sie unterscheiden ihn in nichts von jedem andern Tage, aber an demselben fahren oder reiten möchten sie um keinen Preis, und nicht etwa, weil sie sich nicht frey stellen wollen, dies hört man sie freylich öfters vorschützen, weil sie sich schämen so lächerlich inconsequent zu seyn, sondern weil diese Sünde bey ihnen für viel bedeutender gehalten wird, als sie wirklich ist. Doch, wie schon eben gesagt, es erregt nur Widerwillen aller diese Absurditäten, aller Tollheiten dieser Art zu

[44]The month of Elul, which immediately precedes the New Year.

gedenken; fast jeder Einzelne hat seine eigene Gesetze, oder seine eigene Art die Gesetze auszulegen. Die Strafe der Narren sey ihre Narrheit, könnte man mit Salomo ausrufen.[45]

Man denke sich aber in einer Familie die beysammen wohnt und lebt, einen solchen Mischmasch von Gesinnungen und Denkungsarten, ein lebendiges Quodlibet; die Frau anders als ihr Mann, der Sohn anders als der Vater, der Bruder anders als die Schwester, die Diener anders als die Herrschaft, u.s.w. Was der Mann für die grösste Sünde hält, eben das verlacht oder verspottet öffentlich oder heimlich die Frau; der Mann hält es mit dem Spruche, was in den Mund hineingeht, das sündet nicht, der Frau will dies aber nicht einleuchten, das eine Kind hält es in dergleichen Dingen mit dem Vater, das andere mit der Mutter. Werden sie bey einem ihrer Verwandten oder sonst irgendwo zu Gäste geboten, so müssen sie es bisweilen der Convention wegen annehmen, aber da sitzt dann so mancher an der Tafel und thut nur, als wenn er etwas geniessen möchte. Auch hierin machen sie sich eigene Gesetze, dieses mitzuessen erlauben sie sich, jenes nicht; man isst die Suppe, und die darin befindlichen Krebse lässt man der Sünde wegen liegen, wie ich denn dieses und mehr dergleichen gesehen habe. (Ganz so geht es unter ihnen mit den Fasttagen, der eine hält diesen, der andere wieder jenen für wichtig. So gäbe es meiner Meynung nach unter den Fasttagen keinen, der wichtiger wäre, selbst der Versöhnungstag nicht – als der Tag vor dem Hamansfest[46] – wenn man diese Geschichte für wahr annimmt – und dieser wird am wenigsten geachtet.) So speist denn bisweilen mit vollen Backen der Vater bey solchen Gelegenheiten alles, was ihm vor den Schnabel kommt, die Tochter, die es in diesen Stücken mit der Mutter hält, sieht lüstern zu. So speist denn der Vater oder die Mutter bisweilen bey ihren eignen Kindern nicht das Mindeste, weil sie der Zubereitung der Speisen nicht trauen, und so umgekehrt. Dieses alles, was ich nur gleichsam im Vorbeigehen mitgenommen habe, ging noch an, aber es ist bereits schon viel weiter gekommen, bald sind die Kinder zur christlichen Religion öffentlich übergegangen, und die Eltern sind noch Stockjuden; bald ist der Fall umgekehrt, der Vater oder die Eltern Christen, der Sohn oder die Tochter Juden; auch wohl der Vater Christ, die Mutter Jüdin, und umgekehrt, so dass das Band, welches eigentlich Familien bindet und fest knüpft, das Loos: Freuden und Leiden mit einander zu theilen, unter ihnen ganz gelöst und verwüstet ist. Die Kinder können oft ihren Eltern nicht einmal die letzte Ehre bezeigen, und sie zu Grabe begleiten, oder umgekehrt die Eltern nicht die Kinder. Welche Collision! welche Kluft! welcher bedauernswürdiger Zustand! Und doch habe ich hier nur von Seiten der Absurdität und der Lächerlichkeit geredet, und wir wollen daher eine andere und weit wichtigere Seite aufdecken.

Ernsthaft betrachtet werden diese Possen- und Puppenspiele etwas bedeutender, und es verdiente diese Klasse überhaupt in Rücksicht der Gesellschaft und des bürgerlichen Lebens mehr berücksichtigt zu werden, und ein Gegenstand der Sorge der Regierung zu seyn! – Die erste Klasse, die orthodoxen Gelehrten, wird vermöge der Grundsätze der Religion, die den Grundsätzen jeder andern Religion wenigstens gleich gestellt werden können, von unedlen

---
[45] Proverbs 16:22.
[46] The Fast of Esther.

Handlungen abgehalten, wenigstens so viel als es Religion überhaupt vermag; die 2te Klasse, die blossen Nachahmer, wird zwar weniger von der eigentlichen Religion geleitet, doch aber immer noch durch dieselbe zu moralischen Handlungen eingehalten und von unmoralischen abgehalten, doch ist dies sehr wankend und äusserst schwach, sie werden wie das Rohr am Meer vom Winde hin und her gebogen. Der 3ten Klasse, die wirklich gelehrten Aufgeklärten, wie wir sie eben geschildert haben, ist ächte Moralität das, was nur immer irgend eine Religion den Menschen seyn kann –; sie mögen über Religion, Unsterblichkeit ja selbst über Gott nach diesem oder jenem Systeme denken, sie mögen zu dieser oder jener Fahne geschworen haben, so handeln sie überall moralisch gut; und es kann dem Staate und der bürgerlichen Gesellschaft ganz gleich seyn, nach welchen Principien und Gründen man eine gute gesittete Lebensart führt; – wenn man sich nur ruhig verhält, und wenn man seine Art zu denken keinem Andern aufdrängen will.

Diese 4te Klasse aber, die weder ächte Religion noch ächte Aufklärung kennt, diese muss durchaus dem Staate und der bürgerlichen Gesellschaft gefährlich werden, und mich dünkt, die Erfahrung lehrt es. Man forsche nach, und man wird allgemein finden, dass Verbrechen aller Art von Menschen die zu dieser Klasse von Nachahmern, After-Aufgeklärten, Pseudophilosophen, u.s.w. gehören, begangen worden sind und noch begangen werden; ich brauche wol nicht erst zu erinnern, dass ich hier sowol als an mancher andern Stelle nicht etwa die jüdische Religion allein vor Augen gehabt habe, – ja dass selbst meine Klassifikation mehr oder weniger auf jede andere Religion anzuwenden sey. Ich nehme keinen Anstand, zu behaupten, dass diese letzte Klasse und die 2te, die orthodoxen Nachahmer, es waren, und noch sind, die den Nahmen *Jude* gebrandmarkt haben; die wahre ächte, reine jüdische Religion, man kann es nicht genug wiederhohlen, enthält auch wahre ächte Moralität; ihre Gesetze und Gebräuche sind weder dem Staate noch der bürgerlichen Gesellschaft entgegen; überall gebietet sie Gehorsam und Unterwürfigkeit den Landesgesetzen und Bruderliebe ohne Ausnahme; ihr Gottesdienst, ihre Gebete enthalten nichts Anstössiges gegen jede andre Religion, wohl aber gegen die damaligen Heiden – daher ein Theil dieser Gebete für unsere Zeiten unpassend und unschicklich sind, und daher füglich abgeschafft werden sollten, ja von Seiten des Staates sogar müsste darauf gedrungen werden, solche abzuschaffen, und gewiss würden solche längst schon gereinigt worden seyn, wenn der grosse Haufe das Ungereimte, was sie enthalten, nur verstehen möchte, – wenn man es ihm nur begreiflich machen könnte, dass er es nicht einmal weiss, dass er viel ungereimtes, abgeschmacktes Zeug herplappert; doch ich muss hier schliessen. Es empfiehlt Dich dem Schutze des Allmächtigen Dein Freund.

7tes Schreiben

Theuerster Freund

Der wahre Stein des Anstosses, wenn die Rede war von Umformung, von Abschaffung der Missbräuche, von Verbesserungen überhaupt, war meiner

Meynung nach der, dass man auf diese hier aufgestellte Klassifikation nie gehörig Rücksicht genommen hat. Man betrachtete sie alle als sämmtlich zu einer Klasse gehörig, und wählte daher ganz verkehrte Mittel, die dann auch jedes Mal statt zu nützen, vielmehr schadeten.

Ob wir gleich die 4 Klassen nur oberflächlich dargestellt haben, so könnte man doch daraus zur Genüge einsehen, dass die 2te und 4te Klasse es fast nur allein sind, die verändert und verbessert werden sollten, und das dies durchaus weder von der ersten Klasse, der gelehrten Orthodoxen, wenn sie sich auch dazu bereit finden liessen, – geschehen, noch von der 3ten Klasse, den wahren Aufgeklärten, allein geschehen kann; denn die erste Klasse hat eben so wenig auf die 4te Klasse irgend einen Einfluss, wie die 3te Klasse auf die 2te, diese Klassen sind beständige Antagonisten, ja ich behaupte sogar, dass sie sich bisweilen gegen einander intoleranter betragen, als die beyden Hauptklassen, die ich aufgestellt habe, die ächten Orthodoxen und die ächten Aufgeklärten, und selbst intoleranter noch, als wenn sie 2 verschiedene Religionspartheyen wären. Es ist und bleibt daher eine höchst schwierige Aufgabe, diesem Uebel abzuhelfen, und vorzüglich ohne Gewalt anzuwenden.

So viel ist einleuchtend und geht deutlich hervor, ich muss es wiederholen, dass erstens Alles, was geschehen soll und geschehen kann, nur durch die beyden Hauptklassen geschehen kann und darf, und das 2tens diese beyden Klassen vereinigt seyn müssen, wenn man etwas dauerhaftes erwarten soll, und dass die besten und hellsten Köpfe aus diesen Klassen dazu gehören. Und hier werden wir unmittelbar auf den grossen Fehler stossen, den man sowohl hier als in Hamburg bey dem Versuch einer Umbildung und Herstellung eines vernünftigen Gottesdienstes begangen hat. So wie dieser Versuch begonnen ist, kann und wird es nie zu Stande kommen, und noch weniger bestehen; es sind fromme Wünsche und weiter nichts, und dabey wird es bleiben. Die Orthodoxen, und wie gesagt, die Köpfe unter ihnen, müssen als Repräsentanten nicht nur der sämmtlichen Orthodoxen sondern auch der Nachahmer ihrer Klasse auftreten, denn auch diese muss man sehr vorsichtig angreifen, so wie die besten Köpfe der Aufgeklärten nicht nur als Repräsentanten ihrer eigenen Klasse, sondern selbst der Nachahmer ihrer Klasse; diese müssen mit noch weit mehr Vorsicht behandelt werden, weil sie ohnehin schon wenig oder gar kein Interesse für die Sache haben. Dieses ist aber ganz übersehen und vernachlässigt worden.

Wir wissen es sehr wohl, dass, nachdem der bessere Gottesdienst in einigen Privat-Synagogen versucht worden und Beifall gefunden hatte, man auch mit einigen Rabbinern und Assessoren darüber sprach, aber nun war es zu spät, ihre Autorität war schon beleidigt, sie hatten sich schon dagegen erklärt, konnten, wollten und durften ihre geäusserte Meynung nicht mehr zurücknehmen. Ja man hatte sie von der allerempfindlichsten Seite angegriffen, man hatte sie nicht nur zurückgesetzt, und dadurch offenbar beleidigt, nicht nur Eingriffe in die ihnen bis dahin zukommenden Rechte gethan, sondern hier und da wurden zum Theil ihre Einkünfte und gewisse Sporteln geschmälert, oder sie mussten doch wenigstens fürchten, dass dies künftig geschehen würde. Zum Beyspiel bey Trauungen und Einsegnungen, und was bedarf es wohl mehr? ...

Neuntes Schreiben[47]

Liebster Freund!
Wir kehren nun zu den beyden Hauptfragen zurück nemlich
I. Ist dem Uebel allgemein abzuhelfen? ist eine allgemeine Verbesserung zu hoffen und zu erwarten und
II. Wie ist zu helfen? wie ist eine Verbesserung zu bewerkstelligen?

Was die erste Frage betrifft, so glaube ich aus dem, was bisher gesagt, und wie die Sachen dargestellt worden, dass sich diese Frage nicht anders als mit nein beantworten lässt. Eine allgemeine Verbesserung, die für alle 4 Klassen gleich gut und anpassend seyn soll, so dass sie sich alle dabey beruhigen und zufrieden stellen können, übersteigt die Grenze der Möglichkeit; es kann eine solche allgemeine Verbesserung nicht existiren. Beweist ihnen aus dem Talmud und dergleichen Schriften, dass es nicht nur keine Sünde sey, in der Landessprache zu beten und einer Orgelbegleitung sich zu bedienen, sagt ihnen wie es Herr Dr. Auerbach wirklich gethan und bewiesen, dass es Pflicht sey in der Sprache zu beten, die man versteht,[48] so können sie dies nicht lesen, oder wollen es nicht, sie fürchten sich der Sünde dergleichen zu lesen. Sind solche Schriften in Hebräischer Sprache geschrieben, wie viele verstehen auch dann selbst diese Sprache? und man würde sich selbst widersprechen, ihnen auf Hebräisch zu sagen, dass sie kein Hebräisch verstehen; schreibt ihr in deutscher Sprache, so verliert ihr schon das Zutrauen, und habt noch oben drein nichts als ihren Fluch und das ewige Verdammniss, wie es mir wohl nicht besser gehen wird, zu erwarten, und dies ist alles, was ihr bewirken könnt. Sie werden uns gegen die Stellen aus dem Talmud und dergleichen Schriften auch mit andern Stellen ebenfalls aus dieser Quelle überschwemmen, die das Gegentheil beweisen und für sie sprechen. Der Talmud etc. ist in dergleichen Stücken ein wahres Camäleon, man darf nur einigermassen mit der Art und Weise wie darin manövrirt wird, bekannt seyn, um einzusehen, dass man alles, was man will sowohl heraus als hinein demonstriren kann. Ich habe seit länger als 50 Jahr keinen Blick hinein gethan,[49] und dennoch unterfange ich mich, wenn es darauf ankäme, daraus zu beweisen, einmal dass es nicht erlaubt sey irgend eine Abänderung, sey sie noch so unbedeutend, zu machen, dann wieder, dass es erlaubt, und schon öfter geschehen sey, also daraus zu beweisen, dass beyde Partheyen, die sich gegenwärtig in den Haaren liegen, Recht haben; ferner daraus zu beweisen, dass beyde Unrecht haben, und dass ich dies zu behaupten vollkommen Recht habe, und endlich daraus zu be-

---

[47] In the remainder of the seventh letter and in the eighth, Wolff gives a detailed description of the traditional worship service. He stresses the disorder, the *Schreien*, the exclusion of the female sex, the lack of attendance, the use of inappropriate profane melodies, the public auction of honours. No moral sermons are preached in the synagogue, no confirmations held there. Wedding ceremonies are meaningless to the bride and groom, an embarrassment to the guests when Christians are present. The Jews' existing religious institutions and practices contrast sharply with their civil and cultural status. While the orthodox should not be disturbed, a new reformed service must be allowed to exist alongside the old.

[48] See above, n. 10.

[49] If Wolff wrote this sentence in 1819, then he would have been twelve years old fifty years earlier.

haupten, dass ich Unrecht habe. Denn sobald es erlaubt ist, einzelne abgerissene Stellen, Sentenzen bald aus dem Talmud und dergleichen Büchern, bald aus der heiligen Schrift und den Propheten, aus verschiedenen Psalmen u.s.w. die jeder nach seiner Phantasie erklärt und auslegt, zu Belegen aufzuführen; – wie es denn von diesen Herrn sammt und sonders, von denen, die dafür, und die dawider sprechen, geschieht, – so kenne ich nichts, was sich nicht behaupten, und eben so wohl widerlegen liesse. – Ja es giebt eine unendliche Anzahl dergleichen Stellen, die an und für sich wider und für eine Sache sich sehr wohl brauchen lassen. Wir wollen nur einige solche zum Beweise aufstellen. Sagt z.B. einer zu den angeführten orthodoxen Nachahmern, dass der grösste Theil ihres Gleichen Gott wohl schwerlich durch ihre Gebete gefällig seyn könnte, die sie nicht verstehen, und sie werden auch auf der Stelle mit einem angeerbten Spruch zu besiegen glauben und werden zurufen: *rachamana liba ba'e*.[50] Umgeschrieben heisst dies: Gott sieht nicht auf das Formelle, sieht im Herzen selbst, ob die Absicht rein sey. Sie bedenken es aber nicht, dass man sich derselben Sentenz bedienen kann, um zu beweisen, dass man beten und Gott dienen kann, in welcher Sprache man will, – ja dass man aus dieser Sentenz sogar beweisen kann, dass man zu beten ganz und gar nicht nöthig hat; Gott sieht ja nur auf das Innere und verlangt das Herz und ihm ist reine, ächte, innere Dankbarkeit bey weitem wohlgefälliger, als eine Stunden lange Bewegung der Lippen und der Sprachorgane überhaupt, und besonders, wenn das Herz nichts dabei fühlt und der Kopf nichts denkt.

Sagt Einer einem solchen orthodoxen Nachahmer, dass es einem gebildeten Menschen höchst lächerlich vorkommen muss, wenn im Gottesdienst solcher Unfug getrieben wird, dass selbst in erhabenen Gebeten, z.B. dem Kadischgebet, Melodien aus Operetten, Märsche, ja, Melodien von gemeinen Liedern gehört werden, sagt er, dass dies mehr Gott entehren, als ihn ehren heisst; so werden sie auch aus den Psalmen zurechtweisen und auch zurufen: *ivdu et adonai besimchah*, "Dienet Gott mit Freuden."[51] Aber sie werden auch nicht erlauben wollen, diesen Spruch auf die Orgel oder andere musikalische Begleitung anzuwenden. Doch wo sollte ich ein Ende finden wenn ich fortfahren wollte, alle dergleichen Absurditäten in Erwähnung zu bringen? Zudem kommt es hier wohl nicht auf die Menge an, da sie alle zu einem und demselben Resultate führen, dass eine allgemeine Abänderung für alle vier erwähnten Klassen im Gottesdienst durchaus ein Unding ist, wenn nicht zuvor ein Vereinigungspunkt gegeben werden kann, wenn nicht dergleichen Abänderungen unter gewissen Autoritäten unternommen werden, wenn nicht Männer an der Spitze stehen, die der Sache gewachsen sind. Ein einziger gelehrter und mit allen dazu gehörenden Kräften ausgestatteter Mann wird in diesen Stücken mehr wirken als eine Million Millionairs. Nicht auf einzelne Städte, Provinzen und Länder, sondern auf ganz Israel, wo es auch sei, muss gewirkt werden. Denn obgleich hier und dort die solidarische Verbindung, Gott sei Dank, aufgehört hat, so hat sie doch in Rücksicht des Seelenheils nicht ganz aufgehört: hier will der Israelit überall einer für den andern Bürge sein *kol yisrael arevim* [sic] *zeh bazeh*. Alle Israeliten bürgen einer

[50] Sanhedrin 106b.
[51] Psalms 100:2.

für den andern.⁵² Einen von mir ausgestellten Solo-Wechsel wird keiner acceptieren, wenn er nicht Sicherheit hat, aber für meine Seele zu sorgen wird jeder sich berechtigt fühlen, und wenn es nur einigermassen in seiner Macht steht, wird er mich verfolgen, sobald ich nicht ganz so denke und handle, wie er, – nicht Gott, so wie er, anrufe, und ich werde in seinen Augen als ein Ungeheuer erscheinen.

Und hiermit sei die erste Frage von uns verneinend zurückgewiesen. Wir setzen nur noch hinzu, dass man bei weitem besser thut, Mummerei, Gaukelei, blinde Vorliebe, blosse Anhänglichkeit an alte Gebräuche, National-Orthodoxie in Ruhe zu lassen, wenn man sich nicht stark genug fühlt, ein allgemein Besseres, für ganz Israel anpassend aufstellen zu können. Wo das nicht sein kann, da sind alle Eure Abänderungen nichts, als Meteore; man unterlasse lieber das Aufregen, man nehme ihnen nichts, weil sie nichts anderes haben. Man lasse ihnen den eingebildeten Schatz: er ist besser, als die Überzeugung, gar keinen zu besitzen. Lebewohl.

Zehntes Schreiben

Theuerster Freund!

Ich danke herzlich für Deine bisherige Geduld, und um Dich dafür zu belohnen, sei dieses das letzte Schreiben.

Die Beantwortung der zweiten Frage: wie trotz aller eben aufgestellten Schwierigkeiten, eine Verbesserung zu bewerkstelligen und zu erwarten sei? Diese Beantwortung ist durch Negationen, nämlich dadurch, dass wir gesehen haben, was nicht geschehen kann, nicht geschehen darf, wie ich glaube, sehr erläutert worden.

Ob ich gleich dafür halte, dass eine nur einen Theil berücksichtigende Verbesserung nicht hinreiche, sondern zu einer Radikalkur das Einwirken auf das Ganze erforderlich und höchst nothwendig sei, so bin ich doch nicht weniger der Meinung, dass von der Hauptstadt, aus der schon so manches und so vielfältig Gutes aller Art ausgegangen ist und sich verbreitet hat, auch in diesen Stücken das erste Beispiel ausgehen muss, und zwar nicht nur desswegen, weil die Gesammtheit daselbst am stärksten ist, sondern weil vorzüglich Berlin mit Recht überall in dieser Hinsicht längst schon, besonders seit Mendelssohn auftrat, in sehr vortheilhaftem gutem Ruf, wenigstens bei dem gebildeten Theil der Nation steht.

Die erste Bedingung aber, die grösste, ist, nicht nur die Einwilligung der hohen Regierung zu erflehen, sondern selbst eine Hülfleistung derselben ist unentbehrlich, wenn gleich schon das Wesentliche aus der Nation selbst hervorgehen muss. Die Talmudisten selbst erlauben nicht nur unerlaubte Dinge, d.h. solche, die die Religion verbietet, sobald es die Regierung verlangt, sondern sie befehlen unbedingt, zu gehorchen, wenn unsere hohe Regierung sich der Lage der Sachen anzunehmen geruhen und sich geneigt finden lassen wollte, beide Partheien durch eine dazu gewählte Kommission anzuhören.⁵³ Dann würde so

---
⁵²Shevuot 39a.
⁵³Such a commission was actually formed in 1818, but achieved no results. See Geiger, *op. cit.*, p. 223.

manche Schwierigkeit gehoben sein, und die Bedenklichkeit, dass eine neue Sekte daraus entstehen könnte, gänzlich verschwinden, denn eine solche ist eben so wenig zu befürchten, als dies bei den zeither vorgenommenen Abänderungen in der christlichen Religion der Fall war.

Ein Auszug aus einem Schreiben des Rabbiners zu Pressburg, worin er sein Gutachten über jene Fragen niederlegt, gehört hierher. Es ist zugleich das vorzüglichste von allen andern, weil es das vernünftigste ist.

Nachdem er über die von den Hamburger Assessoren vorgelegten Fragen sein Gutachten, es versteht sich – verneinend – abgelegt sagt er zum Schluss:

> Nur in einer Versammlung aller israelitischen Gelehrten des Zeitalters, unter dem Beistand des Hocherhabenen Weltregierers – und wenn die erhabenen regierenden Fürsten eine solche Versammlung erlauben sollten! – nur alsdann könnten einst die Einwendungen jener Unzufriedenen angehört, und wenn von allen Weisen Israels einiger Grund dazu gefunden wird, darüber gestimmt werden, ob wir ermächtigt sind, eine Veränderung in unseren heiligen Gebräuchen vorzunehmen, ohne gegen das Gesetz zu verstossen: ja nur alsdann würde man wissen was zu thun sei.[54]

Ob ich gleich mir bewusst bin, dass ich diesen Gegenstand nicht nur nicht erschöpft habe, sondern dass alles, was ich darüber gesagt, gleichsam nur Skizze ist, so schmeichle ich mir doch, manchen zu nützen den Wink gegeben zu haben. Die obige Klassifikation, glaube ich auch, giebt hinlängliches Licht, dass sich der Grund zu der gegenseitigen Feindschaft der Christen gegen Juden und Juden gegen Christen, die man hier und dort wahrnimmt, in einer der von mir aufgestellten vier Klassen befinden muss. Ich frage aber: in welcher Klasse ist er zu suchen?

In der ersten Klasse die ich als gelehrte Orthodoxe aufgestellt habe, dürfen wir die gegenseitige Anfeindung nicht suchen, noch weniger in der Klasse, die ich als ächte, gelehrte, aufgeklärte Heterodoxe darstellte. Denn eine gegenseitige Anfeindung ist weder im ächten Judenthum, noch im ächten Christenthum enthalten: Ich trage kein Bedenken, zu behaupten, dass aus diesen beiden Klassen, wenn sie anders so ächt waren, wie ich sie mir denke, nie eine gegenseitige Feindschaft entstanden sei; wo dies jemals der Fall war, da fehlte es gewiss an ächter Gelehrsamkeit, Schwärmerei trat an die Stelle der Religiosität, und der Fanatismus hatte dann offenes Feld, seine Rolle zu spielen. Doch will ich auch nicht in Abrede sein, dass es auch hierin Ausnahmen gegeben haben mag oder geben könnte, dass nicht selbst ächt gelehrte Männer von beiden Klassen von Privathass geblendet, von Privatabsichten geleitet werden könnten. Da ich aber diese Fälle als Ausnahme betrachte, so schadet dies meiner Behauptung nicht, dass in der Regel feindselige Gesinnung in diesen beiden Klassen nicht gefunden wird. Der ächte gelehrte, orthodoxe Jude, der ächt gelehrte Orthodoxe christlicher Religion können und müssen Freunde sein, indem sie sich klar und deutlich bewusst sind, dass sie beide nach ein und derselben Scheibe zielen: sie heisst Glückseeligkeit der Menschen.

Bei weitem weniger wird man die gegenseitige Anfeindung in der Klasse der

[54] Moses Sofer, the "Chatam Sofer", in *Eleh Divre Haberit*, Hamburg 1819, p. 98.

ächten gelehrten Aufgeklärten finden. Ja, ich halte es sogar nicht einmal für nöthig, diese meine Behauptung erst mit Gründen zu belegen, und Beweise dafür aufzustellen.

Noch nie hat es sowohl den gelehrten orthodoxen als den ächten aufgeklärten Juden an christlichen Freunden gefehlt, sofern diese nur zu ein und derselben Klasse gehörten. Der ächt orthodoxe Jude, der ächt orthodoxe Christ, ich wiederhole es, feinden sich nicht an, viel weniger noch, auch dies sei wiederholt gesagt, die aufgeklärten Juden und aufgeklärten Christen. Maimonides, Manasseh Ben Israel,[55] Spinoza, und in neueren Zeiten Moses Mendelsohn, Maimon, Ben David, Wesly,[56] Friedländer, Herz,[57] Bloch u.s.w., so verschieden diese Männer auch unter sich selbst, ihren Meinungen nach, gewesen sein mögen, so hat es ihnen an christlichen Freunden nie gefehlt.

Von Seiten der Juden war dies derselbe Fall; ja, dem orthodoxen Juden befiehlt der Talmud sogar, wenn er einen Weisen der auch nicht seiner Religion ist, zum ersten Mal sehe so wohl eine Segensformel zu sprechen, als wenn er einen König zum ersten Mal sieht.

Da aber in diesen beiden Klassen die gegenseitige Anfeindung nicht zu erwarten ist, und auch nicht gefunden wird, so wagen wir zu schliessen, dass das wo dergleichen Anfeindung noch angetroffen wird, sie durchaus in den beiden Klassen der Nachahmer, und zwar in der Klasse der Nachahmer der Orthodoxen sowohl, als in der der Nachahmer der Aufgeklärten, under Juden und Christen zugleich gefunden wird. Denn was lässt sich wohl von denjenigen anders erwarten, die weder ihre eigne und noch weit weniger das Wesentliche einer andern Religion kennen, und daher nur die gegenseitigen Flecken, nicht aber das Gute sehen?

Ein nicht unbedeutender Wink, glaube ich, wird hierin liegen für den achtungswerthen Verein, der sich neuerdings zur Bekehrung von Juden gebildet hat, wenn derselbe auf diese meine Klassifikation Rücksicht nehmen will.

Eben so, was kann man von solchen Menschen erwarten die Religion verlassen, und Aufklärung, wie Moralität bloss nachahmen? Ja, wahrlich, alles was man will, nur nichts Gutes! Was ich am Schluss einer kleinen Schrift, die ich 1791 herausgab, bei einer solchen Gelegenheit sagte, kann ich hier wiederholen: Kerker, Eisen und Henker mögen mich vor solchen Menschen bewahren.

Da nun aber zu diesen beiden Klassen der grosse Haufen und der Pöbel gehört, so kann es nicht befremden, wenn Kabale, Bosheit, abscheuliche Grausamkeit, Neid, Missgunst, Habsucht, Intoleranz und Verfolgung von Zeit zu Zeit ihr Haupt noch erheben, bis der Tag – kommen wird, wo alle Menschen nicht eben nothwendig eine und dieselbe Religion haben werden, sondern wo alle Menschen in der Religion, zu der sie sich bekennen, entweder ächte Orthodoxe, oder ächte Aufgeklärte, keinesweges aber blosse Nachahmer sein werden!

Wenn ich Kinder hätte so würde ich ihnen wünschen, dass es ihre Urenkel erleben mögten!! –

---

[55]Seventeenth-century Amsterdam rabbi who maintained an active correspondence with Christian scholars.
[56]Naphtali Herz Wessely (1725–1805), enlightener and proponent of Jewish educational reform.
[57]Marcus Herz (1747–1803), Berlin physician and disciple of Kant.

From the Wilhelminian Era to Nazi Rule

Why was there a Jewish Question in Imperial Germany?

BY PETER PULZER

Despite Leopold von Ranke's famous warning, we are liable to assess the importance of historical questions with hindsight. Indeed, we cannot help doing so: part of our knowledge of an epoch is our knowledge of what came next. If an observer at the turn of the century had been asked where in Europe antisemitism was at its strongest, he would probably have answered Russia, the homeland of pogroms and the Black Hundreds, possibly France, where the Dreyfus Case was at its climax, conceivably Austria where Karl Lueger had just been elected mayor of the capital city. It is unlikely that he would have answered Germany. On the other hand, there is little doubt that more has been written about the pre-1914 antisemitism of Germany than of all other countries combined. The reasons for this are to be found in post-1933 experience.

The same applies to the slightly different problem of why there was a Jewish Question in Imperial Germany.* Here the trend in the volume of writing has been reversed. The first publications bearing the title "Die jüdische Frage" appeared in 1838; in 1842 no fewer than five articles or pamphlets (including Bruno Bauer's) appeared, bearing the word "Judenfrage" in their title. For the next century or so a vast literature was published, claiming to deal with this topic.[1] Since the Second World War the notion that the mere existence of Jews might be the cause of a problem has been considered tasteless or even embarrassing; but historical treatment of the phenomenon, again with an emphasis on Germany, has flourished.

Consideration of the Jewish Question is not, of course, entirely separate from that of antisemitism. Both phenomena illustrate not merely aspects of Jewish life and Jewish-Gentile group relations; they also illuminate aspects of state, society and nationality in general, in this case in Imperial Germany. But the Jewish Question is sufficiently distinct to warrant separate treatment and to divide consideration of it into a number of components:

(1) Are Jews a race, a nation or a religious community?
(2) What, if any, are the terms on which Jews should have rights of citizenship?

---

*This is a revised and expanded version of a lecture given at the University of Bonn on the occasion of the Oxford–Bonn Colloquium in April 1979. The author gratefully acknowledges grants from the Leverhulme Foundation and the Historische Kommission zu Berlin to finance research on this topic.
[1]Although this particular expression was used sporadically in English and French from the middle of the eighteenth century onwards, the instances cited are those of their first usage in German. On this whole question see Jacob Toury, ' "The Jewish Question". A Semantic Approach', in *LBI Year Book* XI (1966), esp. pp. 85–93; also, Ulrich Eichstätt, *Bibliographie zur Geschichte der Judenfrage*, Hamburg 1938, Nos. 1033, 1035, 1259, 1825, 1843, 1846.

(3) What, if anything, should be done about the peculiar occupational distribution of Jews?

(4) Does the international scattering of Jews make them peculiar as a race, nation or religious community?

(5) Would it help anyone, including Jews, if they were encouraged to settle somewhere else?

In the light of these criteria, one can see why there was a "Jewish Question" in some countries, but not in others. Its existence is not surprising in states with large and distinctive Jewish populations, such as pre-1914 Russia and Austria–Hungary, or inter-war Poland and Romania. In these regions the first three of our questions remained largely unresolved, with the result than an increasing number of Jews and Gentiles were attracted to an affirmative answer to question 5. Equally, one can see why, despite the Dreyfus Case and the agitation against Jewish immigration in Britain[2] at the beginning of the twentieth century, there was no Jewish Question in Western Europe. It was not a question of numbers – the Jews of Germany amounted, after all, to 1 per cent of the population – rather that the problems raised by the relationship between nationality and citizenship and the citizen's rights *vis-à-vis* the state had (at any rate for the time being) been solved in the developed countries of Western Europe. Barriers of birth and religion to the enjoyment of political rights and social facilities had been removed not only *de jure* but to a large extent *de facto*. These problems had not been settled in Germany and the barriers not removed. That is why the Jewish Question had not disappeared.

The Jewish Question in Germany was a function of the German concepts of the nation and of political rule. The particular roles that Jews played in German society and the development of the German economy certainly caused tensions. They are central to any consideration of antisemitism and the existence of antisemitism made the Jewish Question more important than it would otherwise have been. But these socio-economic factors were at most secondary, aggravating elements in the Jewish Question as we have defined it. They were not the causes of its existence.

The concept of nationality in Germany is central to our whole subject, for the nineteenth century was characterised by the struggle to create and define a German national consciousness. The modern origins of this consciousness are to be found in the wars of liberation against Napoleon, and the nature of this political mass experience was decisive to the German people's sense of common identity.[3] It would be wrong to deduce from this that German nationalism was inherently hostile to Jews: the relationship was more complex. One can, of course, make a catalogue of early German nationalists and their antisemitic utterances; nothing is easier and it has been frequently done. But one can equally

---

[2]On the latter question, see Lloyd P. Gartner, *The Jewish Immigrant in England 1807–1914*, London 1960; Bernard Gainer, *The Alien Invasion*, London 1972.

[3]For recent scholarly treatment of this topic, see Gerhard Schulz, 'Der späte Nationalismus im deutschen politischen Denken des neunzehnten Jahrhunderts', in *Das Judentum in der deutschen Umwelt 1800–1850. Studien zur Frühgeschichte der Emanzipation*, herausgegeben von Hans Liebeschütz und Arnold Paucker, Tübingen 1977 (Schriftenreihe wissenschaftlicher Abhandlungen des Leo Baeck Instituts 35).

point to the part Jewish writers played in "Das Junge Deutschland" and to the antisemitism of such diverse opponents of the nationalist movement as Ludwig von der Marwitz and Wolfgang Menzel. The role of nationalist ideology in defining the position of the Jew is different. Nationalism was a defensive creed – in Karl Dietrich Bracher's phrase an *Abwehrideologie*.[4] It preached unity directed at a common enemy, an enemy who was Western and identified with beliefs in the rights of man, individualism and political rationalism. It coincided with the romantic movement, with its emphasis on the cultural component of nationality and the sanctity of unique traditions. Because it was defensive and romantic, German nationalism was exclusive; the need to ensure the internal cohesion of the tribe put a high premium on internal loyalty; it also put a high premium on rigorously defining the outsider. The debate in the *Burschenschaften*, which began as early as 1817, as to whether a Jewish student could belong to them, illustrates the strength of this obsession.[5]

What the ideology of nationalism contributed to the German "Jewish Question", therefore, was not some congenital antisemitism, but the search for all-embracing definitions, for all-or-nothing criteria of what, or who, is German.

Doctrines concerning the state, though different in content, were similar in their impact. Early German nationalism had been the ideology of a people that lacked a state; contemporaneous theories of the state did not define citizens or territory in ethnic terms. Only extreme nationalists, like Friedrich Ludwig Jahn, insisted that *Volk* and *Staat* should be co-terminous. For the moment, therefore, it will suffice for our purpose if we concentrate on those doctrines current in the first half of the nineteenth century that bore directly on administrative practice, in other words, on theories of citizenship.

Just as political nationalism in Germany had its origins in French doctrines of national self-determination, so the modernisation of the state followed French enlightenment models. Both, however, developed hostility to the French and, indeed, Western European, emphasis on the rights and value of the individual. What characterised the orthodoxy of the Prussian and later of the German bureaucracy was a dogmatic enlightenment, which saw superstition, ignorance, prejudice and all local peculiarities as obstacles to good citizenship. The ideal was a direct relationship between the individual and the state, unimpeded by the pluralism of autonomous groups or the retention of traditionalist practices.

The implications of these attitudes came out clearly in the debate on Jewish emancipation which lasted from the end of the eighteenth century until the 1860s. Both Christian Wilhelm Dohm and Wilhelm von Humboldt saw, as the ultimate aim of any policy of emancipation, the abandonment by Jews of their religion. A change in the situation of the Jews was for them inseparable from the reform of society in general: "[The government] will have realised its great intention," wrote Dohm, "when the nobleman, the peasant, the scholar, the

---

[4]Karl Dietrich Bracher, *Die Auflösung der Weimarer Republik. Eine Studie zum Problem des Machtverfalls in der Demokratie*, 4th edn., Villingen–Schwarzwald 1964, p. 4.

[5]Oskar Scheuer, *Burschenschaft und Judenfrage. Der Rassenantisemitismus in der deutschen Studentenschaft*, Berlin 1927; also, Monika Richarz, *Der Eintritt der Juden in die akademischen Berufe. Jüdische Studenten und Akademiker in Deutschland 1678–1848*, Tübingen 1974 (Schriftenreihe wissenschaftlicher Abhandlungen des Leo Baeck Instituts 28), pp. 150–157.

artisan, the Christian and the Jew is more than all of this, a citizen."⁶ For Humboldt, Minister for Education and Religious Affairs at the time of the Prussian government's emancipation proposals in 1809, equal citizenship would remove the stigma of opportunism from conversions. The Jews' embracing of Christianity would then become "desirable, pleasing and beneficial".⁷ For State Councillor Koehler, who shared Humboldt's sentiments, "the final purpose of our legislation must surely remain to banish totally all differences in civil rights between Christians and Jews", so as "to assimilate the Jews totally to us".⁸

The same sentiments characterised the majority of the reports that the heads of provincial governments submitted to the Prussian Ministry of the Interior in 1842. The *Regierungspräsident* of Breslau commented that military service for Jews "must inevitably contribute materially to [their] most desirable general fusion with the rest of the nation".⁹ The Silesian *Regierungspräsidenten* jointly acknowledged that "since 1812 it has been the task of the state to neutralise the separatist peculiarities of the Jewish character".¹⁰ Their colleague in Posnań echoed this interpretation:

> "It is most desirable that the Christian population should progressively lose its concept of the Jews as a foreign nation, imposed on the state and only to be tolerated as a necessary evil, and that we should rather accustom ourselves to considering the Jews as a section of the population distinguished only by their religion, but in all other respects as fellow-citizens and fellow-subjects similar to the Christians."¹¹

The culmination of this philosophy found expression in the North German Federation's law of 3rd July 1869 on the freedom and equality of religion.

In its generosity, its optimism, its faith in the highest standards of human behaviour this philosophy seems at first sight to be the opposite of the integral, exclusive nationalism of the Romantics. But the two attitudes shared certain characteristics, as the more wide-awake Jewish advocates of emancipation noticed. Gabriel Riesser was aware that there were some who

> "wished to lay the foundations of German nationality, instead of on the fundamentals of common liberty, common rights and common welfare, on large-scale hatred of the French, and small-scale hatred of the Jews."¹²

And Abraham Geiger dissociated himself from those who, in sympathy with the wishes of the enlightened dogmatists, "would like to give up everything in order to gain only one thing".¹³ These doubts illustrate that the Law of 3rd July 1869

---

⁶Christian Wilhelm Dohm, *Über die bürgerliche Verbesserung der Juden*, Berlin 1781–1783, vol. I, p. 26.
⁷Gutachten der Sektion des Cultus zum Schroetter'schen Entwurf, 17.7.1809, in Ismar Freund, *Die Emanzipation der Juden in Preussen unter besonderer Berücksichtigung des Gesetzes vom II. März 1812. Ein Beitrag zur Rechtsgeschichte der Juden in Preussen*, Berlin 1912, vol. II, p. 276.
⁸Gutachten des Staatsrats Koehler zum Schroetter'schen Entwurf, 13.5.1809, in Freund, *op. cit.*, p. 253.
⁹Berichte über das Judenwesen. Z St A Merseburg, Rep. 77, XXX, ad 117, vol. II, pp. 10–11 (27.7.1842).
¹⁰*Ibid.*, vol. II, p. 232 (8.10.1842).
¹¹*Ibid.*, vol. II, p. 20 (1.4.1842).
¹²Gabriel Riesser, 'Betrachtungen über die Verhandlungen der zweiten Kammer des Grossherzogtums Baden über die Emanzipation der Juden', *Gesammelte Schriften*, Frankfurt a. Main 1867–1868, vol. II, p. 361.
¹³Abraham Geiger, 'Das Judentum unserer Zeit und die Bestrebungen in ihm' (1835), *Nachgelassene Schriften*, Breslau 1875–1878, vol. I, p. 454.

far from settling the Jewish Question, in some respects helped to exacerbate it. There are a number of reasons for supposing this to be so.

First, with the creation of the Empire, *Volk*, as defined in the earlier decades of the century, merged with *Staat*, as defined in these decades. Ethnic and civic criteria now coincided. Nationality could no longer be defined without citizenship, nor citizenship without nationality. In the non-national state, the citizen had been defined by his loyalty: there was therefore a strong incentive to minimise the number of outsiders and to integrate Jews into the state. That had indeed been the aim of the enlightened dogmatists in the bureaucracy. In the national state there was a temptation to define loyalty by nationality: this created an incentive to maintain a distinction with outsiders and therefore to exclude Jews, or at least treat them with suspicion. The effect of this was to strengthen the barriers to social pluralism and cultural heterogeneity and to weaken the element of enlightenment in the principles on which the state was run.

Second, the Law of 3rd July 1869 constituted some kind of bargain between the state and the existing nation on the one hand, and the Jews on the other. But since the terms of the bargain were never clarified, accusations never ceased that both sides were failing to honour it. As far as governments were concerned, the aims of "fusion", "assimilation" and "neutralisation" remained unchanged and unqualified. But what would constitute assimilation? The abandonment of peculiar forms of speech and dress? Renunciation of special dietary laws, festivals and days of worship? An occupational distribution indistinguishable from the rest of the population? The abandonment of the Jewish religion altogether? All of these criteria found their advocates. To be fair, there were those on the Jewish side who did not disagree, sometimes in terms that now strike us as ridiculous and even pathetic. On the other hand, beside the undoubted Jewish success in some of the occupations associated with the triumph of Liberalism, there was the equally undoubted failure to pursue other careers, especially in education and public service. As a consequence, there ensued a dialogue of the deaf: as long as Jews were not prepared to abandon all forms of separate culture, said some, they could not demand complete acceptance. As long as they were not offered complete acceptance, said others, they could scarcely be expected to renounce their traditions.

Third, the question of entry to the public service raised, in turn, that of interpreting the 1869 law which, in due course, became an Imperial Law. The law presupposed a secular, liberal political order and the Constitution of the *Reich* was an entirely secular document. It contained no mention of God or religion. It also declared, in Article 2, that *Reich* legislation had precedence over that of the states. Against that, most of the states also had constitutions dating from the 1850s and even where these underwent amendment after 1871 their assimilation to the *Reich* constitution tended to be incomplete. In matters relevant to the rights of Jewish citizens they were apt to be ambiguous. Two examples: while Article 12 of the Prussian constitution guaranteed freedom of religion and outlawed discrimination, Article 14 emphasised the Christian character of state schools. Similarly the "oath of a Christian" required in courts of law made the courts to some extent Christian institutions. The Christian character of the states was further emphasised by the episcopal roles of Protestant crowned heads. Since the most sensitive areas in Jewish public employment, education and the judiciary, remained the province of the states and since others, such as the military, remained largely under royal prerogative, the contradiction between the secular Empire and the Christian member-states was an important contributor to the perpetuation of the Jewish Question after 1871.

The difficulties created by the 1869 law need to be seen in a wider context. Our hypothesis has been that while antisemitism could not be understood without the socio-economic factors, the Jewish Question was largely a constitutional one. But, of course, the two do not inhabit separate vacuums. We need to ask why the German Empire was a less secularised state than contemporary France or Belgium were *de jure*, or Britain *de facto*. The answer is to be found in the manner of German unification, which in turn is to be explained by the balance of forces during the 1860s within and between the German states. The creation of a German nation-state was an aspiration of the middle class, but the Empire was a creation of the Prussian army. The wars of the 1860s brought victories not only by Prussia against Austria and France but by the dynasty over parliament, by the army over the middle class, by autocracy over self-government. This is so well known that one hesitates to mention it at all; nevertheless its relevance is obvious. One reason why there was a Jewish Question after 1871 is that the process of unification scarcely affected the constitutions of the states. The other is that the social structure of the Empire affected the expectations of the Jewish community and their response to it.

As Reinhard Rürup has emphasised, the slow progress of emancipation in Germany, accompanied by a public debate lasting almost ninety years, made the "Jewish Question" an apparently permanent feature of political life.[14] Contemporary observers were fully aware of this. Ludwig Philippson, replying in the middle of the "liberal decade" to the Catholic publicist Freiherr von Loë remarked:

> "If the author rests his case on the writings by Christian authors in favour of emancipation, we are entitled to catalogue ten against emancipation for every one of the former. Indeed, precisely the fact that so much has been written and said demonstrates that it took the Germans an extraordinary effort to acknowledge equality of rights, which even today has been completely achieved in only a few states. In North America, France, Holland, Belgium, England, Denmark and Italy there have been few written exchanges on the subject, but it was carried out in the briefest time."[15]

But progress was further retarded by the kind of Germany that emerged from the wars of unification. This explains what happened to the twin Jewish aspirations of emancipation and assimilation. For most Jews, emancipation was negatively defined: it consisted of the removal of legal barriers to equal citizenship.

---

[14]Reinhard Rürup, 'Kontinuität und Diskontinuität der "Judenfrage" im 19. Jahrhundert. Zur Entstehung des modernen Antisemitismus', in *Sozialgeschichte Heute. Festschrift für Hans Rosenberg zum 70. Geburtstag*, hrsg. von Hans-Ulrich Wehler, Göttingen 1974, p. 398; also, 'Emancipation and Bourgeois Society', in *LBI Year Book XIV* (1969), pp. 86–88.

[15]Ludwig Philippson, 'Judentum und Deutschtum', *Gesammelte Abhandlungen*, Leipzig 1911, vol. I, p. 162.

So, too, assimilation was predominantly negative – the abandonment of peculiarities as a prerequisite for social and intellectual, as opposed to merely commercial or professional, intercourse with Christian citizens. But the satisfaction of these aspirations also pre-supposed a change in the structure of Gentile society. What Jews wanted, though they did not always make this clear, was assimilation not to the German nation but to the German middle class. A necessary condition for success, therefore, was the domination of German society by the middle class. In so far as this did not happen at any time before 1914 – in contrast with the states of Western Europe – the desire to assimilate was bound to meet frustration.

In this respect the revival of antisemitism within a decade of the emancipation law becomes relevant. It has been argued that this in turn breathed new life into the Jewish Question and prevented it from expiring, as mid-century Liberals might reasonably have expected it to.[16] But it could equally be argued that the opposite was true – that it was the survival of the Jewish Question which stimulated the resurgence of antisemitism. In so far as antisemitism in Imperial Germany had economic causes and in so far as the Jew, in his capacity as the successful capitalist became the hate-object of the discontented, this demonstrated the continuation of pre-emancipation roles. Because the change-over from a feudal-absolutist to a bourgeois-capitalist order had been incomplete, Jews continued to perform economic tasks that were both distinctive and widely disliked. Because in the society of Imperial Germany Jews continued to form an "estate",[17] they could evoke the jealousy of other estates. Because the civil equality, proclaimed by the 1869 laws, did not correspond with the constitutional theory and political reality of the majority of the individual states, it was easy to agitate, not merely for the revocation of emancipation, but against its practical implementation. That antisemitism in Imperial Germany was as much the consequence as the cause of a continuing Jewish Question is shown by the experience of Germany's more bourgeois Western neighbours. There, too, there were epidemics of antisemitism, but they did not lead to a revival of the Jewish Question. It was because Germans failed to solve the Jewish Question in the period of emancipation that antisemitism there could become politically dangerous.

How did Jews react to the obstacles to assimilation in the German Empire? For the initial period, Jews sought refuge in the formula of the German citizen of the Jewish faith ("deutsche Staatsbürger jüdischen Glaubens"), the public German and private Jew. Nowhere was this formulation propagated more fervently than in the principal organ of liberal Judaism, the *Allgemeine Zeitung des Judentums*. In 1878, at the height of the first wave of antisemitism, it claimed: "In

---

[16]E.g., Rürup, 'Kontinuität und Diskontinuität', *loc. cit.*, p. 403. The terms of the debate were further confused by the insistence of many antisemites that what they were discussing was the "Jewish Question".

[17]As argued by Lawrence Schofer, 'Emancipation and Population Change. German Jewry in the Nineteenth Century', paper presented at the Symposium 'Revolution and Evolution in German-Jewish History. 1848 in Historical Perspective' of the Leo Baeck Institute London, Oxford, July 1979. The Conference volume of the Symposium, edited by Werner E. Mosse, Arnold Paucker and Reinhard Rürup, will be published in 1981 as an English-language volume in the Schriftenreihe wissenschaftlicher Abhandlungen des Leo Baeck Instituts.

vain have Jews demonstrated, theoretically and practically, that apart from their worship and their charitable institutions, they have no special and common concerns."[18] Thirty years later it could still speak in the same vein: "Jewish citizens may believe or not believe what they wish in their synagogues, in political life they are German citizens and not Jews."[19] Nor was this version of the place of the Jew in modern society restricted to Jews. Hermann Oncken in many ways spoke for the academic generation of his day in a message to Jewish youth in 1911:

> "The process of growing together into one organism has taken longer than idealists in both camps had expected. Amalgamation is more difficult and ... it is perhaps to be considered complete only after a number of generations. It remains the ideal from the point of view of German culture and the German nation, and therefore also of those Jews who have roots in both."[20]

By the eve of the First World War, such sentiments had an old-fashioned ring to them. But in the 1870s and 1880s most Jews and most liberal supporters of civic equality would insist that in fighting discrimination or prejudice they were concerned not with a Jewish question but a constitutional question. This explains in particular the reluctance of Jews to organise to defend their interests in the early decades of the Empire and their slow response to the revival of antisemitism.[21] The antisemitic campaign of the late 1870s raised, among other questions, the one that Jews were most sensitive to – were they really Germans, could they ever really become Germans?* The overwhelming pressure on Jews was to abjure all distinctiveness: on this point antisemites and Liberals agreed. Treitschke's demand, "Let them become Germans, let them feel themselves simply and properly as Germans,"[22] was echoed by the Liberal Alfred Dove, "Remain what you are, but not as you are! ... Be Germans with us."[23]

The response to this from Jewish "assimilationist" spokesmen was entirely defensive. It denied not the premises – that Jews ought indeed to be complete Germans – but the conclusion – that they had failed to fulfil their part of the emancipation bargain. Such organisations as existed within the Jewish community, e.g., the *Deutsch-Israelitischer Gemeindebund* issued advice to Jews: to be modest in their public bearing, diligent in their work and restrained in public controversy. Yet to argue like this was to concede that the terms of equality were to be defined by the emancipator alone. It evaded the hypothesis that equal rights also meant equal rights to agitate, to litigate and to offend against good taste. It acknowledged, in the words of the first chairman of the *Centralverein*, Maximilian Horwitz, that "step-children must be doubly well-behaved".[24]

---

[18]*Allgemeine Zeitung des Judentums*, 11th July 1878, p. 371.
[19]*Ibid.*, 13th December 1907, p. 589.
[20]An den Verband jüdischer Jugend, cit. *Berliner Börsen-Courier*, 10th April 1911.
[21]On this topic see in particular Michael A. Meyer, 'The Great Debate on Antisemitism. Jewish Reaction to New Hostility in Germany 1879–1881', in *LBI Year Book XI* (1966) and Ismar Schorsch, *Jewish Reactions to German Anti-Semitism 1870–1914*, New York 1972, ch. 2.
*See also the essay by Walter Zwi Bacharach, 'Jews in Confrontation with Racist Antisemitism, 1879–1933', in this volume of the Year Book – (Ed.).
[22]Heinrich von Treitschke, 'Unsere Ansichten', *Preussische Jahrbücher*, 15th November 1879, p. 573.
[23]Alfred Dove, 'Humboldt als Judengenoss', *Im Neuen Reich*, vol. I, 1 (1871), p. 390.
[24]"An unsere Glaubensgenossen', *Mitteilungen des deutsch-israelitischen Gemeindebundes*, October 1880, cit.

The same unwillingness to attract attention informed the reaction of Jewish leaders and journals to the revival of antisemitism. The general tendency was to play it down, to let it blow over. The reason for this was not merely the hope, perhaps reasonable in the 1870s, that Stoecker and Treitschke were the terminal symptom of a dying prejudice and not the first indication of a new wave. It was also the conscious decision not to appear as an organised group with special interests to defend. To have done so would have cast doubt on the efficacy of emancipation and the reality of assimilation.

Such attitudes were based on self-deception. To accept the all-inclusive definitions of nationality common to liberal and illiberal advocates of national unification, to accept the all-inclusive definitions of citizenship common to monarchist conservatives and enlightened bureaucrats, was to ignore that belonging to a religious denomination had its social implications, and that belonging to a social group with a long history and distinctive culture were bound to influence the personal and spiritual characteristics of its members.

By the 1890s this particular self-deception was beginning to become more difficult to maintain, though it was replaced by others, just as unhelpful. By the 1890s it was obvious that the advance of civilisation would not, by itself, consign antisemitism to oblivion, nor that the mere passage of legislation would end discrimination. Not only was publicly proclaimed antisemitism flourishing, but state authorities failed to prosecute even the most extreme agitators. With the exception of the SPD, political parties were reluctant to adopt Jews as parliamentary candidates. Perhaps most seriously, it was more difficult in 1893 than in 1873 for a Jew to gain public appointment on his merits. All this forced a revision of the principle that Jews should not organise. This change of policy, which resulted in the formation of the *Centralverein deutscher Staatsbürger jüdischen Glaubens*,[25] was helped by a general evolution in political activism and the multiplication of interest organisations. The *Centralverein* was created in 1893, the same year as the *Agrarian League* and the *Pan-German League*. One of its founders, Eugen Fuchs, commented that in an age of interest groups Jews would have to form their own lobby.[26]

But there were also reasons specific to the situation of Jews for a change of policy. The first was the renewal of antisemitism. Although there had been a Gentile counter-attack to this, in the form of the *Verein zur Abwehr des Antisemitismus*, Jews increasingly deviated from the view, current since the days of Moses Mendelssohn, that the Jewish case should be pleaded by disinterested Gentiles. The second was the continuation of discrimination. Here, too, Jewish leaders felt that they had to take on governments and the courts themselves and

---

Jehuda Reinharz, *Fatherland or Promised Land. The Dilemma of the German Jew, 1893–1914*, Ann Arbor 1975, p. 27; Arnold Paucker, 'Zur Problematik einer jüdischen Abwehrstrategie in der deutschen Gesellschaft', in *Juden im Wilhelminischen Deutschland 1890–1914*, Ein Sammelband hrsg. von Werner E. Mosse unter Mitwirkung von Arnold Paucker, Tübingen 1976 (Schriftenreihe wissenschaftlicher Abhandlungen des Leo Baeck Instituts 33), p. 529, esp. n. 139.

[25]For the origins and evolution of the *Centralverein*, see Schorsch, *op. cit.*, ch. 4 and 5 and Paucker, *loc. cit.*

[26]*Im deutschen Reich*, March 1896, p. 170, cit. Marjorie Lamberti, *Jewish Activism in Imperial Germany. The Struggle for Civil Equality*, New Haven 1978, p. 15.

to shed any embarrassment at doing so. Rather more controversially, they pressed for Jews to be nominated as parliamentary candidates by non-Socialist parties in districts with good prospects, with the Jews so elected to act in a representative capacity:* the Jewish community, it was argued, needed Jews to speak out against antisemitism and discrimination.[27]

In the course of time the *Centralverein* went further; slowly and perhaps unconsciously it redefined, through its activities, the terms of assimilation. It took up a campaign against apostasy, to the extent of branding converts as deserters. It encouraged the study of Jewish religion and history, especially among Jewish children. In other words by 1914 it was emphasising the value of precisely those attributes that had in 1870 been regarded as obstacles to German Jews becoming Jewish Germans. Where, then, did the self-deception lie? It was revealed by the name that the *Centralverein* chose for itself. Though its activities, indeed its very existence, implied a break with the unqualified assimilationism of the 1870s, its vocabulary did not adapt to this break. Its leaders hovered uneasily between the earlier orthodoxy of "we are Germans like everyone else" and a frank recognition that there could and should not be only one kind of German. It would be unfair to blame them too strongly for this. The failure of their self-definition reflected the failure of the German nation at large to arrive at a satisfactory relationship between nationality and citizenship. This dual failure was illustrated by the constant battle that Jewish representative organisations fought with the governments over the legal status of Jews. This battle was fought along many sectors: the appointment of Jews as judges and the Prussian educational reform of 1905–1906 will serve as well as any.

Of all the public positions that Jews aspired to, of all the denials of equal opportunity that they most resented, those in the judiciary loomed largest. In the twenty years before 1914 the states' policies in judicial appointments and promotion were constantly debated. Policies varied from state to state, although all acknowledged that they were bound by the law of 1869. Baden and Hamburg were the most liberal in their policies, Saxony the least so. Prussia, Bavaria, Württemberg and the Grand Duchy of Hesse occupied intermediate positions.[28] Problems arose under a number of headings: denominational parity, individual suitability and public opinion.

The position of critics of the state governments was straightforward. It was obvious that Jewish candidates were not being treated on their merits. In Prussia in 1904 27 per cent of all lawyers were Jewish, but only 10 per cent of all articled clerks (*Referendare*), 5 per cent of court clerks (*Gerichtsassessoren*), 4 per cent of magistrates and 0·3 per cent of the higher ranks of the judiciary. Protestants represented between 67 and 79 per cent of all judicial appointments, rising according to grade, compared with 47 per cent of all lawyers. Catholics provided

---

*Further to the recent literature already quoted see also the following essay by Marjorie Lamberti, 'Liberals, Socialists, and the Defence against Antisemitism in the Wilhelminian Period', pp. 147–162, in this volume of the Year Book – (Ed.).

[27] E.g., *Allgemeine Zeitung des Judentums*, 27th October 1893, p. 505.

[28] Ernest Hamburger, *Juden im öffentlichen Leben Deutschlands. Regierungsmitglieder, Beamte und Parlamentarier in der monarchischen Zeit 1848–1918*, Tübingen 1968 (Schriftenreihe wissenschaftlicher Abhandlungen des Leo Baeck Instituts 19), pp. 40–53.

a consistent 21–26 per cent in all categories.²⁹ However, it was also argued that far from being discriminated against, Jews who made up only 1 per cent of the population were over-represented; if anyone, it was Catholics, who made up one-third, who were badly done by. This was not the only instance where the Jewish Question overlapped with the Catholic Question. The circumstances also explain why on this matter, in contrast with some others, Jews and Catholics were on opposite sides. The Centre Party demanded denominational parity, i.e., a quota, determined by the Catholic share of the population, not by the availability of Catholic law graduates. The Progressive parties supported the Jewish claim to consideration by individualist, secular criteria.

Beneath this lay another consideration which surfaced whenever the topic was debated. The appointment of judges and court officials was so delicate a matter, involving as it did public confidence, that not only should the confessions be represented proportionately, but local sensitivities be respected. As the Hessian Justice Minister Dittmar put it:

> "If somebody were not appointed because he was Jewish then . . . a breach of the constitution would have been committed. But if somebody were not appointed, because he appeared to be for some reason unsuited to the post, there could be no objections."³⁰

Both the Hessian and Bavarian ministers of justice made it clear that Jews were unsuitable as judges in rural areas or in courts presided over by single magistrates.³¹ And whatever else may have been the euphemisms of public phraseology, there is no doubt that officials saw themselves entitled to operate a quota against Jewish applicants: the provincial Chief Justice of Hesse-Nassau reported to the Prussian minister of justice that the number of Jewish applicants for judicial posts was "excessive" ("Der Andrang zur Justiz ist . . . seitens der jüdischen Bevölkerung ein übergrosser.").³² Jewish lobbyists and their allies and government officials performing a tight-rope act were not alone in feeling the frustrations of a constitution that proclaimed norms widely evaded and objectionable to many. One antisemitic paper said of Prussian ministers:

> "These gentlemen are subject to the constitution . . . The constitution requires them to turn their hearts into a murderer's den . . . It is a sign of our own weakness that ministers may no longer say openly what they feel in their hearts . . . The constitution is the enemy, because it contains the emancipation of the Hebrews."³³

For some years after the 1901 debate in the Prussian parliament, officials were required to comment whether local conditions made the nomination of a Jewish judge advisable and the files are filled with minutes such as "no objections in the light of local conditions", "court clerks of the Jewish faith may be employed without undermining the interests of the service".³⁴ This exercise may

²⁹Konfessionsverhältnisse der höheren Beamten, G St A Dahlem. Rep. 84a, 11944, 171–173.
³⁰Cit. *Kreuzzeitung*, 17th October 1899.
³¹Minister of Justice Jakob Finger. 2. Kammer der Landstände, Grossherzogtum Hessen, 7th April 1894; Minister of Justice Freiherr von Leonrodt, Bayr. Abgeordnetenhaus, 29th September 1901.
³²Der Oberlandesgerichtspräsident Dr. Hagens an den Herrn Justizminister in Berlin, 9. September 1901. G St A Dahlem, Rep. 84a, 11944, 141.
³³*Deutsche Hochwacht*, 22nd February 1905.
³⁴Ernennung von Land- und Amtsrichtern und Staatsanwälten, Z St A Merseburg, 2.2.1., 17031, *passim*.

have been an empty formality, since Jewish appointees were posted to Stallupönen and Hechingen as well as Berlin and Breslau. But nothing points more convincingly to the existence of a Jewish Question than the mere fact that these debates took place so frequently and that ministers and their officials were required to have policies on a matter that the 1869 law would have settled long ago if that law had been the only criterion for action.

The debate on the Prussian School Bill of 1905 illustrated these dilemmas even more graphically.* The existing law dated from 1847. It provided for Christian, but not Jewish, religious instruction in state schools, and made it optional for local authorities to subsidise Jewish denominational schools and Jewish religious teachers in state schools. It is evident that though most Jewish pupils attended denominational or interdenominational Christian schools, virtually no Jewish teachers were employed in them. Even before the introduction of the 1905 Bill, Jewish leaders faced dilemmas of both principle and practice. Should they, along with the Liberal parties, demand completely interconfessional schools without religious instruction, or should they demand equal status for Jewish denominational schools and for Jewish religious instruction in state schools? Should they risk offending their political allies in the Progressive parties, whose policy was to demand secular education, or acknowledge that, given the electoral system in Prussia, there was no prospect of a majority for such a demand? Yet to make the best of generally confessionalised educational systems seemed to most of them a bad bargain: it was the first step towards re-segregation and away from assimilation.

In the end the attitude of the Catholic Centre Party was crucial to the shape in which the bill finally passed. The Centre was not in favour of discrimination against Jews, but neither was it in favour of driving Christianity out of the schools. It therefore supported amendments that made subsidies to Jewish religious instruction mandatory and under certain circumstances entitled a rabbi to sit on the school board.[35]

What the debates on the judiciary and education illustrated – and one could choose plenty of other examples – was that in matters of everyday importance Germany after 1871 was still governed by the member states, not the Imperial government.

The attitude of the Centre Party to the Prussian schools bill showed not that it was antisemitic (though some of its members and journals were), but that its political universe was bounded by the assumptions of the 1850 Prussian constitution. It was based on the notion that an individual's religious faith was a matter of public policy and that churches had a right and duty to participate in the formulation of that policy. The evasions of the various ministers of justice showed not that they were antisemitic (though some of them, and quite a few of their officials, were) but their evaluation of the rights of religious denominations was based in the pre-liberal era. They served, for the most part, states in which

---

*See also the essays by Max P. Birnbaum, 'On the Jewish Struggle for Religious Equality in Prussia 1897–1914'; and Geoffrey G. Field, 'Religion in the German Volksschule, 1890–1928', in this volume of the Year Book – (Ed.).

[35]For a full account of these debates, see Lamberti, *op. cit.*, ch. 7.

Christians collectively had legitimate claims and Jews collectively did not. It is the states, more than the Empire, that support the often-made contention that though Germany underwent a revolutionary economic change between 1871 and 1914 this was not accompanied by the changes in social and political attitudes normally associated with urbanisation and industrialisation. Hence the 1869 law, which presupposed an open, bourgeois society, remained, if not a dead letter, then an inadequate guide.

There is a further reason why the 1869 law proved contentious, namely the German predilection for legal positivism, the tendency to take essentially normative legislation literally and to litigate on that basis, to demand of the due process of law that it should solve human relationships. That the spirit and the letter of the law on religious equality were systematically broken in Imperial Germany is undeniable. Whether all such breaches were best dealt with by the same type of formal protest is an open question. In Britain, too, for instance, there were no Jewish members of the Foreign Office[36] before 1914, and being a Jew was undoubtedly an obstacle to gaining an Oxford or Cambridge college fellowship.[37] Yet there is no record of parliamentary questions on the subject, although there was no shortage of Jewish MPs or Gentile sympathisers with Jewish civic aspirations. One can offer only tentative explanations as to why this should be so. One is that unwritten rules and conventions covered areas of social life in Britain larger than in Germany. Another is that social mobility was at this period greater in Britain and this opened other, compensatory avenues to the ambitious Jew. The suggestion of one recent historian of English antisemitism that "Anglo-Jewry's . . . lay leadership provided a catching example of successful integration into Gentile society"[38] is seductive but valid only because the barriers to integration were in any case weak. English Jews were never subject to special legislation. They were excluded from certain privileges as non-Protestants or aliens; therefore their legal emancipation was a less traumatic experience for the host society.

In Germany the Jewish Question remained on the agenda but some aspects were more salient than others. Those who held that Jews were a separate, unassimilable race were a small, though growing and noisy minority. So, too were those who felt that emigration was the only solution to the dilemma of German-Jewish co-existence. The question had a narrower scope: it arose out of the unfulfillable and contradictory prescriptions for the conditions of post-emancipation Jewish life. Most Germans, Gentile and Jewish, agreed that Jews had ceased to be a nation but remained a religious denomination. Some argued that they should cease to be the latter as well; others that as long as they did they could not escape the disadvantages of living in a predominantly Christian state. As for the occupational distribution of Jews, which worried Jewish reformers as much as antisemites, this was a problem only if one wanted it to be one. It is not self-

---

[36]Zara S. Steiner, *The Foreign Office and British Foreign Policy, 1898–1914*, Cambridge 1969, p. 19.

[37]Cf. A. F. Pollard's letter after L. B. Namier failed to be elected to a fellowship at All Souls College in 1911: "The Warden and the majority of Fellows shied at his race, and eventually we elected the two next best." J. Namier, *Lewis Namier: A Biography*, Oxford 1971, p. 101.

[38]Gisela C. Lebzelter, *Political Anti-Semitism in England 1918–1939*, London 1978, p. 179 n. 11 and pp. 6–7.

evident that every religious or ethnic minority should in this respect be a microcosm of the larger unit. The problem arises only if the minority concerned is especially associated with socio-economic transformations that arouse suspicion and fear, and associated with interests on whose merits there is no consensus.

There were, then, two aspects of the Jewish Question in Imperial Germany that ensured its survival. The first was constitutional. As long as articles like No. 14 of the Prussian constitution existed side by side with the 1869 law, the very norms of public policy were in doubt. It has become fashionable to downgrade the importance of constitutions and statutes in ordering relations within society. Of course, such documents are not drafted in vacuums. They reflect the real relations of forces in societies as well as their intellectual and legal traditions. But because they tend to change more slowly than economic or social relations, because they possess a normative force, because a great deal of public conflict is about their interpretation, there is much to be gained from occasionally looking at the super-structures that govern men's lives.

The second was social and ideological. It deals with the relationship between the emergence of bourgeois society and the evolution of secular notions of citizenship. Imperial Germany corresponded neither with the fully-developed bourgeois societies of Western Europe, nor with the semi-patriarchal societies of Eastern Europe, where the bourgeoisie was still a subordinate force. The peculiar way in which the Empire was created led to a mixture of conservative, non-secular notions of citizenship, equating non-conformity with disloyalty, and revolutionary notions of nationality, equally inclined to be intolerant of awkward and anomolous categories. The demands which this made on a non-Christian minority, whose political ideal had to be one of libertarian Enlightenment and what Max Weber called "formal rationality" in administration, could not be satisfied. Those who governed Germany, and those who increasingly influenced her public opinion, could not decide between the insistence that Jews should assimilate more and the conviction that they were incapable of ever doing so. If Nietzsche was right in observing that the question "What is German?" never dies out among Germans,[39] it is easy to see why the question "Can a Jew be a German?" never received a satisfactory answer. Comprehensive definitions of nationality and citizenship, designed to solve problems of allegiance, invariably intensify them, by drawing attention to the outsider. This conclusion is as valid in 1979 as in 1879.

Each country's history is unique, and so is the history of each religious or ethnic minority within it. But such histories are not self-contained.

"Germany's Jews," a recent contributor to the unending debate has written,

> "indignantly rejected all talk of a 'Jewish Question' as a survival of primitive politics. In retrospect we know that in a sense, and a sense they did not intend, they were right: the so-called Jewish Question had no reality in isolation. It was part of, and a clue to, the larger question: the German Question."

To which he wisely added: "German questions ... are not German questions alone." [40]

---

[39] Friedrich Nietzsche, *Jenseits von Gut und Böse* (Kröners Taschenbuchausgabe), Stuttgart 1976, p. 175.
[40] Peter Gay, *Freud, Jews and Other Germans. Masters and Victims in Modernist Culture*, New York 1978, pp. 19, 28.

Liberals, Socialists and the Defence against Antisemitism in the Wilhelminian Period

BY MARJORIE LAMBERTI

The failure of Jewish emancipation in Germany has obscured links that the Jews had with groups in German society that opposed antisemitism, criticised Christian exclusiveness and defended the equality of rights of citizens of the Jewish religion.* In much post-Holocaust reflection and historical research on the defence against antisemitism and on the relations of Jews and Christians in Imperial Germany, there is a tendency to criticise the Liberals and to downgrade the part played by Liberals in the Jewish struggle for civil equality. Implicit in these interpretations is the view that the faith German Jewry put in liberalism was a tragic self-deception and that the Progressive Parties never proved worthy of the optimistic hopes and trust of their Jewish followers. The statement by John Snell and Hans Schmitt that "the left liberals played the genteel echo to socialism . . . as opponents of antisemitism" is an evaluation widely shared and seldom challenged.[1] They add, "Social Democracy, which did everything more dogmatically and emphatically, opposed the anti-Semites more consistently than did the Progressives".

The grounds for a severe judgment of the Liberals in the Progressive Parties were laid in Jacob Toury's analysis of the politics of the Jewish defence organisation founded in 1893, the *Centralverein deutscher Staatsbürger jüdischen Glaubens*. Toury's central thesis is that the leaders of the Jewish defence made the fatal mistake of aligning with the Progressives, a strategy that restricted their freedom of political action and prevented them from pursuing an emphatically Jewish policy.[2] Toury quotes Zionist radicals and Julius Moses, a pro-Zionist Socialist, who contended that the Left Liberals were unreliable opportunists on the "Jewish Question" and only paid lip service to liberal principles. The Progressive Parties lived off Jewish campaign contributions but were not willing to speak out for Jewish interests. Before the 1903 *Reichstag* election Moses, who edited a small Jewish newspaper, warned the Jews about "disguised antisemitism under the liberal flag" and declared that the Social Democrats consistently defended equality of rights for the Jews and had a better claim to Jewish votes than the Pro-

---

*This essay is an expanded and revised version of a paper read at the New York Leo Baeck Institute Faculty Seminar on 18th January 1979. I wish to express appreciation to the seminar participants whose comments enabled me to improve the manuscript.

[1] John L. Snell and Hans A. Schmitt, *The Democratic Movement in Germany, 1789-1914*, Chapel Hill 1976, p. 319.

[2] Jacob Toury, *Die politischen Orientierungen der Juden in Deutschland. Von Jena bis Weimar*, Tübingen 1966 (Schriftenreihe wissenschaftlicher Abhandlungen des Leo Baeck Instituts 15), pp. 205-209. A more recent work belittling the political dimension of the Jewish defence is Jehuda Reinharz's analysis of the *Centralverein* in *Fatherland or Promised Land. The Dilemma of the German Jew, 1893-1914*, Ann Arbor 1975.

gressives.³ Toury reproaches the notables of the *Centralverein* for sticking to the Progressives through thick and thin, even when party officials adopted opportunistic tactics in run-off elections, and the abstention or votes of the Liberals helped antisemitic candidates defeat the Social Democrats.

In Wilhelminian Germany Toury sees three political strategies open to the Jews as alternatives to an alignment with the Progressives: (1) supporting the Social Democrats; (2) collaborating with the Catholic Centre Party; and (3) forming an independent Jewish block or *Zentrum*.⁴ He criticises the *Centralverein* leaders for fearing to chart a new course when Zionists, beginning in 1901, called for a break with the Progressives and the creation of a Jewish *Zentrum*. From the Zionist newspaper *Die Welt*, Toury cites the argument:

> "Utopians are those who can observe every day the deterioration of our position in the country and still persist in expecting 'that conditions will improve'. Precisely because the Progressives [der Freisinn] weaken us, because they prevent the weak and shortsighted from fighting for their threatened interests, because they prevent or regard with a jealous eye the independent organisation of the Jews, it must be taught again and again: *Los von Rickert und Richter*."⁵

Toury thinks that a Jewish secession from the Progressive camp and the formation of a Jewish *Zentrum* came close to realisation in 1907–1908, when Jewish confidence in the Left Liberals was shaken. At this time the Progressives were partners with the Conservatives in the pro-government coalition of Chancellor von Bülow. The three alternatives remained, in Toury's phrase, "unrealised possibilities", and he blames the leaders of the *Centralverein* for missing this opportunity to establish a base for Jewish political power. They could not summon the courage to cut their ties with the Progressives. They restricted the *Centralverein* to a "negative" and "passive" defence against antisemitism and were not interested in the representation of specifically Jewish interests in parliament.⁶

Toury's analysis is based on a Zionist perspective. He looks at the *Centralverein* through the lens of Zionist radicals and Julius Moses who were embittered critics of its liberal leadership and vehement adversaries of the Progressives. The Zionists rejected the liberal view that Jewry was just a religious confession, and they were convinced that relations with the Progressives blinded the *Centralverein* leaders to the estrangement of the Germans and the Jews and made them fall victim to the illusion that social integration and civil equality could be achieved.⁷

Accepting the Zionist contention that the Jewish notables remained bound to the Progressives out of German nationalist sentiment and assimilationism, Toury misses the political reasons for the *Centralverein*'s strategy. His book gives no account of what the *Centralverein* and the *Verband der Deutschen Juden* did in political life. Nor does it relate how the Progressives participated in the fight against discrimination. Toury's thesis about the "unrealised possibilities" of the Jews in

³Toury, *op. cit.*, pp. 221–222.
⁴*Ibid.*, p. 212.
⁵*Ibid.*, p. 210.
⁶*Ibid.*, pp. 291–293.
⁷Yehuda Eloni, 'Die umkämpfte nationaljüdische Idee', in *Juden im Wilhelminischen Deutschland 1890–1914. Ein Sammelband herausgegeben von Werner E. Mosse unter Mitwirkung von Arnold Paucker*, Tübingen 1976 (Schriftenreihe wissenschaftlicher Abhandlungen des Leo Baeck Instituts 33), pp. 668–669.

German politics rests on assumption and speculation. No evidence or argument demonstrates that these options would have been acceptable to the Jews and politically advantageous for the Jewish defence. It is characteristic that he describes in detail Zionist proposals for a Jewish *Zentrum* and gives little notice to objections raised by Jewish Liberals.

Before any valid judgment can be made about the Liberals and the Jewish defence, several questions need to be answered. Why did the *Centralverein* align with the Progressives? Why did the Progressives take up the unpopular Jewish cause? The odds of ending discrimination in the Hohenzollern state establishment were not favourable, and the Progressives brought down on themselves the epithets of *Judenknechte* and *Judenschutztruppe*. What were the circumstances of friction between the Jews and the Left Liberals? Were the Social Democrats more conscientious and consistent than the Progressives in the fight against antisemitism? Is the opinion that "the Social Democrats were the only reliable defenders of Jewish civil equality" grounded in fact?[8]

The historic significance of the *Centralverein* in Imperial Germany was that it waged a politically activist defence against antisemitism.* Historians have been slow to recognise this achievement because at the start it restricted the choice of its weapons to counter-propaganda and the prosecution of antisemites in the courts.[9] The *Centralverein* became an activist movement due to the political aptitude of two lawyers who headed its board of directors. From the start Maximilian Horwitz and Eugen Fuchs had big ambitions for the *Centralverein* and wanted to fight on a second front an enemy more powerful than the factious antisemitic parties – antisemitism in the government bureaucracy, the judiciary and the officer corps. They persisted in arguing that the *Centralverein* had to lobby in parliament to protect Jewish rights. The Jews needed political spokesmen who could compel government ministers to be accountable for discrimination in the area of their jurisdiction and could put pressure on them to redress the injustices. Horwitz and Fuchs were confident that once Jewish grievances were aired in parliament and publicised in the daily press, state officials under pressure would carry out guarantees of civil equality in the Prussian constitution of 1850 and in the Federal Law of 3rd July 1869.[10]

In the spring of 1898 the board of directors made the momentous decision to participate in the impending elections for the *Reichstag* and Prussian parliament.[11] Besides campaigning against the antisemitic parties, the *Centralverein* pro-

---

[8]Robert S. Wistrich, *Revolutionary Jews from Marx to Trotsky*, London 1976, p. 24.

*See also the preceding essay by Peter Pulzer, 'Why was there a Jewish Question in Imperial Germany?', pp. 141–142, in this volume of the Year Book – (Ed.).

[9]On the history of the *Centralverein* in Imperial Germany, see Marjorie Lamberti, *Jewish Activism in Imperial Germany. The Struggle for Civil Equality*, New Haven 1978; Arnold Paucker, 'Zur Problematik einer jüdischen Abwehrstrategie in der deutschen Gesellschaft', in *Juden im Wilhelminischen Deutschland*, pp. 479–548; Reinharz, *op. cit.*; Ismar Schorsch, *Jewish Reactions to German Anti-Semitism, 1870–1914*, New York 1972.

[10]The Federal Law of 3rd July 1869 abolished all restrictions on the political and civil rights of citizens based on religion and made eligibility to hold office independent of religious confession. Article 4 and Article 12 of the Prussian constitution of 31st January 1850 stated that all citizens were equal before the law and enjoyed the full exercise of political and civil rights.

[11]Lamberti, *Jewish Activism in Imperial Germany*, pp. 23 ff.

moted the election of Jewish candidates nominated by the Progressives. After 1898 the involvement of the Jewish defence in German politics grew steadily. Once its leaders set out to combat government antisemitism, they needed allies in parliament. They disregarded the *Centralverein*'s initial policy of nonpartisanship and aligned the Jewish defence with the Progressives.

The *Centralverein*'s reliance upon the Progressives raises troubling questions about the political acumen and judgment of its leaders. These questions cannot be dismissed lightly. After 1878 liberalism ceased to be a power factor in German politics. Bismarck ended his alliance with the National Liberals and found a new parliamentary majority in the Conservative and Centre Parties. Schism debilitated the forces of liberalism. In 1880 the left-wing National Liberals seceded from the party. The National Liberals retreated from liberalism and, as the party of the Protestant upper bourgeoisie, sought influence with the government by entering parliamentary cartels with the Conservatives. The secessionists merged with the Liberals in the Progressive Party in 1884. This union did not survive disagreements over whether to support an army appropriations bill, and in 1893 the Left Liberals split into two parties, the Progressive People's Party and the Progressive Union.[12]

During these years left-liberal strength at the polls declined. The Progressives won only 36 of the 397 *Reichstag* seats in the election of 1893.[13] Their representation remained at this low level until the election of 1912 when it rose slightly to 42 seats. The Progressives did not command the support of a mass constituency and became a party of the educated bourgeoisie – journalists, lawyers and teachers. Their reform platform and eternal opposition to government bills alienated blocs of middle-class voters. Apprehensive about the rapid growth of the Social Democratic Party, the previously liberal middle classes now saw a benevolently conservative government as the best safeguard of social order. In industrial regions the Progressives could not match Social Democracy's appeal to the workers. Their share of the popular vote never came close to the millions of votes that swept 110 Social Democrats into the *Reichstag* in 1912.[14]

The *Centralverein* found among the Progressives the most reliable and conscientious, if not always the most zealous, defenders of Jewish rights. Many Progressives of the Christian faith, especially Richard Eickhoff in the Prussian parliament and Georg Gothein in the *Reichstag*, were willing to collaborate with the lobbyists of the *Centralverein* and the *Verband der Deutschen Juden*. These politicians were prominent figures on the executive board of the *Verein zur Abwehr des Antisemitismus*. This association, founded in 1891 as a Christian defence against antisemitism, campaigned against the antisemitic parties in elections and published pamphlets and a weekly newspaper refuting antisemitic lies and half-

---

[12]On the history and organisation of the Progressive Parties, see Thomas Nipperdey, *Die Organisation der deutschen Parteien vor 1918*, Düsseldorf 1961, pp. 176 ff.; James J. Sheehan, *German Liberalism in the Nineteenth Century*, Chicago 1978, pp. 204 ff.

[13]Snell and Schmitt, *op. cit.*, pp. 306–307.

[14]Dieter Fricke, *Die deutsche Arbeiterbewegung 1869–1914. Ein Handbuch über ihre Organisation und Tätigkeit im Klassenkampf*, Berlin 1976, pp. 526, 568.

truths and publicising the crimes and disreputable character of the antisemites.¹⁵

The initiative in founding the *Abwehrverein* came from Heinrich Rickert, a Progressive deputy in the *Reichstag* who believed that Christian Liberals bore the obligation to protect the rights of Jewish citizens and to stop the antisemitic pollution of German public life and culture. A man of moral courage and with a strong sense of justice, Rickert throughout his political career was never deterred from defending a just cause when the fight had unfavourable prospects.¹⁶ He knew that the membership of the *Abwehrverein*, 13,338 in 1893, was not impressive in comparison with the 163,000 members of the Agrarian League, and he conceded that "with the limitations of our means the results cannot be as great as we had hoped".¹⁷

Rickert and the other organisers intended the *Abwehrverein* to cross party lines and selected Rudolf von Gneist, an elderly and highly respected National Liberal, to be the first chairman. Apart from the Left Liberals, other Germans did not join the organisation in large numbers. When Gneist died in 1895, the leadership of the *Abwehrverein* fell on the Left Liberals entirely. Rickert headed the organisation until his death in 1902. His successor was Theodor Barth, who edited a liberal weekly named *Nation*. A deputy in the *Reichstag* and Prussian parliament until his defeat in 1903, Barth was once described as a *"Kampfhahn"* because his political career had been spent in opposition, fighting for democratic reform and for the rights of the oppressed.¹⁸ When Barth died in 1909, the executive committee was intent on having a parliamentary deputy lead the *Abwehrverein* and elected as the new chairman Georg Gothein, a Progressive who held a seat in the *Reichstag* since 1903.

Mixed feelings were the first reaction of these Liberals to the founding of the *Centralverein*. The leaders of the *Abwehrverein* expressed misgivings that a second organisation might fragment and lessen the effectiveness of the Christian and Jewish forces opposing antisemitism.¹⁹ Nonetheless, they gave moral support to the *Centralverein* during difficult times in 1894 and 1895, when its libel lawsuits provoked criticism and antisemitic newspaper editors were posing as martyrs. The *Abwehrverein* stated that the *Centralverein* was justified in hauling the antisemites into court because they had abused freedom of the press more than any other party. It criticised state attorneys for refusing to prosecute the antisemites and to give legal protection to the Jewish community.²⁰

Also in the Progressive caucus were Jewish deputies willing to work with the Jewish defence movement. In 1903 seven Progressives of the Jewish faith were elected to the Prussian House of Deputies, and again in 1908 seven out of the thirty-six Progressive seats were held by Jews. This generation of Jewish politi-

---

¹⁵For two different interpretations of the work of the *Abwehrverein*, see Richard S. Levy, *The Downfall of the Anti-Semitic Parties in Imperial Germany*, New Haven 1975, pp. 146 ff.; Schorsch, *op. cit.*, pp. 80 ff.
¹⁶Theodor Barth, *Politische Porträts*, ed. by Ernst Feder, Berlin 1923, pp. 77–80.
¹⁷*Mitteilungen aus dem Verein zur Abwehr des Antisemitismus* (hereafter cited as *Mitteilungen*), 3rd December 1893, p. 440. The newspaper had around 8,000 subscriptions in 1898. Its objective was to gain a wider circulation by encouraging local newspaper editors to reprint the articles.
¹⁸*Berliner Tageblatt*, 3rd June 1909, No. 276.
¹⁹*Mitteilungen*, 18th February 1894, p. 52.
²⁰*Ibid.*, 4th August 1894, p. 244; 20th October 1894, pp. 333–334.

cians in the Progressive Parties was more ready to speak out on Jewish issues than Jewish National Liberals had been in the 1870s; Bamberger and Lasker saw themselves as Jews only in private life.[21] The Jewish Progressives were party men and always maintained that they had been elected as German citizens and not as "confessional candidates". But their allegiance to the party and their relationships with fellow Progressives did not weaken their Jewish group identity. Hermann Cohn accepted election to the executive board of the *Centralverein*, and Oskar Cassel sat on the executive committee of the *Verband der Deutschen Juden*. In the years between 1901 and 1914 Oskar Cassel and Martin Peltasohn were the most frequent spokesmen for Jewish interests in the committees and on the floor of the Prussian parliament.

The Progressives seized the occasion of budget debates to confront government ministers with the evidence of discrimination compiled by the *Centralverein* and the *Verband der Deutschen Juden*. From 1904 on, the Progressives raised almost annually the issue of antisemitism in the officer corps and demanded that the Minister of War end the practice of disqualifying Jews from officer commissions in the reserve army.[22] In the Prussian parliament in 1901 and 1905 the Progressives interpellated the Minister of Justice about the practice of barring Jewish lawyers from appointments as notaries and from advancement to high offices in the judiciary.[23] At one budget committee session Peltasohn demanded that the Minister of Justice reprimand law clerks who were forming professional associations that excluded Jews. On the floor of the house a non-Jewish Progressive criticised the Christian exclusiveness of civil servants in Breslau who had organised the *Vereinigung christlicher Referendare*.[24] The grievances of Jewish physicians were publicised in 1910 and 1911. Presenting specific cases, the Progressives charged that hospital directors rejected Jewish doctors applying for internships.[25] Moved by shame, Christian Left Liberals condemned in 1906 the forcible expulsion of unnaturalised Russian Jews ordered by the Berlin *Polizeipräsident*, and they asked Minister of Interior Bethmann Hollweg what he intended to do to stop the arbitrary and harsh actions of the police.[26]

Jewish lobbying attained a high level of political sophistication after 1905 when the *Verband der Deutschen Juden* was founded. From December 1905 to April 1906 the new Jewish pressure group worked with Oskar Cassel to revise the Prussian school bill.[27] The Progressives introduced amendments to prevent interdenominational schools from being converted to Catholic and Protestant schools, to safeguard the rights of Jewish children attending Christian confessional

---

[21]Peter Pulzer, 'Die jüdische Beteiligung an der Politik', in *Juden im Wilhelminischen Deutschland*, p. 184.

[22]Werner T. Angress, 'Prussia's Army and the Jewish Reserve Officer Controversy before World War I', in *LBI Year Book XVII* (1972), pp. 31 ff.

[23]*Stenographische Berichte über die Verhandlungen des preussischen Abgeordnetenhauses*, 31st January 1901, pp. 927 ff.; 30th January 1905, pp. 9235 ff.

[24]*Ibid.*, 17th February 1906, p. 1752; see also *Mitteilungen*, 21st February 1906, pp. 61–63; 28th February 1906, p. 66.

[25]*Stenographische Berichte über die Verhandlungen des preussischen Abgeordnetenhauses*, 30th April 1910, pp. 5172 ff.; 2nd May 1910, pp. 5301–5302; 18th February 1911, pp. 2371 ff.

[26]*Ibid.*, 12th May 1906, pp. 4636 ff.; see also 19th February 1907, p. 1019.

[27]Lamberti, *Jewish Activism in Imperial Germany*, pp. 141 ff.

schools, and to strike out of the bill discriminatory clauses affecting Jewish teachers and the admission of rabbis to the local school boards.

The Progressives expressed the grievances of the Jews with dignity, discretion and moral earnestness. Their speeches were well-reasoned appeals for justice and fair treatment. They were capable of seeing the sense of honour moving the Jews to protest discrimination in the army that stigmatised them as inferior.[28] Knowing that the antisemites were looking for any excuse to turn these debates into a "satiric comedy", the Progressives refrained from answering their preposterous allegations and fuelling antisemitic demagoguery.[29] They tried to prevent the antisemites from diverting the debate away from legal issues and from debasing parliament into a platform for ridicule. Without resorting to invective, the Progressives rejected the transparent excuses offered by government ministers to side-step charges of discrimination and kept these officials on the defensive. Their interpellations aimed at positive action and remedy. Their tactics were to expose the unconstitutional practices of the state authorities and to put pressure on them to comply with the letter of the law.

Why did the Progressives defend Jewish rights, an issue that seemed at times to be a "lost cause"? The Progressives believed that "the emancipation of the Jews was an achievement of the Liberals and its preservation must be seen as an honour-bound obligation for liberalism".[30] Early in the nineteenth century the Liberals spoke out for the political equality of the Jews against the mainstream of public opinion. Many Liberals were not enthusiastic or consistent in supporting the Jewish cause; they knew that the electorate disapproved of laws granting citizen status to the Jews and had given them no mandate to vote for emancipation. Other Liberals argued that on the issue of Jewish emancipation popular opinion represented passion and prejudice and that parliamentary representatives were obliged to "recognise as public opinion only that which is recognised by the people as consonant with the eternal principles of justice".[31] By the 1860s liberal majorities in the state parliaments were convinced that a modern society could no longer deny the full rights of citizenship to the Jews. Withstanding arguments from opponents that emancipation would be rejected if a plebiscite was ever held, the Liberals passed legislation guaranteeing equality of rights to all citizens unconditioned by religious faith.

The Liberals championed emancipation as part of Germany's transformation

[28] In the *Reichstag* sitting of 22nd March 1905 Richard Eickhoff read to the deputies a letter written to him by a Jewish physician, Dr. Siegmund Lachmann, who had resigned from the reserve army in 1904, following a *Reichstag* debate in which the antisemites Böckel and Liebermann von Sonnenberg had insulted and ridiculed Jewish soldiers for cowardice, unfitness for combat and dodging military service. The doctor's resignation was an act of protest against the silence of Minister of War von Einem during the debate. Lachmann wrote in his letter that the minister's failure to refute these untenable charges was an offence to his honour as a Jew. See *Stenographische Berichte über die Verhandlungen des Reichstages*, 22nd March 1905, pp. 5501–5502.
[29] *Stenographische Berichte über die Verhandlungen des preussischen Abgeordnetenhauses*, 12th May 1906, p. 4686. The Progressive deputy Robert Gyssling made this remark. David Waldstein gave the same reason for refusing to reply to the speech made by the antisemite Werner in the *Reichstag*. See *Stenographische Berichte über die Verhandlungen des Reichstages*, 20th June 1913, p. 5658.
[30] *Mitteilungen*, 13th April 1895, p. 114.
[31] Reinhard Rürup, 'German Liberalism and the Emancipation of the Jews', in *LBI Year Book XX* (1975), p. 66.

from a corporate-feudal to a bourgeois-liberal society. The civil equality of the Jews was for the Liberals a touchstone of progress towards a *Rechtsstaat*, a state governed by a written constitution that safeguarded the fundamental liberties of every citizen.[32] Tying the principle of constitutional government to freedom of religion, they repudiated the Conservative notion of the "Christian state" and insisted that religion was a private matter. Freedom of religion meant more than toleration; its corollary was the principle that the exercise of civil rights could not be conditioned or limited by religious belief.

In the Wilhelminian era a close relationship between the *Centralverein* and the Progressives was made possible by a change in the liberal position on the "Jewish Question". Throughout the 1880s Liberals treated populist antisemitism as a temporary threat. Antisemitic oratory seemed too vulgar to appeal to a nation as civilised as the Germans. The founding of the *Abwehrverein* in 1891 was an honest confession by Rickert and his liberal friends that their hopes that the antisemitic movement would not take deep roots and last long had been "too optimistic".[33] The weekly newspaper of the *Abwehrverein* declared in 1893: "The Jewish Question stands once again on the agenda of public life. Being silent and passive will not make it recede."[34] By the end of the 1890s the leaders of the *Abwehrverein* warned the Liberals not to think that the danger of antisemitism had declined because the antisemitic parties had lost steam and momentum. "The danger has become greater," said Rickert, "because now the disseminators of antisemitism are political and economic organisations like the Agrarian League."[35] The Liberals were also awakened to the threat to emancipation and the *Rechtsstaat* posed by discrimination in the civil service and the army.

A parliamentary debate in 1901 revealed to the Progressives the extent to which antisemitism had eroded the bureaucracy's respect for the *Rechtsstaat*. Martin Peltasohn interpellated Minister of Justice Schönstedt about discrimination against Jewish lawyers in the appointment of notaries. Schönstedt replied haughtily that he was not obliged to give the House of Deputies an accounting of how notaries were appointed. He added that many Christians did not have confidence in Jewish lawyers and that the Ministry of Justice had to take into account these feelings.[36] In a second speech the minister argued that government required a degree of administrative discretion and that the constitution could not be the decisive and binding legal norm. There were times when officials had to depart from the letter of the law out of consideration for the needs and wishes of the people.[37]

The lack of scruple with which the Minister of Justice justified practices that stood in violation of the Prussian constitution of 1850 outraged the Progressives. Theodor Barth, Eugen Richter and Heinrich Rickert assailed his speeches. Barth

[32]Reinhard Rürup, 'Emanzipation und Krise. Zur Geschichte der "Judenfrage" in Deutschland vor 1890', in *Juden im Wilhelminischen Deutschland*, p. 22.
[33]*Mitteilungen*, 3rd December 1893, p. 439.
[34]*Ibid.*, 26th February 1893, p. 82.
[35]*Ibid.*, 6th March 1897, p. 74; 22nd July 1899, pp. 225–226.
[36]*Stenographische Berichte über die Verhandlungen des preussischen Abgeordnetenhauses*, 30th January 1901, pp. 929–930.
[37]*Ibid.*, 8th February 1901, p. 1226.

argued that the constitution would have no value if the minister's canons on government administration were accepted, and if any official could dispense with the law and act on the basis of his arbitrary interpretation of the needs of the people.[38] Referring to Studt's attempt to intimidate Jewish lawyers with the advice that it would be prudent not to raise protests, Barth declared:

> "In view of the justification of an unjust practice, what concerns us, to speak frankly and plainly: do we live in a *Rechtsstaat* or not? Of what importance is it ... whether a few more Jews are appointed notaries, whether a few more Jews are appointed judges; this is in itself immaterial. What is alone of importance is that, not without protest, can it be said by the Minister of Justice before the entire country that Article 12 of the constitution does not exist for the Jews."[39]

The Progressives believed that antisemitism was a German problem and not a Jewish concern alone. To defend Jewish rights was to safeguard the *Rechtsstaat*. Christian Liberals in the *Abwehrverein* insisted that they were "not philo-semitic".[40] They championed the principle of equality of rights for all religious communities

> "not out of preference for a particular confession which is oppressed, but because a modern state founded on tolerance, morality and freedom cannot exist if this principle is not carried out in actuality and with honesty".[41]

Disappointments were bound to come because the Progressive politicians were not willing to represent Jewish interests to the extent that the Jews wished. The priorities of the party politicians and the Jews were not set alike. The Progressives did not consider the antisemitic splinter parties a greater danger than the Social Democrats. The antisemites were a tiny caucus in parliament, and their motions for exceptional laws throughout the 1890s had been defeated. The Social Democrats were a party with a bureaucratic organisation and a disciplined following. The increase in the Social Democratic vote and the loss of electoral districts to the Social Democrats were matters more alarming to the Progressives than the oratory of the contemptible antisemites. In run-off matches between the Social Democrats and the antisemites, Progressive Party leaders before 1912 were loath to support their Socialist competitors and took a noncommittal stance.[42] What determined their tactics were considerations of party interests and not a disguised antisemitism as the Zionists charged. Rivalry between the two parties on the Left was fierce in cities like Berlin, Breslau, Danzig and Frankfurt a. Main, and in run-off elections the Progressives fought the Social Democrats more frequently than any other party.

Despite the opportunism of liberal election tactics and other letdowns, the leaders of the *Centralverein* made a pragmatic decision when they aligned the Jewish defence with the Progressives. The alternatives postulated by Toury did not have the slightest prospects of realisation. They were not acceptable to the majority of Jews and would not have been politically more advantageous.

---

[38]*Ibid.*, 31st January 1901, p. 934 ff.
[39]*Ibid.*, 8th February 1901, p. 1275.
[40]*Mitteilungen*, 19th April 1904, p. 121.
[41]*Ibid.*, p. 122.
[42]Lamberti, *Jewish Activism in Imperial Germany*, pp. 45 ff.

The appeal of the Social Democrats for the Jews was limited. Although Jews were prominent names in the Socialist press and *Reichstag* caucus, the growth of the Jewish vote for the party was slow.[43] Middle-class Jews wanted no link with a party that had a Marxist revolutionary ideology, attacked capitalism and was suspected of being unpatriotic. The *Centralverein* reproached Jews for abstaining in run-off elections between Social Democrats and antisemites. They ignored appeals from the *Centralverein* and more explicitly from Barth in the *Abwehrverein* urging Liberals "to vote for the counter-candidate even if he is a Social Democrat".[44]

The Social Democratic Party prevented the antisemitic populists from recruiting the working class and by its existence acted as a stumbling block to the expansion of the antisemitic parties. But out of the party's verbal denunciations against antisemitism could not come a special relationship with the Jewish defence movement. The common interests that the Social Democrats and the Jews shared in opposing exceptional laws could not overcome the chasm separating them. The *Centralverein* fought government antisemitism from a position of loyal opposition. Its leaders believed with good reason that the Jewish struggle for equal rights would have been compromised if it was associated with the Socialist Left.[45]

---

[43] Pulzer, *loc. cit.*, p. 198.

[44] *Mitteilungen*, 10th June 1903, pp. 177-178. From the by-elections in 1910 on, the *Centralverein* endeavoured to soften hostility towards Social Democracy so that Left Liberals would vote for Social Democratic candidates instead of abstaining or voting for the antisemitic and right-wing contenders as they had been doing in the second ballot. At the same time within the Progressive Party was a growing opinion in favour of cooperation between the two parties, which led to an electoral accommodation in the *Reichstag* election of 1912.

[45] Paucker, *loc. cit.*, p. 504. In recent historical scholarship there are different viewpoints on the relationship of the Jews and the *Centralverein* with the Social Democratic Party in the years before the First World War. Arnold Paucker states that there was a marked tendency of Jewish voters to shift to the Social Democratic Party. He contends that a growing number of *Centralverein* members were Social Democrats and that this "socialist component" was making its weight felt. In the *Centralverein*'s monthly journal, beginning around 1903, Paucker sees signs of greater esteem for the Social Democrats, which suggest that it sought to build, in the words of Jacob Toury, "ideological bridges to the SPD". Paucker infers that "the possibility of a closer tie to the SPD must have preoccupied at least theoretically the C.V., for the Social Democrats in Wilhelminian Germany had become undoubtedly *the* main obstacle to a greater spread of antisemitism". See Paucker, *loc. cit.*, pp. 496, 501-502. See also Toury, *op. cit.*, p. 224.

Peter Pulzer stresses the limits of the party's appeal for Jewish voters. He argues that the *Centralverein* "could state correctly" that the Social Democrats could not be expected to go beyond a stand against antisemitism and to speak out for Jewish interests. Quoting the assertion made in 1903 by Hugo Sonnenfeld, a member of the executive board, that Socialist sympathy for the Jews "adds up to zero", Pulzer remarks that "few Social Democrats would not have confirmed this judgment". See Pulzer, *loc cit.*, pp. 192, 201-202.

In the pre-war years the leaders of the *Centralverein* had an uneasy confidence in the Social Democrats and expressed grave doubts. They saw limited possibilities for political cooperation and no basis for close ties between the Jewish defence movement and the Social Democratic Party. In a speech entitled 'The *Centralverein* and the Political Elections' in 1903, Sonnenfeld praised the Social Democratic Party for opposing exceptional laws that would restrict the civil rights of the Jews. "I must qualify my favourable judgment somewhat," he added. He pointed out how ambivalent and indifferent the Social Democrats were on matters affecting the Jews and how antisemitic slips appeared occasionally in their propaganda against capitalism. "By no means do the Jews find an ardent defence, a reliable defence, among the Social Democrats," he asserted. During the Prussian parliamentary election campaign in 1908, the *Centralverein* declared that the Social Democratic

The Defence against Antisemitism

The Social Democrats viewed the *Centralverein* with disdain and displayed this attitude in parliamentary debates on Jewish issues. In April 1913, speaking on two consecutive days in the Prussian House of Deputies, Adolf Hoffmann ridiculed the Jews in the *Centralverein**as bourgeois social climbers who aspired after the prestige of being a *Geheimer Justizrat* and a *Kommerzienrat*. Accusing them of hurrah-patriotism and fawning respect for the state authorites, he declared:

> "I judge very objectively a segment of Jews who do not appeal to me because they believe that equality of rights can be achieved not by fighting but by fawning and cringing."[46]

Less tempestuous than Hoffmann was Georg Schöpflin whose scornful remarks about the *Centralverein*'s purpose in fighting discrimination in the officer corps showed that contempt for the Jewish defence movement was widely felt among the Social Democrats in the *Reichstag*. Georg Gothein opened the debate in 1911 with the evidence of specific cases passed on to him by the *Centralverein*. In his speech Schöpflin gibed:

> "Now I have neither the inclination nor the commission to exert myself for those circles of the Jewish bourgeoisie who aspire covetously to have their sons become reserve officers. That also the Jews are overcome by this epidemic, this obsesssion to have by all means their male sprigs play the part of reserve officers arouses certainly no sympathy."[47]

Having embraced the cause of universal human emancipation, Jewish luminaries in the Social Democratic Party rejected the particularism of Jewish group identity.[48] They could not bring themselves to join any Jewish organisations. One year after the founding of the *Centralverein*, Eduard Bernstein said that

> "with the formal emancipation of the Jews, every excuse for exclusiveness, for a special Jewish solidarity against non-Jews ... has been eliminated and where anything of the kind exists, it must be fought against as energetically as possible".[49]

Jews in the Socialist caucus in the *Reichstag* and, after the election of 1908, in the Prussian parliament showed a callous indifference to the blows struck at the dignity of their co-religionists and sat through debates on the "Jewish Question" in stony silence. Eduard Bernstein attributed their reluctance to speak out against antisemitism to "an exaggerated conscientiousness". Because of their

---

Party, having suffered itself under exceptional legislation, could be relied upon to oppose attempts to curtail the rights of Jewish citizens. Qualifying this statement, it added: "But when it is a question of the threatened religious interests of the Jews, the Social Democrats in view of their party principles cannot speak out for them, and the Social Democrats also will not ignore the fact that they may hope for a rich harvest wherever antisemitism has ploughed the soil.' *Im Deutschen Reich*, November 1903, pp. 628–631; June 1908, p. 350. See also Lamberti, *Jewish Activism in Imperial Germany*, pp. 42–43, 80–81.

*For a differing assessment see the following contribution by Max P. Birnbaum, 'On the Jewish Struggle for Religious Equality in Prussia 1897–1914', pp. 170–171, in this volume of the Year Book – (Ed.).

[46]*Stenographische Berichte über die Verhandlungen des preussischen Abgeordnetenhauses*, 2nd April 1913, p. 13188. Hoffmann repeated his criticism on 3rd April 1913; see p. 13234. In his speeches Hoffmann opposed a motion, introduced by the Progressives, asking the government to appropriate funds to assist poor synagogue congregations just as the state budget had over the years provided money for the Christian churches.

[47]*Stenographische Berichte über die Verhandlungen des Reichstages*, 27th February 1911, p. 4990.

[48]Wistrich, *Revolutionary Jews from Marx to Trotsky*, p. 9.

[49]*Ibid.*, p. 67; see also p. 74.

Jewish origins, he wrote, they "consider it their special duty to protect the party from all suspicion of favouring Jewish interests" and from being stigmatised as a *Judenschutztruppe*.[50]

Ambivalence towards antisemitism accounts for the behaviour of the Social Democrats in debates on Jewish grievances far more than "the otherwise honourable motives" mentioned by Bernstein. Party leaders and ideologists like August Bebel, Heinrich Braun and Franz Mehring saw populist antisemitism as a radical, anti-capitalist movement that would "ultimately benefit" Social Democracy.[51] They thought that plebeian, antisemitic agitators who incited discontented artisans, shopkeepers and peasants against Jewish money-power were conducting a protest movement against the capitalist establishment. In election campaigns the Social Democrats tiptoed past the anti-Jewish platform of the antisemitic parties and blasted the antisemites in the *Reichstag* for voting for army and navy bills and for supporting imperialist aims.[52]

From the Socialist perspective discrimination against the Jews was not one of the great injustices of Imperial Germany; it was insignificant in comparison with the oppression of the working class in a capitalist society. Social Democrats accused the liberal dailies owned by Jewish publishers of giving extensive coverage to the Dreyfus Affair in France and ignoring the problem of class justice under which the workers suffered in Germany.[53] For the Social Democrats the "Jewish Question" was a phase in the development of capitalism, and its solution would come with the advent of a new society in which Socialism and the dissolution of the Jews as a distinctive group would remove all cause for antisemitism.[54]

Combating antisemitism in the army and government bureaucracy was not a political or moral obligation fulfilled by the Social Democrats with earnestness. The tactics of the party in parliamentary debates on the "Jewish Question" could hardly help the cause of Jewish rights. Regarding parliament as a tribune for disseminating propaganda, Social Democrats like Karl Liebknecht seized the issue of antisemitism to assault militarism, Pan-German nationalism and feudal caste privilege.[55] The aim of their speeches was agitation. They did not see any possibility for positive action in parliamentary debates with the Minister of War. The Social Democrats turned *Reichstag* debates on discrimination in the army into a farce in 1911, 1912 and 1913. They provoked laughter and heckling by needling antisemitic politicians and by making jokes at the expense of the dignity of the Jews. Their ironical humour about Prussian aristocrats who married "rich

---

[50]*Ibid.*, pp. 65, 67.

[51]Edmund Silberner, 'German Social Democracy and the Jewish Problem Prior to World War I', *Historia Judaica*, XV (1953), pp. 13–15; Robert S. Wistrich, 'Anti-Capitalism or Antisemitism? The Case of Franz Mehring', in *LBI Year Book XXII* (1977), pp. 47–48.

[52]*Handbuch für Sozialdemokratische Wähler. Der Reichstag 1893–98*, herausgegeben vom Sozialdemokratischen Parteivorstand, Berlin 1898, pp. 25–30; *Handbuch für Sozialdemokratische Wähler anlässlich der Reichstagsauflösung 1906*, herausgegeben vom Sozialdemokratischen Parteivorstand, Berlin 1906, p. 141.

[53]Pulzer, *loc. cit.*, pp. 201–202.

[54]Wistrich, *Revolutionary Jews from Marx to Trotsky*, pp. 15–20.

[55]*Stenographische Berichte über die Verhandlungen des preussischen Abgeordnetenhauses*, 5th April 1913, pp. 13447–13448; *Stenographische Berichte über die Verhandlungen des Reichstages*, 20th June 1913, pp. 5659 ff.

Rebeccas" and about "the blood of the sons of Abraham, Isaac and Jacob flowing in the veins of these gentlemen" trivialised the problem of antisemitism.[56]

The derision and levity with which the Social Democrats treated Jewish grievances suggest that they were not concerned about the constitutional rights of a religious minority. In their speeches they quickly dropped the Jewish issue and went on to a long catalogue of complaints about the army's black-listing of Social Democratic pubs and the harshness of military discipline. The Social Democrats were concerned about the pariah treatment and second-class citizenship status accorded to the workers.[57] Their libertarian impulses were concentrated on opposition to exceptional laws repressing the Social Democratic Party and restricting the workers' rights of association. Despite the fact that the Social Democrats denounced feudal caste privilege and championed the principle of equality, they had an indifference towards Jewish efforts to protect their civil rights and to attain for Judaism legal equality alongside the Christian religions. Social Democrats like Adolf Hoffmann had an antagonistic view of religion and saw it functioning as the cornerstone of an exploitative and authoritarian society.[58] They saw equality in terms of the socialisation of the means of production and the economic emancipation of the working class.

The close identification of the Centre Party with Catholic confessional interests limited its appeal for Jewish voters. Apart from a handful of Zionists who were hostile to the Progressives, there is no evidence for Toury's contention that "an approach to the Catholic Centre Party was repeatedly considered among the efforts to find an alternative to the parties of the Left".[59] Catholic hostility to modernism and liberalism, monumentalised in the Syllabus of Errors of 1864, did not make the party popular with the Jews, except for the Orthodox Jewish voters.

The identity of interests between the two religious minorities in Imperial Germany was more apparent than real. In the 1870s the Catholic bourgeoisie and clergy commonly blamed the *Kulturkampf* on liberalism and used the code words of "Jewish influences" and "Jewish press" to smear liberalism. In the following decade the agrarian wing of the Centre Party, identified with the vehemently anti-Jewish *Bauernvereine*, favoured measures curtailing the economic activity of the Jews. What kept the Centre Party from joining the antisemitic campaign in the 1880s was the strong leadership and integrity of Ludwig Windhorst, who insisted on speaking out for the rights of all religious communities and prevailed against the antisemitic faction by threatening to resign his parliamentary seat.[60] Ernst Lieber, who succeeded Windhorst, condemned antisemitic motions for exceptional legislation throughout the 1890s. The steadfast commitment of both leaders to the ideal of toleration silenced but did not convert the anti-Jewish elements in the Centre Party.

[56]*Stenographische Berichte über die Verhandlungen des Reichstages*, 27th February 1911, p. 4991.
[57]Guenther Roth, *The Social Democrats in Imperial Germany*, Totowa 1963, pp. 127 ff.
[58]Susanne Miller, *Das Problem der Freiheit im Sozialismus*, Frankfurt a. Main 1964, pp. 162–163, 252.
[59]Toury, *op. cit.*, p. 246.
[60]Rudolf Lill, 'Katholizismus nach 1848', in *Kirche und Synagoge. Handbuch zur Geschichte von Christen und Juden*, ed. by Karl Heinrich Rengstorf and Siegfried von Kortzfleisch, Stuttgart 1970, II, pp. 381–383. See also Hermann Greive, 'Die gesellschaftliche Bedeutung der christlich-jüdischen Differenz. Zur Situation im deutschen Katholizismus', in *Judentum im Wilhelminischen Deutschland*, pp. 383–385.

The tradition of Windhorst and Lieber did not prevail in the Centre Party after the turn of the century, and Centre politicians were now unsympathetic or evasive in debates on Jewish issues. In the debate following Peltasohn's interpellation in 1901, Felix Porsch argued that antisemitism was not the reason for objections to the appointment of Jewish notaries. He stated that Catholics preferred to have lawyers of their own faith handle their estates and notarise their wills, and he complained that there were too many Jewish notaries in cities in Silesia heavily populated by Catholics. The Centre deputy scolded the Jews for making accusations of antisemitism:

> "You are mistaken if you think that it is only antisemitism which would not let your demands be fully accepted. The gentlemen should not deceive themselves. The majority of our population, the overwhelming majority, cherishes the urgent desire to live in a Christian state and to be governed by Christians."[61]

Implied in Porsch's speech was a distinction between toleration and equality of rights. Porsch and other Centre politicians followed the Protestant Conservatives in viewing the Jewish community as a "tolerated sect" in a "Christian state", and they thought that in public life the Jews were not on an equal footing with the Christian confessions.[62] Precisely because this theory was not challenged by Orthodox Jews claiming separate rights, Centre politicians were disposed to act as champions of Orthodox Jewry in the debates on the Prussian school bill in 1906.[63] A favourite manoeuvre of Centre deputies was to make references to the division and disagreement between Orthodox and Liberal Jewry in order to evade Jewish demands for equal rights.

Jewish and Catholic interests conflicted in two political controversies in the years before 1914. Since 1890 the Centre Party used its leverage position in pro-government majorities in parliament to attain legislation giving the public elementary schools a pronounced Christian confessional character. Most Jews opposed the confessionalisation of the *Volksschule*. During the deliberations on the Prussian school bill in 1906, Centre politicians voted down amendments that the *Verband der Deutschen Juden* demanded for the maintenance of interdenominational schools.[64] Also straining relations between Jews and Catholics was the Centre Party agitation for "parity". Over the years educated middle-class Catholics resented the Protestant monopoly in the academic professions and in the high offices of government and complained about a bias against the employment of Catholics in the state bureaucracy.[65] Around 1901 Centre politicians began to argue that Catholics should enjoy "parity" in status with the Protestants in the civil service and that the proportion of the German population that was Catholic should be a guideline in making appointments to public offices. In Catholic demands for "parity" the Jews saw a crude system of quotas incompatible with

---

[61]*Stenographische Berichte über die Verhandlungen des preussischen Abgeordnetenhauses*, 8th February 1901, p. 1237.

[62]*Ibid.*, p. 1232; Marjorie Lamberti, 'The Jewish Struggle for the Legal Equality of Religions in Imperial Germany', in *LBI Year Book XXIII* (1978), pp. 107, 111.

[63]Lamberti, *Jewish Activism in Imperial Germany*, pp. 147–148, 155.

[64]*Ibid.*, pp. 152–153.

[65]Ronald J. Ross, *Beleaguered Tower: The Dilemma of Political Catholicism in Wilhelmine Germany*, Notre Dame 1976, pp. 20–22.

the principle of equality of rights.[66] They contended that "parity" could not be official policy because the Federal Law of 3rd July 1869 stipulated that eligibility to hold public office should not be conditioned or restricted by religious faith.

The prospects for organising a Jewish *Zentrum*, Toury's third alternative, were slight. Jewish Left Liberals had many sound political reasons for rejecting this strategy.[67] The Jewish population constituted 0·95 per cent of the German population in 1910. The Jewish vote was too small to elect representatives to the *Reichstag* and Prussian parliament on a Jewish platform. Even in cities where the Jews were heavily concentrated, only in two or three districts could they hope to tip the scale in favour of any candidate by voting as a bloc.[68] The majority of Jews did not wish to constitute a separate bloc in German politics. They felt themselves to be German and were striving for social integration and equal rights and not for separate rights as a distinctive group. Politically-conscious Jews were convinced that the Jews could fight antisemitism effectively only within the German party system. A Jewish *Zentrum* would accomplish a prime goal of the antisemites by isolating the Jews in public life. But apart from the "Jewish Question", there was a host of interests and issues, principles and ideals, that determined how Jews voted and what political parties they joined.

To view the history of the Jews in Imperial Germany as a problem of the psychology of self-delusion – explaining why the Jewish Liberals misread political reality and engaged in politics on an unrealistic basis – is to assume that the Jews had many political options and that the Jewish defence movement missed opportunities to be more effective. The strategy of the *Centralverein* casts in relief the dilemma of German Jewry in political life. The predicament of the Jews was described with sober realism by Fabius Schach, a Jewish journalist, in 1912:

> "We have often called it an unhealthy situation that the Jews in Germany are forced to belong to the Progressive Parties because the others are almost all imbued with antisemitism. As circumstances stand today, a change cannot be contemplated for the time being."[69]

Except for the Left Liberals, Germans on all sides of the political spectrum lacked the will to oppose antisemitism. The Conservative, Centre and National Liberal Parties had their own brand of antisemitism. The Social Democrats did not go beyond verbal blasts against the antisemitic Pan-German nationalists and feudal reactionaries and did not participate in earnest in the fight for Jewish civil equality. Regarding the menace of antisemitism lightly, Social Democrats were joking in the *Reichstag* by 1913 that "the antisemitic movement has collapsed in such a lamentable and pitiful way".[70] The Progressives were the most conscientious defenders of Jewish rights, but at times they were half-hearted and were not willing to put Jewish interests in the forefront of their concerns. Besides the

---

[66]Fabius Schach, 'Parität', *Im Deutschen Reich*, January 1902, pp. 2–7. See also *Im Deutschen Reich*, December 1901, pp. 652 ff.

[67]Hermann Cohn, 'Die deutschen Juden und die Reichstagswahl', *Allgemeine Zeitung des Judentums*, 5th April 1907, pp. 162–163; Lamberti, *Jewish Activism in Imperial Germany*, pp. 62–63; Paucker, *loc. cit.*, pp. 505–506.

[68]Pulzer, *loc. cit.*, p. 191.

[69]*Israelitisches Wochenblatt*, 25th October 1912, No. 43.

[70]*Stenographische Berichte über die Verhandlungen des Reichstages*, 20th June 1913, p. 5652.

nightmare of revolutionary workers, antisemitism did not seem to liberal voters as imminent a danger as Socialism.

Jewish options in politics were limited. Middle-class Jews did not shift to the Right when nationalism and fear of Social Democracy changed the political orientation of the liberal bourgeoisie.[71] Antisemitism made it impossible for the Jews to come to an accommodation with the Hohenzollern political establishment and to affiliate with any of the parties to the right of the Left Liberals. The Jewish bourgeoisie remained in the vanguard of democratic liberalism and supported the declining Progressive Parties, which stood for a free-enterprise economy and a pluralistic and free society based on equal rights.

The idea of a Jewish *Zentrum* was an unrealistic response to the Jewish dilemma in politics. The Jews could not advance demands from a leverage position as did the Catholic minority. The Jewish vote was insignificant; for no party, including the Progressives, was it worthwhile to make a special bid for the Jewish vote.[72] The Catholic Centre Party could exert influence because it commanded a mass constituency and was in a position to form governmental coalitions in parliament.

The most acceptable and pragmatic political choice available to the Jews in Imperial Germany was a small party of Liberals whose power to change government policy was limited and whose rational argumentation and appeals for justice could not influence those people most vulnerable to antisemitic rhetoric. In the parties on the Right the Jew was usually a baptised Jew. In the Social Democratic Party the Jew cast off his Jewish group identity when he ascended to the heights of Marxist universalism. Only in the ranks of the Progressives did the Jew fight for political equality and retain his loyalty to the Jewish community. Christian Left Liberals expected the Jews to look and talk like Germans and continued to express disapproval of Jewish "separateness" in social life. But they also had the rare honesty to criticise Christian exclusiveness and a rudimentary respect for social pluralism not found elsewhere on the German political spectrum. The fact that the Liberals made the defence of Jewish rights a matter of conscience and principles did much to sustain the faith of the Jews in the fair-mindedness of the Germans and made their political isolation seem less ominous.

---

[71]Paucker, *loc. cit.*, p. 494.

[72]Pulzer, *loc. cit.*, p. 196. Pulzer estimates that Jewish voters provided 7–10 per cent of the total Progressive vote.

On the Jewish Struggle for Religious Equality in Prussia 1897–1914

BY MAX P. BIRNBAUM

I

Ismar Freund, the historian and Jewish activist, pronounced in 1911 the goal which he was to pursue in the next twenty years:

> "The road to the complete emancipation of the Jew leads by way of the emancipation of Judaism."[1]

Marjorie Lamberti in her recent studies has directed much of her research to the illumination of the beginnings of this political struggle in Wilhelminian Germany.[2] Since its successful culmination during the Weimar Republic is one of the main subjects of my own research,[3] I would like to add a few notes to her excellent presentation.

To gain the right perspective one fact must be stressed: the problem of religious equality became most acute in Germany's largest state: Prussia. Religious affairs and education were left to the individual states, some of which – like Baden and Württemberg – created central Jewish organisations comparable to the hierarchies of the Christian churches. Lamberti deals only with Prussia where 75 per cent of the German Jews lived, and I will do likewise.

II

The efforts to attain recognition of Judaism on an equal footing with the two main Christian churches antedate the *Verband der Deutschen Juden* (VDJ) which was founded only in 1904. Before that time the *Deutsch-Israelitischer Gemeindebund* (DIGB) had represented the interests of the Jewish communities *vis-à-vis* the State since 1869. The VDJ was created with the full consent and cooperation of the DIGB, because the latter was by its statute forbidden to pursue "political discussions" and the forthcoming School Law made such political and parliamentary intervention necessary.[4]

---

[1]'Staat, Kirche und Judentum in Preussen', in *Jahrbuch für jüdische Geschichte und Literatur*, XIV, Berlin 1911, pp. 109–138.
[2]These notes will mainly refer to her essay 'The Jewish Struggle for the Legal Equality of Religions in Imperial Germany', in *LBI Year Book XXIII* (1978), pp. 101–116, and to ch. 7 'Lobbying and Government School Policies', in *Jewish Activism in Imperial Germany. The Struggle for Civil Equality*, New Haven 1978, pp. 130–175.
[3]A history of the *Preussischer Landesverband jüdischer Gemeinden* which is to be published in the Schriftenreihe wissenschaftlicher Abhandlungen des Leo Baeck Instituts.
[4]Cf. Walter Breslauer, 'Der Verband der Deutschen Juden (1904–1922)', in *Bulletin des Leo Baeck Instituts*, VII (1964), No. 28, p. 349.

Its statutory limitations, however, did not hinder the DIGB from expanding and intensifying its activities in the late 1890s under the leadership of Martin Philippson.[5] One result was the creation of the *Verband der jüdischen Lehrervereine im Deutschen Reich* in 1895. This led to a more active involvement in the problems of Jewish religious instruction in the smaller Jewish communities. Following a resolution of its *Gemeindetag* in Frankfurt a. Main in 1896, the DIGB on 8th January 1897 submitted a petition to the Prussian Ministry for Religious Affairs and Education to introduce Jewish religious instruction in all state schools with Jewish students.[6]

From 1886 rules regarding religious instruction for Christian minorities had been promulgated by the Ministry. These rules applied to Catholic children in Evangelic schools and vice versa. Religious instruction for such minorities in public elementary schools was mandatory, if there were at least twelve such children in a school. No such obligation existed for Jewish children.[7] The situation in the secondary school system was different. Generally, these schools were not confessionally separated and provided Jewish religious instruction, if there was a sufficient number of Jewish students. But this applied mostly to larger towns and cities with relatively many Jewish high school students. The main purpose of the petition of the DIGB was therefore to bring a similar relief to the hundreds of financially distressed smaller Jewish communities.

True to the method of the Prussian ministerial bureaucracy, so vividly depicted by Lamberti, the petition was left unanswered. After almost two years – in the autumn of 1898 – three board members of the DIGB were received in audience by the Ministerial Director Dr. Kügler, head of the Education Department.[8] He seemed to show great understanding, but the high expectations raised by this audience proved to be unfounded. After prolonged negotiations the Ministry finally issued a decree to all its *Regierungs-Präsidenten*, the so-called *Kügler'sche Erlass*, of 13th May 1899 – U III E 2265, U III D.[9] Referring to the Law of 1847 governing the Jewish communities, Kügler repeated the obligation of these communities to provide and pay for the religious instruction of Jewish schoolchildren. He acknowledged that – in cases where no public Jewish elementary school existed – this involved the hiring of a special religious instructor

---

[5]Cf. Johanna Philippson, 'The Philippsons, a German-Jewish Family 1775–1933', in *LBI Year Book VII* (1962), pp. 110–111, and Jacob Toury, 'Organizational Problems of German Jewry. Steps towards the Establishment of a Central Organization (1893–1920)', in *LBI Year Book XIII* (1968), pp. 59–66.

[6]*Mittheilungen vom DIGB*, No. 48 (August 1898). I am using Lamberti's translation of the name of the Ministry: *Ministerium der geistlichen und Unterrichtsangelegenheiten*.

[7]A few larger local communities, however, provided Jewish religious instruction in their public elementary schools on a voluntary basis. In the Rhineland and Westphalia a number of towns even had communal Jewish elementary schools, although the Law of 1847 did not envisage such institutions.

[8]This audience was arranged by the journalist Max Adalbert Klausner. More about him and Kügler in Lamberti, 'The Prussian Government and the Jews. Official Behaviour and Policy-Making in the Wilhelminian Era', in *LBI Year Book XVII* (1972), pp. 6–12.

[9]For the full text of this decree see Ismar Freund, *Die Rechtsstellung der Juden im preussischen Volksschulrecht*, Berlin 1908, pp. 240–241. This comprehensive work was commissioned by the VDJ for its negotiations regarding the *Volksschulunterhaltungsgesetz* of 1906. It contains in over 400 pages all relevant laws, decrees and regulations.

who had to have the qualifications of an elementary schoolteacher. The Ministry fully recognised that this obligation constituted a heavy burden on many small and distressed Jewish communities, and Kügler even mentioned their repeated petitions for support. Nevertheless he blandly declared: "However, I have no means at my disposal for subventions to the Jewish communities to hire religious teachers." Instead he proposed that the local (Christian) school-societies should voluntarily introduce religious instruction for their Jewish pupils. In that case he would be ready to subsidise these school-societies, provided they and the Jewish communities were found to be needy. Even this promise was further hedged by the condition that such a subsidy could only be granted, if there were at least twelve Jewish children in any one school.

The decree displays the hypocrisy typical of the Prussian government. It insisted on the different treatment of Jewish and Christian religious minorities in the schools and, while professing the will to help, imposed plainly impossible conditions on such assistance. It was obvious that there would hardly be any school-society – itself needy – willing to assume the responsibility suggested in the decree, especially since the small and poor Jewish communities almost never had the required minimum of twelve children in any one school. The decree therefore remained without practical significance. Nevertheless it contained for the first time the official acknowledgment – vague and circumscribed as it was – that the State, in imposing the obligation for religious instruction upon all Jewish communities,[10] also assumed a certain responsibility to help them fulfill this obligation if they were financially unable to do so. Thus it was the basis on which the VDJ and DIGB proceeded in 1906–1908 when the new *Volksschulunterhaltungsgesetz* ("School Law" in Lamberti's paper) gave them the opportunity to assert the Jewish claims again.* Lamberti mentions the result of these efforts: the acceptance by the government of a resolution in the Prussian House of Deputies in 1906 requesting it to subsidise Jewish communities with regard to Jewish religious instruction. She again touches on this subject in connection with the Cassel–Campe proposal and a suggestion by the Undersecretary of State Dr. von Chappuis.[11] Although in chapter 7 of her book[12] the fate of this resolution is dealt with at some length, the following details may further illuminate its role in the continuing struggle for state subsidies.

The 1908 state budget of the Ministry for Religious Affairs and Education contained under chapter 121, title 43 for the first time a budgetary position in support of Jewish communities. Because this happened in response to the above mentioned resolution, the budgetary position was generally called the *Resolutionsfonds*. Out of it needy Jewish communities would receive subsidies to the cost

[10]Section 62 of the Prussian 'Law regarding the Conditions of the Jews' of 23rd July 1847, exempted Jewish schoolchildren from participation in Christian religious instruction, but explicitly stipulated: "Every *Synagogengemeinde* is bound to take such measures that no Jewish child of school age will be without the necessary religious instruction."

*See also the essays by Peter Pulzer, 'Why was there a Jewish Question in Imperial Germany?', pp. 144–145; and Geoffrey G. Field, 'Religion in the German Volksschule, 1890–1928', pp. 67–69, in this volume of the Year Book – (Ed.).

[11]*LBI Year Book XXIII* (1978), pp. 104 and 114. Lamberti refers to "Chappius", but he is listed in the Minutes of the House of Deputies 1913 (col. 13126 and 13169) as "Chappuis".

[12]*Jewish Activism* . . ., pp. 153–154 and 160–163.

of Jewish religious instruction for children in elementary schools. The amount – 40,000 Mark – was small enough, but what made it almost as ineffective as the *Kügler-Erlass* were the conditions attached to its distribution, the most damaging one being again the demand for a minimum of twelve children. Although the Ministry changed its previous narrow interpretation and allowed the collection of children from several adjoining communities in one place of instruction,[13] the thin distribution of the Jewish population in the rural districts and small towns made the creation of such district installations very difficult. Therefore the DIGB could submit claims for only seventy-four Jewish communities and request subsidies in the aggregate amount of only 21,280 Mark.[14] Not even this amount, however, was granted. On 14th November 1908, the Ministerial Director von Schwartzkopff, the "father" of the School Law, authorised the provincial governments to check these claims and allow the necessary subsidies (U III E 3408 U III D). The results were minimal.

The DIGB, therefore, asked the Ministry on 27th January 1909, to reduce the minimum from twelve to eight children in view of the different demographic situation in the Jewish as against the Christian communities. But Schwartzkopff refused any further concession (Decree U III E 1395 of 23rd June 1909). A treatment of the Jewish communities more favourable than that for the Christian minorities could not be justified and would lead to remonstrations by the churches.[15]

A report of the DIGB – probably for the year 1910 – comes to the conclusion that only about 6,000 Mark of the *Resolutionsfonds* were distributed in that year: 2,800 Mark for seven communities in East Prussia, 2,100 Mark for eleven communities in the province of Hessen-Nassau and 1,200 Mark for a few communities in Pomerania. In view of the hundreds of Jewish communities which had to raise extremely high taxes and were in desperate need of financial support, this was really a dismal result.

Nevertheless the *Resolutionsfonds* or rather the considerations which led to its creation were to play a significant role in the ultimate success of the struggle for state subsidies. Already in 1913 – in the debate about the Cassel–Campe proposal – several deputies hinted at the possibility of expanding this budget position and widening its applicability. Cassel accepted this suggestion under the condition that the amount of 40,000 Mark would be raised very considerably.[16] Lamberti mentions that even Chappuis adopted the idea in 1914.[17]

When under the Weimar Republic – and after renewed struggles and setbacks – state subsidies were finally granted in 1925, they were divided into two budget provisions. The one for the remuneration of rabbis, analogous to the large

[13]The different attitude Lamberti reports for the district of Cassel (*Jewish Activism* . . ., p. 162) was later overruled.
[14]The VDJ directed the parliamentary negotiations in connection with the School Law. The practical implementation, however, was left in the hands of the DIGB. The Ismar Freund Archive at the Central Archives for the History of the Jewish People in Jerusalem, file No. IX T/4, contains a comprehensive report of the Secretary General of the DIGB, Dr. Wilhelm Neumann, about these negotiations.
[15]*Mitteilungen vom DIGB*, No. 74 (September 1909), pp. 148–150. Cf. *Jewish Activism* . . ., p. 163.
[16]*Minutes of the Prussian House of Deputies 1913*, col. 13170 and 13245.
[17]*LBI Year Book XXIII* (1978), p. 114.

Struggle for Religious Equality 167

amounts the State spent for the two main Christian churches, was distributed by the Ministry itself. Although the budget provided 200,000 Reichsmark (RM) annually for this purpose, the Ministry distributed in the eight years 1925–1932 a yearly average of only 125,000 RM, a trifling amount compared to the church subventions. The second budgetary position, however, not only showed in its formulation a clear reference to the *Resolutionsfonds*, but was originally planned as a mere extension of it.[18] It was listed as "Subsidies for needy Jewish communities for the purpose of meeting their obligation to provide religious instruction" and amounted to 250,000 RM which from 1927 on were raised to 400,000 RM annually. The amount was divided between the two central associations of Jewish communities in Prussia for distribution among their members.[19]

Since the restrictive conditions of the *Resolutionsfonds* no longer applied, almost the entire amount was utilised; only in 1931 and 1932 did the government reduce the subsidies in the course of its general austerity measures. Thus considerable relief could be brought to hundreds of needy Jewish communities and their religious teachers.

III

Marjorie Lamberti mentions that the split between the liberal and the orthodox elements among the Jewish population was cited in 1913 and 1914 by Chappuis and his subordinates as one of the reasons against the granting of state subsidies.[20] In an earlier essay[21] she has shown how these same officials together with their counterparts in the Ministry of the Interior manipulated the internal Jewish differences already in the years 1905–1909 in order to hide the true intentions and tendencies of the government. In this connection she could demonstrate that the extreme orthodox circles played right into the hands of the government. Since this same scenario was repeated time after time and lasted well into the period of the Weimar Republic, it should be noted that also in 1913 the separatist orthodoxy remained true to style. During the debate in the Prussian House of Deputies on 2nd April 1913, the Social Democrat Adolf Hoffmann hinted at the opposition of orthodox Jews against the Cassel initiative and even mentioned numerous letters to this effect which he had received.[22] He certainly was not the only recipient of such protests. But this was not all. In the continua-

---

[18]Ismar Freund prevented this, mainly because the pre-war *Resolutionsfonds* was in the meantime submerged in a general discretionary fund. Freund, therefore, insisted on a clearly marked, separate budget position.

[19]Those associations were both founded in 1922. They were the *Preussischer Landesverband jüdischer Gemeinden* with 650–700 members of all religious persuasions (liberal or reform, conservative and orthodox), representing over 90 per cent of Prussian Jewry, and the *Preussischer Landesverband gesetzestreuer Synagogengemeinden* with about ninety members including the ultra-orthodox four secessionist congregations in Berlin, Cologne, Frankfurt a. Main and Wiesbaden, and representing approx. 5 per cent of the Jewish population. The budget position was divided among them on the basis of 7:1 and later 5:1 in consideration of the relatively greater need of the smaller organisation.

[20]*LBI Year Book XXIII* (1978), pp. 111 and 115.

[21]*LBI Year Book XVII* (1972), pp. 12–13.

[22]*Minutes of the Prussian House of Deputies 1913*, col. 13183/13184 and 13188.

tion of the same debate on 3rd April von Campe himself suggested the formation of a central organisation of the Jewish communities in Prussia as a pre-requisite for the granting of subsidies.[23] This prompted the *Freie Vereinigung für die Interessen des orthodoxen Judentums* (FVJ) in Frankfurt a. Main as the representative of the separatist movement to address a petition to the House of Deputies on 9th April 1913.[24] The FVJ could support the Cassel–Campe proposal only, "if the subsidies are directly distributed by the government to the various Jewish communities". Every central organisation of the Jewish communities in Prussia would imply the worst violation of the freedom of conscience ("schlimmster Gewissenszwang"). It added disparaging remarks about the DIGB and advised again against "impossible conditions" for the granting of subsidies. Although the early dissolution of the House of Deputies made this petition obsolete,[25] it shows that the Ministry could always count on the backing of Jewish ultra-orthodox opinion in its own desire to frustrate constructive measures for the Jewish community in Prussia.

IV

The position of the Orthodoxy during the debates about the *Volksschulunterhaltungsgesetz* of 1906 was a different matter. Lamberti, in dealing with this law in chapter 7 of her book on Jewish activism in Germany, goes deeply into the intricacies of the inner-Jewish differences in religious and political outlook. This is a dangerous field, and it would require a long and comprehensive analysis to arrive at a balanced and objective picture. Without going into a detailed critique, it may suffice to cite a few facts which show the complexity of the background against which the controversies about the desirability of separate Jewish schools developed.

(a) The importance of Jewish elementary schools for the Jewish communities and consequently their interest in them was greater in the rural districts and smaller communities than in the larger cities, especially the four big Jewish communities of Berlin, Breslau, Frankfurt a. Main and Cologne which already in 1910 comprised almost 50 per cent of the Jewish population in Prussia. One of the main reasons was that the more affluent Jews in these cities sent their children mostly to high schools.[26]

(b) The VDJ was dominated by these four largest Jewish communities and by a preponderance of liberal Jews, many of the reform persuasion, whereas the

---

[23] *Ibid.*, col. 13240. See also Viereck (col. 13170) and Winckler (col. 13242). This suggestion was originally made by Chappuis in the Budget Commission, although the same Chappuis had tried to prevent such an effort by the DIGB in 1909, another example of the dishonest and deceitful tactics of this official.

[24] *Der Israelit*, No. 21 (22nd May 1913), pp. 1–3.

[25] For the same reason the Cassel–Campe proposal was not actually "defeated" as Lamberti states in *LBI Year Book XXIII* (1978), p. 112, but never came to a vote.

[26] The figures, cited by Lamberti (*Jewish Activism* . . ., p. 164) refer only to children in elementary schools. For the relatively high percentage of Jewish children in High and *Mittel* Schools see the source cited by Lamberti (*ibid.*, p. 217 n. 152). That the situation was the same in other German states is shown in her note 157.

DIGB historically and by its statutes was more concerned with the fate of the hundreds of smaller communities many of which tended to be religiously conservative or orthodox.

(c) The secessionist ultra-orthodox movement which never comprised more than 5 per cent of the Jewish population in Prussia had its centre in Frankfurt a. Main and the surrounding territory of the Cassel district. Here was also the greatest concentration of small rural Jewish communities which therefore were of prime concern to the orthodox FVJ. They were governed by laws of the former Electorate of Kur-Hessen, dating from 1823 and 1833, and maintained many elementary Jewish schools, most of the one-classroom category. Their teachers were also – in the absence of a rabbi – the religious leaders and cantors of these communities.

To secure the existence of these schools was for them therefore not only a question of education but of crucial importance for their whole religious life. That under these circumstances the FVJ could not accept the position of the VDJ with regard to the desirability of separate Jewish schools is obvious. Moreover, their initial effort to coordinate the procedures of the two organisations was repudiated by the VDJ.[27] The latter, therefore, must in this case share the responsibility for the disarray in the Jewish opposition to the government's proposals.

(d) According to Lamberti the leaders of the VDJ were motivated by the liberal idea of interconfessional schools. There is no doubt that this was their ideological underpinning. But the true motivation goes deeper. In their desire to merge into the overly nationalistic German landscape the Jewish school became for them the symbol of Jewish separateness. Lamberti herself cites enough evidence for the fatuity of this argument.[28] The claim of a Berlin high school teacher that those educated in Jewish schools "would be at a disadvantage later in pursuing certain vocations"[29] totally ignores the real situation in Germany at that time. Antisemitic attitudes directed against the employment of Jews were certainly not influenced by the type of school the candidate had attended. The fact that the Jewish Community of Berlin had kept a *Mittelschule* since 1826 and Frankfurt a. Main a Jewish *Gymnasium* since 1804, in both cases under a liberal régime and despite the generally interconfessional character of German high schools shows the inconsistency of the arguments against Jewish elementary schools. In fact, the leaders of the VDJ, far from being champions of civic equality, in the case of the School Law turned out to be champions of inequality. What really motivated them was the fear that the Jewish schools and their teachers would strengthen the Zionist movement among the younger generation. This almost panic fear of Zionism and the resultant polarisation of Jewish organisational activities lasted until the very advent of Nazi rule.[30] That – several years

[27] *Ibid.*, p. 147.
[28] *Ibid.*, pp. 138–139 and 167–168.
[29] *Ibid.*, p. 169.
[30] The Leo Wolff Collection of the archives of the New York Leo Baeck Institute contains under II 19 No. 2 a letter of Bruno Woyda to the leader of the Liberal Fraction in the *Repräsentantenversammlung* of the Berlin Jewish Community, dated 1st February 1933, in which he vehemently argues against the continuance of several elementary Jewish schools which the previous Zionist administration of the community had founded in 1927.

after the issuance of the School Law – it also affected the DIGB which had been basically a defender of the Jewish schools was in part due to the "Richtlinien" debate of 1912–1913 and the heightened animosity it engendered between the Liberal majority and the Conservative–Orthodox–Zionist minority.[31]

V

Majorie Lamberti's presentation gives the impression that Article 40 of the School Law of 1906 initiated the obligation of the communes to contribute to the costs of elementary schools which were maintained by Jewish communities.[32] This obligation, however, and the criteria for computing such contributions were stipulated already in Section 67 No. 3 of the Law of 1847, governing the Jewish communities. Article 40 of the new School Law maintained "the existing regulations regarding the creation, maintenance and administration" of public Jewish elementary schools with the one significant improvement that Section 67 No. 3 of the Law of 1847 should now be applied to the entire territory of the State.[33] This affected mostly the former Electorate of Kur-Hessen (practically identical with the district of Cassel) with its many small Jewish schools. Here the new law offered indeed for the first time the opportunity to obtain contributions from the local communes. This explains the preponderance of cases from this district which needed the attention of the Ministry, as Marjorie Lamberti reports.

VI

In one respect I feel Marjorie Lamberti is open to correction and that is in her judgment of the Social Democrat Adolf Hoffmann (1858–1930),* whom she accuses of "antisemitic rhetoric" and "crude antisemitic humour".[34] One cannot take his remarks out of the context of his speeches on that day which were part of his general struggle for the separation of State and Church and the main thrust of which was directed against the close relations between the Ministry for Religious Affairs and the central institutions of the Evangelic Church, a relationship which Marjorie Lamberti herself confirms.[35] Hoffmann, called "The Ten Commandments Hoffmann" because of his pamphlet *Die Zehn Gebote und die besitzende*

[31] Cf. Walter Breslauer, 'Die "Vereinigung für das liberale Judentum in Deutschland" und die "Richtlinien zu einem Programm für das liberale Judentum"', in *Bulletin des Leo Baeck Instituts*, IX (1966), No. 36, pp. 302 ff.
[32] *Jewish Activism* . . ., pp. 156 ff.
[33] The territories Prussia acquired after 1847 (mainly the provinces of Hannover, Hessen-Nassau and Schleswig-Holstein) kept their older laws and regulations regarding the Jewish communities (cf. Lamberti in *LBI Year Book XVII* (1972), p. 6). For the text of these laws and of the Law of 1847 see Ismar Freund, *Die Rechtsstellung der Synagogengemeinde in Preussen und die Reichsverfassung*, Berlin 1926, pp. 47 ff.
*For Marjorie Lamberti's differing assessment see also her essay 'Liberals, Socialists, and the Defence against Antisemitism in the Wilhelminian Period', pp. 157–159, in this volume of the Year Book – (Ed.).
[34] *LBI Year Book XXIII* (1978), pp. 111–112.
[35] *Ibid.*, p. 102.

*Klasse*³⁶ was anything but an antisemite. He was loved by his friends and feared by his opponents for his earthy Berlin humour, and his speeches elicited laughter from all sides of the house. His argumentation against Cassel was certainly full of exaggerations and errors, especially when he counselled the Jewish communities to keep their "independence" from the State in contrast to the Churches. These communities were subject to considerable state supervision and even interference under the laws applying to them and quite justified in asking for compensating help from the State. But basically Hoffmann took the established position of the Social Democratic Party which was opposed to all state subsidies and the entire involvement of the State in religious affairs (a position which has found its strongest expression in the First Amendment to the American Constitution). Hoffmann had a longstanding personal animosity against Cassel from their encounters in the Berlin municipality where Cassel used his dominating influence against the Social Democrats,³⁷ and because Cassel often professed his German patriotism in an excessive way, as was not unusual among Jewish Liberals in those days.³⁸ But all this has nothing to do with antisemitism against which Hoffmann had fought vigorously on previous occasions, especially during the Stoecker period. The crude joke in verse which he quoted was not directed against professing Jews but against Jewish careerist converts to Christianity and can hardly be termed "antisemitic". The present author will attempt to show in his forthcoming publication that Hoffmann was more sympathetic towards Jewish interests in the early days of the Weimar Republic than his fellow ministers and that he was the only one who in this respect antagonised the bureaucrats in his ministry.

---

³⁶Berlin 1891.
³⁷Ernest Hamburger, *Juden im öffentlichen Leben Deutschlands. Regierungsmitglieder, Beamte und Parlamentarier in der monarchischen Zeit 1848–1918*, Tübingen 1968 (Schriftenreihe wissenschaftlicher Abhandlungen des Leo Baeck Instituts 19), pp. 368–369.
³⁸Werner T. Angress, 'The German Army's "Judenzählung" of 1916', in *LBI Year Book XXIII* (1978), pp. 133–134.

Zionism and Jewish Orthodoxy

BY HERMANN GREIVE

In the scholarly literature on the early history of Zionism the relationship of the young Jewish national movement to religious Jewry – generally treated as an entity, with little regard for the diversity of religious attitudes – is depicted consistently as one of clear-cut antagonism. This applies equally to specialised investigations dealing with a particular phase or aspect of the development – such as David Vital's *The Origins of Zionism*[1] or Jehuda Reinharz's *Fatherland or Promised Land*[2] – and to comprehensive studies, such as Walter Laqueur's handbook, *A History of Zionism*.[3] The treatment of the issue in Walter Laqueur's book may be regarded as typical, reflecting as it does the perplexities involved in approaching this problem:

> "If the liberals found, however reluctantly, some redeeming feature in Zionism, the leading East European Rabbis regarded it as an unmitigated disaster, a poisonous weed, more dangerous even than Reform Judaism ... A few orthodox Rabbis such as Reines gave it their blessing and established a religious faction within the Zionist movement. But Orthodoxy in Germany, Hungary and countries of Eastern Europe rallied in order to be able to fight the national movement more effectively [inter alia by founding the Agudat Jisrael]."[4]

There is undoubtedly a great deal of truth in this statement, and yet, it is wrong. Was it really the liberals who by and by discovered some "redeeming feature" in Zionism? And precisely what brand of liberalism is supposed to have arrived at such a conclusion? Should it be the liberalism exemplified in Herzl's life style? He, indeed, believed in religion – not, to be sure, in its dogmas nor yet in its laws and customs as a binding code for his personal conduct – be believed in religion as a living power capable of moving the masses, moving the "people" (whatever that may mean). As for Jewish Orthodoxy in Germany, what were its real objectives? And just what does the term designate? Is it the German rabbis as a whole? Or perhaps only the fairly liberal managing board of the Rabbinical Association (*Rabbinerverband*)? Treated in so cursory a manner, it is not surprising that the significance of the relationship between religion and nationalism in terms of Jewish history, and, more particularly, the ambivalence of that relationship were not properly understood. A superficial reading of the anti-Zionist comments from religious quarters creates the overwhelming impression of a straightforward antagonism, with exceptions such as the *Misrachi* and its supporters only serving to prove the rule.

[1]Oxford 1975.
[2]*The Dilemma of the German Jew, 1893–1914*, Ann Arbor 1975.
[3]London 1972. See also Stephen M. Poppel, *Zionism in Germany 1897–1933*, Philadelphia 1977. This author ignores the problem altogether, which is at least as unsatisfactory.
[4]Laqueur, *op. cit.*, p. 407.

Yehuda Eloni, in his essay, 'Die umkämpfte nationaljüdische Idee',[5] departs from this accepted interpretation. Brief as his remarks on the subject are – compressed into four pages of his lengthy paper – they adumbrate a new and more differentiated approach, leading to a far better appreciation of the multifaceted character of both Zionist and anti-Zionist utterances and to a clearer picture of the vicissitudes of the Zionist movement in Germany. We shall return to this point in the course of the present study, which in several respects is using Eloni's observations as a starting point for an exploration of the subject in more detail and at greater depth.

I

Beginning in the era of absolutism and mercantilism, the expansion of trade and production brought about a drastic shrinkage of the domain in which religion ruled supreme. It was a practical critique of religion in the realm of hard facts, which in the realm of ideas went hand in hand with the theoretical critique by the philosophers of the Enlightenment, presenting a momentous challenge – the greatest challenge since the time of the Reformation – to the representatives of the religious institutions as well as to the flock of the faithful, to the people at large, whose organisational ties and emotional commitment to the institutions tend to be far more enduring than is commonly assumed. The magnitude of this challenge emerges clearly, even for the modern reader, in the accounts given by ecclesiastical historiography of trends such as Gallicanism or Josephinism. The process by which important spheres, notably politics and economic life, as well as culture (with the accent on its secular elements) were freed from religious supervision – or by which, seen from a different angle, the individual was set free as a political, economic and cultural agent – must have appeared in Christian eyes as something utterly destructive both for religion (the meaning of which was about to be redefined in terms unacceptable to the traditionalists) and for the spheres now divorced from it. And much time was to elapse before it came to be realised not only by individuals but by the religious communities, too, that this freeing from religious control could also be interpreted as a freeing of religion itself. Indeed, this learning process is still in progress. The trend of secularisation was most clearly manifested in the abolition of ecclesiastical principalities, abbeys of princely status and similar institutions, accompanied by a drastic curtailment of the landed property of the Church. This substantial loss of power on the part of the religious authorities would appear to be a welcome development from the point of view of a critique of religion, and it has in fact been welcomed more or less outspokenly by historiography; yet, it should not be forgotten that it was not the individual citizen who benefited by a corresponding relaxation of tutelage and oppression, but that the powers lost by the ecclesiastical authorities were taken over by the secular state and the groups controlling it.

[5]In *Juden im Wilhelminischen Deutschland 1890–1914*. Ein Sammelband herausgegeben von Werner E. Mosse under Mitwirkung von Arnold Paucker, Tübingen 1976 (Schriftenreihe wissenschaftlicher Abhandlungen des Leo Baeck Instituts 33), pp. 633–688.

This loss of tangible powers was paralleled by developments at the grass roots: there was a growing tendency to flout the spiritual authority of the Churches; their dominant role at parish level became progressively weakened; and there were signs of an incipient trend to discard moral notions and behaviour patterns traditionally associated with Christianity. In the face of such trends, hardline attempts to defend and preserve the *status quo* proved ineffective. This prompted endeavours to redefine the boundaries of the religious sphere in the light of the changed situation, so as to build a solid basis for the re-establishment of religious influence, this time with the assistance of the new State and its legislation. It goes without saying that this could not be achieved without compromising on decisive issues. On the other hand, the Churches saw themselves obliged to test and apply new methods, adapted to the changed circumstances, in order to safeguard religious interests. In the sphere of religious practice, a notable development was the extension and intensification of private worship to supplement the traditional classical liturgy (the psychological impact of which was in any case weakened within the orbit of the Catholic Church by the use of the alien Latin language). This trend, fostering the emotional ties that bind the faithful to the religious institutions, went a long way towards compensating for the loss of the Churches' external authority by a far-reaching internalisation of religious influence. The press, too, played an increasing part in moulding public opinion. Finally, in keeping with the development in other social spheres, various groups and organisations were formed with the aim of safeguarding and advancing religious interests and objectives; in the Catholic camp this development led eventually to the emergence of a separate political party. In the Evangelical camp there was no need for that, at any rate not in Prussia where the leading churchmen moved freely in the circles of the political and military élite and thus were able to exert their influence most effectively.

The Churches, in brief, had managed not merely to survive the tremors of the closing years of the eighteenth and the first half of the nineteenth century, but to adjust to the changed circumstances and thus hold their own to a surprising extent in the face of the critique of religion put forward by the Enlightenment and the radical Young Hegelian philosophers. Nevertheless, the idea of a secular state practising indifferentism in religious matters remained suspect to all Orthodoxies.

These upheavals had a profound effect on the position of the Jews and Judaism. Jewishness, up to that time, had been defined in terms of religious affiliation, but on the basis of a very wide concept of religion, covering almost the entire legal sphere, social conduct and vital sections of "private" life. The growth of state control affected the Jewish communities, if anything, even more deeply than it did other religious groupings, and the impact was greatest where old forms of Jewish self-government had remained intact. The dismantling of the Jewish "state within the state" – a precise parallel to the dissolution of the guilds and corporate Estates – was bound to cause anxiety and alarm among the exponents of traditional Judaic culture and learning, who carried considerable weight in the counsels of the communities, for they saw that the whole edifice of Jewish life – and that included the religious life of Judaism – was being shaken to its foundations. Hardest hit by the crisis were the men in whom traditional authority had been vested, the rabbis who derived their credentials from the mastery of traditional Jewish learning, from a knowledge of Judaic law. They stood most to lose, as under the old dispensation their privileged position had been underwritten by the State, in Prussia, for instance, by the *General-Juden-Reglement* of 1750, which set the seal of the sovereign's approval on the rabbi's exercise of authority.[6]

The outward manifestations of decline were in many respects much alike in the Jewish and Christian communities, although some features emerged more starkly in the former owing to the exceptional status of the Jews. More and more communities, especially in the East, were brought to financial ruin, while individuals, on whom the State now made direct claims, tended to break away from what was felt to be the tutelage of religion and religious institutions. The intellectual armoury for this trend was provided by the philosophy of the Enlightenment. Old rules, rooted in the autonomous constitution of the communities, such as the ban on resorting without need to non-Jewish courts of law, were increasingly disregarded. There was no way of halting this development, especially as certain spheres of modern life, above all the economy, characterised as it was by the industrial revolution and the upsurge of capitalism, clearly eluded regulation by the traditional Talmudic law. Moses Mendelssohn's contention that religious bodies and their representatives had in principle no right to impose sanctions on individuals was wholly consistent and in keeping with this development.[7]

In Prussia the traditional order was undermined by the Edict of 11th March 1812, which thus permitted the Jewish communities to be considered as private associations and by so doing put an end to the royal endorsement of rabbinical authority. This change did not only mark a further step on the road of "freeing the individual", it also introduced an important shift in the balance of power within the communities, which of course continued to exist under the new dispensation. The managing boards of the communities, already strong, now acquired a dominating position at the expense of the rabbis. Naturally, the boards welcomed the change. In Leopold Auerbach's words, they looked upon "this freedom from constraint, this liberation from interference either by the state or by a spiritual leader, a so-called rabbi ... as a boon".[8] One could manage without the rabbi: that was the message widely proclaimed and partly acted upon. It meant a decisive weakening of Jewish traditionalism, and at the same time a further strengthening of the economically strong, for it was the rich, the upper stratum, who invariably controlled the community boards. Accordingly, the communities now showed a far greater readiness to compromise on questions of Jewish separateness and the acceptable limits of adaptation to non-Jewish life styles. In such decisions the boards were markedly influenced by economic interests. Thus, the progress was not so much emancipatory as econo-

[6]Leopold Auerbach, *Das Judentum und seine Bekenner in Preußen und in andern deutschen Bundesstaaten*, Berlin 1890, p. 294.
[7]Cf. Mendelssohn's preface to Menasseh Ben Israel, *Rettung der Juden*, Berlin 1782, and Mendelssohn's *Jerusalem oder über religiöse Macht und Judentum*, Berlin 1783.
[8]Auerbach, *op. cit.*, p. 292.

mic, with the upper stratum the main beneficiary. The subsequent development
– at least till the middle of the century – consolidated the position of the boards
yet further. The Prussian Law of 23rd July 1847 on the status of the Jews recognised the Jewish communities as "synagogue congregations" with the character of bodies corporate; it reintroduced compulsory membership and conferred
upon the members of the boards the status of civil servants in the employment of
state-sponsored bodies, whereas the rabbis remained private individuals, "private officials of a corporation" (*Privatbeamte einer Korporation*).[9] This state of affairs
was not changed by the subsequent Prussian Constitutional Act of 1850.[10]

No wonder this trend was viewed by the traditionalist sections of Jewry with
great misgivings and regret, feelings that are still echoed even today in traditional-religious historiography:

> "After the promulgation of the Law [of 23rd July 1847] the synagogue congregations were
> in a position to enshrine the constitutional influence of the rabbi in their own statutes in the
> traditional form as 'ancestral heritage'. They made no use of that opportunity; they refused to
> grant the rabbi the position due to him. Boards and delegates became the administrators of
> religious affairs and education. The rabbis were denied even the right to participate in the
> decisions of the relevant institutions ... Under the Law, the synagogue statutes could have
> vested the rabbi with the rights of a clergyman. Yet, this provision was ignored, and instead,
> full powers were granted to a lay administration of which the rabbi was not even a member.
> The demand for endowing the rabbi with priestly authority was frowned upon as redolent of
> sectarian tendencies."[11]

Thus, unfavourable as the law was from the point of view of religious traditionalism, the Jewish communities went further still.

This situation inevitably engendered a growing mistrust of the mostly "enlightened" liberal boards on the part of the orthodox and pious Jews, especially
in the communities of the large cities. Under the new régime Jews were compelled, according to Munk, to "comply with all decisions of the community
administration, however flagrantly in breach of religious tradition", and they
were even made to "contribute financially towards the cost of community
schemes for cultural purposes proscribed by the religious laws".[12] This was
bound to lead to unmanageable tensions. After a while, the pious Jews were
simply no longer prepared to tolerate such conditions. Tradition still had an
emotional hold on numerically significant sections of Jewry, and their attachment was strong enough to mobilise resistance against the liberal erosion of tradition. And it was precisely the new liberties, above all the religious freedom of
the modern state, that provided the means to that end. Thus a somewhat paradoxical situation arose, in which the circles wedded to tradition, the very people
to whom the ideas of liberalism and the liberal state were alien if not abhorrent,
saw themselves compelled to invoke the liberal principles in defence of their
group interests. It was a stance adopted by both Jews and Christians, and in the

---

[9]*Ibid.*, p. 307; see also pp. 301 f.
[10]*Ibid.*, p. 320.
[11]Michael L. Munk, 'Austrittsbewegung und Berliner Adass Jisroel-Gemeinde 1869–1939', in *Gegenwart im Rückblick, Festgabe für die Jüdische Gemeinde zu Berlin 25 Jahre nach dem Neubeginn*, eds. Herbert A. Strauss and Kurt R. Grossmann, Heidelberg 1970, pp. 134 f.
[12]*Ibid.*, pp. 133 f.

Catholic camp (as noted before) this response culminated in the foundation of a political party to represent religious interests.

The orthodox Jewish groupings, then, organised religious associations of their own, where that seemed necessary and practicable. Thus, *Adass Jisroel* was formed in Berlin in 1869 as a "law-abiding Jewish religious society" (*gesetzestreue jüdische Religionsgesellschaft*). Later, after the so-called Secession Act (*Austrittsgesetz*) of 28th July 1876, separate congregations (*Separatgemeinden*) were set up at several places, notably in Berlin and Frankfurt a. Main. The endeavour of the orthodox groups to run their own affairs was helped by the tendency of the reactionary state in the second half of the century to draw on the support of religion – and this meant religion in its traditional form – for the maintenance of law and order. Under *Reich* legislation, the authority of the rabbi was to some extent restored: the new provisions, "applying within the sphere of validity of the Prussian law of 23rd July 1847 as elsewhere, treated the rabbis in several respects on a par with Christian clergymen".[13]

Thus, religious traditionalism, among Jews and Christians alike, was able in the end to adjust to the changed circumstances. The new order turned out to be less hostile to tradition than had been assumed at first. Orthodox no less than liberal interests benefited from the new principles of the freedom of religion, of opinion, of the press and so forth (to the extent that those freedoms actually existed). Indeed, it was on the strength of those freedoms that it proved possible to overcome the relegation of religion to the private sphere and make it again a matter of public concern.

This was not achieved without prolonged efforts, especially as far as the Jews were concerned. The specific difficulties facing the Jewish traditionalists were largely due to the rapid pace of urbanisation, a process that worked far more slowly among the Christian population than among the Jews. Notwithstanding their partial success, the traditionalists were not really reconciled to the new situation in which all values had become relative from the standpoint of public policy. The new state of affairs was least acceptable to the rural communities with an unbroken orthodox tradition, such as those of Bavaria, whereas the secessionist congregations in the large cities and the surviving relatively autonomous orthodox congregations in the major communities, as for instance in Hamburg, found it less hard to come to terms with the changed circumstances. But all traditionalists, irrespective of such distinctions, were bound to look with profound suspicion upon the principle of the relativity of spiritual values now adopted as a matter of public policy, because it reinforced tendencies to abolish the separation of the Jews from the non-Jewish environment and thus threatened to disrupt Jewry's inner cohesion. Ambivalent as was the attitude of the orthodox to the new situation, their misgivings would predispose them to welcome the idea behind the Zionist rallying cry, and in particular its anti-assimilationist implications. Herzl undoubtedly touched a chord in the hearts of the pious Jews when he poured scorn on the conditions prevailing in the large urban congregations with their liberal boards, characterised by the:

[13]Auerbach, *op. cit.*, p. 308.

"role of the rich, the pliability of some priests, the two-faced striving to combine the old tradition with an exaggerated imitation of indigenous customs, the shameless mendicancy of the economically weak . . ."[14]

That the sally came from non-orthodox quarters did not make it less welcome. Orthodoxy, after all, was not alone in suffering others, outside the fold, to advance its interests whenever possible.

It does not follow, however, that the objectives pursued by the Zionists did not in other respects run counter to those of the orthodox. Such was indeed the case, precisely because Orthodoxy had come to terms with the new order (as will be explained later). But this divergence does not detract from the fundamental affinities; the Zionists, in fact, proclaimed something which Orthodoxy had not so long ago relinquished, most reluctantly and with trepidation lest it lead to a loss of identity: the collective independence of the Jews, transcending the narrow boundaries within which religion had been (or was to be) confined in the course of liberalisation, in other words, Jewish political–social autonomy. Yet, in the traditionalist view this autonomy did not transcend the religious sphere, for the Talmudic religious laws were based on a concept of religion incompatible with that of the Enlightenment. Bearing in mind, then, that that political–social autonomy had been given up only under pressure and not without more or less serious pangs of conscience, it will be readily understood that the renewed demand for it – raised in a secular rather than religious context – posed a deeply disturbing threat to the orthodox self-image. Thus, the alarm and anxiety aroused by the aims of Zionism points to the existence at a deeper level of agreement in principle.

II

The foregoing general remarks on the principles involved are confirmed by contemporary comments on Zionism from religious quarters. In this context I attach particular importance to a number of statements in Hebrew, which have been scarcely noticed in the discussion up to date. The private character of these statements – all but one made in the course of private correspondence – and the fact that they were written in a language intelligible only within a narrow circle justify the assumption that they expressed the true interests of the writers as well as of the groups they represented with greater candour than did the public statements made in German on the same subject.[15]

As a matter of fact, the public statement by the managing board of the *Rabbinerverband in Deutschland*[16] also appears to bear out, or at any rate not to con-

[14]'Der Baseler Kongreß', in *Theodor Herzl's Zionistische Schriften*, ed. Leon Kellner, Berlin–Charlottenburg n.d., pt. I, p. 248.
[15]For German polemics against Zionism see, apart from the statement by the managing board of the Rabbinical Association (to be briefly discussed below), especially Moritz Güdemann, *National-Judenthum*, Leipzig/Vienna 1897, and David Leimdörfer, 'Gegen den Zionismus', in *Allgemeine Zeitung des Judentums*, No. 27 (2nd July 1897), pp. 316 f.
[16]Published in a number of German papers, including *Kölnische Zeitung*, No. 653 (16th July 1897); also quoted in full in Herzl's reply, 'Protestrabbiner', published in *Die Welt*, 16th July 1897, reprinted in *Theodor Herzl's Zionistische Schriften*, I, pp. 211 f.

tradict, the reasoning outlined in the preceding section. To begin with, it should be noted that the initiative in making this public stand came from religious-liberal rather than orthodox circles, a fact clearly indicated by the person of the responsible leading signatory, the Berlin rabbi Sigmund Maybaum. The wording of the statement points in the same direction. The first point made is a religious one, rejecting Zionism on the ground that the foundation of a Jewish state could not be reconciled with the Messianic promise of Judaism. This was a rather threadbare religious argument, easily refuted by religious Zionists, and thus was hardly more than a pretext. Later on, after the First World War, it was rarely repeated, even by religious-liberal quarters. In any case, although in his pamphlet of 1896 Herzl speaks of the "Jewish state", the Basle programme refers only to a "home secured by public law".

The crucial message of the rabbinical statement is undoubtedly contained in the second sentence:

> "Judaism lays upon its professed disciples the obligation to serve with utter devotion the fatherland to which they belong, and to promote its interests wholeheartedly and to the best of their ability."

In so far as this amounts merely to an avowal of loyalty towards the State, the declaration could have been readily endorsed both by religious traditionalists and by Zionists. But in so far as the reference to the fatherland and its national interests was based on the narrow definition of religion in terms of *Konfession*, a bureaucratic denominational category; in so far as it fostered the tendency to work towards the highest possible degree of assimilation and integration of the Jews within the host country, the statement was a typical expression of liberal, and in particular religious-liberal, thinking and thus was not only clearly anti-Zionist, but at the same time also problematical in the eyes of the representatives of traditional Jewish religiosity, most of all those of the old Orthodoxy.

The dispute which flared up in 1897 about the proposal to hold the First Zionist Congress in Munich was followed, according to Reinharz, by a prolonged period during which Zionism was not the subject of major controversies, a lull said to have lasted till 1912, or at least till the Cohn affair of 1906.[17] This statement can be accepted with some reservations, that is to say only in respect of controversies openly conducted in the press. But within the ranks of Jewry, and in particular among Jewish religious circles, the debate on and with Zionism had not ceased, as the documents to be discussed here show.

There is first the letter from the Hamburg rabbi Amram Hirsch to the Vienna rabbis Moritz/Moses Güdemann, Jakob Fleißig and Joseph Samuel Bloch, dated 1899. But it was especially in the years 1902 to 1904 that the controversy was bound to flare up again following the establishment of the religious-Zionist group of *Misrachi*. The organisation was founded at Wilna (Vilnius) in 1902 on the initiative of Isaak Reines; the second conference was held in 1903 at Lida, where Reines was rabbi, followed in 1904 by the first major Congress of the group at Bratislava. At least three, possibly four of the statements to be discussed here

---

[17]On the suspension of Rabbi Emil Cohn from his office in the Berlin Jewish Community because of the propagation of his Zionist views see Reinharz, *op. cit.*, pp. 177–178 and Eloni, *loc. cit.*, pp. 670–672.

date from that period. There is a lengthy letter, dated 1902, addressed by the historian Abraham Berliner to the aforementioned Vienna rabbi Joseph Samuel Bloch, a man who managed to combine his religious function with scholarly pursuits and political activity as a parliamentarian; a further letter from Abraham Berliner to Moritz Güdemann, another of the previously mentioned Vienna rabbis, dated 1903; two letters written in 1904, one from Sinai Schiffer (Karlsruhe) to Dov Bär Ritter (Rotterdam) and one from Nathan Halevi Bamberger (Würzburg) to an unknown addressee; finally a statement by the Görlitz rabbi Baruch Halberstam(m), undated but – as indicated before – most likely belonging to the same period.[18]

The regional spread of these documents will lead us to expect from the outset that the various authors will express a variety of views in their assessment of Zionism: the situation in Berlin was undoubtedly very different from that, say, in Würzburg. These regional differences may possibly provide a basis for drawing further conclusions. In spite of such differences, the arguments displayed in the various statements turn in the main on the same basic points and problems, although the scale of priorities may differ and not every author deals with the whole range of the basic issues. The objections can be classified as (A) *religious* or (B) *existential* or, in terms of the group's status and survival, as *political–social*. Arguments falling primarily into the second category are sometimes linked with religious issues.

As was to be expected, the main irritant from the religious point of view was invariably (1) the "godlessness" of the individuals who set out to deal with the Jewish problems under the aegis of Zionism. Herzl and Nordau could hardly be accepted as leaders of Jewry by people to whom Jewishness had a religious meaning. Berliner, for instance, who repeatedly discusses this point, speaks of "aliens" who "through their deeds are estranged from God and his Torah; who spurn all that is sacred to us", and he notes that "both Herzl and Nordau have repudiated the faith and the law of our people".[19] One is left to wonder how seriously such accusations were meant to be taken, except as expressions of regret over the tardiness of the pious in taking action for Jewry's cause. As Bamberger put it with fine religious ardour:

> "Are we not ready also to receive those who wish to return home, and is not our heart eager also to impart knowledge to the people, and our mouth full as the sea, brimming with praise for the land of Israel?"[20]

The indictment, however, was not confined to the a-religiosity of individuals; behind it there was (2) the a-religiosity of the cause, of the enterprise promoted by Herzl and Nordau, and it seems that this was the main target. To the extent that the two aspects were linked, it may be said that the individuals were attacked for the sake of the cause rather than the other way round. In other words: if only one could become reconciled to the idea, one might come to terms about personalities.

---

[18]The statements are published in *Dovev Sifte Jeschenim*, I and II, ed. Mose Haim Efraim Bloch, New York 1959/1960.
[19]*Ibid.*, I. pp. 82 f.
[20]*Ibid.*, II, p. 253.

The first religious objection to Zionism was put forward on the ground that the ingathering of the people of Israel was destined to come in the Messianic age ushered in not by man but by the hand of God, and that according to religious tradition man must not presume even to accelerate the coming of that age, except by fidelity to the Law. Berliner refers starkly to the "bidding of the King of the World" that man "shall not speed the end".[21] The injunction is accepted here not merely as rabbinical opinion but as the will of God. During the initial stages of the debate a great deal was made of this argument. As we have seen, it was put forward as the very first point in the declaration by the managing board of the *Rabbinerverband*. Yet, it was a poor debating point, easily countered by religious-Zionist spokesmen. They disclaimed any intention to "speed the end", since their object, irrespective of any eschatological significance, was very simply organised immigration and the organisation of collective life in Palestine, activities which, after all, were paralleled by the non-Zionist Orthodoxy. The Messianic argument continued to be used, but as a rule only incidentally and without pressing the point or entering into detail.

The crucial religious objection, however, was not concerned with any partial objective but with Jewish nationalism as such, nationalism as an all-embracing ideology, as the last word on the Jewish question, challenging the primacy of Judaism, of Jewry's religious destiny. An examination of the way in which this objection is formulated yields two points worthy of note. For one thing, direct criticisms of nationalism are less prominent than expected in the Hebrew-language comments with which we are mainly concerned. Second, and no less important, it is on this point that the differences between the various authors emerge most conspicuously and revealingly. It is not possible in the space available here to elucidate these differences in detail. Even so, they are striking enough. When Amram Hirsch in Hamburg speaks of the "national(ist) scandal" and "Zionism run riot", this amounts to a harsh rejection – an emotional rejection at any rate – of that particular form of Jewish self-identification.[22] On religious grounds? Presumably – though he does not say it in so many words. The context in which these remarks are made would appear to point to non-religious rather than religious motives. Berliner, in a similar vein, opens his letter with an emphatic denunciation of the "national" character of the enterprise, "the infamy of the national Zionists".[23] But here again, the context of the remark is concerned chiefly with the existential, political–social peril posed by the movement.

Sinai Schiffer of Karlsruhe also condemns "nationalism", and in particular the combination of nationalism with religion. Yet, by comparison with the rest of his utterances, his comments on this point seem to strike an almost conciliatory note. "As if the living God were not among us, God forbid!" is his only religious response in this connection, after which he hastens to turn to the argument of "security and protection", that is what he considers the dangerous Zionist illusion that Israel would find security and protection in a state of her own.[24] In

[21] *Ibid.*, I, p. 83.
[22] *Ibid.*, II, p. 267.
[23] *Ibid.*, I, p. 82.
[24] *Ibid.*, II, p. 264.

contrast, Nathan Bamberger of Würzburg, who like his father, Seligmann Baer, can be regarded as a spokesman for the regional Jewry of Southern Germany, avoids any attack on nationalism as such. At a point in the course of his remarks where this opportunity offered he confined himself to a sarcastic remark about the Zionist propensity to wax eloquent about "the people". "I have noted with amazement," Bamberger said, "that Rabbi Reines never stops writing about the people; for does it not say (in the Midrash) . . .: the people consists only of sinners." [25] That Baruch Halberstam(m) of Görlitz, son of the *Hasidic* Zaddik, Hajjim ben Leibusch of Sandez, does not raise the issue of nationalism as such in his relatively brief statement appears to be less significant.[26] His rejection of Zionism is decisive enough, though prompted not by religious reservations in the face of the national idea as such, but by other motives which will be discussed later.

It is in quite a different context that the religious aspect of the debate comes into its own, and that is where it concerns the claim of the religious Zionists to be acting not merely in a way permissible under the religious laws, but – in contrast to those holding aloof – to have chosen the one and only course sanctioned by religious tradition. It is at this point, where the pious non-Zionist Jews have to answer the charge of infidelity to tradition, that the argument becomes really animated as well as discursive. And here the anti-Zionist disputants are clearly on the defensive. Striving laboriously, they are hard put to it to refute the contentions of the religious Zionists whose case, seen in retrospect, seems anything but cast-iron. One has the impression that behind a show of utter confidence in the rightness of their own position and the fallacy of the religious-Zionist theses, these writers were beset by gnawing doubts, and were driven on by their anxiety to prolong the argument. In the light of religious tradition it is perfectly clear that living or settling in the land of Israel – which is the point at issue here – is preferable by far to living outside the land, so that the pious Jew cannot lightly dismiss the idea. The only line of reasoning open to him is to show that it is not the right step to take here and now. But some doubt remains as to whether those who go are not after all the better, and those staying behind the less conscientious Jews.

The question of settling in *Erez Israel* is broached in all five statements. Halberstam(m) takes up a rabbinical dictum cited by the religious Zionists: "He that walks but four ells in the land of Israel will be pardoned all his sins." It is significant that this traditional saying is concerned above all with the individual's innermost feelings of guilt and how to overcome them. In criticising the use of this maxim in the Zionist cause, Halberstam(m) writes accordingly:

---

[25] *Ibid.*, II, p. 254.

[26] Yet, there were prominent *Hasidic* figures who saw more clearly than most that the propagation of national unity might accelerate the breakdown of religious unity, and that in this respect nationalism and Zionism posed a threat to religion. Thus, the Lubbawitscher Rebbe Schalom ben Schneersohn said in the course of a statement in 1903: "It is clear, therefore, on ideological grounds that the Zionist ideal has not only failed to bring near those who were far from Israel, but has even driven them further away. Moreover, it has even led right-thinking Jews to uproot from their hearts every concern with the holiness of the Torah, faith in God and the fulfilment of the active commandments. By that it has taken from them the basis of the obligation of Torah and commandments altogether, and has planted instead the belief that through nationalism they are complete Jews." (*Zionism Reconsidered. The Rejection of Jewish Normalcy*, ed. Michael Selzer, London 1970, p. 13.)

> "Does not the essence of all redemption and salvation ... reside in the salvation and redemption of the soul from the bond of evil desires coming from the 'other side' [i.e., the side of evil] ... and as for those who are not in the least willing to cease from their malice out of reverence for God, how can living in the land of Israel help them?"[27]

The other four writers discuss the question of settling in Palestine with reference to another traditional saying cited by the defenders of Zionism: "Whoever lives outside the land [of Israel] is like a worshipper of graven images." This saying, it should be noted, is directed in the main to the social aspect, to the collective function of religion: the worshipper of graven images stands here not so much as a private sinner, but rather as one guilty of disloyalty, one who breached the solidarity of the chosen people, thus causing scandal. The rabbis appear to be harassed by the thought of the obligation implied in that saying, which they discuss at length, from the quasi-enlightened Abraham Berliner to the *Landjude* Nathan Bamberger, rooted in a long and almost unbroken tradition. Berliner returns twice to the subject and seems to be more deeply touched by it than Bamberger, who dismisses the supposed obligation with relatively calm assurance:

> "What point is there in raising the question of settling in the land of Israel? There is no disagreement among our authorities as to whether settling in the land of Israel is a duty in this age [of the diaspora] ..."[28]

And, whatever some authoritative commentators may have said, Bamberger continues, it is no use invoking their testimony, for "they themselves, indeed, did not immigrate".[29] This "proof" in the name of authority also appears in the statements by Hirsch[30] and Berliner.[31]

Nevertheless, despite such sharp rejections of these Zionist arguments, not one of the pious authors considers the matter closed. This is particularly striking in the cases of Hirsch and Schiffer, both of whom confirm the religious significance of settling (or residing) in the land of Israel and go on to interpret this obligation in a peculiar manner. Sinai Schiffer discusses in this context the awkward position of Ramban (Rabbi Mose ben Nahman, 1194–1270) and arrives at the following conclusion:

> "Thank God, I too have looked into the books and immersed myself in the study of this Halakhah; and I found something which to my knowledge has not been noted either by the earlier or the later Ramban commentators: it is the fact that our rabbi, does not cite the version of the six orders [of the Mishna and the Talmud], [Tractate of] Ketubbot, available to us, but that the text he saw said: Whoever *leaves* the land [of Israel] and lives outside it is as a worshipper of graven images."[32]

From this it follows that "according to Ramban's system, the duty to live in the land of Israel is indeed prescribed by Torah, and this applies to our age as well, but only to those already residing in the land".[33] Amram Hirsch reasons along similar lines.[34]

---

[27] *Dovev Sifte Jeschenim*, I, p. 208.
[28] *Ibid.*, II, p. 254.
[29] *Ibid.*, II, p. 255.
[30] *Ibid.*, II, p. 269.
[31] *Ibid.*, I, p. 84.
[32] My italics. H.G. Cf. Keth 110b.
[33] *Dovev Sifte Jeschenim*, II, p. 265.
[34] *Ibid.*, II, p. 269.

This revealing turn in the argument, this tortuous "yes-but" in the defensive campaign against Zionism, setting out to prove that immigration, though permissible, was not mandatory, suggests that those pious Jews felt deeply stirred and boldly challenged by the message of Zionism, and that the strength of their reaction – which seemed to grow in vehemence the more concessions they had made already in the compromise with the "modern world" – betokened close affinity rather than an unbridgeable gulf between the two trends.

Only when leaving the religious for the secular sphere do the rabbis in their critique of Zionism muster sufficient detachment from the object of their assessment. The change is tangible in all the statements here under review. It is expressed even by the old-orthodox Bamberger, more clearly by Berliner and most emphatically of all by Halberstam(m) whose piety bears the stamp of East European *Hasidism*.

Berliner in his letter refers to it repeatedly (and he returns to the topic elsewhere). The Zionists, he points out, have nothing better to do than

> "to make us into enemies and revolutionaries in the countries in which we live, and to spread among all peoples the fear that Jews are a menace to them. That is why I am in great fear."[35]

And it seems that it was that fear in the first place that impelled him to write. This has little to do with religion, except perhaps indirectly. "The danger is great," he goes on musing: "Who can fail to see that the tiniest tittle of slander against Israel is enough to spread over the whole world?" All too often, Berliner writes, an "unholy alliance" is conjured up, under which

> "the antisemites, with Zionist support, will in turn intensify their activities in order to eliminate and exterminate the Jews, God forbid. Who knows what the day will bring for us."[36]

In conclusion and as the crowning touch of his plea, he combines the criticism of the religious-Zionist settlement idea (be it noted, from a purely defensive posture, lest the existence of a great deal of common ground become too obvious) with the danger theme:

> "In my study of Meiri [on the Tractate of] Berakhot, Chapter 3, I found precious words, which the Zionist rabbis, too, ought to hear. They run as follows: There are things in the face of which Torah authorises us to override injunctions laid down in writing in the Torah itself – out of respect for living creatures. I devoured his words like a premature fruit before the summer. And I have to add: even if the injunction to return to the land of Israel, to restore the rule and to make common cause with reprobates were written in Torah, be it in the most rigorous terms, it should be far from us to observe such an injunction in the face of peril to life."[37]

This is one of the most revealing passages in any of the statements here under review. One notes Berliner's profound relief at his find (as he "devoured his words like a premature fruit"). At last he feels able to shed the religious misgivings about the rejection of the Zionist settlement demand; at last he has found in the religious literature, in an authoritative commentary, a text that justifies his opposition. And what appears to be the true reason for his negative attitude – whether or not Berliner himself understood and acknowledged this – that is, the

---

[35] *Ibid.*, I, p. 84.
[36] *Ibid.*, I, p. 85.
[37] *Ibid.*

danger posed by Zionism and his grim forebodings of fateful consequences, now turns out to be a legitimate ground for rejecting the demand: for danger overrides the religious injunction. Both elements are here thrown into sharp relief: the weight of the duty implied by the religious laws, however controversial, and the weight of the envisaged danger.

The consideration of the danger to Jewry appears in all the statements, and there is no need to cite the individual formulations of this theme.[38] At a first glance it may seem surprising that Baruch Halberstam(m) of Görlitz, son of a *Hasidic* Zaddik, should be scarcely less exercised than Berliner about the danger conjured up by Zionism. Had he adjusted as much as the others to the liberal order (to the extent that it had actually been established) so that the abolition of the equality of legal status posed an equal threat? (In his letter to Güdemann, Berliner uses the German term, referring to "bittul ha-Gleichberechtigung".[39]) Berliner speaks of the "viper-like snake" of Zionism, which would throw Israel into unprecedented confusion, and he goes on:

> "With my heart weighed down by worry, I ask my Jewish brethren: who will stand by us in the time of need, when the peoples will call to us: Out with you, fomenters of sedition, there is no room for rebels in our land!"[40]

This argument is markedly less prominent only in the statement by Nathan Bamberger. (There is, of course, no objective yardstick for minor differences of emphasis.) Bamberger, like Berliner, uses the same argument to refute the obligation to settle in Palestine. Yet, his approach is substantially different, and not only because he does not invoke the fear of death. The common point of departure reveals all the more clearly the divergent development of the argument. Those who held the settlement injunction to be binding must abide by it, Bamberger said. For the rest,

> "Rabbi Reines is in duty bound to announce to the Israelite community the names of all those who have decided that it is permissible to set at nought the words of all our teachers who have warned us not to return to the land [of Israel] and found a state there, and that it is permissible also, for the sake of complying with the injunction to settle in Israel and founding a Jewish state, to kindle the flames of hate in the hearts of the inhabitants of the country [in which we live] and to provide leadership for the antisemites by giving them useful advice on how to transport the Jews in chains to the land of Israel."[41]

This statement is vigorous enough, and yet, it has a different ring. Bamberger, too, disagrees with the Zionists; but it seems that the religious-Zionist interpretation of the settlement injunction does not strike him to the same degree as abstruse, and he is less perturbed than, say, Berliner by the Zionist call for the national rallying of the Jews. As for the crucial question regarding the fundamental relationship between nationalism (as an ideology) and religion, Bamberger does not even mention it.

It goes without saying that the political–social argument relating to the existential threat can be presented with a religious hue, and that it is genuinely of

---

[38]Cf. in particular *ibid.*, II, pp. 271 and 263 f. for relevant comments by Hirsch and Schiffer respectively.
[39]*Ibid.*, I, p. 90.
[40]*Ibid.*, I, p. 209.
[41]*Ibid.*, II, p. 255.

religious significance in the minds of theologians like the authors of the statements here under review. Whenever the existence of the people of Israel is at stake, then, viewed from the religious angle (Jewish and Christian alike) the fate of religion hangs in the balance also. This point needs no elaboration here, the less so as it does not figure prominently in those statements. None the less, it is touched upon, for example by Amram Hirsch, who writes:

> "If, God forbid, the devil's handiwork were to come to fruition, and we were to return to the land [of Israel], then, God forbid the threats of punishment and curses would be fulfilled. I cannot believe it could be the will of God that an alien, one who does not belong, should sit on David's throne . . ."[42]

Hirsch argues that the Zionist activities, noxious in themselves, are endowed with a particularly ominous and menacing quality by the fact that Zionism is set against the will of God and represented by men notorious for their infidelity to the law.

Amram Hirsch's observation points to what may be an even more significant aspect: the threat to the Jews is seen in relation to the situation not only in the diaspora but also in Israel itself. Berliner is most explicit on this point. In his letter to Güdemann he declares roundly "that the Islamic and Christian inhabitants of Palestine will never agree to bow to the yoke of a Jewish government".[43] In his letter to Bloch he expresses the same fear in the form of a question: "Does it not appear that if the peoples truly hate us, we have to be doubly afraid if, God forbid, we are gathered in one place?"[44]

All these objections to Zionism were based on the liberal premise of the need for integration in the host country, now seen as fatherland. Where the ideas of the Enlightenment had been absorbed and assimilation had reached an advanced stage – as in the cases of Berliner and Schiffer – this reasoning led naturally to an open and explicit avowal of the formula propagated by the *Centralverein*:

> "I and all members of my community are with our hearts and our minds devoted to our homeland. In accordance with the laws of the state, we are sons of the German people and the Israelite religion."[45]

Summing up the results of our analysis, it emerges that the rabbis' critique of Zionism clearly is not what it has generally been held to be, namely a predominantly religious critique. Moreover, in so far as it is religious it is less radical than it is in its secular strictures. It emerges that the rabbis' stand was prompted above all by the fear of the "grave peril" to which they kept referring, the political–social threat to Jewish existence which in their view was bound to materialise in response to a unifying anti-assimilationist movement such as the Zionist one. Misgivings of this kind invariably appeared wherever the liberal state and social pluralism had been accepted in principle, that is to say primarily in the liberal camp. But the traditionalist religious circles, too, and even sections of the old Orthodoxy had resigned themselves to the new order and come to terms with it in varying degrees. If this interpretation is right, the criticisms of the Zionist revival of a separate group consciousness will be the sharper and the

[42] *Ibid.*, II, p. 269.
[43] *Ibid.*, I, p. 92.
[44] *Ibid.*, I, p. 83.
[45] *Ibid.*, II, p. 265 (Schiffer) and I, p. 91 (Berliner).

more fundamental, the more liberal the critic's own point of view. And this is precisely the trend that can be observed, and increasingly so with the passage of time: it was liberalism that became the foremost adversary of Zionism.

This relationship is reflected in the statements here under review, notably in the difference between the statements by Bamberger and Berliner. On the other hand, it must be remembered that it had been a very bitter pill for the traditionalist circles to have had to acquiesce in liberalisation and its consequences: the loss of power by the communities, the downgrading of religion to a denominational category and concomitantly the end of the primacy of Judaism and Jewishness as an all-embracing influence dominating both social life and the conduct of the individual. Now that Zionism was proposing to reinstate Jewishness as the dominant attribute of the individual Jew and to re-establish Jewry (like the congregation of old) as a community embracing all spheres of life and thus transcending the bonds of religion in the narrow sense of the Enlightenment, it is understandable that the emotional (rather than principled) reaction of the traditionalists was the more vehement the more painful the loss of the old order had been for them. If what Zionism wanted to achieve was feasible, then the surrender of the old positions had been unnecessary and the accommodation to the new circumstances fruitless. Accordingly it was felt that it *must not* be feasible, for the sacrifice rendered to modern development simply *must not* have been in vain. As in the controversy about settlement in Palestine, strident criticism cannot conceal the fact that at a deeper level there is a great deal of common ground between Zionism and its traditionalist critics. In both cases the tenor of the critique is liberal–religious rather than traditionally religious.

The existence of that common ground, which can be inferred only indirectly from the political–social critique, is made more clearly manifest in the religious discussion, in particular the settlement controversy. No one denies that an obligation exists; the point at issue is whether it is binding here and now. And here again, the vehemence of the reaction appears to be in proportion to the concessions made – with a bad conscience – to modernity. In some respects, the Zionists demanded precisely what the orthodox should have demanded in loyalty to their own principles, and herein lay the challenge. That, shocked and shaken, they responded with charges of "calumny and malicious slander"[46] illuminates both the common elements and the gulf between Zionism and Orthodoxy.

III

There was no inclination in the Zionist camp to accept the need for antagonism with Orthodoxy. Quite to the contrary, prominent Zionists tended from the outset to bank on orthodox support. Were they mistaken? If so, then – at least to some extent – precisely because Orthodoxy was no longer as orthodox as it used to be. Even before Herzl, Bodenheimer had attempted to work in that direction, partly – in the Cologne Circle – with success. In spite of his upbringing in a highly assimilated Stuttgart family, and although he was not religious in the

[46]*Ibid.*, I, p. 82 (Berliner); II, p. 253 (Bamberger); II, p. 271 (Hirsch).

dogmatic sense nor an observant Jew, he joined forces in 1890 with the Cologne rabbi Abraham Salomon Frank in founding the Association for Jewish History and Literature (*Verein für jüdische Geschichte und Literatur*) with the intention of promoting "national" aims.⁴⁷ How far the rabbi was able and willing to proceed along that path – in view both of external circumstances and the mood in the liberal-religious camp – is another question. At any rate, Bodenheimer was not deflected from his determination to make common cause with the orthodox. Undeterred by the quarrel over the venue of the Congress, he wrote to Ernst Kalmus on 20th September 1897, shortly after the Basle Congress:

> "I hope . . . you will not be discouraged in the pursuit of the noble aim of attracting Orthodoxy more closely to our cause. Thanks be to God, there still are orthodox Jews in Germany as elsewhere who will follow the dictate of their sensitive hearts and join the ranks of our movement."⁴⁸

Up till now, it has been customary in assessing this reaction to point out that, though such Jews existed, there were not many of them. It may be opportune to look more closely into the question why, in the face of liberalisation imposed from above (by the governing boards of the communities), there were any orthodox Jews who responded to the Zionist call.

Herzl – also assimilated and not committed religiously, although he was in touch with religious tradition through his parental home and in particular the person of his father⁴⁹ – felt and acted no differently than did Bodenheimer. "What! you do not understand the imponderable? And what is religion? Consider, if you will, what the Jews have endured for the sake of this vision over a period of two thousand years", he wrote in a letter to Baron Hirsch in 1895.⁵⁰ That was his kind of religious faith and to this he held on. That he did not get very far with the fairly liberal Moritz Güdemann, whom he repeatedly approached,⁵¹ nor later on with the neo-orthodox Hirsch Hildesheimer is hardly surprising. Both of them had come to accept the idea of integration – no matter whether out of conviction or necessity – as well as the Enlightenment's concept of religion, and thus could not be expected to cross over into the other camp. In the course of the development outlined in the opening section of this study, the necessity of learning to think on new lines had been turned into the virtue of an essentially universal (that is to say, emphatically not national) prophetic religion of inwardness, admitting of any kind of pluralism. (Seen in perspective, there was a parallel development in the Christian camp. It is no accident that the *völkisch* reaction of Germanic Christendom began to gain ground at the very time when Jewish nationalism gathered strength.)

Herzl wrote in 1895:

⁴⁷Cf. Hans Martin Klinkenberg, 'Zwischen Liberalismus und Nationalismus. Im Zweiten Kaiserreich (1870–1918)', in *Monumenta Judaica (Handbuch)*, ed. Konrad Schilling, Cologne 1963, p. 343, and Henriette Hannah Bodenheimer, *Der Durchbruch des politischen Zionismus in Köln 1890–1900*, Cologne 1978, p. 87.

⁴⁸Quoted by Eloni, *loc. cit.*, p. 680.

⁴⁹Leon Kellner relates: "Jakob [Theodor Herzl's father] . . . inherited [his father's] piety. Even as a married man he used to say his prayers daily in *tallith* and *thephillin*." In *Theodor Herzls Lehrjahre (1860–1895)*, Vienna-Berlin 1920, p. 7.

⁵⁰Cf. *The Complete Diaries of Theodor Herzl*, ed. Raphael Patai, transl. Harry Zohn, New York-London 1960, I, p. 28.

⁵¹Cf. *ibid.*, pp. 76 ff., 108 ff.

"That I am not planning anything contrary to religion, but just the opposite, is shown by the fact that I want to work with the rabbis, with *all* rabbis."[52]

In writing this, Herzl – possibly influenced by the all too vivid memory of his father – appears to have underestimated the full extent and depth of the changes that had already taken place. As is shown by his article 'Protestrabbiner', in which he sought to drive a wedge between the protesters and the others whom he still hoped to win over, he did not abandon his attempt to appeal to religious Jewry, but only drew the lesson of the unexpected results of his initial approaches. At the Second Zionist Congress in 1898, he openly and explicitly called for the "conquest of the congregations". Was it just a tactical gambit, as Jehuda Reinharz believes?[53] No doubt it was. But what does that mean? It clearly implies that he believed – rightly or wrongly – in the prospects of such an enterprise.

Herzl's demand was taken up later by Max Kollenscher, who devoted two pamphlets to this topic. The first, *Aufgaben jüdischer Gemeindepolitik*, was published in 1905,[54] the second, *Jüdische Gemeindepolitik*, four years later, following the 1908 Breslau delegate conference of the German Zionist Association, which carried five theses submitted by him.[55] In the latter publication he demanded the transformation of the synagogue congregations into "Jewish people's communities".[56] The *Jüdische Volkspartei* under the leadership of Max Kollenscher and Alfred Klee vigorously pursued these demands, although these activities were viewed rather critically by the official leadership of the Zionist Association, including Bodenheimer himself. Their misgivings were aroused not so much by the aspiration to establish contact with religious Jewry and its institutions, but by the party's confrontation tactics.

Looking at the situation from the other side, what was the attitude adopted in practice by religious Jewry, and Orthodoxy in particular, towards Zionism? Generally negative; the prevailing trend was towards integration – out of conviction or out of fear. Nevertheless, there are some differences of emphasis, which closely correspond to the attitude of the theologians discussed in the preceding section. As Yehuda Eloni noted, "whereas conservative and orthodox circles in the local communities were more approachable in their attitude to Zionism, Neo-orthodoxy [in this respect, it may be added, at one with the liberal-religious circles] . . . rejected the Zionist ideology".[57]

The broader outlook of the conservatives and the old Orthodoxy and their readiness to condone the religious laxity of leading Zionists for the sake of the Jewish cause were noted for the first time at the Basle Congress, when Herzl – who was clearly interested (and not only for tactical reasons) in consecrating this venture with a solemn religious touch – attended the Sabbath morning service on the eve of the Congress (a Saturday) and was called upon to read the week's

---

[52]Letter to Güdemann, dated 16th/17th July 1895, *ibid.*, p. 109; see also *Kitve Herzl*, 9: *Iggerot mereschit ha-pe'ulah ha-zionit ad ha-Kongreß ha-rischon*, ed. Alexander Bein, Jerusalem 1961, p. [17].
[53]Reinharz, *op. cit.*, p. 112.
[54]Posen 1905.
[55]Berlin–Charlottenburg 1909, p. 23.
[56]See also Reinharz, *op. cit.*, p. 121, and Eloni, *loc. cit.*, p. 671.
[57]*Ibid.*, p. 681.

Bible passage.[58] And he was undoubtedly happy to be able to announce in his report 'Der Baseler Kongreß':

> "The Rabbi of Basle [Dr. Arthur Cohn], who was not a delegate but attended the Congress as an observer, requested permission to address the gathering at the last sitting and declared solemnly that he had been a firm opponent of Zionism but had now been converted. And this honest man, whom we respected before, while he was our adversary, has since then been an apostle of our movement."[59]

The differences in the approach to Zionism on the part of various communities and sections of communities and their representatives were tellingly demonstrated on the occasion of the Ninth Zionist Congress, held in 1909 in Hamburg, the only one ever to take place on German soil. The liberal governing board of the community disowned the Congress (how seriously that was meant was to come out only later) on the ground of "a total divergence of views in the political field". That was at least more honest than the Messianic argument against Zionism advanced twelve years before by the managing board of the *Rabbinerverband*. The *Repräsentantenkollegium*, the – reformed – *Tempelverband* and the Portuguese congregation similarly refused to attend the opening session. The traditionalist *Synagogenverband* however marked the occasion with a festive service. The Federation's Chairman, Dr. B. Levy, welcoming the delegates, declared his solidarity with the supporters of Zionism in their common yearning for Zion and their proud avowal of Jewishness: "Together with all of you, let us come out loud and clear in praise of our Jewishness, with you we will proudly proclaim before the whole wide world: I am an *Ivri* . . ." After that, Levy was no longer acceptable as a member of the community board. When the question of his election arose three months later, part of the governing board refused.[60] The significance of the events in Hamburg is not diminished by the fact that one of the Hamburg rabbis, Dr. Nehemia Anton Nobel, was a Zionist. In fact, it is revealing that in a religious community headed by Mordechai Amram Hirsch as Chief Rabbi, whose uncompromising anti-Zionist statement was discussed in the foregoing (he died in 1909, before the Congress), a Zionist like Nobel should have had any chance at all.

In Berlin's neo-orthodox breakaway congregation, too, there were some Zionist tendencies, in spite of Abraham Berliner who, as we have seen, had attacked Zionism no less virulently than Amram Hirsch. *Jüdische Presse*, the paper of Esriel and Hirsch Hildesheimer, which was respected in circles of Germany's Jewish Orthodoxy, became the organ of the religious-Zionist *Misrachi*,[61] a striking development illustrating the ambivalence of the relationship between Orthodoxy and Zionism.

After the First World War Aron Barth, a Berlin *Misrachi* supporter, grandson

---

[58]Vital, *op. cit.*, p. 355.
[59]*Theodor Herzl's Zionistische Schriften*, I, p. 247.
[60]Helga Krohn, *Die Juden in Hamburg, 1848–1918*, Hamburg 1974, pp. 164 f., and *Jüdische Rundschau*, XV, No. 15 (15th April 1910), p. 175.
[61]Jacob Toury, *Die politischen Orientierungen der Juden in Deutschland. Von Jena bis Weimar*, Tübingen 1966 (Schriftenreihe wissenschaftlicher Abhandlungen des Leo Baeck Instituts 15), p. 259; and Mordechai Eliav, 'Ha-"Jüdische Presse". Ittono schel ha-Rab Esriel Hildesheimer', in *Sinai*, 65 (1969), pp. 221–233, in particular p. 223.

of Esriel Hildesheimer and a leading contributor to *Jüdische Presse*, was able to report in his pamphlet *Orthodoxie und Zionismus*[62] that the Zürich Conference of Orthodox Jews, at which the anti-Zionist wing of Orthodoxy had been well represented, had decided to "engage in common activities with the Zionists and seek an understanding with them".[63]

Yet, such examples of accommodation tell only half the story of the orthodox-Zionist relationship. On the one hand, after the foundation in 1912 of an independent orthodox political organisation, the *Agudat Jisrael*, some tensions were bound to arise between two separate organisations with overlapping aims; on the other hand, what the two movements had in common went far deeper than the official statement on cooperation and understanding suggests. The official statement deals with the relationship on the organisational plane and allows only indirect, if any, inferences about the socio-psychological conditions that led to the emergence of Zionism.

It is the situation of East European Jewry that provides the key for an understanding. Here, the underlying pattern can be seen far more clearly. In Eastern Europe, where Judaism and the Jewish community had far longer than in the West remained the most powerful force, dominating all spheres of life, the whole body of Jewry, including the sections given to religious criticism, continued to be strongly committed to tradition and thus provided a mass basis for Zionism. That does not mean that the nature of Zionism was fundamentally different in the West, where it had no chance of becoming a mass movement. The regional distinctions were characterised by Güdemann as early as 1897 with the formula: national Jewishness in the West, political Zionism in the East.[64] In other words, the Western trend of national Jewishness and the political Zionism of East Europe's Jewry alike are inconceivable without religious tradition. Felix Rosenblüth (later Pinchas Rosen), brought up in a strictly orthodox family, described his "conversion" to Zionism in a way that illuminates the traits of identity as well as of divergency, the common basis as well as the element of novelty and thus of strangeness:

> "What happened to me, and later to my brothers and sisters was a kind of sublimation. That is, Zionism was for us a substitute for religion. Our religious fanaticism was recast in the

---

[62]Berlin 1920.

[63]*Ibid.*, p. 58. This conference, convened by the Central Bureau of *Agudat Jisrael*, was held from 18th to 25th February 1919. In its report on the occasion, *Jüdisches Jahrbuch für die Schweiz*, vol. 4, Basle 1919/20, said: "It was an impressive gathering, to which the participants, braving the acute difficulties of travelling in those days, had come from various countries." On the position adopted by the conference with regard to Jewish nationalism, the report said: "The resolutions carried at the conference revealed the remarkable fact that there are no opposing parties in respect of Palestine, the land of our fathers, and that indeed all Jews are at one in wishing to take an active part in the efforts to settle in the Holy Land. However, in the face of a one-sided nationalism, which looks upon the Jews simply as a people like any other of the world's peoples, the conference declared emphatically that the Jewish people is essentially a people of God, for which religion can never be a private or subsidiary affair, a people for which Torah is and remains the basis of life. It remains to be wished and hoped that the circles faithful to Torah – and it is they who constitute the core of the Jewish people – will be allowed the influence due to them in the reconstruction of the Holy Land." (*Ibid.*, pp. 29 f.)

[64]Güdemann, *op. cit.*, p. 4.

mould of Zionism. It was not a flight from religion. The transition from religion to Zionism was fairly natural ... It was simply idealism taking on a new shape."[65]

The possibility of such a transition was given not only for Jews with an orthodox background; it existed wherever the emotional attitude linked with traditional religiosity had retained some of its vitality. A typical case is that of the Berlin barrister Arthur Hantke, rightly described by Richard Lichtheim as a "central figure of German Zionism". From 1909 he was head of the Berlin Central Bureau, from 1910 Chairman of the German Zionist Association. He came from a Jewish middle-class family that was not orthodox, yet attached to religious tradition.[66] A transition of that kind ceases to be possible – or at any rate presupposes a far more radical spiritual transformation – only where another transition has already taken place: the transition to the post-Enlightenment religion of private inwardness, the forerunner of which was *Hasidism* (and among the Christians pietism), and to national identification with a non-Jewish group.

This gives an inkling of what is implied in the statement that Zionism, and in particular the Zionist leadership, manifested in essence a liberal trend. Looking at the first Congress, David Vital said: "Overwhelmingly, they were liberal and modernist in their social and religious tendencies."[67] Modern, no doubt, they were, in the sense that nationalism in general must be held to be a modern movement. And they were liberal also in their own way, though vastly different from the picture of the "typical" liberal Jew accepted by contemporary literature as well as by later writings on the period. Indeed, the typical liberal Jew is characterised by the wish to become integrated with the non-Jewish environment and – provided he is religious – by the interpretation of his Jewishness in terms of one religious denomination among others. Seen from this angle, then, Zionism is anti-liberal, and in the German context forms part of the anti-liberal trend of the closing years of the nineteenth and the first half of the twentieth century. That most of the Zionists were liberal thus implies no more than that they did not feel bound by any dogma or religious law and that they had largely adjusted to the life style of their environment. Yet, in that sense the majority of contemporary antisemites were no less liberal: it is the liberalism of some of the activists of 1848, like Richard Wagner or Wilhelm Marr. And this brand of liberalism is by no means incompatible with a spirit of genuine religiosity at a deeper level, a spirit equally present among non-Jewish anti-liberals of the period. Following the above quotation, David Vital presented an apt thumb-nail sketch of the Zionists assembled in Basle for the first Congress:

> "There were some agnostics. There were a few socialists, notably among the Russian-Jewish students from Berlin. But most were much less interested in social problems than in the problem of the Jews and, having been brought up in the tradition, had an ingrained respect for – or, at the very least, a certain wariness of – religious orthodoxy."

Though only tenuously represented at Basle as well as later, Orthodoxy proper was not the main opponent of Zionism, as is often assumed, but rather its rival.

---

[65] Quoted by Eloni, *loc. cit.*, p. 680.
[66] Richard Lichtheim, *Rückkehr. Lebenserinnerungen aus der Frühzeit des deutschen Zionismus*, Stuttgart 1970, Veröffentlichung des Leo Baeck Instituts, p. 124.
[67] Vital, *op. cit.*, p. 358.

Moreover the group cohesion that played so vital a part in the constitution, development and successful propagation of Zionism – reflected from the outset in the choice of name for the movement – a cohesion that embraced but transcended the consciousness of belonging to the same people, was largely (though not solely) derived from the religious tradition of Jewish Orthodoxy, in particular the old Orthodoxy.

As pointed out on an earlier occasion, the intimate interdependence of Jewish religion and nationalism, whether pulling together or diverging, springs ultimately from the identity of the national reference group. Non-Jewish nationalism as a rule is related not to any one religious grouping but to a minor or major entity comprising several religions or denominations and its emotional appeal is based on the very fact that it transcends religious boundaries. Jewish nationalism, on the other hand must of necessity always remain Jewish, appealing to the same group already defined as Jewish by its religion. The a-religious Jew still remains a Jew, he belongs, whereas the Christian Jew does not. Notwithstanding the subjective a-religiosity of many individuals, Jewish nationalism rests objectively on the Jewish religion, on Judaism.[68]

A similar conclusion was reached in 1916 by Hermann Cohen in his essay 'Religion and Zionism', where he points out in the opening passage that "Zionism equates religion with nationality".[69] This was anything but a philosopher's abstract thesis conceived in an ivory tower without reference to the empirical world. In disputing this identification, Cohen re-interprets the national-religious nexus without dissolving it, and thus presents a description of contemporary reality from a new angle, pointing out

> "that we non-Zionists do not by any means divorce religion from nationalism. Only, we do not consider the two identical, but look upon nationality as an anthropological means for the reproduction of religion. Thus, the other religions are at the same time assured of the tolerance that we claim for ourselves."[70]

The historical truth of either position – the one criticised by Cohen and the one outlined by him – lies in the contemporary efficacy, in the historical action of the national-religious nexus during the relevant period, operating not solely nor primarily (though successfully enough) through the medium of the religious community, but in the first place and more fundamentally through the family:

> "The family is the cradle of religion. Religion does not establish a fellowship of cogitators but it strikes root in the family, and it is out of the family that it raises its progeny. Thus nationality provides the natural condition and foundation for the survival of religion."[71]

The recognition of the familial roots of religion casts light on its emotional character. Religion signifies binding, the establishing of bonds which, through internalisation in the family ambiance, commit the individual to certain acts of identification and certain patterns of conduct accepted as meaningful. The emo-

---

[68]Cf. Hermann Greive, 'On Jewish Self-Identification. Religion and Political Orientation', in *LBI Year Book XX* (1975), p. 45.
[69]Reprinted in *Jüdische Schriften*, II, Berlin 1924, p. 321. The essay was first published under the (inverted) title 'Zionismus und Religion' in *K.-C.-Blätter*, No. 11 (May/June 1916), pp. 643–646.
[70]*Jüdische Schriften*, II, pp. 321 f.
[71]*Ibid.*, p. 322.

tive charge of these patterns of thought and behaviour is group-related, attached to the group as a haven of security, and is thus at least potentially political. It is not surprising, then, that when religion was to be made non-political – that is, the private concern of the individual – political aspiration promptly took on a religious form. The emotive potential of religion remained a political powder keg.

Thus the scene was set for the rise of political antisemitism – post-liberal and anti-liberal – during the latter part of the nineteenth and the first half of the twentieth century, for the corresponding rise of Jewish nationalism, and indeed for many more socio-historical developments over the years, down to the present.

Jews in Confrontation with Racist Antisemitism, 1879–1933

BY WALTER ZWI BACHARACH

I

What was the reaction of Jews to the growing racial antisemitism in Germany? What means were at their disposal, what was the basis from which they could take action against the attacks of the racists?* In order to answer these questions, we must analyse first of all the position taken by various Jewish spokesmen and the reaction of the influential Jewish bodies in Wilhelminian Germany and the decade or so preceding it for it was then that racial antisemitism, both in political groupings and in other national associations began to show itself in an organised form.[1]

There has been much research on the question of Jewish reaction to German antisemitism,[2] but in most of these studies the researchers have dealt with the cultural, religious, social, organisational and political aspects of the question without concentrating specifically on the Jewish stand in the face of the theory of racism.

Among those who inscribed on their banner of antisemitism the renewed claim of "Purifying the Race" from the Jews was first and foremost the journalist and publicist, Wilhelm Marr. Little is known of him personally, but his anti-Jewish fulminations were published widely,[3] the best known of them being *Der Sieg des Judenthums über das Germanenthum*.[4] It has been well established that Marr, with

---

*This essay forms part of a comprehensive work of research on racist ideology in modern German history and German Jewry's reaction thereto. The research has been made possible through grants by courtesy of the Israel Academy of Sciences and the Wurzweiler Foundation, New York.

[1] For more details on *völkisch* nationalism and its organised manifestations, see my dissertation: *The Development of the Race Theory from the View of Ideology toward the Instrument of Political Action – From Chamberlain to Hitler*, Tel-Aviv University 1973, ch. II, pp. 29–56.

[2] See the following essays contributed to three symposiums edited by Werner E. Mosse in collaboration with Arnold Paucker in the Schriftenreihe wissenschaftlicher Abhandlungen des Leo Baeck Instituts, 13, 25, 33; Eva G. Reichmann, 'Diskussionen über die Judenfrage 1930–1932', in *Entscheidungsjahr 1932. Zur Judenfrage in der Endphase der Weimarer Republik*, Tübingen 1965, 1966, pp. 406–407, in particular; Eva G. Reichmann, 'Der Bewußtseinswandel der deutschen Juden', in *Deutsches Judentum in Krieg und Revolution 1916–1923*, Tübingen 1971, pp. 511–613; Arnold Paucker, 'Zur Problematik einer jüdischen Abwehrstrategie in der deutschen Gesellschaft', in *Juden im Wilhelminischen Deutschland 1890–1914*, Tübingen 1976; and see Ismar Schorsch, *Jewish Reactions to German Antisemitism, 1870–1914*, New York, London 1972; Sanford Ragins, *Jewish Responses to Antisemitism in Germany, 1870–1914*, Diss. Brandeis University 1972.

[3] See Paul Massing, *Vorgeschichte des politischen Antisemitismus*, Frankfurt a. Main 1949, p. 7 ff.; Peter G. J. Pulzer, *The Rise of Political Anti-Semitism in Germany and Austria*, New York–London 1964, pp. 44 ff.

[4] *Vom Nicht-confessionellen Standpunkt aus betrachtet, Vae Victis*, 10th edn., Berne 1879.

his innovatory notion of regarding the Jews as a power whose strength was greater than that of Germany's, instituted a marked change in the form of attack against the Jews.[5] For Marr it was not the existence of religious prejudices, but blood, which was the motivating power which lay behind the struggle between Jew and German. "The question we are faced with is not that of exposing the religious prejudices when the problem is a racial one and the differences are inherent in the blood,"[6] he observed. Moreover, Marr specifically avoided attacking the Jewish religion.[7]

Among those Jews who raised their voices against Marr's onslaught was Ludwig Stern, principal of a Würzburg school who published a pamphlet on the subject[8] and, without discussing in detail the apologetics which characterise his writings, it is worth while examining his opening remarks, which reveal the general orientation which motivated him to take his stand:

> "Only a heretic and a fanatic Jew-hater such as Herr Marr, would compare Judaism with the hordes of Chingiz Khan or with the Longobards who settled in the midst of other nations, as Herr Marr claims. Judaism will never assimilate another nationality, nor will it become assimilated. It is not the race, it is not the nationality, which are at the heart of Judaism, rather it is the concept of the single God which is anchored in Judaism, the concept of absolute monotheism. This is an eternal concept, and its bearers will exist for as long as the earth and skies exist. Judaism will assimilate ideas but not nations . . ."[9]

It is somewhat puzzling that Stern presented the idea of monotheism, as embodied in Judaism, against the anti-religious, pagan claim of the power of race and the primary factor of blood, when Marr had not attacked the religious singularity of Judaism. It was important for Stern to point out the authenticity of Jewish history as opposed to what he called "the un-true and the absurd".[10]

One can detect both a feeling of humiliation and a tone of anger in the Jewish reaction. Adolf Lewin, the Coblenz rabbi, strongly refuted a racist attack on Judaism which had been published anonymously.[11] He attacked the "Naturhistoriker" who made typical racist statements and accusations against the Jews. All the non-racist antisemitic declarations of earlier periods were now being revived under the guise of anthropological findings:

> "After the destruction of Jerusalem, the Jews, in their Diaspora, continued to develop within their race according to that which they had inherited at birth and to the teachings of their fathers of two thousand years: segregation from other races, marriage within their own tribe, preservation of their mode of life and their customs (the Statutes of Moses), their tendency for strife, criticism, wandering, trade, and their aversion to physical labour."[12]

Lewin quoted this excerpt from an anonymous pamphlet, in which the "aversion to

---

[5]Massing, *op. cit.*, p. 6; Pulzer, *op. cit.*, p. 50.
[6]Wilhelm Marr, *Vom Jüdischen Kriegsschauplatz. Eine Streitschrift*, Berne 1879, p. 19.
[7]Wilhelm Marr, *Der Sieg des Judenthums*, pp. 7–8.
[8]Ludwig Stern, *Die Lehrsätze des neugermanischen Judenhasses, mit besonderer Rücksicht auf Wilhelm Marr's Schriften, historisch und sachlich beleuchtet*, Würzburg 1879. In addition to Stern, Israel Frederick wrote against Marr in *Die Juden und das deutsche Reich. Offener Brief an das Deutsche Reich*, von F. Sailer (Pseud.), Berlin 1879.
[9]Stern, *op. cit.*, p. 5.
[10]*Ibid.*
[11]Dr. Adolf Lewin, *Separatdruck aus Rahmers Jüdischem Literaturblatt*, Breslau 1880.
[12]Lewin, *op. cit.*, pp. 8–9.

physical labour" was attributed to the "unique Jewish physiology".[13] He rejected these assumptions, and in a defensive posture tried to refute the claim for a "unique physiology" of the Jews. He especially pointed out the contribution of Jews to creativity and manual labour. He was quite aware of the vicious conflict between Jews and their enemies which would arise as a result of the theory of racism. From now on, anyone who did not have German blood flowing in his veins would be considered an enemy of the German people. In this way, the ostracised Jews would paradoxically be joined by many allies who would also be classified in this category of "impure blood".[14]

Moritz Lazarus, the Jewish liberal, who from 1879 on, was active in the Jewish counter-struggle against antisemitism,[15] also contended with biological antisemitism. He denied the deterministic racial principle because:

> "The spiritual similarities and differences are independent of the genealogical factor . . . and what a nation does to them is not mainly inherent in certain objective factors such as origin, language, etc. . . . but rather it is inherent in the subjective views of individuals in the nation, who see themselves as belonging to one unified nation . . . if we were to discuss plants and animals, an expert on wildlife would be the one to classify these according to their different objective markings . . . but with people, we ask them which nation would they like to belong to . . . a nation is a pure spiritual entity . . . it is a spiritual product of individuals, who themselves belong to this product. They are not being a nation, rather they are continuously creating a nation . . ."[16]

Lazarus rejects the theory of race and blood, which he dismisses as vulgar and materialistic.[17]

On the one hand, he espouses a demand for the cultivation of the feeling of belonging to the German people thereby regarding the creativity and heritage of the German nation as being dependent on an arbitrary decision. The contribution of the Jews to such national creativity would serve as a clear-cut answer to those who proudly elevated themselves in the name of the purification of the German blood, at the expense of making the Jews inferior. On the other hand, Lazarus raised an argument which did not differ much from "spiritual racism". This was even more noticeable when voiced by one such as himself, who advocated the integration of Jews and Germans. According to him, the Jew had to preserve his Jewishness in order to attain a high level of German creativity. And this was not a question of prerogatives, rather:

> "We must preserve what is ours as a unique, spiritual race (*als Stamm an geistiger Eigenart* . . .) so as to place it at the disposal of the German national spirit, as a part of its strength . . ."[18]

This attitude has rightly been called "a form of spiritual chauvinism".[19]

Lazarus was the founder of a new scientific school known as *Völkerpsychologie*.[20]

---

[13] *Ibid.*, p. 17.
[14] *Ibid.*, p. 29.
[15] On Lazarus see Schorsch, *op. cit.*, pp. 59–69; Pinchas Rosenblüth, 'Die geistigen und religiösen Strömungen in der deutschen Judenheit', in *Juden im Wilhelminischen Deutschland*, pp. 567–574.
[16] *Was heisst national?* Ein Vortrag von Prof. Dr. M. Lazarus, Berlin 1880, pp. 5, 13, 17.
[17] Lazarus, *op. cit.*, p. 21.
[18] *Ibid.*, p. 38.
[19] Rosenblüth, *loc. cit.*, p. 570.
[20] M. Lazarus, *Über den Begriff und die Möglichkeit einer Völkerpsychologie*, 1851. See also Moritz Lazarus und Heymann Steinthal, *Die Begründer der Völkerpsychologie in ihren Briefen. Mit einer Einleitung hrsg.*

According to this theory, individual psychology could not explain and characterise the cultural creativity of a nation. Such creativity originated in the *Volksgeist*. It is impossible to ignore the Herderist element in Lazarus's views. Herder, in his philosophical writings, added individual characteristics to the "corporative personality", that is to say, *Volk*. According to him, the cultural facts forming a nation were the means used by the nation to express its originality. Herder believed both in the harmony between the general and the particular and between a nation and mankind in its entirety.[21]

The philosopher, Hermann Cohen, criticised Lazarus's view on religion and ethics. His argument cannot be discussed in detail here,[22] but Cohen yearned for national unity where "racial unity" (*Raceneinheit*) would prevail. He disagreed with Lazarus and with the empirical ruling which defined a nation according to external signs, such as language, territory and statistics.[23] Cohen aspired to

> ". . . a more sublime inner unity than that which the statistician will conclude from given experimental material. I desire a representation for my people which will respect the independent, physical singularity (*leibliche Eigenart*) and which will elevate the racial type to the most splendid level of development."[24]

According to Cohen's ideal, the nation would be recognised by the uniform, material physiognomy of its members, for "The Bible was not given to Angels".[25] In order to establish the ideal national character, one which would thrive on the basis of a unifying monotheistic religion, Cohen relied to some extent on the racist argument as well:

> "We must accept the fact that the racial instinct is not mere barbarism – rather, it is a normal longing which can be justified nationally. This natural feeling will become barbaric only if allowed to sink to the level of the political and national removal of those citizens who have another homeland, or those who do not wish to have one . . ."[26]

Cohen went further when he said that the Jews, themselves, believed in this racist theory, and they would have liked to emulate the external expression of German nationalism.[27] Naturally we must not attribute to Hermann Cohen racist trends of thought such as those spread by racial antisemitism. But we cannot ignore his use of this dangerous form of argument. The vagueness and the undefined quality of these phrases led to an ambivalent understanding of

---

von Ingrid Belke, Tübingen 1971 (Schriftenreihe wissenschaftlicher Abhandlungen des Leo Baeck Instituts 21).

[21] J. G. Herder, *Sämtliche Werke*, Hrsg. Bernard Suphan, Berlin 1887, Hildesheim 1967, Bd. II, pp. 131 ff., Bd. XIII, pp. 354–375.

[22] For this see Uriel Tal, *Judaism and Christianity in the Second Reich 1870–1914. Historical Processes on the Road to Totalitarianism*, Jerusalem 1970, pp. 33–36; Hans Liebeschütz, *Das Judentum im deutschen Geschichtsbild von Hegel bis Max Weber*, Tübingen 1967 (Schriftenreihe wissenschaftlicher Abhandlungen des Leo Baeck Instituts 17), pp. 212–219; Rosenblüth, *loc. cit.*, pp. 559–574; Emil L. Fackenheim, *Hermann Cohen – After Fifty Years*, The Leo Baeck Memorial Lecture 12, New York 1969.

[23] Hermann Cohen, *Ein Bekenntnis in der Judenfrage*, Berlin 1880, in Walter Boehlich (ed.), *Berliner Antisemitismusstreit*, Frankfurt a. Main 1965, pp. 136–137.

[24] *Ibid.*, p. 137.

[25] *Ibid.*

[26] *Ibid.*, p. 140.

[27] *Ibid.*

Cohen's words, and it is this very ambiguous, mystical quality which comprises the theory of national racism.[28]

The biological factor was not the main, exclusive factor in the theory of the racial antisemites. They did not regard anthropology as a *science* – they were more interested in an anthropological outlook on life which could be shaped as a weapon in the campaign against the Jews and Judaism.[29] The distinction between the supposedly inferior physiological signs of identification in the Jews and their mental characteristics was not important for this campaign. Ludwig Jacobowski (a Jew) discussing this lack of distinction in the news bulletin of the *Verein zur Abwehr des Antisemitismus*[30] (*Abwehrverein*) warned in a letter to Friedrich Lange that the latter "... was not arguing against the unique external racial characteristics of Jews, but instead, he was opposing the infamous idea of 'The Jewish Spirit' proclaimed by all ..."[31]

Even a liberal personality such as Ludwig Bamberger understood the sociopolitical connotations of the rise of antisemitism. He felt that the growing racism would jeopardise that Jewish-German integration which so many Jews were heavily relying on as the answer to the racist accusation which portrayed them as inferior outsiders.[32]

The Zionists opposed the idea of Jewish-German integration, but this was not always as a result of their recognition of Jewish nationalism as an immanent factor in Jewish history, but rather as a result of the need to find an answer to growing antisemitism. Bernhard Cohn in his pamphlet *Vor dem Sturm*,[33] showed an awareness of the unique quality of racial antisemitism. It was clear to him that the very essence of this hatred was enmity to the State itself, for this antisemitism was not interested in the correction and adaptation of the Jewish citizen but in his dispossession, his exile and even his annihilation.[34]

At the same time, Cohn was aware of the existing racial differences. "If Judaism would want to, and would be able to forego everything, to denude itself of everything, even with the best of intentions, it would never be able to free itself of its racial singularity ..."[35] Judaism is not merely an acquired religion. It is also characterised by its nationalism and its genetic origin (*Abstammung*).[36]

---

[28]See the criticism of Cohen regarding the integration of Jews and Germans: Fackenheim, *op. cit.*, pp. 6–10; Peter Gay, 'Begegnung mit der Moderne. Deutsche Juden in der deutschen Kultur', in *Juden im Wilhelminischen Deutschland*, p. 263.

[29]For this see my dissertation (n. 1), ch. III, pp. 57–116.

[30]On the history of the *Abwehrverein* and the part played by the Jews in it, see Schorsch, *op. cit.*, pp. 80–101.

[31]Ludwig Jacobowski, 'Offener Brief an Herrn Dr. Friedrich Lange', in *Mitteilungen aus dem Verein zur Abwehr des Antisemitismus* (*Mitteilungen*) 1892, No. 44, p. 359.

[32]Stanley Zucker, 'Ludwig Bamberger and the Rise of Antisemitism in Germany, 1848–1893', in *Central European History*, vol. III, No. 4 (December 1970), pp. 332–352. See esp. p. 342: "The major significance of the essay is found in Bamberger's ability to see antisemitism in terms of German politics and emerging racism."

[33]Bernhard Cohn, *Vor dem Sturm. Ernste Mahnworte an die deutschen Juden*, Berlin 1896, p. 5. See also his essay: 'Jüdisch-politische Zeitfragen. Über den Werth des jüdischen Volksthums', pp. 1, 4.

[34]Cohn, *Vor dem Sturm*, p. 5.

[35]*Ibid.*

[36]*Ibid.*, p. 28.

This approach of Cohn's can perhaps be understood as an attempt to persuade his fellow Jews to recognise their natural uniqueness, and to perceive that this singularity would cause the surrounding Gentile society to rise up against them. From here, Cohn reached the gloomy and for those days somewhat revolutionary conclusion, that the Jews of Germany must abandon their country and emigrate elsewhere.[37]

General developments in Germany from the foundation of the *Reich* naturally left their mark on the stance and the reaction of the Jews of Germany to antisemitism in general, and to racial antisemitism in particular.[38] As this type of antisemitism began to penetrate German public affairs only during this period, so, too, the process of forming a political organisation only began then. The theories and views of the racists were already being voiced, but it was still too early to talk of the established policy of antisemitic bodies and organisations. As a result of this Jewish reaction was also essentially academic and apologetic.[39] Such a prophetic outcry as Bernhard Cohn's, to awake now and take drastic action, was rare.

The reaction of the Zionists was different from that of both orthodox and liberal Jews. Liberal Jews rejected the possibility of regarding Jews as a nation having unique ethnological and racial characteristics. They did recognise the religious-cultural singularity of the "Jewish Spirit" but did so as *citizens of the German nation*, or upholders of the idea of universal monotheism. There were those among the Zionists who made use of the current racist theories to present a case for the right of the Jewish people to self-determination. They assumed that "... we do not regard the Jews as a pure race but as a nation having many racial-anthropological characteristics".[40]

Once the political nationalists in Germany began to form themselves into different associations, the Jews in their turn formed organisations, in particular the mainstream *Centralverein deutscher Staatsbürger jüdischen Glaubens**** and the minority *Zionistische Vereinigung für Deutschland*. There was by now an ever-growing awareness in wide Jewish circles of the imminent danger inherent in racial antisemitism, i.e., "scientific antisemitism". This theory, in its new scientific guise, was now acceptable in intellectual circles and Houston Stewart Chamberlain's book *The Foundations of the Nineteenth Century* (1899) is a classic example of the rise

[37]*Ibid.*, pp. 34–37, Bernhard Cohn was more extreme and pessimistic than Leopold Auerbach who was of the opinion that legal action should be taken against antisemitism. Cohn saw the danger such a struggle would entail, for a ruling in favour of the Jews would cause them to forget their awareness of the dangers of antisemitism.

[38]On this development, see my study, chs. I, II, III.

[39]See the reaction of the orthodox Rabbi Heinrich Galandauer, for example. He tried to contradict the attacks and accusations against the Jews with counter-proofs taken from the Bible. His views were published in instalments under the heading: 'Stammesvorzüge und Semitische Racenfehler', in *Der Israelit*, 1893, No. 96; 1894, Nos. 7, 11, 12, 13, 14, 17.

[40]Leopold Laufer, 'Sind die Juden eine Race?', in *Die Welt*, 30th July 1897, p. 10. Max Nordau discussed 'Jüdische Rasseneigenschaften' in his address at the Zionist Congress: *Die Welt*, 3rd September 1897, p. 6.

*See also the essays by Peter Pulzer, 'Why was there a Jewish Question in Imperial Germany?', pp. 141–142; and Marjorie Lamberti, 'Liberals, Socialists, and the Defence against Antisemitism in the Wilhelminian Period', pp. 147–162, in this volume of the Year Book – (Ed.).

of this "scientific" antisemitism.[41] For as Bernhard Elsass wrote, a book such as Chamberlain's was infinitely more harmful than the one-sided and prejudiced opinions lately aired and therefore it was more important at that time to concentrate specifically on Chamberlain's writings.[42]

The suggestion made to the Jewish public to study a certain anti-Chamberlain pamphlet in depth, shows us just how worried some Jews were about the effect Chamberlain's writings would have even on Jews for:

> "The arrogant way in which he makes his assumptions may lead Jewish readers themselves to believe ... that those who belong to the Jewish community are an inferior race, from a cultural point of view.' (*Kulturell minderwerthige Rasse.*)[43]

The racial inferiority of the Jews became the agreed-upon slogan of the different antisemitic political factions and the organ of the *Centralverein* never tired of pointing out the distinctly opportunistic use that racists made of the Jewish Question.

The Gentile *Abwehrverein* supported the major Jewish defence organisation in its struggle against racism. Even though the *Abwehrverein*'s avowed objective – the gradual breakdown of the Jewish community in Germany and its eventual integration with the German people[44] – was not acceptable to most Jews, the two were still in perfect accord when it came to the possible dangerous effects racial determinism would have on the education of the younger generation. Many articles in the association's weekly newspaper were devoted to the refutation of the racist theory in general and of Chamberlain's theory in particular.[45]

Friedrich Hertz, who had devoted a comprehensive study to refuting the racist theory,[46] had his findings published in various periodicals including the paper of the *Abwehrverein*, where they received particularly favourable criticism.[47] Hertz spoke out against researchers who ignored the pseudo-scientific anthropology and in this way left the public prey to the political propagandists. Sometimes not only the public but scientists themselves tended to regard the assumptions of the racist ideologies as acceptable.[48]

Centralverein and *Abwehrverein* were united in their opposition to Zionism. In a series of articles bearing the title 'Isolation and Rejection' a comparison was made between racial antisemitism and Zionism:

> "Zionism plays into the hands of racial antisemitism, for as a result of similar assumptions, it, too, demands that Jews, who are German citizens, be stamped as foreigners in their home country."[49]

[41]On Chamberlain, see my study, ch. III.
[42]Bernhard Elsass, 'Ein Buch zur Abwehr. Die jüngsten Urtheile über das Judenthum, kritisch untersucht von Martin Schreiner', in *Im deutschen Reich*, 1902, pp. 327–328, 330.
[43]Bücherschau, 'Houston Stewart Chamberlain, Die Grundlagen des neunzehnten Jahrhunderts', besprochen von H.C. (Berlin), in *Im deutschen Reich*, 1902, p. 595.
[44]Schorsch, *op. cit.*, p. 98.
[45]*Mitteilungen*, 1900, p. 161; 1901, pp. 381–382; 1902, pp. 105–108; 1904, pp. 244–247, 251–253; 1905, pp. 142–144, 298–300, 306–308, 345–346; 1906, pp. 166–167, 317–318, 365–367.
[46]Friedrich Hertz, *Moderne Rassentheorien*, Wien 1904.
[47]*Mitteilungen*, 1904, pp. 190–192, 217–219, 244–247, 251–253; 1905, pp. 142–144.
[48]Friedrich Hertz, 'Moderne Rassentheorien', in *Mitteilungen*, 1905, p. 142.
[49]*Mitteilungen*, 1903, pp. 290, 297–301, 305–309, 338–341, 346–347, 396–398; 1904, pp. 2–3, 18–19.

The Zionists in their turn, in order to contradict the negative picture of the "degenerated" Jew drawn by racist ideology, decided to counter it with the development of the physical abilities of the Jews, so as to emphasise the "regenerated" type. These motives led to the establishment of the sports association *Bar Kochba* and to the publication of a Jewish sports newspaper.[50] This independent organisation not only stood in opposition to antisemitism but it also stressed the positive road to the exclusive and independent national strength and consciousness of the Jews.[51]

However, without intending to develop any national feeling of superiority, the Zionist writers were drawn into racist terminology themselves. Dr. Max Besser's writings for instance are unpleasantly similar to those of Chamberlain's. In his opinion:

> "It does not make any difference if people choose to point out a race, type, variation etc. . . . No one dares deny that the subject itself has caught everyone's interest, and it is as real a phenomenon as electricity. It is of little importance that there is a disagreement as to what this phenomenon should be called . . ."[52]

Other Zionist writers pointed to the singularity of the Jews, basing their writings on anthropological views and terms which were made to serve the Jewish national claims.[53]

The question of intermarriage also was not discussed solely from the point of view of Jewish Law. Intermarriage was not only regarded as a danger to national unity, but those who opposed it relied upon a sort of "Theory of the Jewish Race" to emphasise the importance of the purity of the race. "Shared memories of history and a common religion" were not the only components of the Jewish society – the unifying factor was a "racial partnership" (*Rassengemeinschaft*). So claimed Dr. Aron Sandler, who went so far as to declare that "our racial blood, as it flows in our veins now, bears our unique Jewish characteristics, and we must safeguard its purity".[54] Intermarriage was disapproved of because of the "penetration of blood from a foreign race".[55]

---

[50]*Die Welt*, 15th June 1900; *Jüdische Turnzeitung*, May 1900, pp. 1, 4, 8; November 1900, p. 74; and see also George L. Mosse, 'The Influence of the *Völkisch* Idea on German Jewry', in *Studies of the Leo Baeck Institute*, New York 1967, p. 109; and M. Zirker 'Der Antisemitismus und die deutsche Turnerschaft', in *Israelitische Rundschau*, Berlin 1901.

[51]For this, see Ragins, *op. cit.*, pp. 262–263; George L. Mosse, *loc. cit.*, p. 110.

[52]Dr. Max Besser, in *Jüdische Rundschau*, 6th February 1903, No. 6, and also Dr. Max Besser, *Die Juden in der modernen Rassentheorie*, Köln-Leipzig 1911; and compare this with H. S. Chamberlain, *Dilletantismus, Rasse, Monotheismus*, Vorwort zur 4. Auflage der Grundlagen des XIX. Jahrhunderts, München 1903, p. 17: "Ein jeder muss zugeben, dass Rasse . . . von hohem Werte für das Leben der Nationen ist . . . Dagegen braucht das praktische Leben vor allem Tatsachen . . . sichere Tatsachen . . ."

[53]Dr. Alfred Friedmann, 'Forschungen über Rasse und Degenerationen', in *Jüdische Rundschau*, 1903, p. 80. Here, the author praises Waldenburg's study which pointed out the "Uniqueness of the Jewish Race"; Dr. Elias Auerbach, 'Rassenmischungen der Juden', in *Jüdische Rundschau*, 1907, p. 113: "Die jüdische Rasse ist aus zweitausendjähriger Zerstreuung fast *rein* hervorgegangen . . ."; Dr. Max Jungmann demanded the purification of the Jewish Race in the Diaspora, in *Jüdische Rundschau*, 1907, p. 122: "Damit während des Exils wenigstens die rassenhygienischen Forderungen erfüllt werden."

[54]Aron Sandler, 'Mischehe und jüdisch-nationale Gesinnung', in *Jüdische Rundschau*, 1904, pp. 161–164.

[55]*Ibid.*, p. 163. Sandler published a book entitled *Anthropologie und Zionismus*, Brünn 1904, in which, although he questioned the concept of "positive signs of a race", a great deal is left unclear, even

There was an additional tension in Germany in the relationship between the "German" and the East-European Jews. Very often the superior attitude adopted towards the alien *Ostjuden* was attributed to differences in mentality and origin.

The economist, Franz Oppenheimer, distinguished between the West-European Jews' awareness of their *origin* and the East-European Jews' awareness of their *nationality*.[56] The German Jews regarded Germany as their national home but at the same time they were aware of their Jewish origin (*Stammesbewusstsein*).[57] On the other hand, the long-suffering East-European Jews, who had been the victims of pogroms and constant suppression, had a practical Jewish national consciousness (*Volksbewusstsein*), while the Zionist desires of German Jews were purely idealistic and altruistic.[58]

There was strong reaction to Oppenheimer among the Jews. On the one hand he was accused of dogmatism, and on the other, of blurring the terms and disregarding the need to define clearly such terms as national consciousness, consciousness of origin, of state and others which follow from this.[59] Yet there were certainly those who saw in Oppenheimer's writings a decisive answer to the views of such extreme racist theorists as H. S. Chamberlain.[60] These different stances accentuated the need to define the Jewish nation as an anthropological entity, particularly in light of the attacks on Jewish identity from outside. Ignaz Zollschan dealt with the question of the "Jewish Race" from the point of view of the Zionists.[61]

Zollschan had opted for the Zionist solution as a necessary condition for the preservation of the purity of the Jewish race and he wanted to prove that there existed such a "Pure Jewish Race", not inferior as claimed by the antisemites, which knew how to safeguard its inherent cultural abilities (*Kulturfähigkeit*). Thus, in answer to crude racism, he presented the Jewish national idea in an anthropological light.[62] Zollschan felt that the cosmopolitan importance of the Jewish people could be recognised in its cultural singularity. It constituted a *hochgezüchtete Rasse* and as such, it required territorial autonomy which would guarantee its regeneration.[63]

---

though in the appendix to the book he warned against "chauvinistic racism" which was spreading in society (*ibid.*, p. 51). See also L. Eisenberg, 'Darwinismus und Judentum', in *Jüdische Rundschau*, 1909, p. 88.

[56]Franz Oppenheimer, 'Stammesbewusstsein und Volksbewusstsein', in *Die Welt*, 1910, p. 139.

[57]*Ibid.*

[58]*Ibid.*, p. 141. See also Oppenheimer's views expressed in the Zionist Trustees Committee in Berlin 1913: "Ich kann ganz gut zugleich jüdisch-national und deutsch-national sein." (CAFHJP, 15th July 1926, Protokoll der Internen Tagung der Zionistischen Vertrauensmänner, Berlin, 1st May 1913, p. 13.)

[59]Jakob Klatzkin, 'Die Grundlagen', in *Die Welt*, 1910, p. 259.

[60]Dr. H. Kadisch, 'Klassen, Rassenpolitik und Antisemitismus', in *Selbstwehr, Unabhängige Jüdische Wochenschrift*, (Böhmen, Mähren, Schlesien), 1907, No. 25.

[61]Dr. Ignaz Zollschan, *Das Rassenproblem, unter besonderer Berücksichtigung der theoretischen Grundlagen der jüdischen Rassenfrage*, 1910, Wien–Leipzig 1911.

[62]*Ibid.*, p. 426.

[63]*Ibid.*, p. 427 and see also Zollschan's articles in *Jüdische Rundschau*, 1911, pp. 394 ff.; *Die Welt*, 1911, p. 898.

We find certain parallels to Ahad Ha'am's evolutionary ideas on Zionism in this way of thinking, but Zollschan particularly stresses the anthropological basis.[64] At the close of his book he warns his generation that "without Zionism there will be only two possibilities – the breakdown of the race or its physical degeneration".[65] A choice between "national-jüdisch" and "national-deutsch" became more real with the approach of the First World War.

These problems were discussed in Moritz Goldstein's provocative article on the place of Jewish culture in the general culture of Germany.[66] Here he speaks of his "natural nationalistic feeling of belonging to Judaism", though these double loyalties threatened to tear him apart. He was faced with the decision of either being a Jew to all intents and purposes, or a German.[67] In his famous essay 'Deutsch-jüdischer Parnass', Goldstein reached a solution similar to that of Oppenheimer's.

However, whereas Oppenheimer had called the Zionism of the German Jews purely idealistic and altruistic[68] Goldstein saw it as a situation forced upon the Jews by the times. It was neither voluntary nor ideal that the Jewish culture was taking root in the German one – rather it was a result of historical facts to which the Jews had to resign themselves. In Goldstein's words – "The bleak words 'resign yourselves' hang over our heads."[69]

Goldstein's attitude to the Theory of the Race was more sophisticated than that of his contemporaries. Unlike Zollschan who devoted many chapters of his book to the contradiction of erroneous anthropological hypotheses, Goldstein did not use such tactics. He dismissed Chamberlain's racism as being the act of a conjuror (*Taschenspielertrick*) which could easily be disproved,[70] and he was not concerned with the anthropological controversy but with "the hatred which it was impossible to deny". He was shocked by the fact that thousands believed in the anti-Jewish calumnies and that Chamberlain's book was constantly being reprinted, and he feared its social implications.[71]

Different Jewish factions and parties which opposed racism had come to realise that integration into the surrounding Gentile world had not been altogether successful and there were many Jews who now saw a need to foster and en-

---

[64] For Ahad Ha'am's belief in the principle of evolution, see Baruch Kurzweil's article 'Judaism as an Expression of the Biological-National Will to live – A Criticism of Ahad Ha'am's Theory of Continuity', in *Luach HaAretz*, Tel-Aviv 1955, pp. 144–170.

[65] Zollschan, *op. cit.*, p. 491. There also existed an approach opposite to that of Zollschan's. Just as Zollschan tried to prove the cultural singularity of the "Jewish Race", so, too, there existed a non-Zionist tendency to rely on the anthropological theory in order to prove that there was no Jewish racial singularity – neither cultural nor anthropological. See Dr. G. Wittkowsky, 'Maurice Fishberg. Die Rassenmerkmale der Juden', in *Jüdische Rundschau*, 1913, pp. 1–2.

[66] Moritz Goldstein, 'Deutsch-jüdischer Parnass', in *Der Kunstwart*, XXV, München 1912, pp. 281–294. See the contribution of Moritz Goldstein, 'German Jewry's Dilemma before 1914. The Story of a Provocative Essay', in *LBI Year Book II* (1957), pp. 236–254.

[67] Moritz Goldstein, *Ein Mensch wie ich*, p. 176, Collection of Memoirs, 133, Archives of the New York Leo Baeck Institute.

[68] See note 58.

[69] Goldstein, 'Deutsch-jüdischer Parnass', p. 290.

[70] *Ibid.*, p. 284.

[71] *Ibid.*, p. 285.

courage a Jewish uniqueness and exclusiveness. The German nationalists made use of the Theory of the Race for purely negative reasons. Their strategy was to portray a negative picture of the Jew in opposition to that of the German, thereby emphasising the latter's positive qualities.[72] Until the start of the twentieth century, the Zionists also made use of the Theory of the Race in their writings, but there was a very important difference between their reasons for using this theory and the objectives of the German racists. Even if they relied on anthropological-biological evidence, they did not regard race as the primary decisive factor, and the theory of a Jewish race was not presented negatively, so as to detract from the importance of other ethnic groups. Instead it was employed to show the Jewish people in a positive light.[73]

Although certain similarities are clearly discernible in the terminology used by the racist-*völkisch* groups and by some Zionist spokesmen, it is misleading to conclude that there was a close affinity between racial antisemitism and *Völkisch-Zionism* and in their stressing the community of blood.[74] It is difficult to accept this combination of terms *Völkischer Zionismus*. Zionism was the positive recognition of the independent national existence of the Jews alongside other nations, while the word *Volk*, as understood by the Germans, implied the national racial exclusiveness of the German nation at the expense of the existence of other nations.

Until the end of the nineteenth century the conflict between the Jews and the German nationalists on the question of "The German Race" and its place in general history, was mainly an academic, theoretical one. Both Judaism and Germanism were regarded as abstract entities. Peter Pulzer pointed out in his study that as a generation's nationalistic feelings grew, the real problems dealing with the relationship of the Jews to their surroundings became less clear. The antisemitic arrows were aimed mainly at "mystic" Judaism, at "abstract" Judaism and not at the real Jew.[75] The Jews responded to this attack in kind. In answer to the racist anti-Jewish attacks they presented monotheism as proof of the authenticity of Judaism. In this context, the Jewish nation was represented as a purely spiritual entity.

At the turn of the century this conflict became more concrete. This change can be accounted for by the socio-political organisation of *völkisch* circles into different parties and associations. This, in turn, led to a change in the Jewish response. In place of theoretical apologetics, Jewish bodies now demanded legal self-defence and at the same time there were many who previously had favoured

[72]On the negation of the German Jews, see my study, ch. VI, pp. 211–239; and Geoffrey G. Field's article 'Antisemitism and Weltpolitik', in *LBI Year Book XVIII* (1973), p. 77: "In later years Chamberlain admitted that the 'Foundations' was in a sense a political confession. The social and political underpinnings of his ideas are clear. To each negative 'Semitic' trait, he counterposed a German virtue ..."

[73]For this see Ragins, *op. cit.*, pp. 251–259.

[74]Egmont Zechlin, *Die deutsche Politik und die Juden im Ersten Weltkrieg*, Göttingen 1969, p. 73: "Der Rassenantisemitismus und dieser völkische Zionismus behaupteten die unlösliche Bindung an die 'Gemeinschaft des Blutes' und die objektive Bestimmung des Menschen durch seine Abstammung aus Rasse, Volkstum und Geschlechterzusammenhang."

[75]Pulzer, *op. cit.*, p. 71.

the complete socio-cultural integration of Jews and Germans, and now instead strongly opposed it or even advocated emigration.

Both the *Centralverein* and the Zionist organisation increasingly fought against the racial opportunism which was being voiced in the different *völkisch* organisations, and by 1914 the "anthropological controversy" between the two sides began to resemble a real battle. The different lines were sharply defined and such practical suggestions and solutions as for instance the national solution propagated by the Zionists or the preservation of the "exclusiveness of the race" demanded by German nationalists were voiced in attack and counter-attack.

II

After a slight lull at the outbreak of the First World War, the weakening of Germany's military and political power and the approach of defeat and the growing social tensions tended to aggravate the animosity against the Jews still further. The injury to Germany's national pride also found expression in renewed racist plaints. The myth of Jewish "internationalism" now came to be served up in "biological" guise. Such "internationalism" was, "in common antisemitic parlance, in the blood of all Jews".[76]

If in 1919 Ludwig Holländer, one of the leaders of the *Centralverein* voiced his alarm at the danger which the *völkisch*-racist organisations and associations held in store for the Jewish population, and consequently demanded that the Jews fight these energetically within the framework of regional and national associations, he nevertheless continued to stress German Jewry's avowed identification with *Deutschtum*, for "we are anchored in our *Deutschtum*, with all our heart and soul . . .". He also expressed his dismay at the existence of Jewish elements which did not regard such an identification as something to be taken for granted.[77]

And it is against the background of such an identification that we have to understand the tendency of some Jews as well to look for other "culprits", to blame for Germany's defeat. An attempt of this kind was made in 1921 when responsibility for the war was attributed to "the effects of the English Darwinist Theory"! "Perfidious" England was here represented as the carrier of the materialism that had subdued "innocent", idealistic, Germany. Biological–materialistic criteria, such as the one concerning "natural selection", were portrayed by this German-Jewish writer as alien British concepts.[78]

[76]Ansprache der Mitglieder des Badischen Oberrats der Israeliten an die Angehörigen der Badischen Landessynagoge, Karlsruhe, 1st October 1919, Bundesarchiv Koblenz (BA), Reichskanzlei, Fol. 1 – R 431/2192.

[77]Ludwig Holländer, 'Der Antisemitismus der Gegenwart', in *Zeitfragen. Eine Broschürensammlung des C.V.*, II, Berlin 1919, pp. 5–13. See also Leo Wolff, 'Von den deutschen Juden', in *"Krisis", Ein politisches Manifest*, 1922, p. 240. Here the writer, who was chairman of the Berlin Jewish Community (1924–1927), warned against antisemitism appearing in the German political party platforms, notwithstanding German Jewry's contribution to Germany's national, cultural and war effort.

[78]Dr. C. S. Engel, 'Zur Verständigung zwischen christlichen und jüdischen Deutschen', in *Im deutschen Reich*, 1921, pp. 42–49. On the substance of Social Darwinism, see the preface to Richard Hofstädter's *Social Darwinism in American Thought*, Boston (1944), revised ed., 1955, pp. 1–12.

The assassination of Walther Rathenau, in 1922, rallied a broader Jewish front in the struggle against *völkisch* racism. Both Zionists and members of the *Centralverein* were aware of the new undertone to the antisemitic onslaught. Despite differences in outlook, the cry was now raised for a common stand against it, as after all the C.V. and the Zionists had common cause in the demand for equal rights for the Jewish citizen in a Gentile society. Yet, as one observer put it, it had not yet been learned – especially by the *Centralverein* – that the heart of the problem was the question of origin, the Jewish race.[79] The *völkisch* camp and bodies such as the *Schutz- und Trutzbund* and the *Deutschnationale Volkspartei* denying equal rights and demanding the social and economic isolation of the Jew, focused their activities on an antisemitism which blatantly rested on racist foundations.[80]

This racist antisemitism continued to be evaluated by most Jews from the viewpoint of a German citizen. Sometimes the yardstick was the good of the German cause, and not necessarily the harm caused to the Jews themselves. There was certainly something of an element of self-abasement about an intellectual like Kurt Hiller who readily admitted that there were "worthless Jewish characteristics", which had to be eradicated. He distinguished between the "Moses Jew" – the positive spiritual type, and the "Aaron-Jew" – the negative self-seeking type, the moneymaker. Such typology was reflected in the difference that existed, so far as he was concerned, between a personality like Gustav Landauer and the random "Jew of the Bourse". Hiller's conclusion was that

> "... it is only possible to fight antisemitism as long as it is given justification in those areas where it has right on its side, as well as support in its war against the profiteers and speculators".

And his hope was that under this banner "good Jews and good antisemites will find a way to one another ..."![81]

The Germanic tone of the Jewish response even gained in intensity after the sensational trial of Hitler in 1923. It could be argued that the total identification with the German nation and its culture created a distorted perspective of the true ends and aims of racist antisemitism. In the ranks of the C.V. the view was expressed that the Jew as a German could not possibly remain unperturbed by *völkisch* manifestations, for it was his supreme duty to the German fatherland to take up the defensive struggle.[82] And it is symptomatic that a leading personality

---

[79]David Baumgardt, *Wie bekämpft der CV und wie bekämpfen die Zionisten den Antisemitismus?* Unpublished manuscript, n.d., Baumgardt-Collection, Archives of the New York Leo Baeck Institute.

[80]See Dr. Alfred Wiener, 'Wir klagen an! Rathenau, das Opfer der deutschvölkischen Hetze', in *C.V.-Zeitung*, 1922, p. 109. See also David G. Williamson's comments on this article in his essay 'Walther Rathenau: Patron Saint of the German Liberal Establishment (1922–1972)', in *LBI Year Book XX* (1975), p. 215, in which Williamson interprets Wiener's statements as a struggle against antisemitism within a German context, as was customary with members of the C.V.; however, Wiener's emphasis on the *völkisch* element should be noted as well as the fact of his warning against racist antisemitism being organised on a party basis.

[81]*Neue Methode des Kampfes gegen den Antisemitismus* von Dr. Kurt Hiller, Berlin 1923, Archives of the New York Leo Baeck Institute.

[82]Hugo Sonnenfeld, 'Tagesprobleme. Rede gehalten im Herrenhaus zu Berlin anlässlich der Hauptversammlung des Central-Vereins deutscher Staatsbürger jüdischen Glaubens', in *Kulturspiegel*, Heft 2, 12th April 1924, Berlin 1925, p. 3.

of the *Centralverein*, Hugo Sonnenfeld, though he exposed the pseudo-scientific nature of racist antisemitism, nevertheless declared that "even for racist incitement it is possible to feel understanding",[83] without, however, explaining precisely what he meant by this.

Perplexing too is the distinction that was here made between the concepts *völkisch* and *rassisch*. As seen by some Jews, this distinction implied that the *völkisch* outlook had to be understood not as entailing hatred of the Jews alone, but essentially as hostility to Christian religion in particular, and to all monotheistic religions in general. They tended to discern in *völkisch* thought a new religion, a substitute for Christianity, which could not be grasped rationally. This religion would rise from the ruins of the existing order – religious, scientific and rational-creative, and this "*völkisch* Religion" was the foe of the German fatherland.[84] The Jews as staunch Republican Germans often assessed racist antisemitism as being more of a threat to the Republican order (in which they were rooted) than as a threat to their very existence.[85]

There was something paradoxical in the sight of Jews and Christian Germans united in a struggle for the German cause against the demonstratively anti-Republican *völkisch* force. And there is also a tragic element in the determination of Jews to remain impervious to the fact that *völkisch* thought and racism were after all cut from the same cloth and poised for total war against the Jew who, in the eyes of the *völkisch* nationalists personified the anti-German.

Now when Jews set out to protest against the racist doctrine, they did so not first of all as Jews to whom injury had been done – for "it is not merely a Jewish matter that concerns us here, but also a German matter" – they reacted to racism as Germans by presenting opposition thereto in the character of enlightened Germans. Efforts were made to portray and explain *völkisch* antisemitism not merely as it was seen from the Jewish viewpoint, but also, and mainly, as beheld by non-Jews both in pre-Republican times and in the time of the Republic itself.[86] Thus under the heading *Rassenforscher* negative Jewish characteristics mentioned by antisemites were enumerated alongside "Teutonic" characteristics held objectionable by others. This parallel was designed to prove how arbitrary and hollow "race research" was, and that it was a weapon by no means employed by the antisemites alone.[87]

However, the defensive struggle was waged in a constructive manner as well. An example is the initiation by Rudolf Seiden, an Austrian journalist and a Zionist, of a literary enterprise through which non-Jews were invited to comment on and express their appreciation of the cultural values of Judaism. Noted and respected personalities would here paint a true picture of Judaism, *sine ira et studio*, so it was claimed in the introduction to this publication.[88] Its inception

---

[83]*Ibid.*, p. 4.
[84]*Ibid.*, pp. 16–17.
[85]*Ibid.*, p. 15.
[86]H[einemann] Stern, *Angriff und Abwehr. Ein Handbuch über die Judenfrage*, Berlin 1924, p. 255; see in particular p. 258.
[87]*Ibid.*, pp. 85, 94.
[88]Rudolf Seiden, *Judentum, Judenvolk, Judenland. Eine Sammelbroschüren-Reihe, Nicht-Juden über den Kulturwert des Judentums*, 1. Folge, Brünn–Wien 1924.

was attributed to necessity, the Jewish Question having become a burning issue due, on the one hand, to flourishing antisemitism and, on the other, to the realisation of the Zionist ideal which had just then acquired the support of the League of Nations.[89]

After the First World War Jewish reaction came to be more clearly based on social and political reality which was at times shown as proving the utter worthlessness of racist theory.[90] The First World War was interpreted by a spokesman of the C.V. as actually contradicting the racist argument, since contrary to it, an internecine struggle had been waged between two peoples

> "who were racially related to each other, the English and the Germans ... Germans fought against Germans, Austro-Romanians against Romanian-Italians, Slavs against Slavs ... thus racial theories had never before so visibly collapsed".[91]

Also the Zionist demand for the recognition of Jewish national rights took on greater force after the Treaty of Versailles. The Zionist politician Georg Landauer advocated the Jewish right to self-determination in accordance with the policy concerning minorities as embodied in the Treaty on the ground that in Jewish racial uniformity unique characteristics, especially spiritual ones had been preserved.

Until the First World War this Zionist demand had generally been presented as a theoretical claim, but with the post-war changes the demand was renewed and the "racial-cultural-unity" was now presented in a political context.[92] The cultural anthropology on which Landauer relied fortified the Zionists, who pointed to real political achievements after the Balfour Declaration on the one hand and, on the other, to the Jewish minorities in the Diaspora struggling for recognition of their civil rights.[93]

The consolidation and expansion of the Jewish settlement in Palestine, conferred on the Zionist movement the standing of a real and defined political entity. In the eyes of German antisemites the Jews, as both lovers of Zion and German citizens, were persons of "dual loyalty", and the Zionist call for settlement in Palestine was converted by them into a cry for the removal and expulsion of the Jews.

The antisemitic attacks stressed the *natural* differences allegedly separating Jews from Germans, and the demand that the Jew uproot himself from Germany and settle in Palestine, was accompanied by racist arguments. Jakob Wassermann recorded the debate that was conducted between himself and "a young German philosopher" reacting to his autobiography, *Mein Weg als Deutscher und Jude*. This "philosopher", after reading Wassermann's work, categorically demanded that the latter leave Germany and emigrate to Palestine, since

---

[89]Among the contributors to the publication were: Walter Bloem, Michael Georg Conrad, Karl Hauptmann, Ferdinand Tönnies. Seiden himself challenged racist antisemitism in the pages of *Die Selbstwehr* in an article entitled 'Erst kommt die Rasse, dann das Hirn'. His statements were also quoted in *Die Wahrheit* (2nd January 1924), pp. 10–11.
[90]Felix Goldmann, *Das Wesen des Antisemitismus*, Berlin, n.d., p. 78.
[91]*Ibid.*, p. 79.
[92]Georg Landauer, 'Die Juden als Träger nationaler Rechte', in *Quellen und Studien*, Erste Abteilung, Recht und Wirtschaft, 9. Heft. Das geltende jüdische Minderheitenrecht mit besonderer Berücksichtigung Ost-Europas, Leipzig–Berlin 1924, pp. 1–13.
[93]*Ibid.*, p. 12.

"he, the German and avowed nationalist, desired a united and purified German nationalism, and for that reason it seemed essential to him that the Jews be removed from Germany".[94]

This argument he tried to reinforce with an absolute and arbitrary premise that blood was the true measure of pure Germanhood. The demagogic nature of this argument was very well delineated by Wassermann.[95]

The extremist attitude of the antisemites in basing their political demands on the racist theory, provoked a more extreme reaction from the Jews as well. Thus Wassermann responded that he recognised neither "Germans" nor "Jews" as nations, but only as human beings; the biological approach seemed to him no more than a "diversionary theory". As regards his opponents' demand that he return to the land of his fathers, Wassermann replied ironically that to speak of "Fatherland" was sheer mockery; any Italian marketplace, any German cathedral stirred deeper feelings in him than did the soil of Palestine.[96] While Wassermann like most German Jews rejected the Zionist solution, he was not prepared to deny the fact of his Jewishness – in which he saw the manifestation of human ideal – if only out of a feeling of solidarity, as long as "the disgrace of antisemitism lasts".[97]

Increasing attention now began to be paid to the exposure and rejection of the racist theory as a result of the ever more frequent attacks made by the *völkisch* movement. A new awareness on the part of the Jews became especially marked during the latter years of the Weimar Republic. The "anti-biological" campaign was termed by the *Centralverein* as supportive of scholars and scientists in the publication of their conclusions "insofar as their conclusions disqualify the pseudo-scientific claims of the antisemitic race-researchers".[98] In the effort to discount the authenticity of the racist doctrine special emphasis and prominence was given to the belonging of the Jews to the German nation, thanks to their participation in the social and cultural life of Germany throughout a long history. It was argued that one could not speak of a German race, just as there existed no Jewish race. The Jew had the right as well as the duty to regard himself as an integral part of the German nation. It was only correct that this historical right should override the historical justification for being considered a Zionist who wishes to settle among his people in Palestine.

In his six essays directed to German-Jewish youth the educationalist Heinemann Stern sought to contend with the question of race. He rejected the notion

---

[94] Jakob Wassermann, 'Judentum', in *C.V.-Zeitung*, No. 37 (14th September 1928).
[95] *Ibid.*
[96] *Ibid.* Wassermann described the significance of being a modern Jew as "a duty of noble conduct", see 'Zum Rassenproblem', in *Europäische Revue*, Sonderheft, Die Judenfrage, Berlin 1932, p. 26. See also the criticism of Wassermann's conception of Judaism by Felix Weltsch, 'Jakob Wassermanns Kampf mit dem Judentum', in *Jüdische Rundschau*, Nos. 78/79; Nos. 80/81 (1928).
[97] "Offener Brief an den Herausgeber einer Monatsschrift für "Kulturelle Erneuerung" (1925)', in *Lebensdienst. Gesammelte Studien, Erfahrungen und Reden aus drei Jahrzehnten*, Leipzig–Zürich 1928, p. 157. As regards Wassermann's identification with Judaism, see Hans Tramer, 'Der Beitrag der Juden zu Geist und Kultur', in *Deutsches Judentum in Krieg und Revolution*, pp. 349–352; Rainer S. Elkar, 'Jakob Wassermann, ein deutscher Jude zwischen Assimilation und Antisemitismus', in *Jahrbuch des Instituts für Deutsche Geschichte*, III, Tel-Aviv 1974, pp. 289–311.
[98] Organisationen, C.V. (1926) Arthur Lehmann Collection, Archives of the New York Leo Baeck Institute.

of a "pure race", Jewish or German. "The Germans of today, as well as the Jews, are a mixed race like all other peoples."⁹⁹ As far as he was concerned, the choice between a Zionist fatherland and a German fatherland was not a practical necessity, but a matter of free will. Ancient Jewish national history existed solely as a matter of memory, and was "dead" in reality. The Jewish present was in Germany and hence the question "German or Jew?" had thus been firmly answered.¹⁰⁰

Wherever *völkisch* feeling in Weimar found expression in political organisation, its irrationalist and anti-intellectual tone became more marked among the populace. The anti-rationalist trend asserted itself especially at the political level, in the framework of "the constructive revolution".¹⁰¹ The revolutionary process in advanced industry had undermined the conservative historical identity of an important segment of the German population, with existing values in all fields of life bowing to the "onslaught of technology". The guilt for the collapse of the old world was laid at the door of liberalism.¹⁰² This liberalism, in all its social implications, was according to Conservative and *völkisch* thinking defined as letting loose the forces that were undermining and destroying their own concepts of life and world-order. If this pessimistic perception had driven them to see modernisation as endangering their existence, both as individuals and as a body, they now came to be fortified by the racist-anthropological outlook in its optimistic guise: that the laws of the modern-mechanistic world were incapable of changing the validity of the natural order. Thus racist anthropology became central to the outlook of the nationalist circles.¹⁰³ They relied on it to point out the distortions in liberalism, in the doctrine of man's natural and equal rights. The principle of civil equality was rejected as an illusion, as a phenomenon contradicting the laws of nature. It was not equality that these laws determined, so it was argued, but a natural selection between the strong and the weak.¹⁰⁴ This social-Darwinist¹⁰⁵ approach became interwoven with the anti-rationalist criticism of liberalism, and such conservative criticism was converted into an anti-liberal political programme.¹⁰⁶

⁹⁹H[einemann] Stern, *Warum sind wir Deutsche? Sechs Aufsätze für die deutsch-jüdische Jugend*, Berlin 1926, pp. 22, 23.

¹⁰⁰*Ibid.*, pp. 28–29.

¹⁰¹On the conservative anti-rationalist atmosphere see Kurt Sontheimer, *Antidemokratisches Denken in der Weimarer Republik. Die politischen Ideen des deutschen Nationalismus zwischen 1918–1933*, München 1962, 1968; Martin Greiffenhagen, *Das Dilemma des Konservatismus in Deutschland*, München 1977. See also George L. Mosse's article 'Die Deutsche Rechte und die Juden', in *Entscheidungsjahr 1932*, p. 184, in which he quoted a Bavarian Police Report of 1919 concerning the preservation of military discipline in relation to antisemitism, to the effect that the conflict between the Jews and the German people originated from the soul, from the inner consciousness, so that the mistrust was a national consequence.

¹⁰²Greiffenhagen, *op. cit.*, p. 241.

¹⁰³"We do not regard anthropology as an auxiliary science to history. It is in fact the centre of the science of history," *Politisch-Anthropologische Revue*, Monatsschrift für das soziale und geistige Leben der Völker, Hrsg. Ludwig Woltmann, 1902–1907 (1903/4), p. 12.

¹⁰⁴Ludwig Woltmann, *Politische Anthropologie*, Leipzig 1903 (1936), p. 316.

¹⁰⁵On Social Darwinism in Germany, see Hans Günther Zmarzlik, 'Der Sozialdarwinismus in Deutschland als geschichtliches Problem', in *Vierteljahrshefte für Zeitgeschichte*, 11 (1963), pp. 246–273.

¹⁰⁶Greiffenhagen, *op. cit.*, p. 242; Sontheimer, *op. cit.*, p. 54. See also Peter Gay's penetrating research on cultural life in the Weimar Republic: "The Hunger of Wholeness turns out . . . to be a great

Even Jews, many of them fully conversant with intellectual developments, became caught up in the anti-rationalist fever to find themselves, sometimes quite unaware, ranged alongside the opponents of liberalism and propagators of irrationalism. The dilemma of the Jews, and the problematics of their approach, is well illustrated by the public debate conducted after 1930 between the writer, Julius Bab, and a teacher called Stern. The debate centred around contemporary intellectual trends and the place of antisemitism.[107] Stern described the crisis of the time as a revolt of intuition and emotion against the rule of reason. "The consciousness which regulates life, is challenged by the subconscious passion." The connection between irrationalism and the Jewish Question, according to Stern, could be traced to the substance of Judaism which, in his opinion, was "explicitly rationalistic". The Jew, as a personification of the rational being, was seen by the disciples of vitalism, by the supporters of the blood theory, as one who endangered Western culture. Stern found in the anti-rationalist thinking the explanation why so many enlightened Germans supported the racist-*völkisch* movement. This anti-rationalism was romantic and, in his opinion, had to be accepted as a mark of the time and expressive of the longing for a new spirit. "It is interesting," he added, "that the Jews, despite their essential tie to rationalism, are partners thereto [i.e., to the romantic trend]."[108] Stern's remarks not only characterise him as a "romantic Jew" who was carried along by the mood of the time, but also reveal a reproach against the Jewish literati who were to be held responsible, in his view, for the gulf that existed between Jewry and the Christian-bourgeois intellectual stratum.[109] This was true with regard not only to philosophy and literature, but also applied to political orientations. Stern argued that "especially in the political sphere our Jews are trapped in the fetters of the old mechanistic liberalism and democracy, so that they have no understanding of the new ideas as propagated by the . . . *Jungdo*".[110]

Liberalism as an antithesis to the organistic outlook, was commonly termed "mechanistic" by *völkisch* thought and Stern's adoption of the term in condemnation of liberalism is distinctly revealing. The *Jungdo*'s[111] surprising alignment with the Democratic Party in 1930, also had its effect on Jews, as is well illustrated by Stern's cry that "one of the urgent tasks is gradually and without drawing attention to ourselves but with a clear aim in view to steer those who follow us into the new intellectual paths". This new intellectualism was to free

---

regression born from a great fear: the fear of modernity . . . The hunger for wholeness was awash with hate, the political and sometimes the private world of its chief spokesman was a paranoid world filled with enemies: the dehumanizing machine, capitalist materialism, godless rationalism, rootless society, cosmopolitan Jews, and that great all-devouring monster, the city . . .", Peter Gay, *Weimar Culture, The Outsider as Insider*, Penguin book, 1968, 1974, p. 100.

[107]'Gedanken über die geistige Bewegung der Gegenwart und ihre Beziehungen zum Antisemitismus', gezeichnet Mittelschullehrer Dr. Stern, n.d., Julius Bab Collection, Archives of the New York Leo Baeck Institute.

[108] *Ibid.*, p. 4.

[109] *Ibid.*

[110] *Ibid.*, p. 5.

[111] *Jungdo* = *Jungdeutscher Orden*, an antisemitic body par excellence with a strong racist consciousness, which in 1930 made an alliance with the Democratic Party in order to gain a parliamentary political basis for its struggle towards a new "organic" Germany.

"the urban Jews" from "the asphalt-intellectualism" and to implant, instead of the latter, a new conception of culture, freedom and progress.[112]

Julius Bab disputed Stern's premises and warned against the danger of evaluating the Jewish anti-rationalist inclination in a manner detracting from the substance of Judaism. In strong terms Bab rejected Stern's call for Jews either to conceal their own essential being before the German anti-rationalists, or to change it. Bab spoke in the name of those Jewish intellectuals who believed that the irrational blood-cult could only be countered by the force of rationalism.[113]

It was in a like spirit for instance that the debate between the Jewish philosopher Julius Goldstein and the *völkisch* writer, Wilhelm Stapel, on the meaning of the term *Volk* was held. Stapel claimed to reject the concept of race and to prefer speaking of *Volk*, but in actual fact attributed a biologic-naturalist significance to the latter term as well. Goldstein sought by rational argument to expose the fallacy in the racist approach, a fallacy to which both *völkisch* and Marxist theorists had fallen victim: "Both explain the spiritual as a product of the non-spiritual; in the one case the factor is blood, in the other economics . . ."[114]

So too Werner Cahnmann, in yet another *Centralverein* pamphlet, directed against the racist Hans Günther, addressed himself to "the most important representatives of enlightened Germany" with a view to proving that while Jews and Germans were indeed different, the difference was not one of "foreignness".[115]

Even almost a year after the establishment of Nazi rule the writer Lion Feuchtwanger, in a polemic from abroad, continued to dwell on the blatant inconsistencies of racist doctrine. Thus, the physiognomy of many of the leading Nazis quite obviously did not conform to racist norms or standards:

> ". . . for instance in the Nazi party which in principle is based on the doctrine of race, it is found that only one tenth of its members display the characteristic traits of the German race – extended crown, blue eyes and blond hair".

With a naïvety of approach characteristic of many Weimar Jewish intellectuals Feuchtwanger determined that "a doctrine so cheap as the race theory is inadequate to explain the substance and continuity of Judaism".[116]

The fact that a writer of Feuchtwanger's stature could believe that there was still room, after Hitler's rise to power, for "explaining Judaism", is no less per-

[112]'Gedanken über die geistige Bewegung . . .', *op. cit.*, p. 6.
[113]'Skizze für eine Entgegnung zu den Grundgedanken des Herrn Stern', n.d., Julius Bab Collection (see note 107), pp. 1–2.
[114]Julius Goldstein, *Volksidee und Deutsch-Völkische Idee*, Berlin 1927, p. 48.
[115]Werner Cahnmann, *Völkische Rassenlehre. Darstellung, Kritik, Folgerungen*, Berlin 1932, p. 30. Both Cahnmann's and Goldstein's brochures played an important part in the *Centralverein*'s onslaught on racism. Their, of necessity, cursory mention here certainly does insufficient justice to the contents. This in no way exhausts the C.V.'s anti-racialist arsenal. Furthermore in both the *Anti-Anti. Tatsachen zur Judenfrage*, hrsg. vom Centralverein deutscher Staatsbürger jüdischen Glaubens, 6th and 7th edn., Berlin 1932, and the *Anti-Nazi. Handbuch im Kampf gegen die NSDAP*, hrsg. vom Deutschen Volksgemeinschaftsdienst (camouflaged propaganda!), Berlin 1932, handbooks for activists and functionaries, much prominence was given to the refutation of racist "theories". Cf. *Anti-Anti*, 7th edn., 'Rassenfrage', 45b, 48a, 51–56, 69; 'Rassenschwindel', 45b; 'Rassenunsinn', 54d, 55; 'Rassereine Völker', 51, etc., etc.
[116]Lion Feuchtwanger, 'Nationalismus und Judentum', in *Die Streitschriften des Europäischen Merkur*, Paris (Oktober 1933), Heft 1, *Die Aufgabe des Judentums*, pp. 13–14, 16.

plexing than the marked inclination, displayed even among Zionists, to disregard the real danger posed by racism. At one and the same time, a clear awareness of the content and substance of the racist doctrine existed alongside a tendency to gloss over its full implications. It was believed sufficient to define anew the Jewish identity, in anthropological style, as an answer to racist antisemitism, and it was hoped that a determination of the substance of "the Jewish race", as compared with "the Aryan race", could lead to coexistence between the two peoples:

> "The prominent place of the race theory in present-day German life compels us Jews also to re-examine the concept of race. We, who live here as 'a foreign race' (*fremdrassige*), must at all cost respect the German nation's consciousness and fostering of its race. But this does not exclude peaceful co-existence between persons of different racial belonging."

Such coexistence with the Germans was possible if Jews would profess their Judaism and proudly identify themselves with their "own kind and race". The Jew had to reassess his relationship with the German nation in order to determine his own place within the new racial-ideological line-up.[117] All this in the autumn of 1933.

In the introduction to an article entitled 'The Voices of Blood', in which extracts from the literature and poetry of Richard Beer-Hofmann, Ernst Wiechert, Stefan Zweig and Hugo Salus were published, the hope was expressed that by "rediscovery of the Jewish ties, and by reflecting on the force of blood, we shall not be intolerant nor reject persons of different blood".[118] Despite the fact that the anti-Jewish legislation and the events subsequent to January 1933 provided clear proof of the uncompromising Nazi attitude, there existed a tendency among Jews to blur the grave import of the victory of racism.

The fact that the racial-biological substantiation of Nazi antisemitism was a constant and consistent feature of the anti-Jewish campaign, does not, of course, mean that the theory concerned became an integral part of the officially declared ideology. It is clear from the official publications which served as the mouthpieces of the Nazi leaders, that the implications of the race theory, or the inferences therefrom, were not always fully reckoned with, nor consistently drawn. Ideologically speaking there was no revolutionary innovation in Nazi antisemitism. The novelty lay in the practical implementation, at the pragmatic-political level, of ideas and approaches that had long been in existence. The Jews, with their rationalistic approach, failed to recognise the pragmatic political considerations which lay behind the prevalent irrationalism.

Julius Bab had sought a practical political solution in an alignment of the Jews with that "true Germany" whose voice was raised on behalf of the values of reason and humanity, and against *völkisch* racism. The anti-rationalist intellectual atmosphere, the urge to reveal irrational motivations in human conduct, influenced Jewish thinkers when they formulated their world view. The attitudes reflected in the Bab–Stern controversy were prevalent among enlightened Jews, particularly during the latter stages of the Weimar Republic. Thus Wassermann identified himself with the "philosophising" of Graf Keyserling on race as a value when he said that:

[117]'Rasse als Kulturfaktor', in *Jüdische Rundschau*, 4th August 1933, p. 392.
[118]*Ibid.*, p. 393.

> "Race is a very real value, not in the sense of better or worse blood, but in the sense of a memory that has been created in outcome of what was and is ... and has become a physiological fact ..."[119]

With reference to the irrational elements of a person's origin, his shaping and racial ties, Wassermann too came to hold that the force of memory was decisive – "not memory of the spirit, but memory of blood ..."[120] It is true that Wassermann warned against "romantic generalisation" and called for self-restraint in order not to be impelled by "naked instinct", but the inherent dangers of such views were echoed in the very warning he sounded.

What fascinated the minds of Wassermann and others like him, were the mysticism and magic which enveloped the concept of blood; blood being considered the factor that had shaped the history of mankind. While they recoiled from the notion of blood- or racial-"purity", and explicitly campaigned against the biological blood-theory and crude racism, their arguments nevertheless testify to their mystical bent, to their attraction towards the undefined and the intuitive, towards those irrational elements which in fact constituted the substance of the race theory.

Even the Zionists, as we have seen, were not immune to the seductions of the *Zeitgeist*. At the conference of Z.V.f.D. delegates in September 1932, Kurt Blumenfeld contended that many Zionists erred in thinking that the Zionist phenomenon depended for its existence on rational historical evidence and justification, and discounted the substantiation of Jewish nationalism on rational grounds: "Zionism can thrive on irrational grounds alone, out of the Jewish instinct ..."[121] The presentation of this view at a public forum, by the chairman of the German Zionist Association, testified to the translation of irrational consideration into pragmatic political arguments. With great emphasis Krojanker traced the romantic components of nationalism in general, and of Jewish nationalism in particular. At the 24th Zionist Conference the latter referred to the remarks made by Blumenfeld in his address. 'The Zionist Task in Present-Day Germany'.[122] Krojanker, more so than Blumenfeld, valued

> "... the romantic components of nationalism which represent a synthesis of the ideals of the French Revolution and those of German romanticism. These two components are present in every nationalism, also in our own. *They can neither be bridged nor separated*, and we must speak in favour of both."[123]

These remarks disclose the very substantial differences between the German nationalist and the Jewish national outlooks. The Zionist was committed to "the ideas of the French Revolution", whereas in German perception they constituted a serious obstacle to the shaping of the national consciousness. Therein lay the extremism of German nationalism which led to anti-humanism and racism. The national concept as propounded by Krojanker, the thesis of com-

---

[119]Jakob Wassermann, 'Zum Rassenproblem', *loc. cit.*, p. 24.
[120]*Ibid.*, p. 25.
[121]'Der 24. Delegiertentag der Z.V.f.D.', in *Jüdische Rundschau*, Nos. 73/74 (16th September 1932), p. 355.
[122]*Ibid.*, 'Zionistische Aufgabe im heutigen Deutschland', pp. 353–354.
[123]*Ibid.*, p. 354.

ponents which contradict and supplement each other at the same time, is perplexing, and it is difficult to fathom the minds of those Jews who sought to merge rational elements with irrational-romantic ones in the Jewish national outlook. They were remote from the exclusive barbarity of German nationalism, but all the same were seduced by the contemporary romantic attraction. The statements of both Krojanker and Blumenfeld reflected views that were prevalent among the Jewish public.

It is not easy to distinguish between pessimism and the despair that overtook the spirit of German Jewry in 1933. *Audiatur et altera pars*, cried the writer, Georg Hermann, in a plea to allow the Jews under attack by the Nazis to make their attitude heard. In gloomy terms he complained of the Jews having been denied the possibility of existence because it was a non-Aryan minority in German society. Georg Hermann, unlike Jewish intellectuals such as Lazarus, Wassermann and Goldstein who preceded him, and many others who regarded German culture as their own, was ashamed to be considered part of this German world, for he felt that he shared responsibility for the results of a culture which had given birth to racial hatred directed towards fellow men.[124]

The writer Ephraim Frisch termed the racist ideology "philosophical speculations on race", an ideology which had value and validity only as evidencing the psychology of a majority's judgment and evaluation of a minority. And since this majority espoused preconceived notions formulated in the race theory against the minority, there had never been room for balanced discussion and debate between them, for "behind the questions of the majority lurked expulsion, the pogrom and the stake". The contemporary antisemitism was a corrupt phenomenon, an instrument of *Realpolitik* which had to be "evaluated as mainly an instigation to pogroms".[125] The apprehension of violence was to become replaced inexorably by the realisation that the physical extermination of the Jews was intended, that the true objective of the Nazis was the annihilation of "inferior" races with the Jews at the head of their victims. Blumenfeld, for instance, expressed this fear in unequivocal terms a few months before the coming of the Third *Reich*:

> "The annihilation of the Jews is one of the primary objectives . . . the murder of human beings of a different race, particularly of the Jewish race, is the avowed purpose . . ."[126]

The dispossession of the Jews and their expulsion from Germany might have been interpreted as the ultimate outcome of "conventional" antisemitism, as expressed in their elimination from the economic, social and political fields. It was, however, the labelling of the Jews as racially inferior that gradually awoke them to the realisation that their very lives might be at stake. Eventually Jewish activists became convinced that the racist antisemitism purveyed by the Nazis

---

[124]'Antisemitismus! Ach ja, Antisemitismus!' An unpublished essay apparently written after 1933, pp. 3, 9. Georg Hermann Collection, Archives of the New York Leo Baeck Institute.

[125]Ephraim Frisch, *Jüdische Aufzeichnungen*, n.d., pp. 3–4, 6. Frisch Collection, Archives of the New York Leo Baeck Institute.

[126]Kurt Blumenfeld, 'Die Zionistische Aufgabe im heutigen Deutschland', in *Jüdische Rundschau*, Nos. 73/74 (16th September 1932), pp. 353–354.

had closed the door to any active response on their part; for the antisemites who, although prejudiced, were still open to a dialogue with the Jews, had dwindled to insignificant numbers. By 1932 there were not many illusions left about the waging of a successful struggle against racist ideology.[127]

We have sought, in this essay, to elucidate some of the Jewish responses to racist antisemitism from the foundation of the *Reich* until the advent of Nazi rule. The picture that emerges is indeed one of Jewish bewilderment and misconception of the changing situation, of much confusion, with only occasional glimpses of the mortal danger which confronted German Jewry. What was insufficiently understood was the pragmatic-political aspect of racism. It was not theoretical consistency but arbitrary opportunism that lay behind racist agitation, whereas the Jews endeavoured, on the whole, by way of rational argument by disputing racist premises and by unmasking the contradictions inherent in racial thought to fight an attitude nurtured by a theory that had from the outset declined to assume the mantle of rationalism.

Jewish apologetics were such that non-Jewish intellectual support was relied upon to expose the anti-State, anti-Christian and later anti-Republican elements inherent in racist determinism, but the anti-Jewish *Realpolitik* and the true aspirations of the *völkisch* propagandists were all too often glossed over. It was only when the Nazi pragmatists became entrenched that the racist ideology, which had in fact abandoned theory in favour of practice, came to be fully comprehended in all its implications.

[127]This was extensively dealt with by Arnold Paucker. See *Der Jüdische Abwehrkampf gegen Antisemitismus und Nationalsozialismus in den letzten Jahren der Weimarer Republik*, Hamburg 1968, 1969, pp. 72–73, 146–147.

Equality – Egality
Jews and Sport in Germany

BY PAUL YOGI MAYER

"As nations develop in different ways, the function which physical education plays in their history varies. The past only becomes history when the mosaic of events is considered from a certain viewpoint and so it is possible to examine and evaluate the history of physical education within nations. This has been done previously in relation to Jewish history: it has been considered as a national regeneration or as a manifestation of the emancipation of a people or as an emancipation of the individual."

Those sentences are a translation from the opening remarks of an essay 'Geschichte der Leibesübungen im Judentum' which this author wrote in 1937 for a volume on Jewish sport in Germany *Das Jüdische Sportbuch. Weg, Kampf und Sieg*,[1] and returning to this theme now more than forty years later, it must be stated from the outset that for the present survey it was not possible to cover all the essays and books written on the subject of physical education of Jews in Germany, nor to make use of all the detailed material which had been collected for this purpose. Those who wish to acquaint themselves in greater detail with the history of the *Maccabi World Union* or for instance with the events leading to the expulsion of Jewish sportsmen and women from their clubs and associations after the advent of Nazi rule or who may desire to study the relevant documents and letters in the original German will have to resort to the source material listed below. I shall try to present the most important facts in chronological order and will add some of my own personal experiences. My evaluation is likely to differ from that presented in a number of essays and books published over the years in Germany, Israel and America.

Moreover it must be said that even the more recent surveys on Jews and sport are in many instances still based on material first issued prior to 1936 where certain details really have to be corrected in the light of further evidence then not available. Both the meritorious *Sammelwerk, Juden im Deutschen Kulturbereich* and the *Lexikon des Judentums*[2] can be faulted to some slight extent as they perpetuate here and there earlier information which should be subjected to further scrutiny. Still, it is with numerous publications in mind that I returned to my own involvement in German-Jewish sport in the 1930s, and reviewing the relationship between German Jews and the German sports movement as well as the achievements of Jewish champions and organisations, I arrived at certain conclusions which may well be contrary to those I reached over four decades ago.

[1]Martha Wertheimer-Siddy Goldschmidt – Paul Yogi Mayer, *Das Jüdische Sportbuch*, Berlin 1937, pp. 8–9. An earlier contribution on 'Sport' was written by me for the *Philo Lexikon. Handbuch des Jüdischen Wissens*, Berlin 1935, cols. 682–687.
[2]Willy Meisl/Felix Pinczower, 'Sport' in Siegmund Kaznelson (ed.), *Juden im Deutschen Kulturbereich. Ein Sammelwerk*, 2nd edn., Berlin 1959, pp. 926–936; 'Sport', in John F. Oppenheimer (ed.), *Lexikon des Judentums*, Gütersloh 1967, cols. 767–772.

Most publications on the theme of Jews in sport and the achievements of individuals have been written in German or Hebrew. Those in English mainly emanate from America and are therefore written with a bias towards baseball, basketball and American football. Obviously, recent Israeli publications have been, as must be expected, in support of a National Jewish concept.[3] And there are also a number of publications by non-Jews in Germany which investigate the unique achievements of Jewish sports organisations during the Third *Reich*. The most noteworthy and comprehensive of these is undoubtedly Hajo Bernett's *Der jüdische Sport im nationalsozialistischen Deutschland*.[4]

There are two aspects to our topic which will require separate investigation and evaluation: first the role which individual Jewish sportsmen and women played within the modern German sports movement, and second the collective efforts and achievements of Jewish organisations since their inception in Wilhelminian Germany. (Of course the involvement of the individual Jew in physical education, training and competition goes back to the remote historical past of German Jewry, in fact, as far back as Roman times.)

Now whether Jews lived as individuals among a predominantly non-Jewish community or faced an aggressive anti-Jewish population, whether Jews had egalitarian or segregational aims, whether they considered themselves "deutschjüdisch" or "national-jüdisch", whether they believed in integration, assimilation or a more segregated existence as a minority, it appears that the main drive of German Jews was the deep yearning to prove their *Gleichwertigkeit*, their equality as individuals or as a group. It had been the dream of the individual Jew even before the emancipation to be *gleichwertig* to his neighbour, and it was the national dream of men like Max Nordau and Max Mandelstamm who at the II. Zionist Congress called for a *Muskeljudentum* to prove the collective equality of the Jewish people, and its right to a new nationhood.

Looking back at the history of Jewish sport in Germany one is naturally conscious of one's own later experiences of physical education (mainly in England but also in Israel and America). However one cannot discount the fact that political concepts have crept into many publications on Jewish sport and one must be aware of an ingrained bias when striving to achieve an objective survey and evaluation.

Now it cannot be denied that the achievements of Jews in all aspects of German sport are far less impressive than those unique contributions made by German Jews to the sciences, arts, medicine, technology, painting, music, theatre, films and writing. German Jews may pride themselves on having won National Championships, even a few medals at the Olympic Games, but how can these accomplishments stand up in comparison with the number of Nobel prizes won by Jews before and after Hitler's advent to power?

[3]Robert Atlasz, *Aufstieg und Untergang des jüdischen Sports. Bar-Kochba –Makkabi*, Tel-Aviv 1978.
[4]Hajo Bernett, *Der jüdische Sport im nationalsozialistischen Deutschland 1933–1938*, Schorndorf 1978 (Schriftenreihe des Bundesinstituts für Sportwissenschaft 18). Professor Bernett of the *Sportwissenschaftliches Institut der Universität Bonn* contacted me two years ago to obtain an eye-witness account for his book. In return I am indebted to him for a number of valuable suggestions for this essay. At the same time a television producer, Itzchak Pruschnowski, of the Sender Freies Berlin prepared a documentary, *Dornen am Lorbeer*, finally screened in November 1978, in which I also assisted.

Does the fact that relatively few Jews were members of the German Olympic Games' teams support in any way the Nazi theory of Jewish decadence, lack of courage and endurance? Or are these relatively limited successes caused by certain sociological factors which must be considered first? Or did the "final solution" come at a time when a new generation was just reaching for a new height of physical attainment?

We shall here look above all at the history of modern German sport and the involvement and exploits of individual Jews, paying special attention to the Olympic Games and to the events leading up to the Berlin Games in 1936. In addition we shall review the story of the Jewish sports organisations and afterwards add some of the contributions of German-Jewish refugees from Nazi oppression.

Maimonides, as is well known, appealed for physical fitness and the systematic pursuit of physical exercises. Historical records attest to the "Judentournier zu Weissenfels" in 1384 which is reported in the *Mansfelder Chronik* "wo Juden stachen und tournierten", of the book by "Ott", the "tauft Jud" as mentioned in the *Gothaer Handschrift* in 1443. The brothers Andreas (Andres Jud) and Jakob Liegnitzer wrote a book *Das Fechten mit dem Schwerd* and one Thalhoffer followed Ott's version with his own book on wrestling. In certain towns free association and sporting activities of Jews are recorded as including hunting and horse-racing. But all these are rather modest claims to physical prowess.

With the coming of emancipation as in other spheres of national life participation in physical education and leisure-time pursuits by Jews came to be all-embracing, ranging from gymnastics to mountaineering, from fencing to tennis, from horse-racing to motor-racing.

The number of those who participated in sport and leisure activities without being organised in Jewish clubs or who decided to affiliate to a specific one-activity club was very considerable. The majority of the mainly middle-class Jewish population went swimming, hiking, did their "daily dozen" (*Freiübungen*), joined a dance class or rowed and sailed, etc., conscious of the physical and social values of those pursuits. Still, they had no intention of joining an élite to produce "best performances", *Höchstleistungen* – actually these were attitudes which were not seldom belittled as "Gojim naches". Achievements in the field of sport were often considered of secondary importance to an academic career or to commercial success.

I cannot remember anyone of our large family, apart from myself, who joined a sports club. I was considered something of a freak. My father believed in his "daily dip" and long Sunday hikes, but never encouraged me to join a club and I must have been one of the youngest ever, when I started my *Reichsjugendabzeichen* (a National Youth Sports Award) when I was only thirteen. I had joined the *Schwimmclub Wiesbaden* which had quite a number of Jewish officials and members. Among these was Lolo Baer, who was to win the Students' World Championship in the 100 metres breast-stroke in 1930 at the same games where Helene Mayer, Lolo's close friend "Hee" gained a first in fencing. But already two years earlier, in 1928, Helene, when only seventeen and still at school, was to win the Olympic gold medal for Germany at Amsterdam.

In 1932 in my first year as a freshman at the University of Berlin and as a member of the *Berliner-Sport-Club* (B.S.C.), which had also many Jewish members, I received personal coaching in athletics from various German champions who belonged to the same team representing the University. There was a number of Jewish sportsmen and women who had become *Deutscher Hochschulmeister* and among those were Ernst Jokl, 400 metres hurdles (later to become a well-known American professor of sports medicine),[5] Lolo Baer (later a professor of medicine at a Californian University), Helene Mayer and her brother Eugen, also a fencer and Theo Levy, a sprinter and others. None of these was the product of any Jewish sports organisation, but many belonged to a Jewish student fraternity, others to a Jewish sports club in their hometown or were – as I was myself – active in the Jewish youth movement.

We have already named some Jews who became *Deutsche Hochschulmeister* but it is impossible to give a complete list of all those who gained championship status, broke records, belonged to the Olympic Games' teams or excelled otherwise. First of all, there are some who are not known to us as Jews but were of the Jewish faith, others who had one Jewish parent (*Mischlinge, Reichsbürger zweiter Klasse*) or a few non-Jews who were mentioned in previous publications because of hearsay or their "Jewish"-sounding name. The question "who is a Jew" has been put on so many occasions and the answers have been so divergent that we shall refer in the following to those who have Jewish parents and/or belonged to the Jewish community.

In Judo, or rather ju-jitsu – Europe's first encounter with what is today referred to as the martial arts – the R.j.F. (*Reichsbund jüdischer Frontsoldaten*) Sports group, Berlin, distinguished itself in the twenties by not only winning the *Adlerplakette des Reichspräsidenten*, but also by producing a number of German champions such as Walter Beck (later on *Sportdezernent* of the *Sportbund Schild*), Ernst Joachimsthal, Hans Rosenthal, Louis Unger, Egon Wittenberg, Rudolf Zadek and others, quite a unique achievement for a Jewish sports club.

In athletics, Elias Katz, a Finn by birth, won the gold medal at the 1924 Paris Olympic Games in the team event and a silver medal in the individual obstacle race. Later he joined *Bar Kochba Berlin* for some time. He found at *Bar Kochba Berlin* a strong team of sprinters, most of whom had been members of the record breaking *S.C. Charlottenburg*: Georg Kurz, Fritz Gerber, Heinz Nathan, Kurt Lewin and others. Lilly Henoch, who belonged to the *Berliner-Sport-Club*, was German discus champion in 1923 and 1924 and runner-up in 1925, and also excelled in putting the shot and the pentathlon. Martha Jacob (Martl), *S.C. Charlottenburg* won the German javelin-throwing title in 1929.[6] Lilly joined a *Schild Club*; and Martl started for *Makkabi*.

Jewish boxers of renown in Germany were few in comparison with the large

---

[5]See Ernst Jokl's contribution to the *Bulletin des Leo Baeck Instituts*, XII (1969), No. 48, p. 314, on Salomon Mendelssohn, 1813–1892. Mendelssohn was a sports teacher in Oldenburg who also had publications on sport songs and a history of sport to his credit.

[6]Fritz Steinmetz, *Deutsche Leichtathletik-Meisterschaften 1898–1968*, Berlin–München–Frankfurt a. Main 1969, pp. 155–159.

number of world champions who came from the Jewish proletariat of the East End of London and from Manhattan and the Bronx in New York. Still, there were Ernst Weiss, the professionals Erich Seelig, Harry Stein and others.

But, significantly, tennis shows quite a different picture being a much more middle-class activity. Daniel Prenn, now in London, has a collection of awards which must be unique. As a student at the *Technische Hochschule Charlottenburg* he had gained two championships on the same day: in the morning he played handball, in the afternoon football and both teams won the *Hochschul-Meisterschaft* (student championship). He was German tennis champion on a number of occasions and was ranked number one in European tennis. Oppenheim and Fuchs, both Jews from Mannheim, were thirteenth and fifteenth respectively. Ilse Friedleben and Paula Reznicek shared the number one position, Nellie Neppach was placed sixth and Richter-Weiherman seventh. Never before had three Jewish players occupied the leading positions in one sport. Some of these players joined Jewish clubs after the fall of the Weimar Republic, i.e., Ilse Friedleben played in the 1937 *Maccabiah*. Daniel Prenn after he had left Germany received a telegram from the *Reichssportführer* asking him not to participate in international tennis but to return to Germany. In 1933 however, Prenn did not return but his wife received the *Reichsmedaille* on his behalf from Franz von Papen, as he together with his friend Gottfried von Cramm had defeated Perry and Austin in England to win the *Europa-Zone* of the Davis Cup, but lost the final in the United States. The *Deutsche Tennisbund* added a gold medal. But tennis lost its importance for him in his struggles to make a new life in England. (In later years, his oldest son excelled in tennis and was a junior champion at Wimbledon and the youngest son John became one of the world's leading racket players.)

Fencing appears to be a sport in which Jews, as we have seen, apparently shone and even in the Middle Ages. Jewish student fraternities like the K.C. (*Kartell-Convent*) belonged to the group of "schlagende Verbindungen", duelling fraternities, but their fencing with the "Schläger" was more an expression of courage and self-discipline than a sporting achievement, especially where the "Schmiss" took the place of medals and titles. Apart from the well-known Olympic medallist Helene Mayer, daughter of a Christian mother, there were her brother Eugen and club-comrades Hans Halberstadt and Fritz Stark who became a junior champion.

As to football, with the exception of the famous *Hakoah Wien* in Austria, no Jewish team excelled in Germany, but Gottfried Fuchs and Julius Hirsch represented Germany before the First World War. Many Jews became officials, coaches, referees and the brothers Meisl occupied a leading position in world football, Hugo as an organiser and Willy as a leading sports writer in Germany until 1933.

Mountaineering may not be considered a competitive sport, but surely it is as demanding as many track and field events. The Wiener Library in London has in its possession a manuscript *Jewish Mountaineers* by George Bergman,[7] which gives a most detailed and knowledgeable account, extremely well documented,

---

[7] George Bergman (Sidney, Australia), *Jewish Mountaineers*. A study about a particular aspect of Jewish emancipation and assimilation in Central Europe.

of the many achievements of German-Jewish mountaineers. Speaking of men such as Gottfried Merzbacher, Siegmund Porges, Guido Mayer, Paul Preuss, Fritz Pflaum, Otto Margolis and many others, he writes: "We have found that there are Jewish mountaineers of world rank and renown and there are some who have profoundly influenced the development of mountaineering before the First World War. At least 80 per cent of the enumerated prominent Jewish mountaineers are members of the academic professions, scientists, doctors and lawyers." The Jew Sigmund Porges was the first German to climb the Jungfrau in 1856 and scaled the Mönch in 1859. Merzbacher is credited with the first ascent of the Totenkirchl and a hut in the Alps bears his name. He also climbed in the Caucasus and in 1893 in the Himalayas, reaching heights of over 20,000 feet. But the *Deutsch-Oesterreichischer Alpenverein* already in the early twenties showed strongly marked antisemitic tendencies and Bergman reports in detail on clashes with the *völkisch* element. According to Bergman, former Nazis such as Bauer, the President of the German Himalaya Foundation, Dr. von Schmidt and Wellenger were still in the forefront of German mountaineering organisations well after the Second World War.

Little is known about outstanding Jewish oarsmen. Nathan, a leading member of the R.j.F., had been a member of a championship crew in his youth. Some took up sailing successfully at the "Kieler Woche".

Jewish wrestlers there were; as a child I watched the return of the wrestling team of my home town, Kreuznach, the new German champions and among them were our two Jewish upholsterers Hermann and Julius Baruch, and Felix Marx.

Flying was a new sport which was of particular attraction to German Jews. Some won special events as did Willy Rosenstein, Simon Schendel, Lissauer, Grunder, Wertheimer, Heilbrunn, but the risks they ran led to many deaths, among others von Mieses, Neufeld, Dunetz and Dr. Fränkel were killed flying, the latter was a member of the Andrée Arctic Expedition 1897. A Dr. H. Berliner held the Free Balloon record in 1912 and A. Berson the altitude record. Some of Germany's leading aeroplane constructors were Jewish, among these Edmund Rumpler, the designer of the *Rumpler Taube*, Wiener of Albatros, Katzenstein of Raab-Katzenstein. Schwarz and Arnstein were both very closely associated with the Zeppelin enterprise.[8] (Approximately 50 out of 200 Jews who served in the German Airforce in the First World War were killed in action. One of those, Wilhelm Frankel, received the *Pour le Mérite*, the equivalent to the Victoria Cross.) There were many Jews who had excelled in gliding before and after the First World War. Among these was the Austrian-born Robert Kronfeld, who was awarded the *Adlerplakette des Deutschen Reiches* for his high altitude and distance records. He was the first glider pilot to cross the English Channel. (Kronfeld later served with the British Army, gaining the honorary rank of Colonel and Squadron Leader and was killed gliding in 1947.)[9] Freiherr von Huehnefeld, a member of the famous Köhl team which first crossed the Atlantic from East to West, was half-Jewish.

[8]Felix A. Theilhaber, *Jüdische Flieger im Weltkrieg*, Berlin 1924.
[9]Norman Bentwich, *I understand the Risks. The Story of the Refugees from Nazi Oppression who fought in the British Forces in the World War*, London 1950, p. 101.

Within a few months of Hitler's appointment as *Reichskanzler*, everything had drastically changed. Sport, as Hajo Bernett observed,[10] represented a medium for the German Jews to integrate into society, but in 1933 there was no longer any integration into German society and those many thousands who were expelled from their sports clubs and cut off from lifelong friends, gave up sport altogether or at least for some time until they joined the swelling ranks of the Jewish clubs.

The exclusion of Jewish sportsmen and women in 1933 from the various associations often went further than even the law required and the existence of one Jewish grandparent was sufficient for some over-enthusiastic official to expel loyal members who had served the clubs and organisations for forty years and more. Bernett reports in detail in his book on the attitude of the various Sports organisations in Germany in 1933; and I recollect that for many years there had been an ideological difference between the *Deutsche Turnerschaft* (DT) with its "frisch-fromm-fröhlich-frei" mentality and *völkisch* tendencies and the more open-minded *Deutsche Reichsausschuss für Leibesübungen* (DRA), an organisation similar to the Sports Council in Britain. The DT was considered by many as *petit bourgeois*, old-fashioned and rather narrow-minded. The percentage of Jewish membership of the DT had been decreasing over the years and in the later years its composition was more that of the older generation or of rural districts. Until 1933, only a minority of German Jews had enrolled with entirely Jewish sports associations but this picture altered dramatically within a few months of the usurpation of power by the Nazis.

Bernett states:

> "Jewish sport in National Socialist Germany has suffered all forms of degradation: dishonourable exclusion from the German sport community; being deprived of self determination by the *Reichssportführer*; control and suppression by the Gestapo; collision with hostile surroundings; the narrowing of one's living space and room for action; the destruction of organisations; the requisition of property and finally expulsion. This process is without parallel in history and in the history of sport. It can only be analysed with empathy 'teilnehmender Erkenntnis' (Dolf Sternberger) with a sense of shame and a feeling of guilt. But that a suppressed and persecuted minority did not give up sport in spite of all pressures must be encouraging ... Notwithstanding all differences in ideology, *Makkabi* and *Schild* practised in an identical manner sport as it had been shaped by the cultural, political and sociological conditions of Germany and Europe."[11]

The majority of Jewish sportsmen and women belonged to non-denominational organisations and to them sport as such was no justification for segregation. Others had found reasons to form their own Jewish sports organisations already at the turn of the century. It is generally assumed that it was Max Nordau with his demand for *Muskeljudentum* who inspired the first Jewish sports organisations. Actually, the first reports of Jewish sports associations lead us back into the Middle Ages, but the North American Young Men's Hebrew Associations, the "Y"s, were founded in the 1850s and recorded a membership of over a million in early 1970, thus being by far the largest Jewish sports organisation in the world today. The Jewish Athletics Association in England (now Association for Jewish Youth) has affiliated clubs which were founded before the end of the last century.

---

[10]Bernett, *op. cit.*, p. 17.
[11]*Ibid.*, p. 119.

Nordau had demanded: "We must again create a strong, muscular Judaism. We shall renew our youth in our old age, and with broad chest, powerful limbs and valiant gaze – we shall be warriors. For us Jews, sport has a great educational significance. It has to bring about the health not only of the body but also of the spirit." Thus his appeal to the Zionist Congress.[12]

Renewed outbreaks of antisemitism in Germany at the end of last century[13] led to the formation of a number of Jewish clubs, the first being *Bar Kochba Berlin* in 1898. Some years later, the first amalgamation of Jewish clubs in the form of the *Jüdische Turnerschaft* took place. At the first *Jüdischer Turntag*, in 1907, sixteen clubs with 1,215 members and 1,500 *Zöglinge* (juniors) had affiliated,[14] but there were a number of Jewish clubs which did not wish to join. About 1½ to 2 per cent of the *Deutsche Turnerschaft* were Jewish, i.e., approximately "ten thousand" of its members. In May 1909, a *Festschrift* entitled *Körperliche Renaissance der Juden*[15] stated "that there are a number of Jewish *Turnvereine* in Germany and Austria which engage in 'Turnen'[16] but do not pursue Jewish aims", and later: "It is for us Jews a humiliating fact that the difficulties which are at many places created for newly-formed Jewish *Turnvereine* can be traced back to those Jewish assimilationists who work in the dark and do not fight shy of misusing official positions." But even worse is the case which happened on a number of occasions "that the Jewish community refused our clubs the use of the gymnasia belonging to a Jewish school, because the clubs were Zionist or National Jewish". And so from the beginning, a duality was created between the so-called National-Jewish and the German-Jewish groups. (This is a Jewish phenomenon which also exists in England between the more Anglo-Jewish orientated AJY and the more national-Jewish *Maccabi* or in Israel between *Hapoel* and *Maccabi*.)

In contrast to Austria (*Hakoah Wien*) and Czechoslovakia (*Hagibor Prag*), Jewish clubs in Germany – with few exceptions such as the R.j.F. *Sportgruppe Berlin* – did not provide the backgrounds which were likely to lead to records and championships. Jewish clubs, whether Zionist or non-political were affiliated to the appropriate German sports organisations and participated in their leagues, cups and other competitions. Prior to 1933, there was no need for special Jewish leagues and most clubs had at their disposal, as did everybody else, the use of municipal and other facilities. Still, many years before Nazi rule, Jewish clubs began to form their own associations, the *Deutscher Makkabi-Kreis* and the *Sportbund des Reichsbundes jüdischer Frontsoldaten*, later on called *Sportbund Schild*.

Following the rousing appeals of Nordau and Mandelstamm *Bar Kochba Berlin* was formed on the 22nd October 1898 with the slogan: "Openly facing the

---

[12]In B. Postal, J. Silver and P. Silver, *Encyclopedia of Jews in Sports*, New York 1965 (dedication).
[13]Among the many who then emigrated to the United States was Richard Genserowsky, one of Germany's leading gymnasts who gave outstanding service to the Y's.
[14]Isidor Wolff, *Die Verbreitung des Turnens unter Juden. Referat –Dritter Jüdischer Turntag*, Wien 1907.
[15]*Körperliche Renaissance der Juden. Festschrift anlässlich des 10jährigen Bestehens des Jüdischen Turnvereins Bar-Kochba, Mai 1909*, Verlag der Jüdischen Turnzeitung.
[16]"Gymnastics" is too narrow as a substitute for "Turnen" in its wider concept as introduced by *Turnvater* Jahn.

Alfred Flatow and the victorious gymnastics team representing Germany at the 1896 Olympic Games in Athens

Ellen Preiss (Austria)   Ilona Elek-Schacherer (Hungary)   Helene Mayer (Germany)
Bronze   *Gold*   *Silver*
at the awards ceremony of the 1936 Olympic Games in Berlin

By courtesy of Professor Hajo Bernett, Bonn

Maccabiah, Tel-Aviv 1935
The German Makkabi team marching into the stadium

By courtesy of Maccabi World Union, Ramat Gan, Israel

Football at Theresienstadt
From the Nazi film 'Der Führer schenkt den Juden eine Stadt'

Alfred Flatow and the victorious gymnastics team representing Germany at the 1896 Olympic Games in Athens

Ellen Preiss (Austria) Ilona Elek-Schacherer (Hungary) Helene Mayer (Germany)
Bronze *Gold* *Silver*
at the awards ceremony of the 1936 Olympic Games in Berlin

By courtesy of Professor Hajo Bernett, Bonn

Gretel Bergmann, equalling German high jump record; Helene and Eugen Mayer, fencing champions; Daniel Prenn, German tennis champion; Martel Jacob, German javelin champion

Makkabi and Schild championships

Maccabiah, Tel-Aviv 1935
The German Makkabi team marching into the stadium

By courtesy of Maccabi World Union, Ramat Gan, Israel

Football at Theresienstadt
From the Nazi film 'Der Führer schenkt den Juden eine Stadt'

world, we confirm our nationality which we want to retain but we are also conscious of our duties as citizens." In 1900, the first issue of the *Jüdische Turnzeitung* appeared and Heinrich Loewe produced a special Jewish song book. At the time of publication, the second Jewish *Turnverein* was founded in Halberstadt in addition to nine clubs in districts in the East. Finally on the 21st August 1903, ten clubs formed an association to be called *Jüdische Turnerschaft*, Berlin, Freiburg, Köln, Mannheim in Germany, and Bielit-Biala, Mährisch-Ostrau, Prosnitz, Sofia and Hungar-Heradisch beyond the German borders. And at the *Burgvogtei* in Basel at the VI. Zionist Congress in 1903, the first gymnastics display with thirty-five performers took place. Soon other Jewish clubs were formed, some joined the association. Hamburg, Frankfurt a.d Oder, Leipzig, München, Breslau and Frankfurt a. Main and some in the Eastern districts took their time to decide on affiliation, among these *Hannover 04* which in later years joined the *Sportbund Schild*. April 1905 saw another *Turntag* in Berlin and by 1908, the *Jüdische Turnerschaft* consisted of twenty-nine clubs in five districts. In 1909 the famous *Hakoah Wien* was formed. Still, a number of Jewish clubs decided to remain "neutral", i.e., to leave the question of Jewish allegiance to their individual members. However, the First World War interrupted the growth of the National-Jewish Sports-movement (the concept "Sport" slowly began to replace "Turnen" and over the years "Turnen" found its equivalent in the term "Gymnastics").

Finally in 1921 at the XII. Zionist Congress in Karlsbad, the *Maccabi World Union* replaced the *Jüdische Turnerschaft*. Two years later in 1923, eighteen countries met, with 1,500 competitors and 6,000 spectators, for the first Jewish Sports Festival, still without support from Western Europe, America and countries of the Commonwealth.

But the pattern widened in 1932, when the first *Maccabiah*, modelled on the Olympic Games, took place at Tel-Aviv with over 500 competitors apart from those of the host nation. A Winter *Maccabiah* in Zakopane followed in 1933, but events in Germany soon required the transfer of the Presidium of *Maccabi* from Berlin to London and, years later, to Israel.

The expulsion of individual Jews from the German sports organisations during 1933 brought also a break-up of international links. The fact was that the 1936 Olympic Games which were planned to take place in Berlin were still under international consideration. This made it possible to receive permission for a German *Makkabi* team to participate in the second *Maccabiah* in 1935, again at Tel-Aviv. The German *Makkabi* team gained eight medals. The team comprised *Makkabi* members only and did not include members of other Jewish sports organisations. Twenty-seven countries took part with 2,100 competitors in addition to a further 2,400 participants from Palestine. The marching in of the teams with their national flags (with the exception of the team from Germany) was a most impressive sight.[17] And finally the Kfar-ha-Maccabi was established, *Maccabi*'s

---

[17]Since the Second World War, the *Maccabiah* has been open to all Jewish sportsmen whether they belong to *Maccabi* or any other organisation as well as to all citizens of Israel, Jewish or non-Jewish. *Hapoel*, the largest sport organisation in Israel celebrates the *Hapoel Games*, open to the whole international labour movement.

own kibbuz. Some members of the team stayed in the country, others left only to return later. In 1936 the second Winter-*Maccabiah* took place in Banska Bistrica (CSR).

By now, the German *Makkabi* had reached its maximum with 120 clubs and over 20,000 members. But from the outset, that is as soon as Jewish sportsmen and women were cast out from German sport, both *Makkabi* and *Schild* competed for those thousands not yet sure where to go. Many communities were too small to support two organisations, in others a well-known Jewish club was already in existence. And so Zionists joined *Schild* clubs and non-Zionists found their way into *Makkabi* groups. The existing, neutral Jewish clubs had to decide whom to join to be able to carry on with league matches and other competitions.

In its "apartheid" form German sport, *Makkabi* – as well as *Schild* – created nation-wide sports organisations. There were football and handball leagues which led to cup-finals as well, area and national championships in athletics, swimming, gymnastics, boxing, etc. Training courses were organised and schemes introduced which involved participants in studying Hebrew and Jewish history as well as setting targets for achievements in the field of sport. Full-time officials and coaches were employed and there was a sports-supplement of the *Jüdische Rundschau* which was mainly involved in the promotion of *Makkabi* sport and ideology. Some clubs had their own facilities, often built by their own members. But for quite some time, those competitions were confined to members of *Makkabi*. Obviously, the colours chosen everywhere were blue and white. The same applies to *Makkabi Ha-Tzair*, the *bündische* youth movement linked closely to *Makkabi* (with approximately 2,000 members). Water sports as well as winter sports, tennis tournaments and indoor athletics meetings with *Makkabi* clubs from Austria and Czechoslovakia participating were the highlight of the sporting calendar. Where clubs settled down to practical work, the differences with *Sportbund Schild* subsided and a much closer cooperation could be achieved.

The *Sportbund Schild* had been formed by the *Reichsbund jüdischer Frontsoldaten* which was founded by Hauptmann Leo Löwenstein in 1919 to preserve the traditions of "frontline" soldiers. The R.j.F. did not only aim at promoting the investigation and propagation of statistics on the Jewish war-effort, the care for the handicapped and war orphans and widows, etc., but also fostered the physical education of its members and their families, and promoted agricultural settlements in Germany and abroad. Its weekly *Der Schild* had a special sports and youth supplement *Die Kraft*. There have also been a number of books and essays on the R.j.F.,[18] but very little has been published about its *Sportbund*. When in 1933 the expulsion of Jews from German sport occurred, the *Sportbund* with the help of some of the so-called "neutral" clubs with long traditions, such as JTV Köln (1903), TC Karlsruhe (1903), JTV Hannover (1904), ITC Berlin (1905) and others such as *Schild* Frankfurt a. Main grew within a short time into an organisation of 216 affiliated clubs with a membership of over 20,000. The organisation which in numbers was at least equal to if not larger than *Makkabi* had the support of the many *Ortsgruppen* of the R.j.F. and it was relatively easy

---

[18]Especially Ulrich Dunker, *Der Reichsbund jüdischer Frontsoldaten 1919–1938. Geschichte eines jüdischen Abwehrvereins*, Düsseldorf 1977.

to offer shelter to the many thousands of youngsters who just wanted to continue with a wide range of activities but without any ideological involvement. The range was extremely wide and even horse-riding, cycling and mountaineering were among the many popular pursuits, and some of the Jewish clubs near Berlin organised a Regatta in which a number of eights participated. There were thirty-five tennis sections with 120 tennis courts at their disposal, and the boxers had their own twenty-three clubs. *Schild*, like *Makkabi*, organised its own *Reichsmeisterschaften*, association-championships, in a number of sports such as swimming, athletics, ju-jitsu, gymnastics, etc., as well as in football, handball and table tennis. Again similar to *Makkabi*, *Schild* organised training-courses, classes for referees, etc., and it also produced a scheme for a *Leistungsabzeichen*, a sports award similar to the *Reichssportabzeichen* but restricted to sport only. It also published a *Sportleitfaden*, a training compendium.

Arising from the special interest of the parent body, the R.j.F., the *Sportbund* participated actively in the establishment of Gross-Breesen, an agricultural training centre which remained in operation until 1942, the psychologist Curt Bondy acting as its director.[19] In addition, a special holiday programme as well as language classes in English and Spanish were organised. The *Sportbund* promoted the physical education and character formation of its members so that its members would develop into healthy, strong and conscious Jews, capable of succeeding wherever fate would send them. And here appears an important difference to *Makkabi* with its Palestine-orientated *Aliyah* and *Hachscharah* programme. The preparation for emigration was open-ended which meant that a considerable number of *Schild* members left for Palestine as well.

Obviously, the two sports organisations needed each other inasmuch as *VINTUS*, the association of South German Jewish clubs, could not carry on on its own. And so, following the example of the youth organisations, which under the guidance of Ludwig Tietz in 1926 formed the *Reichsausschuss der jüdischen Jugendverbände* as a central organisation, now, and under pressure from the *Reichssportführer*, finally the *Reichsausschuss der jüdischen Sportverbände* was established in 1934.[20] This umbrella organisation was formed with the following objects: "The *Deutsche Makkabi-Kreis* and the *Sportbund* of the *Reichsbund jüdischer Frontsoldaten*, being the only Jewish sports associations in Germany, have founded the *Reichsausschuss der jüdischen Sportverbände*. In accordance with the instruction of the *Reichssportführer* . . . all sport clubs must affiliate." Three members of the *Makkabi* (Rabau, Friedenthal and Paul Lewinsohn) and three of the *Schild* (Loewenstein, Elsbach and Beck) together with two nominees of the *Reichsvertretung* formed its board with Walter Beck and Paul Lewinsohn acting as officers (*Geschäftsführer*). As requested by the *Reichssportführer*, the *Reichsausschuss* commenced to administer the ever-narrowing field of Jewish sport in Germany and also strove to close the gap between the two major organisations and some South

---

[19] See Werner T. Angress, 'Auswandererlehrgut Gross-Breesen', in *LBI Year Book X* (1965), pp. 168–187.

[20] As the *Sportbund* was very much linked to the Jewish Youth Service, I was appointed *Jugenddezernent* first for South Germany but later in 1935 for the whole of Germany, being involved in training courses, holiday schemes, preparation for emigration, etc., as well as editing *Die Kraft*. But these activities came to an end, like so many others, when I was subjected to a *Redeverbot* by the Gestapo.

German-Jewish sports organisations *JTUS*, *VINTUS* which were not members of *Makkabi* or *Schild*. It was not until 1937 that these organisations linked up with the *Reichsausschuss*.

Many details about the differences between the various Jewish organisations come to light when one follows the collection of written evidence, letters, rules and regulations discovered in German and Israeli archives by Bernett and his students of the *Sportwissenschaftliches Institut* of Bonn University. Bernett has unearthed documentary evidence which was unknown to many of us who were so much involved in Jewish sport in Germany. His book is an exceptionally well-informed, objective and non-partial account of Jewish sport in Germany by an author who also shows, in another publication, the damaging influence of the Nazi State on German sport in general. Bernett has covered the events from 1933 to 1938. The *Sportbeilagen* of the *C.V.-Zeitung*, the *Israelitisches Familienblatt* which were perhaps less party-linked than the *Schild* and the *Jüdische Rundschau* provide much further material on this phase as all these papers devoted up to two pages every week to Jewish sport.

Long before the exclusion of Jewish schoolchildren from German schools, Jewish schools had been established in many parts of Germany, well before the formation of Jewish sports clubs in 1898. After the exclusion of Jewish pupils from the German educational system the Jewish school movement grew into 130 schools with 18,500 pupils. In addition, there were a number of private Jewish schools, especially in Berlin. These Jewish schools were recognised, supervised and regularly inspected by the authorities, school attendance remained compulsory for all Jewish children of school age. To overcome an acute shortage of teachers of physical eduction a special qualifying course was arranged by the *Reichsvertretung der deutschen Juden* termed the *Sportpädagogische Lehrgang*. The qualifying certificate had to be approved by the county eduction authorities. Among the students were Lolo Baer as well as myself. Kurt Marx, a graduate of the *Hochschule für Leibesübungen* took charge. This was an institution which had a number of lecturers who were Jewish. (Carl Diem, the Pro-rector of the DHFL insists in his memoirs that at the college there was never even the faintest trace of antisemitism to be noticed.[21]) The P.E. teachers' short course linked up with the *Jüdische Lehrerbildungsanstalt* in Berlin which had physical education as one of the qualifying subjects as well. Finally, a one-year course was arranged by extending the existing *Gymnastikinstitut* (later *Sportschule*) *Bloch* in Stuttgart into a recognised training centre for Jewish physical training specialists.[22] Edwin Halle was appointed to act as its director, the control rested with the local authority. It closed

---

[21] Carl Diem, *Handschriftliche Tagebuchaufzeichnungen*, Carl Diem Institute, p. 4 (supplied by Karl Heinz Fink, Dipl. Arb. DSH Köln 1969). I have used the manuscript, but the diary has been published under the title: *Ein Leben für den Sport. Erinnerungen aus dem Nachlass*, Rattingen–Kastellaun–Düsseldorf 1974, cf. p. 129.

[22] The *Jüdische Erwachsenenbildung* provided adult education courses under Martin Buber, Ernst Simon, Curt Bondy, Karl Adler and others, and including myself for physical education. (It is one of my most memorable recollections to have had Martin Buber actively participating in the daily *Frühsport* during a course at Lehnitz.)

down in 1939. As Jewish sports organisations arranged their own training and competitions so did Jewish schools. The Berlin Jewish community organised the "Day of the Jewish School" at the Stadium in the Grunewald in 1935[23] and at its last festival in 1938, 6,000 youngsters from all over Germany participated in various athletic competitions, one of the very last demonstrations of Jewish vitality before the *Kristallnacht* descended.

The Olympic Games in Berlin in 1936 form the centrepiece of the period 1933–1939, the six years of Jewish sport from the beginning of the Third *Reich* until the outbreak of the war. One can say that the achievements of German Jewry in the field of physical education in this period are without parallel, in conditions of oppression only comparable with the apartheid forced on South Africa's black population.

To understand the impact of the Olympic Games on Jewish sport in Germany one must go back to the beginning.

The story of Alfred Flatow, the gymnast, who won distinction in the First Olympic Games in Athens in 1896 has been investigated by Bernett in some detail.[24] I published an interview with the sixty-six-year-old Alfred Flatow in 1936 in the sports supplement of the *Schild, Die Kraft*,[25] at the time just before the Berlin Games, as otherwise Jewish papers were instructed not to report events connected with the games. Alfred Flatow, who was first on the horizontal bar and second on the parallel bars had gained in addition the team award together with another Jew, Felix Flatow whom he described to us as his "Namensvetter" (cousin in name only). He received a laurel wreath from the holy grove in Olympia (*Heiliger Hain*) together with a gilded medal and a certificate as an award which would be registered as "two gold and one silver" in modern terms. Obviously, Flatow distinguished himself in other gymnastic competitions (Winner of the *Deutsche Turnfest* in Hamburg) and was for many years one of the most honoured members of the *Deutsche Turnerschaft*. In 1933 he was finally asked to resign when the so-called *Arierparagraph* was implemented.

This was his letter of resignation:

20. Oktober 1933

Sehr geehrter Turnbruder Naumann!
   Im Besitze Ihres Briefes vom 18. Oktober habe ich heute meinen Austritt aus der Berliner Turnerschaft schriftlich mitgeteilt.
   Für den Ausdruck Ihrer persönlichen Gefühle danke ich verbindlichst. Über meine eigenen Gedanken und Empfindungen bitte ich schweigen zu dürfen.

Mit turnerischem Gruss.
Ergebenst!

Alfred Flatow

[23]The Stadium in the Grunewald became later on the Sportscentre for the SS.
[24]Bernett, *op. cit.*, pp. 29–30.
[25]'Wie sie die Meisterschaft erkämpften. Ein Olympia Sieger erzählt. Besuch bei Alfred Flatow', *Die Kraft*, Nr. 22 (29th May 1936), p. 4.

"May I be permitted to remain silent about my own thoughts and sentiments,"[26] how much is hidden in those words of farewell. Some years later, Alfred Flatow was murdered in a concentration camp.

Baron Pierre de Coubertin re-established the Olympic Games "of the modern era", when twelve countries representing forty-nine sports organisations met two years prior to the Athens Games at the amphitheatre at the Sorbonne in Paris. They accepted the symbol of the five multicoloured interwoven rings and the motto: "The important thing in the Olympic Games is not to win but to take part, just as the most important thing in life is not the triumph but the struggle. The essential thing is not to have conquered but to have fought well."[27] In 1896, Alfred Flatow was a member of a nineteen-man-strong German team. Dr. Ference Mezö, a Hungarian Jew, himself a member of the International Olympic Committee, reports that both Flatows together won four Olympic medals.[28] In later years, there were other Jewish gymnasts from various countries who followed the successes of Flatow. But he was the first. (One was the Hungarian Jewess Agnes Keleti who won three gold, three silver and two bronze medals in 1948, 1952 and 1956. She now teaches gymnastics at the Wingate Institute in Israel.) From the outset, Jews distinguished themselves in the Olympic Games, but none more so than the Jews from Hungary who altogether won over fifty gold medals and other honours, a feat which even American Jewry will find difficult to surpass.

It is of course a fallacy to state that the Olympic Games were free from politics or international pressures. Germany was excluded from the 1920 and 1924 Games after the First World War, being condemned as *kriegsschuldig*. Russia joined the Olympic Community later but it was not until the Berlin Games of 1936 that a government considered the games as an international and political issue involving a number of other countries. Following the Second World War Germany was again debarred from the 1948 Olympic Games in London, and many examples of suspension and political conflict can be adduced from the post-war period.

But apart from a few individuals, nobody walked out or declined to participate when Adolf Hitler in his capacity as the Head of the German State opened the Berlin Games in 1936. Before relating my own experiences the valuable report of a non-Jewish writer, Monique Berlioux, should be quoted. She was a semi-finalist in the 100 metres back-stroke in 1948 and became in 1976 the Director of the International Olympic Games Committee.[29] Her article is one of a number published in the most reliable book on the Olympic Games by Lord Killanin, since 1972 President of the International Committee (as successor to the late Avery Brundage) and John Clinton Rodda, the distinguished sports writer of the *Manchester Guardian*.[30]

---

[26]Hajo Bernett not only discovered this letter but also the lengthy correspondence between the various officials of the DT which finally led to Flatow's resignation.
[27]Lord Killanin and John Rodda, *The Olympic Games. 80 Years of People, Events and Records*, London 1976, p. 14.
[28]Ference Mezö, *The Modern Olympic Games*, Budapest 1956, p. 40.
[29]*British Olympic Association. Official Report of the London Olympic Games*, London 1948.
[30]Killanin and Rodda, *op. cit*. Permission to quote from this section is hereby gratefully acknowledged

Jews and Sport in Germany

> "Adolf Hitler acquired power on 30 January 1933. The thirty-first Sesseion of the IOC was held in Vienna on 7–9 June of that year. Baillet-Latour officially asked the representatives of the Reich to guarantee their country's observance of the Olympic Charter or to forgo the Games. They gave the requested guarantee. The Vienna Session noted the fact that 'in principle the German Jews would not be excluded from the Games of the XIth Olympiad'. Of the two German members of the IOC, one, Theodore Lewald, half Jewish by birth, was President of the Organizing Committee of the Berlin Games; the other, Dr. Karl Ritter von Halt, was President of the Organizing Committee of the Garmisch Games. Von Halt, born in Munich in 1891 and son of a locksmith, had taken part in the Games of the fifth Olympiad in Stockholm. Knighted during World War I, the tall and statuesque Bavarian became an IOC member in 1929.
>
> Hardly had the thirty-first Session closed when Hitler decided to replace Lewald and von Halt at the head of the two Organizing Committees by the State Director of Sport he had just appointed, Hans von Tschammer und Osten. Baillet-Latour immediately requested an audience with Hitler, who felt obliged to comply. 'It was in consideration of the statures of His Excellence Dr. Lewald and Ritter von Halt that the IOC granted the organization of the Games to Berlin and Garmisch,' the IOC President told the German Führer. 'If our two colleagues should cease to be Presidents of the Organizing Committees, the IOC would be obliged to withdraw the Games from the two cities conditionally elected and to award them to other candidates.' Hitler gave in.
>
> The campaigns against staging the Games in two cities of the Third Reich nevertheless grew to a frenzy. Baillet-Latour invited von Halt and Lewald to confirm publicly their promises regarding the observance of the undertakings they had made in Vienna on behalf of Germany. The two delegates repreated their statements on the Third Reich's 'loyalty' towards German Jewish athletes who, according to them, were in no way at a disadvantage compared with their 'Aryan' comrades. Certainly at that time, racial persecutions were proliferating, giving a faint hint of the horrors to come in 1938–45. But the systematic killings had not begun; the world's strange passivity towards the regime was to continue for several years."

Ritter von Halt, it may be of interest to note, was employed in a leading position with the Jewish bankers Aufhäuser in Munich.[31]

> "Ernest Lee Jahncke, the member for the United States, violently opposed American participation. In doing so he made a stand against Avery Brundage, then President of both the US Olympic Committee and the Amateur Athletic Union. Brundage accused the opponents of American participation in the Games of 'betraying the athletes of the United States'. On 15 September 1935 Hitler proclaimed the 'Nuremberg laws' which made Jews 'sub-humans' and these were followed by a mass of persecutions . . .
>
> At the foot of the Zugspitze the two villages of Garmisch and Partenkirchen were arranged with characteristic Bavarian *Gemütlichkeit*. But signs 'Dogs and Jews are not allowed' had been placed outside the toilet facilites at Olympic sites. Baillet-Latour saw them and again requested an interview with Hitler. After the customary courtesies, he said, 'Mr. Chancellor, the signs shown to the visitors to the Games are not in conformity with Olympic principles.' Hitler replied, 'Mr. President, when you are invited to a friend's home, you don't tell him how to run it, do you?' Baillet-Latour thought a minute and replied, 'Excuse me, Mr. Chancellor, when the five-circled flag is raised over the stadium, it is no longer Germany. It is Olympia and we are masters there.' The signs were removed."

The story can be continued with the report by the Americans, Postal and the two Silvers:[32]

---

to the publishers, The Rainbird Publishing Group Limited, and to Macdonald & Jane's, who are about to publish a second revised edition of this book.

[31] Karl Ritter von Halt, who succeeded Hans von Tschammer und Osten as *Reichssportführer*, could however not really be described as pro-Jewish. When he demanded the removal of anti-Jewish posters, he stated expressly that he did not do so to assist the Jews in any way but in order to save the Games at Garmisch–Partenkirchen.

[32] *Encyclopedia of Jews in Sports, op. cit.*, pp. 399, 400. In addition to those mentioned by Silver, there was the weightlifter Max Seligmann.

"... All Jewish athletic clubs, which were under the supervision of the Reich Sports Commissioner could function only if the local police had not outlawed them as 'enemies of the state'. Thus, German Jewish athletes were being systematically hindered in their efforts by being denied adequate training facilities and opportunities to test themselves in actual competition...

.... In June, 1934, the AOC again postponed official acceptance of the German invitation and instructed Avery Brundage, its chairman, to make an on-the-spot study of the status of Jewish athletes in the Third Reich. Alarmed at the delay in American acceptance, the Reich Fields Sports Organization in June, 1934, nominated 21 Jewish athletes for the German Olympic training camps, but none was ever invited to attend.

Among the 21 were: Helene Mayer, fencer; Gretel Bergmann, high jumper; Erich Lorch, Hanne Manne, Erich Schild, Rudi Marx, Paul Y. Mayer, Werner Schattmann, Kurt Sternlieb and Franz Orgler, track and field men; Bernd Meysel, a swimmer; and a canoeist named Baer. Brundage returned from Germany in Sept. 1934 with a favorable report. On the strength of his findings, the AOC accepted the invitation to participate in the Berlin Olympics..."

The exploits of German-Jewish sportsmen and women gave the answer to the question of *Gleichwertigkeit*. But *Gleichwertigkeit* can only be attained on the basis of *Gleichberechtigung*. Where equality is taken away, achievements must suffer and the picture becomes distorted. With the increasing ghettoisation of Jewish sport in Germany, the participation of German Jews in the Berlin Olympic Games in 1936 became a political issue. One can only compare their situation with the deplorable principle of apartheid in South Africa, which led to the embargo on South Africa in many fields of sport. The blindness of many leading personalities and their political naïvity within the Olympic movement had its best example in the person of Avery Brundage, later the President of the Olympic Games Committee. With his complete dedication to the non-political idea of the Olympic Games, he was only too willing to accept German assurances regarding the equal chances of German-Jewish sportsmen and women. Here my own experiences may help to illustrate the situation during the years prior to 1936 and at the Games.

In October 1934, I received an invitation from the *Reichssportführer* von Tschammer-Osten to report to the *Führerschule-Wilhelmshöhe* near Ettlingen, Baden in the Black Forest together with a number of other Jewish athletes. Nominees had been requested from *Makkabi* and *Schild* and accepted by the German authorities. In 1978, Itzchak Pruschnowski in his television documentary *Dornen am Lorbeer* took great care in tracing former participants of this training course and even revisited Wilhelmshöhe. He interviewed Rüssmann, who had been the German coach appointed to take charge of this all-Jewish course, who said about the participants that "they were not concerned to compete for the honour of the *Reich*" and Werner Schattmann, the sprinter, added "the treatment in the camp was the best one can imagine". As to our attitude towards participation in the Games, it was clear to us, from the very beginning that in no way would we be willing to take part in the Olympic Games. None of us was prepared to compete under the swastika, to strive for Germany's honour. But we were also aware that for political reasons we had to prove, until the last moment, by our personal best performances our equality in relation to other sportsmen.[33]

There was a second training camp in Ettlingen in 1935 for *Schild* members,

---

[33]From the soundtrack of the Film *Dornen am Lorbeer*, Sender Freies Berlin, 1978. Interview given by the author to Pruschnowski.

but at that time, only Gretel Bergmann proved to be a kind of "Probable' while most of us presented a talented pool of "Possibles", to use English selector terms. With the poor facilities for training, limited coaching and lack of real competitions, the Jews in Germany certainly suffered in their apartheid similarly to the black South Africans. But how very different has been the reaction of the world of sport thirty, forty years later! It appears that our experiences have helped others in a similar predicament and produced a common attitude towards offending countries, a position which nobody was willing to take against the increasing might of Nazi Germany in 1936.

Gretel Bergmann, whose family came from Laupheim in South Germany, was asked to participate in the Württemberg Championships. In a recent letter to me, she stated: "I do not remember how the condition of the track was in Stuttgart. I think it was a bit soft but no matter what the state of the track was, it could not compare to the climate as far as the officials were concerned – pretty grim." Still, Gretel equalled the German record for Ladies High Jump with 1·60 metres and was ordered to report to Hanover for a special training course where she shared a room with Dora Rathjen who was the second choice for the German Olympic Games team. I remember meeting Gretel in Hanover when she emphatically stated in her broad Swabian dialect that this girl was a boy. Many years after the games, Rathjen was "unmasked" and confessed that she was planted in the women's team,[34] probably to stop Gretel from keeping up a challenge for a place in a team until the last moment. But Germany selected only two instead of three girls and Gretel received a letter from the *Reichssportführer* in which he stated that she could not be included in the German team as her performances were "zu unbeständig", too inconsistent. But he enclosed a complimentary ticket for her. I remember that Gretel and I discussed the letter and she decided to return the ticket to him marked "personal' but with nothing else, not even a note of explanation. And was it just irony of fate that the event was won by an Hungarian Jewess Ibolya Czák[35] with the same height reached by Gretel in Stuttgart under such adverse conditions?

But two "half-Jews", Helene Mayer and Rudi Ball became, on the invitation of the *Reichssportführer*, members of the German team. Rudi played ice-hockey for Germany in the Winter Games. He and Helene were both asked to return to Germany. Helene had emigrated to the United States. She was the daughter of Dr. Ludwig Mayer, a medical practitioner in Offenbach near Frankfurt a. Main but she accepted the defence of her title which she had won in 1928 for Germany. Some Nazi papers then stooped so low as to suggest that Helene's mother had indicated that Helene was actually born as the result of an affair with an "Aryan". Helene gained a silver medal, gave the obligatory *Deutsche Gruss* on the winners' rostrum, wearing the white uniform of the German team with the swastika badge.[36] As soon as the ceremony was over, she returned to the United States (where she won eight national titles – 1934 to 1946). But again irony

---

[34]*Life Magazine*, 7th October 1966, and *Time Magazine*, September 1966.
[35]*Encyclopedia of Jews in Sports, op. cit.*, p. 402.
[36]There is reason to believe that, by threats to her family in Germany, pressure was exerted on Helene Mayer to return for the Games. This cannot now be substantiated.

gained an upper hand: the gold medal was won by another Hungarian Jewess Ilona Elek-Schacherer, still one of the leading figures in Hungarian fencing circles, Helene Mayer came second and Ellen Preiss, a Jewish girl from Vienna, third. Ellen had won the 1932 Games and came third again in 1948. But Ilona Elek was perhaps the greatest woman fencer ever, as she won the 1948 London Games when already forty-two in addition to having won eleven world championships. (And so in 1948 again three Jewish girls stepped on to the winners' rostrum, this time as third, Karel Lachmann from Denmark.) Bela Komyádi, the Hungarian water polo coach died shortly before the Berlin Games. But his team which included a number of Jewish players won a gold medal. Returning to Budapest, the team planted a tree – so it is said – on his grave at the Jewish cemetery. Recently, a new competition pool has been built in Buadapest which is named the Bela Komyádi-pool.

There were a number of Jewish sportsmen and women who participated in Berlin in the American, Hungarian and other teams as well as members of *Hagibor Prag*[37] while others such as Ruth Langer and Judith Deutsch of *Hakoah Wien* refused to compete. Others still felt it as a special challenge to compete and rejoiced when Jesse Owens won four gold medals and this black American became an idol for many of us who watched the games. Harold Abrahams who had won the 100 metres in 1924 and had become a figure of international standing, shared Brundage's opinion that "the Games had to go on".[38]

As soon as the games were over, the breathing space gained for a short time came to an end. Within two years came the *Kristallnacht*. In the fight for individual and collective survival Jewish sport lost its impetus and was finally wiped out by the icy winds of the final solution.

Bernett has summed up the reasons for his book with these words:

> "As there is a danger that a tragic chapter of the German history of sport may be forgotten, the theme demanded an investigation for the reasons why a dynamic sports movement had been decimated by force and finally extinguished. Under the pressure of the police state and its propaganda policy, the public conscience had failed to react to what was happening. The attempt to reconstruct from a residue of sources and scraps of memory displays the picture of sport in the Third *Reich* from its negative side. Sport does not manifest itself here as the showpiece of the nation, but as the deliberately restricted field of action of a suppressed and persecuted minority."[39]

And it is with his words as a reminder that I have recollected my own experiences in connection with the Olympic Games in Berlin in 1936.

No assessment of the role Jews played and could have played in German sport and physical education can be complete without some evaluation of the war years and the years of emigration.

---

[37] *Encyclopedia of Jews in Sports, op. cit.*, p. 402.
[38] A Captain Wolfgang Fuerstner, who was of Jewish descent, acted as Adjutant to the Commander of the Olympic village. After the Games, on being informed that he would be dismissed from the German army because of his Jewish origin, he committed suicide. He did nevertheless receive a military funeral with full honours.
[39] Bernett, *op. cit.*, p. 7.

Jews and Sport in Germany

Jewish sport in Germany may have lingered on in small groups until 1940, but finally ended in the scenes shot for the grotesque film *Der Führer schenkt den Juden eine Stadt*. Kurt Gerron, the well-known Jewish cabaret artist and actor was ordered to produce this film of the Ghetto Theresienstadt. From the many books and reports in various languages,[40] it appears that there were eleven football teams for seven-a-side. "Football was liked best and was first played in the courtyard ... One attempted even to form a Theresienstadt football league. The results were made known by display of league tables."[41] Apart from former club membership and countries of origin, various workers formed their own teams as the electricians, gardeners, youth service, clothing stores, cooks, butchers, etc....[42] Every Saturday, matches were played at the Südberg, for example: at 15.30 hrs. Holland opposed the Protectorat in handball and at 16.30 hrs. Bohemia played Mähren and finally at 18.00 hrs. the main attraction: Prag versus Wien. Those were weekly events which were taken up in the film in a distorted form, processed by *Aktualita Wochenschau*. The film which is now in the possession of the *Bundesarchiv*, Koblenz, shows a scene in which a former Czech champion is shown giving a diving display at the SS-pool in the River Eder which was handed over for the showing of this one scene only for this vile propaganda film. Those of "non-Jewish" appearance were not enrolled for the task but "since the 60,000 film extras were no longer needed, the Ghetto was liquidated down to 12,000 people while the extras received their payment in the gas chambers of Auschwitz".[43]

Some of those who emigrated proved that if they could not be champions of sport in Germany, they could accomplish this goal abroad. First of all, before the war, Gretel Bergmann became English high-jump champion in 1934 and later gained fame in America where she won the championship in 1937 and again in 1938, as well as in putting the shot, and Ruth Caro excelled in throwing the javelin in England. Henry Laskau represented the United States as a walker in the Olympic Games and at the *Maccabiah*, and Inge Mello (de Preiss) met me in London in 1948, where we trained together in preparation for her Olympic Games début in discus and putting the shot. She qualified – as an Argentinian citizen – for the final in 1948 and came twelfth in Helsinki in 1952. In addition to those four "champions" were Daniel Prenn, Helene Mayer and others.

Finally, perhaps the most remarkable achievements by German Jews in the field of sport are not to be measured by stop-watch and tape, but these two made an outstanding contribution to physical education not only to England but also in the wider world; i.e., Kurt Hahn and Sir Ludwig Guttmann (both born in Breslau). Lord Hunt (who, by the way, took the title for his book on Everest and

---

[40] *Theresienstadt*, Wien 1968.
[41] Hans Hofer, *Der Film über Theresienstadt*, p. 184.
[42] H. G. Adler, *Theresienstadt 1941–1945. Das Antlitz einer Zwangsgemeinschaft*, Tübingen 1960, pp. 183–184.
[43] *Ibid.*, p. 567.

other encounters *Life is Meeting* from Martin Buber)[44] describes Kurt Hahn as "a passionate advocate of developing outdoor adventurous activities as personal tests of youthful character, which he believed to be a necessary complement to the academic aspects of formal education", and continues, "that remarkable Jewish Refugee from Germany who, under duress, had left his own school at Salem, the shores of Lake Constance (1920–1933), and founded a new public school in Britain (Gordonstoun) in Scotland, 1934–1953)", and states, "the essence of his creed was that each boy needed a challenge personal to and attainable by himself, rather than being assessed in competition and comparison with the performances of others". Thus the new concept "competition with yourself and not with others" brought a new philosophy to the playing-fields of Eton and Harrow. As Hunt says, "Dr. Hahn, Headmaster of Gordonstoun, was already making his mark on the British academic scene." Prince Philip, the Duke of Edinburgh, had moved with Hahn from Salem to Gordonstoun, and his sons, Prince Charles and Prince Andrew followed father's footsteps at the same school. Soon, based on a paper of Hunt's, Kurt Hahn introduced the "County Badge Scheme", the forerunner of the "Duke of Edinburgh Awards Scheme". I joined Prince Philip's Council in its initial stages, the so-called "Pilot scheme" with the Brady Clubs, and soon Jewish boys from the East End of London, instead of taking up boxing as had their grandfathers, took up the scheme and won the gold award. Shortly after Hahn founded the "Outward Bound" movement, a group of residential adventure schools in the mountains or near the sea. Years later, Hahn added to his schemes, now internationally acclaimed, and in operation in various countries overseas as well, the Sixth Form College at St. Donath's Castle in South Wales, known as "The Atlantic college" with pupils from over forty countries. Over a million boys – and girls – have participated and benefitted from the scheme, and there are today six Outward Bound schools in the United Kingdom and over twenty abroad.

Many honours and decorations have been awarded to Kurt Hahn,[45] whose philosophy of "competing with yourself" has a certain affinity to the work of Sir Ludwig Guttmann who by request of the government founded a special hospital in 1944 at Stoke Mandeville near London to treat war casualties.[46] Based on his work at this Paraplegia Centre, he created the Olympic Games for the paralysed, the Paraplegic Games. In 1969, the Queen opened the Stoke Mandeville Games, which were attended by many nations. Guttmann became the Director, then the President, and so the embodiment of the paraplegic movement, holding many honorary appointments in Britain and all over the world. No wonder that a former pupil of Hahn's Gordonstoun, the Prince of Wales, agreed to launch an

[44]John Hunt, *Life is Meeting*, London 1978, pp. 62, 70, 128–139. Permission to quote is gratefully acknowledged to Lord Hunt and the publishers, Hodder & Stoughton.

[45]Peter Carpenter, 'Kurt Hahn and the Salem Tradition', *The New Era. World Education Fellowship*, vol. 55, No. 7 (1974).

[46]Sir Ludwig Guttmann, CBE, FRS, FRCP, FRCS, born 3rd July 1899, died on 18th March 1980, while this volume of the Year Book was in the press. For a full obituary, see *The Times* (London) of 20th March 1980; and the further note by Dr. Raymond Greene in *The Times* of 29th March 1980 which describes how Dr. Guttmann as Director of the Jewish Hospital in Breslau protected fellow Jews by concealing them in the guise of fictitious patients. See also the obituary in *AJR Information*, vol. XXXV, No. 3 (May 1980).

appeal for the "Disabled Sports Foundation" aiming to provide a permanent Olympic Village for the disabled in Stoke Mandeville. The achievements of these two German Jews in England can be said to have set the seal on the contribution German Jews have made to sport and physical education.

The Verband nationaldeutscher Juden 1921–1933

BY CARL J. RHEINS

On 30th October 1920, an essay entitled 'Vom nationaldeutschen Juden' appeared in the *Kölnische Zeitung*, a newspaper affiliated to the right-of-centre *Deutsche Volkspartei* (DVP).* The essay was written by Dr. Max Naumann, a Berlin lawyer and former captain in the Bavarian army.[1] Naumann's decision to use the *Kölnische Zeitung* as a forum to express his views on the "Jewish Question" was not surprising in view of his political orientation and military background. Born in Berlin on 12th January 1875 to an old-established West Prussian family,[2] Naumann's youth was typical of that of many of the offspring of assimilated Jews. As a student, he attended the Friedrichs-Werdersche Gymnasium, an institution which catered to the Jewish middle class,[3] and later received a law degree from the University of Berlin.[4] Following his admission to the bar, Naumann became an active member of both the pre-war National Liberal Party and its political successor, the DVP.[5] His military career began in 1897 as an *Einjähriger* stationed in Munich. Five years later, he received a Reserve officer's commission in the Bavarian army.[6] Called to active duty on 4th August 1914, Nau-

---

*The author wishes to express his appreciation to Professor Werner T. Angress of the State University of New York at Stony Brook and to Dr. Eva G. Reichmann of the Leo Baeck Institute, London, who read earlier drafts of this essay and made many valuable suggestions; and to Dr. Ulrich Dunker, Berlin, for sharing with me data from his own research.

[1] This essay soon appeared as a brochure. See Max Naumann, *Vom nationaldeutschen Juden*, Berlin 1920. On the DVP's attitude towards the "Jewish Question" see P. B. Wiener, 'Die Parteien der Mitte', in *Entscheidungsjahr 1932. Zur Judenfrage in der Endphase der Weimarer Republik*. Ein Sammelband herausgegeben von Werner E. Mosse unter Mitwirkung von Arnold Paucker, Tübingen 1966 [2] (Schriftenreihe wissenschaftlicher Abhandlungen des Leo Baeck Instituts 13), pp. 290, 292, 314–320.

[2] Information on Naumann's personal life remains sketchy. His father listed his occupation as *Kaufmann*. His mother, Mathilde Naumann née Herrmann, had a hard life, giving birth to thirteen children. Oral information from Dr. Klaus J. Herrmann, 14th May 1974. She died in 1920 at the age of eighty-five. Max Naumann Collection, Leo Baeck Institute, New York (hereafter cited as L.B.I.) A.R. C.Z. 66–226. Naumann's own marriage, marred by tragedy, was eventually dissolved. Hans Heinrich Peyser to Dr. Herrmann, 9th July [illegible] L.B.I. A.R. C.Z. 66–226. Of his three children, the eldest Hilde, was a Communist and eventually went to the Soviet Union. The two younger children were killed in fatal accidents. Oral information from Mrs. Hans E. Baum, 24th October 1973. Mrs. Baum served as both Naumann's personal secretary and V.n.J. *Geschäftsführer* from 1925 to 1935.

[3] Of the sixteen students who graduated with Naumann on 17th March 1893, ten listed their religion as Jewish. Naumann was among them. Letter of 25th July 1974 from Klaus J. Herrmann to the author.

[4] See Max Naumann, *Der Erbeinsetzungsvertrag in seinen Beziehungen zum Noterbenrechte* (Inaugural dissertation, University of Berlin 1899?).

[5] Alfred Peyser, *Nationaldeutsche Juden und ihre Lästerer. Eine Streitschrift*, Berlin 1925, p. 7. No more than 4 per cent of German Jews supported the DVP. Arnold Paucker, 'Jewish Defence against Nazism in the Weimar Republic', *Wiener Library Bulletin*, XXVI, No. 1/2 (1972), pp. 26–27.

[6] Anon. *Klärung, 12 Autoren und Politiker über die Judenfrage*, Berlin 1932, p. 68.

mann demonstrated his German patriotism by distinguishing himself in combat. As an infantry commander during the First World War, he was awarded the Iron Cross First and Second Class,[7] the Bavarian *Militärverdienstorden* Fourth Class with swords, and was promoted to the rank of captain (*Landwehr* I).[8] Following the armistice, Naumann chose to remain on active duty, serving as *Abteilungsführer* to the Charlottenburg *Einwohnerwehr*.[9] It was during this period that he published his first essay on the "Jewish Question", 'Vom nationaldeutschen Juden'.

In this treatise, Naumann rejected the Zionist argument that Jews were bound together by common ties of history and religion.[10] Instead, he saw the post-war Jewish community in Germany as being divided into three major camps: National-German Jews, who were wholeheartedly committed to the German nation; the Zionists, who were wholeheartedly committed to the Jewish nation; and the *Zwischenschichtler* (in-betweens) by whom he meant members of the *Centralverein deutscher Staatsbürger jüdischen Glaubens* (C.V.).[11] It was this last and largest group that Naumann hoped to reach. The Zionists by definition were "verdrehte Kerle"[12] devoid of any true German feeling. Committed to the establishment of a "new Jewish *Reich*",[13] Naumann saw them playing directly into the hands of antisemites by openly acknowledging the existence of a separate Jewish *Volk*.[14] On the other hand, the vast majority of German Jews were still redeemable. Their fault lay in their failure to divest themselves of the last vestige of "Jewish tribal feeling[s]".[15] One way in which these feelings were manifested, according to Naumann, was in the financial and political support which the *Hilfsverein der deutschen Juden* and the C.V. had provided for Jewish immigrants from Eastern Europe.[16] The National-German Jew, on the other hand, rejected any feelings

---

[7]Max Naumann to President von Hindenburg, Berlin 31st March 1933, p. 3. Bundesarchiv Koblenz (hereafter cited as B.A.) R 43 II/600. Prior to the First World War unbaptised Jews were systematically denied commissions in the Prussian Reserve Officer Corps. On the other hand, between fifty and one hundred unbaptised Jews from Prussia and other North German states were able to secure Reserve commissions in the Bavarian Army. Werner T. Angress, 'Prussia's Army and the Jewish Reserve Officer Controversy before World War I', in *LBI Year Book* XVII (1972), pp. 39–40. In addition to Naumann, Dr. Leo Löwenstein, the head of the R.j.F. also received a pre-war Bavarian commission. Leo Brandt, 'Zur Erinnerung an Leo Löwenstein', *Allgemeine Wochenzeitung der Juden in Deutschland*, vol. XV, No. 25 (16th September 1960), p. 49.
[8]Letter of 8th June 1974 from Klaus J. Herrmann to the author.
[9]*Klärung*, p. 68. For a discussion of the political attitudes of the *Einwohnerwehr* see Robert G. L. Waite, *Vanguard of Nazism. The Free Corps Movement in Postwar Germany 1918–1923*, New York 1969, pp. 54, 68–69, 197–200. See also James M. Diehl, *Paramilitary Politics in Weimar Germany*, Bloomington, Indiana 1977, pp. 32–38, 5967.
[10]Naumann, *Vom nationaldeutschen Juden*, pp. 6–7.
[11]Ruth L. Pierson, *German Jewish Identity in the Wemar Republic* (unpublished doctoral dissertation, Yale University 1970), p. 316.
[12]Naumann, *Vom nationaldeutschen Juden*, p. 3.
[13]*Ibid*.
[14]*Ibid*., p. 7.
[15]Pierson, *German Jewish Identity*, p. 316.
[16]For a discussion of the *Hilfverein*'s activities on behalf of Eastern Jews see Paul Nathan, *Ostjuden in Deutschland*, Berlin 1921. See also S[halom] Adler-Rudel, 'East European Jewish Workers in Germany', in *LBI Year Book II* (1957), pp. 136–165. This essay was later incorporated as part of Adler-Rudel's *Ostjuden in Deutschland 1880–1940. Zugleich eine Geschichte der Organisationen, die sie betreuten*, Tübingen 1959 (Schriftenreihe wissenschaftlicher Abhandlungen des Leo Baeck Instituts 1). On the

of kinship with the *Ostjuden*.[17] Describing them in his essay as "pitiful creatures ... of a not quite human level",[18] Naumann hoped to demonstrate to his readers that the National-German Jew was spiritually and racially different from the Jewish masses in the East and thus worthy of a position within the German *Volksgemeinschaft*.[19] German *völkisch* ideology was thus modified by Naumann to accommodate those Jews who were thoroughly German in feeling. As for continued German-Jewish assistance for the new immigrants, Naumann argued that consideration for Germany came first:

> "[Whereas] a healthy body can tolerate and assimilate many a bacillus, a weakened body is destroyed by one. Germany is too sick to be able to grant the right of asylum to the dangerous guests from the East, whether they are of Jewish or Slavic descent. And the National-German Jew is too much of a German to desire special treatment for the benefit of the Jews who are among these noxious persons."[20]

Implicit in this analysis was an attack against the Jewish establishment's apparent lack of patriotism.[21] More importantly, Naumann's attitude towards the *Ostjudenproblem* was no different from that of most right-wing antisemites.

Despite extremely hostile reviews in the Jewish press,[22] Naumann continued to go ahead with plans to rally other German Jews who shared his sentiments. On 20th March 1921, he announced in Berlin the formation of the *Verband nationaldeutscher Juden* (V.n.J. – League of National-German Jews).[23] Eighty-eight other

---

attitude of the C.V. towards Eastern Jewish Immigration see Kurt Alexander, 'Ostjudenfrage', *Mitteilungen des Syndikus des Centralvereins deutscher Staatsbürger jüdischen Glaubens*, II, No. 7 (17th May 1920), pp. 89–91; Ludwig Holländer, *Denkschrift über die Bestrebungen des Rechtsanwalts Dr. Max Naumann in Berlin auf Begründung eines Verbandes nationaldeutscher Juden*, Berlin 1921, pp. 7–8; and Adler-Rudel's *Ostjuden in Deutschland*, pp. 71–72, 76, 82–83. See also Eva G. Reichmann's 'Der Bewusstseinswandel der deutschen Juden', in *Deutsches Judentum in Krieg und Revolution 1916–1923*. Ein Sammelband herausgegeben von Werner E. Mosse unter Mitwirkung von Arnold Paucker, Tübingen 1971 (Schriftenreihe wissenschaftlicher Abhandlungen des Leo Baeck Instituts 25), pp. 538–545; and Egmont Zechlin, *Die deutsche Politik und die Juden im Ersten Weltkrieg*, Göttingen 1969, pp. 167–176.

[17] Pierson, *German Jewish Identity*, p. 317; Adler-Rudel, *Ostjuden in Deutschland*, pp. 29–30.
[18] Naumann, *Vom nationaldeutschen Juden*, p. 21.
[19] George L. Mosse, 'The Influence of the *Völkisch* Idea on German Jewry', in Max Kreutzberger (ed.), *Studies of the Leo Baeck Institute*, New York 1967, p. 112. This essay was later reprinted by Mosse in *Germans and Jews. The Right, the Left and the Search for a 'Third Force' in Pre-Nazi Germany*, New York 1970, pp. 77–115.
[20] Naumann, *Vom nationaldeutschen Juden*, p. 22, as quoted in Pierson, *German Jewish Identity*, p. 317.
[21] As early as the summer of 1920, Naumann had accused the C.V. of lacking sufficient "national-German" consciousness, citing as evidence the political support shown by the C.V. for candidates of the DDP and SPD. Holländer, *op. cit.*, pp. 1–2.
[22] See, for example, 'Vom nationaldeutschen Juden', *Israelitisches Familienblatt* (Hamburg), XXII, No. 46 (11th November 1920), p. 1; and [Kurt Alexander] K.A. "Zeitschau", *Im deutschen Reich. Zeitschrift des Centralvereins deutscher Staatsbürger jüdischen Glaubens*, XXVI, No. 12 (December 1920), pp. 372–378. See also Gustav Krojanker, 'Deutschland. Der Fall Naumann', *Jüdische Rundschau*, XXVII, No. 26 (31st March 1922), pp. 165–167.
[23] 'Zehn Jahre Verband nationaldeutscher Juden', *Der nationaldeutsche Jude. Mitteilungsblatt des Verbandes nationaldeutscher Juden e.V.*, No. 4 (April 1931), p. 8. A definitive study of the history, ideology and organisation of the V.n.J. during the Weimar Republic is lacking. The only contemporary account of the early history of the League is Peyser's *Streitschrift*. During the period 1945–1965, most scholars working in the field of German-Jewish history tended to minimise the importance of the V.n.J. The sole exception was Trude Weiss Rosmarin's 'It Was Thus in Germany, Too', *Congress Weekly*, 21st December 1945, pp. 8–10, which attempted to draw a comparison between the anti-

Jewish professionals and businessmen joined him in signing this announcement.[24]

Unlike the *Reichsbund jüdischer Frontsoldaten* (R.j.F.), the new organisation was not concerned with refuting the charge that Jews had been responsible for Germany's defeat in the First World War. Instead, the V.n.J. was prepared to criticise Jewish behaviour in terms defined by antisemites[25] and to ascribe the resurgence of post-war antisemitism to the failure of the Jewish community to integrate itself completely within a nationalist German *Volksgemeinschaft*.[26] To

---

Zionist attitudes of the League and the attitudes held by the American Council for Judaism. The first attempt to explain the origins of the V.n.J. came in 1965 with the publication of Klaus J. Herrmann's 'Political Response to the Balfour Declaration in Imperial Germany. German Judaism', *Middle East Journal* XIX (Summer 1965), pp. 303–320. Two years later, George L. Mosse attempted to analyse the V.n.J. in his 'The Influence of the *Völkisch* Idea on German Jewry', pp. 111–114. Since that time a growing literature on the League has begun to appear. The Jewish content of the V.n.J. has been analysed in Pierson's *German Jewish Identity*, pp. 54–56, 70–71, 315–318. On the relationship between the Berlin *Reformgemeinde* and the League see *ibid.*, pp. 54–56; and Klaus J. Herrmann's 'Weltanschauliche Aspekte der Jüdischen Reformgemeinde zu Berlin', *Emuna. Horizonte zur Diskussion über Israel und das Judentum*, IX, No. 2 (March/April 1974), p. 90. On the attitudes of the League towards Germany's Marxist parties see Hans Helmuth Knütter, *Die Juden und die deutsche Linke in der Weimarer Republik 1918–1933*, Düsseldorf 1971, pp. 101–106. For a psychoanalytic interpretation of Naumann's political attitudes see Kurt Lewin, 'Self-Hatred Among Jews', *Contemporary Jewish Record*, IV, No. 3 (June 1941), pp. 218–232. See also Sidney M. Bolkosky, *The Distorted Image. German Jewish Perceptions of Germans and Germany, 1918–1935*, New York 1975, pp. 6, 31, 41–44, 155–156, 161–164, 170, 187, 207. This is a slightly revised version of his doctoral dissertation (State University of New York at Binghamton, 1973).

It should be stressed that despite continuing claims by historians, there is no evidence whatsoever that the V.n.J. emerged as a result of a split within the C.V.

[24]'Alphabetische Liste der 89 Gründungsmitglieder des Verbands nationaldeutscher Juden (März 1921)', in Klaus J. Herrmann, *Das Dritte Reich und die Deutsch-Jüdischen Organisationen 1933–1934*, Schriftenreihe der Hochschule für politische Wissenschaften München, Heft 4, Munich 1969, pp. 36–38. During the Republic, the V.n.J. numbered 3,500 members. Oral information from Mrs. Hans E. Baum. Albert Grzesinski's statement that "tens of thousands" of Jews were members of the V.n.J. is without foundation. Albert Grzesinski, *Inside Germany*, trans. Alexander S. Lipschitz, New York 1939, p. 195. Claims by Klaus J. Herrmann and Zosa Szajkowski that Professor Franz Oppenheimer of the University of Frankfurt was a member of the League are also without foundation. In 1965, in his 'Political Response to the Balfour Declaration in Imperial Germany', p. 310, Herrmann wrote: "Oppenheimer's disillusion with radical Zionism led him ... to enroll as a founding member of the out-spokenly anti-Zionist 'Association of National-German Jews' ... led by Dr. Max Naumann". Szajkowski repeated this charge in his 'The Komitee für den Osten and Zionism', *Herzl Yearbook* VII (1971), p. 236. Their confusion centres around Professor Oppenheimer's namesake, Dr. Franz Oppenheimer of Berlin, who was a founding member of the V.n.J. and later served on its National Executive Committee. Professor Oppenheimer, on the other hand, while disagreeing with the more radical views of Kurt Blumenfeld, never ceased to be a Zionist according to his own interpretation. "In 1926, he went to Palestine at the invitation of the Zionist Executive in order to give an expert opinion on the state of Jewish agricultural settlement at that time." Letter of 18th February 1975 from Dr. Michael Heymann to the author. See also Arthur Ruppin, *Memoirs, Diaries and Letters*, London 1971, p. 222. Other evidence which would indicate that we are dealing with *two* men is the fact that in August 1931 the V.n.J. *Hauptvorstand* sent birthday greetings to Dr. Oppenheimer of Berlin on the occasion of his sixtieth birthday. This would make his date of birth 1871. 'Verbandsnachrichten', *Der nationaldeutsche Jude*, No. 8 (August 1931), p. 5. Professor Oppenheimer of Frankfurt was born on 30th March 1864. Finally, Dr. Oppenheimer of Berlin is never referred to by the title, "Professor" in any V.n.J. publication, an unlikely event in the Weimar Republic.

[25][Henry Wasserman] H.W. 'Verband nationaldeutscher Juden', *Encyclopaedia Judaica*, vol. XVI, New York 1971, col. 106. See also Alfred Peyser, *Der Begriff "nationaldeutsch" in unserer Erziehungsarbeit*, Berlin 1925, p. 16.

[26]*Satzung des Verbandes nationaldeutscher Juden e.V. (Fassung vom 26. April 1921)*, Berlin 1921, p. 1.

correct this Jewish failing, the founders of the V.n.J. sought to create a new movement within German Jewry that would monitor the ideological and political activities of the two principal Jewish defence organisations in Weimar Germany, the C.V. and R.j.F. Specifically, the V.n.J. hoped to force the *Zwischenschichtler* to abandon all external traces of Jewish identity. In an effort to demonstrate their identity with Germany still further, the V.n.J. resolved to combat all "unassimilable" elements within the Jewish community, a position which called for the expulsion of Eastern European Jewish immigrants, revocation of citizenship for all German Zionists and the public rejection of Jewish left-wing intellectuals and politicians.[27] By adopting these objectives, the V.n.J. placed itself outside the mainstream of German-Jewish life. By 1932, it was the only Jewish organisation in Germany prepared to endorse a Nazi-led National Revolution.[28]

To realise their goals, the founders of the V.n.J. restricted their membership to those German citizens[29] of Jewish descent who, while they had not cut themselves off from Judaism (*Judentum*), were nevertheless in full agreement with the declared aims of the League and were particularly opposed to the Zionist ideology.[30] By originally excluding baptised Jews and *Dissidenten* (i.e., those without a declared religious affiliation) from membership, the V.n.J. hoped to avoid the charge that it was composed of renegades.[31] Nevertheless, the exact nature of the League's relation to Judaism remained vague and ill-defined.[32] Both Naumann and his first deputy chairman, Dr. Alfred Peyser, were members of the Berlin *Reformgemeinde*.[33] For others, membership in the V.n.J. was "the only expression of their Jewish identity".[34] In an effort to demonstrate that antisemitism could only be eliminated by total assimilation, the V.n.J. campaigned against those aspects of Jewish religious observance which either emphasised the separate historical nature of the Jewish people, or which tended to separate assimilated Jews

[27]Knütter, *op. cit.*, p. 104.
[28]See, for example, Max Naumann, *Sozialismus, Nationalsozialismus und nationaldeutsches Judentum*, Berlin 1932, pp. 8–10. See also Jacob M. Marcus, *The Rise and Destiny of the German Jew*, Cincinnati 1934, pp.. 295–296; and Bolkosky, *Distorted Image*, pp. 161–163.
[29]In February 1922, the V.n.J. expanded its provisions for membership to include both citizens of the new Austrian Republic (*Deutsch-Österreich*) and residents of former German areas (e.g., Danzig). *Satzung des Verbandes nationaldeutscher Juden e.V.* (*Fassung vom 5. Februar 1922*), Berlin 1922, p. 1. B.A. R 43 II/600.
[30]*Satzung des Verbandes nationaldeutscher Juden e.V.* (*Fassung vom 26. April 1921*), p. 1.
[31]Based on the evidence available, it appears that this policy was later revised. See Max Naumann, 'Von nationaldeutschen Juden, Ostjuden, und Dissidenten', *Mitteilungen der Jüdischen Reformgemeinde zu Berlin*, No. 4 (15th December 1921), p. 4.
[32]See, for example, Verband nationaldeutscher Juden e.V. *Brennende Fragen für den deutschen Juden*, Berlin 1921, p. 3.
[33]Naumann eventually broke with the *Reformgemeinde* over its failure to adopt a truly German religion. See below, n. 43. Peyser, on the other hand, played an active role in Jewish communal affairs. In 1925, he was elected as a Liberal to the Assembly of the Prussian Federation of Jewish Communities and later served as chairman of the Berlin *Reformgemeinde*. He was also an active member of the R.j.F. 'Aus unserer Gemeinde: Sanitätsrat Dr. Alfred Peyser zum Vorsitzenden der Jüdischen Reformgemeinde gewählt', *Mitteilungen der Jüdischen Reformgemeinde zu Berlin*, No. 6 (15th June 1934), p. 10.
[34]Jehuda Reinharz, *Deutschtum and Judentum. Jewish Liberalism and Zionism in Germany 1893–1914* (doctoral dissertation, Brandeis University 1972), p. 117. A revised version of this dissertation has been published as *Fatherland or Promised Land. The Dilemma of the German Jew 1893–1914*, Ann Arbor 1975.

from their German *Volksgenossen*. Of the three Jewish pilgrimage festivals, none was celebrated by the V.n.J. as an organisation and neither were the five Jewish fast days. Instead, the V.n.J. offered an alternative interpretation of Judaism designed to allow assimilated Jews to merge eventually with a German *Volksgemeinschaft*. While this interpretation was never specifically spelled out as a cohesive religious philosophy, certain ideas about the nature of religious observance emerged from the V.n.J. speeches and publications. Thus in an address before the V.n.J.'s Berlin *Ortsgruppe*,[35] Max Naumann argued that the God of Israel no longer existed for the National-German Jew, who should place his religious faith in a "German God".[36] Holidays devoted to honour this "German God" would no longer have to follow the Jewish religious calendar. A further topic of debate within the V.n.J. was whether the Sabbath should be observed on Saturday or Sunday.[37] Those who advocated the observance of Sunday as the Sabbath hoped to eliminate an important difference between German and Jewish religious observance. Another way to mask the difference between Germans and Jews was the celebration of Christmas, a move which was seen as a positive reaffirmation of one's national German identity.[38] This was a major departure from official Jewish religious policy in Germany. While many German Jews had privately adopted the custom of celebrating Christmas, no Jewish organisation in Germany had ever publicly condoned this practice. To have done so would have been tantamount to admitting that the revelation of God through Moses and the Prophets was now superseded by the teachings and person of Jesus. In short, while rejecting conversion, the V.n.J. hoped to reduce Jewish identity to a mere question of descent (*Stamm*).[39]

This attempt to eliminate the religious differences which separated Germans and Jews was not a new phenomenon. As early as 1845 the Berlin *Reformgemeinde* had tried to secure its place in German society by abandoning many of the basic traditions of Judaism. The Berlin *Reformgemeinde* was the only Jewish congregation on the European continent which celebrated the Sabbath on Sunday, thus contravening biblical prescriptions for Saturday worship.[40] With the exception of the *Sh'ma*, the watchword of Judaism, and the *Kedushah*, the sanctification of God's name, the use of Hebrew was eliminated from religious services on the grounds that it was inappropriate to ask German Jews to pray in a language other than their German *Muttersprache*. The wearing of prayer shawls was also

---

[35] In addition to the Berlin *Ortsgruppe*, the V.n.J. also established chapters in Breslau, Danzig, Frankfurt a. Main, Halle, Hamburg, Hanover, Königsberg i. Pr., Munich, Regensburg and Vienna. Peyser, *Streitschrift*, p. 11. In those areas where the League was too weak to establish an *Ortsgruppe*, it was represented by a *Vertrauensmann*. 'Der Verband nationaldeutscher Juden'. *Israelitisches Familienblatt*, XXIII, No. 16 (21st April 1921), p. 2.

[36] Max Naumann as quoted in S[iegmund] Ginsberg, 'Der "deutsche Gott"', *Mitteilungsblatt des Verbandes nationaldeutscher Juden e.V.*, No. 3 (August/September 1924), p. 3. In 1925, the periodical was renamed *Der nationaldeutsche Jude*. See below, n. 71.

[37] Fritz Wachsner, 'Sabbat am Sonntag', *Der nationaldeutsche Jude*, No. 10 (October 1929), p. 5.

[38] Miles, 'Deutsche Weihnacht', *Der nationaldeutsche Jude*, No. 1 (January 1930), p. 6. See also 'Naumann unter dem Weihnachtsbaum', *Jüdische Rundschau*, XXXIX, No. 104 (28th December 1934), p. 4.

[39] Pierson, *German Jewish Identity*, p. 72.

[40] Klaus J. Herrmann, 'Weltanschauliche Aspekte der Jüdischen Reformgemeinde zu Berlin', pp. 86–87.

abolished.⁴¹ According to the founders of the congregation, this "oriental" custom had no place in a German religious service. Most likely, it was felt that the wearing of prayer shawls would cause embarrassment for the assimilated in the event that non-Jews were invited to attend services. By adopting these changes in Jewish liturgy and ritual, the Berlin *Reformgemeinde* hoped to demonstrate that it was prepared to take its place within a German *Volksgemeinschaft*.

Like the V.n.J., the leaders and rabbis of the Berlin *Reformgemeinde* were in the forefront of the struggle against Zionism in Germany.⁴² Nevertheless, their interpretation of what it meant to be a Jew clashed with Naumann's own "ultra-German" version of Judaism. The *Reformgemeinde* never advocated belief in a "German God". Nor was it prepared to abandon the Jewish pilgrimage festivals.⁴³ The fact that prominent members of the congregation participated in the V.n.J. suggests that at least in the area of religion Naumann did not speak for all members of his organisation. Just how many members of the V.n.J. shared Naumann's religious views remains a problem for future research.⁴⁴ What is certain is that Naumann was never censured publicly by the V.n.J. for his views on Judaism. This suggests that religiously observant Jews, including members of the Berlin *Reformgemeinde*, were either a minority within the *Verband* or, because of the League's political isolation, were reluctant to criticise their national chairman publicly.⁴⁵

The relations of the V.n.J. with both the C.V. and R.j.F., organisations which together contained the bulk of German Jewry, were also strained from the outset. This was due to the V.n.J.'s position *vis-à-vis* the Jewish religion, its rejection of the concept of a symbiosis of German and Jew as espoused by both major Jewish defence organisations, and its ultra-nationalist stance which at times bordered on outright antisemitism. By refusing to accept the Jewish community as a *Religionsgemeinschaft* and by defining themselves as "Jews, who while frankly admitting [our] origin, feel so totally integrated into the intrinsic German nature and culture that [we] cannot but think and feel as Germans".⁴⁶ the members of the V.n.J. made it clear that they considered the observance of Jewish religious law

---

⁴¹*Ibid.*

⁴²In 1929, for example, the leaders of the congregation, including its rabbis, opposed the creation of an expanded Jewish Agency for Palestine. 'Erklärung deutscher Juden', *Vossische Zeitung*, No. 236 (3rd October 1929), p. 14. See below, n. 115.

⁴³On the religious differences which separated Naumann from the Berlin *Reformgemeinde* see F[elix] Coblenz, 'Vom mosaischen und nichtmosaischen Juden', *Mitteilungen der Jüdischen Reformgemeinde zu Berlin*, No. 1 (1st March 1922), pp. 5–9. See also Pierson, *German Jewish Identity*, pp. 55–56.

⁴⁴V.n.J. membership lists were seized by the Gestapo in November 1935 and are now presumably in the Deutsches Zentralarchiv in Potsdam. My application to visit Potsdam was rejected by the East German authorities in April 1974.

⁴⁵Naumann served as chairman of the V.n.J. from 1921 to 1926 at which time he was awarded the title, *Ehrenvorsitzender*. Knütter, *op. cit.*, p. 101. He, nevertheless, remained the chief ideologue and spokesman for the League during the remaining years of the Weimar Republic. Conversely, his two successors as chairman, Dr. Alfred Peyser (January 1926?–September 1926) and *Justizrat* Georg Siegmann (September 1926–December 1933) had little impact on the political orientation of the League. In December 1933, under pressure from the Nazi régime, Naumann was again elevated to the post of chairman.

⁴⁶*Satzung des Verbandes nationaldeutscher Juden e.V. (Fassung vom 26. April 1921)*, p. 1.

solely as a private matter for the individual. In adopting this self-definition, the V.n.J. sought to make a clear distinction between membership of the Jewish *Religionsgemeinschaft* and continued adherence to *Judentum*. While this self-definition had been consistent with the views held by many of the C.V.'s founders in 1893, it was no longer acceptable in Jewish circles in the immediate post-war period.[47] As a result of frequent acts of vandalism against synagogues and the appearance in Germany of such notorious antisemitic works as the *Protocols of the Elders of Zion*, the Jewish community in general and the post-war C.V. leadership in particular considered any rejection of the *Religionsgemeinschaft* by a Jew an act of cowardice and desertion. The C.V. also realised the dangerous implications which a dismantling of the Jewish *Religionsgemeinschaft* would have on the ties that linked the Jewish community in Germany with the rest of the Jewish diaspora. As early as 1919, the C.V. had based its defence of Eastern European Jewish immigrants on the grounds that German and Eastern European Jews were both members of the same *Religionsgemeinschaft*.[48] The positive attitude of many C.V. members towards Zionist fund-raising activities was also based on the belief that the conditions of the Jewish community in Palestine were of direct concern to German Jews since both communities were inseparably linked by religion and common descent. Neither German antisemites nor Naumann's V.n.J. could dislodge the C.V. from this attitude.

It follows, therefore, that the real danger which the V.n.J. posed was not seen in an eventual triumph of its interpretation of *Judentum* among liberal Jews, but rather in its publicly avowed attitudes which threatened to weaken the C.V.'s campaign against antisemitism.* By acknowledging "the truth of some antisemitic charges"[49] in the right-wing press, and by casting aspersions on the patriotism of the C.V.'s leadership for having supported the legal rights of new Jewish immigrants from the East, the C.V. was forced, as early as 1921, to divert part of its efforts to neutralising the impact of the V.n.J. on public opinion. This campaign was complicated by the fact that a number of V.n.J. members, including Max Naumann, held concurrent membership in the C.V.[50] This meant that

---

[47]Pierson, *German-Jewish Identity*, pp. 44–45. As early as 1908, Felix Goldmann from the *Centralverein* "suggested that Jews avoid all social contact with converts and above all that they prevent their children from associating with them and their children. Two years later the Centralverein began sponsoring a series of mass meetings to dramatize the danger of apostasy." Ismar Schorsch, *Jewish Reactions to German Anti-Semitism, 1870–1914*, New York 1972, p. 141. See also Arnold Paucker, 'Zur Problematik einer jüdischen Abwehrstrategie in der deutschen Gesellschaft', in *Juden im Wilhelminischen Deutschland 1890–1914*. Ein Sammelband herausgegeben von Werner E. Mosse unter Mitwirkung von Arnold Paucker, Tübingen 1976 (Schriftenreihe wissenschaftlicher Abhandlungen des Leo Baeck Instituts 33), pp. 514–518.

[48]See, for example, [Kurt Alexander] K.A., 'Zeitschau', *Im deutschen Reich*, XXV, No. 12 (December 1919), p. 517. See also Pierson, *German Jewish Identity*, p. 132.

*On the *Centralverein*'s propaganda against Nazism and racism in the Weimar Republic see the second part of the essay by Walter Zwi Bacharach, 'Jews in Confrontation with Racist Antisemitism, 1879–1933', pp. 208–219, in this volume of the Year Book – (Ed.).

[49]Wasserman, *loc. cit.*, col. 106.

[50]Ludwig Foerder, *Die Stellung des Centralvereins zu den innerjüdischen Fragen in den Jahren 1919–1926. Eine Denkschrift für die Vereinsmitglieder von Rechtsanwalt Ludwig Foerder in Breslau*, Breslau 1927, pp. 18–19. Naumann was still a member of the C.V. as late as November 1926. Fritz Weinberg to Geh. Legationsrat Frhr. von Richthofen, Berlin, 24th November 1926, pp. 1–2. Auswärtiges Amt, Bonn (hereafter cited as A.A.), Pol. Abt. III Jüd. Pol. Ang. Allg. Bd. 8.

any attack on the V.n.J. exposed the C.V. to possible internal strife and division. Nevertheless, on 10th April 1921, the C.V.'s National Executive Committee (*Hauptvorstand*) issued a statement of opposition to the League:

> "The *Centralverein* warns German Jews against joining the Naumann [organisation]. It is dangerous and [it is] dedicated to causing confusion both from within and without. Moreover, it is superfluous because the German ideal has always been unmistakably represented in the C.V."[51]

In an effort to maintain Jewish dignity in the face of the V.n.J.'s capitulation to antisemitic thinking, the C.V. felt compelled to expand its denunciation of the *Verband*. On 30th December 1921, the C.V.'s national chairman, Julius Brodnitz, condemned the V.n.J. as an organisation of self-hating Jews: "[This] movement is, consciously or unconsciously, antisemitic . . . Antisemites could not wish for a better ally".[52] Underlying this attack was the fear that the V.n.J.'s programme of abolishing all external traces of Judaism in Germany would endanger the position of the religiously observant Jew, the Eastern European Jewish immigrant and the philanthropic Zionist, all of whom, according to the C.V., had a legitimate place within a German *Volksgemeinschaft*.[53] In short, the C.V. saw the V.n.J. as an organisation which by its avowed objectives threatened its hopes of seeing religious and ethnic pluralism take root in Germany.

The C.V.'s charge of the V.n.J. being a Jewish antisemitic organisation was lent credence by the *Verband*'s persistent defence of right-wing politicians and antisemites. In 1923, the student group of the V.n.J.'s Munich *Ortsgruppe* denounced Dr. Alfred Wiener, the C.V. *Syndikus*, for his "unfounded and repeated attacks" against General Erich Ludendorff. In view of the general's outspokenly antisemitic stance and his close ties to the *Deutschvölkische Freiheitspartei*, the C.V. found it shocking that any German Jew would choose to identify with him.[54] In April 1924, the C.V. also criticised the V.n.J. for having invited Major Kurt Anker, an author "well known in right-wing circles", and the former press secretary to Crown Prince Wilhelm, to address a recent meeting of its Berlin *Ortsgruppe*.[55]

The effect of these criticisms was to isolate the V.n.J. still further within the Jewish community. By the autumn of 1924, the chairman of the C.V.'s *Landesverband* Lower Silesia was prepared to expel V.n.J. members from his section.[56] A few weeks later, the Berlin delegation to the C.V.'s National Executive Committee introduced a resolution prohibiting an alliance with the V.n.J. in the approaching election for the Assembly of the Prussian Federation of Jewish Communities. In spite of the possibility that this resolution might strengthen the

---

[51]Ludwig Holländer, 'Verband nationaldeutscher Juden und Centralverein deutscher Staatsbürger jüdischen Glaubens', *Im deutschen Reich*, XXVII, No. 4 (April 1921), p. 112. See also Foerder, *op. cit.*, p. 16.
[52]Julius Brodnitz as quoted in *ibid.*, p. 16.
[53]Alfred Hirschberg, 'Ludwig Hollaender, Director of the C.V.', in *LBI Year Book VII* (1962), p. 52.
[54]'Die Münchener Jugend- und Studentengruppe nationaldeutscher Juden', *C.V.-Zeitung*, II, No. 30 (26th July 1923), p. 243.
[55]'Der Brief des Major Anker', *C.V.-Zeitung*, III, No. 14 (3rd April 1924), p. 161. See also Knütter, *op. cit.*, pp. 105–106.
[56]Foerder, *op. cit.*, p. 19.

chances for a Zionist victory, the motion was carried by a vote of thirty-seven to eight.[57] Given the choice between a Zionist victory and an electoral coalition with the V.n.J., the C.V. was prepared to see the non-Zionists lose the election rather than legitimise the V.n.J.'s standing within the Jewish community.

This rebuff did not deter the V.n.J. from continuing its feud with the C.V. which in March 1930 it accused of having betrayed its commitment to *"deutsche Gesinnung"* when it admitted such leading Jewish nationalists as Hermann Badt,[58] Hans Goslar[59] and Arnold Zweig into its organisation.[60] The decision to admit these men as members did not imply an endorsement of political Zionism by the C.V., but reflected merely a growing awareness among non-Zionists of the need for a Jewish *Einheitsfront* to combat antisemitism.[61] This, however, was exactly the kind of Jewish political objective in Germany which Naumann despised. A Jewish *Einheitsfront*, according to him, would only serve to reinforce the image already held by antisemites that the Jews were a separate nation incapable of being integrated into the German body politic. In early 1932, it lashed out at the C.V. for its failure to realise that the problem facing the Jewish community in Germany was not the *Antisemitenfrage* but rather the *Judenfrage*.[62]

A few months later, Naumann virtually broke with the German-Jewish community when he personally endorsed Hitler's National Socialist Party as the only

[57]*Ibid.*, p. 20. This resolution had little practical effect. Two members of the V.n.J. were nominated and elected on the non-Zionist Liberal list. See above, n. 33. See also 'Das Wahlergebnis', *Der nationaldeutsche Jude*, No. 2 (February 1925), p. 1.

[58]Badt was a prime target of the V.n.J. Born in Breslau in 1887, he maintained orthodox religious traditions and became an active member of the *Mizrachi* Religious Zionist party. [Ernest Hamburger] E.H. 'Hermann Badt', *Encyclopaedia Judaica*, vol. IV, New York 1971, col. 76–77. Following the armistice, Badt served as an SPD deputy in the Prussian Diet (1922–1926) and as *Ministerialdirektor* for constitutional matters in the Prussian Ministry of the Interior. He was also one of two Prussian representatives to the *Reichsrat*. Arnold Paucker, 'Searchlight on the Decline of the Weimar Republic. The Diaries of Ernst Feder', in *LBI Year Book XIII* (1968), p. 222n. See also [Max Naumann] M.N. 'Der Zionist als Preussischer Ministerialdirektor', *Der nationaldeutsche Jude*, No. 11/12 (November/December 1926), p. 9. In 1933, Badt emigrated to Palestine where he died.

[59]Like Badt, Goslar was an observant Jew and a member of the *Mizrachi* Religious Zionists. He served the *Mizrachi* as a member of its German Executive and European Central Committee. Samuel Hubner, 'Hans Goslar', *Encyclopedia of Zionism and Israel*, I, New York 1971, p. 404. He was also an active Social Democrat. Paucker, 'Searchlight on the Decline of the Weimar Republic ...', p. 216n. Following the Nazi seizure of power Goslar emigrated to the Netherlands where he was a "neighbour of Anne Frank's family and his daughter was Anne's friend". In 1944, he was transported from Westerbork to Bergen Belsen where he died of starvation shortly before liberation. [Getzel Kressel] G.K. 'Hans Goslar', *Encyclopaedia Judaica*, vol. VII, New York 1971, col. 817. See also Martin Broszat, 'Dokumentation. Kritische Bemerkungen Herbert Weichmanns zu den Briefen Brünings an Sollmann', *Vierteljahrshefte für Zeitgeschichte*, XXII, No. 4 (October 1974), pp. 458–460; and Joseph Walk, 'Das "Deutsche Komitee Pro Palästina" 1926–1933', in *Bulletin des Leo Baeck Instituts*, XV, No. 52 (1976), pp. 178, 181.

[60]'Jüdischnationaler Sieg im Centralverein', *Der nationaldeutsche Jude*, No. 3 (March 1930), pp. 5–6. As early as May 1921, the League had accused the C.V. of being Zionist infiltrated. *Brennende Fragen*, p. 4. According to Dr. Eva G. Reichmann, Badt, Goslar and Zweig were never members of the C.V. although they may have been proposed for membership. Dr. Reichmann to the author, 20th December 1978.

[61]On the attempts to form a Jewish United Front in Germany prior to Hitler's accession to power see Arnold Paucker, *Der jüdische Abwehrkampf gegen Antisemitismus und Nationalsozialismus in den letzten Jahren der Weimarer Republik*, Hamburger Beiträge zur Zeitgeschichte, Bd. IV, Hamburg 1969, pp. 40–44.

[62]Max Naumann, 'Grüne Fragen und gelbe Antworten', in *Klärung*, p. 72.

political organisation capable of bringing about a "rebirth of Germandom".[63] This move, coming as it did prior to the imminent *Reichstag* elections, prompted the C.V. to denounce Naumann in unequivocal terms:

> "We are [also] *nationaldeutsch* because we desire the reestablishment and greatness of Germany. We know, however, that ... atrocities and agitation against Jews are not the way to Germany's *Wiederaufstieg*."[64]

These remarks were symptomatic of the C.V.'s continued belief in the viability of a German-Jewish symbiosis, despite the increasing isolation which Jews then faced in German political life.

If Naumann's opposition to a Jewish *Einheitsfront* made it impossible for him to win over the C.V., his public position also prevented a possible alliance with the R.j.F. Like the V.n.J., the Jewish veterans' organisation did not support Zionism, nor did it question the religious commitment of its members. The R.j.F. also opposed the activities of Jewish leftists. Nevertheless, the political differences which separated the two Jewish organisations far outweighed any similarities in political outlook. In May 1922, supporters of Naumann protested against a decision taken by the Jewish veterans' organisation to exclude the national chairman of the V.n.J. from participating in an R.j.F. forum on the "Jewish Question".[65] Dr. Paul Nathan, the head of the *Hilfsverein der deutschen Juden*, defended the R.j.F.'s decision on the grounds that the V.n.J. had denied the patriotism of the greater part of German Jewry, including large numbers of Jewish frontline veterans.[66] The R.j.F.'s national chairman, Leo Löwenstein, was more conciliatory. At the conclusion of the forum, Löwenstein expressed his regrets that what had been such a productive meeting had ended with a debate on internal Jewish political affairs.[67]

This attempt to bridge the differences separating the two organisations ended in failure. Between 1922 and 1933, the V.n.J. repeatedly attacked the R.j.F. for its lack of German patriotism. In late 1922, one V.n.J. member bitterly criticised the R.j.F. leadership for having changed the original name of the Jewish veterans' organisation.[68] In November 1923, while R.j.F. men were protecting the shops and homes of Eastern European Jews in North Berlin from antisemitic

---

[63]Max Naumann as quoted in Ludwig Holländer, 'Hitler und Max Naumann. Ein Wort zur Klärung', *C.V.-Zeitung*, XI, No. 24 (19th August 1932), p. 350. Naumann later attempted to clarify his position, namely, that his devotion was not only to the National Socialist Party but also to the *Volksbewegung* which may include the Nazi circle but encompasses far more than this one party. Max Naumann, *Sozialismus, Nationalsozialismus und nationaldeutsches Judentum*, p. 9, as quoted in Bolkosky, *Distorted Image*, p. 162.

[64]Holländer, 'Hitler und Max Naumann ...', *loc. cit.*, pp. 350–351. See also Kurt Loewenstein, 'Die innerjüdische Reaktion auf die Krise der deutschen Demokratie', in *Entscheidungsjahr 1932*, pp. 371–372.

[65]'Die Juden im Heere', *Der Schild*, I, No. 7 (May 1922), p. 2.

[66]*Ibid*. See also Paul Nathan, 'Eine Antwort an Herrn Max Naumann', *C.V.-Zeitung*, I, No. 3 (18th May 1922), p. 38. On Nathan's career as head of the *Hilfsverein* see Ernst Feder, 'Paul Nathan, the Man and his work', in *LBI Year Book III* (1958), pp. 60–80.

[67]'Die Juden im Heere', *loc. cit.*, p. 2. Based on the tentative evidence available, it appears that Löwenstein's remarks were designed to prevent a walkout by R.j.F. men who were followers of Naumann. 'Briefkasten', *Der Schild*, I, No. 7 (May 1922), p. 3.

[68]C. S. Engel, ' "Vaterländischer Bund" und "Reichsbund jüdischer Frontsoldaten" ', *Der nationaldeutsche Jude*, No. 6 (June 1925), p. 11.

agitators,[69] Naumann was attacking the victims of this pogrom as economic parasites whose presence in Germany only served to weaken the German *Volk*.[70] By 1925, the R.j.F.'s alleged lack of *"deutsche Gesinnung"* had become a persistent theme in V.n.J. propaganda. In June of that year, for example, an editorial in *Der nationaldeutsche Jude*, the official organ of the V.n.J.,[71] argued that the failure of the R.j.F. to endorse Field Marshal von Hindenburg's campaign for President was clear evidence of the Jewish veterans' organisation's move to the Left.

Nor did the last years of the Republic see much improvement in the relations between these two Jewish organisations. The fact that such leading Zionists as Hermann Badt and Felix A. Theilhaber[72] continued to participate in R.j.F. activities served to underscore the unwillingness of the Jewish veterans' organisation to abandon their Zionist comrades to Naumann's attacks. The close relationship which the R.j.F. maintained with the C.V. also aroused the V.n.J.'s anger.[73] The only recognition which the V.n.J. was prepared to grant the Jewish veterans' organisation was over its decision to retrain Jews for careers in agriculture.[74] Any attempt to alter the occupational distribution of German Jews the V.n.J. considered an improvement.[75] Nor had the *Verband* any serious objection to the publication of the book *Die jüdischen Gefallenen* as a means of refuting charges that Jews had been malingerers during the war. This tactic the V.n.J. viewed as a legitimate move to demonstrate the contribution which German Jews had made in war-time to their fatherland.[76] However, this tacit endorsement of the R.j.F.'s campaign did not erase the essential political difference which separated the two Jewish organisations, primarily as the R.j.F. was never prepared to abandon the Jewish community in order to placate antisemites.

Whereas the V.n.J.'s policies towards the C.V. and R.j.F. were based on the

---

[69]On the R.j.F.'s defence of Eastern European Jews during this pogrom see Ulrich Dunker, *Der Reichsbund jüdischer Frontsoldaten 1919–1938. Geschichte eines jüdischen Abwehrvereins*, Düsseldorf 1977, pp. 51–56. See also Ruth L. Pierson, 'Embattled Veterans. The Reichsbund jüdischer Frontsoldaten', in *LBI Year Book XIX* (1974), p. 146; Adolph Asch, 'Fight for German Jewry's Honour. Reminiscences about the R.j.F.', *AJR Information*, XVI (August 1961), p. 8; and Donald L. Niewyk, 'Jews and the Courts in Weimar Germany', *Jewish Social Studies*, XXXVII, No. 2 (Spring 1975), p. 109.

[70]M. S. Dik, 'Unvergessenes', *Jüdische Rundschau*, XXX, No. 8 (28th January 1925), p. 74.

[71]Nachwort der Schriftleitung', *Der nationaldeutsche Jude*, No. 6 (June 1925), p. 6. *Der nationaldeutsche Jude* had a circulation of 5,000 in 1925. Margaret T. Edelheim-Muehsam, 'The Jewish Press in Germany', in *LBI Year Book I* (1956), p. 170. See also Pierson, 'German Jewish Identity', p. 40n. The paper was edited by Dr. Manfred Blochert, a Berlin industrialist and neighbour of Naumann's. Jacob Jacobson (ed.). *Jüdisches Jahrbuch für Gross-Berlin*, 2nd edn., Berlin 1928, p. 134.

[72]For a discussion of Theilhaber's role in the R.j.F. see Pierson, 'Embattled Veterans . . .', *loc. cit.*, p. 150.

[73]See, for example, 'Echo der Presse. Der Schild', *Der nationaldeutsche Jude*, No. 12 (December 1925), p. 9.

[74]The V.n.J. was apparently divided on this point. In 1927, Dr. Alfred Peyser became one of the founding members of the Siedlungsausschuss des Reichsbundes jüdischer Frontsoldaten, Central Zionist Archives, Jerusalem (hereafter cited as C.Z.A.) A 142/90/3b. The editorial staff of *Der nationaldeutsche Jude*, on the other hand, opposed the creation of purely Jewish agricultural settlements. 'Das Landwirtschaftliche Ghetto', *Der nationaldeutsche Jude*, No. 7 (July 1931), p. 5, B.A. E/81.

[75]On the R.j.F.'s plan to settle Jews on the land see Dunker, *op. cit.*, pp. 81–95.

[76]See, for example, 'Jüdische Frontsoldaten aus Württemberg und Hohenzollern', *Der nationaldeutsche Jude*, No. 1/3 (January/March 1927), p. 15. On the book, see Pierson, 'Embattled Veterans . . .', *loc. cit.*, pp. 143–144.

premise that the *Zwischenschichtler* could be persuaded to abandon all external traces of Jewish behaviour, its attitude towards the *Ostjuden*, the Zionists and the Jewish Left was one of total rejection. Afraid that they would reinforce popular antisemitic stereotypes and thus prevent assimilation, the V.n.J. devoted the major part of its efforts to disassociate itself from these Jewish groups.

Like the German Right, the V.n.J. perceived Eastern European Jewish immigration as a threat to the German nation. Between 1910 and 1920, the Eastern European Jewish population in Germany had doubled from 79,000 persons in 1910 to 160,000 by the end of the decade.[77] This increase was due primarily to two factors: the importation of Jewish conscript labour by the German army during the First World War, and the need of Jewish refugees to find asylum from post-war pogroms in Poland and the Ukraine.[78] Dubbed the *Ostjudengefahr* by racial antisemites, most "ultra-German" Jews considered the new immigrants with their orthodox religious practices, kaftans, sidelocks and Yiddish pronunciation an embarrassment. In Berlin, according to Adolf Leschnitzer,

> "[Ultra-German] ... Jews ... recoiled from any contact with them ... [They] were in fact disgusted. They felt they had nothing, absolutely nothing, in common with the bearded Hebrews of [Poland]; the earlocks and the kaftans struck them as funny and they did not hesitate to laugh."[79]

Underlying this reaction was their belief that the new immigrants were the last obstacle which prevented assimilated German Jews from being accepted by their fellow countrymen.

The V.n.J.'s attitudes towards the Eastern European Jewish immigrants went beyond mere rejection. Fearful lest the new immigrants should add to a revitalisation of Jewish cultural life in Germany as well as strengthen the ranks of the Zionists, the V.n.J. strenuously attempted not only to disassociate themselves from the *Ostjuden*, but also to disparage them. In 1921, Max Naumann referred to them as stemming from "Halbasien", in contrast to the National-German Jew whom he defined as a "German [and a] European".[80] The political implications of Naumann's remarks were obvious. In March 1923, the V.n.J. claimed that most Eastern European Jewish workers in Germany either were Communists or

---

[77] Adler-Rudel, *Ostjuden in Deutschland*, pp. 60, 164. For the best existing study of Eastern European Jewish migration to Germany prior to the First World War see Jack. L. Wertheimer, *German Policy and Jewish Politics. The Absorption of East European Jews in Germany (1868–1914)* (unpublished doctoral dissertation, Columbia University, 1978).

[78] Zechlin, *op. cit.*, pp. 260–277; H. G. Adler, *The Jews in Germany. From the Enlightenment to National Socialism*, South Bend, Indiana 1969, p. 126. Zosa Szajkowski, 'East European Jewish Workers in Germany During World War I', in Saul Lieberman (ed.), *Salo Wittmayer Baron Jubilee Volume on the Occasion of his Eightieth Birthday*, vol. II, Jerusalem 1974, pp. 887–918.

[79] Adolf Leschnitzer, *The Magic Background of Modern Anti-Semitism. An Analysis of the German-Jewish Relationship*, New York 1969, p. 11. This antipathy towards Eastern European Jews was widespread within Germany and certainly not limited to members of the V.n.J. alone. See also Julius Hirsch, 'Polnisch, Jiddisch oder Deutsch?, *Allgemeine Zeitung des Judentums*, LXXIX, No. 49 (3rd December 1915), pp. 580–582; and Zosa Szajkowski, 'The Struggle for Yiddish during World War I', in *LBI Year Book IX* (1964), p. 131. For a fictional account of the clash between Eastern European Jewish immigrants and assimilated Berlin Jews see I. J. Singer's *The Family Carnovsky*, trans. Joseph Singer, New York 1973.

[80] Max Naumann, 'Von nationaldeutschen Juden, Ostjuden, und Dissidenten', *Mitteilungen der Jüdischen Reformgemeinde zu Berlin*, No. 3 (15th September 1921), pp. 7–8.

belonged to organisations hostile to *Deutschtum*.[81] Subsequently, its Munich *Ortsgruppe* endorsed Bavarian *Ministerpräsident* Gustav von Kahr's efforts to expel Eastern European Jews from Bavaria.[82] The only qualifications which the V.n.J. added was that in the deportation process "unnecessary hardships [be] avoided, and that complaints from antisemitic sources [be] first submitted to careful investigation".[83]

During the last years of the Weimar Republic, the members of the V.n.J. went to even greater lengths in their abuse of Eastern Jews, in some instances by pillorying those among them who had become defendants in criminal cases.[84] In March 1930, the V.n.J. advocated the boycott of a Jewish theatrical performance in Berlin with the argument that Kaftans worn by the actors would reinforce the unfavourable image that many of "our non-Jewish *Volksgenossen* have of present day Jewry".[85] In order to dramatise its boycott the V.n.J. published the first of several photo-articles in which Eastern European Jews were depicted in degrading poses.[86] These and related acts revealed the high level of anxiety which the V.n.J. felt with regard to its own position within German society.

Next to the *Ostjudenproblem*, the V.n.J. saw Zionism as an equally grave, if not even greater threat to the assimilated. With its stress on the separate nature of the Jewish *Volk* and its emphasis on the importance of building a national Jewish homeland in Palestine, Zionism was depicted as a movement likely to undermine the traditional allegiance of assimilated Jews towards the nations which had granted them citizenship.[87] Such an analysis of the dangers of Zionism was not new. As early as 1897, Rabbis Heinemann Vogelstein and Sigmund Maybaum had opposed Herzl's plans to convene the First World Zionist Congress in Munich because "there are no Jews who do not want to be assimilated into the nations in whose midst they live".[88] On 6th July 1897, the Executive Committee of the "Association of Rabbis in Germany" had declared:

> "The efforts of the so-called Zionists to found a Jewish national state in Palestine contradict the messianic promises of Judaism as contained in the Holy Writ and in later religious sources

[81]'Die Legende von den ostjüdischen Bergarbeitern', *Mitteilungsblatt des Verbandes nationaldeutscher Juden e.V.*, No. 2 (March/April 1923), p. 2.

[82]For the best existing study of van Kahr's actions against Eastern Jews see George and Roberta Earley, 'Bavarian Prelude, 1923. A Model for Nazism?', *Wiener Library Bulletin*, XXX, Nos. 43/44 (1977), pp. 53–60. See also Werner Jochmann, 'Die Ausbreitung des Antisemitismus', in *Deutsches Judentum in Krieg und Revolution*, pp. 506–507.

[83]Jewish Telegraphic Agency (J.T.A.) (National-German Jews Have No Objection to Expulsion of Jews from Bavaria', *Daily News Bulletin* (21st November 1923), (mimeo), p. 2. Altogether thirty foreign Jewish families were expelled. Another twelve families avoided deportation only by winning legal appeals. Gordon Jr., *op. cit.*, p. 224.

[84]See, for example, 'Von den "Brüdern aus dem Osten" ', *Der nationaldeutsche Jude*, No. 3 (March 1925), pp. 6–7.

[85]Margo Wolff, 'Gefahr im Westen! "Kaftan", das Ostjudenkabarett', *Der nationaldeutsche Jude*, No. 3 'March 1930), p. 6.

[86]' "Talmudschule". Eine Szene aus dem Kabarett "Kaftan" ', *ibid.*, p. 3. See also 'Ghetto in Amerika', *Der nationaldeutsche Jude*, No. 6 (June 1930), p. 5.

[87]Max Naumann, *Von Zionisten und Jüdisch-nationalen*, Berlin 1921, p. 8.

[88]Heinemann Vogelstein and Sigmund Maybaum, 'Gegen den Zionismus', *Allgemeine Zeitung des Judentums*, LXI, No. 24 (11th June 1897), p. 277, as quoted in Reinharz, *Fatherland or Promised Land*, p. 174.

The Verband nationaldeutscher Juden

... Judaism obligates its adherents to serve with all devotion the fatherland to which they belong, and to further its national interests with all their heart and with all their strength."[89]

Underlying this early German-Jewish opposition to Zionism was the fear that the establishment of a national Jewish homeland in Palestine would expose the Jewish community in Germany to the charge of dual loyalty, and that Zionism itself was nothing more than a Jewish version of Pan-Germanism.

In 1910, Zionism had begun in earnest to make converts among the Jewish community in Germany. Proceeding from Herzl's belief that it was the Zionists' duty in the West to "conquer the communities", the Z.V.f.D. joined with the *Verband der Synagogenvereine* to challenge the liberals for control of the governing bodies of the Jewish communities of Berlin, Munich and the city of Poznań.[90] Running on a platform that called for "the preservation of the Hebrew language and the establishment of Jewish religious schools",[91] the Zionist-led coalition demonstrated remarkable political strength. In Berlin, the nationalist-religious bloc polled 40 per cent of the vote.[92] This success, coupled with the resolution adopted at the 1912 annual congress of the Z.V.f.D. which obliged "every Zionist ... to incorporate into their life's programme personal immigration to Palestine",[93] led to the formation of the first exclusively anti-Zionist organisation in Germany. In October 1912, a group of prominent Jewish liberals under the leadership of a Berlin lawyer, Hermann Veit Simon, formed the *Reichsverband zur Bekämpfung des Zionismus*.[94] Two months later the organisation was expanded and renamed the *Antizionistisches Komitee*. Like the "Association of Rabbis" in 1897, the *Antizionistisches Komitee* was motivated by

> "the fear that ... political circles which hitherto have seen the solution of the Jewish Question in the granting of full emancipation ... will henceforth, like the Zionists, see the solution ... in the separation of Jews from other German citizens".[95]

In 1913, relations between the Z.V.f.D. and the liberal Jewish establishment came to a head. On 30th March of that year, the C.V.'s National Executive Committee declared that Jewish nationalism and C.V. membership were incompatible:

> "We do not want to solve the German-Jewish question internationally. We want to participate in German culture as Germans and on the soil of the German fatherland. At the same time we want to remain loyal to our Jewish community which has been sanctified by our religion and history. As long as the German Zionist strives to find a secure home for the dispossessed Jews of the East or to enhance the pride of Jews in their history and religion, he is welcome as a member. We must separate ourselves, however, from the Zionist who denies a

---

[89]Statement of the Association of Rabbis in Germany as quoted in Ben Halpern, *The Idea of the Jewish State*, Cambridge, Massachusetts 1961, p. 144.
[90]Reinharz, *Fatherland or Promised Land*, p. 189.
[91]*Ibid.*, p. 190.
[92]*Ibid.*
[93]*Ibid.*, p. 161. For a discussion of the background to this resolution see Kurt Blumenfeld, *Erlebte Judenfrage. Ein Vierteljahrhundert deutscher Zionismus*, Stuttgart 1962, Veröffentlichung des Leo Baeck Instituts, pp. 88–92.
[94]Reinharz, *Fatherland or Promised Land*, p. 206.
[95]*Jüdische Rundschau*, XVII, No. 50 (13th December 1912), p. 483 as quoted by Reinharz, pp. 206–207. At least five members of the *Antizionistisches Komitee* became founders of the V.n.J.: Carl Alexander, Siegmund Breslauer, Georg Guttmann, Alfred Peyser and Professor Georg Schlesinger. *Das Antizionistische Komitee*, Berlin 1912?, pp. 2–4.

German national feeling, who regards himself only as a guest within a foreign host-country, and who affirms only a Jewish national feeling."[96]

While the C.V. took an anti-Zionist stance, it nevertheless qualified it at the same time. The resolution indicates a willingness to distinguish between two types of German Zionists: philanthropic Zionists who were merely concerned with finding a homeland for the oppressed Jewish masses in the East, and the more openly avowed and active Jewish nationalists who had no desire whatsoever to be part of a German *Volksgemeinschaft*. Furthermore, by reaffirming their ties to Judaism and Jewish history, the C.V. rejected any weakening of Judaism as the price for Jewish emancipation in Germany.

The proclamation of the Balfour Declaration on 2nd November 1917, followed by the decision taken by the Allies at San Remo on 24th April 1920 to assign the Palestine Mandate to Great Britain, changed the nature of Jewish anti-Zionism in Germany, for in the post-war period its exponents were forced to confront the fact that the establishment of a national Jewish homeland was no longer a merely theoretical question. To meet this new situation, the V.n.J. took up the banner of anti-Zionism in Germany by combining the traditional liberal arguments against a Jewish state with a new more Machiavellian analysis which held that support for Zionist endeavours in Palestine served to advance British colonial interests in the Mediterranean region.[97] For more politically aware German Jews, the implications of this argument were clear: to be a Zionist meant aiding Germany's war-time enemy and traditional imperial rival.

The V.n.J. also rejected the nineteenth-century liberal distinction between philanthropic Zionists and those actually committed to emigrate to Palestine by insisting that both groups were "dangerous". In May 1921, the V.n.J. advocated that German Zionists either migrate to Palestine or accept the status as aliens (*Ausländer*) living in the country.[98] A year later, Max Naumann denounced a recent Berlin visit of Dr. Chaim Weizmann, the President of the World Zionist Organisation, particularly since Weizmann had been received by the Executive Committee of the Berlin Jewish Community.[99] In an attempt to demonstrate to his readers that this meeting between Zionists and non-Zionists was essentially subversive, Naumann charged that Weizmann was a "protégé" of the British, and argued that German Zionists' efforts on behalf of Weizmann's visit were clear evidence that the "Jewish nationalist element was a foreign body within the German *Volk*".[100]

In a further effort to expose the subversive nature of Zionism, Naumann laun-

---

[96]Ludwig Holländer, 'Centralverein und Zionismus. Zur Klarstellung', *Im deutschen Reich*, XIX, No. 5/6 (May 1913), p. 200, as quoted in Reinharz, *Fatherland or Promised Land*, p. 213.

[97]See, for example, Max Naumann, *Von Zionisten und Jüdisch-nationalen*, pp. 16–17. See also Naumann's *Von deutscher Zukunft. Zwei Aufsätze*, Berlin 1924, p. 23.

[98]*Brennende Fragen*, p. 3. See also Hans Julius Schoeps (ed.), *Zionismus. Vierunddreissig Aufsätze*, Munich 1973, p. 29.

[99]Max Naumann, 'Liegt Berlin in Deutschland?', *Kölnische Zeitung*, No. 212 (24th March 1922), pp. 1–2.

[100]*Ibid.*, p. 2. The arrangements for Weizmann's visit included an invitation to *Reich* Chancellor Josef Wirth to attend a reception in honour of the Zionist leader on 21st December 1921. Zionistische Vereinigung für Deutschland to Reichskanzler Josef Wirth, Berlin, 16th December 1921. B.A. R 43 I/2192.

ched attacks on Zionists who held official positions in the German central government or in the Prussian state government. One of these was Dr. Hans Goslar, the chief of the Press Office of the Prussian *Staatsministerium*, who according to Naumann had privately published laudatory articles on Zionist achievements in Palestine. This, according to Naumann, deprived Goslar of the right to accept a post in what for a Zionist was a foreign country. "Let those who are Zionists go to Jerusalem. They have no right to occupy government positions in Berlin."[101] By emphasising Goslar's Zionist connections, Naumann hoped to expose the hypocrisy of German Zionists who refused to emigrate, and to point out the danger which they represented in laying the Jewish community open to the charge of dual loyalty. Moreover, by linking Zionist activities in Germany with British interests, the V.n.J. sought to counteract the internal threat which Zionism allegedly posed to Jewish communal affairs.

This became particularly evident in the V.n.J.'s campaign against Zionist fund-raising activities in Germany which had already attracted sizeable numbers of non-Zionist supporters. In March 1923, the V.n.J. opposed Jewish contributions for reconstruction work in Palestine on the grounds that funds were desperately needed for victims of the Ruhr occupation.[102] The V.n.J.'s message to the liberal Jewish community was simple: "Charity begins at home." The persistent refusal of liberal Jews to heed this call prompted the V.n.J. to adopt a new set of tactics. In March 1925, the V.n.J. protested to German Foreign Minister Gustav Stresemann against the proposed fund-raising tour of Chaim Weizmann because, so the argument went, Jewish contributions to the *Keren Hajessod* (Palestine Foundation Fund) strengthened British interests in Palestine while at the same time draining Germany of its financial resources.[103] The V.n.J. hoped to secure from the Foreign Minister a condemnation of the *Keren Hajessod*, thereby intimidating non-Zionist contributors to this fund. This condemnation was not forthcoming. On the contrary, Stresemann made it clear that a strong Jewish community in Palestine was in Germany's national interests. He did concede, however, that funds collected for Palestine reconstruction work should be spent in Germany and not sent out of the country.[104] The V.n.J. thus had to continue its campaign against the *Keren Hajessod* alone.

---

[101] Jewish Correspondence Bureau News and Telegraphic Agency, 'Dr. Naumann at it Again', *Daily News Bulletin* (2nd February 1922), (mimeo), p. 2. On Goslar's role in Jewish communal affairs see above, n. 59.

[102] 'Nationaldeutsche Juden!', *Mitteilungsblatt des Verbandes nationaldeutscher Juden e.V.*, No. 2 (March/April 1923), p. 1.

[103] Verband nationaldeutscher Juden e.V., Hauptvorstand to *Reich* Foreign Minister Gustav Stresemann, Berlin, 30th March 1925, pp. 2–3. A.A. Pol. Abt. III. Jüd. Ang. Allg. Bd. 6. For a discussion of Stresemann's attitude towards the League see below, p. 263. See also Aaron Abrahamson, 'Keren Hayesod', *Encyclopedia of Zionism and Israel*, II, New York 1971, pp. 658–660.

[104] Gustav Stresemann to Hauptvorstand, Verband nationaldeutscher Juden, Berlin, 25th April 1925, pp. 3–4, A.A. Pol. Abt. III Jüd. Pol. Ang. Allg. Bd. 6. As early as January 1918, Freiherr von dem Bussche-Haddenhausen, the Deputy Secretary of State of the German Foreign Office, had expressed his support "for the free immigration of Jews to Palestine, so as to further the prospering Jewish settlements there 'within the limits of absorptive capacity' ". Herrmann, 'Political Response to the Balfour Declaration in Imperial Germany . . .', *loc. cit.*, p. 317. See also Zechlin, *op. cit.*, pp. 413–448; and Isaiah Friedman, *Germany, Turkey, and Zionism 1897–1918*, New York 1977, pp. 382–383.

During the last years of the Weimar Republic, the V.n.J. intensified its efforts to portray Zionism as a threat to Jewish integration. It opposed plans to establish community funded Jewish schools in Berlin because such institutions would only increase Zionist consciousness among Jewish youth.[105] In an effort to combat the growing impact of Zionism on the German-Jewish youth movement, the V.n.J. established its own national youth organisation.[106] The venture was not a success, as the groups were composed for the most part of the sons and daughters of V.n.J. members.[107]

The League's most significant attempt to confront Zionism came in 1930, when its Executive Committee voted to enter for the first time its own batch of candidates in the elections for the Assembly of the Berlin Jewish Community.[108] Running on a platform that called for opposition to "Jewish parochial schools (*Ghettoschulen*)", "Jewish nationalist propaganda efforts" (i.e., a Hebrew-language theatre in Berlin)[109] and the "Eastern European-Jewish nationalist tyranny",[110] the V.n.J.'s candidates hoped to alert the Berlin Jewish Community to "the dangers of Zionism". They specifically hoped to capture the *Zwischenschichtler* who normally supported the non-Zionist Liberal Party. This attempt to woo liberal Jews failed. On 30th November 1930, the V.n.J.'s *Deutsche Liste* polled only 1,344 out of a total of 77,398 votes cast, 256 votes short of the minimum required for one seat in the Assembly.[111] The Liberal Party, on the other hand, regained its majority in the Assembly, winning twenty-four seats and 41,797 votes. The Zionist orientated *Jüdische Volkspartei* ran a strong second, capturing fourteen seats and 25,526 votes.[112]

For Naumann, these results were "deplorable"[113] and made his efforts to oppose Zionism even more imperative. In 1931, he launched another campaign in which he branded Zionism as a racist ideology. In a series of essays written for primarily non-Jewish audiences, Naumann portrayed the Z.V.f.D. as a group of "racial fanatics" ready to condemn as a renegade any Jew who rejected the

---

[105] See, for example, Fritz Wachsner, 'Hebräischer Sprachunterricht', *Der nationaldeutsche Jude*, No. 4/6 (June 1927), pp. 6–7.

[106] Margo Wolff and Walter Laaser, 'Zusammenkunft der Jugend', *Der nationaldeutsche Jude*, No. 12 (December 1929), p. 6. Prior to this date, many V.n.J. *Ortsgruppen* had established their own youth groups.

[107] Oral information from Mrs. Hans E. Baum.

[108] In 1926, the V.n.J. had endorsed the Liberal Party. The Zionist *Jüdische Volkspartei* seized on this endorsement to embarrass their liberal opponents. Handbills appeared in Berlin with the slogan: "Gebt keine *Stimme* den mit dem Verband nationaldeutscher Juden verbündeten Liberalen! ... Liste Klee-Badt", C.Z.A. A 142/87/6. On the organisation of the Assembly of the Berlin Jewish Community see David Philipson, *The Reform Movement in Judaism*, New York 1931, p. 398. See also [Joseph Meisl] J. Mel. 'Berlin', *Encyclopaedia Judaica*, IV, New York 1971, col. 646.

[109] 'Deutsche Liste: Unsere Kandidaten', [political handbill], Berlin 1930. On the Zionist commitment to Jewish religious schools in Germany prior to Hitler see Hans Gaertner, 'Problems of Jewish Schools in Germany during the Hitler Régime', in *LBI Year Book I* (1956), pp. 124–126.

[110] 'Mitglieder und Freunde!', *Der nationaldeutsche Jude*, No. 11a (November 1930), p. 1.

[111] Kurt Blumenfeld, 'Das Wahlergebnis', *Jüdische Rundschau*, XXXV, No. 95 (2nd December 1930), p. 639. See also Meisl, *loc. cit.*, col. 646.

[112] Blumenfeld, 'Das Wahlergebnis', *loc. cit.*, p. 639.

[113] Max Naumann, 'Keine Leichenrede', *Der nationaldeutsche Jude*, No. 12 (December 1930), p. 1.

Max Naumann (on horseback) with his regiment during the First World War

From the Archives of the Leo Baeck Institute, New York

concept of a Jewish *Volksgemeinschaft*.[114] Naumann's new offensive tactics were probably in response to the resurgence of Jewish self-awareness during the closing years of the Weimar Republic, including the increased support for a Jewish homeland among non-Zionists.[115] This was particularly the case among the younger generation of German Jews who found themselves shunned by their non-Jewish peers.[116] By 1932, Naumann was faced with the reality that the establishment of a national Jewish homeland in Palestine as a solution to the "Jewish Question" was gaining strength within German-Jewish circles, that the *Zwischenschichtler* refused to abandon their Jewish identity in the face of growing right-wing attacks.[117]

The V.n.J.'s campaign against Eastern European Jewish immigrants and German Zionists was designed to purge the Jewish community in Germany of at least two segments which it considered to be unworthy of participating in a German *Volksgemeinschaft*. But in addition, the V.n.J. attacked Jewish intellectuals and politicians who openly sympathised with left-wing causes. According to the V.n.J., these individuals reinforced the image of the rootless, cosmopolitan Jew devoid of any true German feeling. In order to counteract this stereotype, the V.n.J. made it clear that it was prepared to combat all forms of "political internationalism" within German life, but especially those internationalist elements within the Jewish community.[118]

One of the earliest targets of this campaign was Kurt Tucholsky, the chief

---

[114]See, for example, Max Naumann, 'Grüne Fragen und gelbe Antworten', in *Klärung*, p. 71; and Max Naumann, 'Der Weg zum Deutschtum', in *Der Jud ist Schuld* . . . ? *Diskussionsbuch über die Judenfrage*, Basel–Berlin–Leipzig–Vienna 1932, p. 306.

[115]In 1929, the Sixteenth World Zionist Congress voted to expand the Executive Committee of the Jewish Agency in order " 'to give adequate representation to non-Zionists . . .' The expanded . . . Agency was to be based on the principle of parity between Zionists and non-Zionists, that is, prominent Jews and organizations supporting the building of the Jewish national homeland without identifying themselves with the political aspirations of Zionism." Aaron Zwergbaum, 'Jewish Agency for Israel', *Encyclopedia of Zionism and Israel*, I, New York 1971, p. 612. Seven German non-Zionists were members of the new Executive Committee: Rabbi Leo Baeck (Berlin), Oscar Wassermann (Berlin), Bruno Asch (Frankfurt a. Main), Justizrat Dr. Blau (Frankfurt a. Main), Dr. Bernhard Kahn (Berlin), Gerson Simon (Berlin) and Rabbi Isak Unna (Mannheim). *Jüdisches Jahrbuch 1930*, Berlin 1930, pp. 82–83. The C.V., on the other hand, opposed participation in the expanded Agency. Pierson, *German Jewish Identity*, p. 126. See also Reichmann, *loc. cit.*, p. 568; and Walk, *loc. cit.*, pp. 178, 189, 190.

[116]H. G. Adler, *op. cit.*, pp. 134–135.

[117]Jehuda Reinharz, 'Deutschtum and Judentum in the Ideology of the Centralverein deutscher Staatsbürger jüdischen Glaubens 1893–1914', *Jewish Social Studies*, XXXVI, No. 1 (January 1974), pp. 37–39.

[118]*Brennende Fragen*, p. 2. In conducting this campaign, the V.n.J. was careful to distinguish between those Jewish Social Democrats who had abandoned Marxism and a smaller group of Jewish leftists who still looked to the failed revolutions of 1918–1919 for political inspiration. Thus in 1929, an article in *Der nationaldeutsche Jude* praised Ludwig Frank as a "Nationaldeutsche Jude der Vergangenheit". Frank, a leading Social Democrat from Baden, was the first member of the *Reichstag* to die in combat in the First World War. 'Nationaldeutsche Juden der Vergangenheit', *Der nationaldeutsche Jude*, No. 8 (August 1929), pp. 2, 5. See also Hermann Samter, 'Ist der Verband nationaldeutscher Juden eine rechtsstehende Organisation?', *Der nationaldeutsche Jude*, No. 2 (February 1930), p. 7. Samter was a member of both the V.n.J. and the SPD. On the SPD's attitude towards the League see Donald L. Niewyk, *Socialist, Anti-Semite and Jew. German Social Democracy Confronts the Problem of Anti-Semitism 1918–1933*, Baton Rouge, Louisiana 1971, p. 115. See also Carl Eisfeld, *Jüdischer Antisemitismus und Arbeiterschaft*, Hagen 1922.

satirist of the independent left-wing weekly, *Die Weltbühne*.[119] Embarrassed by Tucholsky's frequent criticisms of the German officer corps, the V.n.J. sought to brand him as an enemy of Jewish integration. In late 1921, the V.n.J. coined the phrase that "a single Tucholsky breeds millions of antisemites".[120] This slogan was consistent with the V.n.J.'s policy of condemning any Jew whose political attitudes offended the sensibilities of the German Right, a position to which many other German Jews, including members of the C.V. also adhered. In attacking Tucholsky, the V.n.J. ironically ignored the fact that as a baptised Jew, married to a Christian, Tucholsky had long since abandoned any formal ties with the organised Jewish community in Germany. Nevertheless, he was still considered to be as dangerous to the goal of full Jewish assimilation as was the Polish-Jewish immigrant.

Tucholsky was not the only member of the *Weltbühne* circle who was singled out for attack by the V.n.J. Between 1921 and 1933, such prominent Jewish writers as Siegfried Jacobsohn,[121] Heinz Pol and Arnold Zweig[122] were denounced for having caused the Jewish community irreparable harm because of their opposition to German militarism. Thus in 1928, the V.n.J. bitterly condemned the publication of Zweig's anti-war novel, *Der Streit um den Sergeanten Grischa*.[123] This kind of novel seriously embarrassed the V.n.J. As a patriotic organisation, the League was opposed to any form of anti-militarist literature, particularly if such works were produced by Jews. For this reason, it condemned the novel in order to demonstrate to the German Right that not all Jews were pacifists.

Besides the pacifist sentiments of the *Weltbühne* circle, the V.n.J. condemned the Jewish press in Germany for ignoring the threat which Jewish Communists posed in the struggle against antisemitism. Naumann in particular was incensed that the *Israelitisches Familenblatt*, German Jewry's second most widely read newspaper, had identified Iwan Katz and Werner Scholem[124] as "semitic" members of the newly elected *Reichstag*.[125] Warning that this kind of ethnocentrism was bound to reinforce the image that all Jews were Communists, Naumann announced that his organisation would oppose any attempt to portray Katz and Scholem as

---

[119]For a discussion of Tucholsky's career see Harold L. Poor, *Kurt Tucholsky and the Ordeal of Germany 1914–1935*, New York 1968, and Istvan Deak's *Weimar Germany's Left-Wing Intellectuals. A Political History of the Weltbühne and Its Circle*, Berkeley–Los Angeles 1968. See also Walter Z. Laqueur, 'The Tucholsky Complaint', *Encounter*, XXXIII, No. 4 (October 1969), pp. 76–80.

[120]Briefwechsel mit dem Reichskriegerbund "Kyffhäuser" ', *Der Schild*, II, No. 15 (February 1923), p. 2. See also Max Naumann, 'Zur Judenfrage. Der Kernpunkt der Judenfrage', *Deutsche Rundschau*, CCXXVII (April 1931), p. 69.

[121]See, for example, 'Jude', *Die Weltbühne*, XXII, No. 48 (30th November 1926), p. 872; and 'Siegfried Jacobsohn', *Der nationaldeutsche Jude*, No. 11/12 (November/December 1926), pp. 13–14. On Jacobsohn's career as editor of *Die Weltbühne* see Deak, *op. cit.*, pp. 30–36.

[122]Zweig's Zionist sentiments made him a prime target of the V.n.J., see above, p. 252.

[123]Max Naumann, 'Grischa-Kunst', *Der nationaldeutsche Jude*, No. 5/10 (October 1928), pp. 3–4. See also 'Polemik, wie sie nicht sein soll', *Der nationaldeutsche Jude*, No. 5 (May 1929), p. 8.

[124]On Katz's and Scholem's role in the early years of the German Communist Party see Ossip K. Flechtheim, *Die KPD in der Weimarer Republik*, Frankfurt a. Main 1969, pp. 38–39, 43–44, 47, 220, 222; and Werner T. Angress, *Stillborn Revolution. The Communist Bid for Power in Germany 1921–1923*, Princeton 1963, pp. 254, 276.

[125]Max Naumann, *Von deutscher Zukunft*, p. 11.

representative of the German-Jewish community. Following the expulsion of the Ruth Fischer faction from the German Communist Party in 1926, the number of Jews holding prominent positions within the KPD decreased.[126] But although the V.n.J. was thus denied one of its principal targets, it still remained virulently anti-Communist.[127]

Throughout its existence, the entire thrust of the V.n.J.'s campaign against Eastern Jews, Zionists and Jewish leftists was designed to demonstrate to the German Right that, despite their Jewish origins, National-German Jews were still prepared to take their place within a nationalist German *Volksgemeinschaft*. The League hoped, specifically, to force the Right to admit that a distinction had to be made between the vast majority of German Jews, who were thoroughly German in feeling, and a minority who, because of their affinity to Zionism or Marxism, were unworthy of continued participation in German life. As a result of mounting racial antisemitism in Germany in the post-war period, this proved to be an impossible task. Of the principal nationalist parties in the Weimar Republic, only the right-of-centre DVP was prepared to accept the League as an organisation of "anständige" Jews whose political stance made them eligible for acceptance as part of a German *Volksgemeinschaft*. Thus in December 1921, for instance, DVP *Reichstag* member Adolf Kempkes praised the League for its campaign against the *Ostjuden*.[128] A few days later, DVP national chairman Gustav Stresemann announced, after having attended a V.n.J. briefing, that he was prepared to use his influence within government circles on behalf of the new Jewish organisation.[129] While there is no evidence to indicate that Stresemann ever used his post as party chairman to oppose Zionist activities in Germany,[130] newspapers closely affiliated with his party did provide space for Naumann's anti-Zionist polemics.[131] This editorial policy suggests that the DVP saw Naumann, a member of that party, as a dedicated German patriot whose

[126]Scholem, for example, was dropped from the KPD Central Committee in 1925. A year later, he was expelled from the party. He eventually perished in the Buchenwald concentration camp. Hermann Weber, *Die Wandlung des deutschen Kommunismus. Die Stalinisierung der KPD in der Weimarer Republik*, Bd. 2, Frankfurt a. Main 1969, pp. 285–287. See also Gershom Scholem, *On Jews and Judaism in Crisis. Selected Essays*, Werner J. Dannhauser (ed.), New York 1976, p. 3.

[127]See, for example, Peyser *Streitschrift*, p. 7; and Max Naumann, *Sozialismus, Nationalsozialismus und nationaldeutsches Judentum*, pp. 6–7. See also Knütter, *op. cit.*, p. 103.

[128]Adolf Kempkes as quoted in 'Nationaldeutsche Juden', *Vorwärts*, XXXVIII No. A 294 (10th December 1921), p. 2. For a discussion of Kempkes's role in the DVP *Reichstag Fraktion* see Wolfgang Hartenstein, *Die Anfänge der Deutschen Volkspartei 1918–1920. Beiträge zur Geschichte des Parlamentarismus und der politischen Parteien*, Bd. 22, Düsseldorf 1962, pp. 152, 268, 278. Other members of the DVP's *Reichstag Fraktion* were impressed by the League's stand against Jewish leftists. In 1924, for example, Albrecht Morath praised the League for its campaign against SPD deputy Dr. Oskar Cohn. Like the DVP, the *Verband* viewed Cohn as a rootless internationalist unworthy of the support of patriotic Germans, 'Reichstagsabgeordneter Morath (DVP)', *Mitteilungsblatt des Verbandes nationaldeutscher Juden e.V.*, No. 1 (January/March 1924), pp. 7–8.

[129]Jewish Correspondence Bureau News and Telegraphic Agency Dispatch, 'Position of the Union of National-German Jews' (12th December 1921), (mimeo), p. 2. See also Viator, 'Nationaldeutsche Juden', *Die Weltbühne*, XVII, No. 4 (27th January 1921), pp. 114–116.

[130]See above, p. 259.

[131]See, for example, Max Naumann, 'Liegt Berlin in Deutschland', and his 'Zionismus und Alljudentum', *Deutsche Allgemeine Zeitung*, LXII, No. 362 (7th August 1923), pp. 1–2. The D.A.Z. was owned by Hugo Stinnes, a member of the DVP's *Reichstag Fraktion*. See also Max Naumann, 'Freude in Zürich - Pogrom in Palästina', *Kölnische Zeitung*, No. 475b (31st August 1929), p. 7.

views on Zionism were worthy of a national German audience. It also indicates that Naumann's programme of total assimilation was perceived by the DVP as a reasonable approach to solving the "Jewish Question" in Germany. It was inconceivable to moderate rightists that fifty years after Jews had received full legal and constitutional rights, a small minority would still insist on identifying themselves as part of a "foreign" *Volksgemeinschaft*. In January 1925, for example, the DVP organ *Hamburgischer Correspondent* denounced the efforts of the Zionist orientated *Jüdische Volkspartei* to gain control of the Prussian Federation of Jewish communities. The editor argued, "It is entirely clear that no State can tolerate a special group of citizens wishing to organise itself along foreign religious or national lines."[132] On the other hand, Albert Ballin and Max Naumann were heralded, by the author, as models of what German Jews should be. Underlying this praise was the fact that Naumann, unlike the C.V. leadership, had no qualms about questioning the political loyalty of German Zionists or of making known his desire to see German Jewry "merge into *Deutschtum*". Unfortunately, there is little direct evidence on the relationship between the DVP and the *Verband* during the last years of the Republic. What evidence is available suggests that relations between the two organisations cooled. In November 1929, the V.n.J. eulogised Stresemann, carefully omitting any references to the DVP. Instead, the V.n.J. chose to remember the DVP leader as a statesman capable of rising above party politics for the good of the German *Volk*.[133] Underlying this eulogy was the realisation of the increasing political gains of the National Socialists at the expense of the moderate Right and the need to be counted as participants in a National Revolution. From this point on, the V.n.J. concentrated its efforts on winning the approval of right-wing, antisemitic parties.

The treatment which the V.n.J. suffered at the hands of German racists was in marked contrast to the favourable reception which it had received in moderate right-of-centre circles. Unable to shed the "stigma" of Jewish descent, the V.n.J.'s ultra-nationalist stance made no impression whatsoever on the leadership of the *völkisch* movement. As early as April 1921, the *Deutsche Zeitung*, the official organ of the Pan-Germans, denounced the V.n.J.'s programme of assimilation – arguing that Zionism was the only solution to the "Jewish Question" in Germany.

> "When Dr. Naumann rejects the question as to race and claims that 'not the political community or that of social status, but only a community based on cultural and personal bonds [*Gefühlsgemeinschaft*] makes a people a people', then we cannot agree. Our history demonstrates the harmful influence of Jewry upon our people; we owe to it the ideas of internationalism and fraternisation of peoples which have ruined us. In all the left-wing parties, including the Democratic Party, the Jews predominate. Now there is the great danger that 'National-German' Jews – and there is no doubt that Jews with a German outlook exist – will gain influence in the national camp. This must be opposed; the Jew must not be allowed, on principle, to have a voice in German affairs. It must be emphasised over and over again: the law of heredity shows that the basic traits of races which are of alien blood cannot be eradicated; they will always remerge anew, even if only in a subsequent generation. A 'merging of

---

[132]'Ein Preussisches Judenparlament', *Hamburgischer Correspondent* (31st January 1925), as quoted in 'Echo der Presse', *Der nationaldeutsche Jude*, No. 4 (April 1925), pp. 8–9.
[133]'Ein Deutscher', *Der nationaldeutscher Jude*, No. 11 (November 1929), p. 1.

Jewry into Germandom' of which Dr. Naumann is dreaming is an impossibility ... For this
reason Zionism is for us the suitable form of subsequent Jewish development."[134]

In short, unlike most moderate rightists, the Pan-Germans saw Palestine as a convenient dumping ground for German Jews.

The leadership of the right-wing *Deutschnationale Volkspartei* (DNVP) was also opposed to mass assimilation as a solution to the "Jewish Question". In July 1919, the *völkisch* wing of the party advocated the creation of a national Jewish homeland in Palestine as a means of eliminating "Jewish domination" of German life.[135] Two years later, the DNVP officially defined itself as a "racist party",[136] thus further weakening the possibility of Jewish participation in right-wing politics. In spite of this stance, some spokesmen within the DNVP were still prepared to accept National-German Jews within a nationalist German *Volksgemeinschaft*. Friedrich von Oppeln-Bronikowski, a self-styled "konservativer Kulturpolitiker" and a non-racist, was a frequent contributor to *Der nationaldeutsche Jude*, a point upon which the League took great pride.[137] Alfred Hugenberg, the right-wing press magnate, also employed Jewish rightists as editors of his newspapers, one of them being Dr. Siegmund Breslauer, a V.n.J. founder and editor-in-chief of the *Berliner Lokalanzeiger*.[138] Oppeln-Bronikowski and Hugenberg proved, however, to be exceptions. Like the Pan-Germans, most German Nationalist leaders saw the V.n.J. as a clever Jewish device to infiltrate the German *Volk*.

These rebuffs forced the V.n.J. to redouble its efforts to gain acceptance from the radical Right. Believing that "cranial dimensions and hair colour"[139] did not determine one's true feeling for Germany, the V.n.J. continued to demonstrate its willingness to reach an accommodation with racial antisemites. This policy placed the V.n.J. in the unenviable position of defending political circles which had already defined National-German Jews as members of an "inferior race". During the 1924 *Reichstag* election campaign, for example, Max Naumann praised the DNVP's stand against Eastern European Jewish immigration while

---

[134]*Deutsche Zeitung*, n.d. as quoted in 'Verband nationaldeutscher Juden', *Allgemeine Zeitung des Judentums*, LXXXV, No. 9 (28th April 1921), pp. 99–100. For a discussion of the Pan-German attitude towards the "Jewish Question" see Shaul Esh, 'Designs for Anti-Jewish Policy in Germany up to the Nazi Rule', *Yad Vashem Studies*, VI (1967), pp. 83–120.

[135]*Ibid.*, p. 104. See also 'Ein neues Pro-Palästina Komitee!', *Der nationaldeutsche Jude*, No. 11/12 (November/December 1926), p. 1. See also Walk, *loc. cit.*, pp. 169–173.

[136]The attitude of the DNVP towards the "Jewish Question" is discussed in Lewis Hertzman, *DNVP Right-Wing Opposition in the Weimar Republic 1918–1924*, Lincoln, Nebraska 1963, pp. 124–164. See also Jochmann, *loc. cit.*, pp. 487–493; and George L. Mosse, 'Die deutsche Rechte und die Juden', in *Entscheidungsjahr 1932*, pp. 183–245.

[137]See, for example, 'Stimmen vom anderen Ufer', *Der nationaldeutsche Jude*, No. 1/3 (January/March 1924), pp. 5–6. For a discussion of Oppeln-Bronikowski's role in the DNVP see Jochmann, *loc. cit.*, pp. 488, 491n; and Arnold Paucker, ' "Gerechtigkeit!" The Fate of a Pamphlet on the Jewish Question', in *LBI Year Book VIII* (1963), pp. 238–251. See below, n. 143.

[138]'Zeitungsschreiber', *Die Weltbühne*, XXII, No. 33 (17th August 1926), p. 278; Werner Liebe, *Die Deutschnationale Volkspartei 1918–1924*. Beiträge zur Geschichte des Parlamentarismus und der politischen Parteien, Bd. 8, Düsseldorf 1956, pp. 46, 65. See also Knütter, *op. cit.*, pp. 104–105. On Breslauer's attitude towards the Jewish Left, see Werner T. Angress, 'Juden im politischen Leben der Revolutionszeit', in *Deutsches Judentum in Krieg und Revolution*, p. 247.

[139]Max Naumann, *Von Zionisten und Jüdisch-nationalen*, pp. 30–31. See also Pierson, *German Jewish Identity*, p. 315.

at the same time ignoring the fact that the Nationalist campaign against "Jewish domination" of German life did not exclude National-German Jews from attack.[140] Most likely, Naumann was motivated by the hope that German racists would look to the example of Mussolini's Italy "where Jews are part of the leadership of the fascist movement and where Mussolini with refreshing clarity has declared his opposition to Zionism".[141]

This attempt to reach an accommodation with the radical Right was never accomplished. During the last years of the Weimar Republic, the League was repeatedly rebuffed by *völkisch* circles. In 1931, Wilhelm Stapel, the editor of the right-wing *Deutsches Volkstum*, rejected a plea by Naumann that National-German Jews be included as part of the German *Volk*.[142] The DNVP leadership likewise refused to reverse its position on the "Jewish Question".[143] These rebuffs did not alter the V.n.J.'s determination to try and persuade the Right to accept nationalist feeling as the sole criteria for acceptance within a German *Volksgemeinschaft*. In August 1932, Naumann called upon the liberal Jewish community in Germany to ignore the "regrettable side effects"[144] of Nazi antisemitism and to join the National Socialists "even if they behave as if they are our enemies".[145] This endorsement probably proceeded from the premise that antisemitism was merely a device which Hitler used to rally the masses, and that once the nationalist revolution had succeeded, the Nazis would have little reason to exclude National-German Jews from their movement.[146] Based on the fragmentary evidence available it appears that by early 1933 Naumann had begun to have second thoughts about the likelihood that his course was realistic and feasible. On 24th February 1933, he backed away from his previous endorsement of Hitler and called upon German Jews to support a conservative coalition of the DNVP, the antisemitic *Stahlhelm* and several smaller parties on the Right in the forthcoming *Reichstag* elections.[147] Given the political situation in Germany at the time, even this position was utterly unrealistic.

[140]Max Naumann, 'Wahlkampf und Judenfrage', *Der nationaldeutsche Jude*, No. 5 (November 1924), pp. 1–2. This article originally appeared in the *Berliner Börsen Zeitung*, No. 529 (9th November 1924). See also Jakob Marx, *Das deutsche Judentum und seine jüdischen Gegner*, Berlin 1925, p. 33.

[141]Max Naumann, *Von deutscher Zukunft*, p. 9. For a discussion of the formation of pronounced right-of-centre Italian-Jewish organisations and the anti-Zionist attitudes of the Mussolini régime see Gene Bernardini, 'The Origins and Development of Racial Anti-Semitism in Fascist Italy', *Journal of Modern History*, XLIX, No. 3 (September 1977), pp. 431–453.

[142]'Briefwechsel mit einem Deutschvölkischen', *Der nationaldeutsche Jude*, No. 5 (May 1931), pp. 2–3. See also Mosse, 'Die Deutsche Rechte ...', *loc. cit.*, p. 217. The Austrian Social-Conservative Othmar Spann was more sympathetic to the dilemma of the National-German Jew. See John Haag, 'The Spann Circle and the Jewish Question', in *LBI Year Book XVIII* (1973), p. 101.

[143]One of the few exceptions to the DNVP's increasing antisemitism was Oppeln-Bronikowski. "In the summer of 1932 he took up the cudgels on behalf of the Jews in a radio debate with a virulently antisemitic deputy of the ... DNVP." Paucker, 'Gerechtigkeit! ...', *loc. cit.*, pp. 238–239. See also Friedrich von Oppeln-Bronikowski, *Gerechtigkeit. Zur Lösung der Judenfrage*, Berlin-Wilmersdorf 1932.

[144]Max Naumann, *Sozialismus, Nationalsozialismus und nationaldeutsches Judentum*, p. 10, as quoted in Bolkosky, *Distorted Image*, p. 162.

[145]*Ibid.*

[146]See, for example, Fred Bon, 'Können Juden Nationalsozialisten sein?', *Der nationaldeutsche Jude*, No. 1 (January 1931), p. 7; and 'Können Juden Nationalsozialisten sein?', *Der nationaldeutsche Jude*, No. 2 (February 1931), p. 5.

[147]Joining Naumann in this endorsement were: Manfred Blochert, the editor of *Der nationaldeutsche*

The V.n.J.'s strategy towards the Right was a reflection of its own mistaken notions about the nature of post-war German antisemitism. The entire thrust of the V.n.J.'s campaign was based on nineteenth-century assumptions that antisemites could be impressed by the *Verband*'s disavowal of all external traces of "Jewish behaviour".[148] This can be attributed in part to the social background and political orientation of many of the V.n.J.'s founders. Prior to 1921, some right-wing Jews had been accepted as members of German nationalist organisations. These individual successes blinded the V.n.J. to the changing nature of German antisemitism. By 1921, most rightists in Germany had accepted the elements of racist thinking and thus were no longer prepared to accept mass assimilation as a solution to the "Jewish Question".

This unwillingness or inability to comprehend the changing nature of antisemitism in Germany also explains the V.n.J.'s total failure within the Jewish community. From the point of view of the Z.V.f.D., the League was a prime example of the naïveté of assimilationist ideology. Accepting racial antisemitism as a fact of life, the Zionists sought to develop a national Jewish homeland in Palestine as a solution to the "Jewish Question" in Europe. The Z.V.f.D. also sought to develop Jewish national consciousness among those German Jews not prepared to emigrate to Palestine as a means of providing a buffer against insults in daily life. Even the C.V., which regarded the Jews as a part of the German nation, had no mistaken notions about the nature of German antisemitism. As early as 1919, the C.V. had recognised that the Weimar Constitution was the

---

Jude and *Justizrat* Georg Siegmann, the V.n.J.'s national chairman. 'Political Realignment of Jewish Leaders Noted', *Jewish Daily Bulletin*, New York, 24th February 1933, p. 4.

Historians have devoted considerable attention to various aspects of the League's lamentable activities under the Nazis. On the attempt by Naumann and the V.n.J. leadership to seek an accommodation with leading officials of the Hitler régime see Abraham Margaliot's, *The Political Reaction of German Jewish Organizations and Institutions to the Anti-Jewish Policy of the National Socialists 1932–1935* (unpublished doctoral dissertation [in Hebrew], Hebrew University of Jerusalem, 1971), pp. VII, 153–158. See also Margaliot's 'The Dispute over the Leadership of German Jewry (1933–1938)', *Yad Vashem Studies*, X (1974), pp. 131–132. A Jewish-Marxist analysis of the V.n.J.'s attitudes and actions under the National Socialist régime can be found in Louis Harap's 'German Jewry Under Hitler', in Louis Harap (ed.). *Jewish Life Anthology, 1946–1956*, New York 1956, pp. 170–178. On the refusal of the V.n.J. to join the *Reichsvertretung* see K. Y. Ball Kaduri, 'The National Representation of Jews in Germany. Obstacles and Accomplishments at its Establishment', *Yad Vashem Studies*, II (1958), p. 160. Valuable documents pertaining to the V.n.J.'s history under the National Socialist régime have been published in Herrmann, *Das Dritte Reich und die Deutsch-Jüdischen Organisationen 1933–34*, pp. 11–14, 21–38, 69–80. Excerpts from other post-1933 V.n.J. publications have been translated by Weiss-Rosmarin, *loc. cit.*, pp. 9–10. On the V.n.J.'s relationship with other pronounced Jewish assimilationist organisations during the first months of the Hitler régime see Carl J. Rheins, 'The Schwarzes Fähnlein, Jungenschaft, 1932–1934', in *LBI Year Book XXIII* (1978), pp. 173–197; esp. pp. 186–189. Finally, on the V.n.J.'s dissolution in November 1935 and Naumann's subsequent arrest and imprisonment see this author's *German Jewish Patriotism 1918–1935* (unpublished doctoral dissertation, State University of New York at Stony Brook, 1978), pp. 184, 284–285.

[148]See, for example, the series 'Nationaldeutsche Juden der Vergangenheit', which appeared in *Der nationaldeutsche Jude* in 1929. This series was designed to strengthen the League's position *vis-à-vis* the Zionists by demonstrating the possibility of assimilation. Among the "typical" Jews featured in this series were Dr. Raphael Löwenfeld, the founder of the C.V.; Moritz Ellstätter, the first unbaptised Jew to become minister of a German state; and Albert Ballin, the German shipping magnate and adviser to Wilhelm II.

only barrier which protected the Jewish community from racist demagogues. It is not surprising, therefore, that the C.V. saw the V.n.J.'s attempt to find a political accommodation with the radical Right as nothing less than an attack against the Jewish community itself.

Erich Mühsam's Jewish Identity

BY LAWRENCE BARON

One hundred years after his birth,* the German anarchist Erich Mühsam (1878–1934) has become the subject of a growing number of scholarly studies.[1] These recent works have highlighted his activities as a Bohemian intellectual, socialist author, radical journalist, anarchist theorist and prominent participant in the Bavarian Revolutions of 1918/1919. Yet almost all of them have disregarded or minimised Mühsam's relationship to his Jewish lineage as a significant factor in his development.[2] This oversight is understandable. Mühsam ostensibly epitomised the "non-Jewish Jew"[3] who transcends Jewry for the sake of humanity. His avowed atheism and internationalism should have excluded any special feeling of attachment to his religious and ethnic background. Contemptuous of the spurious solidarity generated by nationalistic sentiments, Mühsam pronounced himself free of such emotional allegiances: " 'We Jews' have as much and as little in common with one another as 'we Germans', as 'we French', as 'we riders in the same bus'!"[4]

Notwithstanding this blunt denial, there is considerable evidence to belie Müh-

---

*This article is based on a lecture originally presented at the Leo Baeck Institute of New York on 14th December 1978 to commemorate Erich Mühsam's centenary year. The author would like to express his gratitude to Professor Werner T. Angress of the State University of New York at Stony Brook, N.Y., and to Professor Lothar Kahn of Central Connecticut State College, New Britain, Conn., for their valuable suggestions. He would also like to record here his debt to Prof. George L. Mosse, Wisconsin/Jerusalem, for his constant inspiration.

[1]Lawrence Baron, *The Eclectic Anarchism of Erich Mühsam*, New York 1976; Heinz Hug, *Erich Mühsam. Untersuchungen zu Leben und Werk*, Glashütten im Taunus 1974; Wilhelm Lukas Kristl, 'Zwischen Cabaret und Barrikade', in *Börsenblatt für den Deutschen Buchhandel*, XXIX (29th June 1973), No. 51, pp. A221–A230; Roland Lewin, 'Erich Mühsam 1878–1934', supplement to *Le monde libertaire*, (June 1968), No. 143; Ulrich Linse, *Organisierter Anarchismus im Deutschen Kaiserreich von 1871*, Berlin 1969; N. Pawlowa, *Tvorchestvo Erikha Miuzama*, Moscow 1965; Fritz J. Raddatz, *Erfolg oder Wirkung. Schicksale politischer Publizisten in Deutschland*, Munich 1972, pp. 53–80; 'Erich Mühsam: zum 40. Todestag', in *europäische ideen* (1974), No. 5/6; *Erich Mühsam. Scheinwerfer oder Färbt ein weisses Blütenblatt sich schwarz*, Fidus (ed.), Berlin 1978. This list is by no means exhaustive.

[2]For example, Hug writes, "Though the family descended from Judaism, this fact played no great role.' (Hug, *op. cit.*, p. 2). Sterling Fishman asserts: "Mühsam, too, was from a Jewish background but rejected it as he had his bourgeois roots." (Sterling Fishman, *Prophets, Poets and Priests. A Study of the Men and Ideas That Made the Munich Revolution of 1918/1919*. Ph.D., University of Wisconsin/Madison 1960, p. 200.) Kristl also maintains that Mühsam "accepted no religious or racial ties". (Kristl, *loc. cit.*, p. A223.) Hans Tramer, on the other hand, believes that Mühsam's Jewishness did have a considerable impact on his writing. Unfortunately, Tramer does not develop this thesis. (Hans Tramer, 'Der Beitrag der Juden zu Geist und Kultur', in *Deutsches Judentum in Krieg und Revolution 1916–1923*, Ein Sammelband herausgegeben von Werner E. Mosse unter Mitwirkung von Arnold Paucker, Tübingen 1971 [Schriftenreihe wissenschaftlicher Abhandlungen des Leo Baeck Instituts 25], pp. 332–333.)

[3]See Isaac Deutscher, *The Non-Jewish Jew and Other Essays*, New York 1968, pp. 25–41.

[4]Erich Mühsam, 'Zur Judenfrage', in *Die Weltbühne*, XVI (2nd December 1920), No. 49, p. 644.

sam's pose as a cosmopolitan socialist who had shed all traces of his origins. Throughout his life he sensed that society treated him as an outsider because he was Jewish. This personal uneasiness, as well his ideological analysis, alerted him to the dangers inherent in antisemitism. Thus, he resolutely combated manifestations of it when they flared up in Eastern Europe and Germany. Mühsam presupposed that the precarious isolation of the Jews would drive them into the ranks of revolutionary movements dedicated to the abolition of the causes of religious, nationalistic and racial prejudices. As a disciple of Gustav Landauer, Mühsam learned to appreciate the Jews as a genuine *Volk* which had the lofty mission of actualising the Prophetic vision of social justice and universal brotherhood in the present world. He approved of the Zionist factions which promoted these goals. Although he rejected those elements of Jewish faith and life which contradicted his anarchist principles, he never lapsed into the self-hatred or self-effacement which characterised the mentality of many German-Jewish radicals.[5] In the end the Nazis tortured and murdered Mühsam because he symbolised the Jewish subversive whose indefatigable activism they associated with treason and defeat.

He grew up in a prosperous middle-class family whose Jewish identity constituted a balancing act between a Jewish past and a German future. As the undisputed master of the household,[6] Erich's father, Siegfried, set the tone on these matters. On the one hand, he warmly reminisced about his boyhood in a traditional Jewish family living in a small Silesian village. He carefully preserved documents from this period of his life and wrote a nostalgic novel, *Die Killeberger*, about it.[7] At the least he expected his children to marry other Jews.[8] On the other hand, Siegfried had experienced the gradual removal of legal barriers to Jewish equality in his own lifetime and strove to make the fruits of emancipation more accessible to his children by cautioning them against conduct that would differentiate them from their Christian neighbours in Lübeck. He circumspectly avoided uttering the word Jew in front of Gentiles and even fostered the impression that he was one of them by celebrating Christmas. Politically he was a National Liberal who cherished his memories as a pharmacist for the Prussian army in the war against Austria in 1866.[9] Like so many of his Jewish contemporaries, Siegfried earnestly believed that the unification of Germany would accelerate the fusion of *Deutschtum* with *Judentum*.[10]

---

[5]See Theodor Lessing, *Jüdischer Selbsthass*, Berlin 1930; Peter Gay, *Freud, Jews and Other Germans*, New York 1978, pp. 189–230; Robert S. Wistrich, *Revolutionary Jews From Marx to Trotsky*, New York 1976, pp. 23–130.

[6]SNM (Schiller Nationalmuseum in Marbach am Neckar), Paul Mühsam, *Ich bin ein Mensch gewesen*, vol. 1, p. 25; DAK-EMA (Deutsche Academie der Künste der DDR-Erich Mühsam Archiv), III 3037, Erich Mühsam, *Tagebücher* (hereafter *T*), 2nd September 1910.

[7]Onkel Siegfried (Mühsam), *Die Killeberger*, Leipzig 1904. The Löwenherz family in the book is modelled after the Mühsam family. Also see LBIA (Leo Baeck Institute Archives, New York) – Sammlung Siegfried Seligmann Mühsam, AR-C 3059/7112, I (A) Familienbriefe 1801–1854, I (B) Familienpapiere seit 1852, XI Kinder und Schwiegersohn des SM.

[8]DAK-EMA, III 3047, Erich Mühsam, *T*, 9/10th June 1915.

[9]SNM, Paul Mühsam, *op. cit.*, vol. 1, pp. 5–13, 24–29.

[10]Jacob Toury, *Die politischen Orientierungen der Juden in Deutschland. Von Jena bis Weimar*, Tübingen 1966 (Schriftenreiher wissenschaftlicher Abhandlungen des Leo Baeck Instituts 15), pp. 131–153.

Though Siegfried's assimilationist guise seemed appropriate for his generation, it must have struck his children as anachronistic in the era of mounting Judeophobia which was the backdrop of their youth. Between 1873 and 1900 religious, political, economic and racial antisemitism rapidly spread in Germany through the campaigns of demagogues like Adolf Stoecker, Wilhelm Marr and Otto Bökkel.[11] This intolerance infected the predominantly Lutheran population of Lübeck too. By looking at Thomas and Heinrich Mann's depictions of their native city in these years, one can gauge the depth of anti-Jewish bias among its citizens. The following passage from Heinrich Mann's *Der Untertan* illustrates the sort of humiliation a Jewish student might have endured at the Katharineum Gymnasium, the school which both the Mann and Mühsam brothers attended:

> "As was the usual and approved custom, he [Diederich Hessling] had bullied the only Jew in the class, but then he proceeded to an unfamiliar manifestation. Out of the blocks which were used for drawing he built a cross on the desk and forced the Jew on his knees before it. He held him tight, in spite of his resistance; he was strong! What made Diederich strong was the applause of the bystanders, the crowd whose arms helped him, the overwhelming majority within the building and in the world outside. He was acting on behalf of the whole Christian community of Netzig [Lübeck]."[12]

Even if they personally had not undergone such harassment, Siegfried's sons and daughters must have been aware of similar incidents and of the antisemitic attitudes which triggered them. Consequently, Hans, Grete and Charlotte Mühsam repudiated their father's preoccupation with being accepted into German society and zealously embraced the Zionist cause.[13] As Roy Pascal has noted, the espousal of Zionism by younger German Jews often represented "a reaction against the self-mutilation that the desire for assimilation brought". [14] To Erich, however, the ubiquitous hostility towards Jews was just another reason for his eventual revolt against the German state.[15]

After he had embarked on his career as a writer, Mühsam often sensed that he was ostracised for being Jewish. When he was denied entry into a Zürich tavern in 1904, he lashed out at the proprietor for "kicking out the stranger who is a Jew as well as a German".[16] By 1908 he admitted that there was no way to escape one's Jewish extraction: "The antisemites simply scream, 'It makes no

---

[11]Paul W. Massing, *Rehearsal for Destruction*, New York 1949; George L. Mosse, *The Crisis in German Ideology*, New York 1964, pp. 126–145; Peter Pulzer, *The Rise of Political Anti-Semitism in Germany and Austria*, New York 1964.

[12]Heinrich Mann, *Man of Straw*, London 1972, pp. 9–10. Thomas Mann's accounts of antisemitism in Lübeck are more subtle. Nevertheless, he reveals a general dislike of Jews among members of the business community and even portrays a Professor Mühsam who is a typical "clever" Jewish intellectual and an aficionado of Heine, "that cynical and sickly poet". Thomas Mann, *Buddenbrooks*, trans. H. T. Lowe Porter, New York 1952, pp. 361, 583–584.

[13]Paul Mühsam, 'Erich Mühsam: Vorwort', (manuscript in possession of Else Levi-Mühsam), p. 1. Although I have not been able to find any conclusive evidence, it is possible that Erich's brother Hans was the same Hans Mühsam who led the pro-Zionist *Jüdischer Volksverein* of Berlin, see Toury, *op. cit.*, pp. 280, 284–285; and Marjorie Lamberti, *Jewish Activism in Imperial Germany. The Struggle for Civil Equality*, New Haven 1978, p. 61.

[14]Roy Pascal, *From Naturalism to Expressionism*, London 1973, p. 77. Also see Jehuda Reinharz, *Fatherland or Promised Land. The Dilemma of the German Jew, 1893–1914*, Ann Arbor 1975; and Stephen M. Poppel, *Zionism in Germany 1897–1933*, Philadelphia 1976.

[15]Baron, *op. cit.*, pp. 2–4; and Linse, *op. cit.*, pp. 96–97.

[16]Erich Mühsam, 'Brief aus Zürich', in *Der arme Teufel*, III (13th December 1904), No. 13, p. 5.

difference, Jewish or baptised, in the race the foulness lies!' "[17] Mühsam's thinly disguised autobiographical story 'Carmen' (1912) reveals his rage towards a culture which consigns Jews to be outcasts. Therein a struggling Jewish poet seethes with hatred against bourgeois society and intentionally shocks its sensibilities with his poems. A girl from an aristocratic family becomes attracted to this iconoclast and accepts an invitation to meet him at his apartment. He ravishes her and interprets his sexual exploit as a victory of the "pariah" Jew over an inimical society.[18] This sort of crude retribution reminds one of Eldridge Cleaver's obsession with raping white women back in the days when he was a black militant.[19] In both cases sexual defilement of women belonging to the oppressing group serves as a means to avenge discrimination.

In typical anarchist fashion Mühsam argued that the ruling classes of each country welcome and encourage antisemitic movements to deflect legitimate discontent away from the institutions of the capitalist nation state. He excoriated the German purveyors of such bigotry for beclouding the systemic causes of economic exploitation:

> "They spout the dumbest racial theories of the Frenchman Gobineau and the Englishman Houston Stewart Chamberlain as the most German of all German doctrines against the usurious Jews (who comprise one half per cent of the population, but are feared like the devil by the Teutonic heroes as the stranglers of the remaining ninety-nine and one half per cent) without taking umbrage at the usurious business transactions of high finance as a whole."[20]

Mühsam accused governmental leaders of practising the same diversionary tactic to obscure the undemocratic nature of the modern state. He contended that they indoctrinate their subjects with a sense of national superiority to compensate for their political impotence:

> "The hair, eye, or skin colour of one's ancestors, the question whether someone was born on this or that side of a river, whether his language and life style were shaped by this or that set of historical, geographical, and climatic conditions, can be utilised as a measure for human worth only by those who lust for or possess power."[21]

According to Mühsam the Germans were particularly susceptible to this ethnocentric hubris because it had been drummed into their heads for over a century by the élites who benefited from the sacrifice of liberty on the altar of German unity.[22]

Since Jews faced recurrent persecution under the existing system, Mühsam

[17]Erich Mühsam, *Die Jagd auf Harden*, Berlin 1908, p. 18.
[18]Erich Mühsam, 'Carmen', in *Kain Kalender für das Jahr 1912*, Munich 1912, pp. 65–73. Mühsam develops the theme of the Jewish man enticing the Gentile woman in two other poems: Erich Mühsam, 'Meta und der Finkenschafter', in *War einmal ein Revoluzzer, Bänkellieder und Gedichte*, Helga Bemmann (ed.), Berlin 1970, pp. 36–40; and Erich Mühsam, 'Aufforderung zum Tanz', *Der Krater*, Berlin 1909, p. 87.
[19]Eldridge Cleaver, *Soul on Ice*, New York 1968, pp. 10–17. For a conflicting interpretation of "the sexual power of the stranger", see Ernest van den Haag, *The Jewish Mystique*, New York 1969, pp. 214–223.
[20]Erich Mühsam, 'Romantischer Materialismus', in *Aufruf: Organ der Liga der Menschenrechte in der Tschechoslowakei*, III (November 1932), No. 1, p. 11. At a much earlier date Mühsam had reached similar conclusions, DAK-EMA, III 3048, Mühsam, *T*, 23rd November 1915.
[21]Erich Mühsam, *Die Befreiung der Gesellschaft vom Staat. Was ist kommunistischer Anarchismus?*, Berlin–Britz 1933, pp. 24–25.
[22]Mühsam, 'Romantischer Materialismus', pp. 8–11.

concluded that they should align themselves with the communist anarchists who sought the abolition of both capitalism and the state. The anarchist conception of the class struggle recognised only socio-economic status and ideological commitment as the main criteria that divide mankind. Mühsam stressed this ecumenical spirit: "There is no demarcation by race, confession, and genealogy in the social stratification of society."[23] The decentralisation of state authority into small democratic communities as envisaged by the anarchists would maximise individual freedom. This, in turn, would eliminate the xenophobia which had been manipulated by governments to consolidate their power.[24] With these goals in mind, Mühsam wondered why more Jews did not rally around the anarchist banner: "If the Jews would have finally grasped that they by nature belong to the opposition, then things would have gone better for them long ago."[25]

Although his primary allegiance was to the emancipation of the proletariat, Mühsam repeatedly came to the defence of the *Ostjuden* when they faced antisemitic oppression. He correctly perceived that he too was vulnerable to the calumnies directed against other Jews. This attitude is well articulated in his commentary on the Beilis trial of 1913. Noting that the German antisemitic press had cited this case as proof of Jewish perfidy in general, Mühsam felt that as a Jew he had to counter such charges:

> "The Beilis trial is actually a concern of international Jewry since the abominable accusation of ritual murder affects everyone who is a Jew ... That is why it is the duty of all of us who are Jews to remember our descent and membership at such a moment and to demand that the charge against which Beilis must defend himself be raised against us all ... At this moment I am aware of my solidarity with every Galician horse trader just as Spinoza or Heinrich Heine would have been aware of it."[26]

In 1915 Mühsam voiced his anxieties over the plight of Eastern European Jews who might become the targets for the misdirected fury of nascent nationalistic and insurrectionary movements in Poland and Russia.[27] Shortly thereafter his lawyer, Hugo Caro, solicited his support for a plan to convince both German Jews and the German government to start a relief programme for Russian Jews. Sympathising with this project, Mühsam advised Caro to contact Martin Buber and Gustav Landauer before approaching the reactionary leaders of Imperial Germany.[28] Though there is no further mention of this undertaking in his diary, Mühsam continued to believe that Western European Jews were under an obligation to aid their Eastern brethren.[29] When his earlier fears materialised in the Lwow pogrom of 1918, he categorically denounced that massacre despite his

---

[23]Mühsam, 'Zur Judenfrage', p. 644. For an earlier statement of this sort of internationalism, see Erich Mühsam, 'Die Proletarierlied', in *Die Canaille. Monatsbeilage zur Wochenschrift Der freie Arbeiter*, II (March 1906), p. 2.
[24]Mühsam, *Die Befreiung der Gesellschaft*, pp. 24–25.
[25]DAK-EMA, III 3048, Mühsam, *T*, 23rd November 1915.
[26]Erich Mühsam, 'Ritualmord', in *Kain*, III (November 1913), No. 8, p. 126.
[27]DAK-EMA, III 3047, Mühsam, *T*, 30th June 1915 and 21st August 1915.
[28]DAK-EMA, III 3047, Mühsam, *T*, 20th August 1915. For information about Buber's and Landauer's efforts to aid the *Ostjuden* during the First World War, see S[halom] Adler-Rudel, *Ostjuden in Deutschland. 1880–1940. Zugleich eine Geschichte der Organisationen, die sie betreuten*, Tübingen 1959 (Schriftenreihe wissenschaftlicher Abhandlungen des Leo Baeck Instituts 1).
[29]DAK-EMA, III 3048, Mühsam, *T*, 14th October 1915.

involvement in the Bavarian Revolution at this time.[30] After the acquittal of Samuel Schwarzbard in 1927, Mühsam praised the vindication of the assassin of Simon Petlyura, the instigator of the pogroms which raged in the Ukraine between 1918 and 1921.[31]

The upsurge of antisemitism in Germany during the First World War greatly disturbed Mühsam too. By 1915 he detected the emergence of antimsemitic tendencies among all classes of the German populace. His apprehensions fed on the off-hand comments he overheard or exchanged with passers-by. One Munich civil servant whom he met confidently augured that "the next war will be against the Jews". Another man reported that antisemitic acts and remarks by German soldiers were becoming widespread. Piecing together these bits of information, Mühsam foresaw an impending disaster in the making: "It is by no means out of the question that this mood will transform itself into a regular massacre. Russia's sorrow is Germany's sorrow."[32] With so many Germans apportioning the guilt for prolonging the war on the Jews, Mühsam bitterly censured German Jews for flocking to the battlefields under the illusion that this demonstration of patriotism would prove once and for all that they were a loyal part of the national community.[33]

Germany's defeat and the ensuing upheaval in Bavaria thrust Mühsam into the centre of the antisemitic tempest which had been brewing in the years before 1918. The conspicuous role of Jewish radicals like Mühsam in the Bavarian Revolution, the extremism of their socialist rhetoric and the lingering sting of military and economic collapse exacerbated the biases of diehard chauvinists and conservative Catholic Bavarians. Antisemitic invective soon became the staple fare dished up by counter-revolutionary propagandists.[34] Undaunted by this acrimonious climate of opinion, Mühsam frenetically agitated for the establishment of a federated Soviet Republic. To this end he called for the censorship of the press and then temporarily occupied the offices of four Munich newspapers.[35] Though not one of Mühsam's express intentions in this incident, the muzzling of antisemitism coincided with his demands for the suppression of reactionary

---

[30]Erich Mühsam, 'Der Judenmord in Lemberg', in *Kain*, V (10th December 1918), No. 1, p. 4.
[31]Erich Mühsam, 'Schwarzbard und Machno', in *Fanal*, II (December 1927), No. 3, pp. 68–69.
[32]DAK-EMA, III 3048, Mühsam, *T*, 23rd November 1915. For an overview of the spread of antisemitism in Germany during the First World War, see Werner Jochmann, 'Die Ausbreitung des Antisemitismus', in *Deutsches Judentum in Krieg und Revolution*, pp. 409–447.
[33]DAK-EMA, III 3048, Mühsam, *T*, 23rd November 1915; Mühsam, 'Zur Judenfrage', pp. 645–646.
[34]For background on these developments, see Jochmann, *loc. cit.*, pp. 451–510; Saul Friedländer, 'Die politischen Veränderungen der Kriegszeit und ihre Auswirkungen auf die Judenfrage', in *Deutsches Judentum in Krieg und Revolution*, pp. 27–65; Werner T. Angress, 'Juden im politischen Leben der Revolutionszeit', in *Deutsches Judentum in Krieg und Revolution*, pp. 137–316; Hans Helmuth Knütter, *Die Juden und die deutsche Linke in der Weimarer Republik*, Düsseldorf 1971; Georg Franz, 'Munich: Birthplace and Center of the National Socialist German Workers' Party', in *The Journal of Modern History*, XXIX (December 1957), No. 4, pp. 319–326.
[35]Erich Mühsam, 'Mein Putsch gegen die Münchner Zeitungen', in *Kain*, V (17th December 1918), No. 2, p. 4. Although Mühsam claimed that the occupation of the newspaper offices was a spontaneous act, he had informed an associate of his one week earlier that he might undertake such actions, see LC-RS (Library of Congress-Rehse Sammlung), Container 422, Mühsam to Johann Knief, 1st December 1918.

groups and the "pogrom inciting propaganda"[36] which they spewed forth. After a right-wing fanatic had assassinated Kurt Eisner in what Mühsam regarded as part of a broader conspiracy to murder Gustav Landauer, Max Levien and himself,[37] Mühsam stepped up his campaign for the formation of a Communist *Räterepublik* which would energetically repress its arch enemies. Both before and after the creation of the first Munich Soviet Republic in early April of 1919, he proposed the taking of hostages, preferably reactionary aristocrats and army officers, as a way to intimidate their cohorts from planning any further counter-revolutionary actions.[38] Kidnapped on 13th April by supporters of the SPD régime in Bamberg, Mühsam played no role in the subsequent detention and execution of political captives at the Luitpold Gymnasium by guards loyal to the second Munich Soviet Republic. The Nazis, nevertheless, blamed Mühsam for instigating this bloodbath which took the lives of seven members of the Thule Society, a forerunner of the NSDAP.[39] In retrospect Mühsam interpreted the *Geiselmord* as an understandable, albeit regrettable, reprisal for the atrocities committed by the "white" armies which were then overrunning Munich. He was also quick to point out that the Thule Society was hardly an innocent bystander in this tumult, but rather a "clique of antisemitic nobles and nationalists" which had poisoned the minds of Bavarians with its inflammatory vilifications of the revolution.[40]

Some observers and historians have rebuked Mühsam and the other Jewish activists in the forefront of the Munich débâcle for irresponsibly pushing the course of the revolution ever leftward without considering the antisemitic backlash they were provoking.[41] Werner Angress is right when he comments that the violent tone and themes of Mühsam's revolutionary speeches and writings were bound to infuriate the average Bavarian who distrusted the revolution and its leaders from the outset.[42] Mühsam, however, scoffed at the suggestion that he should have acted more moderately because he was a Jew. One purpose of the insurrection, as he saw it, was to break down the arbitrary distinctions, whether religious or racial, which blurred the battle lines of the class struggle. When he nominated Gustav Landauer for educational commissioner of the first Soviet Republic, Mühsam reminded his comrades that Landauer's Jewishness should have no bearing on his appointment to the post because only reactionaries are offended by "*landfremd* literati and Jews".[43] Responding directly to the charge

[36]Erich Mühsam, *Von Eisner bis Leviné*, Berlin–Britz 1929, p. 19.
[37]Mühsam, *Von Eisner bis Leviné*, pp. 25–26; Erich Mühsam, 'Arco und Linder', *Fanal*, I (January 1927), No. 4, pp. 55–59.
[38]Linse, *op. cit.*, p. 362; Angress, *loc. cit.*, pp. 271–272.
[39]Kreszentia Mühsam, *Der Leidensweg Erich Mühsams*, Paris–Zürich 1935, pp. 21–22; SNM, Paul Mühsam, *op. cit.*, vol. 3, pp. 252–253. For background on the Thule Society, see Franz, *loc. cit.*, pp. 326–331.
[40]Erich Mühsam, 'Der Münchener Geiselmord', in *Fanal*, I (March 1927), No. 6, pp. 88–92.
[41]Sigmund Fraenkel, 'Offener Brief an die Herren Erich Mühsam, Dr. Wadler, Dr. Otto Neurath, Ernst Toller und Gustav Landauer', in *Von Juden in München*, Hans Lamm (ed.), Munich 1959, pp. 304–306; Franz, *loc. cit.*, pp. 319–324; Willehad Paul Eckert, 'Wie links darf ein Jude sein?', in *Emuna*, IV (April 1969), No. 2, pp. 73–74.
[42]Angress, *loc. cit.*, p. 274. Angress is also correct when he notes that Mühsam was far less violent than his rhetoric indicated. Cf. Baron, *op. cit.*, pp. 68–73, 110–111, 131–132.
[43]Ernst Niekisch, *Gewagtes Leben. Begegnungen und Begebnisse*, Cologne–Berlin 1958, pp. 68–69.

that Jewish insurgents had jeopardised the entire Jewish community, Mühsam militantly proclaimed that he would not let "the distribution of antisemitic leaflets in the streets, the cries of hatred from cursing Jew baiters, and the whipping up of pogroms by petty Teutonic heroes" deter him from pursuing his ideals. To do otherwise was a tacit recognition that Jews were aliens whose civil liberties should be curtailed. Finally, he added that antisemites would have found grist for their propaganda mills even if his Jewish associates and himself had done nothing.[44]

After his release from prison at the end of 1924, Mühsam attempted to organise a united front of revolutionary groups to oppose the rise of fascism in Germany. In his analysis of recent history, the First World War had revealed the moral bankruptcy of the capitalist nation state and thereby ushered in an epoch of world revolution. Caught in their death throes, the ruling classes of the old system resorted to naked brutality to preserve their dominance.[45] Applying this explanation to developments in Germany, Mühsam accused the SPD of opportunistically stabilising the post-war crisis there by allying itself with the Free Corps, the *Reichswehr* High Command and big business to crush genuine socialist movements.[46] Should this arrangement fail to maintain order, Nazism, the most extreme manifestation of capitalist and statist hegemony, might seize power and liquidate the leftist threat.[47] To avert this frightening prospect Mühsam urged all true revolutionaries, a category which excluded the Social Democrats, to formulate a common strategy to combat Hitler and the pseudo-democracy of the Weimar Republic which had paved the way for him. Given the polarisation of German politics by 1933, Mühsam should have postponed his ideological war with the Republic and the SPD for the sake of broadening the base against the Nazi menace.[48]

Although Mühsam interpreted the racist antisemitism of the Nazis as a ruse to obfuscate class antagonisms and deflect criticism away from existing institutions, he took its ominous implications seriously. The war, in his opinion, had raised the level of racial hatred to a feverish pitch.[49] The counter-revolutionary forces of the Weimar Republic capitalised on this mania in defence of their vested interests. With his experiences of 1918 and 1919 still fresh in his memory, Mühsam had reached the conclusion that "antisemitism is always a symptom of the highest stage of reactionary conjuncture".[50] In the pages of his journal *Fanal* he denounced Hitler's vulgar demagoguery for teaching the Germans "that the trans-

---

[44]Mühsam, 'Zur Judenfrage', pp. 643–647.
[45]Ulrich Linse, 'Die Transformation der Gesellschaft durch die anarchistische Weltanschauung. Zur Ideologie und Organisation anarchistischer Gruppen in der Weimarer Republik', in *Archiv für Sozialgeschichte*, XI (1971), pp. 318–320.
[46]*Ibid.*, pp. 299–308.
[47]*Ibid.*, pp. 315–318.
[48]Linse, *Organisierter Anarchismus*, pp. 374–376; Linse, 'Die Transformation', pp. 346–351; Baron, *op. cit.*, pp. 153–161.
[49]Erich Mühsam, 'Zwölf Jahre Republik', in *Fanal*, V (November 1930), No. 2, p. 32.
[50]Mühsam, 'Zur Judenfrage', p. 647; Mühsam, 'Zwölf Jahre Republik', p. 32. Mühsam expressed a similar opinion in a letter to his sister, Charlotte, and her husband Leo Landau, LBIA-Erich Mühsam Collection, AR-C.Z.420/1806, IX.7, Mühsam to Charlotte and Leo Landau, 18th December 1922.

The three Mühsam brothers in 1889
From the left: Marcus (father of Paul Mühsam), Samuel (Chief Rabbi of Steiermark) and Siegfried (father of Erich Mühsam)

By courtesy of Mrs. Else Levi-Mühsam, Konstanz

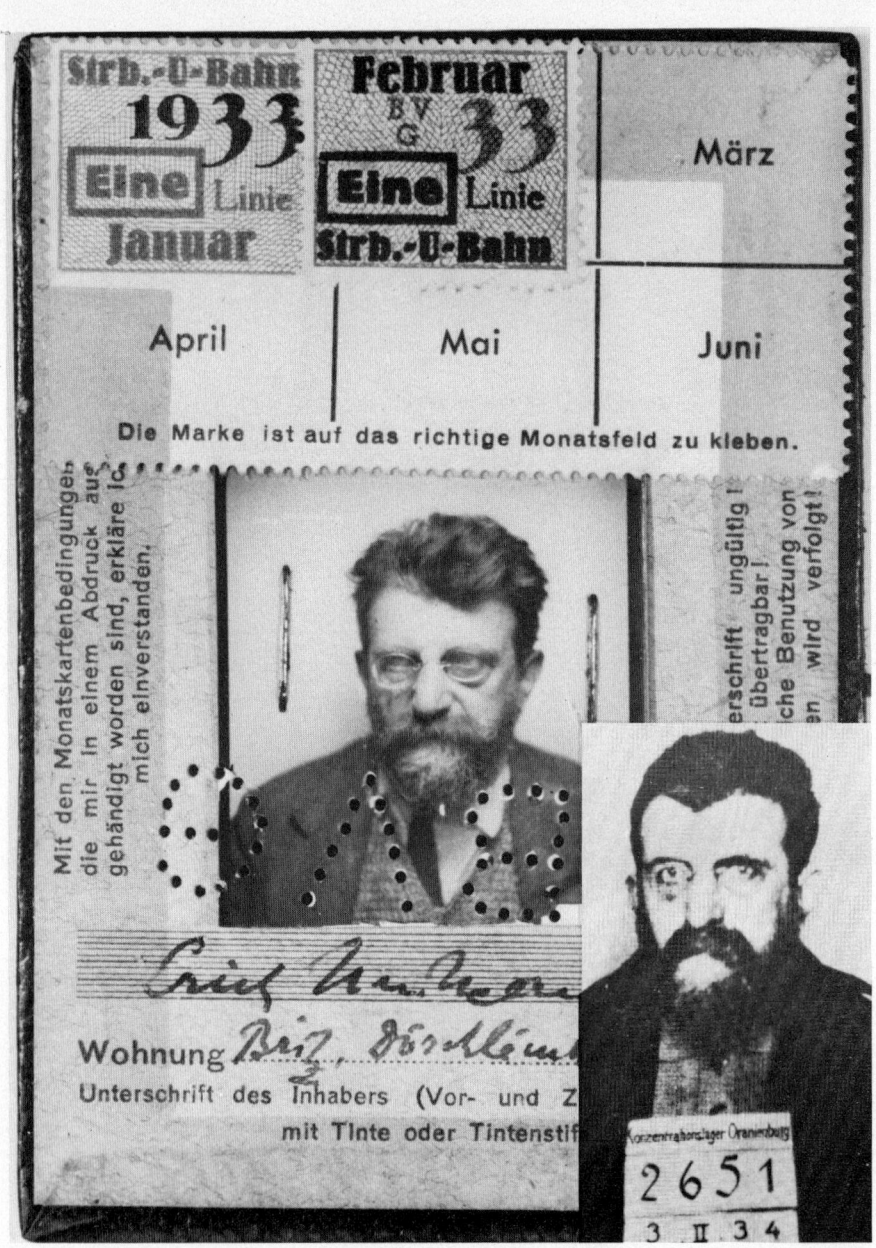

ERICH MÜHSAM
Public transport season ticket not renewed for March 1933 ... lower right inset: Mühsam as inmate of Oranienburg concentration camp

From the Archives of the Leo Baeck Institute, New York

gressors of their welfare were not only those who were not born between certain mountains and rivers, but, above all, those whose ancestors lacked the prescribed skull shape".[51] The strong showing of the NSDAP in the *Reichstag* elections of 1930 provided Mühsam with additional evidence of how effective the appeal of antisemitism could be in times of economic crisis.[52] The next year he reported on Hitler's plans to expropriate all the possessions of German Jews.[53] When *Fanal* was prohibited by a presidential order in 1931, Mühsam left his readers with a warning against being fooled by Nazi "nationalistic, antisemitic, and pseudo-socialistic slogans".[54] As conditions worsened in Germany, he exhorted the working classes to stage a general strike to stave off a Nationalist Socialist future fraught with "martial law shootings, pogroms, plundering, and mass arrests".[55]

Several of Mühsam's literary works from the Weimar period satirise the danger presented by the growth of Nazism and its racist doctrines. His chanson 'Republikanische Nationalhymne' (1924) exposes the politicised judicial system that severely punished left-wing revolutionaries, but coddled right-wing putschists like Ludendorff, Hitler and von Kahr, and the *Feme* murderers who shot down Walther Rathenau for being a treasonous "*Judensau*".[56] The farcical story 'Die Affenschande' (1923) tells the tale of an anthropologist who crossbreeds human beings with gorillas to see if the evolutionary missing link between man and ape can be reproduced. Mühsam succeeds in making monkeys of the Nazis by having one of the offspring of these unnatural unions become a stickler about racial purity and a parliamentary deputy for the *völkisch* party.[57] In his last play *Alle Wetter* (1930) Mühsam concocts a possible scenario for a Nazi seizure of power. Sometime in the not so distant future a libertarian village invents a machine that can control the weather. The state government wants to nationalise this technological marvel and use it for military purposes. When the villagers resist this demand, a delegate of the "Workers' Racial Party" gains support from the army and the other establishment parties by promising to restore order and purge the administration of the weather machine until it is "judenrein". Mühsam's peasants ultimately prevail by conjuring up a storm to blow away their enemies.[58] This was one of the few happy endings which Hitler's foes would enjoy in the coming years.

Until now this article has dealt solely with Mühsam's sensitivity to antisemitism insofar as he comprehended that Jews shared a predicament imposed on them by a hostile Gentile majority. This sort of consciousness constitutes a negative identity because it is a response to external forces rather than a positive

[51] Erich Mühsam, 'Parteien und Massen', in *Fanal*, IV (March 1930), p. 125.
[52] Mühsam, 'Zwölf Jahre Republik', p. 37; Erich Mühsam, 'Das Jahr der Entscheidung', in *Fanal*, V (January 1931), No. 4, pp. 79–80; Erich Mühsam, 'Der politische Hexenkessel', in *Fanal*, V (February 1931), No. 5, pp. 97–101.
[53] Erich Mühsam, 'Das Diktaturprogramm', in *Fanal*, V (April 1931), No. 7, p. 160.
[54] Erich Mühsam, 'Vierter Rundbrief des *Fanal*', in *Erich Mühsam. Scheinwerfer*, p. 135.
[55] Erich Mühsam, 'Aktive Abwehr', in *Die Weltbühne*, XXVII (15th December 1931), No. 50, p. 880.
[56] Erich Mühsam, 'Republikanische Nationalhymne', in *Freie Jugend*, VI (July 1924), No. 7, p. 3.
[57] Erich Mühsam, 'Die Affenschande', in *Erich Mühsam Sammlung 1898–1928*, Berlin 1928, pp. 255–269. The story originally appeared in *Die Muskete* (20th March 1923).
[58] Erich Mühsam, *Alle Wetter. Volksstück mit Gesang und Tanz*. Berlin 1977, pp. 79–80.

assessment of Judaism *per se*.⁵⁹ If Mühsam's relationship to Jewry had consisted of nothing beyond his awareness of a common fate, then it would be merely a logical assertion of defensive self-interest. But through the influence of Gustav Landauer and, to a lesser extent, of Martin Buber he developed an admiration for several secular aspects of Jewish ethics and history.

According to Landauer's conception of the Jewish heritage, the Jews existed to fulfil the messianic mission of bringing peace and brotherhood to all nations as God had ordained in the covenant with Abraham. Landauer infused this calling with his own idiosyncratic *völkisch* and communitarian perspective. He insisted that the Jews were a genuine nation with rich cultural, moral and historical traditions. Drawing on the cosmopolitan legacy of the early romantic nationalists like Herder, Landauer posited that each *Volk* had a unique contribution to make to mankind. By virtue of being scattered in every corner of the earth, the Jews were destined to promote cooperation among the peoples of the world. This universal task emerged not only from the global dispersion of the Jews, but also from the ethical injunctions to achieve social justice as preached in the Old Testament. Inspired by the egalitarian spirit of Jewish law and by the Prophets' crusades against materialism and inequity, Landauer hoped that modern Jews would champion the same progressive causes. By doing their utmost to remove the sources of friction which set country against country and class against class, the Jews would serve as models for their host nations and discharge their divine role as the harbingers of international harmony in the process.⁶⁰

Mühsam's views on the meaning of Jewish history bear the unmistakable imprint of Landauer whom he once described as "the man to whom I am most intellectually indebted".⁶¹ Mühsam respected "the enormous value of the Jewish race as an element of fermentation in the different nationalities and cultures".⁶² Besides the physical danger which antisemitism posed for the Jews, he also detested it as a threat to world peace "since it systematically opposes a *Volk* which is dispersed among all nations and which has strongly participated in the cultures of all peoples".⁶³ When Sigmund Fränkel, a Jewish *Kommerzienrat* from Munich, condemned the Jewish leaders of the first Soviet Republic for precipitating a ground swell of antisemitism with their reckless actions, Mühsam replied that the Jewish tradition could be invoked to justify the struggle for socialism. He reminded his Jewish critic that the Jubilee Year of the ancient Hebrews had been a "communist venture" involving property redistribution and the manumission of slaves,⁶⁴ a point Landauer often had made.⁶⁵ Mühsam also

---

⁵⁹This type of negative identity has been analysed brilliantly by Jean-Paul Sartre, *Anti-Semite and Jew*, trans. George J. Becker, New York 1965, pp. 100–109.

⁶⁰Paul Breines, 'The Jew as Revolutionary: The Case of Gustav Landauer', in *LBI Year Book XII* (1967), pp. 75–84; Heinz Joachim Heydorn, 'Vorwort', in Gustav Landauer, *Aufruf zum Sozialismus*, Frankfurt a. Main 1967), pp. 5–46; Eugene Lunn, *Prophet of Community: The Romantic Socialism of Gustav Landauer*, Berkeley 1973, pp. 267–274; Ruth Link-Salinger (Hyman), *Gustav Landauer, Philosopher of Utopia*, Indianapolis 1977, pp. 72–82, 94–103.

⁶¹DAK-EMA, III 2534, Erich Mühsam to Kreszentia Mühsam, 7th May 1919.

⁶²Mühsam, *Die Jagd auf Harden*, p. 19.

⁶³Mühsam, 'Ritualmord', p. 126.

⁶⁴Mühsam, 'Zur Judenfrage', p. 646.

⁶⁵Gustav Landauer, *op. cit.*, p. 171.

noted that the Mosaic statute requiring that a tenth of the surplus from each harvest be set aside for the poor clearly acknowledged the "necessity for ameliorating social misery". Whereas Fränkel had rationalised his reprimand of Munich's Jewish radicals by citing the biblical passage commanding the Jews to promote the peace and welfare of the peoples in whose midst they dwelt; Mühsam construed the same quotation as a "splendid motto of internationalism to which all of us Socialists, Communists, Bolsheviks, and Anarchists adhere whether we are Jewish or not".[66]

Unlike many Jewish secularists of his generation, Mühsam did not look favourably upon the gradual dissolution of Jewry by either conversion or assimilation. While he empathised with someone like Maximilian Harden whose turn to Christianity was a consistent extension of his political convictions, Mühsam doubted whether this approach or that of nominal Jews who blended in perfectly with their surroundings was desirable because both hastened the disappearance of a nation which had advanced the march of freedom wherever it resided. He added that this exercise in committing ethnic suicide would extinguish the creativity and resilience that the Jews had cultivated for millennia to survive against constant adversity. Having stated his case against the vanishing of Jewry through attrition, Mühsam made this surprising declaration in 1908:

> "For these reasons it appears to me that Zionism, especially the cultural Zionism advocated by Martin Buber, is by far more appropriate for us Jews than Harden's ideas of amalgamation even though I certainly refuse to have anything to do with customary Zionism and its founding of a state."[67]

Mühsam's sudden attraction to Zionism was limited to his approval of the agricultural collectives being started under Zionist auspices. Although he knew of Buber's work on the *Hasidim*,[68] Mühsam probably appreciated only the spirit of *Gemeinschaft* which they exuded rather than their religious mysticism. It was the promise that this spirit of cooperation might be recaptured by the Zionist settlers which impressed him.[69] As early as 1904 he had endorsed Landauer's proposal to a Zionist meeting for starting communities based on the economic principles of mutualism in Palestine with the ultimate aim of forming a decentralised socialist federation there.[70] When this strategy eventually informed the efforts of some of the *kibbutzniks*,[71] Mühsam applauded their attempt to create "a community of work and exchange which would bring to life a socialis-

[66]Mühsam, 'Zur Judenfrage', p. 647.
[67]Mühsam, *Die Jagd auf Harden*, pp. 18–19.
[68]Erich Mühsam, *Unpolitische Erinnerungen*, Berlin 1961, p. 34. Although Mühsam and Buber were never close friends, they do seem to have been congenial to one another, see the reproduction of a postcard from Mühsam to Buber dated 31st December 1907 in *europäische ideen* (1974), No. 5/6, p. 75.
[69]Walter Laqueur, *A History of Zionism*, New York 1976, pp. 167–169; Martin Buber, *Paths in Utopia*, trans. R. F. C. Hull, Boston 1958, pp. 46–57, 139–149.
[70]Erich Mühsam, 'Die Befreiungskampf der Arbeiterschaft', in *Kampf*, I (21st April 1904), No. 11, p. 284; LBIA-Erich Mühsam Collection, AR 1806, II, Erich Mühsam, 'Ascona: Eine Broschüre', p. 20. Landauer's plan for socialist settlements eventually became the platform of the Socialist *Bund* which he founded in 1908. Mühsam headed the Munich chapters of this organisation. See Lunn, *op. cit.*, pp. 190–200; Baron, *op. cit.*, pp. 65–75.
[71]Elkana Margalit, 'The Social and Intellectual Origins of the Hashomer Hatzair Youth Movement, 1913–1920', in *Journal of Contemporary History*, IV (April 1969), pp. 25–46.

tic-communistic society that ignored the capitalist world market". Moreover, their endeavours enabled Jews to set an example for the proletariat to follow.[72] Of course, as Mühsam's earlier statement indicates, he categorically rejected the building of a Jewish state along hierarchical lines which he equated with the establishment of a "capitalistic economy, the rights of exploitation, private ownership of the means of production, bourgeois parliamentary prattle, and proletarian destitution".[73]

Landauer once had suggested to Mühsam that he emulate the impassioned style of the Prophets to enhance the persuasiveness of his writings.[74] This partly accounts for the apocalyptic tone which pervades many of his works.[75] More importantly, Mühsam used various Old Testament figures in his poems to illustrate his iconoclastic reading of the Scriptures. He named his first journal *Kain* to celebrate the rebellious indignation of the misunderstood brother who murdered Abel to protest the unequal treatment the two brothers had received at the hands of God. Thus, Mühsam's Cain wanders the earth to bring the message of revolution to the oppressed:

"I stand upright before you and demand my fair share! Give me freedom and land! – And as an eternal brother, Cain returns to you for the benefit of humanity!"[76]

Mühsam's portrayal of Moses follows a similar pattern. The dying liberator of the Jews feels betrayed by an authoritarian God who will not permit him to enter the Promised Land. Denied his last wish, Moses warns the Lord that some day mankind will revolt against his tyranny.[77] Mühsam later pictured Lenin as a Russian Moses who had destroyed the "sacrilegious madness of the golden calf", but also died before he witnessed the advent of a truly communist society.[78]

Just as Landauer admired Jesus as a Jewish prophet who was martyred for the sake of love and peace,[79] Mühsam depicted Jesus as the "Jew who embarked from Nazareth/To make the poor happy".[80] In another poem he laments over his inability to redeem the sufferings of the downtrodden as Jesus did.[81] *Judas*

---

[72]Mühsam, 'Zur Judenfrage', p. 643.
[73]Mühsam, 'Zur Judenfrage', p. 643; Mühsam, *Die Jagd auf Harden*, p. 19. Mühsam found it difficult to believe the KPD's doctrinaire analysis of the Arab opposition to Zionists as just a legitimate resistance to agents of British imperialism, see Erich Mühsam, 'Der Kampf in Palästina', in *Fanal*, III (September 1929), No. 12, p. 287.
[74]Lunn, *op. cit.*, p. 10.
[75]Linse, *Organisierter Anarchismus*, p. 104. Linse attributes Mühsam's emotional language to an affinity with Expressionism. Yet this quality was present in Mühsam's writings long before Expressionism had entered on to the German literary scene. Moreover, Mühsam rejected the formalistic experimentation of the Expressionists even though he appreciated their activism, see DAK-EMA, III 2526, Erich Mühsam to Kreszentia Mühsam, 27th August 1918. For more information on Mühsam's literary style, see Hug, *op. cit.*, pp. 129–149; and Lawrence Baron, 'Erich Mühsam: Anarchistischer Realismus und Irrealismus', in *Ideologiekritische Studien zur Literatur Essays II*, Volkmar Sander (ed.), Berne–Frankfurt a. Main 1975, pp. 5–28.
[76]Erich Mühsam, 'Kain', in *Kain*, I (April 1911), No. 1, pp. 1–4; Mühsam used the same allusion in 'Ewige Wiederkunft' in *Erich Mühsam Auswahl: Gedichte Drama Prosa*, Berlin 1961, pp. 170–171.
[77]Erich Mühsam, 'Moses', in *Erich Mühsam Auswahl*, p. 106.
[78]Erich Mühsam, 'Lenin', in *Erich Mühsam Auswahl*, pp. 259–260.
[79]Link-Salinger (Hyman), *op. cit.*, pp. 27, 31, 74–75.
[80]Erich Mühsam, 'Golgatha', in *Erich Mühsam Auswahl*, p. 107.
[81]Erich Mühsam, 'Ich weiss von allem Leid', in *Erich Mühsam Auswahl*, p. 108.

(1921), Mühsam's drama about the anti-war strikes of January 1918, vindicates the apparent treachery of its latter-day Judas, a revolutionary named Raffael Schenk. Schenk betrays his pacifist mentor, Mathias Seebald, only out of a desire to fulfill Seebald's quest for peace. Hence, Schenk arranges for the public arrest of Seebald to provoke a confrontation between demonstrators and the police which will show the masses that they can attain peace only by overthrowing their government which continues to wage war. As he lies dying after the bloody incident, Seebald absolves Schenk of any guilt by telling him: "You wanted it to turn out differently, – I know that, Raffael."[82] The irony that a Jew became the saviour of a religion which displaced Judaism on the stage of world history provides the major theme of Mühsam's delightful doggerel about Christmas:

> "Geboren ward zu Bethlehem
> ein Kindlein aus dem Stamme Sem.
> Und ist es auch schon lange her,
> seit's in der Krippe lag,
> so freun sich doch die Menschen sehr
> bis auf den heutigen Tag.
> Minister und Agrarier,
> Bourgeois und Proletarier –
> es feiert jeder Arier
> zu gleicher Zeit und überall
> die Christgeburt im Rindviehstall.
> (Das Volk allein, dem es geschah,
> das feiert lieber Chanukah.)"[83]

As his pronouncements on Judaism and contemporary Jewish movements indicate, Mühsam appreciated only those facets of Jewish life which were commensurate with his anarchist outlook. Conversely, he took issue with Jewish theology and the Jewish community over those areas which conflicted with his ideology.

Mühsam's critique of Judaism stemmed from his rejection of religion in general and of the claim of the Jews to being the chosen people in particular. From his libertarian perspective, faith in an omnipotent God conditioned the masses to defer to all forms of authority:

> "When Judaism first centralised the idea of God, when the Judeo-Christian religion placed the Almighty above mankind, it created the concept of servility to God and renounced its thoughts, feelings, and actions relating to the removal and questioning of the unassailable laws of every distant and unitary authority."[84]

In short, obedience to God the Father prefigured obedience to one's biological father and ultimately to one's fatherland. Furthermore, Mühsam inveighed against Jewry's insistence on being God's chosen people because he deemed such ethnocentrism to be the prototype for modern nationalism and racism: "Whoever speaks of the fatherland speaks in a Jewish manner (*Denkweise*) for he espouses the glorification of his own nation which he professes to be the chosen people." Mühsam, however, discerned the tragic irony that had cast the Jews as

---

[82] Erich Mühsam, *Judas*, in *Erich Mühsam Auswahl*, p. 432. For an analysis of *Judas*, see Baron, *loc. cit.*, pp. 9–10, 15–16.
[83] Erich Mühsam, 'Heilige Nacht', in *Erich Mühsam Auswahl*, p. 76.
[84] Mühsam, *Die Befreiung der Gesellschaft*, pp. 18–19.

the victims of the idea of exclusiveness they had introduced to the world.[85] Yet Mühsam failed to realise that the Jewish universal mission which he extolled was the duty incumbent on the chosen people.

Notwithstanding his generalisations about Judaism, Mühsam did not impute any specific traits to Jews as the heirs of such a religious tradition. As he put it: "The Jews are naturally not a whit better than others, but they are also not worse."[86] His esteem for other Jews depended on whether they were allies or enemies in the continuous struggle for individual and social liberation. He venerated the Jewish freedom fighters of the past like Baruch Spinoza and Heinrich Heine and those of the present like Rosa Luxemburg and Gustav Landauer. But he vehemently dissociated himself from wealthy and powerful Jews who stood on the opposite side of the barricades:

> "The reminder of a rich Jew to other Jews who align themselves with the poor – 'Hello! You belong on our side! We Jews must be united! You are compromising us! – is humbug ... In social matters there are only two groups: the capitalists with those who are tied lock, stock, and barrel to (economically) interested and unscrupulous partisans and the proletarians with those who have a life and death stake in the revolutionary ideal of the proletariat."[87]

Mühsam's treatment of the few recognisable Jewish characters in his fictional works reflects his ideological criteria. He obviously sympathises with the rebelliousness of the angry Jewish poet in the aforementioned story 'Carmen'. But in two of his minor plays, *Die Hochstapler* (1906) and *Im Nachthemd durchs Leben* (1914), he depicts the greed of a Jewish real estate broker[88] and a Jewish pedlar respectively. In the latter Hörschel the *Handelsjude*, whose dialogue is peppered with Yiddish colloquialisms, has elevated the principle of buying cheap and selling dear to an art. Nevertheless, the presentation of Hörschel is more humorous than malicious. Upon completion of a particularly profitable round of bargaining, Hörschel places his shrewd transaction in the context of Jewish history by commenting: "The pogroms are redressed."[89]

As Peter Gay recently has written,

> "A Jewish-born socialist could attack Jewish capitalists from class-hatred rather than self-hatred because they were capitalists rather than because they were Jews. Or he might single out for special vituperation those whom he uncomfortably, perhaps unconsciously, identified as his own kind."[90]

Mühsam belongs to the first category. Excepting the rare instances where he created a stereotypical Jew like Hörschel, he consistently veered away from the tactic of channelling anti-capitalist discontent on to the Jewish bourgeoisie. Though he admired Eugen Dühring for his libertarian critique of Marxism, Mühsam chided him for unjustly stigmatising all Jews as rapacious capitalists.[91] In a

---
[85]*Ibid.*, pp. 19–25.
[86]DAK-EMA, III 3048, Mühsam, *T*, 23rd November 1915.
[87]Mühsam, 'Zur Judenfrage', pp. 644–647; Mühsam, 'Ritualmord', p. 126.
[88]Erich Mühsam, *Die Hochstapler*, Munich 1906, pp. 77–96, 129–131.
[89]Erich Mühsam, C. G. von Maasen and R. Köster, *Im Nachthemd durchs Leben*, Munich 1914, pp. 15–20. James Steakley of the German Department of the University of Wisconsin/Madison provided me with this reference.
[90]Gay, *op. cit.*, p. 198.
[91]Erich Mühsam, 'Eugen Dühring', in *Kain*, II (February 1913), No. 11, pp. 174–175. Mühsam was more charitable about Bakunin's antisemitic comments about Karl Marx. Mühsam dismissed these

telling reply to a letter which advised Mühsam to redirect his rancour against capitalism towards the Jews, he conscientiously refused to exploit antisemitic sentiments for socialist ends:

> "I am an internationalist; my journal [*Kain*] carries the subtitle 'a magazine for humanity'. There is no place in it for provocations. I would have answered you like this even if I were not a Jew. But I am one and believe that I myself am a refutation to your generalisations."

Mühsam continued his response by denying that Jews controlled the bulk of Germany's wealth. Admitting that Jews might be over represented in certain sectors of the German economy like the stock exchange, Mühsam still counselled his misguided correspondent "not to fight against the Jews who profit from the infamous institutions of capitalism just as much as the Aryans do".[92]

Considering Mühsam's ideological priorities, it is significant that he neither disaffiliated himself from Judaism nor concealed his Jewish ancestry from the public. As many of the preceding quotations indicate, Mühsam often drew attention to his Jewishness in one way or another.[93] The only time he ever contemplated officially severing his ties to Judaism occurred in 1915 after the death of his father.[94] His thinking at that moment represented the culmination of a bitter dispute with his father who on his deathbed had threatened to disinherit Erich if he did not marry a Jewish woman and resume his original career as a pharmacist.[95] Although Mühsam married a Catholic and continued to be a writer, he decided to remain a Jew to insure the right of his future children to claim a portion of their grandfather's estate.[96] In 1920 he clarified his position by defining his Jewishness as an existential condition which he could not elude in an antisemitic society:

> "I am a Jew and will remain a Jew as long as I live. I have never disavowed my Judaism and have never withdrawn from the Jewish religious community (because I would not cease being Jewish in that way and because I am totally indifferent to what rubric I am listed under in the state's registry). I regard being Jewish as neither an advantage nor a liability; it is simply part of my essence like my red beard, my body weight, or my interests and talents."[97]

In this sense Mühsam's Jewish identity corresponds to that of a few German-Jewish Socialists who, "despite their loss of any inward commitment to Judaism, were not willing to renounce their descent as long as Jews in Germany were treated as second-class citizens".[98] Indeed, Mühsam's close friend, Martin Ander-

---

comments as Bakunin's mistaking Marx's Jewishness, rather than his Germanness, as the source of his authoritarianism, Erich Mühsam, 'Bismarxismus', in *Fanal*, I (February 1927), No. 5, p. 69.

[92]LC-RS, Container 423, Erich Mühsam letter, 13th January 1918. This letter has been published in Erich Mühsam, *Briefe an Zeitgenossen*, Gerd. W. Jungblut (ed.), Berlin 1978, pp. 88–89.

[93]For other examples of how Mühsam called attention to his Jewishness in his writings, see Erich Mühsam, 'Das Verhör', in *Der Krater*, Berlin 1909, p. 148; and Erich Mühsam, 'Reise an die österreichische Grenze', in *Die Weltbühne*, XXI (11th August 1925), No. 32, pp. 219–224.

[94]DAK-EMA, III 3047, Mühsam, *T*, 27th July 1915.

[95]DAK-EMA, III 3047, Mühsam, *T*, 9th/10th June 1915.

[96]DAK-EMA, III 3047, Mühsam, *T*, 27th July 1915. For background on Mühsam's marriage to Kreszentia Mühsam, see Baron, *op. cit.*, pp. 32–33, 102, 116.

[97]Mühsam, 'Zur Judenfrage', p. 645; Mühsam, *Die Jagd auf Harden*, p. 18.

[98]Angress, *loc. cit.*, p. 149. Angress characterises Mühsam's Jewish identity as "dissidentisch" (p. 314). This may be somewhat misleading in light of Mühsam's denunciations of antisemitism and his socialistic interpretation of the Jewish tradition.

sen-Nexö, has observed that Mühsam's openness about his Jewish roots was refreshing in comparison to the embarrassed reticence of most Jewish Socialists.[99]

Mühsam's pessimism about the indelibility of his Jewishness was confirmed by the vilification and persecution to which he was subjected by the Nazis and other antisemites. In the wake of the suppression of the Munich Soviet Republic, one right-wing publicist asserted that Mühsam's participation in that uprising was part of a coordinated B'nai B'rith plot to seize control of Germany.[100] Goebbels subsequently marked Mühsam as one of the Jewish subversives who would be liquidated when the National Socialists came to power. Never one to mince words, Goebbels ranted: "This Jewish louse must perish!"[101] In 1932 a DNVP campaign poster juxtaposed photographs of prominent Jewish bankers with those of infamous Jewish revolutionaries like Mühsam and posed the rhetorical question: "Who has led us into calamity?"[102] Thus, it came as no surprise when the Nazis arrested Mühsam several hours after the *Reichstag* building had burnt down.[103] For the next year Mühsam endured every sort of indignity, torture and torment at the hands of his captors. As a Jew and as one of the few surviving leaders of the Munich Soviet Republic, he was doubly damned by guards who beat and taunted him for both of his sins:

> "Hey, Mühsam, *mühsame Judensau*, act like the Munich Soviet dictator! – Little Mühsam, do you want a ticket to Palestine? Look, look, that is the king of the commune! What king? *Mistbalg einer Judensau!*"[104]

Other guards ripped out pieces of Mühsam's beard to make him resemble a caricature of an orthodox Jew. On 10th July 1934 his battered corpse was found hanging in a latrine at Oranienburg Concentration Camp.[105] Mühsam may never have lived his life as an exemplary Jew, but he assuredly died as a Jewish martyr.

[99] Martin Andersen-Nexö, *Kultur und Barbarei*, Berlin 1957, p. 193. There are a number of letters from Mühsam to Andersen-Nexö in the Martin Andersen-Nexö Archiv of the DAK.
[100] Friedrich Wichtl, *Weltfreimauerei, Weltrevolution, Weltrepublik*, Munich 1921, p. 261.
[101] Kreszentia Mühsam, *op. cit.*, p. 13; Hug, *op. cit.*, p. 74.
[102] George L. Mosse, 'Die deutsche Rechte und die Juden', in *Entscheidungsjahr 1932. Zur Judenfrage in der Endphase der Weimarer Republik*. Ein Sammelband herausgegeben von Werner E. Mosse unter Mitwirkung von Arnold Paucker, Tübingen 1966 (Schriftenreihe wissenschaftlicher Abhandlungen des Leo Baeck Instituts 13), p. 230.
[103] Mühsam knew that the Nazis would arrest him sooner or later and had purchased train tickets to Prague to escape this fate. Unfortunately, he decided to delay his departure until he received the payment for a lecture he had recently given because he did not want to go into exile without any money, see Henry Marx, 'Mühsams letzte Tage', in *europäische ideen*, (1974), No. 5/6, p. 13.
[104] Ernst Gronau, 'Rätsel um Erich Mühsams Tod', in *Horizont*, II (11th May 1947), No. 10, p. 21.
[105] For other accounts of Mühsam's captivity between 1933 and 1934 in Sonnenburg, Brandenburg and Oranienburg, see Kreszentia Mühsam, *op. cit.*, pp. 10–31; Andersen-Nexö, *op. cit.*, pp. 191–198; Kurt Hiller, *Köpfe and Tröpfe, Profile aus einem Vierteljahrundert*, Hamburg–Stuttgart 1950, pp. 309–317; Stefan Szende, 'Mit Mühsam in Oranienburg', in *europäische ideen*, (1974), No. 5/6, pp. 7–9; Wilhelm Girnus, 'Brandenburg, Oranienburg', in *europäische ideen*, (1974), No. 5/6, pp. 10–11; Fritz Küster, 'Häftling in Oranienburg', in *europäische ideen*, (1974), No. 5/6, pp15–17; Rudolf Rocker, 'Zensl Mühsam', in *Erich Mühsam: Scheinwerfer*, pp. 137–146; Otto Weber, 'Erich Mühsams Tod', in *Harizont*, II (19th January 1947), No. 2, p. 23.

Martin Buber

Martin Buber and Judaism

BY ARTHUR A. COHEN

Death seals with finality even the most fluent tongues, but death only begins the work of silence. Posterity accomplishes what death has begun: passing the whole work in review, determining what is enduring, what insubstantial, what lives beyond the reinforcement and polemic of the life and what dies with the death itself. So it has come to Martin Buber, the centenary of whose birth is recalled.*
His mouth was stopped by death and so for more than a decade has been the resonation of his work. Never particularly popular among his own constituency, always more highly regarded by others than his own Jews, he was nonetheless one of the most influential Jews of our time. It was he, as much as any other, who gave initiative and vitality to the cultural and spiritual Zionism of the early part of this century and it was his writings and discourses prior to the First World War which motivated young Jews of Western Europe – principally the constituency of German-speaking Jews – to reinvest the enterprise of Jewish life with a significance and value which the ideology of assimilation had virtually denied it. He was a moving and evocative rhetorician, a stylist who mastered cadence and interval, whose dress and gesture were as carefully chosen as his language. He was an immensity and a presence. Any who knew him could not forget him; however, to retain his person in memory is not the same as to read him, to study him, to be transformed or converted by his work. It is the work rather more than the presence which has effected the eclipse of his reputation since his death and which augurs a restoration to life of that part of his reputation which deserves to endure.

I

What then is alive and what is dead in Martin Buber's conception of Judaism? To determine this with any degree of credibility requires that I first take a stand respecting the measure, the criterion by which contemporary Jewish intelligence approaches and passes judgment on its past.

The generation of German Jews which came to maturity during the first two decades of the century was (to the extent that it was Jewishly self-aware) moulded by the enlightenment and the emancipation, either enmeshed and snarled by the illusion of German receptivity and cultural accommodation or else critically self-distanced by the recognition that the lines of intellectual influ-

---

*This is a revised and expanded version of a paper originally delivered at a symposium held on the 29th October 1978 at the New York Leo Baeck Institute to mark the centenary of Martin Buber's birth.

ence went more directly from the Jewish philosophers of the *Aufklärung* to Hermann Cohen's virtual identification of German humanism and Jewish prophetism than it did to mystical epistemologists like Franz Rosenzweig, apocalyptic littérateurs like Walter Benjamin, or revisionist historians like Gershom Scholem. I have no doubt any longer that the enlightenment and emancipation as it unfolded – not in its essential conviction, but in its historical ideology – devastated the vitality and interior certitude of Western European Jewry, depriving it of both spontaneity and continuity, while successfully persuading it that the gains were greater than the cost.

The initial impulse of Martin Buber's return to Jewry, signalled by his youthful Zionism, his turning away from the Stefan George *Kreis*, his critical *volte face* from Nietzsche (whose *Thus Spake Zarathustra* he had translated into Polish as a young man) was no simple crisis of assimilation. I have always been immensely curious about Buber's childhood and youth – although available information regarding his youth in the home of his paternal grandfather Salomon Buber is lean and not quite persuasive.[1] Buber was raised in Galicia. He was by natal determination a Polish Jew, an *Ostjude*. Although he knew German early; he also knew Polish, Yiddish and, of course, Hebrew which he had mastered as a young boy, studying Bible and *Midrash* under the aegis of his eminent grandfather. It is the case, however, as Buber attested in a famous letter to Franz Rosenzweig,[2] that shortly after his *Bar Mitzvah* he ceased all formal religious observance, never being seen even once, as Scholem noted with some amazement, in any Jerusalem synagogue during the thirty years of his residence in Israel.[3] And yet, after a period of seven years, during which he wrote poetry, read Nietzsche and Schopenhauer, absorbed the somewhat hot-house atmosphere of pre-war Vienna romanticism, he returned not to religious Judaism but to Zionism, not to a Zionism of territory, but to a Zionism of holy space. Deriving much impetus from the work of Ahad Ha'am, with whom Buber was in communication, the framework of his Zionist formulation derived in considerable measure from heating up, inflaming so to speak, the rationalist assumptions of Ahad Ha'am's cultural Zionism,[4] driving those assumptions from their grounding in Jehudah Ha'Levi's con-

---

[1]Buber, who was not reticent about the currents that bathed his intellectual and spiritual growth, obviously confided little to his first biographer, Hans Kohn. There is scant reference to his parents, his reminiscence of them and their divorce, and of his youth in the household of his paternal grandfather, Salomon Buber. The awe and respect Buber felt towards his grandparents is palpable in the few letters he addressed to them (cf. *Martin Buber. Briefwechsel aus sieben Jahrzehnten*, I, 1897–1918. Heidelberg 1972, p. 152 and the moving letter to Salomon Buber of 31st January 1900, pp. 153–154), but one feels deprived by the absence of an intellectual autobiography of those lonely Galician years. Cf. Hans Kohn, *Martin Buber. Sein Werk und seine Zeit*, Hellerau 1930, 'Ursprünge', pp. 13–18.
[2]*Martin Buber. Briefwechsel aus sieben Jahrzehnten*, II, 1918–1938, p. 141. Cf. also Gershom Scholem, 'Martin Buber's Conception of Judaism', *On Jews and Judaism in Crisis*, New York 1976, particularly pp. 133–134 for discussion of Buber's views of *halakhah* in the light of his biography.
[3]Gershom Scholem, 'Martin Buber's Conception of Judaism', *loc. cit.*, p. 129, although several life-long Jerusalemites whom I have consulted, contest this statement, they are hard-pressed to recollect more than one occasion on which they observed Buber in a synagogue.
[4]The earliest recorded contact between Ahad Ha'am (Asher Ginzburg) and Buber appears in their correspondence where Ahad Ha'am writes to Buber from Odessa during July 1903. Obviously Buber's Zionism was formed of several elements, not the least being the personal influence of Herzl

cept of Israel as "supernation" and Maimonides's rational nation to occupy intellectual territory which he reclaimed from a transformational reading of Nietzsche, Feuerbach, Dilthey and Simmel, all of whom had sought to reconstitute the image of the whole person, the healthy spirit, the integrated man whose life is openness, whose medium is spontaneity and truthfulness, whose goal is relationship.

The diagnosis of the ailing Jew that Buber proposed in his famous Prague lectures of 1909–1911 entailed a series of critical estimations and judgments, which despite numerous refinements and alterations, remained virtually unchanged throughout his life.[5] The Jew was, in his view, a fractured spirit – vulnerable to the assumptions of bourgeois optimism, European materialism, cultural deracination. Whatever the gifts and talents of the Jew, they had been placed at the service of a world which at best manipulated them advantageously and at worst corrupted them. In such a view, the Jew was merely a shadow of himself, a spectral presence that reminded and underscored his intrinsic marginality and historical irrelevance. And yet, Buber reminded his hearers, the Jew of the present had deeper roots than those he had sunk in the shallow soil of Western culture. Those roots were the existential substratum of his contemporary predicament, for hard as he might try to evade the Biblical past, the Jewish historical travail, or the arcana of the mystical tradition, which effected their translation into the intimacy and directness of ordinary life, he was still their creature. Western culture – precisely the same Western culture – owed a profound debt to exactly the Jewish roots the Jew was trying to cut away. Buber's polemic in these lectures was profound and shattering. It is a justifiable contention that these *Drei Reden über das Judentum* were the single most impressive document of Jewish renewal in the fading years of Wilhelminian German culture. Buber called for renewal – an honest recognition of the free spirituality of Jewish sources, a search for the natural ethos of Jewish self-integration, culminating in a call for the establishment of a Jewish spiritual centre in the renewed land of Zion.

At that juncture in Jewish history, Buber's was a perfectly plausible dialectic of rejoining the Jew to the Jewish community. Although Buber, already at this early date, had begun to inveigh against the petrifactions of orthodoxy, the dry-as-dust Talmudism of the schools, the weary attention to the details of Jewish mundaneness, it was an antinomianism less objectionable to disaffected young Jews than was the stern literalism of Jewish othodoxy. It worked and worked profoundly. New centres of Jewish study were convened, new leaders made their appearance, Jewish books were published, the *Jüdischer Verlag* was founded by Buber and his associates, lectures and symposia multiplied, and it became clear, as we now recognise, that the solid strength of the first significant *aliyah* of

---

and Weizmann, but its intellectual stimulation derives in greatest measure from Moses Hess and Ahad Ha'am as Kohn indicates (*Martin Buber. Sein Werk und seine Zeit*, pp. 14–16, also, pp. 43–45). Cf. *Martin Buber. Briefwechsel aus sieben Jahrzehnten*, I, 1897–1918, Letter 65, p. 203.
[5]Martin Buber. *On Judaism*, Nahum N. Glatzer (ed.), New York 1967, which contains Eva Jospe's trans. of *Die Drei Reden über das Judentum* according to the revised text of 1923. It contains as well Buber's controversial essays, *Vom Geist des Judentums*, Leipzig 1916.

German-Jewish intellectuals, teachers and converts from the bourgeoisie was made ready to leave for Palestine in the aftermath of the First World War.

No one denies to Buber the pre-eminence of his leadership in this period. He was the inspired publicist of Jewish renewal, documenting that renewal by the evolution of his own intellectual materials – moving as he did from the translation and editing of Christian and Eastern mystics to those of *Hasidism*, leaving behind Jakob Böhme, Meister Eckardt, Nicolas of Cusa, Lao-Tzu, for his famous compendia of *hasidic* tales, retellings and reworkings which enabled him to extend to *hasidic* sources a cultural imprimatur already stamped by him upon materials of the international religious spirit. It was as though Buber had found in an authentic Jewish souurce the exemplification of personal preferences which enabled him to persevere as a Jew, not only without *ressentiment*, but with joyful celebration. The fact that his reading of *hasidic* sources has been virtually destroyed by the critiques of Scholem and others,[6] who have shown that his view of *Hasidism* as uninfluenced by the *Kabbalah*, unformed by traditional normative Judaism, and disengaged from eschatological and apocalyptic interests is on all three counts false, does not detract from the invincible charm, tenderness and love with which Buber recounted the *hasidic* tales, infecting them with his own self-enchantment while encouraging all the *hasidic* masters to sound finally like Buberians. Scholem's own confrontation with Buber on this point late in his life echoes a particular kind of horror and pathos, for all that Buber could say to Scholem's critique was that a whole life – his own – had been wasted on his misreadings if Scholem were correct.[7] It was a not untypical response and one, coupled with others that Buber has naïvely recounted, which discloses a disappointing streak in Buber's character, healthy pride verging on the illusion of omniscience.

II

The outbreak of the First World War marked a stasis in the development of Buber's thinking about the Jew and Jewish destiny. He was bonded to a formulation of personal religious enterprise in which the principal distinctions of his argument marked off the creative from the formed, the productive and future-orientated from the dead past, the history of Jewish diaspora as one of alienation, timorousness and capitulation, and the new future in Zion as one which augured new beginnings, the recovery of deeper realities, the meeting with God on an ancient soil that nonetheless remained eternally young. He had, to his view, succeeded in formulating his primordial Judaism – a Judaism not of essence, but of eruption, not of constituted historical forms, but of continuously fresh and innovative outburst and encounter. The Buber of the pre-war period had em-

[6]Gershom Scholem, 'Martin Buber's Interpretation of Hasidism', *The Messianic Idea in Judaism*, New York 1971, pp. 227–250. Also Scholem's essay, 'Martin Buber's Conception of Judaism', *loc. cit.* As well, note Jerome Mintz's modest footnote in his *Legends of the Hasidim*, Chicago 1968, p. 2 n. 4.

[7]"If what you are now saying were right, my dear Scholem, then I would have worked on Hasidism for forty years absolutely in vain, because in that case, Hasidism does not *interest* me at all." Gershom Scholem, 'Martin Buber's Conception of Judaism', *loc. cit.*, pp. 166–167.

ployed a vocabulary assumed from German philosophy and mysticism and carried it with him like a bronze mirror into the dark places of his Jewish past, where whatever buried light it contained would flash upon its burnished surface, illuminating resemblances and corroborations. Buber knew what he, wished to find in Judaism even before he had undertaken the search. What he found he always knew existed. It was there awaiting only his bidding to be renewed, as though the magic words were his and the resting princess of the ages needed only to hear those words to come alive once more. The vocabulary was already described in the *Drei Reden*, but as well in his little mystical tractate, *Daniel* (1913), and no less elaborated in his early writings on *Hasidism*.

Judaism was not a history of unfolding and emergence; nor a history of unresolved tension between internal dialectic and obdurate reality, between the wish for reasonableness and the passion for prophecy; nor between the stubborn givenness of the Law and the spinning dreams of the imagination, but rather a permanent state of warfare between the settled, the conventional, the organised, the institutional, the law and the administration of law, the priests, legists and rabbis and the Jewish underground, the heretical, the spontaneous, the untrammelled and unconfined, the aggadists and storytellers, the mythomane and the mystic. With such a view it is no wonder that Buber's reading of Jewish history should have but few mountain tops, few valleys and endless plains, flat and arid, under continuous cultivation but producing stunted and crimped crops. The peaks were the prophets, the kings of Israel, Jesus of Nazareth, and with ambivalence kabbalists and *Hasidim*; the valleys were the gnostics and the demonic antinomians, Sabbatai Zwi, Jakob Frank and Spinoza, and the plains, those endless plains, the ordinary history of Jewish traditionalism and endurance. Clearly a personal, an uncompromisingly personal, reading of Jewish history and one, which not surprisingly, received a more affectionate response from non-Jewish readers than from Jews. It was a reading which treated Jewish belief not as a continuity of tradition whose sense of *kehillah* and unity arose not from the common travail of survival and the shared espousal of an historical faith, but from the wish to achieve an enriched personal identity, an exalted experience of personal value and meaning.

Buber's appeal in the days before the First World War is easily understood against the background of the Wilhelminian German bourgeoisie. That age – drearily conservative, patriotic, smug and self-assured – found many Jews ill-at-ease with an historical faith which employed an ancient liturgy and custom, a foreign language, a bond of suffering coupled with the grim and often despairing historiography of *Wissenschaft des Judentums*. It was no wonder that Jews ran from Judaism, but it is no less a source of wonderment that they ran to German *Kultur*. Buber's critique both of bourgeois Western culture on the one hand, and the polemics of German Orthodoxy and Reform on the other, in the interest of an integral cultural Zionism of self-discovery and creativity struck home. It was a critique which elicited response precisely as long as the teacher was able to maintain the coherence of his teaching and the clarity of his acts. It was a teaching held together by the power of the teacher, by the authenticity of his word and deed.

The First World War and its aftermath and Buber's interpretation of both had a shattering effect upon that coherence. In the opening issue of *Der Jude* which Buber founded in 1916,[8] there appears the first of many editorials which were to be published over the next eighteen months in which Buber gave his support to the war and the justification of its being fought to victory by the German *Volk*. Buber's arguments — in measure limned by Hermann Cohen's no less distraught essays on *Deutschtum und Judentum* – turn on the conviction of the mighty authority of German culture and the sense of its beleaguerment by Anglo-French civilisation.[9] How Buber managed to construe support for the war as part of the legitimate espousal of *Der Jude* remains something of a mystery since in all other respects that remarkable periodical maintained an aloofness to the world beyond Jewry and Jewish preoccupations. Nonetheless it is the case that Buber wrote in September 1914 in a recently uncovered letter to Hans Kohn:

> "Never has the concept of *Volk* been such a reality for me as during the last weeks. A sincere and great feeling also prevails among the Jews. Among the millions who have volunteered were Karl Wolfskehl and Friedrich Gundolf ... I myself, alas, have no prospect of being accepted; but in my own way I shall try to contribute ... Addressed to anyone willing to accommodate himself to these times are the words of John: 'He that loveth his life shall lose it.' If we Jews really felt, thoroughly felt, what this means then we would no longer need our ancient motto: 'Not by might, but spirit' – might (*Kraft*) and spirit (*Geist*) would become one. *Incipit vita nova*."[10]

What is remarkable about this passage and the subsequent argument which broke out between himself and his socialist mentor, the remarkably heroic Gustav Landauer, is that Buber employed the whole of his *Erlebnis* mysticism to underscore his reading of the war. The war binds Jews together in a transcendent cause and even though (as he acknowledged) Jews face each other over the trenches and indeed kill each other, their mutual suicide is justified by the fact that they are living real life, avoiding shadow life and insubstantiality, but sharing the challenge of a consummated risk. Although Buber tried to keep himself distant from a simple racism, from mere patriotic jingoism, anybody examining the letters and documents of the period will find that Buber carries to war the doctrine of his *Daniel*, turning such passages as, "the nameless spark ... through which the deed from being the experience (*Erlebnis*) of an individual becomes an

---

[8] Originally conceived by Buber as a project to be undertaken by himself and Weizmann in 1902 (the original prospectus for *Der Jude* appears in Hans Kohn, *Martin Buber. Sein Werk und seine Zeit*, pp. 296–300), it appeared under Buber's editorship as a monthly from 1916 to March 1924 when Buber relinquished editorship to a board. It was published thereafter as a series of *Sonderhefte*, concluding in 1928 with the publication of an issue consecrated to honouring Buber's fiftieth birthday. Cf. the author's introductory essay to *The Jew. Essays from Martin Buber's Journal Der Jude (1916–1928)*, forthcoming from the University of Alabama Press during 1980.

[9] Hermann Cohen's *Deutschtum und Judentum* appeared in two instalments during 1915 and 1916 and is included in *Hermann Cohen's Jüdische Schriften*, Bruno Strauss (ed.), Berlin 1924, II, pp. 237–318. A small selection from Cohen's essay, trans. by Eva Jospe, appears in *Reason and Hope. Selections from the Jewish Writings of Hermann Cohen*, New York 1917, pp. 176–189. Jacob Klatzkin's extended reply to Hermann Cohen, published in *Der Jude* (II, pp. 245–252, 358–370) appears in trans. in my reader, *The Jew. Essays from Martin Buber's Journal Der Jude (1916–1928)*.

[10] Paul Robert Flohr. *From Kulturpolitik to Dialogue. An Inquiry into the Formation of Martin Buber's Philosophy of I and Thou* (Doctoral Dissertation), Ann Arbor 1974, p. 136; also n. 2, p. 206. Flohr discovered the letter in the Jerusalem Martin Buber Archive, 376/I (Correspondence between Martin Buber and Hans Kohn, September 30th 1914).

event given to all", into a justification of the combat.[11] Precisely this language of sparks which ignites the kinesis of which Buber talks frequently in *Daniel* (to transcribe the movement from potentiality to act) dominates his political journalism of the period. How Buber could have argued in 'Die Losung' (The Watchword)[12] that despite the fact that Jews kill each other, "they are nonetheless fighting for their Jewishness", remains something of a mystery, although it is absolutely coherent with the predominant vagueness of his metaphysical thinking. Buber is always, to my mind, magnificent when he is interpreting a text, for one can then perceive the matrix against which the scalpel rubs – there is something to compare with the exegesis. But when Buber tries to lift from himself and others the incubus of bourgeois morality, by holding on to the bars of abstraction as he ascends the ladder towards the transcendent, he continuously risks a disappearance into abstract cant and ecstatic effusion. It is no wonder that when Landauer replied furiously to Buber's editorial, Buber claimed that he was misunderstood. Landauer disdained this new person – "der Kriegsbuber"[13] – the "war Buber" as he called him – and particularly attacked Buber's famous lecture on 'The Spirit of the Orient and Judaism',[14] claiming that its attempt to link the creative power of the ancient world with the contemporary German is flagrant and wholly unjustified nationalism.

Buber rethought his war years' doctrine, recognising that there was a dangerous and corrupting link between his *Erlebnis*-mysticism and nationalism which demanded revision. It came after the war. Moreover it saved the moral credibility of *Der Jude* and cleansed in some measure Buber's own tarnished reputation. But that revisionism – the re-editing of certain of Buber's books to remove offending passages and the shift in Buber's teaching from *Erlebnis* to *Begegnung* mysticism and the philosophy of dialogue only served to shift doctrinal emphasis, to clarify and make explicit dimensions of Buber's philosophic doctrine which had been made obscure by his first war-time attempt to give it concrete application. The fact is that in the aftermath of the war when it might have been thought the time had come to put behind him the hated diaspora, the desiccated Jewry of the alien exile and turn towards Zion *redivivus*, Buber – who had trained his generation – stayed behind. It is easy to understand why Buber stayed behind from 1933 to 1938, but it is difficult to understand why this early and progenitive Zionist inspired others to leave while he elected to remain another generation.

III

The publication in 1923 of Buber's most famous and undoubtedly least read work, *I and Thou* marks a significant advance in his emergence from the murky

[11] Martin Buber, *Daniel. Dialogues on Realization.* Translated, with an introduction by Maurice Friedman, New York 1964, p. 115 (with minor editorial modifications.)
[12] Martin Buber, 'Die Losung', *Der Jude*, I, Heft 1 (April 1916), p. 2.
[13] Martin Buber, *Briefwechsel aus sieben Jahrzehnten*, 1897–1918, I, Letter No. 306, pp. 433–438. Cf. as well the excellent discussion of the controversy and its aftermath in Paul Robert Flohr, *From Kulturpolitik to Dialogue, op. cit.*, pp. 143–149.
[14] Martin Buber, 'The Spirit of the Orient and Judaism', *On Judaism*, pp. 56–78.

teachings of *Daniel* – teachings which had prompted the linguistic theorist, Fritz Mauthner, to describe the Buber of those years as an "atheistic Zionist"[15] intending by this acute and not wholly untrue assertion that the grounds of Buber's mysticism were not God nor any theologically grounded teaching, but rather a conception of the polarity and struggle which each person reflects in his coming into relation with the world and otherness. Each individual, in Buber's *Erlebnis* mysticism, either orientates himself to the world, mastering the means of manipulating the real by constraining it with laws of order and institutions of control or else, by the modes of actualisation (or *Verwirklichung* – realisation), effects a seizing of that unity which removes duality, partitiveness, the split character of things. The cognitive intuition of this early mysticism of experience – that all things are manifest in separateness, but that the world is finally one and that only through a descent and submersion into that unity is the fracture of the world mended – is a teaching which can be held without a divinity. It is akin to a Zen insight, a wisdom of healing and reconciliation which requires no God, no creation nor revelation, redemption into the unity of actualisation being sufficient.

It was a weak teaching for Jews precisely because there was nothing remarkably or palpably Jewish in its presentation. Although it was reinforced by his early telling of the *hasidic* tales, Buber had in this early work succumbed to the temptation of all wise men which is to imagine that wisdom is general, indeed universal, stripped of the skin of particularity which marks any specific wisdom as having antecedents and sources that make for the discrimination of Jewish, Christian or Zen truth in precisely the same way that it makes for Jewish, Christian or Zen mysticism, rather than mysticism in general. Methodologically it was a shallow doctrine; metaphysically it produced more confusion – particularly as Buber manipulated its language during the war years – and needed to be superseded. It is this supersession he believed he had accomplished in *I and Thou*, a work which no longer turns on the explicit usage of *Erlebnis*, but transfers from epistemology to ontology the basic categories of his teaching, shifting the language from fluidities of perception and cognition to fundamental attitudes of being. Man is the creature who can address the world with two modes of speech – he can construct the world as an It, reifying nature and persons in such a way as to manage and contain them, draining them of life, compelling them to submit, or else as a Thou, wholly present in meeting, fully acknowledged and regarded. Every man is possessed of this two-fold attitude towards the world, but the inborn Thou of every creature is now grounded in the eternal and unconditioned Thou of God and the It of the world is now the silence of nature. This short work, full of difficulties and compelling formulations, stands every test of time as a work endlessly suggestive, drawing together lines of reflection and argumentation which had preoccupied the German tradition from Schelling, Hamann and others to Rosenstock-Huessy and Ferdinand Ebner, while no less

---

[15]Cited by Scholem in his essay, 'Martin Buber's Conception of Judaism', *loc. cit.*, p. 149. It is quoted by Scholem from a letter of Mauthner's included in Gershon Weiler's essay, 'Fritz Mauthner. A Study in Jewish Self-Rejection', in *LBI Year Book VIII* (1963), p. 147.

attempting to effect through the life of dialogue a response to the despair of Kierkegaard.[16]

The rhythm of Buber's work reached a metric evenness with *I and Thou* and from that work to the end of his life, each new book and each new reworking of an old book, was a continuous effort to make the materials of historical faith and traditional belief cohere with his intuition or else be cast to the sidelines of life and relevance. For a thinker who had, throughout his life, maintained an ambivalent connection with the mysterious and the wonderful, Buber's thought allowed for precious little that was unresolved, whose essence remained unplumbed, for the mystery that appeared simply, nakedly and without interpretation.

It is absolutely logical that with the completion of *I and Thou*, Buber was armed with the means of interpreting Judaism and the Jewish world. The life of dialogue originated pre-eminently with ancient Israel for "Israel has understood – or, rather, lived – life as being-spoken-to and answering, speaking-to and receiving answers".[17] The God of monotheism is a divinity translucent in all things. Whereas the pagan makes of each thing he grasps a little god, dividing the world into small principalities of power, the ancient Hebrew saw through all things to the eternal Thou that is its source. The eternal Thou, above all, is not Idea, not a logical premise of our coherence and integrity, but is unitary person, nearing and approaching in dialogue, vanishing and eclipsed by confusion – always Thou, despite the mixed propensity of man to make of Thouness an *objectivum*. From such a criterion, it is possible for Buber to vindicate his critique of historical religion, of Jewish religion most immediately, for the living Thou struggles against the veils by which the hardened spirit of man wishes to conceal him. All ritual, all formal prayer, all law and observance, all institutional structure are human means of keeping the Thou in place, so to speak, under the human thumb.

It is no wonder then that Buber's conception of the creation is notably defective, confined to the analogy of the creative rather than to the exposition of the *bereshit* as such; no less wonder that Buber's doctrine of revelation draws virtually no distinction between the Sinaitic and the prophetic, indeed cannot, precisely because the content of the revelation at Sinai is specific, while the inspiration of the prophet is always the call to turning and renewal. Clearly Buber can impose upon prophetic revelation his pneumatic exegesis more readily because the prophet comes to God with a trained ear – one already familiarised by a history of the People hearing, but Buber's insistence that Mosaic revelation is of the same order, that all revelation is the same, is to mistake what historical religions cannot fail to accredit – that the revelation to the prophets returns the People to its task while the original revelation constitutes the People in the first place and makes known to it its task. The fact is that in Buber's thought it is the ineffaceable human propensity to deafness, to the construction of the world as a

---

[16]Cf. Harold Stahmer's important study, *"Speak that I may See". The Religious Significance of Language*, New York 1968, where the theories of Hamann, Rosenstock-Huessy, Rosenzweig, Buber, Ebner are carefully examined.

[17]Martin Buber, 'Spinoza, Sabbatai Zevi and the Baal Shem', *Hasidism*, New York 1948, p. 95.

hoarding of dead things, to the speech of reification and the fabrication of the It, that conserves for him the hope of redemption and the continuous challenge of conversion and renewal. The speaking of the Thou is a creative apprehension of self-unity and a willingness to open oneself in trust to the world – that therapeutic ontology inspires, heals and renews. The fractured world of loving service and backsliding, of miscreant kings and provocative prophets, of heartfelt service and stiff-necked prideful disobedience – the systole and diastole of Biblical rhythm – leaves open the future of redemption to an ultimate optimism. Buber's doctrine of the Messiah, for me the weakest link in an otherwise thin but delicately wrought chain of argument, is as Scholem has observed from his own impregnable citadel, not "revolutionary" at all.[18] The Messiah is as Buber has written:

> "the fulfiller, he who at last fulfills the function of the viceregent, through whose agency the ordering of the people under YHVH's leadership will be realised. He is anointed to set up with human forces and human responsibility the divine order of human community."[19]

The Messiah and the messianic order is linked to creation as its consummation; it is the ontological gloss of creation, that which fills the black holes of creation, ransoming its lostness and deprivation, bringing it to consummation. Messianic Judaism in Buber's view is not defined simply

> "by the belief in a unique event at the end of time and in a unique human being as the centre of this event. The certitude of the collaborating force which is accorded to man connected the end of time with present life."[20]

The Messiah completes what each man undertakes to do in the fullness of the Thou.

IV

I cannot hope to have compassed all the relevant aspects of Buber's thinking regarding Judaism. I have specifically omitted discussion of his remarkable work of translation, both of the mystic literature and of the Bible, since my language is not German and I cannot hope to appraise, except at second-hand, what Rosenzweig called the impossible undertaking of translation; nor have I taken issue with Buber's interpretation of the Law and traditional Jewish institutions, since this is better done by those whose commitment to the Law is more complete than mine. I feel myself obliged however to raise a number of critical questions regarding Buber's teaching which are implicit in the exposition I have offered of his principal doctrine. I would like to divide these remarks into three parts: first, a consideration of what I take to be Buber's defective, indeed romantic, notion of evil; second, Buber's refusal of the historical; and third, Buber's religious anarchism.

[18] The controversy between Scholem and Buber is set forth by Scholem in 'The Neutralization of the Messianic Element in Early Hasidism', *The Messianic Idea in Judaism and Other Essays on Jewish Spirituality*, New York 1971, pp. 176–202. Cf. also the discussion of the controversy in David Biale's important book, *Gershom Scholem. Kabbalah and Counter-History*, Cambridge 1979, pp. 148–170. Also, Scholem, 'Martin Buber's Conception of Judaism', *loc. cit.*, pp. 160–161.
[19] Martin Buber, *The Prophetic Faith*, New York 1949, p. 153.
[20] Martin Buber. 'Spinoza, Sabbatai Zevi and the Baal Shem', *Hasidism*, p. 112 f.

It is exceedingly difficult to speak of evil in this age and to Jews. And yet to acknowledge this is enough. We are obliged to speak of evil, to understand it as the mountain we cannot scale and to recognise as well that the rock and earth of which it is composed we walk upon no less surely. There is no man who is innocent of evil or its existence, who can speak of it in our time without sickening intimacy, and who, perceiving it, feels nonetheless helpless before its face. The evil is so monstrous. I say all this because I have no intention of challenging Buber's sustained and unbroken doctrine of evil – a mild and I believe pathetic vision – in the aftermath of the holocaustal *tremendum*.[21] Buber did much before the full weight of the axe had fallen. His essay 'The Land and Its Possessors', his open 'Letter to Gandhi', is a masterpiece of ethical clarification, making clear to the Mahatma what no one else could have dared say, that Gandhi had no understanding of the situation of the Jews of Germany or the Jews of Palestine, that he spoke from the assurance of the soul-power of hundreds of millions and knew nothing of the state of beleaguerment which was that of the minuscule Jewish people.[22] Buber could understand suffering and human pathos, but his notion of evil remained without persuasive substance.

It is clear that Buber's conception of evil must be distinguished from a personalist doctrine of sin. The sinful man projects the *imitatio dei*, but misses it. He strives but turns himself back, falling away from the image before which he stands, repents his sin and strives once more. This is the condition of ordinary creaturehood before the Lord who projects his will and makes plain his way. But of evil – the turning away from God which is principled and oppository, wholly constrained by a law of otherness and what Kierkegaard has called "shut-upness",[23] Buber takes account, but late account, the concept of evil occupying significant weight in his thinking only after his interpretation of the rebellion of Korah described in his *Moses* (1940) where Korah's repudiation of the humility and instruction of Moses is described by Buber as a demonic misconstruction.[24] We move beyond sin to wickedness, beyond wrong-doing to evil, beyond even miscreancy to the demonic. There is a virtual pressing to the limit of radical evil, but Buber draws back, struggling to maintain the narrow ridge where the dialectic achieves paradoxicality, radical evil amenable even at the last to the optimism of redemption. In the volume of essays, *Pointing the Way* (1957), Buber's discussion of Hitler in his essay 'People and Leader' declares that Hitler has come forward to assert with finality the condition of "the man without conscience". And even for Hitler Buber has a Jewish analogue, Jakob Frank, who was

---

[21] I first used the term *tremendum* to evoke the Holocaust in my lecture, *Thinking the Tremendum. Some Theological Implications of the Death-Camps*, The Leo Baeck Memorial Lecture 18, New York 1974. The term has been employed by me as indicative of a fundamental ontological structure in the lectures given at Brown University during April 1979, to be published under the title, *The Holocaust as Tremendum*, Seabury Press, New York 1981 (forthcoming).
[22] Martin Buber, 'The Land and Its Possessors', an extract from Buber's reply to the criticism of Jewish claims in Palestine put forward by Mahatma Gandhi. *Israel and the World*, New York 1948, pp. 227–233. The full text appears in Martin Buber's *Pointing the Way*, New York 1957, 'A Letter to Gandhi (1939)', pp. 139–147.
[23] Sören Kierkegaard, *The Concept of Dread*, Princeton 1944, p. 110 ff.
[24] Martin Buber, *Moses*, London 1946, 'The Contradiction', pp. 182–190.

not simply a wicked man, but incarnate wickedness.[25] This seems on the face of it, an accounting, a reckoning with the reality of ontological evil, evil which is an order of being, but it suffers in my view, as all of Buber's ontology suffers, from being tied to persons. The personalism holds up the image of the conscienceless man as a modality of instruction – evil, even evil is a pedagogue, pointing the way of ultimate rebellion, warning and guarding those who have in their hearts the mixed imagination of the twin inclinations of ordinary humanity, to do good and to sin, but such a pedagogic intention, however much it is a heroic struggle against dualism, against twin kingdoms of God and the devil, sacrifices too much for the equanimity of a monistic resolution. We are not able any longer to enjoy the ancient luxury of an ultimately victorious divinity.

The array of history – not merely the array of persons – compels us to acknowledge a kingdom of evil fabricated from the lives of inattentive persons. Persons who sin by turning away, by unclarity, by decisionlessness, by protestation of unknowing and innocence – all these innocent sinners of the twentieth century, formed by the unity of terror, by the threat to life which ends without resurrection and consummation beyond death – all these innocents are of the machinery of the kingdom of evil. Substantive evil (that metaphysical constellation) and ontological evil (that metaphysical abstraction) yield place to a demonism which has no place. What we are obliged to recognise (which I am persuaded eludes Buber) is that the reality of evil, its immensity, its capacity to overwhelm, engulf and transform the innocent into its servant derives from the factuality of historical evil, evil as the kingdom of events, not personal deeds.

History was always for Buber the medium by which myth is echoed through the ages – its outer shell is the constellation of persons and events, actions and upheavals, but its interior meaning is to be limned through the predominant and formative *mythos* of culture. Biblical *mythos* is supervenient to history, supplying it with its implicative significance because it affords each historical witness with the criterion by which to appraise its meaning and self-referential relevance. History is then part of the dialogue between man and God – it is, despite its obvious circumstantiality, always of the portion of *Heilsgeschichte*, endlessly inseminated with the divine, aborted and come to birth, but always the medium through which God and man meet.

> "What we are permitted to know of history comes to this: 'This in one way or another, is history's challenge to me; this is its claim on me; and so this is its meaning as far as I am concerned.' This meaning, however, is not 'subjective' ... It is the meaning I perceive, experience, and hear in reality ... It is only with my personal life that I am able to catch the meaning of history, for it is a dialogical meaning.'[26]

The predicament of such a treatment of history is that the historical as such is never as real as what it conceals and echoes. The murder is not simply murder but meaning; the devastation of nations and peoples, not simply that, but also an echoing of ancient trials and turbulence. Such a view of history makes it impossible to deal with the historical as such, for it lends itself too readily to a kind of reflexivity and pacifism, a modus of patient hearing and awaiting, until the

---
[25] Martin Buber, *Pointing the Way*, pp. 148–160.
[26] Martin Buber, *Israel and the World*, pp. 78–82.

right hour for each man, the right moment for the deed. Buber insists that his doctrine of history is not subjective, but the charge of subjectivism with which he dealt all his life and which he never succeeded in dispelling holds here as well. The charge of subjectivism is in one sense unfair, since objectivity is a robber of human passion and commitment which the real requires ever as much as it requires clarity and precision. Objectivity, subjectivity – these are the obligatory terms of argumentation. The dialectic of persons and events requires that judgment catch hold of the publicly received and held as much as it succours its roots in the internal life of understanding. The difficulty of Buber's teaching on the nature of history is that the inner core of history, its echo of the archetypal myth and its resonation within the continuous hearing of man, leaves history without a criterion by which to appraise its unfolding. History stretches from creation to redemption. It has no centre. Its centre is everywhere that a man stands open before it. Revelation is no centre for Buber, since revelation to become a fixed centre must have fixed meaning and content, but as Buber had stated repeatedly, the content of revelation is within the *vaydeber* and not within the *naaseh v'nishma*. God reveals in speech, but what God says is altered by the hearing. The Thou is always Thou, but manifests itself differently to each I. There is no permanent I; there is only eternal Thou. History can have no centre but the promise, no guideland and hence no *ceasura*, no Thou shalt, only Thou.

It is against this background that one may speak of Buber's religious anarchism, a criticism levelled most ardently and profoundly by Gershom Scholem, whose knowledge of anarchism is no less intimate than Buber's, although it takes its point of departure from a different manifestation of the religious reality.[27] And is religious anarchism a criticism? There are many today who would regard Judaism as over-defined, over-legislated, over-particularised, for whom shattering the shells of historical incrustation would be a service, not a defect. In part I would share with them, feeling often that it would be best if Judaism were to enjoy an age underground, bonded to heretical enquiry and dangerous speculation, but I would recognise nonetheless that it demanded no less a clear and responsible reading of its public, historical manifestation. Buber is surely wrong in thinking that the best ages of Judaism were when everything was being sown and nothing reaped. Surely reaping, that is consolidating and holding fast, making the way straight and safe, is as indispensable as the endangering enterprise of those who dare to face the abyss and do not shrink from its vastness and its threat. Buber was all too comfortable on the mountain peaks, alone with the eagles, when most of us are obliged to live not in the cracks, but in open spaces, the flat plain of history where the prayer of the ordinary, the candles and *kiddushim* and fasts of ordinary Jews are recognised for what they are – holding the sane centre of tradition. Buber was all too often contemptuous of the simple way, thinking of the centre as a narrow ridge between paradoxicalities. The centre is, in truth, a large, broad and grand highway of immense way stations and spir-

---

[27]"To put it bluntly, Buber is a religious anarchist and his teaching is religious anarchism." Gershom Scholem, 'Martin Buber's Interpretation of Hasidism', *loc. cit.*, p. 245. As well see the discussion of Scholem's own religious anarchism in David Biale, *Gershom Scholem. Kabbalah and Counter-History*, pp. 94–100, *passim*.

itual hostels, while beneath the beating hooves that bear us from life to death, it is natural that pebbles, rocks, a multitude of pedestrian obstacles require the endless effort of surmounting. The anarchism of Buber's religious thinking is a measure of its vision and its intolerance – its celebration of dialogue and its hostility to those who would speak through other's words and texts, through the history of descents to ordinariness as well as the climbing to the peaks.

Martin Buber was a romantic pedagogue fated to be misunderstood and misconstrued, while he talked ceaselessly to his people, making his word and the sequence of his books into the tradition by which his own anarchy would become code and be transmitted. He was not content with leaving a gnomic work, a single document, nor was he satisfied to say as another said, "*Into Life*" at the conclusion of his solitary theological preamble. Rather Buber thought of his teaching as healing doctrine, a modus of therapy by which broken spirits would be made whole, Jewish broken spirits, but also Christian broken spirits, for Buber spoke not from the centre of Judaism, but Judaism was at his centre; he spoke not out of being a Jew, but being a Jew was contained by him. He was larger than what he was able to teach and so he taught over and over again in the effort to fill his own lineaments. His person and his presence exceeded his word, however much he would have wished the word to echo within the narrow determination of person. This complexity ensures that insofar as Buber addresses the human spirit which may be Jewish he will endure, but insofar as he addressed the Jew as Jew, he must be constantly revised or qualified, or forgotten.

Reflections on Buber's Impact on German Jewry

BY NAHUM N. GLATZER

In speaking of Buber's impact on German Jewry, we must remember that, indeed, Buber started in Germany and continued to use both the German language and the German mode of expression.* But he wanted to reach beyond German Jewry and beyond Germany. I still remember when, in his advanced years, he complained to me that he was not well known in the world at large. At that time some of his works had been translated into English and I was able to point out to him that people did know him. But he was not satisfied. That satisfaction came later. Hence, if we speak about Buber's impact, we must qualify the term to mean that it was only the starting point that Germany provided; his activity and impact did not end there.

In Germany proper, Buber, in the early years, used to attend conferences of theologians and philosophers. At one such conference he sat next to Edmund Husserl, the phenomenologist. The latter turned to him with the words: "Ach, das ist der Buber. Den gibts ja garnicht." "Yes", said Buber, "I do exist." "Nein, der ist doch eine Legende."[1] So Buber had to fight against this kind of image. He was indeed existent, and one of the major concerns in his thought was to fight for the affirmation of man's existence, an existence which precedes thinking and thought.

A few years ago, an article on Buber appeared in the American magazine, *Commentary*,[2] discussing him as a man who had placed himself outside the Jewish community, who did nothing to be known as representative of the Jewish community. Buber was more appreciated among Protestants, the article said. Jews regarded him as being outside the mainstream. His rejection of *Halakhah* made him suspect. His treatment of Jesus was considered much too positive for a normal Jew. His individualistic definition of revelation was highly untraditional. In sum, Buber was rejected as a spokesman for Jewry. Sooner or later, I believe, this attitude will change and Buber will be fully recognised as a true son of his people.

I have the feeling that the strange style in some of Buber's works – a certain obliqueness, a veiled expression which sometimes makes you ask: What does he really want to say? – is a device employed in order to accentuate an indirectness, a suggestiveness, that was more important to him than a definitive doctrine. He

---

*This is a revised and expanded version of a paper originally delivered at a symposium held on the 29th October 1978 at the New York Leo Baeck Institute to mark the centenary of Martin Buber's birth.
[1] Private communication; also, Werner Kraft, *Gespräche mit Buber*, Munich 1966, p. 139.
[2] Chaim Potok, 'Martin Buber and the Jews', *Commentary*, 41, No. 3 (March 1966), pp. 43–49.

said: "I have no doctrine to teach." If you asked him what *is* this or that in Judaism, or, what is the task of modern man, he could not give a straight answer. "All I can do is to point the way," – the title of one of his books of essays.³

Therefore, Buber avoided making disciples. This great man could have had disciples, in the strict sense of the word. He had listeners, audiences. He had a few men who attached themselves to him; but he did not want his personal life, his personality, to be invaded by disciples. He wished to withdraw from the community-at-large and be for himself, to write whatever he could write, discuss issues of the past and of the day, make errors plain, but no more. Here is a master who avoided creating a circle of disciples. Nevertheless, a master he was. Originally, in the early 1920s, Buber hesitated, but finally accepted an invitation to come to the newly founded *Lehrhaus* of Franz Rosenzweig in Frankfurt and there offer a course of studies.⁴

His hesitancy is expressed in a style which cultivated indirectness, obliqueness, an attempt to conceal rather than express. Some Buber critics wondered: Why did he do so? After all, he wrote for people and people should be able to understand what it is he wants. But if you could not find your way through his style you were lost.

Buber called himself a Polish Jew.⁵ But there was little of the typical Polish Jew in him. He had become a German Jew. His first language may have been Polish, but when he came to the universities of Germany, he became more and more German, to the point that he was recognised as one of the few prominent German stylists. His writings were quoted as products of German culture.

In October 1913, Ludwig Geiger, son of the famous liberal rabbi Abraham Geiger, wrote in the *Allgemeine Zeitung des Judentums*:

> "For us free thinking German Jews, the question of assimilation does not exist. We are completely assimilated. By this we mean a total integration into *Deutschtum*, into its nationality, language, culture, without, however, giving up our religious beliefs. We are Germans according to our *Gesinnung* and language. Yet we remain Jews. Our assimilation has been completed."

That was in 1913. Soon it became clear that assimilation was by no means complete, that although Jews had become fully-fledged citizens of the *Reich*, there were certain disparities (and they became ever stronger, ever deeper) between the normal Christian and the German Jew. The German Jew realised it, sometimes too late. Geiger's position that "our assimilation is completed ... We are Germans" was challenged by Buber who raised some questions in order that Jews should start thinking about their status in Germany. He helped to revise the complicated issue of emancipation.

One term used by Buber offers a clue to this thought. He spoke of himself as an atypical man,⁶ a man who cannot be categorised. To be atypical meant being

---

³*Pointing the Way*, Maurice S. Friedman (ed.), New York 1957, based mainly on *Hinweise. Gesammelte Essays*, Berlin 1953.
⁴See letter to Rudolf Hallo, beginning of December 1922; *Briefe*, Edith Rosenzweig and Ernst Simon (eds.), Berlin 1935, pp. 461 ff. Rosenzweig on Buber: "Das Sprechen werde ich ihn in Frankfurt richtig lehren", *ibid.*, p. 414.
⁵Private communication.
⁶Buber, *Werke*, I, *Schriften zur Philosophie*, Heidelberg-München 1962.

a dissenter, a nonconformist, heterodox, at times Utopian; an atypical man was independent, unique. One could not characterise Buber as a liberal Jew or a Conservative Jew, though he reopened the treasury of Conservative Judaism; and through him the great works of the Jewish classical past suddenly became available. Only as an atypical Jew could he address himself to the Jewish community as it existed at the time. He belonged to the vast European culture – with all that this implied. Within Judaism he was a loner and atypical. As such he achieved more than he could have done had he been a typical man.

His language was not the language of a characteristic German thinker or writer. In a letter to me he spoke of *meine Liebschaft mit der deutschen Sprache*.[7] Now, *Liebschaft* is not *Liebe*. It does not mean "my love" for the German language; it means a love affair. Many people could speak of their love of the German language. Buber does not say *meine Liebe*, but *meine Liebschaft*, "my love affair", which implies that he came to that language from the outside – came to it rather than grew up in it. A man who grows up in the German language does not speak of his love affair with that language. Here then, is another aspect of the atypical man.

Buber spoke of his deep faith in the "Eternal Thou".[8] There is the simple "thou" that means "you", and the ultimate, absolute, eternal Thou, for which we normally use the term God. He did not originally want to use the term God, which was what he really meant. He avoided this term, substituting for it "the absolute". Later his attitude changed, and he was emboldened to utter the term God and then qualify what he meant by it. He abandoned the obliqueness of the "Eternal Thou", and by doing so succeeded in breaking the complacency of the modern agnostic, the superficiality of social critics, the nihilism of the existentialists. He addressed all of them. As an atypical man he was free from all constraints, free from the need to conform. As a radically free man he was able to reopen the discussion about the relevance of faith in our day.

Anent Jewish traditional observance he was often asked, "Why can't you accept normative Jewish behaviour?"[9] He refused to do so. It was a part of his religion not to observe Jewish ritual – and without concession. I understand that in the last years after 1933 he was seen occasionally conforming to Jewish ceremonial.[10] He gave no reason. The fact remains, however, that throughout his life, up to 1933, he refused to conform. Another example of a greatly atypical person.

Now, what, as an atypical thinker did Buber teach? He taught God as a reality, not as an idea. He is a personal being. For the sake of the human person, he stated, God himself must appear as a person.[11] Again we have an unusual formulation of God. Hermann Cohen said that it is the glory of Judaism that it

---

[7]3rd November 1949. *Briefwechsel aus sieben Jahrzehnten*, Grete Schaeder (ed.), III, p. 223, Heidelberg 1975.
[8]*I and Thou*, Walter Kaufmann (ed.), New York 1970, Third Part (p. 123 *et seq.*).
[9]Franz Rosenzweig, 'Die Bauleute: Über das Gesetz' (1923), in *Kleinere Schriften*, Berlin 1937, pp. 106–121. English: 'The Builders. Concerning the Law', in *On Jewish Learning*, N. N. Glatzer (ed.), New York 1955, pp. 72–92. See Ernst A. Simon, 'Martin Buber and the Faith of Israel' (in Hebrew), *Divre Iyyun*, Jerusalem 1958, pp. 13–56.
[10]Private communication.
[11]'The Love of God and the Idea of Deity', in *The Eclipse of God*, New York 1952, p. 83.

teaches an impersonal God.[12] In this context, Cohen, who was identified with liberal Judaism in Germany, did not accept the idea of a personal God, whereas Buber, the outsider, did accept it and fought for its place in modern religious thought.

Buber also proffered an unusual distinction between religion and religiosity.[13] Religion, he stated, denotes the external institutional aspects of faith, while religiosity refers to the personal element of religion. That he made such a distinction is in itself both interesting and significant.

He turned his attention to Christianity – he had many Christian friends and many Christian discussants – and criticised the core of Christian faith.[14] He went far beyond Rosenzweig's work *vis-à-vis* Christianity. Rosenzweig considered the reality of Christianity of importance in the scheme of things.[15] Buber respected the faithful adherent to the Christian belief. But he criticised Christianity's belief that the redeemer has come once and that he is to come for a second time to complete the work of redemption, but that we are already living in a redeemed world.[16] In the Jewish view, as expounded by Buber, we are working at redemption. We are doing our share, so that the Messianic era may come "soon in our days". But it is not here yet. We wait for the redeemer to come. All we can do is wait.

Redemption is preceded by the event of revelation.[17] In revelation God establishes or re-establishes the contact between himself and man. God comes near to man; this nearness turns a society of men into a religious community. But if you had asked Buber, "What did God reveal?," the answer would have been: "The content of revelation is not relevant." To Buber, laws are the evidence of the human hand. Revelation, as such, is divine. Then comes man and fills in the empty spaces in the script and puts into them what God supposedly said and commanded. That is a part of Buber's system.[18] It is repeated in his comments on the book of Job. Job is presented as suffering, a man in anguish, experiencing evil. He asks: "Why do you do this to me? Answer me!" This cry is the last of Job's demands: Answer me![19] And God does the unexpected: he answers. In Chapters 38 to 41, God answers Job. Buber exclaims: There it is. God answers men. He makes himself present and addresses himself to man. That is the answer. However, one may quibble that there are four chapters in which God speaks to Job. What was it then that God said to him in answer? But Buber is not concerned with the content of the answer; the presence of God is all that counts.

---

[12] *Ibid.*, p. 82.
[13] 'Jüdische Religiosität' (1916), in *Reden über das Judentum*, Berlin 1932; *On Judaism*, N. N. Glatzer (ed.), New York 1967, pp. 79–94.
[14] Especially in *Zwei Glaubensweisen*, Zürich 1950. English, *Two Types of Faith*, London 1951.
[15] E.g. letter to Rudolf Ehrenberg, 1st November 1913, in *Briefe*, pp. 73–76. English in N. N. Glatzer, *Franz Rosenzweig. His Life and Thought*, New York 1953, pp. 341–344. More explicitly, *Der Stern der Erlösung*, (*The Star of Redemption*), pt. 3, Book 2.
[16] 'The Two Foci of the Jewish Soul' (1930), in *Israel and the World*, New York 1948, pp. 28–37, esp. p. 35.
[17] Martin Buber and Franz Rosenzweig, 'Revelation and Law' (Letters, 28th September, 1st October 1922, 24th and 29th June, 1st, 5th, 13th and 16th July 1924, 3rd and 5th June 1925), in *On Jewish Learning*, pp. 109–124.
[18] *Ibid.*

To him this factor of God making himself present to Job was the answer – and is the only possible answer to the survivors of the concentration camps. You cannot quote to them the Psalm: "Praise God for he is good and his mercy endureth for ever", he maintained. They will not accept that. Remind them of Job. What was it that kept Job alive? His ability to wait. The trust in God who will again reveal himself, that is what made it possible for God to speak to Job. Herein one sees Buber at work between tradition and innovation – between what is classical in Judaism and what is his own interpretation.[20] The very intensity of his religious thought left a deep impact on parts of German Jewry and on religious existentialists the world over.

Buber was, of course, an early Zionist; in 1898 the twenty-year-old Buber attached himself to Herzl.[21] Herzl noticed him and put him in charge of the Zionist party organ, *Die Welt* (1901). Soon, Buber became critical of Herzl: He objected to Herzl's political Zionism, and advocated a spiritual, cultural Zionism, a movement which would suffuse a person's entire humanity.[22] His idea, namely a Zionism which would embrace the whole human personality was to be with him throughout his mature writing life. The Zionism included a deep concern with the Arab problem.[23] Something radical must be done to solve that question, and without delay, he maintained. He went to the Zionist Congresses – starting with the Twelfth in 1921 – and pleaded with the representatives of Zionism to act then and there, or it would be too late. Not only is it politically right to do so, he argued, but it is a moral obligation. As Jews the obligation is on us to follow the moral principle of neighbourliness. He introduced a relevant resolution in one of the Congresses but the resolution was watered down; it became merely a vague expression of "our willingness to cooperate", etc.[24] Buber lost, but his valiant stand had not failed to make an impact even on the most "practical" of Zionists.

When, in 1918, General Allenby conquered Palestine, Buber wrote a leading article in *Der Jude*, the periodical edited by him from 1916 to 1924.

> "They tell me that Palestine has been conquered. I do not believe it and I am prepared to continue not to believe it. You cannot conquer a land. You have to work on a land. And through your dedicated work, you come into the possession of the land. You cannot conquer it."[25]

The very term "conquest" (*Eroberung*) was repugnant to Buber. If we ask whether he succeeded in making an impact on German Jewry, we must say that in

---

[19]*Job* 32:35.
[20]*On Judaism*, pp. 224 ff. *At the Turning*, New York 1952, pp. 61 ff. *The Prophetic Faith*, New York 1949, pp. 188–197.
[21]Cf. letter to Herzl, 6th January 1899, *Briefwechsel*, pp. 146 ff.; and letters of later date, *op. cit.* See also Introduction to *Briefwechsel* by Grete Schaeder, I, 31 ff.
[22]*Die jüdische Bewegung*, Berlin 1920, I, pp. 29 and 125.
[23]E.g. 'Address at the 12th Zionist Congress at Carlsbad', 2nd September 1921; *Kampf um Israel*, Berlin 1933, pp. 327–341. *Der Jude und sein Judentum*, Köln 1963, pp. 467–475. See also Introduction to this volume by Robert Weltsch.
[24]Robert Weltsch, 'Postscript to Hans Kohn', *Martin Buber. Sein Werk und seine Zeit*, Köln 1961, Veröffentlichung des Leo Baeck Instituts, pp. 435–438.
[25]'Die Eroberung Palästinas', Heft 10/11 (Januar/Februar 1918), p. 633; *Der Jude*, II, *Der Jude und sein Judentum*, pp. 505 ff.

a majority of cases there was not necessarily a direct influence; but there was definitely an indirect one. He worked on this indirectness, rather than on making a direct impact. What he wanted was to suggest, to point a direction, and then let people struggle with the problem.

That Buber was a polemicist is often forgotten, but polemics is a significant aspect of his intellectual life. We have already mentioned Hermann Cohen's *Deutschtum* and anti-Zionism; Buber wrote a pamphlet refuting Cohen.[26]

He polemicised against Kierkegaard,[27] who sent away his betrothed Regina, maintaining that she was obstructing his way to God. Said Buber: "The way to God leads via your betrothed, via marriage, through the world, not bypassing the world, trying to communicate with the divine 'directly'." Did Buber understand Kierkegaard on this point? Maybe not. Kierkegaard was too anguished a man, and this psychological factor is important if we want to realise why he did what very few others do – consider the women they love as obstacles in the way of communicating with God.

Buber polemicised against Nietzsche,[28] whom he had initially admired, at University, as did many intellectuals, both Jewish and Christian. Nietzsche's new style of life and thought appealed to young thinkers. But the "God is dead" idea Buber had to reject. The *concept* of God may be dead, he postulated. The notion of the death of God was deeply offensive; God does not die.

Buber joined in the fight against Hegel[29] as the man who opined that what happens to an individual is unimportant. What matters is the idea. Buber had to reject this view; he fought Hegel, as did his friend Rosenzweig.[30] In their view man was most definitely important.

He fought Sartre.[31] Sartre said that we create our own ethics. Buber replied, one cannot create morals. They are given to us. Note Buber's indirectness. He would not say that God revealed the moral law, but "*it is* revealed to us". Now, personal ethics is one of Sartre's main points and it is on this point that Buber attacked him.

Spinoza[32] came late into Buber's view of things. But once he detected Spinoza's view of God, he fought him. A God that does not answer man is no God, Buber opined. Whereas Spinoza said, if I pray, I do not care whether or not God hears. This implied that God is not a God who hears; therefore no answer is possible. Buber, on the other hand, believed that God is an answering God if we turn in our speech and our deed to the divine. A dialogue between man and God is going on all the time; Spinoza does not accept this view. He posits an impersonal God, a God who is *sive natura*.

---

[26] *Völker, Staaten und Zion*, Wien 1917 (based on articles in *Der Jude*).
[27] 'On the Suspension of the Ethical', in *The Eclipse of God*, pp. 149–156.
[28] 'Autobiographical Fragments', introduction to *The Philosophy of Martin Buber*, P. A. Schilpp and Maurice Friedman (eds.), La Salle, Illinois 1967, pp. 12ff. *The Eclipse of God*, pp. 142–146.
[29] *Ibid.*, pp. 28–31.
[30] *The Star of Redemption*, trans. by William W. Hallo, New York 1970, pp. 3–7.
[31] *The Eclipse of God*, pp. 87–94.
[32] 'Spinoza, Sabbatai Zvi and the Baal-Shem', in the *Origin and Meaning of Hasidism*, Maurice Friedman (ed.), New York 1960, ch. III.

Gandhi[33] came in for rebuke for suggesting that German Jewry under Hitler should commit mass suicide as the only possible answer to its plight. Said Buber:

> "You cannot compare the Jewish situation with the position of the Hindus in South Africa. If something happened to the Hindus in South Africa, there are 100 million Hindus who would support you and the tiny group of Hindus in South Africa. But if we Jews commit suicide no one will notice. It would leave no impact and therefore, Mahatma, that cannot be our answer. You fail to understand the situation of the German Jews."

What did Gandhi answer? Nothing. There was no answer.

Then there were those antisemites among the Christians of Germany who were at times quite subtle in their opposition to Jews. One of them said: the Jews do not know how to die; we Christians do.[34] No, Buber answered, we, too, know how to die. But we are commanded to live before we die. Underneath this notion that the Jew does not know how to die lay the wish that he would be better dead. Buber detected this underlying wish and stressed the individual Jew's profound desire to live.[35] In a special issue of *Der Jude* (1925) Buber answered the question Who is the Pharisee? Some of the Christian contributors to the issue characterised the Pharisee as the Jew who killed Jesus and who is stubborn in his observance of the law. Buber, who was not a Pharisee, who was not observant, proffered information on the true identity of the Pharisees. He pointed to the deep humanitarian aspect of Pharisaism, the Pharisee's profound social concern, the readiness to die, as symbolised by the "ten martyrs" who are remembered in Judaism as men willing to die for the sake of God. Thus suddenly, Buber became a defender of Pharisaism from within.[36]

In 1911 Buber was invited to address the Prague Jewish Student Organisation Bar Kochba.[37] The young men were in a quandary. They knew that they were Jews. They did not sympathise with their bourgeois parents. But what did it really mean to be a Jew? They invited Buber, who was already prominent among the intellectuals, to elucidate. He accepted, came to Prague and offered the 'Addresses on Judaism' that became a classic in modern Jewish thought. In answer to the question "Who is a Jew?" Buber differentiated between official and unofficial Judaism. There have always been official representatives of Jewry. They sat in the temple and preserved the priestly hierarchy; they sat in the various councils and propounded doctrine. In contrast a subterranean Judaism is actively at work not openly but secretly, so to speak. There is critical tension between this group and the so-called official Jews. Who are these subterranean Jews?[38] The Rechabites in the Bible, a group of ascetics; the Essenes, who left

---

[33]M. Buber and Judah Magnes, *Two Letters to Gandhi*, Jerusalem 1939; abridged in *Israel and the World*, pp. 227–233. See also my foreword to *On Zion. The History of an Idea*, New York 1973.

[34]Wilhelm Michel, 'Deutsche und Juden', *Der Jude*, Sonderheft: *Antisemitismus und jüdisches Volkstum*, Berlin 1925, pp. 54 ff.

[35]"Pharisäertum"', *ibid.*, pp. 129 ff.

[36]*Ibid.*, pp. 123–131.

[37]Hans Kohn, *Martin Buber. Sein Werk und seine Zeit*, Hellerau 1930, pp. 90–104; Introduction by Robert Weltsch to *Der Jude und sein Judentum; Reden über das Judentum. Gesamtausgabe*, 2. Auflage, Berlin 1932; *On Judaism*, N. N. Glatzer (ed.), New York 1967; this edn. includes also 'The Later Addresses' (1939–1951). See also: Leo Herrmann, 'Erinnerungen an Bubers "Drei Reden" in Prag', *Der Jude. Zu M. Bubers fünfzigsten Geburtstag*, Berlin 1928, pp. 158–164.

[38]Subterranean Jews: *On Judaism*, pp. 45 *et. seq.*

Jerusalem, established themselves in the desert and are identical or close to the Dead Sea sectarians; the early Christians – a sectarian Jewish movement which stressed imminent Messianism. In the Middle Ages we find the so-called early German *Hasidim*, the mystics, and later the Polish *Hasidim* of the eighteenth and nineteenth centuries. Throughout Jewish history runs an underground stream of Jews who denied the validity, the rightfulness, of official institutional Jewry. You, too, students of the University of Prague, Buber implied, are Jews of the unofficial kind. You belong to a legitimate form of Jewry. You are Jews and very much so, while your parents (not stated overtly in the addresses but implied) – are Jews only formally. To the young men of Prague, Buber's message was relevant and full of impact.

Buber found in East-European *Hasidism*, its lore, legend and way of life, much of what is meaningful to modern religious man: a personal God, an attitude of faith on the part of the human person, a dialogical relationship to man and to the divine, community, joy of life, trust in the next day, a sanctification of every day. From *The Stories of Rabbi Nahman* (1906) to the collection of *Tales of the Hasidim* (1947–1948) Buber tirelessly brought the religious and humanist message of *Hasidism* to the world. His efforts were not a scholarly, critical presentation, but rather an artistic paraphrase of selected *hasidic* materials. The impact, especially on West-European Jewry, was extraordinary. The West in general saw in Buber's *Hasidica* an enrichment of folklore and religious expression.

Buber's last activity to have a profound impact was his decision to stay on in Germany after 1933 to take care of the educational needs of German Jewry, and to organise this effort under the Nazis.[39] At that time, this was still possible. He had people who cooperated with him and younger persons who helped him. On the whole, this dedication to the survival orientation of German Jewry was his last important task on behalf of his adopted country.

In 1938 he came to Palestine and settled there with his family. During the post-1938 period, when the war was over, he came twice to the United States (in 1951 and 1957) for lectures. He continued to criticise the Jews who had left the ranks of Judaism – people like Henri Bergson,[40] who obviously lacked sufficient knowledge of Jewry and Judaism. Similarly Simone Weil.[41] Her critique of Judaism was simply based on her lack of knowledge. Buber tried to argue with persons of this bent – and they were many. He spoke up as a free man and an atypical Jew.

Buber continued teaching well into his old age. When he visited Brandeis University in 1957, he agreed to answer questions from the audience. Professor Paul Tillich, the pre-eminent Protestant theologian, was there. The animated discussion finally centred on one issue: Should we employ concepts or not? Buber advocated a negative position because "concepts step between myself and the thou, the other person. Sometimes I may have to use concepts, but we should

---

[39]Ernst Simon, *Aufbau im Untergang. Jüdische Erwachsenenbildung im nationalsozialistischen Deutschland als geistiger Widerstand*, Tübingen 1959 (Schriftenreihe wissenschaftlicher Abhandlungen des Leo Baeck Instituts 2).
[40]*On Judaism, op. cit.*, pp. 205–213.
[41]Ibid.

avoid them as much as possible." Rejection of concepts was to Buber a sign of the free man, the atypical thinker. Tillich defended concepts as simplifying intellectual communication. At the end of the evening Buber was outside the lecture hall, still arguing, when Tillich came out; Buber shook his finger: "Tillich, Sie haben noch viel zu lernen!"[42]

[42]Writer's recollection.

In the Third Reich

Jewish Emigration from Germany
Nazi Policies and Jewish Responses (I)

BY HERBERT A. STRAUSS

I. MIGRATION AND THE ANTISEMITIC TRADITION

The archetype at the core of Jew-hatred is controlled by the dialectics of ethological fantasies. Stereotyped hatred thrives on distance from its object.* Greater closeness creates invidious fear, competition, spatial constriction. The "solution" to emotional tension lies in increasing the distance to the reputed source of the discomfort. Greater distance, in the vague miasma of hate fantasies, takes all forms known to xenophobia. The "final solution" represents the ultimate distancing – death.[1]

Migration, movement by the minority towards and away from the majority, has historically embodied the dynamics in this dialectics of space. Like acculturation, migration has been generally characteristic of populations in modern industrialising societies. There has been a momentous *Binnenwanderung* from countryside to city over the past two hundred years. National unifications have uprooted previously isolated and regional cultures and created new syntheses through acculturation. The great East-West trek of labour and impoverished

---

*The author acknowledges gratefully the assistance of Dr. Daniel Schwartz, Hebrew University and University of the Negev, Beersheva, in researching parts of this essay, and the unflagging encouragement received from Dr. Curt C. Silberman and the Board of the Research Foundation for Jewish Immigration, New York. It grew out of a contribution he is preparing for the forthcoming M. Dobkowski and H. A. Strauss, *A Social and Intellectual History of the Jewish Immigrant from Nazi Germany in the U.S.A.* (*The Jewish Immigrant of the Nazi Period in the U.S.A.*, H. A. Strauss (ed.), sponsored by the Research Foundation for Jewish Immigration, New York, vol. VI). Research and writing was supported by a grant of the National Endowment for the Humanities, Washington, D.C. in the summer of 1977. Lack of time dictated the limitations and omissions of subject matter areas such as the international Jewish communal effort to aid Jewish émigrés from Germany. The author thanks the American Federation of Jews from Central Europe, New York, for granting him a two months' leave of absence to work on this essay in the summer of 1977.

[1]The *völkisch* tradition on which Nazi antisemitism was based appeared, quite properly to observers, as no more than a fantastic and vaporous miasma as long as its protagonists retained their marginal or crackpot positions in German society and culture. The idea of extermination was blended with eugenics, justifications for war or racial imperialism. It was summarised following the First World War in a Bavarian infantryman's letter to Bavarian Ministerpräsident von Kahr in which the internment of Jews in concentration camps, their murder in reprisal for allied advances into Germany and their complete despoliation are proposed as serious possibilities. Bayerisches Hauptstaatsarchiv, Allgem. StA, M Inn 66 138: cf. Werner Jochmann, 'Die Ausbreitung des Antisemitismus', in *Deutsches Judentum in Krieg und Revolution 1916–1923*. Ein Sammelband herausgegeben von Werner E. Mosse unter Mitwirkung von Arnold Paucker, Tübingen 1971 (Schriftenreihe wissenschaftlicher Abhandlungen des Leo Baeck Instituts 25), p. 450, n. 144. For a recent review of the same see E. Goldhagen, 'Weltanschauung und Endlösung', in *Vierteljahrshefte für Zeitgeschichte* (*VfZ*), 24 (October 1976), No. 4, pp. 379–405. Both extermination and emigration were present simultaneously in some minds at some time in this tradition.

rural migrants from Europe across the seas led forty to sixty million emigrants from Europe to America alone between 1830 and 1939. The Second World War has uprooted about sixty million people. The ebb and flow of migrant labour in post-war Europe, legal and illegal immigration to America, the arrival of ethnically different migrants in Great Britain, the peopling of Palestine/Israel, to quote a few examples culturally close to Western readers, have continued the migratory trend. Movement has surpassed rootedness in the experience of industrial man.[2]

Jewish migration has partaken in both of these worlds, the archetypical tension and the structured rationality. German Jews have been part of the East-West trek and the urbanisation movements of the nineteenth and twentieth centuries. Their acculturation in Germany, the moving closer of two cultural traditions, has been accompanied by movement in physical space. Roots the young believed to be centuries deep had extended to no more than the usual two urban generations in one locality. Jewish urban concentration had been recent, like that of the German environment. The Jewish population reservoirs of Germany's Eastern region (Posen-Poznań, Silesia) and of the Russian and Austro-Hungarian empires (Poland, Galicia) have kept Germany's Southern and Western Jewish populations from the steep decline demographic developments had in store for them.[3]

Structural, i.e., economically motivated, migration, had aroused the concern of governments from early on. Prussian governments of the *Vormärz* period instituted elaborate enquiries to search for immigrants, e.g. from Hesse, Holland or Bavaria, that might have caused a disproportionate growth in the Jewish population. Jewish cultural movements into the coveted preserves of government, university or professional services and occupations were fended off as trespasses on inner space. Throughout modern Jewish history in Germany, the immigrant *Ostjude* cast his shadow over the state governments' migration policies.[4]

In the anti-Jewish movements of the nineteenth and twentieth centuries, preoccupations such as these fixated the spatial theme in minds and literature. The *Ostjude* was to be barred from "moving into" economy and society. Immigration was to be prohibited. He was to be placed under *Fremdenrecht*. Jewish immigrants from Eastern Europe were expelled at regular intervals in spite of German-Jewish resistance to such government action. Police raids (*Razzias*), internment

---

[2]For a review of the literature concerning migration and acculturation see H. A. Strauss, 'Changing Images of the Immigrant in the U.S.A.', in *Amerikastudien/American Studies*, 21, No. 1 (1976), pp. 119–137.

[3]For an excellent review of demographic trends immediately prior to the Nazi period see E. Bennathan, 'Die demographische und wirtschaftliche Struktur der Juden', in *Entscheidungsjahr 1932. Zur Judenfrage in der Endphase der Weimarer Republik*. Ein Sammelband herausgegeben von Werner E. Mosse unter Mitwirkung von Arnold Paucker, Tübingen 1965 (Schriftenreihe wissenschaftlicher Abhandlungen des Leo Baeck Instituts 13), pp. 87–134.

[4]Prussian government enquiry, 1840: cf. H. A. Strauss, 'Prussian Policies towards the Jews 1815–1847', in *LBI Year Book XI* (1966), pp. 112–116; *Ostjuden*: S. Adler-Rudel, *Ostjuden in Deutschland 1880–1940. Zugleich eine Geschichte der Organisationen, die sie betreuten*, Tübingen 1959 (Schriftenreihe wissenschaftlicher Abhandlungen des Leo Baeck Instituts 1). Other information, Ostjuden; courtesy Dr. Jack Wertheimer, New York, N.Y.

at concentration points, threatened expulsions punctuated the disturbed domestic peace after the First World War.[5]

The *Ostjude* turned into the paradigm for his Western brother. The *völkisch* hate literature sprouting after the depression of 1873 called for the placing of Jews in Germany under *Fremdenrecht*. Some writers demanded that all Jews be forced to leave and resettle abroad. By 1912, placing German Jews under *Fremdenrecht* and restricting Jewish cultural and economic freedom became the *alldeutsche* means to force Jews to leave Germany: "Glaubst du," said Heinrich Class, "daß ein ehrenhafter Jude sich solchen Gesetzen unterwirft? Er wird den Staub des unwirtlichen deutschen Bodens von den Füßen schütteln und sich anderwärts eine Heimat suchen. Hart, aber unvermeidlich."[6]

The rise of Social Darwinism, eugenicism and racism created the "racial Jew". Antisemitism was rationalised into race science. Spatial fantasies of removing the Jew covered a wide variety of means to this end. *Fremdenrecht*, the destruction of Jewish participation in public life, the curtailing of Jewish economic activities, were incorporated into the Nazi anti-Jewish programme. Their esoteric intent – the removal of Jews, expulsion, emigration. The killing of the Jew as a hostage for German collective misfortunes or in revenge for alleged misdeeds of "World Jewry" was only marginally present as yet in the miasma of these fantasies. Emigration and extermination were points in the esoteric continuum, means to the spatial ends. Extermination as goal remained unstated in Nazi propaganda until years of persecution had passed, but was present as an insane *ultima ratio* in radical thought, subdued by the *reality* principle of economics and politics. The practical programmes elaborated by Nazi party and (in part former) government officials between 1930 and 1933 reflect the structure of antisemitic programming. They aimed at discriminatory and exclusionary *Fremdenrecht* legislation and at creating a situation that would force Jews out of Germany. Emigration as the immediate goal remained unstated in the unfolding anti-Jewish legislation.[7]

[5]The "Ostjuden" theme recurs in pre-1914 German *völkisch* antisemitism, e.g., in Ahlwardt (1895); Debates in the Prussian Abgeordnetenhaus 20th November and 21st November 1880; Böckel (1887): Dühring (1881); the *Antisemiten-Petition* to Bismarck (1881); *Bund der Landwirte* (1893); Sigl (1896); Schneider (1890); Paasch (1892); the programme of the *Soziale Reichspartei* and other publicists or writers; Treitschke attacks Eastern Jews as well as the urbanisation-migration of German Jews, but considers restrictions on immigration as ineffective for the desired full national and social integration of Jews in Germany, i.e., Jewish self-destruction. (*Preussische Jahrbücher*, 1879–1880). Cf. G. L. Mosse, *The Crisis of German Ideology. Intellectual Origins of the Third Reich*, New York 1964 (pb. edn.), pp. 126–145; L. S. Dawidowicz, *The War against the Jews 1933–1945*, New York 1975 (pb. edn.), pp. 42–62, and printed materials, *sub voce* authors mentioned above.
[6]The emigration-expulsion theme in German antisemitism as linked with demands for placing Jews in Germany under *Fremdenrecht* recurs frequently in conjunction with the theme of removing or barring Jews from participation in German life. A typical example is offered by Konstantin Freiherr von Gebsattel (1913): cf. Jochmann, *loc. cit.*, p. 466. The above quotation is trans. from D. Frymann (pseud. for H. Class), *Wenn ich der Kaiser wär' – Politische Wahrheiten und Notwendigkeiten*, 3rd edn., Leipzig 1912, p. 77. Class summarises pre-war *völkisch* thought on *Fremdenrecht* propagandised after 1918 by the *Völkische Schutz- und Trutzbund*, Count Reventlow and other political figures on the nationalist Right and feeding into the twenty-five-point programme of the Nazi party of 1920. For a (critical) appraisal of the use of police and administrative justice in dealing with aliens in Germany see Ernst Isay, *Das Deutsche Fremdenrecht. Ausländer und Polizei*, Berlin 1923.
[7]Hitler's first recorded antisemitic utterance speaks of "planmässige gesetzliche Bekämpfung und

II. MIGRATION AND RESISTANCE

In response, emigration became the only effective means available to German Jewry in opposing Nazi persecution.[8] It was caused by this persecution, and must be interpreted, in its ebb and flow, as closely related to the ebb and flow of this persecution. It was not planned by the Jewish community, only one of whose segments, the minority Zionist group, had demanded of Jews in Germany that they emigrate to Palestine in existential commitment to the Jewish nation and people. The emigration of Jews from Germany began as a spontaneous movement in 1933, and, as will be argued below, remained largely unaffected by the social planning or policies of Jewish representatives in Germany or abroad. It was the only available means, as it turned out, to save the lives of a considerable part of the Jewish minority in Germany, and to transfer its cultural substance abroad, there to enter into new links with the cultures and societies that had the foresight to receive them.

In spite of its crucial role for the history of German Jewry, the scholarly study of this migration movement, as emigration as well as immigration, has taken a back seat in institutionally sponsored research compared to the pre-1933 period of German-Jewish history, and to the Holocaust period, primarily for Eastern Europe. As a result, many questions remain unanswered. The observations presented in this essay were limited by the lack of *Vorarbeiten*. They should be read with these limitations in mind.

III. DEMOGRAPHIC ASPECTS OF GERMAN JEWRY 1933–1945

Between 1933 and 1945 German Jewry declined from an estimated 525,000 Jews (by religion) to an estimated 25,000 (by "race"). This decline is documented in Table I.

The actual number of persons threatened by the "racial laws" of the Nazi régime exceeded these figures. This group was made up of persons married to a Christian spouse and not of the Jewish religion, and persons of varying degrees of Jewish ancestry, so-called *Mischlinge* not of the Jewish religion. *Mischlinge* of the Jewish religion were considered Jews (*Geltungsjuden*) and exposed to precisely the same measures as Jews. The number of *Mischlinge* remains subject to considerable insecurity. Tables IIa and IIb present some of the estimates and data available.

Beseitigung der Vorrechte des Juden ... (Fremdengesetzgebung). Sein [des Antisemitismus der Vernunft] letztes Ziel muss unverrückbar die Entfernung aller Juden überhaupt sein." (Hitler to Adolf Gemlich, 16 September 1919, in E. Deuerlein, 'Hitlers Eintritt in die Politik und die Reichswehr', *VfZ*, 7 (April 1959), No. 2, p. 204). For the programmes elaborated by Nazi officials 1930–1932 see U. D. Adam, *Judenpolitik im Dritten Reich*, Düsseldorf 1972, pp. 28–46, esp. the programme first published by the late Shaul Esh in *Ha'aretz* (1st April 1963) which aims at the expulsion of the Jews from German life with the hoped-for effect of Jewish emigration "if the laws would be harsh enough". (Adam, *op. cit.*, p. 33).

[8]On this see Konrad Kwiet, 'Problems of Jewish Resistance Historiography', in *LBI Year Book XXIV* (1979), esp. pp. 55–56.

TABLE I
Decline of German Jewry

Year	Number of Jews
1925	564,379
January 1933	525,000 (estimated)
June 1933	499,682
May 1939	213,390
September 1939	185,000
October 1941	164,000
1942	139,000
1st January 1943	51,257
April 1943	31,910
1st September 1944	14,574
mid-1945	25,000 (estimated)

Sources: German census data (1925, June 1933, May 1939); data published by *Reichsvertretung* (*Reichsvereinigung*) *der Juden in Deutschland* (October 1939 to September 1944); estimates (1945).[9] NB: Data for 1939–1944 include "full Jews by race" since they were placed under the jurisdiction of the Jewish *Reichsvereinigung* by decree of 14th July 1939, i.e., including Jewish spouses of "mixed marriages" whose children were Christians.

TABLE IIa
Jews living in mixed marriages

Year	Number of Jewish-Gentile marriages
1933	35,000 (estimate)
May 1939	20,000
1st December 1942	16,760
1st April 1943	16,658
1st September 1944	12,487

TABLE IIb
Persons of Jewish descent (Mischlinge)

Year	Estimated number
1933	292,000
1935	200,000
17th May 1939	84,674 (German census based on self-declarations and probably understated)

Sources: Y. Bauer, p. 114 (1933); Lösener (1935).[10]

[9]*Statistik des Deutschen Reiches*, vol. 451, No. 5; vol. 453, Nos. 2 and 4; 451, No. 5; *Statistisches Jahrbuch für das Deutsche Reich*, 59 (1941/1942); K. Drobisch, *et al.*, *Juden unterm Hakenkreuz. Verfolgung und Ausrottung der deutschen Juden 1933–1945*, Berlin (East) 1973; H. Genschel, *Die Verdrängung der Juden aus der Wirtschaft im Dritten Reich*, Göttingen 1966 (for other sources see tables, *ibid.*, pp. 274–291).

[10]Y. Bauer, *My Brother's Keeper. A History of the American Jewish Joint Distribution Committee 1929–1939*, Philadelphia 1974, p. 114; B. Lösener, 'Als Rassereferent im Reichsministerium des Innern', *VfZ* 9 (July 1961), No. 3, pp. 277–282; Adam, *op. cit.*, p. 136 (quoting Lösener Memorandum, 10th

If the (estimated) number of Jews not affiliated with the Jewish religion (15,000) is added to the total number of Jews by religion, in mixed marriages and by descent, Nazi "racial measures" affected a total of about 867,000 persons living in Germany in 1933 to a greater or lesser degree.

The Jewish population in Germany, long before the rise of Nazism, had "been abnormal in its age structure – compared to the German age structure – in a way bordering on the grotesque". Tables III a, III b and III c indicate the steep acceleration of this "abnormality".

TABLE III a

Changes in the age structure of Jews in Germany, 1933 and 1939

Age	June 1933	September 1939	% Decrease
60 and over	81,400	59,700	27
40–59	157,400	76,600	51
25–39	119,700	24,100	80
16–24	58,600	9,700	83
0–15	82,700	15,000	82
Total	499,800	185,100	

Sources: Genschel, based on *Jüdisches Nachrichtenblatt* (interview with Hirsch); census data 1933; *Reichsvereinigung* statistics 1939.[11]

TABLE III b

Persons 60 years and over

Year	Number	Per cent
1933	81,444	16·30
1938 (beginning)	96,200	27·49
1938 (end)	90,500	30·17
September 1939	59,700	32·25
31st July 1941	60,941	36·44

Source: Adler-Rudel, *Jüdische Selbsthilfe*, pp. 216 f.

November 1935). The figure for 17th May 1939 was obtained by German census takers: "Mischlinge" were to report the Jewish descent of grandparents in closed envelopes to be added to the census form, i.e., incriminate themselves in Nazi eyes, hardly a reliable census situation. The figure is thus probably far below the actual number of such persons.

[11]Genschel, *op. cit.*, p. 263 (the figures in Table IIIa for 1939 from *Jüdisches Nachrichtenblatt* (Berlin), (30th November 1939), interview with Dr. Otto Hirsch; S. Adler-Rudel, *Jüdische Selbsthilfe unter dem Naziregime 1933–1939 im Spiegel der Berichte der Reichsvertretung der Juden in Deutschland*, Tübingen 1974 (Schriftenreihe wissenschaftlicher Abhandlungen des Leo Baeck Instituts 29), pp. 216f. At the Wannsee Conference 15th–17th January 1942, Heydrich estimated that 30 per cent of Jews in Germany were sixty-five years or older: cf. Drobisch, *op. cit.*, p. 306.

TABLE IIIc

Jews age 0–18, 1933–1941

Age	1933	%	1938a	%	1938b	%	9/1939	%	7/1941	%
0–6	24,318	4·87	7,200	2·06	6,000	2				
0–16	86,219	17·26	35,700	10·20						
0–17					36,600	12·20				
0–15							15,000	8·1		
0–18									20,669*	12·36

*About 15,400 Jews by religion. *Source:* Adler-Rudel, *Jüdische Selbsthilfe*, pp. 218 f.

TABLE IVa

Children born to Jews, 1933–1939

Year	Jews by race	Jews by religion
1933	1,246	1,146
1934	1,001	903
1935	1,139	1,046
1936	1,109	992
1937	1,174	1,076
1938	1,230	1,117
1939*	325	284
Total	7,218	6,564

*January to 31st May 1939.

TABLE IVb

Children born to Mischlinge (with two Jewish grandparents), 1933–1939

Year	Number born	Jews by religion
1933	1,095	180
1934	1,052	147
1935	992	157
1936	715	108
1937	647	102
1938	614	69
1939*	174	16
Total	5,289	779

*January to 31st May 1939.

An additional illustration of the steep demographic decline of German Jews is provided by the number of births and the (partly estimated) excess of deaths over births for the period. This is outlined in Tables IV a–d.

TABLE IV c

Children born to Mischlinge (with one Jewish grandparent), 1933–1939

Year	Number born	Jews by religion
1933	920	4
1934	979	6
1935	1,044	3
1936	998	4
1937	936	5
1938	973	4
1939*	388	3
Total	6,238	29

*January to 31st May 1939.
Source for Tables IV a–c: German census, 1939.[12]

TABLE IV d

Excess of births over deaths among Jews in Germany, 1933–1935

Years	Number
1933–1938	29,500
1938–1939	18,000
1940–1941	12,000
1942–1945	13,500
Total	72,000

Sources: Genschel; R. Korherr, 'Der Inspekteur für Statistik' of the RSHA reported a total of 61,693 for 1933–1942. See S. Klarsfeld (ed.), *The Holocaust and the Neo-Nazi Mythomania*, New York 1978, App. (The first Korherr Report), p. 169. The figures for Jewish births quoted by Korherr, *op.cit.*, p. 181 combine Tables IV a to d, and use slightly different base figures. His total for Jewish births, 1933–1942 is 15,221.[13]

[12]*Statistik des Deutschen Reiches*, vol. 552, No. 4 (1944), pp. 40–41.
[13]Genschel, *op. cit.*, p. 291. The late Hanns Reissner, in personal communication with the author, argued that the figures compiled in Table IVb exaggerated the excess of deaths over births by a factor of 2 (72,000 as compared to 35,000) and estimated both emigration and extermination figures correspondingly higher. (285,000 émigrés over against 270,000.) In view of the age structure of Jews in Germany, and the excessive suicide rate prior to the assembly of Jews for deportation in Berlin (10 per cent according to my information, obtained at the time from the *Jüdische Gemeinde*

TABLE Va

Jews of German and foreign nationality in Germany, 1925, 1933 and 1939

	1925			1933			1939		
	Tot. Jews	For. nat.	%	Tot. Jews	For. nat.	%	Tot. Jews	For. nat.	%
Total	564,000	107,747	19·1	499,682	98,747	19·8	221,763	25,783	11·6
Prussia	403,969	76,387	18·9	361,826	84,801	23·4	165,897	17,000*	10·2*
Berlin	172,672	43,838	25·4	160,564	48,075	29·9	78,713	15,000*	19·0*
Saxony	23,000*	15,000*	65·2*	20,584	13,716	66·6	7,017	4,000*	57·0*
Leipzig	12,700*	10,250*	80·7*	11,564	8,547	73·9	5,000*	2,500*	50·0*
Munich	10,000*	2,700*	27·0*	9,005	2,408	26·7	5,000*	1,000*	20·0*
Dresden	5,000*	3,000*	60·0*	4,397	2,671	60·7	2,000*	1,000*	50·0*

* Estimated. *Source:* Adler-Rudel.[14]

TABLE Vb

Nationalities of foreign Jews in Germany, 1925, 1933 and 1939

Nationality	Total foreign Jews 1925		Total foreign Jews 1933		Total foreign Jews 1939	
	No.	%	No.	%	No.	%
Poland	50,993	47·3	56,480	37·2	10,000	38·8
Austria	13,509	12·5	4,647	4·7		
Czechoslovakia	5,620	5·2	4,275	4·3	500	1·9
Hungary	3,179	3·0	2,280	2·3	800	3·1
Romania	3,240	3·0	2,210	2·2	500	1·9
USSR (Russia)	9,505	8·8	1,650	1·7	100	0·4
Latvia/Lithuania	3,063	2·9	1,730	1·8	100	0·4
Other	7,776	7·2	5,515	5·6	600	2·3
Stateless	9,908	9·2	19,746	20·0	13,000	50·4
No information	954	0·9	214	0·2	200	0·8
Total	107,747	100·0	98,747	100·0	25,800	100·0

Source: see Table Va.

German Jews, the introduction makes clear, had been kept from steeper demographic decline by the immigration of foreign Jews which had set in in larger numbers with 1880. The process of their naturalisation as German citizens had been much impeded since the state governments, to whose jurisdiction naturalisation proceedings in part belonged, had been slow in granting naturalisation to foreign Jews. As a result, significant numbers of German-born and acculturated children of foreign Jewish immigrants continued to bear foreign passports. Nationality and acculteration did not coincide.

Tables Va and Vb indicate the decline in the number of foreign Jews in Germany, and their national origin.

Foreign Jews in Germany thus did not completely compensate for the decline in fertility among German Jews by number of immigrants. Fertility among foreign Jews has been presumed as being higher than among German Jews whose number would have diminished further without immigrants. Their decline 1933–1939 was steeper than that of German Jews (from 19·1 per cent of all Jews in 1933 to 11·6 per cent in 1939).

Berlin up to 1943, a 25 per cent according to B. Blau, 'Die Juden in Deutschland von 1939– (sic) 1945', in *Judaica* 7 (1951), pp. 271–284) the higher death figure appears more likely, although a margin of error in these estimates (were suicides of persons on deportation lists counted as deportees or suicides?) cannot be excluded.

[14] Adler-Rudel, *Ostjuden in Deutschland*, p. 165. Asterisked figures are estimates. Figures for 1939 based on German census data: cf. *Wirtschaft und Statistik*, 31 (May 1941) No. 9.

Information on the social and economic development of German Jewry during the Nazi period will have to be deferred at this point, since the basic trends cannot be properly understood without a consideration of Nazi policies and the Jewish responses evolved in reaction to these policies. The census data of 1939, obtained following the complete destruction of Jewish economic activities on 9th/10th November 1938 (semi-ironically dubbed *"Kristallnacht"* (*Reichskristallnacht*), fail to reveal socio-economic changes prior to that destruction. No cohesive analysis of the period based on the published or new archival data is known to this writer. However, some aspects of Jewish socio-economic conditions at the beginning of the period under discussion appear relevant for developments during the period and thus for emigration.[15]

The urbanisation of the German-Jewish population, like its demographic development, had anticipated the trend towards leaving the countryside among the general population for some time prior to the Nazi period. (It had corresponded in extent to the urban drift of similar socio-economic groups in the general population.) In 1933, this trend, accentuated by the economic dislocations of the depression, had concentrated 49·6 per cent of the entire Jewish population in six major cities. This is shown in Table VI.

TABLE VI

The Jewish population in six German cosmopolitan cities
(Großstädte), 1933

	Population	% pop. general	% Jews
Berlin	160,564	3·8	32·1
Frankfurt a. Main	26,158	4·7	5·2
Breslau	20,202	3·2	4·0
Hamburg	16,885	1·5	3·4
Cologne	14,816	2·0	3·0
Leipzig	11,564	1·6	2·3
Totals six cities	250,189	33·36	49·6[16]

In all other forty-six German *Großstädte* (over 100,000 inhabitants) lived 103,931 Jews, or 0·9 per cent of the population of these cities, and 20·8 per cent of the Jewish population.

Thus, the total percentage of Jews living in major cities in 1933 amounted to 354,121 persons or 67·8 per cent of the Jewish population.

---

[15]See also below, pp. 338 ff.
[16]M. P. Birnbaum, 'Die jüdische Bevölkerung in Preussen. Verteilung und Struktur im Jahre 1931', in *Gegenwart im Rückblick. Festgabe für die Jüdische Gemeinde zu Berlin 25 Jahre nach dem Neubeginn*, H. A. Strauss and Kurt R. Grossmann (eds.), Heidelberg 1970, p. 118.

By 1937, 200 of the 1,600 Jewish *Gemeinden* (congregations, corporations under public law until 1st January 1938[17]) had ceased to exist, while the rate of Jewish concentration in seven major *Großgemeinden* (cosmopolitan Jewish congregations) had reached 63 per cent of the Jewish population. Eighty-five per cent of all Jews in Germany now lived in fifty-two *Gemeinden*, while only 15 per cent resided in the remaining 1,348 congregations.[18]

Already prior to 1933, the cities had attracted economically more viable and younger members of the Jewish community in search of economic advance or careers closed to talent in the confinement of the village or small town. Exceptions to this general observation, leaving special local conditions aside, rural and small-town Jewish *Gemeinden* contrasted sharply in per capita income with their larger sister congregations. Persecution-related conditions continued this trend during the Nazi period. Emigration was paralleled by internal migration. In October 1938, 42 per cent of all Jews in Germany (127,600 persons) lived in Berlin alone. Jewish welfare agencies furthered the trend away from small Jewish settlements because concentration allowed more effective social care. The rural Jew of the Nazi period was an impoverished Jew in many sectors of the country.[19]

Statistics do not reveal the qualitative role Jews played in German economic life, some of whose sectors were led by Jewish firms (branch-leadership) while others (textiles, furs, the metal trade, the – declining – private banking industry) were characterised by significant concentration of Jewish businesses or professionals. Compared to the Christian environment, the German-Jewish group had distinct economic characteristics. More than the Christian population, Jews had engaged in *Handel und Verkehr* (trade and commerce), 61·3 per cent of the Jewish, as compared to 19·4 per cent of the general population in 1933. Jews were also strongly represented in professions and public or private service jobs (12·5 per cent, as compared to 8·4 per cent). Fewer Jews had been occupied in industry or the crafts (32·1 per cent, as compared to 40·4 per cent), in agriculture and forestry (1·7 per cent, as compared to 28·9 per cent – all data for 1933). Almost half of the Jewish population (46 per cent, as compared to 16·4 per cent) were self-employed. One third of the Jewish population were white-collar employees, and only 8·7 per cent classified themselves as workers (as compared to 46·4 per cent of the general population). In Bennathan's description Jews were primarily

> "by profession economically independent breadwinners or employees in the commercial departments and the administration of commercial enterprises. The self-employed, too . . . commercially trained and active as businessmen. In every branch of industry Jews were employed in the office, in sales, as travelling salesmen, or commercial administrators (*kaufmännische Direktoren*). The only exception to this rule were craftsmen (like tailors and butchers) and the legal and medical professions . . . Of 240,000 breadwinners (1933) (and their employed families) about 200,000 belonged to the major 'Jewish' categories (self-employed and leaseholders (66,891), commercial employees (83,398), textile and leather industries (11,651), health-related professions (8,006), and legal profession (4,442), teaching and academic pursuits (4,885), the arts, film and photography (4,245). Only 12,972 Jews were workers, mechanics, employed in the food industry or related clerical positions."[20]

[17]See below, p. 342.
[18]Adler-Rudel, *Jüdische Selbsthilfe*, pp. 150 ff.
[19]*Ibid.*, pp. 150–158.
[20]H. A. Strauss, 'The Immigration and Acculturation of the German Jew in the United States of America', in *LBI Year Book XVI* (1971), pp. 76 f.; Bennathan, *loc. cit.*, pp. 112 f.

Although the average income of the Jewish appears to have exceeded that of the general population, including wage earners in 1931 and subsequently,[21] the majority of German Jews in 1933 belonged socially to the lower middle and working classes (33·5 per cent employees, 8·7 per cent workers including immigrant workers, and a substantial – unknown – percentage of the self-employed). The numbers of the indigent and people on public assistance had increased with the onset of the depression. Structural factors increasingly barred the classical route of commercial employees towards independence:

> "As a result of growing state capitalism and an increase in the number of cartels and trusts, more and more Jews were eliminated from their economic positions, especially in commerce, and many lost their independence as employers."

Precise data are as yet unavailable to estimate the number of persons belonging to the middle and upper middle classes among German Jews, either in terms of the German status system and its (partly pre-modern) ascriptive values, in terms of income, or in regional or local status and class contexts. The census data suggest a relatively stronger representation of these classes among Jews – although on somewhat different status-value terms than among the general population.[22]

IV. DEMOGRAPHIC ASPECTS OF GERMAN-JEWISH EMIGRATION

American folklore and most American immigration research institutions and archives perceive post-1880 immigrants as young adult workers or as families with a respectable number of children passing through Ellis Island on the way to an ethnic ghettto, a steel mill, the railroads or a sweatshop, to become the subject, in the 1970s, of the new American labour history, recently attuned to its ethnic components.[23]

German-Jewish realities did not correspond to this classic image. In numbers and social type, the Jewish immigrant from Germany resembled more the 300,000 French Huguenots expelled from France in the wake of the revocation of the Edict of Nantes in 1685, or the 150,000 Jews estimated to have lived in Castile prior to 1492. Basically urban, an ageing and over-aged group, concentrated in commerce and selected professions, their occupational structure reflected choices made long before the emigration crisis had brought home that industrial concentration and large-scale merchandising and sales organisations

---

[21]Birnbaum, *loc. cit.*, p. 113. The "self-employed" included considerable numbers of small establishments (agents, salesmen, repairmen, petty retailers of all kinds and similar businesses). Persons who lost their jobs would characteristically gravitate towards independence, apart from the trend towards independence observed as characteristic of Jewish economic attitudes. Jewish over-representation in this category dwindles if it is compared to the parallel occupational group. Bennathan, *loc. cit.*

[22]R. Stahl, 'Vocational Retraining among Jews in Nazi Germany, 1933–1938', in Jewish Social Studies (1939), p. 169.

[23]For a concise statement of the new orientation of American labour history towards ethnicity see H. G. Gutman, 'Work, Culture and Society in Industrializing America, 1815–1919', *American Historical Review* 78 (1973), No. 3, pp. 531–587.

were relegating their small-scale entrepreneurial or crafts' skills to a backwater. The major obstacle to Jewish mass emigration lay probably as much in the occupational and age structure of the Jewish community, as it derived from Jewish perceptions of themselves in their relationship to German society and politics, or in restrictionism in immigration countries.

The total number of all persons leaving Germany on account of "racial" persecution cannot be established. Up to 867,000 Jewish and "non-Aryan" Germans were affected by Nazi decrees barring officials, students, university teachers, pastors, actors, writers, journalists or political activists from exercising their professions, pursuing studies at universities, completing their examinations, doing business or entering upon their careers.[24] Statistics on aid given to them, when available in the limited literature on the subject, are insufficient. Considerable numbers of "non-Aryan" Christian Germans may be presumed to have been active in government, politics, the professions, industry or commerce, and if they emigrated at all, to have gone unrecorded by any census, without the aid of the Protestant, Catholic or Society of Friends agencies that aided their co-religionists. Estimates of the total number of émigrés from Germany, Austria and

TABLE VII

Total number of émigrés

Year	Jew. pop.	1,000 Emigr.	1,000 Excess deaths	1,000 Deport.
1933	525,000(est.)	37	5.5	
1934		23	5.5	
1935		21	5.5	
1936		25	6.0	
1937		23	7.0	
1938		40	8.0	
17th May 1939	213,390			
31st December 1939		78	10	
1940		15	8	10
1st May 1941	169,000			
1st October 1941	164,000	8	4	25
1942	139,000 ⎫		7.5	73
1943	51,000 ⎬	8.5	5	25
1944	14,500 ⎭			1
1945	20–25,000			
Total		278,500	72,000	134,000

Sources: Genschel; Rosenstock; Blau.[26]

[24]See, e.g., L. E. Reutter, *Die Hilfstätigkeit katholischer Organisationen und kirchlicher Stellen für die im nationalsozialistischen Deutschland Verfolgten*, 2nd edn., Hamburg 1970.

Czechoslovakia range up to 500,000, including persons not of the Jewish religion.[25]

The total number of Jewish émigrés can be estimated from German census data, Jewish sources and the reports periodically submitted to Nazi authorities by the *Reichsvereinigung* during the Second World War. Table VII summarises these data.

Given a certain margin of error, an estimate of between 270,000 and 300,000 Jewish émigrés from Germany appears a reasonable approximation, born out by cross-checks with the available census totals. About 30,000 of these are estimated to have been interned in their countries of refuge in occupied Europe during the Second World War, and to have perished in the Holocaust. Comparisons with the official statistics of immigration countries are inconclusive because of the frequent double-counts of persons re-emigrating from their first country of settlement, the lumping together of all Central European refugees into one category, the use of visitors' visas for immigration in the expectation of converting them into permanent residence permits following arrival, and of illegal entry. Thus, about three-fifths of German Jewry succeeded in leaving the country. About 10,000 Jews (5,000 in hiding, and 5,000 returnees from concentration camps) or less than 1·5 per cent of the original 525,000 German Jews of 1933 survived in Germany.

The age composition of émigrés as implied by Tables IIIa to c was weighted towards the young and the productive middle-aged cohorts, as would be expected. The ratio of persons over sixty years of age climbed from 16·54 per cent in 1933 to 36·44 per cent in July 1941, while persons between nought and thirty-nine years of age decreased by 80–83 per cent. In contrast, the ratio of children under eighteen years of age (the available data are not entirely comparable) suggests a smaller relative decline in spite of the steep decrease in absolute numbers.

[25] W. Röder, Institut für Zeitgeschichte, München (personal communication), 1976/1977.

[26] Adjusted from Genschel, *op. cit.*, p. 291; German census data (see n. 9); W. Rosenstock, 'Exodus 1933–1939. A Survey of Jewish Emigration from Germany', in *LBI Year Book I* (1956), p. 377 (Rosenstock's are the most precise and reliable of the available estimates); Blau, *loc. cit.* These data, it should be stressed, rest to some extent on estimates. Possible changes concern individuals who had left the Jewish religion and succeeded in changing to "privileged status" in passing into the non-Jewish community, or emigrated as "non-Aryan" Christians. (Conversions for the period were estimated by one source – Blau – as 3,319.) Emigration figures are based in part on estimates, especially for the first few years of the period, where flight and the repatriation of foreign nationals as well as returns by persons who had left Germany and returned subsequently (see below p. 357) made precise recording difficult. Precise Jewish statistics on émigrés are available only for the period January 1937 to June 1938, and in the unpublished reports submitted periodically by the *Reichsvereinigung* to Nazi authorities during the Second World War. These reports had been used by Blau, *loc. cit.* and by Drobitsch, *op. cit.*, SS statistics on emigration are based on unrefined calculations. Korherr in Klarsfeld, *op. cit.*, p. 182, includes Sudetenland Jewish emigration in his figure of 352,534 for 1st January 1943. Heydrich, at the Wannsee Conference of January 1943, spoke of 360,000 émigrés from the *Altreich*. Suicides to avoid being deported to concentration camps were estimated at 10 per cent of the number called up for deportation, as this writer learned in Berlin in 1941–1942. Other estimates place the ratio of such suicides as high as 25 per cent (Blau). The number of "non-Aryans" found in 1945 in Germany includes about 14,000 living "legally in mixed marriages not subject to deportations" (and not included in the census figure for 16th June 1933 for "Jews by religion"). The number of Jews surviving in hiding in Germany until 1945 estimated at 5,000 is equally subject to insecurities. Finally, one estimate had placed the number of émigrés at 254,000 (Blau, *loc. cit.*), another at 236,000 (Adler-Rudel, *Jüdische Selbsthilfe*).

The emigration of children of school-leaving age had been one of the first priorities of the *Reichsvertretung* in 1933,[27] and at least 18,000 children had left Germany as "unaccompanied children" to be placed in foster homes or families.[28] The relatively large number of children aged nought to six in 1938 suggests the hypothesis that families with infants tended to postpone emigration. The 1938 figure presumably includes the 7,200 children born 1933/1938. Additional factors contributing to the relatively large percentage of children remaining in July 1941 (to which 2,270 "non-Aryan" Christian children must be added) may have been the failure of major countries, above all the U.S.A. and the British Colonial Office and the High Commissioner for Palestine, to permit the non-quota immigration of unaccompanied children. In the U.S.A., the German-Jewish Childrens' Aid Committee asked that only children from well-to-do families be selected from among German Jews for placement in U.S. foster homes. This was designed to minimise the social problems expected from poorer children. Placement also bogged down in the interminable bureaucratic paper-shuffling characteristic of some social agencies. A bill to admit German-Jewish children outside the U.S. quota, the Wagner–Rogers bill, was never reported out of Committee since Congressional support for lifting immigration restrictions was missing in 1939. Following the *Kristallnacht*, the *yishuv* in Palestine offered to arrange for the adoption of 10,000 Jewish children from Germany, and to receive 100,000 German Jews still of productive age. This was rejected by the Colonial Secretary who offered to admit Jewish children to Great Britain instead, if Jewish aid organisations would guarantee their maintenance. The admission of about 8,000 unaccompanied children to Great Britain after November 1938 was thus "firmly linked" with British immigration policies on Palestine. 3,262 children were brought by emigration to Palestine through the good offices of the *Youth Aliyah*, whose German branch (*Arbeitsgemeinschaft für Kinder- und Jugend-Alijah*) cooperated with Palestine's childrens' village "Ben Shemen", childrens' homes and the kibbutz organisations to resettle them following preparatory training. Finally, reluctance among German-Jewish families to part with children, and to have children complete their schooling before emigrating may have been a further influence on the low number of emigrating unaccompanied children.[29]

Foreign Jews, i.e., Jews of foreign nationality, as may be inferred from Table V a, were concentrated heavily in the major cities of Prussia and Saxony. The attack on their residence in Germany had been a continuous programme point of *völkisch* antisemitism since the 1880s. In consequence, when the Prussian Conser-

[27]See the forthcoming Pt. II of this essay in *LBI Year Book XXVI* (1981).
[28]For regulations governing the selection of unaccompanied children to the U.S.A. see *The Jewish Immigrant of the Nazi Period in the U.S.A.*, vol. I: *Archival Resources*, comp. S. W. Siegel, New York 1979; H. L. Feingold, *The Politics of Rescue. The Roosevelt Administration and the Holocaust, 1938–1945*, New Brunswick, N.J. 1970, pp. 148–155. For the admission of unaccompanied children to Great Britain see A. J. Sherman, *Island Refuge. Britain and the Refugees from the Third Reich 1933–1939*, Berkeley–Los Angeles 1973, p. 211 (House of Commons Debate 14th December 1938). See also Adler-Rudel, *Jüdische Selbsthilfe*, pp. 97–100.
[29]H. Gärtner, 'Problems of Jewish Schools in Germany during the Hitler Regime', in *LBI Year Book I* (1956), pp. 126–129, 138–141, records that parents tended to keep their children in German schools to complete their education before emigration, even where equivalent Jewish schools were available.

vative coup of 20th July 1932 ousted the elected Social Democratic administration, they came under attack even before Hitler's ascendance to power. The Conservative Prussian Minister of the Interior, von Gayl, had prepared a decree allowing for the revocation of their acquired German nationality for persons naturalised between 9th November 1918 and 30th January 1933. This decree was enacted by the Nazi government 14th July 1933. By 1936, 2,200 naturalisations had been revoked in Saxony alone.[30]

As far as can be gathered from the available information, foreign Jews formed strong components of the crafts, especially in the textile, cigarette, shoe, beauty, leather and cleaning industries, while their entrepreneurial and commercial classes were active in these fields and in the arts (theatre, opera, music) and in real estate ownership and management.[31] In 1933, Jews of foreign nationality are said to have left small or middle-sized towns in appreciable numbers and joined the *Binnenwanderung* of German Jews.[32] About 10,000 to 12,000 Jews of foreign, mostly Eastern and South-eastern European nationality, were assisted by the *Hauptstelle für jüdische Wanderung*, Berlin, which had cared for Jews of foreign nationality since the First World War to return to their country of origin or nationality. Repatriates thus represented almost 30 per cent of all Jewish émigrés from Germany in 1933. In 1936, the number of trans-migrants of foreign nationality (present in smaller numbers earlier on) "increased". The first group of émigrés among Jews of foreign nationality had a preponderance of younger men (age and sex distribution among this group appeared to have differed from that of German Jews as a whole in having more youth and an excess of men over women)[33] and included primarily persons marginally integrated into the German economy. By 1936, *Hauptstelle* statistics suggest, 24,200 Jews had been assisted in their repatriation, i.e., if these figures are correct and their number is included in the totals for émigrés, of a total of 106,000 émigrés, almost one fourth had been repatriates of foreign nationality by 1936.

The role of foreign Jews in emigration patterns from Germany, aside from isolated information and repatriation figures, has not been analysed at this writing. The number of foreign Jews included in émigrés to other countries than Palestine has never been determined. It would have to be added to the number of repatriates to arrive at more precise determinations of the ratio of foreign Jewish to German-Jewish emigration. Their position in Nazi Germany was ambivalent, since they were protected by their status as foreign nationals and made the occasion for numerous intercessions at the *Auswärtiges Amt* by foreign diplomats when their rights were violated. Fearing reprisals against Germans abroad (*Auslandsdeutsche*), the Foreign Office remained sensitive to such intercessions. However, it did reject all protests against the mistreatment of German Jews as "interference in German domestic affairs". On the other hand, foreign Jews were strongly represented in sectors of the economy that were accessible to informal radical and terror pressures (workers and employees, retails and crafts,

[30]*Rasse und Recht*, Ristow (ed.), I (1937), p. 423, as quoted by Adam, *op. cit.*, p. 81 n. 65.
[31]Bennathan, *loc. cit.*, p. 122.
[32]Information courtesy Prof. Henry Huttenbach, Department of History, The City College New York (unpublished study), 1978.
[33]Adler-Rudel, *Jüdische Selbsthilfe*, pp. 94–99; Bennathan, *loc. cit.*, p. 99 n. 19.

travelling salesmen and fair-going) and to administrative discriminations in granting or renewing licence. No data have so far come to light to assess the importance of these factors for the group's pattern of emigration.

By 1939, the ratio of foreign Jews had declined more steeply than that of Jews of German nationality (from 19·8 per cent of all Jews to 11·6 per cent of all Jews in Germany). Among the factors that may have contributed to this result were the brutal expulsion of 14,000 to 17,000 Jews of Polish nationality on 28th October 1938, the younger age structure, wider links with relatives abroad and marginality in the economy.

The ratio of immigrants of foreign nationality among immigrants from Germany to Palestine, 1933–1945 appears to have remained below the ratio of such Jews in the German-Jewish population.[34]

V. NAZI PERSECUTION: PATTERN AND POLICIES

The truism that the pattern of Nazi persecution was the root cause of the pattern of Jewish emigration presents complex problems at closer analysis, because the factors that made Nazi policies towards Jews polymorphous also created a confused reality, and led to confused perceptions among almost all parties to the deed, including the victims whose emigration is the subject of this essay.

The statistical pattern reviewed above shows that Jewish emigration from Germany fell from a peak of 37,000 in 1933, to 21,000 in 1935, rose to 25,000 in 1936, fell once again in 1937 and reached its final crescendo in 1938 before and after the pogroms of 9th/10th November, the *Kristallnacht*, to continue through 1940.

Nazi persecution was equally divided into periods if nation-wide trends and *Reich*-level measures are considered.[35]

The first period, from 30th January 1933 to mid-1933, was dominated by the multiple violence occurring across Germany. It was mainly perpetrated by the SA which, in several states, had been drafted as auxiliary policemen. The main targets of this violence were political enemies of the régime, persons against whom local Nazi individuals harboured political – sometimes personal – grudges, lawyers, physicians, members of the *Reichstag*, persons considered guilty of past misdeeds, etc. On 1st July 1933, the Ministry of the Interior recorded that 26,789 persons were held in "protective custody", the euphemism for the internment of political opponents.[36] All of these victims included persons of the

[34]See Tables Va and Vb, pp. 321–322 above.
[35]Coherent accounts of Nazi policies: Adam, *op. cit.* (for internal decision-development and policy), and Genschel *op. cit.* (economic policy). The following is based on these two accounts and: Adler-Rudel, *Jüdische Selbsthilfe*; Bauer, *op. cit.*; Blau, *Das Ausnahmerecht für die Juden in Deutschland 1933–1945*, 2nd edn., Düsseldorf 1954 (collection of laws); Dawidowicz, *op. cit.*; R. Hilberg, *The Destruction of European Jews*, Chicago 1961, pp. 43–124; H. Krausnick, 'The Persecution of the Jews', in H. Krausnick *et al.*, *Anatomy of the SS State*, New York 1968, pp. 1–126; H. Buchheim, 'The SS-Instrument of Domination', *ibid.*, pp. 127–302; M. Broszat, 'The Concentration Camps 1933–1945', *ibid.*, pp. 397–460. F. Neumann, *Behemoth. The Structure and Practice of National Socialism 1933–1944*, revised edn. (pb. reprint), New York 1963. Also consulted for background social history: *Oral History Collection*, Research Foundation for Jewish Immigration, New York.
[36]M. Broszat, *op. cit.*, p. 410.

Jewish religion. Sadistic tortures, beatings and gangster-like killings characterised these events. They went on in a highly charged atmosphere of street demonstrations, marches, elections, the take-over of state and local governments and the dissolution of the political parties, workers' associations and trade unions.

For the Jewish minority *qua* Jews this terror phase brought legislative exclusion primarily from "public life" – *öffentliches Leben* – including the removal of certain categories of civil servants, lawyers and judges, a curtailment of the activities of Jewish physicians, etc. The "boycott day" of 1st April 1933, and widespread local pressures brought attacks on Jewish retail stores and large-scale dismissals of Jewish employees, partly (under pressure) by Jewish-owned firms. Jews began to be excluded from cultural activities, the press and the arts. As associations were brought in line with Nazi principles – *gleichgeschaltet* – numerous Jews lost their positions. Antisemitic propaganda and harassment were intense, but did not lead – they never did in Germany – to non-organised, spontaneous pogrom-style attacks on Jews. The passivity of broad strata of the population in Germany remained a constant throughout the period of persecution.[37]

Phase II began during the summer of 1933. Sadistic SA brutalities were confined and institutionalised in the newly founded concentration camps. Legislative activity against Jews continued. It affected primarily professionals, students, foreign Jews, Jewish employees and workers, the legal position of Jews, the theatre and Jewish business. Characteristic for this phase of creeping persecution was the announced intention not to interfere with Jewish economic activities. This was declared *Reich*-policy. Numerous attacks and pressures of many kinds by local Nazi organisations and propaganda agencies as well as intense defamation continued.

Phase III divided into two sub-periods. In April 1935, a new wave of street terror and propaganda attacks began nation-wide, culminating in July in pogrom-like mass attacks by Hitler Youth and SA on Jews on the Berlin Kurfürstendamm. This sub-phase was stopped by the party leadership on Hitler's orders. The Nuremberg Laws passed on 12th September 1935 and subsequent *Verordnungen* deprived Jews of German citizenship rights and led to the exclusion of all remaining Jewish civil servants, artists, university teachers, judges and other public servants. The activities of other professionals like lawyers and physicians continued to be curbed, and Jewish art dealers prohibited from pursuing their business. Legal and local economic pressures to force the sale of Jewish business continued, but Jewish business kept being assured by *Reich* agencies that its activities would be protected.

Phase IV, covering most of 1936 and extending into the autumn of 1937, once again saw creeping persecution, primarily through continued Nazi pressures on local levels. *Reich* decrees excluding Jews from the economy extended to occupations considered "semi-public" or "quasi-public" in Germany, such as accountants, consultants on foreign currency or tax matters, apothecaries, veterinarians, book-dealers, publishers and similar groups. Creeping pressures were also exerted

[37]See also Kwiet, *loc. cit.*, esp. p. 45.

on rural cattle and produce traders, Jewish representatives of large companies working abroad and on Jewish private banks. (Some large companies had shifted Jewish managers abroad to promote business and protect them and their employers from Nazi harassment.)

In the autumn of 1937, Phase V opened with a concerted drive to force the sale of the remaining (1st April 1938: 39,552) business establishments, an estimated 50 per cent of the number existing in 1933.[38] The drive to "Aryanise" (enforce the transfer of business from a Jewish to a German owner at depressed prices) now extended systematically to big Jewish business and manufacturing. Persons owning more than RM 5,000 were obligated to register all their holdings with the government in April 1938, and a series of *Berufsverbote* and decrees sharply narrowed the sphere of Jewish economic activities. Physicians and lawyers lost their remaining practices. Licences were withdrawn from salesmen and agents. Jewish communal institutions suffered a change in legal status and severe disadvantages in their economic and service activities. In mid-1938, the synagogues of Munich, Düsseldorf and Nuremberg were torn down as part of "urban renewal" or to make way for subway construction. On 28th October 1938, between 14,000 and 17,000 Polish-Jewish nationals were expelled to Poland under inhuman conditions. Following the pogroms of 9th/10th November 1938, all Jewish activities in the German economy were prohibited, Jews were forced to make good the damage they suffered through the organised vandalism of SA units across Germany and to pay RM 1·25 billion to "atone" for the murder of German diplomat Ernst vom Rath at the hands of a Jewish student in Paris. About 30,000 Jewish men were interned in German concentration camps.

The last phase, VI, of the emigration period lasted until October 1941. Jews were now forced to live off their savings or receive social asssistance. They were drafted into forced labour in factories or had to accept low menial jobs. The first deportations began in 1940 (Baden, Stettin, Vienna, Prague, Moravska-Ostrava). On 1st October 1941, the RSHA prohibited further emigration, although exceptions to this prohibition continued throughout the later war years.

Already this first review suggests that, in its framework of defamation and anti-Jewish propaganda, Nazi persecution was selective in the groups whose economic or professional activities it curtailed or destroyed. The periodisation of this summary reveals two kinds of influence patterns: an interplay between terror and street pressure and legislative measures, and between *Reich* level measures and local or regional pressures. Both in its "on-again-off-again" timing, and in the action patterns occurring on the different levels of German social and political space, persecution policy was polymorphous.

The political activities from which the pattern of persecution derived tend to support this observation.

---

[38]A. Krüger, *Die Lösung der Judenfrage in der deutschen Wirtschaft. Kommentar zur Judengesetzgebung*, Berlin 1940, p. 44. Krüger was a *Ministerialrat* in the Economics Ministry. The figure 39,552 is based on the Nazi registration of Jewish business decreed on 26th April 1938. The figure for 1933 was an Economics Ministry estimate.

It has often been pointed out, in part with apologetic intent, that even under the extreme propagandistic and terror pressures accompanying the German elections of 5th March 1933, the Nazi vote rose only to 43·9 per cent from its earlier high (in completely free elections) of 37·3 per cent (1932a). Phrased differently, the about 51·9 per cent of Nazi and German nationalist voters supporting Hitler outright in March 1933 saw no hindrance in the antisemitic policies with which the Nazi party had interlaced its electoral appeals with varying degrees of salience and intensity. German right-nationalist antisemitism, the literature has made abundantly clear, rested on older anti-Jewish traditions. Conservatives had accepted an antisemitic platform for their party as early as 1892 (Tivoli Programme). The ready acceptance of Hitler's chancellorship by Conservatives, Catholic political leaders, church dignitaries and the *Beamtenschaft* rested to a considerable extent on a common anti-liberal and anti-modernist political mood for which Jews exemplified the enemy, especially in such highly visible fields as journalism, films, literature and the arts (the cosmopolitan avant-garde minority culture misnamed "Weimar culture").[39]

Thus, in 1933, not one but several antisemitic strains coexisted within the broad consensus of centre-right government and politics. Programmes for anti-Jewish action prepared by Nazi "shadow" ministerial and party officials before 1933, and the legislative programme dated 6th April 1933, first published by the late Israeli scholar Shaul Esh in 1963, summarise the consensus among the several strains of antisemitism in Germany.[40]

The administrative travail from whose strained intra-governmental and intra-party quarrels the over 400 anti-Jewish *Reich* laws and decrees were born, reflect, in part, the disintegration of the *völkisch*-centrist consensus of 1933. These administrative quarrels – which do not indicate opposition to antisemitism, or philo-semitic trends within the ministerial bureaucracy – explain changes in policy only to a limited degree and derive from several sources. They originate, for one, in the "*institutionelle Bewahrungspolitik*" typical of polycentric administrative patterns. They originate also with the differences among the Nazi coalition in granting priority to antisemitism as contrasted with such priorities as domestic economic recovery, foreign trade and international relations. They denote differences in form, and contrasts between, the "*bekoved* antisemitism" (Hebrew for "honourable", an ironic folk-term used in Germany) of conservative moderates and the vulgarities of the violence and murder squads among Nazi extreme radicals. In sum, they reflect unstable balances between the members of the government coalition of 1933.[41]

[39]See above, notes 5–7 for references and literature.
[40]The draft programme published by Esh foreshadows the course of anti-Nazi measures, not because it was followed as a blueprint but because it summarises the mutual accommodations of the several strains of anti-Jewish *völkisch* and Nazi thought with some accuracy. See also n. 7.
[41]For the story of intra-ministerial and party-government cooperation and conflict on anti-Jewish measures see Adam, *op. cit*. Of special significance is his summary of constitutional developments which provide the background for the decision-making process in anti-Jewish legislation. The *Reich* cabinet stopped meeting in 1935. Individual ministries, although theoretically gaining power through the (never completed) *Reichsreform*, were reduced, in consequence, to a process of negotiations in initiating and drafting laws. The (equally unresolved) position held by Nazi party agencies *vis-à-vis* the government extended the number of agencies whose input was taken into consideration

The influence of non-Nazi power centres on antisemitic policy diminished in step with their general loss of influence (denoted by the Röhm affair of 30th June 1934, the assumption of the president's office by Hitler on 2nd August 1935, and the Nazification of the military high command and the foreign office leadership). The dismissal of Hjalmar Schacht as economics minister in 1937, and the rise of SD, Gestapo and RSHA were the most influential components of these shifts in power for Jews in Germany.

A summary review of the policy background of the periodisation introducing this chapter will substantiate these general observations.

In 1933, the first phase, numerous anti-Jewish terror attacks accompanied legislative exclusions or restrictions imposed on Jews in the professions, the civil service, universities or other public positions. Terror against Jews was far exceeded by the universal violence and terror unleashed against Communists, Socialists and other enemies of the régime. Politically, it served to put "revolutionary" pressures on local and state governments and administrations by using or threatening violence unless legal or constitutional changes were effected. The laws incorporating terror-induced changes *ex-post-facto* failed to establish uniform conditions for Jews, since states and localities, courts and education authorities enacted different laws and decrees on Jewish restrictions.

Legislative restrictions, in this situation, were perceived as "normalisations" and "moderate policies" by Jews and ministerial officials alike. That a Jewish agency, the *Reichsbund jüdischer Frontsoldaten* (R.j.F.), for the first and only time during the period, succeeded in having a law amended prior to its promulgation indicates the initial fluidity of the Jewish situation.[42] (This fluidity should cau-

---

in drafting laws. The much discussed "polycentrism" of administration in the Third *Reich* thus pitted the several policy-making agencies against each other and permitted Hitler to manipulate agencies and policies as the ultimate arbiter in cases of dispute.

This control pattern continued, on another level, methods that had proven successful in Hitler's manipulation of conflicts within the NSDAP prior to 1933: cf. J. Nyomarkay, *Charisma and Factionalism in the Nazi Party*, Minneapolis, Minn. 1967. Hitler's power rested, of course, on his control of the physical means of coercion – army, police – his dictatorial monopoly of political power through the Party, and his charismatic effect on public opinion, see M. Broszat, *Der Staat Hitlers. Grundlegung und Entwicklung seiner inneren Verfassung* (pb.), München 1969.

Care must be taken, however, to assess properly the role of these agencies *vis-à-vis* Jewish policies. Since these agencies, especially radical Nazi party groups, maintained their independent initiatives, they set the framework for policy options and thus exercised considerable influence on substantial issues of policy. Adam's view that ministries had no influence on policy after 1935 may be somewhat misleading. Concentration on administrative controversy is to be related consistently to the socio-economic structures, whose interest was served by the ideologically rationalised policy proposals. One of these structures was represented by the career interests of ministerial bureaucracies. Others reflect the shift towards big business and away from the lower-middle-class economic romanticism that had been one of the professed goals of Nazi social policy prior to 1933. The shift, in 1938, to radical expulsion of Jews from economic life was inherent in the increase of state control over business and industry, i.e., the alliance with big business was shifting into a more state-capitalistic phase. The acquisition of Jewish productive and other capacities and entitlements by industry represents a dialectic counterpart to the simultaneous loss of business independence to increased state control. Thus, Jewish policies played a central role in the socio-economic evolution of the Nazi power system and can not be divorced from the *historic Faschismusbegriff*.

[42]The law in question, *Gesetz zur Wiederherstellung des Berufsbeamtentums* of 7th April 1933, provided exemptions for Jewish war veterans, the fathers or sons of Jewish soldiers killed in action in the First World War, and officials in service since before 1st August 1914 from forced dismissal from the civil

tion against using Jewish documents of the early period as basis for reconstructing the policy of Jewish communal agencies in Germany for the entire period.) Policy was controlled by, and was part of, domestic political considerations during the *Gleichschaltungs*-period. Whether anti-Jewish terror was initiated or merely used by Hitler to effect the desired changes remains unclear. It was tolerated, defended, or, certainly in the case of the abortive anti-Jewish boycott of 1st April 1933, initiated by Hitler and Goebbels.

Phase II coincided with the Nazi government's decision to use the political gains achieved by the terror phase to ease German economic problems and initiate rearmament. Programmes for either area brought an alliance with conservative power centres. Rearmament was to proceed in an orderly fashion, i.e., the military high command was entrusted with reconstructing the armed forces (and a new air-force was to be built up clandestinely) along the lines of military technology. It was to be based on the necessary military and industrial infrastructures. With this programme, Hitler and the generals had rejected the option of a "people's army" proposed by *SA-Führer* Ernst Röhm. His opposition to the new army led, one year later, to his and his henchmen's murder, and the political decline of his military-political troopers. In its rearmament drive, the Nazi government had obtained the cooperation of German industry and big business and a representative of big finance, Schacht (a "Christian-conservative" antisemite of long standing) was appointed economics minister (2nd August 1934).[43]

Reich-level policy to keep Jews unmolested in the economic sphere originated in this conservative turn. Jewish economic activity was as yet considered vital for German domestic recovery and foreign trade. The Economics Ministry under Schacht, by promoting this policy, acquired the image of a "moderating influence" in intra-government competition with other ministries. It found Hitler's (tactical) support, i.e., economic consideration and rearmament took priority over Nazi party promises of relief to the *Mittelstand* and attacks on monopolies, trusts and banking. As a result of the turn to big business and industry, the Nazi *Mittelstand* organisations lost political power and were submerged in the Labour Front. Their disappointment was deflected into sporadic terror acts, widespread local Nazi party pressures and numerous propaganda attacks against Jewish retail business across the country. Effective especially on local levels where Jewish business was highly visible, the *Mittelstand* eliminated Jewish competition, managed to take over Jewish stores at bargain prices and drove Jews into the bigger cities. Central authorities, including the Ministries of Foreign Affairs,

---

service. The clause had been inserted on the insistence of President Hindenburg in response to a petition submitted by the Jewish War Veterans Association. All such exemptions for Jews were rescinded following the Nuremberg Laws of 12th September 1935. The fluidity of this early period is also indicated by the fact that Jewish dignitaries were made to publish protests against "atrocity stories" abroad, see the forthcoming Pt. II of this essay in *LBI Year Book XXVI* (1981).

[43]Cf. K. D. Bracher, W. Sauer, G. Schulz, *Die nationalsozialistische Machtergreifung. Studien zur Entwicklung des totalitären Herrschaftssystems in Deutschland 1933–1934*, Köln–Opladen 1960; K.-J. Mueller, *Das Heer und Hitler. Armee und nationalsozialistisches Regime 1933–1940*, Stuttgart 1969, pp. 88–141.

Interior and Economics, attempted to assert "legality" against such wild actions.[44]

The Nuremberg Laws, which placed Jews under *Fremdenrecht,* had fulfilled a traditional programme point of the German antisemitic tradition. They were by no means a legislative coup sprung by Hitler on unsuspecting *Judenreferenten* in the ministries, as suggested in the literature. Like earlier measures, they were designed to fix in law what the street violence and terror occurring in the spring and summer of 1935 had aimed at, a further step in the radical exclusion of Jews from German life. Their racism linked them with the ideology of Nazi radicals, while their quality as "laws" passed by the *Reichstag* appeased the moderate demands of the Economics Ministry for "legal solution". That official Jewish declarations supported "law and order" as preferable to street terror reflects this constellation.[45]

Phase IV, 1936–1937 reflected not only the delicate state of foreign affairs reached by German expansionism with the occupation of the demilitarised zone of the Rhineland (March 1936) and by Germany's military unpreparedness against possible Western interventions, but also the propaganda purpose of presenting the image of an orderly, anti-Communist Germany to the world while attention was riveted on the Olympic Games in Garmisch-Partenkirchen and Berlin in 1936.* The near-total lack of reaction by Nazidom to the murder of a German *Gauleiter* (Wilhelm Gustloff) in Switzerland in February 1936 must be compared to the violent "reaction" following the murder of vom Rath in November 1938. Intra-government disputes now centred on fine points in the definition of the Jew. In education, the law, medicine and, especially the economy, Jewish activities were restricted progressively while major steps were postponed. Gestapo and SD began to compete with government and Party agencies for influence on Jewish policy, and embraced radical emigration as the openly acknowledged goal of Nazi policy.[46]

The next phase begun in the autumn of 1937 was linked with major changes in the policies and perceptions of the Nazi government. Domestically, economic preparation for war was intensified as war in Europe entered the practical calculations of the Nazi government.[47] Industry, under this stimulus, approaching limits in its productive capacities, stood to gain from additional allocations of raw material or foreign currency by absorbing Jewish big business, even if the increased cartellisation derived from "Aryanising" Jewish firms met with hostility from the Nazi *Mittelstand.* In foreign trade, the bilateral arrangements entered into with South-eastern Europe, Latin America and Asia by Schacht had

---

[44]Genschel, *op. cit.*, pp. 139–150; A. Schweitzer, *Big Business in the Third Reich*, Bloomington, Ind. 1964. For documentation on regional economic pressures throughout the period see *Dokumente über die Verfolgung der jüdischen Bürger in Baden-Württemberg durch das nationalsozialistische Regime, 1933–1945*, 2 vols., P. Sauer (ed.), for Archivdirektion Stuttgart, Stuttgart 1966, *passim.*

[45]For the text of the Declaration of the central Jewish representation, the *Reichsvertretung der Juden in Deutschland*, see Adler-Rudel, *Jüdische Selbsthilfe*, pp. 191–193.

*In this connection see the essay by P. H. Y. Mayer, 'Equality – Egality. Jews and Sport in Germany', pp. 233–238, in this volume of the Year Book – (Ed.).

[46]For the rise of the SD and the *Reichssicherheitshauptamt* (RSHA) in the determination of Jewish policy see Buchheim, *op. cit.*; Krausnick, *op. cit.*; H. Höhne, *Der Orden unter dem Totenkopf. Die Geschichte der SS.* (pb.), vol. 2, Frankfurt a. Main–Hamburg 1969, pp. 343–367.

[47]Cf. the date of the Hossbach-Memorandum, 5th November 1937.

increased Germany's independence from markets controlled by the liberal-democratic industrial nations of the West. The anti-German boycott resulting from persecution could be disregarded. Schacht's dismissal from office (September–November 1937) signalled the first of several major new concentrations of government power in the hands of the Nazi hierarchy (Hitler, Göring, Ribbentrop).

Under such changed conditions, the fixations on the "*zersetzende Einfluß*" of Jews on morale in the First World War revived: Hitler's Memorandum on the Four-Year Plan (most likely dated August 1936) implied fear of sabotage directed against Germany's intensified rearmament and autarky drive on the part of the Jews, and called for laws providing collective reprisals against all Jews should this contingency arise.[48]

Finally, the events surrounding the *Anschluß* in Austria added another element and changed the condition of Jews in Germany. Austrian atrocities and greed had resulted in a fast take-over of numerous Jewish firms and had led to the mass exodus of Jews. In 1938, the SD's *Zentralstelle für jüdische Auswanderung* was founded in Vienna to force a mass emigration of the Jewish community. Compared to the Austrian exodus, German emigration figures were low. A memorandum by a *Bankdirektor* in charge of "Aryanisation" (Dr. Binder, Dresdner Bank) notes as of 23rd May 1938 that prices for Jewish property were still too high since Jews showed "strong reluctance" to put them on the market.[49] The *Kristallnacht* pogroms of November 1938 thus stand at the end of a planned long-range policy. They offered an immediate occasion for the long-prepared final exclusion of Jews from the last area they were still active in, the German economy.

With the destruction of the Jewish economic position, the semi-independence enjoyed by the community during the first six years of Nazi rule and Nazi policies against Jews sunk to a low priority. Diplomacy and war took the centre of the stage. From now on, not policy but police measures shaped persecution. The drafting of Jews for forced labour owed probably as much to the Nazi fear of having to make welfare payments for the Jewish poor as to their desire to humiliate and proletarianise Jews by forcing them to work under degrading conditions. Robbing and despoiling powerless victims needed no policy, and found no opposition within government or party. The rapidly diminishing number of Jews had been brought under the control of unified anti-Jewish policies directed by the RSHA and its SD, much as, after the destruction of all Jewish voluntary associations, only one central Jewish agency, the *Reichsvereinigung der Juden in Deutschland* established 4th July 1939, coordinated what remained of Jewish communal life. In Berlin, the SD set down a *Reichszentrale für jüdische Auswanderung* modelled on its Vienna *Zentralstelle* to centralise "all work for Jewish emigration" until the war, the changing age and social structure of the Jewish population, and increased immigration restrictions abroad made their work redundant.

---

[48]Text of Hitler's *Denkschrift*: W. Treue, 'Hitlers Denkschrift zum Vierjahresplan', in *VfZ*, 3 (1955), No. 2, pp. 184–210.
[49]Genschel, *op. cit.*, pp. 153 ff., quoting Nuremberg documents NG 1526 and NI 13, 462.

VI. ECONOMIC IMPACT OF NAZI PERSECUTION

The emigration of Jews from Germany was a social movement of individuals and families. The decision to leave had to be made by individuals and families, not by a government, a social agency, a communal representation or the religious community of the *Gemeinde*. In line with the tradition of close family cohesion among Jews (and, of course, other ethnic groups or nationalities), family ties abroad and mutual aid between members of the extended family played a major role in the selection of the immigration country: the social support derived from the family tradition was also required by the laws of immigration countries (including and especially the U.S.A.). They recognised the family as a safe guarantee of immigrant support during the first steps of resettlement and thus prescribed prior declarations by (preferably close) resident relatives of the prospective immigrant that he would be received by his primary social group. Where exception to this rule of family-centred migration occurred, they concerned the young of working age whose traditional severance of ties to the nuclear family coincided with their age upon emigrating. Having children of school age may have been a factor in delaying the date of emigration. Family cohesion may also have played a role in the small number of children placed by German Jews in foster and home-care placement programmes initiated in foreign countries prior to the *Kristallnacht*, when the situation had become sufficiently threatening to outweigh family cohesion and the emotional strain of separating from young children.[50]

Beyond social ties such as these, which transcended class and occupational determinants of behaviour, both the emigration and the immigration movement of Jews from Germany were strongly influenced by the economic impact of persecution and the economics of immigration countries. As has been pointed out above, the polymorphous character and discontinuous timing of major persecution and extrusion measures directed against Jews in Germany created confusing and contradictory stimuli for the several groups affected by Nazi persecution. Nonetheless, the terror and defamation welling up – or called up – from time to time remained constant in official propaganda, the radio, the newspapers, posters and antisemitic literature and created an atmosphere of persecution even where Jewish-German relations had continued on personal or professional levels,

---

[50]The basic family character of Jewish emigration emerges clearly from the interviews collected by the Oral History Project of the Research Foundation for Jewish Immigration, New York, U.S. immigration statistics, and the immigration statistics of other countries (number of dependents) where available. Exceptions concern the migration, in 1933–1934, of Jews of foreign nationality returning to their country of origin; the unaccompanied children; the men migrating prior to their families to ICA colonies in Brazil; and *chaluzim*, primarily male (there was a reported scarcity of women entering *hachscharah*). The immigration to the U.S. in the early to mid-thirties, before larger numbers began to arrive, also included single men – a tradition typical also for the Jewish immigration from Germany of the 1920s – Gärtner, *loc. cit.* (see n. 28), as we have seen, comments on the slow shift of Jewish pupils from German to Jewish schools and the parental desire to complete their children's education before leaving Germany. An unknown (but probably small) number of young couples emigrating, e.g., to Palestine concluded fictitious marriages to use the provisions of certain types of certificate that admitted couples under one certificate.

or, as was more usual, where the general population remained passively silent, rather than aggressively active in support of Nazi defamation.[51]

The major factor – except for the two extreme periods of persecution, 1933 and 1938 – that influenced the timing of emigration was thus the threat to economic survival, anticipated or actual, that resulted from persecution measures, anticipated or actual, and correspondingly, the availability of the opportunity to emigrate to another country not as a temporary exile but with the intention of permanent settlement. Persecution and defamation, mass imprisonment in concentration camps, the din of harassment as much as the resurgence of Jewish identification among large groups, especially the young, had helped Jewish leadership to shift the emphasis in the German-Jewish equation from the German to the Jewish and turn the challenge of exile into the opportunity of striking roots in a more responsive and humane environment, wherever possible, and begin another cycle of acculturation – even in the homeland Palestine-Israel. The following chapters of this essay will relate economic factors to the emigration process and point out the economics of the admission policies of countries that, collectively, added up to the "closed world" facing the German Jew in the 1930s.

The economic development of Jews in Nazi Germany appears to have followed two divergent directions, increasing impoverishment, unemployment and loss of professional capacity on the one hand, and relative economic recovery from depression levels on the other. Impoverishment stimulated emigration, recovery tended, in many cases, to retard it. To begin with the first: some impoverishment was caused by the exclusion of Jews from public and semi-public functions due to Nazi legislation, although professionals having middle-class status may be presumed to have had financial reserves adequate enough to prepare for emigration, transfer funds (e.g., through *Haavara*) or find substitute employment in the Jewish organisations (primarily lawyers, health personnel, academicians, teachers, law students).[52] Legal exclusion does, of course, not ade-

---

[51]This observation on the attitude of the German public towards "legal" or terror measures against Jews, or Nazi party pressures for forced sales of Jewish property, has not been subjected to a systematic, nation-wide analysis. It rests, in part, on the personal observations of the author, 1933–1943. The two major physical attacks on Jewish persons or property punctuating the steady pressures of the period were either carried out by SA radicals (1933) or by Party and SA units ordered to burn the synagogues while the police rounded up Jews for internment in concentration camps (1938) – on orders. Silent passivity did not exclude the frequently commented upon termination of personal and social contacts between Jews and Christians or expressions of personal protest, see Ian Kershaw, 'Antisemitismus und Volksmeinung. Reaktion auf die Judenverfolgung', in M. Broszat und E. Froehlich (eds.), *Bayern in der NS-Zeit. II: Herrschaft und Gesellschaft im Konflikt*, Munich-Vienna 1979, pp. 281–348. No doubt, fear of Nazi reprisals for being a "Jew-lover" played a role in some cases of such withdrawal. The Gestapo files extant (e.g., Düsseldorf) were reported to contain a number of cases (upward of 400) concerning support for Jews or breaches of the provisions against sexual relations with Jews.

[52]A relatively large number of Jewish physicians was reported to have emigrated to Palestine 1934–1936. A list published by the *Notgemeinschaft deutscher Wissenschaftler* (Zürich) listed over 600 persons in all fields and professions seeking positions abroad. The placement of Jewish lawyers and public officials removed from their positions in 1933/1935 is reported by Adler-Rudel, *Jüdische Selbsthilfe*. A book published by the Council of Jews from Germany in memory of martyred Jewish communal officials in Germany includes persons who had entered Jewish service after losing their professional positions or had been unable to complete their studies, including some of the 2,000 *Referendare*

quately reflect extra-legal boycotts, local pressures or terror measures. Among the groups so excluded were the following:

University personnel (all kinds): 800, 7th April 1933; 2,000 (estimate), 14th November 1935.

Physicians: Number of practising physicians: 7,800–8,000, 1933; about 6,000, 1st January 1935; about 3,300, 1st January 1937; about 3,150, 1938; 709, 1st October 1938 (restricted to Jewish patients).

Dentists: Number of practising dentists: about 1,150, 1933; about 750, November 1936.

Apothecaries: Number: 657 (200 forced to close), 1936.

Lawyers: About 5,400, number prior to 7th April 1933 (estimate for Prussia); 3,030, June 1933; 1,735, 1st January 1938; 200 (admitted for practice among Jews as "legal counsels"), December 1938.

Referendare: Number about 2,000, 1933.

Civil service: Total number of "non-Aryan" *Beamte* estimated at 6,000 in 1933 of whom 5,000 were dismissed in 1933 and 1,000(?) in November 1935.

Writers, journalists, etc. [no estimates available].

Artists: Number of persons engaged in "cultural and artistic professions": 4,245, June 1933; in 1935 persons not self-employed – with few exceptions – barred from membership in professional organisations, number unknown; in 1936 2,357 performing and plastic artists were registered with the Jewish *Kulturbund.*

All occupations not identified as agriculture, industry and crafts, commerce and transportation (Öffentlicher Dienst und private Dienstleistungen): 29,974, June 1933.[53]

Loss or restriction of occupational function led a substantial ratio of these (and other) professionals to seek substitute employment. Others prepared their emigration. They became part of the "intellectual migration". Precise data on the religious or professional division of this group are not available at this time. The 7,500 academics and professionals reported by the High Commissioner for re-

---

(lawyers in public-training positions – obligatory for being licensed as lawyers). *Bewährung im Untergang*, E. G. Lowenthal (ed.), Stuttgart 1965, *passim*. In 1933/1934, the German Zionist leaders emigrated to Palestine, and were replaced by younger men who may be presumed to have included persons formerly employed in the German sector. The *Reichsvertretung*, especially in its managerial personnel (as different from its political leadership) also included such persons, e.g., Cora Berliner, Otto Hirsch, Paul Eppstein, Friedrich Brodnitz, Arthur Lilienthal, Paul W. Meyerheim, Paula Fürst, Richard Joachim and others.

[53]The available sources present some difficulties since not all people who could be identified by Jewish names belonged to the Jewish religion. Thus counting persons excluded for example under para. 3 of the *Gesetz zur Wiederherstellung des Berufsbeamtentums* of 7th April 1933 and its enabling legislation ("non-Aryan" descent as reason for dismissal) will not automatically yield the number of Jews extruded. The above figures are based on the following sources: Adler-Rudel, *Jüdische Selbsthilfe*, pp. 139–141, 143, 146; Bauer, *op. cit.*, p. 113; Blau, *Ausnahmerecht*, Nos. 3, 78; Krüger, *op. cit.*, p. 46; German census, 1933.

fugees as having been placed by mid-1934 included about 5,500 professionals, some 700 academic teachers and students.[54]

Figures for Jewish unemployment for the period vary considerably from observer to observer. The German census of 16th June 1933, counted 34,000 presumably not including "dependents", as without gainful employment. For 1935, an estimate placed Jewish unemployment in Germany at 48,000 for employees and workers, and 37,000 for "independents". German-Jewish sources placed the figure at 40,000 for 1936 and 1937, in spite of the decline in the population due to emigration and excess of deaths over births.[55]

The total number of persons in receipt of one of the several forms of public welfare at some time during the period is not known. However, in 1935/1936, Jews were excluded from receiving *Winterhilfe*, i.e., support from a special German fund financed by contribution drives, made quasi-obligatory by public pressure, including prescribed deductions from business earnings and wages. The Jewish community then organised its own *Jüdische Winterhilfe* sanctioned by the authorities, and based on a similar collection principle each year from 1935/1936 to 1939.

As Table VIII indicates, between one fifth and one fourth of German Jews received welfare support from the fund. In absolute numbers, school-age children, store owners, commercial employees and persons without occupation headed the list. Needs were above average in North and North-East German rural areas, the *Hanse* cities (Hamburg, Bremen) and the Palatine, below average in Bavaria and Berlin.

If small loans and other forms of social aid are included in the estimate of

TABLE VIII

Jewish recipients of support from Jüdische Winterhilfe

Years	No. supported	No. of Jew. pop.	Percentage supported
1935/36	83,761	409,000	20·5
1936/37	82,067	389,000	21·0
1937/38	77,231	375,000	20·6
1938/39	70,000	286,000	25·0
end of 1939	52,000	204,000	26·0

[54]The best single source for the emigration of persons in politics, public life, the sciences and the arts on a world-wide basis is the *International Biographical Dictionary of Central European Émigrés 1933–1945*, vol. I: *Öffentliches Leben* (in German), 1979, vol. II: *The Arts and Sciences* (in English), München–New York (vol. II in preparation). The Dictionary was initiated by this author and carried out jointly by the Research Foundation for Jewish Immigration and the *Institut für Zeitgeschichte*, München. It is based on a collection of about 25,000 life histories housed at the Foundation and the Institute in New York and Munich in identical copies.

[55]The higher estimate for 1935 is quoted in Bauer, *op. cit.*, p. 137, based on a report by Bernhard Kahn, the then European Director of the American Jewish Joint Distribution Committee. For other estimates (based on *Reichsvertretungs* statistics see Adler-Rudel, *Jüdische Selbsthilfe*, p. 132.

supported persons, as many as 33 per cent of the German-Jewish population may have received some form of social assistance in 1935 – about 52,000 Jews received assistance from the government welfare system. In 1935, about 35 per cent of Jewish public funds were used for social assistance, and of the 1,400 Jewish congregations left in Germany in 1937 (of 1,600 in 1933), 610 could no longer meet their needs without assistance from regional organisations.[56]

Thus, while these figures add up convincingly to proof of the increasing impoverishment of Jews in Nazi Germany, at the other end of the socio-economic scale German Jews shared in the recovery brought about by Nazi policies of economic pump-priming and rearmament. The data documenting this trend are less precise. The basic index: size and distribution of tax revenues from the *Gemeindesteuer* (tax) has not been investigated. It was paid as a percentage of the income tax by Jews until Jewish *Gemeinden* lost their traditional status as *Körperschaften des öffentlichen Rechts* (corporations under public law) on 1st January 1938.[57] Indirect data, however, permit some tentative conclusions.

In 1933, the number of indirect Jewish businesses and craft-workshops was estimated as between 75,000 and 80,000. This possibly inflated number included a considerable number of middling and marginal stores, craft-workshops and similar enterprises and does not reveal the significance of Jewish branch leadership in the characteristically "Jewish" sector (textile, metal trade, produce trade, art dealing, banking and related fields and others). Attempts to estimate the value of Jewish business property for 1933 remain highly tentative. On 1st April 1938, Nazi sources reported 39,552 establishments of all kinds still in being. The Nazi census of Jewish property of 26th April 1938 recorded total Jewish property as 7,050 billion *Reichsmark* (8,426 billion minus 1,376 billion debts and other debits) exclusive of property owned by foreign and stateless Jewish owners (about 0·5 billion *Reichsmark*).[58] Between April 1938 and April 1939, the removal of Jews from industry was reported to have progressed "especially well". The

---

[56]For *Winterhilfe* figures see A. J. Phiebig, 'Statistische Tabellen', in *Almanach des Schocken Verlags auf das Jahr 5699*, Berlin 1938/1939, pp. 145 f.; Adler-Rudel, *Jüdische Selbsthilfe*, pp. 161–165. An excellent overview of the social aid given by German Jews during the Nazi period in different forms and to different groups is found *ibid.*, pp. 121–182. For *Kleingemeinden* see *ibid.*, pp. 150–158.

[57]*Gesetz über die Rechtsverhältnisse der jüdischen Kultusgemeinden vom 28. März 1938*. The law was retroactive to 1st January 1938.

[58]Authorities (Dr. Kurt May, Director of United Restitution Organization, Frankfurt a. Main, and Dr. Walter Schwarz, the editor-in-chief of the authoritative *Rechtsprechung zur Wiedergutmachung*) have confirmed in letters to the author the difficulty of arriving at near-precise figures for Jewish-held property. Dr. Schwarz has estimated the amount at "10 bill. RM and probably considerably more" for 1933. (W. Schwarz, *Rückerstattung nach den Gesetzen der Alliierten Mächte*, Die Wiedergutmachung nationalsozialistischen Unrechts durch die Bundesrepublik Deutschland, Bd. I), München 1974, p. 365 s. tit. 10. A lower estimate (RM 7·2 billion) was offered by Nehemia Robinson (*Beraubung und Wiedergutmachung*, 1962, p. 13). Both figures appear low: a Nazi census of Jewish property instituted by the *Reich* Economic Ministry in April 1938 claimed RM 7·05 billion as total Jewish assets (after deducting liabilities). *Reichswirtschaftsministerium. Vertrauliches Rundschreiben* dated 21st November 1938, signed A. Krüger, MinRat (on face sheet). (Photocopy of typewritten original in the possession of the author, courtesy Dr. K. May, Frankfurt a. Main. Provenance unknown.) The number of Jewish firms still extant in 1938 is reported by Krüger, *op. cit.*, p. 44. (Krüger's figures are based on reports on Jewish property by Jews who had no conceivable interest in 1938 in using accounting methods maximising their holdings. This figure must be considered on the low side as well.)

exclusion *in toto* and *by decree* of Jews from entire branches of business – as distinct from continuous informal pressures to liquidate ("Aryanise") by forced sales – began on 6th July 1938.[59] As has been pointed out above, the government had begun its drive to "Aryanise" large Jewish business firms following the Economics Minister, Schacht's retirement, 5th September 1937, when the rearmament economy had begun to produce at capacity and the government's initiative to "Aryanise" the large Jewish firms met with their economic interest. Until that time, the attitudes of Nazi economic authorities had been ambivalent towards the placing of orders with Jewish traders and manufacturers, and government agencies on municipal, state or *Reich* levels as well as the army had been under consistent attack by party radicals for placing government orders with Jewish firms. Similar controversies arose over the Economics Ministry's practice of permitting the establishment of new Jewish enterprises (August 1935) – surely an indication that such enterprises were still being founded. Three major Jewish banks remained members of the *Reichsanleihekonsortium* (a group of banks charged with the marketing of government financial instruments) until 1938. Major Jewish firms were "Aryanised" in 1937–1938, in part before the *Kristallnacht* destroyed all Jewish retail business and enforced the liquidation of the rest.[60]

In line with this trend – the maintenance of Jewish economic positions and

TABLE IX

Flight tax paid by all emigrants

Year	Amount
1932/1933	1 million
1933/1934	45 million
1934/1935	70 million
1937/1938	81 million
1938/1939	342 million

Source: *Wirtschaftliche Mitteilungen*, ed. Deutsche Bank, 5 (1939); (30th May 1939), p. 143; see Hilberg, *op. cit.*, pp. 90 f.

[59]*Gesetz zur Änderung der Gewerbeordnung für das deutsche Reich vom 6. Juli 1938*, RGBl 1938, p. 823. Krüger, *op. cit.*, p. 44.
[60]No systematic analysis of the pattern of "Aryanisation" and the progressive liquidation of Jewish firms has been attempted to date on a *Reich* level. The available literature restricts itself to single firms or illustrates general trends by example. Allied and German restitution files should offer primary materials for such a study. (Examples of such approaches are provided by Hilberg, *op. cit.*, pp. 66–82; Genschel, *op. cit.*, pp. 144–176 and *passim*; Drobisch, *op. cit.*, pp. 164–167; for the attack on newly-founded Jewish firms see Adam, *op. cit.*, pp. 123 f.) For bank participation in the *Reichsanleihekonsortium* see Max M. Warburg, *Aus meinen Aufzeichnungen*, New York 1972, p. 154 (privately printed). A study of such "Aryanisations" would, of course, have to be supplemented by the inclusion of firms liquidated under Nazi pressures, or firms which had been "pseudo-Aryanised" by being taken over and continued by loyal employees or non-Jewish partners.

their participation in the German economy under the weakening protection of the Economics Minister, Schacht – figures for the flight tax to be paid by all persons leaving Germany permanently since 1931, shown in Table IX, suggest that major Jewish firms continued to function until 1937–1938.

This tax – *Reichsfluchtsteuer* – was originally imposed on persons owning upward of RM 200,000 or owning RM 20,000 in property in 1931. In 1934, the tax base was changed to include those owning RM 50,000 at any time since 1931, or having earned RM 20,000 and above per annum since that date. It was paid for capital exported above the minimum amounts and was assessed at 25 per cent of the transferred property. The amounts reported as having been transferred via *Haavara* to Palestine 1937 to 1939 (RM 31·4 million, RM 18·8 million and RM 8·2 million respectively) peaked in 1937 and near-equalled the years 1935 and 1936 for the year 1938. The figure for 1939 constitutes a significant drop-off.[61]

In the absence of break-downs for the flight tax and the *Haavara* data, the ratio of number of émigrés to amount of flight tax or *Haavara* transfer, or the distribution of tax payments and transfers by size cannot be determined. The increase in flight taxes by 422 per cent paid by émigrés in 1938/1939 corresponds roughly to the increase in emigration from Germany following the *Kristallnacht*. In spite of this lack of conclusive evidence, the data suggest clearly that more wealthy German Jews emigrated in 1937/1938 and 1939 than in the earlier years of the Nazi régime.

Further indirect evidence for German-Jewish business recovery may be deduced from the following: the contributions to the *Jüdische Winterhilfe* which were collected in parallel to the general Nazi *Winterhilfe* rose proportionately in three collections, i.e., the amounts collected remained equal in spite of the declining numbers of Jews in Germany (1935/1936, RM 3.644 million; 1936/1937, RM 3.630 million; 1937/1938, RM 3.316 million). The per-capita income of Jewish wage earners based on tax deductions from salaries remained higher than the income of Catholic or Protestant wage earners in 1936 (RM 2,234 for Jews compared to RM 2,017 for Protestants, RM 1,921 for Catholics). However, Jews reporting represented only 0·2 per cent of total reports compared to 0·8 per cent Jews in the total population.[62]

[61] For the breakdown of *Haavara* transfers by year see Feilchenfeld, *op. cit.*, p. 75. A search made in the German microfilm materials at the National Archives, Washington D.C. has not yet turned up material relevant to the *Kirchensteuer* (church tax) collected at varying ratios of the income tax, or their breakdown. A manuscript by M. P. Birnbaum on the *Preussische Landesverband jüdischer Gemeinden* which presumably includes data on this expanding tax on which had been reported by that author only in part in previous publications was not available to me when this article was completed. A search for the breakdown of the flight tax by size of individual payment or source has been equally unsuccessful to date, and the German archives (which presumably contain the files of the *Finanzämter*) could not be searched due to limitations of time. The *Haavara* archives should also contain breakdowns of the annual transfer figures not reported in Feilchenfeld, *op. cit.*

[62] Data for *Winterhilfe* contributions are cited in Adler-Rudel, *Jüdische Selbsthilfe*, p. 164. They contrasted sharply with the falling income reported for contributions to *Blaue Karte*, the broad-based collection scheme for welfare aid. (The American immigrant fund "Blue Card" constituted a direct transfer of the scheme, including its name, to the U.S.A. It has continued to this date to support extremely indigent immigrants beyond the funds available to them from U.S. Social Security payments or German *Wiedergutmachung* pensions.) It may be conjectured that the falling contributions

Jewish Emigration from Germany

On a similar level, the repayment rate of loans granted by *Jüdische Wirtschaftshilfe* to marginal commercial and crafts enterprises rose from near zero in 1933 to 50 per cent in 1935, 65 per cent in 1936 and 75–80 per cent in 1937/1938.[63] In 1934, the Jewish vocational guidance agencies advised that Jewish business needed apprentices and that commerce offered promising careers to suitable young Jews. While this advice[64] reflects the policy of the *Reichsvertretung* to maintain Jewish economic positions in Germany as a matter of reason and self-preservation, it also indicates at least continued business activities among Jewish firms.

Details like these illustrating the participation of Jewish business of several kinds in the recovery need to be related to the history of local persecution and pressures described above. While small and middling Jewish communities, employees and those excluded from their occupations fought marginality, and between 20 and 25 per cent of all Jews received public assistance, Jewish business and manufacturing, especially the larger establishments, succeeded in maintaining their economic positions and, presumably, shared in the upswing of the economy.

For the pattern of Jewish emigration from Germany, the existence of "two Jewish economies" offers an additional clue in explaining its flow and timing. Clearly, social strata among Jews who had lost their foothold in the economy were not absorbed by the "Jewish sector". In 1933, about two-thirds of Jewish employees had been employed by Jewish firms, and the dwindling of the number of Jewish firms by about 50 per cent in about five years is clearly reflected in the persistent unemployment figures. For this group, retraining for settlement abroad in crafts or agriculture constituted a constructive response to being extruded from the German economy. The strong *chaluz* movement of the first years (1933–1936) and the rapid build-up of retraining facilities in Germany, as well as *Youth Aliyah* emigration, study abroad and the beginning of overseas migration would appear to reflect this condition. A limiting consideration in explaining the relatively slow decline (50 per cent in five years in spite of persistent publicity and local pressures) in the number of firms registered, may have been the fact, mentioned above, that new firms were established by Jews during the Nazi period. This may, however, reflect in part, the tendency among Jews, observed for the pre-1933 period as well, to respond to a loss of jobs by founding a tiny independent, door-to-door, one-man sales agency, or by taking to peddling and middlemen positions for which no or minuscule capital was needed. Unless more

---

to *Blaue Karte*, reflect precisely the "two economies" characteristic of German Jews during the period, since contribution to *Blaue Karte* came from the Jewish population at large beset by increasing impoverishment and unemployment. Data for the income of Jewish employees are included in *Statistik des Deutschen Reiches*, vol. 492, 1937, p. 20, and *ibid.*, vol. 530, p. 22 (for 1934 and 1936, respectively). They reflect, of course, the previously reported higher levels of income among Jews, see Birnbaum, *loc. cit.* Another reflection of this contrast may be found in the fact that Jews in Germany funded an overwhelming part of Jewish welfare costs through their own contribution. See Bauer, *op. cit.*, p. 127 and see the forthcoming Pt. II of this essay in *LBI Year Book XXVI* (1981). Adler-Rudel, *Jüdische Selbsthilfe*, pp. 180–181, considerably understates the ratio contributed by German Jews to their *Selbsthilfe* if his data are compared with the expenditures reported for foreign aid by Bauer, *loc. cit.*

[63]For loan repayment figures for the Berlin *Wirtschaftshilfe* see A. Szanto, 'Economic Aid in the Nazi Era. The Work of the Berlin Wirtschaftshilfe', in *LBI Year Book IV* (1959), p. 212.

[64]Adler-Rudel, *Jüdische Selbsthilfe*, pp. 49 f.

information is available, conclusions drawn from these figures remain tentative in view of other intervening factors, including the policies of immigration countries towards admitting Jews from Germany who had no visible means of support.

The figures for capital transfers also suggest that although the pattern of emigration cannot be related precisely to continued Jewish business activities in Germany – as will be seen below, and as is indicated by flight tax and *Haavara* figures – a strong group of Jewish firms had remained active until, in the last pre-*Kristallnacht* phase, Nazi measures set in and forced sales or liquidations. That this was in line with the polymorphism of Nazi policies and its deceptive signals to Jewish business has been made clear above. While it would be quite unrealistic to expect that conditions characterised by business expansion were conducive to the realism or pessimism that was needed to unmask Nazi polymorphism as temporary expediencies, and exchange the known miseries of selective persecution for the rigours of pulling up stakes and re-starting a new cycle of life and work in unknown surroundings, no doubt the lack of political acumen and the comfortable *embourgeoisement* of life in Germany blocked early insight into the Nazi threat as much as economic considerations. The tendency to consider oneself immune to measures affecting other members of the community as long as Nazi policies, for historic reasons or by design, practised selective persecution, remained a constant characteristic in the reaction of Nazi victims during the Holocaust phase as well.

VII. RESTRICTIONISM IN HISTORIC PERSPECTIVE

If these data and their interpretation are correct, stabilisation and, possibly economic expansion as well as economic decline and impoverishment were characteristic of the first four and a half years of Jewish life in Nazi Germany. The pattern of persecution described earlier, the timing of persecution measures and the selective ways in which such measures affected different social and economic groups explain this divergence of socio-economic trends in the context of Nazi policies.

The economic pattern relates to the timing and the group breakdown of émigrés from Germany in a number of ways – although intervening variables and the paucity of immigration data for many countries make the relationship considerably less than precise. Generally, groups pushed into marginality could be expected to react to their plight with preparations for emigration. Among these groups, however, were a considerable number of professionals of all kinds who had been the first target of Nazi attacks. Thus economic class and displacement by persecution did not coincide, and the early wave of émigrés in 1933–1934 included intellectuals, artists, academics, physicians, lawyers, students and other groups from the public or "semi-public" sectors of the economy. For the entire period, local displacement fed into the emigration pattern to an extent that is impossible to determine since the *Binnenwanderung* remained unrecorded until 1937. This erased the possibility of differentiating numerically for geographic and social origin if rural displacement, as has been assumed, did indeed move lower income or economically as yet unestablished younger groups from country to city.

In attempting to break down the Jewish emigration of the years 1933/1934 and 1937/1938 into its social components, however, the economic policies of admission in *immigration* countries has to be reviewed. This policy tended to strengthen the economic selectivity of the emigration process, but it also counterbalanced it in important respects.

The Nazi government, as has been made clear, had no interest at any time in an orderly emigration of Jews from Germany, even if, as noted above, the moderate attitudes of several ministries are taken into consideration, and their intentions and humane effects are acknowledged. They did not create an *immigration* policy or plan. "Plans" amounted to no more than empty talk. The government never cooperated with the League of Nations' High Commission for Refugees. It aborted negotiations initiated by the Intergovernmental Committee for Refugees set up by the Evian Conference. Diplomatic feelers and SD "plans" concerning a resettlement of German Jews on the island of Madagascar (a Utopian idea broached by the Polish government and private groups for Jewish citizens in the 1920s and 1930s) remained in the realm of fantasy. The emigration, not the immigration or resettlement of German Jews, were Nazi goals prior to the deportations and genocide. Nazi efforts on all levels concentrated on making Germany "judenrein".

Ideologically, the Nazi leaders rationalised their chaotic policies in propaganda and diplomatic conversations. Germany, it was said, expected foreign public opinion to understand and sympathise with Nazi antisemitism better the more "the world gained first-hand experience with the Jewish question" created by unregulated Jewish immigration.[65]

In consequence, the Nazi government refused to respond to whatever protests were lodged publically or through diplomatic channels by other governments against the expulsion of Jews from Germany, and against the chaos created by robbing Jews of most of their property before permitting them to leave. Diplomatic protests against Nazi measures concerned primarily the mistreatment of foreign nationals residing in Germany. Foreign governments, in turn, proved reluctant to yield to pressures and entreaties by Jewish and liberal groups for policy-level intervention in Germany on behalf of a more orderly or planned Jewish emigration. Such intervention, it was argued, would not only legitimise Nazi persecution of German Jews by helping in their removal from Germany; it would also tend to encourage the governments of Poland, Romania and Hungary to follow the Nazi example and force their Jewish nationals into emigration. In addition, such planning presupposed an available area of settlement, or changes in the restrictions applied by governments to immigration. Fear of the economic and social problems, including increased antisemitism that would be

---

[65]Hitler saw antisemitic tendencies grow in Poland, Czechoslovakia, France, Great Britain, Holland, South America and other countries, and boasted that his "export of antisemitism" and the arrival of Jewish émigrés from Germany had caused a new universal hostility to Jews. Hitler–Pirow conversations, 24 November 1938 DGFP, ser. D., vol. IV, pp. 338–340; Hitler–Csáky conversation, 16th January 1939, DGFP, ser. D., vol. V, p. 366; Schumburg (Referat Deutschland) Circular to all diplomatic representations 25th January 1939, DGFP, ser. D., vol. V, pp. 931–932. See E. Ben Elissar, *La Diplomatie du IIIe Reich et les Juifs (1933–1939)*, Paris 1939, pp. 400 f.

created by "Jewish mass immigration" had added domestic considerations to diplomatic calculations.[66]

To some extent, this policy of creating chaos in immigration countries succeeded in turning the dispersal of Jews from Germany into a national problem in each country accepting, or asked to accept, German Jews, and into an international problem on the level of international organisations.

The League of Nations proved ineffective to do more than draw attention to and, to some extent, alleviate some problems connected with the search of German Jews for a haven. As early as 1933, the League of Nations Assembly had created a "High Commission for Refugees (Jewish and other) coming from Germany". It was set up as a quasi-separate body and housed away from Geneva (in Lausanne). Pending the return of Nazi Germany to the League which, in self-deception, European diplomats as yet hoped for, it was felt that German feelings were to be respected. (In addition, the legally effective date for Germany's renunciation of membership in the League occurred only in 1935.) The League expected member states to help in solving the "economic, financial, and social problems created by the large number of persons from Germany, Jewish and other, seeking refuge". Handicapped by its separation from the League's structure, and by the restrictive policies of member states, the Commission's work remained limited to remedial action. James G. McDonald, its first High Commissioner resigned on 31st December 1935 expressing in his letter of resignation his frustration over the unwillingness of governments to "subordinate considerations of diplomatic correctness to . . . humanity".[67]

It would be a-historical, however, to see the (already moribund) League's failure to act on behalf of planned emigration apart from the policies pursued by the major immigration countries to which, theoretically, German Jews might have turned for admission. Whatever Utopian schemes of "natural law" may have exercised the minds of international lawyers through the centuries in postulating a law of nations that would enjoin states to admit aliens to their territory, the admission of aliens had been regulated by economic, political or demographic considerations as perceived by governments defining their *raison d'état* in response to national socio-political interest structures.[68]

---

[66] See Bauer, *op. cit.*, pp. 105–179 *passim*, for the role of this motive in American-Jewish discussions concerning large-scale planning for emigration from Germany. For reference to the diplomatic issues involved see Sherman, *op. cit.*, p. 202; Feingold, *op. cit.*; Wyman, *op. cit.*; Ben Elissar, *op. cit., passim*.

[67] The League had played a major role in population transfers affecting Greeks, Turks and Bulgarians following the First World War. See H. A. Strauss, 'Greek-Turkish and Greek-Bulgarian Population Transfers after World War One', paper delivered at the American Historical Association Annual Convention, Washington D.C., December 1976 (unpubl.). Its "Nansen-Office" had successfully alleviated some of the post-war refugee problems, and had created the "Nansen-passport" for stateless refugees.

[68] See R. Plendes, *International Migration Law*, Leiden 1972, pp. 38–70, for a review of these principles and the historic practices of states disregarding them. Several supreme courts or administrative agencies (Poland 1927, Austria 1922, Argentina 1935, U.S.A. 1931), the Convention on the Status of Aliens adopted by the Sixth International Conference of American States (1928), and the Draft Convention adopted at the International Conference on the Treatment of Foreigners held under the auspices of the League of Nations (Paris 1929) are examples of immediate pre-Hitler affirmations of state sovereignty over the admission of aliens to national territory. Plendes, *ibid.*, pp. 62 f., notes 148–150.

Historically, population policies affecting the admission of aliens had expressed themselves in rationalisations of these interest structures by economic theoreticians. Mercantilists had stressed the significance of strong productive populations for the economic and political power of states. As a result, eighteenth-century absolutist governments tended to encourage the selective immigration of population groups considered assets to their developing economies. Jewish migrations had selectively profited from mercantilist policies, as had Christian dissenters expelled *en masse* from their homelands (Huguenots, Salzburg Protestants). With the French Revolution, fear of political subversion appeared first as a motive in national migration policies (U.S. Aliens and Sedition Act, British Alien Bill, Swiss legislation, Canadian supervision of immigrants). For Jews (e.g., during the Napoleonic, or Metternich period) the fear of governments of their "excessive increase" was both a stimulus (to emigrate) and a barrier (to constructive immigration) within Europe, including the Germany Confederacy. Following a period of relatively free immigration policies after 1815, the Revolution of 1848, once again, led to restrictive policies by governments fearing political subversion. Several European governments date the beginning of their immigration legislations to 1848/1849, while such immigration countries as the U.S.A., Latin-American countries or Canada maintained relatively free admission policies for aliens, in line with their interest in demographic and economic development. Jewish immigration from Eastern Europe after 1880 profited from these policies. During the last quarter of the nineteenth century, however, racist moods, combined with nationalist and protectionist interests in Western Europe, led to the beginning of restrictionist immigration legislation. Western European states, never "open-hearted receivers of foreign nationals",[69] progressively tightened admission policies, introduced police supervision (registration) of aliens and restrcted their economic activities, especially employment by licensing and work permit requirements. Government legislation also reflected prevailing views as to which immigrant populations might be "desirable" or "undesirable" for a national economy. (Oriental exclusion policies directed against Chinese and Japanese immigrant labour in the U.S.A. and Canada, quota systems, hostility to Jewish immigration, e.g., in Great Britain, the U.S.A. or late nineteenth- or early twentieth-century Germany are examples of a general trend.) Finally, the First World War, the outbreak of which was accompanied by widespread spy and anti-foreign hysteria in Europe, led to further tightening of restrictions on the admission and free movement of aliens. The war inaugurated the broad policies of restrictionism that characterised the 1920s:

> "La première guerre mondiale précipita le movement. Successivement atteints par les crises économiques et sociales, les États crurent y parent en applicant une politique étroitement nationaliste et protectionniste."[70]

Thus, when Hitler struck, and forced German Jews to seek havens abroad, international migration restrictions had reached one of their peaks. The depression that had led German voters to ultra-nationalism or ultra-leftism and to substantial anti-liberal protest- and frustration-voting had also induced potential

[69]*Ibid.*, pp. 43–44.
[70]D. Visscher, as quoted *ibid.*, pp. 58 f.

target countries for Jewish immigration from Germany to tighten admission and employment requirements for prospective immigrants.

The ideology used to justify such policies reflects pre-Keynesian values. Nineteenth-century economic theory had viewed the fluctuations of business increasingly as crises of purchasing power (i.e., imbalances between the supply and demand for goods) rather than as results of speculation or financial misdealings by banks or exchanges. As a result, the preservation or increase of purchasing power of national populations, and thus the admission of immigrants, became focal points of public economic policy. Industrial slowdowns, and the unemployment of native labour began to be added to earlier concerns with political subversion as a prime motive in restricting immigration. The dates of new decrees restricting immigration in European states appear to be linked with political or economic crises: 1849, 1857, 1882, 1920, 1929. In the words of an American expert (1931):

> "The limit of production is, in one sense, determined by the buying population or consumer. In another sense immigration is limited by land-absorptive capacity. The addition to a nation's population of such [immigrant] poor buying power does not improve business conditions but rather impoverishes them by adding to those who must be given food for consumption without the means, even through no fault of their own."[71]

In traditional development-immigration countries (Latin America, Canada, Australia/New Zealand), the depression was related to the steep fall in international raw material prices, their main export article. There, restrictionism in admission policies took the form of differentiating between occupations desirable for national development, and occupations considered undesirable for immigrants, or adequately filled by natives or residents. In these countries, as in the U.S.A., economic arguments were reinforced by (admitted or implied) ethnic or racial biases. "Ethnic homogeneity", "desirable genetic endowment", the "proper demographic mixture of high-quality immigrants" are easily recognisable code words for the racist element in the restrictionism of the period.[72]

Government policies of this kind generally were supported by labour unions defending native workers against increased unemployment or the competition of cheaper foreign labour, by industry wary of additional social problems, or by professional or occupational groups protected by legislation against the competition of foreign nationals or financial burdens. Middle-class liberal governments, in accordance with long-standing fears of "foreign subversive elements", had no desire to aggravate social conflicts by sharpening labour or lower-middle-class unemployment. A survey done in 1931, for example, revealed that in the U.S.A. "three out of every five jobs are closed to aliens ... four out of every five memberships in labor unions are open to citizens only, and ... innumerable laws in each of the states deter an alien from entering many occupations".[73] In a differ-

---

[71]H. Fields, 'Closing Immigration throughout the World', *American Journal of International Law*, vol. 26 (1936), p. 675.

[72]H. H. Laughlin, *The Codification and Analysis of the Immigration-Control Laws of each of the Several Countries of Pan-America*. Analysis Volume, Carnegie Institute Washington D.C., Eugenics Research Office, 1936 (mimeo.) reflects quite explicitly the racist and cultural-nationalist background of restrictionism for the period under discussion.

[73]Fields, *op. cit.*, p. 674, quoted from Harold Fields, 'Unemployment and the Alien', *South Atlantic Quarterly*, I (1931).

ent political climate, where awakening nationalisms competed for power, economic arguments of a similar nature were advanced by Great Britain in its role as the mandatory power for Palestine. While the basic rationale for restricting Jewish immigration was political, it took the form of linking immigration with the "economic capacity" of that country to absorb immigrants, presumed to be a fixed quality independent of demographic or socio-economic stimulation, the world market, capital import or labour and entrepreneurial skills.

For the German Jew contemplating emigration as a necessity, a precaution, or an act of faith (Zionism), the combined impact of immigration restrictions and economic discrimination he would face in his quest for security from oppression supplied the second series of factors influencing the timing of his emigration. His information about historic details, or about the world-wide migration crisis was, no doubt, incomplete. It was derived from sources of varying reliability, subject to his educational and linguistic proficiencies, his grasp of world affairs or his provincialism. How intensely information on immigration opportunities was sought was related to the pattern of persecution, the intensity of defamation and the deprivation of livelihood experienced as their result. The pursuit of immigration opportunities had primarily depended on personal initiatives in establishing contacts with relatives abroad and overseas. Once the decision was made, however, solid information was available to him. It was provided by the network of emigration advisors established in major Jewish centres by the Jewish aid organisations, by several types of literature at his disposal, the increasingly frequent reporting of the Jewish press on immigration countries or letters from relatives abroad.[74]

VIII. THE EUROPEAN COUNTRIES OF REFUGE

If these general observations are tested against the actual migration situation, i.e., if restrictionism in a given country is matched with the flow of Jewish (or "political") emigration, however, the correlation is less clear-cut, and not applicable in all cases as a factor in emigration.

This applies particularly to Europe and to the years 1933–1935, the first three years of Jewish emigration from Germany. During these years, European countries headed the list of migration targets. The two most reliable estimates (based on the figures of a German and a U.S. Jewish aid organisation) suggest that 72 to 77 per cent of Jewish émigrés resorted to European countries in 1933; 35 to 40 per cent in 1934; 26 to 31 per cent in 1935; and 20 to 25 per cent in 1936. In 1937, and during the first six months of 1938, European countries were chosen by 25 per cent of Jewish émigrés, including 4 per cent repatriates (i.e., primarily

[74]These sources of the "images" of immigration countries are as yet unanalysed. Reports in the Jewish press reflect changes in immigration goals, beginning with Europe and Palestine (1933–1935) and increasing emphasis on overseas countries from 1936 on. The press and *Jüdische Auswanderung, Korrespondenzblatt des Hilfsvereins der Juden in Deutschland* also reprinted selected letters, sometimes from former journalists. For a classified list of references to migration issues see 'Emigration and Immigration in the German Jewish Press, 1933–1939', in *Jewish Immigrants of the Nazi period in the U.S.A.*, vol. III–2, comp. Daniel Schwartz, N.Y. 1980 (in print).

residents of foreign, mostly Eastern European, nationality). These ratios were upset by the pressure felt by émigrés following the November 1938 pogroms in Germany, and eight months earlier, by the panic flight of Viennese Jews across the Austrian frontiers into Switzerland and other neighbouring countries, and into Western Europe generally. (Yugoslavia, Italy and Czechoslovakia had closed their frontiers as soon as Austrian-Jewish migration pressures became evident in March/April 1938.) With the invasion of Czechoslovakia, the Nazi-Soviet Pact, the Second World War and the fall of Poland, France, Holland and Belgium to Axis conquest, Eastern as well as Western European countries ceased to be targets for German-Jewish immigration and became centres of rescue and flight. Only neutral countries (Spain, Portugal, Switzerland, Sweden) or overseas havens remained to save Jews from incarceration and deportation to death camps when legal emigration from Germany ended in October 1941.[75]

Table X, compiled from a variety of sources, reflects the *entry* or *presence* of Jewish émigrés from Germany or Austria at a given time based on estimates for selected European countries made at the time. The table reflects the "refugee" character of Jewish emigration within Europe. Each major advance of violent persecution brought about the entry of larger numbers of Jewish persecutees. Great Britain, France, Holland, Belgium and Switzerland as well as the Czechoslovak Republic were heirs to liberal traditions concerning the "right of asylum" for political and religious persecutees. Some of these traditions had been anchored in constitutional provisions. In the past they had been accepted by public opinion as part of the national self-image (*Staatsidee*), and in periods of persecution, had been followed with honourable liberality. This tradition had remained a factor throughout the 1930s in these countries, and had become part of the internal government (or public opinion) assessment of immigration policies. Politically, parties of the liberal centre and the left were more prone than rightist-nationalist parties to combine the humanitarianism inherent in the idea of asylum for persecutees with the defence of the economic interests of their constituents in time of depression. For small countries, concern with pressure on the part of Nazi Germany at times also played a part in their attitude towards Jewish immigration from Germany. As a result, domestic political and government changes affected the degree of restrictionism or liberality towards the refugee-immigrant residing in the country or asking for a visa. In most countries, the Jewish welfare establishments or representative Jewish bodies cooperated with government agencies and with the representatives of overseas immigrant Jewish aid agencies to ease the admission of Jewish refugees by working for their re-migration to final destinations. In other countries, fear of increasing anti-semitism or *Überfremdung* led such Jewish bodies to accept restrictionist trends in national policy. (Frequently, both motives were present in Jewish attitudes.) The impact of such policies, from whatever sources or for whichever motive, turned most European countries into countries of transient migration, and considerable government and police pressures were exerted to reduce the number of

---

[75]Rosenstock, *loc. cit.*, based on material of the *Zentralausschuß für Hilfe und Aufbau*, the social welfare arm of the *Reichsvertretung*; Bauer, *op. cit.*, based on published and archival materials engendered by the American Jewish Joint Distribution Committee.

resident émigrés through re-migration. In most countries this situation changed only following the outbreak of the Second World War.

In general, caution is indicated in estimating the number of Jewish refugees for some of the countries included in Table X. This is especially true of the figures for France, possibly also for Belgium and Italy and, to a minor extent and for limited periods, for Switzerland. The pressure of persecution, especially in 1933 for political refugees, and 1938–1939 for Jewish refugees from post-*Anschluß* Austria and post-November Germany often forced refugees to cross borders illegally, i.e., to avoid either the exit controls of passports (which would have led to their arrest and worse), or the procurement of an entrance visa in a passport if available (which made contact with Nazi control agencies like police or Gestapo necessary, with similar consequences). Another form of illegality (most typically in France) was brought about by the fact that residence permits of various kinds carried time limits at the end of which the refugee was expected to have left the country or face arrest, imprisonment or, the worst contingency, deportation to his country of origin. For numerous refugees of the middle- and later 1930s in Europe, the refusal of German authorities to renew German passports for émigrés, especially for visible and activist political enemies of the régime, and the lengthening list of émigrés being deprived of their German nationality by the Nazi authorities created the personal and political nightmare of "statelessness".[76] For refugees ready to re-migrate to overseas countries, some countries of intermediate settlement in Europe had followed a policy providing travel documents in lieu of passports. The League of Nations High Commission for Refugees also had worked for the provision of such papers for stateless post-1933 refugees (Convention of Geneva, 4th July 1936).

However, all such identity papers presupposed that the immigrant had been granted legal residence in a country of refuge – and such residence was contingent on the alien's proof of nationality. Through provisions such as these, persecutees were forced to enter illegally or stay on beyond the time granted originally. In situations such as these, refugees, at times supported by political friends, sympathetic officials or "lenient" interpretations of government regulations, were forced to exist in the loose interstices of immigration, residence or work rules governing their stay. In European countries of refuge, illegality and humanitarianism thus formed a functional corrective to breaches of the tradition of asylum, and, once the emergency had passed, were recognised as justified mitigations of harsh national policies.

In 1933, when Hitler struck and Europe was still at, or near, the peak of the world depression, the countries bordering Germany had long had provisions on

---

[76]*Gesetz über den Widerruf von Einbürgerungen und die Aberkennung der deutschen Staatszugehörigkeit*, 14th July 1933, RGB I, S. p. 480. The passport system controlling the movement of people across frontiers had been universally adopted only with the First World War. Previously, even where provisions for passports as basis for transnational travel existed, "legislation was allowed to pass into desuetude" (Plendes, *op. cit.*, p. 59). For such immigration countries as the U.S.A., the then valid provisions for naturalisation required a "declaration of intention" (first papers) which, in practice, permitted the issuance of travel papers, in any event hardly a pressing need for recent immigrants struggling in entry-level jobs to make ends meet.

TABLE X

Estimated numbers of Jewish refugees from Germany/Austria having entered (ent.) or present (pr.) in selected European countries, 1933–1939.

Year	Belgium	Czechoslovakia	France
1933		4,000 ent.	8,900–9,500 ent.
1934			10,000–12,000 pr. 2,400–3,000 re-emigrated.
1935		800 pr.	9,000 pr. of whom 2,000 illegal residents.
1936		6,500 ent. (1933–1936)	
1937			7,000 pr. of whom 2,500 supported.
1938	15,000 ent. (1933 to Sept. 1938). 13,300 pr. Nov. 1938. 3,000 ent. illegally (Nov./Dec. 1938).	5,000–6,000 pr.	10,000 pr. beginning 1938. 13,500 ent. to Dec. 1938-January 1939. 25,000 pr., incl. 2,000 Czechoslovaks.
1939	25,000 pr. (March). 400 per week illegal entrants (March 1939).		7,500 Baden deportees to Gurs (22nd October 1940)

Year	Netherlands	Great Britain	Italy
1933	3,682 ent.	300–400 per month.	
1934	1,200–1,500 returned to Germany, 1933/1934. Total 9,000 ent. 1933/1934.	100 per month.	
1935			
1936		"Several thousand" pr. (8th Sept. 1936).	1,000 pr.
1937	600 ent. per month (late 1936).		
1938	11,000 pr. 1933–1938 of whom 2,000 on relief. 2,000 ent. (elderly relatives of resident immigrants).	11,000 total entry 1933–Sept. 1938 + 400 transit.	6,000 pr. 7th Sept. 1938: Italian race laws.

Year	Netherlands	Great Britain	Italy
1939	10,000–12,000 pr. Feb. of whom 3,000 supported. 7,000–8,000 pr. Sept.	46,458 ent. 1933–Sept. 1939 of whom: aged 1–18 9,028 trainees 1,707 elderly 877 domestics 4,461 at Richborough camp 1,700 residents 28,685	(?) 10,000 left by Sept. 1939.

Year	Switzerland
1933	10,000 ent. Bad. Bahnhof Basle, March–Sept. (all kinds, German nationals). 5,000 pr.
1934	
1935	2,000 pr.
1936	
1937	
1938	3,000 ent. from Austria March–April. 2,000 enter illegally (after April 1938). 3,000 enter from Italy (to Sept. 1938).
1939	2,300 enter from Austria (July–August 1938). 10,000–12,000 pr. (late 1938/ early 1939). 5,000 pr. (Sept. 1939). 300 children ent.

Compiled from Bauer, *op. cit.*; R. Fabian/C. Coulmas, *Die deutsche Emigration in Frankreich nach 1933*, Munich–New York–Paris–London 1978; *Aid to Jews Overseas. Report for 1939*, Am. Jew. Joint Distribution Committee, New York 1940; C. Ludwig, *Die Flüchtlingspolitik der Schweiz seit 1933 bis zur Gegenwart* (1957), Bern 1966; A. J. Sherman, *Island Refuge. Britain and Refugees from the Third Reich 1933–1939*, Berkeley–Los Angeles, Cal. 1973.

their statute books, and worked out administrative procedures, controlling the admission, residence and gainful work of aliens.[77]

The restrictive potential of "alien laws" affected alien workers except where seasonal work or workers indispensable for a branch of industry dictated otherwise. Unemployment figures suggest the obvious motives for the restrictionist interpretations generally applied at the time: France – 400,000 (1936); Great Britain – 2,224,000 (1933), 1,804,000 (1938); Switzerland – 68,000 (average between monthly fluctuations of 101,000 and 49,000, 1933), 93,000 (average 1936); the Netherlands – 451,000 (1936); Czechoslovakia – 70,000 (1933).[78]

Disregarding national differences in police practice or the local, state (canton) or federal authorities concerned, practically all European countries established at least one of the following conditions for the residence permits of aliens: a work permit from a government authority or a government-approved contract with a native employer; "sufficient means" to support the immigrant and his family; an occupation considered useful or desirable (i.e., non-competitive with native occupations); a wealthy relative or sponsor able to guarantee the livelihood of the alien while in the country. Admission generally called for pre-entry visa procedures based on various proofs of health, non-criminality, trustworthiness or economic viability; all countries demanded registration of aliens within specified periods following their arrival. In several countries (France, Switzerland, Holland) residence permits were granted in cooperation between central (federal) and local or regional authorities. Loss of nationality (i.e., statelessness and thus non-deportability to the home country) represented reasons (e.g., in France and Switzerland) for withdrawal of residence permits and were grounds for either forced return to home country, or expulsion across a frontier. Enforcement of these provisions was handled with consideration, however, during several periods of the refugee emergency, or was subject to political and media pressures for liberalisation. There were several refinements of the web of restrictive measures to which aliens found themselves subjected, and the administration of restrictive policies varied from one country or period to another. Governments, however their policies may have appeared at the time, and however they appear in the retrospective light of the Holocaust or post-war immigration policies towards political refugees (e.g., Hungarians, 1956; Czechs, 1968) or "guest workers", were conscious of the sensitive issues related to immigration, and of the cross-pressures created by political and economic interests. And many governments failed to live up to their professed ideals or political traditions and employed harsh restrictive measures to keep Jewish refugees from entering their countries.

In sum, alien laws in liberal-democratic Northern and Western Europe and in liberal-democratic Czechoslovakia hovered between traditions of asylum, the right–left political divisions within the country and the "national interest" defined as balances between public opinions, political traditions, the economic nationalism dictated by business and employment conditions, and, for Jews coming from Germany, and more strongly, from Austria, real or anticipated fears of xenophobic and antisemitic reactions. For Jews or political refugees in panic

[77]For these provisions concerning aliens see Appendix.
[78]Bauer, *op. cit.*, p. 170 and *passim*; Ludwig, *op. cit.*, (see Table X), p. 62.

flight, however, it may safely be presumed that considerations such as these hardly entered into the decision to leave Germany in early 1933. The extent of this flight cannot be determined with precision: as terror unfolded following the Nazi takeover, a considerable number of Jews used the opportunity to travel, presumably as tourists, to such countries where the easy admission of such tourists had been an interest of the tourist industry. That 10,000 persons entered Switzerland between April and September 1933 at one frontier railroad station alone (*Badischer Bahnhof*, Basle) suggests the extent of the temporary escape to safety, and the widespread return movement from such havens.[79] The economic problems created for émigrés by their inability to secure gainful employment in European countries of refuge explains adequately the relatively uniform decline in absolute and relative numbers of Jewish refugees in Western Europe and Czechoslovakia. In 1933–1934, Jewish opinion as well as the Jewish press in Germany had gained a clear view of the increasing misery of middle-class émigrés and their families in Western countries sliding into marginality and, ultimately, poverty and dependence on welfare. Return migration appears to have persisted through early 1935 when a Nazi threat of internment in a concentration camp for returnees appears to have put a stop to such return movement. (Pupils or students studying abroad, however, were able to return for visits even after that date.) For the bulk of émigrés, however, re-emigration to a final destination beyond Europe was the only acceptable solution for their difficulties. It is in this light that German-Jewish emigration to European countries in absolute or relative numbers is to be evaluated. Aggravated persecutions of Jews in Upper Silesia, Austria, Germany, Danzig and Czechoslovakia, once again introduced mass pressures for admission, especially in 1938–1939. In response, most countries tightened restrictions for the admission of refugees once again, closed their frontiers or pushed émigrés strongly into re-migration.[80] In spite of these new restrictions, however, considerable numbers of refugees succeeded in crossing the frontiers to European countries of refuge. Public opinion, revolted by the orgy of brutality and despoliation, began to understand that the emigration of Jews from Germany had been more than a *Wirtschaftsemigration* all along. Parliamentary debates, the press, the churches and liberal organisations overcame bureaucratic or ministerial scruples and reasserted traditions of asylum in spite of continued economic difficulties. One country (Great Britain) changed its earlier restrictionism and admitted a considerably larger number of refugees, including unaccompanied children, than any other country in a ten-month period. The outbreak of the war in Europe led belligerents to close their frontiers to German nationals and thus stop emigration, except for transit visas to ports or neutral countries. Of occupied countries, only immigrants to Denmark were spared major involvement in the Holocaust when Danish resistance succeeded in saving

[79] For Netherlands, see Bauer, *op. cit.*, pp. 170 f.; for Switzerland, see Ludwig, *op. cit.*, p. 65; no corresponding figures are available for other countries. The movement included also German Jews of foreign nationality as indicated by the figures of émigrés – returnees of this group assisted by the *Hauptstelle für jüdische Wanderfürsorge*, Berlin, which was charged with care for Jews of foreign nationality, see Adler-Rudel, *Jüdische Selbsthilfe*, pp. 94–97.

[80] Switzerland, for example, succeeded in halving the number of émigrés present from 10,000 to 5,000 between January and September 1939, Bauer, *op. cit.*, p. 268.

most Jewish refugees by ferrying them to neutral Sweden. Substantial numbers were also saved in France, Belgium and Holland in underground operations, while about 21,000 Jewish refugees (including 9,119 German and 3,655 Austrian nationals) survived the war in Switzerland. In spite of the efforts of many individuals and organisations, however, an estimated 30,000 Jewish refugees residing in Axis-occupied Western Europe were deported to Eastern Europe and perished there.[81]

(END OF PART I)

[81] In France, their internment was aided by the police and administration of Vichy France; the documentary material bearing on the involvement of the French bureaucracy in these events is said to have been destroyed following the Second World War.

Jewish Emigration from Germany

APPENDIX

The legal provisions concerning aliens provide only a framework for often widely varying interpretations and applications by administrative departments, and their language permits considerable adaptability to changing social, economic or political conditions. The major applicable legal provisions for major European countries *prior to 1933* are:

Belgium: (for texts see H. Bekaerd, *Le Statut des Etrangers en Belgique* 2 vols. (vol. Ia and Ib) Brussels 1940; reprints of all provisions 1830–1939 pp. 475–668.)

Netherlands: Law 13th of August 1849 concerning admission and expulsion of aliens, *State Journal* No. 39; Act of 4th June 1858, *State Journal* No. 46; Royal Decree of 7th July 1887; *State Journal* No. 141; Revision of Royal Decree of 7th July 1887; Law of 17th June 1918, *State Journal* No. 410; Law of 16th August 1918, *State Journal* No. 52; Royal Decree of 11th August 1920, *State Journal* No. 669; and of 12th December 1922, *State Journal* No. 671. Regulations concerning Foreigners, article 27 and Criminal Code Art. 438, as amended by Royal Decree of 31st March 1922, 12th December 1922.

France: Loi sur la naturalisation et le séjour des étrangers en France, 3 décembre 1849, *Collection Complète des Lois* (C.C.L.) 1894, pp. 415–420; Décret relatif aux étrangers résidants en France, 2 octobre 1888, C.C.L., 1888, pp. 279–280; Lois relatives au séjour des étrangers en France et à la protection du travail national, 8 août 1893, C.C.L., 1893, pp. 371–373; Lois sur l'exercice des professions ambulantes et réglementation de la circulation des Nomades, 16 juillet 1912, C.C.L., 1912, pp. 408–415 (Art. 9: "Les art. [?] et 3 de la loi du 8 août 1893 sont modifiés et complèts comme il suit"); Décret portant à création d'une carte d'identité a l'usage des étrangers, 2 avril 1917, C.C.L., 1917, pp. 137–139; Décret réglementant la délivrance des cartes destinées aux étrangers, 10 juillet 1929, C.C.L., pp. 504–505; Décret complementant le décret du 10 juillet 1929 etc., 21 mai 1932, C.C.L., 1932, pp. 242–243.

Switzerland: Bundesratsverordnung vom 21. November 1917 betreffend die Grenzpolizei und die Kontrolle der Ausländer; Verordnung vom 29. November 1921 über die Kontrolle der Ausländer, as amended by Bundesratsbeschluß vom 7. September 1925 und Bundesratsbeschluß vom 16. Oktober 1928. (See Ludwig, *op. cit.*, pp. 14–27, includes historic review); Bundesgesetz vom 26. März 1931 über Aufenthalt und Niederlassung der Ausländer, und Vollziehungsverordnung vom 5. Mai 1933. (Provisions concerning military deserters or objectors, and references to Art. 70 a. 120 of the Federal Constitution are not included.)

Austria: Inlandarbeiterschutzgesetz vom 19. Dezember 1925, BGB No. 457.

Czechoslovakia: Law of 13th March 1928, Collection of Czechoslovakian Laws and Decrees, 1928, No. 39.

Great Britain: Aliens Act of 1905 (5 Edw. 7, c.13); Aliens Restrictions Act of 1914 (4 and 5 Geo. 5, c. 12); Aliens Restriction (Amendment) Act of 1919 (9 and 10 Geo. 5, c. 92); Order in Council of 1920 (Aliens Order). (S.R.O. No. 448.) For additional references to pre-Hitler restrictionist laws or decrees see Fields, *op. cit.*, pp. 675–699, and Plendes, *op. cit.*, p. 63, n. 151.

For the period following the Nazi seizure of power in Germany, the interpretation of administrative legislation concerning aliens reflected the leniency or harshness of public policies. A comprehensive scholarly analysis of the legislative and administrative history of alien law remains a *desideratum*. The monographic studies for several countries (France, Switzerland, Netherlands, United Kingdom, U.S.A.) quoted throughout section VIII illustrate the complex patterns of domestic and foreign influences that shaped the admission of Jews from Germany and Austria in the 1930s. Among the basic decrees or laws, applicable to the immigration of Jewish refugees and developed in response to the economic and political situation as perceived by changing governments during the period, were the following:

Belgium: Royal Decree 15th December 1930; the Belgian ratification of the Convention on Refugees of the League of Nations of 25th May 1936 (11th October 1936); ratification of the Statute of the League of Nations for Refugees coming from Germany of 4th July 1936 (5th December 1936); Instructions Générales pour l'application des arrêts royaux ... relatives aux étrangers en Belgique 29 octobre 1936; Convention concernant le statut des refugiés provenant de l'Allemagne, 10 février 1938.

Netherlands: Government Declaration 30th May 1934; Circulars, Ministry of Justice, 3rd July 1934; 10th October 1934; 15th March 1935; 23rd March 1938; 7th May 1938.

France: Décret modifiant la réglementation de la délivrance des cartes d'identité destinées aux étrangers, 6 février 1935, 35 C.C.L., pp. 53–56; Décret sur les marchands ambulants étrangers, 30 octobre 1935, C.C.L., p. 787; Décret tendant à protéger les artisans français contre la concurrence des artisans étrangers, 8 août 1935 (Bull. annote des lois 1935, p. 338); Le président de la République Française, ... l'arrangement conclus à Genève le 4 juillet 1936 – ... les articles 196, 197 et 351 du code du timbre fixant ... du droit exigible pour la délivrance et le visa des passeports, 17 septembre 1936 (le Bull. législatif Dalloz, 1936, p. 759; Décret sur la police des étrangers, 2 mai 1938, 38 C.C.L., pp. 310–311; Décret réglementant les conditions de séjour des étrangers en France, 14 mai 1938, 39 C.C.L., pp. 344–348; Décret tendant à assurer la protection du commerce français, 17 juin 1938, 38 C.C.L.; Décret-Loi relatif à la situation et à la police des étrangers, 12 novembre 1938 (Bull. annoté des lois, 1938, pp. 396–400; Décret-Loi relatif à la carte d'identité de commerçant pour les étrangers, 12 novembre 1938 (Bull. annoté des lois, pp. 400–401).

For a more detailed discussion of the legal provisions governing the nationality, naturalisation, immigration, work and other aspects of French legislation on refugees see now B. Vormeier, 'Dokumentation zur französischen Emigrantenpolitik (1933–1944). Ein Beitrag'. in H. Schramm, *Menschen in Gurs. Erinnerungen an ein französisches Internierungslager (1940–1941)*, Worms 1977, pp. 259–274 (Anhang C: Analytische Liste der wichtigsten französischen Gesetze betreffend die Ausländer), and *passim*.

Switzerland: Weisung des Eidgenössischen Justiz- und Polizeidepartments (EJPD) an die kantonalen Polizeidirektionen, 31st March 1933; Beschluß des Bundesrats (BBR) über die Behandlung der politischen Flüchtlinge, 7th April 1933; Kreisschreiben des EJPD, 20th April 1933; dto., 14th September 1933; dto., 8th August 1937; BBR, 28th March 1938; BBR, 19th August 1938; BBR, 10th October 1938; BBR, 20th January 1939 (for other Kreisschreiben und Weisungen see Ludwig, *op. cit.*, *passim*).

For the Swiss-SD agreement to stamp the letter "J" (for *Jude*) in red into German passports following the *Anschluß* of Austria, see Ludwig, *op. cit.*, pp. 94–134. (For the British reaction to the proposal of identifying Jews in this manner see Sherman, *op. cit.*, pp. 89 f.)

Great Britain: Foreign Office, Passport Control Division, Circular Visas for Holders of German and Austrian passports entering the United Kingdom, 27th April 1938, Sir Samuel Hoare (Home Secretary), House of Commons, 21st November 1938, Hansard, pp. 1428–1483. Internal Home Office Memoranda (unpublished). See Sherman, *op. cit., passim*, esp. pp. 213, 215 for 1938–1939.

Post-War Publications on German Jewry

A Selected Bibliography of Books and Articles 1979

Compiled by
IRMGARD FOERG and ANNETTE PRINGLE

Leo Baeck Institute
4 Devonshire Street
London W.1.

CONTENTS

		Page
I.	**HISTORY**	
	A. General	365
	Linguistics/Western Yiddish	369
	B. Communal and Regional History	370
	1. Germany	370
	1a. Alsace	374
	2. Austria	374
	3. Czechoslovakia	375
	4. Hungary	376
	C. German Jews in Various Countries	376
II.	**RESEARCH AND BIBLIOGRAPHY**	
	A. Libraries and Institutes	378
	B. Bibliographies and Catalogues	379
III.	**THE NAZI PERIOD**	
	A. General	381
	B. Jewish Resistance	390
IV.	**POST WAR**	
	A. General	391
	B. Restitution	393
	C. Antisemitism, Judaism, Nazism in Education and Teaching	394
V.	**JUDAISM**	
	A. Jewish Learning and Scholars	395
	B. The Jewish Problem	400
	C. Jewish Life and Organisations	401
	D. Jewish Art and Music	402
VI.	**ZIONISM AND ISRAEL**	402
VII.	**PARTICIPATION IN CULTURAL AND PUBLIC LIFE**	
	A. General	404
	B. Individual	408
VIII.	**AUTOBIOGRAPHY, MEMOIRS, LETTERS, GENEALOGY**	431
IX.	**GERMAN-JEWISH RELATIONS**	
	A. General	435
	B. German-Israeli Relations	435
	C. Church and Synagogue	436
	D. Antisemitism	438
	E. Noted Germans and Jews	439
X.	**FICTION, POETRY AND HUMOUR**	440
	INDEX	442

BIBLIOGRAPHY 1979

I. HISTORY

A. General

15815. BEN-SASSON, HAIM HILLEL, ed.: *Geschichte des jüdischen Volkes.* 1–2. München: Beck, 1978–1979. 2 vols. *Bd. 1: Von den Anfängen bis zum 7. Jahrhundert.* Von Abraham Malamat. Übers. von Siegfried Schmitz. 1978. IX, 515 pp., 44 illus., 13 maps, bibl. *Bd. 2: Vom 7. bis zum 17. Jahrhundert, das Mittelalter.* Von Haim Hillel Ben-Sasson. Übers. von Modeste zur Nedden Pferdekamp. 1979. IX, 434 pp., 37 illus., 5 maps, bibl. [Orig. title: 'Toldot 'am Jisrael', publ. in 1969. For Engl. edn. see No. 13589/YB. XXII.]

15816. BRODY, STANTON: *Seeds of the Holocaust. The German economy 1916–23.* Ed. by Don Venes. Glencoe, Ill., 1979. V, 42 pp., bibl. (pp. 41–42).

15817. CARLEBACH, JULIUS: *The forgotten connection. Women and Jews in the conflict between enlightenment and romanticism.* [In]: LBI Year Book XXIV, London, 1979. Pp. 107–138, bibl. footnotes.

15818. COHN, WILLY: *Juden und Staufer in Unteritalien und Sizilien.* Aufsätze zur Geschichte der Juden im Mittelalter, über ihr Verhältnis zu den Stauferkaisern und den Königen von Sizilien, sowie zur allgemeinen Staufergeschichte. Eine Sammlung verstreut erschienener Schriften aus den Jahren 1919–1936. Aalen: Scientia, [1978]. 131 pp., illus., bibl. (pp. 7–8), bibl. footnotes.

15819. ENDELMAN, TODD M.: *The Jews of Georgian England, 1714–1830. Tradition and change in a liberal society.* Philadelphia, Pa.: The Jewish Publication Society of America, 1979. 365 pp., illus., notes, bibl. [The author challenges the Germano-centric orientation of the bulk of modern Jewish historiography and argues that the modernisation of European Jewry encompassed far more than an intellectual revolution.]

15820. *Epistolae obscurorum virorum.* Hrsg. von Aloys Bömer. Neudr. der Ausg. Heidelberg 1924. 1–2. Aalen: Scientia, 1978. 2 vols. in 1 (164, 191 pp.). (Stachelschriften, Ältere Reihe, 1.) [Anonymously published satire, written mainly by Crotus Rubianus and Ulrich von Hutten to assist Johannes Reuchlin in the 'Battle of the Books' against Johannes Pfefferkorn and his backers.]

15821. FABRY, PHILIPP W.: *Mutmassungen über Hitler. Urteile von Zeitgenossen.* Unveränd. Nachdr. des erstmals 1969 erschienenen Werkes. Königstein/Ts.: Athenäum, 1979. 265 pp., bibl. (pp. 254–260). (Athenäum–Droste-Taschenbücher, Nr. 7227: Geschichte.) [Incl. chap. '*Die deutschen Juden und das heraufdämmernde Dritte Reich*', pp. 125–137. For 1st edn. see No. 7606/YB. XV. Cf. in this connection the article: Jewish defence against Nazism in the Weimar Republic (Arnold Paucker) [in]: The Wiener Library Bulletin, Vol. 26, Nos. 1/2 (New Series Nos. 26/27), London, 1972, pp. 21–31 (see No. 10166/YB. XVIII).]

15822. GRUNFELD, FREDERIC V.: *Prophets without honour. A background to Freud, Kafka, Einstein and their world.* New York: Holt, Rinehart and Winston, 1979. XIII, 349 pp., ports., bibl. (pp. 323–334). [Cf.: Eine Kulturgeschichte des Exils (Gert Niers) [in]: Aufbau, New York, Dec. 7, 1979, p. 20. Review (John Leonard) [in]: Internat. Herald Tribune, Zürich, Sept. 25, 1979, p. 14. See also excerpts: The Jews in the Weimar Republic (F. V. Grunfeld) [in]: Midstream, Vol. 25, No. 8, New York, Oct. 1979, pp. 29–31. Prophets without honour. The lost world of German-Jewish intellectuals (F. V. Grunfeld) [in]: Present Tense, Vol. 6, No. 4, New York, Summer 1979, pp. 27–35, ports., illus.]

15823. *Jews and Germans from 1860 to 1933. The problematic symbiosis.* Ed. by David Bronsen. Heidelberg: Winter, 1979. 383 pp., tabs., curricula vitae. (Schriftenreihe der Gesamthochschule Siegen, Reihe Siegen, Beiträge zur Literatur- u. Sprachwissenschaft, Bd. 9.) [Cont.: Foreword (David Bronsen, pp. 1–7). On the social psychology of the Jews in Germany, 1900–1933 (Gershom Scholem, pp. 9–32). Anti-Semitism as a reflection of social, economic and political tension in Germany, 1880–1933 (Hans-Joachim Bieber, pp. 33–77). Jewish participation in Wilhelmine politics (Peter Pulzer, pp. 78–99. Concise version of 'Die jüdische Beteiligung an der Politik' [in]: Juden im Wilhelminischen Deutschland 1890–1914, see No. 13387/YB. XXII). Walther Rathenau and the tensions of Wilhelmine society (Peter Loewenberg, pp. 100–128). 'Germanism and Judaism', Hermann Cohen's normative paradigm of the

German-Jewish symbiosis (Steven S. Schwarzschild, pp. 129–172). Tradition als Revolution: Gustav Landauers 'gewordenes-werdendes' Judentum (Norbert Altenhofer, pp. 173–208). Defense and introspection: German Jewry, 1914 (Stephen Magill, pp. 209–233). Assimilation and the demise of liberal political tradition in Vienna, 1860–1914 (Dennis Klein, pp. 234–261). Melting pot or witch's cauldron? Jews and anti-Semites in Vienna at the turn of the century (Egon Schwarz, pp. 262–287). Mahler: German romantic or Jewish satirist? (Henry A. Lea, pp. 288–305). Jews in German society: Prague, 1860–1914 (Gary B. Cohen, pp. 306–337). The rediscovery of the Eastern Jews. German Jews in the East, 1890–1918 (Sander Gilman, pp. 338–365).

15824. JOSPE, ALFRED: *German Jewry was different.* [In]: Judaism, Vol. 28, No. 2, New York, Spring, 1979. Pp. 237–247. [Review essay of 'Freud, Jews and other Germans. Masters and victims in modernist culture' by Peter Gay, New York, 1978, see No. 14996/YB. XXIV.]

15825. *Juden im Wilhelminischen Deutschland 1890–1914.* Ein Sammelband. Hrsg. von Werner E. Mosse unter Mitwirkung von Arnold Paucker. Tübingen: Mohr, 1976. XIV, 786 pp., tabs., bibl. (pp. 703–754). (Schriftenreihe wissenschaftlicher Abhandlungen des Leo Baeck Instituts, 33.) [See No. 13387/YB. XXII.] *Selected reviews:* Between recognition and discrimination (Robert S. Wistrich) [in]: AJR Information, No. 6, London, June 1977. (Giuseppe Bevilacqua) [in]: Belfagor, No. 6, Florence, 30. Nov. 1977, pp. 732–734. (Gerd Fesser) [in]: Deutsche Literaturzeitung, H. 718, Berlin/East, 1979, pp. 461–463. (Ernst Walter Zeeden) [in]: Historisches Jahrbuch, Bd. 97/98, Freiburg i. Br., 1978, pp. 597–600. (Peter Steinbach) [in]: Jahrbuch für die Geschichte Mittel- u. Ostdeutschlands, Bd. 27, Berlin, 1977, pp. 318–321. Der Anfang vom Ende der Illusionen (Gabriel Ilan) [in]: MB, Nr. 12/13, Tel Aviv, 1. April 1977, p. 9. Juden in Deutschland. Historische Analysen deutscher Politik (Ursula Hüllbüsch) [in]: Politische Vierteljahresschrift, Nr. 2, Opladen, 1978, pp. 282–287 (also on 'Deutsches Judentum in Krieg und Revolution 1916–1923'. Schriftenreihe wissenschaftlicher Abhandlungen des Leo Baeck Instituts, 25, Tübingen, Mohr, 1971, see No. 9225/YB. XVII). Assimilation und Antisemitismus (Immanuel Birnbaum) [in]: SZ, München, 5./6. März 1977. Kaiser Wilhelm II. u. die Juden (Karl Kupisch) [in]: Der Tagesspiegel, Berlin, 6. April 1977, p. 15. Jews and the Fatherland (F. L. Carsten) [in]: Times Literary Supplement, London, March 11, 1977, p. 268. (Wilhelm Treue) [in]: Vierteljahrschrift für Sozial- u. Wirtschaftsgeschichte, Bd. 65, H. 2, Wiesbaden, 1978, pp. 285–287. (Joachim Streisand) [in]: Zeitschrift für Geschichtswissenschaft, H. 5, Berlin/East, 1977, p. 600.

15826. *Judentum im Zeitalter der Aufklärung.* Hrsg. vom Vorstand der Lessing-Akademie. (Red.: Ingeborg Wiesbach.) Bremen, Wolfenbüttel: Jacobi, 1977. 407 pp. (Wolfenbütteler Studien zur Aufklärung, Bd. 4.) [Incl.: Judentum im Zeitalter der Aufklärung (Karl Heinrich Rengstorf, pp. 11–37). Zur historischen Deutung der Aufklärung. Probleme u. Perspektiven (Rudolf Vierhaus, pp. 38–54). Toleranz u. Judenrecht in der öffentlichen Meinung von 1783 (Jacob Toury, pp. 55–73). Aufklärung, Judentum u. Emanzipation (Julius H. Schoeps, pp. 74–102). Antijudaistische Phänomene in der Aufklärung (Ludwig Borinski, pp. 103–117). 'Primat der Ethik' oder 'erkenntnistheoretische Begründung der Ethik'? Thesen zur Kant-Rezeption in der jüdischen Philosophie (Friedrich Niewöhner, pp. 118–162). Moses Mendelssohn u. Immanuel Kant im Gespräch über die Aufklärung (Frieder Loetzsch, pp. 163–186). Moses Mendelssohn u. Hermann Samuel Reimarus (Gerhard Alexander, pp. 187–209). Joseph von Sonnenfels als Patriot (Grete Klingenstein, pp. 210–228). Lessing u. das Judentum. Rezeption, Dramatik u. Kritik, Krypto-Spinozismus (Karl S. Guthke, pp. 229–271). 'Die Erziehung des Menschengeschlechts' u. jüdisches Selbstbewusstsein im 19. Jahrhundert (Michael Graetz, pp. 273–295). Friedrich Schleiermacher über das Sendschreiben jüdischer Hausväter (Gunter Scholtz, pp. 297–351). Schrifttum über Salomon Maimon. Eine Bibliographie mit Anmerkungen (Noah J. Jacobs).]

15827. *Das Judentum in der Deutschen Umwelt 1800–1850. Studien zur Frühgeschichte der Emanzipation.* Hrsg. von Hans Liebeschütz und Arnold Paucker. Tübingen: Mohr, 1977. XII, 445 pp., tabs., bibl. (pp. 391–420). (Schriftenreihe wissenschaftlicher Abhandlungen des Leo Baeck Instituts, 35.) [See No. 14181/YB. XXIII.] *Selected reviews:* Jews in German Society (Erwin Rosenthal) [in]: AJR Information, Vol. 30, No. 12, London, Dec. 1978, p.1. (Michael A. Meyer) [in]: The American Historical Review, Bloomington, In., June 1978, pp. 745–746. (Ernst Walter Zeeden) [in]: Historisches Jahrbuch, Bd. 97/98, Freiburg i. Br., 1978, pp. 597–600. (Guido Kisch) [in]: Historische Zeitschrift, Bd. 226, München, 1978, pp. 733–734. (Stefi Jersch-Wenzel) [in]: Jahrbuch für die Geschichte Mittel- u. Ostdeutschlands, Bd. 27,

Berlin, 1977, pp. 317–318. (Lamar Cecil) [in]: Journal of Modern History, Vol. 51, No. 2, 1979, pp. 368–370. (Rudolf Pfisterer) [in]: Judaica, No. 1, 1979, pp. 40–42. Geschichtsprobleme im Zeitalter der Emanzipation (Naftali H. Sonn) [in]: MB, Nr. 15/16, Tel-Aviv, 21. April 1978, pp. 17–18. (Ruth Wolf) [in]: Studia Rosenthaliana, Vol. 13, No. 1, 1979, pp. 119–121.

15828. KAMPMANN, WANDA: *Deutsche und Juden. Die Geschichte der Juden in Deutschland vom Mittelalter bis zum Beginn des Ersten Weltkrieges.* Frankfurt a. Main: Fischer, 1979. 449 pp. (Fischer-Taschenbücher, 3429.) [1st edn. 1963, see No. 3679/YB. IX.]

15829. KATZ, JACOB: '*Entscheidungsjahr 1932*'. [Introductory essay to the following contributions, now publ. for the first time though they are reprints from the 'Festschrift Herrn Rabbiner Dr. Leo Baeck zu seinem sechzigsten Geburtstag', Berlin [23.] Mai 1933, which, due to the circumstances, exists only in a few privately mimeog. copies]: An Leo Baeck, 20. Mai 1933 (Max Kreutzberger, pp. 11–15). Zur wirtschaftlichen Lage u. Haltung der deutschen Juden (Alfred Marcus, pp. 16–34, diagr.). Das Geschlecht zwischen gestern und morgen (Max Wiener, pp. 35–49). Die pädagogische Situation (Max Grünewald, pp. 50–56). Tel Aviv: Bitaon, 1979. 58 pp. (Bulletin des Leo Baeck Instituts, Jg. 18, N.F., Nr. 55.) [Jacob Katz, chairman of the board of the Leo Baeck Institute Jerusalem. Cf.: Professor Katz zum 75. Geburtstag (Pinchas E. Rosenblüth) [in]: MB, Nr. 42, Tel Aviv, 16. Nov. 1979, p. 7.]

15830. KISCH, GUIDO: *Forschungen zur Rechts-, Wirtschafts- und Sozialgeschichte der Juden.* Mit einem Verzeichnis der Schriften von Guido Kisch zur Rechts- und Sozialgeschichte der Juden. Sigmaringen: Thorbecke, 1979. 495 pp., 4 illus. (Kisch, Guido: Ausgewählte Schriften, Bd. 2.) [Cont. essays under the following section-titles: I. Studien zur Rechts-, Sozial- u. Wirtschaftsgeschichte der Juden in Deutschland während des Mittelalters. II. Die Universitäten u. die Juden. III. Biographie. IV. Bücherkunde u. Bibliographie. V. Kritische Beiträge. VI. Nachrufe. For vol. 1 of Guido Kisch: 'Ausgewählte Schriften' see No. 15002/YB. XXIV. Vol. 3 will follow in 1980. G. Kisch, born Jan. 22, 1889 in Prague, emigrated to the U.S.A., now living in Basle. Cf. birthday tributes: [in]: AJR Information, Vol. 39, No. 2, London, Febr. 1979, p. 7. (E. G. Lowenthal) [in]: 'Allgemeine', Düsseldorf, 23. Febr. 1979, p. 4. Der Lebensweg eines Rechtshistorikers. Zum 90. Geburtstag von G. Kisch (E. G. Lowenthal) [in]: Isr. Wochenblatt, Nr. 3, Zürich, 19. Jan. 1979, p. 33, port.]

15831. LEUSCHEN-SEPPEL, ROSEMARIE: *Neuere Studien zur deutsch-jüdischen Geschichte im 19. Jahrhundert.* Forschungsberichte u. Rezensionen. [In]: Archiv für Sozialgeschichte, Bd. 19, Bonn, 1979. Pp. 643–659. [Review article, also of Leo Baeck Institute publications.]

15832. LOW, ALFRED D.: *Jews in the eyes of the Germans from the Enlightenment to Imperial Germany.* Philadelphia: Institute for the Study of Human Issues, 1979. X, 509 pp., illus., ports., bibl. (pp. 462–494).

15833. MAGILL, STEPHEN: *Defense and introspection. The First World War as a pivotal crisis in the German Jewish experience.* Los Angeles, Univ. of California, Phil. Diss., 1977. 435 pp.

15834. MEYER, MICHAEL: *The question of continuity in Jewish history.* [Hebrew with Engl. summary.] [In]: Gesher, No. 1–2 (96–97), Tel Aviv, Spring–Summer 1979. Pp. 14–21. [Refers to Abraham Geiger, Heinrich Graetz, Leopold Zunz and others.]

15835. MILLER, SUSANNE: *Deutsche Juden und jüdische Deutsche.* [In]: Die Neue Gesellschaft, Nr. 7, Bonn, Juli 1979. Pp. 644–647. [Review article.]

15836. MOSSE, GEORGE L.: *Towards the Final Solution. A history of European racism.* London: Dent, 1979. XVI, 277 pp. [For previous edn. with different sub-title, publ. in 1976, see No. 14188/YB. XXII.]

15837. MOSSE, WERNER E.: *Judaism, Jews and capitalism. Weber, Sombart and beyond.* [In]: LBI Year Book XXIV, London, 1979. Pp. 3–15, bibl. footnotes.

15838. RICHARZ, MONIKA, ed.: *Jüdisches Leben in Deutschland. Bd. 2: Selbstzeugnisse zur Sozialgeschichte im Kaiserreich.* Hrsg. u. eingeleitet von Monika Richarz. Stuttgart: Deutsche Verlags-Anstalt, 1979. 494 pp., illus., facsims., ports., biogr. notes, bibl. notes. (Jüdisches Leben in Deutschland, Bd. 2.) (Veröffentlichung des Leo Baeck Instituts.) [Cont.: Einführung: 1. Auswahl u. Edition der Selbstzeugnisse; 2. Die jüdische Bevölkerung Deutschlands; 3. Berufliche u. soziale Schichtung; 4. Wirkungen des Antisemitismus; 5. Religiöse u. soziale Entwicklung. Quellentexte: I. Reichshauptstadt Berlin; II. In Dörfern u. Kleinstädten; III. An der Reichsgrenze; IV. Firmengeschichten; V. Anwalt u. Politik; VI. Frauen; VII. Als Deutscher u. Jude; VIII. Zionismus u. Antizionismus; IX. Im Ersten Weltkrieg. Cf.: The Kaiser's Jews (Egon Larsen) [in]: AJR Information, London, Oct. 1979, p. 5. So lebten sie einmal (Hans Steinitz) [in]: Aufbau, New York, Dec. 7, 1979, p. 19. [In]: deutschland-berichte, Jg. 15, Nr. 7, Bonn, Juli 1979, p. 24. Als Deutschland den Juden He mat war (Martin Broszat) [in]: FAZ, Frankfurt a. Main, 16. Nov. 1979, p. 10. (Martin Broszat) [in]: Geschichte in Wissenschaft u. Unterricht, Jg. 31, H. 1, Stuttgart, Jan. 1980, p. 26. Blick zurück auf die 'gute alte Zeit'. Dokumente zur Sozialgeschichte der Juden im Wilhelminischen Reich [in]: MB, Nr. 47, Tel Aviv, 21. Dez. 1979, pp. 6–7. (Salcia Landmann) [and correction] (E. G. Lowenthal) [in]: Das Neue Israel, Jg. 32, H. 3 (p. 163) & H. 5 (p. 263), Zürich, Sept. & Nov. 1979. Deutsche Juden, jüdische Deutsche im Wilhelminischen Reich (Gerhard Frick) [in]: NZZ, Zürich, 20. Juli 1979. Ehe das Unheil kam. Wie Juden einmal in Deutschland lebten, in Glück u. Frieden (Julius H. Schoeps) [in]: Die Zeit, Nr. 46, Hamburg, 9. Nov. 1979, p. 65. For vol. 1 see No. 13397/YB. XXII; Vol. 3, Selbstzeugnisse 1918–1945, in preparation.]

15839. ROTHSCHILD, ELI: *König Davids Kinder. Eine Heimkehr-Chronik der Juden*. Mainz: v. Hase u. Köhler, 1979. 144 pp., bibl. (pp. 137–144). [Cf.: Review [in]: deutschland-berichte, Jg. 16, Nr. 1, Bonn, Jan. 1980, p. 27. Bilder aus der jüdischen Vergangenheit (Abraham Tobias) [in]: Das Neue Israel, Jg. 32, H. 5, Zürich, Nov. 1979, p. 268. See also: Glückwunsch für Eli Rothschild zum 70. Geburtstag (Hans Capell) [in]: MB, Nr. 45, Tel Aviv, 7. Dez. 1979, p. 6.

15840. SCHOEPS, JULIUS H.: *Autoemanzipation und Selbsthilfe. Die Anfänge der nationaljüdischen Bewegung in Deutschland, 1882–1897*. [In]: Zeitschrift für Religions- u. Geistesgeschichte, Bd. 31, H. 4, Köln, 1979. Pp. 345–365.

15841. SCHOFER, LAWRENCE: *The history of European Jewry. Search for a method.* [In]: LBI Year Book XXIV, London, 1979. Pp. 17–36, bibl. footnotes.

15842. SCHRÖCKER, ALFRED: *Jüdische Finanziers des Fürstbischofs Lothar Franz von Schönborn (1655–1729)*. [In]: Jahrbuch für Fränkische Landesforschung, Bd. 37, Erlangen, 1977. Pp. 125–137.

15843. SCHUBERT, KURT: *Die Kultur der Juden. Teil 2: Judentum im Mittelalter*. Wiesbaden: Athenaion, 1979. 188 pp., 105 illus., 2 tabs. (Handbuch der Kulturgeschichte. Hrsg. von Eugen Thurnher. Abt. 2: Kulturen der Völker.) [Part 1, 'Israel im Altertum', was publ. in 1977.]

15844. SCHWARZFUCHS, SIMON: *Napoleon, the Jews and the Sanhedrin*. London: Routledge & Kegan Paul, 1979. 218 pp., bibl. (The Littman Library of Jewish Civilization.)

15845. SPITZER, SHLOMO: *Die jüdische Gemeinde im Mittelalter: Institutionen, Kompetenzen und Aufgaben.* [In]: Kairos, N.F. 21, H. 1, Salzburg, 1979. Pp. 48–59, bibl. footnotes.

15846. STEMBERGER, BRIGITTE: *Zu den Judenverfolgungen in Deutschland zur Zeit der ersten beiden Kreuzzüge.* In: Kairos, N.F. 20, H. 1 & 2, Salzburg, 1978. Pp. 53–72, 151–157.

15847. STERN, FRITZ: *Gold and Iron. Bismarck, Bleichröder and the building of the German Empire*. London: Allen & Unwin, 1979. 620 pp., illus., bibl. (Paperback.) [Cf.: Ein Bankier im Halbdunkel zwischen Politik, Finanzen u. Geschäft. Bemerkungen zu: Fritz Stern, Gold and Iron (Jacob van Klaweren) [in]: Bankhistorisches Archiv, Jg. 5, H. 1. Frankfurt a. Main, Juli 1979, pp. 51–66. Review (Ivo N. Lambi) [in]: Canadian Journal of History, Vol. 13, Saskatoon/Canada, April 1978, pp. 85–93. For earlier English and German edns. and reviews see No. 13400/YB. XXI, No. 14192/YB. XXIII, No. 15012/YB. XXIV.]

15848. STRAUS, RAPHAEL: *Die Juden im Königreich Sizilien unter Normannen und Staufern*. [Nachdr. der Ausg.] Heidelberg, Winter, 1910. Nendeln/Liechtenstein: Kraus, 1977. 115 pp. (Heidelberger Abhandlungen zur mittleren u. neueren Geschichte, H. 30.)

15849. SUCHY, BARBARA: *Lexikographie und Juden im 18. Jahrhundert. Die Darstellung von Juden und Judentum in den englischen, französischen und deutschen Lexika und Enzyklopädien im Zeitalter der Aufklärung*. Köln: Böhlau, 1979. 323 pp. (Neue Wirtschaftsgeschichte, Bd. 14.) Zugl.: Marburg, Univ., Wirtschaftswiss. Diss., 1976.

15850. TALMON, SHEMARYAHU/SIEFER, GREGOR, eds.: *Religion und Politik in der Gesellschaft des 20. Jahrhunderts*. Ein Symposion mit israelischen u. deutschen Wissenschaftlern. Bonn: Keil, 1978. 221 pp. [Contributions by the two eds. and Ernst Simon, Hans Jochen Margull, Yehoshua Arieli, Alexander Schwan, Shlomo Aronson, Werner Jochmann, Nathan Rotenstreich, Christian Krockow.]

15851. VAGTS, ALFRED: *Die Juden im amerikanisch-deutschen imperialistischen Konflikt vor 1917.* [In]: Amerikastudien, Jg. 24, H. 1, Stuttgart, 1979. Pp. 56–71, bibl. footnotes.

15852. VAGTS, ALFRED: *Bilanzen und Balancen. Aufsätze zur internationalen Finanz und internationalen Politik.* Hrsg. von Hans-Ulrich Wehler. Frankfurt a. Main: Syndikat, 1979. 307 pp., bibl. (pp. 303–306). [Incl. reprints of: *M. M. Warburg und Co. Ein Bankhaus in der deutschen Weltpolitik 1905–1933* (see No. 1460 a/YB. IV) and: *Die Juden im englisch-deutschen Imperialismuskonflikt vor 1914* (see No. 13843/YB. XXII).]

15853. WASSERMANN, HENRY: *Jews, 'Bürgertum' and 'bürgerliche Gesellschaft' in a liberal era (1840–1880)*. [Hebrew with Engl. summary (pp. III–XXIV).] Jerusalem, Hebrew Univ., Phil. Diss., 1979. XXIV, 315 pp., stats. [Incl. sections on: 'Bürgertum' as a society, and the Jews. From 'traditional society' to a 'Jüdisch-bürgerliche Gesellschaft'. New images and attitudes in the 'Gartenlaube' (see No. 15017/YB. XXIV) and 'Fliegende Blätter'.]
15854. WERTHEIMER, JACK L.: *German policy and Jewish politics. The absorption of East European Jews in Germany, 1868–1914*. New York, Columbia Univ., Phil. Diss., 1978. 604 pp., bibl. [Incl. chaps.: The inhospitable milieu. German responses to Jewish immigration (pt. I). Characteristics of the immigrant group. The relationship between image and reality (pt. II). Eastern Jews and native society. Peripheral groups (pt. III). Eastern and native Jews. The communal absorption of immigrants (pt. IV).]

Linguistics/Western Yiddish

15855. BIRNBAUM, [SOLOMON] A.: *Grammatik der Jiddischen Sprache*. Mit einem Wörterbuch und Lesestücken. [Von] Salomo A. Birnbaum. 3., ergänzte Aufl. Hamburg: Buske, 1979. IV, 199 pp.
15856. BIRNBAUM, SOLOMON A.: *Yiddish. A survey and a grammar*. Toronto: Univ. of Toronto Press, 1979. XVI, 400 pp., 2 facsims., 1 map, bibl. [Incl.: Origin of Yiddish in Germany. Old Yiddish or middle high German. Western Yiddish. 'Jargon', 'Judaeo-German'. See also: Soviet Yiddish (Solomon A. Birnbaum) [in]: Soviet Jewish Affairs, Vol. 9, No. 1, London, 1979, pp. 29–41 (incl. chap. 'The German element').]
15857. FREIMARK, PETER: *Language behaviour and assimilation. The situation of the Jews in Northern Germany in the first half of the nineteenth century*. [In]: LBI Year Book XXIV, London, 1979. Pp. 157–177, bibl. footnotes.
15858. HUTTERER, CLAUS JÜRGEN: *Die germanischen Sprachen. Ihre Geschichte in Grundzügen*. Budapest: Akadémiai Kiadó, 1975. XX, 543 pp., illus., maps. [Incl.: Jiddisch (Geschichte; Quellen; Entwicklung u. Dialekte des Jiddischen; Die jiddische Sprache; Sprachverbindungen; Textproben), pp. 347–361, bibl. (pp. 457–478).]
15859. *Jiddische Volkslieder. Liebeslieder*. Für Singstimmen mit Klavier oder Gitarre eingerichtet von Andre Asriel. Dt. Nachdichtung u. phonetische Transkription von Werner Günzerodt. Berlin/East: Verlag Neue Musik, 1978. 36 pp.
15860. KAPLAN, ANATOLI L.: *Variationen zu jiddischen Volksliedern*. Hrsg. u. mit einem Nachwort von Beate Jahn-Zechendorff. Leipzig: Insel, 1976. 47 pp., 32 colour plates.
15861. LANDMANN, SALCIA: *Jiddisch, das Abenteuer einer Sprache*. Nachwort von F. J. Beranek. Wiesbaden: Limes, 1979. 474 pp. [For previous edns. see No. 3011/YB. VIII; also No. 3693/YB. IX and No. 4352/YB. X].
15862. LOCKWOOD, W. B.: *Herabsetzendes shm- im Jiddischen*. [In]: Zeitschrift für vergleichende Sprachforschung. Bd. 92, H. 1 & 2, Göttingen, 1978. Pp. 300–305.
15863. LOWENSTEIN, STEVEN M.: *The Yiddish written word in nineteenth-century Germany*. [In]: LBI Year Book XXIV, London, 1979. Pp. 179–192, bibl. footnotes.
15864. MIESES, MATTHIAS: *Die Entstehungsursache der jüdischen Dialekte*. Nachdr. der Ausg. Wien 1915. Mit einer Einleitung von Peter Freimark. Hamburg: Buske, 1979. XI, 120 pp.
15865. RUBIN, RUTH: *Voices of a people. The story of Yiddish folksong*. Philadelphia, Pa.: The Jewish Publication Society of America, 1979. 558 pp., illus. [Incl. also songs that came out of the Nazi concentration camps.]
15866. SCHACK, INGEBORG-LIANE: *Der Mensch tracht un Got lacht. 450 jiddische Sprichwörter*. Mainz: Krach, 1977. 128 pp., illus., bibl. (pp. 119–121).
15867. SILVERMAN-WEINREICH, BEATRICE: *Towards a structural analysis of Yiddish proverbs*. [In]: YIVO Annual of Jewish Social Science, Vol. XVII, New York, 1978. Pp. 1–20, bibl. notes (pp. 19–20). [See also: International conference on research in Yiddish language and literature [at the University of Oxford, from Aug. 6 to 9, 1979. A report]. [In]: News of the YIVO, No. 150, New York, Sept. 1979, pp. 1–3, port.]

Bibliography

B. Communal and Regional History

1. Germany

15868. ALTENKIRCHEN/Westerwald. HEUZEROTH, GÜNTER: *Jüdisch-deutsche Bürger unserer Heimat.* I. Altenkirchen. II. Altenkirchen und Hamm/Sieg. III. Wissen, Betzdorf, Kirchen, Herdorf. IV. Die Zeit der Vernichtung. [In]: Heimat-Jahrbuch des Kreises Altenkirchen/Westerwald u. der angrenzenden Gemeinden, Bd. 1–4. Altenkirchen: Dieckmann, 1975–1978. Pp. 48–59 (Bd. 1, 1975); 45–59 (Bd. 2, 1976); 118–128 (Bd. 3, 1977); 137–147 (Bd. 4, 1978). [Also offprint under the title]: Jüdisch-deutsche Mitbürger unserer Heimat, hrsg. vom Heimatverein des Kreises Altenkirchen. Altenkirchen/Westerwald: Dieckmann, n.d. [1978]. 52 pp.

15869. ALZEY. BÖCHER, OTTO: *Zur Einführung in Samuel Adlers 'Worte der Weihe'* [zur Einweihung der neuen Synagoge in Alzey] 1854. [In]: Alzeyer Geschichtsblätter, H. 14, Alzey: Rheinhessische Druckwerkstätte, 1979. Pp. 58–73.

15870. — WEILAND, LINDE B.: *In memoriam. Das Alzeyer Memorbuch.* [In]: Alzeyer Geschichtsblätter, H. 14, Alzey: Rheinhessische Druckwerkstätte, 1979. Pp. 132–141.

15871. AUGSBURG. GROOS, WALTER: *Juden in Augsburg.* [In]: Augsburger Blätter, Jg. 5, H. 1, Augsburg, 1979. Pp. 11–18. Also about the 'Kristallnacht'.

15872. BADEN. ROSENTHAL, BERTHOLD: *Heimatgeschichte der badischen Juden seit ihrem geschichtlichen Auftreten bis zur Gegenwart.* Mit 11 Beilagen. Nachdr. der Ausg. Bühl/Baden, 1927. Magstadt b. Stuttgart: Bissinger, 1979. 532 pp.

15873. — WEISS, ELMAR: *Jüdisches Schicksal im Gebiet zwischen Neckar und Tauber* [Kreis Buchen, Mosbach u. Tauberbischofsheim]. Heidelberg (Postfach 103728), 1979. 32 pp., illus., map, bibl. footnotes. (Veröffentlichung der Landeszentral für politische Bildung Baden-Württemberg, Aussenstelle Nordbaden.) [Cover title.]

15874. BAVARIA. OPHIR, BARUCH Z./WIESEMANN, FALK, eds.: *Die jüdischen Gemeinden in Bayern 1918–1945. Geschichte und Zerstörung.* München: Oldenbourg, 1979. 511 pp., 9 maps, bibl. (pp. 492–497). (Veröffentlichung im Rahmen des Projekts 'Widerstand und Verfolgung in Bayern 1933–1945' im Auftrag des Bayerischen Staatsministeriums für Unterricht u. Kultus bearb. vom Institut für Zeitgeschichte in Verbindung mit den Staatlichen Archiven Bayerns.) [Based on the original edn. in Hebrew by B. Z. Ophir in collaboration with Shlomo Schmiedt and Chasia Turtel-Aberzhanska: *Pinkas Hakehillot.* Encyclopaedia of Jewish communities from their foundation till after the Holocaust: Germany–Bavaria, Jerusalem: Yad Vashem, 1972, see No. 10184/YB. XVIII.]

15875. BERLIN. GAY, PETER: *Der 'Berlinisch-jüdische Geist'. Zweifel an einer Legende.* [In]: Der Monat, Jg. 31, H. 1 (Nr. 273), Berlin, Febr./März 1979. Pp. 5–18. [This essay is a transl. chapter of the author's 'Freud, Jews and other Germans', New York, 1978, see No. 14996/YB. XXIV.]

15876. — HERTZ, DEBORAH: *Salonières and literary women in late eighteenth-century Berlin.* [In]: New German Critique, No. 14, Milwaukee, Univ. of Wisconsin, Spring 1978. Pp. 97–108. [On the prominence of Jewish women in the Salon.]

15877. — LOWENTHAL, ERNST G.: *Von Moritz Veit bis Heinrich Stahl. Gemeindevorsteher 1845–1943.* Ein Beitrag zur Geschichte der Juden in Berlin. [In]: Der Bär von Berlin, Jahrbuch des Vereins für die Geschichte Berlins, 28, Berlin, 1979. Pp. 79–92. [E. G. Lowenthal, born 1904. See birthday tributes: (Hans Steinitz) [in]: Aufbau, New York, Dec. 21, 1979, p. 4, port. (Werner Rosenstock) [in]: AJR Information, London, Dec. 1979, p. 7.]

15878. — MEYER, MICHAEL A.: *The religious reform controversy in the Berlin Jewish Community, 1814–1823.* [In]: LBI Year Book XXIV, London, 1979. Pp. 139–155, bibl. footnotes.

15879. BONN. ENNEN, EDITH: *Die jüdische Gemeinde in Bonn.* In: Bonner Geschichtsblätter, 29 (1977). Pp. 81–94.

15880. BRANDENBURG (Mark). SIMON, HEINRICH: *Ein Beschneidungsbuch des 19. Jahrhunderts aus der Mark Brandenburg.* Quellentext zur jüdischen Gemeinde. 3. Forts. [In]: Nachrichtenblatt der Jüd. Gemeinde von Berlin u. des Verbandes der Jüd. Gemeinden in der D.D.R., Dresden–Berlin, Juni 1979. Pp. 9–12. [For pt. 1 and 2 see No. 15227/YB. XXIV.]

15881. BUTTENHAUSEN. PEISER, FRANZ: *Besuch in deutsch-jüdischer Vergangenheit.* Buttenhausen 1979. [In]: Die Mahnung, Jg. 26, Nr. 6, Berlin, 1. Juni 1979. Pp. 3 & 5, illus. [Also in]: Aufbau, New York, July 13, 1979, p. 20, illus.

15882. COLOGNE. LOWENTHAL, ERNST G.: *100 Jahre Synagoge in Köln.* [In]: MB, Nr. 13, Tel Aviv, 30. März 1979. P. 6.

15883. — JOSEPH, ARTUR: *Meines Vaters Haus*. Ein Dokument. Mit einer Vorrede von Heinrich Böll. Köln: Kiepenheuer u. Witsch, 1979. 143 pp. [Reminiscences of a Cologne businessman, first publ. in 1959, see No. 1615/YB. V.]
15884. — MÜLLER, ALWIN: *Die Geschichte der Juden in Köln zu Beginn des 19. Jahrhunderts*. [In]: Geschichte in Köln, Studentische Zeitschrift am Historischen Seminar, H. 5, Köln, 1979. Pp. 16–47, bibl. notes (pp. 44–47). (Beiträge zur Kölner Stadtgeschichte, 2.)
15885. EAST PRUSSIA. KRÜGER, HANS JÜRGEN: *Juden in Ostpreussen im Jahr 1720*. [In]: Preussenland, Jg. 6, Nr. 1/2, Marburg/Lahn, 1978. Pp. 14–26, bibl. footnotes.
15886. FRANCONIA. HERDE, PETER: *Probleme der christlich-jüdischen Beziehungen in Mainfranken im Mittelalter*. [In]: Würzburger Diözesan-Geschichtsblätter, Bd. 40, Würzburg, 1978. [16] pp. [Lecture held at the opening of the Staatsarchiv, Wertheim, 10. Febr. 1978. Excerpts also in: Wertheimer Panorama, Nr. 1, Wertheim/Main, Dez. 1978, pp. 19–24, illus.]
15887. FRANKFURT a. MAIN. DIETZ, ALEXANDER: *Stammbuch der Frankfurter Juden*. Nachdr. der Ausg. Frankfurt a. Main 1907. Frankfurt a. Main: S. Bodenheimer (Postfach 2342), [1978?]. XII, 481 pp., fold-out plan of the 'Judengasse'. [Cf.: A classic on Frankfurt's Jews (Frank J. Adler) [in]: Toledot, the Journal of Jewish Genealogy, Vol. 2, No. 2, New York, Fall 1978, pp. 4–6.]
15888. — EISENMAN, JOSEPH F.: *Erinnerungen an Frankfurt am Main*. [In]: Mitteilungen des Verbandes ehemaliger Breslauer u. Schlesier in Israel, No. 45, Tel Aviv, April/Mai 1979. Pp. 25–27, illus., ports. [On Salomon and Josef Breuer, Benno Pessachowitz.]
15889. — KARASEK, HORST: *Der Fedtmilch-Aufstand oder: Wie die Frankfurter 1612/14 ihrem Rat einheizten*. Berlin: Wagenbach, 1979. 141 pp., illus., ports., facsims., bibl. (pp. 139–141). (Wagenbachs Taschenbücherei, 58.)
15890. — LOEWENSTEIN, ISRAEL EGON: *Frankfurts Messe in jüdischen Quellen*. [In]: 'Allgemeine', Düsseldorf, 15. Juni 1979. P. 4.
15891. — RUDOLPH, MARIA: *Die Frauenbildung in Frankfurt am Main*. Geschichte der privaten, der kirchlich-konfessionellen, der jüdischen und der städtischen Mädchenschulen. Hrsg. von Otto Schlander. Teil 1: Historische Darstellung der Frankfurter Mädchenschulen. Frankfurt a. Main: Lang, 1978. 296 pp., illus. (Eruditio, Bd. 6.)
15892. FREUDENTAL. BÄCHLE, GÜNTER: *Württembergs ältester Synagoge* [in Freudental bei Ludwigsburg] *droht der Abbruch*. [In]: 'Allgemeine', Düsseldorf, 30. Nov. 1979. P. 4, illus. [and] 14. Dez. 1979, p. 4.
15893. GENTHIN. DIAMANT, ADOLF: *Geschichte eines jüdischen Friedhofes* [in Genthin]. [In]: 'Allgemeine', Düsseldorf, 9. Nov. 1979. P. 4, illus.
15894. HAMBURG. FREIMARK, PETER: *Juden auf dem Johanneum*. [In]: 450 Jahre Gelehrtenschule des Johanneum zu Hamburg 1979 (Sonderheft der Zeitschrift 'Das Johanneum'). Hamburg: Christians, 1979. Pp. 123–130, 224–226, illus.
15895. — HAMMER-SCHENK, HAROLD: *Hamburgs Synagogen des 19. und frühen 20. Jahrhunderts*. Hamburg: Hower, 1978. 46 pp., 24 pp. illus., bibl. references.
15896. — MALEACHI, RUBEN: *Die Synagogen in Hamburg*. [In]: Mitteilungen des Verbandes ehemaliger Breslauer u. Schlesier in Israel, No. 44 (Tel Aviv, 1978), pp. 26–28 & 40; No. 45 (Tel Aviv, April/Mai 1979), pp. 18–20, illus. [Will be continued.]
15897. — ZIMMERMANN, MOSHE: *Hamburgischer Patriotismus und deutscher Nationalismus. Die Emanzipation der Juden in Hamburg 1830–1865*. Hamburg: Christians, 1979. 266 pp., ports., notes, list of names (pp. 263–266), bibl. (pp. 239–261). (Hamburger Beiträge zur Geschichte der deutschen Juden, Bd. 6.) [Part. cont.: Die Juden Hamburgs am Anfang des 19. Jahrhunderts. I. Zwischen zwei Krisen (1830–1842): Eine neue Strategie, Gabriel Riesser; Die öffentliche Diskussion der Judenfrage; Riesser contra [Eduard] Meyer. II. Der grosse Hamburger Brand und seine Folgen (1842–1848): Das Programm der sozialen Integration, Anton Rée, Eduard Cohn u. seine Zeitschrift. III. Revolution u. Emanzipation (1848–1865): Die Hamburger Reform von 1849; Die rechtliche Gleichstellung der Juden; [Wilhelm] Marr contra Riesser; Frühantisemitismus.]
15898. HANAU. *675 Jahre Altstadt Hanau*. [Katalog zu einer Ausstellung.] Hanau: Peters, 1978. 286 pp., illus. [References in text and illus. to the Jewish ritual bath, the synagogue, the deportation of Jews.]
15899. HEMSBACH. SCHUBSKY, KARL: Die Hemsbacher Synagoge, ein Relikt jüdischer Kultur. Hemsbach, Sept. 1979. 6 pp., 1 illus. [Mimeog.]
15900. HESSE. HENTSCH, GERHARD: *Gewerbeordnung und Emanzipation der Juden im Kurfürstentum Hessen*. Wiesbaden (Mainzer Str. 80): Kommission für die Geschichte der Juden in Hessen,

1979. 204 pp. (Schriften der Kommission für die Geschichte der Juden in Hessen, 4.)

15901. — *Juden in Hessen.* Ausstellung der hessischen Staatsarchive. [Katalog.] Wiesbaden: Hessisches Hauptstaatsarchiv (Mainzer Str. 80), n.d. [June 1979]. 66 pp., illus., facsims., bibl. (pp. 63–65).

15902. HINDENBURG O/S. BRILLING, BERNHARD: *Die jüdische Gemeinde in Hindenburg O/S.* [In]: Hindenburg O/S., Stadt der Gruben und Hütten. Bearb. von Joseph Pollok, hrsg. vom Vertretungsausschuss der Hindenburger bei der Patenstadt Essen. Essen, 1979. Pp. 318–324.

15903. KAISERSLAUTERN. FRIEDEL, HEINZ: *Aus der Geschichte der Kaiserslauterner Judengemeinde.* [In]: Pfälzer Heimat, Jg. 27, H. 3, Speyer, 1976. Pp. 99–103.

15904. KOBLENZ. DIAMANT, ADOLF: *Koblenzer Grabsteine von 1420 gefunden.* [In]: 'Allgemeine', Düsseldorf, 15. Juni 1979. P. 4.

15905. LANGEN. GREIN, GERD J.: *Geschichte der jüdischen Gemeinde zu Langen und ihrer Synagoge.* Eine Dokumentation [zu einer] Ausstellung des Magistrates der Stadt Langen, Kulturabteilung, aus Anlass des 40. Jahrestages der Zerstörung der Synagoge in der 'Reichskristallnacht' 1938. Langen, 1978. [58] pp., bibl. [Incl. also: Geschichte der Juden im Rhein-Main-Gebiet bis 1900.]

15906. LOWER SAXONY. ASARIA, ZVI: *Die Juden in Niedersachsen. Von den ältesten Zeiten bis zur Gegenwart.* Leer: Rautenberg, 1979. 676 pp., illus., bibl. (pp. 641–653).

15907. — DIETERICHS, HEINZ E. [et al.]: *Nachrichten zur Geschichte der Juden in Niedersachsen.* Eine Sammlung von Gelegenheitsfunden. [In]: Norddeutsche Familienkunde, Jg. 26, H. 3, Neustadt/Aisch: Degener, Juli–Sept. 1977. Pp. 70–72.

15908. LÜNEBURG. MENTZSCHEL, ERIKA: *Notizen über die jüdischen Bürger in Lüneburg.* [In]: Jahrbuch des baltischen Deutschtums, 23, Lüneburg, 1976. Pp. 145–158.

15909. MAINZ. *Juden in Mainz.* Rückblick auf eine stadthistorische Ausstellung im Mainzer Rathaus-Foyer Nov. 1978; Okt./Nov. 1979. Bearb. von Friedrich Schütz, gestaltet von Valy Schmidt-Heinecke. Mainz, 1979. 135 pp., illus., facsims., plans, ports. [For catalogue of this exhibition, on display for the second time in 1979, see No. 15051/YB. XXIV.]

15910. MEPPEN. LEMMERMANN, HOLGER: *Geschichte der Juden im alten Amt Meppen bis zur Emanzipation (1848).* Meppen: Emsländ. Heimatbund, 1975. V, 156 pp., illus. (Schriftenreihe des Emsländischen Heimatbundes, Bd. 2.)

15911. MUNICH. CAHNMAN, WERNER J.: *Die Juden in München 1918–1943.* [In]: Zeitschrift für bayerische Landesgeschichte, Bd. 42, H. 2, München, 1979. Pp. 403–461. [Incl. sections on the structure of the Munich Jewish community, the activities of the Bavarian regional organisation of the 'Centralverein deutscher Staatsbürger jüdischen Glaubens', Bavarian antisemitism and Jewish responses.]

15912. — LAMM, HANS: *Von Juden in München.* Ein Gedenkbuch. 3, unveränd. Aufl. Darmstadt: Verlag Darmstädter Blätter, 1979. 406 pp., illus. [1st edn. 1958, see No. 1372/YB. IV.]

15913. MÜNSTER. ASCHOFF, DIETHARD: *Die Stadt Münster und die Juden im letzten Jahrhundert der städtischen Unabhängigkeit (1562–1662).* [In]: Westfälische Forschungen, Jg. 27, Münster, 1975. Pp. 84–113.

15914. OLDENBURG. MENDELSSOHN, JOSEPH: *Eine Ecke Deutschlands.* Reisesilhouetten, Oldenburger Bilder, Charaktere und Zustände. Unveränd. Nachdr. der Ausg. Oldenburg 1845, mit einem Nachwort von Harald Schieckel. Leer: Schuster, 1979. VIII, 122, [5] pp. (Schuster-Reprint.) [Incl.: Die Juden. Toleranz u. Intoleranz. Das Schutzverhältnis. Der Landrabbiner Wechsler (pp. 93–97).]

15915. OSTFRIESLAND. MAHRENHOLTZ, HANS: *Literatur über Juden in Ostfriesland.* [In]: Norddeutsche Familienkunde, Jg. 26, H. 3, Neustadt/Aisch: Degener, Juli–Sept. 1977. Pp. 75–79.

15916. — MESTDAGH, J. H. de vey/JONGELING, DOOR, K./BRILLEMAN, J., eds.: *Joodse begraafplaatsen in Groningen en Oost-Friesland.* Vol. 1. Groningen, 1977. 127 pp., illus. (62 pp.), bibl. (Nedersaksische Studies, 2.) [Text in Dutch, transcriptions of the epitaphs in Hebrew. Refers to cemeteries in Holland and in Bunde in Ostfriesland, Germany. Cf.: Erinnerung an die Väter. Jüd. Friedhöfe in Holland u. Ostfriesland (Adolf Diamant) [in]: 'Allgemeine', Düsseldorf, 7. Sept. 1979, p. 4.

15917. PALATINATE. ARNOLD, HERMANN: *Materialien zur Volkskunde der pfälzischen Juden.* [In]: Blätter für pfälzische Kirchengeschichte u. religiöse Volkskunde, Jg. 43, Grünstadt, 1976. Pp. 59–67.

15918. POSEN. MEYER, CHRISTIAN: *Geschichte des Landes Posen.* Ein Nachdr. [der Ausg.] Posen, Jolowicz, 1881. Osnabrück: Ackerstaff u. Kuballe, 1979. 483 pp. [Also about Jews in the province of Posen.]

15919. RECKLINGHAUSEN. REUTER, HEINZ: *Die Juden im Vest Recklinghausen.* Sonderdruck aus: Vestische Zeitschrift, Bd. 77/78 (1978–79). 132 pp. [Cf.: Dokumentation über die Juden Recklinghausens (Adolf Diamant) [in]: 'Allgemeine', Düsseldorf, 28. Sept. 1979, p. 11, illus.]

15920. REGENSBURG. STRAUS, RAPHAEL: *Die Judengemeinde Regensburg im ausgehenden Mittelalter.* Auf Grund der Quellen kritisch untersucht u. neu dargestellt. Nachdr. der Ausg. Heidelberg 1932. Nendeln/Liechtenstein: Kraus, 1979. VIII, 147 pp. (Heidelberger Abhandlungen zur mittleren u. neuen Geschichte, H. 61.)

15921. RHEDA. WEINBERG, WERNER: *Die Geschichte einer Tora.* Aus dem Engl. übers. von Walter Wolf in Zusammenarbeit mit Lisi Weinberg. Rheda-Wiedenbrück: Stadtarchiv, 1978. 21, 7 pp. [Orig. title: 'Tale of a Torah scroll'. Refers to the Jewish community in Rheda.]

15922. RHINELAND. BATTENBERG, FRIEDRICH: *Zur Rechtsstellung der Juden am Mittelrhein im Spätmittelalter und früher Neuzeit.* [In]: Zeitschrift für historische Forschung, Bd. 6, H. 2, Berlin, 1979. Pp. 129–183.

15923. — *Dokumentation zur Geschichte der jüdischen Bevölkerung in Rheinland-Pfalz und im Saarland von 1800 bis 1945.* Hrsg. von der Landesarchivverwaltung Rheinland-Pfalz in Verbindung mit dem Landesarchiv Saarbrücken. Bd. 2: *Der Weg zur Gleichberechtigung der Juden.* Bearb. von Anton Doll [*et al.*]. Koblenz: Landesarchivverwaltung Rheinland Pfalz, 1979. VII, 472 pp., maps, bibl. (Veröffentlichungen der Landesarchivverwaltung Rheinland-Pfalz, Bd. 13.) [For vols. 3, 4, 6 & 7 of this *Dokumentation* see Nos. 11951–11954/YB. XX; vol. 5 see No. 12690/YB. XXI. Vols. 1, 8 & 9 not yet published. Cont.: Teil 1: Die südlichen Bezirke der preussischen Rheinprovinz. Teil 2: Die nördlichen Teile des Herzogtums Nassau, Fürstentum Lichtenberg, Oberamt Meisenheim u. Fürstentum Birkenfeld. Teil 3: Die bayerische Pfalz. Teil 4: Die linksrheinischen Teile des Grossherzogtums Hessen.]

15924. ROSENTHAL. HAMMANN, GUSTAV: *Die Rosenthaler Judentaufe von 1735.* Nach einem Bericht von Pfarrer Joh. Ägigius Ruppersberger d.Ä. (1722–1747). Bottendorf: Evang.-Luther. Pfarramt, 1977. 23 pp. (Bottendorfer Brief, 43.)

15925. SEESEN. BALLIN, GERHARD: *Geschichte der Juden in Seesen.* (Hrsg. von der Stadt Seesen.) Seesen: Flentje-Druck, 1979. XI, 286 pp., illus., facsims., plans, ports., bibl. notes (pp. 142–149). [Incl.: Genealogische u. persönliche Angaben über die einzelnen Familien (pp. 153–242).]

15926. SILESIA. LOWENTHAL, ERNST G.: *Zur Demographie der Juden im früheren Oberschlesien.* [In]: Zeitschrift für Ostforschung, Jg. 28, H. 1, Marburg/Lahn, März 1979. Pp. 81–84.

15927. — *Mitteilungen des Verbandes ehemaliger Breslauer und Schlesier in Israel.* Hrsg.: Erich Lewin. No. 45. Tel Aviv, April/Mai 1979. 44 pp. [*No. 45* incl.: Vorübergehend in Schlesien: Dichter, Künstler, Geistige (A. Tobias). Das Johanneum (Ernest Mitschel). Die Geschichte der Familie Goldstein u. der Oberschlesischen Holz-Industrie A.G. Beuthen O/S (Ulrich Skaller, pp. 9–10). Erinnerungen (Hans Margolius). Erinnerung aus den dunklen Tagen des 9. u. 10. Nov. 1938 (Fritz Tau). Rabbiner Dr. Moses Hoffmann s.A. (Erich Lewin). Mein Leben, Deutsch-Krone–Ramat Gan (Edwin Landau s.A., pp. 21–24). Dr. Conrad Cohn, eine Auktion erinnert (E. G. Lowenthal). Nora Hauben, Interview (Redaktion). Freunde meiner Eltern San. Rat Dr. Albert Sachs u. Clara, geb. Goldstein (Julius Sachs). Further contributions are listed according to subject.]

15928. SPEYER. SALLIS-FREUDENTHAL, MARGARETE: *Jüdische Kindheit in Speyer und Edenkoben.* [In]: Pfälzer Heimat, Jg. 30, H. 1, Speyer, 1979. Pp. 30–34, 2 illus.

15929. — STEIN, GÜNTER: *Judenhof und Judenbad in Speyer am Rhein.* München: Dt. Kunstverl., 1978. 15, 1 pp., illus., plan, Engl. summary, bibl. (pp. 14–15). (Grosse Baudenkmäler, H. 238.)

15930. SPRENDLINGEN (Kreis Offenbach). DIAMANT, ADOLF: *Alte Mikwa in Sprendlingen entdeckt.* [In]: 'Allgemeine', Düsseldorf, 24. Aug. 1979. P. 8, illus. [And in]: Aufbau, New York, Sept. 14, 1979, p. 14.

15931. STADE. BOHMBACH, JÜRGEN: *Die Juden im alten Regierungsbezirk Stade.* [In]: Stader Jahrbuch, 67 (1977). Pp. 31–75.

15932. TRIER. LOWENTHAL, ERNST G.: *Er war ein angesehener Trierer. Zum 100. Geburtstag von Rabbiner Dr. Adolf Altmann.* [In]: Trierischer Volksfreund, Nr. 206, Trier, 5. Sept. 1979. [A. A., 1879 Hungary–1944 Auschwitz, rabbi and scholar, officiated 1907–1914 in Salzburg, 1920–1938 in Trier, emigrated to Holland in 1938. See also: A great German rabbi, Adolf Altmann centenary [in]: AJR Information, London, Sept. 1979, p. 2. Trier honours Rabbi Altmann [in]: AJR Information, London, Nov. 1979, p. 7. Der letzte Oberrabbiner von Trier. Zum 100. Geburtstag von Dr. A. A. (H. Istor) [in]: 'Allgemeine', Düsseldorf, 31.

Aug. 1979, p. 5. Erinnerungen an A. A. (Hans Steinitz) [in]: Aufbau, New York, Aug. 31, 1979, p. 4. See also No. 15949.]

15933. TÜBINGEN. ZAPF, LILLI: *Die Tübinger Juden*. Eine Dokumentation. 2. Aufl. Tübingen: Katzmann, 1978. 288 pp., illus., port., bibl. (pp. 279–282). [1st edn. 1974, see No. 11958/ YB. XX.]

15934. WARBURG. EVERS, MARTHA: *Die Geschichte der Juden in der Stadt Warburg zur fürstbischöflichen Zeit*. Mit einem Vorwort und einer aktualisierten Bibliographie. Calenberg: Hermes, 1978. 87 pp.

15935. WENNIGSEN-HOLTENSEN. WEBER-OLDECOP, DIETER WILHELM: *Juden und ihre getauften Nachkommen im KB [Kirchenbuch] von Wennigsen-Holtensen*. [In]: Norddeutsche Familienkunde, Jg. 26, H. 3, Neustadt/Aisch, Juli–Sept. 1977. Pp. 72–74.

15936. WERTHEIM. EHMER, HERMANN: *Wertheim im Grossherzogtum Baden. Bilder aus einer alten Stadt*. Wertheim: Buchheim, 1979. 191 pp., illus., plan. [Incl. references to Jews in Wertheim. English and French summaries.]

15937. WÖRRSTADT. ZAHN, RALF: *Die Geschichte der jüdischen Gemeinden in Wörrstadt und Nieder-Wiesen*. [In]: Alzeyer Geschichtsblätter, H. 14, Alzey: Rheinhessische Druckwerkstätte, 1979. Pp. 142–151.

15938. WORMS. LEONHARDT-KÖNIG, CHRISTIANE: *Jahrhunderten getrotzt und doch vergangen. Verwitterte Grabsteine in Worms, Zeugen uralter Geschichte*. [In]: 'Allgemeine', Düsseldorf, 14. Dez. 1979. Pp. 4 & 6.

15939. — *Stadtsanierung Worms: Die Judengasse. Die Geschichte des Judenviertels*. Hrsg.: Stadtplanungsamt Worms unter Mitarbeit des Stadtarchivs. Worms, Dez. 1978. 40 pp., many plans, illus. (Bürgerinformation der Stadtverwaltung Worms zur Altstadtsanierung, 5.)

15940. WÜRZBURG. STERN, WILLIAM: *Drei alte Steine an der Würzburger Synagoge*. [In]: 'Allgemeine', Düsseldorf, 13. Juli 1979. P. 5, illus. [And in]: Neue Jüd. Nachrichten, Nr. 27, München, 20. Juli 1979, p. 7, illus.

15941. ZITTAU. DIAMANT, ADOLF: *Zur Geschichte der Juden im sächsischen Zittau*. [In]: 'Allgemeine', Düsseldorf, 21. Sept. 1979. P. 19.

1a. Alsace

15942. TRESCHAN, VICTOR: *The struggle for integration. The Jewish community of Strasbourg 1818–1850*. Madison, The Univ. of Wisconsin, Phil. Diss., 1978. 212 pp.

15943. WEYL, ROBERT/RAPHAEL, FREDDY: *L'imagerie juive d'Alsace*. (Préface de Max Warschawski, Grand-Rabbin du Bas-Rhin.) Strassburg: Editions des Dernieres Nouvelles d'Alsace, n.d. [1979]. 82 pp., illus.

2. Austria

15944. BERGER, MAX: *Judaica. Die Sammlung Berger: Kult und Kultur des europäischen Judentums*. Text: Wolfgang Häusler, Bild: Erich Lessing, Katalog: Max Berger. Wien: Jugend u. Volk, 1979. 298, [1] pp., illus., bibl. (pp. 297–299). [English, French, Spanish and Hebrew summaries, 4 pp., inserted. Incl.: Zur Geschichte und Kulturgeschichte des österreichischen Judentums (Wolfgang Häusler).]

15945. CAHNMAN, WERNER J.: *Adolph Fischhof and the problem of reconciliation of nationalities*. [In]: East European Quarterly, 12, Boulder, Colorado, Spring 1978. Pp. 44–56. [For German version see No. 11964/YB. XX.]

15946. GALICIA. HÄUSLER, WOLFGANG: *Das galizische Judentum in der Habsburgermonarchie im Lichte der zeitgenössischen Publizistik und Reiseliteratur von 1772–1848*. Wien: Verlag für Geschichte u. Politik; München: Oldenbourg, 1979. 89 pp., bibl. (Österreich-Archiv.) (Schriftenreihe des Instituts für Österreichkunde.)

15947. LADOR-LEDERER, J. J.: *Jews in Austrian Law*. 1–2. [In]: East European Quarterly, 12, Boulder, Colorado, Spring and Summer 1978. Pp. 27–41; 129–142.

15948. MAGENSCHAB, HANS: *Josef II. Revolutionär von Gottes Gnaden*. Graz: Styria, 1979. 300 pp., illus., bibl. (pp. 292–295). [Refers also to Josef's policy towards Jews. Cf.: Review [in]: Neue Jüd. Nachrichten, Nr. 30, München, 10. Aug. 1979, p. 7.]

15949. SALZBURG. BREUSS, EDGAR: *1100 Jahre jüdische Geschichte*. Salzburger Rabbi [Adolf] Alt-

mann gebührt ein Ehrenplatz. Kultusgemeinde zählt 120 Seelen. [In]: Salzburger Nachrichten, Salzburg, 8. Sept. 1979. P. 9.
15950. TIROL. SELLA, GAD HUGO (orig. Hugo Silberstein): *Die Juden Tirols. Ihr Leben und Schicksal.* Tel Aviv: Japhet Press, 1979. 166 pp.
15951. VIENNA. BRASSLOFF, FRITZ L.: *Die Wiener Leopoldstadt, heute und einst.* [In]: Das Neue Israel, Jg. 32, H. 5, Zürich, Nov. 1979. Pp. 257 & 259.
15952. — HERZ, PETER: *Requiem für das jüdische Villenviertel 'Cottage' in Wien.* [In]: Isr. Wochenblatt, Nr. 4, Zürich, 26. Jan. 1979. Pp. 45 & 46, ports.
15953. — SCHUBERT, KURT, ed.: *Der Wiener Stadttempel 1826–1976.* Im Auftrag des Vereins Österreichisches Jüdisches Museum in Eisenstadt hrsg. Eisenstadt: Edition Roetzer, 1978. 103 pp., illus., facsims., ports., bibl. references. (Studia Judaica Austriaca, Bd. 6.) [Cover title]: Bethhaus der Israeliten in Wien. [Cont.: Die Rabbiner des Stadttempels von I. N. Mannheimer bis Z. P. Chajes (J. Allerhand, pp. 5–28. Refers also to Adolf Jellinek and Moritz Güdemann). 'Orthodoxie' u. 'Reform' im Wiener Judentum in der Epoche des Hochliberalismus (W. Häusler, pp. 29–56). Zur sozialen Situation der Wiener Juden im Jahre 1857 (P. Schmidtbauer, pp. 57–89). 150 Jahre Stadttempel, Bilder u. Dokumente (N. Vielmetti, pp. 91–103 & 32 illus.]
15954. — SPITZER, SHLOMO: *Das Wiener Judentum bis zur Vertreibung im Jahre 1421.* [In]: Kairos, N.F. 19, H. 2, Freilassing-Salzburg, 1977. Pp. 134–145.
15955. — WISTRICH, ROBERT S.: *Dilemmas of assimilation in fin de siècle Vienna.* [In]: The Wiener Library Bulletin, Vol. 32, new ser. Nos. 49/50, London, 1979. Pp. 15–28, bibl. notes (pp. 27–28).
15956. VORARLBERG. BURMEISTER, K. A.: *Die Juden im Vorarlberg im Mittelalter.* [In]: Schriften des Vereins für Geschichte des Bodensees und seiner Umgebung, H. 94, Friedrichshafen, 1976. Pp. 1–18. [See also: Wanderungen der Juden nach Vorarlberg (Leo Brod) [in]: Neue Jüd. Nachrichten, Nr. 27, München, 20. Juli 1979, p. 8.]

3. Czechoslovakia

15957. *Judaica Bohemiae.* Vol. 15, Nos. 1–2. Publication du Musée juif d'Etat, Prague. Rédacteur en chef: Miroslav Jaroš. Praha: Státní židovské muzeum v Praze, 1979. 60 pp., illus. (4 pp.); pp. 63–131, illus. (4 pp.), facsims. [2 issues.] [*No. 1* incl.: Das Theresienstädter Familienlager in Birkenau (Miroslav Kárný, pp. 3–26). Rabbi Loew. Sa vie, héritage pédagogique et sa légende (Vladimír Sadek, pp. 27–41). The old Jewish cemetery at Mikulov (Bedřich Nosek, pp. 42–55). *No. 2:* Der Lyriker Vlastimil Artur Polák (orig. Salomon Arthur Pollak). Zu seinem 65. Geburtstag (Ludvík Václavek, pp. 63–73). From the MSS collections of the State Jewish Museum in Prague. The Scrolls of Esther (Jiřina Šedinová, pp. 74–85). Auswahlkatalog hebräischer Drucke Prager Provenienz: Druckerei M. I. Landau, 1824–1853 (Bedřich Nosek, pp. 86–121). Cimetière juif de Holešov (Vlastimila Hamáčková et Jarmila Škochová, pp. 122–125).
15958. *Jüdisches Jahrbuch 5740, 1979/1980.* Hrsg. vom Rat der Jüd. Religionsgemeinden in der Tschechischen Sozialistischen Republik. [In Czech, title transl.] Red.: Tomáš Tieber. Prag: Kirchenzentralverlag, 1979. 159 pp. [Orig. title: 'Židovská ročenka'. Incl. (titles transl.): Karl IV und die Juden (František Kafka, pp. 28–35). Pogrome in Holešov in den Jahren 1774–1918 (Josef Svátek, pp. 36–44, bibl. footnotes).]
15959. PRAGUE. BRILLING, BERNHARD: *Die Prager jüdische Gemeinde als Fürsprecherin und Vertreterin des deutschen Judentums im 16. und 17. Jahrhundert.* [In]: Theokratia, Jahrbuch des Institutum Judaicum Delitzschianum, 3 (1973–1975), Leiden, 1979. Pp. 185–198.
15960. — BRUTSCHER, LUDWIG: *Der Rabbi von Prag. Leben und Leiden des Jomtow Lipmann Heller-Wallerstein* [1579–1654]. [In]: Das Neue Israel, Jg. 32, H. 4, Zürich, Okt. 1979. Pp. 189–192, bibl. (p. 192).
15961. — ECKHARDT, PAUL: *Ermittlungen über den Golem. Die Golemgeschichten des Chajim Bloch.* Stuttgart: Collispress, 1977. 39 pp., illus. (Collisbibliothek, Nr. 1.)
15962. — MEYRINK, GUSTAV: *Der Golem.* Mit Illustrationen von Hugo Steiner-Prag und einem Nachwort von Eduard Frank. München: Langen-Müller, 1979. 333 pp., 25 illus. [H. Steiner-Prag, 1880 Prag–1945 New York.]
15963. — PAZI, MARGARITA: *Der 'Prager Kreis'. Ein Kapitel der deutsch-jüdischen Symbiose.* [In]: Tribüne, H. 70, Frankfurt a. Main, 1979. Pp. 110–127.
15964. — SCHWARZ, STEFAN: *Der Hohe Rabbi Löw Mahral (1525–1609).* Zu seinem 370. Todestag. [In]: Neue Jüd. Nachrichten, Nr. 46, München, 14. Dez. 1979. P. 2.

4. Hungary

15965. FISCH, HEINRICH: *Zum 120jährigen Bestehen der Dohàny-Synagoge in Budapest.* [In]: Neue Jüd. Nachrichten, Nr. 28, München, 27. Juli 1979. P. 3.
15966. HODIK, FRITZ PETER: *Beiträge zur Geschichte der Mattersdorfer Judengemeinde im 18. und in der ersten Hälfte des 19. Jahrhunderts.* Eisenstadt: Burgenländisches Landesarchiv, 1975. 286 pp., illus., tabs., map. (Burgenländische Forschungen, H. 65.) [Zugl. Wien, Univ., Phil. Diss., 1972, see No. 10240/YB. XVIII.]

C. German Jews in Various Countries

15967. ALEXANDER, MARCUS: *The letter of Marcus Alexander, an early migrant from Germany.* (Transl. by A. Fabian.) [In]: Australian Jewish Historical Society, Vol. 8, pt. 5, Sydney, 1978. Pp. 277–281. [M. Alexander, born 1820.]
15968. *Les Barbelés de l'exil. Études sur l'émigration allemande et autrichienne (1938–1940).* [Par] Gilbert Badia [et al.]. Grenoble: Presses universitaires de Grenoble, 1979. 443 pp., facsims., maps, plates, bibl. footnotes. (Actualités–recherche.) [Collection of papers on the fate of refugees from Nazi persecution in France. Cf.: Stacheldraht im Exil. Emigrantenlos in Frankreich (Rolf Schneider) [in]: Die Zeit, Hamburg, 15. Juni 1979, pp. 33–34, illus.]
15969. BERGAS, HANNA: *Fifteen years lived among, with and for refugee children.* Palo Alto, California, 1979. 74 pp. [Priv. mimeog.]
15970. BLUMENTHAL, W. MICHAEL. COWAN, EDWARD: *His old home in China seen by Blumenthal.* [In]: The New York Times, March 4, 1979. [United States Treasury Secretary W. Michael Blumenthal in Shanghai where he and his family lived as refugees from Nazi Germany.]
15971. BRUNO, GUIDO [orig. Curt Josef Kisch]. KISCH, ARNOLD I.: *The romantic ghost of Greenwich Village. Guido Bruno in his garret.* Frankfurt a. Main: Lang, 1976. 154 pp., illus., bibl. (pp. 129–131). [G.B., Oct. 15, 1884 Jungbunzlau/Bohemia–Dec. 31, 1942 U.S.A., eldest son of rabbi Dr. Alexander Kisch, came to New York in 1906. His book-store 'Bruno's Garret' in Greenwich Village was a meeting-place for writers and artists.]
15972. DIEZEL, PETER: *Exiltheater in der Sowjetunion 1932–1937.* Berlin/East: Henschelverlag, 1978. 334 pp. (Veröffentlichung der Akademie der Künste der D.D.R.) [Refers also to Jewish emigrants from Nazi Germany.]
15973. *Exil in der UdSSR.* Von Klaus Jarmatz, Simone Barck, Peter Diezel [et al.]. Leipzig: Reclam, 1979. 661 pp., illus., ports., facsims., bibl. notes (pp. 577–632), list of names (pp. 633–656). (Kunst und Literatur im antifaschistischen Exil 1933–1945, Bd. 1.) (Reclams Universal-Bibliothek, Bd. 806: Kunstwissenschaften.) [Cont. chaps.: 1. Das Asylland Sowjetunion. 2. Arbeitsfelder der deutschen antifaschistischen Künstler in der Sowjetunion (Schriftsteller; Theaterarbeit; Architekten; Rundfunk). 3. Wichtige Ergebnisse in den verschiedenen Künsten.]
15974. *Exil in den USA, mit einem Bericht 'Schanghai, eine Emigration am Rande'.* Von Eike Middell [et al.]. Leipzig: Reclam, 1979. 589 pp., illus., ports., facsims., bibl. notes (pp. 521–555), list of names (pp. 556–587). (Kunst und Literatur im antifaschistischen Exil 1933–1945, Bd. 3.) (Reclams Universal-Bibliothek, Bd. 799: Kunstwissenschaften.) [Cont. chaps.: 1. Die gesellschaftliche Situation in den U.S.A. u. die Bedingungen für die antifaschistische deutsche Emigration. Die politische Situation. 2. Politisches Engagement deutscher Emigranten in den U.S.A. 3. Künstlerisches Schaffen im U.S.A.-Exil.]
15975. FREEDLAND, MICHAEL: *New roots for old.* [In]: Jewish Chronicle, London, Jan. 19, 1979. Illus. [On the life of German refugees in Gt. Britain.]
15976. GREFFRATH, MATHIAS: *Die Zerstörung einer Zukunft. Gespräch mit emigrierten Sozialwissenschaftlern.* Reinbek: Rowohlt, 1979. 351 pp. (Das neue Buch, 123.) [Interviews with: Günther Anders, Hans Gerth, Marie Jahoda, Leo Löwenthal, Adolph Lowe, Toni Oelsner, Alfred Sohn-Rethel, Karl August Wittfogel.]
15977. GUTTMANN, LUDWIG (Sir). *Birthday tribute:* Sir Ludwig Guttmann 80. Two tributes to his life and work (Joan Scruton and Lothar Nelken). [In]: AJR Information, London, July 1979. P. 7. [L. G., born July 3, 1899 in Königshütte/OS, founder director of the National Spinal Injuries Centre at Stoke Mandeville Hospital, creator of the Stoke Mandeville Games, the

'Olympics of the paralysed'.] [L. G. died on March 18, 1980. For obits. see: 'The Times', London, March 20 & 29, 1980 and AJR Information, No. 5, London, May 1980.]

15978. HARRIS, LEON: *Merchant princes. An intimate history of Jewish families who built great department stores.* New York: Harper & Row, 1979. 411 pp. [Incl. many families of German-Jewish origin. Cf.: Review (Christopher Lehmann-Haupt) [in]: 'The New York Times', Dec. 27, 1979, p. C17.]

15979. HEINEMANN, HEINZ EGON. KURTZE, GERHARD: *Zum Tode des Buchhändlers und Antiquars Heinz Egon Heinemann.* Wiesbaden, Shanghai, Montreal. Auf vielfache Weise als Mittler zwischen Deutschland und Kanada tätig gewesen. [In]: Börsenblatt für den Dt. Buchhandel, Nr. 91, Frankfurt a. Main, 13. Nov. 1979. P. 2246, port. [H.E.H., March 23, 1912 Wiesbaden–Sept. 20, 1979, Montreal.]

15980. HELBRONNER, JULES. ROME, DAVID: *On Jules Helbronner.* With an introduction by Saul Hayes. Montreal: National Archives, Canadian Jewish Congress, 1978. 105 pp. (Canadian Jewish Archives, New Series, No. 11.) [J. H., Alsatian Jew, was editor of the Montreal paper 'La Presse', the target of antisemitic attacks.]

15981. HERZBERG, STEVEN: *Strangers within the Gate City. The Jews of Atlanta 1845–1915.* Philadelphia: Jewish Publication Society of America, 1979. 324 pp., tabs., charts, notes. [Also on German-Jewish immigrants in Atlanta.]

15982. HUGHES, H. STUART: *The sea change. The migration of social thought, 1930–1965.* New York: Harper & Row, 1975. X, 283 pp. [Incl. Theodor Adorno, Hannah Arendt, Erich Fromm, Max Horkheimer, Karl Mannheim, Herbert Marcuse, Hans Meyerhoff, Franz Neumann, Ludwig Wittgenstein and others.]

15983. KISSINGER, HENRY: *White House years.* Boston: Little, Brown, 1979. 1521 pp., illus. [Engl. edn.]: *The White House years.* London: Weidenfeld and Nicolson, 1979. 1582 pp., illus. [German edn.]: *Memoiren 1968–1973.* (Aus dem Amerikan. von Hans-Jürgen Baron von Koskull.) München: Bertelsmann, 1979. 1632 pp. [Cf.: Kissinger's crises (Christopher Serpell) [in]: The London Review of Books, Dec. 20, 1979, pp. 11–12. The case of Dr. Kissinger (Stanley Hoffmann) [in]: The New York Review of Books, Dec. 6, 1979, pp. 14–29. Kissingers Jahre im Weissen Haus. Memoiren als Zeitgeschichte [in]: NZZ, Zürich, 13. Dez. 1979, p. 7. Geopolitical attitudes (D. C. Watt) [in]: 'The Observer', London, 18. Nov. 1979. Die Jahre des Triumphs (Dieter Schröder) [in]: SZ, München, 20./21. Okt. 1979, pp. 149–150, port.]

15984. KRAUS, HANS PETER: *A rare book saga. The autobiography of H. P. Kraus.* New York: Putnam, 1978. XVII, 386 pp., illus., facsims., plates, ports. [H.P.K., born 1907 in Vienna, founded a second-hand book-shop in Vienna in 1932, emigrated to Sweden and, 1939, to New York. See also: Kraus hat's. Das 3,7-Millionen-Geschäft mit der Gutenberg-Bibel nennt Hans P. Kraus ein Missgeschick (Alexander Wischnewski) [in]: Börsenblatt für den Dt. Buchhandel, Nr. 6, Frankfurt a. Main, 19. Jan. 1979, pp. 133–135, illus., ports.]

15985. MASCHLER, KURT. LARSEN, EGON: *Adventures of a bookman.* [In]: AJR Information, London, July 1979. P. 5. [The story of the literary agent Kurt Maschler, Austrian citizen, born in Berlin, living in London since 1939 who controls Stefan Zweig's copyrights and those of other authors.]

15986. MAYER, ROBERT (Sir): *My first hundred years.* With a foreword by Bernard Levin and 100th birthday address by Geraint Evans. Gerrads Cross, Bucks.: Van Duren, 1979. 120 pp., ports., illus. [Enlarged edn. of No. 14251/YB. XXIII. See also No. 13468/YB. XXII. Cf. reviews: (Alex Hamilton) [in]: 'The Guardian', London, June 2, 1979, p. 11. (Kenneth Harris) [in]: 'The Observer', London, June 3, 1979, p. 33. Born in Mannheim 1879 R.M. emigrated to England in 1896. He inaugurated and financed the 'Robert Mayer Concerts for Children'. For his services to music he was knighted in 1938, made a companion of Honour in 1973. Cf. birthday tributes: England feierte einen 100jährigen Mannheimer. Sir Robert Mayer: Herkunft, Wirken, Bedeutung (Ernst G. Lowenthal) [in]: Mannheimer Hefte, H. 2, Mannheim, 1979, pp. 105–106, port. Sir R.M. 100 on June 5, 1979 (E. G. Lowenthal) [in]: AJR Information, London, June 1979, p. 11.]

15987. SELL, HANS JOACHIM: *Briefe einer Jüdin aus Cuzco.* Dokumentarische Erzählung aus dem heutigen Peru. Wien: Herold, 1978. 136 pp. [A German Jewess, emigrant from Berlin, describes Jewish life in modern Peru.]

15988. SHAPIRO, EDWARD S.: *German and Russian Jews in America.* [In]: Midstream, Vol. 25, No. 4, New York, April 1979. Pp. 42–51.

15989. STRAUSS, HERBERT A., ed.: *Jewish immigrants of the Nazi period in the USA.* Sponsored by the

Research Foundation for Jewish Immigration, New York. *Vol. 1: Archival resources.* Comp. by Steven W. Siegel. New York, München, London, Paris: Saur, 1979. XXVIII, 279 pp., bibl. [This reference work will comprise 6 vols.: Vol. 2: An annotated bibliography of books and articles on Jewish refugees 1933–1945. Vol. 3: Oral history. Vol. 4: Source book on emigration and persecution in Germany and Austria 1933–1945. Vol. 5: Source book on emigration of Jews from Central Europe to the U.S.A. 1933–1945. Vol. 6: Social and intellectual history of Jews in the U.S.A. See also No. 16017.]

II. RESEARCH AND BIBLIOGRAPHY

A. Libraries and Institutes

15990. DEUTSCHES LITERATURARCHIV, Marbach am Neckar. *Jahrbuch der Deutschen Schillergesellschaft.* Jg. 20–23. Im Auftrag des Vorstands hrsg. von Fritz Martini, Walter Müller-Seidel, Bernhard Zeller. Stuttgart: Kröner, 1976–1979. *Jg. 20* (1976) [with]: *Gesamtregister für die Jahrgänge 1–20* (1957–1976), bearb. von Jutta Salchow. 638 pp. & VIII, 75 pp. *Jg. 21* (1977), 575 pp. *Jg. 22* (1978), 782 pp. *Jg. 23* (1979), XI, 659 pp. [Individual contributions relevant to German Jewry are listed according to subject. Furthermore each vol. incl. a section 'Aus der Arbeit des Schiller-Nationalmuseums und des Deutschen Literaturarchivs' in Marbach a. N. with information on new acquisitions especially for the archives, referring frequently to German-Jewish personalities. For previous vol. see No. 13479/YB. XXII.]

15991. — *Aus dem Marbacher Magazin gehobene Daten & Fakten, Reden, Verlautbarungen & Veröffentlichungen. Zur Geschichte der Deutschen Schillergesellschaft, des Schiller-Nationalmuseums, des Deutschen Literaturarchivs & der Sammlungen in den Jahren 1953 bis 1979.* Extra-Ausgabe des Marbacher Magazins (Bernhard Zeller überreicht von seinen Mitarbeitern, 19.9.1979). Marbach a. N.: Dt. Schillergesellschaft, 1979. 238, (10) pp., illus., ports., facsims. [Title from cover.] [Refers to many German-Jewish authors and their documentation in the archives of the 'Dt. Literaturarchiv'. Cf.: Wo die Vergessenen unvergessen sind. Besuch im Dt. Literaturarchiv (Schalom Ben-Chorin) [in]: 'Allgemeine', Düsseldorf, 14. Sept. 1979, p. 7. Marbach erschliesst Manfred Georges Nachlass. Auch Tucholsky-Sammlung im Dt. Literaturarchiv [in]: Aufbau, New York, June 15, 1979, p. 24.]

15992. GERMANIA JUDAICA. Kölner Bibliothek zur Geschichte des deutschen Judentums. Leitung Jutta Bohnke-Kollwitz, ed.: *Arbeitsinformationen über Studienprojekte auf dem Gebiet der Geschichte des deutschen Judentums und des Antisemitismus.* Ausgabe 10. Köln, 1977. 38, XXI pp. [Mimeog.]

15993. INSTITUT FÜR DEUTSCHE GESCHICHTE. *Jahrbuch des Instituts für Deutsche Geschichte, Universität Tel Aviv.* Bd. 8. Hrsg. u. eingeleitet von Walter Grab. (Red. Sekretär: M. Techniczek.) Tel Aviv: Nateev-Printing, 1979. 527 pp., XVI pp. summaries in Hebrew. [Incl.: Unehrlichkeit, Vagantentum u. Bettelwesen in der vorindustriellen Gesellschaft (Karl-Ludwig Ay, pp. 13–17. Refers also to Jews). Der Deutsche Republikanische Lehrerbund in der Weimarer Republik (Chaim Seeligmann, pp. 365–387). Himmler's doctrine of the SS-leadership (Yoash Meisler, pp. 389–432). Das 'Dritte Reich' und das Judentum in Rumänien Anfang 1938 (Haim Shamir, pp. 433–444). Further contributions relevant to German Jewry are listed according to subject.]

15994. LEO BAECK INSTITUTE. *Bulletin des Leo Baeck Instituts.* Jg. 18, N.F., Nr. 55. Gründer-Hrsg. des Bulletins 1957–1978: Hans Tramer s.A. [Gedenkheft.] Tel Aviv: Bitaon, 1979. 58 pp., front. port. Hans Tramer [1908 Bunzlau–6. Jan. 1979 Tel Aviv, executive vice president of the Leo Baeck Institute], list of names, biogr. notes (p. 58). For contributions see No. 15829.

15995. — *Year Book XXIV.* The transformation of German Jewry. An annual collection of essays on the history and activity of Jews in Germany during the past century. Founder ed.: Robert Weltsch. Co-ed.: Arnold Paucker. London: Secker & Warburg, 1979. VII, 472 pp., front. port. (Moses Mendelssohn), ports. (Hans Liebeschütz, 1893–1978; Max Kreutzberger, 1900–1978; Hans Tramer, 1908–1979, Jochanan Ginat, 1908–1979), illus., ports., facsims., bibl. (pp. 375–458). [Individual contributions are listed according to subject. Cf.: Review (Margot Pottlitzer) [in]: AJR Information, No. 3, London, March 1980, pp. 1–2. *Obituaries:* Yochanan Ginat, orig. Hans Gaertner [in]: AJR Information, London, June 1979, p. 10. J. Ginat zum Gedächtnis (Reuven Golan) [in]: MB, Nr. 14/15, Tel Aviv, 11. April 1979, p. 18

Max Kreutzberger, see No. 15113/YB. XXIV [and]: (H. Steinitz) [in]: Aufbau, New York, Dec. 1, 1978, p. 4. (E. G. Lowenthal) [in]: Isr. Wochenblatt, Nr. 49, Zürich, 8. Dez. 1978, p. 18/19. Hans Liebeschütz, see No. 15006 & 15113/YB. XXIV. Hans Tramer, see No. 15110/YB. XXIV.]

15996. — LBI NEW YORK. *Library and Archives News.* Ed.: Gabrielle Bamberger. No. 10 (May) – No. 11 (December). New York: Leo Baeck Institute, 1979. 8; 8 pp. [2 issues.]

15997. — — *LBI News.* Ed.: Gabrielle Bamberger. Vol. 20, Nos. 38 (Summer 1979)–39 (Winter 1980). New York: Leo Baeck Institute, 1979–1980. 16; 16 pp., front. illus., illus., ports., facsims. [2 issues.] [*No. 38* incl.: Moses Mendelssohn at the gate of the Royal Palace in Potsdam (engraving by Daniel Nicolaus Chodowiecki). Moses Mendelssohn and eighteenth-century Berlin Jewry (illus.). The divorce of Mendelssohn's daughter Brendel (Dorothea). Jewish community newspapers. Reports on LBI events: East European Jews in pre-World War I Germany (lecture by Jack Wertheimer); The Einstein exhibition at the LBI; Erich Muehsam's Jewish identity (lecture by Lawrence Baron). Obituaries: Hans Tramer, vice president of the LBI, 1908–1979, (port.); Yochanan Ginat, director of the LBI in Israel, 1908–1979. *No. 39*: Reconstructing a tragic past, 1933–1945 (illus.). The voyage of the S.S. 'Navemar'. The memoirs of Ludwig Bendix (abstract). Art in the concentration camp (illus.). Reports on LBI events: The political philosophy of Moses Mendelssohn (lecture by Alexander Altmann); The first news of the Holocaust (Leo Baeck Memorial Lecture by Walter Laqueur); 1848 in historical perspective (Seminar at Oxford Univ., July 1979). Congratulatory tribute to Rabbi Max Gruenewald, President of the LBI. For further birthday tributes see: Dr. Max Gruenewald 80 (Fritz Bamberger) [in]: AJR Information, London, Dec. 1979, p. 7. (E. G. Lowenthal) [in]: Aufbau, New York, Nov. 30, 1979, p. 4. 'Ein Jude unter Juden'. Dem 80jährigen Max Gruenewald zum Gruss (Ernst Simon) [in]: MB, Nr. 44, Tel Aviv, 30. Nov. 1979, pp. 5–6.]

15998. YIVO INSTITUTE FOR JEWISH RESEARCH. *YIVO Annual of Jewish Social Science.* Vol. XVII. Ed.: David G. Roskies. New York: YIVO, 1978. 289 pp. [Incl.: From paternalism to cooptation: The French Jewish Consistory and the immigrants, 1906–1939 (Paula E. Hyman, pp. 217–237, notes). From controversy to conversion: Liberal Judaism in America and the Zionist movement, 1917–1941 (Stuart E. Knee, pp. 260–289, notes). See also No. 15867.]

B. Bibliographies and Catalogues

15999. ALLIANCE ISRAÉLITE UNIVERSELLE: *Catalogue des manuscrits de la bibliothèque.* Tome 1: Manuscrits Judaica (non hébraïques) No. 103 à 522. Avec une introduction historique par Georges J. Weill. Avec la collaboration de Samuel Kerner et Richard Ayoun. Paris: Alliance Israélite Universelle, 1979. 107 pp. [Lists many manuscripts appertaining to German-Jewish history.]

16000. BLUMENKRANZ, BERNHARD, ed.: *Documents modernes sur le Juifs XVI–XX siècles, réunis par l'Équipe de recherche 208, 'Nouvelle Gallia Judaica',* sous la direction de Bernhard Blumenkranz. T. 1: Dépôts parisiens. Toulouse: Edouard Privat, 1979. 667 pp., facsims. (Collection Franco-Judaica, 7.) [Annotated list of Jewish documents in public archives in Paris.]

16001. EISENBERG-BACH, SUSI: *Ergänzungen zur Bio-Bibliographie der deutschen Exilliteratur.* [In]: Aus dem Antiquariat, [Beilage zum] Börsenblatt für den Dt. Buchhandel, Nr. 96, Frankfurt a. Main, 30. Nov. 1979. Pp. A411–A413. [List of about 80 new titles or corrected entries as supplement to the bio-bibliography 'Deutsche Exil-Literatur 1933–1945', ed. by Wilhelm Sternfeld and Eva Tiedemann, 2. Aufl., Heidelberg, 1970, see No. 8525/YB. XVI.]

16002. *Florence Guggenheim Archiv zur Geschichte, Sprache und Volkskunde der Juden in der Schweiz: Ergänzungs-Katalog.* (Nachträge 1974 bis 31. Dez. 1978.) Zürich: Bibliothek der Isr. Cultusgemeinde Zürich, 1979. 35 pp. [mimeog.]. [Incl. also bibl. of Florence Guggenheim, pp. 29–33. For main catalogue see No. 11994/YB. XX. See also: Ehrendoktor für Dr. Florence Guggenheim (von der Theologischen Fakultät in Zürich). [In]: Isr. Wochenblatt, Zürich, 14. Sept. 1979, pp. 27–28.]

16003. HARVARD UNIVERSITY. LIBRARY: *German Judaica pamphlets.* Judaica serials and ephemera microfilmed under the strengthening Research Library Resources Program, Title II–C of the Higher Education Act of 1965, checklist No. 3. Cambridge, Mass.: Harvard Univ. Library, 1979. 74 pp.

16004. HOLOCAUST. ANTI-DEFAMATION LEAGUE OF B'NAI B'RITH: *Holocaust information center. A selected and annotated resource list of materials on the Holocaust.* New York, 1978. 64 pp.

16005. — ARAD, YITZHAK/GUTMAN, YISRAEL/MARGALIOT, ABRAHAM: *Documents on the Holocaust.* Selected sources on the destruction of the Jews of Germany and Austria, Poland and the Soviet Union. [Hebrew.] Jerusalem: Yad Vashem, 1978. 402 pp.

16006. — BROSZAT, MARTIN: *Holocaust-Literatur (1979) im Kielwasser des Fernsehfilms.* [In]: Geschichte in Wissenschaft und Unterricht, Jg. 31, H. 1, Stuttgart, Jan. 1980. Pp. 21–29. [Review article.] [And abridged version]: Der Schock und seine Folgen. Literatur im Kielwasser des Holocaust-Filmes [in]: FAZ, Frankfurt a. Main, 4. Sept. 1979, p. 25.

16007. — *Guide to unpublished materials of the Holocaust period. Vol. 5.* Ed. by Yehuda Bauer, Shmuel Krakowski and Aharon Weiss. Jerusalem: The Hebrew University, The Institute of Contemporary Jewry, Division of Holocaust Studies, Yad Vashem Martyrs' and Heroes' Remembrance Authority, 1979. 436 pp. [This is the last volume in the series to be devoted to the Yad Vashem Archives; Vol. 6 will list the materials at 'Moreshet'. See also No. 8559/YB. XVI (Vol. 1); No. 10261/YB. XVIII (Vol. 2); No. 13492/YB. XXII (Vol. 3); No. 15118/YB. XXIV (Vol. 4).]

16008. — *Judenverfolgung im Dritten Reich. Literaturverzeichnis* anlässlich des 40. Jahrestages der Reichskristallnacht. Hrsg.: Stadtbücherei Solingen. Solingen: Stadtbücherei, [1979?]. 5 pp.

16009. — *On the Holocaust. Bibliographies. Vol. 1.* Philadelphia: National Institute on the Holocaust, 1978. Various pagings.

16010. —PIEKARZ, MENDEL, comp.: *The Holocaust and its aftermath as seen through Hebrew periodicals. A bibliography.* [Hebrew.] Jerusalem: Yad Vashem, 1978. 492 pp.

16011. JEWISH THEOLOGICAL SEMINARY OF AMERICA, New York. ARCHIVES: *Preliminary listing of holdings* [of archival collections]. New York, n.d. [1979]. 11 pp. [mimeog.] [Lists prints and photographs spanning the seventeenth to twentieth centuries, communal records also from Germany, documents from the Nuremberg Trial, and others.]

16012. *Judaica. A short-title catalogue of the books, pamphlets and manuscripts relating to the political, social and cultural history of the Jews and to the Jewish question in the library of Ludwig Rosenberger, Chicago, Ill.* Expanded supplement. Cincinnati: Hebrew Union College Press, 1979. 66 pp. (Bibliographica Judaica, 4. A bibliographic series of the Library of Hebrew Union College.) [Incl.: Judaica Germanica; Emancipation in Germany and Austria; Jewish question in Germany and Austria; Books on prominent German Jews. Expanded version of No. 12000/YB. XX. For main catalogue see No. 10267/YB. XVIII.]

16013. LEO BAECK INSTITUTE NEW YORK. MILTON SYBIL: *German-Jewish genealogical research: selected resources at the Leo Baeck Institute, New York.* [In]: Toledot, the Journal of Jewish Genealogy, Vol. 2, No. 4, New York, Spring 1979. Pp. 13–18, facsims., notes (pp. 17–18).

16014. — MILTON, SYBIL: *The Leo Baeck Institute in New York and its holdings in the era of the Second World War.* [In]: American Committee on the History of the Second World War. Newsletter, No. 20, Department of History, Southern Illinois Univ., Carbondale, Ill., Fall 1978. Pp. 7–11, bibl. (pp. 10–11).

16015. *Österreichisches Biographisches Lexikon 1815–1950.* Hrsg. von der Österr. Akademie der Wissenschaften. Redigiert von Eva Obermayer-Marnach. Bd. 7: Music – Petra Petrescu. Wien: Verlag der Österr. Akademie der Wissenschaften, 1979. [For previous vols. see No. 10274/YB. XVIII and No. 15122/YB. XXIV.]

16016. *Post-War publications on German Jewry. A selected bibliography of books and articles 1978.* Compiled by Bertha Cohn. [In]: LBI Year Book XXIV, London, 1979. Pp. 375–458.

16017. SPALEK, JOHN M.: *Guide to the archival materials of the German-speaking emigration to the United States after 1933. Verzeichnis der Quellen und Materialien der deutschsprachigen Emigration in den U.S.A. seit 1933.* By John M. Spalek in collaboration with Adrienne Ash and Sandra H. Hawrylchak. Charlottesville: Univ. Press of Virginia, 1978. XXV, 1133 pp. (Publ. for the Bibliographical Society of the University of Virginia.)

——— STRAUSS, HERBERT A., ed.: *Jewish immigrants of the Nazi period in the USA. Vol. 1: Archival resources.* [See No. 15989.]

16018. TRUMPP, THOMAS/KÖHNE, RENATE, comps.: *Archivbestände zur Wirtschafts- und Sozialgeschichte der Weimarer Republik. Übersicht über Quellen in Archiven der Bundesrepublik Deutschland.* Mit Beiträgen von Jens Flemming [et al.]. Boppard: Boldt, 1979. 380 pp. (Schriften des Bundesarchivs, 29.) [Lists also archival material pertinent to German Jewish personalities.]

16019. WININGER, S[ALOMON]: *Grosse jüdische National-Biographie mit mehr als 12000 Lebensbeschreibungen namhafter jüdischer Männer und Frauen aller Zeiten und Länder. Ein Nachschlagewerk für das jüdische Volk und dessen Freunde.* Bd. 1–7 [no more published]. Nachdr. der Ausg. Cernauti 1925–1936. Nendeln/Liechtenstein: Kraus Reprint, 1979. 7 vols.

III. THE NAZI PERIOD

A. General

16020. ADAM, UWE DIETRICH: *Judenpolitik im Dritten Reich*. Königstein/Ts.: Athenäum, 1979. 382 pp. (Athenäum-Droste Taschenbuch, Nr. 7223: Geschichte.) [First publ. 1972, see No. 10283/YB. XVIII.]

16021. ALEXANDER, EDWARD: *The incredibility of the Holocaust*. [In]: Midstream, Vol. 25, No. 3, New York, March 1979. Pp. 49–58.

16022. ALGAZY, JOSEPH: *The summary of the 'Final Solution' and the literature denying the Holocaust*. In appendices: The 'Korherr File' and selected excerpts from the 'anti-Holocaust' literature. [Hebrew, preface in English (pp. A–I).] Tel Aviv, Univ., submitted to the Faculty of Humanities, the Aranne School of History, March 1979. 190 pp., facsims., bibl. (pp. 165–187). [Mimeog.]

16023. *Anatomie des SS-Staates*. Gutachten des Instituts für Zeitgeschichte. 1–2. München: Dt.-Taschenbuch-Verl., 1979. 2 vols. (dtv, 2915–2916: dtv-Dokumente.) *Bd. 1:* BUCHHEIM, HANS: *Die SS, das Herrschaftsinstrument. Befehl und Gehorsam*. 2. Aufl. 323 pp. *Bd. 2:* BROSZAT, MARTIN: *Nationalsozialistische Konzentrationslager 1933–1945*. [And]: JACOBSEN, HANS-ADOLF: *Kommissarbefehl und Massenexekutionen sowjetischer Kriegsgefangener*. [And]: KRAUSNICK, HELMUT: *Judenverfolgung*. 2. Aufl. 370 pp. [First publ. 1965.]

16024. ANDERS, GÜNTER: *Besuch im Hades: Auschwitz und Breslau 1966; nach 'Holocaust' 1979*. München: Beck, 1979. 218 pp. (Beck'sche schwarze Reihe, Bd. 202.)

16025. ANTONI, E.: *KZ. Von Dachau bis Auschwitz*. Faschistische Konzentrationslager 1933–1945. Frankfurt a. Main: Röderberg, 1979. 144 pp., illus.

16026. ARENDT, HANNAH: *German guilt*. [In]: Jewish Frontier, Vol. 47, No. 10, New York, Dec. 1979. Pp. 36–41. [Reprint from Jewish Frontier, Jan. 1945.]

16027. ARONSFELD, C. C.: *Extermination and war*. Hitler's 'prophecy' in 1939. [In]: AJR Information, London, Jan. 1979. P. 1.

16028. ARTZT, HEINZ: *Mörder in Uniform*. Organisationen, die zu Vollstreckern nationalsozialistischer Verbrechen wurden. Mit einem Vorwort von Gert Bastian. München: Kindler, 1979. 205 pp., illus., diagrs., bibl. (pp. 202–204). [Cf.: Keiner war Kain? Warum die Trauerarbeit notwendig ist (Dietrich Strothmann) [in]: Die Zeit, Hamburg, 16. Nov. 1979, pp. 23 & 24.]

16029. AUSCHWITZ. ADLER, H[ANS] G. *[et. al.]*. eds.: *Auschwitz. Zeugnisse und Berichte*. 2., überarb. Aufl. Köln: Europäische Verlagsanstalt, 1979. 316 pp.

16030. — BIER, JEAN-PAUL: *Auschwitz et les nouvelles littératures allemandes*. Bruxelles: Editions de l'Université de Bruxelles, 1979. 232 pp. (Centre national des hautes études juives.)

16031. — CONWAY, JOHN S.: *Frühe Augenzeugenberichte aus Auschwitz*. Glaubwürdigkeit und Wirkungsgeschichte. [In]: Vierteljahrshefte für Zeitgeschichte, Jg. 27, H. 2, München, April 1979. Pp. 260–284.

16032. — DEMANT, EBBO, ed.: *Auschwitz–'direkt von der Rampe weg...'. Kaduk, Erber, Klehr: drei Täter geben zu Protokoll*. Mit einer Einführung von Axel Eggebrecht. Reinbek: Rowohlt, 1979. 143 pp., bibl. (pp. 142–143). (rororo, 4438: rororo aktuell.)

16033. — HEUBNER, CHRISTOPH/MEYER, ALWIN/PIEPLOW, JÜRGEN: *Lebenszeichen. Gesehen in Auschwitz*. Bornheim-Merten, Lamuv, 1979. 183 pp.

16034. — MÜLLER, FILIP: *Auschwitz Inferno. The testimony of a Sonderkommando*. Literary collaboration by Helmut Freitag. Ed. and transl.: Susanne Flatauer. Foreword: Yehuda Bauer. London: Routledge & Kegan Paul, 1979. XII, 180 pp., illus., plans. [Also German edn. under the title]: *Sonderbehandlung. Drei Jahre in den Krematorien und Gaskammern von Auschwitz*. Dt. Bearb. von Helmut Freitag. München: Steinhausen, 1979. 287 pp., diagrs. [Cf.: 'Sonderbehandlung' (Manfred Bosch) [in]: Tribüne, H. 71, Frankfurt a. Main, 1979, pp. 151–154.]

16035. — STÄGLICH, WILHELM: *Der Auschwitz-Mythos. Legende oder Wirklichkeit?* Eine kritische Bestandsaufnahme. Tübingen: Grabert, 1979. XI, 467 pp., illus., bibl. (pp. 451–458). (Veröffentlichungen des Institutes für Deutsche Nachkriegsgeschichte, Bd. 9.) [Neo-Nazi attempt to prove that Auschwitz is a myth. Attempts to stop the sale of this book did not succeed. Cf.: Nicht indiziert [in]: SZ, München, 12. Okt. 1979, p. 9.]

16036. — WYMAN, DAVID S.: *Why Auschwitz was never bombed*. [In]: Commentary, Vol. 65, No. 5, New York, 1978. Pp. 37–46. [See also: Bombing Auschwitz (letters to the editor) [in]: Commentary, Vol. 66, No. 1, New York, 1979, pp. 7–12.]

16037. AUSTRIA. MAASS, WALTER B.: *Country without a name. Austria under Nazi rule 1938–1945.* New York: Ungar, 1979. X, 178 pp., illus., maps, bibl. (pp. 165–167). [Incl.: The Final Solution in Austria, pp. 41–50.]
16038. — NEUGEBAUER, WOLFGANG, ed.: *Widerstand und Verfolgung im Burgenland, 1934–1945.* Eine Dokumentation. Auswahl, Bearb. u. Zusammenstellung: Wolfgang Neugebauer unter Mitarbeit von Erica Fischer [*et al.*]. Wien: Österr. Bundesverlag, 1979. 486 pp., illus., facsims., ports. [Incl.: Die Juden, pp. 294–341.]
16039. — *Wien 1938.* Wien: Verein für Geschichte der Stadt Wien, 1978. 326 pp., bibl. (pp. 312–322). (Forschungen u. Beiträge zur Wiener Stadtgeschichte, Bd. 2.) (Wiener Geschichtsblätter, Sonderreihe. Hrsg.: Felix Czeike.) [Incl.: Das Schicksal der Wiener Juden in den März- u. Apriltagen 1938 (Jonny Moser, pp. 172–182). Arisierungen in Wien (Georg Weis, pp. 183–189). Die Situation an der Universität Wien, März/April 1938 (Albert Massiczek, pp. 216–229. Refers also to Jews).]
16040. BAVARIA. BROSZAT, MARTIN/FRÖHLICH, ELKE, eds.: *Bayern in der NS-Zeit. Bd. 2: Herrschaft und Gesellschaft im Konflikt.* Teil A. München: Oldenbourg, 1979. XXV, 517 pp., 52 illus. (Veröffentlichung im Rahmen des Projekts 'Widerstand und Verfolgung in Bayern 1933–1945' im Auftrag des Bayerischen Staatsministeriums für Unterricht u. Kultus bearb. vom Institut für Zeitgeschichte in Verbindung mit den Staatlichen Archiven Bayerns). [For vol. 1 see No. 15135/YB. XXIV. Vol. 2 incl.: Antisemitismus und Volksmeinung (Ian Kershaw, pp. 281–348, illus.). Das Konzentrationslager Dachau (Günther Kimmel). Cf.: Bayern in der NS-Zeit. Notwendige Anmerkungen zu einer Neuerscheinung (Ernst G. Lowenthal) [in]: 'Allgemeine', Düsseldorf, 21. Sept. 1979, p. 36.
— OPHIR, BARUCH Z./WIESEMANN, FALK, eds.: *Die jüdischen Gemeinden in Bayern 1918–1945.* [See No. 15874.]
16041. BEHREND-ROSENFELD, ELSE R.: *Ich stand nicht allein. Erlebnisse einer Jüdin in Deutschland 1933–1944.* 3. Aufl. Köln: Europäische Verlagsanstalt, 1979. 263 pp. (Zeugnisse unserer Zeit.) [Incl. details about the deportation of the Jews from Munich.]
16042. BENDORF. SCHABOW, DIETRICH: *Zur Geschichte der Juden in Bendorf.* Bendorf (D-5413, Hedwig-Dransfeld-Haus e.V., in Verbindung mit dem ökumenischen Arbeitskreis in Bendorf), November 1979. 32 pp., illus., map. [Refers to the 'Heil- u. Pflegeanstalt für jüdische Nerven- u. Gemütskranke', also called 'Jacoby'sche Anstalt', founded in 1869 in Bendorf-Sayn/Rhineland. In 1941/42 the inmates were killed by the Nazis.]
16043. BERGEN–BELSEN. LÉVY-HASS, HANNA: *Vielleicht war das alles erst der Anfang. Tagebuch aus dem KZ Bergen-Belsen 1944–1945.* Hrsg. von Eike Geisel. Berlin: Rotbuch-Verl., 1979. 110 pp., facsims., tabs., map. (Rotbuch, 191.) [Incl. also: Ein Gespräch mit Hanna Lévy-Hass, Tel Aviv/Genf, 1978.]
16044. — ROSENSAFT, MENACHEM Z.: *The mass-graves of Bergen-Belsen.* Focus for confrontation. [In]: Jewish Social Studies, Vol. 41, No. 2, New York, Spring 1979. Pp. 155–186.
16045. BERLIN. GOLDSTEIN, HEINZWERNER: *Untergrund in Berlin.* [In]: Mitteilungen des Verbandes ehemaliger Breslauer und Schlesier in Israel, No. 45, Tel Aviv, April/Mai 1979. Pp. 7–8.
16046. BILLIG, JOSEPH: *Die Endlösung der Judenfrage. Studie über ihre Grundsätze im III. Reich und in Frankreich während der Besatzung.* Übers. aus dem Franz.: Eva Schulz. Dokumentationszentrum für Jüd. Zeitgeschichte CDJC Paris. New York: Beate-Klarsfeld-Foundation; Frankfurt a. Main: Jewish Young Leadership, 1979. 240 pp. [Orig. title: 'La solution finale de la question juive'. Incl.: Teil 1: Die Judenfrage im Dritten Reich bis 1941. Teil 2: Die Befehle zur Endlösung der Judenfrage. Teil 3: Die Endlösung der Judenfrage in Frankreich.]
16047. BRENNER, HANS: *Zur Frage der Ausbeutung von KZ-Häftlingen durch den Osram-Konzern 1944/45.* [Dokumentation.] [In]: Zeitschrift für Geschichtswissenschaft, Jg. 27, H. 10, Berlin/East, 1979. Pp. 952–965. [See also No. 16060.]
16048. BROWDER, GEORGE C.: *Die Anfänge des SD.* Dokumente aus der Organisationsgeschichte des Sicherheitsdienstes des Reichsführers SS. [In]: Vierteljahrshefte für Zeitgeschichte, Jg. 27, H. 2, München, April 1979. Pp. 299–324. [Incl. Referat IV/2 Judentum and Greuelpropaganda, etc.]
16049. BROWNING, CHRISTOPHER R.: *The Final Solution and the German Foreign Office.* A study of Referat D III of Abteilung Deutschland 1940–1943. New York: Holmes & Meier, 1979. 276 pp., map, bibl. [Incl. initial chaps on: The evolution of the German Jewish policy and the background; Referat Deutschland, Jewish policy and the German Foreign Office 1933–1940. For 1975 Diss. see No. 14286/YB. XXIII.]

16050. BUSCH, EBERHARD: *Juden und Christen im Schatten des Dritten Reiches.* Ansätze zu einer Kritik des Antisemitismus in der Zeit der Bekennenden Kirche. München: Kaiser, 1979. 76 pp. (Theologische Existenz heute, Nr. 205.)
16051. CASTLE STANFORD, JULIAN [orig. Julius Schloss]: *Tagebuch eines deutschen Juden im Untergrund 1938–1945.* Darmstadt: Verlag Darmstädter Blätter, 1979. 181 pp.
16052. CHAGOLL, LYDIA, ed.: *Im Namen Hitlers. Kinder hinter Stacheldraht.* Köln: Pahl-Rugenstein; Frankfurt a. Main: Röderberg, 1979. 136 pp., mostly illus.
16053. CZECHOSLOVAKIA. LIPSCHER, LADISLAV: *Die Juden im slowakischen Staat 1939–1945.* München: Oldenbourg, 1979. 210 pp. (Veröffentlichungen des Collegium Carolinum, Bd. 36.)
16054. — SCHNEIDER, HANSJÖRG: *Exiltheater in der Tschechoslowakei 1933–1938.* Berlin/East: Henschel, 1979. 358 pp., illus., bibl. notes (pp. 243–345). (Deutsches Theater im Exil.) (Veröffentlichung der Akademie der Künste der D.D.R. in Zusammenarbeit mit der Sektion Ästhetik in Kunstwissenschaft der Humboldt-Univ. zu Berlin.) [Incl. chap.: Die Tschechoslowakei als Asyl der antifaschistischen deutschen Emigranten (pp. 16–54).]
16055. DACHAU. *Nauseated by the sights and odors.* [In]: American Jewish Archives, Vol. 31, No. 1, Cincinnati, April 1979. Pp. 51–61. [Letter by an unknown American-Jewish soldier, giving his first impressions, conversations and interviews with Jewish survivors at Dachau.]
16056. DAENE, WILHELM: *Ein Werkmeister erzählt.* Bericht eines Mannes und einer Frau über ihre engagierte Hilfe bei der Rettung von Menschenleben jüdischer Mitbürger in der Zeit der Naziherrschaft. Veröffentlicht von der Gustav-Heinemann-Oberschule, Berlin-Tempelhof, Okt. 1979. 40 pp. [Mimeog.]
16057. DAHM, VOLKER: *Das jüdische Buch im Dritten Reich. Teil 1: Die Ausschaltung der jüdischen Autoren, Verleger und Buchhändler.* Frankfurt a. Main: Buchhändler-Vereinigung, 1979. 300 cols., illus., bibl., summaries in English, French and German. (Sonderdruck aus: Archiv für Geschichte des Buchwesens, Bd. 20, Lfg. 1–2.) [Cont.: 1. Das 'jüdische' Buch als Volksfeind. 2. Die Ausschaltung jüdischer Autoren, Verleger und Buchhändler durch Berufsverbot. 3. Die Ausschaltung 'jüdischen' Schrifttums durch Buchverbot. Pt. 2: 'Salman Schocken und sein Verlag' will be publ. in 1980. This edn. in two vols. is based on a Munich dissertation 1976/77. Corrected entry of No. 13510/YB. XXII. Cf.: Jüdische Literatur in der NS-Zeit (Adolf Diamant) [in]: 'Allgemeine', Düsseldorf, 13. Juli 1979, p. 6. Jüdische Verleger u. Buchhändler 1933–1943 (E. G. Lowenthal) [in]: MB, Tel Aviv, 10. Aug. 1979, p. 6.]
16058. DANZIG. LICHTENSTEIN, ERWIN: *Abiturententag. Reminiszenzen an die letzten Tage der Juden in der Freien Stadt Danzig.* [In]: MB, Nr. 11, Tel Aviv, 16. März 1979. P. 4.
16059. DAWIDOWICZ, LUCY S.: *Der Krieg gegen die Juden, 1933–1945.* Aus dem Amerikan. übersetzt. München: Kindler, 1979. 441 pp., bibl. (pp. 429–438). [Orig. title: 'The war against the Jews', 1975. Last Engl. edn. see No. 15140/YB. XXIV.]
16060. DEMPS, LAURENZ: *Die Ausbeutung von KZ-Häftlingen durch den Osram-Konzern 1944/45.* [Dokumentation.] [In]: Zeitschrift für Geschichtswissenschaft, Jg. 26, Nr. 5, Berlin/East, 1978. Pp. 416–437. [See also No. 16047.]
16061. DEUTSCHKRON, INGE, ed.: *Denn ihrer war die Hölle. Kinder in Gettos und Lagern.* Neuaufl. Köln: Verlag Wissenschaft u. Politik, 1979. 157 pp., illus. (children's drawings). [1st edn. 1965, see No. 5074/YB. XI.]
16062. DIWALD, HELLMUT: *Geschichte der Deutschen.* Frankfurt a. Main: Propyläen, 1978. 767 pp., illus. (4th edn., 1979, 760 pp.) [Incl. controversial statements about persecution of the Jews. Cf.: Axel Springer apologises [in]: AJR Information, London, April 1979, p. 9. 'Ein ausgesprochenes Missgeschick'. Axel Springer über Diwalds 'Geschichte der Deutschen' [in]: 'Allgemeine', Düsseldorf, 9. Febr. 1979, p. 3. War Hitler die zentrale Gestalt der dt. Geschichte? Eine Frage an Hellmut Diwald (Hans Lamm) [in]: 'Allgemeine', Düsseldorf, 2. Nov. 1979, p. 6. Diwald oder das System der Geschichtsverdrehung (Hans Kühner) [in]: Basler Zeitung, 7. Juli 1979, p. 39. Geschichte im Widerstreit. Hellmut Diwald antwortet seinen Kritikern [in]: Börsenblatt für den Dt. Buchhandel, Jg. 35, Nr. 1, Frankfurt a. Main, 2. Jan. 1979, pp. 25–28. Ein Gegenchronologe am Werk: H. Diwalds Geschichtsklitterung (Hermann Glaser) [in]: Tribüne, H. 71, Frankfurt a. Main, 1979, pp. 92–101.]
16063. *Le Dossier juif.* Documents. Paris: S.N.R.A., 1979. 80 pp., ports., illus., facsims. (France 1940–1945, No. 2.)
16064. ERMREUTH. KIRSCHNER, KLAUS: *'Da brennt's in Ermreuth!' Juden und Nazis in einem fränkischen Dorf.* [In]: Frankfurter Hefte, Jg. 34, H. 10, Frankfurt a. Main, Okt. 1979. Pp. 37–44. [History of the Jewish community of Ermreuth, Franconia, persecution, 'Kristallnacht', and post-war re-emergence of Nazi elements in the area.]

16065. *Essays in Holocaust history.* Jerusalem: The Hebrew University, Institute of Contemporary Jewry, Division of Holocaust Studies, 1979. 113 pp. (Publication of the Alexander Silberman Internat. Scholarship Foundation in Contemporary Jewry, 1.) [Incl.: Trends in Holocaust research (Yehuda Bauer). The reaction of the Jewish public in Germany to the Nuremberg Laws (Abraham Margaliot).]

16066. FEIN, HELEN: *Accounting for genocide. National responses and Jewish victimization during the Holocaust.* New York: Free Press, 1979. XXI, 468 pp., charts, maps, tables.

16067. FEINGOLD, HENRY L.: *Who shall bear guilt for the Holocaust. The human dilemma.* [In]: American Jewish History, Vol. 68, No. 3, Waltham, Mass., March 1979. Pp. 261–282.

16068. FOX, JOHN P.: *The Holocaust in historical perspective.* [In]: The Jewish Quarterly, Vol. 27, Nos. 2/3, London, Summer/Autumn 1979. Pp. 30–33.

16069. FRANK, ANNE. FRANK, ANNE: *Das Tagebuch der Anne Frank. 12. Juni 1942 bis 1. August 1944.* Mit einer Einführung von Marie Baum. 11., durchgesehene Aufl. Heidelberg: L. Schneider, 1979. 295 pp., illus., ports., facsims. [Also paperback edn.]: Mit einem Vorwort von Albrecht Goes. (Aus dem Holländ. übertr. von Anneliese Schütz.) 46. Aufl. Frankfurt a. Main: Fischer, 1979. 200 pp. (Fischer-Taschenbücher, 77.) [Cf.: Im Juni 1979 wäre Anne Frank 50 Jahre alt. Zum Erscheinen der 11. Aufl. des 'Tagebuch der Anne Frank' [in]: deutschland-berichte, Jg. 15, Nr. 2, Bonn, Febr. 1979, pp. 18 & 19. Vor allem ein politisches Dokument. 'Das Tagebuch der Anne Frank' im Düsseldorfer Schauspielhaus (Boike Jacobs) [in]: 'Allgemeine', Düsseldorf, 5. Okt. 1979, p. 7, illus.]

16070. — *Anne Frank. Eine Dokumentation.* Hrsg. von der Anne-Frank-Stiftung, Amsterdam. Heidelberg: L. Schneider, 1979. 70 pp., 135 illus., ports., facsims.

16071. — *Birthday tributes, 50th anniversary* (12. Juni 1929): Gedanken über Anne Frank. Zum 12. Juni 1979 (Hans Lamm) [in]: 'Allgemeine', Düsseldorf, 8. Juni 1979, p. 3, port. New York ehrte Anne Frank [in]: Aufbau, New York, June 22, 1979, p. 2, port. Ich möchte mal eine bedeutende Frau werden (Robert M. W. Kempner) [in]: Die Mahnung, Jg. 26, Nr. 7, Berlin, 1. Juli 1979, p. 6.

16072. — FREIMARK, PETER/KOPITZSCH, WOLFGANG: *Anne Frank, ein jüdisches Schicksal. Texte und Materialien für die politische Bildung.* Hamburg: Landeszentrale für politische Bildung, 1979. 31 pp., bibl. (pp. 29–31).

16073. — JALDATI, LIN: *Erinnerungen an Anne Frank.* [In]: Nachrichtenblatt der Jüd. Gemeinde von Berlin u. des Verbandes der Jüd. Gemeinden in der D.D.R., Dresden–Berlin, Juni 1979. Pp. 3–5. [Personal report about the last months of Anne Frank whom the author met in Belsen.]

16074. — KUGLER, VICTOR: *The reminiscences of Victor Kugler, the 'Mr. Kraler' of Anne Frank's diary, as told to Eda Shapiro.* [In]: Yad Vashem Studies, 13, Jerusalem, 1979. Pp. 353–385, facsims.

16075. — THOMMEN, ANDREAS: *Otto Frank erzählt.* [In]: Isr. Wochenblatt, Nr. 5, 6 & 7, Zürich, 2., 9., & 16. Febr. 1979. Pp. 45 & 47 [in each issue], illus., ports. [Reminiscences of Anne Frank's father, aged 90, living in Basle.]

16076. FREEDEN HERBERT: *Menetekel im November. Ein deutscher Jude zwischen 'Reichskristallnacht' und englischem Exil.* Zwei Features. Hrsg.: Deutschlandfunk, Abt. Presse- u. Öffentlichkeitsarbeit (Postfach 510640, D-5000 Köln 51). Köln: Deutschlandfunk, 1979. 48 pp., port. (Deutschlandfunk, 25/79.) [Transcript of two radio-transmissions: 'Menetekel im November. Erinnerungen eines Betroffenen', 9. Nov. 1978 (pp. 5–21), and 'Wie ich Brite wurde. Als Emigrant in England', 20. Dez. 1977 (pp. 23–44).

16077. FRIEDMAN, PHILIP: *Their brothers' keepers.* New York: Holocaust Library, 1978. 232 pp. (Paperback.) [This tribute to the gentiles who helped persecuted Jewry during World War II incl. a chap. 'We let God wait ten years' on Germans who assisted German Jews. First publ. 1958, see No. 1069/YB. III.]

16078. GERSTEIN, KURT: *Dokumentation zur Massen-Vergasung.* [Augenzeugenbericht.] [In]: Freiburger Rundbrief, Folge 30, Freiburg i. Br., 1978. Pp. 130–135 [footnote].

16079. GILBERT, MARTIN: *Final journey. The fate of the Jews in Nazi Europe.* London: Allen & Unwin, 1979. 224 pp., 280 illus. [Largely composed of eye-witness accounts.]

16080. GLEIWITZ O/S. BIENEK, HORST: *Zeit ohne Glocken. Roman.* München: Hanser, 1979. 411 pp. [Refers also to Arthur Kochmann, the last representative of the Jewish community and the deportation of Jews from Gleiwitz O/S; fictitious description of the last days of the poet Arthur Silbergleit (see also No. 16704).]

16081. *Gott nach Auschwitz. Dimensionen des Massenmords am jüdischen Volk.* [Von] Eugen Kogon [et al.]. Freiburg i. Br.: Herder, 1979. 144 pp. [Orig. title: 'Dimensions of the holocaust'. Cf.:

Vom Gebot des Misstrauens. Gedanken zum Holokaust (Max Schoch) [in]: NZZ, Zürich, 18. Juli 1979, p. 27.]

16082. GROBMAN, ALEX: *What did they know?* The American Jewish press and the Holocaust, 1. Sept. 1939–17. Dec. 1942. [In]: American Jewish History, Vol. 68, No. 3, Waltham, Mass., March 1979. Pp. 327–352.

16083. GRÖBZIG. HOBUSCH, ERICH: *Jugenderinnerungen.* [Jüdische Gemeinde Gröbzig, 1939.] [In]: Nachrichtenblatt der Jüd. Gemeinde von Berlin u. des Verbandes der Jüd. Gemeinden in der D.D.R., Dresden–Berlin, Juni 1979. Pp. 6–9, illus. [And]: Berichtigung [in]: Dez. 1979, pp. 8–9.

16084. GROPPE, LOTHAR, SJ.: *Kirche und Juden im Dritten Reich.* (Erweiterte Fassung eines Vortrags vor der Wiener Kath. Akademie am 5.3.1979.) Wien (Freyung 6): Wiener Kath. Akademie, 1979. 19 pp. (Wiener Kath. Akademie, Miscellanea. Arbeitskreis für kirchl. Zeit- u. Wiener Diözesangeschichte, 66.)

16085. HAUSNER, GIDEON: *Die Vernichtung der Juden, das grösste Verbrechen der Geschichte.* [Dokumentation der 1967 erschienenen Darstellung des Eichmann-Prozesses 'Gerechtigkeit in Jerusalem' von Gideon Hausner. Übers. aus dem Amerikan. von Peter de Mendelssohn. 2. Aufl.] München: Kindler, 1979. 349 pp., illus. [Orig. title: 'Justice in Jerusalem', abridged version.]

16086. HILBERG, RAUL: *In search of special trains.* [In]: Midstream, Vol. 25, No. 8, New York, Oct. 1979. Pp. 32–38. [Also]: *German railroads, Jewish souls* (Raul Hilberg) [in]: Society, Vol. 14, No. 1, Rutgers State Univ., 1976/77, pp. 60–74. [Hilberg's research on the part the German railways played in the destruction of the Jews and his impressions of post-war Germany. See also No. 16111.]

16087. HIRSCH, HELMUT: *Vor 40 Jahren.* [Persönliche Erinnerungen.] [In]: Erziehen heute, Jg. 6 (29), H. 3, Duisburg, 1979. Pp. 23–26, bibl. notes (p. 26).

16088. HITLER. BROSZAT, MARTIN: *Hitler and the genesis of the 'Final Solution'. An assessment of David Irving's theses.* [In]: Yad Vashem Studies, 13, Jerusalem, 1979. Pp. 73–125, bibl. footnotes. [Refers to 'Hitler's war' by David Irving, London, 1977, and the expurgated German transl. under the title 'Hitler und seine Feldherren', Frankfurt a. Main, Ullstein, 1975. See also Nos. 16092, 16098.]

16089. — EBON, MARTIN: *Why did Hitler hate the Jews?* [In]: Midstream, Vol. 25, No. 8, New York, Oct. 1979. Pp. 19–24.

16090. — FOX, JOHN P.: *Adolf Hitler. The continuing debate.* [In]: International Affairs, Vol. 55, No. 2, London, April 1979. Pp. 252–264. [Review article of new books on Hitler.]

16091. — HAFFNER, SEBASTIAN: *The meaning of Hitler.* London: Weidenfeld and Nicolson; New York: Macmillan, 1979. 172 pp. [Orig. title: 'Anmerkungen zu Hitler', 1st edn. München, 1978.]

16092. — IRVING, DAVID: Hitlers Weg zum Krieg. (Aus dem Engl. übers. von Georg Auerbach.) München: Herbig, 1979. 529 pp., illus. [Orig. title: 'The war path'. In his second Hitler book as well as in his first one ('Hitler und seine Feldherren', Engl. edn. 'Hitler's war', see No. 14310/YB. XXIII) Irving negates the prime responsibility of Hitler for the liquidation of German and European Jewry. Cf.: The selling of Adolf Hitler: David Irving's Hitler's war (Charles W. Sydnor jr.) [in]: Central European History, Vol. 12, No. 2, Atlanta, Ga., June 1979, pp. 169–199. 40 Jahre nach Ausbruch des 2. Weltkrieges: Viel Lärm um nichts. Kritische Anmerkungen zu Irvings jüngstem Erfolgsbuch (Hans-Adolf Jacobsen) [in]: Die Zeit, Hamburg, 28. Sept. 1979, p. 55. See also Nos. 16088, 16098.]

16093. — ZENTNER, CHRISTIAN: *Adolf Hitler.* Texte, Bilder, Dokumente. München: Delphin, 1979. 144 pp., illus., facsims. [Incl.: 'Antisemitismus vor Hitler; Hitlers Wandlung zum Antisemitismus; Der Judenmörder; Holocaust'.]

16094. HOLOCAUST-ART. INTERNATIONAL CONFERENCE ON THE LESSONS OF THE HOLOCAUST: *The living witness. Art in the concentration camps.* [Exhibition] under the auspices of the Coordinating Council on the Holocaust, Memorial Committee for the Six Million Jewish Martyrs, National Institute on the Holocaust [at the] Museum of American Jewish History, 55 North Fifth Street, Philadelphia, Penn., Oct. 18–Nov. 19, 1978. [Catalogue ed. by Richard Firster and Nora Levin.] Philadelphia, 1978. 48 pp., illus., biogr. of artists. [The LBI New York contributed to this exhibition with loans from its archives.]

16095. — MILTON, SYBIL: *Art and artists in Nazi Europe, 1933–1945.* [In]: International Conference on the Lessons of the Holocaust, Oct. 18–20, 1978. Philadelphia, Pa. (Suite 500, 260 S. 15th Str.): National Institute on the Holocaust [1979]. Pp. 87–136, illus., bibl. footnotes (pp. 123–136). [Mimeog.] [Refers also to works of art in the archives of the LBI New York.]

16096. — MILTON, SYBIL: *Concentration camp art and artists.* [In]: Shoah. A Review of Holocaust Studies and Commemorations, Vol. 1, No. 2, New York, Fall 1978. Pp. 10–15, illus., bibl. footnotes (pp. 14–15). [Refers also to the relevant art-collection of the LBI New York.]
16097. — *Überleben und widerstehen. Zeichnungen von Häftlingen des Konzentrationslagers Auschwitz 1940–1946.* Hrsg.: Deutsch-Polnische Gesellschaft. Düsseldorf, 1979. 86 pp., illus.
16098. HOLOCAUST TV-FILM. MÄRTHESHEIMER, PETER/FRENZEL, IVO, eds.: *Im Kreuzfeuer: der Fernsehfilm 'Holocaust'. Eine Nation ist betroffen.* Hrsg. unter Mitarbeit von Hellmuth Auerbach u. Walter H. Pehle. Frankfurt a. Main: Fischer, 1979. 331 pp., illus., facsims., maps, bibl. (pp. 327–330). (Fischer-Taschenbücher, 4213: Informationen zur Zeit.) Besides contributions on the reaction to the Holocaust-film, this volume incl. also documentary articles: Zeitgeschichtliche Dokumente (pp. 82–115). Chronik der Judenverfolgung 1933–1945, Übersichtskarte der KZ (Wilhelm van Kampen, pp. 82–129). Der politische Antisemitismus in Deutschland, Entstehung u. Funktion (Iring Fetscher, pp. 133–150). Hitler u. der Mord an den europäischen Juden, Widerlegung einer absurden These; Noch einmal: Irving, Hitler und der Judenmord (Eberhard Jäckel, pp. 151–166). Organisierter Massenmord an Juden ... ein Beitrag zur Richtigstellung apologetischer Literatur (Ino Arndt/Wolfgang Scheffler, pp. 167–206). For literature on the reaction to the Holocaust TV-film see Nos. 16181–16185.
16099. HUNGARY. ELON, AMOS: *Schrei ohne Antwort. Die Mission des Joel Brand, 1 Million Juden gegen 10.000 Lastkraftwagen zu tauschen.* Roman-Bericht. Wien: Molden, 1979. 360 pp.
16100. — HOLZTRÄGER, HANS: *Judenverfolgung in Ungarn 1941–1944.* Gewaltmassnahmen gegen Juden im Spiegel der ungarndeutschen Presse. [In]: Tribüne, H. 70, Frankfurt a. Main, 1979, Pp. 94–108.
16101. IG FARBENINDUSTRIE. BORKIN, JOSEPH: *The crime and punishment of IG Farben.* London: Deutsch; New York: The Free Press, 1979. 264 pp., 8 pp. illus. [German edn. under the title]: BORKIN, JOSEPH: *Die unheilige Allianz der IG Farben. Eine Interessengemeinschaft im Dritten Reich.* (Übers. von Bernhard Schulte.) Frankfurt a. Main: Campus-Verl., 1979. 232 pp. [Cf.: Review [in]: The American Zionist, Vol. 69, No. 4, New York, April/May 1979, pp. 5–10. Im Dienst des Diktators. Industrie auf grausamen Abwegen (Gerd Bucerius) [in]: Die Zeit, Hamburg, 11. Jan. 1980, pp. 12–13 (review article which also deals with IG Farben's earlier history and the chemist Fritz Haber). IG Farben, founded in 1925, gained its importance after the fusion with the Jewish firm Leopold Cassella & Co., Frankfurt a. Main, whose owners, Carl and Arthur von Weinberg, became members of the board of directors. After 1933 Carl von Weinberg emigrated to Rome where he died in 1943, Arthur von Weinberg perished in Theresienstadt.]
16102. — SCHREIBER, PETER WOLFGANG: *IG Farben. Die unschuldigen Kriegsplaner. Profit aus Krisen, Kriegen und KZs. Geschichte eines deutschen Monopols.* Stuttgart: Verlag Neuer Weg, 1979. 283 pp.
16103. ITALY. MICHAELIS, MEIR: *Mussolini and the Jews. German–Italian relations and the Jewish question in Italy, 1922–1945.* Publ. for the Institute of Jewish Affairs. Oxford: The Clarendon Press, 1978. 472 pp. [Cf.: Half-hearted cynicism. Mussolini's racial politics (Andrew M. Canepa) [in]: Patterns of Prejudice, Vol. 13, No. 6, London, Nov.–Dec. 1979, pp. 18–27, bibl. footnotes. Juden unter Mussolini (Julius H. Schoeps) [in]: Tribüne, H. 70, Frankfurt a. Main, 1979, pp. 140–142.]
16104. — POMMERIN, REINER: *Rassenpolitische Differenzen im Verhältnis der Achse Berlin-Rom 1938–1943.* [In]: Vierteljahrshefte für Zeitgeschichte, Jg. 27, Heft 4, Stuttgart, Okt. 1979. Pp. 646–660.
16105. *Justiz und NS-Verbrechen.* Sammlung deutscher Strafurteile wegen nationalsozialistischer Tötungsverbrechen 1945–1966. Bearb. von Irene Sagel-Grande, H. H. Fuchs, C. F. Rüter. *Bd. 20*: Die vom 12.04.1964 bis zum 03.04.1965 ergangenen Strafurteile, Lfd. Nr. 569–590. *Bd. 21*: Die vom 03.04.1965 bis zum 21.08.1965 ergangenen Strafurteile, Lfd. Nr. 590–596. Amsterdam: University Press, 1979. 854 pp; 900 pp. [2 vols. For previous vols. see No. 15166/YB. XXIV. See also Nos 16191–16193.]
16106. KÖNIG, JOEL: *David. Aufzeichnungen eines Überlebenden.* Frankfurt a. Main: Fischer, 1979. 331 pp. (Fischer-Taschenbücher, 2196.) [1st publ. 1967 under the title: 'Den Netzen entronnen', see No. 6329/YB. XIII. Author's real name: Esra Ben Gershôm.]
16107. KOGON, EUGEN: *Der SS-Staat. Das System der deutschen Konzentrationslager.* 6. Aufl. München: Heyne, 1979. 427 pp. (Heyne-Bücher, Nr. 7027.)
16108. KORMAN, GERD: *Trivialising the Holocaust.* [In]: Jewish Chronicle, London, Oct. 5, 1979. P. 27.

Bibliography

16109. KOSELLECK, REINHART: *Terror und Traum*. Methodologische Anmerkungen zu Zeiterfahrungen im Dritten Reich. [In]: NZZ, Zürich, 3./4. Febr. 1979. Pp. 65–66. [Refers especially to the book by Charlotte Beradt: 'Das Dritte Reich des Traums', München, 1966, see No. 6995/YB. XIV.]

16110. KÜHNL, REINHARD, ed.: *Der deutsche Faschismus in Quellen und Dokumenten*. 3., unveränd. Aufl. Köln: Pahl-Rugenstein, 1978. 530 pp., illus., bibl. (pp. 503–512). (Kleine Bibliothek, 62.) [Incl. chaps.: Die Behandlung der Juden bis zum Beginn der Massenmorde (pp. 269–279); Die Konzentrationslager u. die industrielle Verwertung der Häftlinge (pp. 369–383); Massenmord (pp. 384–397).]

16111. *Kursbuch für die Gefangenenwagen*. Gültig vom 6. Oktober 1941 an. (Nachdr.) Mit einem Anhang: Nummernplan und Übersichtszeichnung eingesetzter Gefangenenwagen. Mainz: Dumjahn, 1979. 224 pp., 5 photos, 9 plates, 2 fold-outs. (Dokumente zur Eisenbahngeschichte, Bd. 10.) [Reprint from the only known copy in possession of the Deutsche Bücherei, Leipzig. This 'Kursbuch' (i.e., time-table) gives a survey on Nazi concentration camps. See also No. 16086.]

16112. LAQUEUR, WALTER: *The first news of the Holocaust*. New York: Leo Baeck Institute, 1979. 32 pp. (Leo Baeck Memorial Lecture, 23.)

16113. LAQUEUR, WALTER: *Jewish denial and the Holocaust*. [In]: Commentary, Vol. 68, No. 6, New York, Dec. 1979. Pp. 44–45.

16114. LEIBFRIED, STEPHAN/TENNSTEDT, FLORIAN: *Berufsverbote und Sozialpolitik 1933*. Die Auswirkungen der nationalsozialistischen Machtergreifung auf die Krankenkassenverwaltung und die Kassenärzte. Analyse. Materialien zu Angriff und Selbsthilfe. Erinnerungen. Bremen: Universitätsdruckerei, 1979. XIX, 325 pp. [Mimeog.] (Arbeitspapiere des Forschungsschwerpunktes Reproduktionsrisiken, soziale Bewegungen und Sozialpolitik, Nr. 2.) [First publ. in shortened version under the title]: TENNSTEDT, FLORIAN: *Sozialpolitik und Berufsverbote im Jahre 1933*. Mit einem Vorwort von Stephan Leibfried. [In]: Zeitschrift für Sozialreform, Jg. 25, H. 3 & 4, Wiesbaden, 1979, pp. 129–153, 211–238, biogr. & bibl. footnotes. [Mentions many Jewish physicians and psycho-analysts and gives ample biographical data. On the resistance to Nazi measures aimed at exclusion of Jewish physicians see also: Auf Spuren unserer Vergangenheit. Neue Literatur zur Geschichte der Juden in Deutschland. Widerstand durch Selbsthilfe 1933/39 (E. G. Lowenthal) [in]: MB, Nr. 3, Tel Aviv, 18. Jan. 1980, pp. 3 & 4.]

16115. MAJDANEK. BURG, J. G. [orig. Josef Ginsburg]: *Majdanek in alle Ewigkeit?* München: Ederer, 1979. 121, 22 pp., illus. [Negates the Nazi crimes. Cf.: Polizei beschlagnahmt Majdanek-Buch (Johann Freudenreich) [in]: SZ, München, 21. Dez. 1979, p. 14. Anklage gegen den Verfasser des Majdanek-Buches [in]: SZ, München, 15. Febr. 1980, p. 14.]

16116. — *KZ Majdanek*. Report über das Vernichtungslager und über den Majdanek-Prozess. Hrsg. vom Präsidium der VVN, Bund der Antifaschisten, u. des Kreisverbandes Düsseldorf der VVN. 3., erweiterte Aufl. Frankfurt a. Main: Röderberg, 1979. 71 pp., illus.

16117. — LICHTENSTEIN, HEINER: *Majdanek. Reportage eines Prozesses*. Mit einem Nachwort von Simon Wiesenthal. Frankfurt a. Main: Europäische Verlagsanstalt, 1979. 188 pp., maps. [See also: Beobachtungen beim Majdanek-Prozess (Rupert Neudeck) [in]: Frankfurter Hefte, Jg. 34, H. 5, Frankfurt a. Main, Mai 1979, pp. 46–52.]

16118. MORLEY, JOHN FRANCIS: *Vatican diplomacy and the Jews during the Holocaust, 1939–1943*. New York University, Phil. Diss., 1979. 601 pp. [See also: Weizsäcker, the Vatican, and the Jews (Owen Chadwick) [in]: Journal of Ecclesiastical History, Vol. 28, London, April 1977, pp. 179–199 (review article). Le Vatican et le problème juif, 1941–1942 (L. Papeleux) [in]: Revue d'Histoire de la Deuxième Guerre Mondiale, Vol. 27, Paris, July 1977, pp. 75–84.]

16119. MÜNDEN. PEZOLD, JOHANN DIETRICH von, ed.: *Judenverfolgung in Münden 1933–1945*. Eine Dokumentation aus dem Archiv der Stadt Münden, bearb. u. hrsg. im Auftrag der Stadt Münden. Münden: Stadtverwaltung, 1979. [48] pp., fascims., list of names.

— MUNICH. CAHNMAN, WERNER J.: *Die Juden in München 1918–1943*. [See No. 15911. Also No. 15912 (Hans Lamm), and No. 16041 (Else R. Behrend-Rosenfeld).]

16120. NORDEN, GÜNTHER van: *Der deutsche Protestantismus im Jahr der nationalsozialistischen Machtergreifung*. Gütersloh: Mohn, 1979. 438 pp., bibl. (pp. 393–402). [Incl. documentation on the reaction of German Protestantism to the discrimination against Jews.]

16121. NOVEMBER POGROM. FLEHINGER, ARTHUR: *Flames of fury*. [In]: Jewish Chronicle, London, Nov. 9, 1979. P. 27, illus. [First-hand account, never before publ., by the late Dr. A. Flehinger about the events on Nov. 9, 1938, the 'Kristallnacht', in Baden-Baden.]

16122. — HELMICH, HANS: *Zwischen Kreuz und Davidstern als die Synagogen brannten. Kristallnacht und Kirche in Wuppertal.* [In]: Bergische Blätter, Nr. 11, Wuppertal, Nov. 1978. Pp. 4–10, illus., facsims., ports.
16123. — MEYER, ENNO: *Die Reichskristallnacht in Oldenburg.* [With]: FLEISCHER, HANS: *Die Verantwortung einer Stadt für alle ihre Bürger 1938/1978.* Oldenburg: Holzberg, 1979. 28 pp., 1 illus.
16124. NUREMBERG. *Schicksal jüdischer Mitbürger in Nürnberg 1933–1945.* Dokumentation bearb. vom Stadtarchiv Nürnberg. Hrsg. vom Schul- u. Kulturreferat der Stadt Nürnberg. Nürnberg: Stadtrat, 1978. 69 pp. [Partial reprint of 'Schicksal jüdischer Mitbürger in Nürnberg 1850–1945', catalogue with documentation, publ. 1965, see No. 5084/YB. XI.]
16125. PAEPCKE, LOTTE: *Ich wurde vergessen. Bericht einer Jüdin, die das 3. Reich überlebte.* Mit einem aktuellen Nachwort. Freiburg i. Br.: Herder, 1979. 128 pp. (Herderbücherei, Bd. 733.)
16126. PENKOWER, MONTY NOAM: *The World Jewish Congress confronts the International Red Cross during the Holocaust.* [In]: Jewish Social Studies, Vol. 41, Nos. 3–4, New York, Summer–Fall 1979. Pp. 229–256.
16127. REFUGEE POLICY. ABELLA, IRVING/TROPER, HAROLD: *'The line must be drawn somewhere'. Canada and Jewish refugees 1933–1939.* [In]: Canadian Historical Review, Vol. 60, No. 2, Toronto, 1979. Pp. 178–209, bibl. footnotes.
16128. — DRAPER, PAULA JEAN: *The accidental immigrants. Canada and the interned refugees.* [In]: Canadian Jewish Historical Society Journal, Vol. 2, Nos. 1 & 2, Toronto, 1978. Pp. 1–38, 1–112.
16129. — DRUKS, HERBERT: *The failure to rescue.* New York: Speller, 1977. 108 pp., bibl. (pp. 102–106). [Documentary study of the United States and United Kingdom governmental policy resulting in the failure to save Jews from Nazi persecution.]
16130. — GILBERT, MARTIN: *British Government policy towards Jewish refugees (November 1938–September 1939).* [In]: Yad Vashem Studies, 13, Jerusalem, 1979. Pp. 127–167, bibl. footnotes.
16131. — HALLIE, PHILIP: *Lest innocent blood be shed. The story of the village of Le Chambon and how goodness happened there.* New York: Harper and Row; London: Michael Joseph, 1979. 291 pp. [A documentary report how the inhabitants of a small Protestant village in southern France rescued many Jewish and non-Jewish refugees between 1940 and 1944.]
16132. — ISOLANI, GERTRUD: *Stadt ohne Männer. Roman.* 3. Aufl. Basel: Buchverl. Basler Zeitung, 1979. 336 pp. [Refers to the French women's-KZ Gurs where the author was interned.]
16133. — MICHMAN, DAN: *The Jewish refugees from Germany in the Netherlands 1933–1940.* [Hebrew with English summary.] Jerusalem, 1978. 2 vols. (XXXIII, 625 pp.), illus., charts, facsims., tables, bibl. (in English). Jerusalem, Hebrew Univ., Thesis.
16134. — PATKIN, BENZION: *The Dunera internees.* Stanmore, N.S.W.: Cassell Australia, 1979. 185 pp., illus., facsims. [The transport from England to Australia of 2,542 internees, mainly German-Jewish refugees, and their time of internment in Australia.]
16135. — STEIN, JOSHUA B.: *Britain and the Jews of Danzig, 1938–1939.* [In]: The Wiener Library Bulletin, Vol. 32, new ser. Nos. 49/50, London, 1979. Pp. 29–33, bibl. notes (p. 33).
16136. — STÖSSINGER, FELIX: *Flucht aus Frankreich.* [In]: NZZ, Zürich, 31. Aug. 1979. P. 39. [F. St., 1889 Prag–Aug. 31, 1954 Zürich, author and journalist, emigrated after 1933 from Berlin to France and in 1942 to Switzerland.]
16137. — TOKAYER, MARVIN/SWARTZ, MARY SAGMASTER: *The Fugu Plan. The untold story of the Japanese and the Jews in World War II.* New York, London: Paddington Press, 1979. 287 pp., illus., map. [Documented story of the survival of European Jewish refugees in Japan.]
16138. — WASSERSTEIN, BERNARD: *Britain and the Jews of Europe 1939–1945.* Publ. for the Institute of Jewish Affairs. Oxford: Oxford Univ. Press, 1979. VIII, 389 pp., 1 illus., bibl. (pp. 363–378). [Cf.: Indolence of the heart (Margot Pottlitzer) [in]: AJR Information, London, Dec. 1979, pp. 1–2. Grossbritannien und die Juden. Niederschmetternde Enthüllungen aus dem Zweiten Weltkrieg (H. G. Alexander) [in]: Aufbau, New York, Aug. 3, 1979, p. 7. Review [in]: Jewish Chronicle, London, July 27, 1979, p. 14. Mean spirits (Elie Kedourie) [in]: The New York Review of Books, Nov. 22, 1979, pp. 6–10. Verschlossene Heimstätte Palästina. Grossbritannien und Hitlers Judenausrottung [in]: NZZ, Zürich, 3. Sept. 1979, p. 29. The F.O. and the Holocaust (Hyam Maccoby) [in]: 'The Observer', London, Aug. 5, 1979. Vorwürfe gegen Grossbritannien (Nachum Orland) [in]: SZ, München, 2. Okt. 1979, p. 9.] See also: Der letzte Kindertransport [nach England] verlässt Deutschland [1939] (Raanan Melitz) [in]: 'Allgemeine', Düsseldorf, 21. Sept. 1979, pp. 24–25.
16139. REICHE, E. G.: *From 'spontaneous' to legal terror: SA, police and the judiciary in Nürnberg, 1933–34.* [In]: European Studies Review, Vol. 9, No. 2, London, April 1979. Pp. 237–264.

16140. RHINELAND. GORDON, SARAH ANN: *German opposition to Nazi anti-Semitism measures between 1933 and 1945, with particular reference to the Rhine–Ruhr area*. State Univ. of New York at Buffalo, Phil. Diss., 1979. 502 pp.

16141. ROSENTHAL, LUDWIG: '*Endlösung der Judenfrage*', *Massenmord oder Gaskammerlüge*. Eine Auswertung der Beweisaufnahme im Prozess gegen Hauptkriegsverbrecher vor dem Internationalen Militärgerichtshof Nürnberg vom 14. Nov. 1945 bis 1. Okt. 1946. Darmstadt: Verlag Darmstädter Blätter, 1979. 154 pp., illus. (Judaica, [Nr. 2].)

16142. SEFTON, W. VICTOR: *The European Holocaust. Who knew what and when*. A Canadian aspect. [In]: Canadian Jewish Historical Society Journal, Vol. 2, No. 2, Toronto, Fall, 1978. Pp. 121–133.

16143. SERENY, GITTA: *The men who whitewash Hitler*. [In]: New Statesman, London, Nov. 2, 1979. Pp. 670–673. [Deals with the claim by the Neo-Nazis (National Front) that the Holocaust is a hoax.]

16144. SHERWIN, BYRON L./AMENT, SUSAN G., eds.: *Encountering the Holocaust*. An interdisciplinary survey. Chicago: Impact Press, [1979]. X, 502 pp., bibl.

16145. SIEGELE-WENSCHKEWITZ, LEONORE: *Die Evangelische Kirche in Deutschland während des Zweiten Weltkriegs 1939–1945*. [In]: Evangelische Theologie, Jg. 39, H. 5, München, Sept./Okt. 1979. Pp. 389–409. [Incl. attitude of the German Protestant Church to Jews and Judaism.]

16146. SIEGELE-WENSCHKEWITZ, LEONORE: *Die Evangelisch-Theologische Fakultät Tübingen in den Anfangsjahren des Dritten Reichs. 2: Gerhard Kittel und die Judenfrage*. Tübingen: Mohr, 1978. 80 pp. (Zeitschrift für Theologie und Kirche. Beiheft 4: Tübinger Theologie im 20. Jahrhundert.)

16147. SILESIA. JONCA, KAROL: *The attitude of the Evangelical Church in Silesia to the racist policies of the NSDAP*. [Polish with German and English summaries. Title transl.] [In]: Studia Slaskie, Seria nowa, tom. 35, 1979. Pp. 131–179. [Orig. title: 'Kościół Ewangelicki na Śląsku wobec polityki rasistowskiej NSDAP'.]

16148. STONE, ADOLF: *The last years of German Jewry*. One man reminiscences [In]: Reconstructionist, Vol. 45, No. 1, New York, March 1979. Pp. 7–12.

16149. STRAUSS, WALTER: *Mein Schicksal, die Nürnberger Rassendiskriminierung*. (Böse Erinnerungen an 1938–1945.) Wien (Freyung 6): Wiener Kath. Akademie, 1979. 26 pp. (Wiener Kath. Akademie, Miscellanea, Arbeitskreis für kirchliche Zeit- u. Wiener Diözesangeschichte, 74.)

16150. SWITZERLAND. HÄSLER, ALFRED A.: *Das Boot ist voll ... Die Schweiz und die Flüchtlinge 1933–1945*. Neuaufl., ergänzt durch ein Vorwort u. einen Anhang. Zürich: Exlibris, 1979. 364 pp., ports., illus., facsims. [First publ. in 1967, see No. 6339/YB. XIII. Engl. edn. see No. 8567/YB. XVI.]

16151. — ISOLANI, GERTRUD: *Flucht in die Schweiz im Herbst 1942*. [In]: NZZ, Zürich, 19./20. Mai 1979. Pp. 7–8. [G.I., born 1899 in Dresden, journalist, writer. Cf.: G. Isolani feiert ihren 80. Geburtstag am 7. Febr. 1979 (Heinz Badt) [in]: Isr. Wochenblatt, Nr. 5, Zürich, 2. Febr. 1979, pp. 29–30, port.]

16152. — MITTENZWEI, WERNER: *Exil in der Schweiz*. Frankfurt a. Main: Röderberg, 1979. 446 pp., ports., illus., facsims., notes (pp. 386–425), list of names (pp. 426–444). (Kunst u. Literatur im antifaschistischen Exil 1933–1945, Bd. 2.) (Röderberg Taschenbuch, Bd. 89: Kunstwissenschaft.) [Cont. chaps.: 1. Die Zerstörung der Illusion vom klassischen Land des Exils. 2. Wege u. Stationen antifaschistischer deutscher Literatur u. Kunst. 3. Das Zürcher Schauspielhaus. Cf.: Exilanten in der Schweiz (Manfred Bosch) [in]: Tribüne, H. 72, Frankfurt a. Main, 1979, pp. 154–157.]

16153. — MITTENZWEI, WERNER: *Das Zürcher Schauspielhaus 1933–1945 oder Die letzte Chance*. Berlin/East: Henschel, 1979. 211 pp., 128 illus., bibl. notes (pp. 195–205), list of names (pp. 206–211). (Deutsches Theater im Exil.) [Many Jewish refugees in Zürich had the chance to continue their career. Incl. also: 'Die Schweiz als Exilland' (pp. 14–19).]

16154. — SCHMID, MAX: *Schalom – wir werden euch töten*. Texte und Dokumente zum Antisemitismus in der Schweiz 1930–1980. Zürich: eco-Verlag, 1979. [Cf.: Schweizer Regierung war gut informiert (Nathan Kadezki) [in]: Isr. Wochenblatt, No. 19, Zürich, 11. Mai 1979, pp. 9–12. Antisemitism in Switzerland [in]: Patterns of Prejudice, Vol. 13, No. 4, London, July-Aug. 1979, pp. 14–15.]

16155. THERESIENSTADT–TEREZIN. OELZE, REGINA: *Mein dreijähriger Aufenthalt im KZ Theresienstadt vom 20.7.1942 bis zum 20.7.1945*. Hrsg. von Alida Oelze. Recklinghausen: Bitter, 1978. 28 pp.

16156. — STANIĆ, DOROTHEA, ed.: *Kinder im KZ ... und draussen blühen Blumen*. Mit Kinderzeichnungen aus Theresienstadt, Zeichnungen der Theresienstädter Maler Leo Haas u. Fritz Fritta, Fotos u. Dokumenten. [Katalog zu einer] Wanderausstellung. Berlin: Elefanten-Press-Verl., 1979. 167 pp., illus., diagrs.

16157. TRUNK, ISAIAH: *Jewish responses to Nazi persecution*. Collective and individual behavior in extremis. New York: Stein and Day, 1979. XII, 371 pp., illus., maps.

16158. WIESEL, ELIE. ROSENFELD, ALVIN H./GREENBERG, IRVING, eds.: *Confronting the Holocaust. The impact of Elie Wiesel*. Bloomington: Indiana Univ. Press, 1978. XIII, 239 pp. [See also: Nur die, die dabei waren, wissen, was war. Die anderen werden es niemals wissen (Elie Wiesel) [in]: Isr. Wochenblatt, Nr. 19, Zürich, 11. Mai 1979, pp. 7–9. Elie Wiesel bleibt die Antwort schuldig (Roland Gradwohl) [in]: Isr. Wochenblatt, Nr. 20, Zürich, 18. Mai 1979, pp. 11 ff. (Both contributions also in): Freiburger Rundbrief, Folge 30, Freiburg i. Br., 1978, pp. 126–129. Witness and rebellion: the unresolved tension in the works of Elie Wiesel (Maurice Friedman) [in]: Judaism, Vol. 28, No. 4, New York, Fall 1979, pp. 484–491.]

16159. WOLFFENSTEIN–FAMILY, Berlin. *Erinnerungen* von Valerie Wolffenstein bis 1945 [und] Andrea Wolffenstein 1938 bis 1945. [D-8918 Diessen/Ammersee, Wohnstift Augustinum], 1979. 203 pp. [Privately printed recollections, illegal existence in Nazi Germany, assistance by Germans.]

16160. *Yad Vashem Studies*. 12 [&] 13. Ed. by Livia Rothkirchen. Jerusalem: Yad Vashem Martyrs' and Heroes' Remembrance Authority 1977 [&] 1979. 2 vols. (387 pp., bibl. footnotes [&] 424 pp., bibl. footnotes). [*Vol. 12* incl.: In memoriam Jacob Robinson, 1889–1977 (1 p., port.). Trends in Holocaust research (Yehuda Bauer, pp. 7–36). Referat Deutschland, Jewish policy and the German Foreign Office, 1933–1940 (Christopher R. Browning, pp. 37–73). The reaction of the Jewish public in Germany to the Nuremberg Laws (Abraham Margaliot, pp. 75–107). The treatment of Hungarian Jews in German-occupied Europe (Randolph L. Braham, pp. 125–146).]

[*Vol. 13* incl.: On the study of the Holocaust and genocide (Uriel Tal, pp. 7–52). On racism and anti-Semitism in Occultism and Nazism (Jeffrey A. Goldstein, pp. 53–72). Zionist policy and the fate of European Jewry, 1939–1942 (Yoav Gelber, pp. 169–210). Czech attitudes towards the Jews during the Nazi Regime (Livia Rothkirchen, pp. 287–320). Attempts to obtain Shanghai permits in 1941. A case of rescue priority during the Holocaust (Efraim Zuroff, pp. 321–351). Pre-war reactions to Nazi anti-Jewish policies in the Jewish press (Nana Sagi and Malcolm Lowe, pp. 387–408). Further contributions are listed according to subject.]

16161. ZENTNER, CHRISTIAN, ed.: *Anmerkungen zu 'Holocaust'. Die Geschichte der Juden im Dritten Reich*. Berichte, Texte, Dokumente. München: Delphin, 1979. 144 pp., illus. [Cf.: Noch ein 'Holocaust'-Buch (Hans Lamm) [in]: Tribüne, H. 70, Frankfurt a. Main, 1979, pp. 142–145.]

B. Jewish Resistance

16162. CENTRO DI DOCUMENTAZIONE EBRAICA CONTEMPORANEA: *Aspetti di una resistenza ebraica al nazismo. Comunicazioni visive dai campi di concentramento*. Guida alla mostra, Milano, Biblioteca Trivulziana, Castello Sforzesco, 17 gennaio–7 febbraio, 1979. [Milano, 1979.] 69 pp., 7 maps, 8 plates.

16163. KWIET, KONRAD: *Problems of Jewish resistance historiography*. [In]: LBI Year Book XXIV, London, 1979. Pp. 37–57, bibl. footnotes.

16164. PIKARSKI, MARGOT: *Jugend im Berliner Widerstand. Herbert Baum und Kampfgefährten*. Berlin: Militärverlag der D.D.R., 1978. 235 pp., illus., ports., facsims., bibl. (pp. 221–223). [Herbert Baum, born in 1912, and twenty-one members of his Jewish anti-Fascist resistance group were executed by the Nazis after 1942.]

16165. PINGEL, FALK: *Häftlinge unter SS-Herrschaft. Widerstand, Selbstbehauptung und Vernichtung im Konzentrationslager*. Hamburg: Hoffmann u. Campe, 1978. 338 pp., bibl. (pp. 318–336). (Historische Perspektiven, 12.) [Incl. chaps.: Jüdische Häftlinge (pp. 91–96). Antisemitismus zwischen Ideologie und Ökonomie (pp. 139–144).]

IV. POST WAR

A. General

16166. AUSTRIA. KONRAD, HELMUT, ed.: *Sozialdemokratie und 'Anschluss'. Historische Wurzeln, Anschluss 1918 und 1938, Nachwirkungen.* Eine Tagung des Dr.-Karl-Renner-Instituts, Wien, 1. März 1978. Wien: Europaverl., 1978. 150 pp. (Schriftenreihe des Ludwig Boltzmann Instituts für Geschichte der Arbeiterbewegung, 9.) [One chapter deals with post-Fascist 'antisemitism without antisemites' in Austria, another with the treatment of Fascism in Austrian schoolbooks. See also: 'Antisemitismus ohne Antisemiten?' Zum nachfaschistischen Antisemitismus in Österreich (Bernd Tichatschek-Marin) [in]: Österr. Zeitschrift für Soziologie, Jg. 1, Nr. 1, Wien, 1976, pp. 1–14.]

16167. — VOGEL, ROLF, ed.: *Das Echo. Widerhall auf Simon Wiesenthal.* Stuttgart: Seewald, 1979. 154 pp., port. [See also: Für Sühne, nicht für Rache. Zum 70. Geburtstag von Dipl.-Ing. Simon Wiesenthal (Hermann Lewy) [in]: 'Allgemeine', Düsseldorf, 12. Jan. 1979, p. 4. Die Jagd nach Dr. Mengele geht weiter. Ein Interview mit Simon Wiesenthal (Nathan Kadezki) [in]: Isr. Wochenblatt, Nr. 30, Zürich, 27. Juli 1979, pp. 5–7.]

16168. — WISTRICH, ROBERT: *The strange case of Bruno Kreisky. Between Vienna and Jerusalem.* [In]: Encounter, Vol. 52, No. 5, London, May 1979. Pp. 78–85. [See also: Bruno Kreisky and Simon Wiesenthal (Robert Wistrich) [in]: Midstream, Vol. 25, No. 6, New York, June/July 1979, pp. 26–35.]

16169. CZECHOSLOVAKIA. ADAM, PETER: *Antisemitismus ohne Juden. Kontinuität und Wandel in der tschechischen Geschichte.* [In]: Tribüne, H. 70, Frankfurt a. Main, 1979. Pp. 86–92.

16170. — *Informationsbulletin.* Hrsg. vom Rat der Jüd. Religionsgemeinden in der Tschechischen Sozialistischen Republik zu Prag und vom Zentralverband der Jüd. Religionsgemeinden in der Slowakischen Sozialistischen Republik zu Bratislava. Nrs. 1–2 (März & Sept. 1978); [&] Nrs. 1–3 (April, Juni, Okt. 1979). Redakteur [1/79 ff.]: Dezider Galský. Prag: Kirchen-Zentralverlag, 1978 & 1979. 2 issues (1978) & 3 issues (1979). [*Nr. 1/78* incl.: Zum 40-jährigen Jubiläum des jüd. Gemeindeblattes Věstník (pp. 8–32). *Nr. 2/78*: Ansprache zur Gedenkfeier für die Opfer der Nazi-Genozide (František Schwarz, pp. 8–25). Egon Erwin Kisch (František Kafka, pp. 29–35). *Nr. 1/79:* Nazistische Verbrechen dürfen nicht verjähren (pp. 1–5). Eine neue Entdeckung aus Theresienstadt, die Oper 'Kaiser der Atlantis' (pp. 29–31). Max Brod und das Theater D 34 (P. Pavlovský, pp. 32–34). *Nr. 2/79:* Jüd. Schwimmer in der Vorkriegs-Tschechoslowakei (Jan Marek, pp. 20–23). *Nr. 3/79:* Über den Stand jüd. Friedhöfe (pp. 13–15). 100 Jahre Alfred Justitz, Kunstmaler (pp. 29–30).]

16171. FEDERAL GERMAN REPUBLIC. AMERONGEN, MARTIN van: *Deutschland und seine Juden.* Fotos: Oscar van Alphen. Übers. aus dem Niederländ.: E. Mil. (Hrsg.: Unterstützungsausschuss Arbeiterkampf gegen Rosenbaum.) Hamburg: Reents in Komm., 1979. 23 pp., illus. [The Jews in post-war Germany, relations between Germans and Jews.]

16172. — Berlin. JÜDISCHES MUSEUM IM PALAIS EPHRAIM: *Erste Erwerbungen und Stiftungen für das künftige Jüdische Museum im Palais Ephraim.* Berlin, 1978. [12] pp., illus. [See also: Das Jüdische Museum im Palais Ephraim. Eine Bestandsaufnahme, Daten und Fakten (Käthe Kusserow) [in]: Berlinische Notizen, 12, Berlin, 1978, pp. 25–27, illus. Um das Ephraim-Palais in Berlin (Ernst G. Lowenthal) [in]: Aufbau, New York, Nov. 9, 1979, p. 23.]

16173. — BOSCH, MICHAEL, ed.: *Antisemitismus, Nationalsozialismus und Neonazismus.* Düsseldorf: Schwann, 1979. 152 pp., illus., diagrs. (Geschichte u. Sozialwissenschaften.)

16174. — DIAMANT, ADOLF: *Ehemalige Synagogen in Deutschland werden erhalten.* Bemühungen und Erfolge bei der Restaurierung historischer Gebäude. [In]: Das neue Israel, Jg. 32, H. 3, Zürich, Sept. 1979. Pp. 131–137, illus. [Refers to synagogues in Floss, Gau-Algesheim, Gelnhausen, Gross-Umstadt, Gröbzig, Hechingen, Hohenlimburg, Hornburg, Wittlich.]

16175. — Frankfurt a. Main. DIAMANT, ADOLF: *Jüdisches Gemeindezentrum für Frankfurt geplant.* [In]: 'Allgemeine', Düsseldorf, 24. Aug. 1979. P. 11, illus. [See also: Abschied vom Philanthropin (E. G. Lowenthal) [in]: Aufbau, New York, Aug. 10, 1979, p. 4.]

16176. — GINSBURG, HANS JAKOB: *Jüdische Jugend in Deutschland, 1979.* [In]: 'Allgemeine', Düsseldorf, 25. Mai 1979. Pp. 1 & 2.

16177. — Hochschule für Jüdische Studien, Heidelberg, gegr. Herbst 1979. LEWY, HERMANN: *Eine historische Entscheidung.* Schaffung einer Jüdischen Theologischen Hochschule. [In]: 'Allgemeine', Düsseldorf, 9. Febr. 1979. P. 1. [Reports also in]: Jüdischer Pressedienst, Nrs. 4/5,

Düsseldorf, Juli 1979, pp. 22–23; [and in]: deutschland-berichte, Jg. 15, Nrs. 8/9, Bonn, Aug./Sept. 1979, pp. 19–20. [See also]: Ein historischer Tag. Vorlesungsbeginn der Jüd. Hochschule. Bericht (Hermann Lewy) [in]: 'Allgemeine', Düsseldorf, 26. Okt. 1979, pp. 1–4. Hochschule für jüd. Studien eingeweiht [in]: deutschland-berichte, Jg. 15, Nr. 11, Bonn, Nov. 1979, pp. 10–12.

16178. GERMAN DEMOCRATIC REPUBLIC. *Gedenke! Vergiss nie! 40. Jahrestag des faschistischen 'Kristallnacht'-Pogroms.* Eine Dokumentation. Hrsg. vom Verband der Jüd. Gemeinden in der D.D.R. Berlin/East: Union-Verl., 1979. 125 pp., illus. [Collection of addresses and speeches by state-officials (Erich Honecker and others) and officials of the Jewish communities in the G.D.R.; reports of various events and short personal reminiscences.]

16179. — *Nachrichtenblatt* der Jüdischen Gemeinde von Berlin und des Verbandes der Jüdischen Gemeinden in der Deutschen Demokratischen Republik. Red.: Helmut Aris, Peter Kirchner, Herbert Ringer. Dresden, Berlin, März, Juni, Sept., Dez. 1979. 40; 29; 32; 31 pp., illus. [4 issues.] [*March* incl.: Pogromnachtgedenken 1938/1978 (Helmut Aris, pp. 6–15, illus.). *Sept.:* Dr. Max Jacoby, ein Arzt des Volkes, 1845–1912 (Heimatgeschichtliches Kabinett Berlin-Köpenick, pp. 15–16). *Dez.:* Judentum u. Aufklärung. Ein Bericht über die Studientagung in Eisenstadt (Renate Kirchner, pp. 7–8). Each issue also incl. reports on events in the various Jewish communities of the G.D.R. Further contributions are listed according to subject.]

16180. — THOMPSON, JERRY E.: *Jews, Zionism and Israel. The story of the Jews in the German Democratic Republic since 1945.* Washington Univ., Phil. Diss., 1978. 328 pp.

16181. HOLOCAUST TV-FILM. *Discussion* (selection): Anstoss zum Nachdenken. Zur Fernsehserie 'Holocaust' (Hermann Lewy) [in]: 'Allgemeine', Düsseldorf, 2. Febr. 1979, pp. 1 & 3. Das Echo auf die Fernsehserie 'Holocaust' in der Bundesrepublik Deutschland [in]: deutschland-berichte, Jg. 15, Nr. 3, Bonn, März 1979, pp. 5–17. [Incl. contributions by Walter Scheel, Helmut Schmidt, Erik Blumenfeld, Werner Nachmann and others.] Nachüberlegungen zu Holocaust (Felix Messerschmid) [in]: Geschichte in Wissenschaft und Unterricht, Jg. 30, H. 3, Stuttgart, März 1979, pp. 175–178. 'Holocaust' und die Zukunft der Vergangenheitsbewältigung (Heine von Alemann) [in]: Merkur, H. 370, Stuttgart, März 1979, pp. 232 ff. 'Holocaust', so reagieren Prominente, Presse u. Zuschauer [in]: Isr. Wochenblatt, Nr. 4, Zürich, 26. Jan. 1979, pp. 5–9. Weinen oder denken? 'Holocaust' und die Folgen (Erwin Leiser) [and]: Ist Antisemitismus je zu bewältigen (Heinrich Lang) [and]: Leser äussern sich zu 'Holocaust' [in]: Isr. Wochenblatt, Nr. 5, Zürich, 2. Febr. 1979, pp. 5–11. Auf den Spuren der eigenen Vergangenheit (Ernst Ludwig Ehrlich) [in]: Isr. Wochenblatt, Nr. 9, Zürich, 2. März 1979, pp. 17–19. The German conscience. 'Holocaust' on German TV (Andrei S. Markovits) [in]: Jewish Frontier, Vol. 46, No. 4, New York, April 1979, pp. 13–17. Holocaust oder: Konsequenzen nach Auschwitz (Martin Stöhr) [in]: Judaica, Jg. 35, H. 3, Zürich, 1979, pp. 103–112. Im Angesicht von 'Holocaust' (Fritz Bock) [in]: NZZ, Zürich, 19./20 Mai 1979, p. 7. Germans' struggle with their past after the 'Holocaust' film (Eva Kolinsky) [in]: Patterns of Prejudice, Vol. 13, Nos. 2–3, London, March–June 1979, pp. 13–18, bibl. footnotes. 'Holocaust' und die Amnesie (Helmut Dahmer) [in]: Psyche, Jg. 33, H. 11, Stuttgart, Nov. 1979, pp. 1039–1045, bibl. (pp. 1044–1045). Holocaust. Der Judenmord bewegt die Deutschen [in]: Der Spiegel, Jg. 33, Nr. 5, Hamburg, 29. Jan. 1979, pp. 17–34, illus. Ein Jude sieht 'Holocaust' (Hans Lamm) [in]: Tribüne, H. 69, Frankfurt a. Main, 1979, pp. 46–48. 'Holocaust'. Das Gespräch einer Nation mit sich selbst. Die Fernseh-Serie im Spiegel der Presse (Klaus W. Wippermann) [in]: Tribüne, H. 69, Frankfurt a. Main, 1979, pp. 22–45. Die Entdeckung der Leiche im eigenen Keller. Warum 'Holocaust' kein antideutscher Film ist (Yizhak Ahren/Christoph B. Melchers) [in]: Tribüne, H. 72, Frankfurt a. Main, 1979, pp. 46–62, bibl. footnotes.

16182. — FRENZEL, IVO [et al.]: *Im Kreuzfeuer: Holocaust.* [Köln: Westdeutscher Rundfunk, 1979.] 97 pp. [Mimeogr. transcript of discussion.] See also No. 16098.

16183. — HÄRTLE, HEINRICH: *Was 'Holocaust' verschweigt. Deutsche Verteidigung gegen Kollektivschuld-Lügen.* Leoni am Starnberger See: Druffel, 1979. 94 pp. [Nazi historian attempts to deny the Holocaust. See also: German neo-Nazi denunciation of the 'Holocaust' film [in]: Patterns of Prejudice, Vol. 13, No. 1, London, Jan.–Febr. 1979, pp. 9–11.]

16184. — KAMPEN, WILHELM van, ed.: *Holocaust. Ein Medienereignis und die Öffentlichkeit.* Hrsg. in Zusammenarbeit mit der Pressestelle des Westdeutschen Rundfunks. Wuppertal: Hammer, 1979. 260 pp.

16185. — MAGNUS, UWE: *Die Reaktionen auf 'Holocaust'*. I. Ergebnisberichte der Begleitstudien des Westdeutschen Rundfunks u. der Bundeszentrale für politische Bildung. II. 'Holocaust' im Spiegel der Teleskopie-Zahlen. [In]: Freiburger Rundbrief, Folge 30, Freiburg i. Br., 1978. Pp. 118–121.

16186. HOLOCAUST TRAUMA. EPSTEIN, HELEN: *Children of the Holocaust. Conversations with sons and daughters of survivors*. New York: Putnam, 1979. 348 pp., bibl. (pp. 346–348).

16187. — FRANKL, VICTOR E.: *Trotzdem Ja zum Leben sagen. Ein Psychologe erlebt das Konzentrationslager*. Vorwort von Hans Weigel. 4. Aufl. München: Kösel, 1979. 200 pp.

16188. — GRUBRICH-SIMITIS, ILSE: *Extremtraumatisierung als kumulatives Trauma*. Psychoanalytische Studien über seelische Nachwirkungen der Konzentrationslagerhaft bei Überlebenden und ihren Kindern. [In]: Psyche, Jg. 33, H. 11, Stuttgart, Nov. 1979. Pp. 991–1023, bibl. (pp. 1020–1023).

16189. — LAUB, DORI: *Holocaust survivors' adaptation to trauma*. [In]: Patterns of Prejudice, Vol. 13, No. 1, London, Jan.–Febr. 1979. Pp. 17–25, bibl. (pp. 23–25).

16190. — LEMPP, REINHART: *Extrembelastung im Kindes- und Jugendalter*. Über psychosoziale Spätfolgen nach nationalsozialistischer Verfolgung im Kindes- und Jugendalter anhand von Aktengutachten. Bern: Huber, 1979. 158 pp.

16191. PROSECUTION OF NAZI CRIMES. *Die Justiz und die Nazis*. Zur Strafverfolgung von Nazismus und Neonazismus seit 1945. Von Michael Ratz [et al.]. Frankfurt: Röderberg, 1979. 184 pp. [Also about the statute of limitation.]

—— — *Justiz und NS-Verbrechen*. [See No. 16105 and Nos. 16116–16117 (Majdanek-Trial).]

16192. — OPPITZ, ULRICH DIETER: *Strafverfahren und Strafvollstreckung bei NS-Gewaltverbrechen*. Dargestellt an Hand von 542 rechtskräftigen Urteilen deutscher Gerichte aus der Zeit von 1946–1975. [2., erweiterte Aufl.] Ulm: U. Oppitz, 1979. 380, XXIX pp., charts, facsims., tables, bibl. (pp. IV–XIII). (Forschungsunternehmen der Humboldt-Gesellschaft, 9.) [First edn., for the years 1946–1965, see No. 14370/YB. XXIII. See also: Die justizielle Behandlung der NS-Verbrechen (Hermann Langbein) [in]: Frankfurter Hefte, Jg. 34, H. 1, Frankfurt a. Main, Jan. 1979, pp. 23–28.]

16193. — RÜCKERL, ADALBERT: *Die Strafverfolgung von NS-Verbrechen 1945–1978*. Eine Dokumentation. Heidelberg: C. F. Müller, 1979. 148 pp. (Recht, Justiz, Zeitgeschehen, Bd. 31.) [English transl. under the title]: RÜCKERL, ADALBERT: *The investigation of Nazi crimes, 1945–1978*. A documentation. Transl. by Derek Rutter. Heidelberg: C. F. Müller, 1979. 145 pp. (Legal affairs, justice, contemporary events, Vol. 31.) [Report by the head of the Federal Bureau for the Prosecution of Nazi crimes.]

16194. *Report on Jewish communities in Central Europe: Federal German Republic* [and] *German Democratic Republic* (Friedo Sachser, pp. 235–252, 253–254). [Also]: *World Jewish population* (Leon Shapiro, pp. 291–298). [In]: American Jewish Year Book 1979, Vol. 79, New York, 1978.

16195. STATUTE OF LIMITATION. DEUTSCHER BUNDESTAG. *145. Sitzung, Bonn, 29. März 1979.* Inhalt: Beratung des Antrages ... Unverjährbarkeit von Mord ... in Verbindung mit Erste Beratung des ... eingebrachten Entwurfs eines 18. Strafrechtsänderungsgesetzes ... in Verbindung mit der Beratung der Entschliessung des Europäischen Parlaments zur Unverjährbarkeit von Völkermord und Mord. Düsseldorf: Zentralrat der Juden in Deutschland, 1979. 90 pp. (Jüdischer Pressedienst, Nr. 3, April 1979, Sonderdruck.) [Cf.: 'Über Auschwitz wächst kein Gras'. Zur Verjährungsdebatte im Bundestag [in]: MB, Nr. 19, Tel Aviv, 18. Mai 1979, pp. 4 & 7. So votierten die Abgeordneten [in]: Jüdischer Pressedienst, Nrs. 4/5, Düsseldorf, Juli 1979, pp. 35–41.]

16196. — ROTH, STEPHEN J.: *The Statute of Limitation for Nazi crimes*. London: Institute of Jewish Affairs, 1979. 15 pp., tabs. [Mimeog.] (Research Report, Western Europe 79/1.)

B. Restitution

16197. *Ein Antrag in Wiedergutmachungsfragen aus der Fraktion der SPD*. [And]: *Leistungen der öffentlichen Hand auf dem Gebiet der Wiedergutmachung*. [In]: deutschland-berichte, Jg. 15, No. 6, Bonn, Juni 1979. Pp. 11–13, 17–18. [See also]: *Neue Entwicklung auf dem Gebiet der Wiedergutmachung*. [In]: MB, Nr. 47, Tel Aviv, 21. Dez. 1979. P. 5. Reprint of an article from: FAZ, 15. Dez. 1979, referring to a final restitution fund by the Federal German Republic.

16198. PEASE, LOUIS EDWIN: *After the Holocaust. West Germany and material reparation to the Jews, from the Allied occupation to the Luxemburg agreements*. 1–2. Ann Arbor, Mich.: University Microfilms

Internat., 1978. 2 vols. (3, III, 283; 1, II, 284–605 pp.) [Photocopy.] Florida State Univ., Diss., 1976.
16199. PRITTIE, TERENCE: *The velvet chancellors.* London: Frederick Muller, 1979. 286 pp. [West-German chancellors since the war. Incl. references to restitution, German-Israeli relations, etc. Cf.: Germany restored (Richard Grunberger) [in]: Jewish Chronicle, London, Oct. 26, 1979, p. 27.]
16200. SCHMIDINGER, VOLKER: *Zur Frage der Rentenversicherungspflicht jüdischer Jugendlicher auf landwirtschaftlichen Lehrgütern (Hachscharah).* [In]: Rechtsprechung zum Wiedergutmachungsrecht, Jg. 30, H. 5, München, 1979. Pp. 167–170. Also about the history of the Hachsharah.]
16201. SCHWARZ, WALTER: *Die Wiedergutmachung nationalsozialistischen Unrechts in der Bundesrepublik.* [In]: Deutsche Richterzeitung, Köln, Juni 1979. Pp. 178–180.

C. Antisemitism, Judaism, Nazism in Education and Teaching

16202. BOBKE, WOLFGANG: *Jews in West German history textbooks.* A study commissioned by The American Jewish Committee. New York: American Jewish Committee, 1979. 73 pp.
16203. BROSZAT, MARTIN: '*Holocaust*' *und die Geschichtswissenschaft.* [In]: Vierteljahrshefte für Zeitgeschichte, Jg. 27, H. 2, München, April 1979. Pp. 285–298.
16204. CONFERENCE ON THE HOLOCAUST. *The International Conference on: The lessons of the Holocaust, Oct. 18–20, 1978.* Ed. by Josephine Knopp. Philadelphia: National Institute on the Holocaust, 1979. V, 228 pp. [Incl.: Right and wrong teaching of the Holocaust (Yehuda Bauer, pp. 3–15). Reports on textbooks and teaching in the German Federal Republic, France and North America (pp. 35–71). The untold story of the Holocaust (Joseph Borkin, pp. 137–145). Special report on West German Catholic teaching of Jews and Judaism (Peter Fiedler, pp. 222–225). See also No. 16095. For exhibition on the occasion of this Internat. Conference, see No. 16094.]
16205. — *International Theological Symposium on the Holocaust, Oct. 15–17, 1978.* Ed. by Josephine Knopp. Philadelphia: National Institute on the Holocaust, 1979. VI, 134 pp.
16206. GLASER, HERMANN: *Das Dritte Reich, wie es war und wie es dazu kam.* Bericht und Dokumente. 5., überarb. u. ergänzte Neuaufl. Freiburg i. Br.: Herder, 1979. 208 pp., bibl. (pp. 180–204). (Herderbücherei, Bd. 744). [See also: Politische Bildungsarbeit nach Holocaust. Von der Notwendigkeit emotionaler Aufklärung über den Nationalsozialismus (Hermann Glaser) [in]: Tribüne, H. 70, Frankfurt a. Main, 1979, pp. 44–54.]
16207. *Judentum. Ein Modell für die Sekundarstufe II.* Bearb. von Ingeborg Kleinert [*et al.*]. 2., durchgesehene Aufl. Göttingen: Vandenhoeck u. Ruprecht, 1979. 94 pp., diagrs., bibl. (Werte und Normen, Modell 4.) [On *Teaching Judaism* see also]: Das Judentum für den Religionsunterricht kennenlernen. Freiburger Studienwoche an der Hebräischen Universität Jerusalem, März 1979 (Günter Biemer) [and]: Das Judentum, Gottes Minderheit. Ein Unterrichtsversuch für den katholischen Religionsunterricht der Sekundarstufe I (Werner Trutwin) [in]: Freiburger Rundbrief, Folge 30, Freiburg i. Br., pp. 38–47, bibl. notes. Holokaust, Theologie und Religionsunterricht (Herbert Schmid) [in]: Judaica, Jg. 35, H. 1, Zürich, 1979, pp. 5–11.
16208. KERR, JUDITH: *When Hitler stole pink rabbit.* Illus. by the author. Hamburg: ELT-Verl., 1979. 189 pp. (Klassiker des Gebrauchs an Schule und Universität, 4.)
16209. MEYERS, PETER/RIESENBERGER, DIETER, eds.: *Der Nationalsozialismus in der historisch-politischen Bildung.* Mit Beiträgen von Peter Meyers [*et al.*]. Göttingen: Vandenhoeck u. Ruprecht, 1979. 218 pp. (Kleine Vandenhoeck-Reihe, 1457.) [See also: Zur Behandlung des Nationalsozialismus im Unterricht (Harold Kästner) [in]: Tribüne, H. 71, Frankfurt a. Main, 1979, pp. 36–42.]
16210. *Sammlung. Jahrbuch für antifaschistische Literatur und Kunst.* 1 (1978) [&] 2 (1979). Hrsg. von Uwe Naumann. Frankfurt a. Main: Röderberg, 1978–1979. 2 vols. (223, 260 pp., illus.) [*Bd. 1* incl.: Das Faschismusverständnis im Deutschlandroman der Exilierten. Untersucht am Beispiel von Anna Seghers 'Das siebte Kreuz', Lion Feuchtwanger 'Die Geschwister Oppermann' und Ödön von Horvath 'Ein Kind unserer Zeit', einschliesslich eines Vorschlags für die Behandlung im Unterricht (Reinhold Jaretzky u. Helmuth Taubald, pp. 12–36). Faschismusbewältigung in Kinder- u. Jugendbüchern (Dieter Bongartz, pp. 53–61).

Unterrichtsvorschläge (pp. 147-179). Bd. 2: Zur Behandlung antifaschistischer Literatur im Unterricht. Ergänzt durch zwei Unterrichtsvorschläge zu E. Langgässers 'Saisonbeginn' u. L. Ossowskis 'Stern ohne Himmel' (Friedrich Starke, pp. 166-173). Unterrichtsvorschläge (pp. 174-219). Further contributions are listed according to subject.]

16211. STEHLING, JUTTA: *Das Zusammenleben von Deutschen und Juden in der Geschichte des Kreises Heilbronn.* Ein Projekt zur Behandlung der Probleme lokalen Judentums in einem geschichtlichen Leistungskurs der Klassenstufe 2 der Reformierten Oberstufe. [In]: Geschichte in Wissenschaft und Unterricht, Jg. 30, H. 5, Stuttgart, Mai 1979. Pp. 297-314.

16212. STÖHR, MARTIN, unter Mitarbeit von ULRIKE BERGER [et al.], eds.: *Erinnern, nicht vergessen. Zugänge zu Holocaust.* Hrsg. im Auftrag der Arbeitsgemeinschaft Juden und Christen beim Deutschen Evangelischen Kirchentag. München: Kaiser, 1979. 184 pp., facsims. (Kaiser Traktate, 43.) [On *Teaching the Holocaust* see also]: Welchen Beitrag leisten unsere Schulen zur Aufarbeitung des Nationalsozialismus? [and]: 'Holocaust', eine deutsche Geschichtsstunde (Ernst Vogt) [in]: Emuna/Israel-Forum, H. 1/2, Rothenburg o. d. Tauber, 1979, pp. 76-82. Der Unterricht der Holocaust-Periode als Erziehung zu ethischen Werten. Entworfen, redigiert u. vorgetragen anlässlich der Internat. Holocaust-Konferenz in Philadelphia am 19.10.1978 (Arye Carmon) [in]: Freiburger Rundbrief, Folge 30, Freiburg i. Br., 1978. Pp. 52-55. Wie sagen wir es den Kindern? (Günter Grass) [in]: L 76 Demokratie und Sozialismus, H. 2, Köln, 1979, pp. 5-17 [also on the persecution of the Jews]. German debate on how to teach the Holocaust story [in]: Patterns of Prejudice, Vol. 13, No. 4, London, July-Aug. 1979, pp. 20-21 & 31. Holocaust, Emotionen für die Nation – Alptraum für die Geschichtslehrer? (Annelie Flemming-Schmalfeld) [in]: Sozialwissenschaftliche Informationen für Unterricht und Studium, Jg. 8, H. 3, Stuttgart, Juli 1979, pp. 156-159, bibl. (pp. 157-159). Toward a methodology of teaching about the Holocaust (Henry Friedlander) [in]: Teachers College Record, Vol. 80, No. 3, New York, Columbia Univ., Febr. 1979, pp. 519-542. Holocaust und politische Bildung. Ausgewählte Ergebnisse einer repräsentativen empirischen Untersuchung (Tilman Ernst) [in]: Tribüne, H. 70, Frankfurt a. Main, 1979, pp. 64-81 [and in]: Freiburger Rundbrief, Folge 30, Freiburg i. Br., 1978, pp. 122-126.

16213. TRUTWIN, WERNER/WISCHMANN, GÜNTER, eds.: *Juden und Christen.* 7., überarb. u. erweiterte Aufl. Göttingen: Vandenhoeck u. Ruprecht, 1979. 118 pp. (Quellentexte zum Religionsunterricht, 16, Folge 2, Befragter Glaube.)

16214. *Von Holocaust zu uns. Wirkung und Analysen.* [Title from cover.] [In]: Materialien zur Politischen Bildung, H. 2, Bonn: Dt. Bundes-Verl., 1979. Pp. 48-70. [Cont.: Es wird mehr sein als nur ein Strohfeuer. Nach der Ausstrahlung der 'Holocaust'-Serie (Hermann Langbein). Aus der Einsicht zu konkretem Handeln. Von Holocaust über Hadamar u. Altenkirchen zu uns selbst, ein Projektbericht (Heike Bräuer/Friedhelm Zöllner). Holocaust in der Akademie. Überlegungen zu Möglichkeiten politischer Erwachsenenbildung nach einer Tagung in der Evang. Akademie Locum (Michael Bosch). Haben die Historiker versagt? Holocaust u. die deutsche Geschichtswissenschaft (Hans Mommsen). Was müssen wir noch tun? (Dirk Klose). Vergangenheitsbewältigung: Fluchtbewegung oder Reifungsprozess des politischen Bewusstseins (Herbert Eichmann.).]

V. JUDAISM

A. Jewish Learning and Scholars

16215. BAECK, LEO: *Das Wesen des Judentums.* [Nachdr. der] 6. Aufl. [Köln 1960]. Wiesbaden: Fourier, n.d. [1979]. 327 pp.

16216. BAER, FRITZ JIZCHAK. ROSENBLÜTH, PINCHAS E.: *Moderne jüdische Geschichtsschreibung. Der Beitrag von Fritz Jizchak Baer.* [In]: NZZ, Zürich, 3./4. Nov. 1979. P. 65. [F.J.B., born 1888 in Halberstadt, pupil and assistant of Eugen Taeubler, since 1930 professor at the Hebrew University, Jerusalem.]

16217. BERNAYS, JACOB: *Theophrastos' Schrift über Frömmigkeit. Mit Bemerkungen zu Porphyrios' Schrift über Enthaltsamkeit.* Nachdr. der Ausg. Genf 1894. Hildesheim: Olms, 1979. XII, 176 pp.

16218. BREUER, ISAAC: *Weltwende.* Jerusalem: Ahva Co-op. Press, 1979. VIII, 287 pp., port. on back cover. [Cont.: Weltwende (written 1938). Zur Erinnerung an das deutsche Judentum (written 1942). Publ. for the first time. I.B., 1883 Hungary–1946 Jerusalem.]

16219. BRILLING, BERNHARD. BRILLING, BERNHARD: *Jacob Emden (1698–1776)*. [And]: *Jonathan Eybenschütz (1690–1764)*. [In]: Schleswig-Holsteinisches Biographisches Lexikon, Bd. 5, Neumünster, 1979. Pp. 87–89 & 89–91.

16220. — *Bibliographie Bernhard Brilling*. (Fortsetzung) 1968–1978 (Nr. 284–356). [In]: Theokratia, Jahrbuch des Institutum Judaicum Delitzschianum, 3(1973–1975), Leiden, 1979. Pp. 263–270.

16221. BUBER, MARTIN. BUBER, MARTIN, ed.: *Der Jude*. Eine Monatsschrift. Hrsg. von Martin Buber. Jg. 1–10, H. 1. [No further issues.] Nachdr. der Ausg. Berlin, Wien, 1916–1928. Vaduz/Liechtenstein: Topos, 1979. 10 vols. [Jg. 9, H. 1 – H. 4 & Jg. 10, H. 1 (1925–1928) the 5 'Sonderhefte': Antisemitismus u. jüdisches Volkstum; Erziehung; Judentum und Deutschtum; Judentum und Christentum; Zu Martin Bubers 50. Geburtstag. The reprint incl. introduction by Erich Gottgetreu: Martin Bubers 'Jude'. Vom Werden und Wirken einer grossen Zeitschrift. 24 pp.]

16222. — BEN-CHORIN, SCHALOM: *Martin Buber in Jerusalem*. [In]: Tribüne, H. 69, Frankfurt a. Main, 1979. Pp. 80–106.

16223. — BIELANDER, RAPHAEL: *Martin Bubers Rede von Gott*. Versuch einer philosophischen Würdigung des religiösen Denkens. Bern: Lang, 1976. 299 pp. (Basler u. Berner Studien zur historischen u. systematischen Theologie, Bd. 25.)

16224. — COHN, MARGOT/BUBER, RAFAEL, eds.: *Bibliographie der Werke Martin Bubers 1897–1978*. Jerusalem: Magnes Press; München: Saur, 1979. 166 pp.

16225. — DOLINSKY, PAUL LOUIS: *Martin Buber's philosophy of dialogue*. State Univ. of New York at Buffalo, Phil. Diss., 1978. 376 pp.

16226. — GARAVELLI, SILVANA: *Il giovane Martin Buber*. Bologna, Univ., Phil. Diss., 1978/1979. 437, XCI (appendices) pp., facsim., bibl., bibl. M. Buber. [2 vols.] [1. La formazione. 2. Il sionismo. 3. Gli studi chassidici.]

16227. — GOTTGETREU, ERICH: *Buber und Rathenau*. Zu einem wiederentdeckten Briefwechsel. [In]: MB, Nr. 35/36, Tel Aviv, 21. Sept. 1979. P. 9.

16228. — HORN, HERMANN: *Leben und Werk Martin Bubers im Spiegel seines Briefwechsels*. Ausgewählte Probleme, Ereignisse und Gestalten. Rheinstetten: Schindele, 1979. 86 pp. (Dortmunder Studien zur Philosophie, Psychologie, Soziologie u. Erziehungswissenschaft, Bd. 5.)

16229. — KAUFMANN, WALTER: *Martin Buber. Of his failures and triumph*. [In]: Encounter, Vol. 52, No. 5, London, May 1979. Pp. 31–38.

16230. — KOHN, HANS: *Martin Buber, sein Werk und seine Zeit. Ein Beitrag zur Geistesgeschichte Mitteleuropas 1880–1930*. Vorwort 1979 von Julius Schoeps. Nachwort: 1930–1960, von Robert Weltsch. 4., um ein Vorwort erweiterte Aufl. Wiesbaden: Fourier, 1979. 484 pp., bibl. (Publication of the Leo Baeck Institute.)

16231. — KROLL, STANLEY ELI: *Martin Buber's philosophy of dialogue*. St. Louis Univ., Phil. Diss., 1979. 147 pp.

16232. — LANGFUR, STEPHEN JOSEPH: *Death's second self. A response to Heidegger's Question of Being through the insights of Buber and the findings of Freud*. Syracuse Univ., Phil. Diss., 1977. 564 pp.

16233. — MACK, RUDOLF: *Mystik-Chassidismus-Dialog. Zu Martin Bubers Umgang mit der jüdischen Tradition*. [In]: Zeitschrift für Religions- und Geistesgeschichte, Bd. 31, H. 2, Köln, 1979. Pp. 159–172.

16234. — *Martin Buber commemorative issue*. New York: Fordham Univ. Press, 1978. Pp. 239–342, bibl. footnotes. (Thought. A Review of Culture and Idea. Fordham University Quarterly.)

16235. — MENTSHER, ARYEH: *Buber and Herzl*. [Hebrew.] [In]: Gesher, Quarterly Review of Jewish Affairs, No. 3–4 (94–95), Tel Aviv, Fall-Winter 1978. Pp. 82–90.

16236. — RÖHRS, HERMANN/MEYER, ERNST: *Die pädagogischen Ideen Martin Bubers*. Begründungs- und Wirkungszusammenhänge. Wiesbaden: Akademische Verlagsgesellschaft, 1979. 57 pp., illus. (Erziehungswissenschaftliche Reihe, Bd. 18.)

16237. — RÜBNER, TUVIA: *Glossen zu Bubers Recht-und-Unrecht-Deutung einiger Psalmen*. (Ein Vortrag anlässlich des 100. Geburtstages von Martin Buber [1978].) [In:] Das Neue Israel, Jg. 31, H. 7 & 8, Zürich, Jan. & Febr. 1979. Pp. 375–377; 427–430.

16238. — TAL, URIEL: *Mythos und Solidarität im zionistischen Denken und Wirken von Martin Buber*. [In]: Toleranz heute, H. 9, Veröffentlichungen aus dem Institut Kirche und Judentum bei der Kirchlichen Hochschule Berlin, Berlin, 1979. Pp. 116–126, bibl. footnotes.

16239. CHIEL, ARTHUR A., ed.: *Perspectives on Jews and Judaism. Essays in honor of Wolfe Kelman*. New

York: Rabbinical Assembly, 1978. [7], 483 pp. [Incl.: Israel's cultural mission (Nahum Goldmann). The problem of the Given in Buber's conception of the interpersonal (L. J. Goldstein). Zionism in the early days of Conservative Judaism (Simcha Kling). The tale of a niggun (Elie Wiesel).]

16240. COHEN, HERMANN. COHEN, HERMANN: *Religion der Vernunft aus den Quellen des Judentums.* Nach dem MS. des Verfassers neu durchgearb. u. mit einem Nachwort versehen von Bruno Strauss. [Nachdr. der Ausg. Frankfurt a. Main 1929.] Wiesbaden: Fourier, 1978. 629 pp.

16241. — OLLIG, HANS LUDWIG: *Religion und Freiheitsglaube. Zur Problematik von Hermann Cohens später Religionsphilosophie.* Königstein/Ts.: Forum Academicum, 1979. 377 pp. (Monographien zur philosophischen Forschung, Bd. 179.) Zugl. [shortened version]: Freiburg i. Br., Univ., Theol. Diss., 1977/78.

16242. ETTLINGER, JACOB. BLEICH, JUDITH: *Jacob Ettlinger, his life and work. The emergence of modern orthodoxy in Germany.* Ann Arbor, Mich.: University Microfilms Internat., 1979. 387 pp., bibl. (pp. 367–387). [Photocopy.] New York, N.Y. Univ., Thesis, 1974.

16243. GLATZER, NAHUM N[ORBERT]: *Essays in Jewish thought.* Tuscaloosa, Alabama: Univ. of Alabama Press, 1978. VII, 295 pp., bibl. references. (Judaic studies series, no. 8.) [Incl.: The beginning of modern Jewish studies. Leopold Zunz (2 articles). F. Kafka. Buber as an interpreter of the Bible. Franz Rosenzweig (4 articles). The Frankfort Lehrhaus.]

16244. GRAUPE, HEINZ MOSCHE: *The rise of modern Judaism. An intellectual history of German Jewry 1650–1942.* Transl. from German by John Robinson. Huntington, N.Y.: Krieger, 1978. XI, 329 pp., plates, ports., bibl. (pp. 311–318), bibl. of the main thinkers and authors whose works are available in English transl. (pp. 319–322). [Orig. title: 'Die Entstehung des modernen Judentums. Geistesgeschichte der deutschen Juden 1650–1942'. 1st edn. 1969, 2nd edn. 1977, see No. 14411/YB XXIII.]

16245. GRUENEWALD, MAX: *Here, there, and above.* New York: Ktav, 1979. VII, 196 pp. [A collection of articles written for the most part for the 'Bulletin' of Congregation B'nai Israel in Millburn, New Jersey over a period of thirty years, many dealing with German-Jewish affairs. Some articles also written by his wife, Hede Gruenewald.]

16246. GUTTMANN, JACOB: *Die Philosophie des Salomon ibn Gabirol.* Nachdr. der Ausg. Göttingen 1889. Hildesheim: Olms, 1979. IV, 272 pp.

16247. HILDESHEIMER, ESRIEL. ELLENSON, DAVID: *A response by modern Orthodoxy to Jewish religious pluralism. The case of Esriel Hildesheimer.* [In]: Tradition, a Journal of Orthodox Jewish Thought, Vol. 17, No. 4, New York, Spring 1979. Pp. 74–89, bibl. notes (pp. 87–89).

16248. KATZ, STEVEN T.: *Modern Jewish historians.* [In]: Shefa Quarterly, a Journal of Jewish Thought and Study, Vol. 1, No. 3, Jerusalem, April 1978. Pp. 65–80, bibl. [Incl. Jost, Zunz, Graetz, Baron, and others.]

16249. KOHLER, KAUFMANN: *Grundriss einer systematischen Theologie des Judentums auf geschichtlicher Grundlage.* Nachdr. der Ausg. Leipzig 1910. Hildesheim: Olms, 1979. VIII, 383 pp. (Grundriss der Gesamtwissenschaft des Judentums, [4.])

16250. LÖW, LEOPOLD: *Gesammelte Schriften.* Hrsg. von Immanuel Löw. 1–5. Nachdr. der Ausg. Szegedin 1889–1900. Hildesheim: Olms, 1979. 5 vols., bibl. [L.L., 1811–1875, Hungarian rabbi and scholar.]

16251. MENDELSSOHN, MOSES. MENDELSSOHN, MOSES: *Briefwechsel der letzten Lebensjahre.* Eingeleitet von Alexander Altmann. Stuttgart: Frommann, 1979. X, 342 pp.

16252. — MENDELSSOHN, MOSES: *Morgenstunden oder Vorlesungen über das Dasein Gottes.* Hrsg. von Dominique Bourel. *Der Briefwechsel Mendelssohn – Kant.* Stuttgart: Reclam, 1979. 266 pp., diagrs. (Universal-Bibliothek, Nr. 9941.)

16253. — MENDELSSOHN, MOSES: *Phädon oder Über die Unsterblichkeit der Seele.* Mit einem Nachwort hrsg. von Dominique Bourel u. mit einer Einleitung von Nathan Rotenstreich. Hamburg: Meiner, 1979. XXVIII, 178 pp. (Philosophische Bibliothek, Bd. 317.)

16254. — MENDELSSOHN, MOSES: *Selbstzeugnisse.* Ein Plädoyer für Gewissensfreiheit und Toleranz. Hrsg. von Martin Pfeideler. Tübingen: Erdmann, 1979. 214 pp., plates, facsim., ports.

16255. — ALTMANN, ALEXANDER: *Aufklärung und Kultur. Zur geistigen Gestalt von Moses Mendelssohn.* [In]: MB, Nr. 35/36, Tel Aviv, 21. Sept. 1979. Pp. 5–6 & 16.

16256. — BADT-STRAUSS, BERTHA: *Mendelssohn und die Balfour-Deklaration.* [In]: MB, Nr. 34, Tel Aviv, 7. Sept. 1979. Pp. 5 & 8. [Reprint from 'Jüdische Rundschau', 1936.]

16257. — BERGMANN, J[UDA]: *Moses Mendelssohn und die Berliner Jüdische Gemeinde.* Nachdr. aus dem Gemeindeblatt der Jüd. Gemeinde zu Berlin vom Sept. 1929. [In]: Nachrichtenblatt der

Jüd. Gemeinde von Berlin u. des Verbandes der Jüd. Gemeinden in der DDR, Dresden–Berlin, Sept. 1979. Pp. 13–15.

16258. — BERWIN, BEATE: *Moses Mendelssohn im Urteil seiner Zeitgenossen.* Unveränd. Neudr. der Ausg. Berlin 1919. Vaduz/Liechtenstein: Topos, 1978. 92 pp., bibl. (pp. 89–92). (Kant-Studien, Ergänz.-H. Nr. 49.)

16259. — *Tributes, 250. anniversary (6 Sept. 1729)*. Selection: Moses Mendelssohn, 250th anniversary (Fritz Friedlaender) [in]: AJR Information, London, Sept. 1979, pp. 1–2. Tributes to M.M. (E. G. Lowenthal) [in]: AJR Information, London, Nov. 1979, p. 7. M.M., Bruder seiner Brüder (Wolfgang Hamburger) [in]: 'Allgemeine', Düsseldorf, 31. Aug. 1979, p. 4, port. Mendelssohn-Ausstellung in Münster (Hubertus Graf Hoensbroech) [in]: 'Allgemeine', Düsseldorf, 7. Dez. 1979, p. 5, port (relief by H.-G. Bücker). Erinnerungen an M.M. (R.A.) [and]: Vor 50 Jahren: Mendelssohn Zweihundertjahr-Feier (John F. Oppenheimer) [in]: Aufbau, New York, Sept. 7, 1979, p. 28, ports., illus. (tomb-stone). Berlin gedenkt M. Mendelssohns. Feierstunde am 250. Geburtstag des Philosophen (E. G. Lowenthal) [in]: Aufbau, New York, Sept. 21, 1979, p. 21. Zum 250. Geburtstag von M.M. Feier in der Preussischen Staatsbibliothek. [Bericht nebst Ansprachen von Dieter Sauberzweig u. Cécile Lowenthal-Hensel] [in]: deutschland-berichte, Jg. 15, Nr. 10, Bonn, Okt. 1979, pp. 42–47. Der Fremdling aus Dessau (Hilde Spiel) [in]: FAZ, Frankfurt a. Main, 6. Sept. 1979. M. Mendelssohn (Gustav Erdmann) [in]: Nachrichtenblatt der Jüd. Gemeinde von Berlin u. des Verbandes Jüd. Gemeinden in der DDR, Dresden–Berlin, Sept. 1979, pp. 7–11. Der 'Juif de Berlin' (Ernst G. Lowenthal) [in]: Das Neue Israel, Jg. 32, H. 4, Zürich, Okt. 1979, pp. 199 & 201. M.M. und Berlin (Ernst G. Lowenthal) [in]: Mitteilungen des Vereins für die Geschichte Berlins, Jg. 75, H. 4, Berlin, Okt. 1979, pp. 90–97. Philosoph der Toleranz (Ernst-Peter Wieckenberg) [in]: SZ, München, 8./9. Sept. 1979, p. 108. Die unvollendete Aufklärung. Die Hamburger Kath. Akademie gedenkt des 250. Geburtstags von M.M. (Gisela Uellenberg) [in]: SZ, München, 15./16. Sept. 1979, p. 15. Weltbürger, Deutscher u. Jude (Julius H. Schoeps) [in]: Tribüne, H. 72, Frankfurt a. Main, 1979, pp. 92–110.

16260. — ENGEL, EVA: *The emergence of Moses Mendelssohn as literary critic.* [In]: LBI Year Book XXIV, London, 1979. Pp. 61–82, bibl. footnotes, bibl. M. Mendelssohn (pp. 81–82).

16261. — FEUCHTWANGER, LUDWIG: *Der Streit um den Geist Moses Mendelssohns.* [In]: MB, Nr. 34, Tel Aviv, 7. Sept. 1979. P. 5. [Reprint from 'Jüdische Rundschau', 1936.]

16262. — GILON, MEIR: *Mendelssohn's Kohelet Mussar in its historical context.* [Hebrew, English summary pp. V–VIII.] Jerusalem: The Israel Academy of Sciences and Humanities, 1979. 186 pp. (Publications of the Israel Academy of Sciences and Humanities.)

16263. — KNOBLOCH, HEINZ: *Herr Moses in Berlin. Auf den Spuren eines Menschenfreundes.* Berlin/East: Der Morgen, 1979. 475 pp., illus., facsims., plates, ports., bibl. (pp. 460–462). [Cf.: M. Mendelssohn in Ost und West (Hans Jakob Ginsburg) [in]: 'Allgemeine', Düsseldorf, 21./28. Dez. 1979, p. 4. See also: Von Verlusten und Seltenheiten. Auf der Suche nach Bildern von M. Mendelssohn (Heinz Knobloch) [in]: Nachrichtenblatt der Jüd. Gemeinde von Berlin u. des Verbandes der Jüd. Gemeinden in der DDR, Dresden–Berlin, Sept. 1979, pp. 11–13, illus.]

16264. — LEWY, HERMANN: *Moses Mendelssohn und die Zeit der Berliner Salons.* [In]: 'Allgemeine', Düsseldorf, 2. März 1979. Pp. 20 & 25, illus., ports.

16265. — LOWENTHAL-HENSEL, CÉCILE: *Moses Mendelssohn. Gedanken zu Toleranz und Emanzipation.* [In]: Aus Politik und Zeitgeschichte, Beilage zur Wochenzeitung Das Parlament, hrsg. von der Bundeszentrale für politische Bildung, B 36, Bonn, 8. Sept. 1979. Pp. 3–6, bibl. notes.

16266. — *Mendelssohn-Studien.* Beiträge zur neueren deutschen Kultur- und Wirtschaftsgeschichte. Bd. 4: Zum 250. Geburtstag von Moses Mendelssohn. Hrsg. von Cécile Lowenthal-Hensel und Rudolf Elvers. Berlin: Duncker u. Humblot, 1979. 312 pp., port. (M. Mendelssohn). [Cont.: Gewissensfreiheit und Toleranz. Eine begriffsgeschichtliche Untersuchung (Alexander Altmann, pp. 9–46). Tageslektüre in Berlin, 1740–1780 (Bodo Rollka, pp. 47–80). Ist alles gut? Pope, Mendelssohn u. Lessing. Zur Schrift 'Pope ein Metaphysiker!' (Peter Michelsen, pp. 81–109). Die Bedeutung Moses Mendelssohns für die Literatur des 18. Jahrhunderts (Eva J. Engel-Holland, pp. 111–159). Naturrecht u. Ästhetik bei Moses Mendelssohn (Manfred Voigts, pp. 161–198). Fromet Mendelssohn an Elise Reimarus. Abschluss einer theologischen Tragödie (Eva J. Engel-Holland, pp. 199–209). Sprung in die Metaphysik oder Fall ins Nichts. Eine Alternative im Spinozismusstreit, zugleich noch ein Beitrag zu vielen Beiträgen, dies Thema betreffend (Wilhelm Schmidt-Biggemann, pp. 211–221). Moses

Mendelssohn, Markus Herz und die Akademie der Wissenschaften zu Berlin (Dominique Bourel, pp. 223–234). Vor 50 Jahren. Das erste grosse Mendelssohn-Gedenken. Versuch eines Rückblicks (Ernst G. Lowenthal, pp. 235–275). Zur Geschichte der Jubiläumsausgabe von M. Mendelssohns Gesammelten Schriften (Günther Holzboog, pp. 277–292).]

16267. — MEVORAH, BAROUCH: *Johann Kaspar Lavaters Auseinandersetzung mit Moses Mendelssohn über die Zukunft des Judentums.* [In]: Zwingliana, Jg. 14, Nr. 8, Zürich, 1977. Pp. 431–450.

16268. — MICHAEL, REUVEN: *Der hebräische 'Moralprediger'* ['*Kohelet Mussar*'] – *eine Tendenzschrift der jüdischen 'Aufklärung'.* [In]: Saeculum, Bd. 30, H. 1, Freiburg i. Br., 1979. Pp. 86–99.

16269. — SCHOEPS, JULIUS H.: *Moses Mendelssohn.* Königstein/Ts.: Jüdischer Verl., 1979. 193 pp., ports., illus., facsims., chron. [Cf.: M. Mendelssohn in Ost u. West (Hans Jakob Ginsburg) [in]: 'Allgemeine', Düsseldorf, 21./28. Dez. 1979, p. 4.]

16270. — SPIEL, HILDE: *Lessing und Mendelssohn.* [In]: Tribüne, H. 69, Frankfurt a. Main, 1979. Pp. 66–70.

16271. — STAATSBIBLIOTHEK PREUSSISCHER KULTURBESITZ, Berlin: *Moses Mendelssohn, Leben und Werk. Ausstellung zum 250. Geburtstag am 6. Sept. 1979* (geöffnet bis 20. Okt. 1979. [Katalog] bearb. von Rudolf Elvers u. Hans-Günter Klein.) Wiésbaden: Reichert in Komm., 1979. 48 pp. illus., ports., facsims. (Ausstellungskataloge, Staatsbibliothek Preussischer Kulturbesitz, 10.)

16272. — WIECKENBERG, ERNST-PETER: *Der Bekehrungsstreit zwischen Lavater und Mendelssohn.* [In]: Tribüne, H. 69, Frankfurt a. Main, 1979. Pp. 71–79.

16273. PELLI, MOSHE: *The Age of Haskalah. Studies in Hebrew literature of the Enlightenment in Germany.* Köln: Brill, 1979. XII, 255 pp. (Studies in Judaism in modern times, Vol. 5.)

16274. PELLI, MOSHE: *The beginning of the epistolary genre in Hebrew Enlightenment literature in Germany. The alleged affinity between Lettres Persanes and 'Igrot Meshulam.* [In]: LBI Year Book XXIV, London, 1979. Pp. 83–103, bibl. footnotes.

16275. PERL, JOSEPH: *Über das Wesen der Sekte der Chassidim.* Ed. from the manuscript [MS. Var. 293 in the Jewish National- and University Library, Jerusalem] with introduction and annotations by Avraham Rubinstein. Jerusalem, 1977. 174 pp. (Publications of the Israel Academy of Sciences and Humanities.) [First publication of a polemic in German written to inform Austrian authorities against Chassidism. J. Perl, 1773–1839, author of significant satirical works and leading figure in the Galician Haskalah.]

16276. PREUSS, JULIUS: *Biblical and Talmudic medicine.* Transl. and ed. by Fred Rosner. New York: Sanhedrin Press, 1978. XXIX, 652 pp., facsims., port. [On J. Preuss see No. 14428/YB XXIII.]

16277. ROSENZWEIG, FRANZ. ROSENZWEIG, FRANZ: *Briefe und Tagebücher.* Hrsg. von Rachel Rosenzweig und Edith Rosenzweig-Scheinmann, unter Mitwirkung von Bernhard Casper. *Bd. 1: 1900–1918: Bd. 2: 1918–1929.* Haag: Nijhoff, 1979. 2 vols. (XXXI, 1334 pp.), facsims., geneal. tables. (Rosenzweig, Franz: Der Mensch und sein Werk. Gesammelte Schriften, Abt. 1, Bd. 1–2.) [Corrected entry of No. 15311/YB XXIV.] Cf.: Offenbarung u. Sprache des Menschen (Walter Strolz) [in]: NZZ, Zürich, 10. Dez. 1979, p. 18. See also: Zum Tode von Edith Rosenzweig [Nov. 1979 in Baden-Baden] [in]: 'Allgemeine', Düsseldorf, 21./28. Dez. 1979, p. 6.

16278. — *50. Anniversary of Franz Rosenzweig's death (Dec. 10, 1929):* Franz Rosenzweig, unser Lehrer (Schalom Ben-Chorin) [in]: 'Allgemeine', Düsseldorf, 7. Sept. 1979, p. 5, port. Warum ist Rosenzweig so unbekannt? Fragen zu seinem 50. Todestag am 10. Dez. (Hans Lamm) [in]: 'Allgemeine', Düsseldorf, 7. Dez. 1979, p. 6. Ausstellung F. Rosenzweig (in der Frankfurter Stadt- u. Universitätsbibliothek, 12. Dez. 1979 bis 10. Jan. 1980. Kurzbericht) [in]: Börsenblatt für den Dt. Buchhandel, Nr. 101, Frankfurt/M., 18. Dez. 1979, p. 2487. Zum 50. Todestag von F. Rosenzweig, 1886–1929 (Bodo von Maydell) in: Judaica, Jg. 35, H. 1, Zürich, 1979, pp. 1–4. Beiträge zum F. Rosenzweig Gedenkjahr (Bodo von Maydell) [in]: Judaica, Jg. 35, H. 3 & 4, Zürich, 1979, pp. 99–102 & 145–147. F. Rosenzweig, 50 Jahre nach seinem Tode (Zeew Levy) [in]: MB, Nr. 45, Tel Aviv, 7. Dez. 1979, pp. 5–6. Zum 50. Todestag von F. Rosenzweig (Pinchas Lapide) [in]: Das Neue Israel, Jg. 32, H. 4, Zürich, Okt. 1979, pp. 203–205. Der vollkommene Jude (H. E. Blumenthal) [in]: Neue Jüd. Nachrichten, Nr. 47/48, München, 21./28. Dez. 1979, p. 5. Ein jüdischer Denker der Offenbarung. Jüdisches Denken zwischen Schöpfung und Exodus. Ausführungen zum 50. Todestag F. Rosenzweigs (Walter Strolz) [in]: Orientierung, Kath. Blätter für weltanschauliche Information, Jg. 43, Nr. 22 & 23/24, Zürich, 1979, pp. 247–250 & 258–260. Nach Martin Buber jetzt: Franz Rosenzweig und wir (Bodo von Maydell) [in]: Der Quäker, Jg. 53, Nr.

4, Wien, 4. April 1979, pp. 64–65. F. Rosenzweig. Zum 50. Todestag am 10. Dez. 1979 (Schalom Ben-Chorin) [in]: Zeitschrift für Religions- und Geistesgeschichte, Bd. 31, H. 4, Köln, 1979, pp. 338–344.

16279. ROSENZWEIG, RACHEL: *Solidarität mit den Leidenden im Judentum.* (Übers. u. Neubearb. des hebräischen Originals durch die Verfasserin.) Berlin: de Gruyter, 1978. XXVI, 296 pp., 1 map, bibl. (pp. 280–286). (Studia Judaica, Bd. 10.)

16280. SALZBERGER, GEORG. JACOBS, LOUIS: *Rabbi Meir Simhah of Dvinsk.* London: Belsize Square Synagogue, 10. Dec. 1978. 10 pp. (Second annual Rabbi Dr. Georg Salzberger Memorial Lecture.)

16281. SCHOLEM, GERSHOM. SCHOLEM, GERSHOM: *Identifizierung und Distanz.* Abschiedsworte an der Eranos-Tagung 1979. [In]: NZZ, Zürich, 29. Febr. 1980. P. 41. [Excerpts from the author's speech.]

16282. — SCHOLEM, GERSHOM: *Zur Kabbala und ihrer Symbolik.* 2. Aufl. Frankfurt a. Main: Suhrkamp, 1977. 303 pp. (Suhrkamp Taschenbücher Wissenschaft, 13.) [1st edn. Zürich, 1960, see No. 2629/YB VII.]

16283. — BIALE, DAVID: *Gershom Scholem. Kabbalah and counter-history.* Cambridge, Mass.: Harvard Univ. Press, 1979. VI, 279 pp., front. port., bibl. (pp. 217–226). [Hebrew review (J. Dan) [in]: Kirjath Sepher, Vol. 54, No. 2, Jerusalem, April 1979, pp. 358–362.]

16284. SIMON, ERNST: *Mein Judentum. Essays.* Frankfurt a. Main: Suhrkamp, 1979. 402 pp. (Bibliothek Suhrkamp, 641.) [E.S., born March 15, 1899 in Berlin. Cf.: E. Simon – eighty (Eva G. Reichmann) [in]: AJR Information, London, March 1979, p. 8. Wagnis des Glaubens, Pathos der Formulierung. E. Simon zum 80. Geburtstag (Carl Frankenstein. Transl. of the introductory essay to a Hebrew 'Festschrift' for E.S.) [and]: Humanismus und Judentum. E. Simons unkategorischer Imperativ (Naftali H. Sonn) [in]: MB, No. 10, Tel Aviv, 9. März 1979, pp. 4–6. E. Simon und die deutsche Kultur (Werner Kraft) [in]: Neue Deutsche Hefte, 162, Berlin, 1979, pp. 227–267. E. Simon zum 80. Geburtstag (Paul R. Mendes-Flohr) [in]: Freiburger Rundbrief, Folge 30, Freiburg i. Br., 1978, p. 60 (transl. from the English original, publ. [in]: Jerusalem Post, Jerusalem, March 26, 1979).]

16285. STEINSCHNEIDER, MORITZ: *Verzeichnis der hebräischen Handschriften.* Nachdr. der Ausg. Berlin 1878–1897. Hildesheim: Olms, 1979. XVI, 321 pp., 3 plates. (Handschriften-Verzeichnisse der Königl. Bibliothek zu Berlin, Bd. 2, 1. 2.)

16286. TAL, URIEL: *On Judaism and humanism in education.* [In]: Immanuel, No. 9, Jerusalem: The Ecumenical Theological Research Fraternity in Israel, 1979. Pp. 115–121. [Also German transl.]: *Über Judentum und Humanismus in der Erziehung.* [In]: Freiburger Rundbrief, Folge 30, Freiburg i. Br., 1978. Pp. 63–67.

16287. *Tradition und Erneuerung.* Zeitschrift der Vereinigung für religiös-liberales Judentum in der Schweiz. Begr. von Lothar Rothschild. Nr. 43 (Sept. 1977); 44 (Mai 1978); 45 (März 1979). Red.: Lutz O. Zwillenberg. Bern, 1977–1979. 28; 32; 32 pp. [3 issues.] *Nr. 43* incl.: Das religiös-liberale Judentum im Wandel (Lutz Zwillenberg, pp. 1–16). Die Sektion Zürich der Vereinigung für religiös-liberales Judentum und die Isr. Cultusgemeinde Zürich (Jacques Kunstenaar u. Ellen Kaufmann). *Nr. 44*: Geburt einer Gemeinde: Jüdische Liberale Gemeinde 'Or Chadasch', Zürich (Lutz Zwillenberg, pp. 26–29). *Nr. 45:* Der Begriff der Offenbarung (Schalom Ben-Chorin, pp. 1–3). Der jüdische Kalender, seine Bedeutung u. seine Eigenarten (Manfred Rehfeld, pp. 12–19).

16288. WEHR, GERHARD: *Der Chassidismus.* Mysterium und spirituelle Lebenspraxis. Freiburg i. Br.: Aurum Verl., 1978. 121 pp. [Study based on Buber's and Scholem's works.]

B. The Jewish Problem

16289. FACKENHEIM, EMIL L.: *The Jewish return into history.* Reflections in the age of Auschwitz and a New Jerusalem. New York: Schocken Books, 1978. XIII, 296 pp. [Incl.: Jewish faith and the Holocaust, a fragment. The Nazi Holocaust as a persisting trauma for the non-Jewish mind. The human condition after Auschwitz, a Jewish testimony one generation after. Jewish identity, and the centrality of Israel; an essay in the philosophy of history.]

16290. GOLDMAN, EDWARD A., ed.: *Jews in a free society.* Challenges and opportunities. New York: Hebrew Union College Press, 1978. XI, 175 pp. [Incl.: Reform Judaism, evolution or revolution? (Jakob J. Petuchowski). Becoming a friend to myself with a little help from S.

Bibliography

Freud, E. Fromm and M. Buber (Robert L. Katz). Jewish-Christian relations in our time (Samuel Sandmel).]

16291. KANOWITZ, KURT: *Der deutsche Jude und der jüdische Deutsche.* Das Trauma der Vergangenheit. [In]: MB, Nr. 21, Tel Aviv, 31. Mai 1979. Pp. 5–6.

16292. KEMPER, THOMAS: *Über einen deutschen Alp und verlorengegangene Evidenz.* Anlässlich des Sammelbandes 'Mein Judentum' [see No. 15328/YB XXIV]. [In]: Neue Rundschau, Jg. 90, H. 2, Frankfurt a. Main, 1979. Pp. 320–322.

16293. SILBERNER, EDMUND: *Die Kommunistische Partei Deutschlands zur Judenfrage.* In: Jahrbuch des Instituts für Deutsche Geschichte, Bd. 8, Tel Aviv, 1979. Pp. 283–334, bibl. footnotes.

16294. SPERBER, MANÈS: *Churban oder Die unfassbare Gewissheit.* Wien: Europaverl., 1979. 227 pp. [Collection of essays written over 20 years on the themes: Catastrophe and Jewish identity; The meaning and development of Israel; The Yiddish literature.] Cf.: Review (Joachim Günther) [in]: Neue Deutsche Hefte, 164, Berlin, 1979, pp. 846–848. Mit (zu) hohem Anspruch (Corinna Coulmas) [in]: SZ, München, 26./27. Jan. 1980, p. 164. [Sperber received for this book on Nov. 22, 1979 in Geneva the Internat. Essay Prize of the Foundation Charles Veillon. He was also honoured on March 4, 1979 in Hanover with the 'Buber-Rosenzweig-Medaille', see: Buber-Rosenzweig-Medaille für Sperber (Wolfgang Zink) [in]: 'Allgemeine', Düsseldorf, 2. März 1979. Report [in]: deutschland-berichte, Jg. 15, Nr. 3, Bonn, März 1979, pp. 26–28.]

16295. WISTRICH, ROBERT: *Eduard Bernstein and the Jewish problem.* [In]: Jahrbuch des Instituts für Deutsche Geschichte, Bd. 8, Tel Aviv, 1979. Pp. 243–256, bibl. footnotes. [See also: Eduard Bernstein on the Jewish problem (Robert S. Wistrich) [in]: Midstream, Vol. 25, No. 10, New York, December 1979, pp. 8–13.]

C. Jewish Life and Organisations

16296. CENTRALVEREIN (C.V.). ENGEL, DAVID JOSHUA: *Organized Jewish responses to German antisemitism during the First World War.* Ann Arbor, Mich.: University Microfilms International, 1979. X, 449 pp., bibl. (pp. 444–449). [Photocopy.] Los Angeles, Univ. of California, Hist. Diss. (Ph.D.), 1979. [Incl. chaps.: I. The progress of antisemitism. II. The Jewish defense. III. Zionists, antisemites, and Centralverein. Central to this dissertation is an assessment of the activities of the 'Centralverein deutscher Staatsbürger jüdischen Glaubens' in the years 1914–1918.]

16297. — GOLDSCHMIDT, FRITZ: *Meine Arbeit bei der Vertretung der Interessen der jüdischen Ärzte in Deutschland seit dem Juli 1933.* Hrsg. von Stephan Leibfried u. Florian Tennstedt. Bremen, 1979. IV, 179 pp., illus., facsims., ports. (Universität Bremen: Arbeitsberichte zu verschütteten Alternativen in der Gesundheitspolitik, 2.) [Cover title.] [F. Goldschmidt, 1893–1968 London, jurist, describes his activities on behalf of the 'Centralverein deutscher Staatsbürger jüdischen Glaubens' and his negotiations with the Nazi authorities regarding the protection of the interests of Jewish physicians.]

16298. GLÜCKEL VON HAMELN: *Denkwürdigkeiten der Glückel von Hameln.* Aus dem Jüdisch-Deutschen übersetzt, mit Erläuterungen versehen u. hrsg. von Alfred Feilchenfeld. [5. Aufl. Nachdr. der] 4. Aufl. Berlin, Jüdischer Verlag, 1923. Vorwort von Hans Lamm. Darmstadt: Verlag Darmstädter Blätter, 1979, 333 pp., geneal. tables, plates. [For English edn. see No. 15332/ YB XXIV.]

16299. HECHALUZ. BARLEV, JEHUDA [orig. Kurt Herzberg]: *Hechaluz, deutscher Landesverband.* Ein Bericht über seine Arbeit in den Jahren 1933 bis 1938. Köln, Febr. 1979. 25 pp. [Mimeog.]

16300. HERRNSTADT, MARION: *Jüdische Familiennamen.* [In]: Die Mahnung, Jg. 26, Nr. 6 (pp. 6 & 8); Nr. 7 (p. 8); Nr. 8 (p. 6), Berlin, 1. Juni, 1. Juli, 1. Aug. 1979.

16301. HILDESHEIMER, ESRIEL: *Die Versuche zur Schaffung einer jüdischen Gesamtorganisation während der Weimarer Republik 1919–1933.* [In]: Jahrbuch des Instituts für Deutsche Geschichte, Bd. 8, Tel Aviv, 1979. Pp. 335–364, bibl. footnotes.

16302. HILFSVEREIN DER DEUTSCHEN JUDEN. FRIEDMAN, ISAIAH: *The Hilfsverein der deutschen Juden, the German Foreign Ministry and the controversy with the Zionists, 1901–1918.* [In]: LBI Year Book XXIV, London, 1979. Pp. 291–319, bibl. footnotes.

16303. JEWISH SPORT. EISEN, GEORGE: *The Maccabiah Games. A history of the Jewish Olympics.* Univ. of Maryland, Phil. Diss., 1979. IX, 427 pp., 34 illus. [Incl. chap. on the emergence of the Jewish gymnastics and sports movement, 1880–1914; a detailed treatment of the

'Jüdische Turnerschaft'; a survey of the history of the German Makkabi; Jewish sport in Nazi Germany; Jewish sportsmen and the Berlin Olympic Games.]

16304. — LEVINSON, FRITZ A.: *Turn- und Sport-Klub Hakoah-Essen, einer der grössten jüdischen Sportvereine, 1923–1938.* [In]: Das Münster am Hellweg, Jg. 32, H. 1/4, Essen, Jan. 1979. Pp. 42–48.

16305. JÜDISCHER FRAUENBUND. KAPLAN, MARION A.: *The Jewish feminist movement in Germany. The campaigns of the Jüdischer Frauenbund 1904–1938.* Westport, Conn.: Greenwood Press, 1979. VIII, 229 pp., illus., port., bibl. (pp. 209–222). (Contributions in women's studies, 8.) [Incl. chaps.: 2. Bertha Pappenheim. 4. Prostitution, morality crusades, and feminism. 5. The pursuit of influence and equality in Germany's Jewish community. 6. Housework as lifework.]

16306. — KAPLAN, MARION A.: *Women's strategies in the Jewish community in Germany.* [With comments by Nolly Molan.] [In]: new german critique, No. 14, Milwaukee, Univ. of Wisconsin, Spring, 1978. Pp. 109–118; 139–141. [On the policies of the Jüdischer Frauenbund.]

16307. LOEW, IMMANUEL: *Studien zur jüdischen Folklore.* Hrsg. von Alexander Scheiber. Hildesheim: Olms, 1975. IX, 150 pp., illus. (Collectanea, 16.) [I.L., 1854–1944, Hungarian rabbi and scholar.]

16308. REICHSBUND JÜDISCHER FRONTSOLDATEN, ed.: *Die jüdischen Gefallenen des deutschen Heeres, der deutschen Marine und der deutschen Schutztruppen 1914–1918.* Ein Gedenkbuch. Nachdr. der Ausg. 1932. Moers: Steiger, 1979. 425 pp.

16309. THIEBERGER, FRIEDRICH unter Mitwirkung von ELSE RABIN, eds.: *Jüdisches Fest, jüdischer Brauch.* Ein Sammelwerk. Mit Nachträgen und Verbesserungen. 2. Aufl. Nachdr. der im Jahre 1937 von den nationalsozialistischen Behörden beschlagnahmten u. vernichteten Erstaufl. Königstein/Ts.: Jüdischer Verl., 1979. 458 pp. illus., facsims., scores.

16310. UTLEY, PHILIP L.: *Siegfried Bernfeld's Jewish Order of Youth, 1914–1922.* [In]: LBI Year Book XXIV, London, 1979. Pp. 349–368, bibl. footnotes.

D. Jewish Art and Music

16311. AVENARY, HANOCH: *The Ashkenazi tradition of biblical chant between 1500 and 1900.* Documentation and musical analysis. Tel Aviv: Tel-Aviv Univ., Faculty of Fine Arts, School of Jewish Studies, 1978. 87 pp., facsims., music, bibl. (pp. 7–8). (Documentation and studies, 2.)

16312. FRIEDMANN, ARON: *Der synagogale Gesang.* Fotomech. Nachdr. der Originalausg. Berlin 1908. Mit Nachwort u. Registern hrsg. von Leo Roth u. Richard Campbell, in Verbindung mit Helmut Aris. Leipzig, Frankfurt a. Main: Peters, 1978. 148, XXII pp., scores. (Musikwissenschaftl. Bibliothek Peters.) (Peters-Reprints.)

16313. FROMM, HERBERT: *On Jewish music. A composer's view.* New York: Bloch, [1979]. [Cf.: Review [in]: Aufbau, New York, Aug. 17, 1979, p. 9. H.F., born in Kitzingen, since 1937 living in the U.S.A., composer, organist, author.]

16314. HAMMER-SCHENK, HAROLD: *Edwin Opplers Theorie des Synagogenbaus.* Emanzipationsversuche durch Architektur. [In]: Hannoversche Geschichtsblätter, N.F. Bd. 32, H. 1–3, Hannover, 1979. Pp. 99–118, illus. [E. Oppler, 1831 Oels/Silesia–1880 Hanover, architect of synagogues in Hanover and Breslau.]

16315. ROSENAU, HELEN: *The vision of the Temple. The image of the Temple of Jerusalem in Judaism and Christianity.* London: Oresko Books, 1979. 193 pp., 167 illus. [Incl.: The Israelitische Synagoge in Hamburg and the New Hamburg Synagogue. Illus. of neo-Classic and neo-Gothic synagogues, also in Germany. Deals also with mediaeval German manuscripts, with reproductions.]

VI. ZIONISM AND ISRAEL

16316. BAMBUS, WILLY. *Ein vergessener Palästina-Fahrer: Willy Bambus (1863–1904).* [In]: MB, Nr. 41, Tel Aviv, 2. Nov. 1979. Pp. 5–6.

— BARLEV, JEHUDA: *Hechaluz, deutscher Landesverband ... 1933 bis 1938.* [See No. 16299.]

16317. BETHEL, NICHOLAS: *Das Palästina-Dreieck. Juden und Araber im Kampf um das britische Mandat 1935–1948.* (Aus dem Engl. von Klaus Kochmann.) Frankfurt a. Main: Propyläen, 1979. 415 pp., illus., bibl. (pp. 403–406). [Orig. title: 'The Palestine triangle'. Refers also to the immigration of Jews from Nazi-Germany and its consequences for Palestine.]

16318. BOAS, JACOB: *A Nazi travels to Palestine.* [In]: History Today, Vol. 30, London, Jan. 1980 [issued Dec. 1979]. Pp. 33–38. [The journey of a leading SS official and a representative of the Zionist Federation of Germany [Kurt Tuchler, died Tel-Aviv 1979.] to Palestine. This issue of History Today was advertised in The Observer, The Guardian, and other British papers under the heading 'What happened when the Nazis and Zionists joined forces?' displaying the Star of David and the Swastika intertwined. For the protest of the Board of Deputies of British Jews see [in]: Jewish Chronicle, London, Dec. 28, 1979, p. 1 [and]: Jan. 4, 1980, pp. 6 & 18. See also: The lie of Zionist-Nazi collaboration (Jacob Gewirtz) [in]: Jewish Chronicle, London. Jan. 25, 1980, p. 23. See further: Ein Nazi fährt nach Palästina. Rückblende auf 1934 (Robert Weltsch) [in]: MB, Nr. 11, Tel Aviv, 14. März 1980. p. 3.]

16319. BRAATZ, WERNER E.: *German commercial interests in Palestine. Zionism and the boycott of German goods, 1933–1934.* [In]: European Studies Review, Vol. 9, No. 4, Univ. of Lancaster, Oct., 1979. Pp. 481–513.

16320. CARMEL, ALEX: *Palästina-Chronik 1853–1882. Deutsche Zeitungsberichte vom Krimkrieg bis zur ersten jüdischen Einwanderungswelle.* Ulm: Vass Verl., 1978. 374 pp.

16321. DANNHAUSER, WERNER J.: *German Zionism.* [In]: The Jewish Journal of Sociology, Vol. 20, No. 2, London, Dec. 1978. Pp. 173–181. [Review essay of 'Zionism in Germany 1897–1933' by Stephen M. Poppel, Philadelphia, 1977, see No. 14489/YB XXIII.]

16322. FABIAN, KÄTE: *Aus Erinnerungen an die zwanziger Jahre in Palästina.* 1–3. [In]: Das Neue Israel, Jg. 31, H. 9 (pp. 475–479); H. 10 (pp. 533–537); H. 11 (pp. 585–589), Zürich, März, April, Mai 1979.

—— FRIEDMAN, ISAIAH: *The Hilfsverein der deutschen Juden, the German Foreign Ministry and the controversy with the Zionists, 1901–1918.* [See No. 16302.]

16323. FRIESEL, EVYATAR: *The Holocaust and the birth of Israel.* [In]: The Wiener Library Bulletin, Vol. 32, new ser. Nos. 49/50, London, 1979. Pp. 51–60, bibl. notes (pp. 59–60).

16324. GOLDMANN, NAHUM: *The Jewish paradox.* Transl. by Steve Cox. London: Weidenfeld and Nicolson, 1978. 218 pp. [Orig. title: 'Le paradoxe Juif', see No. 13675/YB XXII. For German edn. see No. 15351/YB XXIV.]

16325. HERZL, THEODOR. *75. Anniversary of Theodor Herzl's death (July 3, 1904):* Th. Herzl, der Visionär des Judenstaates. Zum 75. Todestag (Roland Gradwohl) [in]: Isr. Wochenblatt, Nr. 26, Zürich, 29. Juni 1979, pp. 37–38. Mythos und Wirklichkeit. Th. Herzl zum 75. Todestag am 20. Tamus 5739 (Schalom Ben-Chorin) [in]: Das Neue Israel, Jg. 32, H. 2, Zürich, Aug. 1979, pp. 60–62; [also in]: Neue Jüd. Nachrichten, Nr. 27, München, 20. Juli 1979, pp. 1–2, port.

16326. —— BUSI, FREDERICK: *Anti-Semites on Zionism. The case of Herzl and Drumont.* [In]: Midstream, Vol. 25, No. 2, New York, Febr. 1979. Pp. 18–27.

16327. —— ELON, AMOS: *Theodor Herzl. Eine Biographie.* Übertr. von Traudl Lessing. Wien: Molden, 1979. 415 pp., bibl. (pp. 407–410). (Molden Taschenbuch, 143.) [Engl. edn., 1975, see No. 13677/YB XXII; previous German edn. under the title: 'Morgen in Jerusalem', 1975, see No. 12915/YB XXI.]

16328. KATZ, JACOB: *Zionism vs. anti-Semitism.* [In]: Commentary, Vol. 67, No. 4, New York, April 1979. Pp. 46–52. [Also publ. in German under the title]: *Zionismus contra Antisemitismus.* [In]: MB, Nr. 38 & 39, Tel Aviv, 12. & 19. Okt. 1979. Pp. 3–4 & 3–4.

16329. KATZ, JACOB: *Zionismus und Antisemitismus – die Geschichte einer historischen Beziehung.* 1–4. [In]: Isr. Wochenblatt, Vol. 79, Nr. 18 (pp. 61–63); Nr. 20 (pp. 51–52); Nr. 21 (pp. 21–23); Nr. 23 (pp. 19–21), Zürich, 4., 18., 25. Mai & 8. Juni 1979.

16330. KATZBURG, NATHANIEL: *European Jewry and the Palestine question. Appraisals and predictions.* [In]: Yad Vashem Studies, 13, Jerusalem, 1979. Pp. 249–259, bibl. footnotes. [Concerns refugee-policy during World War II.]

16331. MALACHI, RUBEN: *Vor 70 Jahren Zionisten-Kongress in Hamburg. Ein beinahe vergessenes Jubiläum.* [In]: MB, Nr. 48, Tel Aviv, 28. Dez. 1979. Pp. 5–6.

16332. MOSES, SIEGFRIED. HIRSCH, JACOB: *Dr. Siegfried Moses in memoriam. Zu seinem 5. Todestag.* [In]: MB, Nr. 5, Tel Aviv, 2. Febr. 1979. P. 5. [S. Moses, May 3, 1887 Lautenburg–Jan. 15, 1974 Tel Aviv.]

16333. NICOSIA, FRANCIS R. J.: *National Socialism and the demise of the German-Christian communities in Palestine during the nineteen thirties.* [In]: Canadian Journal of History, Vol. 14, No. 2, Saskatoon, Aug. 1979. Pp. 235–255, bibl. footnotes. [Attitude of 'Palästinadeutsche' to Nazi anti-Jewish policies in Germany, etc.]

16334. NICOSIA, FRANCIS R. J.: *Weimar Germany and the Palestine question.* [In]: LBI Year Book XXIV, London, 1979. Pp. 321–345, port., bibl. footnotes.
16335. NICOSIA, FRANCIS R. J.: *Zionism in National Socialist Jewish policy in Germany, 1933–1939.* [In]: The Journal of Modern History, Vol. 50, No. 4, Chicago, Dec. 1978. Pp. D 1253–D 1282. (The demand article of this issue is obtainable on microfiche or xerographic print from Monograph Publishing, University Microfilms International, Ann Arbor, Michigan.) [An analysis of the contacts between the Nazi regime and the German Zionist movement, primarily with regard to promotion of Jewish emigration from Germany.]
16336. PINNER, LUDWIG. KANOWITZ, KURT: *Ludwig Pinner in memoriam.* [In]: MB, Nr. 24, Tel Aviv, 22. Juni 1979. P.5, port. [See also: Persönliche Erinnerungen an L. Pinner (Lotte Cohn) [in]: MB, Nr. 22, Tel Aviv, 8. Juni 1979, p. 7. Agronom L. Pinner gestorben (E. G. Lowenthal) [in]: Aufbau, New York, June 29, 1979, p. 4. L.P., Febr. 2, 1890 Berlin – May 27, 1979 Tel Aviv, agronomist, came to Palestine in 1921, official of the Jewish Agency for Palestine.]
16337. REINHARZ, JEHUDA: *The Esra Verein and Jewish colonisation in Palestine.* [In]: LBI Year Book XXIV, London, 1979. Pp. 261–289, bibl. footnotes. [Refers also to Willy Bambus.]
16338. TAEUBLER, EUGEN: *Die allgemeingeschichtlichen Grundlagen der Palästinabestrebungen im 16. Jahrhundert und in der neuesten Zeit.* (Wiederabdruck aus: Die Welt, Zentralorgan der zionistischen Bewegung, Köln, 1910.) [In]: MB, Nr.37, Tel Aviv, 5. Okt. 1979. Pp. 3–4. [Reprint in memory of the author's 100th birthday. E.T., 1879 Gostyn/Posen–1953 Cincinnati, historian, emigrated in 1941 to the U.S.A., research professor at the Hebrew Union College.]
16339. WALK, JOSEPH: *Profile of a local Zionist association 1903–1904. On the social history of German Zionism.* [In]: LBI Year Book XXIV, London, 1979. Pp. 369–374, bibl. footnotes. [Refers to the Breslau Zionist Association.]
16340. WEIZMANN, CHAIM: *The letters and papers of Chaim Weizmann.* General ed.: Barnet Litvinoff. Series A. Vols. 15–21. Jerusalem: Transaction Books, Rutgers Univ., Israel Universities Press, 1978–1979. 7 vols., illus., ports., facsims., biogr., index. *Vol. 15:* Oct. 1930–June 1933. Ed. Camillo Dresner. 1978. XXXVI, 482 pp. *Vol. 16:* June 1933–Aug. 1935. Ed. Gabriel Sheffer, ass. ed. Bella Stern. 1978. XXXVI, 499 pp. *Vol. 17:* Aug. 1935–Dec. 1936. Ed. Yemima Rosenthal. 1979. XXXIV, 405 pp. *Vol. 18:* Jan. 1937–Dec. 1938. Ed. Aaron Klieman. 1979. XXX, 513 pp. *Vol. 19:* Jan. 1939–June 1940. Ed. Norman A. Rose. 1979. XXVIII, 315 pp. *Vol. 20:* July 1940–Jan. 1943. Ed. Michael J. Cohen. 1979. XXIX, 417 pp. *Vol. 21:* Jan. 1943–May 1945. Ed. Michael J. Cohen. 1979. XXVIII, 333 pp. [For previous vols. see 15370/YB XXIV.]

VII. PARTICIPATION IN CULTURAL AND PUBLIC LIFE

A. General

16341. BERLINISCHE GALERIE: *1913–1933 Bestände: Malerei, Skulptur, Graphik.* (Ausstellung u. Katalog: Ursula Prinz, Eberhard Roters.) Berlin: Berlinische Galerie e.V. (Jebenstrasse 2), [1978]. 211 pp., ports., illus. (Katalog, 1.) [Incl. works by Isidor Aschheim, Charlotte Berend-Corinth, Nikolaus Braun, Joseph Budko, Richard Colin, Dolbin, Georg Ehrlich, Liselotte Friedlaender, Rudolf Jacobi, Bruno Krauskopf, Julio Levin, Max Liebermann, Ludwig Meidner, Felix Nussbaum, Josef Oppenheimer, Max Oppenheimer (MOPP), Emil Orlik, Arthur Segal, Eugen Spiro, Jakob Steinhardt, Lesser Ury, Gert H. Wollheim. Also chap. on 'Reimann Schule' (pp. 53–54).]
16342. BULLIVANT, KEITH, ed.: *Das literarische Leben in der Weimarer Republik.* Königstein/Ts.: Scriptor, 1978. 292 pp. (Monographien: Literaturwissenschaft, 43.) [Incl.: Mythologie u. Allegorie, Selbstverständnis u. satirische Strategie bei K. Tucholsky (Tony Phelan, pp. 114–145). Individuum u. Kollektiv in Döblins Roman 'Berlin Alexanderplatz' (Herbert Scherer, pp. 146–163). Ernst Toller. Vom Aktivismus zum humanistischen Materialismus (Stephen Lamb, pp. 164–191). Die sogenannten 'goldenen zwanziger Jahre'. Zeitkritik u. Kulturgeschichte in E. Blochs 'Erbschaft dieser Zeit' (Tony Phelan, pp. 250–281). English edn. under the title: *Culture and society in the Weimar Republic.* Manchester: Manchester Univ. Press, 1977. 205 pp.]
16343. CAHN, PETER: *Das Hoch'sche Konservatorium in Frankfurt am Main (1878–1978).* Frankfurt a.

Main: Kramer, 1979. 394 pp., illus., bibl. (pp. 374–376). [Many Jewish musicians were teaching at this conservatoire, Alfred Auerbach, Carl Friedberg, Friedrich Gernsheim, Rosy Hahn, Joseph Joachim, Ludwig Rottenberg, Bernhard Sekles (director, 1923–1933), and others.]

16344. ENGELMANN, BERNT: *Deutschland ohne Juden. Eine Bilanz.* München: Goldmann, 1979. 524 pp., bibl. (pp. 501–507), list of names. (Goldmann-Sachbuch, 11240. Ein Goldmann-Taschenbuch.) [1st edn. 1970. The German Jews in cultural and public life before 1933. Incl. documents, also an extensive list of German-Jewish physicians of the 19th and early 20th century.]

16345. europäische ideen, H.45/46: *Faschismus – Stalinismus.* Hrsg.: Andreas W. Mytze. Berlin: Verlag europäische ideen, 1979. 138 pp. [Incl.: Freitod im Exil (Elsbeth Wolffheim, pp. 117–135, on the suicide of Jewish emigré writers); and contributions by H. G. Adler, Alfred Döblin, Erich Fried, Hans Jaeger, Arthur Koestler, Dora Segall, Gabriele Tergit, Alfred Wolfenstein, and others.]

16346. EXILE LITERATURE. BOCK, SIGRID/HAHN, MANFRED, eds.: *Erfahrung Exil. Antifaschistische Romane 1933–1945.* Analysen. Berlin/East: Aufbau, 1979. 500 pp. [Incl. analyses of the novels: Döblin 'November 1918'; Feuchtwanger 'Exil'; Seghers 'Die Toten bleiben jung'; Ernst Weiss 'Der Augenzeuge'; Arnold Zweig 'Das Beil von Wandsbek'.]

16347. — DAHLKE, HANS: *Geschichtsroman und Literaturkritik im Exil.* Berlin/East: Aufbau, 1979. 452 pp.

16348. — *Deutsche Exilliteratur 1933–1945. Bücher, Bilder, Dokumente.* Aus der Sammlung [Hans-Albert] Walter. Begleitheft zur Ausstellung [in der] Stadtbücherei Heilbronn, Deutschordenshof, 6. März bis 8. April 1979. Heilbronn: Stadtbücherei, 1979. 55 pp., ports., facsims., biogr. notes (pp. 37–55).

16349. — DURZAK, MANFRED, ed.: *Deutsche Exilliteratur 1933–1945.* Stuttgart: Reclam, 1979. 600 pp. [Among the 40 contributors are Kurt R. Grossmann (on Czechoslovakia), Alfred Kantorowicz (on Spain), Gabriele Tergit (on Britain).]

16350. — ELFE, WOLFGANG [et al.], eds.: *Deutsches Exildrama und Exiltheater.* Akten des [1.] Exilliteratur-Symposiums der Univ. of South Carolina 1976. Bern: Lang, 1977. 160 pp., bibl. references. (Jahrbuch für internat. Germanistik: Reihe A, Kongressberichte, Bd. 3.)

16351. — ELFE, WOLFGANG [et al.], eds.: *Deutsche Exilliteratur, Literatur im Dritten Reich.* Akten des 2. Exilliteratur-Symposiums der Univ. of South Carolina [in Columbia, SC., Febr. 1977]. Bern: Lang, 1979. 190 pp. (Jahrbuch für internat. Germanistik: Reihe A, Kongressberichte, Bd. 5.)

16352. — FREI, BRUNO: *Heine im Exil. Erinnerungen eines Antifaschisten.* [In]: Sammlung, Jahrbuch für antifaschistische Literatur u. Kunst, Bd. 1, Frankfurt a. Main, 1978. Pp. 48–52. [Refers to the 'Heine-Klub' in Mexico.]

16353. — GOLDNER, FRANZ: *Austrian emigration, 1938–1945.* New York: Ungar, 1979. XII, 212 pp., bibl. [Transl. of the German original, see No. 14497/YB XXIII.]

16354. — HARDT, HANNO [et al.], eds.: *Presse im Exil.* Beitrag zur Kommunikationsgeschichte des deutschen Exils 1933–1945. München: Saur, 1979. 512 pp. (Dortmunder Beiträge zur Zeitungsforschung, Bd. 30.)

16355. — KRISPYN, EGBERT: *Anti-Nazi writers in exile.* Athens, Georgia: Univ. of Georgia Press, 1978. XII, 200 pp., bibl. [Incl.: K. Tucholsky, Arnold Zweig, and others.]

16356. — LOEWY, ERNST, ed.: *Exil. Literarische und politische Texte aus dem deutschen Exil 1933–1945.* Hrsg. unter Mitarbeit von Brigitte Grimm, Helga Nagel, Felix Schneider. Stuttgart: Metzler, 1979. XIV, 1277 pp., bibl. (pp. 1225–1238), bio-bibl. (pp. 1239–1277). [See also: Exil nd Rundfunk (Ernst Loewy) [in]: Rundfunk und Fernsehen, Jg. 25, Nr. 3, Hamburg, 1977, pp. 254–263.]

— — SPALEK, JOHN M.: *Guide to the archival materials of the German-speaking emigration to the United States after 1933.* [See No. 16017.]

16357. — STEPHAN, ALEXANDER: *Die deutsche Exilliteratur 1933–1945. Eine Einführung.* München: Beck, 1979. 376 pp. (Beck'sche Elementarbücher.)

— — STRAUSS, HERBERT A., ed.: *Jewish immigrants of the Nazi period in the U.S.A. Vol. 1: Archival resources.* [See No. 15989.]

16358. — STRELKA, JOSEPH P./BELL, ROBERT F./DOBSON, EUGENE, eds.: *Protest, form, tradition. Essays on German exile literature.* Tuscaloosa, Alabama: Univ. of Alabama Press, 1979. [Incl. essay by Erna Moore on Friedrich Torberg's 'Mein ist die Rache'.]

16359. EXPRESSIONISM. GEERKEN, HARTMUT, ed.: *Märchen des Expressionismus.* Frankfurt a.

Main: Fischer, 1979. 340 pp., bibl. (pp. 327–340). (Fischer-Taschenbücher, 2177.) [Incl.: Albert Ehrenstein, Jakob van Hoddis, F. Kafka, Alfred Mombert, Mynona.]

16360. — GÖBEL, WOLFRAM: *Der Kurt Wolff Verlag 1913–1930*. Expressionismus als verlegerische Aufgabe. Mit einer Bibliographie des Kurt Wolff Verlages u. der ihm angeschlossenen Unternehmen 1910–1930. Frankfurt a. Main: Buchhändler-Vereinigung, 1979. 312 pp., 36 illus.

16361. The FRANKFURT SCHOOL. CRAMER, ERICH: *Hitlers Antisemitismus und die 'Frankfurter Schule'*. Kritische Faschismus-Theorie und geschichtliche Realität. Düsseldorf: Droste, 1979. 280 pp.

16362. — TAR, ZOLTAN: *The Frankfurt School Institute of Social Research. The critical theories of Max Horkheimer and Theodor W. Adorno*. Foreword by Michael Landmann. New York: Wiley, 1977. XX, 243 pp., bibl. (pp. 209–233).

16363. HERMAND, JOST/TROMMLER, FRANK: *Die Kultur der Weimarer Republik*. München: Nymphenburger Verlagshandlung, 1978. 448 pp., 70 illus., ports. [Refers to many Jewish personalities.]

16364. HERMAND, JOST: *Sieben Arten an Deutschland zu leiden*. Königstein/Ts.: Athenäum, 1979. XI, 170 pp., illus. (Athenäum-Taschenbücher, 2141: Literaturwissenschaft.) [Incl. essays: Heines 'Wintermärchen', zum Topos der 'deutschen Misere'. Schreiben in der Fremde, Gedanken zur deutschen Exilliteratur seit 1789. Der Aufmarsch der Dissonanzen, Hanns Eislers 'Deutsche Symphonie'.]

16365. HOFMANN, HANNS HUBERT, ed.: *Bankherren und Bankiers*. Büdinger Vorträge 1976. Limburg/Lahn: Starke, 1978. XVI, 208 pp., illus. (Deutsche Führungsschicht der Neuzeit, Bd. 10.) [Incl.: Entwicklung u. Bedeutung des Frankfurter Bankhauses Erlanger u. Söhne (Norbert G. Klarmann, pp. 27–44). Über Felix Hecht, erster Direktor der Rheinischen Hypothekenbank in Mannheim (Bernhard Kirchgässner, pp. 45–84).

16366. JENS, INGE: *Dichter zwischen rechts und links. Die Geschichte der Sektion für Dichtkunst an der Preussischen Akademie der Künste*. Dargestellt nach den Dokumenten. München: Dt.-Taschenbuch-Verl., 1979. 298 pp. (dtv, 2910: dtv-Dokumente.) [Members were among others Döblin, Mombert, Wassermann.]

16367. JENTZSCH, BERND, ed.: [1.] *Ich sah das Dunkel schon von ferne kommen*. Erniedrigung und Vertreibung in poetischen Zeugnissen. [Exil.] [2.] *Der Tod ist ein Meister aus Deutschland*. Deportation und Vernichtung in poetischen Zeugnissen. [KZ.] [3.] *Ich sah aus Deutschlands Asche keinen Phönix steigen*. Rückkehr und Hoffnung in poetischen Zeugnissen. [Befreiung.] München: Kindler, 1979. 3 vols. (V, 148; VII, 164; X, 180 pp.) [Incl. poems by Günther Anders, Rose Ausländer, Paul Celan, Hilde Domin, Yvan Goll, Erich Fried, Gertrud Kolmar, Else Lasker-Schüler, Walter Mehring, Nelly Sachs, Friedrich Torberg, and others. Cf.: Verse der Verlorenheit. Zu der dreiteiligen Lyrikanthologie von B. Jentzsch (Elisabeth Endres) [in]: SZ, München, 24./25. Dez. 1979, p. 50.]

16368. KLEIN, DENNIS B.: *Jewish origins of the psychoanalytic movement*. Ann Arbor, Mich.: University Microfilms Internat., 1978. XII, 333 pp., bibl (pp. 292–311). [Typescript-photocopy.] Univ. of Rochester, Thesis, 1978.

16369. LANGNER, ILSE: *Drei deutsch-jüdische Dichterinnen*. [In]: Frankfurter Hefte, Jg. 34, H. 5, Frankfurt a. Main, Mai 1979. Pp. 37–45. [Gertrud Kolmar, Else Lasker-Schüler, Nelly Sachs.]

16370. LARSEN, EGON: *Fifty years ago: Weimar climax*. [In]: AJR Information, London, Jan. 1979. Pp. 5–6. [Participation of Jews in cultural life.]

16371. LUTHARDT, WOLFGANG, ed.: *Sozialdemokratische Arbeiterbewegung und Weimarer Republik*. Materialien zur gesellschaftlichen Entwicklung 1927–1933. 1–2. Frankfurt a. Main: Suhrkamp, 1978. 2 vols. (422; 435 pp.) (Edition Suhrkamp, 923. 934.) [Incl. articles from periodicals of that period by Ernst Fraenkel, Rudolf Hilferding, Paul Levi, Fritz Naphtali, Hugo Sinzheimer, and others.]

16372. NACHMANSOHN, DAVID: *German-Jewish pioneers in science, 1900–1933*. Highlights in atomic physics, chemistry, and biochemistry. Berlin, New York: Springer, 1979. XX, 380 pp., illus., ports., bibl. (pp. 381–388). [Cont. chaps.: I. Historical background. II. Atomic physics in the early twentieth century. III. Developments in chemistry and physiology in the nineteenth century. IV. Chemistry and biochemistry in the early 20th century. The Kaiser Wilhelm Institutes in Berlin-Dahlem. V. Worldwide effects on biochemistry due to Nazi persecution. This volume is an extended version of the first *Siegfried Moses Memorial Lecture* given in Jerusalem in November 1976, and it is dedicated to the memory of Siegfried Moses, first President of the Leo Baeck Institute.]

16373. OLLIG, HANS LUDWIG: *Der Neukantianismus.* Stuttgart: Metzler, 1979. 175 pp., bibl. (Sammlung Metzler, M 187: Abt. D, Literaturgeschichte.) [Incl.: The 'Marburger Schule': Hermann Cohen, Ernst Cassirer, Arthur Liebert; also Jonas Cohn, Otto Liebmann, and others.]

16374. *Paris–Berlin, 1900–1933.* Übereinstimmungen und Gegensätze Frankreich–Deutschland. Kunst, Architektur, Graphik, Literatur, Industriedesign, Film, Theater, Musik. [Katalog der Ausstellung im Centre National d'Art et de Culture Georges Pompidou vom 12. Juli–6. Nov. 1978.] München: Prestel, 1979. 632 pp., illus., ports., facsims., biogr. notes (pp. 604–623), list of names (pp. 624–632). [Refers to many German-Jewish authors and artists.]

16375. PERIODICALS (ALMANACS, YEARBOOKS). *Arkadia.* Ein Jahrbuch für Dichtkunst. Hrsg. von Max Brod. Nachdr. der Ausg. Leipzig, Wolff, 1913. [No further issues.] Nendeln/Liechtenstein: Kraus, 1978. 241 pp. [Incl. contributions by Oskar Baum, Martin Beradt, Moritz Heimann, Heinrich Eduard Jacob, Franz Janowitz, Franz Kafka, Willy Speyer, Kurt Tucholsky, Franz Werfel, Alfred Wolfenstein, and others.]

16376. — *Der Bildermann.* Hrsg. von Paul Cassirer. Jg. 1. [No further issues.] Nachdr. der Ausg. Berlin, Cassirer, 1916. Nendeln/Liechtenstein: Kraus, 1979. 1 vol. (114 pp., mostly illus.) [Incl. lithographs by Max Liebermann, and literary contributions by Peter Altenberg, Max Brod, Stefan Grossmann, Walter Hasenclever, Else Lasker-Schüler, Alfred Richard Meyer, Erich Mühsam, Arno Nadel, Alfred Polgar, Stefan Zweig, and others.]

16377. — *Der Blaue Reiter.* Hrsg. von Wassily Kandinsky und Franz Marc. Mit 161 Abb. Dokumentarische Neuausg. von Klaus Lankheit. (3., überarb. Aufl.) München: Piper, 1979. 368 pp., illus., scores, facsims. [1st edn. 1912, 1st reprint 1965. Incl. contributions by Eugen von Kahler, Alfred Mombert, Arnold Schönberg, and others.]

16378. — *Der Gegner.* Blätter zur Kritik der Zeit. Hrsg. von Julian Gumperz, Karl Otten u. Wieland Herzfelde. Jg. 1–3, H. 1–3. [No further issues.] Ab Jg. 2 mit dem satirischen Teil 'Die Pleite'. Reprint der Ausg. Halle, Leipzig u. Berlin 1919–1922. Einleitung von Wieland Herzfelde u. Kommentar von Hans-Jörg Görlich. Leipzig: Zentralantiquariat der DDR; Berlin/East: Das Arsenal, 1979. 806 pp., illus. [Incl. contributions by Kurt Hiller, Gina Kaus, Frida Rubiner, Ludwig Rubiner and others. Julian Gumperz, 1898 New York–1972 New York, German-Jewish parentage, brought up in Germany, became director of the 'Institut für Wirtschaftswissenschaft' Frankfurt a. Main, emigrated with this Institute to the U.S.A. in 1934.]

16379. — *Das Goldene Tor.* Monatsschrift für Literatur und Kunst. Hrsg. von Alfred Döblin. Jg. 1–6. [No further issues.] Nachdr. der Ausg. Lahr, Baden-Baden, 1946–1951. Vaduz/Liechtenstein: Topos, 1979. 6 vols.

— *Der Jude.* Eine Monatsschrift. Hrsg. von Martin Buber. [See No. 16221.]

16380. — *Neue Blätter.* Hrsg.: Carl Einstein [ab Folge 1, H. 7: Jakob Hegner; ab Folge 3, H. 1: Anton Heiderich; ab H. 3: Erich Baron]. Folge 1–3. [No further issues.] Nachdr. der Ausg. Berlin, Hellerau, 1912–1913. Vaduz/Liechtenstein: Topos, 1979. 3 vols. [Incl. contributions by Paul Adler, Max Brod, Martin Buber, Albert Ehrenstein, Carl Einstein, Gustav Landauer, Else Lasker-Schüler, Georg von Lukács, Georg Munk, Stefan Zweig and others.]

16381. — *Ost und West.* Beiträge zu kulturellen und politischen Fragen der Zeit. Hrsg. von Alfred Kantorowicz. 1947–1949. [No further issues.] Vollständiger Nachdr. mit einer Einleitung hrsg. von Alfred Kantorowicz u. Barbara Baerns. Königstein/Ts.: Athenäum, 1979. 5 vols. [Cf. reviews: Parzival im Kalten Krieg (Jürgen Rühle) [in]: SZ, München, 12./13. Jan. 1980, p. 150, port. Auf den Flügeln des Friedens (Fritz J. Raddatz) [in]: Die Zeit, Hamburg, 21. Dez. 1979, p. 46.]

16382. — *Die Schaubühne.* Hrsg.: Siegfried Jacobsohn. Vollständiger Nachdr. der Jahrgänge 1905–1918. Mit einem Begleitband von Rolf Michaelis. Königstein/Ts.: Athenäum, 1979–1980. 14 vols. [Publ. in 1979: Jg. 1905–1909. 'Die Schaubühne' was continued from 1918–1933 under the title 'Die Weltbühne' (for reprint see No. 15395/YB XXIV), and in exile until 1939 under the title 'Die Neue Weltbühne'.]

16383. — *Der Sozialist.* Organ des Sozialistischen Bundes. Hrsg.: Gustav Landauer. Jg. 1–7. [No further issues.] Nachdr. der Ausg. Berlin, Bern, 1909–1915, mit einer Einleitung von Andreas Seiverth u. neu erstellten Inhaltsverzeichnissen. Vaduz/Liechtenstein: Topos, 1979. 3 vols.

16384. — *Der Theater-Teufel.* Humoristisch-satyrischer Almanach für 1848. Hrsg. von Joseph Mendelssohn. Mit Beiträgen von Moritz Saphir, Adolf Glassbrenner, Johann Nestroy [et al.]. Reprint der Ausg. Hamburg 1848. Leipzig: Zentralantiquariat der DDR, 1979/80. 202 pp.

16385. — *Uhu.* Das Magazin der 20er Jahre. Nachdruck der Erstveröffentlichungen aus den Original Uhu-Bänden von 1924–1933. Hrsg. von Christian Ferber. Frankfurt a. Main: Ullstein, 1979. 355 pp., ports., illus. facsims., cartoons. [Incl. contributions by Vicki Baum, Walter Benjamin, Max Brod, Alfred Döblin, Albert Einstein, Friedrich Gundolf, Friedrich Hollaender, Else Lasker-Schüler, Walter Mehring, Alfred Polgar, Erich Salomon, Carl Sternheim, Kurt Tucholsky, Jakob Wassermann, Carl Zuckmayer, Arnold Zweig, Stefan Zweig.]

16386. PRAWER, SIEGBERT: *A new muse climbs Parnassus*. German debates about literature and the cinema 1909–1929. [In]: German Life and Letters, New Ser. Vol. 32, No. 3, Oxford, April 1979. Pp. 196–205.

16387. RADDATZ, FRITZ J.: *Revolte und Melancholie. Essays zur Literaturtheorie*. Hamburg: Knaus, 1979. 330 pp., notes (pp. 291–321). [Incl. essays on Adorno, Benjamin, Bloch, Engels, Lassalle, Lukács, Marx and others.]

16388. SCHÜTTE, WOLFGANG U., ed.: *Unterm Pulverfass glimmt noch der Zunder*. Eine Auswahl aus 'Das Wort' (1923–25) und 'Proletarische Heimstunden' (1923–26). Berlin/East: Tribüne, 1979. 266 pp. [Incl. contributions by Egon Erwin Kisch, Erich Mühsam, Ernst Toller and others.]

16389. SCHUMANN, THOMAS B.: *Plädoyers gegen das Vergessen*. Hinweise zu einer alternativen Literaturgeschichte. Porträts und Aufsätze über vergessene oder unbekannte Autoren und Bücher des 20. Jahrhunderts. Berlin: Verlag europäische ideen, 1979. 132 pp., list of names (pp. 123–129). [Refers to many German-Jewish authors. Incl. also chap. 'Über den Neuen Club und das Neopathetische Cabaret', founded 1909 in Berlin by Kurt Hiller.]

16390. SERKE, JÜRGEN: *Frauen schreiben. Ein neues Kapitel deutschsprachiger Literatur*. Mit Fotos von Stefan Moses. Hamburg: Gruner u. Jahr, 1979. 336 pp., ports. (Ein Stern-Buch.) [On Rose Ausländer, Hilde Domin, Gertrud Kolmar, Nelly Sachs, Anna Seghers and others.]

16391. SERKE, JÜRGEN: *Die verbrannten Dichter*. Berichte, Texte, Bilder einer Zeit. Mit Fotos von Wilfried Bauer. Sonderausg. Weinheim: Beltz u. Gelberg, 1979. 271 pp., illus., ports., facsims., bibl. (pp. 256–269). [Incl. essays on Walter Benjamin, Alfred Döblin, Albert Ehrenstein, Carl Einstein, Salomo Friedlaender (Mynona), Ivan & Claire Goll, Walter Hasenclever, Franz Hessel, Jakob van Hoddis, Gertrud Kolmar, Paul Kornfeld, Theodor Kramer, Else Lasker-Schüler, Walter Mehring, Erich Mühsam, Ernst Toller, Ernst Weiss and others. 1st edn. 1977, see No. 14512/YB XXIII.]

16392. SZEEMANN, HARALD, ed.: *Monte Verità, Berg der Wahrheit*. Lokale Anthropologie als Beitrag zur Wiederentdeckung einer neuzeitlich-sakralen Topographie. [Buch zu einer Ausstellung in Ascona u. auf den Brissago-Inseln, 8. Juli bis 30. Aug. 1978.] Milano: Electa Editrice, 1978. 191 pp., ports., illus., facsims., bibl. (pp. 179–182), list of names. [Refers to many Jewish personalities, authors and artists.]

16393. WEGER, KARL-HEINZ, ed.: *Religionskritik von der Aufklärung bis zur Gegenwart*. Autoren-Lexikon von Adorno bis Wittgenstein. Freiburg i. Br.: Herder, 1979. 319 pp. (Herderbücherei, Bd. 716.) [Incl. articles on Adorno, Bloch, Durkheim, Freud, Fromm, Heine, Hess, Horkheimer, Kafka, Löwith, Mannheim, Marcuse, Marx, Plessner, Popper, Spinoza, Wittgenstein.]

16394. WILLETT, JOHN: *Art and politics in the Weimar period*. The new sobriety 1917–1933. New York: Pantheon Books, 1978. 272 pp., 212 illus., map, ports., bibl. (pp. 260–263). [Refers to many Jewish personalities.]

16395. WINCKLER, LUTZ/FRITSCH, CHRISTIAN, eds.: *Antifaschistische Literatur. Bd.3: Prosaformen*. Königstein/Ts.: Scriptor, 1979. 284 pp., bibl. (Literatur im historischen Prozess, Bd. 12.) [For previous vols. see No. 14514/YB XXIII.]

B. Individual

16396. ADLER, ALFRED. BRANDL, GERHARD, ed.: *Vom Ich zum Wir. Individualpsychologie konkret*. München: Reinhardt, 1979. 190 pp., bibl. [11 contributions referring to A. Adler (1870–1937).]

16397. ADORNO, THEODOR W. ADORNO, THEODOR W.: *Kierkegaard. Konstruktion des Ästhetischen*. Hrsg. von Rolf Tiedemann. 1. Aufl. Frankfurt a. Main: Suhrkamp, 1979. 266 pp. (Adorno, Th. W.: Gesammelte Schriften, Bd. 2.)

16398. — ADORNO, THEODOR W.: *Soziologische Schriften. 1*. Hrsg. von Rolf Tiedemann. Frankfurt a. Main: Suhrkamp, 1979. 587 pp. (Suhrkamp-Taschenbücher Wissenschaft, 306.)

16399. — BEYER, WALTRAUD: *Tradition als 'Spur von Leiden'. Zu Adornos Traditionsauffassung*. [In]:

Weimarer Beiträge, Jg. 25, H. 2, Berlin–Weimar, 1979. Pp. 79–103, bibl. notes (pp. 100–103).
16400. — BOLZ, NORBERT W.: *Geschichtsphilosophie des Ästhetischen. Hermeneutische Rekonstruktion der 'Noten zur Literatur' Th. W. Adornos.* Hildesheim: Gerstenberg, 1979. X, 390 pp.
16401. — HOLL, HANS-GÜNTHER: *Emigration in die Immanenz. Theodor Adorno.* [In]: Neue Deutsche Hefte, 163, Berlin, 1979. Pp. 535–556.
16402. — JONES, MICHAEL TAYLOR: *Constellations of modernity. The literary essays of Th. W. Adorno.* New Haven, Conn., Yale Univ., Phil. Diss., 1978. 331 pp.
16403. — MIRBACH, THOMAS: *Kritik der Herrschaft.* Zum Verhältnis von Geschichtsphilosophie, Ideologiekritik u. Methodenreflexion in der Gesellschaftstheorie Adornos. Frankfurt a. Main: Campus-Verl., 1979. (Campus Forschung, Bd. 118.)
16404. — SAUERLAND, KAROL: *Einführung in die Ästhetik Adornos.* Berlin, de Gruyter, 1979. VI, 172 pp., bibl. (pp. 155–168). (De-Gruyter-Studienbuch.)
16405. AICHHORN, AUGUST. AICHHORN, THOMAS, ed.: *Wer war August Aichhorn?* Briefe, Dokumente, unveröffentlichte Arbeiten. Wien: Löcker u. Wögenstein, 1976. 124 pp. [Prof. A. Aichhorn, noted child-psychoanalyst in Vienna.]
16406. ALTENBERG, PETER [orig. Richard Engländer]. ALTENBERG, PETER: *Diogenes in Wien.* Aphorismen, Skizzen und Geschichten. Auswahl in zwei Bänden. Hrsg. u. mit einer Nachbemerkung versehen von Dietrich Simon. Berlin/East: Volk u. Welt, 1979. 2 vols. (536 pp.) [See also: 'Telegramm-Stil der Seele'. Beim Wiederlesen von Peter Altenberg [in]: NZZ, Zürich, 24./25. März 1979, p. 69.]
16407. — SCHAEFER, CAMILLO: *Peter Altenberg.* Ein biographischer Essay. Wien: Edition Freibord, 1979. 34 pp., illus., ports., bibl. (Freibord Sonderreihe, 10.)
16408. — WYSOCKI, GISELA von: *Peter Altenberg.* Bilder und Geschichten des befreiten Lebens. München: Hanser, 1979. 124 pp., bibl. (pp. 113–124). (Literatur als Kunst.) [See also: Poesie aus den letzten Tagen der Menschheit. Eine Skizze über Peter Altenberg (Gisela von Wysocki) [in]: Die Zeit, Hamburg, 16. Febr. 1979, p. 42, port.]
16409. AMÉRY, JEAN. AMÉRY, JEAN: *In den Wind gesprochen.* [In]: Die zornigen alten Männer, Gedanken über Deutschland seit 1945, hrsg. von Axel Eggebrecht. Reinbek: Rowohlt, 1979. Pp. 258–279. [See also: Der gefährliche Fortschritt. Zu einem Aufsatz von Jean Améry ['In den Wind gesprochen'] (Carl Amery) [in]: Frankfurter Hefte, Jg. 34, H. 8, Frankfurt a. Main, Aug. 1979, pp. 15–18.]
16410. — KESTING, HANJO: *Der Tod des Geistes als Person. Leben und Werk des Jean Améry.* [In]: Frankfurter Hefte, Jg. 34, H. 6, Frankfurt a. Main, Juni 1979. Pp. 51–62.
16411. — SCHMID, BEAT: *Aufklärung als Revision und Selbstbehauptung. Über Jean Améry (1912–1978).* [In]: NZZ, Zürich, 10./11. März 1979. P. 69.
16412. ARENDT, HANNAH. ARENDT, HANNAH: *Vom Leben des Geistes.* 1–2. München: Piper, 1979. 2 vols. Bd. 1: *Das Denken.* 241 pp. Bd. 2: *Das Wollen.* 269 pp. [Orig. title: 'The life of the mind', see No. 15422/YB XXIV. Cf.: Philosophie über die Tätigkeiten des Geistes: kein Erbarmen mit der Unbarmherzigkeit. Ein Vermächtnis. Die Gedanken Hannah Arendts (Monika Plessner) [in]: Die Zeit, Hamburg, 15. Febr. 1980. This review refers also to Julie Braun-Vogelstein (1883–1971).]
16413. — ERLER, HANS: *Hannah Arendt, Hegel und Marx.* Studien zu Fortschritt und Politik. Köln: Böhlau, 1979. IV, 210 pp. (Böhlau philosophica, 5.)
16414. — HILL, MELVYN, ed.: *Hannah Arendt. The recovery of the public world.* New York: St. Martin's Press, 1979. XIII, 362 pp., bibl. of H. Arendt by Elisabeth Young-Bruehl (pp. 341–354).
16415. — LAQUEUR, WALTER: *Re-reading Hannah Arendt.* [In]: Encounter, Vol. 52, No. 3, London, March 1979. Pp. 73–79. [Eichmann controversy, etc.]
16416. — REIF, ADELBERT, ed.: *Hannah Arendt. Materialien zu ihrem Werk.* (Engl. Beiträge übers. von Heinrich Helinek.) Wien: Europaverl., 1979. 371 pp., bibl.
16417. — WASHINGTON, JONNY: *Hannah Arendt's conception of the political realm.* Stanford, Calif., Stanford Univ., Phil. Diss., 1978. 163 pp.
16418. AUERBACH, ERICH. GRONAU, KLAUS: *Literarische Form und gesellschaftliche Entwicklung. Erich Auerbachs Beitrag zur Theorie und Methodologie der Literaturgeschichte.* Königstein/Ts.: Forum Academicum, 1979. 199 pp. (Hochschulschriften: Literaturwissenschaft, Bd. 39.) Zugl.: Bremen, Univ., Phil. Diss., 1977 [E. Auerbach, born 1892, professor of Romanic literature in Marburg, emigrated to Turkey.]
16419. AUSLÄNDER, ROSE: *Ein Stück weiter. Gedichte.* Hrsg.: Berndt Mosblech. Köln: Literar. Verl. Braun, 1979. 155 pp.

16420. BAUER, OTTO. *Otto Bauer und der 'dritte' Weg*. Die Wiederentdeckung des Austromarxismus durch Linkssozialisten und Eurokommunisten. Hrsg.: Detlev Albers [et al.]. Frankfurt a. Main: Campus-Verl., 1979. 182 pp., bibl. Otto Bauer (pp. 165–168).

16421. BAUMGARDT, DAVID: *Das Möglichkeitsproblem der Kritik der reinen Vernunft, der modernen Phänomenologie und der Gegenstandstheorie*. Unveränd. Neudr. der Ausg. Berlin 1920. Vaduz/Liechtenstein: Topos, 1978. 64 pp. (Kant-Studien, Ergänz.-H. 51.)

16422. BEER-HOFMANN, RICHARD. GOTTGETREU, ERICH: *Richard Beer-Hofmanns Abschied*. Das bisher unveröffentlichte Gedicht, das der Dichter vier Monate vor seinem Tode schrieb. [In]: 'Allgemeine', Düsseldorf, 26. Okt. 1979. P. 11.

16423. — LIPTZIN, SOL: *Georg Brandes and Richard Beer-Hofmann*. [In]: Modern Austrian Literature, Vol. 12, No. 1, Ashland, Pittsburgh, Pa., 1979. Pp. 19–29.

16424. BEN-HAIM, PAUL [orig. Frankenburger]. HIRSHBERG, JEHOASH: *Paul Ben-Haim (Frankenburger), the early years*. [In]: Ariel, No. 45–46, Jerusalem, 1978. Pp. 5–26. [P. Ben-Haim, born July 5, 1897 in Munich, composer in Israel. This article deals with his life and work in Germany and his emigration to Palestine in 1933.]

16425. BENJAMIN, GEORG. BENJAMIN, HILDE: *Georg Benjamin. Eine Biographie*. Leipzig: Hirzel, 1977. 360 pp., 65 illus., ports., facsims. [G.B., Sept. 10, 1895 Berlin–Aug. 26, 1942 Mauthausen, physician, brother of Walter Benjamin.]

16426. BENJAMIN, WALTER. BENJAMIN, WALTER: *Goethe. Der Artikel für die Sowjet-Enzyklopädie*. [With]: DREWS, JÖRG: *Nur 12%. Benjamins Auftrag und sein Ergebnis*. [In] : SZ, München, 13./14 Okt. 1979. Pp. 141–142, illus. [Excerpts from Benjamin's article which appeared, mutilated, in Vol. 16 of the Great Sowjet Encyclopaedia in 1929. The complete text was publ. for the first time in Benjamin's 'Gesammelte Schriften', Vol. II/3 ('Aufsätze, Essays, Vorträge'), 1977, see No. 14540/YB XXIII.]

16427. — FIGAL, GÜNTER/FOLKERS, HORST: *Zur Theorie der Gewalt und Gewaltlosigkeit bei Walter Benjamin*. Heidelberg: Forschungsstätte der Evang. Studiengemeinschaft, 1979. V, 69 pp. (Texte u. Materialien der Forschungsstätte der Evang. Studiengemeinschaft: Reihe A, Nr. 10.)

16428. — FULD, WERNER: *Walter Benjamin. Zwischen den Stühlen. Eine Biographie*. München: Hanser, 1979. 323 pp., facsims., plates, ports., bibl. (pp. 311–315). [Cf.: Der Weg in die Sackgasse (Wolf Scheller) [in]: 'Allgemeine', Düsseldorf, 21. Sept. 1979, p. 34. Ein Benjamin-Mosaik aus dritter Hand (Christoph Siegrist) [in]: Basler Zeitung, 8. Sept. 1979, p. 55. Walter Benjamin – fast einen Kopf kürzer (Martin Lüdke) [in]: Merkur, Jg. 33, No. 9, Stuttgart, Sept. 1979, pp. 902–908. Biographie als Physiognomie. Zur ersten Lebensbeschreibung Walter Benjamins (Gerd Henniger) [in]: Neue Rundschau, Jg. 90, H. 3, Frankfurt a. Main, 1979, pp. 470–472. Akzeptable Ansätze, groteske Versäumnisse. Werner Fulds umstrittene Benjamin-Biographie (Jörg Drews) [in]: SZ, München, 4./5. Aug. 1979, p. 116.]

16429. — GAGNEBIN, JEANNE-MARIE: *Zur Geschichtsphilosophie Walter Benjamins. Die Unabgeschlossenheit des Sinnes*. Erlangen: Palm u. Enke, 1978. 159 pp. (Erlanger Studien, Bd. 19.) Zugl.: Heidelberg, Univ., Phil.-Hist. Diss., 1977.

16430. — NIEMEYER, HELMUT: *Gift und Grab im Schatten der Pyrenäen*. Walter Benjamins Tod auf der Flucht 1940 in Port Bou. [In]: Die Zeit, Hamburg, 28. Sept. 1979. Pp. 41–42. [On Benjamin's last days in Sept. 1940 see also the fictitious story 'Die Nacht in den Pyrenäen' [in]: Helmut Heissenbüttel: Wenn Adolf Hitler den Krieg nicht gewonnen hätte, Stuttgart, Klett-Cotta, 1979.]

16431. — QUACK, JOSEF: *Benjamins Spleen. Verabschiedung oder Rettung eines modernen Klassikers*. [In]: Frankfurter Hefte, Jg. 34, H. 9, Frankfurt a. Main, Sept. 1979. Pp. 55–62.

16432. — RADDATZ, FRITZ J.: *Die Kräfte des Rausches für die Revolution gewinnen*. Der Literaturbegriff des Melancholikers Walter Benjamin. Mit einem Postscriptum von Hans Paeschke. [In]: Merkur, Jg. 33, H. 9, Stuttgart, Sept. 1979. Pp. 867–882.

16433. BERADT, MARTIN. BERADT, MARTIN: *Der deutsche Richter*. [Nachdr. der] Erstausg. Frankfurt a. Main, Rütten u. Loening, 1930. Königstein/Ts.: Scriptor, 1979. 241 pp. (Reihe Q, Bd. 8.)

16434. — BERADT, MARTIN: *Die Verfolgten. Novellen*. Mit einem Nachwort von Ingrid Kreuzer. Königstein/Ts.: Scriptor, 1979. 303 pp. (Reihe Q, Bd. 9.)

16435. — BERADT, CHARLOTTE: *Martin Beradt, ein Porträt*. [Funkmanuskript zur Sendung 'Am Abend vorgestellt' am 8. Okt. 1979.] Köln: Westdeutscher Rundfunk, 1979. 13 pp. [Typescript-photocopy.]

16436. — KRANEFUSS, ANNELEN: *Warum er, nicht ich? Zur Erinnerung an den Anwalt und Schriftsteller*

Martin Beradt, gestorben 1949 im Exil. [Funkmanuskript zu einer Sendung am 30. Sept. 1979.] Köln: Westdeutscher Rundfunk, 1979. 30 pp. [Mimeog.]

16437. BERKOWITZ, HORST. BEER, ULRICH: *Versehrt, verfolgt, versöhnt: Horst Berkowitz, ein jüdisches Anwaltsleben.* Essen: Juristischer Fachbuchverlag, 1979. 168 pp., illus.

16438. BERNSTEIN, EDUARD. FLETCHER, ROGER: *Bernstein in Britain. Revisionism and foreign affairs.* [In]: The International History Review, No. 1/3, Toronto, July 1979. Pp. 349–375. [See also: An English advocate in Germany. Eduard Bernstein's analysis of Anglo–German relations 1900–1914 (Roger Fletcher) [in]: Canadian Journal of History, Vol. 13, Saskatoon/Canada, Aug. 1978, pp. 209–235. Russell und Bernstein als sozialistische Berufungsinstanzen (Gerhard Frick) [in]: NZZ, Zürich, 28/29. April 1979, p. 70.]

16439. — HEIMANN, HORST/MEYER, THOMAS, eds.: *Bernstein und der demokratische Sozialismus.* Bericht über den wissenschaftlichen Kongress 'Die historische Leistung und aktuelle Bedeutung Eduard Bernsteins'. Berlin/East: Dietz, 1978. 578 pp. (Internat. Bibliothek, Bd. 114.) [Contains 25 essays and contributions to the discussion.]

16440. — MORGAN, DAVID W.: *The father of Revisionism revisited: Eduard Bernstein.* [In]: The Journal of Modern History, Vol. 51, No. 3, Chicago, Sept. 1979. Pp. 525–532. [Review article of several books on Bernstein, see No. 13755/YB XXII, Nos. 14504 & 14551/YB XXIII.]

— WISTRICH, ROBERT: *Eduard Bernstein and the Jewish problem.* [See No. 16295.]

16441. BETHE, HANS ALBRECHT. BERNSTEIN, JEREMY: *Profiles. Master of his trade: Hans Albrecht Bethe.* Part 1–3. [In]: The New Yorker, Dec. 3, 1979 (pp.50–107); Dec. 10, 1979 (pp. 52–108); Dec. 17, 1979 (pp. 50–99). [H. A. Bethe, born July 2, 1906 in Strassburg, physicist, emigrated to the U.S.A., during the Second World War director at the Atomic Research Center, Los Alamos.]

16442. BETTAUER, HUGO. HALL, MURRAY G.: *Der Fall Bettauer.* Wien: Löcker, 1978. [Cf.: Der Fall Hugo Bettauer, Zeichen an der Wand (Alice Schwarz) [in]: Neue Jüd. Nachrichten, Nr. 14/15, München, 11. April 1979, p. 5. H.B., 1872–1925, Viennese journalist and novelist, worked for one of the Ullstein's newspapers in Berlin, imprisoned several times for offending Emperor William II.]

16443. BETTELHEIM, BRUNO: *Surviving and other essays.* London: Thames and Hudson; New York: Knopf, 1979. 432 pp. [Cf.: After the Holocaust (David Biale) [in]: Commentary, Vol. 66, No. 4, New York, Oct. 1979, pp. 79–82. Wise man from the East (Philip Toynbee) [in]: The Observer, London, 5. Aug. 1979, p. 36. For German edn. under the title: 'Der Weg aus dem Labyrinth' see No. 15438/YB XXIV.]

16444. BLOCH, ERNST. BLOCH, ERNST: *Revolution der Utopie.* Texte von und über Ernst Bloch, hrsg. von Helmut Reinicke. Frankfurt a. Main: Campus Verl., 1979. 114 pp. (Schriftenreihe des Instituts für sozialhistorische Forschungen, Frankfurt a. Main.)

16445. — GRADL, FELIX: *Ein Atheist liest die Bibel. Ernst Bloch und das Alte Testament.* Frankfurt a. Main: Lang, 1979. 288 pp. (Beiträge zur biblischen Exegese u. Theologie, Bd. 12.) Zugl.: Salzburg, Univ., Theol. Diss. 1977.

16446. — RABINBACH, ANSON: *Unclaimed heritage. Ernst Bloch's 'Heritage of our times' and the theory of Fascism.* [In]: New German Critique, No. 4, Milwaukee, Univ. of Wisconsin, Spring, 1977. Pp. 5–21.

16447. — SCHELSKY, HELMUT: *Die Hoffnung Blochs. Kritik der marxistischen Existenzphilosophie eines Jugendbewegten.* Stuttgart: Klett-Cotta, 1979. 234 pp.

16448. — WITSCHEL, GÜNTER: *Ernst Bloch. Literatur und Sprache, Theorie und Leistung.* Bonn: Bouvier, 1978. 152 pp., bibl. (pp. 151–152). (Akademische Vorträge u. Abhandlungen, H. 44.)

16449. BORCHARDT, RUDOLF. BORCHARDT, RUDOLF: *Prosa V. Reden und Schriften zur Politik.* Hrsg. von Marie Luise Borchardt u. Ulrich Ott unter Beratung von Ernst Zinn. Stuttgart: Klett-Cotta, 1979. 606 pp. (Borchardt, Rudolf: Gesammelte Werke in Einzelbänden.) [Corrected entry of No. 14562/YB XXIII. Cf.: Damit wir bildbarer Stoff werden. R. Borchardts politische Schriften (Hans Christian Kosler) [in]: SZ, München, 24./25. Dez. 1979, p. 50.]

16450. BOUVIER. Bookstore and Publishing House in Bonn. GRUNDMANN, HERBERT, ed.: *Bouvier 1828–1978.* Bonn: Bouvier, 1978. 342 pp., illus. [Founded by Max Cohen and Aimé Henry. After 1933 the name of the firm 'Friedrich Cohen' was changed by Friedrich's widow Hedwig, née Bouvier. See also: 150 Jahre Bouvier in Bonn (Gerd Schulz) [in]: Börsenblatt für den Dt. Buchhandel, Nr. 94, Frankfurt a. Main, 24 Nov. 1978, pp. 2407–2409, ports.]

16451. BRAUN, HEINRICH. OSCHILEWSKI, WALTHER G.: *Ein grosses Menschenleben für den Sozialismus. Erinnerung an Heinrich Braun (1854–1927).* [In]: Die Neue Gesellschaft, Jg. 26, Nr. 12, Bonn, Dez. 1979. Pp. 1146–1149.

16452. BROCH, HERMANN. BROCH, HERMANN: *Massenwahntheorie. Beitrag zu einer Psychologie der*

Politik. Frankfurt a. Main: Suhrkamp, 1979. 582 pp., bibl. (Broch, Hermann: Kommentierte Werkausgabe, Bd. 12.) (Suhrkamp Taschenbücher, 502.) [Hitherto publ. vols. 1–5, 9–12. See also No. 15450/YB XXIV.]

16453. — STRELKA, JOSEPH, ed.: *Broch heute*. Bern: Francke, 1978. 154 pp., bibl. references. [Cont.: Broch heute (J. Strelka). 'Die Schlafwandler' als Zeitroman (H. Steinecke). Broch oder die Redlichkeit (F. Torberg). H. Brochs 'Die Verzauberung' im Kontext von Faschismuskritik u. Exilroman (P. M. Lützeler). H. Broch als Volkserzieher (W. Vordtriede). H. Broch: 'Massenpsychologie' u. 'Politik' (H. Pross). Gescheiterte Liebhaber. Erotismus u. Sexualneurose im Werk H. Brochs (W. Rothe). Zwischen Satire u. Pathos. Die Möglichkeiten des Erzählers H. Broch in den 'Schuldlosen' (M. Durzak).]

16454. — WINKEL, MARIA ANGELA: *Denkerische und dichterische Erkenntnis als Einheit. Eine Untersuchung zur Symbolik in Hermann Brochs 'Tod des Vergil'*. Frankfurt a. Main: Lang, 1979. 450 pp. (Europäische Hochschulschriften: Reihe 1, Dt. Literatur u. Germanistik, Bd. 319.)

16455. BROD, MAX. BROD, MAX: *Der Prager Kreis*. Mit einem Nachwort von Peter Demetz. Frankfurt a. Main: Suhrkamp, 1979. 253 pp., illus., bibl. (pp. 247–249). (Suhrkamp-Taschenbücher, 547.)

16456. — BROD, MAX: *Rëubeni, Fürst der Juden*. Ein Renaissance-Roman. Deutsche Neuausgabe. (Nachwort von Nahum Glatzer.) Frankfurt a. Main: S. Fischer, 1979. 430 pp. [Cf.: Mit dem guten und dem bösen Trieb (Egon Schwarz) [in]: FAZ, Frankfurt a. Main, 12. Dez. 1979, p. 24.]

16457. — BROD, MAX: *Tycho Brahes Weg zu Gott*. (Nachwort von Stefan Zweig.) Frankfurt a. Main: Suhrkamp, 1979. (Suhrkamp Taschenbuch, 490.) [Cf.: Unsterblicher Max Brod (Schalom Ben-Chorin) [in]: 'Allgemeine', Düsseldorf, 21. Sept. 1979, p. 15.]

16458. — PAZI, MARGARITA: *Max Brod, Willensfreiheit und ethische Tat*. [In]: Neue Rundschau, Jg. 90, H. 1, Frankfurt a. Main, 1979. Pp. 165–167. [See also: Max Brod in memoriam (Margarita Pazi) [in]: Emuna/Israel-Forum, H. 1/2, Rothenburg o. d. Tauber, 1979, pp. 29–32.]

16459. CANETTI, ELIAS. BARNOUW, DAGMAR: *Elias Canetti*. Stuttgart: Metzler, 1979. XI, 138 pp., bibl. (pp. 115–136). (Sammlung Metzler, M 180: Abt. D, Literaturgeschichte.) [Cf.: Review [in]: NZZ, Zürich, 8./9. Sept. 1979, p. 39.]

16460. CASSIRER, ERNST: *Symbol, myth and culture*. Essays and lectures, 1935–1945. Ed. by Donald Philip Verene. New Haven: Yale Univ. Press, 1979. 304 pp. [See also: Kultur und Symboltheorie. Rückblick auf Ernst Cassirers 'Philosophie der symbolischen Formen' (Reto Luzius Fetz) [in]: NZZ, Zürich, 8./9. Dez. 1979, p. 70.]

16461. CELAN, PAUL. *Paul Celan*. [Gedichte.] (Auswahl dieses Heftes: Richard Pietrass.) Berlin: Verlag Neues Leben, 1979. 31 pp., port. (Poesiealbum, 137.)

16462. — CHALFEN, ISRAEL: *Paul Celan. Eine Biographie seiner Jugend*. Frankfurt a. Main: Insel, 1979. 188 pp., geneal. tabs., map, illus., ports., bibl. notes (pp. 159–176). [Cf.: Spuren P. Celans (Herbert Freeden) [in]: 'Allgemeine', Düsseldorf, 20. Juli 1979, p. 7. Wegmarken, eine Celan-Biographie [in]: NZZ, Zürich, 20./21. April 1979, p. 65, port. Corrected entry of No. 15459/YB XXIV.]

16463. — JACKSON, J. E.: *Le judaïsme divisé de Paul Celan*. [In]: Colloque d'Intellectuels juifs de langue française. 17. Paris: Presses Universitaires de France, 1977. VI, 215 pp.

16464. — KRAMER, HEINZ MICHAEL: *Eine Sprache des Leidens. Zur Lyrik von Paul Celan*. München: Kaiser; Mainz: Grünewald, 1979. 280 pp. (Gesellschaft u. Theologie, Abt. Praxis der Kirche, Nr. 31.)

16465. — SCHULZ, GEORG-MICHAEL: *Individuation und Austauschbarkeit. Zu Paul Celans 'Gespräch im Gebirg'*. [In]: Deutsche Vierteljahrsschrift für Literaturwissenschaft u. Geistesgeschichte, Jg. 53, H. 3, Stuttgart, Okt. 1979. Pp. 463–477.

16466. CHAIN, ERNST, Sir. *Obituaries* (June 19, 1906 Berlin – Aug. 12, 1979 Ireland): [In]: AJR Information, London, Oct. 1979, p. 10. 'Sir Emigrant' (E. G. Lowenthal) [in]: MB, Nr. 41, Tel Aviv, 2. Nov. 1979, p. 8. Sir Ernst Chain, Professor für Biochemie, starb 73jährig [in]: Das Neue Israel, Jg. 32, H. 3, Zürich, Sept. 1979, pp. 141 & 143. Leserzuschrift (Wladimir Vogel) [in]: Das Neue Israel, Jg. 32, H. 5, Zürich, Nov. 1979, p. 263. Sir Ernst Chain, Nobel Prize for penicillin [in]: The Times, London, Nov. 16, 1979, p. VIII of Obituaries Supplement. [E. Ch., biochemist, emigrated to England in 1933, shared a Nobel Prize with Alexander Fleming and Howard Florey in 1945 for work which led to the introduction of penicillin into medicine. He was knighted in 1969.]

16467. COURANT, RICHARD. REID, CONSTANCE: *Richard Courant 1888–1972. Der Mathematiker als Zeitgenosse*. Aus dem Engl. übers. von J. Zehnder. Berlin: Springer, 1979. 420 pp., 40 illus., ports. [Orig. title: 'Courant in Göttingen and New York', 1976, see No. 14574/YB XXIII.]

16468. DESSAU, PAUL: *Leonce und Lena*. [Cf.: Eine 'Antwort' auf Büchners Verzweiflung. Paul Dessaus Alterswerk 'Leonce und Lena' Uraufführung an der Deutschen Staatsoper Berlin (Claus-Henning Bachmann) [in]: Aufbau, New York, Dec. 14, 1979, p. 20. Parabel von Hunger und Ruhm. P. Dessaus Oper 'Leonce und Lena' in Ostberlin uraufgeführt (Wolfgang Schreiber) [in]: SZ, München, 26. Nov. 1979, p. 15, illus. P. Dessau, Dec. 19, 1894 Hamburg – June 1979 Königswusterhausen/GDR. *Obituaries* [in]: MB, Tel Aviv, 10. Aug. 1979, p. 5. Viel geehrt u. immer umstritten. Zum Tod von Paul Dessau (Jens Wendland) [in]: SZ, München, 30. Juni/1. Juli, 1979.]

16469. DÖBLIN, ALFRED. DÖBLIN, ALFRED: *Erzählungen aus fünf Jahrzehnten*. (Hrsg. von Edgar Pässler.) Olten: Walter, 1979. 484 pp. (Döblin, Alfred: Ausgewählte Werke in Einzelbänden.) [Incl. also: 'Die Ermordung einer Butterblume'.]

16470. — DÖBLIN, ALFRED: *Hamlet oder Die lange Nacht nimmt ein Ende*. Roman. München: Dt.-Taschenbuch-Verl., 1979. 578 pp. (dtv, 1484.) [Döblin's last novel, finished 1946.]

16471. — BEST, OTTO F.: *Zwischen Orient und Okzident: Döblin und Spinoza*. Einige Anmerkungen zur Problematik des offenen Schlusses von 'Berlin Alexanderplatz'. [In]: Colloquia Germanica, Bd. 12, H. 1/2, Bern, 1979. Pp. 94–105, notes (pp. 102–105).

16472. — DSCHENG, FANG-HSIUNG: *Alfred Döblins Roman 'Die drei Sprünge des Wang-lun' als Spiegel des Interesses moderner deutscher Autoren an China*. Frankfurt a. Main: Lang, 1979. 272 pp. (Europäische Hochschulschriften: Reihe 1, Dt. Literatur u. Germanistik, Bd. 305.) Zugl.: München, Univ., Phil. Diss., 1978.

16473. — KEIM, ANTON MARIA: *Zwischen 'Alexanderplatz' und Philippsschanze. Mainzer Erinnerungen an Alfred Döblin*. [In]: Aufbau, New York, Aug. 10, 1979. P. 24. [See also: Die Brüder Alfred und Hugo Döblin (Margo H. Wolff) [in]: Aufbau, New York, Oct. 5, 1979, p. 23, port. Literaturskandal um Döblin. Ein Sohn von Alfred Döblin verklagt den Literaturwissenschaftler Robert Minder: Pornoschnüffler oder werkgerechter Interpret? (Fritz J. Raddatz) [in]: Die Zeit, Hamburg, 12. Okt. 1979, p. 45, port., facsims.]

16474. — SCHILLER, DIETER: *Gemeinsamkeiten und Differenzen bei der Sammlung der Kräfte. Zu Döblins Pariser Rede im Januar 1938 und ihrem literaturpolitischen Kontext*. [In]: Sammlung, Jahrbuch für antifaschistische Literatur u. Kunst, Bd. 2, Frankfurt a. Main, 1979. Pp. 16–28.

16475. — THOMANN TEWARSON, HEIDI: *Alfred Döblin. Grundlagen seiner Ästhetik und ihre Entwicklung 1900–1933*. Bern: Lang, 1979. 133 pp., bibl. (pp. 119–126), (Europäische Hochschulschriften: Reihe 1, Dt. Sprache u. Literatur, Bd. 286.)

16476. — WICHERT, ADALBERT: *Alfred Döblins historisches Denken*. Zur Poetik des modernen Geschichtsromans. Mit einem Geleitwort von Walter Müller-Seidel. Stuttgart: Metzler, 1978. XIV, 274 pp. (Germanistische Abhandlungen, 48.) Zugl.: München, Univ., Phil. Diss., 1976.

16477. DOLBIN, BENEDIKT FRED. *Benedikt Fred Dolbin. Kopf-Stenogramme für die Berliner Presse 1926–1933*. [Katalog der Ausstellung im] Historischen Museum der Stadt Heilbronn 9. März bis 20. Mai 1979. (Hrsg.: Andreas Pfeiffer.) Heilbronn: Städt. Museen, 1979. 272 pp., 132 reproductions. (Heilbronner Museumskatalog, Nr. 8.) [Incl.: Notizen über den grossen Kopfjäger (Will Schaber, pp. 10–16). Dolbin als Zeichner (Andreas Pfeiffer, pp. 20–26). Dolbin in eigener Sache (pp. 28–31).]

16478. DOMIN, HILDE. DOMIN, HILDE: *Abel steh auf. Gedichte, Prosa, Theorie*. Hrsg. von Gerhard Mahr. Stuttgart: Reclam, 1979. 96 pp. (Universal-Bibliothek, Nr. 9955.)

16479. — STERN, DAGMAR C.: *Hilde Domin. From exile to ideal*. Bern: Lang, 1979. 100 pp. (Germanic studies in America, No. 33.) Zugl.: Indiana Univ., Phil. Diss., 1977.

16480. EHRENSTEIN, ALBERT: *Briefe an Gott*. Hrsg. u. mit einem Nachwort versehen von Jörg Drews. Frankfurt a. Main: Suhrkamp, 1979. 123 pp. (Bibliothek Suhrkamp, Bd. 642.)

16481. EHRLICH, PAUL. BÄUMLER, ERNST: *Gefärbte Spur zur Chemotherapie. Paul Ehrlichs Lebenswerk eröffnet ein neues Zeitalter der Medizin*. [In]: Höchst heute, 73, Frankfurt a. Main, 1979. Pp. 14–17, illus., facsim., ports.

16482. — BÄUMLER, ERNST: *Paul Ehrlich, Forscher für das Leben*. Frankfurt a. Main: Societäts-Verl., 1979. 370 pp., 48 plates (illus., facsims., ports.), bibl. (pp. 347–361). [Cf.: Paul Ehrlich, der vergessene Forscher. Ein Film [der Farbwerke Höchst in Frankfurt a. Main] u. eine Biographie rufen Erinnerungen wach (Stefanie Zweig) [in]: 'Allgemeine', Düsseldorf, 26. Okt. 1979, p. 11. Schwierige Koryphäen (Heinrich Sattler) [in]: FAZ, Frankfurt a. Main, 9. Okt. 1979, p. L 23.]

16483. — Parnas, Joseph: *In memoriam: Dr. Paul Ehrlich 1854–1915.* Erinnerungen, gewidmet meinem Lehrer Ludwig Hirszfeld. [In]: Neue Jüd. Nachrichten, Nr. 7 & Nr. 19, München, 16. Febr. & 18. Mai 1979. P. 5, port.; pp. 4–5, illus. [See also: Benefactor to mankind. Paul Ehrlich anniversary [125th birthday] (Susanne Liebmann) [in]: AJR Information, London, Oct. 1979, p. 9.]

16484. EINSTEIN, ALBERT. Einstein, Albert: *An appeal by Einstein, Freud, Dubnow and other Jewish scholars to support YIVO.* Reprinted from News of the YIVO, No. 31, April 1930. [And]: *Brief von Albert Einstein an Simon Dubnow,* Berlin, 8. April 1929 [also in English and Yiddish translation]. [In]: News of the YIVO, No. 150, New York, Sept. 1979. Pp. 1–2, port., facsim. of letter (p. 3).

16485. — Einstein, Albert: *Aus meinen späten Jahren.* Stuttgart: Deutsche Verlags-Anstalt, 1979. 271 pp. [Essays, some dealing with Jews and Judaism.]

16486. — Einstein, Albert: *Why war? The correspondence between Albert Einstein and Sigmund Freud.* (Transl. by Fritz and Anna Moellenhoff.) Chicago: Chicago Institute for Psychoanalysis, 1978. [15] pp., facsims. [See also: Albert Einstein, man of peace (Yehuda Blum) [in]: ADL Bulletin (Anti-Defamation League), Vol. 36, No. 4/5, New York, Summer 1979, p. 7.

16487. — Aichelburg, Peter C./Sexl, Roman U., eds.: *Albert Einstein. His influence on physics, philosophy and politics.* With contributions by Peter G. Bergmann [et al.]. Braunschweig: Vieweg, 1979. XV, 220 pp., illus., graphs., ports., bibl. references. [Publ. also in German under the title]: *Albert Einstein. Sein Einfluss auf Physik, Philosophie und Politik.* Braunschweig: Vieweg, 1979. XV, 231 pp.

16488. — *Centenary of Albert Einstein's birthday (March 14, 1879 Ulm).* Selection of tributes and of articles: A. Einstein. Centenary of unique man (Fritz Friedlaender) [in]: AJR Information, London, March 1979, p. 5. Einstein, der Mensch und der Jude (Hans Lamm) [in]: 'Allgemeine', Düsseldorf, 9. März 1979, pp. 1–2, ports., illus. on p. 8. The Zionist Einstein at 50 (Harry Torczyner) [in]: The American Zionist, Vol. 69, No. 4, New York, April/May 1979, pp. 13–14 [Einstein's participation in the 16th Zionist Congress 1929]. The Einstein revolution (Frederic Golden) [in]: Dialogue, Vol. 12, No. 2, Washington, 1979, pp. 3–13. Memories of Einstein (Esther Salaman) [in]: Encounter, Vol. 52, No. 4, London, April 1979, pp. 19–23. A. Einstein in Prague (József Illy) [in]: Isis, 70 (No. 251), Brüssel, 1979, pp. 76–84, bibl. footnotes. A. Einstein als Jude und Zionist (Heinz Badt) [in]: Isr. Wochenblatt, No. 10, Zürich, 9. März 1979, pp. 21–23. Einstein on Zionism (Kurt Blumenfeld) [in]: Jewish Frontier, Vol. 46, No. 3, New York, March 1979, pp. 10–11 [reprint of an article orig. publ. in June 1939 in Jewish Frontier in honour of Einstein's 60th birthday]. Einstein the Zionist (Yosef Gotlieb) [in]: Midstream, Vol. 25, No. 6, New York, June/July 1979, pp. 43–48. A. Einstein zur 100. Wiederkehr seines Geburtstages (Rudolf Lappe) [in]: Nachrichtenblatt der Jüd. Gemeinde von Berlin u. des Verbandes der Jüd. Gemeinden in der DDR, Dresden–Berlin, März 1979, pp. 3–6. Einstein und Jerusalem (E. Gottgetreu) [in]: Das Neue Israel, Jg. 31, H. 10, Zürich, April 1979, pp. 503–505. Zur Erinnerung an A. Einstein (Stefan Schwarz) [in]: Neue Jüd. Nachrichten, Nr. 11, München, 16. März 1979, p. 3. Einstein and Israel (Isaiah Berlin) [in]: The New York Review of Books, Nov. 8, 1979, pp. 13–18. Ein Monument für A. Einstein. Einige Überlegungen über den Nachruhm des Naturforschers (Erwin Chargaff) [in]: Scheidewege, Jg. 9, H. 3, Stuttgart, 1979, pp. 359–376. Warten auf die Gesammelten Werke. Zum 100. Geburtstag Einsteins: viele Bücher, aber das Bedürfnis nach Originaltexten bleibt (Albrecht Fölsing) [in]: Die Zeit, Hamburg, 7. Dez. 1979, p. Literatur 11.

16489. — Clark, Ronald W.: *Einstein. The life and times.* Introduction by Sir Bernard Lovell. London: Hodder and Stoughton, 1979. 672 pp., illus., bibl. [1st edn. 1973. Publ. also in German under the title]: *Albert Einstein. Leben und Werk.* Aus dem Engl. von Monika Raeithel-Thaler. 3. Aufl. München: Heyne, 1979. XV, 507 pp., illus., ports., bibl. (pp. 484–498). (Heyne-Biographien, 30.)

16490. — Dukas, Helen/Hoffmann, Banesh, eds.: *Albert Einstein, the human side. New glimpses from his archives.* Princeton, N.J.: Princeton Univ. Press, 1979. VIII, 167 pp., port.

16491. — Frank, Philipp: *Albert Einstein. Sein Leben und seine Zeit.* [Mit einem Vorwort von Albert Einstein.] Braunschweig: Vieweg, 1979. 468 pp., port.

16492. — French, A[nthony] P[hilip], ed.: *Einstein. A centenary volume.* Cambridge, Mass.: Harvard Univ. Press; London: Heinemann, 1979. XX, 332 pp., illus., ports., diagrs., facsims., bibl. (p. 323).

16493. — HEBREW UNIVERSITY, JEWISH NATIONAL AND UNIVERSITY LIBRARY, Jerusalem: *Einstein, 1879–1979. Exhibition.* (Catalogue and exhibition: Yehuda Elkana, Adi Ophir.) Jerusalem: Jewish National and University Library, 1979. 59, 73 pp., illus., ports., facsims.
16494. — INTERLIBRUM BUCHANTIQUARIAT: *Albert Einstein. An almost complete collection of his publications and two original manuscripts.* (Catalogue 278, compiled by Walter Alicke.) Vaduz/Liechtenstein (Schloss-Str. 6): Interlibrum, 1979. 1 vol. (unpaged, 356 entries), ports., facsims.
16495. — KIRSTEN, CHRISTA/TREDER, HANS-JÜRGEN, eds.: *Albert Einstein in Berlin 1913–1933.* 1–2. Berlin/East: Akademie-Verl., 1979. 2 vols. (287 pp., illus., port., facsims.; 295 pp.) (Studien zur Geschichte der Akademie der Wissenschaften der DDR, Bd. 6–7.) [Cont.: Teil 1: Darstellung u. Dokumente. Teil 2: Spezialinventar: Regesten der Einstein-Dokumente in den Archiven der DDR; Regesten von Sitzungsprotokollen der Berliner Akademie der Wissenschaften; Verzeichnis der Akademie-Schriften u. der Berliner Patentschriften von A. Einstein (pp. 287–291).]
16496. — LEO BAECK INSTITUTE, New York: *Albert Einstein, humanist and Jew.* [Catalog of] A centennial exhibition, April 1st to May 31st 1979 at the Leo Baeck Institute, New York. With the cooperation of the Estate of Albert Einstein and the support of the New York Council for the Humanities. New York: Leo Baeck Institute, 1979. 11 pp., cover port., ports., facsims. [Cf.: Die Einstein-Ausstellung in New York. Streiflichter aus einer Zwischenbilanz [in]: Aufbau, New York, June 15, 1979, p. 11.]
16497. — NATIONAL MUSEUM OF HISTORY AND TECHNOLOGY: *Einstein. A centenary exhibition (March 1979–March 1980).* Publ. for the National Museum of History and Technology. Washington: Smithsonian Institution Press, 1979. 48 pp., illus., ports., facsims.
16498. — SPECKER, HANS EUGEN, ed.: *Einstein und Ulm.* Festakt, Schülerwettbewerb und Ausstellung zum 100. Geburtstag von Albert Einstein. Ulm: Stadtarchiv; Stuttgart: Kohlhammer, 1979. 135 pp., illus., ports., facsims., geneal. table, bibl. (p. 133). (Forschungen zur Geschichte der Stadt Ulm: Reihe Dokumentation, Bd. 1.) [Incl.: 'Die jüdische Gemeinde in Ulm', pp. 49–52.]
16499. EISNER, KURT. EISNER, FREYA: *Kurt Eisner. Die Politik des libertären Sozialismus.* Frankfurt a. Main: Suhrkamp, 1979. 246 pp., bibl. (pp. 240–244). (Edition Suhrkamp, 422.) [Cf.: Der einsame Sozialist, verachtet, verkannt: Kurt Eisner (Ossip K. Flechtheim) [in]: Die Zeit, Hamburg, 26. Okt. 1979, p. 60.]
16500. ETTINGHAUSEN, RICHARD: *Arabische Malerei.* Stuttgart: Skira-Klett-Cotta, 1979. 211 pp., illus., bibl. (pp. 193–198). (Die Kunstschätze Asiens.) [R.E., Febr. 5, 1906 Frankfurt a. Main–April 1, 1979 New York, art historian, expert for Islamic art, emigrated to the U.S.A. in 1934, from 1958–1967 chief curator at the Free Gallery of Art, Smithsonian Institute, advisory boardmember of the Metropolitan Museum New York.]
16501. FERENCZI, SÁNDOR: *Zur Erkenntnis des Unbewussten und andere Schriften zur Psychoanalyse.* Hrsg. u. eingeleitet von Helmut Dahmer. München: Kindler, 1978. (Geist u. Psyche, 2194.) [Cf.: Der Mensch aus dem Meer (Caroline Neubaur) [in]: FAZ, Frankfurt a. Main, 13. Nov. 1979, p. L 10. S.F., orig. Fränkel, 1873 Budapest–1933 Budapest.]
16502. FEUCHTWANGER, LION. FEUCHTWANGER, LION: *Exil. Roman.* Frankfurt a. Main: Fischer, 1979. 790 pp. (Fischer-Taschenbücher, 2128.)
16503. — FEUCHTWANGER, LION: *Die Jüdin von Toledo. Roman.* Berlin/East: Aufbau, 1979. 480 pp. (Taschenbibliothek der Weltliteratur.)
16504. — FISCHER, LUDWIG MAXIMILIAN: *Vernunft und Fortschritt. Geschichte und Fiktionalität im historischen Roman Lion Feuchtwangers, dargestellt am Beispiel Goya.* Königstein/Ts.: Forum Academicum, 1979. 247 pp., bibl. (pp. 239–248). (Hochschulschriften, Literaturwissenschaft, Bd. 45.)
16505. — MOREHOUSE, KEITH HERBERT: *Lion Feuchtwanger. The theory and practise of historical 'fabulation'.* Boston College, Phil. Diss., 1977. 262 pp.
16506. FRANK, BRUNO. FRANK, BRUNO: *Die Monduhr. Erzählungen.* Hrsg. und mit einem Nachwort von Martin Gregor-Dellin. München: Nymphenburger Verl., 1979. 307 pp.
16507. — FRANK, BRUNO: *Die Tochter. Roman.* Mit einem Nachwort von Klaus Hermsdorf. Berlin/East: Der Morgen, 1979. 284 pp. [Incl. details about Frank's family-history, his wife Liesl and his mother-in-law Fritzi Massary.]
16508. — HOYT, WALTER CARL-ALEXANDER: *Conflict in change. A study of the prose-fiction of Bruno Frank.* Rutgers Univ., The State Univ. of New Jersey, Phil. Diss., 1978. 203 pp.
16509. FRANK, RUDOLF. ISOLANI, GERTRUD: *Zum Tode von Rudolf Frank.* [In]: 'Allgemeine', Düsseldorf, 7. Dez. 1979. P. 7 [and in]: Isr. Wochenblatt, Nr. 44, Zürich, 2. Nov. 1979, p.

33. [R.F., Sept. 16, 1886 Mainz–Oct. 25, 1979 Basle, writer, theatre-producer, emigrated to Switzerland in 1938.]

16510. FRANKL, VIKTOR E[MIL]: *Der Mensch vor der Frage nach dem Sinn.* Eine Auswahl aus dem Gesamtwerk. München: Piper, 1979. IX, 312 pp., bibl. (pp. 283–312). [V.E.F., born 1905, psychiatrist, professor in Vienna.]

16511. FRANZOS, KARL EMIL: *Der Pojaz. Eine Geschichte aus dem Osten.* Neugesetzt nach der Aufl. Stuttgart, Cotta 1906. Königstein/Ts.: Athenäum, 1979. 384 pp. [See also: Tradition and modernity in the German ghetto novel. Leopold Kompert and Karl Emil Franzos (Lothar Kahn) [in]: Judaism, Vol. 28, No. 1, New York, Winter 1979, pp. 31–41. L. Kompert, 1822 Bohemia–1886 Vienna. K. E. Franzos, 1848 Galicia–1904 Berlin.]

16512. FREUD, ANNA. PETERS, UWE HENRIK: *Anna Freud. Ein Leben für das Kind.* München: Kindler, 1979. 390 pp., illus., ports.

16513. FREUD, SIGMUND. FREUD, SIGMUND: *Der Mann Moses und die monotheistische Religion.* Neuaufl. Frankfurt a. Main: Suhrkamp, 1979. 174 pp. (Bibliothek Suhrkamp, 131.)

—— — FREUD, SIGMUND: *Why war? The correspondence between Albert Einstein and Sigmund Freud.* [See No. 16486.]

16514. — BATTKE, MARION: *Das Böse bei Sigmund Freud und C. G. Jung.* 1. Aufl. Düsseldorf: Patmos-Verl., 1978. 244 pp. (Patmos-Paperbacks.) Zugl.: Tübingen, Phil. Diss., 1978.

16515. — BOYER, JOHN W.: *Freud, marriage, and late Viennese liberalism.* A commentary from 1905. [In]: Journal of Modern History, Vol. 50, No. 1, Chicago, March 1978. Pp. 72–102.

16516. — EISSLER, K[URT] R.: *Freud und Wagner-Jauregg vor der Kommission zur Erhebung militärischer Pflichtverletzungen.* Wien: Löcker, 1979. 334 pp. (Veröffentlichung des Ludwig-Boltzmann-Institutes für Geschichte der Gesellschaftswissenschaften.)

—— — FROMM, ERICH: *Sigmund Freuds Psychoanalyse, Grösse und Grenzen.* [See No. 16532.]

16517. — HAYMOND, ROBERT: *Roots in the Shtetl. Modern Western thought and the case of Sigmund Freud.* [In]: Journal of Psychology and Judaism, Vol. 3, No. 4, Ottawa, Summer 1979. Pp. 235–267.

16518. — *Jahrbuch der Psychoanalyse.* Beiträge zur Theorie und Praxis. Bd. 11. Bern: H. Huber, 1979. 183 pp. [Incl.: Ansprache zur Denkmalenthüllung am 6. Mai 1977 (Anna Freud). Bericht über die sich in den Vereinigten Staaten befindenden Bücher aus S. Freuds Bibliothek (K. R. Eissler). Zwei Beiträge zur Biographie S. Freuds: S. Freud im Gymnasium [and]: S. Freud und B'nai B'rith (Hugo Knoepfmacher, pp. 51–72 [S. Freud and the B'nai B'rith also in: Journal of the American Psychoanalytic Association, Vol. 27, No. 2, New York, 1979, pp. 441–449, bibl.]) Zeitgenosse Sigmund Freud. Bericht über drei Freud-Korrespondenzen im Archiv des Leo Baeck Instituts, New York (Fred Grubel, pp. 73–80) [and]: Kommentar zu 'Zeitgenosse Freud' (Erich Simenauer, pp. 166–170).]

16519. — KRÜLL, MARIANNE: *Freud und sein Vater. Die Entstehung der Psychoanalyse und Freuds ungelöste Vaterbindung.* Mit einem Geleitwort von Helm Stierlin. München: Beck, 1979. 344 pp., illus., bibl. (pp. 319–336).

—— — MARCUSE, HERBERT: *Triebstruktur und Gesellschaft. Ein philosophischer Beitrag zu Sigmund Freud.* [See No. 16632.]

16520. — ROBERT, MARTHE: *Sigmund Freud zwischen Moses und Ödipus. Die jüdischen Wurzeln der Psychoanalyse.* Aus dem Franz. übers. von Hans Krieger. Frankfurt a. Main: Ullstein, 1977. 192 pp. (Ullstein-Buch, Nr. 3393.) [Orig. title: 'D'Oedipe à Moise', see No. 13041/YB XXI. For Engl. ed. see No. 14604/YB XXIII.]

16521. — *Sigmund Freud 1856–1939. Forty years after.* London: Goethe Institute, 1979. 60 pp., 16 pp. illus., ports., facsims., bibl. (p. 59). [Catalogue of an exhibition held at the Goethe Institute in London to commemorate the 40. anniversary of Freud's death and made possible by the Goethe Institute, Sigmund Freud Copyrights and the European Literature Music and Poetry Association. With a foreword by Clifford Simmons.]

16522. — SULLOWAY, FRANK J.: *Freud, biologist of the mind. Beyond the psychoanalytic legend.* New York: Basic Books, 1979. 612 pp. [Cf.: Was Freud a crypto-biologist? (Richard Wollheim) [in]: The New York Review of Books, Nov. 8, 1979, pp. 25–28. Freud and the myth of the leader (George Steiner) [in]: The Sunday Times, London, 25 Nov. 1979.]

16523. — WEBER, SAMUEL: *Freud-Legende. Drei Studien zum psychoanalytischen Denken.* Olten: Walter, 1979. 211 pp.

16524. FRIED, ERICH: *Liebesgedichte.* Berlin: Wagenbach, 1979. 102 pp. (Quartheft, 103.)

16525. FRIEDELL, EGON. PATTERSON, GORDON MARSHALL: *The misunderstood clown: Egon Friedell and his Vienna.* Los Angeles, Univ. of California, Phil. Diss., 1979. 292 pp.

16526. FRIEDENTHAL, RICHARD. FRIEDENTHAL, RICHARD: *Luther. Sein Leben und seine Zeit.* Neuausg., 5. Aufl. München: Piper, 1979. 680 pp., illus.
16527. — *Obituaries* (June 9, 1896 Munich–Oct. 19, 1979 Kiel): [In]: AJR Information, London, Dec. 1979, p. 8. Erster Herausgeber des Kleinen Knaur: Deutsch-britischer Schriftsteller R. Friedenthal starb [in]: 'Allgemeine', Düsseldorf, 2. Nov. 1979, p. 4. Abschied von R. Friedenthal [in]: Aufbau, New York, Oct. 26, 1979, p. 4. Ein kluger Biograph. Zum Tode R. Friedenthals (Werner Ross) [in]: SZ, München, 22. Okt. 1979, p. 28, port.
16528. FRIEDLÄNDER, LUDWIG: *Darstellungen aus der Sittengeschichte Roms in der Zeit von Augustus bis zum Ausgang der Antonine.* 10. Aufl. Neudr. der Ausg. Leipzig 1921–1923. Bd. 1–4. Aalen: Scientia, 1979. 4 vols., illus. [L.F., 1824 Königsberg–1909 Strassburg, historian.]
16529. FRIEDLÄNDER, MAX J./ROSENBERG, JAKOB: *Die Gemälde von Lucas Cranach.* (Hrsg. von Gary Schwartz.) 2. Aufl. Basel: Birkhäuser, 1979. 205, [362] pp.; 434,18 illus., bibl. (pp. 169–178). [M. J. Friedländer, June 5, 1867 Berlin–Oct. 10, 1958 Amsterdam. J. Rosenberg, born Sept. 5, 1893 in Berlin, since 1936 at Harvard University.]
16530. FROMM, ERICH. FROMM, ERICH: *Arbeiter und Angestellte am Vorabend des Dritten Reiches. Eine sozialpsychologische Untersuchung.* (Erarbeitet in den Jahren 1929/30. Bearb. u. hrsg. von Wolfgang Bonss.) Stuttgart: Deutsche Verlags-Anstalt, 1979. 230 pp.
16531. — FROMM, ERICH: *Die Seele des Menschen. Ihre Fähigkeit zum Guten und zum Bösen.* (Aus dem Amerikan. neu übers. von Liselotte u. Ernst Mickel.) Stuttgart: Deutsche Verlags-Anstalt, 1979. 170 pp., bibl. [Orig. title: 'The heart of man'. For previous German edn. see No. 7257/YB XIV.]
16532. — FROMM, ERICH: *Sigmund Freuds Psychoanalyse, Grösse und Grenzen.* (Aus dem Amerikan. übers. von Liselotte Mickel.) Stuttgart: Deutsche Verlags-Anstalt, 1979. 176 pp., bibl. (pp. 167–169). [The Nelly-Sachs-Prize was received by Erich Fromm on Dec. 9, 1979. Cf.: (E. G. Lowenthal) [in]: 'Allgemeine', Düsseldorf, 20. Juli 1979, p. 4 [and in]: Aufbau, New York, July 27, 1979, p. 4.]
16533. — FUNK, RAINER: *Mut zum Menschen. Erich Fromms Denken und Werk, seine humanistische Religion und Ethik.* Mit einem Nachwort von Erich Fromm. Stuttgart: Deutsche Verlags-Anstalt, 1978. 446 pp., bibl. (pp. 361–412). [See also: Erich Fromm, der Prophet des Untergangs. Ein Portrait [u. Interview] (Heinrich Jaenecke) [in]: Stern Magazin, H. Nr. 17, Hamburg, 19. April 1979, pp. 76–86, ports.] [E.F. died March 18, 1980, Locarno. See obits. [in] *The Times*, London, March 19, 1980 and [in] *The Jewish Chronicle*, London, March 21, 1980.]
16534. GOLL, IVAN/GOLL, CLAIRE: *Die Antirose.* Mit 11 Zeichnungen von Marc Chagall. München: Heyne, 1979. 124 pp., bibl. (pp. 117–119). (Heyne Lyrik, Nr. 17.) [First publ. in 1967, see No. 6878/YB XIII.]
16535. GOMBRICH, ERNST H. SAUERLÄNDER, WILLIBALD: *Warum Kunst eine Geschichte hat.* Zum 70. Geburtstag Ernst Gombrichs. [In]: SZ, München, 30. März 1979. [Sir E. H. Gombrich, born 1909 in Vienna, emigrated to London in 1935, director of the 'Warburg Institute'.]
16536. GOMPERZ, HEINRICH: *Die Lebensauffassung der griechischen Philosophen und das Ideal der inneren Freiheit.* Zwölf gemeinverständliche Vorlesungen. Mit Anhang zum Verständnis der Mystiker. Neudr. der Ausg. Jena u. Leipzig 1904. Aalen: Scientia, 1979. VIII, 322 pp. [H. G., 1873 Vienna–1942 Los Angeles.]
16537. GOMPERZ, THEODOR. *Festschrift Theodor Gomperz.* Dargebracht zum 70. Geburtstage am 29. März 1902 von Schülern, Freunden, Kollegen. Neudr. der Ausg. Wien 1902. Aalen: Scientia, 1979. 499 pp., illus. [Th.G., 1832 Brünn–1912 Baden near Vienna, philosopher and philologist.]
16538. GRAB, WALTER. *Revolution und Demokratie in Geschichte und Literatur. Festschrift für Walter Grab zum 60. Geburtstag.* Hrsg. von Julius H. Schoeps u. Imanuel Geiss. Duisburg: Walter Braun, 1979. 415 pp., port., bibl. W. Grab. (Duisburger Hochschulbeiträge, 12.) [Incl.: Abraham Jacoby und der 'Bund der Kommunisten' (Arno Herzig, pp. 277–306). Berthold Auerbach und seine revolutionäre und literarische Tätigkeit (Margarita Pazi, pp. 355–374).]
16539. GUMBEL, EMIL JULIUS: *Verschwörer. Zur Geschichte und Soziologie der deutschen nationalistischen Geheimbünde 1918–1924.* Mit einem Vorwort zur Neuaufl. von Karin Buselmeier u. 2 Dokumenten zum Fall Gumbel. Reprint [der Ausg.] Wien, Malik, 1924. Heidelberg: Verlag Das Wunderhorn, 1979. XXV, 224, 8 pp., bibl. (pp. 220–224). [E. J. G., 1891 Munich–1966 New York, mathematician, statistician, pacifist, dismissed from his university post at Heidelberg in 1932. Cf.: Mathematicians under Hitler (Max Pinl and Lux Furtmüller) [in]: LBI Year Book XVIII, London, 1973, pp. 132–164 passim.]

16540. GUMPLOWICZ, LUDWIG: *Grundriss der Soziologie.* Mit einem Vorwort von Franz Oppenheimer. Neudr. der Ausg. Innsbruck 1926. Aalen: Scientia, 1978. XXX, 269 pp. (Gumplowicz, Ludwig: Ausgewählte Werke, Bd. 2.) [L. G., 1838 Krakau–1909 Graz.]

16541. GURLAND, ARCADIUS R. L. DAHMER, HELMUT/EMIG, DIETER: *Arcadius R. L. Gurland. Ein Nachruf.* [In]: Internat. wissenschaftliche Korrespondenz zur Geschichte der deutschen Arbeiterbewegung, Jg. 15, H. 2, Berlin, Juni 1979. Pp. 187–188. [A. R. L. Gurland 1905–March 27, 1979, political scientist. In 1945 he wrote a critical analysis of Central-Verein policy in Germany for the Institute of Social Research, New York.]

16542. HAASE, HUGO. CALKINS, KENNETH R.: *Hugo Haase, democrat and revolutionary.* Durham, N.C.: Carolina Academic Press, 1979. X, 254 pp., bibl. (pp. 247–254). [For German edn., see No. 13837/YB XXII. H.H., 1863 Allenstein–1919 Berlin.]

16543. HAMBURGER, KÄTE: *Wahrheit und ästhetische Wahrheit.* Stuttgart: Klett-Cotta, 1979. 152 pp.

16544. HARDEN, MAXIMILIAN. GOEBEL, HANS JOACHIM: *Maximilian Harden als politischer Publizist im Ersten Weltkrieg.* Frankfurt a. Main: Lang, 1977. 406 pp., bibl. (pp. 393–406). (Europäische Hochschulschriften: Reihe 3, Geschichte u. ihre Hilfswissenschaften, Bd. 85.)

16545. HEINE, HEINRICH. HEINE, HEINRICH: *Deutschland, ein Wintermärchen.* Mit 60 Zeichnungen von H[anns] E. Köhler. Frankfurt a. Main: Societäts-Verl., 1979. 140 pp., illus.

16546. — HEINE, HEINRICH: *The Lazarus poems.* Transl. by Alistair Elliot. Chester Springs, Pa.: Carcanet Press, 1979. 79 pp.

16547. — HEINE, HEINRICH: *Säkularausgabe.* Werke, Briefwechsel, Lebenszeugnisse. Hrsg. von den Nationalen Forschungs- u. Gedenkstätten der Klassischen Dt. Literatur in Weimar u. dem Centre National de la Recherche Scientifique in Paris. Berlin/East: Akademie-Verl.; Paris: Editions du CNRS, 1972–1979 ff. [Survey of vols. publ. during 1978/1979; also short references to the vols. publ. in earlier years which were not listed in previous bibliographies for reason of space]: *Bd. 1: Gedichte.* Bearb.: Hans Böhm. 272 pp. 1979. *Bd. 2: Gedichte 1827–1844 und Versepen.* Bearb.: Irmgard Möller u. Hans Böhm. 384 pp. 1979. *Bd. 8: Über Deutschland, 1833–1836.* 1972. *Bd. 9: Prosa, 1836–1840.* Bearb.: Fritz Mende. 399 pp. 1979. *Bd. 10: Pariser Berichte, 1840–1848.* Bearb.: Lucienne Netter. 296 pp. 1979. *Bd. 11: Lutezia.* 1974. *Bd. 13: Poèmes et légendes.* Bearb.: Pierre Grappin. 456 pp. 1978. *Bd. 14: Tableaux de voyage.* Bearb.: Claude David. 320 pp. 1978. *Bd. 15: Tableaux de voyage. 2: Italie.* Bearb.: René Anglade. 230 pp. 1979. *Bd. 16: De l'Allemagne. 1.* Bearb.: Claude Pichois. 215 pp. 1978. *Bd. 19: Lutèce.* 1977. *Bd. 20: Briefe, 1815–1831.* 1970. *Bd. 20 K: Kommentar.* 1976. *Bd. 21: Briefe, 1831–1841.* 1970. *Bd. 21 K: Kommentar.* 1975. *Bd. 22: Briefe, 1842–1849.* 1972. *Bd. 22 K: Kommentar.* 1976. *Bd. 23: Briefe, 1850–1856.* 1972. *Bd. 23 K: Kommentar.* 1976. *Bd. 24: Briefe an Heine, 1823–1836.* 1974. *Bd. 24 K: Kommentar.* Bearb.: Renate Francke. 340 pp. 1978. *Bd. 25: Briefe an Heine, 1837–1841.* 1974. *Bd. 25 K: Kommentar.* Bearb.: Christa Stöcker. 298 pp. 1979. *Bd. 26: Briefe an Heine, 1842–1851.* 1975. *Bd. 26 K: Kommentar.* Bearb.: Christa Stöcker. 345 pp. 1979. *Bd. 27: Briefe an Heine, 1852–1856.* 1976. *Bd. 27 K: Kommentar.* Bearb.: Christa Stöcker. ca 400 pp. 1980.

16548. — ANGLADE, RENÉ: *Eine Begegnung, die nicht stattfand. Heines 'Der weisse Elefant'. Eine Interpretation.* [In]: Jahrbuch der Dt. Schillergesellschaft, Jg. 20, Stuttgart, 1976. Pp. 464–491, facsim., bibl. footnotes.

16549. — BELLER, JACOB: *Heinrich Heine, 1797–1856.* [In]: Midstream, Vol. 25, No. 4, New York, April 1979. Pp. 28–33.

16550. — *Heine-Jahrbuch 1979.* Jg. 18. Hrsg. von Joseph A. Kruse, Heinrich-Heine-Institut der Landeshauptstadt Düsseldorf. Hamburg: Hoffmann u. Campe, 1979. 291 pp., illus., ports., facsims., bibl. (pp. 259–274). (Heine-Jahrbuch. Begründet von Eberhard Galley. Hrsg. in Verbindung mit der Heinrich-Heine-Gesellschaft.) [Incl.: Heine und Kant (Rudolf Malter, pp. 35–64). Versuch über Heines 'Jehuda ben Halevy' (Ruth Wolf, pp. 84–98). Rollenspiel oder Ichbezogenheit? Zum Problem der Selbstdarstellung in Heines Werk (Michael Werner, pp. 99–117). Dichtung als Provokation. Heine u. seine Kritiker, 1821–1856 (Eberhard Galley, pp. 118–138). Liliencron u. Heine im Urteil von Karl Kraus (Uta Schaub, pp. 191–201). Heine-Literatur 1977/78 mit Nachträgen (Heike von Berkholz, pp. 259–274). See also: Das Heinrich-Heine-Archiv in Düsseldorf und seine Archivbestände (Joseph A. Kruse) [in]: Der Archivar, Siegburg, Nov. 1978, pp. 475–480.]

16551. — *Heinrich Heine und die Zeitgenossen. Geschichtliche und literarische Befunde.* Hrsg.: Akademie der Wissenschaften der DDR, Zentralinstitut für Literaturgeschichte, Centre National de la Recherche Scientifique, Centre des Manuscrits Modernes. Berlin/East: Aufbau, 1979. ca. 500 pp.

16552. — KÄFER, KARL-HEINZ: *Versöhnt ohne Opfer. Zum geschichtstheologischen Rahmen der Schriften Heinrich Heines 1824–1844.* Meisenheim am Glan: Hain, 1978. XI, 260 pp. (Hochschulschriften: Literaturwissenschaft, Bd. 36.) Zugl.: Hamburg, Univ., Sprachwiss. Diss., 1977.
16553. — KIRSCH, HANS-CHRISTIAN: *. . . und küsste des Scharfrichters Tochter. Heinrich Heines erste Liebe.* Frankfurt a. Main: Krüger, 1978. 277 pp. [Heine's love for Josefa Goch.]
16554. — KRÄMER, HELMUT: *Heinrich Heines Auseinandersetzung mit zeitgenössischer Philosophie.* Eine Studie an ausgewählten Beispielen. Frankfurt a. Main: Lang, 1979. 116 pp. (Europäische Hochschulschriften: Reihe 1, Dt. Literatur u. Germanistik, Bd. 335.)
16555. — MAYSER, ERICH: *Heinrich Heines 'Buch der Lieder' im 19. Jahrhundert.* Stuttgart: Heinz, 1978. 229, XIX pp. (Stuttgarter Arbeiten zur Germanistik, Bd. 58.) Zugl.: Heidelberg, Univ., Phil. Diss.
16556. — RADDATZ, FRITZ J.: *Heine, ein deutsches Märchen.* Essay. Frankfurt a. Main: Fischer, 1979. 139 pp., bibl. (pp. 97–100). (Fischer-Taschenbücher, 2216.)
16557. — WERNER, MICHAEL: *Genius und Geldsack. Zum Problem des Schriftstellerberufs bei Heinrich Heine.* Hamburg: Hoffmann u. Campe, 1978. 164 pp., illus. (Heine-Studien.)
16558. HEINE, THOMAS THEODOR. STÜWE, ELISABETH: *Der 'Simplicissimus' Karikaturist Thomas Theodor Heine als Maler.* Mit einem kritischen Katalog der Gemälde. Frankfurt a. Main: Lang, 1978. 243 pp., illus. (Europäische Hochschulschriften: Reihe 28, Kunstgeschichte, Bd. 7.) Zugl.: Hamburg, Univ., Diss., 1978.
16559. HERMANN, GEORG [orig. Georg Hermann Borchardt]: *Grenadier Wordelmann. Ein Roman aus friderizianischer Zeit.* Nachdr. der Orig.-Ausg. Berlin, Ullstein, 1930. Frankfurt a. Main: Ullstein, 1979. 279 pp. (Ullstein-Bücher, Nr. 20011.)
16560. HERMLIN, STEPHAN: *Gesammelte Gedichte.* München: Hanser, 1979. 109 pp.
16561. HERZ, HENRIETTE. WIPPERMANN, KLAUS: *Henriette Herz.* Eine Skizze aus der preussischen Frühromantik. [In]: Tribüne, H. 72, Frankfurt a. Main 1979. Pp. 112–117.
16562. HERZ, IDA. MAYER, HANS-OTTO: *Ida Herz, eine Weggenossin Thomas Manns.* [In]: Aus dem Antiquariat, [Beilage zum] Börsenblatt für den Dt. Buchhandel, Nr. 96, Frankfurt a. Main, 30. Nov. 1979. Pp. A 402-A 405. [See also: Undiminished vigour. 85th birthday of Ida Herz (W. Rosenstock) [in]: AJR Information, London, Oct. 1979. p. 12. I.H., born Oct. 18, 1894 in Nürnberg, catalogued Th. Mann's private library. Emigrated to Zürich, then London, worked as librarian at the Warburg Institute.]
16563. HESS, MOSES. ROSEN, ZVI: *Der Einfluss von Moses Hess auf die Frühschriften von Karl Marx.* [In]: Jahrbuch des Instituts für Deutsche Geschichte, Bd. 8, Tel Aviv, 1979. Pp. 143–174, bibl. footnotes.
16564. HEYM, STEFAN. HEYM, STEFAN: *Collin.* Roman. München: Bertelsmann, 1979. 400 pp. [See also: Schriftsteller zwischen zwei Welten. Vortragszyklus Stefan Heyms in Pittsburgh (Klaus W. Jonas) [in]: 'Allgemeine', Düsseldorf, 5. Jan. 1979, p. 6.]
16565. — HEYM, STEFAN: *Der König-David-Bericht.* Roman. (Aus dem Amerikan. übers. vom Autor.) 36.–60. Tsd. Frankfurt a. Main: Fischer, 1979. 211 pp. (Fischer-Taschenbücher, 1508.)
16566. — HEYM, STEFAN: *Lassalle.* Roman. 2., vom Autor besorgte Fassung. 1. Aufl. München: Goldmann, 1979. 334 pp. (Sammlung moderne Literatur.) (Ein Goldmann-Taschenbuch.)
16567. — ZACHAU, REINHARD KONRAD: *Stefan Heym in Amerika.* Eine Untersuchung zu Stefan Heyms Entwicklung im amerikanischen Exil 1935–1952. Univ. of Pittsburgh, Phil. Diss., 1978. 273 pp.
16568. HILDESHEIMER, WOLFGANG. HILDESHEIMER, WOLFGANG: *Exerzitien mit Papst Johannes. Vergebliche Aufzeichnungen.* Frankfurt a. Main: Suhrkamp, 1979. 139 pp. (Bibliothek Suhrkamp, 647.)
16569. HIRSCH, ROBERT VON. *The Robert von Hirsch Collection, sold at auction by Sotheby Parke Bernet June 20.–27., 1978.* Catalogue. 1–4. London: Sotheby, 1978. 4 vols., mostly illus. [R. v. Hirsch, 1883 Frankfurt a. Main–1977 Basle, industrialist, art-collector, emigrated to Switzerland in 1933. See also No. 15535/YB XXIV.]
16570. — *Meisterwerke aus der Sammlung [Robert] von Hirsch, erworben für deutsche Museen.* Wissenschaftszentrum, Bonn-Bad Godesberg, 10. Mai–4. Juni 1979. (Ausstellung, im Auftrag des Bundesministers des Innern vorbereitet u. durchgeführt von der Stiftung Preuss. Kulturbesitz, Berlin. Katalog u. Ausstellung Red.: Dietrich Kötzsche.) Berlin: Stiftung Preuss. Kulturbesitz, 1979. 76 pp., illus., bibl.
16571. HOCHWÄLDER, FRITZ. HOCHWÄLDER, FRITZ: *Dramen 3.* Mit einem Nachwort von Martin Esslin. Graz: Styria, 1979. 307 pp. [Cont.: Die unziemliche Neugier (1934); Der

Flüchtling (1945); Donnerstag (1959); '1003' (1962/63); Lazaretti oder Der Säbeltiger (1968/73). For vols. 1 and 2, publ. 1975, see No. 13077/YB XXI.]

16572. HOLITSCHER, ARTHUR: *Ansichten. Essays, Aufsätze, Kritiken, Reportagen 1904–1938*. Hrsg. u. mit einer Vorbemerkung u. einem Nachwort von Frank Beer. Berlin/East: Volk u. Welt, 1979. 365 pp.

16573. HORKHEIMER, MAX. HORKHEIMER, MAX/ADORNO, THEODOR W.: *Dialektik der Aufklärung. Philosophische Fragmente*. 51.–55. Tsd. Frankfurt: Fischer, 1979. 229 pp. (Fischer-Taschenbücher, 6144: Bücher des Wissens.)

16574. HUSSERL, EDMUND. HUSSERL, EDMUND: *Aufsätze und Rezensionen, 1890–1910*. Hrsg. von B. Rang. The Hague: Nijhoff, 1979. 485 pp. (Husserliana, 22.)

16575. — BERSLEY, WILLIAM JOHN: *The origins of consciousness. Husserl and Sartre on the cogito*. Univ. of Colorado at Boulder, Phil. Diss., 1978. 309 pp.

16576. — DERRIDA, JACQUES: *Die Stimme und das Phänomen. Ein Essay über das Problem des Zeichens in der Philosophie Husserls*. Aus dem Franz. übers. u. mit einem Vorwort versehen von Jochen Hörisch. Frankfurt a. Main: Suhrkamp, 1979. 173 pp. (Edition Suhrkamp, 945.)

16577. — SCHUHMANN, KARL: *Heideggers Verhältnis zu Husserl im Dritten Reich*. [And]: MARX, WERNER: *'Zu den Sachen selbst!' Über Edmund Husserl*. [In]: NZZ, Zürich, 8./9. Sept. 1979. P. 66 [&] p. 65, port.

16578. — STAPLETON, TIMOTHY JOHN: *Husserl and Heidegger. The question of a phenomenological beginning*. The Pennsylvania State Univ., Phil. Diss., 1978. 235 pp.

16579. JACOB, HEINRICH EDUARD. *Heinrich Eduard Jacob 1889–1967, der Begründer des modernen Sachbuchs*. Katalog einer Ausstellung der Neuen Gesellschaft für Literatur, Kunstamt Schöneberg, 26. Sept.–19. Okt. 1979. Berlin, 1979. 48 pp., illus.

16580. JESSNER, LEOPOLD: *Schriften. Theater der zwanziger Jahre*. Hrsg. von Hugo Fetting. Berlin/East: Henschel, 1979. 400 pp., 83 illus. [L. J., 1878–1945.]

16581. KAFKA, FRANZ. BÄNZIGER, HANS: *Das namenlose Tier und sein Territorium. Zu Kafkas Dichtung 'Der Bau'*. [In]: Deutsche Vierteljahrsschrift für Literaturwissenschaft und Geistesgeschichte, Jg. 53, H. 2, Stuttgart, Juni 1979. Pp. 300–325.

16582. — BIER, WOLFGANG: *Franz Kafka in der Strafkolonie*. Berlin: Anabis Verl., 1979. 30 pp., illus.

16583. — BINDER, HARTMUT, ed.: *Kafka-Handbuch*. Unter Mitarbeit zahlreicher Fachwissenschaftler hrsg. 1–2. Stuttgart: Kröner, 1979. 2 vols. Bd. 1: *Der Mensch und seine Zeit*. 611 pp. Bd. 2: *Das Werk und seine Wirkung*. 951 pp.

16584. — BORN, JÜRGEN, ed.: *Franz Kafka, Kritik und Rezeption zu seinen Lebzeiten, 1912–1924*. Hrsg. unter Mitwirkung von Herbert Mühlfeit u. Friedemann Spicker. Frankfurt a. Main: S. Fischer, 1979. 213 pp., facsims.

16585. — BUBER-NEUMANN, MARGARETE: *Milena, Kafkas Freundin*. München: Heyne, 1979. 221 pp. (Das besondere Taschenbuch, 33.) [Account of a friendship in the KZ Ravensbrück where Milena Jesenská died in 1944. 1st edn. 1963, see No. 4087/YB IX.]

16586. — KAUF, ROBERT: *Franz Kafka. Human and divine justice*. [In]: Colloquia Germanica, H. 4 (1976/77), Bern: Francke. Pp. 308–316, notes (pp. 315–316). [Part III of a symposium on 'Human and divine justice in the works of German Christian and German Jewish authors'.]

16587. — MOSES, STEPHANE: *Das Kafka-Bild Gershom Scholems*. [In]: Merkur, Jg. 33, H. 9, Stuttgart, Sept. 1979. Pp. 862–867.

16588. KAHN-FREUND, OTTO: *Arbeit und Recht*. Aus dem Engl. übers. von Franz Mestitz. Köln: Bund-Verl., 1979. XXXI, 315 pp. (Schriftenreihe der Otto-Brenner-Stiftung, 13.) [Sir O. Kahn-Freund, Nov. 17, 1900 Germany–Aug. 16, 1979 England, emigrated to England in 1933, professor of comparative law at Oxford and Cambridge, knighted for services to labour law in 1976. *Obituaries*: [In]: AJR Information, London, Oct. 1979, p. 10. 'Sir Emigrant' (E.G. Lowenthal) [in]: MB, Nr. 41, Tel Aviv, 2. Nov. 1979, p. 8. Sir O. Kahn-Freund, scholar who was Nazi victim [in]: The Times, London, Nov. 16, 1979, p. VII of Obituaries Supplement.]

16589. KAHNWEILER, DANIEL-HENRY. GLOZER, LASZLO: *Geburtshelfer des Kubismus. Zum Tod des grossen Kunsthändlers Daniel-Henry Kahnweiler*. [In]: SZ, München, 15. Jan. 1979. P. 22, port. [Cf. also: Henry Kahnweiler, der Verfechter des Kubismus, ist gestorben (Rebecca Libermann) [in]: Isr. Wochenblatt, Nr. 3, Zürich, 19. Jan. 1979, pp. 18–19, port. D.-H. K., 1884 Mannheim–Jan. 12, 1979 Paris, noted art dealer and art historian.]

16590. KANTOROWICZ, ALFRED. KANTOROWICZ, ALFRED: *Deutsches Tagebuch*. (Hrsg.: Andreas W. Mytze.) Teil 1–2. Berlin: Verlag Anpassung u. Widerstand (Teil 1); Berlin: Guhl (Teil 2), 1979. 750; 739 pp., illus. (Bibliothek Anpassung u. Widerstand, 3.)

16591. — Kantorowicz, Alfred: *Spanisches Kriegstagebuch*. Mit einem neuen Vorwort des Verfassers u. einem Anhang bisher unveröffentlichter Dokumente u. Briefe von Theodor Balk [et al.]. Hamburg: Konkret-Literatur-Verl., 1979. 504 pp., illus. (Bibliothek der verbrannten Bücher.)

16592. — *In memoriam Alfred Kantorowicz*. [12. Aug. 1899 Berlin–27. März 1979 Hamburg.] Berlin: Verlag europäische ideen, 1979. 35 pp., port., select. bibl. Kantorowicz (p. 35). (europäische ideen, H. 44.) [Incl. obituaries by various friends, excerpts from letters by Kantorowicz. See also: Ein Streiter für die Freiheit. Zum Tode von Prof. Dr. A. Kantorowicz [in]: 'Allgemeine', Düsseldorf, 6. April 1979, p. 7. Zum Tode von A. Kantorowicz (E. G. Lowenthal) [in]: MB, No. 16/17, Tel Aviv, 27. April 1979, p. 8.]

16593. KAUTSKY, KARL. Steenson, Gary P.: *Karl Kautsky, 1854–1938. Marxism in the classical years*. Pittsburgh, Pa.: Univ. of Pittsburgh Press, 1979. 336 pp.

16594. KERR, ALFRED. Schöllmann, Traute: *Ein Weg zur literarischen Selbstverwirklichung: Alfred Kerr. Zur Eigenart und Wirkung seiner kritischen Schriften*. München: Bahmann, 1977. 160 pp., facsims. Zugl.: München, Univ., Phil. Diss., 1977.

16595. Kerr, Judith: *Eine Art Familientreffen*. Aus dem Engl. übertr. von Annemarie Böll. (Die Übersetzung wurde überarb. von Judith Kerr u. Hans-Christian Kirsch.) Ravensburg: Otto Maier, 1979. 183 pp. [Orig. title: 'A small person far away'. Last vol. in a semi-biographical trilogy by Alfred Kerr's daughter. For the first two vols., English and German editions, see No. 9385/YB XVII, No. 12024/YB XX, Nos. 12724, 12772/YB XXI, and also No. 16208, (German school edn). Cf.: J. Kerrs Familientreffen oder Anna zum dritten Mal (Albert von Schirnding) [in]: SZ, München, 10. Okt. 1979, p. XIII. Abschiedstage in Berlin (Cornelia Wrangel) [in]: Die Zeit, Hamburg, 16. Nov. 1979, p. L 12.]

16596. Kesten, Hermann: *Meine Freunde, die Poeten*. [In]: Tribüne, H. 72, Frankfurt a. Main, 1979. Pp. 122–139. [Essays on Schalom Asch, Alfred Döblin, Walter Hasenclever. See also in the same issue, pp. 118–120: Für Hermann Kesten. Zum 80. Geburtstag des Dichters [28. Jan. 1980] (Wolfgang Buhl).]

16597. KISCH, EGON ERWIN. Kisch, Egon Erwin: *Nichts ist erregender als die Wahrheit. Reportagen aus 4 Jahrzehnten*. 1–2. Hrsg. von Walther Schmieding. Köln: Kiepenheuer u. Witsch, 1979. 2 vols. (320 pp., 1 illus.; 288 pp., 1 illus.)

16598. — Kronberger, Johann: *Egon Erwin Kisch. Seine politische und publizistische Entwicklung vom bürgerlichen Journalisten zum Schöpfer der literarischen sozialistischen Reportage*. Wien, Univ., Grund- u. integrativwiss. Diss., 9. Juni 1979. 249 pp. [See also: Egon Erwin Kisch und die Besetzung der 'Neuen Freien Presse' (Hans Kronberger) [in]: Publizistik, Jg. 23, Nr. 1–2, München, 1978, pp. 99–105.]

16599. — Pem [orig. Paul E. Marcus]: *Reporter und Dichter*. [Bisher unveröffentlichtes Manuskript aus dem Nachlass von Pem, geschrieben 1965 anlässlich des 80. Geburtstages von E. E. Kisch.] [In]: 'Allgemeine', Düsseldorf, 28. Sept. 1979. P. 7.

16600. Klieneberger-Nobel, Emmy: *Pionierleistungen für die medizinische Mikrobiologie*. Stuttgart: Gustav Fischer, 1977. X, 144 pp. [Report of childhood and early professional career in Frankfurt a. Main. The author emigrated to England, worked at the Lister Institute. Cf.: Two women from Frankfurt (Margot Pottlitzer) [in]: AJR Information, London, April 1979, pp. 8–9 (refers also to the memoirs of Mathilde Maier, see No. 16784).]

16601. Koestler, Arthur: *Ein spanisches Testament*. Mit Vorwort des Verfassers u. der Herzogin von Atholl sowie Pressestimmen von Walter A. Berendsohn u. Alfred Döblin. Berlin: Guhl, 1979. 240 pp. (Bibliothek Anpassung und Widerstand, 4.)

16602. Kofler, Leo: *Zur Geschichte der bürgerlichen Gesellschaft*. 7., neu bearb. u. ergänzte Aufl. Darmstadt: Luchterhand, 1979. 367 pp. (Soziologische Texte, Bd. 38.) [L. K., born 1907 in Chocimierz/Poland, studied in Vienna with Max Adler, now living in the Federal German Republic.]

16603. Kohn, Adolph: *Politische Tagebücher 1848–1851*. Bearb. von Günter Richter. [In]: Denkwürdige Jahre 1848–1851. Wien: Böhlau, 1978. Pp. 97–346. (Veröffentlichungen aus den Archiven Preussischer Kulturbesitz, Bd. 13.)

16604. KOHN, HANS. Wolf, Kenneth: *Hans Kohn's liberal nationalism. The historian as prophet*. [In]: Journal of the History of Ideas, Vol. 37, New York, Oct.–Dec. 1976. Pp. 651–672. [H. Kohn, 1891–1971.]

16605. Kracauer, Siegfried: *Von Caligari zu Hitler. Eine psychologische Geschichte des deutschen Films*. Übers. aus dem Amerikan. von Ruth Baumgarten u. Karsten Witte. Frankfurt a. Main: Suhrkamp, 1979. 632 pp. (Kracauer, Siegfried: Schriften. Hrsg. von Karsten Witte. Bd. 2.) [1st German edn. 1958 was abridged.]

16606. KRAUS, KARL. KRAUS, KARL: *Frühe Schriften 1892–1900.* Hrsg. von Johannes J. Braakenburg. 1–2. München: Kösel, 1979. 2 vols. *Bd. 1: 1892–1896.* 306 pp. *Bd. 2: 1897–1900. Die demolierte Literatur. Eine Krone für Zion.* 324 pp. [Cf.: K. Kraus' satirische Gehversuche (Fritz L. Brassloff) [in]: 'Allgemeine', Düsseldorf, 17. Aug. 1979, p. 7.]

16607. — MAYER KÖNIG, WOLFGANG: *Karl Kraus als Theaterkritiker und Schauspieler.* Wien: Gesellschaft der Kunstfreunde, 1978. 28 pp., 4 pp. illus., bibl. (Separatumdruck zu den 'Wiener Kunstheften'.)

16608. — SANDER, EMIL: *Gesellschaftliche Struktur und literarischer Ausdruck. Über 'Die letzten Tage der Menschheit' von Karl Kraus.* Königstein/Ts.: Scriptor, 1979. 336 pp. (Theorie, Kritik, Geschichte, Bd. 18.)

16609. — SCHNEIDER, MANFRED: *Die Angst und das Paradies des Nörglers. Versuch über Karl Kraus.* Frankfurt a. Main: Syndikat, 1977. 208 pp., bibl. (pp. 202–208).

16610. KUCZYNSKI, JÜRGEN: *Studien zu einer Geschichte der Gesellschaftswissenschaften. Bd. 10: Gegenwartsprobleme. Briefe und Vorträge.* Berlin/East: Akademie-Verl., 1978. 238 pp. [For vols. 1–9 see No. 15577/YB XXIV. Cf.: Review (Gerd Hardach) [in]: German Historical Institute, Bulletin, Issue 3, London, Winter 1980, pp. 15–16.]

16611. LANDAUER, GUSTAV: *Aufruf zum Sozialismus.* Nachdr. der Ausg. Köln, Marcan-Block-Verl., 1923. Wetzlar: Verlag Büchse der Pandora, 1978. XIX, 155 pp. [See also No. 16383.]

16612. LASKER-SCHÜLER, ELSE. LASKER-SCHÜLER, ELSE: *Ichundich. Ein Drama.* [Cf.: Ein Höllenspiel mit allegorischem Ausgang. Uraufführung von Else Lasker-Schülers 'Ichundich' (Hermann Lewy) [in]: 'Allgemeine', Düsseldorf, 16. Nov. 1979, p. 6, illus. [and in]: Isr. Wochenblatt, Nr. 47, Zürich, 23. Nov. 1979, pp. 32–33. Else Lasker-Schüler und der 'Kraal' (Erich Gottgetreu) [in]: Aufbau, New York, Dec. 14, 1979, p. 21. Höllenspiel auf einer Herzensbühne. 'Ichundich' von E. L.-Sch. Uraufführung in Düsseldorf (Georg Hensel) [in]: FAZ, Frankfurt a. Main, 12. Nov. 1979, p. 21. E. Lasker-Schüler und das Urböse (Erich Gottgetreu) [in]: MB, Nr. 46, Tel Aviv, 14. Dez. 1979, pp. 6–7. Die Poesie in der Hölle. Zur Uraufführung von E. Lasker-Schülers nachgelassenem Stück (Heinrich Vormweg) [in]: SZ, München, 14. Nov. 1979, p. 11.]

16613. — PAZI, MARGARITA: *Else Lasker-Schüler in Jerusalem.* Zur Nuancierung einer allgemeinen Meinung. [In]: Deutsche Vierteljahrsschrift für Literaturwissenschaft und Geistesgeschichte, Jg. 53, H. 1, Stuttgart, März 1979. Pp. 115–124.

16614. — SIMA, MIRON: *Lebensabend und Abschied von Else Lasker-Schüler in Jerusalem.* Zeichnungen und Erinnerungen. Wuppertal: Baedecker'sche Verlagsbuchhandlung, 1979. 62 pp.

16615. LASSALLE, FERDINAND. BLEUEL, HANS PETER: *Ferdinand Lassalle oder Der Kampf wider die verdammte Bedürfnislosigkeit.* München: Bertelsmann, 1979. 301 pp., illus., ports., chronol.

16616. — VAHLTEICH, JULIUS: *Ferdinand Lassalle und die Anfänge der deutschen Arbeiterbewegung.* Mit einer Rezension von Franz Mehring aus der Neuen Zeit und einer Erwiderung von Julius Vahlteich im Anhang sowie einer Einleitung zum Nachdruck von Toni Offermann. Nachdr. der 1904 erschienenen 1. Aufl. Berlin/East: Dietz, 1978. XII, 86, XI pp., port. (Reprints zur Sozialgeschichte.)

16617. LESSING, THEODOR. POETZL, HERBERT: *Confrontation with modernity. Theodor Lessing's critique of German culture.* Univ. of Massachusetts, Phil. Diss., 1978. 328 pp. [See also: Begegnung mit Prof. Dr. Theodor Lessing (Stefan Schwarz) [in]: 'Allgemeine', Düsseldorf, 8. Sept. 1978.]

16618. LEVY, RUDOLF. THESING, SUSANNE: *Der Maler Rudolf Levy (1875–1944?). Monographie und Werkverzeichnis.* München, Univ., Phil. Diss., 1979. 253 pp. bibl. (pp. 236–250).

16619. LIEBERMANN, MAX. *Max Liebermann in seiner Zeit.* Eine Ausstellung der Nationalgalerie Berlin, Staatl. Museen Preuss. Kulturbesitz, 6. Sept.–4. Nov. 1979 [und im] Haus der Kunst, München, 14. Dez. 1979–17. Febr. 1980. (Ausstellung u. Katalog: Sigrid Achenbach, Matthias Eberle.) München: Prestel (in Komm.), 1979. 687 pp., illus., ports., bibl. Liebermann (pp. 679–684).

16620. LIEPMAN, HEINZ: *Das Vaterland. Ein Tatsachenroman aus Deutschland.* Vorwort: Heinrich Böll. Hamburg: Konkret-Literatur-Verl., 1979. 214 pp. (Bibliothek der verbrannten Bücher.)

16621. LUKÁCS, GEORG. LUKÁCS, GEORG: *Geschichte und Klassenbewusstsein.* Studien über marxistische Dialektik. Sonderausg., 6. Aufl. Darmstadt: Luchterhand, 1979. 518 pp. (Lukács, Georg: Politische Aufsätze, 4.) (Sammlung Luchterhand, 11.) [For vols. 1–3 and 5 of 'Politische Aufsätze' see No. 15589/YB XXIV.]

16622. — ARATO, ANDREW/BREINES, PAUL: *The young Lukács and the origins of Western Marxism.* New York: The Seabury Press, 1979. 256 pp. [See also: Young Lukács, old Lukács, new Lukács

(Paul Breines) [in]: The Journal of Modern History, Vol. 51, No. 3, Chicago, Sept. 1979, pp. 533–546. Review article.]
16623. — István, Hermann: *Die Gedankenwelt von Georg Lukács.* Aus dem Ungar. von Endre Kiss. Budapest: Akadémiai Kiadó, 1978. 403 pp. [Cf.: Review (Günther K. Lehmann) [in]: Deutsche Literaturzeitung, Jg. 100, H. 10, Berlin/East, Okt. 1979, cols. 611–613.]
16624. — Miles, David H.: *Portrait of the Marxist as a young Hegelian. Lukács theory of the novel.* [In]: PMLA (Publications of the Modern Language Association of America), Vol. 94, No. 1, New York, Jan. 1979. Pp. 22–35, bibl. notes (pp. 33–35).
16625. LUXEMBURG, ROSA. Geras, Norman: *Rosa Luxemburg. Kämpferin für einen emanzipatorischen Sozialismus.* (Aus dem Engl. von Klaus Kochmann.) Berlin: Olle u. Wolter, 1979. 189 pp. [For Eng. edn. see No. 13921/YB. XXII.]
16626. — Radczun, Evelyn & Günter: *Wirklichkeitsbewältigung in den Briefen Rosa Luxemburgs aus dem Gefängnis 1915–1918.* [In]: Zeitschrift für Geschichtswissenschaft, Jg. 27, H. 2, Berlin/ East, 1979. Pp. 99–110.
16627. — Stadler-Labhart, Verena: *Rosa Luxemburg an der Universität Zürich 1889–1897.* Zürich: Rohr, 1978. 92 pp., facsims., ports., bibl. (pp. 77–78). (Schriften zur Zürcher Universitätsu. Gelehrtengeschichte, Bd. 2.)
16628. MAHLER, GUSTAV. *Gustav Mahler, Werk und Interpretation: Autographe, Partituren, Dokumente.* 30. Okt. 1979–6. Jan. 1980. [Katalog zu einer] Ausstellung ... aus Anlass des Mahler-Zyklus des Landes Nordrhein-Westfalen in Verbindung mit der Internat. Gustav-Mahler-Gesellschaft (Wien) im Heinrich-Heine-Institut (Düsseldorf). Zusammengestellt u. kommentiert von Rudolf Stephan. Mit einem Beitrag von Bruno Walter. [Hrsg.: Joseph A. Kruse.] Köln: Volk, 1979. 120 pp., scores, bibl.
16629. — Karbusicky, Vladimir: *Gustav Mahler und seine Umwelt.* Darmstadt: Wissenschaftl. Buchgemeinschaft, 1978. viii, 158 pp., illus., scores. (Impulse der Forschung, Bd. 28.)
16630. — Willauer, Franz: *Gustav Mahler und die Wiener Oper.* Ein Band der Wiener Themen. Wien: Jugend u. Volk, 1979. 230 pp., illus.
16631. MARCUSE, HERBERT. Marcuse, Herbert: *Aufsätze aus der Zeitschrift für Sozialforschung, 1934–1941.* Frankfurt a. Main: Suhrkamp, 1979. 320 pp. (Marcuse, Herbert: Schriften, Bd. 3.)
16632. — Marcuse, Herbert. *Schriften. Bd. 5: Triebstruktur und Gesellschaft. Ein philosophischer Beitrag zu Sigmund Freud.* Übers. von Marianne von Eckardt-Jaffe. 1. Aufl. Frankfurt a. Main: Suhrkamp, 1979. 232 pp. [Orig. title: 'Eros and civilisation'.]
16633. — Brown, Alison Pogrebin: *Herbert Marcuse. The path of his thought.* Ithaca, N.Y., Cornell Univ., Phil. Diss., 1978. 199 pp.
16634. — Herlyn, Heinrich: *Heinrich Böll und Herbert Marcuse. Literatur als Utopie.* Lampertheim: Kübler, 1979. 148 pp., bibl. (pp. 144–148).
16635. — *Obituaries* (July 19, 1898 Berlin–July 29, 1979 Starnberg/Bavaria): [In]: AJR Information, London, Sept. 1979, p. 2. Für Freiheit und Freizügigkeit. Zum Tod von H. M. (Meir Faerber) [in]: 'Allgemeine', Düsseldorf, 10. Aug. 1979, p. 7. Gedanken zum Tode von H.M. [in]: Aufbau, New York, Aug. 3, 1979, p. 4. Ein Träumer kluger Träume. Nach dem Tode H.M. (Jens Fischer) [in]: Evang. Kommentare, Jg. 12, Nr. 9, Stuttgart, Sept. 1979, p. 502. Denkspiele gegen eindimensionales Leben (Werner Post) [in]: Herder Korrespondenz, Jg. 33, H. 9, Freiburg i. Br., Sept. 1979, pp. 475–479. Philosopher of revolt Herbert Marcuse, radical hero, dies [in]: 'Internat. Herald Tribune', Zürich, July 31., 1979, pp. 1 & 5, port. Zum Tode von H.M. (Julius Jitzchak Loewenstein) [in]: MB, Nr. 30, Tel Aviv, 10. Aug. 1979, p. 5. H. Marcuse als Jude (Hans Lamm) [in]: Neue Jüd. Nachrichten, Nr. 33, München, 7. Sept. 1979, p. 2. Pied piper of protest (Anthony Quinton) [in]: 'The Observer', London, Aug. 5, 1979. Denken u. Schreiben gegen das tägliche Entsetzen. Über meine Begegnungen mit H.M. (Reinhard Lettau) [in]: Stern Magazin, H. Nr. 33, Hamburg, 9. Aug. 1979, pp. 100–101, port. Freiheit für alle, Glück für jeden. Zum Tode des Philosophen H.M. (Ivo Frenzel) [in]: SZ, München, 31. Juli 1979, p. 8, port. Ein undogmatischer Denker. Zum Tode des Philosophen H.M. (Iring Fetscher) [in]: Die Zeit, Hamburg, 3. Aug. 1979, p. 40.
16636. — Sahmel, Karl-Heinz: *Vernunft und Sinnlichkeit. Eine kritische Einführung in das philosophische und politische Denken Herbert Marcuses.* Königstein/Ts.: Forum Academicum, 1979. 268 pp. (Monographien zur philosophischen Forschung, 187.)
16637. MARCUSE, LUDWIG: *Essays, Porträts, Polemiken.* Ausgewählt aus 4 Jahrzehnten von Harold von Zofe. Zürich: Diogenes, 1979. 479 pp.

16638. MARX, HEINRICH. Monz, Heinz: *Advokatanwalt Heinrich Marx. Die Berufsausbildung eines Juristen im französischen Rheinland.* [In]: Jahrbuch des Instituts für Deutsche Geschichte, Bd. 8, Tel Aviv, 1979. Pp. 125–141, bibl. footnotes. [H.M., 1777–1838, father of Karl Marx.]

16639. MARX, KARL. Andréas, Bert: *Marx' Verhaftung und Ausweisung, Brüssel, Febr. März 1848.* Trier: Karl-Marx-Haus, 1978. 148 pp. (Schriften aus dem Karl-Marx-Haus Trier, Nr. 22.)

16640. — Carlebach, Julius: *The Jewishness of Karl Marx.* [In]: Jewish Spectator, vol. 44, No. 3, Santa Monica, Ca., Fall 1979. Pp. 37–43.

16641. — Longuet, Robert-Jean: *Karl Marx, mein Urgrossvater.* (Aus dem Franz. übers. von Günter Kluge.) Berlin/East: Dietz, 1979. 207 pp.

16642. — *Marx-Engels-Jahrbuch.* 1[&] 2. Hrsg. vom Institut für Marxismus–Leninismus beim Zentralkomitee der Kommunistischen Partei der Sowjetunion u. vom Institut für Marxismus–Leninismus beim Zentralkomitee der Sozialistischen Einheitspartei Deutschlands. Berlin/East: Dietz, 1978 [&] 1979. 2 vols. (486 [&] 580 pp.) [Yearbook founded in connection with the Marx-Engels-Gesamtausgabe (MEGA) to publish new results in research based on the MEGA. *Bd. 1* incl.: Entstehungsgeschichte der Marxschen politischen Ökonomie; Probleme der weltanschaulichen Entwicklung von K. Marx, 1841–1843; Bedeutung des ersten Briefbandes der MEGA für die Erforschung der frühen Lebens- u. Schaffensperiode von Marx u. Engels u. zur Geschichte der 'Neuen Rheinischen Zeitung'. *Bd. 2* contains articles on Engels' 'Anti-Dühring'.]

16643. — Neubauer, Franz: *Marx-Engels-Bibliographie.* Boppard: Boldt, 1979. XV, 417 pp., bibl. (pp. 377–401). [Cf.: Marx–Engels, vollständige Bibliographie [in]: Börsenblatt des Dt. Buchhandels, Nr. 43, Frankfurt a. Main, 29. Mai 1979, p. 1046.]

16644. — Pachter, Henry: *Marx and the Jews.* [In]: Dissent, New York, Fall 1979. Pp. 450–467.

16645. — Rosen, Zvi: *Der Einfluss von Moses Hess auf die Frühschriften von Karl Marx.* [See No. 16563.]

16646. — Steiner, Herbert: *Karl Marx in Wien. Die Arbeiterbewegung zwischen Revolution und Restauration 1848.* Wien: Europaverl., 1978. 223 pp., illus., bibl. (pp. 211–220).

16647. — Wistrich, Robert S.: *Karl Marx, the enlightenment, and Jewish emancipation.* [In]: Jewish Frontier, Vol. 46, No. 4, New York, April 1979. Pp. 9–12.

16648. — Wygodski, W. S.: *Wie 'Das Kapital' entstand.* Berlin/East: Verlag Die Wirtschaft, 1979. 224 pp. [See also: Existiert noch das 'Kapital'-Manuskript? Nachforschungen zu Karl Marx' Hauptwerk, 1. Band (Edgar Klapperstück) [in]: Börsenblatt für den Dt. Buchhandel, Jg. 146, H. 23, Leipzig, 5. Juni 1979, pp. 426–428, illus., notes. Eine Dokumentation der Entstehungsgeschichte des 'Kapitals' (Wolfgang Jahn) [in]: Zeitschrift für Geschichtswissenschaft, Jg. 26, Nr. 2, Berlin/East, 1978, pp. 134–143 (review article).]

16649. Mehring, Walter: *Höllische Komödie. Drei Dramen.* Düsseldorf: Claassen, 1979. 272 pp. (Mehring, Walter: Werkausgabe, Bd. 4.) [Cont.: 'Die Frühe der Städte' and 'Höllische Komödie' (never performed) and 'Der Kaufmann von Berlin'.]

16650. MEIDNER, LUDWIG. *Ludwig Meidner. Zeichnungen aus dem Nachlass.* [Katalog zu einer] Ausstellung in der Galerie Ruchti, Köln, [Frühjahr 1979]. Leutkirch: Druck Rud. Roth, [1979]. [18] pp., illus., port.

16651. Mendelssohn-Family. *Mendelssohn-Studien. Beiträge zur neueren deutschen Kultur- und Wirtschaftsgeschichte. Bd. 3.* Hrsg. von Cécile Lowenthal-Hensel und Rudolf Elvers. Berlin: Duncker u. Humblot, 1979. 248 pp., 8 illus. [Cont.: Unpublished letters of Abraham Mendelssohn and Fanny Hensel (Boyd Alexander, pp. 9–50). Karl August Varnhagen von Ense: Sieben Briefe an Rebekka Dirichlet [Schwester von Felix Mendelssohn Bartholdy] (Konrad Feilchenfeldt, pp. 51–79). Georg Benjamin Mendelssohn im Spiegel seiner Korrespondenz. Mit unveröffentlichten Briefen von Alexander von Humboldt, Ernst Moritz Arndt u. Clemens Theodor Perthes (Ingeborg Stolzenberg, pp. 81–161). Um das Eiserne Kreuz von 1813. Wilhelm Hensel in den Freiheitskriegen (Karl Johann v. Schroeder, pp. 163–173). Wilhelm Hensels 'Lebenslauf' von 1829 (Cécile Lowenthal-Hensel, pp. 175–179). Theodor Fontane über Wilhelm Hensel (pp. 181–199). Albrecht Mendelssohn-Bartholdy. Ein Lebensbild (Alfred Vagts, pp. 201–225).] [For vol. 4 see No. 16266. Vol. 1 see No. 10805/YB. XVIII; Vol. 2, see No. 13175/YB. XXI.]

16652. MENDELSSOHN BARTHOLDY, FELIX. Krummacher, Friedhelm: *Mendelssohn, der Komponist. Studien zur Kammermusik für Streicher.* München: Fink, 1978. 612 pp., scores, bibl. (Werkeverzeichnis pp. 574–576). Zugl.: Erlangen, Univ., Phil. Habil.-Schrift, 1972.

16653. — Kurzhals-Reuter, Arntrud: *Die Oratorien Felix Mendelssohn Bartholdys.* Untersuchungen zur Quellenlage, Entstehung, Gestaltung und Überlieferung. Tutzing: Schneider, 1978. 251 pp., diagrs., scores. (Mainzer Studien zur Musikwissenschaft, Bd. 12.) Zugl.: Mainz, Univ., Geschichtswiss. Diss., 1976.

16654. MERCHAV, PERETZ: *Linkssozialismus in Europa zwischen den Weltkriegen*. Mit einer Einleitung von Helmut Konrad. Wien: Europaverl., 1979. XXVI, 129 pp., port. (Ludwig Boltzmann Institut für Geschichte der Arbeiterbewegung: Materialien zur Arbeiterbewegung Nr. 14.) [Peretz Merchav, orig. Paul Marchfeld, 1913 Vienna–1978 Israel, historian of the labour movement.]

16655. MERZ, KONRAD [orig. Kurt Lehmann]: *Ein Mensch fällt aus Deutschland*. Nachdr. der Ausg. Amsterdam, Querido, 1936. Hamburg: Konkret-Literatur-Verl., 1978. 173 pp. (Bibliothek der verbrannten Bücher.)

16656. METZGER, ARNOLD: *Phänomenologie der Revolution. Frühe Schriften*. Mit einem Nachwort von Ulrich Sonnemann. Frankfurt a. Main: Syndikat, 1979. 247 pp. [Incl. letter by Edmund Husserl to the author, Sept. 4, 1919. A. Metzger, 1892 Landau/Pfalz–1974 Bad Gastein, philosopher, assistant of Edmund Husserl, 1934–1937 lecturer at the 'Lehranstalt für die Wissenschaft des Judentums', emigrated to Paris in 1938, later to England and the U.S.A., returned to Germany after the war.]

16657. NADEL, ARNO. KEMP, FRIEDHELM: *Der Spaziergang. Arno Nadel zum Gedenken (geb. 3. Okt. 1878 in Wilna, gest. 1943 in Auschwitz)*. [Funkmanuskript zur] Sendung am 8. Okt. 1978. München: Bayerischer Rundfunk, 1978. 12 pp. [Mimeog.]

16658. NEUMANN, ALFRED. *Alfred Neumann. Eine Auswahl aus seinem Werk*. Mit einer Einführung hrsg. u. kommentiert von Guy Stern. Wiesbaden: Steiner, 1979. 215 pp., port., bibl. (Verschollene und Vergessene.)

16659. NEUMANN, ROBERT: *Die Kinder von Wien. Roman*. Mit einer Einführung von Christine Nöstlinger. Weinheim: Beltz u. Gelberg, 1979. 176 pp. [Engl. edn. 1946. 1st German edn. 1948.]

16660. PANOFSKY, ERWIN: *Die Renaissancen der europäischen Kunst*. Aus dem Engl. von Horst Günther. Frankfurt a. Main: Suhrkamp, 1979. 463 pp., 157 illus. [Orig. Engl. edn., publ. 1960. Cf.: Die Renaissance und die Renaissancen. Zwei Jahrzehnte nach seiner Entstehung liegt E. Panofskys grosses Werk deutsch vor (Willibald Sauerländer) [in]: SZ, München, 2./3. Febr. 1980, p. 168.]

16661. PAULI, WOLFGANG: *Wissenschaftlicher Briefwechsel mit Niels Bohr, Albert Einstein, Werner Heisenberg [et al.]. Bd. 1: 1919–1929*. Hrsg. von A. Hermann, K. von Meyem, V. F. Weisskopf. Berlin: Springer, 1979. 624 pp. [W.P., April 25, 1900 Vienna–Dec. 15, 1958 Zürich, physicist, Nobel Prize for physics in 1945.]

16662. PLESSNER, HELMUTH: *Zwischen Philosophie und Gesellschaft. Ausgewählte Abhandlungen und Vorträge*. Frankfurt a. Main: Suhrkamp, 1979. 382 pp. (Suhrkamp-Taschenbücher, 544.) [See also: Die Unergründlichkeit des Menschenmöglichen. Helmuth Plessners 'Die Stufen des Organischen und der Mensch' (Helmut Holzhey) [in]: NZZ, Zürich, 10./11. Nov. 1979, p. 69, port.]

16663. POLAK, ERNST [orig. Pollak]. BINDER, HARTMUT: *Ernst Polak, Literat ohne Werk. Zu den Kaffeehauszirkeln in Prag und Wien*. [In]: Jahrbuch der Dt. Schillergesellschaft, Jg. 23, Stuttgart, 1979. Pp. 366–415, illus., ports., notes. [Refers to many Jewish writers. E. Polak, Aug. 4, 1886 Jičin/Czechoslovakia–Sept. 21, 1947 London, literary critic and agent.]

16664. — SULZER, DIETER: *Der Nachlass von Ernst Polak im Deutschen Literaturarchiv* [Marbach a.N.]. Bericht, Verzeichnis und Edition von Briefen Polaks, Werfels und Brochs. [In]: Jahrbuch der Dt. Schillergesellschaft, Jg. 23, Stuttgart, 1979. Pp. 514–548, notes.

16665. POLGAR, ALFRED: *Taschenspiegel*. Hrsg. u. mit einem Nachwort versehen von Ulrich Weinzierl. Wien: Löcker, 1979. 262 pp. [Incl. essay by Ulrich Weinzierl 'Alfred Polgar im Exil'.]

16666. POPPER, KARL. POPPER, KARL: *Creative self-criticism in science and in art*. [In]: Encounter, Vol. 53, No. 5, London, Nov. 1979. Pp. 10–14. [See also: Verleihung der Ehrendoktorwürde an Sir Karl Popper am 8. Juni 1979 in der Aula der Johann-Wolfgang-Goethe-Univ. Frankfurt a. Main. Frankfurt a. Main: Pressestelle der Univ., 1979. 31 pp.]

16667. — ALBRECHT, REINHARDT: *Sozialtechnologie und ganzheitliche Sozialphilosophie. Zu Karl R. Poppers Kritik der ganzheitlichen Sozialphilosophie*. 2., durchgesehene Aufl. Bonn: Bouvier, 1979. 235 pp. (Abhandlungen zur Philosophie, Psychologie u. Pädagogik, 82.)

16668. — LIEBERSON, JONATHAN SEARS: *Critical control and objectivity in Popper's theory of scientific method*. New York, Columbia Univ., Phil. Diss., 1978. 301 pp.

16669. — ROTHBART, DANIEL: *Conjectures and refutations. A critique of Popper's theory of corroboration.* Washington Univ., Phil. Diss., 1978. 245 pp.

16670. RATHENAU, EMIL. PINNER, FELIX: *Emil Rathenau und das elektrische Zeitalter.* Nachdr. der Ausg. Leipzig, Akademische Verlagsgesellschaft, 1918. New York: Arno Press, 1977. IX, 408 pp., port.

16671. RATHENAU, WALTHER. BORELLI, GIORGIO: *Rathenau e la crisi del primo dopoguerra.* [In]: Economia e Storia, Vol. 24, No. 2, Roma, 1977. Pp. 213–216.

16672. — SCHULIN, ERNST: *Walther Rathenau, Repräsentant, Kritiker und Opfer seiner Zeit.* Göttingen: Musterschmidt, 1979. 140 pp., illus., ports., bibl. (p. 140). (Persönlichkeit und Geschichte, Bd. 104/104a.)

16673. REINHARDT, MAX. REINHARDT, GOTTFRIED: *The genius. A memoir of Max Reinhardt.* New York: Knopf, 1979. 420 pp. [Orig. title see No. 11718/YB. XIX.]

16674. RHEINSTEIN, MAX: *Gesammelte Schriften. Collected works.* Hrsg. von Hans G. Leser. 1–2. Tübingen: Mohr, 1979. 2 vols. *Bd. 1: Rechtstheorie und Soziologie. Rechtsvergleichung und Common Law (USA).* XXIV, 506 pp. *Bd. 2: Kollisionsrecht, Familienrecht, Anhang und Bibliographie.* IX, 471 pp., bibl. (pp. 432–471). [Contrib. in German and English. M. Rheinstein, 1899 Berlin–1977 U.S.A., professor of comparative law at the University of Chicago Law School from 1935.]

16675. ROSENBERG, HANS: *Machteliten und Wirtschaftskonjunkturen.* Studien zur neueren deutschen Sozial- und Wirtschaftsgeschichte. Göttingen: Vandenhoeck u. Ruprecht, 1978. 344 pp. (Kritische Studien zur Geschichtswissenschaft, Bd. 31.) [Incl.: 'Rückblick auf ein Historikerleben zwischen zwei Kulturen'. H.R., born 1904, professor of history in Cologne, emigrated in 1933 to England, later to the U.S.A., since 1977 living in Germany.]

16676. ROSENTHAL, PHILIPP, AG., China-manufacture. KOCH, THOMAS R.: *Anfangs weisses Porzellan bemalt. Rosenthal hat seine Unabhängigkeit über 100 Jahre bewahrt.* [In]: SZ, München, 14. Sept. 1979. P. 22. [See also: Vom Aschenbecher zur Porzellanmanufaktur [in]: Aufbau, New York, Nov. 2, 1979, p. 28, illus. 100 Jahre Rosenthal. Es begann mit einem Aschenbecher [in]: Das Neue Israel, Jg. 32, Nr. 6, Zürich, Dez. 1979, pp. 318–319, port., illus.]

16677. ROTH, JOSEPH. ROTH, JOSEPH: *L'auto-da-fé de l'esprit. Das Autodafé des Geistes.* (Aufsatz, erstmals veröffentlicht in 'Cahiers Juifs', Paris 1933. Wiederveröffentlicht u. übers. von Brita Eckert.) [In]: *Joseph Roth.* Frankfurt a. Main: Buchhändler-Vereinigung, 1979. 66 pp., ports. (Kleine Schriften der Deutschen Bibliothek, 5.) [This vol. 'Joseph Roth' incl. also]: REICH-RANICKI, MARCEL: *Vortrag zur Eröffnung der Ausstellung 'Joseph Roth 1894–1939' in der Deutschen Bibliothek, 29. März 1979.*

16678. — ROTH, JOSEPH: *Die Rebellion. Ein Roman.* (Hrsg. von Hubert Witt mit einem Nachwort 'Joseph Roths Rebellion'.) Leipzig: Insel, 1979. 123 pp. (Insel-Bücherei, 1028.)

16679. — *Joseph Roth 1894–1939.* Eine Ausstellung der Deutschen Bibliothek Frankfurt a. Main, 1979. (Ausstellung u. Katalog: Brita Eckert u. Werner Berthold. Mitarb.: Mechthild Hahner u. Jutta Braun.) Frankfurt a. Main: Buchhändler-Vereinigung, 1979. XXIII, 551 pp., illus., ports., facsims., bibl. 1945 ff. (pp. 492–530). (Sonderveröffentlichungen der Dt. Bibliothek, Nr. 7.) [Exhibition assisted by loans from the archives of the Leo Baeck Institute New York. Cf. reviews: Joseph Roth zum 40. Todestag (Fritz Brassloff) [and]: 'Ich kenne die Welt nur wenn ich schreibe', Vortrag (Marcel Reich-Ranicki) [in]: 'Allgemeine', Düsseldorf, 25. Mai 1979, p. 7 [and]: 13. April 1979, p. 7. Der Mythomane Joseph Roth (Erich Gottgetreu) [in]: Das Neue Israel, Jg. 32, H. 4, Zürich, Okt. 1979, pp. 209 & 211. 'Er hatte Leidenschaft, Geist, Mut' [in]: NZZ, Zürich, 21. Mai 1979, p. 21.]

16680. — KRISPYN, EGBERT: *Joseph Roth and the art of adaption.* [In]: Protest, form, tradition, Tuscaloosa, Alabama, 1979. Pp. 97–109, bibl. references.

16681. — ZAMPA, GIORGIO: *Joseph Roth. Una fuga senza fine.* [In]: Epoca, No. 1504, Milano, 4. Agosto 1979. Pp. 7–13, illus. [Refers also to the archives of the Leo Baeck Institute New York.]

16682. SACHS, NELLY. BAHR, EHRHARD: *Nelly Sachs.* München: Beck, 1979. 160 pp. (Autorenbücher, 16.)

16683. SCHELER, MAX. SCHELER, MAX: *Problems of a sociology of knowledge.* Transl. by Manfred S. Frings. Ed. and with an introduction by Kenneth W. Stikkers. London: Routledge & Kegan Paul, 1979. 232 pp. (International library of sociology.)

16684. — SCHELER, MAX: *Die Zukunft des Kapitalismus. Tod und Fortleben. Zum Phänomen des Tragischen.* Hrsg. mit einem Nachwort von Manfred S. Frings. München: Francke, 1979. 131 pp. (Uni-Taschenbücher, 871.)

16685. SCHNABEL, ARTUR. WOLFF, KONRAD: *Interpretation auf dem Klavier. Was wir von Artur*

Schnabel lernen. Einführung von Alfred Brendel. (Übers. aus dem Engl. von Tamara Trykar-Lu.) München: Piper, 1979. 219 pp., scores.

16686. SCHNITZLER, ARTHUR. SCHNITZLER, ARTHUR: *Gesammelte Werke in Einzelausgaben: Das erzählerische Werk, Bd. 1–7; Das dramatische Werk, Bd. 1–8.* Frankfurt a. Main: Fischer, 1977–1979. 15 vols. (Fischer-Taschenbücher, 1960–1974.)

16687. — ELFVING VOGEL, MARGOT: *Schnitzler in Schweden. Zur Rezeption seiner Werke.* Stockholm: Almqvist och Wiksell (in Komm.), 1979. 223 pp. (Acta Universitatis Upsaliensis, Studia Germanistica Upsaliensia, 23.) Zugl.: Uppsala, Univ., Phil. Diss., 1979.

16688. — MORSE, MARGARET ELIZABETH: *The works of Arthur Schnitzler as an index of cultural change.* Relationship between the sexes in society, ideology and the imagination. Berkeley, Univ. of California, Phil. Diss., 1977. 365 pp.

16689. — SCHNEIDER-HALVORSON, BRIGITTE-LINA: *The late dramatic works of Arthur Schnitzler.* Riverside, Univ. of California, Phil. Diss., 1978. 350 pp.

16690. SCHÖNBERG, ARNOLD. SCHÖNBERG, ARNOLD: *Die Grundlagen der musikalischen Komposition.* Übertr. von Rudolf Kolisch. Hrsg. von Rudolf Stephan. a–b. Wien: Universal Edition, 1979. 125 pp., bibl., & 102 pp. scores. [a.: Text; b.: Notenbeispiele.]

16691. — *Moses und Aron. Zur Oper Arnold Schönbergs.* Bergisch Gladbach: Thomas-Morus-Akademie, 1979. 98 pp., scores. (Bensberger Protokolle, Nr. 28.) [Cont.: Moses und der unvorstellbare Gott (Hans-Joachim Kraus). Der unvorstellbare Gott (Eugen Biser). Arnold Schönberg (H. G. Adler). A. Schönbergs Oper 'Moses und Aron' (Rudolf Stephan).]

16692. SCHOEPS, HANS-JOACHIM. SCHOEPS, HANS-JOACHIM: *Deutsche Geistesgeschichte der Neuzeit. Ein Abriss in 5 Bänden.* Mainz: v. Hase u. Koehler. *Bd. 3: Von der Aufklärung zur Romantik.* 1978. 400 pp. *Bd. 4: Die Formung der politischen Ideen im 19. Jahrhundert.* 1979. 419 pp. [For vols. 1 and 2, publ. 1977, see No. 15672/YB. XXIV.]

16693. — SCHOEPS, HANS-JOACHIM: *Üb immer Treu und Redlichkeit. Preussen in Geschichte und Gegenwart.* Die besten Vorträge, Reden, Aufsätze zum 70. Geburtstag von H.-J. Schoeps. Düsseldorf: Rau, 1979. 200 pp., bibl. (pp. 192–200). [Cf. also: Geisteswissenschaftler auf vielen Gebieten. Zum 70. Geburtstag von H.-J. Schoeps (Yizhak Ahren) [in]: 'Allgemeine', Düsseldorf, 26. Jan. 1979, p. 6.]

16694. — *Zeitschrift für Religions- und Geistesgeschichte. Bd. 31, H. 1.* Dieses Sonderheft ist dem Begründer u. Herausgeber dieser Zeitschrift Hans-Joachim Schoeps zum 70. Geburtstag (30. Jan. 1979) gewidmet. Köln: Brill, 1979. 117 pp. [Incl.: H.-J. Schoeps 70 (Kurt Töpner, pp. 1–6). H.-J. Sch. als preussischer Geschichtsschreiber (Manfred P. Fleischer, pp. 7–26). Der Beitrag von H.-J. Sch. zur Paulusforschung (Gösta Lindeskog, pp. 27–47). Johann Wolfgang Brenks Stellung in der Geschichte des 'Philosemitismus' des 18. Jahrhunderts (Friedrich Wilhelm Kantzenbach, pp. 78–98). Bibliographie H.-J. Sch. (p. 116).]

16695. SCHWARZWALD, EUGENIE. HERDAN-ZUCKMAYER, ALICE: *Genies sind im Lehrplan nicht vorgesehen.* Frankfurt a. Main: S. Fischer, 1979. 287 pp., illus. [Memoirs especially referring to Eugenie Schwarzwald, born 1873 in Galicia, pedagogue and early fighter for women's rights in Vienna.]

16696. SEGHERS, ANNA. SEGHERS, ANNA: *Der Ausflug der toten Mädchen. Erzählungen.* Darmstadt: Luchterhand, 1979. 91 pp. (Sammlung Luchterhand, 288.)

16697. — SEGHERS, ANNA: *Die Macht der Worte. Reden, Schriften, Briefe.* (Auswahl von Sina Witt.) Leipzig: Kiepenheuer, 1979. 255 pp. (Gustav-Kiepenheuer-Bücherei.)

16698. — BILKE, JÖRG BERNHARD: *Ein überschaubares Werk. Literatur von und über Anna Seghers.* [In]: Deutsche Studien, H. 62, Hamburg, 1978. Pp. 155–162, bibl. references.

16699. — BUNTEN, KATHLEEN ANNE: *Isolation and solidarity in the early works of Anna Seghers.* The Ohio State Univ., Phil. Diss., 1978. 170 pp.

16700. — ROGGAUSCH, WERNER: *Das Exilwerk von Anna Seghers 1933–1939.* Volksfront und antifaschistische Literatur. München: Minerva-Saur, 1979. IV, 424 pp. (Minerva-Fachserie, Geisteswissenschaften.) Zugl.: Bremen, Univ., Phil. Diss. 1977.

16701. SERNER, WALTER [orig. Seligmann]. SERNER, WALTER: *Angst. Frühe Prosa.* Mit fünf Illustr. von Christian Schad. Hrsg. u. Nachwort von Thomas Milch. Erlangen: Renner, 1979. 70 pp. [W.S., born about 1889, disappeared in 1933, place and date of death not known. Dadaist and writer.]

16702. — SERNER, WALTER: *Hirngeschwür. Walter Serner und Dada.* Texte u. Materialien. Hrsg. von Thomas Milch. Erlangen: Renner, 1979. 166 pp.

16703. — SERNER, WALTER: *Sämtliche Kriminalgeschichten. Bd. 1: Zum blauen Affen. Bd. 2: Der Pfiff um* die Ecke. Erlangen: Renner, 1979. 2 vols. (292; 281 pp.) (Serner, Walter: Das gesamte Werk. Hrsg. von Thomas Milch. Bd. 4. 5.)

16704. SILBERGLEIT, ARTHUR. BIENEK, HORST: *Arthur Silbergleit. Hinweise auf einen vergessenen Dichter.* [In]: SZ, München, 17./18. März 1979. P. 130. [See also: Eine kleine Spur genügt. Erinnerungen an den Lyriker Arthur Silbergleit (Karl Krolow) [in]: NZZ, Zürich, 24./25. Febr. 1979, p. 70. A.S., poet, born 1881 in Gleiwitz O/S., arrested in March 1943 in Berlin and deported, date of death uncertain. Silbergleit, together with Arthur Kochmann, the last representative of the Jewish community Gleiwitz, play leading parts in Horst Bienek's novels 'Septemberlicht' and 'Zeit ohne Glocken', see No. 16080.]

16705. SILBERMANN, ALPHONS: *Kein Brett vor dem Kopf. Ketzereien eines Soziologen.* Düsseldorf: Econ, 1979. 304 pp. [A.S., born 1909, sociologist, emigrated in 1933 to the Netherlands, later to Australia, now prof. of sociology at Cologne univ. Cf.: Alphons Silbermann 70 [in]: SZ, München, 11./12. Aug. 1979.]

16706. SIMMEL, GEORG. CHRISTIAN, PETRA: *Einheit und Zwiespalt. Zum hegelianisierenden Denken in der Philosophie und Soziologie Georg Simmels.* Berlin: Duncker u. Humblot, 1978. 158 pp. (Soziologische Schriften, Bd. 27.)

16707. SINZHEIMER, MAX. MEYER, HERBERT: *Max Sinzheimer. Ein Beitrag zur Mannheimer Musikgeschichte.* [And]: Nochmals Max Sinzheimer (Ernst G. Lowenthal). [In]: Mannheimer Hefte, H. 1 (pp. 14–15, port.) [&] H. 2 (p. 91), Mannheim, 1979. [M.S., June 20, 1894 Frankfurt a. Main–Oct. 16, 1977 Elm Grove/Wisconsin, conductor, 1917–1938 in Mannheim.]

16708. STERNHEIM, CARL. DEIRITZ, KARL: *Geschichtsbewusstsein, Satire, Zensur. Eine Studie zu Carl Sternheim.* Königstein/Ts.: Forum Academicum, 1979. 230 pp. (Hochschulschriften: Literaturwissenschaft, Bd. 43.) Zugl.: Hamburg, Univ., Sprachwiss. Diss., 1979.

16709. — LINKE, MANFRED: *Carl Sternheim in Selbstzeugnissen und Bilddokumenten.* Reinbek: Rowohlt, 1979. 173 pp., illus., ports., facsims., bibl. (pp. 164–170). (Rowohlts Monographien, 278.)

16710. — WENDLER, WOLFGANG, ed.: *Carl Sternheim Materialienbuch.* Darmstadt: Luchterhand, 1979. 400 pp. (Sammlung Luchterhand, Bd. 245.)

16711. — WILLIAM, RHYS W.: *Carl Sternheim's image of Marx and his critique of the German intellectual tradition.* [In]: German Life and Letters, New Ser. Vol. 32, No. 1, Oxford, Oct. 1978. Pp. 19–29.

16712. STOLPER, GUSTAV. STOLPER, TONI: *Ein Leben in Brennpunkten unserer Zeit. Gustav Stolper 1888–1947.* Neuausg. mit einem Vorwort von Hildegard Hamm-Brücher. Stuttgart: Klett-Cotta, 1979. 508 pp., facsim., bibl. [G.St., political economist and chief editor of the 'Berliner Börsen-Courier'. For earlier edn. see No. 2323/YB. VI.]

16713. TÄUBLER, EUGEN: *Tyche.* [Bound with]: *Die Archäologie des Thukydides* von Eugen Täubler. Nachdr. der Ausgaben Leipzig, Berlin, Teubner, 1926 u. 1927. Hildesheim: Olms, 1979. IV, 240, IV, 139 pp. [E.T., 1879–1953, historian, see also No. 16338.]

16714. TIETZ, LEONHARD. Department Store. KRÖGER, JOST J.: *Hundert Jahre Kaufhofkonzern. Der 'Tietze Leienad', ein Kölner von Weltrang.* [In]: Köln, Vierteljahresschrift für die Freunde der Stadt, Nr. 3, Köln, 1979. Pp. 28–33. [See also: Den wahren Tatsachen die Ehre geben. Zum 'Kaufhof'-Jubiläum (H. Istor) [in]: 'Allgemeine', Düsseldorf, 20. Juli 1979, p. 4 [and in]: Isr. Wochenblatt, Nr. 30, Zürich, 27. Juli 1979, pp. 25–27 (E. G. Lowenthal). Tietz-Enkel kamen nach Köln. Prominenz aus Politik u. Wirtschaft feierte '100 Jahre Kaufhof' [in]: 'Allgemeine', Düsseldorf, 14. Sept. 1979, p. 4, port. Leonhard Tietz u. der 'Kaufhof' (Ernst G. Lowenthal) [in]: Aufbau, New York, June 29, 1979, p. 19. Hundert Jahre 'Kaufhof'. Die Revolution des Leonhard Tietz [in]: Isr. Wochenblatt, Nr. 49, Zürich, 7. Dez. 1979, pp. 33 & 34, port. Die Wende kam nach 100 Jahren. Warenhäuser auf Rollensuche im Einzelhandel. Kaufhof-Jubiläum [vorm. Leonhard Tietz] (Norbert Sturm) [in]: SZ, München, 28. Aug. 1979, p. 15, facsim. 100 Jahre Warenhaus. Die Tempel der Konsumgesellschaft [in]: Zeit Magazin, Nr. 51, Hamburg, 14. Dez. 1979, pp. 28–34, illus.]

16715. TOLLER, ERNST. TOLLER, ERNST: *Prosa, Briefe, Dramen, Gedichte.* Mit einem Vorwort von Kurt Hiller. Reinbek: Rowohlt, 1979. 331 pp., bibl. (p. 331). (rororo, 4417.)

16716. — EICHENLAUB, RENÉ: *Ernst Toller et l'expressionnisme politique.* 1–2. Lille: Atelier de reproduction des thèses de l'Université de Lille III; Diffusion Champion, 1978. 2 vols.

16717. — FRÜHWALD, WOLFGANG/SPALEK, JOHN M., eds.: *Der Fall Toller. Kommentar und Materialien.* München: Hanser, 1979. 300 pp., illus., bibl. (pp. 233–240). [Supplementary vol. to Ernst Toller: Gesammelte Werke, München, 1978, 5 vols., see No. 15686/YB. XXIV. Incl.: Lebens- u. Werkchronik (pp. 11–24). Dokumentation: Revolution u. Räterepublik; Flucht, Verhaftung u. Prozess; Festungshaft; Kampf für die Weimarer Republik; Exil (pp. 27–232).

Cf.: Der Fall Toller. Hinweis auf einen Dokumentationsband (Ernst Nef) [in]: NZZ, Zürich, 1./2. Dez. 1979, p. 68.]

16718. TORBERG, FRIEDRICH [orig. Friedrich Kantor Berg]. TORBERG, FRIEDRICH: *Der Beifall war endenwollend. Theaterkritiken und Glossen.* Hrsg. von Eberhard Gaupp. München: Dt.-Taschenbuch-Verl., 1979. 245 pp. (dtv, 1488.) [In Oct. 1979 Torberg received the 'Grosser Österr. Staatspreis für Literatur'.]

16719. — TORBERG, FRIEDRICH: *Hier bin ich, mein Vater.* Roman. Reinbek: Rowohlt, 1979. 220 pp. (rororo, 4373.) [1st edn. Stockholm, Bermann-Fischer, 1948.]

16720. — *Obituaries* (Sept. 16, 1908 Vienna–Nov. 10, 1979 Vienna): Dem Gedenken F. Torbergs (Hans Lamm) [in]: 'Allgemeine', Düsseldorf, 23. Nov. 1979, p. 6, port. Letzte Ehren für Torberg (Hans Lamm) [in]: 'Allgemeine', Düsseldorf, 7. Dez. 1979, p. 7. F. Torberg gestorben (Hans Steinitz) [in]: Aufbau, New York, Nov. 16, 1979, p. 4, port. Zum Tode von F.T. (Marcel Reich-Ranicki) [in]: FAZ, Frankfurt a. Main, 12. Nov. 1979, p. 21, port. Judesein war der Kern seines Wesens [in]: Isr. Wochenblatt, Nr. 46, Zürich, 16. Nov. 1979, pp. 28–29, port. Aus Torbergs frühen Jahren u. letzten Wochen (Erich Gottgetreu) [in]: MB, Nr. 43, Tel Aviv, 23. Nov. 1979, p. 7. Zum Tode von F.T. (Leo Brod) [in]: Neue Jüd. Nachrichten, Nr. 44, München, 23. Nov. 1979, p. 4. In seinem Werk ist Österreich. Zum Tode von F.T. [in]: NZZ, 13. Nov. 1979, p. 23. Ein Stück Österreich. Zum Tode von F.T. (Otto F. Beer) [in]: SZ, München, 12. Nov. 1979, p. 16, port. Obituary [in]: 'The Times', 21. Nov. 1979. Obituary (Gabriel Laub) [in]: Die Zeit, Hamburg, 16. Nov. 1979.

16721. TUCHOLSKY, KURT. BRADY, P. V.: *The writer and the camera. Kurt Tucholsky's experiments in partnership.* [In]: The Modern Language Review, Vol. 74, pt. 4, Cambridge, Oct. 1979. Pp. 856–870. [K. Tucholsky and John Heartfield, orig. Helmut Herzfelde.]

16722. — ZWERENZ, GERHARD: *Kurt Tucholsky. Biographie eines guten Deutschen.* München: Bertelsmann, 1979. 335 pp., illus., ports., facsims. [Cf.: Eine typische Verfalls-Erscheinung. Was Zwerenz u. Bertelsmann als Tucholsky-Biographie anbieten (Claus Heinrich Meyer) [in]: SZ, München, 28./29. Juli 1979, p. 144. Plädoyer für einen 'guten Deutschen' (Norbert Schachtsiek-Freitag) [in]: Tribüne, H. 71, Frankfurt a. Main, 1979, pp. 164–167. Besprechung (Fritz J. Raddatz) [in]: Die Zeit, Hamburg, 1. Juni 1979. '... nun haben die Anwälte das Wort'. Die Kontroverse zwischen Tucholsky-Biograf Zwerenz u. der 'Zeit'. Was die Hamburger 'Zeit' nicht abdrucken mag, jetzt im Wortlaut (Gerhard Zwerenz) [in]: Börsenblatt für den Dt. Buchhandel, Nr. 56, Frankfurt a. Main, 13. Juli 1979, pp. 1367–1369.]

16723. ULLSTEIN VERLAG. HAACKE, WILMONT: *Hundert Jahre Ullstein als Spiegelung der Geistesgeschichte.* [In]: Zeitschrift für Religions- u. Geistesgeschichte, Bd. 32, H. 2, Köln, 1979. Pp. 185–194.

16724. URZIDIL, JOHANNES: *Die verlorene Geliebte.* [Erinnerungen an Prag.] Mit einem Nachwort von Oskar Holl. München: Langen-Müller, 1979. 374 pp., bibl. (pp. 372–374). [1st edn. in 1956.]

16725. VALENTIN, VEIT: *Geschichte der Deutschen.* Mit einem ergänzenden Abriss zur deutschen Geschichte von 1945 bis zur Gegenwart von Erhard Klöss. Köln: Kiepenheuer u. Witsch, 1979. 772 pp., 140 illus. [1st publ. New York, Knopf, 1946. V. Valentin, 1885–1947, professor of history in Heidelberg, 'Reichsarchivar' during the Weimar Republic, emigrated to the U.S.A. in 1933.]

16726. WARBURG, ABY M. WARBURG, ABY M.: *Ausgewählte Schriften und Würdigungen.* Hrsg. von Dieter Wuttke in Verbindung mit Carl Georg Heise. Baden-Baden: Koerner, 1979. 638 pp., illus., tabs., bibl. Aby M. Warburg (pp. 517–598). (Saecula spiritalia, Bd. 1.) [Incl. also articles on Aby M. Warburg by Gertrud Bing, Leopold D. Ettlinger, Ernst Hans Gombrich, Carl Georg Heise, Fritz Saxl, Edgar Wind, pp. 313–516. Corrected entry of No. 15700/YB. XXIV.]

16727. — *Aby Warburg. Aus Anlass der 50. Wiederkehr seines Todestages.* [Prospekt, verfasst von Georg Syamken, zur Ausstellung in der] Hamburger Kunsthalle, 14. Okt. 1979 bis 6. Jan. 1980. Hamburg, 1979. [8 pp.], ports., illus. [Cf.: Erinnerungen an Aby M. Warburg. Gedenkstunde in der Hamburger Kunsthalle (Arie Goral) [in]: 'Allgemeine', Düsseldorf, 26. Okt. 1979, p. 8, port.]

16728. — FÜSSEL, STEPHAN, ed.: *Mnemosyne. Beiträge zum 50. Todestag von Aby M. Warburg.* Mit Beiträgen von Ernst Cassirer, Erwin Panofsky, Max J. Warburg [*et al.*]. Göttingen: Gratia-Verl., 1979. 63 pp. (Gratia, H. 7.) [See also: Der Entdecker der klassischen Unruhe. Zum 50. Todestag Aby M. Warburgs (Henning Ritter) [in]: SZ, München, 27./28. Okt. 1979, p. 150.]

16729. M. M. WARBURG & CO., Banking-House. ROSENBAUM, EDUARD/SHERMAN, A. J.: *M. M. Warburg & Co. 1798–1938. Merchant bankers of Hamburg.* London: Hurst, 1979. 190 pp., illus., ports., facsims., bibl. (pp. 179–183). [For German edn. see No. 15702/YB. XXIV.] [Dr. Eduard Rosenbaum, economist, sociologist, member of the Executive of the London Board of the Leo Baeck Institute, born 1887 in Hamburg, died May 22, 1979 in London. *Obits.*: In memoriam (Werner Rosenstock) [in]: AJR Information, London, July 1979, p. 10. The late Eduard Rosenbaum (Sir Otto Kahn-Freund) [in]: AJR Information, London, Sept. 1979, p. 11. Nachruf [in]: Die Zeit, Hamburg, 1. Juni 1979.]

16730. WARBURG, OTTO. KREBS, HANS unter Mitarbeit von ROSWITHA SCHMID: *Otto Warburg, Zellphysiologe, Biochemiker, Mediziner, 1883–1970.* Stuttgart: Wissenschaftl. Verlagsgesellschaft, 1979. 167 pp., facsims., plates, ports., bibl. (pp. 130–133). (Grosse Naturforscher, Bd. 41.) ['Verzeichnis der Arbeiten aus dem Warburgschen Laboratorium' pp. 134–161. Cf.: Erfolge u. Irrtümer eines grossen Biochemikers. Die erste Biographie über Otto Warburg (Rainer Flöhl) [in]: FAZ, Frankfurt a. Main, 9. Okt. 1979, p. L23.]

16731. WASSERMANN, AUGUST PAUL von. COHN, ERICH: *August Paul von Wassermann.* [In]: Nachrichtenblatt der Jüd. Gemeinde von Berlin u. des Verbandes der Jüd. Gemeinden in der DDR, Dresden–Berlin, Dez. 1979. Pp. 4–6, port., illus. (Berühmte jüdische Ärzte, 4.)

16732. WASSERMANN, JAKOB. WASSERMANN, JAKOB: *Etzel Andergast. Roman.* Mit einem Nachwort von Henry Miller. München: Langen-Müller, 1979. 666 pp. [Cf.: Wassermann, der Bestsellerautor von gestern (Marcel Reich-Ranicki) [in]: 'Allgemeine', Düsseldorf, 16. Febr. 1979, p. 7.

16733. — GARRIN, STEPHEN HOWARD: *The concept of justice in Jakob Wassermann's [Andergast-] trilogy.* Bern: Lang, 1979. 107 pp., bibl. (pp. 95–107). (Europäische Hochschulschriften: Reihe 1, Dt. Sprache u. Literatur, Bd. 267.) Zugl.: State Univ. of New York at Stony Brook, Thesis, 1976. [Refers to 'Der Fall Maurizius', 'Etzel Andergast' and 'Joseph Kerkhovens dritte Existenz'.]

16734. WEISS, PETER: *Aufsätze, Journale, Arbeitspunkte. Schriften zu Kunst und Literatur.* Hrsg. von Manfred Haiduk. Berlin/East: Henschel, 1979. 187 pp.

16735. WERFEL, FRANZ. WERFEL, FRANZ: *Die vierzig Tage des Musa Dagh. Roman.* Frankfurt a. Main: Fischer, 1979. 869 pp. (Fischer-Taschenbücher, 2062.)

16736. — COOK, KATHLEEN MAYHEW: *The drama of Franz Werfel.* Houston, Texas, Rice Univ., Phil. Diss., 1979. 273 pp.

16737. WITTGENSTEIN, LUDWIG. AMÉRY, JEAN: *An den Grenzen des Scharfsinns. Zu den 'Vermischten Bemerkungen' Ludwig Wittgensteins.* [In]: Neue Rundschau, Jg. 90, H. 1, Frankfurt a. Main, 1979. Pp. 86–95.

16738. — CAVELL, STANLEY: *The claim of reason. Wittgenstein, skepticism, morality, and tragedy.* Oxford: Oxford Univ. Press, 1979. 500 pp.

16739. — FROMM, SUSANNE: *Wittgensteins Erkenntnisspiele contra Kants Erkenntnislehre.* Freiburg i. Br.: Alber, 1979. 267 pp. (Symposion, 61.) Zugl.: Kiel, Univ., Phil. Diss. [See also: Lauter Sprachspiele. Ludwig Wittgensteins 'Philosophische Untersuchungen' (Jean-Pierre Leyvratz) [in]: NZZ, Zürich, 10./11. Nov. 1979, p. 68, port.]

16740. — HERINGER, HANS-JÜRGEN/NEDO, MICHAEL, eds.: *Wittgensteins geistige Erscheinung.* Frankfurt a. Main: Suhrkamp, 1979. 116 pp. (Wittgenstein, Ludwig: Schriften, Beiheft 3.) [Incl.: Freud u. Wittgenstein (Brion McGuinness).Wittgenstein u. seine Zeit (Georg Henrik von Wright).]

16741. — HÜLSER, KARLHEINZ: *Wahrheitstheorie als Aussagentheorie. Untersuchungen zu Wittgensteins Tractatus.* Königstein/Ts.: Forum Academicum, 1979. X, 244 pp. (Monographien zur philosophischen Forschung, Bd. 117.) Zugl.: Konstanz, Univ., Phil. Diss., 1977.

16742. — WUCHTERL, KURT/HÜBNER, ADOLF: Ludwig Wittgenstein in Selbstzeugnissen und Bilddokumenten. Reinbek: Rowohlt, 1979. 156 pp., illus., ports., facsims., bibl. (pp. 145–156). (Rowohlts Monographien, 275.)

16743. ZADEK, PETER. CANARIS, VOLKER: *Peter Zadek, der Theatermann und Filmemacher.* München: Hanser, 1979. 284 pp., illus. (Theaterbuch, 2.) [P.Z., born in Berlin, emigrated to London in 1933, now stage-director in Germany.]

16744. ZONDEK, HERMANN. *Hermann Zondek in memoriam.* [In]: MB, Nr. 27, Tel Aviv, 20. Juli 1979. Pp. 5–6. [See also No. 11819/YB. XIX. H.Z., 1887 Wronke/Posen–1979 Jerusalem, professor of endocrinology, emigrated to England, later to Jerusalem, member of the Royal Society of Medicine in London.]

16745. ZUCKMAYER, CARL. FISCHER, BRIGITTE B.: *'Zuck' und sein Verleger [Samuel Fischer].* Erinnerungen. [With]: Zuckmayer auf der Bühne [by several authors]. Mainz: Carl-Zuckmayer-Ges., 1979. Pp. 157–208. (Blätter der Carl-Zuckmayer-Gesellschaft, Jg. 5, H. 3.)

16746. ZWEIG, ARNOLD: *Das Beil von Wandsbek. Roman.* Königstein/Ts.: Verlag Autoren-Edition im Athenäum-Verl., 1979. 544 pp. (Republikanische Bibliothek.)

16747. ZWEIG, STEFAN. ZWEIG, STEFAN: *Balzac. Eine Biographie.* (Aus dem Nachlass hrsg. u. mit einem Nachwort versehen von Richard Friedenthal.) Frankfurt a. Main: Fischer, 1979. 399 pp., bibl. (pp. 387–395). (Fischer-Taschenbücher, 2183.)

16748. — ZWEIG, STEFAN: *Ein Gewissen gegen die Gewalt. Castellio gegen Calvin.* Frankfurt a. Main: S. Fischer, 1979. 201 pp.

16749. — ZWEIG, STEFAN: *Legenden.* Mit einem Nachwort von Alexander Hildebrand. Frankfurt a. Main: S. Fischer, 1979. 238 pp. (Fischer-Bibliothek.)

16750. — ZWEIG, STEFAN: *Verwirrung der Gefühle und andere Erzählungen.* Ausgewählte Ausg. Frankfurt a. Main: Fischer, 1979. 200 pp. (Fischer-Taschenbücher, 2129.)

VIII. AUTOBIOGRAPHY, MEMOIRS, LETTERS, GENEALOGY

16751. ARONSFELD, C. C.: *Memories of a childhood in Posen.* [In]: Jewish Frontier, Vol. 46, No. 2, New York, Febr. 1979. Pp. 26–28.

16752. BALLIN, GÜNTHER: *Es war ja erst gestern. Erinnerungen.* (Erstes Bändchen.) Buenos Aires, Mai 1979. 64 pp. [Priv. print.] [G.B., born 1909 in Berlin.]

16753. BAMBERGER FAMILY. ESH, SHAUL, ed.: *The Bamberger family. The descendants of Rabbi Seligmann Bär Bamberger, the 'Würzburger Rav'* (*1807–1878*). 2nd, revised edn. Jerusalem: Priv. print. by the Bamberger Family, 1979. 112, 56 [Hebrew] pp., geneal. tabs. [1st edn. 1964, see No. 4838/YB. X. See also: The 'Wuerzburger Rav'. Centenary of his death, Oct. 17th, 1978 (William Stern) [in]: AJR Information, London, April 1979, p. 5 (see also No. 15247/YB. XXIV).]

16754. BEHREND, ITZIG: *The family chronicle.* (Foreword by William Bonwitt.) London, 1978. XI, 23 pp., geneal. tab., illus., ports., notes. [Priv. mimeog.] [Orig. written about 1829, partly publ. in the 1909 issue of 'Jahrbuch für Jüd. Geschichte u. Literatur'. Transl. now into English by Caroline Bonwitt, née Behrend. I. Behrend, 1765–1845 Grove-Rodenberg, near Kassel, trader.]

16755. BEN-CHORIN, SCHALOM: *Ich lebe in Jerusalem.* Ein Bekenntnis zu Geschichte und Gegenwart. Gerlingen: Bleicher, 1979. 263 pp. (Aktuelles Taschenbuch.)

16756. BENJAMIN, WALTER. LACKNER, STEPHAN [orig. Morgenroth]: *'Von einer langen schwierigen Irrfahrt'. Aus unveröffentlichten Briefen Walter Benjamins* [an St. Lackner], *1936–1940.* [In]: Neue Deutsche Hefte, 161, Berlin, 1979. Pp. 48–69. [St. Lackner, born 1910 in Paris, grew up in Germany, now living in the U.S.A., author, art-historian.]

16757. BERMANN-FISCHER, GOTTFRIED: *Bedroht, bewahrt: der Weg eines Verlegers.* Frankfurt a. Main: Fischer, 1979. 350 pp. (Fischer-Taschenbücher, 1169.) [1st edn. 1967, see No. 6788/YB. XII.]

16758. BROD, MAX: *Streitbares Leben. Autobiographie 1884–1968.* Neuaufl. Frankfurt a. Main: Insel, 1979. 367 pp., illus. [1st publ. in 1960, now enlarged by diary-notes for the years up to 1968. See also: My escape from Prague (Max Brod) [in]: Jewish Frontier, Vol. 46, No. 10 (500th issue), New York, Dec. 1979. Pp. 30–32 (reprint from Jewish Frontier, May 1939).]

16759. CANETTI, ELIAS: *The tongue set free. Remembrance of a European childhood.* Transl. by Joachim Neugroschel. New York: The Seabury Press, 1979. 268 pp. [Orig. German edn., see No. 14054/YB. XXII.]

16760. EDEL, PETER: *Wenn es ans Leben geht. Meine Geschichte.* 1–2. (Mit Fotos, Dokumenten u. Zeichnungen des Autors.) Berlin/East: Verlag der Nation, 1979. 2 vols. (451; 420 pp., illus.) [P.E., born 1921 in Berlin, artist, journalist and writer, survived Auschwitz, lives in the G.D.R.]

16761. EISENBERG, LOTTE: *Meine Gäste, Tiberias und ich. Memoiren.* Jerusalem: Maass, 1979. 152 pp.

16762. EPHRAIM FAMILY. MICHAELIS, DOLF: *The Ephraim family and their descendants (II).* [In]: LBI Year Book XXIV, London, 1979. Pp. 225–246, ports., bibl. footnotes [Part I was publ. in: LBI Year Book XXI (1976) pp. 201–228, see No. 14055/YB. XXII.]

16763. FEUCHTWANGER, LION. FEUCHTWANGER, MARTA: *The world of Lion Feuchtwanger on tape.* Los Angeles, Univ. of Southern California, [1979]. 32 tapes. [M.F., 87-year-old widow of Lion Feuchtwanger, has recorded her memoirs in a series of interviews conducted by the Univ. of Southern California.]

16764. FRICK, HANS: *Die blaue Stunde*. München: Steinhausen, 1979. 137 pp. [The author, son of a gentile mother and Jewish father, tells of the conflicts of his youth in Frankfurt a. Main during the Nazi years. Cf.: Apokalypse des Grauens (Norbert Schachtsiek-Freitag) [in]: Tribüne, H. 72, Frankfurt a. Main, 1979, pp. 157–161.]

16765. FRIEDLÄNDER, SAUL: *When memory comes*. Transl. from the French by Helen R. Lane. New York: Farrar, Straus and Giroux, 1979. 185 pp. [Also German edn.]: *Wenn die Erinnerung kommt* ... Aus dem Franz. von Helgard Oestreich. Stuttgart: Deutsche Verlags-Anstalt, 1979. 192 pp. [S.F., born 1932 in Prague, escaped to France and spent childhood as a Catholic, now professor of modern history in Israel. Cf.: Drama u. Melancholie einer jüdischen Odyssee (Hilde Marx) [in]: Aufbau, New York, Sept. 14, 1979, p. 29. Between Paris and Jerusalem (Leon Wieseltier) [in]: The New York Review of Books, Oct. 25, 1979, pp. 3–4.]

16766. FRISCH, OTTO R.: *What little I remember*. Cambridge: Cambridge Univ. Press, 1979. 227 pp., illus. [Incl. literary portrait of his aunt Lise Meitner. O. R. Frisch, Oct. 1, 1904 Vienna–Sept. 22, 1979 England, physicist, emigrated to London in 1933, worked also with Niels Bohr and at Los Alamos in the U.S.A. on nuclear fission. Cf. obituary: Professor Otto Frisch, outstanding successes in nuclear physics [in]: 'The Times', London, Nov. 16, 1979, p. VIII of Obituaries Supplement.]

16767. GERNSHEIM FAMILY. GERNSHEIM, HELMUT: *The Gernsheims of Worms*. [In]: LBI Year Book XXIV, London, 1979. Pp. 247–257, ports., illus., bibl. footnotes.

16768. GOLDAMMER, PETER, ed.: *Lebensdaten. Autobiographisches von Gerhart Hauptmann bis Arnold Zweig*. Rostock: Hinstorff, 1979. 431 pp. [Incl. autobiographical essays by: Döblin, Feuchtwanger, Egon E. Kisch, Joseph Roth, Sternheim, Werfel, Arnold Zweig and others.]

16769. GROSSMANN, STEFAN: *Ich war begeistert. Eine Lebensgeschichte*. Mit einem Vorwort von Egon Schwarz u. einem Nachwort von Carel ter Haar. Nachdr. der Erstausg. von 1930. Königstein/Ts.: Scriptor, 1979. 344 pp. (Reihe Q, Bd. 7.) [Refers to Friedrich and Viktor Adler, Peter Altenberg, Theodor Herzl, Gustav Landauer, Walther Rathenau and others. St. G., 1875–1935, journalist, founded the 'Freie Volksbühne' in Vienna, and together with Leopold Schwarzschild 'Das Tagebuch' in Berlin.]

16770. GRÜNFELD, FRITZ V.: *Heimgesucht, heimgefunden. Betrachtung und Bericht*. Berlin: arani, 1979. 232 pp., illus. [F.V.G., last owner of Falk Valentin Grünfeld, linen-factory and shop.]

16771. HANNAM, CHARLES [orig. Karl Hartland]. HANNAM, CHARLES: *Almost an Englishman*. London: André Deutsch, 1979. 208 pp. [Ch.H., born 1925 in Essen. Cf.: Hardly a Jew (Edward Blishen) in: 'The Guardian', Oct. 11, 1979, p. 10.]

16772. — HANNAM, CHARLES: *Und dann musste ich gehen. Die Geschichte eines jüdischen Jungen von 1933–1940*. Würzburg: Arena, 1979. 240 pp. [For Engl. edn. see No. 14895/YB. XXIII. Describes childhood in Essen and emigration to England. Cf.: Ein Junge in deiner Lage (Sophie Fischer) [in]: SZ, München, 10. Okt. 1979, p. XIII.]

16773. HEINE, BETTY. JUNG, HERMANN: *'Wo Deutschland noch Deutschland war ...' Aus Jugendbriefen der Mutter Heinrich Heines*. [In]: Aus dem Antiquariat, [Beilage zum] Börsenblatt für den Dt. Buchhandel, Frankfurter Ausg., Nr. 60, Frankfurt a. Main, 27. Juli 1979. Pp. A244–A248.

—— HEINE, HEINRICH: *Briefe von* [Heine and]: *Briefe an Heine*. [See in No. 16547.]

16774. HERMLIN, STEPHAN: *Abendlicht*. Berlin: Wagenbach, 1979. 120 pp. (Quarthefte, 101.)

16775. KAFKA. FRANZ. BINDER, HARTMUT: *Ein ungedrucktes Schreiben Franz Kafkas an Felix Weltsch*. Edition u. Kommentar. [In]: Jahrbuch der Dt. Schillergesellschaft, Jg. 20, Stuttgart, 1976. Pp. 103–131, facsim., bibl. footnotes.

16776. KAUS, GINA: *Und was für ein Leben ... Mit Liebe und Literatur, Theater und Film*. Hamburg: Knaus, 1979. 288 pp. [G.K., born 1893 in Vienna, living in Hollywood, journalist and writer, friendships with Karl Kraus and other literary figures.]

16777. KERR, ALFRED: *Ich kam nach England. Ein Tagebuch aus dem Nachlass*. Hrsg. von Walther Huder u. Thomas Koebner. Bonn: Bouvier, 1979. 206 pp. (Schriftenreihe Literaturwissenschaft, Bd. 9.)

16778. KOLMAN, ARNOŠT: *Die verirrte Generation. So hätten wir nicht leben sollen. Eine Biographie*. Aus dem Russischen von Elisabeth Mahler-Berger. Frankfurt a. Main: S. Fischer, 1979. 280 pp., illus., ports. [A.K., 1892–1979, Prague-born Communist leader, left the USSR 1976 for the West.]

16779. KREUTZBERGER, MAX: *Eine lebenslange Freundschaft*. [Erinnerungen.] [In]: Des Geistes Gleichmass. Festschrift zum 75. Geburtstag des Ehrwürdigen Nyanaponika Mahathera. Konstanz: Christiani, 1976. Pp. 19–32. [Autobiographical account of the friendship between

M. Kreutzberger (1900 Königshütte–1978 Locarno) and Nyanaponika Mahathera, orig. Siegmund Feniger, born 1901 in Hanau, scholar, emigrated to Ceylon in 1936, co-founder of 'The Buddhist Publication Society' in Kandy. See also in this 'Festschrift' the contribution by Erich Fromm: 'Die Bedeutung Nyanaponika Mahatheras für die Westliche Welt', pp. 35–38.]

16780. LEHRMANN, CUNO CH.: *Als der Grossvater die Grossmutter nahm.* [Aus Lehrmanns] Familienchronik 'Stirb und werde' hrsg. von Graziella Lehrmann. [In]: Neue Deutsche Hefte, 161, Berlin, 1979. Pp. 89–102. [C.Ch.L., 1905–1977, rabbi, professor of Romanic languages, Würzburg.]

16781. LUXEMBURG, ROSA. LUXEMBURG, ROSA: *Comrade and lover. Rosa Luxemburg's letters to Leo Jogiches,* ed. and transl. by Elzbieta Ettinger. Cambridge, Mass.: MIT Press, 1979. 206 pp. [First publ. in Polish. For German edn. 1971 see No. 10043/YB. XVII. Cf.: R. Luxemburg's letters to L. Jogiches [in]: Midstream, Vol. 25, No. 8, New York, Oct. 1979, pp. 50–54. Love and revolution (Neal Ascherson) [in]: The New York Review of Books, March 6, 1980, pp. 14–16.]

16782. — LUXEMBURG, ROSA et al.: *Briefe an Mathilde Jacob (1913–1918).* Bonn: Dietz, 1979. IX, 248 pp. (Reprints zur Sozialgeschichte.) [154 letters by R. Luxemburg written in prison to her secretary M. Jacob. For previous edn. see No. 10938/YB. XVIII.]

16783. MAHLER-WERFEL, ALMA: *Erinnerungen an Gustav Mahler.* [With]: MAHLER, GUSTAV: *Briefe an Alma Mahler.* Hrsg. von Donald Mitchell. Übers. der Einleitung u. des Nachwortes aus dem Engl. von Jürgen Schwab. Frankfurt a. Main: Ullstein, 1978. 392 pp., scores. (Ullstein-Buch, Nr. 3526.) [Engl. edn., 1968, see No. 7369/YB. XIV. Previous German edn. 1971, see No. 9881/YB. XVII.]

16784. MAIER, MATHILDE: *Alle Gärten meines Lebens.* Frankfurt a. Main: Knecht, 1978. 152 pp., illus. [See also No. 10199/YB. XVIII and 12672/YB. XXI.]

16785. MARX, KARL: *The letters of Karl Marx.* Selected and transl. with explanatory notes and an introduction by Saul K. Padover. Englewood Cliffs, N.J.: Prentice-Hall, 1979. 576 pp., illus. [Cf.: Drei unbekannte Marx-Briefe aus den Jahren 1851 u. 1852 (Martin Hundt) [and]: Drei unbekannte Briefe von Karl Marx u. Friedrich Engels (Ursula Herrmann/Jutta Seidel) [in]: Beiträge zur Geschichte der Arbeiterbewegung, Jg. 20, Nr. 3, Berlin/East, 1978, pp. 369–373; 373–386.]

16786. MARX, LEOPOLD: *Jehoshua, mein Sohn. Lebensbild eines früh Gereiften.* Gerlingen: Bleicher, 1979. 311 pp., port. (Bleicher-Bücherbord.) [Memoirs, 1921–1948. L.M., born Dec. 8, 1889 in Stuttgart, emigrated to Palestine in 1939. See also: Gärtner u. Dichter, L. Marx zum Neunzigsten (E. G. Lowenthal) [in]: MB, Nr. 45, Tel Aviv, 7. Dez. 1979, p. 6. L. Marx 90 Jahre alt [in]: Neue Jüd. Nachrichten, Nr. 45, München, 7. Dez. 1979, pp. 5 & 7.]

16787. MASUR, GERHARD: *Das ungewisse Herz. Berichte aus Berlin, über die Suche nach dem Freien.* Mit einem Wegweiser von Wilmont Haacke. Holyoke, Mass.: Blenheim Publ. House, 1978. XXV, 356 pp. [Refers to childhood and years of study in Berlin, emigration to Colombia. See also: Erinnerungen an Gerhard Masur. Wegweiser zu seinem Werk (Wilmont Haacke) [in]: Zeitschrift für Religions- u. Geistesgeschichte, Bd. 31, H. 3, Köln 1979, pp. 263–276. G.M., 1901 Berlin–1975 U.S.A., historian.]

16788. MEHRING, WALTER. MEHRING, WALTER: *Die verlorene Bibliothek. Autobiographie einer Kultur.* Düsseldorf: Claassen, 1978. 320 pp. (Mehring, Walter: Werkausgabe, Bd. 1.)

16789. — MEHRING, WALTER: *Wir müssen weiter. Fragmente aus dem Exil.* (Hrsg. von Christoph Buchwald.) Düsseldorf: Claassen, 1979. 160 pp., bibl. (pp. 157–160). (Mehring, Walter: Werke, [Bd. 3].)

16790. MEIDNER, ELSE. HODIN, JOSEPH PAUL: *Aus den Erinnerungen von Else Meidner.* Eine Würdigung ihres Werkes mit einem Beitrag von Max Peter Maass und einem Nachwort von Heinz Winfried Sabais. Darmstadt: Justus-von-Liebig-Verl., 1979. 132 pp., illus., ports., facsims., bibl. E. Meidner (pp. 130–132). (Darmstädter Schriften, 42.)

— MENDELSSOHN, MOSES: Briefwechsel der letzten Lebensjahre. [See No. 16251.]

16791. MENDELSSOHN BARTHOLDY, FELIX: *Eine Reise durch Deutschland, Italien und die Schweiz: Briefe, Tagebuchblätter, Skizzen.* Mit einem Lebensbild Mendelssohns und seiner Familie. Mit Aquarellen u. Zeichnungen aus Mendelssohns Reiseskizzenbüchern. Hrsg. von Peter Sutermeister. [Nachdr. der Ausg.] Zürich, Niehans, 1958. Tübingen: Heliopolis-Verl., 1979. 384 pp., illus., scores.

16792. MEYER-LEVINÉ, ROSA: *Im inneren Kreis. Erinnerungen einer Kommunistin in Deutschland 1920–1933.* Hrsg. u. eingel. von Hermann Weber. Aus dem Engl. von Barbara Bortfeldt. Köln:

Kiepenheuer u. Witsch, 1979. 404 pp., illus., ports., facsims., bibl. notes (pp. 377–384). [Cf.: Zum Tode Rosa Meyer-Levinés (Hermann Weber) [in]: 'Allgemeine', Düsseldorf, 23. Nov. 1979, p. 6. R.M.-L. died on Nov. 11, 1979 in London.]

16793. MONASCH, BAER LOEW (1801–1876). FRAENKEL, PETER: *The memoirs of B. L. Monasch of Krotoschin*. [In]: LBI Year Book XXIV, London, 1979. Pp. 195–223, notes, ports.

16794. MÜHSAM, ERICH: *Briefe an Zeitgenossen*. Eingeleitet u. hrsg. von Gerd W. Jungblut. Berlin: Guhl, 1978. 274 pp., ports., illus.

—— POLAK, ERNST [orig. Pollak]. SULZER, DIETER: *Der Nachlass von Ernst Polak im Deutschen Literaturarchiv. Bericht, Verzeichnis und Edition von Briefen Polaks, Werfels und Brochs*. [See No. 16664.]

16795. POPPER, KARL R.: *Ausgangspunkte. Meine intellektuelle Entwicklung*. (Aus dem Engl. von Friedrich Griese u. vom Autor. Die dt. Ausg. wurde vom Verfasser überarb.) Hamburg: Hoffmann u. Campe, 1979. X, 371 pp., bibl. (pp. 335–346). [Orig. edn. see No. 14070/YB. XXII. Cf.: Glücklich im Ideenkampf. K. Poppers Autobiographie (Willy Hochkeppel) [in]: Die Zeit, Hamburg, 16. Nov. 1979, p. LI.]

16796. REDLICH, JOSEF: *Dichter und Gelehrter. Hermann Bahr und Josef Redlich in ihren Briefen 1896–1934*. Hrsg. von Fritz Fellner. Salzburg: Neugebauer, 1979. 720 pp., illus. (Quellen zur Geschichte des 19. u. 20. Jahrhunderts, Bd. 2.) [J.R., 1869 Göding/Moravia–1936 Vienna, Austrian minister of finance in 1918 and 1931 to 1934.]

16797. SCHNITZLER, ARTHUR: *The letters of Arthur Schnitzler to Hermann Bahr*. Ed., annotated, and with an introduction by Donald G. Daviau. Chapel Hill: The Univ. of North Carolina Press, 1978. 183 pp.

16798. SCHRAG, PAUL J.: *Heimatkunde. Die Geschichte einer deutsch-jüdischen Familie*. München: Kindler, 1979. 161 pp. [Tells the story of the family Kusel in southern Germany and of the tobacco factory Moll & Schneider, owned 1881–1938 by the Kusel family.]

16799. SCHWARZ, EGON: *Keine Zeit für Eichendorff. Chronik unfreiwilliger Wanderjahre*. Königstein/Ts.: Athenäum, 1979. 190 pp. [E.Sch., born 1922 in Vienna, fled to Czechoslovakia in 1938 and finally came to the U.S.A. in 1949.]

16800. SCHWARZ, STEFAN: *Sage nie, du gehst den letzten Weg. Tatsachenroman um den Leidensweg einer jüdischen Familie*. München: Heyne, 1979. (Heyne-Bücher, Nr. 5552.) [1st edn. 1971, see No. 10148/YB. XVII. See also: Dipl. Ing. St. Schwarz mit hoher, seltener Auszeichnung geehrt [Denkmalschutz-Medaille] (Gerhard E. Habermann) [in]: Neue Jüd. Nachrichten, Nr. 44, München, 23. Nov. 1979, p. 5.]

16801. STEIN, EDITH: *Mein erstes Göttinger Semester*. Mit Nachweisen u. Chronologie. Heroldsberg b. Nürnberg: Glock u. Lutz, 1979. 39 pp. (Nürnberger Liebhaberausgaben, Bd. 3.)

16802. STIEGLITZ FAMILY. MAYDELL, BODO Freiherr von: *Im Banne des Tikkun. Ein wiedergewonnenes geistiges Erbe*. Grafenau: Morsak, 1979. 81 pp., illus., facsims., geneal. tabs., ports.

16803. TUCHOLSKY, KURT. KING, W. J.: *Tucholsky's Q-Tagebücher*. [In]: German Life and Letters, New Ser. Vol. 33, No. 1, Oxford, Oct. 1979. Pp. 61–65. [Review article of 'Die Q-Tagebücher 1934–1935', Hamburg 1978, see No. 15743/YB. XXIV.]

16804. VARNHAGEN, RAHEL: *Briefwechsel*. Hrsg. von Friedhelm Kemp. 2., durchgesehene u. um Nachträge vermehrte Ausg. Bd. 1–4. München: Winkler, 1979. 4 vols. *Bd. 1: Rahel und Alexander von der Marwitz*. 485 pp. *Bd. 2: Rahel und Karl August Varnhagen*. 521 pp. *Bd. 3: Rahel und ihre Freunde*. 500 pp. *Bd. 4: Rahel und ihre Zeit*. 525 pp. [1st edn. 1966–1968, see No. 6822/YB. XIII.]

16805. VIERTEL, SALKA: *Das unbelehrbare Herz. Ein Leben in der Welt des Theaters, der Literatur und des Films*. Mit einem Vorwort von Carl Zuckmayer. (Von der Autorin überarb. Übers. von Helmut Degner.) Reinbek: Rowohlt, 1979. 358 pp., cover ports. (rororo, 4320.) [1st German edn. see No. 9088/YB. XVI.]

16806. WECHSBERG, JOSEPH: *The Vienna I knew. Memories of a European childhood*. Garden City, N.Y.: Doubleday, 1979. 263 pp. [J.W., born 1907.]

16807. ZWEIG, STEFAN: *Die Welt von gestern. Erinnerungen eines Europäers*. Frankfurt a. Main: Fischer, 1979. 317 pp. (Fischer-Taschenbücher, 1152.)

IX. GERMAN-JEWISH RELATIONS

A. General

16808. AKTION SÜHNEZEICHEN. *Polen '78. Stutthof, Białowieża, Warszawa.* Hrsg.: Arbeitsgemeinschaft Friedensdienste, Stuttgart, Rohreckweg 20. Red.: Georg Bopp [*et al.*]. Bad Cannstatt: Druck Evang. Dekanatamt (1978). 108 pp., illus. [Mimeog.] [Diary of 23 young Germans, voluntary labourers in Poland in 1978. Incl. section on the persecution of the German Jews.]

16809. BRODER, HENRYK M./LANG, MICHEL R., eds.: *Fremd im eigenen Land. Juden in der Bundesrepublik.* Mit einem Vorwort von Bernt Engelmann. Frankfurt a. Main: Fischer, 1979. 373 pp. (Fischer-Taschenbücher, 3801.)

16810. ECKSTEIN, GEORGE G.: *Apropos Deutsche und Juden.* [In]: Merkur, Jg. 33, H. 9, Stuttgart, Sept. 1979. Pp. 920–923.

16811. GOLDMANN, NAHUM: *Juden und andere Deutsche.* [1.]: War Hitler unvermeidbar? Reflexionen über eine gemeinsame Geschichte. [2.]: Warum der Nazi-Schock nicht enden darf. Über die Schizophrenie und die Wahlverwandtschaften zweier Völker. [In]: Die Zeit, Hamburg, 26. Jan. [&] 2. Febr. 1979.

16812. MARCH, JOACHIM: *Toleranz heute, 250 Jahre nach Lessing und Mendelssohn.* [In]: Die Mahnung, Nr. 3, Berlin, 1. März 1979. Pp. 1 & 2.

16813. SCHEEL, WALTER, ed.: *Nach dreissig Jahren. Die Bundesrepublik Deutschland.* Vergangenheit, Gegenwart, Zukunft. Stuttgart: Klett-Cotta, 1979. 352 pp., illus. [Incl. contributions by Jean Améry, Alfred Grosser, Richard Löwenthal, Hans Mayer, Toni Stolper and others. Abridged version of H. Mayer's contrib., also [in]: Die Zeit, Hamburg, 18. Mai 1979, illus.]

16814. *Tribüne.* Zeitschrift zum Verständnis des Judentums. Jg. 18, H. 69–72. Hrsg. von Elisabeth Reisch. Frankfurt a. Main: Tribüne-Verl., 1979. [4 issues.] [*H. 69* incl.: Ein Moralist in Deutschland. Zum 250. Geburtstag von G. E. Lessing (Hermann Kesten, pp. 50–64). *H. 70:* Gottesglaube nach Auschwitz (Rudolf Pfisterer, pp. 28–42). Dialog mit der jungen Generation (Hermann Langbein, pp. 56–62). *H. 71:* Nationalsozialismus u. Widerstand als erfahrbare Geschichte (Alfred Krink, pp. 44–68). Die unbewältigte Vergangenheit oder Haben die Deutschen gelernt? (Gerd Renken, pp. 70–90). *H. 72:* Unsere Geschichte mit dem Trivialen (Hermann Glaser, pp. 22–44). 'Mein Kampf' vor Gericht (Ulrich Klug, pp. 70–76). Further contributions are listed according to subject.]

B. German-Israeli Relations

16815. *deutschland-berichte.* Hrsg.: Rolf Vogel. Jg. 15, Nr. 1–12. Bonn, 1979. [11 issues.] [Incl.: 'Politik ist eine psychologische Frage' (Nahum Goldmann, Nr. 8/9, pp. 4–6. Text of a TV-interview concerning the relation between Germany and Israel and the Arabic question). Das deutsch-israelische Verhältnis, Deutsche und Juden (Gershom Scholem, Nr. 8/9, pp. 13–15). Zum deutsch-israelischen Verhältnis. Ein Gespräch mit Dr. Robert M. W. Kempner (Nr. 12, pp. 14–15). Further contributions are listed according to subject.]

16816. GOTTGETREU, ERICH: *Deutsche Studien an israelischen Universitäten.* [In]: MB, Nr. 21, Tel Aviv, 31. Mai 1979. Pp. 3–4.

16817. SCHMIDT, JOSEF: *Germanistik in Jerusalem.* Die Rückkehr der deutschen Sprache. Bescheidene aber solide Normalisierung. [In]: Die Zeit, Hamburg, 5. Okt. 1979. P. 52

16818. SCHWEIGER, RALPH: *Deutsch-jüdisch-israelische Beziehungen.* Ein Seminar des Aspen Instituts Berlin. [In]: 'Allgemeine', Düsseldorf, 21. Sept. 1979. P. 11.

16819. WISTRICH, ROBERT S., ed.: *The Left against Zion. Communism, Israel and the Middle East.* London: Vallentine, Mitchell, 1979. 309 pp. [Compilation of essays, lectures, etc., some already publ. in the Wiener Library Bulletin et al. Incl.: Neues Deutschland and Israel: A diary of East German reactions. Also: Zionism and the new Left (Rudolf Kraemer-Badoni). Anti-Israel extremism in West Germany (Gerd Langguth).]

C. Church and Synagogue

16820. *Aus den Psalmen leben. Das gemeinsame Gebet von Kirche und Synagoge neu erschlossen.* [Mit Beiträgen von Albert H. Friedlander u.a. Schriftleitung: Walter Strolz.] Freiburg i. Br.: Herder, 1979. 223 pp.

16821. BETHGE, EBERHARD: *Autobiographisches zum kirchlichen Antisemitismus und einige Folgerungen.* Stuttgart: Arbeitsgemeinschaft der Evang. Jugend (AEJ) in der Bundesrepublik Deutschland u. Berlin West e.V., [1978]. 16 pp. (Seminarmaterial der AEJ.)

16822. *Christen und Juden.* Eine Studie des Rates der Evang. Kirche in Deutschland, hrsg. im Auftrag des Rates von der Kirchenkanzlei der Evang. Kirche in Deutschland. 3. Aufl. Gütersloh: Mohn, 1979. 55 pp., bibl. (pp. 54–56). [And]: *Arbeitsbuch Christen und Juden.* Zur Studie des Rates der Evang. Kirche in Deutschland hrsg. von Rolf Rendtorff. Mit einem Vorwort des Vorsitzenden des Rates der Evang. Kirche in Deutschland. Gütersloh: Mohn, 1979. 288 pp., bibl.

16823. *Christian Attitudes on Jews and Judaism.* A bi-monthly documentary survey. Ed.: C. C. Aronsfeld. London: Institute of Jewish Affairs in association with the World Jewish Congress, 1979. No. 64–69. [6 issues.] [*No. 64* incl.: The Catholic Church and the Nazis. *No. 65:* Pope John Paul II received the representatives of Jewry. Oberammergau Passion Play discussion. *No. 66:* Christianity and the Holocaust. *No. 67:* The Pope at Auschwitz. East German remembrance. *No. 68:* Pope John Paul II's address to the United Nations. *No. 69:* First meeting in Germany of Catholic-Jewish Liaison Committee.]

16824. *Emuna/Israel-Forum.* Vereinigte Zeitschriften über Israel und Judentum. H. 1–3. Hrsg.: Deutscher Koordinierungsrat der Gesellschaften für Christlich-Jüdische Zusammenarbeit; Deutsch-Israelische Gesellschaft (DIG). Red.: Willehad Paul Eckert, Erika Doerdelmann-Kolbe, Erich Rotter. Rothenburg ob der Tauber: Verlag Israel-Forum, 1979. [2 issues.] [*H. 1–2* incl.: Kult u. Handwerk im Judentum (Schalom Ben-Chorin, pp. 13–17). Die Kristallnacht, ein theologisches Problem (Stefan Schreiner, pp. 23–25). Gegen Verjährung von Naziverbrechen (Meir Faerber and others, pp. 57–74). Die jüdische Herkunft der [Johann] Strauss-Dynastie (K. Karèl, pp. 93–96). *H. 3:* Martin Bubers Glaubensbegriff als Kritik am Christentum (Lorenz Wachinger, pp. 1–10, bibl.). M. Buber u. Hermann Gerson. Paradigma einer Lehrer-Schüler-Beziehung (Friedhelm Logos, pp. 11–19, bibl.). 'Ich und Du', eine mystische Schrift (Kees Waaijman, pp. 20–31, bibl.). Xenophobie oder die Sage vom Ewigen Juden (Leo Brod, pp. 31–36). Judenmord, warum? Versuch einer Motivverklärung (Michael Siegert, pp. 37–45, illus., bibl.). Die Justiz gegenüber den Naziärzten (pp. 59–62). Jesus, ein Sozialrevolutionär? (Salcia Landmann, pp. 64–68). Further contributions are listed according to subject.]

16825. *Freiburger Rundbrief.* Beiträge zur christlich-jüdischen Begegnung. Folge 30, Nr. 113–116. Hrsg. (mit Unterstützung der Deutschen Bischofkonferenz und des Deutschen Caritasverbandes) von Willehad P. Eckert, Rupert Giessler, Georg Hüssler, Ludwig Kaufmann, Gertrud Luckner, Clemens Thoma, Anton Vögtle. Freiburg i. Br.: Freiburger Rundbrief, 1978. 220 pp., 'Literaturhinweise' (pp. 152–187), 'Immanuel' (pp. 198–220, see No. 16832). [1 issue.] [Incl.: Ökumene nach Auschwitz. Zum Verhältnis von Christen u. Juden in Deutschland (J. B. Metz, pp. 7–13). Ansprache von Papst Johannes Paul II. an die Repräsentanten jüdischer Organisationen am 12. März 1979 (pp. 13–15). Ansprache von Kardinal Franz König anlässlich seines Besuches im Heim des Wiener B'nai B'rith am 20. Nov. 1978 (pp. 16–19). 40 Jahre danach: Deutsche Katholiken gedenken des 9. Nov. 1938 (pp. 20–33, illus. Freiburger Synagoge, bibl.). Theologische Schwerpunkte des Jüdisch-Christlichen Gesprächs. Arbeitspapier (pp. 34–38). Ein unbestechlicher Beobachter. Zum Tode Moshe Tavors [orig. Tauber], 1903 Olmütz–1978 Jerusalem (Karl-Alfred Odin, p. 61). Theologische u. historische Thesen u. Diskussionen um Judentum, Christentum u. gemeinsame Weltverantwortung (Uriel Tal/Bertold Klappert/Paul M. van Buren/Martin Stöhr, pp. 63–92). Zum Gedenken an den 9. Nov. 1938 (Helmut Schmidt, pp. 110–114). Zur Erklärung des Sekretariats der Deutschen Bischofskonferenz anlässlich der Holocaust-Fernsehserie, 31.1.1979 (D. A. Seeber, pp. 114–117). Nachklänge zum Holocaust-Film (E. L. Ehrlich, pp. 117–118). Verjährung von NS-Verbrechen, rechtliche Lage u. moralische Verpflichtung (Helmut Just, pp. 129–135). Further contributions are listed according to subject.]

16826. GAHLEN, HEINZ: *Juden und Christen.* Arbeitsheft. Göttingen: Vandenhoeck u. Ruprecht; Düsseldorf: Patmos, 1979. 195 pp. (Analysen u. Projekte zum Religionsunterricht, H. 13.)
16827. GESELLSCHAFT FÜR CHRISTLICH-JÜDISCHE ZUSAMMENARBEIT. *25 Jahre Gesellschaft für Christlich-Jüdische Zusammenarbeit.* Dortmund. *Drei Vorträge.* [Dortmund: Kulturamt der Stadt, 1979.] 45 pp. (Dortmunder Vorträge, 131.)
16828. GOLDSTEIN, HORST, ed.: *Gottesverächter und Menschenfeinde? Juden zwischen Jesus und frühchristlicher Kirche.* Mit Beiträgen von Horst Goldstein, Pinchas Lapide, Nathan Peter Levinson [et al.]. Düsseldorf: Patmos, 1979, 192 pp. (Patmos Paperback.)
16829. GREIVE, HERMANN: *Die nationalsozialistische Judenverfolgung und Judenvernichtung als Herausforderung an Christentum und Kirche.* [Vortrag vom 14. Jan. 1978 an der Paulus Akademie in Zürich.] 1–2. [In]: Judaica, Jg. 35, H. 1 & 2, Zürich, 1979. Pp. 12–22 & 57–62.
16830. HENRIX, HANS HERMANN/STÖHR, MARTIN, eds.: *Exodus und Kreuz im ökumenischen Dialog zwischen Juden und Christen.* Diskussionsbeiträge für Religionsunterricht und Erwachsenenbildung. Aachen: Einhard-Verl., 1978. 256 pp. (Aachener Beiträge zu Pastoral- u. Bildungsfragen, 8.) [A continuation of 'Jesu Judesein als Zugang zum Judentum, hrsg. von Paul Willehad Eckert u. Hans-Hermann Henrix', 1976, see No. 14086/YB. XXII.]
16831. HENRIX, HANS HERMANN: *In der Entdeckung von Zeitgenossenschaft.* Ein Literaturbericht zum christlich-jüdischen Gespräch der letzten Jahre. [In]: Una sancta, Jg. 33, H. 3, Freising, 1978. Pp. 245–259.
16832. *Immanuel.* Dokumente des heutigen religiösen Denkens und Forschens in Israel. Hebräische Veröffentlichungen aus Israel in deutscher Übersetzung. 7/1978. Hrsg.: Ökumenisch-Theologische Forschungsgemeinschaft in Israel und Freiburger Rundbrief. Freiburg i. Br., 1978. Pp. 198–220 (IM 1–23) [in]: Freiburger Rundbrief, Folge 30 [see No. 16825]. [Incl.: Rabbi David Kimchis polemische Auseinandersetzung mit dem Christentum (Frank Talmage, pp. 212–216). Religion u. Wissenschaft in Mittelalter u. Neuzeit (Yeshayahu Leibowitz, pp. 216–220).]
16833. *Israel hat dennoch Gott zum Trost. Festschrift für Schalom Ben-Chorin.* Hrsg. von Gotthold Müller. Trier: Paulinus Verl., 1979. 202 pp., bibl. (Ben-Chorin 1931–1978). [Contributions on: Jüdische Bibel ('Altes Testament'); Christliche Bibel ('Altes' u. 'Neues Testament'); Jüdisches Erbe im Christentum; Jüdische Geistesgeschichte; Jüdisch-christlicher Dialog.]
16834. JOHN PAUL II., Pope: *Auschwitz, ein Golgatha unserer Welt.* [In]: Tribüne, H. 71, Frankfurt a. Main, 1979. Pp. 8 & 10. [Excerpts of the Pope's speech in Auschwitz during his visit to Poland. See also: Papst Johannes Paul II, ein Freund der Juden (Joseph Parnas) [in]: Neue Jüd. Nachrichten, Nr. 40, München, 26. Okt. 1979, p. 7. See also in No. 16825.]
16835. KREMERS, HEINZ: *Judenmission heute? Von der Judenmission zur brüderlichen Solidarität und zum ökumenischen Dialog.* Neukirchen-Vluyn: Neukirchener Verl., 1979. 80 pp. [Cf.: Protestantische Judenmission heute? (Ernst Ludwig Ehrlich) [in]: 'Allgemeine', Düsseldorf, 13. Juli 1979, pp. 5 & 6.]
16836. LAPIDE, PINCHAS/LUZ, ULRICH: *Der Jude Jesus. Thesen eines Juden. Antworten eines Christen.* Zürich: Benziger, 1979. 174 pp.
16837. LAPIDE, PINCHAS E./MOLTMANN, JÜRGEN: *Jüdischer Monotheismus, christliche Trinitätslehre. Ein Gespräch.* München: Kaiser, 1979. 90 pp. (Kaiser-Traktate, 39.)
16838. LUTHER, MARTIN. BOENDERMAKER, JOHANNES PETER: *Der Graben war noch sehr tief. Martin Luthers zwiespältiges Verhältnis zum Judentum.* [In]: Lutherische Monatshefte, Jg. 18, H. 10, Hamburg, Okt. 1979. Pp. 585–589.
16839. MUSSNER, FRANZ: *Traktat über die Juden.* München: Kösel, 1979. 398 pp., diagr. [Cf.: Versuch einer theologischen Wiedergutmachung (Pinchas Lapide) [in]: 'Allgemeine', Düsseldorf, 31. Aug. 1979, pp. 5 & 6.]
16840 OBERAMMERGAU PASSION PLAY. ARONSFELD, C. C.: *Prelude to 1980. The Oberammergau Passion Play.* [In]: AJR Information, London, June 1979. Pp. 1–2. [See also: Beruhigungspille oder echte Reform? Zum Stand der Auseinandersetzungen über die Oberammergauer Passionsspiele (Hans Steinitz) [in]: Aufbau, New York, Aug. 24, 1979, p. 7. Also see in No. 16823.]
16841. — SWIDLER, LEONHARD/SLOYAN, GERARD S.: *A commentary on the Oberammergau Passionsspiel in regard to its image of Jews and Judaism.* New York: Anti-Defamation League of B'nai B'rith, 1978. 110 pp.
16842. PETUCHOWSKI, JAKOB J.: *Melchisedech, Urgestalt der Ökumene.* Mit einem Nachwort von Franz Mussner. Freiburg i. Br.: Herder, 1979. 111 pp.
—— SCHUBERT, KURT: *Die Kultur der Juden. Teil 2: Judentum im Mittelalter.* [See No. 15843. Especially on the relation between Church and Synagogue.]

D. Antisemitism

16843. ALEXANDER, WOLFGANG: *Ludwig Quidde und die Agitation der Antisemiten in Göttingen 1879/80.* [In]: Göttinger Monatsblätter, Jg. 6, Nr. 62, Göttingen, April 1979. Pp. 1–3, ports.
16844. BAHR, HERMANN: *Der Antisemitismus. Ein internationales Interview.* Hrsg. u. mit einem Anhang versehen von Hermann Greive. Königstein/Ts.: Jüdischer Verl., 1979. 154 pp. [Biographical details of those interviewed, pp. 149–154. 1st edn. Berlin, S. Fischer, 1894.]
16845. BERNSTEIN, FRITZ: *Der Antisemitismus als Gruppenerscheinung. Versuch einer Soziologie des Judenhasses.* Mit einem Nachwort von Henri Taifel. Königstein/Ts.: Jüdischer Verl., 1979. 248 pp. [1st edn. 1926.]
16846. BURG, J. G. [orig. Josef Ginsburg]: *Holocaust des schlechten Gewissens unter Hexagramm-Regie.* München: Ederer, 1979. 24 pp. [From]: NS-Verbrechen, Prozesse des schlechten Gewissens unter Zions Regie. [The author was excluded from the Munich Jewish Community.]
16847. BURG, J. G. [orig. Josef Ginsburg]: *Verschwörung des Verschweigens. Die potentiellen Brandattentäter des Münchner israelitischen Altersheimes.* München: Ederer, 1979. 93 pp.
16848. EHRLICH, ERNST LUDWIG: *Judenfeindschaft im 19. Jahrhundert: Hofprediger Stöcker und seine Zeit.* [In]: Tribüne, H. 72, Frankfurt a. Main, 1979. Pp. 78–91.
16849. ENGEL, DAVID JOSHUA: *Organized Jewish responses to German antisemitism during the First World War.* [See No. 16296.]
16850. GELLATELY, ROBERT: *Problems of modern anti-Semitism in Germany.* [In]: Canadian Journal of History, 12, Saskatoon/Canada, Febr. 1978. Pp. 383–388. [Review article.]
16851. GERTZ, ELMER: *Odyssey of a barbarian. The biography of George Sylvester Viereck.* Buffalo, N.Y.: Prometheus Books, 1979. 305 pp. [The story of the German-American poet and novelist, Hitler's chief apologist in America.]
16852. GRIESWELLE, DETLEFF: *Antisemitismus in deutschen Studentenverbindungen des 19. Jahrhunderts.* [In]: Studien zum Wandel von Gesellschaft u. Bildung im 19. Jahrhundert, Bd. 12, Göttingen, 1975. Pp. 366–379.
16853. GROSSER, P. F./HALPTERIN, E. G.: *The causes and effects of anti-Semitism. The dimensions of a prejudice.* New York: Philosophical Library, 1978. 480 pp.
16854. HORKEL, WILHELM: *Israel und wir Christen.* [In]: Christliches ABC, heute und morgen. Loseblattsammlung, hrsg. von W. Horkel. Seeshaupt/Bavaria: Verlag 'Das Besondere', [1979?]. [Cf.: Unchristliches ABC. Judenhass in einem christlichen Ratgeber (Julius H. Schoeps) [in]: Die Zeit, Hamburg, 1. Juni 1979.]
16855. JOCHUM, HERBERT: *'Botschaft des Glaubens' oder zurück zu den 'bösen Juden'? Eine erste Zitatenlese aus dem neuesten Katechismus.* [In]: Freiburger Rundbrief, Folge 30, Freiburg i. Br., 1978. Pp. 47–51, bibl. notes. [Refers to: Botschaft des Glaubens. Ein katholischer Katechismus. Im Auftrag der Bischöfe von Augsburg u. Essen hrsg. von Andreas Baur u. Wilhelm Plöger. Donauwörth-Essen, 1978. 385 pp. Cf. also: Den verborgenen Antijudaismus verlernen (Günter Biemer) [in]: Diakonia, Jg. 10, H. 3, Freiburg i. Br., 1979, pp. 145–148. Ein Buch mit himmelschreienden Sünden (J. Quadflieg) [in]: imprimatur, Nachrichten u. kritische Meinungen aus der katholischen Kirche, Jg. 12, H. 1, Trier, 1979, pp. 16–22. Ein neuer Katechismus von gestern (W. Trutwin) [in]: Stimmen der Zeit, H. 3, Freiburg i. Br., 1979, pp. 203–206.]
16856. KERN, ERICH: *Die Tragödie der Juden. Schicksal zwischen Propaganda und Wahrheit.* Preussisch-Oldendorf: Schütz, 1979. 327 pp., illus., bibl. (pp. 325–327). [Neo-Nazi publ.]
—— KERSHAW, IAN: *Antisemitismus und Volksmeinung. Reaktionen auf die Judenverfolgungen.* See in No. 16040.
16857. MANNZMANN, ANNELIESE, ed.: *Judenverfolgung in Altertum, Mittelalter und Neuzeit. Geschichte der Stigmatisierung einer religiösen Minderheit.* Königstein/Ts.: Scriptor, 1979. 160 pp. (Historie heute, Bd. 2.)
16858. MICHALSKI, GABRIELLE: *Der Antisemitismus im deutschen akademischen Leben in der Zeit nach dem I. Weltkrieg.* Frankfurt a. Main: Lang, 1979. 246 pp. (Europäische Hochschulschriften: Reihe 3, Geschichte u. ihre Hilfswissenschaften, Bd. 128.)
16859. MOGGE, BIRGITTA: *Rhetorik des Hasses. Eugen Dühring und die Genese seines antisemitischen Wortschatzes.* Neuss: Gesellschaft für Buchdruckerei, 1977. 243 pp., bibl. (pp. 201–222). (Aus Zeit u. Geschichte, Bd. 1.)
16860. NAUEN, FRANZ: *Hermann Cohen's concept of the state and the problem of anti-Semitism (1867–1907).*

[In]: Jahrbuch des Instituts für Deutsche Geschichte, Bd. 8, Tel Aviv, 1979. Pp. 257–282, bibl. footnotes.
16861. NOVOGORATZ, HANS: *Sebastian Brunner und der frühe Antisemitismus.* Wien, Univ., Geisteswiss. Diss., 22. März 1979. IX, 319 pp., port. [Typescript.]
16862. *Patterns of Prejudice.* Vol. 13, No. 1–6. Ed.: C. C. Aronsfeld. Publ. bi-monthly. London: Institute of Jewish Affairs, 1979. [5 issues.] [*No. 2–3* incl.: Neo-Nazi youth (pp. 19–21). The treatment of genocide in US sociology textbooks (Helen Fein, pp. 31–38, bibl. pp. 36–38). *No. 4:* Racial prejudice in British society (Richard C. Thurlow, pp. 1–8, review article, refers also to refugee policy). Antisemitism in Switzerland (pp. 14–15). *No. 5:* German neo-Nazi terrorists (pp. 17–18). *No. 6:* Neo-Nazi literature in Germany (pp. 14 & 28). Further contributions are listed according to subject.]
16863. RASSINIER, PAUL: *Was ist Wahrheit? Die Juden und das Dritte Reich.* Übers. aus dem Franz. 3. u. 4. Aufl. Leonie am Starnberger See: Druffel, 1978–1979. 284 pp. [See also: The lies of Paul Rassinier (C. C. Aronsfeld) [in]: AJR Information, London, Nov. 1979, p. 5.]
16864. REZZORI, GREGOR von: *Memoiren eines Antisemiten. Ein Roman in fünf Erzählungen.* München: Steinhausen, 1979. 316 pp. [Cf.: Wie wird man Antisemit? (Armin Ayren) [in]: FAZ, Frankfurt a. Main, 22. Dez. 1979, p. 24. In der Klammer des Ressentiments (Joachim Kaiser) [in]: SZ, München, 29. Nov. 1979, p. III.]
16865. RÜRUP, REINHARD, ed.: *Antisemitismus und Judentum.* Göttingen: Vandenhoeck u. Ruprecht, 1979. Pp. 439–581, bibl. footnotes. (Geschichte und Gesellschaft, Zeitschrift für Historische Sozialwissenschaft, Jg. 5, H. 4.) [Cont.: Frankfurter Schule und Judentum. Die Antisemitismusanalyse der Kritischen Theorie (Martin Jay, pp. 439–454). Antisemitismus und jüdischer Selbsthass. Eine sich wechselseitig verstärkende sozialpsychologische Doppelbeziehung (Peter Loewenberg, pp. 455–475). Generationskonflikt, Selbsthass u. die Entstehung antikapitalistischer Positionen im Judentum. Der Einfluss des Antisemitismus auf das Sozialverhalten jüdischer Kaufmanns- u. Unternehmersöhne im Deutschen Kaiserreich u. in der K. u. K. Monarchie (Hans Dieter Hellige, pp. 476–518). Antisemitismus in Deutschland als Problem jüdisch-nationalen Denkens u. jüdischer Geschichtsschreibung (Shulamit Volkov, pp. 519–544). Ein historisch neuartiger 'Antisemitismus ohne Antisemiten'? Beobachtungen u. Thesen am Beispiel Österreichs nach 1945 (Bernd Marin, pp. 545–569). Anmerkungen zum Fernsehfilm 'Holocaust' und zu Fragen zeithistorischer Forschung (Wolfgang Scheffler, pp. 570–579). Ein 'Zentrum für Antisemitismusforschung' an der Technischen Universität Berlin (Reinhard Rürup, pp. 580–581).]
16866. SCHOEPS, JULIUS H.: *Sozialdemokratie und Antisemitismus.* [In]: 'Allgemeine', Düsseldorf, 21./28. Dez. 1979. Pp. 2 & 3.
16867. VOLKOV, SHULAMIT: *The rise of popular antimodernism in Germany. The urban master artisans 1873–1896.* Princeton, N.J.: Princeton Univ. Press, 1978. IX, 399 pp., bibl. (pp. 355–386). [Refers to Jews and antisemitism in Germany.]

E. Noted Germans and Jews

16868. GROSZ, GEORGE: *Briefe 1913–1959.* Hrsg. von Herbert Knust. Reinbek: Rowohlt, 1979. 598 pp., illus., ports. [Incl. letters to Günther Anders, Ulrich Becher, Alfred Flechtheim, John Heartfield, Wieland Herzfelde, Max Horkheimer, Walter Mehring, Ernst Toller, Berthold Viertel, Franz Werfel and others.]
16869. JUNG, CARL GUSTAV. GROSSMAN, S.: *C. G. Jung and National Socialism.* [In]: Journal of European Studies, Vol. 9, pt. 4, No. 36, London, 1979. Pp. 231–259. [Incl. Jung and Jews, Judaism, antisemitism, racism.]
16870. KESSLER, HARRY, Graf: *Tagebücher 1918–1937.* Hrsg. von Wolfgang Pfeiffer-Belli. 4. Aufl. Frankfurt a. Main: Insel, 1979. 799 pp. [Many leading German-Jewish personalities are mentioned. For 1961 edn. see No. 2688/YB. VII.]
16871. LESSING, GOTTHOLD EPHRAIM. BOHNER, KLAUS: *Nathan der Weise. Über das 'Gegenbild einer Gesellschaft' bei Lessing.* [In]: Deutsche Vierteljahrsschrift für Literaturwissenschaft u. Geistesgeschichte, Jg. 53, H. 3, Stuttgart, Okt. 1979. Pp. 394–416. [See also: Lessings Humanität (Jürgen Jacobs) [in]: Neue Rundschau, Jg. 90, H. 2, Frankfurt a. Main, 1979, pp. 177–185.
16872. — WESSELS, HANS-FRIEDRICH: *Lessings 'Nathan der Weise'. Seine Wirkungsgeschichte bis zum Ende*

der Goethezeit. Königstein/Ts.: Athenäum, 1979. XI, 459 pp. Zugl.: Bochum, Univ., Phil. Diss., 1978.
16873. [LISZT, FRANZ.] GRADENWITZ, PETER: *'Gebt den Juden ihr eigenes Land'. Ein christlicher Aufruf vor 120 Jahren.* [In]: 'Allgemeine', Düsseldorf, 14. Sept. 1979. P. 5, port. [And in]: MB, Nr. 35/36, Tel Aviv, 21. Sept. 1979, pp. 15–16. [Author of the anonymously publ. pamphlet was Franz Liszt.]
16874. MANN, HEINRICH and THOMAS. HAMILTON, NIGEL: *The brothers Mann. The lives of Heinrich and Thomas Mann 1871–1950 and 1875–1955.* London: Secker & Warburg, 1979. 422 pp., bibl., photo of both on dust-jacket. [Incl. matter on the Manns' attitude towards Nazism and the persecution of the Jews, and on their relationship with many German-Jewish writers. See also: Die Brüder Mann und das Judentum (Leo Brod) [in]: Neue Jüd. Nachrichten, Nr. 40, München, 26. Okt. 1979, p. 8.]
16875. MANN, THOMAS. MANN, THOMAS: *Tagebücher 1918–1921.* Hrsg. von Peter de Mendelssohn. Frankfurt a. Main: S. Fischer, 1979. XII, 907 pp. [Incl. reflections on German Jews and on his relations with Jewish writers. Cf.: Die Irrfahrt zum Zauberberg. Th. Manns 'Tagebücher 1918–1921' (Hans Mayer) [in]: Die Zeit, Hamburg, 7. Dez. 1979, p. 3. For 'Tagebücher' 1933–1934 and 1935–1936 see No. 15806/YB. XXIV.]
16876. — MEYER-CRONEMEYER, HERMANN: *Thomas Mann, Tagebücher 1933–1934.* [In]: Jahrbuch des Instituts für Deutsche Geschichte, Bd. 8, Tel Aviv, 1979. Pp. 498–507. [Review article, dealing also with Th.M.'s ambivalent attitude towards Jews.]
16877. — ZELLER, BERNHARD: *Die Thomas-Mann-Sammlung des Deutschen Literaturarchivs [Marbach a.N.].* Mit einer Auswahl unveröffentlichter Briefe durch Gisela von Einem. [In]: Jahrbuch der Dt. Schillergesellschaft, Jg. 20, Stuttgart, 1976. Pp. 557–601, biogr. notes. [Incl. letters to Hermann Broch, Alfred Döblin, Liesl Frank, Manfred George, Jonas Lesser, Herbert Steiner, Jakob Wassermann, Victor Wittkowski.]
16878. MEINECKE, FRIEDRICH. PACHTER, HENRY: *Friedrich Meinecke and the tragedy of German liberalism.* [In]: Salmagundi, No. 43, Saratoga Springs, N.Y., 1979. Pp. 12–42, bibl. footnotes. [See also Nos. 14971–14972/YB. XXIII.]
16879. WAGNER, RICHARD. FEST, JOACHIM: *Richard Wagner. A sketch drawn from Cosima's diaries.* [In]: Encounter, Vol. 53, No. 3, London, Sept. 1979. Pp. 7–17. [On Wagner's antisemitism. For German version see No. 14976/YB. XXIII.]
16880. — GRADENWITZ, PETER: *Assimilation, Antisemitismus und Zionismus.* Professor Jacob Katz' Siegfried Moses Memorial Lecture [des Leo Baeck Instituts Jerusalem über Wagners Schrift 'Judentum in der Musik']. [In]: MB, Nr. 24, Tel Aviv, 22. Juni 1979. P. 4. [Review article. See also: Wie antisemitisch darf ein Künstler sein (Peter Gradenwitz) [in]: Isr. Wochenblatt, Nr. 9, Zürich, 2. März 1979, pp. 21–22.]

X. FICTION, POETRY AND HUMOUR

16881. CHOTJEWITZ, PETER O.: *Saumlos. Roman.* Königstein/Ts.: Verlag Autoren-Edition im Athenäum-Verl., 1979. 161 pp. [A young man, born 1934, returns to his native village in search of the past, refers to occurrences of the 'Reichskristallnacht'.]
16882. EISNER, STEFAN: *Tödliche Liebe.* Ein Schauspiel über die unerlaubte Liebe zwischen einer Jüdin und einem jungen Nazi im Dritten Reich. Köln: Ellermann, 1979. 96 pp.
16883. ELRO [pseud.]: *I did survive.* Short stories by a concentration camp survivor. London: Regency Press, 1979. 77 pp.
16884. ERMANN, LEO: *Die Fliegerjacke, oder Die bedingt ehrenvolle Tragödie der Heimgekehrten. Roman.* Jerusalem: Mass, 1979. 406 pp. [L.E., born 1899.]
16885. FAERBER, MEIR M., ed.: *Stimmen aus Israel. Eine Anthologie deutschsprachiger Literatur in Israel.* Gerlingen: Bleicher, 1979. 272 pp., ports., biogr. of the authors (pp. 254–267), bibl. notes (pp. 268–271). (Bleicher Bücherbord.) [Contributions by Schalom Ben-Chorin, Elazar Benyoetz, Meir Faerber, Leopold Marx, Margarita Pazi, Max Zweig and others.]
16886. GERSHON, KAREN: *Coming back from Babylon.* London: Gollancz, 1979. 58 pp. [Collection of poems based on themes from the Old Testament. K.G., born 1923 in Bielefeld.]
16887. HAKEL, HERMANN, ed.: *Wenn der Rebbe lacht. Anekdoten.* 2. Aufl. München: Dt.-Taschenbuch-Verl., 1979. 124 pp. (dtv, 1318.)
16888. HILSENRATH, EDGAR: *Gib acht Genosse Mandelbaum. Roman.* München: Langen-Müller, 1979. 320 pp.

16889. KOPLOWITZ, JAN: *'Bohemia', mein Schicksal. Eine Familiengeschichte. Roman.* Halle-Leipzig: Mitteldeutscher Verl., 1979. 763 pp. [Story of a Jewish family and their hotel 'Bohemia', reflecting 50 years of German history. J.K., born Dec. 1, 1909, living in the G.D.R.]
16890. LAMPEL, RUSIA: *Als ob wir im Frieden lebten. Ein Mädchen in Jerusalem.* Würzburg: Arena, 1979. 141 pp. (Arena-Taschenbuch, Bd. 1358.) [R.L., born in Eastern Galicia, sister of William S. Schlamm, went to Palestine in 1931, died in Jerusalem.]
16891. LEUKEFELD, PETER: *Meschugge biste, Moses. Jüdische Witze.* Bergisch Gladbach: Lübbe, 1979. 126 pp., illus. (Bastei Lübbe, 18017: Heiteres.)
16892. ROTENBERG, STELLA: *Die wir übrig sind.* Darmstadt: Bläschke, 1978. 76 pp. [St.R., born in Vienna, emigrated to Britain in 1939. Poems reflecting the Holocaust.]
16893. SCHROBSDORFF, ANGELIKA: *Die kurze Stunde zwischen Tag und Nacht. Roman.* Düsseldorf: Claassen, 1979. 432 pp. [Autobiographical novel. A German 'half-Jewess' in search of her Jewish identity.]
16894. UNIKOWER, INGE: *Suche nach dem gelobten Land. Die fragwürdigen Abenteuer des kleinen Gerschon.* Biographie. Berlin/East: Verlag der Nation, 1978. 301 pp., 56 pp. illus. [The fictitious main character in this novel is based on Abraham Pisarek, photographer for the democratic press in Berlin and later for the Reichsvertretung der deutschen Juden.]
16895. VOGEL, MANFRED: *Kopf oder Schrift. Roman.* München: Jugend u. Volk, 1979. 237 pp. [Fictitious report, 1938–1948, of a young Jew's flight from Germany and his experiences in Paris, London and Palestine.]

Index to Bibliography

Abella, Irving, 16127
Achenbach, Sigrid, 16619
Adam, Peter, 16169
Adam, Uwe Dietrich, 16020
ADL Bulletin see Anti-Defamation League
Adler, Alfred, 16396
Adler, Frank J., 15887
Adler, Friedrich, 16769
Adler, H[ans] G[ünther], 16029, 16345, 16691
Adler, Paul, 16380
Adler, Samuel, 15869
Adler, Viktor, 16769
Adorno, Theodor W. (orig. Wiesengrund), 15982, 16362, 16387, 16393, 16397–16404, 16573
Ahren, Yizhak, 16181, 16693
Aichelburg, Peter C., 16487
Aichhorn, August, 16405
Aichhorn, Thomas, 16405
'AJR Information', London, 15825, 15827, 15830, 15838, 15877, 15932, 15977, 15985–15986, 15995, 15997, 16027, 16062, 16138, 16259, 16284, 16370, 16466, 16483, 16488, 16527, 16562, 16588, 16600, 16635, 16729, 16753, 16840, 16863
Akademie d. Künste d. DDR, 15972, 16054
Akademie d. Wissenschaften, Berlin, 16266, 16495
— d. DDR, Veröffentlichungen, 16495, 16551
Aktion Sühnezeichen, 16808
Albers, Detlev, 16420
Albrecht, Reinhardt, 16667
Alemann, Heine von, 16181
Alexander, Boyd, 16651
Alexander, Edward, 16021
Alexander, Gerhard, 15826
Alexander, H. G., 16138
Alexander, Marcus, 15967
Alexander, Wolfgang, 16843
Alexander Silberman Internat. Scholarship Foundation, Publication, 16065
Algazy, Joseph, 16022
Alicke, Walter, 16494
Allerhand, Jacob, 15953
'Allgemeine' Jüd. Wochenzeitung, Düsseldorf, 15830, 15890, 15892–15893, 15904, 15916, 15919, 15930, 15932, 15938, 15940–15941, 15991, 16040, 16057, 16062, 16069, 16071, 16138, 16167, 16175–16177, 16181, 16259, 16263–16264, 16269, 16277–16278, 16294, 16422, 16428, 16457, 16462, 16482, 16488, 16509, 16527, 16532, 16564, 16592, 16599, 16606, 16612, 16617, 16635, 16679, 16693, 16714, 16720, 16727, 16732, 16792, 16818, 16835, 16839, 16866, 16873
Alliance Israélite Universelle, Paris, 15999
Almanacs, Reprints see Periodicals
Alphen, Oscar van, 16171
Alsace, 15942–15943, 15980
Altenberg, Peter (orig. Richard Engländer), 16376, 16406–16408, 16769
Altenhofer, Norbert, 15823
Altenkirchen/Westerwald, 15868, 16214
Altmann, Adolf, 15932, 15949
Altmann, Alexander, 15997, 16251, 16255, 16266
Alzey, 15869–15870
'Alzeyer Geschichtsblätter', 15869–15870, 15937
Ament, Susan G., 16144
American Committee on the History of the Second World War, Newsletter, 16014
'American Historical Review', Bloomington, In., 15827
'American Jewish Archives', Cincinnati, 16055
American Jewish Committee, New York, Publication, 16202
'American Jewish History', Waltham, Mass., 16067, 16082
'American Jewish Year Book', New York, 16194
'(The) American Zionist', New York, 16101, 16488
'Amerikastudien', Stuttgart, 15851
Amerongen, Martin van, 16171
Amery, Carl, 16409
Améry, Jean (orig. Hans Mayer), 16409–16411, 16737, 16813
Anatomie d. SS-Staates, 16023
Anders, Günther (orig. Stern), 15976, 16024, 16367, 16868
Andréas, Bert, 16639
Anglade, René, 16547–16548
Anne-Frank-Stiftung, 16070
Anti-Defamation League of B'nai B'rith, 16004, 16841
— 'ADL Bulletin', New York, 16486
Antifaschistische Literatur, 16395
Anti-Holocaust Literature see Holocaust: Denial
Antisemitism (see also Zionism), 15823, 15826, 15897, 15911, 15914, 15992, 16093, 16098, 16221, 16642, 16843–16867, 16869, 16879–16880
— Austria, 15823, 16166, 16865
— Canada, 15980
— Christian, 16050, 16821, 16855
— Czechoslovakia, 16169

Index to Bibliography 443

— Imperial Germany, 15823, 15838, 16296, 16865
— Nazi, 16040, 16093, 16160, 16361
— Post War, 16173
— Switzerland, 16154, 16862
Antisemitism, Judaism, Nazism in Education and Teaching, 16166, 16202–16214, 16826, 16830, 16855, 16862
Antisemitismus u. Judentum, 16865
Antoni, E., 16025
Arad, Yitzhak, 16005
Arato, Andrew, 16622
Arbeitsgemeinschaft
— d. Evang. Jugend (AEJ), 16821
— Friedensdienste, Stuttgart, 16808
— Juden u. Christen, 16212
Architects, Jewish, 15973, 16314, 16374
'Archiv für Geschichte d. Buchwesens', Frankfurt a. Main, 16057
'Archiv für Sozialgeschichte', Bonn, 15831
'(Der) Archivar', Siegburg, 16550
Archives, Resources in, see Libraries
Arendt, Hannah, 15982, 16026, 16412–16417
'Ariel', Jerusalem, 16424
Arieli, Yehoshua, 15850
Aris, Helmut, 16179, 16312
'Arisierung', 16039
'Arkadia', Jahrbuch für Dichtkunst, 16375
Arndt, Ernst Moritz, 16651
Arndt, Ino, 16098
Arnold, Hermann, 15917
Aronsfeld, C. C., 16027, 16751, 16823, 16840, 16862–16863
Aronson, Shlomo, 15850
Art, Jews in (see also Holocaust Art), 16170, 16341, 16374, 16376–16377, 16392, 16394, 16477, 16558, 16618–16619, 16650, 16760, 16790
Art Collectors, Jewish, 16569–16570
Art Dealers, Jewish, 16589
Art Historians, Jewish, 16500, 16529, 16535, 16660, 16726–16728, 16756
Artzt, Heinz, 16028
Asaria, Zvi (orig. Hermann Helfgott), 15906
Asch, Schalom, 16596
Ascherson, Neal, 16781
Aschheim, Isidor, 16341
Aschoff, Diethard, 15913
Ash, Adrienne, 16017
Aspen Institut, Berlin, 16818
Aspetti di una resistenza ebraica al nazismo, 16162
Asriel, Andre, 15859
Assimilation, 15823, 15955, 16880
Atholl, Herzogin von, 16601
Atlanta, USA, Immigration, 15981
Auerbach, Alfred, 16343
Auerbach, Berthold, 16538
Auerbach, Erich, 16418

Auerbach, Georg, 16092
Auerbach, Hellmuth, 16098
'Aufbau', New York, 15822, 15838, 15877, 15881, 15930, 15932, 15991, 15995, 15997, 16071, 16138, 16172, 16175, 16259, 16313, 16336, 16468, 16473, 16496, 16527, 16532, 16612, 16635, 16676, 16714, 16720, 16765, 16840
Augsburg, 15871
'Augsburger Blätter', 15871
'Aus dem Antiquariat', Frankfurt a. Main, 16001, 16562, 16773
'Aus Politik u. Zeitgeschichte', Bonn, 16265
Auschwitz, 16024–16025, 16029–16036, 16081, 16823, 16834
Ausländer, Rose, 16367, 16390, 16419
Australia, Immigration and Refugees, 15967, 16134
'Australian Jewish Historical Society', Sydney, 15967
Austria, 16012, 16275
— Antisemitism, 15823, 16166, 16865
— Communal History, 15944–15956
— Nazi Period, 16005, 16037–16039, 16353
— Post War, 16166–16168
Autobiographies, Diaries, Letters, 15838, 15883, 15983, 15986, 16251–16252, 16254, 16277, 16340, 16405, 16486, 16547, 16595, 16626, 16651, 16664, 16751–16807, 16893
— Nazi Period, 16041, 16043, 16045, 16051, 16056, 16069, 16106, 16114, 16125, 16159, 16297, 16758, 16764–16765, 16772, 16799–16800
Avenary, Hanoch, 16311
Ay, Karl-Ludwig, 15993
Ayoun, Richard, 15999
Ayren, Armin, 16864

Bachmann, Claus-Henning, 16468
Baden, 15872–15873
Baden-Baden, 16121
Badia, Gilbert, 15968
Badt, Heinz, 16151, 16488
Badt-Strauss, Bertha, 16256
Bächle, Günter, 15892
Baeck, Leo, 15829, 16215
— Memorial Lecture, 16112
Bänziger, Hans, 16581
Baer, Fritz Jizchak, 16216
'(Der) Bär von Berlin', Jahrbuch d. Vereins für d. Geschichte Berlins, 15877
Baerns, Barbara, 16381
Bäumler, Ernst, 16481–16482
Bahr, Ehrhard, 16682
Bahr, Hermann, 16796–16797, 16844
Balfour-Declaration, 16256
Balk, Theodor, 16591
Ballin, Gerhard, 15925

Ballin, Günther, 16752
Bamberger, Family, Würzburg, 16753
Bamberger, Fritz, 15997
Bamberger, Gabrielle, 15996–15997
Bamberger, Seligmann Bär, 16753
Bambus, Willy, 16317, 16337
Bankers, Jewish (see also Financiers), 15847, 15852, 16365, 16729
Bankherren u. Bankiers, 16365
'Bankhistorisches Archiv', Frankfurt a. Main, 15847
Baptism ('Judentaufe'), 15924
(*Les*) *Barbelés de l'exil*, 15968
Barck, Simone, 15973
Barlev, Jehuda (orig. Kurt Herzberg), 16299
Barnouw, Dagmar, 16459
Baron, Erich, 16380
Baron, Lawrence, 15997
Baron, Salo Wittmayer, 16248
'Basler Zeitung', 16062, 16428
Bastian, Gert, 16028
Battenberg, Friedrich, 15922
Battke, Marion, 16514
Battle of the Books, 15820
Bauer, Otto, 16420
Bauer, Wilfried, 16391
Bauer, Yehuda, 16007, 16034, 16065, 16160, 16204
Baum, Herbert, 16164
Baum, Marie, 16069
Baum, Oskar, 16375
Baum, Vicki, 16385
Baumgardt, David, 16421
Baumgarten, Ruth, 16605
Baur, Andreas, 16855
Bavaria (Bayern), 15874, 15911, 16040
— Bayerischer Rundfunk, 16657
— Palatinate, 15923
— Staatliche Archive, 15874, 16040
— Staatsministerium für Unterricht u. Kultus, 15874, 16040
Beate-Klarsfeld-Foundation, New York, 16046
Becher, Ulrich, 16868
Beer, Frank, 16572
Beer, Otto F., 16720
Beer, Ulrich, 16437
Beer-Hofmann, Richard, 16422–16423
Behrend, Itzig, 16754
Behrend-Rosenfeld, Else R., 16041
'Beiträge zur Geschichte d. Arbeiterbewegung', Berlin/East, 16785
Beiträge zur Kölner Stadtgeschichte, 15884
'Belfagor', Florence, 15825
Bell, Robert F., 16358
Beller, Jacob, 16549
Ben-Chorin, Schalom (orig. Fritz Rosenthal), 15991, 16222, 16278, 16287, 16325, 16457, 16755, 16824, 16833, 16885

Bendix, Ludwig, 15997
Bendorf, 16041
Ben Gershôm, Esra see König, Joel [pseud.]
Ben-Haim, Paul (orig. Frankenburger), 16424
Benjamin, Georg, 16425
Benjamin, Hilde, 16425
Benjamin, Walter, 16385, 16387, 16391, 16425–16432, 16756
Ben-Sasson, Haim Hillel, 15815
Benyoetz, Elazar, 16885
Beradt, Charlotte, 16109, 16435
Beradt, Martin, 16375, 16433–16436
Beranek, F[ranz] J[osef], 15861
Berend-Corinth, Charlotte, 16341
Berendsohn, Walter A., 16601
Bergas, Hanna, 15969
Bergen-Belsen, 16043–16044, 16073
Berger, Max, 15944
Berger, Ulrike, 16212
'Bergische Blätter', Wuppertal, 16122
Bergmann, Juda, 16257
Bergmann, Peter G., 16487
Berkholz, Heike von, 16550
Berkowitz, Horst, 16437
Berlin, 15838, 15875–15878, 15997, 16045, 16164, 16172, 16257, 16264, 16266, 16477, 16787, 16818
— Akademie d. Wissenschaften, 16266, 16495
— East, 16179
— Königl. Bibliothek, 16285
— Kunstamt Schöneberg, 16579
— Nationalgalerie, 16619
— Staatsbibliothek Preuss. Kulturbesitz, 16259, 16271
— Stiftung Preuss. Kulturbesitz, 16570, 16603
— Zentrum für Antisemitismusforschung, 16865
Berlin, Isaiah, 16488
'Berliner Börsen-Courier', 16712
Berlinische Galerie, 16341
'Berlinische Notizen', 16172
Bermann-Fischer, Gottfried, 16757
Bernays, Jacob, 16217
Bernfeld, Siegfried, 16310
Bernstein, Eduard, 16295, 16438–16440
Bernstein, Fritz, 16845
Bernstein, Jeremy, 16441
Bersley, William John, 16575
Berthold, Werner, 16679
Berwin, Beate, 16258
Best, Otto F., 16471
Bethe, Hans Albrecht, 16441
Bethel, Nicholas, 16317
Bethge, Eberhard, 16821
Bettauer, Hugo, 16442
Bettelheim, Bruno, 16443
Betzdorf/Westerwald, 15868
Beuthen/ O/S., 15927
Bevilacqua, Giuseppe, 15825

Index to Bibliography

Beyer, Waltraud, 16399
Biale, David, 16283, 16443
Bibliographica Judaica, Series of the Library of the Hebrew Union College, 16012
Bibliographical Society of the Univ. of Virginia, 16017
Bibliographies, Catalogues, 15826, 15830, 15999–16019, 16220, 16224, 16285, 16414, 16495, 16550, 16643
Biblioteca Trivulziana, Milano, 16162
Bibliothek Anpassung u. Widerstand, 16590, 16601
Bibliothek d. verbrannten Bücher, 16591, 16620, 16655
Bieber, Hans-Joachim, 15823
Bielander, Raphael, 16223
Biemer, Günter, 16207, 16855
Bienek, Horst, 16080, 16704
Bier, Jean-Paul, 16030
Bier, Wolfgang, 16582
'(Der) Bildermann', 16376
Bilke, Jörg Bernhard, 16698
Billig, Joseph, 16046
Binder, Hartmut, 16583, 16663, 16775
Bing, Gertrud, 16726
Biochemistry, Jews in, see Science
Biographical Dictionaries, 16015, 16019
Birkenau, 15957
Birkenfeld (Fürstentum), 15923
Birnbaum, Immanuel, 15825
Birnbaum, Solomon A. (Salomo A.), 15855–15856
Biser, Eugen, 16691
Bismarck, Otto von, 15847
'Blätter für pfälzische Kirchengeschichte u. religiöse Volkskunde', Grünstadt, 15917
'(Der) Blaue Reiter', 16377
Bleich, Judith, 16242
Bleichröder, Gerson von, 15847
Bleuel, Hans Peter, 16615
Blishen, Edward, 16771
Bloch, Chajim, 15961
Bloch, Ernst, 16342, 16387, 16393, 16444–16448
Blum, Yehuda, 16486
Blumenfeld, Erik, 16181
Blumenfeld, Kurt, 16488
Blumenkranz, Bernhard, 16000
Blumenthal, H. E., 16278
Blumenthal, W. Michael, 15970
B'nai B'rith, Vienna, 16518, 16825
Board of Deputies of British Jews, 16318
Boas, Jacob, 16318
Bobke, Wolfgang, 16202
Bock, Fritz, 16181
Bock, Sigrid, 16346
Böcher, Otto, 15869
Böhm, Hans, 16547
Böll, Annemarie, 16595

Böll, Heinrich, 16620, 16634
Bömer, Aloys, 15820
Boendermaker, Johannes Peter, 16838
'Börsenblatt für d. Dt. Buchhandel'
— Frankfurt a. Main, 15979, 15984, 16062, 16278, 16450, 16643, 16722
— Leipzig, 16648
Bohmbach, Jürgen, 15931
Bohner, Klaus, 16871
Bohnke-Kollwitz, Jutta, 15992
Bohr, Niels, 16661
Boltzmann, Ludwig see Ludwig Boltzmann Institut
Bolz, Norbert W., 16400
Bongartz, Dieter, 16210
Bonn, 15879
'Bonner Geschichtsblätter', 15879
Bonss, Wolfgang, 16530
Bonwitt, Caroline, 16754
Bonwitt, William, 16754
Book Trade, Jews in (see also Publishers), 15971, 15979, 15984–15985, 16057, 16450, 16663–16664
Bopp, Georg, 16808
Borchardt, Georg Hermann see Hermann, Georg
Borchardt, Marie Luise, 16449
Borchardt, Rudolf, 16449
Borelli, Giorgio, 16671
Borinski, Ludwig, 15826
Borkin, Joseph, 16101, 16204
Born, Jürgen, 16584
Bortfeldt, Barbara, 16792
Bosch, Manfred, 16034, 16152
Bosch, Michael, 16173, 16214
Bourel, Dominique, 16252–16253, 16266
Bouvier, Bonn, 16450
Bouvier, Hedwig, 16450
Boyer, John W., 16515
Braakenburg, Johannes J., 16606
Braatz, Werner E., 16319
Brady, P. V., 16721
Bräuer, Heike, 16214
Braham, Randolph L., 16160
Brand, Joel, 16099
Brandenburg (Mark), 15880
Brandes, Georg, 16423
Brandl, Gerhard, 16396
Brassloff, Fritz L., 15951, 16606, 16679
Bratislava, Zentralverband d. Jüd. Religionsgemeinden, 16170
Braun, Heinrich, 16451
Braun, Jutta, 16679
Braun, Nikolaus, 16341
Braun-Vogelstein, Julie, 16412
Breines, Paul, 16622
Bremen, Univ., 16297
Brendel, Alfred, 16685

Brenk, Johann Wolfgang, 16694
Brenner, Hans, 16047
Brenner, Otto see Otto-Brenner-Stiftung
Breslau, 15927, 16024, 16339
Breuer, Isaac, 16218
Breuer, Josef, 15888
Breuer, Salomon, 15888
Breuss, Edgar, 15949
Brilleman, J., 15916
Brilling, Bernhard, 15902, 15959, 16219–16220
Britain see Great Britain
Broch, Hermann, 16452–16454, 16664, 16877
Brod, Leo, 15956, 16720, 16824, 16874
Brod, Max, 16170, 16375–16376, 16380, 16385, 16455–16458, 16758
Broder, Henryk M., 16809
Brody, Stanton, 15816
Bronsen, David, 15823
Broszat, Martin, 15838, 16006, 16023, 16040, 16088, 16203
Browder, George C., 16048
Brown, Alison Pogrebin, 16633
Browning, Christopher R., 16049, 16160
Brunner, Sebastian, 16861
Bruno, Guido (orig. Curt Josef Kisch), 15971
Brutscher, Ludwig, 15960
Buber, Martin, 16221–16239, 16243, 16278, 16288, 16290, 16380, 16824
Buber, Paula see Munk, Georg
Buber, Raphael, 16224
Buber-Neumann, Margarete, 16585
Buber-Rosenzweig-Medaille, 16294
Bucerius, Gerd, 16101
Buchen/Baden, 15873
Buchheim, Hans, 16023
Buchwald, Christoph, 16789
Budapest, 15965
Buddhist Publication Society, 16779
Budko, Joseph, 16341
Büchner, Georg, 16468
Bücker, H.-G., 16259
Büdinger Vorträge, 16365
Buhl, Wolfgang, 16596
Bullivant, Keith, 16342
Bund d. Antifaschisten, 16116
Bunde/Ostfriesland, 15916
Bundesarchiv Koblenz, Schriften, 16018
Bundeszentrale für Politische Bildung, 16185
Bunten, Kathleen Anne, 16699
Buren, Paul M. van, 16825
Burg, J. G. (orig. Josef Ginsburg), 16115, 16846–16847
Burgenland, 16038
Burgenländische Forschungen, 15966
Burmeister, K. A., 15956
Busch, Eberhard, 16050
Buselmeier, Karin, 16539
Busi, Frederick, 16326
Buttenhausen, 15881

'Cahiers Juifs', Paris, 16677
Cahn, Peter, 16343
Cahnman, Werner J., 15911, 15945
Calendar, Jewish, 16287
Calkins, Kenneth R., 16542
Campbell, Richard, 16312
Canada, Refugees, 15979–15980
— Refugee Policy, 16127–16128
'Canadian Historical Review', Toronto, 16127
Canadian Jewish Archives, New Series, 15980
'Canadian Jewish Historical Society Journal', Toronto, 16128, 16142
'Canadian Journal of History', Saskatoon, 15847, 16333, 16438, 16850
Canaris, Volker, 16743
Canepa, Andrew M., 16103
Canetti, Elias, 16459, 16759
Capell, Hans, 15839
Capitalism and Jews, 15837
Carlebach, Julius, 15817, 16640
Carmel, Alex, 16320
Carmon, Arye, 16212
Carsten, F. L., 15825
Casper, Bernhard, 16277
Cassella & Co., Frankfurt a. Main, 16101
Cassirer, Ernst, 16373, 16460, 16728
Cassirer, Paul, 16376
Castle Stanford, Julian (orig. Julius Schloss), 16051
Catalogues see Bibliographies
Cavell, Stanley, 16738
CDJC see Centre Documentation Juive Contemporaine
Cecil, Lamar, 15827
Celan, Paul, 16367, 16461–16465
Cemeteries, 15893, 15904, 15916, 15938, 15957, 16170
'Central European History', Atlanta, Ga., 16092
Centralverein dt. Staatsbürger jüd. Glaubens (C.V.), 15911, 16296–16297, 16541
Centre Documentation Juive Contemporaine, 16046
Centre National de la Recherche Scientifique, Paris, 16547, 16551
Centro di Documentazione Ebraica Contemporanea, Milano, 16162
Ceylon, 16779
Chadwick, Owen, 16118
Chagall, Marc, 16534
Chagoll, Lydia, 16052
Chain, Sir Ernst, 16466
Chajes, Zwi Perez, 15953
Chalfen, Israel, 16462
Chargaff, Erwin, 16488
Chemistry, Jews in, see Science
Chiel, Arthur A., 16239
China (see also Shanghai), 16472
Chodowiecki, Daniel Nicolaus, 15997
Chodziesner, Gertrud see Kolmar, Gertrud

Chotjewitz, Peter O., 16881
Christen u. Juden, 16822
Christian, Petra, 16706
'Christian Attitudes on Jews and Judaism', London, 16823
Christian–Jewish Cooperation, Society for, 16212, 16824, 16827
Christian–Jewish Relations, 15843, 15886, 16221, 16290
— Nazi Period, 16056, 16077, 16131, 16159
Church and Jews, Nazi Period, 16050, 16084, 16118, 16120, 16122, 16145, 16147, 16823
Church and Synagogue, 16213, 16820–16842
Circumcision, Register of, 15880
Clark, Ronald W., 16489
Cohen, Friedrich, 16450
Cohen, Gary B., 15823
Cohen, Hermann, 15823, 16240–16241, 16373, 16860
Cohen, Max, 16450
Cohen, Michael J., 16340
Cohn, Bertha, 16016
Cohn, Conrad, 15927
Cohn, Eduard, 15897
Cohn, Erich, 16731
Cohn, Jonas, 16373
Cohn, Lotte, 16336
Cohn, Manfred see George, Manfred
Cohn, Margot, 16224
Cohn, Willy, 15818
Colin, Richard, 16341
Collection Franco-Judaica, 16000
Collegium Carolinum, Veröffentlichungen, 16053
'Colloquia Germanica', Bern, 16471, 16586
'Colloque d'Intellectuels Juifs de Langue Française', Paris, 16463
Cologne, 15882–15884, 16714
— Germania Judaica, Kölner Bibliothek, 15992
Colombia, Refugees, 16787
'Commentary', New York, 16036, 16113, 16328, 16443
Communists, 16778, 16792
Community History see Name of Country; Region; Town
Community Officials, 15877
Concentration Camps, 16023, 16025, 16047, 16052, 16060–16061, 16086, 16098, 16101–16102, 16107, 16110–16111, 16162, 16165, 16187–16188, 16367, 16883 (see also Auschwitz; Bergen-Belsen; Birkenau; Dachau; Gurs; Majdanek; Ravensbrück; Stutthof; Theresienstadt; Nazi Crimes: Prosecution)
Conference on the Holocaust, 16204–16205
Congregation B'nai Israel, Millburn, N.J., Bulletin, 16245
Conservative Judaism, 16239
Conway, John S., 16031
Cook, Kathleen Mayhew, 16736

Coulmas, Corinna, 16294
Courant, Richard, 16467
Cowan, Edward, 15970
Cox, Steve, 16324
Cramer, Erich, 16361
Cramer, Heinz Michael, 16464
Critics, Literary, 16594, 16663
Cultural History (see also Weimar Republic), 15843, 16651
Cuzco/Peru, 15987
Czechoslovakia, 15957–15964, 16053–16054, 16160, 16169–16170
— Refugees, 16054, 16349
Czeike, Felix, 16039

Dachau, 16025, 16040, 16055
Dadaists, 16701–16703
Daene, Wilhelm, 16056
Dahlke, Hans, 16347
Dahm, Volker, 16057
Dahmer, Helmut, 16181, 16501, 16541
Dan, J., 16283
Dannhauser, Werner J., 16321
Danzig, 16058, 16135
Daviau, Donald G., 16797
David, Claude, 16547
Dawidowicz, Lucy S., 16059
Degner, Helmut, 16805
Deiritz, Karl, 16708
Demant, Ebbo, 16032
Demetz, Peter, 16455
Demography, 15926
Demps, Laurenz, 16060
Department Stores, 15978, 16714
Derrida, Jacques, 16576
Dessau, 16259
Dessau, Paul, 16468
Deutsche Bibliothek, Frankfurt a. Main, 16677, 16679
Deutsche Bischofskonferenz, 16825
'Deutsche Literaturzeitung', Berlin/East, 15825, 16623
'Deutsche Richterzeitung', Köln, 16201
Deutsche Schillergesellschaft, 15990–15991
'Deutsche Studien', Hamburg, 16698
'Deutsche Vierteljahrsschrift für Literaturwissenschaft u. Geistesgeschichte', Stuttgart, 16465, 16581, 16613, 16871
Deutscher Bundestag, Bonn, 16195
Deutscher Caritasverband, 16825
Deutscher Evang. Kirchentag, 16212
Deutscher Koordinierungsrat d. Gesellschaften für christlich-jüdische Zusammenarbeit, 16824
Deutsches Literaturarchiv, Marbach a. N., 15990–15991
Deutsches Theater im Exil (Series), 16054, 16153
Deutsch–Israelische Gesellschaft, 16824
Deutschkron, Inge, 16061

Deutsch-Krone, 15927
'deutschland-berichte', Bonn, 16815; 15838–15839, 16069, 16177, 16181, 16197, 16259, 16294
Deutschlandfunk, Köln, 16076
'Diakonia', Freiburg i. Br., 16855
'Dialogue', Washington, 16488
Diamant, Adolf, 15893, 15904, 15916, 15919, 15930, 15941, 16057, 16174–16175
Diaries see Autobiographies
Dictionaries, Jews in, 15849
Dieterichs, Heinz, 15907
Dietz, Alexander, 15887
Diezel, Peter, 15972–15973
Dirichlet, Rebecka, 16651
'Dissent', New York, 16644
Dissertations, Univ. of Bochum 16872; Bologna 16226; Boston College 16505; Bremen 16418, 16700; California (Los Angeles) 15833, 16296; California (Berkeley) 16688; California (Riverside) 16689; Colorado (Boulder) 16575; Columbia, New York 15854, 16668; Cornell, Ithaca 16633; Erlangen 16652; Florida State 16198; Freiburg i. Br. 16241; Hamburg 16552, 16558, 16708; Heidelberg 16429, 16555; Indiana 16478; Jerusalem (Hebr. Univ.) 15853, 16133; Kiel 16739; Konstanz 16741; Lille 16716; Mainz 16653; Marburg 15849; Maryland 16303; Massachusetts 16617; Munich 16057, 16472, 16476, 16594, 16618; New York Univ. 16118, 16242; New York State at Buffalo 16140, 16225; New York State at Stony Brook 16733; Ohio State 16699; Pennsylvania State 16578; Pittsburgh 16567; Rice Univ., Houston 16736; Rochester 16368; Rutgers, State Univ., New Jersey 16508; Salzburg 16445; Syracuse 16232; Stanford 16417; St. Louis 16231; Tel Aviv 16022; Tübingen 16514; Uppsala 16687; Vienna 15966, 16598, 16861; Washington 16180, 16669; Yale 16402
Diwald, Hellmut, 16062
Dobson, Eugene, 16358
Döblin, Alfred 16342, 16345–16346, 16366, 16379, 16385, 16391, 16469–16476, 16596, 16601, 16768, 16877
Döblin, Hugo, 16473
Doerdelmann-Kolbe, Erika, 16824
D[okto]r-Karl-Renner-Institut, Wien, 16166
Dokumentation zur Geschichte d. jüd. Bevölkerung in Rheinland-Pfalz, 15923
Dolbin, Benedikt Fred, 16341, 16477
Dolinsky, Paul Louis, 16225
Doll, Anton, 15923
Domin, Hilde, 16367, 16390, 16478–16479
Dortmund, 16827
Dossier Juif, 16063
Draper, Paula Jean, 16128

Dresner, Camillo, 16340
Drews, Jörg, 16426, 16428, 16480
Druks, Herbert, 16129
Drumont, Edouard, 16326
Dscheng, Fang-hsiung, 16472
Dubnow, Simon, 16484
Dühring, Eugen, 16642, 16859
Dukas, Helen, 16490
Dunera, 16134
Dunkelmännerbriefe see Epistolae obscurorum virorum
Durkheim, Emile, 16393
Durzak, Manfred, 16349, 16453

East European Jews and German Jews, 15823, 15854, 15997
'East European Quarterly', Boulder, Colorado, 15945, 15947
East Prussia, 15885
Eberle, Matthias, 16619
Ebon, Martin, 16089
Eckardt-Jaffe, Marianne, 16632
Eckert, Brita, 16677, 16679
Eckert, Willehad Paul, 16824–16825, 16830
Eckhardt, Paul, 15961
Eckstein, George G., 16810
'Economia e Storia', Roma, 16671
Economics (see also Bankers; Book Trade; Department Stores; Industry; Publishers; Trade), 15816, 15829, 15830, 15837–15838, 15890, 16039, 16651, 16712
— and Antisemitism, 15823, 16865, 16867
Edel, Peter, 16760
Edenkoben, 15928
Education, 15829, 15891, 15894, 15927, 16175, 16177, 16221, 16236, 16243, 16286, 16695 (see also Antisemitism, Judaism, Nazism in Education and Teaching)
Eggebrecht, Axel, 16032, 16409
Ehmer, Hermann, 15936
Ehrenstein, Albert, 16359, 16380, 16391, 16480
Ehrlich, Ernst Ludwig, 16181, 16825, 16835, 16848
Ehrlich, Georg, 16341
Ehrlich, Paul, 16481–16483
Eichenlaub, René, 16716
Eichmann, Adolf, 16085, 16415
Eichmann, Herbert, 16214
Einem, Gisela von, 16877
Einstein, Albert, 15822, 16385, 16484–16498, 16661
Einstein, Carl, 16380, 16391
Eisen, George, 16303
Eisenberg, Lotte, 16761
Eisenberg-Bach, Susi, 16001
Eisenmann, Joseph F., 15888
Eisenstadt (Burgenland), 15953, 16179
Eisler, Hanns, 16364

Eisner, Freya, 16499
Eisner, Kurt, 16499
Eisner, Stefan, 16882
Eissler, Kurt R., 16516, 16518
Elfe, Wolfgang, 16350–16351
Elfving Vogel, Margot, 16687
Elkana, Yehuda, 16493
Ellenson, David, 16247
Elliot, Alistair, 16546
Elon, Amos, 16099, 16327
Elro [pseud.], 16883
Elsass see Alsace
Elvers, Rudolf, 16266, 16271, 16651
Emancipation, 15826–15827, 15897, 15900, 15910, 15923, 16012, 16265, 16314, 16647
Emden, Jacob, 16219
Emig, Dieter, 16541
Emigration see Immigration; Refugees
Emsländischer Heimatbund, Schriftenreihe, 15910
'Emuna/Israel-Forum', Rothenburg o.d.T., 16824; 16212, 16458
'Encounter', London, 16168, 16229, 16415, 16488, 16666, 16879
Endelman, Todd M., 15819
'Endlösung' see Final Solution
Endres, Elisabeth, 16367
Engel, David Joshua, 16296
Engel, Eva, 16260, 16266
Engel-Holland, Eva J. see Engel, Eva
Engelmann, Bernt, 16344, 16809
Engels, Friedrich, 16387, 16642
Engländer, Richard see Altenberg, Peter
England see Great Britain
Enlightenment, 15817, 15826, 15832, 15849, 16179, 16255, 16259, 16268, 16273–16275, 16393, 16647, 16692
Ennen, Edith, 15879
Ephraim. Family, 16762
'Epoca', Milano, 16681
Epstein, Helen, 16186
Erber, Josef, 16032
Erdmann, Gustav, 16259
Erfahrung Exil, 16346
Erinnern, nicht vergessen, 16212
Erlanger u. Söhne (Banking House), 16365
Erler, Hans, 16413
Ermann, Leo, 16884
Ermreuth/Franconia, 16064
Ernst, Tilman, 16212
'Erziehen heute', Duisburg, 16087
Esh, Shaul, 16753
Esra Verein, 16337
Essen, 16304, 16772
Esslin, Martin, 16571
Ettinger, Elzbieta, 16781
Ettinghausen, Richard, 16500
Ettlinger, Jacob, 16242

Ettlinger, Leopold D., 16726
'europäische ideen', Berlin, 16345, 16592
European Literature, Music and Poetry Association, 16521
'European Studies Review', London, 16139, 16319
Evangelische Akademie Locum, 16214
'Evangelische Kommentare', Stuttgart, 16635
'Evangelische Theologie', München, 16145
Evans, Geraint, 15986
Evers, Martha, 15934
'Ewige Jude' see Wandering Jew
Exil in d. UdSSR, 15973
Exil in d. USA, 15974
Exile, 15822, 16372
— Literature, 15973–15974, 15989, 16017, 16152, 16345–16358, 16364, 16367, 16389, 16453, 16474, 16479, 16502, 16567, 16571, 16665, 16677, 16700, 16717, 16789
— Theatre, Radio, 15972–15973, 16054, 16152–16153, 16356
Exilliteratur-Symposium, 16350–16351
Expressionism, 16359–16360, 16716
Eybenschütz, Jonathan, 16219

Fabian, A., 15967
Fabian, Käthe, 16322
Fabry, Philipp W., 15821
Fackenheim, Emil L., 16289
Faerber, Meir, 16635, 16824, 16885
Faschismus, Stlanismus, 16345
'FAZ' (Frankfurter Allgemeine Zeitung), 15838, 16006, 16197, 16259, 16456, 16482, 16501, 16612, 16720, 16730, 16864
Federal German Republic, 16171–16177, 16194, 16204, 16808–16814
Feilchenfeld, Alfred, 16298
Feilchenfeldt, Konrad, 16651
Fein, Helen, 16066
Feingold, Henry L., 16067
Fellner, Fritz, 16796
Feniger, Siegmund see Nyanaponika Mahathera
Ferber, Christian, 16385
Ferenczi, Sándor (orig. Fränkel), 16501
Fesser, Gerd, 15825
Fest, Joachim, 16879
Festschrift, 15829, 16239, 16538, 16694, 16833
Fetscher, Iring, 16098, 16635
Fedtmilch-Aufstand, Frankfurt a. Main, 15889
Fetz, Reto Luzius, 16460
Feuchtwanger, Lion, 16210, 16346, 16502–16505, 16763, 16768
Feuchtwanger, Ludwig, 16261
Feuchtwanger, Marta, 16763
Fiedler, Peter, 16204
Figal, Günter, 16427
Final Solution, 16022, 16037, 16046, 16049, 16088, 16141

Financiers, Jewish (see also Bankers), 15842
Firster, Richard, 16094
Fisch, Heinrich, 15965
Fischer, Brigitte, 16745
Fischer, Erica, 16038
Fischer, Jens, 16635
Fischer, Ludwig Maximilian, 16504
Fischer, Samuel, 16745
Fischer, Sophie, 16772
Fischhof, Adolf, 15945
Flatauer, Susanne, 16034
Flechtheim, Alfred, 16868
Flechtheim, Ossip K., 16499
Flehinger, Arthur, 16121
Fleischer, Hans, 16123
Fleischer, Manfred P., 16694
Fleming, Jens, 16018
Flemming-Schmalfeld, Annelie, 16212
Fletcher, Roger, 16438
'Fliegende Blätter', 15853
Flöhl, Rainer, 16730
Florence Guggenheim Archiv, Zürich, 16002
Floss, 16174
Fölsing, Albrecht, 16488
Folkers, Horst, 16427
Folklore, 15917, 16221, 16298, 16307, 16309
Fontane, Theodor, 16651
Forschungen u. Beiträge zur Wiener Stadtgeschichte, 16039
Fox, John P., 16068, 16090
Fraenkel, Ernst, 16371
Fraenkel, Peter, 16793
Fränkel, Sándor see Ferenczi, Sándor
France, 15844
— Immigration and Refugees, 15968, 15998
— Nazi Period, 16046, 16063, 16204
— Refugee Policy, 16131–16132, 16136
Francke, Renate, 16547
Franconia, 15886
Frank, Anne, 16069–16075
Frank, Bruno, 16506–16508
Frank, Eduard, 15962
Frank, Liesl (Elisabeth), 16507, 16877
Frank, Otto, 16075
Frank, Philipp, 16491
Frank, Rudolf, 16509
Franken see Franconia
Frankenburger, Paul see Ben-Haim, Paul
Frankenstein, Carl, 16284
Frankfurt a. Main, 15887–15891, 16175, 16243, 16343, 16365
— Deutsche Bibliothek, 16677, 16679
— Stadt- u. Univ. bibliothek, 16278
— University, 16666
(The) Frankfurt School, Institute of Social Research, 16361–16362, 16541, 16865
'Frankfurter Allgemeine Zeitung' see 'FAZ'
'Frankfurter Hefte', 16064, 16117, 16192, 16369, 16409–16410, 16431

Frankl, Victor E., 16187, 16510
Franzos, Karl Emil, 16511
Freeden, Herbert (orig. Friedenthal), 16076, 16462
Freedland, Michael, 15975
Frei, Bruno, 16352
Freiburg i. Br., 16825
'Freiburger Rundbrief', Freiburg i. Br., 16825; 16078, 16158, 16185, 16207, 16212, 16284, 16286, 16832, 16855
'Freie Volksbühne', Wien, 16769
Freimark, Peter, 15857, 15864, 15894, 16072
Freitag, Helmut, 16034
Fremd im eigenen Land, 16809
French, Anthony Philip, 16492
Frenzel, Ivo, 16098, 16182, 16635
Freud, Anna, 16512, 16518
Freud, Sigmund, 15822, 15824, 16232, 16290, 16393, 16484, 16486, 16513–16523, 16532, 16632, 16740
Freudenreich, Johann, 16115
Freudental near Ludwigsburg, 15892
Frick, Gerhard, 15838, 16438
Frick, Hans, 16764
Fried, Erich, 16345, 16367, 16524
Friedberg, Carl, 16343
Friedel, Heinz, 15903
Friedell, Egon, (orig. Friedmann), 16525
Friedenthal, Herbert see Freeden, Herbert
Friedenthal, Richard, 16526–16527, 16747
Friedlaender, Fritz, 16259, 16488
Friedlaender, Liselotte, 16341
Friedländer, Ludwig, 16528
Friedländer, Max J., 16529
Friedlaender, Salomo (Mynony), 16359, 16391
Friedländer, Saul, 16765
Friedlander, Albert H., 16820
Friedlander, Henry, 16212
Friedman, Isaiah, 16302
Friedman, Maurice, 16158
Friedman, Philip, 16077
Friedmann, Aron, 16312
Friedmann, Egon see Friedell, Egon
Friesel, Evyatar, 16323
Frings, Manfred S., 16683–16684
Frisch, Otto R., 16766
Fritsch, Christian, 16395
Fritta, Fritz, 16156
Fröhlich, Elke, 16040
Fromm, Erich, 15982, 16290, 16393, 16530–16533, 16779
Fromm, Herbert, 16313
Fromm, Susanne, 16739
Frühwald, Wolfgang, 16717
Fuchs, H. H., 16105
Füssel, Stephan, 16728
Fugu Plan, 16137
Fuld, Werner, 16428

Index to Bibliography

Funk, Rainer, 16533
Furtmüller, Lux, 16539

Gabirol, Salomon ibn, 16246
Gaertner, Hans see Ginat, Yochanan
Gagnebin, Jeanne-Marie, 16429
Gahlen, Heinz, 16826
Galicia, 15946, 16275
Galley, Eberhard, 16550
Galský, Dezider, 16170
Garavelli, Silvana, 16226
Garrin, Stephen Howard, 16733
'Gartenlaube', 15853
Gau-Algesheim, 16174
Gaupp, Eberhard, 16718
Gay, Peter, 15824, 15875
Gedenke, vergiss nie, 16178
Geerken, Hartmut, 16359
'(Der) Gegner', 16378
Geiger, Abraham, 15834
Geisel, Eike, 16043
Geiss, Imanuel, 16538
Gelber, Yoav, 16160
Gellately, Robert, 16850
Gelnhausen, 16174
Geneaology (see also Circumcision, Register of; Memorbuch), 15887, 15907–15908, 15925, 15935, 16013, 16298, 16300, 16753–16754, 16762, 16767, 16802, 16824
Genthin, 15893
George, Manfred (orig. Cohn), 15991, 16877
Geras, Norman, 16625
German Democratic Republic, 16178–16180, 16194, 16819, 16823
German Foreign Office, 16049, 16160, 16302
'German Historical Institute, Bulletin', London, 16610
German Jews in Various Countries, 15967–15989
'German Life and Letters', Oxford, 16386, 16711, 16803
German–Israeli Relations, 15850, 16180, 16199, 16815–16819
German-Jewish Relations, 15823, 15826, 15838, 16171, 16211, 16221, 16291, 16344, 16808–16814, 16868–16880
Germania Judaica, Kölner Bibliothek zur Geschichte d. dt. Judentums, 15992
Germany (see also Imperial Germany; Weimar Republic; Federal German Republic; German Democratic Republic)
— Communal History, 15845, 15868–15941
— Northern Germany, 15857
Gernsheim. Family, 16767
Gernsheim, Friedrich, 16343
Gernsheim, Helmut, 16767
Gershon, Karen, 16886
Gerson, Hermann, 16824
Gerstein, Kurt, 16078

Gerth, Hans, 15976
Gertz, Elmer, 16851
Geschichte d. jüd. Volkes, 15815
'Geschichte in Köln', 15884
'Geschichte in Wissenschaft u. Unterricht', Stuttgart, 15838, 16006, 16181, 16211
'Geschichte u. Gesellschaft', Göttingen, 16865
Gesellschaft für Christlich-Jüdische Zusammenarbeit see Christian-Jewish Cooperation, Society for
'Gesher', Quarterly Review, Tel Aviv, 15834, 16235
Gewirtz, Jacob, 16318
Giessler, Rupert, 16825
Gilbert, Martin, 16079, 16130
Gilon, Meir, 16262
Ginat, Yochanan (orig. Hans Gaertner), 15995, 15997
Ginsburg, Hans Jakob, 16176, 16263, 16269
Ginsburg, Josef see Burg, J. G.
Glaser, Hermann, 16062, 16206, 16814
Glassbrenner, Adolf, 16384
Glatzer, Nahum N[orbert], 16243, 16456
Gleiwitz/O/S, 16080
Glozer, Laszlo, 16589
Glückel von Hameln, 16298
Goch, Josefa, 16553
Goebel, Hans Joachim, 16544
Göbel, Wolfram, 16360
Görlich, Hans-Jörg, 16378
Goes, Albrecht, 16069
Goethe, Johann Wolfgang von, 16426
Goethe Institute, London, 16521
Göttingen, 16801, 16843
'Göttinger Monatsblätter', 16843
Golan, Reuven, 15995
Goldammer, Peter, 16768
Golden, Frederic, 16488
'(Das) Goldene Tor', 16379
Goldman, Edward A., 16290
Goldmann, Nahum, 16239, 16324, 16811, 16815
Goldner, Franz, 16353
Goldschmidt, Fritz, 16297
Goldstein. Family, 15927
Goldstein, Heinzwerner, 16045
Goldstein, Horst, 16828
Goldstein, Jeffrey A., 16160
Goldstein, L. J., 16239
Golem, 15961–15962
Goll, Claire, 16391, 16534
Goll, Yvan, 16367, 16391, 16534
Gombrich, Sir Ernst Hans, 16535, 16726
Gomperz, Heinrich, 16536
Gomperz, Theodor, 16537
Goral, Arie, 16727
Gordon, Sarah Ann, 16140
Gotlieb, Yosef, 16488
Gott nach Auschwitz, 16081

Gottgetreu, Erich, 16221, 16227, 16422, 16488, 16612, 16679, 16720, 16816
Grab, Walter, 15993, 16538
Gradenwitz, Peter, 16873, 16880
Gradl, Felix, 16445
Gradwohl, Roland, 16158, 16325
Graetz, Heinrich, 15834, 16248
Graetz, Michael, 15826
Grappin, Pierre, 16547
Grass, Günter, 16212
Graupe, Heinz Mosche, 16244
Great Britain, 15819, 15852, 16438
— Immigration, 15986
— Refugees, 15975, 15977, 15985, 16076, 16349, 16772, 16777
— Refugee Policy, 16129–16130, 16134–16135, 16138, 16862
Greenberg, Irving, 16158
Greffrath, Mathias, 15976
Gregor-Dellin, Martin, 16506
Grein, Gerd J., 15905
Greive, Hermann, 16829, 16844
Griese, Friedrich, 16795
Grieswelle, Detleff, 16852
Grimm, Brigitte, 16356
Grobman, Alex, 16082
Gröbzig, 16083, 16174
Gronau, Klaus, 16418
Groningen, 15916
Groppe, Lothar, 16084
Gross, Walter, 15871
Grosser, Alfred, 16813
Grosser, P. F., 16853
Grossman, S., 16869
Grossmann, Kurt R., 16349
Grossmann, Stefan, 16376, 16769
Gross-Umstadt, 16174
Grosz, George, 16868
Grubel, Fred, 16518
Grubrich-Simitis, Ilse, 16188
Gruenewald, Hede, 16245
Gruenewald, Max, 15829, 15997, 16245
Grünfeld, Falk Valentin, 16770
Grünfeld, Fritz V., 16770
Grunberger, Richard, 16199
Grundmann, Herbert, 16450
Grundriss d. Gesamtwissenschaft d. Judentums, 16249
Grunfeld, Frederic V., 15822
'(The) Guardian', London, 15986, 16318, 16771
Güdemann, Moritz, 15953
Günther, Horst, 16660
Günther, Joachim, 16294
Günzerodt, Werner, 15859
Guggenheim, Florence, 16002
Guide to Unpublished Materials of the Holocaust Period, 16007
Gumbel, Emil Julius, 16539
Gumperz, Julian, 16378
Gumplowicz, Ludwig, 16540

Gundolf, Friedrich, 16385
Gurland, Arcadius R. L., 16541
Gurs, 16132
Gustav-Heinemann-Oberschule, Berlin, 16056
Guthke, Karl S., 15826
Gutman, Yisrael, 16005
Guttmann, Jacob, 16246
Guttmann, Sir Ludwig, 15977

Haacke, Wilmont, 16723, 16787
Haas, Leo, 16156
Haase, Hugo, 16542
Haber, Fritz, 16101
Habermann, Gerhard E., 16800
Hachsharah, 16200
Hadamar, 16214
Härtle, Heinrich, 16183
Häsler, Alfred A., 16150
Häusler, Wolfgang, 15944, 15946, 15953
Haffner, Sebastian, 16091
Hahn, Manfred, 16346
Hahn, Rosy, 16343
Hahner, Mechthild, 16679
Haiduk, Manfred, 16734
Hakel, Hermann, 16887
Hakoah, Turn- u. Sport-Klub, Essen, 16304
Hall, Murray G., 16442
Hallie, Philip, 16131
Halpterin, E. G., 16853
Hamáčková, Vlastimila, 15957
Hamburg, 15894–15897, 16259, 16315, 16331, 16727
Hamburger, Käte, 16543
Hamburger, Wolfgang, 16259
Hamburger Beiträge zur Geschichte d. dt. Juden, 15897
Hameln see Glückel von Hameln
Hamilton, Alex, 15986
Hamilton, Nigel, 16874
Hamm/Sieg, 15868
Hamm-Brücher, Hildegard, 16712
Hammann, Gustav, 15924
Hammer-Schenk, Harold, 15895, 16314
Hanau, 15898
Hannam, Charles (orig. Karl Hartland), 16771–16772
'Hannoversche Geschichtsblätter', Hannover, 16314
Hardach, Gerd, 16610
Harden, Maximilian, 16544
Hardt, Hanno, 16354
Harris, Kenneth, 15986
Harris, Leon, 15978
Hartland, Karl see Hannam, Charles
Harvard Univ., Library, 16003
Hasenclever, Walter, 16376, 16391, 16595
Hasidism, 16233, 16275, 16288
Haskalah see Enlightenment
Hauben, Nora, 15927

Hauptmann, Gerhart, 16768
Hausner, Gideon, 16085
Hawrylchak, Sandra H., 16017
Hayes, Saul, 15980
Haymond, Robert, 16517
Heartfield, John (orig. Helmut Herzfelde), 16721, 16868
Hebrew Literature in Germany, 16262, 16268, 16273–16274, 16285
Hebrew Union College, Cincinnati, Library, 16012
Hebrew Univ., Jerusalem see Jerusalem
Hechaluz, Dt. Landesverband, 16299
Hechingen, 16174
Hecht, Felix, 16365
Hegner, Jakob, 16380
Heidegger, Martin, 16232, 16577–16578
Heidelberg, 16177
Heidelberger Abhandlungen zur mittleren u. neueren Geschichte, 15848, 15920
Heiderich, Anton, 16380
Heilbronn, 16211, 16348, 16477
Heil- u. Pflegeanstalt für jüd. Nerven- u. Germütskranke, Bendorf, 16042
Heimann, Horst, 16439
Heimann, Moritz, 16375
'Heimat-Jahrbuch d. Kreises Altenkirchen/Westerwald', 15868
Heine, Betty, 16773
Heine, Heinrich, 16364, 16393, 16545–16557, 16773
— Heinrich-Heine-Archiv, 16550
— Heinrich-Heine-Institut, Düsseldorf, 16550, 16628
— Heine-Jahrbuch, 16550
— Heine-Studien, 16557
Heine, Thomas Theodor, 16558
Heine-Club, Mexico, 16352
Heinemann, Heinz Egon, 15979
Heise, Carl Georg, 16726
Heisenberg, Werner, 16661
Heissenbüttel, Helmut, 16430
Helbronner, Jules, 15980
Helfgott, Hermann see Asaria, Zvi
Helinek, Heinrich, 16416
Heller-Wallerstein, Jomtow Lipmann, 15960
Hellige, Hans Dieter, 16865
Helmich, Hans, 16122
Hemsbach, 15899
Henniger, Gerd, 16428
Henrix, Hans Hermann, 16830–16831
Henry, Aimé, 16450
Hensel, Fanny, 16651
Hensel, Georg, 16612
Hensel, Wilhelm, 16651
Hentsch, Gerhard, 15900
Herdan-Zuckmayer, Alice, 16695
Herde, Peter, 15886
'Herder Korrespondenz', Freiburg i. Br., 16635
Herdorf/Westerwald, 15868
Herlinger, Hans-Jürgen, 16740
Herlyn, Heinrich, 16634
Hermand, Jost, 16363–16364
Hermann, A., 16661
Hermann, Georg (orig. Georg Hermann Borchardt), 16559
Hermlin, Stephan, 16560, 16774
Hermsdorf, Klaus, 16507
Herrmann, Ursula, 16785
Herrnstadt, Marion, 16300
Herz, Henriette, 16561
Herz, Ida, 16562
Herz, Markus, 16266
Herz, Peter, 15952
Herzberg, Kurt see Barlev, Jehuda
Herzberg, Steven, 15981
Herzfelde, Helmut see Heartfield, John
Herzfelde, Wieland, 16378, 16868
Herzig, Arno, 16538
Herzl, Theodor, 16235, 16325–16327, 16769
Hess, Moses, 16393, 16563
Hesse, 15900–15901, 15923
— Hessisches Hauptstaatsarchiv, 15901
Hessel, Franz, 16391
Hessen see Hesse
Heubner, Christoph, 16033
Heuzeroth, Günter, 15868
Heym, Stefan, 16564–16567
Hilberg, Raul, 16086
Hildebrand, Alexander, 16749
Hildesheimer, Esriel (Rabbi, 1820–1899), 16247
Hildesheimer, Esriel, 16301
Hildesheimer, Wolfgang, 16568
Hilferding, Rudolf, 16371
Hilfsverein d. Dt. Juden, 16302
Hill, Melvyn, 16414
Hiller, Kurt, 16378, 16389, 16715
Hilsenrath, Edgar, 16888
Himmler, Heinrich, 15993
Hindenburg/O/S., 15902
Hirsch, Helmut, 16087
Hirsch, Jacob, 16332
Hirsch, Robert von, 16569–16570
Hirshberg, Jehoash, 16424
Hirszfeld, Ludwig, 16483
Historians, Jewish, 16216, 16220, 16248, 16528, 16538, 16604, 16675, 16694, 16713, 16725, 16787
Historiography, 15819, 15834, 15841, 16160, 16163, 16203
'Historische Zeitschrift', München, 15827
'Historisches Jahrbuch', Freiburg i. Br., 15825, 15827, 15838
'History Today', London, 16318
Hitler, Adolf, 15821, 16088–16093, 16098, 16143, 16361, 16811, 16851
Hobusch, Erich, 16083
Hochkeppel, Willy, 16795

Hoch'sches Konservatorium, Frankfurt a. Main, 16343
Hochschule für Jüd. Studien, Heidelberg, 16177
Hochwälder, Fritz, 16571
Hoddis, Jakob van (orig. Hans Kempner), 16359, 16391
Hodik, Fritz Peter, 15966
Hodin, Joseph Paul, 16790
'Höchst heute', Frankfurt a. Main, 16481
Hoensbroech, Hubertus Graf, 16259
Hörisch, Jochen, 16576
Hoffmann, Banesh, 16490
Hoffmann, Moses, 15927
Hoffmann, Stanley, 15983
Hofmann, Hanns Hubert, 16365
Hohenlimburg, 16174
Holešov, 15957–15958
Holitscher, Arthur, 16572
Holl, Hans-Günther, 16401
Holl, Oskar, 16724
Hollaender, Friedrich, 16385
Holland see Netherlands
Holocaust, 16021, 16023, 16027–16028, 16065–16068, 16078–16079, 16081–16082, 16085, 16098, 16108, 16110, 16112–16113, 16118, 16126, 16140, 16142, 16144, 16157–16158, 16160–16161, 16203–16205, 16212, 16214, 16294
— Art, 15997, 16052, 16061, 16094–16097, 16156
— Bibliographies, 16004–16010
— Denial, 16022, 16030, 16035, 16062, 16088, 16092, 16098, 16115, 16141, 16143, 16183, 16846, 16856, 16862–16863
— Film, 16098, 16181–16185, 16825, 16865
— Prosecution see Nazi Crimes
— Theological Impact, 16081, 16289, 16814, 16829, 16834
— Trauma, 16109, 16186–16190, 16289, 16443
Holocaust Library, 16077
Holzboog, Günther, 16266
Holzhey, Helmut, 16662
Holzträger, Hans, 16100
Honecker, Erich, 16178
Horkel, Wilhelm, 16854
Horkheimer, Max, 15982, 16362, 16393, 16573, 16868
Horn, Hermann, 16228
Hornburg, 16174
Horvath, Ödön von, 16120
Hoyt, Walter Carl-Alexander, 16508
Huder, Walther, 16777
Hübner, Adolf, 16742
Hüllbüsch, Ursula, 15825
Hülser, Karlheinz, 16741
Hüssler, Georg, 16825
Hughes, H. Stuart, 15982
Humboldt, Alexander von, 16651
Hundt, Martin, 16785

Hungary, 15965–15966, 16099–16100, 16160
Husserl, Edmund, 16574–16578, 16656
Hutten, Ulrich von, 15820
Hutterer, Claus Jürgen, 15858
Hyman, Paula E., 15998

IG Farben, 16101–16102
Ilan, Gabriel, 15825
Illy, József, 16488
Im Kreuzfeuer: Holocaust, 16098, 16182
'Immanuel', Freiburg i. Br., 16832; 16286, 16825
Immigration see Australia; France; Great Britain; Refugees
Imperial Germany (see also Antisemitism), 15823, 15825, 15828, 15832, 15838, 15847, 15851–15852, 16302, 16442, 16542, 16544
'imprimatur', Nachrichten u. krit. Meinungen aus d. kath. Kirche, Trier, 16855
Industry, Jews in, 15927, 16101, 16670, 16676, 16770, 16798, 16865
'Informationsbulletin', Prag, 16170
Institut für
— Dt. Geschichte, Univ. Tel Aviv, 15993
— Dt. Nachkriegsgeschichte, 16035
— Marxismus-Leninismus, 16642
— Österreichkunde, 15946
— Zeitgeschichte, München, 15874, 16023, 16040
Institut Kirche u. Judentum, 16238
Institute of
— Contemporary Jewry, Jerusalem, 16007, 16065
— Jewish Affairs, London, 16103, 16138, 16196, 16823, 16862
— Social Research see Frankfurt School
Institutum Judaicum Delitzschianum see 'Theokratia'
Interlibrum Buchantiquariat, Vaduz, 16494
'International Affairs', London, 16090
International Conference on the Lessons of the Holocaust, 16094–16095, 16204, 16212
'International Herald Tribune', Zürich, 15822, 16635
'(The) International History Review', Toronto, 16438
International Red Cross, 16126
International Theological Symposium on the Holocaust, 16205
'Internationale wissenschaftl. Korrespondenz zur Geschichte d. dt. Arbeiterbewegung', Berlin, 16541
Irgun Olej Merkas Europa see 'MB'
Irving, David, 16088, 16092, 16098
'Isis', Brüssel, 16488
Isolani, Gertrud, 16132, 16151, 16509
Israel, State of, 16239, 16294, 16323, 16755, 16885, 16890

Index to Bibliography 455

Israel Academy of Sciences and Humanities, Jerusalem, 16262, 16275
'Israelitisches Wochenblatt', Zürich, 15830, 15952, 15995, 16002, 16075, 16151, 16154, 16158, 16167, 16181, 16325, 16329, 16488, 16509, 16589, 16612, 16714, 16720, 16880
Istor, H. (i.e. Ernst G. Lowenthal), 15932, 16714
István, Hermann, 16623
Italy, 16103–16104

Jackson, J. E., 16463
Jacob, Heinrich Eduard, 16375, 16579
Jacob, Mathilde, 16782
Jacobi, Rudolf, 16341
Jacobs, Boike, 16069
Jacobs, Jürgen, 16871
Jacobs, Louis, 16280
Jacobs, Noah J., 15826
Jacobsen, Hans-Adolf, 16023, 16092
Jacobsohn, Siegfried, 16382
Jacoby, Abraham, 16538
Jacoby, Max, 16179
Jacoby'sche Anstalt, Bendorf, 16042
Jäckel, Eberhard, 16098
Jaeger, Hans, 16345
Jaenecke, Heinrich, 16533
Jahn, Wolfgang, 16648
Jahn-Zechendorff, Beate, 15860
Jahoda, Marie, 15976
'Jahrbuch d.
— Baltischen Deutschtums', Lüneburg, 15908
— Dt. Schillergesellschaft', Stuttgart, 15990; 16548, 16663–16664, 16775, 16877
— Instituts für Dt. Geschichte', Univ. Tel Aviv, 15993; 16293, 16295, 16301, 16563, 16638, 16860, 16876
— Psychoanalyse', Bern, 16518
— Vereins für d. Geschichte Berlins', 15877
'Jahrbuch für
— Fränkische Landesforschung', Erlangen, 15842
— d. Geschichte Mittel- u. Ostdeutschlands', Berlin, 15825, 15827
— Internat. Germanistik', Bern, 16350–16351
— Jüd. Geschichte u. Literatur', 16754
Jaldati, Lin, 16073
Janowitz, Franz, 16375
Japan, Refugee Policy, 16137
Jaretzky, Reinhold, 16210
Jarmatz, Klaus, 15973
Jaroš, Miroslav, 15957
Jay, Martin, 16865
Jellinek, Adolf, 15953
Jens, Inge, 16366
Jentzsch, Bernd, 16367
Jersch-Wenzel, Stefi, 15827
Jerusalem
— Hebrew University, 16007, 16065, 16207, 16216, 16493

— Jewish National and Univ. Library, 16275, 16493
'Jerusalem Post', Jerusalem, 16284
Jesenská, Milena, 16585
Jessner, Leopold, 16580
'Jewish Chronicle', London, 15975, 16108, 16121, 16138, 16199, 16318, 16533
'Jewish Frontier', New York, 16026, 16181, 16488, 16647, 16751, 16758
Jewish Identity see Jewish Problem
Jewish Immigrants of the Nazi Period in the USA, 15989
'(The) Jewish Journal of Sociology', London, 16321
Jewish National- and University Library see Jerusalem
Jewish Problem, 16289–16295, 16865
Jewish Publication Society of America, Philadelphia, 15819, 15865, 15981
'(The) Jewish Quarterly', London, 16068
Jewish Question, 15897, 16012, 16103, 16146, 16293
'Jewish Social Studies', New York, 16044, 16126
'Jewish Spectator', Santa Monica, Ca., 16640
Jewish Theological Seminary of America, New York, Archives, 16011
Jewish Young Leadership, Frankfurt a. Main, 16046
Jews and Germans from 1860 to 1933, 15823
Jews in a Free Society, 16290
Jiddische Volkslieder, 15859
Joachim, Joseph, 16343
Jochmann, Werner, 15850
Jochum, Herbert, 16855
Jogiches, Leo, 16781
Johanneum, Breslau, 15927
— Hamburg, 15894
John Paul II, Pope, 16823, 16825, 16834
Jonas, Klaus W., 16564
Jonca, Karol, 16147
Jones, Michael Taylor, 16402
Jongeling, Door K., 15916
Joodse begraafplaatsen in Groningen, 15916
Josef II, Austrian Emperor, 15948
Joseph, Artur, 15883
Jospe, Alfred, 15824
Jost, Isaak Markus, 16248
'Journal of
— the American Psychoanalytic Association', New York, 16518
— Ecclesiastical History', London, 16118
— European Studies', London, 16869
— the History of Ideas', New York, 16604
— Modern History', Chicago, 15827, 16335, 16440, 16515, 16622
— Psychology and Judaism', Ottawa, 16517
Journalists see Publicists
Juda Loew ben Bezalel (Maharal), 15957, 15964
Judaic Studies Series, 16243

'Judaica', Zürich, (Periodical), 15827, 16181, 16207, 16278, 16829
Judaica (Series), 16141
Judaica (Short-title Catalogue), 16012
'Judaica Bohemiae', Prag, 15957
'Judaism', New York, 15824, 16158, 16511
Judaism see Philosophy and Learning
Judaism in Education see Antisemitism, Judaism, Nazism in Education and Teaching
'(Der) Jude', eine Monatsschrift, 16221
Juden in Hessen, 15901
Juden in Mainz, 15909
Juden im Wilhelminischen Deutschland, Reviews, 15825
Juden u. Christen, 16213
Juden im Zeitalter d. Aufklärung, 15826
Judentum in d. Dt. Umwelt 1800–1850, Reviews, 15827
Judenverfolgung im Dritten Reich, 16008
'Jüdische Rundschau', Berlin, 16256, 16261
Jüdische Turnerschaft, 16303
(Die) Jüdischen Gefallenen d. dt. Heeres, 16308
(Die) Jüdischen Gemeinden in Bayern, 15874
Jüdischer Frauenbund, 16305–16306
'Jüdischer Pressedienst', Düsseldorf, 16177, 16195
Jüdisches Fest, jüd. Brauch, 16309
'Jüdisches Jahrbuch', Prag, 15958
Jüdisches Leben in Deutschland (2), 15838
Jung, Carl Gustav, 16514, 16869
Jung, Hermann, 16773
Jungblut, Gerd W., 16794
Just, Helmut, 16825
Justitz, Alfred, 16170
Justiz u.d. Nazis, 16191
Justiz u. NS-Verbrechen, 16105

Kabbalah, 16282–16283
Kadezki, Nathan, 16154, 16167
Kaduk, Oswald, 16032
Käfer, Karl-Heinz, 16552
Kästner, Harald, 16209
Kafka, František, 15958, 16170
Kafka, Franz, 15822, 16243, 16359, 16375, 16393, 16581–16587, 16775
Kafka-Handbuch, 16583
Kahler, Eugen von, 16377
Kahn, Lothar, 16511
Kahn-Freund, Sir Otto, 16588, 16729
Kahnweiler, Daniel-Henry, 16589
'Kairos', Salzburg, 15845–15846, 15954
Kaiser, Joachim, 16864
Kaiser d. Atlantis, Opera, 16170
Kaiserslautern, 15903
Kampen, Wilhelm van, 16098, 16184
Kampmann, Wanda, 15828
Kandinsky, Wassily, 16377
Kanowitz, Kurt, 16291, 16336
Kant, Immanuel, 15826, 16252, 16550

Kant-Studien, 16258, 16421
Kantor Berg, Friedrich see Torberg, Friedrich
Kantorowicz, Alfred, 16349, 16381, 16590–16592
Kantzenbach, Friedrich Wilhelm, 16694
Kaplan, Anatoli L., 15860
Kaplan, Marion A., 16305–16306
Karasek, Horst, 15889
Karbusicky, Vladimir, 16629
Karèl, K., 16824
Karl IV, German Emperor, 15958
Kárný, Miroslav, 15957
Katholische Akademie, Hamburg, 16259
Katz, Jacob, 15829, 16328–16329, 16880
Katz, Steven T., 16248
Katzburg, Nathaniel, 16330
Kauf, Robert, 16586
Kaufhof, 16714
Kaufmann, Ludwig, 16825
Kaufmann, Walter, 16229
Kaus, Gina, 16378, 16776
Kautsky, Karl, 16593
Kedourie, Elie, 16138
Keim, Anton Maria, 16473
Kelman, Wolfe, 16239
Kemp, Friedhelm, 16657, 16804
Kemper, Thomas, 16292
Kempner, Alfred see Kerr, Alfred
Kempner, Hans see Hoddis, Jakob van
Kempner, Robert M. W., 16071, 16815
Kern, Erich, 16856
Kerner, Samuel, 15999
Kerr, Alfred (orig. Kempner), 16594, 16777
Kerr, Judith, 16208, 16595
Kershaw, Ian, 16040
Kessler, Harry, Graf, 16870
Kesten, Hermann, 16596, 16814
Kierkegaard, Sören, 16397
Kimchi, David, 16832
Kimmel, Günther, 16040
Kinder im KZ, 16156
King, W. J., 16803
Kirchen/Westerwald, 15868
Kirchgässner, Bernhard, 16365
Kirchliche Hochschule, Berlin, 16238
Kirchner, Peter, 16179
Kirchner, Renate, 16179
'Kirjath Sepher', Jerusalem, 16283
Kirsch, Hans-Christian, 16553, 16595
Kirschner, Klaus, 16064
Kirsten, Christa, 16495
Kisch, Alexander, 15971
Kisch, Arnold I., 15971
Kisch, Curt Josef see Bruno, Guido
Kisch, Egon Erwin, 16170, 16388, 16597–16599, 16768
Kisch, Guido, 15827, 15830
Kiss, Endre, 16623
Kissinger, Henry, 15983

Index to Bibliography

Kittel, Gerhard, 16146
Klapperstück, Edgar, 16648
Klappert, Bertold, 16825
Klarmann, Norbert G., 16365
Klarsfeld, Beate, Foundation, New York, 16046
Klaweren, Jacob van, 15847
Klehr, Joseph, 16032
Klein, Dennis, 15823, 16368
Klein, Hans-Günther, 16271
Kleinert, Ingeborg, 16207
Klieman, Aaron, 16340
Klieneberger-Nobel, Emmy, 16600
Kling, Simcha, 16239
Klingenstein, Grete, 15826
Klöss, Erhard, 16725
Klose, Dirk, 16214
Klug, Ulrich, 16814
Kluge, Günter, 16641
Knee, Stuart E., 15998
Knobloch, Heinz, 16263
Knoepfmacher, Hugo, 16518
Knopp, Josephine, 16204-16205
Knust, Herbert, 16868
Koblenz, 15904, 16018 (Bundesarchiv)
Koch, Thomas R., 16676
Kochmann, Arthur, 16080
Kochmann, Klaus, 16317, 16625
Koebner, Thomas, 16777
Köhler, Hanns E., 16545
Köhne, Renate, 16018
Köln see Cologne
'Köln', Vierteljahresschrift, 16714
König, Franz, Kardinal, 16825
König, Joel (i.e. Esra Ben Gershôm), 16106
Koestler, Arthur, 16345, 16601
Kötzsche, Dietrich, 16570
Kofler, Leo,, 16602
Kogon, Eugen, 16081, 16107
Kohler, Kaufmann, 16249
Kohn, Adolph, 16603
Kohn, Hans, 16230, 16604
Kolinsky, Eva, 16181
Kolisch, Rudolf, 16690
Kolman, Arnošt, 16778
Kolmar, Gertrud (orig. Chodziesner), 16367, 16369, 16390-16391
Kommission für d. Geschichte d. Juden in Hessen, Schriften, 15900
Kompert, Leopold, 16511
Konrad, Helmut, 16166, 16654
Kopitzsch, Wolfgang, 16072
Koplowitz, Jan, 16889
Korherr, [Richard]-File, 16022
Korman, Gerd, 16108
Kornfeld, Paul, 16391
Koselleck, Reinhart, 16109
Koskull, Hans-Jürgen, Baron von, 15983
Kosler, Hans Christian, 16449
Kracauer, Siegfried, 16605

Krämer, Helmut, 16554
Kraemer-Badoni, Rudolf, 16819
Kraft, Werner, 16284
Krakowski, Shmuel, 16007
Kraler, Mr. see Kugler, Victor
Kramer, Theodor, 16391
Kranefuss, Annelen, 16436
Kraus, Hans-Joachim, 16690
Kraus, Hans Peter, 15984
Kraus, Karl, 16550, 16606-16609, 16776
Krauskopf, Bruno, 16341
Krausnick, Helmut, 16023
Krebs, Sir Hans, 16730
Kreisky, Bruno, 16168
Kremers, Heinz, 16835
Kreutzberger, Max, 15829, 15995, 16779
Kreuzer, Ingrid, 16434
Krieger, Hans, 16520
Krink, Alfred, 16814
Krispyn, Egbert, 16355, 16680
'Kristallnacht' see November Pogrom
Krockow, Christian, 15850
Kröger, Jost J., 16714
Kroll, Stanley Eli, 16231
Krolow, Karl, 16704
Kronberger, Hans, 16598
Krotoschin, 16793
Krüger, Hans Jürgen, 15885
Krüll, Marianne, 16519
Krummacher, Friedhelm, 16652
Kruse, Joseph A., 16550, 16628
Kuczynski, Jürgen, 16610
Kühner, Hans, 16062
Kühnl, Reinhard, 16110
Kugler, Victor, 16074
Kunst u. Literatur im antifaschistischen Exil, 15973-15974, 16152
Kupisch, Karl, 15825
Kurtze, Gerhard, 15979
Kurzhals-Reuter, Arntrud, 16653
Kusel. Family, 16798
Kusserow, Käthe, 16172
Kwiet, Konrad, 16163
KZ see Concentration Camps

'L 76 Demokratie u. Sozialismus', Köln, 16212
Lackner, Stephan (orig. Morgenroth), 16756
Lador-Lederer, J. J., 15947
Lamb, Stephen, 16342
Lambi, Ivo N., 15847
Lamm, Hans, 15912, 16062, 16071, 16161, 16181, 16278, 16298, 16488, 16635, 16720
Lampel, Rusia, 16890
Landau, Edwin, 15927
Landau, M. I., 15957
Landauer, Gustav, 15823, 16380, 16383, 16611, 16769
Landeszentrale für politische Bildung, 15873 (Baden-Württemberg), 16072 (Hamburg)

Landmann, Michael, 16362
Landmann, Salcia, 15838, 15861, 16824
Lane, Helen R., 16765
Lang, Heinrich, 16181
Lang, Michel R., 16809
Langbein, Hermann, 16192, 16214, 16814
Langen, 15905
Langfur, Stephen Joseph, 16232
Langgässer, Elisabeth, 16210
Langguth, Gerd, 16819
Langner, Ilse, 16369
Lankheit, Klaus, 16377
Lapide, Pinchas, 16278, 16828, 16836–16837, 16839
Lappe, Rudolf, 16488
Laquer, Walter, 15997, 16112–16113, 16415
Larsen, Egon, 15838, 15985, 16370
Lasker-Schüler, Else, 16367, 16369, 16376, 16380, 16385, 16391, 16612–16614
Lassalle, Ferdinand, 16387, 16566, 16615–16616
Laub, Dori, 16189
Laub, Gabriel, 16720
Lavater, Johann Kaspar, 16267, 16272
Lea, Henry A., 15823
Le Chambon (France), 16131
(*The*) *Left against Zion*, 16819
Legal History, Jewish (see also Nuremberg Laws), 15830, 15897, 15914, 15922, 15947
Legal Professions, Jews in, 15838, 16297, 16433, 16437, 16588, 16638, 16674, 16796
Lehmann, Günther K., 16623
Lehmann, Kurt see Merz, Konrad
Lehmann-Haupt, Christopher, 15978
Lehranstalt für d. Wissenschaft d. Judentums, 16656
Lehrmann, Cuno Ch., 16780
Lehrmann, Graziella, 16780
Leibfried, Stephan, 16114, 16297
Leibowitz, Yeshayahu, 16832
Leiser, Erwin, 16181
Lemmermann, Holger, 15910
Lempp, Reinhart, 16190
Leo Baeck Institute, 16372
— Bulletin, 15994; 15829
— Publications, 15831
— Schriftenreihe, 15825, 15827
— Veröffentlichung, 15838,, 16230
— Year Book, 15995; 15817, 15837, 15841, 15857, 15863, 15878, 16016, 16163, 16260, 16274, 16302, 16310, 16334, 16337, 16339, 16539, 16762, 16767, 16793
— Jerusalem, 15829, 16880
— London, Seminar at Oxford Univ., 15997
— New York, Archives, 16013–16014, 16094–16096, 16496, 16518, 16679, 16681
— — Leo Baeck Memorial Lecture (23), 16112; 15997
— — Library and Archives News, 15996
— — LBI News, 15997
Leonard, John, 15822
Leonhardt-König, Christiane, 15938
Leser, Hans G., 16674
Lesser, Jonas, 16877
Lessing, Erich, 15944
Lessing, Gotthold Ephraim, 15826, 16266, 16270, 16814, 16871–16872
Lessing, Theodor, 16617
Lessing, Traudl, 16327
Lessing-Akademie, Bremen, 15826
Lettau, Reinhard, 16635
Letters see Autobiographies
Leukefeld, Peter, 16891
Leuschen-Seppel, Rosemarie, 15831
Levi, Paul, 16371
Levin, Bernard, 15986
Levin, Julio, 16341
Levin, Nora, 16094
Levinson, Fritz A., 16304
Levinson, Nathan Peter, 16828
Levy, Rudolf, 16618
Levy, Zeew, 16278
Lévy-Hass, Hanna, 16043
Lewin, Erich, 15927
Lewy, Hermann, 16167, 16177, 16181, 16264, 16612
Leyvratz, Jean-Pierre, 16739
Libermann, Rebecca, 16589
Libraries and Archives, Resources in, 15989–15991, 15996–15997, 15999–16000, 16003, 16011–16014, 16017–16018, 16094–16096, 16495–16496, 16518, 16550, 16679, 16763
Lichtenberg (Fürstentum), 15923
Lichtenstein, Erwin, 16058
Lichtenstein, Heiner, 16117
Liebermann, Max, 16341, 16376, 16619
Lieberson, Jonathan Sears, 16668
Liebert, Arthur, 16373
Liebeschütz, Hans, 15827, 15995
Liebmann, Otto, 16373
Liebmann, Susanne, 16483
Liepman, Heinz, 16620
Liliencron, Detlev, 16550
Lindeskog, Gösta, 16694
Linke, Manfred, 16709
Lipscher, Ladislav, 16053
Liptzin, Sol, 16423
Liszt, Franz, 16873
Literary Critics see Critics
Littman Library of Jewish Civilization, 15844
Litvinoff, Barnet, 16340
Living Witness, 16094
Lockwood, W. B., 15862
Locum, Evang. Akademie, 16214
Loetzsch, Frieder, 15826
Loew, Immanuel, 16250, 16307

Löw, Leopold, 16250
Löw Juda ben Bezalel see Judah Loew ben Bezalel
Loewenberg, Peter, 16865
Loewenstein, Israel Egon, 15890
Loewenstein, Julius Jitzchak, 16635
Löwenthal, Leo, 15976
Löwenthal, Richard, 16813
Löwith, Karl, 16393
Loewy, Ernst, 16356
Logos, Friedhelm, 16824
'(The) London Review of Books', 15983
Longuet, Robert-Jean, 16641
Lothar Franz von Schönborn, Fürstbischof, 15842
Lovell, Sir Bernard, 16489
Low, Alfred D., 15832
Lowe, Adolph, 15976
Lowe, Malcolm, 16160
Lowenstein, Steven M., 15863
Lowenthal, Ernst G[ottfried] (see also Istor, H.), 15830, 15838, 15877, 15882, 15926–15927, 15932, 15986, 15995, 15997, 16040, 16057, 16114, 16172, 16175, 16259, 16266, 16336, 16466, 16532, 16588, 16592, 16707, 16786
Lowenthal-Hensel, Cécile, 16259, 16265–16266, 16651
Lower Saxony, 15906–15907
Luckner, Gertrud, 16825
Ludwig Boltzmann Institut, Wien, 16166, 16516, 16654
Lüdke, Martin, 16428
Lüneburg, 15908
Lützeler, Paul Michael, 16453
Lukács, Georg, 16380, 16387, 16621–16624
Luthardt, Wolfgang, 16371
Luther, Martin, 16838
'Lutherische Monatshefte', Hamburg, 16838
Luxemburg, Rosa, 16625–16627, 16781–16782
Luz, Ulrich, 16836
Lyric Writers see Poetry

Maass, Max Peter, 16790
Maass, Walter B., 16037
Maccabiah, 16303
Maccoby, Hyam, 16138
McGuinness, Brion, 16740
Mack, Rudolf, 16233
Märthesheimer, Peter, 16098
Magenschab, Hans, 15948
Magill, Stephen, 15823, 15833
Magnus, Uwe, 16185
Mahler, Gustav, 15823, 16628–16630, 16783
— Internat. Gustav-Mahler-Gesellschaft, Wien, 16628
Mahler-Berger, Elisabeth, 16778
Mahler-Werfel, Alma, 16783

'(Die) Mahnung', Berlin, 15881, 16071, 16300, 16812
Mahr, Gerhard, 16478
Mahrenholtz, Hans, 15915
Maier, Mathilde, 16784
Maimon, Salomon, 15826
Mainfranken, 15886
Mainz, 15909
Majdanek, 16115–16117
Makkabi, 16303
Malachi, Ruben see Maleachi, Ruben
Malamat, Abraham, 15815
Maleachi, Ruben, 15896, 16331
Malter, Rudolf, 16550
Mann, Heinrich, 16874
Mann, Thomas, 16562, 16874–16877
Mannheim, 16365
Mannheim, Karl, 15982, 16393
Mannheimer, Isaak Noah, 15953
'Mannheimer Hefte', 15986, 16707
Mannzmann, Anneliese, 16857
'Marbacher Magazin', 15991
Marburger Schule, 16373
Marc, Franz, 16377
March, Joachim, 16812
Marchfeld, Paul see Merchav, Peretz
Marcus, Alfred, 15829
Marcus, Paul E. see Pem
Marcuse, Herbert, 15982, 16393, 16631–16636
Marcuse, Ludwig, 16637
Marek, Jan, 16170
Margaliot, Abraham, 16005, 16065, 16160
Margolius, Hans, 15927
Margull, Hans Jochen, 15850
Marin, Bernd, 16865
Markovits, Andrei S., 16181
Marr, Wilhelm, 15897
Martini, Fritz, 15990
Marwitz, Alexander von der, 16804
Marx, Heinrich, 16638
Marx, Hilde, 16765
Marx, Karl, 16387, 16393, 16563, 16639–16648, 16711, 16785
— Karl-Marx-Haus, Trier, 16639
— 'Marx-Engels-Jahrbuch', 16642
Marx, Leopold, 16786, 16885
Marx, Werner, 16577
Marxism, 16621–16624
— Austria, 16420, 16646
Maschler, Kurt, 15985
Massary, Fritzi, 16507
Massiczek, Albert, 16039
Masur, Gerhard, 16787
'Materialien zur Politischen Bildung', Bonn, 16214
Mathematics, Jews in, 16467, 16539
Mattersdorf (Burgenland), 15966
Maydell, Bodo Freiherr von, 16278, 16802

Mayer, Hans, 16813, 16875
Mayer, Hans see Améry, Jean
Mayer, Hans-Otto, 16562
Mayer, Sir Robert, 15986
Mayer König, Wolfgang, 16607
Mayser, Erich, 16555
'MB' Wochenzeitung des Irgun Olej Merkas Europa, Tel Aviv, 15825, 15827, 15829, 15838–15839, 15882, 15995, 15997, 16057–16058, 16114, 16195, 16197, 16227, 16255–16256, 16261, 16278, 16284, 16291, 16316, 16318, 16328, 16331–16332, 16336, 16338, 16466, 16468, 16588, 16592, 16612, 16635, 16786, 16816, 16873, 16880
Medicine, Jewish, 16276
— Jews in, 15977, 16114, 16179, 16266, 16297, 16344, 16425, 16466, 16481–16483, 16600, 16731, 16744
MEGA (Marx–Engels–Gesamtausgabe), 16642
Mehring, Franz, 16616
Mehring, Walter, 16367, 16385, 16391, 16649, 16788–16789, 16868
Meidner, Else, 16790
Meidner, Ludwig, 16341, 16650
Meinecke, Friedrich, 16878
Meisenheim, 15923
Meisler, Yoash, 15993
Meitner, Lise, 16766
Melchers, Christoph B., 16181
Melitz, Raanan, 16138
Memoirs see Autobiographies
Memorbuch, 15970
Mende, Fritz, 16547
Mendelssohn. Family, 16651
Mendelssohn, Abraham, 16651
Mendelssohn, Brendel, 15997
Mendelssohn, Fromet, 16266
Mendelssohn, Georg Benjamin, 16651
Mendelssohn, Joseph, 15914, 16384
Mendelssohn, Moses, 15826, 15995, 15997, 16251–16272
Mendelssohn, Peter de, 16085, 16875
Mendelssohn-Bartholdy, Albrecht, 16651
Mendelssohn Bartholdy, Felix, 16651–16653, 16791
Mendelssohn-Studien, 16266, 16651
Mendes-Flohr, Paul R., 16284
Mengele, Josef, 16167
Mentzschel, Erika, 15908
Mentsher, Aryeh, 16235
Meppen, 15910
Merchav, Peretz, (orig. Paul Marchfeld), 16654
'Merkur', Stuttgart, 16181, 16428, 16432, 16587, 16810
Merz, Konrad (orig. Kurt Lehmann), 16655
'Messe', 15890
Messerschmid, Felix, 16181

Mestdagh, J. H. de vey, 15916
Mestitz, Franz, 16588
Metz, J. B. 16825
Metzger, Arnold, 16656
Mevorah, Baruch, 16267
Meyem, K. von, 16661
Meyer, Alfred Richard, 16376
Meyer, Alwin, 16033
Meyer, Christian, 15918
Meyer, Claus Heinrich, 16722
Meyer, Eduard, 15897
Meyer, Enno, 16123
Meyer, Ernst, 16236
Meyer, Herbert, 16707
Meyer, Michael A., 15827, 15834, 15878
Meyer, Thomas, 16439
Meyer-Cronemeyer, Hermann, 16876
Meyer-Leviné, Rosa, 16792
Meyerhoff, Hans, 15982
Meyers, Peter, 16209
Meyrink, Gustav, 15962
Michael, Reuven, 16268
Michaelis, Dolf, 16762
Michaelis, Meir, 16103
Michaelis, Rolf, 16382
Michalski, Gabrielle, 16858
Michelsen, Peter, 16266
Michman, Dan, 16133
Mickel, Ernst, 16531
Mickel, Liselotte, 16531–16532
Middell, Eike, 15974
Middle Ages, Jews in the, 15815, 15818, 15828, 15830, 15843, 15845–15846, 15886, 15920, 15922, 15956, 16832, 16857
'Midstream', New York, 15822, 15988, 16021, 16086, 16089, 16168, 16295, 16326, 16488, 16549, 16781
Mieses, Matthias, 15864
Mikulov, 15957
Milch, Thomas, 16701–16703
Milena see Jesenská, Milena
Miles, David H., 16624
Mill, E., 16171
Miller, Henry, 16732
Miller, Susanne, 15835
Milton, Sybil, 16013–16014, 16095–16096
Minder, Robert, 16473
Mirbach, Thomas, 16403
Mitchell, Donald, 16783
Mitschel, Ernest, 15927
'Mitteilungen d. Verbandes ehemaliger Breslauer u. Schlesier in Israel', Tel Aviv, 15927; 15888, 15896, 16045
'Mitteilungen d. Vereins für d. Geschichte Berlins', 16259
Mittenzwei, Werner, 16152–16153
'Modern Austrian Literature', Ashland, Pittsburg, Pa., 16423

Modern Language Association of America, Publications see PMLA
'(The) Modern Language Review', Cambridge, 16721
Moellenhoff, Anna, 16486
Moellenhoff, Fritz, 16486
Möller, Irmgard, 16547
Mogge, Birgitta, 16859
Molan, Nolly, 16306
Moll & Schneider, Tobacco Factory, 16798
Moltmann, Jürgen, 16837
Mombert, Alfred, 16359, 16366, 16377
Mommsen, Hans, 16214
Monasch, Baer Loew, 16793
'(Der) Monat', Berlin, 15875
Monz, Heinz, 16638
Moore, Erna, 16358
Morehouse, Keith Herbert, 16505
Morgan, David W., 16440
Morgenroth, Stephan see Lackner, Stephan
Morley, John Francis, 16118
Morse, Margaret Elizabeth, 16688
Mosbach/Baden, 15873
Mosblech, Berndt, 16419
Moser, Jonny, 16039
Moses, Siegfried, 16332, 16372, 16880
Moses, Stefan, 16390
Moses, Stephane, 16587
Mosse, George L., 15836
Mosse, Werner E., 15825, 15837
Mühlfeit, Herbert, 16584
Mühsam, Erich, 15997, 16376, 16388, 16391, 16794
Müller, Alwin, 15884
Müller, Filip, 16034
Müller, Gotthold, 16833
Müller-Seidel, Walter, 15990, 16476
München see Munich
Münden, 16119
Münster, 15913, 16259
'(Das) Münster am Hellweg', Essen, 16304
Munich, 15911–15912, 16041, 16847
Munk, Georg (orig. Paula Buber), 16380
Museum, Jewish
— Berlin, 16172
— Eisenstadt, 15953
— Prague, 15957
Music, Jewish, 16311–16313
— Jews in, 15823, 16170, 16313, 16343, 16364, 16377, 16424, 16468, 16628–16630, 16652–16653, 16685, 16690–16691, 16707, 16783, 16791, 16824
Mussner, Franz, 16839, 16842
Mussolini, Benito, 16103
Mynona (orig. Salomo Friedlaender), 16359, 16391
Mytze, Andreas W., 16345, 16590

Nach dreissig Jahren, 16813
Nachmann, Werner, 16181
Nachmansohn, David, 16372
'Nachrichtenblatt d. Jüd. Gemeinde von Berlin u.d. Verbandes d. Jüd. Gemeinden in der DDR', 16179; 15880, 16073, 16083, 16257, 16259, 16263, 16488, 16731
Nadel, Arno, 16376, 16657
Nagel, Helga, 16356
Names, Jewish, 16300
Naphtali, Fritz, 16371
Napoleon, 15844
Nassau (Herzogtum), 15923
National Institute on the Holocaust, Philadelphia, Publications, 16009, 16094–16095, 16204–16205
National Museum of History and Technology, Washington, 16497
Nationale Forschungs- u. Gedenkstätten d. Klassischen Dt. Literatur in Weimar, 16547
Nationalgalerie Berlin, 16619
Nationalism, Jewish, 15840
Nauen, Franz, 16860
Naumann, Uwe, 16210
Navemar (Steamship), 15997
Nazi Crimes, Prosecution of (see also Nuremberg Trial; Statute of Limitation), 16105, 16116–16117, 16191–16193, 16824
Nazi Period (see also Zionism: Immigration), 15829, 15868, 15874, 15877, 15898, 15911, 15997, 16004, 16020–16165, 16297, 16299, 16303–16305, 16309, 16318–16319, 16333, 16335, 16395, 16577, 16808
Nazism in Education see Antisemitism, Judaism, Nazism in Education and Teaching
Neckar, Region of, 15873
Nedersaksische Studies, 15916
Nedo, Michael, 16740
Nef, Ernst, 16717
Nelken, Lothar, 15977
Neo Nazism (see also Holocaust: Denial), 16035, 16143, 16173, 16183, 16191, 16862
(Das) Neopathetische Cabaret, 16389
Nestroy, Johann, 16384
Netherlands, 15916
— Refugees, 16069–16075, 16133
Netter, Lucienne, 16547
Neubauer, Franz, 16643
Neubaur, Caroline, 16501
Neudeck, Rupert, 16117
'Neue Blätter', 16380
(Der) Neue Club, 16389
'Neue Deutsche Hefte', Berlin, 16284, 16294, 16401, 16756, 16780
'Neue Freie Presse', 16598
'(Die) Neue Gesellschaft', Bonn, 15835, 16451
Neue Gesellschaft für Literatur, Berlin, 16579
'(Das) Neue Israel', Zürich, 15838–15839,

15951, 15960, 16174, 16237, 16259, 16278, 16322, 16325, 16466, 16488, 16676, 16679
'Neue Jüd. Nachrichten', München, 15940, 15948, 15956, 15964–15965, 16278, 16325, 16442, 16483, 16488, 16635, 16720, 16786, 16800, 16834, 16874
'Neue Rheinische Zeitung', 16642
'Neue Rundschau', Frankfurt a. Main, 16292, 16428, 16458, 16737
'(Die) Neue Weltbühne', 16382
'Neue Zürcher Zeitung' see 'NZZ'
Neugebauer, Wolfgang, 16038
Neugroschel, Joachim, 16759
Neumann, Alfred, 16658
Neumann, Franz, 15982
Neumann, Robert, 16659
'new german critique', Milwaukee, 15876, 16306, 16446
'New Statesman', London, 16143
New York Council for the Humanities, 16496
'(The) New York Review of Books', 15983, 16138, 16488, 16522, 16765, 16781
'(The) New York Times', 15970, 15978
'(The) New Yorker', 16441
Nicosia, Francis R. J., 16333–16335
Niedersachsen, see Lower Saxony
Nieder-Wiesen, 15937
Niemeyer, Helmut, 16430
Niers, Gert, 15822
Niewöhner, Friedrich, 15826
Nöstlinger, Christine, 16659
'Norddeutsche Familienkunde', Neustadt/Aisch, 15907, 15915, 15935
Norden, Günther van, 16120
Normans, 15848
Nosek, Bedřich, 15957
November Pogrom, 15871, 15905, 15927, 16008, 16064, 16076, 16121–16123, 16178–16179, 16824–16825, 16881
Novogoratz, Hans, 16861
Nuremberg, 16124
Nuremberg Laws, 16065, 16139, 16149, 16160
Nuremberg Trial, 16011, 16141
Nussbaum, Felix, 16341
Nyanaponika Mahathera (orig. Siegmund Feniger), 16779
'NZZ' (Neue Zürcher Zeitung), 15838, 15983, 16081, 16109, 16136, 16138, 16181, 16216, 16277, 16281, 16406, 16411, 16438, 16459, 16460, 16462, 16577, 16662, 16679, 16704, 16714, 16717, 16720, 16739

Oberammergau Passion Play, 16823, 16840–16841
Obermayer-Marnach, Eva, 16015
Oberschlesien see Silesia
Oberschlesische Holz-Industrie A. G., Beuthen, 15927

'(The) Observer', London, 15983, 15986, 16138, 16318, 16443, 16635
Odin, Karl-Alfred, 16825
Ökumenisch-Theologische Forschungsgemeinschaft in Israel, 16832
Oelsner, Toni, 15976
Oelze, Alida, 16155
Oelze, Regina, 16155
Österreich see Austria
Österreich-Archiv, 15946
Österreichische Akademie d. Wissenschaften, 16015
'Österreichische Zeitschrift für Soziologie', Wien, 16166
Österreichisches Biographisches Lexikon, 16015
Österreichisches Jüd. Museum in Eisenstadt, Verein, 15953
Oestreich, Helgard, 16765
Offermann, Toni, 16616
Oldenburg, 15914, 16123
Ollig, Hans Ludwig, 16241, 16373
On the Holocaust, 16009
Ophir, Adi, 16493
Ophir, Baruch Z., 15874
Oppenheimer, Franz, 16540
Oppenheimer, John F., 16259
Oppenheimer, Josef, 16341
Oppenheimer, Max (MOP), 16341
Oppitz, Ulrich Dieter, 16192
Oppler, Edwin, 16314
Organisations, 15911, 16296–16297, 16299, 16301–16306, 16308, 16310, 16337
'Orientierung', Zürich, 16278
Orland, Nachum, 16138
Orlik, Emil, 16341
Orthodoxy, Jewish, 16242, 16247
Oschilewski, Walther G., 16451
Osram-Konzern, 16047, 16060
Ossowski, Leonie, 16210
'Ost und West', 16381
Ostjuden see East European Jews
Ostfriesland, 15915–15916
Ostpreussen see East Prussia
Ott, Ulrich, 16449
Otten, Karl, 16378
Otto-Brenner-Stiftung, Schriftenreihe, 16588

Pachter, Henry, 16644, 16878
Pacifists, Jewish, 16539, 16542
Padover, Saul K., 16785
Paepcke, Lotte, 16125
Paeschke, Hans, 16432
Pässler, Edgar, 16469
Painters see Art
Palatinate, 15917
Palestine see Zionism
Panofsky, Erwin, 16660, 16728
Papeleux, L., 16118

Pappenheim, Bertha, 16305
Paris, 15999–16000
'Parlament', Wochenzeitung, Bonn see 'Aus Politik u. Zeitgeschichte'
Parnas, Joseph, 16483, 16834
Passion Play see Oberammergau Passion Play
Patkin, Benzion, 16134
'Patterns of Prejudice', London, 16862; 16103, 16154, 16181, 16183, 16189, 16212
Patterson, Gordon Marshall, 16525
Paucker, Arnold, 15821, 15825, 15827, 15995
Pauli, Wolfgang, 16661
Pavlovský, P., 16170
Pazi, Margarita, 15963, 16458, 16538, 16613, 16885
Pease, Louis Edwin, 16198
Pedagogics see Education
Pehle, Walter H., 16098
Peiser, Franz, 15881
Pelli, Moshe, 16273–16274
Pem (orig. Paul E. Marcus), 16599
Penkower, Monty Noam, 16126
Periodicals, Reprints, 16221, 16375–16385
Perl, Joseph, 16275
Perthes, Clemens Theodor, 16651
Peru, Refugees, 15987
Pessachowitz, Benno, 15888
Peters, Uwe Henrik, 16512
Petuchowski, Jakob J., 16290, 16842
Pezold, Johann Dietrich von, 16119
'Pfälzer Heimat', Speyer, 15903, 15928
Pfalz see Palatinate
Pfefferkorn, Johannes, 15820
Pfeideler, Martin, 16254
Pfeiffer, Andreas, 16477
Pfeiffer-Belli, Wolfgang, 16870
Pfisterer, Rudolf, 15827, 16814
Phelan, Tony, 16342
Philanthropin, Frankfurt a. Main, 16175
Philosemitism, 16694
Philosophy and Learning, Jews in, 16215, 16217–16218, 16221–16247, 16249–16274, 16277–16280, 16284, 16286–16287, 16373, 16393, 16397–16404, 16412, 16421, 16429, 16444–16448, 16460, 16536–16537, 16573–16578, 16617, 16632–16633, 16656, 16662, 16666–16669, 16683–16684, 16706, 16737–16742, 16795, 16801
Photographers, Jewish, 16894
Physics see Science
Pichois, Claude, 16547
Piekarz, Mendel, 16010
Pieplow, Jürgen, 16033
Pietrass, Richard, 16461
Pikarski, Margot, 16164
Pingel, Falk, 16165
Pinkas Hakehillot: Germany Bavaria, 15874
Pinl, Max, 16539

Pinner, Felix, 16670
Pinner, Ludwig, 16336
Pisarek, Abraham, 16894
'(Die) Pleite', 16378
Plessner, Helmuth, 16393, 16662
Plessner, Monika, 16412
Plöger, Wilhelm, 16855
'PMLA' (Publications of the Modern Language Association of America), New York, 16624
Poetry, 16367, 16369, 16375, 16390, 16419, 16422, 16461, 16464, 16478, 16524, 16534, 16545–16547, 16682, 16704, 16885, 16886, 16892
Poetzl, Herbert, 16617
Polak, Ernst (orig. Pollak), 16663–16664
Polák, Vlastimil Artur (orig. Salomon Arthur Pollak), 15957
Poland, 16005
Polgar, Alfred, 16376, 16385, 16665
Politics, Jews in (see also Communists; Revolutionaries; Socialists), 15823, 15838, 15847, 15983, 16168, 16542, 16603, 16671–16672, 16796
'Politische Vierteljahresschrift', Opladen, 15825
Pollak, Ernst see Polak, Ernst
Pollak, Salomon Arthur see Polák, Vlastimil Artur
Pollok, Joseph, 15902
Pommerin, Reiner, 16104
Pope, Alexander, 16266
Poppel, Stephen M., 16321
Popper, Sir Karl R[aimund], 16393, 16666–16669, 16795
Porphyrios, 16217
Posen, 15918, 16751
Post, Werner, 16635
Post-War Publications on German Jewry, 16016
Pottlitzer, Margot, 15995, 16138, 16600
Prague, 15823, 15959–15964, 16663, 16724, 16758
— Rat d. Jüd. Religionsgemeinden, 16170
Prawer, Siegbert, 16386
'Present Tense', New York, 15822
'(La) Presse', Montreal, 15980
Presse im Exil, 16354
Preuss, Julius, 16276
Preussen see Prussia
'Preussenland', Marburg/Lahn, 15885
Preussische Akademie d. Künste, Sektion für Dichtkunst, 16366
Preussische Staatsbibliothek, Berlin, 16259
Prinz, Ursula, 16341
Prittie, Terence, 16199
'Proletarische Heimstunden', 16388
Pross, Harry, 16453
'Protest, Form, Tradition', Tuscaloosa, Alabama, 16680
Prussia, General History, 16693–16694

'Psyche', Stuttgart, 16181, 16188
Psychoanalysts, Psychologists, Jewish, 16114, 16187, 16368, 16396, 16405, 16443, 16501, 16510, 16512–16523, 16531–16533
Publicists, Journalists, Jewish, 15980, 16136, 16170, 16442, 16544, 16597–16599, 16712, 16760, 16769
Publishers, Jewish, 15957, 16057, 16450, 16723, 16745, 16757, 16793
'Publizistik', München, 16598
Pulzer, Peter, 15823

Quack, Josef, 16431
Quadflieg, J., 16855
'(Der) Quäker', Wien, 16278
Quidde, Ludwig, 16843
Quinton, Anthony, 16635

Rabbinical Assembly, New York, Publication, 16239
Rabbis, 15888, 15914, 15927, 15932, 15953, 15960, 15964, 15971, 16242, 16247, 16250, 16280, 16307, 16780
Rabin, Else, 16309
Rabinach, Anson, 16446
Racism, 15836, 16160
Radczun, Evelyn, 16626
Radczun, Günter, 16626
Raddatz, Fritz J., 16381, 16387, 16432, 16473, 16556, 16722
Radio see Theatre
Raithel-Thaler, Monika, 16489
Rang, B., 16574
Raphael, Freddy, 15943
Rassinier, Paul, 16863
Rat d. Evang. Kirche in Deutschland, 16822
Rat d. Jüd. Religionsgemeinden, Tschechoslowakei, 15958
Rathenau, Emil, 16670
Rathenau, Walther, 15823, 16227, 16671–16672, 16769
Ratz, Michael, 16191
Ravensbrück, 16585
'Rechtssprechung zum Wiedergutmachungsrecht', München, 16200
Recklinghausen, 15919
'Reconstructionist', New York, 16148
Redlich, Josef, 16796
Rée, Anton, 15897
Referat Deutschland, 16049, 16160
Referat Judentum, 16048
Reform, Religious, 15878, 15897, 15953, 16290
Refugee Ship, 15997
Refugees see Australia; Canada; Ceylon; Colombia; Czechoslovakia; France; Great Britain; Japan; Netherlands; Peru; Shanghai; Soviet Russia; Spain; Switzerland; U.S.A.; Zionism: Immigration

Regensburg, 15920
Rehfeld, Manfred, 16287
Reich-Ranicki, Marcel, 16677, 16679, 16720, 16732
Reiche, E. G., 16139
Reichmann, Eva G., 16284
Reichsbund Jüd. Frontsoldaten, 16308
Reichsvertretung d. Dt. Juden, 16894
Reid, Constance, 16467
Reif, Adelbert, 16416
Reimann Schule, Berlin, 16341
Reimarus, Elise, 16266
Reimarus, Hermann Samuel, 15826
Reinhardt, Gottfried, 16673
Reinhardt, Max, 16673
Reinharz, Jehuda, 16337
Reinicke, Helmut, 16444
Reisch, Elisabeth, 16814
Religion see Philosophy and Learning
Religion u. Politik in d. Gesellschaft d. 20. Jh., 15850
Religionskritik, 16393
Rendtorff, Rolf, 16822
Rengstorf, Karl Heinrich, 15826
Renken, Gerd, 16814
Renner, Karl see Doktor-Karl-Renner-Institut
Research Foundation for Jewish Immigration, New York, 15989
Resistance, 15874, 16038, 16162–16165
Restitution, 16197–16201
Reuchlin, Johannes, 15820
Reuter, Heinz, 15919
Revolutionaries (see also Socialists), 16538–16539, 16542, 16717
'Revue d'Histoire de la Deuxième Guerre Mondiale', Paris, 16118
Rezzori, Gregor von, 16864
Rheda, 15921
Rheinland see Rhineland
Rheinstein, Max, 16674
Rhineland, 15922–15923, 16140
Rhineland-Palatinate, 15923
Rhine-Main, Region of, 15905
Richarz, Monika, 15838
Richter, Günter, 16603
Riesenberger, Dieter, 16209
Riesser, Gabriel, 15897
Ringer, Herbert, 16179
Ritter, Henning, 16728
Ritual Bath, 15898, 15929–15930
Robert, Marthe, 16520
Robinson, Jacob, 16160
Robinson, John, 16244
Röhrs, Hermann, 16236
Roggausch, Werner, 16700
Rollka, Bodo, 16266
Romania, 15993
Romanticism, 15817, 16561, 16692
Rome, David, 15980

Rose, Norman A., 16340
Rosen, Zvi, 16563
Rosenau, Helen, 16315
Rosenbaum, Eduard, 16729
Rosenberg, Hans, 16675
Rosenberg, Jakob, 16529
Rosenberger, Ludwig, Library, Chicago, 16012
Rosenblüth, Pinchas E., 15829, 16216
Rosenfeld, Alvin H., 16158
Rosensaft, Menachem Z., 16044
Rosenstock, Werner, 15877, 16562, 16729
Rosenthal, 15924
Rosenthal, Berthold, 15872
Rosenthal, Erwin, 15827
Rosenthal, Fritz see Ben-Chorin, Schalom
Rosenthal, Ludwig, 16141
Rosenthal, Philipp, China-Manufacturer, 16676
Rosenthal, Yemima, 16340
Rosenzweig, Franz, 16243, 16277–16278
Rosenzweig, Rachel, 16277, 16279
Rosenzweig-Scheinmann, Edith, 16277
Roskies, David G., 15998
Rosner, Fred, 16276
Ross, Werner, 16527
Rotenberg, Stella, 16882
Rotenstreich, Nathan, 15850, 16253
Roters, Eberhard, 16341
Roth, Joseph, 16677–16681, 16768
Roth, Leo, 16312
Roth, Stephen J., 16196
Rothbart, Daniel, 16669
Rothe, Wolfgang, 16453
Rothkirchen, Livia, 16160
Rothschild, Eli, 15839
Rothschild, Lothar, 16287
Rottenberg, Ludwig, 16343
Rotter, Erich, 16824
Rubianus, Crotus, 15820
Rubin, Ruth, 15865
Rubiner, Frida, 16378
Rubiner, Ludwig, 16278
Rubinstein, Avraham, 16275
Ruchti, Galerie, Köln, 16650
Rudolph, Maria, 15891
Rübner, Tuvia, 16237
Rückerl, Adalbert, 16193
Rühle, Jürgen, 16381
Rürup, Reinhard, 16865
Rüter, C. F., 16105
'Rundfunk u. Fernsehen', Hamburg, 16356
Ruppersberger, Johann Ägigius, 15924
Rural Jews, 15838
Russell, Bertrand, 16438
Russia see Soviet Russia
Rutter, Derek, 16193

Saarland, 15923
Sabais, Heinz Winfried, 16790

Sachs, Albert, 15927
Sachs, Clara née Goldstein, 15927
Sachs, Julius, 15927
Sachs, Nelly, 16367, 16369, 16390, 16682
— Nelly-Sachs-Prize, 16532
Sachser, Friedo, 16194
Sadek, Vladimir, 15957
'Saeculum', Freiburg i. Br., 16268
Sagel-Grande, Irene, 16105
Sagi, Nana, 16160
Sahmel, Karl-Heinz, 16636
Salaman, Esther, 16488
Salchow, Jutta, 15990
Sallis-Freudenthal, Margarete, 15928
'Salmagundi', Saratoga Springs, N.Y., 16878
Salomon, Erich, 16385
Salons, 15876, 16264, 16561, 16804
Salzberger, Georg, 16280
Salzburg, 15932, 15949
'Salzburger Nachrichten', 15949
'Sammlung', Frankfurt a. Main, 16210; 16352, 16474
Sander, Emil, 16608
Sander, Gilman, 15823
Sandmel, Samuel, 16290
Saphir, Moritz, 16384
Sartre, Jean-Paul, 16575
Sattler, Heinrich, 16482
Sauberzweig, Dieter, 16259
Sauerländer, Willibald, 16535, 16660
Sauerland, Karol, 16404
Saxl, Fritz, 16726
Schaber, Will, 16477
Schabow, Dietrich, 16042
Schachtsiek-Freitag, Norbert, 16722, 16764
Schack, Ingeborg-Liane, 15866
Schad, Christian, 16701
Schaefer, Camillo, 16407
Schaub, Uta, 16550
'(Die) Schaubühne', 16382
Scheel, Walter, 16181, 16813
Scheffler, Wolfgang, 16098, 16865
Scheiber, Alexander, 16307
'Scheidewege', Stuttgart, 16488
Scheinmann, Edith, see Rosenzweig-Scheinmann, Edith
Scheler, Max, 16683–16684
Scheller, Wolf, 16428
Schelsky, Helmut, 16447
Scherer, Herbert, 16342
Schicksal jüd. Mitbürger, Nürnberg, 16124
Schieckel, Harald, 15914
Schiller, Dieter, 16474
Schirnding, Albert von, 16595
Schlander, Otto, 15891
Schlegel, Dorothea, 15997
Schleiermacher, Friedrich, 15826
Schlesien see Silesia

'Schleswig-Holsteinisches Biographisches Lexikon', 16219
Schloss, Julius see Castle Stanford, Julian
Schmid, Beat, 16411
Schmid, Herbert, 16207
Schmid, Max, 16154
Schmid, Roswitha, 16730
Schmidinger, Volker, 16200
Schmidt, Helmut, 16181, 16825
Schmidt, Josef, 16817
Schmidt-Biggemann, Wilhelm, 16266
Schmidt-Heinecke, Valy, 15909
Schmidtbauer, Peter, 15953
Schmieding, Walther, 16597
Schmiedt, Shlomo, 15874
Schmitz, Siegfried, 15815
Schnabel, Artur, 16685
Schneider, Felix, 16356
Schneider, Hansjörg, 16054
Schneider, Manfred, 16609
Schneider, Rolf, 15968
Schneider-Halvorson, Brigitte-Lina, 16689
Schnitzler, Arthur, 16686–16689, 16797
Schoch, Max, 16081
Schocken, Salman, 16057
Schöllmann, Traute, 16594
Schönberg, Arnold, 16377, 16690–16691
Schönborn, Lothar Franz von, 15842
Schoeps, Hans-Joachim, 16692–16694
Schoeps, Julius H., 15826, 15838, 15840, 16103, 16230, 16259, 16269, 16538, 16854, 16866
Schofer, Lawrence, 15841
Scholem, Gershom, 15823, 16281–16283, 16288, 16587, 16815
Scholtz, Gunter, 15826
Schools see Education
Schrag, Paul J., 16798
Schreiber, Peter Wolfgang, 16102
Schreiber, Wolfgang, 16468
Schreiner, Stefan, 16824
Schriften see Name of Institution
Schrobsdorff, Angelika, 16893
Schröcker, Alfred, 15842
Schröder, Dieter, 15983
Schroeder, Karl Johann von, 16651
Schubert, Kurt, 15843, 15953
Schubsky, Karl, 15899
Schütte, Wolfgang U., 16388
Schütz, Anneliese, 16069
Schütz, Friedrich, 15909
Schuhmann, Karl, 16577
Schulin, Ernst, 16672
Schulte, Bernhard, 16101
Schulz, Eva, 16046
Schulz, Georg-Michael, 16465
Schulz, Gerd, 16450
Schumann, Thomas B., 16389
Schwab, Jürgen, 16783

Schwan, Alexander, 15850
Schwartz, Gary, 16529
Schwarz, Alice, 16442
Schwarz, Egon, 15823, 16456, 16769, 16799
Schwarz, František, 16170
Schwarz, Stefan, 15964, 16488, 16617, 16800
Schwarz, Walter, 16201
Schwarzfuchs, Simon, 15844
Schwarzschild, Leopold, 16769
Schwarzschild, Steven S., 15823
Schwarzwald, Eugenie, 16695
Schweiger, Ralph, 16818
Science, Jews in, 16101, 16372, 16441, 16466, 16481–16498, 16600, 16661, 16766
Scruton, Joan, 15977
Šedinová, Jiřina, 15957
Seeber, D. A., 16825
Seeligmann, Chaim, 15993
Seesen, 15925
Sefton, W. Victor, 16142
Segal, Arthur, 16341
Segall, Dora, 16345
Seghers, Anna, 16210, 16346, 16390, 16696–16700
Seidel, Jutta, 16785
Seiverth, Andreas, 16383
Sekles, Bernhard, 16343
Seligmann, Walter see Serner, Walter
Sell, Hans Joachim, 15987
Sella, Gad Hugo (orig. Hugo Silberstein), 15950
Sereny, Gitta, 16143
Serke, Jürgen, 16390–16391
Serner, Walter (orig. Seligmann), 16701–16703
Serpell, Christopher, 15983
Sexl, Roman U., 16487
Shamir, Haim, 15993
Shanghai, Refugees, 15970, 15974, 16160
Shapiro, Eda, 16074
Shapiro, Edward S., 15988
Shapiro, Leon, 16194
'Shefa Quarterly', Jerusalem, 16248
Sheffer, Gabriel, 16340
Sherman, A. J., 16729
Sherwin, Byron L., 16144
'Shoah', New York, 16096
Sicily, 15818, 15848
Siefer, Gregor, 15850
Siegel, Steven W., 15989
Siegele-Wenschkewitz, Leonore, 16145–16146
Siegen, Gesamthochschule, Schriften, 15823
Siegert, Michael, 16824
Siegrist, Christoph, 16428
Silbergleit, Arthur, 16080, 16704
Silberman, Alexander see Alexander Silberman Internat. Scholarship Foundation
Silbermann, Alphons, 16705
Silberner, Edmund, 16293
Silberstein, Hugo see Sella, Gad Hugo

Index to Bibliography 467

Silesia, 16147
— Upper Silesia, 15926–15927
Silverman-Weinrich, Beatrice, 15867
Sima, Miron, 16614
Simenauer, Erich, 16518
Simhah, Meir, 16280
Simmel, Georg, 16706
Simmons, Clifford, 16521
Simon, Dietrich, 16406
Simon, Ernst, 15850, 15997, 16284
Simon, Heinrich, 15880
'Simplicissimus', 16568
Sinzheimer, Hugo, 16371
Sinzheimer, Max, 16707
Skaller, Ulrich, 15927
Škochová, Jarmila, 15957
Sloyan, Gerard S., 16841
Social History, 15823, 15830, 15838, 15853, 15953, 16865
Social Science, Jews in, 15976, 15982, 16393, 16398, 16413–16417, 16444–16448, 16452, 16530, 16540–16541, 16602, 16610, 16631–16636, 16666–16669, 16683–16684, 16705–16706, 16729, 16795
Socialists, 15823, 16371, 16383, 16438–16440, 16451, 16499, 16563, 16566, 16593, 16611, 16615–16616, 16625–16627, 16654, 16781–16782, 16794, 16866
'Society', Rutgers State Univ., 16086
Sociologists see Social Science
Sohn-Rethel, Alfred, 15976
Solingen, Stadtbücherei, 16008
Sombart, Werner, 15837
Sonn, Naftali H., 15827, 16284
Sonnemann, Ulrich, 16656
Sonnenfels, Joseph von, 15826
Sotheby Parke Bernet, 16569
'Soviet Jewish Affairs', London, 15856
Soviet Russia, 16005
— Refugees, 15972–15973, 16345
Sozialdemokratische Arbeiterbewegung u. Weimarer Republik, 16371
'(Der) Sozialist', 16383
'Sozialwissenschaftliche Informationen für Unterricht u. Studium', Stuttgart, 16212
Spain, Refugees, 16349
Spalek, John M., 16017, 16717
Specker, Hans Eugen, 16498
Sperber, Manès, 16294
Speyer, 15928–15929
Speyer, Willy, 16375
Spicker, Friedemann, 16584
'(Der) Spiegel', Hamburg, 16181
Spiel, Hilde, 16259, 16270
Spinoza, Baruch, 16393, 16471
Spinozismusstreit, 16266
Spiro, Eugen, 16341
Spitzer Shlomo, 15845, 15954

Sports, Jews in, 16170, 16303–16304
Sprendlingen, 15930
Springer, Axel, 16062
Stade, 15931
'Stader Jahrbuch, 15931
Stadler-Labhart, Verena, 16627
Stäglich, Wilhelm, 16035
Stahl, Heinrich, 15877
Stanford, Julian Castle see Castle Stanford, Julian
Stanić, Dorothea, 16156
Stapleton, Timothy John, 16578
Starke, Friedrich, 16210
Státní Židovské Muzeum v Praze, 15957
Statute of Limitation, 16170, 16191, 16195–16196, 16825
Staufer, 15818, 15848
Steenson, Gary P., 16593
Stehling, Jutta, 16211
Stein, Edith, 16801
Stein, Günther, 15929
Stein, Joshua B., 16135
Steinbach, Peter, 15825
Steinecke, Hartmut, 16453
Steiner, George, 16522
Steiner, Herbert (1892–1966), 16877
Steiner, Herbert, 16646
Steiner-Prag, Hugo, 15962
Steinhardt, Jakob, 16341
Steinitz, Hans, 15838, 15877, 15932, 15995, 16720, 16840
Steinschneider, Moritz, 16285
Stemberger, Brigitte, 15846
Stephan, Alexander, 16356
Stephan, Rudolf, 16628, 16690–16691
Stern, Bella, 16340
Stern, Dagmar C., 16479
Stern, Fritz, 15847
Stern, Günther see Anders, Günther
Stern, Guy, 16658
Stern, William, 15940, 16753
'Stern-Magazin', Hamburg, 16533, 16635
Sternfeld, Wilhelm, 16001
Sternheim, Carl, 16385, 16708–16711, 16768
Stieglitz. Family, 16802
Stikkers, Kenneth W., 16683
Stimmen aus Israel, 16885
'Stimmen der Zeit', Freiburg i. Br., 16855
Stöcker, Adolf, 16848
Stöcker, Christa, 16547
Stöhr, Martin, 16181, 16212, 16825, 16830
Stössinger, Felix, 16136
Stolper, Gustav, 16712
Stolper, Toni, 16712, 16813
Stolzenberg, Ingeborg, 16651
Stone, Adolf, 16148
Strasbourg, 15942
Strauss, Raphael, 15848, 15920

Strauss, Bruno, 16240
Strauss, Herbert A., 15989
Strauss, Johann, 16824
Strauss, Walter, 16149
Streisand, Joachim, 15825
Strelka, Joseph P., 16358, 16453
Strolz, Walter, 16277, 16278, 16820
Strothmann, Dietrich, 16028
Studia Judaica Austriaca, 15953
'Studia Rosenthaliana', Amsterdam, 15827
'Studia Slaskie', 16147
'Studien zum Wandel von Gesellschaft u. Bildung im 19. Jh.', Göttingen, 16852
Studies in Judaism in Modern Times, 16273
Stüwe, Elisabeth, 16558
Sturm, Norbert, 16714
Stuttgart, Arbeitsgemeinschaft Friedensdienste, 16808
Stutthof, 16808
Suchy, Barbara, 15849
'Süddeutsche Zeitung', München, see 'SZ'
Sulloway, Frank J., 16522
Sulzer, Dieter, 16664
'(The) Sunday Times', London, 16522
Sutermeister, Peter, 16791
Svátek, Josef, 15958
Swartz, Mary Sagmaster, 16137
Swidler, Leonhard, 16841
Switzerland, 16002, 16287, 16862
— Refugees, 16150–16154
Syamken, Georg, 16727
Sydnor, Charles W. jun., 16092
Symbiosis, German-Jewish, 15823, 15838, 15963
Synagogues, 15869, 15882, 15892, 15895–15896, 15898–15899, 15905, 15940, 15953, 15965, 16174, 16314–16315, 16825
'SZ' (Süddeutsche Zeitung), München, 15825, 15983, 16115, 16138, 16259, 16294, 16367, 16381, 16426, 16428, 16449, 16468, 16527, 16535, 16589, 16595, 16612, 16635, 16660, 16676, 16704–16705, 16720, 16722, 16728, 16772, 16864
Szeemann, Harald, 16392

Taeubler, Eugen, 16216, 16338, 16713
'(Das) Tagebuch', Berlin, 16769
'(Der) Tagesspiegel', Berlin, 15825
Taifel, Henri, 16845
Tal, Uriel, 16160, 16238, 16286, 16825
Talmage, Frank, 16832
Talmon, Shemaryahu, 15850
Tar, Zoltan, 16362
Tau, Fritz, 15927
Taubald, Helmuth, 16210
Tauber, Region of, 15873
Tauber, Moshe see Tavor, Moshe
Tauberbischofsheim, 15873
Tavor, Moshe (orig. Tauber), 16825

'Teachers College Record', New York, 16212
Teaching see Antisemitism, Judaism, Nazism in Education and Teaching
Techniczek, M., 15993
Tenastedt, Florian, 16114, 16297
Terezin see Theresienstadt
Tergit, Gabriele, 16345, 16349
Ter Haar, Carel, 16769
'(Der) Theater-Teufel', 16384
Theatre, Cabaret, Cinema, Radio, Jews in, 15972–15973, 16054, 16152–16153, 16170, 16356, 16386, 16389, 16509, 16580, 16605, 16607, 16673, 16718, 16743, 16776, 16805
'Theokratia', Jahrbuch d. Institutum Judaicum Delitzschianum, 15959, 16220
Theophrastos, 16217
Theresienstadt, 16101, 16155–16156, 16170
— Birkenau, 15957
Thesing, Susanne, 16618
Thieberger, Friedrich, 16309
Thoma, Clemens, 16825
Thomann Tewarson, Heidi, 16475
Thommen, Andreas, 16075
Thompson, Jerry E., 16180
'Thought', Fordham Univ. Quarterly, 16234
Thurnher, Eugen, 15843
Tichatschek-Martin, Bernd, 16166
Tieber, Tomáš, 15958
Tiedemann, Eva, 16001
Tiedemann, Rolf, 16397–16398
Tietz, Leonhard, 16714
'(The) Times', London, 15977, 16466, 16533, 16588, 16720, 16766
'Times Literary Supplement', London, 15825
Tirol, 15950
Tobias, Abraham, 15839, 15927
Töpner, Kurt, 16694
Tokayer, Marvin, 16137
'Toledot', New York, 15887, 16013
'Toleranz heute', Berlin, 16238
Toller, Ernst, 16342, 16388, 16391, 16715–16717, 16868
Torberg, Friedrich, 16358, 16367, 16453, 16718–16720
Torczyner, Harry, 16488
Toury, Jacob, 15826
Toynbee, Philip, 16443
Trade, Jews in, 15838, 15883, 15900, 16754, 16865
'Tradition', Journal of Orthodox Jewish Thought, New York, 16247
'Tradition u. Erneuerung', Bern, 16287
Tramer, Hans, 15994–15995, 15997
Treder, Hans-Jürgen, 16495
Treschan, Victor, 15942
Treue, Wilhelm, 15825
'Tribüne', Frankfurt a. Main, 16814; 15963, 16003, 16034, 16062, 16152, 16161, 16169,

16181, 16206, 16209, 16212, 16222, 16259, 16270, 16272, 16561, 16596, 16722, 16764, 16834, 16848
Trier, 15932
— Karl-Marx-Haus, 16639
'Trierischer Volksfreund', 15932
Trommler, Frank, 16363
Troper, Harold, 16127
Trumpp, Thomas, 16018
Trunk, Isaiah, 16157
Trutwin, Werner, 16207, 16213, 16855
Trykar-Lu, Tamara, 16685
Tuchler, Kurt, 16318
Tucholsky, Kurt, 15991, 16342, 16355, 16375, 16385, 16721–16722, 16803
Tübingen, 15933
— University, 16146
Turtel-Aberzhanska, Chasia, 15874

Überleben u. widerstehen, 16097
Uellenberg, Gisela, 16259
'Uhu', 16385
Ullstein, (Publisher), 16442, 16723
Ulm, 16498
'Una Sancta', Freising, 16831
Unikower, Inge, 16894
Universities (see also Dissertations)
— Berlin, Humboldt-Univ., 16054
— Bremen, 16297
— Cincinnati see Hebrew Union College
— Fordham, 16234
— Frankfurt a. Main, 16666
— Harvard, 16003
— Jerusalem see Jerusalem
— Köln, 15884
— South Carolina, 16350–16351
— Southern California, 16763
— Tel Aviv, 15993
— Tübingen, 16146
— Vienna, 16039
— Virginia, 16017
— Wisconsin see 'new german critique'
— Zürich, 16627
Universities and Jews, 15830, 16039, 16146, 16858
Ury, Lesser, 16341
Urzidil, Johannes, 16724
U.S.A., 15851, 15998, 16204
— Immigration, 15971, 15978, 15981, 15988
— Refugees, 15969, 15974, 15976, 15982–15984, 15988–15989, 16017, 16129
Utley, Philip L., 16310

Václavek, Ludvík, 15957
Vagts, Alfred, 15851–15852, 16651
Vahlteich, Julius, 16616
Valentin, Veit, 16725
Varnhagen von Ense, Karl August, 16651, 16804

Varnhagen, Rahel, 16804
Vatican, 16118
Veit, Dorothea, 15997
Veit, Moritz, 15877
Venes, Don, 15816
Verband d. Jüd. Gemeinden in d. DDR, see 'Nachrichtenblatt d. Jüd. Gemeinde von Berlin'
Verband ehemaliger Breslauer u. Schlesier in Israel, see 'Mitteilungen d. Verbandes . . .'
Verein d. Verfolgten d. Naziregimes, 16116
Verein für
— d. Geschichte Berlins, Jahrbuch, 15877
— Geschichte d. Bodensees, Schriften, 15956
— Geschichte d. Stadt Wien, Forschungen, 16039
Verein Österr. Jüd. Museum, Eisenstadt, 15953
Verene, Donald Philip, 16460
Verjährung see Statute of Limitation
Verschollene u. Vergessene (Series), 16658
'Vestische Zeitschrift', 15919
'Věstník, Jüd. Gemeindeblatt, Prag, 16170
Vielmetti, Nikolaus, 15953
Vienna, 15823, 15951–15955, 16039, 16515, 16525, 16630, 16646, 16663, 16806, 16825
Viereck, Sylvester, 16851
Vierhaus, Rudolf, 15826
Viertel, Berthold, 16868
Viertel, Salka, 16805
'Vierteljahrschrift für Sozial- u. Wirtschaftsgeschichte', Wiesbaden, 15825
'Vierteljahrshefte für Zeitgeschichte', München, 16031, 16048, 16104, 16203
Vögtle, Anton, 16825
Vogel, Manfred, 16895
Vogel, Rolf, 16167, 16815
Vogel, Wladimir, 16466
Vogt, Ernst, 16212
Voigts, Manfred, 16266
Volkov, Shulamit, 16865, 16867
Vorarlberg, 15956
Vordtriede, Werner, 16453
Vormweg, Heinrich, 16612
VVN (Verein d. Verfolgten d. Naziregimes), 16116

Waaijman, Kees, 16824
Wachinger, Lorenz, 16824
Wagner, Richard, 16879–16880
Wagner-Jauregg, Julius, 16516
Walk, Joseph, 16339
Walter, Bruno, 16628
Walter, Hans-Albert, 16348
Wandering Jew, Tale of, 16824
War and German Jews, 15838, 16308, 16651
Warburg (town), 15934
Warburg, Aby M., 16726–16728
Warburg, Max J., 16728

Warburg, M. M., u. Co., 15852, 16729
Warburg, Otto, 16730
Warburg Institute, London, 16535
Warschawski, Max, 15943
Washington, Jonny, 16417
Wassermann, August Paul von, 16731
Wassermann, Henry, 15853
Wassermann, Jakob, 16366, 16385, 16732–16733, 16877
Wasserstein, Bernard, 16138
Watt, D. C., 15983
Weber, Hermann, 16792
Weber, Max, 15837
Weber, Samuel, 16523
Weber-Oldecop, Dieter Wilhelm, 15935
Wechsberg, Joseph, 16806
Wechsler (Landrabbiner), 15914
Weg zur Gleichberechtigung d. Juden, 15923
Weger, Karl-Heinz, 16393
Wehler, Hans-Ulrich, 15852
Wehr, Gerhard, 16288
Weigel, Hans, 16187
Weiland, Linde B., 15870
Weill, Georges J., 15999
Weimar Republic, 15816, 15821–15822, 15829, 15993, 16018, 16301, 16334, 16342, 16363, 16370–16371, 16374, 16394, 16617, 16671–16672, 16716–16717, 16858
'Weimarer Beiträge', Berlin-Weimar, 16399
Weinberg, Arthur von, 16101
Weinberg, Carl von, 16101
Weinberg, Lisi, 15921
Weinberg, Werner, 15921
Weinzierl, Ulrich, 16665
Weis, Georg, 16039
Weiss, Aharon, 16007
Weiss, Elmar, 15873
Weiss, Ernst, 16346, 16391
Weiss, Peter, 16734
Weisskopf, Victor F., 16661
Weizmann, Chaim, 16340
Weizsäcker, Ernst Heinrich von, 16118
'(Die) Welt', Zentralorgan d. zionist. Bewegung, Köln, 16338
'(Die) Weltbühne', 16382
Weltsch, Felix, 16775
Weltsch, Robert, 15995, 16230, 16318
Wendland, Jens, 16468
Wendler, Wolfgang, 16710
Wennigsen-Holtensen, 15935
Werfel, Franz, 16375, 16664, 16735–16736, 16768, 16868
Werner, Michael, 16550, 16557
Wertheim/Main, 15886, 15936
Wertheimer, Jack L., 15854, 15997
'Wertheimer Panorama', 15886
Wessels, Hans-Friedrich, 16872
Westdeutscher Rundfunk, Köln, 16182, 16184–16185, 16435–16436

'Westfälische Forschungen', Münster, 15913
Weyl, Robert, 15943
Wichert, Adalbert, 16476
Widerstand u. Verfolgung in Bayern 1933–1945, 15874, 16040
Widerstand u. Verfolgung im Burgenland, 16038
Wieckenberg, Ernst-Peter, 16259, 16272
Wien see Vienna
Wien 1938, 16039
Wiener, Max, 15829
Wiener Geschichtsblätter, 16039
Wiener Kathol. Akademie, Publications, 16084, 16149
'Wiener Kunsthefte', 16607
'(The) Wiener Library Bulletin', London, 15821, 15955, 16135, 16323, 16819
Wiener Stadttempel 1826–1976, 15953
Wiesbach, Ingeborg, 15826
Wiesel, Elie, 16158, 16239
Wieseltier, Leon, 16765
Wiesemann, Falk, 15874
Wiesengrund, Theodor see Adorno, Theodor W.
Wiesenthal, Simon, 16117, 16167–16168
Wilhelm II, German Emperor, 15825, 16442
Wilhelminian Germany see Imperial Germany
Willauer, Franz, 16630
Willett, John, 16394
William, Rhys W., 16711
Winckler, Lutz, 16395
Wind, Edgar, 16726
Wininger, Salomon, 16019
Winkel, Maria Angela, 16454
Wippermann, Klaus W., 16181, 16561
Wischmann, Günter, 16213
Wischnewski, Alexander, 15984
Wissen/Westerwald, 15868
'Wissenschaft d. Judentums', 15834, 16243, 16249
Wistrich, Robert S., 15825, 15955, 16168, 16295, 16647, 16819
Witschel, Günter, 16448
Witt, Hubert, 16678
Witt, Sina, 16697
Witte, Karsten, 16605
Wittfogel, Karl August, 15976
Wittgenstein, Ludwig, 15982, 16393, 16737–16742
Wittowski, Victor, 16877
Wittlich, 16174
Wörrstadt, 15937
Wolf, Kenneth, 16604
Wolf, Ruth, 15827, 16550
Wolf, Walter, 15921
Wolfenbütteler Studien, 15826
Wolfenstein, Alfred, 16345, 16375
Wolff, Konrad, 16685
Wolff, Kurt (Publisher), 16360
Wolff, Margo H., 16473
Wolffenstein, Andrea, 16159

Wolffenstein, Valerie, 16159
Wolffheim, Elsbeth, 16345
Wollheim, Gert H., 16341
Wollheim, Richard, 16522
Women, 15817, 15838, 15876, 15891, 16305–16306, 16390, 16695
World Jewish Congress, 16126, 16823
Worms, 15938–15939, 16767
'(Das) Wort', 16388
Wrangel, Cornelia, 16595
Wright, Georg Henrik von, 16740
Wuchterl, Kurt, 16742
Württemberg, 15892
Würzburg, 15940
'Würzburger Diözesan-Geschichtsblätter', 15886
Würzburger Raw, 16753
Wuppertal, 16122
Wuttke, Dieter, 16726
Wygodski, W. S., 16648
Wyman, David S., 16036
Wysocki, Gisela von, 16408

Yad Vashem, Jerusalem, Archives, 16007
— Publications, 15874, 16005, 16007, 16010
— Studies, 16160; 16074, 16088, 16130, 16330
Yiddish, 15855–15867, 16294, 16298
Yivo Institute for Jewish Research, 16484
— Annual, 15998; 15867
— News, 15867, 16484
Young-Brühl, Elisabeth, 16414

Zachau, Reinhard Konrad, 16567
Zadek, Peter, 16743
Zahn, Ralf, 15937
Zampa, Giorgio, 16681
Zapf, Lilli, 15933
Zeeden, Ernst Walter, 15825, 15827, 15838
Zehnder, J., 16467
'(Die) Zeit', Hamburg, 15838, 15968, 16028, 16092, 16101, 16381, 16408, 16412, 16430, 16473, 16488, 16499, 16595, 16635, 16720, 16722, 16729, 16795, 16811, 16813, 16817, 16854, 16875
'Zeit Magazin', Hamburg, 16714
'Zeitschrift für
— Bayerische Landesgeschichte', München, 15911

— Geschichtswissenschaft', Berlin/East, 15825, 16047, 16060, 16626, 16648
— Historische Forschung', Berlin, 15922
— Ostforschung', Marburg, 15926
— Religions- u. Geistesgeschichte', Köln, 15840, 16233, 16278, 16694, 16723, 16787
— Sozialforschung', 16631
— Sozialreform', Wiesbaden, 16114
— Theologie u. Kirche', Tübingen, 16146
— Vergleichende Sprachforschung', Göttingen, 15862
Zeller, Bernhard, 15990–15991, 16877
Zentner, Christian, 16093, 16161
Zentrum für Antisemitismusforschung, Berlin, 16865
'Židovská Ročenka', Praha, 15958
Zimmermann, Moshe, 15897
Zink, Wolfgang, 16294
Zinn, Ernst, 16449
Zionism, 15838–15839, 15840, 16238, 16239, 16256, 16296, 16299, 16302, 16316–16340, 16488, 16880
— and Antisemitism, 16326, 16328–16329
— Immigration during Nazi Period, 16138, 16160, 16317, 16323, 16330, 16335, 16424
— and Nazis, 16318–16319, 16335
— U.S.A., 15998
Zittau, 15941
Zöllner, Friedhelm, 16214
Zofe, Harold von, 16637
Zondek, Hermann, 16744
Zuckmayer, Carl, 16385, 16745, 16805
— Blätter d. C.-Z.-Gesellsch., 16745
Zürcher Schauspielhaus, 16152–16153
Zürich, 16002, 16287, 16627
Zunz, Leopold, 15834, 16243, 16248
Zur Nedden Pferdekamp, Modeste, 15815
Zuroff, Efraim, 16160
Zweig, Arnold, 16346, 16355, 16385, 16746, 16768, 16885
Zweig, Stefan, 16376, 16380, 16385, 16457, 16747–16750, 16807
Zweig, Stefanie, 16482
Zwerenz, Gerhard, 16722
Zwillenberg, Lutz O., 16287
'Zwingliana', Zürich, 16267

List of Contributors

BACHARACH, Walter Zwi, Ph.D., b. 1928 in Hainau a. Main. Senior Lecturer in Modern History and in Educational Science, University of Bar Ilan, Israel. Author of *Thirteen Lectures on Modern Antisemitism in Germany* (1979, in Hebrew); and of essays in English, German and Hebrew on German antisemitism and the Holocaust.

BARON, Lawrence, Ph.D., b. 1947 in Chicago. Associate Professor of History, St. Lawrence University, Canton, New York. Author of *The Eclectic Anarchism of Erich Mühsam* (1976) and of various essays and book reviews. Currently working on a biography of Theodor Lessing.

BIRNBAUM, Max P., b. 1905 in Berlin. Studied law at Friedrich-Wilhelm-University in Berlin. Formerly Assistant Secretary General and Department Head of the Preussischer Landesverband jüdischer Gemeinden in Berlin, active in Zionist and refugee affairs in the United States, since 1969 retired in Jerusalem. Author of numerous articles in German-Jewish journals and American and Israeli periodicals; and of a forthcoming history of the *Preussischer Landesverband jüdischer Gemeinden* to be published in the Schriftenreihe wissenschaftlicher Abhandlungen des Leo Baeck Instituts.

COHEN, Arthur A., M.A., b. 1928 in New York. Formerly a publisher, now a bookseller. Lecturer in Religion and Judaic Theology, Brown University. Author of, a.o., *Martin Buber* (1958); *A People part: Hasidic Life in America* (1970); *In the Days of Simon Stern* (1973); *A Hero in His Time* (1976); *Acts of Theft* (1980); and editor of and contributor to numerous books and author of articles and short stories.

FIELD, Geoffrey G., Ph.D., b. 1944 in London. Associate Professor of European History, State University of New York, Purchase. Author of *Evangelist of Race: The Germanic Vision of Houston Stewart Chamberlain* (1980); and of various essays and reviews. (Contributor to Year Book XVIII.)

GLATZER, Nahum N., Ph.D., Dr. h.c., b. 1903 in Lemberg (Austria). 1950–1973, Professor of Jewish History and Social Ethics, Brandeis University. Now Professor of Judaica and Religion, Boston University. Author of, a.o., *Franz Rosenzweig: His Life and Thought* (1953); *Leopold and Adelheid Zunz. An Account of Letters* (1958); *Leopold Zunz: Jude – Deutscher – Europäer* (1964); *The Dimensions of Job* (1969); *Essays in Jewish Thought* (1978). Editor of *The Judaic Tradition* (1969); *I am a Memory Come Alive: Kafka* (1974); *Modern Jewish Thought* (1977). Fellow of the Leo Baeck Institute, New York and Member of its Board. (Contributor to Year Books I, V and XXII.)

GREIVE, Herman, Dr. phil., b. 1935 in Walstedde (Germany). Professor at the Martin-Buber-Institut für Judaistik, University of Cologne. Author of *Theologie*

und Ideologie. Katholizismus und Judentum in Deutschland und Österreich 1918–1935 (1969); *Studien zum jüdischen Neuplatonismus* (1973); 'Die gesellschaftliche Bedeutung der christlich-jüdischen Differenz – Zur Situation im deutschen Katholizismus', in *Juden im Wilhelminischen Deutschland 1890–1914* (1976); *Die Juden. Grundzüge ihrer Geschichte im mittelalterlichen und neuzeitlichen Europa* (1979); Editor of *Hermann Bahr, Der Antisemitismus. Ein internationales Interview* (1979); and author of numerous essays on historical and philosophical subjects. (Contributor to Year Book XX.)

LAMBERTI, Marjorie, Ph.D., b. in Connecticut, U.S.A. Professor of History, Middlebury College, Vermont. Author of *Jewish Activism in Imperial Germany. The Struggle for Civil Equality* (1978); 'The Attempt to Form a Jewish Bloc: Jewish Notables and Politics in Wilhelmian Germany', in *Central European History* (1970) and other historical essays. (Contributor to Year Books XVII and XXIII.)

LIDTKE, Vernon, Ph.D., b. 1930 in Avon, South Dakota. Professor of History, Johns Hopkins University, Baltimore. Author of *The Outlawed Party: Social Democracy in Germany, 1878–1890* (1966); and of numerous essays, a.o., 'Naturalism and Socialism in Germany', in *American Historical Review* (1974); and 'August Bebel and German Social Democracy's Relation to the Christian Churches', in *Journal of the History of Ideas* (1966). Currently working on a study of the political culture of the Social Democratic labour movement in Imperial Germany.

MAYER, Paul Yogi, b. 1912 in Bad Kreuznach (Germany). Qualified teacher and social worker with diplomas from the Universities of Berlin and Frankfurt and the Department of Education, London. Formerly RjF Jugend-Dezernent and sports editor of *Die Kraft* in Germany, later Area Youth Officer in London. Now Lecturer, North London College (Community Studies) and Training Consultant to the London Union of Youth Clubs. Author of various articles and contributions to periodicals and books, in Germany (prior to 1935) and in England, related to youth and community work and physical education.

MEYER, Michael A., Ph.D., b. 1937 in Berlin. Professor of Jewish History, Hebrew Union College-Jewish Institute of Religion, Cincinnati, Ohio. Author of, a.o., *The Origins of the Modern Jew: Jewish Identity and European Culture in Germany, 1749–1824* (1967, 1972); *Ideas of Jewish History* (1974); and of numerous articles on Judaism and Jewish History. Fellow of the LBI, New York, and Member of its Board. (Contributor to Year Books XI, XVI and XXIV.)

PULZER, Peter, Ph.D., Fellow of the Royal Historical Society, b. 1929 in Vienna. Official Student (i.e., Fellow) of Christ Church and University Lecturer in Politics, Oxford. Author of *The Rise of Political Anti-Semitism in Germany and Austria* (1964); 'Die jüdische Beteiligung an der Politik', in *Juden im Wilhelminischen Deutschland 1890–1914* (1976); and of numerous articles in learned journals. Member of the Executive Committee of the LBI, London.

List of Contributors

REZLER-BERSOHN, Nehama, Ph.D., b. 1941 in Israel. Lecturer in the Department of Near-Eastern Studies, Princeton University. Author of numerous essays and articles in Hebrew literary journals.

RHEINS, Carl J., Ph.D., b. 1945 in Cincinnati, Ohio. Formerly Lecturer in Judaic Studies, State University of New York at Stony Brook, 1974–1978, now Assistant to the Academic Vice President, SUNY at Stony Brook. Co-editor with Richard A. Siegel of the forthcoming *The Jewish Almanac*. (Contributor to Year Book XXIII.)

SCHORSCH, Ismar, Ph.D., b. 1935 in Hanover. Dean of Graduate School, 1975–1979, and Rabbi Herman Abramowitz Professor in Jewish History, Jewish Theological Seminary of America, New York. Author of *Jewish Reactions to German Anti-Semitism 1870–1914* (1972); Editor of Heinrich Graetz, *The Structure of Jewish History and other Essays*; and author of numerous articles in scholarly journals. Fellow of the American Academy for Jewish Research. Fellow of the LBI, New York, and Member of its Executive Committee. (Contributor to Year Books XI, XIX and XXII.)

STERN, Fritz, Ph.D., b. 1926 in Germany. Seth Low Professor of History, Columbia University. Author of *The Failure of Illiberalism. Essays on the Political Culture of Modern Germany* (1972 – German edn. 1974); *The Politics of Cultural Despair* (1961, 2nd edn. 1974 – German edn. 1963); *Gold and Iron: Bismarck, Bleichröder and the Building of the German Empire* (1977, 1979 – German edn. 1978; French edn. 1980). Editor of, a.o., *The Varieties of History* (1956, 1970, 1973); and of numerous articles and reviews. (Contributor to Year Books VIII and XX.)

STRAUSS, Herbert A., Dr. phil., b. 1918 in Würzburg. Professor of History, The City College, New York. Executive Vice President, American Federation of Jews from Central Europe, New York. Author of *Staat, Bürger, Mensch* (1948); *Botschaften der Präsidenten der Vereinigten Staaten von Amerika, 1793–1948* (1956); editor of *Conference on Acculturation* (1965): *Conference on Anti-Semitism* (1969); *Conference on American-Jewish Dilemmas* (1971); of series *Jewish Immigrants of the Nazi Period in the U.S.A.* (1979 ff.); co-editor of *Gegenwart im Rückblick. Festgabe für die Jüdische Gemeinde Berlin 25 Jahre nach dem Neubeginn* (1970); *Biographical Dictionary of Central European Emigrés 1933–1945* (1979 ff.); and author of numerous articles. Fellow of the LBI, New York, and Member of its Board. (Contributor to Year Books VI, XI and XVI.)

Corrections to Year Book XXIV

Essay by Dolf Michaelis, p. 229, n. 17
For Language and Science
Read Language and Silence
p. 237, text and n. 51 and index p.469
For Meydell *Read* Bodo Freiherr von Maydell

Essay by Joseph Walk, p. 370 and index p. 471
For Hugo Translateur
Read Salo Translateur

Abstracts of articles in this Year Book are included in *Historical Abstracts* and *America: History and Life*.

General Index to Year Book XXV of the Leo Baeck Institute

Adam, Uwe Dietrich, 333n–334n
Adass Jisroel (Israelitische Synagogen-Gemeinde, Berlin), 178
Adler, Karl, 232n
Adler-Rudel, Shalom (Director of Leo Baeck Institute), 34n, 314–357 *passim*
Agudat Israel (Agudas Jisroel), 173, 192
Ahad Ha'am (Zionist leader, philosopher and Hebrew writer), 206, 288
Ahlwardt, Hermann (antisemitic agitator), 315n
Alexander, Carl, 257n
Alldeutscher Verband, 141, 161, 264–265
Allenby, General Edmund Henry Hynman (British field marshal), 305
'Allgemeine Zeitung des Judentums', 139, 302
Allgemeiner Rabbinerverband in Deutschland, 173, 179, 182, 191, 256, 257
Altenstein, Karl von (Prussian Minister for Religion), 104, 110
American Federation of Jews from Central Europe, New York, 313n
American Historical Association, VII–VIII, 73n
American Jewish Joint Committee, 352n
Anarchists, 269–278 *passim*
Andersen-Nexö, Martin (Danish writer), 283–284
Andreas (Andres Jud) (writer), 223
Andrew, Prince, 240
Angress, Werner T., 275
Anker, Kurt (writer), 251
'Anti-Anti', 215n
'Anti-Nazi', 215n
Antisemiten-Petition, 315n
Antisemitism, 13, 32, 69–70, 76, 93, 106, 133, 134, 135, 139, 140, 141, 142, 145, 147–162, 185, 197–219, 228, 245, 246, 247, 250, 251, 252, 256, 266, 267, 270, 271, 272, 273, 274, 276, 278, 283, 307, 313, 315, 316n, 328, 333, 347; Ahlwardt, 315n; Alldeutscher Verband, 141, 161, 264–265; Antisemiten-Petition, 315n; Bauernvereine, 159; Böckel, 153n, 271, 315n; Bruno Bauer, 3, 9, 12, 133; Bund der Landwirte, 141, 151, 154, 315n; H. St. Chamberlain, 202–203, 204, 205, 206, 207n, 272; 'Christlich-soziale Blätter', 32n; Christlichsoziale Partei, 32n; Class, 315; Adolf Damaschke, 70; Deutsche Turnerschaft, 227; Deutschnationale Volkspartei, 209, 265–266, 284; Deutschvölkische Freiheitspartei, 251; Deutschvölkischer Schutz- und Trutzbund, 209, 315n; Deutschösterreichischer Alpenverein, 226; Gebsattel, 315n; German Liberals and, 147–162; in German students' fraternities, 135; Gobineau, 272; Günther, 215; Heydrich, 318; Jewish defence againsst, 141, 147–162, 197–219; Jungdeutscher Orden, 214; Liberals and, 141–146 *passim*, 147–162; Liebermann von Sonnenberg, 153n; Lueger, 133; Marr, 193, 197–198, 271; Marwitz, 135; Menzel, 135; Paasch, 315n; at Prussian Universities, 3-19 *passim*; Reventlow, 315n, Hans Schemm, 70; Schneider, 315n; Sigl, 315n; Social Democracy and, 147–162, 170–171; Soziale Reichspartei, 315n; Stapel, 215, 266; Stoecker, 141, 171, 271; Streicher, 70; Thule Gesellschaft, 275; Treitschke, 140, 141, 315n; Wagner, 193; Werner, 153n, in Zentrumspartei, 159. *See also* boycott, pogroms, Nazism, racism.
Antizionistisches Komitee, 257
'(Der) Arbeiter', 38
Arbeitsgemeinschaft für Kinder- und Jugend-Alijah, 328
Arnstein (aircraft constructor), 226
Asch, Bruno, 261n
Ascher, Saul (author and translator), 109n
Ashkenazi, Eliezer ben Elia (physician and Talmudist), 94
Assimilation, 10, 137, 138, 139, 141, 142, 180, 247, 287, 302
Aufhäuser (banking house), 235
Auschwitz, 239
Auerbach, Isaak Levin (preacher and educationalist), 104
Auerbach, Leopold (writer), 176, 202n
Auerbach, Elias (physician), 204n
Auslandsdeutsche, 329
Auswärtiges Amt, 259n, 329
Austin, Bunny (tennis champion), 225

Bab, Julius (writer), 214–215, 216
Bach, Hans I. (writer), 18n
Baden, Jewry, 163, 166
Badt, Hermann (Prussian civil servant), 252, 254
Baeck, Leo, 261n
Baer (canoeist), 236
Baer, Bamberger Seligmann (Isaak Dow) (rabbi), 183
Baer, Lola (swimming champion), 223, 232
Baer, Yizhak (historian), XI
Baillet-Latour (Olympic official, sports' organiser), 235
Bakunin, Michael Alexandrowitsch (Russian revolutionary), 282n–283n
Balfour Declaration, 211, 258

Ball, Rudi (ice-hockey player), 237
Ballin, Albert (Director of HAPAG), 264, 267n
Bamberger, Ludwig (Liberal politician), 152, 201
Bamberger, Nathan Halevi (rabbi), 181, 183, 184, 185, 186, 188
Baptism *see* Conversion
Baptists, 24, 37
Bar Kochba Berlin (Jewish sports' club), 204, 224, 228
Bar Kochba (Prague Jewish student organisation), 307-308
Barkow, Hans K. L. (university teacher; Breslau), 15n
Barth, Aron, 191
Barth, Theodor (Liberal politician), 151, 154-155
Baruch, Hermann (wrestler), 226
Baruch, Julius (wrestler), 226
Bauer (President of the German Himalaya Foundation), 226
Bauer, Bruno (Protestant theologian and historian), 3, 9, 12n, 133
Bauernvereine, 159
Baum, Hans E. (Mrs.), 243
Baumgardt, David (philosopher), 209n
Bavarian Jewry, 166, 178, 275-276, 278-279, 314
Bavarian Räterepublik, 269, 274, 275-276, 278-279, 284
Bebel, August (leader of German Socialists), 43n, 45, 158
Beck, Walter, 224, 231
Becker, Carl Heinrich (Prussian Minister for Cultural Affairs), 63n
Beer-Hofmann, Richard (poet), 216
Beilis trial, 273
Bendavid, Lazarus (writer), 84n, 109, 130
Benjamin, Walter (writer), 288
Bennathan, Esra, 324
Ben Shemen (children's village and agricultural school, Palestine/Israel), 328
Bergen Belsen, 252n
Bergman, George (writer), 225
Bergmann, Gretel (high jumper), 236, 237, 239
Bergson, Henri (philosopher), 308
Berlin Jewish community, 82-83, 90, 101-130, 168, 169, 180, 233, 258, 260, 320-322, 323; Austrittsgemeinden, Separatgemeinden, 178; Cohn affair, 180; Freischule, 83; Reformgemeinde, 246n, 247, 248-249
Berliner, Abraham (historian), 181, 182, 184, 185, 186, 187, 188, 191
Berliner, Cora (educationalist and social worker), 340n
Berliner, H. (balloonist), 226
'Berliner Lokalanzeiger', 265
Berliner-Sport-Club (B.S.C.), 224

Berlioux, Monique, 234
Bernays, Jacob (philologist), 12n, 17, 18-19
Bernett, Hajo, 222, 227, 232, 233, 234n, 238
Bernstein, Eduard (Socialist politician), 157-158
Besser, Max (writer), 204
Bethmann Hollweg, Theobald von (German Imperial Chancellor), 152
Binder (banker), 337
Bismarck, Otto von, 76
Bittlinger, Ernst (Protestant clergyman), 26
'Blätter für religiöse Erziehung', 50n
Blau, Dr. (Justizrat), 261n
Bloch, Joseph Samuel (rabbi), 180, 181, 187
Bloch, Mordechai (icthyologist), 117
Blochert, Manfred (industrialist and editor), 254n, 266n
Bloem, Walter (writer), 211n
Blumenfeld, Kurt (German Zionist leader), 217-218, 246n
B'nai B'rith, 284
Bodenheimer, Max Isidor (German Zionist leader), 188,*189, 190
Böckel, Otto (antisemitic politician), 153n, 271, 315n
Böhme, Jakob (theosophist), 290
Bondy, Curt (educationalist), 232n
Bopp, Franz (orientalist), 14
Boycott, anti-Jewish, 1st April 1933, 331, 335
Bracher, Karl Dietrich, 135
Brandis, Christian August (philologist and philosopher), 12n
Brandt, Willy, 77
Braniss, Christian Julius (philosopher), 12n
Braun, Heinrich (Socialist politician), 158
Braun, Otto (Prime Minister of Prussia), 63n
Breslau Jewish community, 101-102, 168, 323
Breslau Rabbinical Seminary, 19
Breslauer, Siegmund (editor of 'Berliner Lokalanzeiger'), 257n, 265
Brodnitz, Friedrich, 340n
Brodnitz, Julius (Chairman of Centralverein), 251
Brundage, Avery (President of International Olympic Committee), 234, 235, 236, 238
Buber, Martin, VII, 232n, 240, 273, 278, 279, 287-309; and Ahad Ha'am, 288-289; Bible translation, 296; and Hermann Cohen, 303-304, 306; 'Drei Reden über das Judentum', 289, 307-308; at Frankfurt Lehrhaus, 302; and German language, 302-303; Hasidism, 290, 291, 294, 308; and Herzl, 305; 'Ich und Du', 293-296, 303; 'Der Jude', 292, 293, 305, 307; and Gustav Landauer, 292-293; Letter to Ghandi, 297, 307; on Nazism, 297-298; on Nietzsche, 306; and Rosenzweig, 296, 304, 306; Scholem on, 296, 299; on Spinoza, 306; and World War I, 292-293; Zionism, 288, 289, 305

General Index

Buber, Salomon (grandfather of Martin Buber), 288
Buchenwald, 263n
Bülow, Bernhard, Fürst von (German Imperial Chancellor), 148
Bund (German Socialist organisation), 279n
Bund der entschiedenen Schulreformer, 56n
Bund freireligiöser Gemeinden, 27n
Bund der Landwirte, 141, 151, 154, 315
Bunsen, Freiherr Christian K. G. von (Prussian diplomat), 18
Bussche-Haddenhausen, Freiherr von dem (Deputy Secretary of German Foreign Office), 259n

Cahnmann, Werner (sociologist), 215
Campe, Rudolf von (Liberal politician), 165, 166, 168
Caro, Hugo, 273
Caro, Ruth (javelin thrower), 239
Cassel, Oskar (Liberal politician), 152, 165, 166, 168, 171
Casserley, J. V. L., 74
Centralverein deutscher Staatsbürger jüdischen Glaubens (C.V.), 140, 141–142, 147, 187, 202, 203, 208, 209, 210, 211, 212, 215n, 244, 245n, 246n, 247, 249, 250, 251, 253, 254, 257, 258, 262, 264, 267, 268
Chamberlain, Houston Stewart (writer), 202–203, 204, 205, 206, 207n, 272
von Chappuis (Prussian Under-Secretary for Religious Affairs and Education), 165, 166, 168n
Charles, Prince of Wales, 240
Chassidism *see* Hasidism
'Christlich-soziale Blätter', 32n
Christlich-soziale Partei, 32n
Class, Heinrich (nationalist politician), 315
Cleaver, Eldridge, 272
Cloer, Ernst, 50
Cohen, Arthur A., VII
Cohen, Hermann (philosopher), 194, 200–201, 288, 292, 303–304, 306
Cohn, Arthur (rabbi), 191
Cohn, Bernhard (writer), 201–202
Cohn, Emil (rabbi), 180
Cohn, Hermann (Liberal politician), 152
Cohn, Oskar (Socialist politician), 263n
Cologne Jewish community, 168, 323
Concentration Camps, 234, 252n, 263n, 284, 327, 332, 339
Condillac, Etienne Bonnot de Mably de (French philosopher), 93
Conrad, Michael Georg (writer), 211n
Conservative Party (Germany), 45, 150, 161, 333
Conversion, 10, 21–36 *passim*, 96, 97, 106, 108, 130, 142, 250n, 327n

Coubertin, Baron Pierre de (First President of International Olympic Committee), 234, 239
Council of Jews from Germany, 339n
Cramm, Gottfried von (tennis champion), 225
Cruse (university teacher; Königsberg), 12
Csáky, Stephan (István) (Hungarian Foreign Minister), 347n
'C.V.-Zeitung', 69, 209n, 212n, 232, 251n–253n
Czák, Ibolya (high jumper), 237

Dahrendorf, Ralf, 75
Damaschke, Adolf (economist and teacher), 70
Deutsch, Judith (sportswoman), 238
Deutsch-Israelitischer Gemeindebund, 140, 163–164, 165, 166, 168, 170
Deutsch-Oesterreichischer Alpenverein, 226
Deutsche Demokratische Partei (DDP), 41, 54, 55, 56, 61, 62, 214, 245n, 264
Deutsche Hochschule für Leibesübungen (DHFL), 232
Deutsche Kulturpartei, 50
Deutsche Turnerschaft (DT), 227, 228, 233, 234n
Deutsche Volkspartei (DVP), 57, 62, 63, 243, 263–264
'Deutsche Zeitung', 264
Deutscher Lehrerverein (DLV), 46–63 *passim*
Deutscher Makkabi-Kreis, 228, 231. *See also* Makkabi.
Deutscher Reichsausschuss für Leibesübungen (DRA), 227
Deutscher Tennisbund, 225
'Deutsches Volkstum', 266
Deutschkatholiken, 24, 27n, 37
Deutschnationale Volkspartei (DNVP), 52, 61, 63n–64n, 209, 265–266, 284
Deutschvölkische Freiheitspartei, 251
Deutschvölkischer Schutz- und Trutzbund, 209, 315n
Diderot, Denis (writer), 3
Diem, Carl (Rector of Deutsche Hochschule für Leibesübungen), 232
Dieters (university teacher; Bonn), 15n
Dilthey, Wilhelm (philosopher), 289
Dittmar (Hessian Minister of Justice), 143
Durkheim, Emile (sociologist), 71
Dohm, Christian Wilhelm von (writer and archivist), 89, 91–92, 93, 97, 135–136
Dohm, Lewin Benjamin (syndic of the Breslau Jewish community), 101
Dove, Alfred (historian), 140
Dreyfus Affair, 133, 134, 158
Dühring, Eugen (philosopher), 282, 315n
Dunetz (aviator), 226

Ebner, Friedrich, 294, 295n
Eckardt, Meister, 290
Education, in Germany, 3–19, 21–36 *passim*, 41–

71, 73–77; and Christian churches, 41–66, 73–77; elementary, 41–66; Jewish "influence" on, 3–19 *passim*, 45, 53, 67; Jewish pupils, 67–71 *passim*, 75–76; secondary, 41; and secularisation, 3–19, 21–36 *passim*, 41–77; reform of, 41–66; Socialists and, 45, 46, 49, 51, 52, 53–66 *passim*; University, 3–19, 42, 76
Education, Jewish in Germany, 67–71, 152–153, 163–170, 232–233, 260, 328, 338
Eichhorn, Johann Albrecht Friedrich (Prussian statesman), 5, 7, 8, 9, 10, 14
Eickhoff, Richard (Liberal politician), 150, 153n
Einem, Karl von (Prussian general and War Minister), 153n
Einheitsschule *see* Education, in Germany
Eisner, Kurt (Socialist politician), 275
Elek-Schacherer, Ilona (fencing champion), 238
Ellstätter, Moritz (Finance Minister of Baden), 267n
Eloni, Yehuda, 174, 190
Elsass, Bernhard, 203
Elsbach (Jewish functionary), 231
Emancipation, 3–19 *passim*, 67, 76, 83, 101–130, 135, 136, 138, 139, 140, 141, 163, 222, 270, 273, 287, 288, 302; Prussian edict of 1812, 3, 4, 101, 176
Emden, Jacob Israel (rabbi and Talmudist), 87, 90–91, 117n
Emigration, Jewish, from Germany, 185, 231, 238–241, 313–361; age structure of emigrants, 318–320, 325; demographic aspects of, 314, 316–318, 323, 324–326; emigration figures, 326–327, 330, 351–352; exclusion policies, 346–351 *passim*; flight tax (*Reichsfluchtsteuer*), 343–344; internment of emigrants in occupied Europe, 327, 358n; Nazi policies and, 315–316, 317–329 *passim*, 330–358; occupational background to, 314, 324–325, 329–330; provisions of European Countries controlling admission of aliens, 353, 356, 359–361; restrictions subjected to, 346–351, 356–357; retraining (assistance) for, 345–351 *passim*; of youth, 327–328, 338n, 345; emigration to individual countries: Belgium, 352, 353, 354, 358, 359, 360; Brazil, 338n; Czechoslovakia, 352, 354, 356, 357, 359; Denmark, 357–358; France, 352, 353, 354, 356, 358, 359, 360; Great Britain, 314, 328, 352, 354, 355, 356, 357, 359, 360–361; Italy, 353, 354, 355; the Netherlands, 352, 354, 355, 356, 358, 359, 360; Palestine (Israel), 314, 316, 328, 338, 339; Sweden, 358; Switzerland, 352, 353, 355, 356, 357, 358, 359, 360–361; United States, 314, 325, 328, 338, 348, 360
Enlightenment, 22, 87, 174, 175, 176, 187, 189, 287, 288
Eppstein, Paul (functionary in Reichsvertretung), 340n

Esh, Shaul (historian), 316n, 333
Esser, Wilhelm (philosopher), 14n
Euchel, Isaac (Hebrew writer and editor), 83, 84n
'Evangelische Kirchenzeitung', 10
Evangelischer Bund, 51
Evangelisch-Sozialer Kongreß, 26
Evans, Ellen L., 63
Evian Conference, 347
Expressionism, 280n
Eybeschütz, Jonathan (rabbi and Kabbalist), 90

Falk (Prussian statesman, Minister for Education), 46
'Fanal' (periodical), 276, 277
Fascism, 276
Feuchtwanger, Lion (writer), 215–216
Feuerbach, Ludwig (philosopher), 289
Field, Geoffrey G., VII, 74, 75, 76
Finger, Jacob (Hessian Minister for Justice), 143n
Fischer, Ruth (Communist politician), 263
Fishman, Sterling, 269n
Flatow, Alfred (gymnast), 233–234
Flatow, Felix (gymnast), 233, 234
Fleissig, Jakob (rabbi), 180
Fischer, Karl (leader of German teachers' organisation), 47
Fortschrittliche Volkspartei (Progressives), 141–146 *passim*, 147
Fränkel (aviator), 266
Frank, Abraham Salomon (rabbi), 189
Frank, Anne, 252n
Frank, Jakob Leibowicz (leader of Frankist movement), 97–99, 291, 297–298
Frank, Ludwig (Socialist politician), 261n
Frankel, Wilhelm (pilot), 226
Frankel, Zacharias (rabbi and religious leader), XI, 19
Frankenheim, Marcus Leo (mathematician), 4–5
Fränkel, Sigmund (Kommerzienrat), 278–279
Frankfurt a. Main Jewish community, 168, 169, 323; Austrittsgemeinden, Separatgemeinden, 178; Lehrhaus, 302
Frankism, Frankist movement, 82, 97
Fraternities, German 135
Fraternities, Jewish, 224, 225; in Prague, 307–308
Frederick, Israel (pseud. F. Sailer), 198n
Frederick II, Frederick the Great (King of Prussia), 82, 106
Freie Vereinigung für die Interessen des orthodoxen Judentums (FVJ), 168, 169
Freisinnige Volkspartei (Progressives), 141–146 *passim*, 147
French Revolution, 217, 349

General Index

Freund, Ismar (Jewish functionary and writer), 163
Freytag, Georg W. (Arabist), 12n
Friedenthal (Jewish functionary), 231
Friedländer, David (reformer of Judaism), 83, 84n, 90, 91, 92, 101–110, 111n, 130
Friedleben, Ilse (tennis player), 225
Friedmann, Alfred, 204n
Friedrich Wilhelm III (King of Prussia), 4, 101, 104, 110
Friedrich Wilhelm IV (King of Prussia), 5, 9, 44
Friedrichsfeld, David (advocate of Jewish emancipation), 109n
Frisch, Ephraim (writer), 218
Fuchs (tennis player), 225
Fuchs, Eugen (Chairman of Centralverein), 141, 149
Fuchs, Gottfried (footballer), 225
Fürst, Paula (head of Theodor-Herzl-Schule), 340n
Fuerstner, Wolfgang (army officer), 238n

Galandauer, Heinrich (rabbi), 202n
Gandhi, Mahatma, 297, 307
Gans, David ben Salomo (chronicler), 86
Gans, Eduard (jurist and philosopher), 4, 16n
Gaupp (university teacher; Breslau), 13n
Gay, Peter, 282
Gayl, Wilhelm von (Prussian Minister of the Interior), 329
Gebsattel, Konstantin Freiherr von (nationalist politician), 315n
Gebser (university teacher; Königsberg), 15n
Geiger, Abraham (religious philosopher), 12n, 136
Geiger, Ludwig (literary historian), 7n, 302
Gemlich, Adolf, 316n
Genserowsky, Richard (gymnast), 228
George, Stefan (poet), 288
Gerber, Fritz (sprinter), 224
Gerlach (university teacher; Halle), 15n
German Jewish Childrens' Aid Committee (U.S.A.), 328
Gerron, Kurt (cabaret artist), 239
Gesamtarchiv der deutschen Juden, 103
Gesamtverband Evangelischer Arbeitervereine Deutschlands, 31–33, 39, 40; for regional organisations see p. 40
Gestapo, 227, 231n, 249n, 334, 336, 339n, 353
Gilbert, Felix, 76
Ginat, Jochanan (Hans Gaertner) (educationalist and Director of Leo Baeck Institute), 71
Glatzer, Nahum N., VII
Gneist, Rudolf von (Liberal politician), 151
Gobineau, Joseph Arthur, Count of (orientalist and poet), 272
Goebbels, Josef, 284, 335

Göhre, Paul (writer), 26, 27, 76
Göring, Hermann, 337
Goldmann, Felix (rabbi), 211n, 250n
Goldschmidt, Ernst Daniel (Hebrew scholar), IX
Goldstein, Julius (philosopher and editor of 'Der Morgen'), 215
Goldstein, Moritz (writer), 206, 218
Gordonstoun, 240
Goslar, Hans (Prussian civil servant), 252, 259
Gothein, Georg (Liberal politician), 150, 151, 157
Graetz, Heinrich (historian), 12n, 105n
Grattenauer (antisemitic writer), 106
Grégoire, Henri (French bishop; Jansenist), 88
Greive, Hermann, 69
Gross-Breesen (agricultural training centre), 231
Gruenewald, Max (President of Leo Baeck Institute), 70
Grunder (aviator), 226
Güdemann, Moritz (Chief Rabbi of Vienna), 179n, 180, 181, 186, 189, 190n, 192
Günther, Hans (racist writer), 215
Gundolf, Friedrich (literary historian), 292
Gustloff, Wilhelm (Nazi politician), 336
Gutteridge, Richard, 69
Guttmann, Georg, 257n
Guttmann, Sir Ludwig (Director of Stoke Mandeville Hospital), 239–241
Gymnastikinstitut (later Sportschule) Bloch, Stuttgart, 232
Gyssling, Robert (Liberal politician), 153n

'Ha-aretz', XI
Haavara, 339, 344
Haeckel, Ernst (natural scientist), 29
Haenisch, Konrad (Socialist politician), 54
Hagibor, Prag (Czech-Jewish sports club), 228, 238
Hahn, Kurt (educationalist), 239–240
Hakoah Wien (Austrian-Jewish sports club), 225, 228, 229, 238
Halberstam(m), Baruch (rabbi), 181, 183, 185, 186
Halle, Edwin (Director of sports institute), 232
Ha'Levi, Jehudah (poet and religious philosopher), 288–289
Ha-Levi, Moses (father of Isaac Satanow), 81
Halberstadt, Hans (fencer), 225
Haller, Karl Ludwig von (Swiss politician and jurist), 5
Hallo, Rudolf, 302n
Hamann, Johann Georg (writer), 294, 295n
Hamburg Jewish community, 102, 103, 104, 178, 323; Portuguese congregation, 191; Synagogenverband, 191; Tempelverband, 191
'Hamburgischer Correspondent', 264

'Hame'asef' (Hebrew periodical), 82n, 83, 86, 93, 94
Hannover 04 (Jewish sports club), 229
Hantke, Arthur (German Zionist leader), 193
Hapoel (Israeli sports organisation), 228, 229n
Hapoel Games, 229n
Harden, Maximilian (journalist, editor of 'Die Zukunft'), 279
Hardenberg, Karl August von (Prussian statesman), 4n
Hasidism, 95n, 183, 185, 186, 193, 279, 290, 291, 294
Haskalah (Hebrew Enlightenment), 81–97, 98
Hauptmann, Karl (writer), 211n
Hauptstelle für jüdische Wanderfürsorge, 357n
Hauptstelle für jüdische Wanderung, Berlin, 329
Haym, Rudolf (literary historian and politician), 7n
Hebrew language, 12n, 81–99 passim, 101, 103, 113n, 126, 179, 182, 248, 257, 288
Hebrew literature, in Germany, 81–99
Hegel, Georg Wilhelm Friedrich (philosopher), 306
Heilbrunn (aviator), 226
Heine, Heinrich, 273, 282
Hellpach, Willy (Liberal politician), 41–42
Helvétius, Claude Adrian (French philosopher), 93
Henke (university teacher; Halle), 15n
Henoch, Lilly (discus champion), 224
Herder, Johann Gottfried (writer), 200, 278
Hermann, Georg (novelist), 218
Herrnhuter (Christian sect), 24, 37
Herz Beer, Jacob (banker), 102, 108n
Hertz, Friedrich (writer), 203
Herz, Marcus (physician and philosopher), 83, 87, 130
Herzl, Jakob (father of Theodor Herzl), 189n
Herzl, Theodor, 173, 178, 180, 181, 188, 189, 190, 256, 257, 288n, 305
Hess, Josef (Catholic politician), 63n
Hess, Moses (Socialist and Zionist writer), 289n
Hesse Jewry, 166, 314
Heydrich, Reinhard (Nazi politician). 318n, 327
Hildesheimer, Esriel (rabbi, leader of orthodoxy), 191, 192
Hildesheimer, Hirsch (leader of orthodoxy), 189, 191
Hilfsverein der deutschen Juden, 244, 253
Hiller, Kurt (writer), 209
Hindenburg, Paul von (Second President of Weimar Republic), 244n, 254, 335n
Hirsch, Amram (rabbi), 180, 182, 184, 186n, 187, 191
Hirsch, Julius (footballer), 225
Hirsch, Baron Maurice de (banker and philanthropist), 189

Hirsch, Otto (Director of Reichsvertretung), 318n, 340n
Hitler, Adolf, 209, 215, 222, 227, 234, 235, 252, 266, 267n, 276, 277, 297–298, 307, 315n, 316n, 333, 334, 335, 336, 337, 347n, 349, 353
Hoare, Sir Samuel (British Home Secretary), 361
Hoffmann, Adolf (Socialist politician), 54, 157, 159, 167, 170–171
Hoffmann von Fallersleben, August Heinrich (poet and Germanist), 9
Hoffmann, Johannes (Socialist politician), 53
Holländer, Ludwig (Director of Centralverein), 208, 251n, 253n, 258n
Horwitz, Maximilian (Chairman of Centralverein), 140, 149
Huehnefeld, Freiherr von (pilot), 226
Hug, Heinz, 269n
Hugenberg, Alfred (nationalist politician), 265
Humboldt, Wilhelm von (Prussian statesman), 135–136
Hunt, Lord John, 239, 240
Husserl, Edmund (phenomenologist), 301

'Im deutschen Reich', 203n, 245n–251n passim
Intermarriage, 21–36 passim, 204, 316–318, 319–320, 327n
'Israelitisches Familienblatt', 232, 262
Itzig, Daniel (banker), 83, 90

Jacob, Martha (javelin thrower), 224
Jacobowski, Ludwig (poet), 201
Jacobsohn, Siegfried (editor of the 'Weltbühne'), 262
Jacobson, Jacob (archivist and historian), 103, 105
Jahn, Friedrich Ludwig (Turnvater), 135, 228n
Jahncke, Ernest Lee (Olympic official, sports organiser), 235
Jatho, Karl (Protestant theologian), 50
Jewish Agency, 261n
Jewish Colonization Association (ICA), 338n
Jewish National and University Library, Jerusalem, 81n
Jewry, Austrian, emigration of, 313–361 passim
Jewry, Eastern, 173, 192, 257, 258, 273–274
Jewry, German, acculturation, 314, 322, 339; adult education, 232n, 308; age structure, 318–320, 325; civil rights for, 90–93, 133, 134, 135, 136, 139; communal reform, 101–130, 163–170 passim, 176–179; defence against anti-semitism, 141–146 passim, 147–162; demographic distribution, 67–68, 143, 161, 314, 316–318, 323; deportations, 320n–322n, 327n, 332, 347, 352; and Eastern Jewry, 205, 244–245, 249, 253–258, 261, 263, 265, 273–274, 314, 315; education, 3–19, 67–71, 93–95, 101–130, 152–153, 163–170, 232–233, 260, 328,

338; emigration, 185, 231, 238–241, 313–361; exclusion from professions and public life, 315, 331–332, 334–336, 339–340, 342–343, 346; extermination of, 313n, 315, 320n, 347, 352; fight for equal rights, 140–146 *passim*, 147–162, 163–170; forced labour under Nazism, 332, 337; at German universities, 3–19; impoverishment of under Nazi rule, 341–342, 345, 346; intermarriage, 316–318, 319–320, 327n; mass suicides, 320n–322n, 327n; migration (*Binnenwanderung*), 314, 315, 329, 346; military service, 98, 153, 157, 243–244, 334n; modernisation, 68; occupational structure, 91–92, 134, 137, 142–143, 145, 314, 324–325, 329–330; and pacifism, 262; patriotism, 274; persecution, 313–358; political allegiances, 147–162, 243n; religious reform, 101–130, 163–170 *passim*, 176–179; revocation of citizenship rights, 331; secularisation, 33–34; social mobility, 4, 67–70; social welfare, 324, 341–342, 344–345, 346–351 *passim*; in sport, 221–241; survival in Nazi Germany, 327; urbanisation, 67–68, 178, 314, 315, 323–324, 325; value of business property, 342; vocational training, 345–351 *passim*; voting patterns, 147–162 *passim*, 243n. *See also* Baden, Bavarian, Hesse, Pomeranian, Poznań, Prussian, Saxonian, Silesian, Westphalian, Württemberg Jewry *and under* individual communities.

Jewry, Italian, 266

Jews, Eastern, in Germany, 33–34, 68, 152, 193, 244–245, 247, 251–256, 261, 263, 265, 314–315

Jews, foreign, in Germany, 321–322, 328–330, 331–357 *passim*; naturalisation of, 322, 329, 338n

Joachim, Richard (functionary of Reichsvertretung), 340n

Joachimsthal, Ernst (sports champion), 224

Jokl, Ernst (sprinter; Professor of Sports Medicine), 224

JTUS (South-German-Jewish sports organisation), 232

Judaism, 8, 10, 13, 15, 70, 99, 106–130, 163, 173–195, 198, 201, 207, 214, 215, 216, 257, 258, 278, 281, 282, 283; and Christianity, 3–19 *passim*, 95, 97. Science of Judaism *see* Wissenschaft des Judentums.

'(Der) Jude', 292, 293, 305, 307

Judenschutztruppe, 149, 158

'Jüdische Auswanderung, Korrespondenzblatt des Hilfsvereins der Juden in Deutschland', 351n

'Jüdische Presse', 191, 192

'Jüdische Rundschau', X–XI, 204n, 205n, 206n, 212, 216n, 217n, 218n, 230, 232, 245n–260n *passim*

'Jüdische Schulzeitung', 69

Jüdische Turnerschaft, 228

'Jüdische Turnzeitung', 204n, 229

Jüdische Volkspartei, 190, 260, 264

Jüdische Winterhilfe, 341, 342n, 344, 345

Jüdischer Kulturbund, 340

Jüdischer Lehrerverband, 70

Jüdischer Verlag, 289

Jüdischer Volksverein, Berlin, 271n

Jungdeutscher Orden (Jungdo), 214

Jungmann, Max, 204n

Jung Spartakusbund, 60

(Das) Junge Deutschland, 135

Kabbalah, 87, 88, 99

Kaempf, Saul Isaak (theologian and orientalist), 17n

Kahn, Bernhard (General Secretary of Hilfsverein), 261n, 341n

Kahr, Gustav von (Bavarian statesman), 256, 277, 313

'Kain' (periodical), 280, 283

Kalisch, M. (writer), 11n

Kalmus, Ernst (physician), 189

Kant, Immanuel (philosopher), 130n

Kartell-Convent der Verbindungen deutscher Studenten jüdischen Glaubens (K.C.), 225

Katholische Arbeiter-Vereine, 31–33, 38

Katholische Gesellenvereine, 31–33

Katholische Schulorganisation, 58

Katz, Elias (sprinter), 224

Katz, Iwan (Communist politician), 262

Katzenstein (aircraft constructor), 226

Keleti, Agnes (sports champion), 234

Kellner, Leon (literary historian and editor of Zionist organ 'Die Welt'), 189n

Kempkes, Adolf (Liberal politician), 263

Keren Hajessod, 259

Keudell, Walter (Conservative politician), 62, 63, 67n

Keyserling, Hermann, Graf (philosopher), 216

Kierkegaard, Sören (philosopher), 295, 297, 306

Killanin, Lord (President of International Olympic Committee), 234

Klatzkin, Jacob (philosopher and publicist), 292n

Klausner, Max A. (journalist and editor of 'Israelitische Wochenschrift'), 164n

Klee, Alfred (jurist and German Zionist leader), 190

Kley, Eduard (preacher and headmaster), 103n

Koch-Weser, Erich (German Minister of the Interior), 61, 62

Koehler (Prussian civil servant), 136

'Kölnische Zeitung', 243

Kohn, Hans (historian), 288n–289n, 292

Kollenscher, Max (jurist and German Zionist leader), 190

Kommunistische Partei Deutschlands (KPD), Communists, 60, 255, 262–263, 279, 280n, 334
Komvádi, Bela (waterpolo coach), 238
'(Die) Kraft', 230, 231n, 233
Kraushaar, A., 98
Kristallnacht see Pogroms, Germany, November 1938
Kristl, Wilhelm Lukas, 269n
Krojanker, Gustav (Zionist politician), 217–218
Kronfeld, Robert (pilot), 226
Krueger, A. (Ministerialrat), 332n, 342n
Krügler (Prussian civil servant), 164, 165, 166
Kulturkampf, 23n, 51, 54, 74, 159
Kurz, Georg (sprinter), 224

La Beaumelle, Laurent de (French writer), 108, 120
Lachmann, Karel (fencing champion), 238
Lachmann, Siegmund (physician), 153n
Lamberti, Marjorie, 67, 68, 163–170
Landau, Leo, 276n
Landauer, Georg (Zionist politician), 211
Landauer, Gustav (Anti-Marxist Socialist), 270, 273, 275, 278, 279, 280, 292, 293
Landsbury, George (British Socialist), 66
Lange, Friedrich (writer), 201
Langer, Ruth (sportswoman), 238
Laqueur, Walter, 173
Lasker, Eduard (Liberal politician), 152
Lazarus, Moritz (philosopher), 19n, 199–200, 218
League of Nations, 347, 348, 353, 360
Left Liberals see Fortschrittliche Volkspartei, Freisinnige Volkspartei and also under Liberals
Lehnerdt (university teacher; Königsberg), 15n
Leibniz, Gottfried Wilhelm (philosopher), 93, 95n
Leibusch, Hajjim ben (Hasidist), 183
Leimdörfer, David (rabbi), 179n
Leipzig Jewish community, 323
Lenin, Vladimir Ilyich, 280
Lenman, Robin, 51
Lenz, Max (writer), 12n
Leo Baeck Institute, VII–XII, 77; Arden House Conference, VII; New York Archives, IX, 77, 103; Oxford Seminar, VII; Schriftenreihe wissenschaftlicher Abhandlungen, VII, IX; Year Book, VII–VIII, IX, X–XI
Leo, Heinrich (historian), 16n
Leonrodt, Freiherr von (Bavarian Minister for Justice), 143n
Leschnitzer, Adolf (historian and educationalist), 255
Levenstein, Alfred (writer), 28, 38, 76
Levien, Max (Communist politician), 275
Levy, B. (Chairman of Hamburg Synagogenverband), 191
Levy, Theo (sprinter), 224

Lewald, Theodor (Staatssekretär; Olympic official), 235
Lewin, Adolf (rabbi), 198–199
Lewin, Kurt (sprinter), 224
Lewinsohn, Paul (Jewish functionary), 231
Liberals, and German antisemitism and the Jewish Question, 141–162
Lichtfreunde (Christian religious movement), 27n
Lichtheim, Richard (Zionist politician), 193
Lidtke, Vernon, VII, 74, 76
Lieber, Ernst (Catholic politician), 159, 160
Liebermann von Sonnenberg, Max (Conservative politician), 153n
Liebknecht, Karl (Leftist Socialist politician), 158
Liebknecht, Wilhelm (Socialist politician), 45
Liegnitzer, Jakob (writer), 223
Lilienthal, Arthur (General Secretary of Reichsvertretung), 340n
Linse, Ulrich, 280n
Lissauer (aviator), 226
Locke, John (philosopher), 88, 89n, 93
Loë, Freiherr von (Catholic publicist), 138
Loewe, Heinrich (writer), 229
Löwenstein, Leo (Chairman of R.j.F.), 230, 231, 244n, 253
Löwenthal, Raphael (writer, theatre director and founder of C.V.), 267n
Lorch, Erich (athlete), 236
Ludendorff, Erich (general, nationalist politician), 251, 277
Lueger, Karl (Lord Mayor of Vienna), 133
Luther, Hans (German statesman), 62
Luxemburg, Rosa (Socialist leader), 282

Maccabi, Maccabi World Union, 221, 228, 229
Maccabiah, 225, 229, 230
MacIntyre, Alasdair, 35
Maimon, Salomon (Shlomo) (philosopher), 82n, 105, 130
Maimonides, 85, 130, 223, 289
Makkabi, 224, 227, 229, 230, 231, 236
Makkabi Ha-Tzair, 230
'Manchester Guardian', 234
Manasseh Ben Israel (Amsterdam rabbi), 130
Mandelstamm, Max (physician and Zionist politician), 222, 228
Mann, Heinrich (novelist), 271
Mann, Thomas (novelist), 271
Manne, Hanne (athlete), 236
Margolis, Otto (mountaineer), 226
Marr, Wilhelm (writer), 193, 197–198, 271
Marwitz, Friedrich August Ludwig von der (Prussian general), 135
Marx, Felix (wrestler), 226
Marx, Karl, 75, 282n–283n
Marx, Kurt (director of sports institute), 232

Marx, Rudi (athlete), 236
Marx, Wilhelm (German Chancellor), 62
Maskilim, 81, 83, 87, 90, 93, 94, 97, 98, 99
Mauthner, Fritz (writer and philosopher), 294
May, Kurt (Director of United Restitution Organization), 342n
Maybaum, Sigmund (rabbi), 180, 256
Maydell, Bodo, Freiherr von, 476
Mayer, Eugen (fencer), 224, 225
Mayer, Guido (mountaineer), 226
Mayer, Helene (fencing champion), 223, 224, 225, 236, 237, 239
Mayer, Ludwig (physician), 237
Mayer, Paul Yogi (athlete), 236
McDonald, James G. (High Commissioner for Refugees), 348
Me'asfim, 82n, 83
Mehring, Franz (writer and Socialist politician), 158
Meisl, Hugo (sports' organiser), 225
Meisl, Willy (sports' writer), 225
Mello (de Preiss), Inge (discus thrower), 239
Mendelssohn, Moses, 3, 5, 12, 82n, 83, 91, 92, 95, 97, 99, 102, 108, 120–121, 128, 130, 141, 176
Mendelssohn, Salomon (sports' teacher and writer), 224n
Mennonites, 24, 37
Menzel, Wolfgang (writer), 135
Merzbacher, Gottfried (mountaineer), 226
Methodists, 24, 37
Mevissen, Gustav (manufacturer and publisher), 7
Meyerbeer, Giacomo (composer), 105n
Meyerheim, Paul Werner (financial adviser of Reichsvertretung), 340n
Meysel, Bernd (swimmer), 236
Mezö, Ference (Olympic official, sports' organiser), 234
Michaelis, Dolf, 476
Middle Ages, 225, 227, 308
von Mieses (aviator), 226
Milberg, Hildegard, 59
Misrachi (Mizrachi), 173, 180, 191, 252n
'Mitteilungen aus dem Verein zur Abwehr des Antisemitismus', 201n, 203n
'Mitteilungsblatt des Verbandes nationaldeutscher Juden e.V.', see '(Der) nationaldeutsche Jude'
'Monatsschrift für Geschichte und Wissenschaft des Judentums', XI
Montesquieu, 93
Morath, Albrecht (Liberal politician), 263n
Moses, Julius (editor, and Socialist politician), 147, 148
Movers, Franz Karl (theologian), 15n
Mühsam, Charlotte, 271, 276n
Mühsam, Erich (writer, anarchist-theorist), 269–284; on antisemitism, 270, 272, 274, 276; in Bavarian Räterepublik, 269, 274, 275, 276, 278–279, 284; and Buber, 273, 279; on Eastern Jewry, 273–274; 'Fanal', 276, 277; on Judaism, 277–278, 281–283; 'Kain', 280, 283; and Gustav Landauer, 270, 273, 275, 279–280; murder in Oranienburg, 284; and Zionism, 270, 279–280
Mühsam, Grete, 271
Mühsam, Hans, 271
Mühsam, Kreszentia, 283
Mühsam, Paul (writer), 270n
Mühsam, Siegfried (apothecary), 270–271, 283
Muhr, Abraham (writer and businessman), 101
Mumm, Richard (Conservative politician), 61
Munchmeyer (Konsistorialrat), 44
Munk, Michael L., 177
Munk, Salomon (orientalist), 12n
Muskeljudentum, 222, 227
Mussolini, Benito, 266

Namier, L. B. (British historian), 145n
Nansen-Office, Nansen-passport, 348n
Napoleon I, 134
Nathan (oarsman), 226
Nathan, Heinz (sprinter), 224
Nathan, Paul (politician and writer), 253
'Nation' (Liberal weekly), 151
National Liberal Party (Germany), 150, 161, 243, 270
'(Der) nationaldeutsche Jude', 245n–252n, 254, 256n–264n, 265, 266n–267n
Nationalism, German, 134
Naumann (gymnast), 232
Naumann, Hilde, 243
Naumann, Mathilde née Herrmann, 243
Naumann, Max (leader of Verband nationaldeutscher Juden), 243–267
Nauwerck, Karl (philosopher), 9
Nazism, X, XI, 19, 59, 61, 169, 215, 216, 218–219, 221, 223, 227, 232, 249n, 250n, 266, 270, 275, 276, 277, 284, 308, 313, 315
Neppach, Nellie (tennis player), 225
Neufeld (aviator), 226
Neumann, Wilhelm (Secretary General of DIGB), 166n
Nicholls, J. A., 51
Nietzsche, Friedrich (philosopher), 74, 146, 288, 289, 306
Nobel, Nehemia Anton (rabbi, religious leader), 191
Nordau, Max (writer and Zionist leader), 181, 202n, 222, 227, 228
Norddeutscher Verband der christlich gesinnten Arbeitervereine, 40
Notgemeinschaft deutscher Wissenschaftler (Zürich), 339n
Nuremberg Laws, 235, 335n, 336

Oestreich, Paul (educationalist), 55, 56n
Olympic Games, 222, 223, 224, 229, 233–238, 239, 336; Jewish sportsmen at, 222–239
Oncken, Hermann (historian), 140
Oppeln-Bronikowski, Friedrich von (writer and translator), 265
Oppenheim (tennis player), 225
Oppenheimer, Franz (Dr.), 246n
Oppenheimer, Franz (economist and sociologist), 205, 206, 246n
Oranienburg, 284
Orgler, Franz (athlete), 236
Orthodoxy, Jewish, 101–130, 159, 160, 167–169, 170, 291; and Zionism, 173–195
Ostdeutscher Verband der katholischen Arbeitervereine, 38
Ott (the "tauft Jud"), 223
Owens, Jesse (sprinter), 238

Paasch (politician), 315n
Pacifism, 262
Papen, Franz von (German Chancellor), 225
Pappenheim, Salomon (Hebraist and dayan), 102
Pascal, Roy, 271
Paucker, Arnold, 156n, 219n
Paulsen, Friedrich (philosopher and educationalist), 19n, 42
Peltasohn, Martin (Liberal politician), 152, 154, 160
Perry, Fred (tennis champion), 225
Petlyura, Simon (Ukrainian nationalist and pogromist), 274
Peyser, Alfred (Deputy Chairman of Verband nationaldeutscher Juden), 247, 249n, 254n, 257n
Pflaum, Fritz (mountaineer), 226
Philip, Prince, Duke of Edinburgh, 240
Philippson, Ludwig (editor of 'Allgemeine Zeitung des Judentums'), 138
Philippson, Martin (historian), 164
Pinson, Koppel S., 71
Pius IX, 22
Planck, Julius Wilhelm von (jurist), 11
Pogroms, Germany, in Berlin, 1923, 253–254; November 1938, 233, 238, 323, 328, 331, 332, 337, 338, 344, 346, 352; in Eastern Europe, 273–274
Pohl, Georg F. (physicist), 14n
Pol, Heinz (writer), 262
Pomeranian Jewry, 166
Porges, Siegmund (mountaineer), 226
Porsch, Felix (Catholic politician), 160
Poznań Jewry, 314
Preiss, Ellen (fencing champion), 238
Prenn, Daniel (tennis champion), 225, 239
Prenn, John (racket player), 225
Preuss, Paul (mountaineer), 226

Preussischer Landesverband gesetzestreuer Synagogengemeinden, 167n
Preussischer Landesverband jüdischer Gemeinden, 163n, 167n, 247n, 251, 264, 344n
'Preussische Lehrerzeitung', 70
Progressives see Fortschrittliche Volkspartei, Freisinnige Volkspartei and also under Liberals
Protestrabbiner, 179n, 190
'Protocols of the Elders of Zion', 250
Pruschnowski, Itzchak, 222, 236
Prussian Jewry, 101–130, 163–170, 328
Pulzer, Peter, 156n, 162n, 207
Purkinje, Johannes Evangelista (physiologist and pathologist), 13n

Quakers, 24, 37

Rabbi, Rabbinate, in Germany, 153, 166, 169, 173–195
Rabau (Jewish functionary), 231
Racism, 69, 197–219, 281, 292, 336; Jewish responses to, 197–219. *See otherwise under* antisemitism.
Rade, Martin (Protestant clergyman), 28, 30
Ramban (Rabbi Mose ben Nahman) (Nachmanides), 184
Ranke, Leopold von (historian), 16n, 133
Rath, Ernst vom (German diplomat), 332, 336
Rathenau, Walther (statesman and philosopher), 209, 277
Rathjen, Dora (high jumper), 237
Raumer, Karl Otto von (Prussian Minister for Education), 18–19
Reformation, 174
Reform Judaism, 10, 173
Reichsausschuss der jüdischen Jugendverbände, 231
Reichsausschuss der jüdischen Sportverbände, 231, 232
Reichsbund jüdischer Frontsoldaten (R.j.F.), 224, 226, 230, 231, 244n, 246, 247, 249, 253, 254, 334, 335n
Reichselternbund, 58, 59
Reichsverband zur Bekämpfung des Zionismus, 257
Reichsvereinigung der Juden in Deutschland, 317, 327, 337
Reichsvertretung der deutschen Juden (der Juden in Deutschland), 231, 232, 267n, 317, 328, 336n, 340, 341, 345, 352n
Reichswehr, 276
Reichszentrale für jüdische Auswanderung, 337
Reines, Isaak Jakob (Talmudist and Zionist leader), 173, 180, 183, 186
Reinharz, Jehuda, 147n, 173, 180, 190
Reissner, Hanns (historian), 320n
Remak, Robert (physician and neurologist), 17
Reuter, Ernst, 76

General Index

Research Foundation for Jewish Immigration, New York, 313n, 330n
Reventlow, Graf Ernst zu (Nazi politician), 315n
Revolution of 1848, 349
Reznicek, Paula (tennis player), 225
'Rheinische Zeitung', 7
Rheinländer (Catholic politician), 62n
Ribbentrop, Joachim (Nazi Foreign Minister), 337
Richarz, Monika, 70
Richter-Weiherman (tennis player), 225
Rickert, Heinrich (Liberal politician), 148, 151, 154
Richter, Eugen (Liberal politician), 148, 154
Riess (mathematician), 5
Riesser, Gabriel (politician), 136
Rissmann, Robert (leader of German teachers' organisation), 47
Ritter, Dov Bär (rabbi), 181
Ritter von Halt, Karl (Reichssportführer), 235
R.j.F. Sportsgruppe Berlin, 228
Rodda, John Clinton, 234
Röhm, Ernst (SA Chief of Staff), 334, 335
Romanticism, 135, 136, 217
Rosenblüth, Felix (Pinchas Rosen), (Zionist leader and Israeli Minister of Justice), 192
Rosenstein, Willy (aviator), 226
Rosenstock-Huessy, Eugen, 294, 295n
Rosenthal, Hans (sports champion), 224
Rosenzweig, Franz (philosopher), 288, 295n, 296, 302, 304, 306
Rousseau, Jean Jacques (philosopher), 93
Rürup, Reinhard, 138
Rüssmann (sports' coach), 236
Rumpler, Edmund (aircraft constructor), 226

SA, 330, 331, 339n
Saalschütz, Joseph (rabbi and orientalist), 17
Sabbatai Zwi (Kabbalist and pseudo-Messiah), 98–99, 291
Sabbatian movement, 98–99
Salomon, Gotthold (preacher), 102
Salus, Hugo (writer), 216
Samter, Hermann, 261n
Sandler, Aron (physician and Zionist politician), 204–205
Sartre, Jean-Paul, 278n, 306
Satanow, Isaac (Hebrew writer), 81–99; on education, 93–95; and Frankism, 97–99; on religion and tolerance, 95–97; on secular knowledge and science, 84–90
Savigny, Friedrich Karl von (jurist), 16n
Saxonian Jewry, 328–329
S. C. Charlottenburg (sports club), 224
Schach, Fabius (journalist), 161
Schacht, Horace Greely Hjalmar (President of the Reichsbank), 334, 335, 337, 343, 344
Schattmann, Werner (athlete), 236

Scheinmann, Dr. (son of Isaac Satanow), 82
Schelling, Friedrich Wilhelm Joseph von (philosopher), 294
Schemm, Hans (teacher), 70
Schendel, Simon (aviator), 226
Schiffer, Sinai (rabbi), 181, 182, 184, 186n, 187
Schild, Erich (athlete), 236
'(Der) Schild', 227, 230, 232, 233, 251n, 253n
Schild Club see Sportbund Schild
Schiller, Friedrich von, 14n
Schleiermacher, Friedrich Ernst Daniel (Protestant theologian and philosopher), 108, 121n
Schlesinger, Georg (engineer), 257n
Schmidt, von (mountaineer), 226
Schmitt, Hans, 147
Schnabel, Franz, 75
Schneemelcher, Wilhelm (General Secretary of Evangelisch-Sozialer Kongreß), 26
Schneersohn, Schalom ben (rabbi), 183n
Schneider, Ernst (antisemitic politician), 315n
Schocken-Verlag, XI
Schönstedt, Karl Heinrich von (Prussian statesman), 154
Schöpflin, Georg (Socialist politician), 157
Scholem, Gershom, 288
Scholem, Werner (Communist politician), 262, 290, 296, 299
Scholl, Carl (religious leader), 27n
Schopenhauer, Arthur (philosopher), 288
Schorsch, Ismar, VIII, 75, 76
Schuckmann, Friedrich, Freiherr von (Prussian Minister of the Interior), 102n, 104
Schulz, Heinrich (Socialist politician), 49, 55, 61, 62
Schwarz (aircraft constructor), 226
Schwarz, Karl (theologian), 9
Schwarz, Walter, 342n
Schwarzbard, Samuel (assassin of Petlyura), 274
von Schwartzkopff (Prussian civil servant), 166
Schwimmclub Wiesbaden, 223
Secularisation, 3–19 passim; and Christian Churches, 21–40, 73–77 passim; conversion, 21–36 passim; and education, 3–19, 21–36 passim, 41–77; intermarriage, 21–36 passim; Jewish, 33–34, 75, 78; and working class, 21–36, 38, 73–77 passim
Seelig, Erich (boxer), 225
Seiden, Rudolf (Austrian journalist), 210–211
Seligmann, Max (weightlifter), 235n
Sermon, Jewish, in Germany, 120
Seyfert, R. (leader of German teachers' organisation), 62n
Sieffert (university teacher; Königsberg), 15n
Siegmann, Georg (V.n.J. national chairman), 267n
Sigl, Joseph (Bavarian politician), 315n
Silesian Jewry, 101–102, 160, 166, 314
Simmel, Georg (philosopher), 289

488 General Index

Simon, Ernst, 232n
Simon, Gerson, 261n
Simultanschulen *see* Education, in Germany
Snell, John, 147
Social Darwinism, 208, 213, 315
Sofer (Schreiber), Moses ("Chatam Sofer") (Talmudist), 108, 129
Sonnenfeld, Hugo (jurist and leader of Centralverein), 156n, 157, 209n, 210, 211
Sozialdemokratische Partei Deutschlands (SPD), Social Democrats, 22, 26, 27, 28, 29, 30, 31, 33, 35, 36, 45, 49, 51, 52, 53, 54, 55, 57, 66, 76, 141, 147–162, 167, 170–171, 245n, 252n, 261n, 263n, 275, 276, 329,, 334; and German antisemitism and the Jewish Question, 147–162, 170–171
Soziale Reichspartei, 315n
'Sozialistischer Erzieher', 58
Spann, Othmar (sociologist), 266n
Spinoza, Baruch, 12, 106, 108, 121, 130, 273, 282, 291, 306
Sport, Jewish, in Germany, 204, 221–241. *See otherwise* under individual sports clubs and sports organisations, Bar Kochba, Jüdische Turnerschaft, Maccabi, Makkabi, Sportbund Schild etc.
Sport, Jewish, in England, 227, 228, 336
Sport, Jewish, in the United States, 227
Sportbund des Reichsbundes jüdischer Frontsoldaten *see* Sportbund Schild
Sportbund Schild, 224, 225, 229, 230, 231, 236
Sportsmen and -women, Jewish in Germany, 221–241; at Olympic Games, 222, 223, 229, 233–238, 239
Sportwissenschaftliches Institut, Bonn University, 232
SS, 327n
Stahl, Friedrich Julius (politician), 10
Stahlhelm, 266
Stapel, Wilhelm (German nationalist writer and editor of 'Deutsches Volkstum'), 215, 266
Stark, Fritz (fencer), 225
Stefan George Kreis, 288
Stein, Harry (boxer), 225
Sterling, Eleonore (historian), 13n
Stern, Heinemann (headmaster, educationalist), 210n, 212–213
Stern, Ludwig (headmaster), 198
Stern (teacher), 214–215, 216
Stern-Täubler, Selma (historian), XI
Sternberger, Dolf, 227
Sternlieb, Kurt (athlete), 236
Stinnes, Hugo (industrialist), 263n
Stoke Mandeville Hospital, 240–241
Stoecker, Adolf (antisemitic leader), 141, 171, 271
Strauss, David Friedrich (Protestant theologian), 74

Streicher, Julius (Nazi leader), 70
Stresemann, Gustav (German statesman), 259, 263, 264
Studt, Konrad von (Prussian statesman), 155
Sudetenland Jewry, 327n

Tal, Uriel, 67
Talmud, 13, 87, 95, 99, 107, 108, 113–114, 115, 117, 127, 130, 176, 179, 184, 289
Teachers, Jewish, in Germany, 70–71, 153
Teller, Wilhelm Abraham (Protestant theologian), 21n
Thalhoffer (writer), 223
Theilhaber, Felix A. (sociologist), 254
Theresienstadt (Terezin), 239
Tholuck, Friedrich A. G. (theologian), 14n
Thule Gesellschaft, 275
Tietz, Ludwig (Jewish functionary and youth leader), 231
Tillich, Paul, 308–309
Tönnies, Ferdinand (philosopher and sociologist), 211n
Toury, Jacob, 147–149, 155, 159, 161
Tramer, Hans (publicist and editor; Vice-President of Leo Baeck Institute), 212n, 269n
Translateur, Salo, 476
Traub, Gottfried (Protestant theologian), 50
Treitschke, Heinrich von (historian), 140, 141, 315n
Trilling, Lionel, 75
Tschammer und Osten, Hans von (Reichssportführer), 235, 236, 237
Tucholsky, Kurt (writer), 261–262
Turnvereine, Jewish *see* Sport, Jewish, in Germany

Unabhängige Sozialdemokratische Partei Deutschlands (USPD), 52, 54
Unger, Louis (sports champion), 224
United Restitution Organization, 342n
Universities, Jewish academics at, 3–19, 75–76
Unna, Isak (rabbi), 261

Verband der Deutschen Juden, 67, 148, 150, 152, 160, 163, 164n, 165, 168, 169
Verband evangelischer Arbeiterinnen-Vereine, 39n
Verband der jüdischen Lehrervereine im Deutschen Reich, 164
Verband der katholischen Vereine polnischer Arbeiter, 38
Verband katholischer Arbeitervereine (Sitz Berlin), 38
Verband katholischer Arbeitervereine Nord-und Ostdeutschlands, 38
Verband katholischer Arbeitervereine Westdeutschlands, 38

General Index

Verband katholischer Vereine erwerbstätiger Frauen und Mädchen Deutschlands, 38
Verband nationaldeutscher Juden (V.n.J.), 243–268; and antisemitism, 250, 251, 252, 256, 264–268; and Centralverein, 244, 247, 249, 250–254; and Deutsche Volkspartei, 263–264; and Deutschnationale Volkspartei, 265–266; and Eastern Jews, 244–245, 247, 251, 253–254, 255–256, 261, 263, 265; and Judaism, 247–251; and Marxists, 246n, 247, 255, 261–263; membership, 246n, 247n, 249n; and Nazism, 247, 252–253, 266; and Reformgemeinde, Berlin, 246n, 247, 248–249; and R.j.F., 247, 249, 253–254; Youth organisation, 260; and Zionism, 244, 245n–246n, 247, 249, 251, 252, 255, 256–261, 263
Verband süddeutscher katholischer Arbeiterinnenvereine, 38
Verband süddeutscher katholischer Arbeitervereine, 38
Verband der Synagogenvereine, 257
Verbände katholischer Arbeitervereine West- und Süddeutschlands, 32n
Verein zur Abwehr des Antisemitismus (Abwehrverein), 141, 150–151, 154, 155, 156, 201, 203
Verein für jüdische Geschichte und Literatur, 189
Verein für religiöse Erziehung, 50
Vereinigung christlicher Referendare, 152
Vincke, Georg, Freiherr von (Liberal politician), 7
VINTUS (Association of South German Jewish sports clubs), 231, 232
Vital, David, 173, 193
Vital, Hayim (Kabbalist), 87
Vogelstein, Heinemann (rabbi), 256
Volksschule, German see Education, in Germany
Volksverein für das katholische Deutschland, 54
Voltaire, 93

Wagner, Richard (composer), 193
Waldstein, David (Liberal politician), 153n
Walk, Joseph, 476
Wannsee Conference, 318n, 327n
Warburg, Max M. (banker), 343n
Wassermann, Oscar (banker), 261n
Wassermann, Jakob (novelist), 211–212, 216–217, 218
Weber, Max (sociologist), 146
Wegscheider, Julius A. S. (theologian), 14n
Weil, Simon (writer), 308
Weimar Constitution, 53–66 passim, 267
Weimar Republic, 53–66, 70–71, 208–219, 266, 276
Weiss, Ernst (boxer), 225
Weizmann, Chaim, 258, 289n, 292n
Wellinger (mountaineer), 226
'(Die) Welt', 148

'(Die) Weltbühne', 262
Weltsch, Felix, 212n
Weltsch, Robert, VIII, X, 305n
Werner, Ferdinand (antisemitic politician), 153n
Wertheimer (aviator), 226
Wessely, Hartwig (Naphtali Herz) (Hebrew writer), 83, 85n, 93, 130
Wessely, Wolfgang (orientalist and jurist), 17n
'Westdeutsche Arbeiter-Zeitung', 38
Westerbork, 252n
Westphalian Jewry, 164n, 166
Wiechert, Ernst Emil (writer), 216
Wiener (aircraft constructor), 226
Wiener, Alfred (Syndicus of Centralverein and founder of Wiener Library, London), 209n, 251
Wiener Library, VIII, 225
Wilhelm (Crown Prince of Germany), 251
Wilhelm II (Emperor of Germany), 45, 267n
Wille, Bruno (writer and religious leader), 27n
Williamson, David G., 209n
Windthorst, Ludwig (Catholic politician), 51, 159, 160
Winterhilfe, 341, 344
Wirth, Josef Karl (German Chancellor and Minister of the Interior), 258n
Wissenschaft des Judentums, XI, XII, 291
De Witte (university teacher; Halle), 15n
Wittenberg, Egon (sports' champion), 224
Wolff, Joseph Sabattia (physician and writer), 104–130; treatise on religious and educational reform, 104–130; text of, 111–130
Wolff, Leo, 208n
Wolfskehl, Karl (poet), 292
Woyda, Bruno (Liberal Jewish leader), 169n
Württemberg Jewry, 163, 166
Wunderlich (university teacher; Halle), 15n

Yiddish, 282, 288
Youth movement, Jewish, in Germany, 224, 230, 231, 260
Youth Aliyah, 328, 345

Zadek, Rudolf (sports' champion), 224
Zedlitz und Trützschler, Graf Robert von (German statesman), 51, 52
Zentralausschuß für Hilfe und Aufbau, 352n
Zentralstelle für jüdische Auswanderung, Vienna, 337
Zentrumspartei (Germany), 51, 52, 53, 54, 55, 61, 62, 63, 143, 144, 148, 150, 159–161, 162; and German antisemitism, 148–162 passim; and Jewish Question, 143, 144, 148–162 passim
Zetkin, Clara (Communist politician), 49, 62n
Zionism, X, 147, 148, 149, 155, 159, 169, 170, 201–218 passim, 228, 229, 230, 244, 250, 256–

261, 263, 264, 270, 271, 279, 287, 288, 305, 316, 340, 351

Zionistische Vereinigung für Deutschland (ZVfD.), 190, 193, 202, 208, 217, 257, 260, 267

Zollschan, Ignaz (writer), 205, 206

Zunz, Leopold (Jewish scholar), XI, 4, 17n, 84

Zweig, Arnold (novelist), 252, 262

Zweig, Stefan (novelist), 216